40°E 60°E 80°E 100°E 120°E 140°E 160°E 180°
80°N
ARCTIC OCEAN
Inset: Below, right
RUSSIA
60°N
KAZAKSTAN
MONGOLIA
UZBEKISTAN
KYRGYZSTAN
TURKMENISTAN
TAJIKISTAN
NORTH KOREA
SOUTH KOREA
JAPAN
40°N
PACIFIC OCEAN
UNISIA
IRAN
AFGHANISTAN
CHINA
KUWAIT
BAHRAIN
QATAR
PAKISTAN
NEPAL
BHUTAN
LIBYA
EGYPT
SAUDI ARABIA
UNITED ARAB EMIRATES
OMAN
BANGLADESH
INDIA
MYANMAR
LAOS
TAIWAN
HONG KONG (U.K.)
MACAO (Port.)
Tropic of Cancer
20°N
NORTHERN MARIANA IS. (U.S.)
GUAM (U.S.)
MARSHALL ISLANDS
CHAD
ERITREA
SUDAN
YEMEN
DJIBOUTI
ETHIOPIA
THAILAND
VIET NAM
CAMBODIA
PHILIPPINES
CENTRAL AFRICAN REPUBLIC
CAMEROON
SRI LANKA
MALDIVES
BRUNEI
MALAYSIA
SINGAPORE
PALAU
FEDERATED STATES OF MICRONESIA
KIRIBATI
0°
NAURU
UGANDA
KENYA
SOMALIA
RWANDA
BURUNDI
CONGO
ZAIRE
TANZANIA
SEYCHELLES
INDONESIA
PAPUA NEW GUINEA
SOLOMON ISLANDS
TUVALU
INDIAN OCEAN
COMOROS
MAYOTTE (Fr.)
ANGOLA
MALAWI
ZAMBIA
ZIMBABWE
MOZAMBIQUE
MADAGASCAR
NAMIBIA
BOTSWANA
MAURITIUS
REUNION (Fr.)
Tropic of Capricorn
VANUATU
FIJI
NEW CALEDONIA (Fr.)
20°S
AUSTRALIA
SWAZILAND
SOUTH AFRICA
LESOTHO
0 1,000 2,000 Miles
0 1,000 2,000 Kilometers
NEW ZEALAND
Antarctic Circle
ANTARCTICA

EUROPE INSET
0 200 400 Miles
0 200 400 Kilometers
10°W 0° 20°E
60°N
SWEDEN
FINLAND
NORWAY
ESTONIA
North Sea
Baltic Sea
LATVIA
RUSSIA
DENMARK
(Russia)
LITHUANIA
UNITED KINGDOM
IRELAND
NETHERLANDS
POLAND
BELARUS
GERMANY
BELGIUM
CZECH. REPUBLIC
UKRAINE
50°N
CHANNEL IS. (U.K.)
LUXEMBOURG
SLOVAK REPUBLIC
LIECH.
AUSTRIA
MOLDOVA
SWITZERLAND
HUNGARY
Bay of Biscay
FRANCE
SLOVENIA
ROMANIA
SAN MARINO
CROATIA
YUGOSLAVIA
ANDORRA
MONACO
ITALY
BOSNIA AND HERZ.
BULGARIA
Black Sea
GEORGIA
MACEDONIA
ARMENIA
SPAIN
ALBANIA
40°N
PORTUGAL
GREECE
TURKEY
AZERBAIJAN
IRAN
MALTA

NINTH EDITION

BUSINESS TODAY

Michael H. Mescon

Founder & Chairman, The Mescon Group
Atlanta, Georgia

Dean Emeritus & Regents Professor of Management
Georgia State University

Courtland L. Bovée

Professor of Business Administration
C. Allen Paul Distinguished Chair
Grossmont College

John V. Thill

Chief Executive Officer
Communication Specialists of America

Prentice Hall, Upper Saddle River, New Jersey 07458

Acquisitions Editor: Don Hull
Editorial Assistant: Paula D'Introno
Editor-in-Chief: Natalie Anderson
Marketing Manager: Debbie Clare
Production Editor: Carol Lavis
Permissions Coordinator: Monica Stipanov
Managing Editor: Dee Josephson
Manufacturing Buyer: Kenneth J. Clinton
Manufacturing Supervisor: Arnold Vila
Manufacturing Manager: Vincent Scelta
Designer: Cheryl Asherman
Design Manager: Patricia Smythe
Interior Design: Donna Wickes
Photo Research Supervisor: Melinda Lee Reo
Image Permission Supervisor: Kay Dellosa
Photo Researcher: Melinda Alexander
Cover Design: Cheryl Asherman
Illustrator (Interior): York Production Services
Cover Illustration/Photo: Mark Jasin
Composition: York Production Services

Illustration and Text Credits and Photo Credits appear on pages R35-R45.

Published by Prentice Hall,
A Simon & Schuster Company
Upper Saddle River, New Jersey 07458
(Previous editions published by McGraw-Hill, Inc.)

Library of Congress Cataloging-in-Publication Data
Mescon, Michael H.
Business today / Michael H. Mescon, Courtland L. Bovée, John V. Thill.—9th ed.
p. cm.
Rev. ed. of: Business Today / David J. Rachman . . . [et al.]. 8th ed. © 1996.
Includes bibliographical references and indexes.
ISBN 0-13-080819-9 (alk. paper)
1. Business. 2. Management—United States. I. Bovée, Courtland L. II. Thill, John V. III. Title.
HF5351.M376 1998
658—dc21 98-33629
CIP

Prentice-Hall International (UK) Limited, London
Prentice-Hall of Australia Pty. Limited, Sydney
Prentice-Hall Canada, Inc., Toronto
Prentice-Hall Hispanoamericana, S.A., Mexico
Prentice-Hall of India Private Limited, New Delhi
Prentice-Hall of Japan, Inc., Tokyo
Simon & Schuster Asia Pte. Ltd., Singapore
Editora Prentice-Hall do Brasil, Ltda., Rio de Janeiro

Printed in the United States of America
10 9 8 7 6 5 4 3 2 1

CONTENTS IN BRIEF

CONTENTS

PROLOGUE

To the Students:

Join Us Behind the Scenes and Explore the Exciting World of Business Today.

Business Today—it's challenging, fast paced, intriguing, and stimulating. Perhaps that's why so many students like yourself choose to study business. Think about it—business is everywhere. Whether you're flying on an airplane, waiting in line at the movies, buying a CD over the Internet, enjoying an ice cream cone, or making a withdrawal at an ATM machine, you're involved in someone else's business. Of course, like many college students, you've been sitting in the audience for most of your life, observing and enjoying the class act that others have tried to perfect. But that's about to change.

In a few moments, *Business Today* will take you backstage, where you'll experience the business world from a different perspective. We'll introduce you to some people who started out just like you—taking a couple of business courses. Through our unique simulation exercises, award-winning videos, and slice-of-life case studies, you'll meet real men and women—on the job—who work at large and small companies, fly around the globe, work outdoors, and telecommute from their homes. You'll see them cope with daily challenges and opportunities, and you'll discover that many of them really aren't so perfect. Some will struggle; others will stumble and fall; most will achieve success by working hard and learning from their mistakes. In fact, that's what makes *Business Today* so exciting; it's one giant learning experience, and a dress rehearsal for the real thing.

Consider this: Most employers today seek job candidates with excellent critical thinking, problem-solving, and communication skills. Furthermore, these skills are not only job-seeking skills, but job-holding skills. By using *Business Today* in your introductory business course, you'll have plenty of opportunities to sharpen your business skills—before the curtain goes up and you're on center stage. For instance, in the "On the Job" simulation in each chapter of this text, you'll become a part of that organization. As a manager, controller, consultant, independent contractor, adviser, or even vice president, you'll get the next best thing to on-the-job training, and the company team will be counting on you to make some important decisions. In addition, the book's actual case stories will involve you in some critical decision making where you'll learn firsthand that problems are never solved in real life as easily as they are on television. You'll even discover that successful businesspeople don't just have great ideas; they have great ideas *and* know how to execute them.

Furthermore, you will use the skills and knowledge you gain from this textbook throughout your life even if you don't major in business. For instance, you'll develop a strong business vocabulary that will make it easier for you to keep up with the latest news. Plus you'll learn how to read a financial report, evaluate a company's stock, apply for a loan, interview for a job, buy the right kind of insurance, market yourself, and so much more. You'll explore some really resourceful "Best of the Web" sites, and you'll learn hands-on how to access, interpret, evaluate, apply, and communicate data. Plus our new Component Chapter on the Internet is a handy resource you'll want to keep referring to so you can continually improve your Internet skills. In addition, by completing our unique, integrated "Exploring the Best of the Web" exercises, you'll gain practical Internet experience that will assist you throughout your college studies, at your job, or whenever you're searching for information.

Of course, one of our favorite Web sites is the new one for our textbook. Once you access our Web site <http://www.philip.marist.edu> you'll be in touch with literally thousands of students—just like you—who will be using this book all over the country. Join them in our study hall where you can chat about the course, ask our tutor a question, pick up some tools at our study skills and writing centers, and of course, contact us. We're there to support you in your efforts.

You'll also find a career center on our Web site that has resources for everyone. In fact, that's another big advantage of taking this introductory business course. Throughout the course you will learn about the many career opportunities in fields such as economics, human resources, accounting, management, finance, marketing, and so on. This will be especially helpful when it's time for you to declare a major or choose your career. You will even see how each of these separate business functions work together to contribute to the success of the company as a whole. In other words, like actors, businesspeople must not only learn their individual parts, but they must become fairly familiar with the roles of everyone in the company. Learning how to work together as a team is a big part of *Business Today*. By understanding everyone's role, and listening for your cues, you'll be able to assist your peers through the difficult scenes. Remember, a great performance by a single actor or actress does not necessarily earn a standing ovation for the company.

Perhaps you're already beginning to see the world of business from a different perspective. It's really quite exciting. And we have so much more to share with you. So join us backstage now, meet our cast, step inside the hundreds of small and large companies we spotlight, and explore the fascinating world of *Business Today*. We think business opportunities have never been greater.

Michael H. Mescon
Courtland L. Bovée
John V. Thill

PREFACE

Literally millions of students have learned about business from *Business Today*, and its popularity continues. *Business Today* is relied on for its consistency of topics covered, content, currency, ancillary package, service, and commitment to students. *Business Today* presents a balanced view of business—the strengths, weaknesses, successes, failures, problems, and challenges. With its vast array of features, it gives students a solid underpinning for more advanced courses, and it explains the opportunities, rewards, and challenges of a business career.

Business Today, Ninth Edition, continues its respected tradition of excellence. Students not only read about business but also experience it firsthand in every chapter through a variety of highly involving activities that no other textbook can match. Students appreciate its up-to-date real-life examples, its carefully integrated in-depth coverage, its lively conversational writing style, and its eye-opening contemporary graphics. With its integration of international examples and concepts throughout the book, coverage of current events, exploration of important ethical and societal issues, activities that foster critical thinking, and wealth of assignments to improve students' business communication skills, this edition implements the guidelines for undergraduate business programs of the American Association of Collegiate Schools of Business.

This Ninth Edition marks a milestone for *Business Today* and is especially exciting because we have a new publisher, Prentice Hall. Instructors and students will be well served by Prentice Hall's commitment to excellence. When preparing this edition, we dedicated ourselves to four important goals: (1) to provide the most current and up-to-date introduction to business textbook in the market, (2) to provide a clear and complete description of the concepts underlying business, (3) to illustrate with real-life examples and cases the remarkable dynamism and liveliness of business organizations and of the people who operate them, and (4) to incorporate the valuable recommendations of instructors who use this book daily.

To achieve our goals, we have completely rewritten or revised all of the book's chapters, and we have added many new special features to give students an even better learning experience. Here is an overview of the major changes of *Business Today*, Ninth Edition. A complete chapter-by-chapter description is provided at the end of this Preface.

Revision Highlights

The following new features have been added to the Ninth Edition:

- A new chapter on the Internet serves as a learning tool and resource.
- Entirely new, exceptionally high-quality, critically acclaimed videos replace existing videos.
- New company examples place greater emphasis on small businesses.
- Three "Best of the Web" features included in each chapter describing resourceful sites that extend chapter material.
- Revised end-of-chapter questions to appeal to three levels of learning: recall, analysis, and higher-level critical thinking skills.
- Thoroughly integrated coverage of the Internet includes special Web-based exercises for the "Best of the Web" features, case studies, and *The Wall Street Journal* and geography exercises.
- A new Web site supports this new edition with hot links and resources and provides threaded conferencing capabilities for students, instructors, and authors, plus much more.
- A new chapter feature—"Is It True?"—focuses on interesting business facts and fallacies.
- Over 80 percent of chapter boxes and case studies are new; all others have been updated.
- Over 50 percent of "On the Job" vignettes and simulations are new; all others have been updated.

The Leader in Currency

For the Ninth Edition of *Business Today*, over 500 professors of business contributed their viewpoints on trends in instructional methodology for the introductory business course. In addition, we have conducted an exhaustive study of the literature of business, including thousands of the very latest reports, monographs, books, and articles. As a quick glance at the extensive References and Acknowledgments sections near the end of this book will show, *Business Today* is the most carefully researched and currently documented introductory business textbook on the market (over 220 resources from 1998 have been added to this edition alone). Topic coverage includes:

South Korea bailout ♦ Hudson's *Workforce 2020* ♦ ethical use of the Internet ♦ World Trade Organization ♦ Europe's new common currency, the euro ♦ Java ♦ cybermalls and virtual storefronts ♦ supply-chain management ♦ 14 points of TQM ♦ Web advertising ♦ direct public stock offerings ♦ smart cards and electronic money ♦ long-term-care insurance ♦ privatization ♦ electronic pricing ♦ one-to-one marketing ♦ Internet publishing ♦ database marketing ♦ teleconferencing ♦ online banking ♦ decimal stock pricing ♦ Internet telephony ♦ e-stamps ♦ electronic catalogs ♦ security on the Internet ♦ price-based pricing ♦ corporate downsizing and outsourcing ♦ the Mercosur ♦ DaimlerChrysler

Some of the new key terms include mass customization, relationship marketing, euro, virtual reality, price-based pricing, co-branding, outsourcing, cross-functional teams, computer viruses, data warehousing, data mining, fiber optic cable, executive information systems, artificial intelligence, multimedia, CD-ROMs, local area network, wide area network, Internet, intranet, download, firewall, domain name, client/server system, bandwidth, multitasking, and derivatives.

IN-DEPTH COVERAGE

The Ninth Edition of *Business Today* continues our long-standing practice of providing the most in-depth coverage of material suitable for an introductory business course compared to any book on the market. This book not only tells what is happening in the world of business today, it explains why (or perhaps why not). Furthermore, our company examples expose students to more than a company name or a person. We make sure that we include a fair amount of detail about each company or person we mention. In addition, we explain difficult concepts by using a variety of interesting examples and metaphors that students can relate to.

In short, we believe that no other textbook in the field is as successful as *Business Today* at drawing students into the subject matter, presenting both sides of the story—the advantages and disadvantages—and preparing students to obtain and pursue satisfying business careers.

MORE REAL-WORLD FOCUS AND REAL COMPANY EXAMPLES

This Ninth Edition offers the most contemporary look at business of any book in the field. In addition to the companies featured in our chapter case studies, vignettes, simulation exercises, special feature boxes, and videos, we spotlight hundreds of small and large companies throughout each chapter, looking closely at the issues their managers and employees struggle with on a daily basis. Each company example has been carefully selected to draw students into the real world of business today, and offers students the opportunity to learn from other people's successes and failures.

Business Today has no examples promoting alcohol. We certainly support companies' rights to market their products, but considering that many students taking this course are not of legal drinking age and that alcoholism among college students is increasing, we believe that an emphasis on alcoholic products in a textbook is inappropriate. *Business Today* also avoids tobacco examples (other than those instances in which tobacco products are the subject of critical discussion). The business literature offers thousands of great examples that students can relate to, and this book takes advantage of those. Some of the examples focusing on real companies include:

Microsoft antitrust case ♦ FedEx Virtual Order System ♦ crisis management: TWA's Flight 800 ♦ Amazon.com ♦ WorldCom/MCI merger ♦ Outback Steakhouse's unique management strategy ♦ United Airlines' ESOP pays off ♦ Boston Chicken—not everything is lip-smacking good ♦ complete financial analysis of Computer Discount Warehouse ♦ mass customization at Andersen Windows and Levi Strauss ♦ Intuit's "follow me home" program ♦ Euro Disney's faux pas ♦ Sky Mall's overstatement of customers' needs ♦ Quaker Oats bailing out of Snapple snafu ♦ Grandmother Calendar's bobbles success ♦ Enterprise Car Rental's astoundingly simple approach for being successful ♦ tomorrow's banks: Security First National and Integrion ♦ drowning in debt at Denny's ♦ Wood Classic's insurance escapade ♦ Rhino Foods' employment policy ♦ environmental self-regulation at Weyerhaeuser ♦ Whirlpool's global lesson ♦ Teamster strike at UPS

NEW! SPOTLIGHT ON FIVE MAJOR BUSINESS CHALLENGES

New to this edition is a special emphasis on the major challenges facing businesses in today's highly competitive, fast-paced, and changing environment. This material is woven into chapter text where explanation and analysis offer students vivid insights into how businesspeople cope with these challenges on a daily basis. A listing of the examples associated with each of the following well-integrated themes can be found in a special Guide to Thematic Examples following this Preface:

Challenge: Supporting Quality Initiatives and Achieving Customer Satisfaction

The Ninth Edition of *Business Today* adds many new examples of both successful and unsuccessful quality initiatives. Chapter 6 adds an entirely new section on total quality management (TQM). Chapter 12 has been entirely rewritten to focus on the importance of understanding customers. Plus numerous company examples have been added throughout the text to demonstrate ongoing efforts to reduce product defects, cut costs and delivery times, and offer customers innovative products.

Challenge: Keeping Pace with Technology and the Internet While Embracing Innovation

Everywhere we look today, powerful new technological forces are reshaping the world. *Business Today*, Ninth Edition, provides hundreds of examples of how businesses are integrating technology and the Internet into their processes. In addition to a thoroughly revised chapter on computers and information technology (Chapter 16) and a completely new chapter on the Internet (see p. xxix), a series of "Understanding the High-Tech Revolution" and "Gaining the Competitive Edge" boxes demonstrate the challenges and opportunities businesses face as they use these new technologies to innovate, differentiate, and leap ahead of competition.

Challenge: Starting and Managing a Small Business in Today's Competitive Environment

Today's business students have strong entrepreneurial interests. Although comparatively few will ever be self-employed, many will work for small enterprises. In either case, they have an obvious need to understand the risks, rewards, problems, and perils of small business. In addition to devoting an entire chapter to this subject (see Chapter 5), we have added many more examples of small companies. In fact, a quick glance at our Guide to Thematic Examples will show that small businesses are indeed a big part of *Business Today.*

Challenge: Behaving in an Ethically and Socially Responsible Manner

By pointing out ethical dilemmas and by reminding students of the responsibilities that accompany the rights of free enterprise, *Business Today* helps prepare the next generation of conscientious businesspeople. In addition to a well-rounded chapter that discusses ethical decision making (Chapter 3), a series of "Thinking About Ethics" boxes and numerous other examples appear throughout the book so students can see that nearly every aspect of business presents ethical questions.

Challenge: Thinking Globally and Committing to a Culturally Diverse Work Force

Companies today are increasingly pursuing markets beyond their borders, and globalization is changing the way we work. *Business Today*, Ninth Edition, integrates hundreds of international and cultural examples throughout the text, including a complete chapter (see Chapter 2) on international business, and a series of "Exploring Global Business" and "Focusing on Cultural Diversity" boxes.

NEW! EXTENSIVE INTERNET COVERAGE

As you know, the Internet hype can get rather intense at times. But you do not need hype to make a business case for the Internet. The reality is compelling enough. It has already begun to change the way we work, and it will inevitably change the way we interact with the world around us. This Ninth Edition demonstrates the power of the Internet by including hundreds of real-world examples that show how businesses today are using the Internet. In addition, specially designed Web-based exercises provide students with hands-on experience in accessing, interpreting, evaluating, applying, and communicating Internet information.

NEW! Internet Component Chapter

In addition to including the Internet as one of our five integrated themes, we have added an entirely new component chapter on the Internet. For many students, this will be their first formal introduction to the Internet. This new chapter explains what you can do on the Internet, how businesses are using the Internet, and how to find information on the Internet—including a special section on search strategies and tips. Many instructors will want to introduce this chapter first; students will want to use this chapter as a resource to assist them with research projects and the new Web-based exercises (marked by a special icon for easy identification). Plus our special end-of-chapter Internet glossary will assist students as they explore on their own.

NEW! "Best of the Web" Internet Resources

To acquaint students with the wealth of valuable information on the World Wide Web that relates to the content of *Business Today*, several "Best of the Web" features are included in each chapter describing resourceful sites that extend chapter material. Students can access each site by using the URL provided or by going to the Web site for this text <http://www.phlip.marist.edu/> where live links will take students straight to the site of their choice. This new feature helps students understand how to achieve greater success in business by using the Internet.

RELIABLE AND EFFECTIVE PEDAGOGY SPARKS STUDENT LEARNING

National test results show a serious weakness in the ability of U.S. students to reason, analyze, interpret, synthesize, and solve problems. According to respected reports on the state of higher education by the National Commission on Excellence in Education, the National Institute of Education, and the Association of American Colleges, fostering students' ability to think critically should be one of the major focuses of an undergraduate education. Critical thinking calls for skills such as observing, classifying, interpreting, criticizing, summarizing, analyzing, comparing, hypothesizing, collecting and organizing information, making decisions, and applying knowledge to new situations.

Business Today includes an extraordinary number of pedagogical devices that simplify teaching, facilitate learning, stimulate critical thinking, maintain interest and enjoyment, and illustrate the practical application of chapter concepts. In short, these devices make this new edition the most effective teaching tool ever published for introductory business.

On the Job: Facing Business Challenges

Each chapter begins with a slice-of-life vignette that attracts student interest by vividly portraying the business challenges faced by a real executive. Each vignette closes with thought-provoking questions that draw the students not only into the chapter material but also into the world of business. Throughout the chapter itself, references to the opening vignette help students see the connection between chapter content and the real world of business.

On the Job: Meeting Business Challenges

Each chapter concludes with an end-of-chapter case study/simulation that (1) elaborates on the real-world actions taken by the executive featured in the opening vignette, and (2) analyzes the results in light of the concepts presented in the chapter. Then the students take over, playing a role in the executive's organization by making business decisions in four carefully chosen scenarios—many of which can be completed using teams.

Chapter vignettes and simulations encourage students to view themselves as part of an actual organization and give students "on-the-job" training applying principles they've just learned. These case studies/simulations (over 50 percent new; all others updated) include companies such as Gateway 2000, AJ Wraps, Top of the Tree Baking Company, Harley Davidson, Starbucks, She's Florists, Black and Decker, The Concrete Doctor, and Holiday Inn.

Special Feature Boxes Revolve Around Five Well-Integrated Themes

Special feature boxes are strategically placed in every chapter to further enhance students' learning by making the world of business come alive. Each box includes two questions for critical thinking that are ideal for developing team or individual problem-solving skills. The themes for these boxes (over 80 percent are new) include Focusing on Cultural Diversity, Thinking About Ethics, Exploring Global Business, Understanding the High-Tech Revolution, and Gaining the Competitive Edge. Boxes include:

Creating a Winning Web Site ♦ Choosing a Company Name ♦ Do Mergers Threaten Management's Responsibility to Shareholders? ♦ How Computer Networks Are Changing the Way We Work ♦ Bribery, Piracy, and Thievery: Understanding the Challenges of Global Corruption ♦ Workers Unite! Travailleurs Univ! Trabajadores Unir! ♦ Cybershopping for Groceries ♦ Web Ads Start to Click ♦ Privacy in the Workplace: Whose E-Mail Is It, Anyway? ♦ Smashing Pumpkins on the Produce Aisle? New Distribution Strategies Boost Sales ♦ Bytes, Bits, Banks, and Bucks: Money and the Internet

A Case for Critical Thinking

At the end of each chapter, "A Case for Critical Thinking" reinforces points made in the chapter. This classic device assists students in evaluating situations, using good judgment, learning to make decisions, and developing critical thinking skills. Over 80 percent of the case studies are new; all others have been updated. Case topics include:

Molex: The Billion Dollar Globetrotter ♦ Kiva Container: All in the Family ♦ Continental Airlines: Coffee, Tea, and On-Time Arrival ♦ America Online: Losing the Battles, but Winning the War ♦ SSI Services: Labor and Management Bury the Hatchet ♦ Staples: The Price of Success ♦ Working Assets: Dialing Up Social Responsibility ♦ Southwest Airlines: Flying High on Employee Morale ♦ Sears: From Turnaround to Transformation ♦ Entrepreneurs Clean Up in South Africa.

NEW! "Exploring the Best of the Web" Exercises

To give students practice in experiencing the rich resources of the World Wide Web, end-of-chapter exercises, "Exploring the Best of the Web," are directly tied to the "Best of the Web" sites showcased within the chapters. These exercises help students understand how the Internet is changing business by giving them hands-on experience using the Internet to research and evaluate a variety of business topics. The exercises provide navigational directions as well as student guidance and hints. Students who complete these exercises will learn how to use the Internet proficiently and productively.

NEW! "Is It True?"

Each chapter includes three intriguing business facts or fallacies, closely related to the chapter material and strategically placed in the margin. The statements are designed to stimulate student interest by challenging some commonly accepted beliefs about business. Students are asked whether the statements presented are true or false. The answers—many of them surprising—are located at the end of the chapter. These brief exercises are fun, challenging, and informative.

Keeping Current Using The Wall Street Journal

To emphasize the link between today's business news and *Business Today*, a "Keeping Current Using *The Wall Street Journal*" exercise is provided at the end of each chapter. Students are asked to choose an article they are interested in and are provided a structure for analyzing the article in the context of the material covered in the chapter. These exercises offer interesting and useful ways to use *The Wall Street Journal* in the classroom and give students practice in the critical skill of interpreting business news.

Building Your Business Skills

The ability to communicate well—whether listening, speaking, reading, or writing—is a skill students must possess to have a successful career. Because of their extensive research and writing in the area of communication, the authors are especially equipped to help your students develop these skills. You'll find unique "Building Your Business Skills" exercises near the end of each chapter. Students are called on to practice a wide range of communication activities, including one-on-one and group discussions, class debates, personal interviews, panel sessions, oral and written reports, and letter-writing assignments.

Mastering the Geography of Business

Now that so many businesses are affected by global affairs, students need a stronger understanding of geography. You'll find a "Mastering the Geography of Business" exercise at the end of each major part of this text. Each of these new exercises describes a real-world business situation and asks students to complete an activity that requires geographic knowledge or research.

NEW! Integrated Web Exercises

To further integrate the use of the World Wide Web throughout this course, we have added Web-based questions to all chapter case studies and *The Wall Street Journal* exercises as well as to the geographic exercise that appears at the end of each major part of the text.

NEW! Integrated Videos Teach Important Concepts

The ability to drive home a point—to excite the human mind and to stimulate action—is what makes videos so incredibly powerful. Now you can harness this power and bring the drama and immediacy of real-world business into your classroom. Entirely new, exceptionally high-quality Small Business 2000 Videos by Hattie Bryant accompany this text. The videos allow students to meet, on location, a cross section of real people who have created some of the country's most fascinating companies. These critically acclaimed videos have been shown on PBS stations throughout the country, and they surpass those offered with any other text.

NEW! PHLIP Web Site

Join our new Web-based learning environment that includes live links to all URLs in the Ninth Edition of *Business Today*, plus numerous links to discipline-specific Web sites. In addition to download areas and threaded bulletin board capacity, PHLIP features current events articles that are updated about every two weeks and a faculty support section that provides instructors with access to textual and media material in the Prentice Hall Business Publishing archives. Students will find the computerized Interactive Study Guide, Writing Center, Study Skills Center, Career Center, Research Area, and threaded conference message board, "Ask the Tutor," especially helpful. The purpose of PHLIP is to furnish up-to-date classroom support through state-of-the-art technology and resources. Instructors and students can access PHLIP at <http://www.phlip.marist.edu/>.

Lively, Conversational Writing Style Motivates Students

Read a few pages of this textbook and then read a few pages of another textbook. We think you will immediately notice the difference. The lucid writing style in *Business Today*, Ninth Edition, makes the material pleasing to read and easy to comprehend. It stimulates interest and promotes learning. We have also carefully monitored the reading level of *Business Today* to make sure it is neither too simple nor too difficult.

Tools That Help Develop Skills and Enhance Comprehension

Business Today uses a variety of helpful learning tools to reinforce and apply chapter material as well as stimulate higher-level thinking skills. These include:

- *Learning Objectives to Establish Benchmarks for Measuring Success.* Each chapter begins with a list of objectives summarizing what students should learn after studying the chapter. These objectives guide the learning process and help motivate students to master the material. The end-of-chapter "Summary of Learning Objectives" restates these learning objectives and summarizes chapter highlights to reinforce learning of basic concepts.
- *End-of-Chapter Questions.* Each chapter includes five review and five analysis questions to reinforce and apply chapter learning. New to this edition are two questions for application that prompt students to stretch their learning beyond the chapter content. Not only will students find these questions useful when studying for examination, but the instructor may also draw on them to promote classroom discussion of issues that have no easy answers.
- *Four-Way Approach to Vocabulary Development.* Because business has its own special terminology, an important goal of this textbook is vocabulary development. Our four-way method of vocabulary reinforcement helps students learn basic course terminology with ease. First, each key term is printed in boldface within the text. Second, a definition appears in the margin adjacent to the term. Third, an alphabetical list of key terms appears at the end of each chapter, with convenient cross-references to the pages where the terms are defined. Fourth, all marginal definitions are assembled in an alphabetical Glossary at the end of the book.
- *Team Building.* Many of the exercises included in *Business Today* are designed to encourage students to work in teams to solve business issues. This is especially true for application and critical thinking questions, as well as all simulation and Web-based exercises.
- *Integrated Interactive Exercises.* Available on our new Web site are a series of self-administered interactive chapter quizzes that allow students to assess their chapter knowledge. Immediate feedback makes these exercises excellent pretest and posttest learning tools.
- *Real-Company Photographs.* Most of the photographs used in this book are from real companies. Each picture is accompanied by a caption that describes how it relates to business today. The photos cover a rich assortment of people, organiza-

tions, and events, and all of them give students an intimate glimpse into the real-life application of the topic being studied.

An Unsurpassed Instructional Resource Package

The instructional resource package accompanying this text is specially designed to simplify the task of teaching and learning. The supplementary package for the Ninth Edition of *Business Today* has been thoroughly revised, and several new and exciting elements have been added.

Instructor's Resource Manual

This one-volume comprehensive paperback book by Judith Bulin, Monroe Community College, is a set of completely integrated support materials. It is designed to assist instructors in finding and assembling the resources available for each chapter of the text. Also available electronically from the book's Web site, the *Instructor's Resource Manual* for the Ninth Edition of *Business Today* includes:

Revision Highlights
Course Planning Guide
In the News (one for each part)
Summary of Learning Objectives
Lecture Outlines and Teaching Suggestions
Boxed Inserts: Write Focus, and Team Talk
Answers to End-of-Chapter Questions, Text Cases, Boxes, and Simulations
Answers to "Exploring the Best of the Web"
Project Ideas
Instructor's Notes for the Video Series
Instructor's Notes for the Study Guide

Introduction to Business Insights Newsletter

Delivered exclusively by e-mail every month, this newsletter provides interesting materials that can be used in class, and it offers a wealth of practical ideas about teaching methods. To receive a complimentary subscription, simply send a message by e-mail to <majordomo@po.databack.com>. In the message area, insert the following two lines:

subscribe ibi
end

Test Bank

A master test item file of over 3,000 questions is available for use with *Business Today*, Ninth Edition. The test file consists of multiple-choice (60 percent), true/false (30 percent), and essay items (10 percent). Over half of the questions in the revised *Test Bank* are new for this edition. Each test question is followed by a code indicating the corresponding text page on which the answer can be found and whether the question is factual or applied. The *Test Bank* was prepared by Morgan Bridge of Mesa State College.

Prentice Hall Custom Test (Windows Version)

Based on a state-of-the-art test generation software program developed by Engineering Software Associates, *Prentice Hall Custom Test* is suitable for your course and can be customized to your class needs. This user-friendly software allows you to originate tests quickly, easily, and error-free. You can create an exam, administer it traditionally or online, and analyze the success of the examination—all with a simple click of the mouse.

Color Acetate Transparency Program

A set of 150 large-type entirely new color transparency acetates, available to instructors on request, highlight text concepts or supply additional facts and information to help bring concepts alive in the classroom and enhance the classroom experience. All are keyed to the *Instructor's Resource Manual.* The transparencies were created by Cathleen Golden of Indiana University of Pennsylvania.

PowerPoint Presentation Software

The overhead transparency program is also available on PowerPoint 4.0. The software is designed to allow you to present the overhead transparencies to your class electronically. PowerPoint slides can be downloaded from the text's Web site or are available on disk from your Prentice Hall representative.

*Prentice Hall/*New York Times "Themes of the Times" *for Business*

This mini version of the newspaper includes excerpts of recent *New York Times* articles that are compiled especially for introductory business students. Copies are distributed directly to the professor and are free to students.

Guide for Non-Native Speakers

This popular supplement by J. Marcia Le Roy responds to the special needs of the fast-growing population of non-native-speaking students whose English language skills are limited. The major focus of this guide is terminology and includes a dictionary-like ESL glossary that corresponds chapter for chapter with *Business Today.* This guide contains high-level instructor tips to assist students in making adjustments to U.S. classroom culture—especially our lively debate/discussion format.

Threshold Competitor: A Management Simulation, Second Edition

This team-based introduction to business simulation gives students the opportunity to manage small manufacturing companies competing in the same marketplace. Each student team decides on company missions, goals, policies, and strategies in areas ranging from marketing to finance and manufacturing. Students practice skills in planning, organizing, directing, and controlling, and they get responses to both questions and decisions. Group performance is rated and ranked according to criteria determined by the instructor.

Additional Instructional and Student Resource Materials

Additional instructional materials available include:

- *Free CD-ROM!* A free CD-ROM is packaged with each copy of *Business Today,* Ninth Edition. This desktop resource presents video clips to help students address and apply key concepts from the text. The CD is both engaging and interactive. It goes beyond the text and requires analytical thinking. Your students will find this resource a valuable learning tool. For example, using this CD, students can link to a Web site for dynamic case resources. The *Business Today* CD reflects current cutting-edge business topics as well as traditional business concepts. It contains the following sections:

  Q&A: This section illustrates 12 hot business issues. Each video is introduced by a question or statement. For example, by clicking on "Going International—It's Easy, Isn't It?" students are presented a video featuring a manager's experience with international markets.

Small Business 2000 Videos: This section features video clips that are directly related to the text. Several videos relate to each part. Next to the on-screen video clips, corresponding contextual information tells students what to look for in the clip and explains the clips's relevancy to the text.

- *Study Guide* by Douglas Copeland of Johnson Country Community College is designed to increase your students' comprehension of the concepts presented in this text. The guide provides chapter-by-chapter explanations and exercises designed to reinforce comprehension of key terms and concepts, and to promote concept-application skills.
- *Beginning Your Career Search* by James S. O'Rourke IV is a concise book offering some straightforward, practical advice on how to write a résumé, where and how to find company information, how to conduct yourself during an interview, and tips on the interview process. Included in the book are copies of sample introductory, cover, follow-up, and thank-you letters. This book is provided at no charge to students using *Business Today*, Ninth Edition.
- *Surfing for Success on Business Internet Guide,* Third Edition, shows in detail how to make the Internet work to your advantage. This book is provided at no charge to students using *Business Today*, Ninth Edition.

A Thorough Revision

When preparing the Ninth Edition of *Business Today*, we dedicated ourselves to a thorough revision. For example, we have entirely rewritten the chapters on technology, banking, finance, accounting, marketing, small business, and insurance. We have added a new Internet component chapter, and we have converted our chapters on risk management and insurance, and government regulations, taxation, and business law to component chapters to maximize your flexibility in teaching the course. Moreover, in each chapter we emphasize the growing influence of technology and the Internet.

Members of the academic and business community have carefully reviewed this Ninth Edition and have all praised its competent coverage of subject material, its depth, its up-to-date examples, its flexible organization, and its authentic portrayal of business. Here is an overview of the major content changes in the Ninth Edition:

Chapter 1: Foundations and Challenges of Business Now examines the step-by-step process involved in going from a domestic to an international company and then a global entity; discusses the shift of planned economies to more market-driven systems; updates insights into why the communist system is breaking down; gives a clearer explanation of the CPI and GDP as economic tools including their misleading nature; explains how the four traditional factors of production are becoming less of a competitive advantage in the global marketplace; highlights the five major challenges that businesses are facing in the twenty-first century.

Chapter 2: Global Business Updates the discussion of international business activity, including importing and exporting, licensing, franchising, wholly owned facilities, joint ventures, and strategic alliances; adds material on regional trading blocs and agreements; explains developments in the EU, NAFTA, Mercosur, ASEAN, WTO, and APEC; shows how intrafirm trade obscures the balance of trade as a measure of a country's performance; presents material on how information technology and the Internet are making it easier for companies to effectively expand their global reach.

Chapter 3: Business Ethics and Social Responsibility Condenses discussion about the history of social responsibility and affirmative action to allow for more current discussion of diversity initiatives; strengthens the discussion of how consumers, investors, and managers are placing more and more value on ethical and socially responsible behavior; increases emphasis on the role of management in creating a corporate culture that values socially responsible and ethical behavior; provides international perspectives on gender issues, pollution, and employee safety.

Chapter 4: Forms of Business Ownership Condenses discussion of company categorization by industry sector; updates changes in the regulatory environment affecting both public and private corporations; cites recent trends including the naming of experienced managers to boards, creating diverse boards, and compensating directors with shares of stock; examines industry consolidation and the quest for synergies in today's mergers, acquisitions, and joint ventures; explains why 50 percent of mergers fail; adds more real-life company examples to illustrate why businesspeople choose one form of ownership over another.

Chapter 5: Small Business, New Ventures, and Franchises Elaborates on the challenges, issues, advantages, and disadvantages small companies face in a competitive, global marketplace; transfers sections on obtaining financing to Chapter 18; now describes the many issues confronting small, family business today; adds a new section on expanding globally and doing business on the Internet, all from the perspective of the small-business owner; includes management and exit strategy as two new business plan elements; adds a new section on current issues in franchising to explain why the pendulum has begun its swing toward the franchisee.

Chapter 6: Management Fundamentals Now highlights the need for managerial tasks to revolve around supporting and achieving a corporate vision, mission, and goals; adds an entire section on total quality management (TQM); expands on TQM's relationship with each of the four management functions (planning, organizing, leading, and controlling); transfers the discussion of mentoring and corporate culture from Chapter 7; includes new discussion on promoting a corporate culture that values diversity; points out the importance of forecasting to the planning process; presents current thinking on leadership and elaborates on whether effective leadership differs from effective management.

Chapter 7: Organization, Teamwork, and Communication Condenses the information included in the previous edition into a major section titled "Organization"; adds a major section on teamwork in organizations; expands significantly the discussion of organizational communication, the various forms of communication and their proper use, and barriers to effective communication; discusses how computer networks are changing the way companies organize and explains how companies use telecommuting to cut costs and accomplish more; presents more examples to illustrate how companies today are organizing for flexibility and working in teams.

Chapter 8: Producing Quality Goods and Services Emphasizes quality as the focal point of the chapter and as the main objective of efficient production; expands discussion of flexible manufacturing to explain how small companies are using FMS to compete on a global scale; includes new discussion that examines supply-chain management and logistics; clarifies discussion of JIT to emphasize that it is an entire production strategy and not just a method for managing inventory; adds new material on the role of information systems in production, including EDI; increases company examples showing the relationship between quality and superior customer service.

Chapter 9: Human Relations, Motivation, and Performance Condenses the discussions of scientific management; emphasizes how globalization, technology, and the shift to a service economy have created a surplus of low-skilled employees and a demand for highly skilled employees; points out the growing gap between highly skilled and low-skilled labor as a major trend that managers and employees will have to contend with in the twenty-first century; expands motivation techniques to include innovative and nonfinancial incentives; adds real-company examples to demonstrate the challenges of motivating employees in a team-oriented workplace.

Chapter 10: Human Resource Management Examines new value-based pay systems that link executive pay to overall company performance; discusses broadbanding as an alternative to traditional promotion-based raises for today's flatter, more flexible organizations; expands the discussion of employee stock ownership programs to explain stock options in detail; now defines the two most common types of pensions; presents a new section that explores the challenges of managing human resources in the global business environment; focuses on the ethical implications of employee drug, personality, and genetic testing.

Chapter 11: Employee-Management Relations Explores how labor unions differ around the world; discusses new tactics being used by unions to gain publicity, increase membership, and exert influence; updates discussion of job security to include outsourcing as a major concern of unions today and a major reason for recent strikes in the automobile industry; examines how labor and management are forging cooperative relationships based on teamwork and problem solving; completely revises discussion of the future of unions by explaining how many unions are focusing more on helping management to meet company goals while maintaining union standards.

Chapter 12: Marketing and Customer Satisfaction Now focuses on understanding customers, relationship marketing, segmentation, one-to-one marketing, database marketing, customer loyalty, and the influence of technology and the Internet on marketing; transfers mass customization to an earlier chapter; adds four new exhibits: customer satisfaction, keeping customers loyal, database marketing, and how the Internet enhances customer relations; highlights deficiencies inherent to customer surveys; presents new discussion of virtual reality; includes new material on Internet usage and privacy concerns.

Chapter 13: Product and Pricing Decisions Now includes all discussions of strategic marketing planning in addition to product management and pricing strategies; adds discussion of market leader strategies; substantially reduces discussion of markup pricing method and various pricing strategies to allow greater emphasis on price-based versus cost-based pricing methods; introduces concept of value pricing; adds discussion on co-branding, electronic pricing, and international marketing strategies; increases discussion on service-based products and choosing a company name.

Chapter 14: Distribution Expands discussion on Internet and nonstore retailers; includes new section on electronic catalogs and retailing, cybermalls and virtual storefronts, and home shopping; now emphasizes importance of modifying channel design to meet new conditions in the marketplace; expands discussion on channel selection and channel conflict; includes additional examples of the ethical dilemma suppliers face when they change their channels; highlights challenges facing the retail industry; adds new discussion on using physical distribution to gain a competitive advantage.

Chapter 15: Promotion Expands discussion on integrated marketing communications; adds two new key terms: interactive advertising and cross-promotion; incorporates textual material on advantages and disadvantages of major media types into an expanded exhibit; now includes a discussion of Web advertising; provides new material on sales force automation and how it is changing the job of sales personnel.

Chapter 16: Computers and Information Technology Completely reorganizes chapter structure; eliminates much of the technical information to make room for more discussion of current business computing applications and networks; expands the discussion of the role of the Internet in business computing to include Internet publishing, Java-based applications, and the future of Internet commerce; discusses privacy in the information age and emerging technologies such as virtual reality and biometrics; discusses the widespread use of client/server systems; explains the convergence of telecommunications, television, and computer networks.

Chapter 17: Accounting Now places more emphasis on the conceptual understanding of how accounting is used by businesses today; focuses on the changing role of accountants—especially their involvement in strategic decision making; deemphasizes distinction between management and financial accounting, because the division of work is weakening; puts less emphasis on calculations and more emphasis on exhibits to show calculations and numerical detail; uses an actual company example (Computer Discount Warehouse) to provide a unifying thread when explaining analytical tools and financial statement components; places greater emphasis on financial analysis and the use of financial statements for decision making.

Chapter 18: Banking and Financial Management Reduces the finance material from three chapters to two, integrating a company's need for financing with the sources for money and loans; discusses electronic cash and tiered lending; deemphasizes the history and traditional roles of banks to allow more focus on the competitive environment of banking in the future; places greater emphasis on the global environment, international currencies, and international banks; introduces new terms—Eurodollar and euro (Europe's planned unified currency); adds new material on the changing role of community banks and branches; elaborates on how the Internet is changing the role and functions of banks; discusses the problems of regulating the money supply in the global banking environment.

Chapter 19: Securities Markets Broadens the discussion about the Dow Jones Industrial Average; condenses the discussion of options and financial futures; adds a discussion of the Internet and its impact on security exchanges, brokers, trading, government regulation, and investment information; expands discussion of investment choices by combining material previously discussed in other chapters; strengthens discussion of the regulation of securities trading; includes new discussion of trading online, global markets, decimal pricing, and derivatives.

Component Chapter A: Government Regulations, Taxation, and Business Law Condenses the discussion about how the government regulates business to protect consumers, employees, investors, and the natural environment into a brief section; analyzes the effects of deregulation in the telecommunications industry; presents material on IRS and Labor Department investigations into the use of contract employees.

Component Chapter B: Risk Management and Insurance Expands discussion of basic concepts of insurance including the advantages and disadvantages of self-insurance; updates chapter with the most current industry terminology; removes discussion of endowment insurance; adds discussion of functional replacement cost coverage; expands discussion of disability insurance to include long-term care; adds new discussion of the Internet, showing how some insurers are using Web sites to provide information and assistance to customers.

Component Chapter C: The Internet and Business Success Adds a totally new chapter to the Ninth Edition to be used by students as a resource and learning tool; understanding that each student's exposure to and experience with the Internet is different, provides both a "how to use" approach for beginning users and some advanced tools to assist students who have already mastered the basics.

ACKNOWLEDGMENTS

A key reason for the continued success of *Business Today* is an extensive market research effort. In this revision, the advice of hundreds of instructors around the country aided us in out attempt to create a textbook suited to the unique needs of the introductory business market. Our sincere thanks are extended to the individuals who responded to our market questionnaires.

Survey Reviewers

Lee Adami, Northern Wyoming College; **Robert Alliston,** Davenport College of Business; **Lorraine Anderson,** Marshall University; **Doug Ashby,** Lewis and Clark Community College; **Fay Avery,** Northern Virginia Community College; **Sandra Bailey,** Indiana Vocational Technical College; **James Baskfield,** Northern Hennepin Community College; **Gregory Baxter,** Southeastern Oklahoma State University; **Charles Beavin,** Miami-Dade Community College; **Larry Beck,** Colin County Community College; **Joseph Berger,** Monroe Community College; **James Boeger,** Rock Valley College; **Riccardo Boehm,** Hostos Community College; **Mary Jo Boehms,** Jackson State Community College; **Glennis Boyd,** Cisco Junior College; **Jeffrey Bruehl,** Bryan College; **Carl Buckel,** College of the Canyons; **Howard Budner,** Borough of Manhattan Community College; **John Bunnell,** Broome Community College; **Van Bushnell,** Southern Utah University; **William Carman,** Bucks County Community College; **Paul Caruso,** Richard Bland College; **Eloise Chester,** Suffolk County Community College; **Carmin Cimino,** Mitchell College; **Ellen Clemens,** Bloomsburg University of Pennsylvania; **James Cleveland,** Sage Junior College of Albany; **Debra Clingerman,** California University of Pennsylvania; **Herbert Coolidge,** Southern College of Seventh-Day Adventists; **Gary Cutler,** Dyersburg State Community College; **Giles Dail,** Edgecombe Community College; **Joe Damato,** Cuyamaca College; **James Day,** Shawnee State University; **Patrick Ellsberg,** Lower Columbia College; **Alfred Fabian,** Indiana Vocational College; **Jennifer Friestad,** Anoka-Ramsey Community College; **Joan Gailey,** Kent State University, East; **Joyce Goetz,** Austin Community College; **Barbara Goza,** Southern Florida Community College; **Phyllis Graff,** Kauai Community College; **Hugh Graham,** Loras College; **Vance Gray,** Bishop State Community College; **Gary Greene,** Manatee Community College; **Marciano Guerrero,** LaGuardia Community College; **Delia Haak,** John Brown University; **Maurice Hamington,** Mount St. Mary's College; **E. C. Hamm,** Tidewater Community College; **Carnella Hardin,** Glendale Community College; **Marie Hardink,** Anne Arundel Community College; **Diana Hayden,** Northeastern University; **Elizabeth Haynes,** Haywood Community College; **Sheila Devoe Heidman,** Cochise College; **Diana Henke,** University of Wisconsin at Sheboygan; **Norman Humble,** Kirkwood Community College; **Liz Jackson,** Keystone Junior College; **Michael Johnson,** Chippewa Valley Technical College; **Carol Jones,** Cuyahoga Community College; **Lonora Keas,** Del Mar College; **Sylvia Keyes,** Northeastern University; **Sharon Kolstad,** Fort Peck Community College; **Ken LaFave,** Mt. San Jacinto Community College; **Richard Larsen,** University of Maine at Machias; **Philip Lee,** Campbellsville College; **Richard Lenoir,** George Washington University; **Martha Leva,** Pennsylvania State University; **Kathy Lorencz,** Oakland Community College; **James Loricchio,** Ulster County Community College; **Tricia McConville,** Northeastern University; **Cheryl Macon,** Butler County Community College; **Ann Maddox,** Angelo State University; **Marie Madison,** Harry S. Truman College; **Barry Marshall,** Northeastern University; **George Michaelides,** Franklin Pierce College; **Norman Muller,** Greenfield Community College; **Lucia Murphy,** Ursinus College; **Alita Myers,** Copiah-Lincoln Community College; **Eric Nielsen,** College of Charleston; **Patricia Parker,** Maryville University of St. Louis; **Clyde Patterson,** Shawnee State University; **Corey Pfaffe,** Marantha Baptist Bible College; **Noel Powell,**

West Georgia College; **Allen Rager,** Southwestern Community College; **Roy Roddy,** Yakima Valley Community College; **Ehsan Salek,** Virginia Wesleyan College; **Bernard Saperstein,** Passaic County Community College; **Kurk Schindler,** Wilbur Wright College; **Mark Schultz,** Rocky Mountain College; **Arnold Scolnick,** Borough of Manhattan Community College; **David Shepard,** Virginia Western Community College; **Stephanie Smith,** Lander University; **Susan Smith,** Finger Lakes Community College; **George Stook,** Anne Arundel Community College; **David Stringer,** DeAnza College; **Ben Tanksley,** Sul Ross State University; **John Taylor,** University of Alaska, Fairbanks; **Chris Tomas,** Northeast Iowa Community College; **Palmina Uzzolino,** Montclair State University; **Martha Valentine,** Regis University; **Juanita Vertrees,** Sinclair Community College; **Ingo Von Ruckteschel,** Long Island University; **Chuck Wall,** Bakersfield College; **Jay Weiner,** Adams State College; **Lewis Welshofer,** Miami University of Ohio; **Charles White,** Edison Community College; **Richard Williams,** Laramie County Community College; **Clay Willis,** Oklahoma Baptist University; **Ira Wilsker,** Lamar University; **Ron Young,** Kalamazoo Valley Community College; **Sandra Young,** Jones County Junior College; **Harold Zarr,** Des Moines Area Community College; **Nancy Zeliff,** Northwest Missouri State University; and **Gene Zeller,** Jordan College.

Market Reviewers

Harvey Bronstein, Oakland Community College; **Debra Clingerman,** California University of Pennsylvania; **Bill Dempkey,** Bakersfield College; **John Heinsius,** Modesto Junior College; **Alan Hollander,** Suffolk Community College; **Bob Matthews,** Oakton Community College; **Jerry Myers,** Stark Technical College; **Dianne Osborne,** Broward Community College; **Mary Rousseau,** Delta College; **Martin St. John,** Westmoreland Community College; **Patricia Setlik,** William Rainey Harper College; **Richard Shapiro,** Cuyahoga Community College; and **Shafi Ullah,** Broward Community College.

Reviewers for Ninth Edition

Randy Barker, Virginia Commonwealth University; **James D. Bell,** Southwest State University; **Joe Brum,** Fayetteville Technical Community College; **Steven Cassidy,** Howard University; **Jan Feldbauer,** Austin Community College; **Lorraine Hartley,** Franklin University; **Donald Johnson,** College for Financial Planning; **Jeffery Klivans,** University of Maine-Augusta; **Paul Londrigan,** Mott Community College; **Ted Valvoda,** Lakeland Community College; and **William Warfeld,** Indiana State University.

A very special acknowledgment goes to Barbara Schatzman and Patrick Batson for their remarkable talents and valuable contributions. Their wealth of real-world experience and creativity helps provide the book with a true reflection of the business world. Our deep gratitutde is extended to Terry Anderson, Jackie Estrada, and Joe Glidden, whose stellar communication and organizational skills aided throughout the preparation of this project.

We wish to extend a sincere appreciation to the devoted professionals at Prentice Hall. They include Sandra Steiner, president; James Boyd, vice president/editorial director; Natalie Anderson, editor-in-chief; Donald Hull, senior editor; all of the Prentice Hall Business Publishing group; product manager Debbie Clare; and the outstanding Prentice Hall sales representatives. Finally, we thank Dee Josephson, managing editor, and Carol Lavis, production editor, for their dedication; we are grateful to photo researcher Melinda Alexander, copyeditor Nancy Marcello, and designer Cheryl Asherman for their superb work.

Michael H. Mescon
Courtland L. Bovée
John V. Thill

GUIDE TO THEMATIC EXAMPLES

SUPPORTING QUALITY INITIATIVES AND ACHIEVING CUSTOMER SATISFACTION

CHAPTER	EXAMPLE	PAGE
9	Japanese motivation techniques treat employees like family	263–264
	Southwest Airlines commitment to employees is a competitive advantage	284
10	Innovative compensation plans improve quality, teamwork, and productivity	308
11	Marriott International reduces employee turnover with its employee friendly policies	346
	Ford builds communication and trust with autoworkers	346–347
	Employee stock ownership gives United Airlines a competitive edge	347
	Xerox employees find innovative ways to cut costs	347
	Unions reinvent themselves to be leaner, more efficient, and more effective	348–349
	Saturn's unique partnership with the United Auto Workers	350
	Labor and management solve problems together at SSI Services	352
12	Database of Asian American immigrants turns flower shop into gold mine	357
	Building relationships with customers pays off	361
	The importance of understanding customers	363–372
	SkyMall gets in trouble because it doesn't understand customers	363
	Saturn knows satisfied customers are the best kind of advertisement	364–365
	The problem with customer satisfaction surveys	365
	Why customers are less loyal today	366
	Customer value disciplines	366–367
	One-to-one marketing	370
	Learn more about customers by storing key customer attributes and preferences in databases	375–376
13	Turning around Continental Airlines	410–411
14	Today's consumer has more choices and information	430–431
	Balancing customer service with distribution costs	432–433
	Sears' transformation—quality and customer service win back shoppers	440–441
15	Catering to different customers at Ikea	445
16	Groupware improves employee collaboration and customer service	497–498
17	Motorola applies TQM to accounting processes	526–527

KEEPING PACE WITH TECHNOLOGY AND THE INTERNET WHILE EMBRACING INNOVATION

CHAPTER	EXAMPLE	PAGE
1	Innovation at Intel	14
	Technology and innovation spur 50 years of global leadership ping-pong	18–20
2	Singapore uses information technology to dramatically increase shipping capacity	33–34
3	Modern technology reduces pollution and waste	74–75
5	Tips for creating a winning Web site	150–151
7	Electronic links allow companies to outsource key functions	200–201
	Costs and benefits of employee e-mail	214–215
	Teleconferencing enables distant employees to hold virtual meetings	215–216

STARTING AND MANAGING A SMALL BUSINESS IN TODAY'S COMPETITIVE ENVIRONMENT

CHAPTER	EXAMPLE	PAGE
1	Ted Waitt started Gateway 2000 with a $10,000 loan from grandmother	1, 24–25
4	Low barriers to entry make many service business start-ups attractive	102–103
	Smaller firms responsible for many technological advances	103
	Choosing the right form of business ownership	104–110
	Mergers and acquisitions are increasing among small businesses	120
	AJ Wraps develops a plan for business growth	123–125
5	Using friends and relatives to finance small business start-ups	131
	Intrapreneurs imitate small business innovative spirit	132–133
	Trends and characteristics of small businesses	132–136
	How entrepreneurs spend their time	133
	Technology levels the playing field for small companies	135
	Downsizing and outsourcing fuel growth in number of small-business start-ups	136
	Minority business owners are fastest-growing segment of small-business economy	136
	Key entrepreneurial success factors	136–138
	Business start-up checklist	139
	Outback Steakhouse's unconventional management strategy	140–141
	Meineke Discount Muffler Shops turn pendulum in franchisees favor	143
	Things to consider before signing a franchise agreement	143–145
	Strict requirements for SBA-backed loans	145–146
	MIT Enterprise Forum's criteria for winning business plans	148
	Rapid success of Grandmother Calendar causes company's own demise	149
	Company size doesn't matter on the Internet	152
	Internet forums are a great resource for small business owners	152
	Gordon Weinberger's entrepreneurial pie odyssey	152–153
	The saga of a small family business—Kiva Container	155–156
	ISO 9000 is tough hurdle for small businesses	156
6	Granite Construction improves customer service through the control cycle	180
7	Simple organization structure for small companies	192
	Technology and outsourcing enable Attainment Marketing Partners to compete with large firms	200–201
8	Smaller firms develop competitive advantages with flexible manufacturing	230–231
9	J.W. Pepper & Son inspires commitment and productivity through work sharing	279–280
12	Small companies like Mi Amore Pizza and Pasta and Speedy Car Wash use marketing databases to track customer purchases	361
13	RDP uses computer modeling to design jewelry—cuts design time by 75 percent	396–397
	Choosing a name for your new company	400–401
14	Independent card shops are victimized by Hallmark's new distribution strategy	420–421
	Fresh Picks outfits supermarkets with CD racks	428
	Amazon.com—the world's smallest and largest bookstore	428
	Cybermalls offer many advantages for small businesses	430–431

CHAPTER	EXAMPLE	PAGE
	Home shopping networks are an effective way to launch your product	431
15	Small companies handle advertising differently from larger organizations	456
17	The Concrete Doctor pumps up revenue by automating accounting and financial systems	534–535
18	Private financing alternatives for small entities	552
	Small corporate offering registrations	553
19	Why many small companies don't pay dividends	575
	E*Trade catches Wall Street flat-footed	588–589
Component B	Managing risk in small companies	626
	Wood Classics underestimated its insurance needs	629
	Zebra Technologies joins insurance cooperative to save money	629

BEHAVING IN AN ETHICALLY AND SOCIALLY RESPONSIBLE MANNER

CHAPTER	EXAMPLE	PAGE
1	Price fixing—who's paying the price?	6
2	Paying bribes is business-as-usual in some countries	50–51
	Understanding the challenges of global corruption	50–51
	The Foreign Corrupt Practices Act; its impact on the ability of U.S. businesses to compete in foreign countries	51–52
3	Finding the balance between profitability, ethics, and social responsibility	64–66
	Businesses must balance the diverse needs of their stakeholders	66–67
	Companies appoint ethics officers and conduct social audits	67
	Socially responsible behavior can improve a company's bottom line	67–70
	Standards for ethical use of the Internet	68–69
	The evolution of social responsibility	68–70
	After paying steep pollution fines, Weyerhaeuser becomes a role model for clean manufacturing	73
	Major Federal environmental and consumer legislation sets standards for business	74–77
	A legal product is not necessarily a safe or an ethical product	78
	Women continue to face discrimination in the workplace	82–83
	Mitsubishi faces the EEOC's largest sexual harassment lawsuit ever	84
	Companies face consumer backlash at home for unfair labor practices abroad	86
	Levi's maintains high ethical standards in tough times	90–91
	Working Assets turns social responsibility into a strategy for success	93–94
4	Companies face lawsuits over misrepresenting financial performance	126–127
6	Common business decisions often carry ethical implications	168–169
9	Employees today want a better balance between work and personal life	276
10	Do background checks on job candidates violate privacy?	297–299
	Compensation differences between CEOs and employees	307
	Many single employees work more but receive fewer benefits than colleagues with families	311–312
	The number of paid vacation days is shrinking for U.S. workers	312
	Xerox employees take paid leaves of absence to work for charities	312

THINKING GLOBALLY AND COMMITTING TO A CULTURALLY DIVERSE WORKFORCE

■ PART I

Introducing Business Today in a Global Environment

CHAPTER 1

FOUNDATIONS AND CHALLENGES OF BUSINESS

OBJECTIVES

After studying this chapter, you will be able to

1 Explain what an economic system is
2 Name the three major types of economic systems and differentiate their identifying characteristics
3 Identify the four major economic roles of the U.S. government
4 List three ways companies compete
5 Explain how supply and demand interact to influence price
6 Name the four factors of production and discuss why they are becoming less of a competitive advantage in the global marketplace
7 Define the gross domestic product and explain what it is used for
8 Identify five trends that will influence the economy in years ahead

ON THE JOB: FACING CHALLENGES AT GATEWAY 2000

From Farm Boy to Billionaire

Computers. The odds are slim you will survive, much less thrive, in this industry. You have to guess what customers will want more than a year in advance, even though technology is changing at an incredibly fast pace. It's hardly a business for cowboys—unless you're Ted Waitt.

Son of a fourth-generation cattle broker, Waitt (currently 34 and worth an estimated $1.7 billion) rides herd over Gateway 2000. They tell stories about Waitt, and not just in Sioux City, South Dakota—Gateway's homeland. They talk about how he built a fortune by trusting his instincts and making gutsy calls that led the industry. How he borrowed $10,000 from his grandmother to start a mail-order computer business, and how he turned a two-man, farmhouse operation into a global giant—in only ten years. And they talk about the pony-tailed farm boy clad in deck shoes and a polo shirt who knew that someday he was going to run his own company.

It all began while Waitt was working for a local computer store; he was amazed by how easy it was to sell computer equipment to knowledgeable computer users over the phone. So in 1985 Waitt (the marketer) teamed up with his buddy Mike Hammond (the technical whiz), and the two started a small mail-order computer business of their own. Waitt and Hammond worked long hours—from their upstairs office in Waitt's family farmhouse.

Their big break came in 1987, when Texas Instruments (TI) decided to stop manufacturing its own computers and instead sell only industry-standard IBM-compatible personal computers (PCs). Of course, owners of TI computers could trade in their equipment for newer IBM-compatible computers, but first they would have to cough up $3,500. Waitt and Hammond knew they could provide the same computer equipment TI was offering—and at a much cheaper price ($1,995). They did this by finding the best deals on cutting-edge computer components, and assembling the components to build top-quality custom PCs. Because all sales were made-to-order and transacted over the phone, Gateway could afford to give customers more computer for their money—a strategy from which the company has never veered.

Within three short years, the company was shipping 225 PCs a day (each one in a black-and-white cow-spotted box), and sales reached $70 million. By 1993 sales topped $1.7 billion, and the company sold its stock to the investing public. In spite of Gateway's speedy trip to the top, the company was at a treacherous intersection. Gateway was run essentially by one guy—Ted Waitt—who relied on his instincts. And the company was getting too big to depend on only one man's judgment. In order to survive in this competitive industry, Gateway would have to find ways to expand its customer base and manage the company's growth.

If you were Ted Waitt, what steps would you take to beef up business? Would you compete on price, speed, quality, or innovation? Would you consider other sales approaches besides telephone selling?[1]

Success in a Free-Market System

business
Activity and enterprise that provides goods and services that an economic system needs

Like Ted Waitt, many people start a new **business**—a profit-seeking activity that provides goods and services that consumers want. In fact, compared with many countries, the United States makes it pretty easy to start a business. All you have to do is change the message on your answering machine, buy a personal computer, create a Web site, or sell computers over the telephone—like Waitt did. In some countries it can take 6 months to create a charter (the equivalent of a U.S. corporation), and the minimum investment needed to start a corporation can be high: $35,000 in Germany and $60,000 in South Korea.[2]

free-market system
Economic system in which the way people spend their money determines which products will be produced and what those products will cost

Of course, starting a new business doesn't guarantee that you'll be successful. That takes plenty of hard work. Many factors contribute to the success of a business—like management, research, innovation, timing, location, product appeal, pricing, money, and customer satisfaction, to name a few. But in a **free-market system,** business owners can influence these factors, for the most part. They are free to charge any price they want and to sell to anyone willing to pay that price. They have the chance to succeed—or fail—by their own efforts. Other economic systems sometimes limit the freedom of choice in order to accomplish government goals.

Types of Economic Systems

economic system
Means by which a society distributes its resources to satisfy its people's needs

An **economic system** is a basic set of rules for allocating a society's resources to satisfy its citizens' needs. The link between economy and society is crucial; every nation's economic system is shaped by its political and social values. Regardless of exactly how each economic system operates, they all compete in the same world economy, and all must deal with the same basic questions: How should limited economic resources be used to satisfy society's needs? What goods and services should be produced? Who should produce them? How should these goods and services be divided among the population? Such questions are addressed differently by the three main economic systems: capitalism, communism, and socialism. The best way to distinguish between these systems is in terms of the freedom they give individuals to pursue their own economic interests. (Keep in mind that even though capitalism, communism, and socialism are discussed here as economic systems, they can be political and social systems as well.)

capitalism
Economic system based on economic freedom and competition

Capitalism Permitting a high degree of individual freedom, **capitalism** owes its philosophical origins to eighteenth-century philosophers such as Adam Smith. According to Smith, in the ideal capitalist economy (pure capitalism), the *market* (an arrangement between buyer and seller to trade goods and services) serves as a self-correcting mechanism—an "invisible hand" to ensure the production of the goods that society wants in the quantities that society wants, without anyone's ever issuing an order of any kind.[3]

Because the market is its own regulator, Smith was opposed to government intervention. He believed that if anyone's prices or wages strayed from acceptable levels that were set for everyone, the force of competition would drive them back. In reality, however, the government sometimes intervenes in business to influence prices and wages or to change the way resources are allocated. This type of intervention is called *mixed capitalism,* and it is the economic system of the United States. Other countries with variations of this economic system include Canada, Germany, and Japan. Under mixed capitalism, private individuals are allowed to determine what is produced, by whom, and for whom. In addition, the pursuit of private gain is regarded as a worthwhile goal that ultimately benefits society as a whole.

profit
Money left over after expenses and taxes have been deducted from revenue generated by selling goods and services

Under mixed capitalism, most firms operate to earn a **profit**—the difference between what it costs to produce something and what customers are willing to pay for it. However, sometimes firms are willing to sacrifice short-term profits for the sake of long-term goals. This strategy is frequently adopted by the Japanese, whose companies are willing (and able) to postpone initial profits in order to keep their prices lower and thereby penetrate global markets to a greater degree. As you can imagine, this is not an easy strategy to implement; you need deep pockets and patient investors.

Of course, not all businesses operate to earn a profit. Some businesses—like museums, schools, public universities, symphonies, libraries, and government agencies—exist to provide a valuable service rather than to make a profit. They are **not-for-profit organizations.** Even though these businesses do not have a profit motive, the business concepts discussed throughout this textbook—such as competition, marketing, finance, quality, and so on—apply to not-for-profit organizations as well.

not-for-profit organization Firm whose primary objective is something other than returning a profit to its owners

Communism The system that allows individuals the least degree of economic freedom is **communism,** which is characterized by (1) state ownership of the factors of production and (2) planned resource allocation. The second feature is so important in these economies that they are frequently called planned economies. In a planned economy, social equality is a major goal, and private enterprise is generally regarded as wasteful and exploitative. Planned economies exist in such countries as North Korea and Cuba.

communism Economic system in which all productive resources are owned and operated by the government, to the elimination of private property

The degree to which communism is actually practiced varies from country to country. In its purest form, almost all resources are under state control. Private ownership is restricted largely to personal and household items. Resource allocation is handled through rigid centralized planning by a handful of government officials who decide what goods to produce, how to produce them, and to whom they should be distributed. Thus the managers of a communist factory produce not what they want but what the plan wants; nor can they shop around for materials, pick and choose customers, hire or fire labor without authorization, or go out to buy an unauthorized lightbulb if one blows out. Everything is arranged by the government.[4]

Socialism The third major type of economic system is **socialism,** which lies somewhere between capitalism and communism in the degree of economic freedom that it permits. Like communism, socialism involves a relatively high degree of government planning and some government ownership of land and capital resources (like buildings and equipment). Unlike communism, government involvement is limited to key industries considered vital to the common welfare, such as transportation, utilities, medicine, steel, and communications. In these industries, the government owns or controls all the facilities and determines what will be produced and how the output will be distributed. Private ownership is permitted in industries that are not considered vital, and both businesses and individuals are allowed to benefit from their own efforts. However, taxes are high in socialist states because the government absorbs the costs of medical care, education, subsidized housing, and other social services. Varying degrees of socialism are practiced today in countries like Mexico and Sweden, but even this is changing.

socialism Economic system characterized by public ownership and operation of key industries combined with private ownership and operation of less vital industries

The Changing Nature of Economic Systems

Although pure communism still has its supporters, the future of communism is dismal. According to economists Lester Thurow and Robert Heilbroner, "it's the plan from above that eventually caused the Soviet communist system to break down. It's a great deal easier to design and assemble the skeleton of a mighty economy than to run it."[5] For example, in a free-market system, mistakes are repaired and remedied as soon as possible because they cost the factory owners money. Thus, suppliers are told to hurry up or hold back on shipments, unprofitable items are canceled, and profitable ones run overtime. None of this happens in a society planned from top to bottom because the pursuit of private gain is nonexistent.

privatization
Trend to substitute private ownership for public ownership

Because of such economic failure and the associated social unrest, the republics that were formerly part of the Soviet Union have now restructured their communist economies by shifting to market-driven systems. Many other planned economies are adopting free-market policies as well. They are selling off their government-owned enterprises to privately held firms to raise badly needed cash or to compete more effectively in the global marketplace. This trend is known as **privatization** and is occurring in countries like Great Britain, Mexico, Argentina, Israel, and France. In fact Israel plans to sell 50 of its 140 government-owned companies over the next 4 years, and the chairman of Air France is hopeful he can convince the French socialist government to privatize the airline.[6] Even Sweden, one of the most committed socialist countries in the world, has been forced to trim its generous social role and push for more market-based competition among businesses, diminishing the role of its government in industry.

Likewise, China is taking steady steps toward a more market-based economy. In spite of hard-line communists who are trying to prevent political reform, China's president wants to convert most of the country's 305,000 state-owned companies into shareholder-owned corporations and open them to foreign competition—while keeping key industries under state control. But turning state-owned enterprises into world-class corporations is a huge task with no blueprint. Even so, China is making progress. In fact, *Business Week* projects that by 2003, one-tenth of all the goods produced in the world will come from developing nations of Asia (including India and China).[7] China's ability to carry out such reform will have a profound impact on the shape of the global economy in the twenty-first century.[8]

Of course, in spite of China's progress, some businesspeople in Hong Kong are concerned. Hong Kong ceased being a British colony in 1997 and was returned to communist China. Many are worried that China's preoccupation with the mainland may well erode

Capitalistic fever is gripping almost every one of Shanghai's 13 million citizens.

the open, internationalist mentality that has long been Hong Kong's chief advantage in Asia. As a result, hundreds of thousands of businesspeople and their families are leaving Hong Kong.[9]

THE ROLE OF GOVERNMENT

Historically, government has played an important role in capitalism. The government collects involuntary taxes to raise funds to provide for public goods like education, national defense, and public highways. In addition, the economy sometimes needs a boost; at other times it needs to be slowed down a bit. That's because although the free-market system generally works well, it's far from perfect. If left unchecked, the economic forces that make capitalism succeed may also create severe problems for some groups or individuals. The solution to these problems often requires governments to intervene by enforcing laws and regulations, fostering competition, contributing to economic stability, and spending for the public good.

Enforcing Laws and Regulations

The U.S. federal government creates thousands of new laws and regulations every year.[10] Moreover, state and local governments are adding their own provisions to the body of regulations that limit what businesses and consumers can and cannot do. Thus the hand of government affects business activities, from applying for permits and licenses to starting a business and all the way through to advertising the product.

Sometimes government laws and regulations restrict the freedom of the marketplace. As a consumer, you can't buy some medications without a doctor's prescription; you can't buy alcoholic beverages without a certificate proving that you're old enough; and you can't buy certain products lacking safety features, such as cars without seatbelts and medication without childproof tops. Some legislation, such as the Clean Air Act and the Nutrition Labeling and Education Act, forced businesses to enact changes that cost millions and perhaps billions of dollars. The burden of regulation falls particularly hard on small companies, which often lack the legal and administrative resources to keep up with new rules. But just as government bodies create new regulations year after year, they sometimes seek to remove or relax existing regulations through the process of **deregulation** in order to foster competition.

Is It True?

The Gulf War cost the United States billions of dollars.

Note: "Answers to 'Is It True?'" are at the end of each chapter.

deregulation
Removal or relaxation of rules and restrictions affecting businesses

Fostering Competition

Competition is the situation in which two or more suppliers of a product are rivals in the pursuit of the same customers. The theoretical ideal is **pure competition,** in which no single firm or group of firms in an industry is large enough to influence prices and thereby distort the workings of the free-market system. In practice, however, pure competition works better in some industries than in others. Compare the dry-cleaning business with the auto industry. The nature of dry cleaning is such that small, independent firms operating on a local level are efficient. This is not the case in the auto industry, in which large manufacturers are favored by **economies of scale** (cost efficiencies made possible by making or buying large quantities of an item).

If you set out to sell a product or service in a free-market society, chances are that someone else will be trying to sell something similar. Most of the competition in advanced free-market economies is **monopolistic competition,** in which a large number of sellers (none of which dominates the market) offers products that can be distinguished from competing products in at least some small way.

competition
Rivalry among businesses for the same customer

pure competition
Situation in which so many buyers and sellers exist that no single buyer or seller can individually influence market prices

economies of scale
Savings from manufacturing, marketing, or buying large quantities

monopolistic competition
Situation in which many sellers differentiate their products from those of competitors in at least some small way

oligopoly
Market dominated by a few producers

When an industry (such as the auto industry) is dominated by just a few producers, it is called an **oligopoly.** Although oligopolies themselves are not illegal, the government has the power to prevent combinations of firms that would reduce competition and lead to oligopolistic conditions in an industry. For example, in 1997 the government opposed the $4 billion merger of Staples and Office Depot, asserting that the combination would substantially impair competition and force consumers to pay higher prices for office supplies.[11] However, months earlier the government allowed Boeing, the world's largest commercial aircraft maker, to purchase McDonnell Douglas, the world's largest military aircraft maker, because the two served different markets.[12]

In addition, the U.S. government prohibits oligopolists from artificially setting prices by agreeing among themselves. This is not the case in many foreign governments like Japan, where company directors hold monthly meetings to strategically plot both the Japanese and U.S. markets. If U.S. executives held such meetings, they would swiftly find themselves in jail or paying steep fines, regardless of what market they were plotting. Look at Archer Daniels Midland (ADM). When executives of that company and three of its competitors pleaded guilty to conspiring to fix prices in the then $454 million global market for lysine (a feed additive), they paid a record $100 million fine.[13]

monopoly
Market in which there are no direct competitors so that one company dominates

Because competition generally benefits the U.S. economy, the government has laws to ensure that no single enterprise becomes too powerful. A **monopoly** is a company that has total control over products and prices and that keeps other companies from competing. (Some monopolies, such as utilities, are legal but closely regulated.) Because true monopolies undermine the principle of competition, they are prohibited by federal antitrust laws and have been a subject of continuing government concern since the turn of the century.

One of the highest-profile antitrust cases of the 1990s involved the software giant Microsoft, which makes both the operating-system software used by most personal computers and a wide array of application software that runs on those operating systems. The

For the world. By the world

The commercial aircraft industry, led by Seattle-based Boeing, is an example of an oligopoly market.

U.S. Justice Department accused Microsoft of using its vast clout with operating systems to give itself an unfair advantage in the application-software business. The Justice Department could have gone as far as splitting the company in two but settled for some relatively minor changes in the demands Microsoft can make on companies that want (or don't want) to buy its operating systems. However, the Justice Department continued to keep a close watch on Microsoft, and in December 1997, a federal judge ordered Microsoft to stop requiring computer makers to install its Internet Explorer Web browser as a condition of licensing the Windows 95 operating system. Competitors such as Netscape had complained that this practice gave Microsoft an unfair advantage in Internet software and online commerce.[14]

Contributing to Economic Stability

Another important role that the U.S. government plays in mixed capitalism is to contribute to the country's economic stability. An economy never stays exactly the same size. Instead, it grows and contracts in response to the combined effects of such factors as technological breakthroughs, changes in investment patterns, shifts in consumer attitudes, world events, and basic economic forces. These up-and-down swings are known as the **business cycle.** Although such swings are natural and to some degree predictable, they cause hardship. During periods of downward swing, or **recession,** consumers buy less, and factories produce less, so companies must lay off workers, who in turn buy less—and so on.

In an attempt to avoid such problems and to foster economic stability, the government can adjust the tax system, the interest rates, and the total amount of money circulating in our economy. These government actions have two facets: **Fiscal policy** involves changes in the government's revenues and expenditures to stimulate or dampen the economy. **Monetary policy** involves adjustments to the nation's money supply by increasing or decreasing interest rates to help control inflation. In the United States, monetary policy is controlled primarily by the Federal Reserve Board, a group of appointed government officials who oversee the country's central banking system. (Monetary policy is discussed more fully in Chapter 18.)

business cycle
Fluctuations in the rate of growth that an economy experiences over a period of several years

recession
Period during which national income, employment, and production all fall

fiscal policy
Use of government revenue collection and spending to influence the business cycle

monetary policy
Government policy and actions taken by the Federal Reserve Board to regulate the nation's money supply

inflation
Economic condition in which prices rise steadily throughout the economy

disinflation
Economic condition in which the rate of inflation declines

Inflation and Disinflation **Inflation** is a steady rise in the prices of goods and services throughout the economy. When prices in the overall economy decline, economists use the term **disinflation.** Although prices in the overall economy tend to increase year after year, not all industries and product categories necessarily follow this trend. In the electronics industry, for instance, technological advances have the opposite effect—prices tend to drop as production increases.

One way economists measure the rate of inflation is by comparing the change in prices of goods and services over a period of time. The *consumer price index (CPI)* is a tool used to measure this price change. Although far from a perfect measure, the CPI keeps track of the prices of a representative basket of goods and services (like clothing, food, housing, and utilities) and applies weights to specific items to account for their relative importance in the market. The problem with this measure is that the representative basket of goods may not accurately represent the prices and consumption patterns of the area in which you live. In addition, the mix in this basket may not include new innovations that become key economic players in the future. Nonetheless, many industries use the CPI to adjust rent increases and employees' wages to keep them in line with the pace of inflation.

Employment and Unemployment When the U.S. economy is strong, it has historically been able to employ about 95 percent of the people who are willing and able to work. During downturns in the business cycle, however, unemployment may become a major economic and social problem. The most extreme case in this century came during the Great Depression of the 1930s, when unemployment affected as much as 25 percent of the labor force.

BEST OF THE WEB

..A tip for finding Web sites:
If you get an error message when you try to get to a site, go to <http://www.inference.com>. Insert the name of the site or the URL in the space provided, and press "search." If the site you're seeking is still operating, the results of this search will usually provide a hot link to it.

What's in the CPI?

The CPI is an important tool that allows us to track the change in prices over time. But the CPI doesn't always match a person's inflation experience. Find out why by visiting the official CPI Web site maintained by the U.S. Bureau of Labor Statistics. Be sure to check out how the CPI measures homeowner's cost, and don't leave without getting some data. Click on the *Most Requested Series*, find your region, and trace the CPI for your area by entering some information in the boxes.
http://stats.bls.gov/cpihome.htm

Spending for the Public Good

Although everybody hates to pay taxes, most of us are willing to admit they're a necessary evil. If the government didn't take your tax money and repair our nation's roads, would you be inclined to fix them yourself? Similarly, it might not be practical to rely on individual demand to provide police and fire protection, or to launch satellites. Instead, the government steps in and supplies such *public goods.*

In addition, U.S. society recognizes that some individuals aren't capable of supplying enough labor to provide themselves a decent standard of living. Instead of individuals each contributing voluntarily to care for these people, the government collects "contributions" in the form of taxes from those who are capable of supporting themselves and distributes the money to the less self-sufficient in the form of **transfer payments** such as Social Security, food stamps, welfare, and unemployment compensation. The individuals who receive these allocations are usually not required to provide any goods or services in return.

transfer payments
Payments by government to individuals that are not made in return for goods and services

The United States is currently facing a problem with spending. For many years the U.S. government has spent more than it takes in. Each year this excess spending creates an annual budget deficit—on the order of several hundred billion dollars (see Exhibit 1.1).

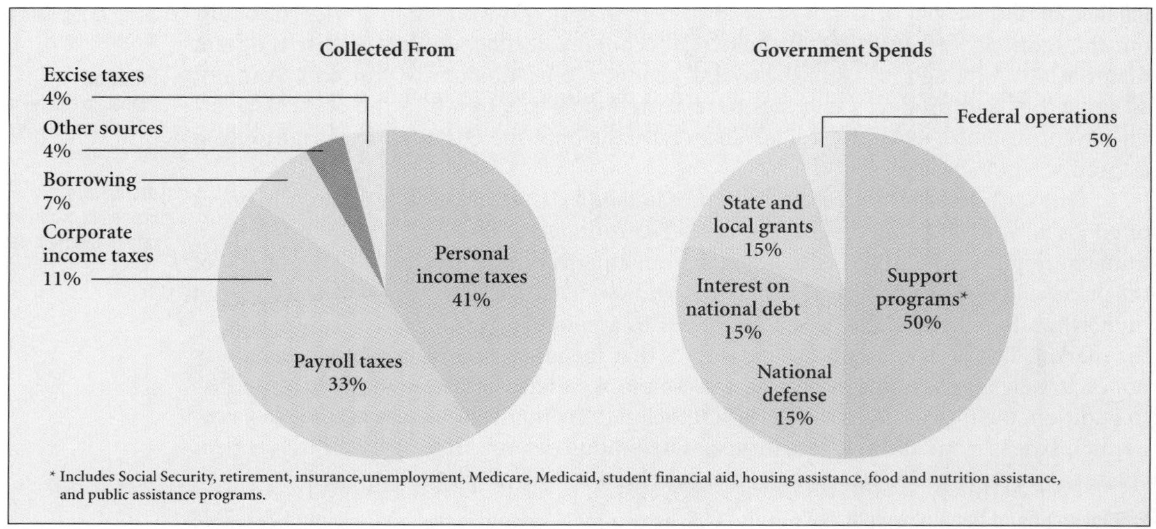

EXHIBIT 1.1

The Federal Dollar

The annual federal budget document for 1998 was 5 volumes and 2,424 pages. Here's a breakdown of the federal dollar—how it's collected and how it's spent.

When combined over time, these deficits have swelled the amount owed by the U.S. government (the national debt) to almost $5 trillion. As a result, interest payments alone on this debt cost U.S. taxpayers $250 billion a year—or $8,000 per second. In 1997 Congress approved a plan to pare down future deficits in order to balance the budget by 2002.[15]

However, reductions in government spending can have rippling consequences. For instance, government spending boosts the economy, and it has a *multiplier effect* as it makes its way through the economy. Here's how it works. If the government decides to fund new highway projects, then thousands of construction people will work on the project and earn wages. If some of these workers decide to spend their extra income to buy new cars, car dealers will have more income. The car dealers, in turn, might spend this income on new clothes, and the sales clerks (who earn commissions) might buy compact disks, and so on. This *circular flow* of money through the economic system shows that all elements of the U.S. economy are linked. Just as the bloodstream carries oxygen to the body's cells and carbon dioxide from those cells back to the lungs, the economy carries goods and services, which are exchanged for money.

BEST OF THE WEB

Learn About Your Benefits

U.S. workers pay a lot of money to the Social Security program each year. Do you know what that money is used for? Why not visit the Social Security Administration (SSA) Web site and satisfy your curiosity. Learn what *FICA* stands for. Find out the real truth to some myths about this program. Begin your discovery now by clicking on the *History of the SSA* (from the SSA home page). Be sure to play some *Fun and Games* before you leave.
http://www.ssa.gov

Economic Forces Affecting Business

For many, the role of government is a reasonably constant fact of economic life—as are such economic forces as competition, supply and demand, and scarcity of resources. Businesspeople take these forces into account when planning how to operate a business, even though they can't control their economic impact. By matching data from recent trends with fundamental economic forces, forecasters try to project trends into the future, but this is becoming more difficult (see Exhibit 1.2). That's because globalization is happening at an unprecedented speed, and it's changing the way we conduct business. Consequently, businesspeople must work smarter today. To compete in the twenty-first century, they must play a new game with new rules. Some will win; others will lose.

Competition

In a free-market economy, customers are free to buy whatever and wherever they please. Therefore, companies must compete with rivals for potential customers. They might choose to compete in one of three ways: price, quality, or innovation.

Competition and Price Southwest Airlines competes on price. It offers the lowest fares of any of its competitors. So does Dell Computer. Each time Compaq loses a sale, it's either because of Dell's low price or because of Hewlett-Packard's and IBM's service and support.[16] In fact, evidence of price competition is everywhere you look. Fast-food restaurants sell special meal deals at reduced prices, Coke sells 24-pak cans at $3.99, carmakers offer rebates and discounts, and stereo stores offer to beat any other price in town. These are all

EXHIBIT 1.2

Facing the Future

Businesspeople can use predictions such as these to devise strategies and get their companies ready for the future.

	1994	2010
Our planet		
World population	5.607 billion	7.32 billion
World economy	$26 trillion	$48 trillion
World trade	$4 trillion	$16.6 trillion
Consumer inflation	4.3 percent	2.5 percent
Average income per capita		
Developed countries	$16,610	$22,802
Emerging market nations	$950	$2,563
Number of nations	192	202
Number of people living in poverty	2.7 billion	3.9 billion
Number of AIDS cases	20 million	38 million
Average number of children per woman	3.2	2.7
Average life expectancy		
Men	63	67
Women	67	71
Work and play		
World telephone lines		
Wired	607 million	1.4 billion
Wireless	34 million	1.3 billion
Personal computers		
Worldwide	150 million	278 million
Desktop computers	132 million	230 million
Mobile computers	18 million	47 million
Communications satellites	1,100	2,260
Cars produced annually		
Developed countries	20 million	30 million
Emerging market nations	8 million	30 million
McDonald's restaurants	14,000	30,000
Credit-card transactions	1.5 trillion	2 trillion
Air-travel miles	1.5 trillion	3 trillion
U.S. golf courses	14,648	16,800
Movie screens		
United States	25,105	74,114
Worldwide	86,902	162,766
U.S. gambling revenues	$39.5 billion	$125.6 billion
What we'll pay		
Dollar's value abroad	1.0	9.33
U.S. single-family home	$153,000	$287,000
Wharton School of Business M.B.A.	$ 84,200	$257,200
Mercedes E320 Sedan	$ 43,975	$ 70,600
Ford Contour	$ 13,310	$ 21,000

competitive advantage
Ability to perform in one or more ways that competitors cannot match

examples of using price to gain a **competitive advantage**—something that sets you apart from your rivals and makes your product more appealing to customers. When markets become filled with competitors and products start to look alike, price often becomes a company's key competitive weapon.

Competing on price seems an obvious and easy choice to make, but the consequences can be devastating to individual companies and to entire industries. During a 3-year period in the early 1990s, price wars caused the U.S. airline industry to lose more money than it had made since the Wright brothers' first flight. The harsh truth of many price wars is that sooner or later, everybody will be selling at a loss. Companies that are vulnerable to price wars are desperately looking for ways to survive. They seem to have only two alternatives: They can structure their company in a way that lets them produce goods or services at a lower cost, or they can find ways to add unique value to their products so that they can compete on something other than price, such as quality, service, or innovation.

Competition, Quality, and Service Dominos Pizza was built on the convenience of home delivery. FedEx's Virtual Order system allows businesses to link their online catalog sales directly with FedEx so that customer orders are automatically shipped and tracked through the FedEx delivery system. Enterprise car rental has blown past its competitors. Instead of massing 10,000 cars at a few dozen airports, Enterprise sets up inexpensive rental offices just about everywhere. And as soon as one branch grows to 150 cars, the company opens another a few miles away. Enterprise's approach is astoundingly simple. If your car breaks down or needs service, Enterprise will provide you with a spare family car right at the dealer's service center. And it bets that you won't be in the mood to quibble about prices. These companies compete on quality and service, and may well end up with a total profit that's equal to or greater than the profit of a business that competes on price.[17]

Competition and Innovation Innovation has always been a way of life at 3M. For nearly a century, 3M's management has fostered creativity and given employees the freedom to take risks and try new ideas. Beginning with the invention of sandpaper in 1904, 3M has produced such staples as masking tape, cellophane tape, magnetic tape, and videotape—not to mention Scotchgard fabric and Post-it Notes.

Innovation not only drives growth, but it can also revolutionize an industry. Think of products like Rollerblades, AbFlex, Atomic hour-glass skis, and Burton & Sims snowboards. Each of these innovations revolutionized the sporting goods industry by creating new market opportunities and market demand.

Supply and Demand

Demand refers to the amount of a good or service that consumers will buy at a given time at various prices. It is the immediate driving force of the economy. On the other hand, **supply** refers to the quantities of a good or service that producers will provide on a particular date at various prices. In other words, *demand* is a shorthand way of describing the behavior of buyers, whereas *supply* refers to the behavior of sellers. Both work together to impose a kind of order on the market system.

demand
Buyer's willingness and ability to purchase products

supply
Specific quantity of a product that the seller is able and willing to provide

On the surface, the theory of supply and demand seems little more than common sense. Consumers would buy more when the price is low and less when the price is high. Producers would offer more when the price is high and less when the price is low. In other

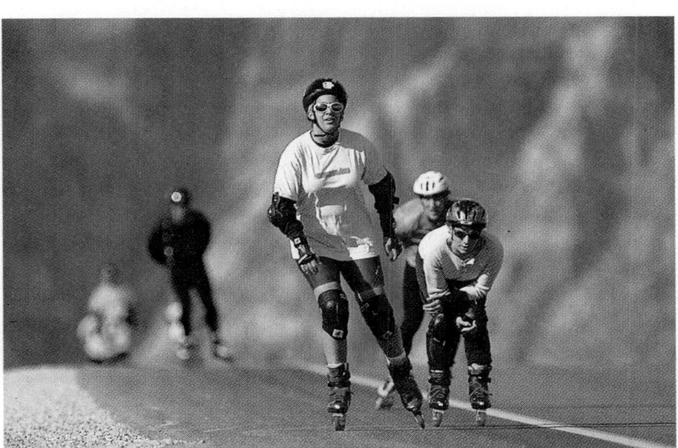

It doesn't take long before innovative products like in-line skates catch on. In fact, just rolling out a "me-too" product in today's competitive marketplace will no longer work. Companies looking to enter the market must bring something new to the table to survive.

words, the quantity supplied and the quantity demanded would continuously interact, and the balance between them at any given moment would be reflected by the current price on the open market.

However, a quick look at any real-life market situation shows you that pricing isn't that simple. To a large degree, pricing depends on the type of product being sold. When the price of gasoline goes up, consumers may cut down a little, but most won't stop driving, even if the price were to double. In the same way, you're not going to stop taking your medicine just because the price goes up—and you wouldn't take more just because the price happened to go down. Likewise, suppose a rise in airline ticket prices sets off rumors that prices will rise even more. You might witness a mad rush for available seats forcing the prices to rise higher still.

Nevertheless, in broad terms, supply and demand regulate a free-market system by determining what is produced and in what amounts. For example, a movie studio might produce more comedies if ticket sales for similar films are brisk. On the other hand, it might decide to produce fewer comedies and more action adventure movies if attendance at comedies lags. The result of such decisions—in theory, at least—is that consumers will get what they want and producers will earn a profit by keeping up with public demand.

Buyer's Perspective The forces of supply and demand determine the market price for products and services. Say that you're shopping for blue jeans, and the pair you want is priced at $35. This is more than you can afford, so you don't make the purchase. When the store puts them on sale the following week for $18, however, you run right in and buy a pair.

But what if the store had to buy the jeans from the manufacturer for $20. It would have made a profit selling them to you for $35, but it would lose money selling them for $18. What if the store asks to buy more from the manufacturer at $10 or $15 but the manufacturer refuses? Is there a price that will make both the supplier and the customer happy? The answer is yes—the price at which the number of jeans demanded equals the number supplied.

This relationship is shown in Exhibit 1.3. A range of possible prices is listed vertically at the left of the graph, with the lowest at the bottom and the highest at the top. Quantity of blue jeans is represented along the horizontal axis. The points plotted on the curve labeled **D** indicate that on a given day the store would sell 10 pairs of jeans if they were priced at $35, 15 pairs if they were priced at $27, and so on. The curve that describes this relationship between price and quantity demanded is a **demand curve.** (Demand curves are not necessarily curved; they may be straight lines.)

demand curve
Graph of relationship between various prices and the quantity demanded at each price

EXHIBIT 1.3

The Relationship Between Supply and Demand

In a free-market system, prices aren't set by the government; nor do producers alone have the final say. Instead, prices reflect the interaction of supply (**S**) and demand (**D**). The equilibrium price (**E**) is established when the amount of a product that producers are willing to sell at a given price equals the amount that consumers are willing to buy at that price.

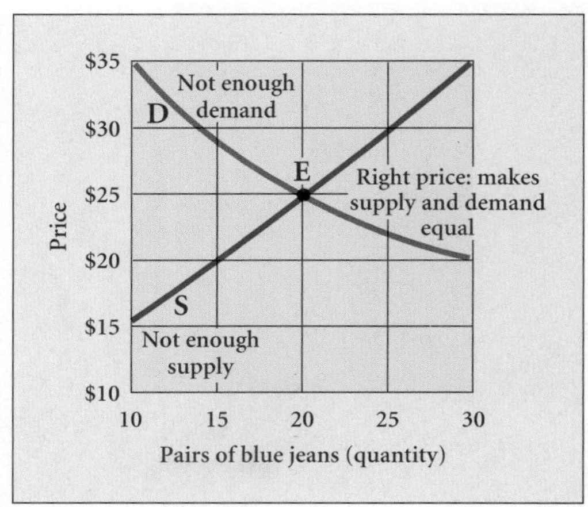

Seller's Perspective Now think about the situation from the seller's point of view. In general, the more profit the store can make on a particular item, the more of that item it will want to sell. This relationship can also be depicted graphically. Again, look at Exhibit 1.3. The line labeled **S** shows that the store would be willing to offer 30 pairs of jeans at $35, 25 pairs at $30, and so on. The store's willingness to carry the item increases as the price it can charge and its profit potential per item increase. In other words, as price goes up, quantity supplied goes up. The line tracing the relationship between price and quantity supplied is called a **supply curve.**

supply curve
Graph of relationship between various prices and the quantity supplied at each price

As much as the store would like to sell 30 pairs of jeans at $35, you and your fellow consumers are likely to want only 10 pairs at that price. If the store offered 30 pairs, therefore, it would probably be stuck with some that it would have to mark down. How does the store avoid this problem? It looks for the point at which the demand curve and the supply curve intersect, the point at which the intentions of buyers and sellers coincide. The point marked **E** in Exhibit 1.3 shows that when jeans are priced at $25, consumers are willing to buy 20 pairs of them and the store is willing to sell 20 pairs. In other words, at the price of $25, supply and demand are in balance. The price at this point is known as the **equilibrium price.**

equilibrium price
Point at which quantity supplied equals quantity demanded

Note that this intersection represents both a specific price—$25 in our example—and a specific quantity of goods—here, 20 pairs of jeans. It is also tied to a specific point in time. Note also that it is the mutual interaction between demand and supply that determines the equilibrium price. In a purely free-market economy, no outside interference disrupts that interaction.

As time passes, equilibrium points between supply and demand may shift. In the blue-jeans business, clothing styles may change or other retailers may mark down their jeans and attract your customers. When supply and demand shift, you need to reevaluate the profit potential of the jeans and adjust your buying and pricing policies accordingly.

Increasing supply to meet demand is not always easy. A company's productivity is often determined by its access to resources, its stock of machinery, the skills and talents of its people, and overall morale. Often these are not controllable factors. For example, what if Ted Waitt could not find enough skilled employees to assemble Gateway computers? What if the equipment used in Gateway's assembly operation were obsolete? Or what if Waitt wasn't willing to take the necessary risks to start his business in the first place? Labor, equipment, and risk takers are inputs that all societies use to produce goods and services. Economists call these inputs **factors of production.**

factors of production
Basic inputs that a society uses to produce goods and services, including natural resources, labor, capital, and entrepreneurship

Guessing consumer demand is tricky, and mistakes are costly—especially when selling to this group of young adults. Tired of being labeled Generation Xers, these 18- to 24-year-old buyers are some of the most complex and savvy consumers in today's marketplace.

GAINING THE COMPETITIVE EDGE

Intel Is Betting Its "Chips" on Demand

Speed. Power. Today's computers have plenty of it. But for Andy Grove, chairman of Intel, there's never enough. So Grove's entire company depends on the fact that you'll want more speed and power too. Consider this. It cost $2 billion to build a new Intel chip plant, or "fab," and the company builds a new one every nine months. That's two years in advance of needing them and long before the company knows whether the industry is going to grow. "Our fabs are fields of dreams. We build them and hope people will come," says Grove. But this could stop.

For years Intel held to the high ground, pushing pricey chips that could run the newest, coolest software, and lowering their price only after demand subsided. But Compaq changed everything overnight when it began hawking powerful, dirt-cheap computers using a rival's chip. A new class of sub-$1,000 PCs opened the doors to competitors and forced Intel to lower its prices. Intel responded by offering unique chip designs for each market. Still Grove knows that he will have to increase sales to compensate for lower profits. But how? "From here on," declares Grove, "Intel will create the demand."

Grove wants to make the PC the central appliance in your life. He wants you to use it to watch TV, play complex games on the Internet, store and edit family photos, manage the appliances in your home, and stay in regular video contact with family, friends, and co-workers. If Grove's vision comes to pass, Intel will thrive; if not, it will fall apart. That's why he's willing to spend more than $500 million for projects that contribute to market development and demand—even though they have nothing to do with microprocessors.

For example, Intel Architecture Labs (IAL) employs 600 programmers whose primary function is to expand the market for all products, not just Intel. Many of the labs' projects involve creating new software—like IAL's new add-in circuit card that enables a computer to broadcast video. But guess what—the card will work properly only with a fast microprocessor. Or consider Intel's software for Internet videophones. This kind of innovation could persuade computer users to keep paying $1,500 or more every few years for a new PC.

Intel has even invested big money in some 50 new companies like Digital Planet, which creates virtual communities on the Internet, or OZ Interactive, a Web browser that lets you walk around in 3-D spaces and meet other people. Grove is even willing to spend on some pretty esoteric projects if they have a chance of sparking demand for the processing power only Intel can provide. After all, Intel builds large factories and must create the demand to fill them.

QUESTIONS FOR CRITICAL THINKING

1. Why would Intel want to invest in companies whose primary function is to expand the market for *all* computer products?
2. Using the concept of supply and demand, explain why Intel decided to lower the price of its computer chips faster than usual.

natural resources
Land, forests, minerals, water, and other tangible assets usable in their natural state

human resources
Organization's employees

capital
The physical, human-made elements used to produce goods and services, such as factories and computers; can also refer to the funds that finance the operations of a business

entrepreneurs
People who accept the risk of failure in the private enterprise system

Factors of Production

Historically, individuals, firms, and countries become rich if they possess more of the following four factors of production than their competitors:

- **Natural resources**—things that are useful in their natural state, such as land, forests, minerals, and water
- **Human resources**—anyone (from company presidents to grocery clerks) who works to produce goods and services
- **Capital**—resources (such as money, computers, machines, tools, and buildings) that a business needs to produce goods and services
- **Entrepreneurs**—people like Ted Waitt who are willing to take risks to create and operate businesses

In the past, putting some combination of these four factors together with reasonable management was the route to success. In fact, historians trace much of U.S. economic success to a combination of the country's cheap, plentiful, well-located raw materials and farmland; its supportive environment for entrepreneurship; and its compulsory public education system (see Exhibit 1.4). Together these factors have given the United States an economic edge.[18]

Today, new technologies and modern transportation allow companies like electronic-connector manufacturer Molex to draw their supplies from one part of the world, locate their production facilities in another, and sell their products in a third. As a result, the natural resources factor, for all practical purposes, has dropped out of the competitive equation: Having natural resources is not the way to become rich, and not having them is not a barrier to becoming rich. For example, even though the Japanese have the world's best steel industry, they have neither iron ore nor coal.

Likewise, businesses today can shop around the world for labor. Many U.S. computer-software factories have opened up offices in India, and some insurance companies process their claims in the Caribbean. In addition, many businesses today no longer require

EXHIBIT 1.4

Rags to Riches

Not all start-up companies are resource rich. In fact, sometimes companies become great because ingenuity is substituted for capital.

THE COMPANY	ITS START
Clorox	In May 1913, five men pooled $100 each and started Clorox. The group had no experience in bleach-making chemistry but suspected that the brine found in salt ponds in San Francisco Bay could be converted into bleach.
The Limited	In 1963, 26-year-old Leslie Wexner left his family's retail store after having an argument with his father. He opened one small store in a strip mall in Columbus, Ohio. Today the company operates more than 5000 stores in the United States.
Gateway 2000	Using $10,000 he borrowed from his grandmother, Ted Waitt started the company in his father's South Dakota barn in 1985. Because a typical computer-industry campaign would have been too costly, Waitt invented its now-famous faux-cowhide boxes. Today Gateway's revenues exceed $5 billion.
Coca-Cola	Pharmacist John Pemberton invented a soft drink in his backyard in 1886. Asa Chandler bought the company for $2,300 in 1891. Today it is worth over $170 billion.
E & J Gallo Winery	The brothers invested $6,000 but had no wine-making experience when they rented their first warehouse in California. They learned wine making by studying pamphlets at the local library.
Marriott	Willard Marriott and his fiancee/partner started a 9-seat A&W soda fountain with $3,000 in 1927. They demonstrated a knack for hospitality and clever marketing from the beginning.
Nike	In the early 1960s, Philip Knight and his college track coach sold imported Japanese sneakers from the trunk of a station wagon. Start-up costs totaled $1,000.
United Parcel Service	In 1907 two Seattle teenagers pooled their cash, came up with $100, and began a message and parcel delivery service for local merchants.
William Wrigley Jr.	In 1891 young Wrigley Jr. started selling baking soda in Chicago. To entice new customers, he threw in two packages of chewing gum with every sale. Guess what the customers were more excited about?
FedEx	In 1971 Fred Smith started a bicycle messenger service pedaling packages around Memphis. In 1973 a customer requested next-day delivery to Knoxville, Tennessee; Smith agreed, unsure of how he'd do it.

heavy investments in plants and equipment. Consider Amazon.com, the Internet bookstore. Even though this multimillion-dollar business employs 110 people, the company keeps very little inventory in its warehouse—yet it claims to be the world's biggest bookstore. That's because Amazon is a virtual store; it exists only on the Internet. Amazon's customers search a database of over 1 million books by title, author, subject, or key word. If they find a book they want to buy, they use online forms to order it. Then Amazon requests the books from a distributor or publisher, which will deliver them to the company's warehouse in Seattle, and the order is immediately packed and shipped to the customer.[19]

Even a country full of inventors has no guaranteed success. In the past, countries with new products were the economic winners. Yet today, new products can be easily reproduced. The Americans invented video cameras and the fax machine. The Dutch invented the CD player. But measured in terms of sales, employment, and profits, all three have become Japanese products. The moral of the story is clear. Those who can make a product cheaper can take it away from the inventor. Today the historical factors of production are being superseded by one key economic resource—knowledgeable workers.[20]

How important will knowledgeable workers be in the future? Consider this: Economists agree that the seven key industries of the next few decades will be microelectronics, biotechnology, composite materials, telecommunications, civilian aviation, robotics, and computers plus software.[21] All of these are brainpower industries. Each could be located anywhere in the world. Of course, Microsoft recognizes this. The company has never needed other people's money to expand, yet in 1986, the company sold *stock* (shares of ownership) so that the company could share its success with its employees by making them part owners. Why? Because Microsoft knows that its employees create the company's key property—lines and lines of software code. And Microsoft recognizes that its employees own the company's most important asset—the knowledge of how to write more code.[22] Furthermore, Microsoft recognizes that knowledgeable workers own the means of production and can easily move from company to company or country to country.

Even if a country is rich in industry and knowledgeable workers, how do economists evaluate whether a government's policies and economic systems are working? And how do they compare the performance of one nation to another? One way to measure the productivity of a nation is to see whether the goods and services it produces are more or less than what was produced in the past.

Economic Measurements

macroeconomics
Study of the economy as a whole

microeconomics
Study of specific entities in the economy, such as households, companies, or industries

In order to evaluate a country's performance, economists view the business world at two levels: **Macroeconomics** deals with the "big picture," as if looking down at a country from a plane. On the other hand, **microeconomics** focuses on the specific details of the economy—like companies, households, or industries. For example, we might want to examine how a change in price would affect the demand for a product, or we might want to look at the relationship between the number of new businesses started and the availability of resources such as labor or supplies.

Sometimes economists want to know which country is the most productive. So they try to keep economic score, as if it were a contest. One way to do this is by computing a nation's gross domestic product.

gross domestic product (GDP)
Dollar value of all the final goods and services produced by businesses located within a nation's borders; excludes receipts from overseas operations of domestic companies

Computation of the Gross Domestic Product **Gross domestic product (GDP)** is the sum of all goods and services produced for final use in a market during a specified period (usually a year). The goods may be produced by either domestic or foreign companies as long as these companies are located within a nation's boundaries. So sales from a Honda assembly plant in California would be included in the GDP. Another less popular measure is the

gross national product (GNP). This measure excludes the value of production from foreign-owned businesses within a nation's boundaries (like Honda U.S.), but it includes receipts from the overseas operations of domestic companies—like McDonald's in Switzerland. Put another way, GNP considers *who* is responsible for the production; GDP considers *where* the production occurs.

gross national product (GNP)
Dollar value of all the final goods and services produced by domestic businesses including receipts from overseas operations; excludes receipts from foreign-owned businesses within a nation's borders

One way to understand the calculation of the GDP is to visualize our economy as a river of outputs from farms, factories, offices, and agencies. This river is then divided into four separate streams:

- *Consumption products*—goods and services bought mostly by households for their personal use or consumption (such as cars, haircuts, jewelry, and meat).
- *Investment goods*—goods that are not consumed but used mostly by businesses (such as machines, trucks, office buildings, and office furniture). These goods typically last a long time and are replaced when they wear out.
- *Government spending*—the amount of money spent by the government, excluding transfer payments (which are made for social purposes such as Social Security, unemployment compensation, and subsidies of various kinds).
- *Net exports*—the amount of production sold abroad minus the amount of foreign production brought in.

When we compute GDP, the output from each of these four streams is totaled separately (as if they pass through four separate, imaginary dams) and then combined to produce an aggregate figure. This total is then divided by a nation's population to produce a per capita figure in order to account for the different population sizes of nations.

Uses of the Gross Domestic Product In the United States,,government policymakers and businesspeople use the GDP to forecast trends and to analyze the economy's performance. But some complain that the GDP (as well as GNP) are misleading because their computations do not include output for which money does not change hands—such as voluntary and charitable work, or the underground economy (income that is legal but not reported to the government). In addition, using the GDP to calculate a nation's wealth can be misleading. For example, a nation can pollute the clean air and then spend money cleaning it up, all of which the GDP would count as an increase in the nation's wealth—but which would certainly not indicate how comfortable or well off that nation's people are.

Economists point out that the GDP was never meant to measure quality of life, nor does it measure a country's ability to keep producing in the future.[23] Like many economic measures (including the CPI), the GDP and GNP are only gauges—tools for comparison. Although far from perfect, they allow a nation to evaluate its economic policies and compare its current performance to prior periods or to the performance of other nations (see Exhibit 1.5). For example, the Institute of Management Development (IMD) uses the GDP to evaluate world competitiveness and rank nations accordingly. For the past 5 years, the United States has been ranked number one by that measure, which has not always been the case.[24]

U.S. Economic Growth and the Challenges Ahead

By any objective measure, the U.S. economy is thriving today. GDP, jobs, trade, output productivity, and purchasing power all show the United States in the midst of a robust expansion. New technologies, the end of the Cold War, and industry reinvention have put the United States back in the driver's seat. However, a look into the history of the country's economic growth will show that getting there has been a long journey and a very rough ride.

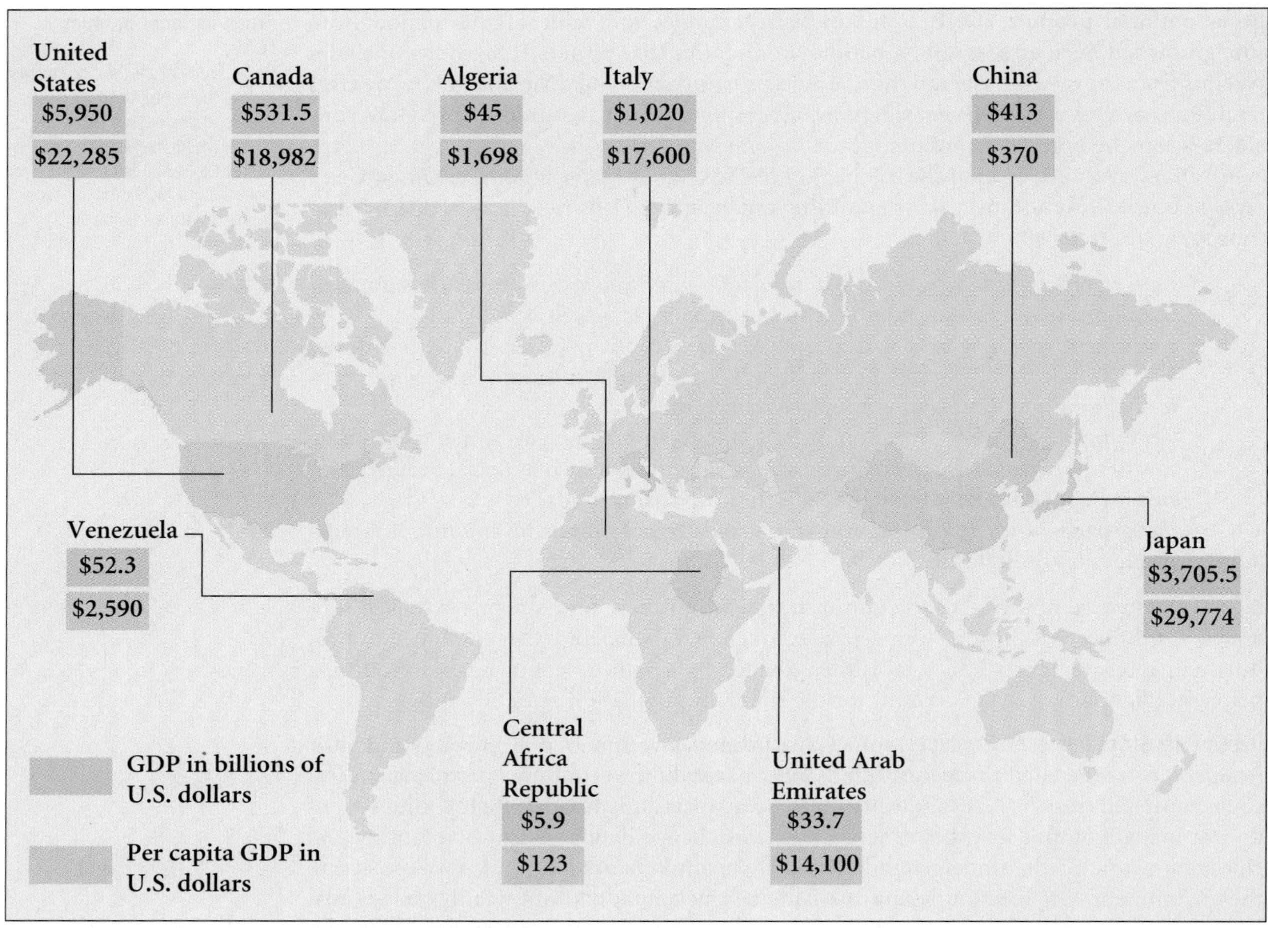

EXHIBIT 1.5

Total and Per Capita GDP in Ten Nations

The free-market system is one of the factors that contributes to the productivity of a nation, as measured by per capita GDP.

Is It True?

The median household income in the United States is increasing.

History of U.S. Economic Growth

The first economic base in the United States was the small family farm. People grew enough food for their families and used any surplus to trade for necessary goods provided by independent craftspeople and merchants. Business operated on a small scale, and much of the population was self-employed. With fertile, flat terrain and adequate rainfall, farmers soon prospered, and their prosperity spread to the townspeople who served them.

In the early nineteenth century, people began making greater use of the rivers, harbors, and rich mineral deposits. Excellent natural resources helped businesspeople accumulate the capital they needed to increase production—fueling the transition of the United States from a farm-based economy to an industrial economy.

technology
Knowledge, tools, techniques, and activities used in the production of goods and services

Age of the Entrepreneur: 1900 to 1944 During the nineteenth century, people in the United States were encouraged to take risks and become entrepreneurs. Businesses prospered in the United States as entrepreneurs industrialized by bringing together labor, capital, and **technology** (the knowledge and processes used in the production of goods and services). As a result, the scale of business began to shift. Millions of new workers came to the United States from abroad, fueling the trend toward mass production. Independent craftspeople were replaced by large-scale factories in which each person did one simple task over and over.

As businesses increased in size, they increased in power. More and more industrial assets were concentrated in fewer and fewer hands, putting smaller competitors, workers, and consumers at a disadvantage. By popular mandate, the government passed laws and regulations to prevent the abuse of power by big business. At the same time, workers began to organize into unions to balance the power of their employers. Meanwhile, U.S. businesses enjoyed such an enormously diverse market within its borders that they didn't need to trade overseas.

The era that began with big savings accounts soon witnessed one of the worst financial panics and the Great Depression of the 1930s—throwing millions of people out of work. By 1941, one in ten workers remained unemployed, the birthrate was stagnant, and the hand of the government strengthened as people lost confidence in the power of business to pull the country out of hard times.

Postwar Golden Era: 1945 to 1979 World War II and the postwar reconstruction revived the economy and renewed the trend toward large-scale enterprises. Anyone with a bit of capital could rent a brick building and pay immigrants to make shirts or shoes. The GI bill opened advanced education to the working classes. The middle class grew and prospered. By 1950 the birthrate jumped, and the baby boom was on.

Accustomed to playing a major role in the war effort, the government continued to exert a large measure of control over business and the economy. President Eisenhower's highway system fueled expansion and the growth of the suburbs. American cars ruled the roads. Stimulated by a boom in world demand and an expansive political climate, the United States prospered throughout the 1960s. Expanding world trade provided limitless markets for U.S. goods. General Electric found ready markets abroad for its televisions and toasters, IBM sold electric typewriters, and Coca-Cola took the world by storm. Then the world recovered from the war and began challenging U.S. industries—Italy with shoes, Switzerland with watches, and Japan with cameras. By the end of the 1960s, Japanese transistor radios dominated the world market, but the more advanced technological industries and their products—televisions, copying machines, and aircraft—remained U.S. preserves.

In the early 1970s inflation depressed demand and economic growth began to slump. In 1973 the price of oil went from $3 to $11 per barrel. This forced companies to invest in ways to save energy instead of investing in new equipment. The U.S. economy barely recovered from the 1973 oil shock when it got hit again in 1979 (oil jumped from $13 to $23 per barrel), resulting in galloping inflation and sky-high interest rates. Exports from Asia began to pour into the United States—some bearing U.S. labels—and U.S. companies shifted production abroad. Western Europe and Japan gradually grew stronger. Auto companies continued to manufacture larger cars (despite customer preferences for smaller cars), and the United States entered an era of diminishing growth.[25]

Rise of Global Competition: 1980s During the 1980s global competition crept up slowly on the United States. Since the 1950s, Japanese firms had been refining their manufacturing processes and by 1980 they had a 30-year head start on the United States. (Ironically, the United States had supplied its foreign competitors with the resources and know-how to stake a claim in the world marketplace.) Meanwhile, U.S. goods were expensive and foreign goods were dirt cheap. So while U.S. manufacturers took it on the chin, Japanese machines hummed even faster. Sony introduced the Walkman and the compact disk player. *Time* magazine put the VCR on its cover. One day Indonesia was making sweaters; the next, it was making semiconductors. By the mid-1980s, it became almost impossible to buy a consumer electronic device that was made in the United States.

Today, CDs account for roughly 75 percent of the market for recorded music. Many consumers own multiple CD players and listen to their favorite recording artists in their cars, homes, offices, or wherever they go, thanks to portable CD players.

In the mid-1980s foreign companies began to buy up U.S. assets. Sony opened factories in the United States, and suddenly the global economy was setting up shop inside U.S. borders. IBM was driving toward the future while looking out the rearview mirror, and Eastern Airlines fell asleep at the wheel. Some giant corporations gobbled up one another; others splintered into fragments. And hundreds of thousands of jobs were eliminated. During this period of upheaval, a subtle shift occurred. Small companies began reasserting their role in the economy, generating new jobs to employ some of the workers abandoned by large corporations.

Decade of Reinvention: 1990s In 1991 the U.S. economy went into full-blown recession. Companies that had loaded up on debt in the 1980s went bankrupt. Unemployment soared. General Motors layoffs numbered 130,000 workers—enough to fill two football stadiums. Had the United States continued in the direction it was headed at the beginning of the 1990s, it might well have experienced the disaster that many economists feared. But it didn't. Motorola struck back with its pagers. Hewlett-Packard took over the high-volume market in low-cost printers, and once-sleepy Kodak challenged the Japanese with digital and disposable cameras.[26]

Today, many U.S. companies have reasserted themselves through improved product quality and a focus on productivity. The computer industry, one of the largest segments of the global economy, is led by U.S. companies such as Compaq. The U.S. auto industry, led by Chrysler and Ford, has pushed itself through a remarkable turnaround and is poised for a positive future. The vast U.S. service sector is also reaching around the world, offering banking, telecommunications, and other services to a growing list of customers. In short, the economic revival of the United States is broad based and has taken the world by storm.

The Challenges Ahead

Even though the United States is beginning a new century with a position second to none, it has lost the big lead it once had in the twentieth century. Doing business in the twenty-first century means working in a world of increasing uncertainty as the very nature of work, organizations, and economics is changing. Businesses today are already facing a raft of new challenges. In the coming chapters we will explore many of these challenges in greater depth and provide real-life examples of how companies are meeting these challenges and dealing with them on a daily basis.

Supporting Quality Initiatives and Achieving Customer Satisfaction Competitiveness today means speed and quality. For many businesses like Gateway 2000, the challenge in the future will

EXPLORING GLOBAL BUSINESS

Doing Everybody's Wash—Whirlpool's Global Lesson

Everybody is talking about going global these days, but most people don't understand what it really means. As chairman and CEO of Whirlpool David Whitman does. In less than a decade, Whirlpool has gone from being essentially a U.S. company to being a global company—manufacturing 12 major brands in 140 countries.

It all started with Whirlpool's purchase of N. V. Philips's floundering European appliance business in 1989. Whitman could have chosen to "fix" Philips by cutting costs and changing operations. After all, Wall Street analysts expected the company to ship 500 people over to Europe, plug them into the plants, and turn the business around within 6 months to a year by imposing the "superior American way" of operating on the European operation. Instead Whitman followed a more ambitious path.

Whitman knew that sooner or later the appliance industry would become global. He had three choices: Ignore the inevitable and condemn Whirlpool to a slow death, wait for globalization to begin before reacting and put Whirlpool in catch-up mode, or control the company's own destiny and shape the very nature of the industry. Whitman chose to lead the industry. But first Whirlpool had to find a way to marry its feature-rich German products with its efficient, low-cost Italian products, and then use this technology in its North American products.

At first, Whitman sent the engineers and manufacturing people from the United States to Europe. However, the engineers spent all their time walking around the plants and saying to themselves, "We do all of these things better at home." Of course the Europeans who toured the U.S. facilities had the same parochial attitude. As a result, neither group spent any time looking at what they could learn from each other. So Whitman took 150 senior managers to Montreux, Switzerland, where they spent one week developing the company's global vision. Then he made those 150 people responsible for educating all 38,000 employees around the world. Instead of imposing one approach on the entire organization, the company created cross-cultural teams with members from Europe and North America, and together they examined operations and designed a program for ensuring quality—one of the best programs in the world.

Still, Whitman knew that selling products in the European market would pose many new challenges—like the need to customize products for the various European countries. For instance, clothes washers sold in northern countries like Denmark must spin dry clothes much better than those sold in southern Italy, where consumers often line dry clothes in warmer weather. Whitman was also caught off guard by the poor economic conditions in Europe, which forced consumers to buy cheaper appliances—cutting into Whirlpool's profit. So instead of piling up the profits, Whirlpool racked up big losses. And the process of going global became a learning experience from top to bottom—ending with the entire restructuring of Whirlpool's business.

For instance, prior to the restructuring, Whirlpool had always thought of itself as being in the refrigerator business or the washing-machine business or the range business. But today Whirlpool is in "the fabric-care business" and the "food-preparation business." As a result, the company is studying consumer behavior from the time people take off their dirty clothes at night until the clothes have been cleaned, ironed, and hung in the closet. "The hard part," notes Whitman, "is when you take your clothes out of the dryer and you have to do something with them—iron, fold, hang them up." And by using insulation technology from its European business, compressor technology from its Brazilian affiliate, and manufacturing design expertise from its U.S. operations, who knows—maybe someday Whirlpool will solve that problem too.

QUESTIONS FOR CRITICAL THINKING

1. What are some of the advantages of doing business overseas?
2. How did global expansion affect Whirlpool's products?

be to compete on the basis of *time* (getting products to market sooner), *quality* (doing a better job of meeting customer expectations), and *customer satisfaction* (making sure buyers are happy with every aspect of the purchase, from the shopping experience until they're through using the product).

Keeping Pace with Technology and the Internet While Embracing Innovation Everywhere we look today, powerful new forces are reshaping the world. For the most part, these forces are technological. Each day millions of transactions zip across computers all over the world. It takes only seconds to transmit hundreds of pages from Australia to the United States. And it's almost impossible to keep up with what *is,* let alone what *will be.*

Companies are spending billions of dollars on computer-based information systems to collect, organize, and use information more effectively. In fact, information technology (technology used in computer-based information systems) accounts for a quarter to a third of today's economic growth.[27] Not only does the world contain a vast amount of information, but that amount roughly doubles every 2 years. Managing information effectively, integrating technology into processes, innovating, offering things in different ways, and using the Internet as a creative resource to expand one's market—these are challenges that all businesses will need to tackle to compete successfully in the future.

Is It True?

The labor-saving devices and technology we have at home today reduce the amount of time spent on household chores.

Starting and Managing a Small Business in Today's Competitive Environment Small business owners are a growing and powerful economic force. But starting a new business or successfully managing a small company in today's global economy will require creativity and a willingness to exploit new opportunities. Small companies often lack the sheer resources to buffer them from competition. That's why their biggest challenge is to find a position or make a product that is hard to imitate—or that competitors choose not to imitate—because if something is easy for the large competitors to do, they will.

Using technology to level the playing field, meeting an unsatisfied consumer need through better service or a higher-quality product, and thinking globally are some of the ways small businesses can compete successfully against industry Goliaths. Many are already meeting this challenge.

Behaving in an Ethically and Socially Responsible Manner As businesses become more complex through global expansion and technological change, they face an increasing variety of ethical issues, from the marketing of unhealthful products to the questionable tactics used in computing financial results. Environmental issues are high on the list of consumer concerns, and many businesses today get blamed for causing environmental troubles. The horrific pollution problems in the former communist countries illustrate how a healthy environment and a healthy economy are not only compatible but interdependent. In the future, businesses can expect continued pressure from both environmental groups and government regulators to act responsibly.

Thinking Globally and Committing to a Culturally Diverse Work Force Experts agree that the skills of the labor force are going to be the key competitive weapon in the twenty-first century. The U.S. Labor Department estimates that service organizations will create 20 million jobs in the next 10 years; after home health care, information services will grow fastest. In contrast, manufacturing will shed about 40,000 jobs per year.[28]

BEST OF THE WEB

Find the Right Stuff

Getting information on a specific company can be a challenge, especially if you don't know where to begin. One of the best starting points is Hoover's Online. This Web site provides an incredible gateway to over 10,000 companies and provides their latest information (such as profiles, financial, history, and current events). So log on and do some power searching. Type in the full name of a company and check it out. Be sure to explore the *Other Features* such as the *List of Lists.* You might want to read about some of the emerging companies.
http://www.hoovers.com

OUT WITH	IN WITH
Bigness	Smallness
Stability	Change
Predictability	Uncertainty
Continuity	Flexibility
Hierarchy	Empowerment
Mass production	Specialty shops
Hiring	Outsourcing and contracting
Production orientation	Customer orientation
Unionization	Independent contracting
Seniority an asset	Seniority a liability
Management	Leadership
Human labor	Automation
Middle managers	Computers
9-to-5 work schedules	Telecommuting
Gold as currency	Information as currency

EXHIBIT 1.6

Bracing for the Twenty-first Century

Job definitions and responsibilities will change dramatically in the twenty-first century as technology advances.

Computers and sophisticated telecommunications equipment make it possible for employees to work in scattered locations. Tomorrow's workers will be freelancers, contractors, and analysts-for-hire. Their work will be brain-intensive instead of labor-intensive (see Exhibit 1.6). And they will be more diverse in race, gender, age, physical and mental abilities, lifestyles, culture, education, ideas, and backgrounds. Corporate commitment to employee diversity will require programs such as those enacted by Wisconsin Power and Light, and Xerox. These companies view diversity as something more than a moral imperative or business necessity. They see it as a business opportunity—a competitive edge.[29]

Globalization will not only change the way we work but also open new markets for our goods and services. As companies continue to expand overseas, the economies of the world will continue to merge, and the lines between exports and imports will blur. It's already difficult to define just what "U.S. car" means when so many parts come from other countries. The companies that will boom in the future are not the ones that insulate themselves from foreign competition; rather, they are the ones that take the lead in expanding internationally. Only global standards of excellence, honed through fierce competition in overseas markets, can ensure a company's success in the years ahead.

Summary of Learning Objectives

1. **Explain what an economic system is.**
   An economic system is a society's way of producing, distributing, and marketing the goods and services desired by its population.
2. **Name the three major types of economic systems and differentiate their identifying characteristics.**
   Under capitalism, the factors of production are owned by individuals, who make the business decisions. Citizens have a high degree of economic freedom but also face considerable economic risk. Under communism, the government owns all factors of production and makes all the business decisions. Distinctions between rich and poor are minimized. Under socialism, the state owns and operates certain key industries but allows private ownership of many businesses. Relatively high taxes permit the government to provide many social services.
3. **List the four major economic roles of the U.S. government.**
   The U.S. government enforces rules and regulations, fosters competition, contributes to economic stability, and provides public goods and transfer payments.
4. **List three ways companies compete.**
   Companies compete on the basis of price, quality and service, and innovation.

5. **Explain how supply and demand interact to affect price.** In the simplest sense, supply and demand affect price in the following manner: When price goes up, the quantity demanded goes down, but the supplier's incentive to produce more goes up. When price goes down, the quantity demanded increases, whereas the quantity supplied may (or may not) decline. When the interests of buyers and sellers are in balance, an equilibrium price is established. However, price is more than simple notions of supply and demand, as the examples of medicine and gasoline illustrate.
6. **Name the four factors of production and discuss why they are becoming less of a competitive advantage in the global marketplace.** The four historical factors of production are natural resources, human resources, capital, and entrepreneurship. Technology and modern transportation have made it possible for countries to shop around the world for these factors. The key industries of the future will place a greater emphasis on having knowledgeable workers than on these traditional factors.
7. **Define the gross domestic product and explain what it is used for.** The gross domestic product (GDP) is the sum of all goods and services produced by both domestic and foreign companies as long as they are located within a nation's boundaries. The GDP is used to measure the productivity of a nation and to evaluate the effectiveness of a government's policies and economic systems.
8. **Identify five trends that will influence the economy in the years ahead.** The five trends identified in the chapter are (1) the need to compete on the basis of time, quality, and customer satisfaction; (2) the accelerating pace of technological change and the resulting emergence of a new information-based economy; (3) the competition small business faces from industry giants and the global economy; (4) the continued public and government scrutiny of business's social, ethical, and environmental performance; and (5) the increasingly global nature of the economy and the challenges of meeting the needs of a diverse work force.

On the Job: Meeting Business Challenges at Gateway 2000

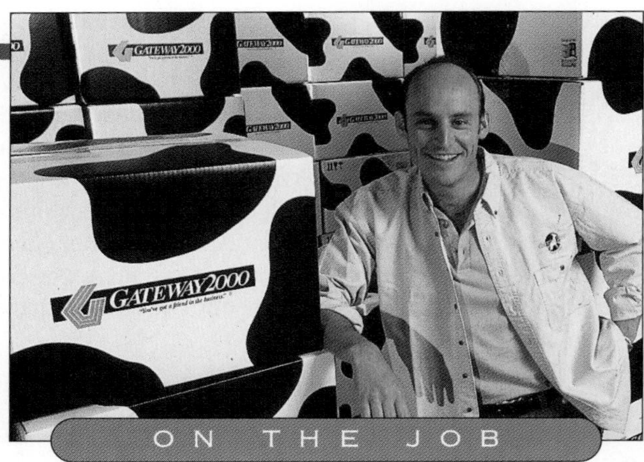

Relying on his instincts, Ted Waitt made a number of critical calls that put Gateway in the lead. Of course, Waitt was no longer a one-man show. Beginning in 1991, he brought in experienced executives (from top companies like Digital Equipment, Texas Instruments, and IBM) to help manage the company's growth. Together they brought Gateway to new heights while sticking with its efficient, bare-bones assembly operation—no showroom, little inventory, and no retail outlets. In fact, Gateway's simple direct-sales operation allows the company to compete on speed, quality, and price.

Speed and quality in manufacturing give Gateway the biggest advantage. Not only can speed and quality win customers, but they win the right kind of customers—those who are willing to pay a bit more for computer equipment. Gateway moves like lightning: It gets new computers out the door in a hurry. They include all the latest technology—like top-quality color monitors, the latest operating system and software, and the most powerful computer chip.

Of course, buying a computer over the telephone and not seeing the equipment until the truck delivers the cow-spotted boxes to your doorstep is not for everyone. Gateway attracts computer-savvy buyers who need a lot less hand-holding and are comfortable purchasing from a catalog or an advertisement. Here's how it works: The customer calls in and, over the phone (or Internet), designs a custom-configured computer system using cutting-edge technology. In about five days, the custom system is built and shipped. Because there is no inventory to speak of (computers are made-to-order), as technology gets cheaper, Gateway can compete on price by changing prices daily and passing the savings on to customers.

Relying on word of mouth and a strong advertising campaign (about $90 million a year), Gateway rode a wave of success fueled by computer buyers hunting for good equipment at bargain prices. Gateway's success, however, did not come without its share of growing pains. Gateway's first portable laptop computer was a disaster. Failing to recognize that customers had to see and touch the product to appreciate its smaller size and capabilities, Gateway ran into a wall because the company's computers were not sold in retail stores where customers could experience the product's features. This lesson would not be forgotten. Other mishaps included sending out machines that did not work and busy phone lines that kept customers waiting—sometimes for hours. Fortunately, Waitt corrected these problems early on by instituting various quality-control measures to increase customer satisfaction. And his efforts paid off. By 1996 Gateway was shipping 5,000 to 6,000 computers daily and sales skyrocketed to roughly $5 billion.

That same year Gateway launched a product that was way ahead of its time. Called Destination, it was a combo PC and 31-inch television set with a wireless keyboard, a mouse, and a home-theater sound system. Learning from past mistakes, Waitt knew he would have to get the product in front of consumers so that they could see its features. This time Gateway cut deals with retail stores. None had ever carried Gateway's stuff before.

But Waitt's biggest challenge has been trying to crack the corporate market. Whereas Gateway sold most of its computers to individual users and small businesses, rival Dell set its sights on the lucrative Fortune 1000 corporate accounts and made some expensive investments—like $22 million in research and development (Gateway spent practically zip). Despite doubling its sales force, Gateway discovered that selling computers to corporate customers was not an easy task. First of all, competitors like IBM and Hewlett-Packard (HP) have large, well-trained sales and service staffs who have been doing business with big companies for years. Furthermore, IBM and HP products can be purchased at traditional retail stores.

Still, relying on a cost-efficient, bare-bones, direct-sale operation is Gateway's stronghold in this cutthroat industry. The company has no plans to alter its fundamental selling strategy. "If you come see us in the next century, we'll be bigger, better, and smarter, but fundamentally we'll be the same," notes Waitt. That is, Gateway will stick to what it does best: churning out huge volumes of PCs that are equipped with the latest technology at affordable—but not rock bottom—prices and selling them to customers over the phone.

Your Mission: You are a member of the executive team at Gateway, helping your colleagues make the decisions that will keep the company growing into the future. Using what you know about business in a free-market economy—and your own experience as a consumer—decide how the company should respond to the following scenarios. Like real business decisions, some of these scenarios have more than one good answer, so be sure you can defend the answer you choose.

1. Gateway's sales are skyrocketing. The company is outgrowing its present South Dakota location and must expand to a larger facility in order to meet consumer demand. Using your knowledge about factors of production and Gateway's operation, which of the following courses sounds best for Gateway over the long term?
   a. Taxes and building costs are the cheapest in South Dakota. The company can save a bundle of money each year by adding on to its present South Dakota facility, even though the current labor shortage in the area is predicted to continue for quite some time.
   b. Open up a new production facility overseas. Skilled labor is plentiful and wages are substantially lower overseas. Building costs are relatively inexpensive too. This looks like the most economical alternative.
   c. Build an additional facility to handle the increased demand in a state with a plentiful supply of skilled labor—even if labor and facility costs are higher there. Because this is the most expensive alternative, it might force Gateway to keep its prices a bit higher than those of its competitors.
2. Like every other product category, computers can be influenced by a multiplier effect. Which of the following events in the economy is likely to generate the most product sales for Gateway 2000 over the long term?
   a. Lowering of credit-card interest rates.
   b. Increased government funding for rebuilding the nation's major highway system.
   c. An increase in the minimum hourly pay rate (minimum wage).
3. During last week's executive team meeting, several team members got into a heated argument over Gateway's current pricing policies. Several comments were made. Which long-term pricing strategy sounds best for Gateway?
   a. "The PC business is not about price, it's about value, or what you can give customers for their money. Customers want the latest technology, even though it costs more, and they are willing to pay for it."
   b. "Gateway has always been a trustworthy company that offers near rock-bottom prices. Because technology keeps improving, nobody wants to sink pots of money into hardware that is sure to be obsolete in a couple of years."
   c. "The most important factor for this industry is price, price, and price. We must lower our prices before our competitors force us to by taking away our business."
4. Information plays a key role in all your business decisions; the more and better information you have, the better decisions you can make. Which of the following approaches to collecting information would be the most beneficial in laying out Gateway's strategy for the future?
   a. Regularly interviewing people in the marketplace to see what features are most important to them when using a computer.
   b. Watching what competitors do to see what kind of products Gateway should come out with next.
   c. Keeping a close eye on new technology, emerging trends, and product innovations in the marketplace.[30]

Key Terms

business (2)
business cycle (7)
capital (14)
capitalism (2)
communism (3)
competition (5)
competitive advantage (10)
demand (11)
demand curve (12)
deregulation (5)
disinflation (7)
economic system (2)
economies of scale (5)
entrepreneurs (14)
equilibrium price (13)
factors of production (13)
fiscal policy (7)
free-market system (2)
gross domestic product (GDP) (16)
gross national product (GNP) (17)
human resources (14)
inflation (7)
macroeconomics (16)
microeconomics (16)
monetary policy (7)
monopolistic competition (5)
monopoly (6)
natural resources (14)
not-for-profit organization (3)
oligopoly (6)
privatization (4)
profit (2)
pure competition (5)
recession (7)
socialism (3)
supply (11)
supply curve (13)
technology (18)
transfer payments (8)

Questions

For Review

1. How is capitalism different from communism and socialism in the way it achieves key economic goals?
2. What role does competition play in a free-market economy?
3. Define the demand curve, the supply curve, and the equilibrium price.
4. What are the two principal ways of looking at the economy and how do they differ?
5. What is the difference between the federal deficit and the national debt?

For Analysis

6. Why do governments intervene in a free-market economy?
7. How does a free-market system regulate itself?
8. How has the globalization of businesses changed the nature of economic systems?
9. Why will knowledgeable workers be the key economic resource in the future?
10. What is the Consumer Price Index and how is it used?

For Application

11. Explain how a product like Rollerblades revolutionized the sporting goods industry and how the economy as a whole benefits from new products like Rollerblades.
12. How would a decrease in Social Security benefits to the elderly affect the economy?

A Case for Critical Thinking ■ Molex: The Billion-Dollar Globetrotter

It began as goo, a mixture of ingredients nobody wanted—at least not until John Krehbiel Sr. discovered that this goo was also an inexpensive electrical insulator. That was 60 years ago. Today, Molex (named after that black gooey substance) is a $1.5 billion company and the second largest maker of electronic connectors in the world.

Run by the third generation of Krehbiels, the company manufactures more than 50,000 types of electronic-connector products used in just about every electronic gadget imaginable—cameras, computers, telephones, televisions, pagers, and printers. Molex builds these products in 46 plants located in 21 countries on 6 continents. Still, until 1967 Molex was strictly a domestic company. That's when Krehbiel Sr. sent his son (now CEO Fred Krehbiel) to Japan to drum up foreign sales.

STUMBLING UPON SUCCESS

With a budget of $25,000 (including his salary), CEO Fred Krehbiel took off for Tokyo. "I didn't speak Japanese, and very few of them spoke English. But through sign language and a little bit of English, I got the impression that the Japanese were interested in our products," he recalls. But their way of doing business was far different from what Molex was used to. For example, the Japanese would consider Molex as a supplier only if the company opened up a manufacturing plant in Japan. So it did. And the Japanese insisted that Molex meet their quality production standards. So it did that too.

NAVIGATING THE GLOBE

Of course, setting up shop in Japan was only the beginning. For years, Molex simply followed the lead of its customers. When General Electric took its television production to Singapore, Molex trailed behind. When RCA moved production to Taiwan, Molex tagged along too. Soon there were few places in the world where Molex wasn't. That gave the company an enormous advantage over many of its competitors. For example, when the disk-drive business migrated to Singapore, Molex was already there.

In spite of the company's success, Krehbiel admits that Molex made every possible mistake. Fortunately, the company learned from its mistakes. For instance, Molex learned that if you are going to survive in today's global economy, you have to be where your customers are. You have to listen to your customers and make what they want the way they want it. Also Molex figured out that to be successful in foreign markets, you have to create a decentralized company that is not afraid to grant lots of freedom to its foreign offices. Plus you have to staff those offices with local managers who understand the market and business culture of the country they are in. "You have to be a local company no matter where you are in the world," says Krehbiel. And Molex was everywhere. But that also became a problem.

GETTING CONNECTED

"Our information systems were local and regional, and couldn't communicate back and forth with each other," recalls Krehbiel. "We needed to make a transition from a decentralized international model in which each site runs autonomously to a global orientation with a single face in a worldwide location."

Today, Molex's global computer network links engineering departments around the world. As a result, Molex Japan can collaborate with Molex Alabama and get input from Molex Italy, and so on. More important, the company's customers don't know whether the product they are purchasing was manufactured in Singapore or the United States. That's because Molex understands that the world is their market, and to be successful today, you have to change people's attitudes from thinking regionally to thinking globally.

1. Would you classify CEO Fred Krehbiel as an entrepreneur in the 1970s? Why or why not?
2. If Molex were just beginning to expand overseas today, what might they want to know about the economies of the countries in which they intend to do business?
3. What do you think Fred Krehbiel meant when he said, "You have to be a local company no matter where you are in the world"?
4. Go to the Molex Web site at <http://www.molex.com> and click on *financial* at the top of its home page. How many new-product patents did Molex acquire last year? How much did the company spend on research and development last year? What do these figures tell us about the company?

Building Your Business Skills

Examine how the various economic forces (such as competition, factors of production, and supply and demand) affect a business operation by interviewing the owner or manager of a local business. If that is not possible, consult the journals and periodicals available in your library, and select an article that profiles a business. Present a brief discussion of your findings to several class members or write a brief summary, as directed by your instructor. Be prepared to discuss the method you used to locate information for the analysis.

Keeping Current Using *The Wall Street Journal*

Gaining a competitive advantage in today's marketplace is critical to a company's success. Look in recent issues of *The Wall Street Journal* and find a company whose practices have set that company apart from its competitors.

1. What products or services does the company manufacture or sell?
2. Does the company compete on price, quality, service, or innovation?
3. How does the company set its goods or services apart from its competitors?
4. 3M is a company that competes on innovation. The company manufactures or sells over 50,000 products. Find out about its innovative culture by visiting its Web site at <http://www.mmm.com>. At the top of its home page, click on *News and Profile,* then on *Overview* to find *Our Values.* What percentage of 3M's annual sales must come from products less than 4 years old?

Exploring the Best of the Web

What's in the CPI?, page 8

Find out what's in the Consumer Price Index (CPI) and how it is calculated by visiting the CPI Web site at <http://stats.bls.gov/cpihome.htm>.] Click on the *FAQs (frequently asked questions)* to answer these questions (hint: sometimes you will need *more* information).

1. How is the CPI used?
2. What goods and services does the CPI cover, and how are they categorized?
3. Using the inflation calculator at the Web site <http://www.westegg.com/inflation/>, see the power of inflation by answering the following: If you had $100 in 1900, how much would it be worth today? (Use the latest year available.)

Learn About Your Benefits, page 9

Social Security takes a big bite out of your paycheck. Find out what this government program is all about. Visit the Social Security Administration (SSA) Web site at <http://www.ssa.gov>, scroll down, and click on *History of the SSA*. Click on the *FAQs* to answer the following questions.

1. Is there any significance to the numbers assigned in your Social Security number? Are Social Security numbers reused after a person dies?
2. Approximately how much has Social Security paid out in benefits since its inception?
3. Explore the Web site. Besides history, what types of helpful information does this site offer?

Find the Right Stuff, page 22

Hoover's Online provides a wealth of company information. Browse Hoover's Online to learn about the following companies: Gateway 2000, Wrigley, and Marriott International. (Be sure to enter the company name as shown under the *power search*.) Use the information provided for these companies to answer the following.

1. Find the names of the three main competitors for each company.
2. Review several press releases or current news articles for these companies. Explore the other data given. How is Hoover's Online an effective tool for gathering information about companies?
3. Return to the Hoover's Online home page (click *Home*) and under *Other Features*, click on the *List of Lists*, click *Select*, and click on the *Social Responsibility and Workplace* link. Click on *America's 100 Most Admired Companies (Fortune)*, and click on any of the companies listed. What are the eight categories that these companies are judged on? Which of these categories are discussed in this chapter?

Answers to "Is It True?"

Page 5. False. Assuming the United States is able to collect all the money owed, the country made a profit. The war cost the United States $38 billion, but foreign contributions totaled $52 billion—so the United States actually turned a profit.

Page 18. False. When adjusted for inflation, median family income in the United States has not changed since 1969.

Page 22. False. Among the many appliances in the home, only the microwave oven has saved time. Although some labor-saving devices save time on one task, they create work in others. For example, the refrigerator saved time by eliminating the need for daily shopping and for storing ice at home, but it resulted in the loss of door-to-door vendors and increased the time needed to travel to the supermarket and shop. Other modern appliances have increased working time by raising standards of cleanliness or perfection.

CHAPTER 2

GLOBAL BUSINESS

OBJECTIVES

After studying this chapter, you will be able to

1 Differentiate between absolute, comparative, and national competitive advantage

2 Distinguish between the balance of trade and the balance of payments

3 Identify four techniques that countries use to protect their domestic industries

4 Outline the arguments for and against protectionism

5 Explain how trading blocs, the GATT, and the WTO affect trade

6 Define foreign exchange and discuss the effect of a weaker U.S. dollar on U.S. companies that do business abroad

7 Discuss five forms of international business activity

8 Identify six ways to improve communication in an international business relationship

ON THE JOB: FACING BUSINESS CHALLENGES AT HOLIDAY INN WORLDWIDE

Sending Invitations Across the Globe

In the 1960s a family vacation in the United States usually meant loading the kids into the station wagon and driving off down the highway toward a tourist destination. And when weary vacationers needed to rest for the night, they often looked for the familiar green signs with "Holiday Inn" written in script and a colorful star for emphasis. All across the United States, this sign welcomed travelers to Holiday Inn hotels with promises of quality, comfort, and value.

By 1968 Holiday Inn was so well known in the United States that it began opening franchises in Europe. In 1973 the company opened its first Asian hotel in Japan, and in 1984 it became the first U.S.-based hotel to open for business in China. For 25 years Holiday Inn enjoyed great success in the European and Asian markets, opening 600 hotels and earning a reputation as upscale, professional, and well run.

However, in the 1980s Holiday Inn's fortunes were beginning to fade in the United States. Many of the franchises were outdated and substandard. Family vacationers were being replaced by business travelers as the hotel industry's bread and butter, and aggressive competitors with superior marketing strategies were targeting this growing segment. In addition, overbuilding had set off a wave of price discounting. As a result, both Holiday Inn's share of the lodging market and its image took a nosedive.

But in the 1990s this icon of the U.S. highway was brought back to life after being purchased by Bass PLC, a British conglomerate. Bass moved quickly to make Holiday Inn Worldwide the leading hotel chain, not just in the United States but around the globe. In the United States, Holiday Inn pursued a strategy that segmented the market into different types of travelers and created a unique type of lodging for each group. Under names like Holiday Inn Express, Holiday Inn Select, SunSpree Resorts, and Crowne Plaza, the company offered different accommodations and amenities at different prices to suit the diverse needs of business and leisure travelers. Combined with a campaign to bring all of the franchises back up to a high standard of quality, the strategy quickly began to pay off.

Even so, the top brass at Holiday Inn Worldwide knows that the greatest growth potential is not in the saturated U.S. market but in the evolving markets of Europe, Asia, and Latin America. With increasing tourism and business development in these regions, the demand for comfortable, consistent, and affordable accommodations is booming. Holiday Inn needs a strategy for tapping this vast potential. Would the strategies that fueled Holiday Inn's turnaround in the United States bring similar results internationally? Large-scale construction of new hotels will play a major role, so what kinds of hotels should they be? How can the company best meet the needs of a wide variety of international travelers? Should Holiday Inn expand through franchises or by opening company-owned hotels? Should the same type of promotion be used for the entire global market, or should it be localized to each geographic area? These are questions that Raymond Lewis faces daily as vice president of marketing. If you were Lewis, how would you answer them?[1]

The Globalization of Business

Like Holiday Inn, more and more enterprises are recognizing that pursuing opportunities in the global marketplace is the key to their present and future success. If you work for a U.S. manufacturer, the chances are better than 75 percent that some of your toughest competitors will be companies based in other countries.[2] The chances are also good that your employer will buy, sell, or manufacture at least some products abroad. Hundreds of U.S. corporations have invested in overseas operations, and they now look to those markets for future sales and profit growth (Exhibit 2.1). At the same time, companies based in other countries are expanding their operations around the globe.

The shift to a worldwide focus poses obvious problems for managers like Raymond Lewis. Each country has unique ways of doing business, and these must be learned. Consumer preferences, government regulations, ethical standards, labor skill, and political stability all vary from country to country, and all have the potential to affect a firm's international prospects. Nevertheless, the opportunities of a global marketplace greatly outweigh the risks. A few of the advantages of going global include new markets and new sources of capital abroad, swifter technological advancement through collaboration, efficiencies in production, and greater consumer choices at home. Jean-Pierre Rosso is president and CEO of Case, a major worldwide manufacturer of construction and agricultural equipment. Rosso knows the importance of a global perspective. When he realized that Case derived 90 percent of its revenues from sales in the United States and western Europe,

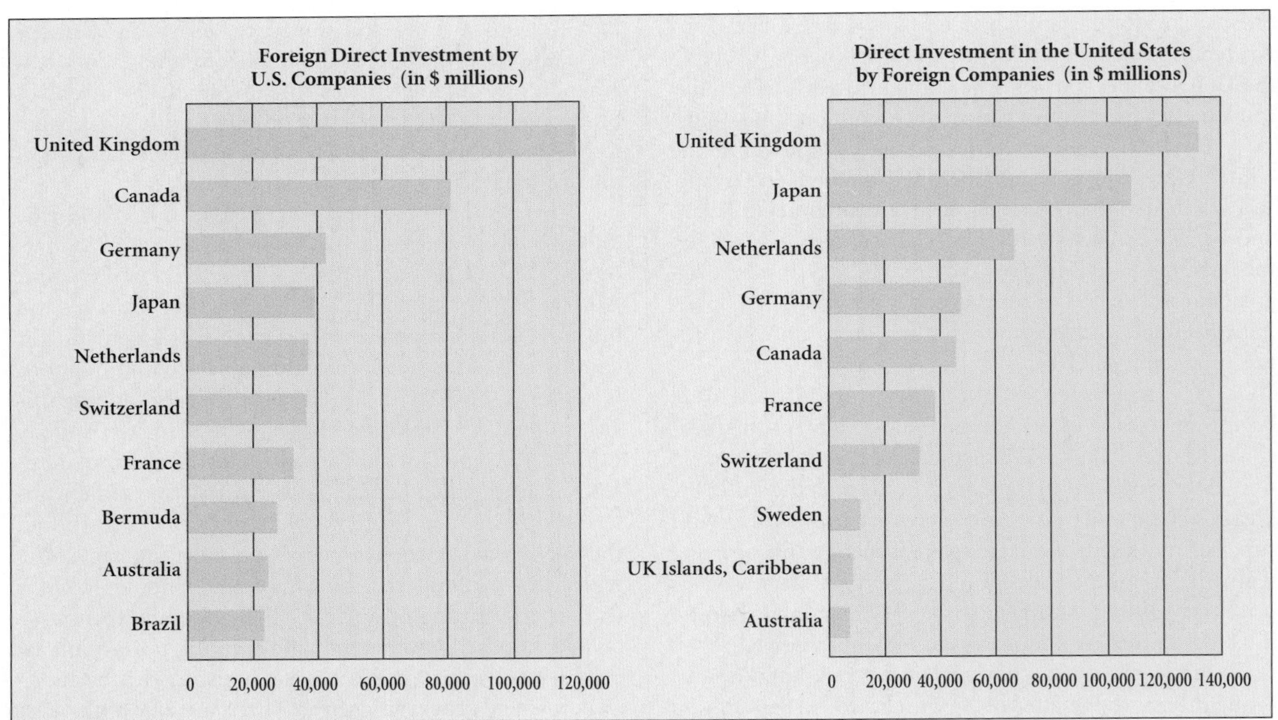

EXHIBIT 2.1

United States Involvement in International Business

These charts show the amount of foreign direct investment by U.S companies and the amount invested in the United States by foreign companies.

Rosso expanded Case's marketing efforts to include Asia and the countries of the former Soviet Union.[3]

As the scope of international business expands, government policymakers also face new issues. What should national objectives be with respect to international business? For example, when countries negotiate international trade agreements, should they try to promote the interests of domestic companies and protect them from foreign competitors? For the past few years, one of the most popular cars in the United States has been the Honda Accord, a "Japanese import" manufactured not in Tokyo but in Marysville, Ohio. If the U.S. government tries to protect GM from Honda, is it doing the United States a favor? Consider also the fact that shifting production to developing nations where wages are lower has cost some U.S. workers their jobs. Should the government be concerned? And what about the transfer of U.S. technology to foreign companies. For example, the Chinese government requires companies to share their technology before they can enter China's huge market.[4] Should the U.S. government try to limit such activity? You can see the difficulties in developing a national trade policy that serves equally well for global corporations, their workers, and consumers around the world.

Why Nations Trade

International trade occurs because no single country has the resources to produce everything well. Nations specialize in the production of certain goods and trade with other nations for those they do not produce. A nation has an **absolute advantage** when it can produce a particular product using fewer resources per unit of output than any other nation. For example, Saudi Arabia is seen as having an absolute advantage in crude oil production because of its huge, developed reserves.

absolute advantage
Nation's ability to produce a particular product with fewer resources per unit of output than any other nation

Even if a country cannot claim an absolute advantage in any product, it is still advantageous for it to trade with other nations. When a nation achieves international success in a particular industry, that nation is traditionally said to have a **comparative advantage,** an ability to produce certain products more efficiently and at a lower cost than other products, compared to other nations. For example, imagine two countries, A and B. Country A can produce bread three times more efficiently than Country B and can produce milk twice as efficiently. Although Country A has an absolute advantage in both products, it realizes a greater advantage by specializing in bread, where it is most efficient. Country B is less efficient than Country A in both products but can produce milk relatively more efficiently than it can produce bread. Therefore, Country B should focus its resources on milk production. Both countries will benefit economically when each focuses on producing the product for which it has a comparative advantage and trading for the other product.

comparative advantage
Nation's ability to produce certain items more efficiently and at a lower cost than other items, relative to other nations

However, these two concepts don't explain how many nations are able to compete successfully on a global level in industries that don't depend on naturally occurring raw materials or large labor pools. To explain this phenomenon, Harvard Business School professor Michael E. Porter points to the theory of **national competitive advantage**, the ability of a country's industries to innovate and upgrade to a higher level of technology and productivity. According to this theory, a nation can be competitive in the world market by making the best use of innovation and technology.[5]

national competitive advantage
Ability of a nation's industries to be innovative and move to a higher level of technology and productivity

Consider Singapore. This city-state of only 239 square miles is not rich in natural resources. Therefore, the government established The National Computer Board, which works with private industry to exploit information technology for a national competitive advantage. By developing computer networks that enable companies involved in shipping to share information, Singapore has dramatically increased its capacity to handle the number of ship containers that pass through its ports. Moreover, the time it takes to process

Singapore's commitment to developing cutting-edge electronic data interchange (EDI) systems has helped to give the country a national competitive advantage as a major Asian port.

customs documents has been reduced from over 2 days to just 4 hours. The port of Singapore now processes no fewer than 8.5 million containers annually, and Singapore's position as one of the major ports in the Far East has been greatly strengthened.[6]

Because no nation can make everything it needs, each nation trades the products it makes most efficiently for products that other countries produce more efficiently. Specialization expands the total supply of products and reduces their total cost. However, most countries try to remain reasonably self-sufficient in certain essential industries, such as agriculture and energy. In this way, countries are able to provide for the basic needs of their citizens in the event of an international conflict.

The Growing Importance of World Markets

Never before have organizations been able to cross national borders so easily or so inexpensively. Efficient transportation makes it easier than ever before for companies to bring raw materials to their production plants and to ship their products to foreign markets. E-mail allows employees around the globe to communicate with each other almost as easily as if they were next door. And the Internet permits companies to advertise, research markets, buy raw materials, and recruit employees worldwide from within their domestic headquarters. For example, Hewlett-Packard has linked its buyers with 200 suppliers through a computer network that has reduced the costs and simplified the process of procuring parts.[7]

Initially, most U.S. companies approached their growing foreign markets from bases in the United States. However, as international business became an increasingly important source of sales and profits, U.S. companies wanted to be closer to foreign customers. Therefore, they began to open foreign branches and sales offices that were staffed by local workers. One step led to another, and soon U.S. companies were opening production and assembly operations abroad to minimize transportation expenses, capitalize on lower labor costs, and take advantage of local raw materials. Sometimes plants were built to bypass local tariffs (import taxes), or to meet the requirements set by local governments for selling products in their countries. To utilize the skills of foreign engineers and scientists, research and design facilities were also opened abroad. Such companies are **multinational corporations (MNCs),** businesses with operations in several countries. The nation where a company is headquartered is the home country; any other nation where the company does business is a host country.

multinational corporations (MNCs)
Companies with operations in more than one country

Intel is one MNC that divides its activities among many host countries. The company's well-known computer chips are manufactured in several countries that have strong bases of skilled labor, such as the United States, Israel, and Ireland. The chips are then shipped to countries with a lower-skilled labor pool, such as the Philippines, for testing and packaging. Finally, the chips are shipped to the countries where they will be sold. Intel encourages the development of international markets for its products by investing in projects like the Intel Technology Lab in Delhi, India. The Delhi lab was designed to develop the Indian computer market by increasing technology awareness and strengthening local computer expertise.[8]

Is It True?

India is a poor and technologically backward nation.

Forms of International Business Activity

Any company can become involved in world trade through a range of activities that reflect an increasing level of ownership, financial commitment, and risk. Many companies first expand into international trade through *importing* and *exporting*. Four other forms of international business activity are *licensing, franchising,* forming *joint ventures* and *strategic alliances,* and running *wholly owned facilities.*

importing
Purchasing goods or services from another country and bringing them into one's own country

exporting
Selling and shipping goods or services to another country

Importing and Exporting **Importing** is buying goods or services from a supplier in another country; **exporting** is selling products outside the country in which they are produced. Importing and exporting have existed for centuries, but only in the last few decades has such activity caused the economies of the world to become so tightly linked (see Exhibit 2.2).

The level of U.S. exports has grown steadily in recent years to well over $800 billion—providing more than 11.5 million U.S. manufacturing jobs. Ninety-five percent of

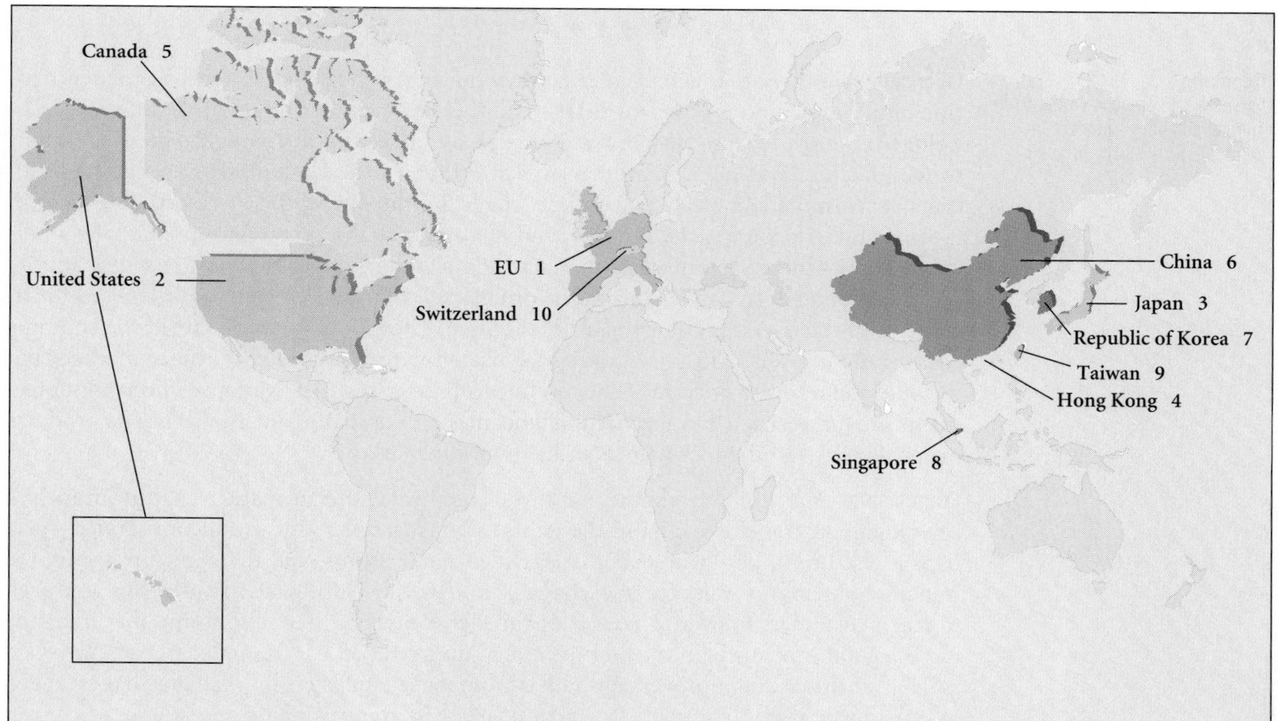

EXHIBIT 2.2

The World's Major Trading Economies

The top ten trading economies of the world include both industrialized and developing nations.

the world's consumers live outside the United States, and in many areas, consumers are only now beginning to buy products for which the U.S. market is saturated, such as home appliances. It is clear, then, that exporting is vital to future U.S. economic growth.[9] Companies that want to export their products may do so directly by calling on potential customers overseas, or they may rely on intermediaries at home or abroad. Working through someone with connections in the target country is often very helpful to both large and small companies alike.[10] Many countries now have foreign trade offices to help importers and exporters interested in doing business within their borders. The International Trade Administration of the U.S. Department of Commerce offers a variety of services, including political and credit-risk analysis, advice on entering other markets, and tips on financing sources. Professional agents and established businesspeople are also primary resources for helping companies establish a local presence in foreign markets.

BEST OF THE WEB

Going Global

Have you ever thought about getting into the world of exporting? Where would you go for information and help? Many small and large companies have gotten valuable export assistance from the U.S. government through the International Trade Administration. You can find a wealth of information about export procedures; foreign markets, industries, companies, and products; export financing; unfair trade practices; trade statistics; and more by visiting the ITA's Web page. The site is also a great starting point for links to many other trade-related sites. Select *Regions and Countries* to find out more about markets all over the world.
http://www.ita.doc.gov

licensing
Agreement to produce and market another company's product in exchange for a royalty or fee

Licensing Another approach to international business is **licensing**. License agreements entitle one company to produce or market another company's product or to utilize its technology in return for a royalty or fee. For example, a U.S. business might obtain the rights to manufacture and sell a Scandinavian skin lotion in the United States, using the Scandinavian formula and packaging design. The U.S. company would be responsible for promoting and distributing the product, and it would pay the Scandinavian company a percentage of its income from sales in exchange for the product rights.

Licensing deals can also work the other way, with the U.S. company acting as the licenser and the overseas company as the licensee. The U.S. firm would avoid the shipping costs, trade barriers, and uncertainties associated with trying to enter other markets, but it would still receive a portion of the revenue from overseas sales. Moreover, licensing agreements are not restricted to international business. A company can also license its products or technology to other companies in its domestic market.

Franchising *Franchising* is another way to expand into foreign markets. With a franchise agreement, the franchisee obtains the rights to duplicate a specific product or service—perhaps a restaurant, photocopy shop, or a video rental store—and the company selling the franchise obtains a royalty fee in exchange. Holiday Inn Worldwide has used this approach to reach customers in over 65 countries. Smaller companies have also found that franchising is a good way for them to enter the global marketplace. For example, Ziebart Tidy-Car, which franchises car-improvement outlets from its headquarters in Michigan, has arranged to open more than 300 outlets in 40 countries.[11] By franchising its operations, a firm can minimize the costs and risks of global expansion and bypass certain trade restrictions.

joint venture
Cooperative partnership in which organizations share investment costs, risks, management, and profits in the development, production, or selling of products

Forming Joint Ventures and Strategic Alliances *Joint ventures* and *strategic alliances* offer another practical approach to international business. A **joint venture** is a partnership in which one company cooperates with other companies or governments to develop, produce, or

Changing eating habits and growing disposable income in Thailand have created new expansion opportunities for companies like Kentucky Fried Chicken.

sell products. A **strategic alliance** is a long-term partnership between two or more companies aimed at helping each to establish competitive advantages. To reach their individual but complimentary goals, the companies may share ideas, resources, and technologies. In contrast to a strategic alliance, companies involved in a joint venture typically share the investment costs, risks, management, and profits of their business venture. For example, U.S.-based Caterpillar and Mitsubishi Heavy Industries of Japan teamed up in a 50–50 venture to build construction equipment. Cat wanted access to the Japanese market to compete against rival Komatsu. Mitsubishi wanted to beat Komatsu at home and expand its export markets. Both companies have benefited from the venture: In addition to catching up with Komatsu, Cat is now able to build most of its equipment for the Asian market in Japan, putting it much closer to Japanese customers. In return, Mitsubishi is able to access Cat's network of independent dealers in over 197 countries.[12]

strategic alliance
Long-term relationship in which two or more companies share ideas, resources, and technologies in order to establish competitive advantages

In some countries, a joint venture may be the only logical form of business because of local restrictions on direct investment. Many countries will not allow foreign companies to own facilities outright, so to do business at all, a local partner is necessary. This has been true for many U.S. companies trying to sell their products in China. For instance, the Chinese government would not allow Boeing to sell airplanes in China until the company agreed to move half of the tail-section production for its 737s to Xian.[13]

Running Wholly Owned Facilities The most comprehensive form of international business is a wholly owned operation run in another country, without the financial participation of a local partner. Many U.S. firms currently do business this way, as do companies based in other countries. These operations vary in form, size, and purpose. Some are started from scratch; others are acquired from local owners. Some are small sales offices; others are full-scale manufacturing facilities. Some are set up to exploit the availability of raw materials; others take advantage of low wage rates or provide the most direct access to markets in other countries. In almost all cases, at least part of the work force is drawn from the local population. Consider Samsung Electronics. This South Korean company moved its production facilities to Tijuana, Mexico, enabling Samsung to take advantage of Mexico's lower wages while providing the company with easy access to the U.S. and Canadian markets. At the same time, the move positions Samsung for future expansion in Latin America. Samsung is currently investing almost $600 million in the facility to increase its capacity for producing televisions, picture tubes, and microwave ovens. It expects to employ over 9,000 people in Tijuana in the coming years.[14]

Overseas Investment in the United States

foreign direct investment (FDI)
Investment of money by foreign companies in domestic business enterprises

While U.S. companies greatly expand their presence overseas, companies based abroad are also moving into the U.S. market by acquiring U.S. companies or building new facilities. The U.S. Commerce Department reports that **foreign direct investment (FDI),** which is the investment of money by foreign companies to acquire an ownership interest in domestic businesses or to establish production and marketing facilities domestically, has been rising steadily over the past few years.[15] These investments boost the U.S. economy by adding jobs and increasing demand for local supplies and services.

Companies from all over the world are doing business in the United States. Some have owned U.S. facilities for years. One example is Unilever, a Dutch-British company that owns Lever Brothers, maker of laundry detergents, margarine, and other consumer products.[16] Others have only more recently set up shop in the United States. Carmakers such as Mazda, Honda, Nissan, and Toyota now make and sell some of their most popular models here. BMW recently began production of its sporty Z3 roadster at its new plant in Spartanburg, South Carolina. By manufacturing in the United States, BMW benefits from comparatively cheap energy and material costs, experienced suppliers, and a skilled and affordable labor force. In addition, because it is producing cars in the United States, the single largest car market in the world, the company pays less to get its products to customers. At the same time, BMW is building goodwill in the United States by employing 1,500 people.[17]

International Business Economics

At any given time, a country may be importing more of one type of product and exporting more of another. As Exhibit 2.3 illustrates, the United States exports more machinery, transportation equipment, and food products than it imports, but it imports more consumer goods, automotive vehicles, and industrial supplies than it exports. The level of a country's imports and exports forms an important part of international business economics.

EXHIBIT 2.3

Leading U.S. Imports and Exports

The United States actively participates in global trade by importing products from other countries and exporting products to other countries.

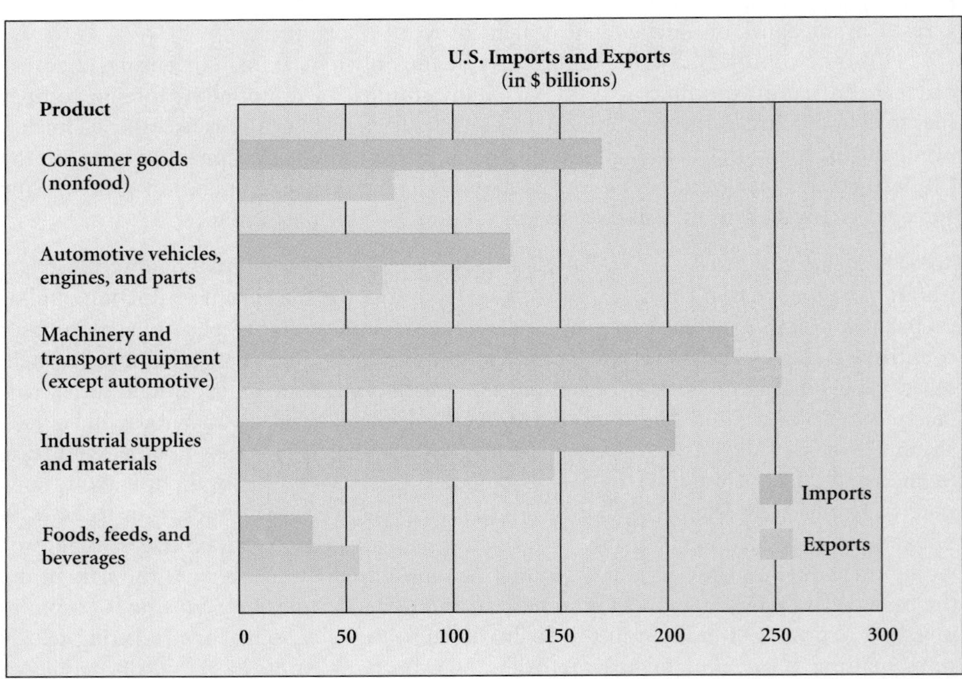

The Balance of Trade The relationship between the value of a country's imports and the value of its exports determines its **balance of trade**. In years when the United States exports more goods and services than it imports, its balance of trade is favorable, creating a **trade surplus**: People in other countries buy more from the United States than it buys from them, and money flows into the U.S. economy. When U.S. imports exceed exports, its balance of trade is unfavorable, creating a **trade deficit**: The United States is buying more from other countries, so money is flowing out from the U.S. economy into the other economies.

balance of trade
Relationship between the value of the products a nation exports and those it imports

trade surplus
Positive trade balance created when a country exports more than it imports

trade deficit
Negative trade balance created when a country imports more than it exports

As Exhibit 2.4 illustrates, the U.S. balance of trade varies from year to year. One reason for the variation is the change in the value of the dollar compared with the value of other currencies. When the dollar is extremely high against other currencies, products from other countries seem relatively inexpensive in the United States, and U.S. products seem relatively expensive overseas. As U.S. consumers buy more of the relatively inexpensive imported goods and consumers overseas buy less of the relatively expensive U.S. goods, the U.S. trade deficit grows. However, when the situation is reversed and U.S. consumers buy fewer imported goods while people in other countries buy more U.S. exports, the U.S. trade deficit narrows and may even turn into a trade surplus.

Bear in mind that the gap between imports and exports does not necessarily mean that U.S. companies are not competitive in the world market. The balance of trade is obscured by several factors. One is **intrafirm trade,** which is trade between the various units of a multinational corporation. Intrafirm trade now accounts for one-third of all the goods traded around the world. Shipments of goods by U.S. companies to their overseas affiliates (related companies) account for over 25 percent of U.S. exports, and another 10 percent of U.S. exports is made up of shipments from the U.S. affiliates of foreign companies. Imports are also affected by intrafirm trade. One-fourth of all U.S. merchandise imports are sent from foreign multinationals to their U.S. operations, and almost one-fifth of U.S. imports are shipments to U.S. companies from their foreign affiliates.[18] Companies like AT&T, Texas Instruments, and General Electric set up factories to make components in countries where wage rates are low. When the parts are shipped back to the United States for assembly, they are counted as imports. Another offsetting factor is that many of the products imported into the United States are made for the U.S. market by U.S.-owned

intrafirm trade
Trade between global units of a multinational corporation

Imports
Exports
$ billions, 1982 dollars
1,100
1,000
900
800
700
600
500
400
300
200
100
0
1975 1977 1979 1981 1983 1985 1987 1989 1991 1993 1995

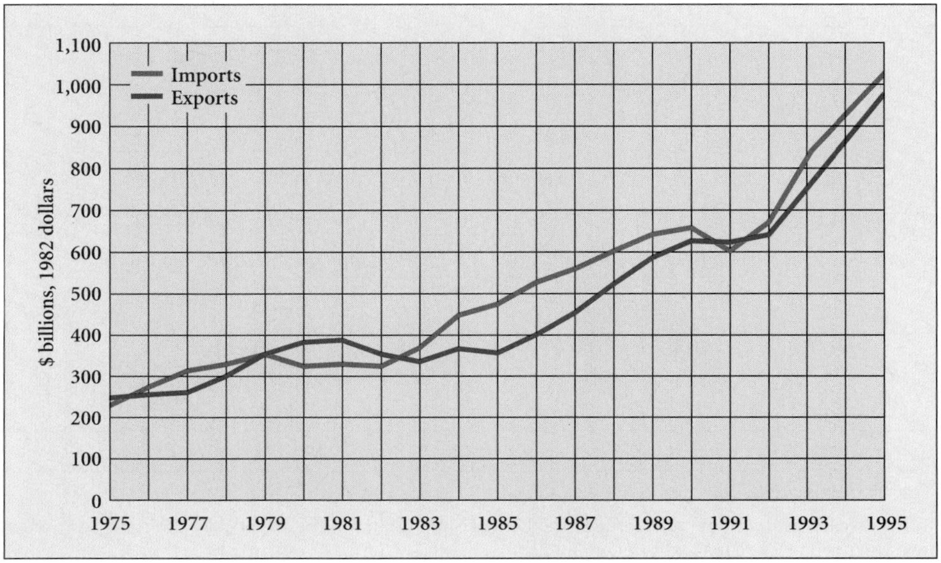

EXHIBIT 2.4

The U.S. Balance of Trade

When the United States imports more than it exports, it experiences a trade deficit. However, when the United States exports more than it imports, it enjoys a trade surplus.

companies operating abroad. In addition, U.S. subsidiaries of foreign companies produce products in the United States for the U.S. market that are not considered imports. As you can see, by itself, the balance of trade does not paint a complete picture of a nation's global competitiveness.

balance of payments
Sum of all payments one nation has made to other nations minus the payments it has received from other nations during a specified period of time

The Balance of Payments The **balance of payments** is the broadest indicator of international trade, measuring the total flow of money into a country minus the flow of money out of the country over a period of time—usually one year (see Exhibit 2.5). The balance of payments includes not only the balance of trade but also payments of foreign aid by governments and direct investments in assets. For example, when a U.S. company buys all or part of a company based in another country, that investment is counted in the balance of payments but not in the balance of trade. Similarly, when foreign companies buy U.S. companies, stocks, bonds, or real estate, those transactions are part of the balance of payments.

Is It True?

The United States buys about half of all of the goods exported by developing nations.

Foreign direct investment in the United States has been increasing in recent years. Germany, Britain, and Canada are among the top investors.[19] At the same time, new investment opportunities have opened up throughout the world. Business investments in eastern Europe and the former Soviet Union continue to draw funds from all around the globe, as do opportunities in the emerging markets of Latin America. Bell South has been one of the most aggressive U.S. investors in Latin America. The company owns large shares of telephone companies in Argentina, Uruguay, Chile, Venezuela, Panama, Peru, Colombia, and Nicaragua.[20]

The biggest investment opportunities in the 1990s, however, are in the developing economies of East Asia, which together receive over 60 percent of the world's private capital flows to developing countries. That is equal to over $100 billion per year. The Chinese

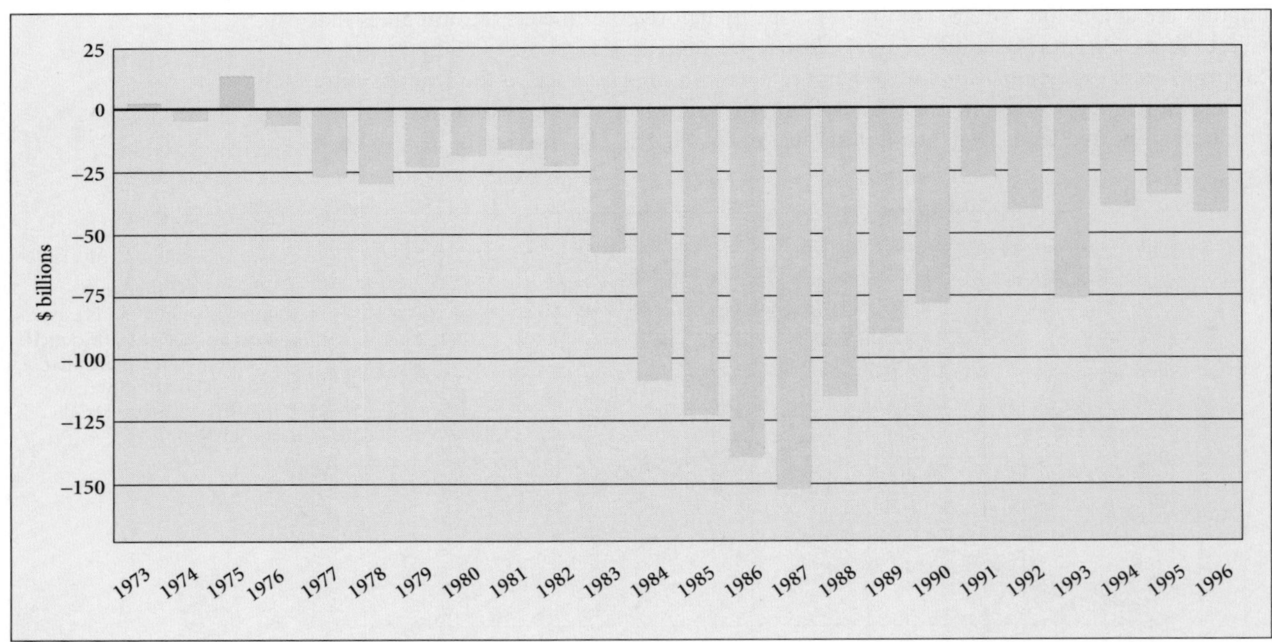

EXHIBIT 2.5

The U.S. Balance of Payments

In most years, more money flows out of the United States than in. This is partially the result of foreign investments by U.S. firms and foreign aid disbursements by the U.S. government.

Economic Area (China, Hong Kong, and Taiwan), South Korea, Singapore, Thailand, Malaysia, and Indonesia have all enjoyed unprecedented economic growth, and Vietnam and India are showing signs of becoming future hot spots for foreign investment.[21] These countries are all known as *Big Emerging Markets.* They have been identified by the U.S. International Trade Administration, along with eight other countries (including Poland, South Africa, Turkey, and Brazil), as having the greatest potential for large increases in U.S. exports over the next two decades (see Exhibit 2.6).[22] Some of the emerging countries of East Asia, including South Korea, Thailand, and Indonesia, experienced severe economic setbacks in late 1997. Saddled with huge amounts of debt, companies and governments could no longer make payments to their banks, forcing some banks out of business. As investors began to lose confidence in the economic stability of the region, they pulled their money out, causing stock markets to tumble and currency values to decline. However, emergency financial support from developed nations like Japan, Germany, and the United States helped keep the crisis from sliding further. Although the crisis means that the region will experience higher unemployment and slower economic growth for some time, many experts agree that East Asia will continue to be an area of future opportunity for business and investment.[23]

Government Actions Relating to International Business

How the United States or any other country fares in its international economic relationships depends to a great extent on government actions that affect trade, foreign investment, and currency values. Basically, the national objective is to devise policies that balance the interests of U.S. companies, U.S. workers, and U.S. consumers. Other countries, of course, are trying to do the same thing. As you might expect, the many players involved in world trade sometimes have conflicting goals.

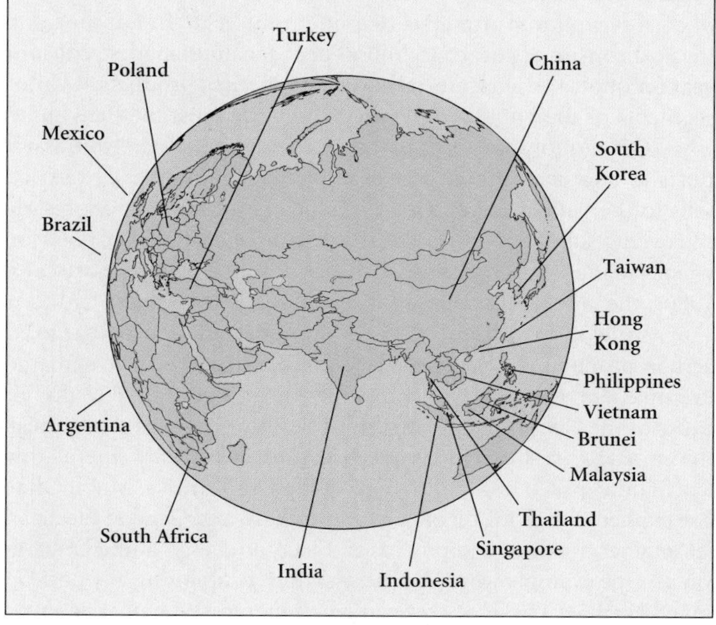

EXHIBIT 2.6

The World's Big Emerging Markets (BEMs)

The countries that hold the greatest potential for U.S. exports in the coming two decades are not our traditional trading partners.

Protectionist Measures

protectionism
Government policies aimed at shielding a country's industries from foreign competition

Every country has the right to control its participation in the global marketplace. All countries practice **protectionism** in one way or another to shield their industries from foreign competition. In the case of some emerging economies, such as China, protectionist measures may also be designed to create industries that previously did not exist.[24] Protectionism is usually broken into two categories: tariffs and nontariff barriers. Nontariff barriers include quotas, subsidies, and restrictive standards.

tariffs
Taxes levied on imports

Tariffs **Tariffs** are taxes levied against imported goods. Sometimes tariffs are put in place to generate revenue for a government. However, most tariffs are protective; they raise the price of imported goods to give domestic producers a cost advantage. Although countries see tariffs as a way to protect their own industries, consumers who want to buy imported goods wind up paying a higher price.[25]

During the depression years of the 1930s, many countries tried to protect jobs at home by increasing tariffs. However, those tariffs stifled world trade and contributed to the downward spiral of the world economy. To avoid repeating the problem, the United States led a movement after World War II to reduce tariffs throughout the world. The effort resulted in an international agreement that has sharply reduced tariffs. This agreement, known as the General Agreement on Tariffs and Trade, is discussed in detail later in the chapter.

quotas
Fixed limits on the quantity of imports a nation will allow for a specific product

Quotas As reliance on tariffs declined, many countries adopted nontariff barriers to discourage imports. One of the most common is to impose **quotas**, which limit the number of specific items that may be imported. These limits raise the price consumers pay for items covered by quotas. For example, only 1.7 million pounds of imported peanuts are allowed into the United States each year. Although that may sound like a lot, it's less than one-tenth of 1 percent of the U.S. crop. The lack of foreign competition allows U.S. peanut growers to charge more for peanuts than they otherwise would. The United States also places stiff quotas on sugar. These quotas cost consumers an additional $1.4 billion each year, with over 40 percent of the benefits going to just 1 percent of the sugar growers. Moreover, the U.S. corn industry enjoys higher profits because sugar quotas make the price of corn syrup more attractive to food producers.[26] In Europe quotas on textiles and clothing cost consumers over $15 billion per year, and Japanese consumers pay $110 billion per year for quotas on agricultural and manufactured products.[27] Unfortunately, it is the poorer segments of the population who are hurt the most by these higher prices.

voluntary export restrictions (VERs)
Self-imposed limits on the amount of certain goods a country exports

Often quotas are negotiated; one trading partner "voluntarily" agrees to limit its exports to another country. For example, Japan voluntarily restricts the number of cars it sells to the United States. However, such **voluntary export restrictions (VERs)** can limit the overall supply of goods, causing the price of domestic goods to rise. Such was the case when Japanese automakers first began limiting their exports to the United States in the 1980s; the cost of U.S. cars went up, and U.S. consumers had to pay.[28]

embargo
Total ban on trade with a particular nation or in a particular product

In its most extreme form, a quota becomes an **embargo**, which prohibits trade in certain products or with specific countries altogether. The embargo against Vietnam is one example. For 19 years, U.S. companies weren't permitted to do business with Vietnam because of the U.S. government's opposition to Vietnam's communist regime. However, when the embargo was lifted in 1994, U.S. companies quickly entered this growing market: Coca-Cola and PepsiCo began distributing their soft drinks, Mobil Oil teamed up with Japanese companies to drill for oil off Vietnam's coast, and General Electric began negotiating to sell jet engines, medical equipment, and locomotives.[29] Some embargoes are politically motivated. One example would be the sanctions prohibiting any new U.S. investment in Mayanmar (Burma). The U.S. government imposed the embargo to protest the human rights

Once the target of a U.S. embargo, Vietnam is now an emerging economy with great potential for U.S. companies.

abuses inflicted by Mayanmar's government on its country's citizens.[30] However, most embargoes are imposed to protect domestic industries or for health or safety reasons. For example, Canada forbids the importation of oleomargarine in order to protect its dairy industry, and the U.S. ban on toys with lead paint is motivated by health concerns.

Subsidies Rather than restrict imports, some countries prefer to subsidize domestic producers so that their prices will be substantially lower than import prices. The goal is often to help build up an industry until it is strong enough to compete on its own in both domestic and foreign markets. For example, Airbus is a subsidized joint venture in aircraft manufacturing supported by Germany, France, England, and Spain. Subsidies help Airbus compete against Boeing, which holds a majority of the world's passenger airplane market. Worldwide, agriculture receives the largest subsidies. However, in the United States new agricultural policies are gradually reducing price supports until the year 2002.[31]

Restrictive Standards One way to restrict imports is to establish standards that give domestic producers an edge. Many countries require special licenses for doing certain kinds of business and then make it difficult for foreign companies to obtain a license. For example, Saudi Arabia restricts import licenses for a variety of products, including chemicals, pasteurized milk, and information technology products.[32] Other countries require imports to pass special tests, which complicates selling products in that country. And some countries encourage companies to purchase parts from domestic suppliers. For instance, Brazil offers car manufacturers reduced import duties on cars assembled in plants outside

Brazil if those manufacturers promise to meet certain targets for including Brazilian parts in vehicles and components they produce in their Brazilian plants for export.[33]

BEST OF THE WEB

Leading the Way to Foreign Trade

How do products from all over the world find their way into the hands of consumers? The process can take a long time, but it may begin with a trade lead—a sort of classified ad to buy or sell products internationally. World Trade Markets lists many current trade leads on its Web page. In them you will find product and contact information from companies and professional agents all over the world. You can view the leads by date, country, or product. Follow the links to products or areas of the world that are of interest to you—who knows what opportunities you will find.
http://www.wtm.com

dumping
Charging less than the actual cost or less than the home-country price for goods sold in other countries

Unfair Trade Practices Sometimes countries engage in trade practices that are deemed unfair by the host country. One example is **dumping,** when a company sells large quantities of its products at a price lower than the cost of production or below what it would charge for the product in its home market. This practice is often used to quickly gain a larger share of the market or to reduce inventories. Dumping puts pressure on competitors to cut their own prices in order to maintain sales. Even though reducing prices may benefit consumers, it can greatly damage a company's competitive position. At least 200 antidumping cases have been brought against China by the United States and the European Union in recent years. Among the products China is accused of dumping are shoes and bicycles.[34]

Like other countries, the United States has legal weapons to use against nations that engage in unfair trade practices. Under Section 301 of the Trade Act of 1988, the U.S. president is legally obligated to retaliate against foreign producers that use questionable tactics in approaching the U.S. market. For example, if a U.S. company can support a dumping claim, the U.S. government typically responds by imposing an antidumping duty on the import, which effectively raises its price to the U.S. level, thereby protecting U.S. producers.

The Pros and Cons of Protectionism Is protectionism a good idea or a bad idea? Proponents of both sides of the issue can make convincing arguments (see Exhibit 2.7). Since World War II, Congress has tended to support those who favor protectionism, usually in response to pressure from manufacturers and workers in their districts who fear the immediate threats of competition and possible loss of jobs. However, many developing countries that once imposed trade barriers to shield their emerging industries are now opening up their markets. These countries found that trade restrictions were stifling their economies. U.S. presidents, looking at the overall long-term economic picture, have also advocated a reduction in trade barriers in recent years. Study after study has shown that in the long run, protectionism hurts everyone.

Trade Agreements and Trade Finance

To prevent trade disputes from escalating into full-blown trade wars, and to ensure that international business is conducted in a fair and orderly fashion, the countries of the world have created a number of agreements. Philosophically, most of these agreements support the basic principles of **free trade**; that is, each nation will ultimately benefit by freely exchanging the goods and services it produces most efficiently for the goods and services it produces less efficiently. The major trade agreements include the GATT, the WTO, APEC, and several regional trading blocs.

free trade
International trade unencumbered by restrictive measures

PRO	CON
Protectionism boosts domestic economies by restricting foreign competition.	Protectionism raises the price of both foreign and domestic goods. This has a negative impact on economic growth in the long run.
Local jobs are saved because demand for domestically produced goods remains strong.	The cost of saving jobs in specific industries is enormous. For example, in the steel industry, each job saved through protectionism costs over $800,000. Moreover, companies that depend on imported parts may have to cut back on production and employment if they can't obtain what they need from overseas suppliers.
Protectionism helps weak domestic industries stay afloat.	Protectionism discourages innovation. The isolated economies of the Soviet Union and its satellites prior to the 1990s demonstrated all too well that shielding domestic industries results in poor quality, outdated technology, and a lack of competitiveness.
Nations must sometimes retaliate against foreign trade restrictions.	A loophole exists for every "protectionist fix." For example, when the United States limited imports of cotton from China, Chinese companies got around the barrier by switching to cotton blends.

EXHIBIT 2.7

Protectionism Pros and Cons

Although arguments can be made both for and against protectionism, most experts agree that it is damaging to a nation's economy in the long run.

The General Agreement on Tariffs and Trade (GATT) The General Agreement on Tariffs and Trade (GATT) is a worldwide trade pact that was first established in the aftermath of World War II. Over the years, each GATT member country has sent representatives to a series of meetings about trade problems. The guiding principle has been one of nondiscrimination: Any trade advantage a GATT member gives to one country must be given to all GATT members, and no GATT nation can be singled out for punishment.

GATT successfully reduced tariff barriers on manufactured goods, which have fallen from an average of 40 percent during pre-GATT days to 5 percent today. The latest GATT agreement, known as the Uruguay Round, was signed in 1994 and implemented in 1995. This agreement cut worldwide tariffs by an average of one-third and brought agricultural products under GATT rules for the first time.[35] It also established the World Trade Organization (WTO), which has now replaced GATT as the world forum for trade negotiations.

The World Trade Organization (WTO) The WTO is a permanent negotiating forum for implementing and monitoring international trade procedures and for mediating trade disputes among its 123 member countries. The WTO's goals include facilitating free trade, lowering the costs of doing business, enhancing the international investment environment, simplifying customs, and promoting technical and economic cooperation. The WTO should ultimately prove to be more effective than the GATT in encouraging free trade because it has a formal legal structure for settling disputes. The WTO also encompasses sectors not previously covered by the GATT, such as services and intellectual property rights.[36]

The Asia Pacific Economic Cooperation Council (APEC) The Asia Pacific Economic Cooperation Council (APEC) is an organization of 18 countries that are making efforts to liberalize trade in the Pacific Rim (the land areas that surround the Pacific Ocean). Among the member nations are the United States, Japan, China, Mexico, Australia, South Korea, and Canada. In 1994 representatives from all member nations met in Bogor, Indonesia, where they agreed to eliminate all tariffs and trade barriers among industrialized countries of the

Pacific Rim by 2010 and among developing countries by 2020. APEC's broad-reaching agreements aim to reduce restrictions and improve reciprocity in market access, investment, standards and customs, intellectual property rights, energy and environmental issues, and dispute mediation.[37] Subsequent APEC meetings have been held to further pursue these goals.

trading blocs
Organizations of nations that remove barriers to trade among their members and that establish uniform barriers to trade with nonmember nations

Trading Blocs One way to encourage trade is through **trading blocs**, regional groupings of countries that agree to remove trade barriers with each other. Although specific rules vary from group to group, trading blocs generally promote trade inside the region while creating uniform barriers against goods and services entering the region from nonmember countries. Some economists are apprehensive about the growing importance of regional trading blocs. They fear that the world is splitting into three camps, revolving around the Americas, Europe, and Asia. Any nation that does not fall into one of these economic regions could suffer, they say, because members of the trading blocs could place severe restrictions on trade with nonmember countries. The critics fear that overall world trade could decline as members become more protective of their own regions. As a result, consumers could find themselves with fewer choices, and many producers could lose sales in lucrative foreign markets. In May, 1998, President Suharto resigned.

On the other side of this issue, the growth of commerce and the availability of customers and suppliers within a trading bloc can be a boon to smaller or younger nations that are trying to build strong economies. The lack of trade barriers in the bloc helps their industries compete with producers in more developed nations, and in some cases, member countries can reach a wider market than before.[38] In addition, alliances with other countries can lead to increased levels of foreign direct investment and greater sharing of technology, both of which can aid future economic development. Moreover, close ties to more stable economies can help shield emerging nations from fluctuations in the global economy. Although it is unlikely that regional trading blocs will cut themselves off from trade with the rest of the world, they are becoming a significant force in the global marketplace. The four most powerful trading blocs today are the European Union, the NAFTA countries, the ASEAN nations, and the Mercosur (see Exhibit 2.8).

EXHIBIT 2.8

Members of Major Trade Blocs

As the economies of the world become increasingly linked, many countries have formed powerful regional trade blocs that trade freely with each other and limit foreign competition.

EUROPEAN UNION (EU)	NORTH AMERICAN FREE TRADE AGREEMENT (NAFTA)	ASSOCIATION OF SOUTHEAST ASIAN NATIONS (ASEAN)	MERCOSUR
France	United States	Brunei	Argentina
Germany	Canada	Indonesia	Brazil
Italy	Mexico	Malaysia	Uruguay
Belgium		Philippines	Paraguay
Netherlands		Singapore	
Luxembourg		Thailand	
Great Britain		Vietnam	
Denmark			
Greece			
Ireland			
Portugal			
Spain			
Austria			
Finland			
Sweden			

The European Union One of the largest trading blocs is the European Union (EU). Originally formed in 1957, the EU began as a loose alliance of six trading partners: France, West Germany (now Germany), Italy, Belgium, the Netherlands, and Luxembourg. Later, the number expanded to 12 through the admittance of Great Britain, Denmark, Greece, Ireland, Portugal, and Spain. And more recently, Austria, Finland, and Sweden have been admitted. Inside the bloc, the EU nations are working to do away with hundreds of local regulations, variations in product standards, and protectionist measures that limit trade between member countries. Eliminating barriers means the nations of the EU can function as a single market, with trade flowing between member countries as it does between states in the United States. In addition, the countries of the EU are working to create a standardized currency.

With a combined gross domestic product (GDP) of over $6.5 trillion and a population of over 367 million, the EU has become a commanding force in the world economy.[39] The EU also has a close economic relationship with four neighboring western European countries (Iceland, Liechtenstein, Norway, and Switzerland). Together, they form a larger trading bloc called the European Free Trade Association (EFTA). Moreover, talks are already under way to admit more countries early in the twenty-first century, including the Czech Republic, Estonia, Hungary, Slovenia, and Poland.[40]

Is It True?

The movement for a unified Europe is a recent development.

The North American Free Trade Agreement (NAFTA) In 1994 the United States, Canada, and Mexico formed a powerful trading bloc, the North American Free Trade Agreement (NAFTA), which incorporates 400 million people and an economic output of $8 trillion. As outlined in the agreement, the three countries have been phasing out all of the tariffs and quotas that formerly restricted trade within the bloc. This process paves the way for the freer flow of goods, services, and capital within the three-nation region. In addition, talks are currently under way to expand NAFTA to include Chile, whose streamlined economy has become the envy of Latin America. Ultimately, NAFTA's supporters would like to see the agreement expanded to include all of Central and South America by 2005.

NAFTA has always been controversial. Debate still continues about whether the agreement is helping or hurting the U.S. economy. Although U.S. exports to Mexico and Canada increased slightly, the balance of trade with Mexico went from a $1.7 billion surplus to a $16.2 billion deficit. However, this shift resulted in part from the massive 1995 *devaluation* of the Mexican peso, reducing the peso's value relative to other currencies and making Mexican goods much less expensive in the United States and Canada. Also of concern has been NAFTA's effect on U.S. jobs. Critics contend that many jobs have been lost because U.S. manufacturers moved production to Mexico and Canada. Supporters, on the other hand, say that U.S. jobs have multiplied as a result of increased exporting. Which side is right? It's still too early to tell whether NAFTA's overall impact on the U.S. economy will be positive or negative.[41] Over the coming years, U.S. trade policy and NAFTA will certainly continue to be watched closely.

The Association of Southeast Asian Nations (ASEAN) In Asia, seven nations make up the Association of Southeast Asian Nations (ASEAN). Together, they have formed the ASEAN Free Trade Area (AFTA) to boost regional trade. This trading bloc consists of Brunei, Indonesia, Malaysia, the Philippines, Singapore, Thailand, and Vietnam—the countries known as the Asian Tigers. Laos is also interested in joining.

Like other trading blocs, ASEAN seeks to reduce barriers to trade within the region. Recently, the ASEAN nations agreed to implement the ASEAN Investment Area (AIA). The AIA aims to enable the free flow of capital among ASEAN member nations, facilitate access to technology and skilled personnel, and promote a larger role for private investment in the area.[42]

The Mercosur The countries of Latin America have developed many smaller trade pacts. However, the largest trade bloc in the region is the Mercosur, a common market established by Argentina, Brazil, Uruguay, and Paraguay. Together, these countries represent more than half of South America's GDP and 40 percent of its foreign trade. In addition to reducing tariffs by 75 percent, these nations are working toward full economic integration. Even more significantly, the Mercosur countries, as well as other countries in Latin America, are negotiating trade agreements with the European Union, Japan, and the NAFTA countries. Many trading nations see Latin America as an area for large-scale economic growth in the future, and they want to establish ties early in the game. Some U.S. officials hope that Mercosur will eventually join NAFTA to form a Free Trade Area of the Americas (FTAA). Experts predict, however, that Mercosur will benefit most from trade agreements with the EU, and French officials have vocalized strong support for this possibility.[43] It remains to be seen whether the Latin American nations will develop a large trading bloc on their own, whether they will become a part of the NAFTA bloc, whether they will partner with the EU, or whether they will opt for less economic integration. Whatever the outcome, Latin America promises to be an increasingly larger player in the global economy.

Unilateral Trade Privileges In addition to forming regional trading blocs, nations often provide each other with special trade privileges on a country-by-country basis. When the United States grants **most favored nation (MFN) trading status** to a country, it greatly simplifies and reduces the import duties that the country pays on goods exported to the United States. MFN status also sends a signal to foreign companies that the U.S. government is committed to building a stable trading relationship with the foreign government. This promotes stronger ties between companies in both countries.

most favored nation (MFN) trading status
A privilege granted by the United States that greatly simplifies and reduces import duties levied on goods from certain countries

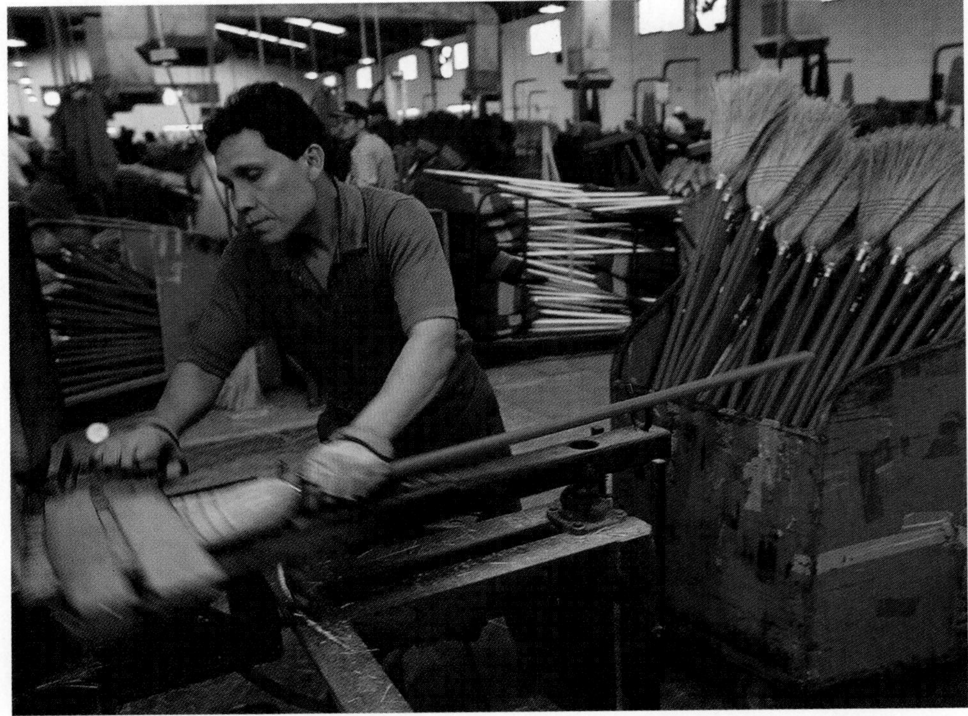

The elimination of tariffs under NAFTA enabled this Mexican broom manufacturer to double its exports. However, sales of U.S. made brooms have decreased about 25 percent each year since NAFTA was signed.

International Trade Finance One of the major problems of international trade is that some less-developed countries are too poor to participate to any great extent in the world economy. They lack both the capital to develop their own industrial potential and the money to pay for much-needed imports. Two international organizations—the International Monetary Fund (IMF) and the World Bank—are especially helpful in channeling funds to these nations.

The IMF was founded in 1945 and is now affiliated with the United Nations. It lends money to countries that are suffering from an unfavorable balance of payments. For example, the IMF provided loans totaling $57 billion to South Korea when the country faced a large economic crisis in 1997.[44] In contrast, the World Bank, officially known as the International Bank for Reconstruction and Development, was founded to finance reconstruction following World War II. It now provides low-interest loans to developing nations for the improvement of transportation, telecommunications, health, and education. Currently the World Bank is focused on bringing the Internet to the less-developed regions of the world, such as Africa. World Bank officials and telecommunication executives hope that Internet connections will attract more companies to the region, which will lead to more rapid economic development.[45] Both the IMF and the World Bank are funded by contributions from 135 member nations. The bulk of the funds come from the United States, western Europe, and Japan.

Companies based in the United States can also receive financial support for their export activities through the government-backed Export-Import Bank of the United States, known as Eximbank. Eximbank arranges loans that enable customers in other countries to buy U.S. goods and services, guarantees repayment of loans made to U.S. exporters, and arranges insurance to cover exporters against nonpayment by overseas customers.[46]

The private banking system is also involved in international lending. However, many banks have become hesitant to make loans to less-developed nations because these countries have had problems repaying their loans. The international debt of developing countries now totals $1.7 trillion. Strapped with large loan repayments, some indebted nations are unable to pay for imports and industrial development. It is estimated that 40 percent to 60 percent of the export earnings from less-developed countries goes to paying off foreign debts. However, 77 of the world's developing nations met in Costa Rica recently to establish new strategies to relieve this burden on their economic growth.[47]

Get the Facts

BEST OF THE WEB

Whether you are trying to spot business trends for your company or write a report for class, at some point you will need information on other countries. Many sources are available on the Internet, but few can rival the Central Intelligence Agency's home page for sheer volume of information. Take a look at the *Handbook of International Economic Statistics* for a glimpse of world GDP, agricultural production, or energy consumption. Check out *Chiefs of State and Cabinet Members of Foreign Governments* to find out who leads countries from Afghanistan to Zimbabwe. And for a wealth of valuable facts and statistics from all over the globe, browse *The World Factbook.* To access these and other resources, select *Publications* when you reach the main menu page.
http://www.odci.gov/cia/

Economic Summit Meetings Apart from participating in formal organizations that facilitate world trade, some countries also hold occasional economic summit meetings with key trading partners. These policy-making sessions are generally attended by the finance ministers of the countries involved, and they usually deal with such issues as exchange rates and trade imbalances. Because they are attended by high-ranking government officials, the meetings can be influential in shaping trade relationships. In recent years, the United States has increasingly relied on such meetings to resolve perplexing trade problems within the Group of Five (the United States, Great Britain, France, Germany, and Japan), the Group of Seven (the Group of Five plus Canada and Italy), and the Group of Ten (the Group of Seven plus Belgium, the Netherlands, Sweden, and Switzerland, which joined later). The Group of Seven (G7) met in Denver in June of 1997. This summit was especially significant because Russia, although not a G7 member, was invited to participate for the first time. The meeting was referred to as the "Summit of the Eight."[48]

U.S. Measures Governing Foreign Trade

In addition to promoting world trade through international groups, the United States has established domestic agencies and policies that help U.S. companies compete abroad. Over 15 federal agencies, including the Commerce Department, the Small Business Administration, and the Agriculture Department, are together spending more than $2 billion to help promote exports.[49] Many of the resources they offer are now accessible via the Internet.

Promotion of Foreign Trade Companies interested in conducting business abroad are affected by a number of U.S. laws passed to encourage participation in international trade. For instance, the Webb-Pomerene Export Trade Act of 1918 allows U.S. companies to cooperate in developing export markets without running afoul of the antitrust laws that limit joint activities in the United States. The Export Trading Companies Act of 1982 extends the Pomerene Act by allowing companies and banks to form export trading companies to market products abroad. In 1988 Congress enacted a sweeping trade bill that gives the president

THINKING ABOUT ETHICS

Bribery, Piracy, and Thievery: Understanding the Challenges of Global Corruption

Conducting business overseas offers companies many new opportunities, but it also presents new challenges. One of those challenges is having to deal with corrupt business practices. In countries such as Indonesia and China, bribing government officials to take care of routine transactions is accepted and expected. However, U.S. law prevents U.S. companies from making such payments.

So how do U.S. companies get things done without breaking the law, especially when competitors show up with briefcases full of cash? Some U.S. companies offer to make financial contributions in other ways. For example, IBM recently donated $25 million in hardware and software to 20 Chinese universities. Another option that the U.S. government supports is to pay for foreign executives to visit the United States. Such trips usually mix both business and pleasure and often involve stops at attractions like Las Vegas and Disneyland.

However, many smaller companies do not have the financial resources to make these types of large "investments." Instead, they have to work hard at cultivating relationships with local leaders without giving them questionable payments. In the long run, solid relationships can be a very valuable asset. One U.S. businessman who worked as a country manager in Latin America for 17 years says that he managed to avoid paying a single bribe in that time. Instead, he relied on relationships, influence, exchange of favors, and legitimate third-party facilitators to accomplish his goals. He admits that sometimes he had to accept delays and other setbacks in order to maintain his ethical standards.

Bribery isn't the only form of corruption U.S. companies face abroad. Theft of intellectual property is on the rise as nations struggle to keep up with rapid changes in technology. Intellectual property includes consumer goods such as music CDs, books, and software, as well as highly

power to block any foreign purchase of U.S. companies that might endanger U.S. security. The act also requires the government to investigate the trade practices of countries that maintain numerous barriers to U.S. exports.

To further encourage exporting, the U.S. government grants tax benefits to companies engaged in international business. Companies can set up **foreign sales corporations (FSCs),** marketing subsidiaries that are partially exempted from paying income taxes on export profits. For example, California Microwave, a major satellite and wireless communications company, receives tax benefits of almost half a million dollars annually through its FSC.[50]

foreign sales corporations (FSCs)
Tax-sheltered subsidiaries of U.S.-based corporations that engage in exporting

The U.S. government also offers insurance against some of the political and economic risks associated with doing business abroad. The government-sponsored Foreign Credit Insurance Association and the Overseas Private Investment Corporation offer coverage for losses due to expropriation (the takeover of a business by a foreign government), war, revolution, credit defaults, and currency-exchange problems.

Promotion of Ethical Business Standards All U.S. companies that do business in other countries must comply with the Foreign Corrupt Practices Act. This U.S. law outlaws actions such as bribing government officials in other nations to approve deals. However, it does allow certain payments, including small payments to officials for expediting routine government actions. Critics of this U.S. law complain that payoffs are a routine part of world trade, so forbidding U.S. companies to follow suit cripples their ability to compete. Others counter that U.S. exports haven't been affected by this law and that companies can conduct business abroad without violating antibribery rules. Regardless of whether they agree with the law or not, some companies have had to forego opportunities as a result of it. For

sensitive trade secrets, technologies, and product formulas. Consumer products are often illegally copied and sold on the streets and in retail outlets of foreign countries. At the same time, increasing numbers of foreign employees of U.S firms are being lured away by local competitors, often taking proprietary information with them. These activities cost U.S. firms billions of dollars each year.

Part of the problem for U.S. companies is that foreign laws protecting intellectual property are often very weak or nonexistent. However, the Uruguay Round of the GATT provided the United States with some new weapons to combat the problem. Under the new rules, the United States is able to file charges with the WTO against offending countries. The United States can also threaten them with unilateral trade sanctions. Such threats recently forced China to crack down on piracy and open its markets wider to legitimate products from the United States. Nonetheless, piracy and theft are still rampant in China and many other countries. The International Intellectual Properties Alliance, an industry group, estimates that illegal copies account for 70 to 90 percent of all U.S. software and music CDs sold in Russia. Although U.S. business leaders and government representatives continue to meet with foreign officials to find ways to curb piracy, any U.S. company conducting business abroad must be aware of the risks, and it should take all measures possible to protect both its products and its technology.

QUESTIONS FOR CRITICAL THINKING

1. Should the U.S. government more closely regulate the practice of giving trips and other incentives to foreign managers to win their business? Is this bribery?
2. What steps can U.S. companies take to protect themselves from theft of intellectual property?

example, a U.S. power-generation company recently walked away from a $320 million contract in the Middle East because government officials demanded a $3 million bribe. The contract went to a Japanese company instead.[51]

Promotion of Foreign Investment in the United States When it comes to encouraging overseas companies to do business in the United States, most of the action occurs on the state and local level. Most U.S. states and many major U.S. cities have agencies that try to persuade foreign companies to open regional facilities. For example, Tuscaloosa, Alabama, competed against cities in 30 states to be selected as the site of the first Mercedes-Benz factory in the United States. Since opening, the plant has hired 1,500 workers and created an additional 1,200 area jobs in related industries.[52]

Adjustments in Currency Values

foreign exchange
Trading one currency for the equivalent value of another currency

exchange rate
Rate at which the money of one country is traded for the money of another

floating exchange rate system
World economic system in which the values of all currencies are determined by supply and demand

Because each country has its own currency, trade between countries involves an exchange of currencies. When a company in one country sells its products abroad, the price must be converted from one currency to another. For example, every time a Japanese trading company buys a ton of soybeans from the United States, it must obtain U.S. dollars to pay for them. The company may do so by exchanging Japanese yen for dollars at one of the international banks that handle **foreign exchange**, the conversion of one currency into an equivalent amount of another currency. The number of yen, francs, or pounds that must be exchanged for every dollar, mark, or won is known as the **exchange rate** between those two currencies.

International traders operate under a **floating exchange rate system**, whereby currency values fluctuate in response to the forces of global supply and demand. The system is actually not completely flexible, as developing countries sometimes base the value of their currencies on the value of more stable currencies, such as the dollar or the yen. Nevertheless, exchange rates change rapidly because supply and demand are always changing. The relationships between the rates are determined in part by what is happening in local economies. For example, if Italy's economy is suffering from severe inflation and unemployment, foreign investment in Italy will decrease, thereby lessening the demand for Italian currency and causing its value to be lower than the currency values in countries not experiencing economic turmoil.

A drop in the value of a nation's currency relative to the value of other currencies is known as *devaluation.* This adjustment in currency values makes domestic products cheaper abroad and increases the price of imports (see Exhibit 2.9). For example, when the U.S. dollar is weak—that is, relatively low in value—fewer units of foreign currency are required to purchase each dollar. Such situations tend to lower U.S. imports and raise U.S. exports. Conversely, a strong dollar boosts imports and dampens exports. The exchange rate also affects the prices for supplies, payroll, and other items that companies have to pay for when they operate in another country. For example, when the dollar is weak relative to the Deutsche mark, it costs more for U.S. companies to conduct business in Germany because more dollars are required to pay for the same amount of paper clips, personnel, or consulting services.

Although a government can manipulate its country's currency value to improve the competitive position of its industries, devaluation typically occurs in response to the forces of supply and demand. Consider the devaluation of the Indonesian rupiah, which traded at 2,500 to the dollar in the summer of 1997. At that time, however, Indonesia's economy was overburdened with debt. Many investors began to lose confidence in their Indonesian securities and subsequently sold them, causing the rupiah to weaken. In simple terms, excess supply and weak demand forced the rupiah's value down. Although the IMF offered a $43 billion bailout to help the country get back on solid financial footing, Indonesian

1997 VALUE	
$1 =	*Currency*
1.53	British pound
1.62	German mark
102.18	Japanese yen
31.39	Indian rupee
806.93	South Korean won
33.43	Belgian franc
25.16	Thai baht
133.88	Spanish peseta
242.50	Greek drachma
.73	Australian dollar

Equation A. 1 British pound $= \frac{\$1}{1.53} = \$0.65$

Equation B. 1 British pound $= \frac{\$1}{1.33} = \$0.75$

EXHIBIT 2.9

The Value of the Dollar

This table lists the average value of ten foreign currencies relative to the dollar in 1997. Equation A shows that $0.65 dollars could be purchased with one British pound at the 1997 exchange rate. As Equation B demonstrates, when the dollar is devalued it will buy fewer pounds, making the denominator in the equation smaller and thus increasing the purchasing power of the pound in the United States.

President Suharto made little attempt to satisfy the IMF's conditions for the loan by reining in government spending. This reduced investor confidence even further, and by early January of 1998, the rupiah was trading at 7,900 to the dollar, a devaluation of almost 300 percent in about 6 months.[53]

The foreign-exchange value of currency issued by countries that have not joined the International Monetary Fund cannot be easily determined, which complicates international trade with those countries. Moreover, some nations don't allow their currencies to cross into other nations. In such situations, a company can turn to **countertrade**, a trading practice in which the company accepts locally produced products instead of cash in exchange for imported products. The products accepted as payment can then be sold for cash. For example, Russia recently offered to sell a fleet of MiG-29 aircraft to the Philippine armed forces in a deal that included partial payment with Philippine commodities.[54]

countertrade
Trading practice in which local products are offered instead of cash in exchange for imported products

MANAGEMENT OF THE GLOBAL CORPORATION

Managing operations in more than one country can be tricky. Traditionally, multinational companies have used a *multidomestic management* approach that allows their local units to act independently. In each country, the local organization is self-contained and acts much like a separate domestic business. Multidomestic management allows local managers to respond quickly to the unique needs and pressures of their host countries.

However, the rapid pace of global expansion has pushed many multinationals to adopt *transnational management*, an approach in which the company coordinates the activities of all its units to achieve worldwide goals—without losing local flexibility. With transnational management, every part of the company shares similar goals, and top management balances the overall use of resources with the opportunities available in each host country. At the same time, local managers are responsible for day-to-day operations in the host countries. In this way, companies are able to operate efficiently on a global level, while maintaining the ability to act and react swiftly on a local level. As mentioned earlier, rapid developments in communication, transportation, and information systems have greatly enhanced the ability of companies to operate transnationally.

Unilever uses transnational management to coordinate the efforts of 500 companies that it controls in 75 countries. Local managers have the freedom to make decisions and

FOCUSING ON CULTURAL DIVERSITY

How to Avoid Business Blunders Abroad

Doing business in another country can be extremely tricky. Here are some issues to consider when you conduct business abroad.

THE IMPORTANCE OF PACKAGING

Numerous problems result from the failure to adapt packaging for other cultures. Sometimes only the color of the package needs to be altered to enhance a product's sales. For instance, white symbolizes death in Japan and much of Asia; green represents danger or disease in Malaysia. Obviously, using the wrong color in these countries might produce negative reactions.

THE LANGUAGE BARRIER

Some product names travel poorly. For instance, the gasoline company Esso found out that its name means "stalled car" in Japan. However, some company names have traveled well. Kodak may be the most famous example. A research team deliberately developed this name after searching for a word that was pronounceable everywhere but had no specific meaning anywhere.

PROBLEMS WITH PROMOTIONS

In its U.S. promotion, one company had effectively used this sentence: "You can use no finer napkin at your dinner table." The U.S. company decided to use the same commercials in England because, after all, the British do speak English. To the British, however, the word *napkin* or *nappy* actually means "diaper." The ad could hardly be expected to boost sales of dinner napkins in England.

LOCAL CUSTOMS

Social norms vary greatly from country to country and it is difficult for any outsider to be knowledgeable about all of them, so local input is vital. For example, one firm promoted eyeglasses in Thailand with commercials featuring animals wearing glasses. However, in Thailand animals are considered a low form of life; humans would never wear anything worn by an animal.

TRANSLATION PROBLEMS

The best translations of an advertising message convey the concept of the original but do not precisely duplicate the original. PepsiCo learned this lesson when it reportedly discovered that its slogan "Come alive with Pepsi" was translated into German as "Come alive out of the grave with Pepsi." In Asia, the slogan was once translated as "Bring your ancestors back from the dead."

THE NEED FOR RESEARCH

Proper market research may reduce or eliminate most international business blunders. Market researchers can uncover needs for product adaptations, potential name problems, promotional requirements, and useful market strategies. Good research may even uncover potential translation problems.

As you can see, doing business in other cultures can be risky if you're unprepared. However, awareness of differences, consultation with local people, and concern for host-country feelings can reduce problems and save money.

QUESTIONS FOR CRITICAL THINKING

1. If you were thinking of marketing a breakfast cereal in Japan, what sorts of issues would you want to consider when you perform your market research?
2. What steps could you take to make sure your product would fit the expectations of the local culture?

take independent action within their companies. At the same time, they are expected to work toward the overall goals set by Unilever's top managers. The sharing of information helps Unilever apply what it learns in one country to operations in other countries. For example, Unilever managers sometimes find that products selling well in one country can be successfully introduced in other countries. However, they realize that a few products (such as steak and kidney pie in the United Kingdom) are uniquely national and therefore not appropriate for other markets.[55]

Cultural Differences in International Business

Unilever, like other multinational corporations, recognizes that each country has its own local tastes and cultural customs. Regardless of whether you work for a U.S. company or one that is headquartered in another country, the best approach you can take in international business is to recognize and respect the differences that distinguish people of other cultures. Cultural differences include social values, ideas of status, decision-making habits, attitudes toward time, use of space, body language, manners, and ethical standards. Such differences can lead to misunderstandings in international business relationships, particularly if language differences also exist.

However, problems can be resolved if you maintain an open mind. The best way to prepare yourself to do business with people from another culture is to study that culture in advance. Learn everything you can about the culture's history, religion, politics, and customs—especially its business customs. Who makes decisions? How are negotiations usually conducted? Is gift giving expected? What is the proper attire for a business meeting? Seasoned international businesspeople suggest the following techniques for improving intercultural communication:

- *Deal with the individual.* Don't stereotype the other person or react with preconceived ideas. Regard the person as an individual first, not as a representative of another culture.
- *Be alert to the other person's customs.* Expect him or her to have differing values, beliefs, expectations, and mannerisms. For instance, don't be surprised when businesspeople in Pakistan excuse themselves in the middle of a meeting to conduct prayers. Moslems pray five times a day.
- *Be aware that gestures and expressions mean different things in different cultures.* The other person's body language may not mean what you think, and he or she may read unintentional meanings into your message. Clarify your true intent by repetition and examples. Ask questions and listen carefully. The Japanese are generally appreciative when foreigners ask what is proper behavior because it shows respect for the Japanese way of doing things.[56]
- *Adapt your style to the other person's.* If the other person appears to be direct and straightforward, follow suit. If not, adjust your behavior to match. In many African countries, for example, people are suspicious of others who seem to be in a hurry. Therefore, you should allow plenty of time to get to know the people you are dealing with.
- *Show respect.* Learn how respect is communicated in various cultures—through gestures, eye contact, and so on. For example, in Spain let a handshake last five to seven strokes; pulling away too soon may be interpreted as a rejection. In France, however, the preferred handshake is a single stroke.

Summary of Learning Objectives

1. **Differentiate between absolute, comparative, and national competitive advantage.**
   A country with an absolute advantage can produce a particular product with fewer resources than any other nation. A country with a comparative advantage produces a particular product more efficiently than other products, relative to other nations. A country with a national competitive advantage has the ability to innovate and upgrade to a higher level of technology and productivity, which makes it more competitive in the world market.

2. **Distinguish between the balance of trade and the balance of payments.**
The balance of trade is the total value of exports minus the value of imports over a specific period. The balance of payments is the total flow of money into the country minus the flow of money out of the country.
3. **Identify four techniques that countries use to protect their domestic industries.**
Four of the most common forms of protectionism are tariffs, quotas, subsidies, and restrictive standards.
4. **Outline the arguments for and against protectionism.**
People who support protectionism believe that building in a preference for a country's home industries can boost local economies and save local jobs. It can also shield domestic industries from head-to-head competition with overseas rivals. Those who argue against protectionism say that it leads to higher consumer prices, high costs of saving jobs and the possibility of losing jobs in other sectors of the economy, damage to U.S. companies that depend on imports, the stifling of innovation, and the existence of many loopholes.
5. **Explain how trading blocs, the GATT, and the WTO affect trade.**
Trading blocs are regional groupings of countries within which trade barriers have been removed. These alliances ease trade between bloc members and strengthen barriers for nonmembers. The World Trade Organization (WTO) is a worldwide forum encompassing 138 nations seeking to reduce certain trade barriers and increase world trade. The WTO also provides a legal framework in which to handle trade disputes. The WTO replaces the GATT, which is a trade agreement that has greatly reduced tariffs in the past 50 years.
6. **Define foreign exchange and discuss the effect of a weaker U.S. dollar on U.S. companies that do business abroad.**
Foreign exchange is the conversion of one currency into an equivalent amount of another currency. When the dollar falls in value relative to other currencies, U.S. products become cheaper on the world market. Because U.S. products cost less, demand rises, and U.S. companies can export more. At the same time, imports become expensive, which puts U.S. products at an advantage in the U.S. market.
7. **Discuss five forms of international business activity.**
Importing and exporting, licensing, franchising, joint ventures and strategic alliances, and wholly owned facilities are five of the most common forms of international business activity. Each entails different levels of risk and provides a company with varying degrees of control.
8. **Identify six ways to improve communication in an international business relationship.**
To improve international communication, learn as much as you can about the cultures of the people you are working with; keep an open mind and avoid stereotyping; be sensitive to other people's customs; anticipate misunderstandings and guard against them; adapt your style to match the style of others; and learn how to show respect in another culture.

On the Job: Meeting Business Challenges at Holiday Inn Worldwide

Part of Raymond Lewis's job is to monitor and predict changes in the ever-evolving global market. Among the trends he has observed is the increasing similarity between the needs and desires expressed by consumers and businesses around the world in certain product categories such as lodging. On the other hand, Lewis knows that various countries and cultures approach purchases differently, and that people of various cultures respond differently to product promotion. His challenge, then, is to figure out how to satisfy both the similar and the diverse needs of each new market.

Lewis also knows that all travelers, regardless of where they are from or where they are going, share many of the same desires, fears, and expectations when they are traveling. They may not speak the same language or live the same lives while at home, but when they're on the road, all travelers are (1) away from home and out of their personal comfort zones, (2) in different and often unfamiliar surroundings, and (3) subject to the same hassles and hardships. Therefore, Holiday Inn focuses on delivering a consistent product around the world. This way, whether the hotel is in South Korea, India, Buenos Aires, or Israel, travelers know that they will always receive a comfortable room at a fair price.

In addition, the strategy of segmenting the market by types of travelers that proved so successful in the United States also works abroad, but in a different way. Segmentation in the hotel industry is a relatively new concept in Europe, and in Asia it is virtually nonexistent. This is largely because in many of the developing nations of Asia, travel has only recently become an option for the majority of people. As a result, not every type of Holiday Inn hotel will be successful in every country. The company must know each market very well before it decides which type of hotel to open. Does the area draw mainly tourists or business travelers? How long do visitors usually stay? Do people from surrounding areas travel often? What types of accommodations do competitors offer in the area? By knowing the answers to questions like these, Holiday Inn is able to decide which type of hotel will best serve the needs of travelers to the area. For example, the company opened a SunSpree Resort in Arequipa, Peru, close to Machu Pichu, a popular international tourist destination. Holiday Inn's management team feels that SunSpree has a great chance for success in this location because the hotel caters to tourists. In the same way, Holiday Inn management expects a mix of business and leisure travelers to visit Seoul, South Korea. Therefore, the new Holiday Inn Seoul appeals to a broad range of travelers by offering a business center, banquet facilities, four restaurants, a fitness center, and a gift shop.

Just as in its early days of expansion in the United States, Holiday Inn is accomplishing its international expansion through a mix of wholly owned facilities and franchises, depending on the availability of resources and potential for profit in each local market. Although franchising agreements place less risk on Holiday Inn Worldwide, they also require the company to give up more control than it would by opening wholly owned facilities. However, franchisees must adhere to strict quality standards if they intend to operate under Holiday Inn's famous name.

Lewis and his team also recognize that even though travelers have similar expectations for the quality and value they get in a hotel, sometimes they like to stay in places that don't feel like hotel chains. Therefore, the company has opened hotels in Europe, Australia, and South Africa that have a style and character unique to their locations. In this way, Holiday Inn is able to tailor its global product to local markets.

Nonetheless, Holiday Inn's promotion strategy is decidedly global, regardless of which markets it enters. Lewis bases the strategy on two themes: "Welcome" and "Stay with somebody you know." Although the ad copy is translated when necessary, even the visual format is the same from country to country. Of course, cultural differences must be accommodated from time to time. For example, travelers in Britain preferred an ad that focused on a friendly doorman, whereas U.S. and German travelers preferred a more sentimental ad showing a businesswoman receiving a fax of a drawing from her child.

The inspiration for this global strategy came to Lewis, not surprisingly, while he was traveling. When boarding a plane at Dulles Airport outside of Washington, D.C., he passed a group of Russian teenagers gathered around a guitar player singing "Puff the Magic Dragon," a folk song that was popular in the United States a few decades ago. This connection between cultures helped convince Lewis that the world's people were alike in many ways, particularly in the field of pleasure and business travel.

It remains to be seen how successful Holiday Inn's global strategy will be in the long run. The company is off to a flying start. However, competitors such as Marriott and Choice Hotels are moving quickly to make sure Holiday Inn doesn't outpace them in the hot new global markets. But one thing is sure, Lewis and the rest of the management team are not content with Holiday Inn being a leading hotel chain in the United States. They want Holiday Inn to be the leader around the world.

Your Mission: You work for a small U.S. company that has opened a Holiday Inn franchise in Jakarta, Indonesia. You're in Jakarta to manage the new hotel. Select the best solution to the following situations, using your common sense and the principles you've learned in the chapter.

1. A large shipment of supplies for the hotel, such as towels, soap, and ashtrays, has been held up in customs for two weeks. A local business associate tells you that you are expected to give customs agents some "incentive money" to see that everything clears easily. How do you handle this issue?
   a. Go to the customs office and explain that you refuse to pay a bribe to have your shipment cleared. Threaten to enlist the help of the U.S. trade representative if customs officials do not comply.
   b. Check the Foreign Corrupt Practices Act to determine how much "incentive money" you are legally allowed to pay in this type of situation and pay the customs officials.
   c. Offer the customs officials vouchers for free stays at Holiday Inn hotels if they will clear the shipment quickly.
2. Because your hotel caters to Western businesspeople and tourists, much of the food you buy for the hotel restaurant is imported from the United States and Europe. Lately, the value of the rupiah (Indonesian currency) has been falling relative to Western hard currencies such as the dollar, the pound sterling, and the Deutsche mark. This makes your food imports much more costly, and your profits are declining. What do you do?
   a. Raise prices across the board.
   b. Accept only Western currencies.
   c. Try to purchase more of your food items locally.
3. Your hotel has been quite successful, so the company is considering opening a second one in Bandung. You have heard, however, that it is often difficult for foreigners to obtain building permits unless they have an Indonesian business partner. Which course of action should you pursue?
   a. Arrange to meet with the proper city officials in Bandung who can help you get the permit. Explain that your hotel will bring tourism and jobs to the area, which will help the local economy.
   b. Recommend to your boss in the United States that the company begin seeking local Indonesian investors who would make good partners in the franchise.

c. Offer to make a financial contribution to a city public works project in exchange for the permit.

4. You have decided to advertise your hotel in airline magazines and on billboards in Indonesia's major cities. You want to appeal to both male and female business travelers. However, Asia is still largely dominated by businessmen, some of whom are offended by the movement of women up the corporate ladder. Which of the following ad concepts should you use?

   a. Although it runs counter to majority opinion elsewhere in the world, you should go with the flow in Asia and feature only businessmen in your ads.

   b. The traveling businesswoman may be a rare sight in Asia, but it is on the increase. You should feature women in your ad because that will position Holiday Inn as an innovative company.

   c. You can't afford to offend either group, so you should focus on the expert hotel staff in your ads, not the guests, and let potential guests of either gender decide that the hotel is for them.[57]

Key Terms

absolute advantage (33)
balance of payments (40)
balance of trade (39)
comparative advantage (33)
countertrade (53)
dumping (44)
embargo (42)
exchange rate (52)
exporting (35)
floating exchange rate system (52)
foreign direct investment (FDI) (38)
foreign exchange (52)
foreign sales corporations (51)
free trade (44)
importing (35)
intrafirm trade (39)
licensing (36)
joint venture (36)
most favored nation (MFN) trading status (48)
multinational corporations (MNCs) (34)
national competitive advantage (33)
protectionism (42)
quotas (42)
strategic alliance (37)
tariffs (42)
trade deficit (39)
trade surplus (39)
trading blocs (46)
voluntary export restrictions (VERs) (42)

Questions

For Review

1. What is the balance of trade, and how does it relate to the balance of payments?
2. What is dumping, and how does the United States respond to this practice?
3. Why do countries join trading blocs?
4. What is a floating exchange rate?
5. How does multidomestic management differ from transnational management?

For Analysis

6. What actions might a government take to help develop a national competitive advantage?
7. What are some of the risks a small company might face by exporting its products directly to another country? How can it avoid some of these risks?
8. How can a company use a licensing agreement to enter world markets?
9. What types of situations might cause the U.S. government to implement protectionist measures?
10. How does the International Monetary Fund differ from the World Bank and the Export-Import Bank?

For Application

11. Suppose you own a small company that manufactures baseball equipment. You are aware that Russia is a large market, and you are considering exporting your products there. What steps should you take? Who might be able to give you assistance? Where can you get financing?
12. Now suppose you are a high-level manager with a large multinational corporation that is searching for a location for a new manufacturing facility. What factors should you consider as you go about your search?

A Case for Critical Thinking ■ Entrepreneurs Clean Up in South Africa

A few years ago, Michael Giles and Bernadette Moffat made what many would consider to be a very bold move. This husband-and-wife team were both successful attorneys living a suburban lifestyle in the United States when they decided to end their corporate careers, move to South Africa, and open a chain of laundry and dry-cleaning stores. Now they have 4 stores, 24 employees, and funding to open 100 more laundries nationwide.

Giles and Moffat are two entrepreneurs who demonstrate that the opportunities of the global marketplace are not just for large companies. They came to Soweto, South Africa, with $150,000 of start-up capital borrowed from friends and relatives in the United States. They were motivated by what they saw as a huge potential market and by the belief that the nation of South Africa will not succeed unless small and medium-sized businesses are established. At first they looked at working with major corporations seeking to do business in the area, but they wanted more control than what the corporations were offering. Next, they investigated consumer goods and service businesses; however, the start-up costs for most of these businesses were too high. Then they hit on the idea of laundromats. Giles admits that at first he thought the idea was boring. But when he considered adding dry cleaning, he realized that customers would come to the business for any fabric-care problem, which would give their company significant market control.

So the couple completed a three-week course at the International Fabric Care Institute in Silver Springs, Maryland, and set out for Johannesburg. Once there, they ordered laundry and dry-cleaning equipment from the United States, found store space in a commercial area, and opened their first store. However, from the start, Giles and Moffat had a growth plan that included over 100 more stores. They knew that obtaining financing would play a large role in making this a reality. They sought a $9 million loan from the Overseas Private Investment Corporation (OPIC), an agency offering loans, guarantees, and political risk insurance to qualified U.S. investors in developing nations. Ruth Harkin, OPIC's president, believed in the couple's ability to make their plan an entrepreneurial success story.

But the success would not come without challenges. Moffat and Giles quickly discovered that doing business in South Africa is much different than doing business in the United States. Some major difficulties are the South African attitudes toward time, deadlines, and details. Giles found that black and white South Africans alike seem to lack the sense of urgency that motivates most people in the United States. He also found that many South Africans are reluctant to challenge authority, which he attributes to decades of authoritarian rule. In addition, he says that even if you know "what you want to do, how you want it done, and when you want it done, you find that—even if you hire first-rate lawyers—you really have to make sure you follow up on them." Another major difference between the United States and South Africa is the lack of an educated work force. Government statistics put the illiteracy rate over 60 percent in South Africa. "The educational system here has not encouraged people to think independently, and we have had to hire employees based on attitude and their willingness to learn," says Giles.

Giles and Moffat have learned to adapt the way they think about business to the special conditions of the South African market. They say that entrepreneurs must have patience, perseverance, and deep pockets if they are to succeed, because things always take longer and cost more money to accomplish in South Africa. But the couple has learned quickly, and they have big plans for the future. Once their laundry and dry-cleaning chain is established, they intend to franchise to other South Africans, making them an even more integral part of the future growth of this emerging market.

1. What are some of the advantages of a small entrepreneur setting up a business venture in an emerging market like South Africa? What are some of the disadvantages?
2. How can entrepreneurs like Giles and Moffat cope with some of the cultural differences that make it more difficult to run their business the way they would in the United States?
3. What benefits might the couple gain from forming strategic alliances with established local businesspeople in South Africa?
4. The Tradeport Trade Directory is a useful Internet resource for finding international trade information. Follow the links at <http://www.tradeport.org> to find market research reports on South Africa and answer the following questions: Which industries have strong growth potential in South Africa? What types of trade restrictions exist in South Africa? What sort of franchising opportunities exist in South Africa? Which communication channels are most successful in reaching South African consumers?

Building Your Business Skills

As directed by your instructor (either in a group of three or four students or on your own), select a U.S.-made good or service that you think might be appropriate for customers outside the United States. Next, choose a country that you believe would be a good place to market that product. Finally, develop a strategy for marketing your selected product in the country of your choice.

- Using the library or the Internet as a resource, write a brief profile of your chosen country; include its geographical location, population, form of government, monetary unit, language, literacy rate, per capita income, political climate, legal environment, availability of transportation, rate of development, and status of communication (number of television sets, radios, newspapers, magazines, and consumers with telephone and Internet access).
- In addition to the information in your profile, identify other factors that would influence the marketing of your selected product in your chosen country. Such factors might include packaging or product color, brand name, potential applications, and social customs.
- Prepare a brief presentation outlining how you would present this product in your chosen country. Would any changes need to be made in the product to bring it to this new market? Would advertising aimed at the U.S. audience be appropriate in the country you've chosen? What competition do you think your product would face?

Keeping Current Using *The Wall Street Journal*

Find a *Wall Street Journal* article describing an experience of a U.S. company or division that conducts business outside the United States. As an alternative, look for an article describing how a company or division based in another country has started doing business in the United States.

1. Describe in your own words the company's experience. Was it positive, negative, or mixed? Why?
2. What legal or political barriers did the company have to overcome? What cultural or business differences did the company encounter? What problems did these differences create for the company? What did the company do to overcome the obstacles?
3. Did the company achieve its objectives? What major changes, if any, did the company have to make in its plans? What conclusions can you draw from this company's particular experience with international trade?
4. Visit the company's Web site and search for information about the company's current or future international plans. Based on your findings, do you think that the past experience has made the company more eager or less willing to engage in international business? What do you think the company will do differently in the future? If the company does not yet have a Web site, search your library databases for other articles about the company's international plans.

Exploring the Best of the Web

Going Global, page 36

There are many factors to consider when you want to export a product, but the information at the International Trade Administration's Web page can help you make sense of it all. Explore the links to information about individual countries found on the *Regions and Countries* page <http://www.ita.doc.gov>. Drawing on this information as well as on what you've learned in the text, answer the following questions about trading with emerging economies.

1. What are the top 5 U.S. exports to India? What are the top 5 U.S. imports from India? What does this say about the comparative advantages enjoyed by each country?
2. What steps is Poland taking to improve transportation throughout the country?
3. How open is Turkey to investment in domestic industries by foreign companies? Why does the Turkish government have an interest in boosting foreign direct investment? Why does the Turkish government limit the amount of foreign ownership in industries such as transportation and communication?

Leading the Way to Foreign Trade, page 44

Trade leads are an excellent way for manufacturers and professional export agents to learn about international trade opportunities. Go to World Trade Markets <http://www.wtm.com>, and follow either the date, country, or product link to trade leads. Select a particular lead that interests you and answer the following questions.

1. What is the company's name, where is it located, and how long has it been in business? What product does the company wish to import or export? How much of the product is needed or is available for sale?
2. Could this particular request be handled by a small company, or does it require the experience and resources of a large firm? What type(s) of business arrangements would be most applicable to handling this request (i.e., direct importing or exporting, joint venture, licensing, franchising, or running a wholly owned facility) and why?
3. What contact information is given for the company? Does the contact person speak English? Does your contact have a fax number or e-mail address? If you were a small importer or exporter, what kind of information would you want to know about this individual or company?

Get the Facts, page 49

The CIA's primary purpose is to gather information. Fortunately for businesspeople, the agency shares a lot of its information about foreign countries on its Web site <http://www.odci.gov/cia/>. Select *The World Factbook* from the list of CIA publications, and click on links to the appropriate countries to answer the following questions.

1. What major industries play a role in Austrialia's economy? What natural resources does Australia possess? How is Australia's economy similar to the western European economies?
2. What current environmental issue does Chile face? What laws and agreements has Chilean government signed to deal with these issues? Why might such information be important to foreign companies locating in Chile?
3. How might a business use the country information in the *World Factbook* when considering its options for global expansion?

Answers to "Is It True?"

Page 35. False. India enjoys the world's third largest scientific and technical work force, trailing only the United States and the former Soviet Union. Spending on consumer goods in India is rising at a rate of 10 percent a year, according to an estimate from India's Planning Commission.

Page 40. True

Page 47. False. Writer and statesman Victor Hugo called for the establishment of a United States of Europe at a Paris peace conference in 1849.

CHAPTER 3

ETHICAL AND SOCIAL RESPONSIBILITIES OF BUSINESS

OBJECTIVES

After studying this chapter, you will be able to

1. Explain the difference between ethical dilemmas and ethical lapses
2. List and explain four philosophical approaches to resolving ethical questions in business
3. Identify four stakeholder groups to which business has a responsibility
4. Name three kinds of pollution and outline actions to control them
5. List the four rights of consumers
6. Discuss the problem of discrimination and explain how government and business are working to end it
7. Discuss two general ways that businesses may cheat investors
8. Identify steps that businesses are taking to encourage socially responsible and ethical behavior

ON THE JOB

On the Job On the Job

ON THE JOB: FACING BUSINESS CHALLENGES AT LEVI STRAUSS

Can a Company Be Socially Responsible and Successful?

Levi Strauss & Company chairman and chief executive officer Bob Haas had some problems on his hands. After taking over leadership of the world-famous blue-jeans maker in 1984, Haas had worked hard to revitalize the company's long-standing commitment to ethical and socially responsible behavior. However, changes in consumer tastes and stiff competition from rival clothing manufacturers were hitting the company hard on all sides. In order to remain competitive, Haas would have to make some tough decisions that could threaten the company's principles.

The original Mr. Levi Strauss had a simple business mission—make and sell quality work pants for San Francisco's gold-rush miners. However, Strauss also demonstrated a strong social conscience and commitment to employees early on. During the Great Depression, workers were paid to lay a new floor in the factory until business picked up. By the 1960s, the company had become a vocal advocate for racial integration and a leader in corporate diversity programs.

However, by the time Bob Haas (great-great-grandnephew of Levi Strauss) took over in 1984, the company seemed to have lost its social conscience. Levi's had expanded aggressively into product lines that were ultimately unprofitable. The company was bloated, profits were falling, and management was more concerned with numbers than with values. Haas believed that public shareholders and stock analysts had blurred the company's vision by demanding short-term profit gains over long-term goals. So with the help of friends and family, Haas bought up the remaining public stock and set out to turn the company around.

Haas began to streamline the company, which meant taking the painful step of cutting the work force by a third. To reward and motivate those who remained, he developed an aspirations statement with companywide goals based on ethics, diversity, environmental stewardship, teamwork, trust, and openness. He backed up his statement by training employees in leadership, diversity, and ethical decision making and also by linking employee compensation to performance in these areas. "A company's values—what it stands for, what its people believe in—are crucial to its competitive success," Haas exhorted. "Indeed, values drive the business." Levi's also spent large sums to reduce the impact of its operations on the environment. At the same time, the company shed unprofitable clothing styles and refocused on traditional jeans and the new casual "Dockers" products. With revitalized company values, soaring staff morale, and revamped product lines, Levi Strauss enjoyed double-digit gains in sales revenues and profits.

However, the 1990s brought new crises. First, reports of widespread human rights abuses in China led the company to question the ethics of its operations there.

Second, Levi's discovered that some of its suppliers in Asia were making Levi's products with child labor. And third, Levi's own failure to spot new clothing trends, modernize its production facilities, and keep retailers happy resulted in declining jeans sales. The situation worsened as new competitors undercut Levi's pricing by manufacturing the majority of their products overseas (Levi's still made half of its products in the United States). With demand shrinking, Levi's again found it had too many plants and employees in the United States. But large-scale layoffs could undermine the social values that had once again become synonymous with the Levi's name. Haas had to find a way to ensure the company's long-term profitability while standing by Levi's principles.

If you were Bob Haas, how would you balance your company's economic needs with its goals for ethics and social responsibility? How would you deal with suppliers who don't adhere to your company's values? Would you take a stand against human rights abuses? How would you handle the problem of excess capacity and employees?[1]

Foundations of Social Responsibility and Ethical Behavior

social responsibility
The idea that business has certain obligations to society beyond the pursuit of profits

Each company functions as part of an interactive system of relationships with individuals and groups in society. However, the ideal relationship between businesses and society is a matter of debate. Those who support the concept of **social responsibility** argue that a company has a greater obligation to society beyond the pursuit of profit or other goals. Managers like Bob Haas agree and strive to create organizations that encourage social responsibility in their policies and among their employees. In fact, businesses such as Tom's of Maine (a producer of natural personal-care products) and Working Assets (a long-distance telephone service provider) link the pursuit of socially responsible goals with their overall growth strategies.[2] Many other managers believe that their primary obligation is to the company's shareholders and that social responsibility is a secondary concern. As you will see, finding the right balance is challenging.

When you think about a business's approach to social responsibility, you probably think about programs and plans executed by the business as a whole. However, the business does not take action or make decisions; only individuals within the business can do that. So the sense of right and wrong that each decision maker brings to the workplace influences a company's policies regarding social responsibility. Are there standards of right and wrong that businesses and individuals should follow? This question is the focus of **ethics,** the study of individual decisions made in the context of a system of moral standards or rules of conduct.

ethics
Study of standards of conduct and individual choices based on rules, values, and moral beliefs

Ethical Dilemmas and Ethical Lapses

ethical dilemma
Situation in which both sides of an issue can be supported with valid arguments

Ethical questions can be divided into two general categories. The first is an **ethical dilemma,** an issue that has two conflicting but arguably valid sides. Boots is the maker of the leading drug to control hypothyroidism, and not long ago, the company paid for a study to determine whether generic versions of its drug worked as well as the Boots version. The study found that the generics are just as good and that, each year, Boots's higher-priced version costs people who need the drug $356 million more than the generic drugs. The primary researcher had signed an agreement stating that the findings would not be published without Boots's consent. Publishing these findings would clearly be bad for profits, and not publishing was the company's right. However, consumers also have the right to be informed.[3] Thus, Boots faced an ethical dilemma. The common theme in all ethical dilemmas is the conflict between the rights of two or more important groups of people. Ultimately, the company decided to withhold permission to publish the study.

An **ethical lapse** occurs when an individual makes an unethical decision. Be careful not to confuse ethical dilemmas with ethical lapses. A company faces an ethical dilemma when it must decide whether to continue selling a product that is suspected, but not proven, to be unsafe. An example of an ethical lapse would be falsely inflating prices for certain customers or selling trade secrets to competitors.

ethical lapse
Situation in which an individual makes an unethical decision

Philosophical Bases for Ethical Decisions

Guided by written policies, unwritten standards, and examples set by top managers, every individual in a corporation makes choices that have moral implications. If everyone behaves ethically, the organization as a whole will act in a responsible manner. The key is for each person to think through the consequences of his or her actions and then make the "right" choice.

Determining what's right in any given situation can be difficult. One approach is to measure each act against certain absolute standards. In the United States, these standards are often grounded in religious teachings, such as "Do not lie" and "Do not steal." However, rules have their limitations. Some situations defy clear-cut distinctions. In such cases, three other philosophical approaches are useful in choosing the most ethical course of action: utilitarianism, individual rights, and justice.[4]

Utilitarianism According to the concept of **utilitarianism,** the right decision is the one that produces the greatest good for the greatest number of people. Using this approach, you would try to figure out how each action affects everyone concerned, and then you would choose the action that creates the most good for the most people. You would reject alternatives that cater to narrow interests or that fail to satisfy the needs of the majority. For example, a company facing hard times might decide to close a plant in one city in order to keep production strong at its remaining plants. Although workers at the closed plant would suffer, the company would be able to continue operating and perhaps to reorganize for future success, thus serving the greater good of the corporation and the communities it's a part of. The value of the utilitarian approach depends on your skill in estimating the effects of your decisions.

utilitarianism
Philosophy used in making ethical decisions that aims to achieve the greatest good for the greatest number

Individual Rights Another approach is to uphold the importance of **individual rights.** A right is an individual's entitlement to something. It may be based on a legal system, such as the right to freedom of speech guaranteed by the U.S. Constitution. Or it may be based on moral norms and principles that apply to all humans, such as the right to work for a decent living. Moral rights are also known as human rights because they are usually thought of as applying universally to all humans.[5]

individual rights
Philosophy used in making ethical decisions that aims to protect rights guaranteed by a legal system or by moral norms and principles

By taking this perspective, you would reject any decision that violated an individual's rights. You would not deceive people or trick them into acting against their own interests. You would also respect their privacy and their right to express their opinion. You would not force people to act in a way that was contrary to their religious or moral beliefs, and you would not punish a person without a fair and impartial hearing. Although you might be guided by a desire to achieve the greatest good for the greatest number of people, you would reject any choice that violated the rights of even one person. In an era when individual workers expect and demand their rights, this philosophy is becoming a practical necessity in some cases. For example, when dealing with issues related to AIDS or drug testing, companies are trying to honor the individual's right to privacy without jeopardizing the group's right to a safe working environment.

Justice When making ethical decisions, you might also apply the principles of **justice.** These principles include a belief that people should be treated fairly and impartially, that rules

justice
Philosophy used in making ethical decisions that aims to ensure the equal distribution of burdens and benefits

should be applied consistently, and that people who harm others should be held responsible and should make restitution. For example, we want everyone to carry a fair share of the burden of paying taxes. We also expect that criminals will be punished for their crimes, and that the punishment will fit the crime. A just decision, then, is one that is fair, impartial, and reasonable in light of the rules that apply to the situation.

These three approaches are not mutually exclusive alternatives. On the contrary, most people combine them to reach decisions that will satisfy as many people as possible without violating any person's rights or treating anyone unjustly. In any case, wanting to be an ethical corporate citizen isn't enough; a business must actively practice ethical behavior. The difficulty in doing so is often the result of the conflicting interests of stakeholders.

Business and Its Stakeholders

stakeholders
Individuals or groups to whom business has a responsibility

A business has many **stakeholders**—groups that are affected by (or that affect) a business's operations. Stakeholders include employees, customers, investors, and society at large (see Exhibit 3.1). If a company's management consistently ignores social responsibilities and shortchanges its stakeholders, the business will suffer and eventually fold. Investors who are unhappy with the company's performance will invest elsewhere. Workers whose needs are not met will be unproductive, or they will quit and find other jobs. Customers whose tastes and values are ignored will spend their money on other things. And if the concerns of society are disregarded, the voters will clamor for laws to limit offensive business activities.

Many business executives sincerely try to respond to the needs of these four groups, and their efforts are often successful. However, the needs of stakeholders sometimes conflict, which means that managers face choices as they try to reconcile competing interests. For example, Ford found evidence that the ignition switch in many of the cars it had produced since the mid-1980s were defective, causing engine fires that damaged not only the cars but also the garages and homes of the car owners. Fearing lost profits, public embarrassment, and a possible decline in stock price, Ford downplayed the problem,

EXHIBIT 3.1

Business and Its Stakeholders

Balancing the individual needs and interests of a company's stakeholders is one of management's most difficult tasks.

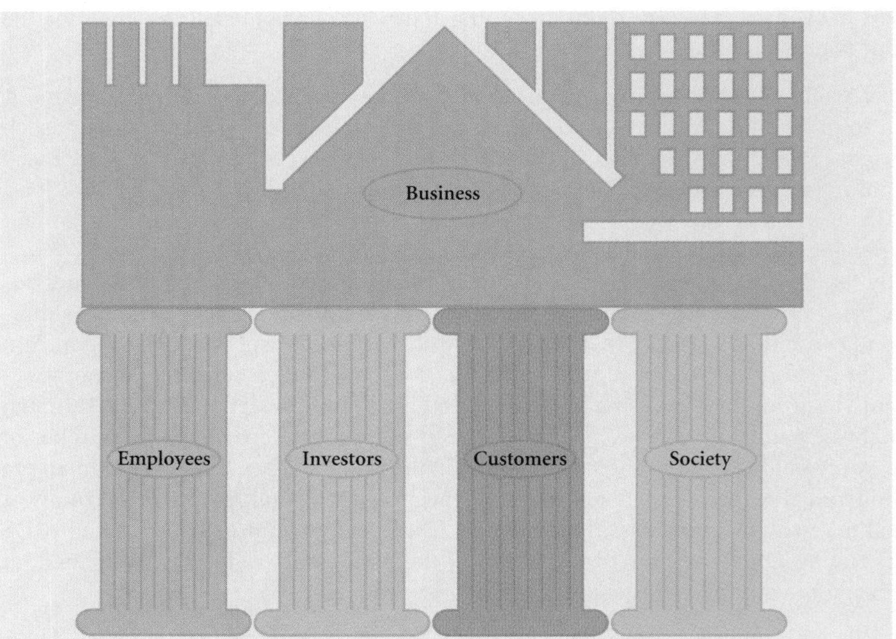

hoping that the fires were just flukes in a few vehicles. But it wasn't long before federal safety investigators became involved and uncovered numerous cases that spanned a period of several years. In 1996 Ford finally admitted the fault and recalled 8.7 million cars. However, by that time more damage had been done, and the cost of reparation was much higher for Ford.[6] Did Ford have an obligation to its customers to take care of the defective switches as soon as possible? Was the company right to protect investors by waiting to see whether a large-scale recall was really necessary? Hindsight tells us that the interests of all parties would have been better served by an early recall. However, it is often difficult for managers to have such a clear perspective when a potential problem arises, especially if the company has no specific guidelines regarding how to deal with such problems.

Business Approaches to Ethical and Socially Responsible Behavior

Many companies are now creating official positions to guide their ethics policies. For example, NYNEX, a telecommunications company that serves the northeastern United States, established the NYNEX Office of Ethics and Business Conduct (OE&BC) and named a vice president of business conduct.[7] This can be an important step, but it is effective only if senior management reinforces the company's commitment to ethics with both words and actions. Furthermore, encouraging ethical behavior often means doing more than simply complying with laws. In the words of Shirley Peterson, head of the ethics program at Northrop, a major defense contractor: "Compliance is what you have to do; ethics is what you should do."[8]

One way companies can evaluate their ethical standards is by conducting a **social audit,** a systematic evaluation and reporting of the company's ethical and social performance. The report typically includes objective information about how the company's activities affect its various stakeholders. For example, once a year Ben & Jerry's Homemade asks an outsider to conduct a social audit that assesses the impact of the company's operations on its employees, customers, communities, suppliers, and shareholders. The company announces the results of the audit in its annual report to shareholders.

social audit
Assessment of a company's performance in the area of social responsibility

Companies like Ben & Jerry's also engage in *cause-related marketing,* in which product sales help to support worthy causes. For instance, MBNA America offers a credit card that contributes 10 cents to charities every time customers use it.[9] Another example is Peaceworks, a New York–based company that markets a product called "spraté." Spratés are uniquely flavored spreads that are produced in Israel by a Jewish-owned company that buys all of its ingredients from Israeli Arabs and Palestinians. When consumers buy a jar of spraté, they not only get a tasty spread, they also support the peace process in the Middle East. Peaceworks founder Daniel Lubetzky says, "There is no better way to create political stability than by having people work together and giving them economic incentives."[10]

Daniel Lubetzky, the founder of Peaceworks, is helping the Middle East peace process on two fronts: by encouraging cooperative business ventures between Jews and Arabs, and by increasing awareness among American consumers.

For some companies, social responsibility extends to *philanthropy,* the donation of money, time, goods, or services to charitable, humanitarian, or educational institutions. Corporations including Microsoft, Oracle, Columbia Healthcare, and VH1 donate billions of dollars in cash and products to charity each year. Many executives also donate their time and their employees' paid work time to community affairs. For example, the discount brokerage firm of Charles Schwab recently spent $1 million to bring 900 executives to San Francisco to build houses and renovate schools in low-income neighborhoods. Shell Oil undertook a similar project in Houston, and Prudential Insurance recently sent its New Jersey employees to clean up local parks and hiking trails. These companies and many others are finding that giving back to their communities leads to a more favorable public image and stronger employee morale.[11]

THINKING ABOUT ETHICS

Ethical Use of the Internet

It's a fact: Today's businesses depend heavily on computer networks to accomplish their goals and remain competitive. The global network we call the Internet is becoming increasingly important to business. Many companies already use the Internet to communicate, advertise, distribute products, purchase materials, and recruit employees. It is estimated that online commerce will exceed $7 billion by the year 2003.

With the growing importance of the Internet to business transactions, companies find it necessary to incorporate standards for Internet ethics into their corporate ethics codes. Ethics experts at St. Cloud University suggest that the following ten areas should be considered:

1. *Contamination and sabotage.* Companies must design appropriate safeguards into their computer systems so that their files are protected from viruses and other forms of sabotage. At the same time, companies must not tolerate sabotage of competitors' systems by employees.
2. *Censorship.* Internet censorship is a much debated issue. Companies must establish clear policies regarding what is acceptable for accessing and downloading information from company computers, as well as what can and cannot be transmitted via company e-mail systems. Downloading pornography or transmitting e-mail messages that contain profanity, sexual references, or off-color remarks may lead to charges of sexual harassment or racial discrimination.
3. *Confidentiality.* Companies must take every precaution to make sure that confidential customer and employee information is not available on the Internet.
4. *Privacy.* Employees must be discouraged from trying to access confidential information that does not pertain to them. Breaking into other systems to retrieve sensitive information amounts to theft and should not be tolerated.
5. *Cost.* Companies pay to provide employees with Internet access and e-mail. Therefore, employees

The Evolution of Social Responsibility

Social responsibility is a concept with decades-old roots. In the nineteenth century, the prevailing view among U.S. industrialists was that business had only one responsibility: to make a profit. Railroad tycoon William Vanderbilt summed up this attitude when he said, "The public be damned. I'm working for the shareholders."[12] *Caveat emptor* was the rule of the day—"Let the buyer beware." If you bought a product, you paid the price and took the consequences. No consumer groups or government agencies would help you if the product was defective or caused harm.

By the early twentieth century, reformers were pushing politicians and government regulators to protect citizens from the abuses of big business. Their efforts paid off. Laws were passed to ensure the purity of food and drugs, limit the power of monopolies, and prevent unfair business practices, among other reforms (see Exhibit 3.2).

The Great Depression, which started in 1929, led to more disenchantment with business. With 25 percent of the work force unemployed, many people lost their faith in capitalism, and pressure mounted for government to fix the system. At the urging of President Franklin D. Roosevelt, Congress passed laws in the 1930s and 1940s to protect workers, consumers, and investors. These laws established the Social Security system, allowed employees to join unions and bargain collectively, set a minimum hourly wage, and limited the length of the workweek. New laws prevented unfair competition and false advertising and started the Securities and Exchange Commission (SEC) to protect investors.

Is It True?

Exploitation of child labor was wiped out in the United States many years ago.

Public confidence in U.S. business revived during World War II, and throughout the 1950s, the relationship between business, government, and society was relatively tranquil.

should not make frivolous use of these valuable but costly resources.

6. *Copyrights.* Copyrights must always be respected. Unwarranted software reproduction is a crime, as is downloading protected documents and images.
7. *Plagiarism.* Companies must discourage employees from plagiarizing (using material without giving credit to the authors) any information published online. Plagiarism amounts to intellectual theft.
8. *Fraud.* Traditional ethics must always apply to any information a company disseminates online. Companies should not falsify information or attempt to defraud Internet users.
9. *Ideology and advertising.* Companies and employees must avoid using the Internet to disseminate propaganda. Internet advertising should adhere to the same standards required of other forms of advertising.
10. *Appropriateness.* Keep in mind that the Internet is not always the right place to share communications. Sometimes telephones, mail, conferences, and publications are more appropriate.

Using the Internet involves certain responsibilities, just as all other rights and privileges do. When using the Internet, if companies and individuals do not maintain the same ethical standards that apply to other areas of business and communications, they risk exposing themselves to lawsuits, consumer backlash, regulation, and sabotage. Ethical behavior will help ensure that the Internet remains an open and safe place to do business.

QUESTIONS FOR CRITICAL THINKING

1. What steps can companies take to ensure that their employees maintain ethical principles when using the Internet?
2. Some employee advocacy groups are concerned about companies monitoring their e-mail and Internet usage. Do you feel that companies have a right to do this? Do employees have a right to privacy when using company computer systems?

However, the climate shifted in the 1960s, as activism exploded on four fronts: environmental protection, national defense, consumerism, and civil rights. These movements have drastically altered the way business is conducted in the United States. Many of the changes

REGULATION	DATE	EFFECT
Interstate Commerce Act	1887	Regulates business practices, specifically railroad operations and shipping rates
Sherman Antitrust Act	1890	Fosters competition by preventing monopolies and noncompetitive mergers; establishes competitive market environment as national policy
Pure Food and Drug Act	1906	Prohibits misbranding and adulteration of food and drugs, specifically those transported across state lines
Meat Inspection Act	1906	Encourages purity of meat and meat products, specifically those transported across state lines
Federal Trade Commission Act	1914	Creates the Federal Trade Commission to control illegal trade practices
Clayton Antitrust Act	1914	Restricts practices such as price discrimination, tying contracts, exclusive dealing, and interlocking boards of directors that give large businesses an advantage over smaller firms

EXHIBIT 3.2

Early Government Regulations Pertaining to Business

Despite their reputation for relentlessly pursuing profits, many early tycoons were also philanthropists. For example, Andrew Carnegie, a pioneer in the steel industry, donated money to build public libraries in towns throughout the United States. Nevertheless, government regulations were needed to ensure fair business practices.

have been made willingly by socially responsible companies, others have been forced by government action, and still others have come about because of pressure from citizen groups.

Social Responsibility versus Profits

Despite the progress that has been made, many people say that U.S. businesses should do much more for society. A recent Business Week/Harris poll found that 95 percent of adults reject the notion that a corporation's only role is to make money. Seventy-six percent say that if price and quality are equal, they would be likely to switch brands and retailers to support socially responsible companies. Successful businesses pay attention to the concerns of their customers. Fifty-eight percent of executives now agree that corporations have a responsibility to address social issues. In addition, an increasing number of firms are adding social responsibility to their list of corporate goals.[13]

Many experts are demonstrating that socially responsible actions can actually contribute to a company's profits. Amory Lovins, co-founder of the Rocky Mountain Institute (RMI), a resource policy center that helps businesses operate more efficiently, has been a consultant for some of the biggest names in business and government. He says that using resources efficiently reduces overhead expenses and saves the company money. Moreover, a study by researchers at Vanderbilt University found that 80 percent of the time, low-polluting companies perform better financially than high-polluting companies.[14]

Businesses are also finding that writing checks to charitable organizations does not have to cut into profits. As president and CEO of Liberty Bank and Trust in New Orleans, Alden J. McDonald Jr. feels that his company is "doing well by doing good." McDonald recognizes that his bank's success is contingent on the success of the community it serves. Therefore, the bank invests portions of its marketing budget in helping to solve community problems. Each time a project is successful, the bank receives lots of favorable publicity, which generates many new customers. Likewise, Shell Oil CEO Philip Carroll suggests that encouraging employees to volunteer for causes, both on company time and on their own time, makes them more productive.[15]

Just how much money does it take for a business to be socially responsible? On the other hand, how much can a business save? The answer is unclear, because no single source of information exists on business's expenditures for socially desirable activities. Although such activities are welcomed by many stakeholders, including shareholders, companies do

Workers in the United States are protected from hazardous, abusive, or unfair work environments by strict labor laws. However, labor laws in many developing countries are often much more lenient. Companies such as Nike have recently come under protest for employing child labor at manufacturing facilities in Southeast Asia.

Build a Better Business

BEST OF THE WEB

One way to distinguish your business as an ethical organization is to join the Better Business Bureau (BBB), a private, nonprofit business group whose members agree to maintain specific standards for operating ethically and for addressing customer complaints. The BBB's Web site is packed with information about the organization, its member businesses, and its programs that will benefit businesses and consumers alike. You can find reports on companies, register complaints, get help resolving grievances, access publications on everything from buying a new car to obtaining financial aid for college, find out about recent business scams and how to avoid them, find information about charitable organizations, and much more.
http://www.bbb.org

not have unlimited resources. Deciding how much money to spend on upgrading facilities and equipment, developing new products, marketing existing products, rewarding employee efforts, and contributing to social causes is a juggling act that every business faces.

BUSINESS AND THE ENVIRONMENT

The difficulty of balancing profits and social responsibility is very apparent when you consider environmental issues. Consumers value the goods and services that businesses produce, but businesses cannot produce goods and services without polluting to some degree. Businesses strive to lower their costs in order to offer products to consumers more efficiently and to make profits for investors, but sometimes it is necessary for businesses to spend more in order to pollute less. When such situations arise, whose interests should be served first—those of society, the consumer, or the investor? Clearly, this question has no easy answer, but examining how businesses pollute may provide some perspective.

The Pervasiveness of Pollution

Economic progress threatens our air, water, and land because these elements can so easily be tainted by **pollution** (the contamination or destruction of the natural environment by humans). Moreover, the pollution in any one element can easily taint the others. This problem is pervasive in industrialized and developing nations alike. In fact, the emerging economies of Asia and Latin America have built much of their growth on very loose environmental standards. But Mexico, Malaysia, and other countries are realizing that their prosperity can be sustained only if their citizens can enjoy a quality of life that comes with a clean environment. At the same time, the countries of eastern Europe are scrambling to reverse the decades of environmental neglect that occurred under communism.[16] As you can imagine, this is no easy task.

pollution
Damage or destruction to the natural environment caused by human activities

Air Pollution The most noticeable form of air pollution, smog, is produced by the interaction of sunlight and hydrocarbons (gases released when fossil fuels are burned). Another damaging air pollutant is acid rain, created when emissions from coal-burning factories and electric utility plants react with air. Acid rain has been blamed for damaging lakes and forests in southeastern Canada and the northeastern United States.

In addition, emissions from factories and cars pollute the air and contribute to global warming through the greenhouse effect, in which heated gases form a layer of unusually warm air around the earth, trapping the sun's heat and preventing the earth's surface from cooling. The United Nations' Intergovernmental Panel on Climate Change (IPCC), which includes over 900 scientists worldwide, recently reported that global warming will cause worldwide temperatures to rise by 1 to 3.5 degrees centigrade in the next century. This is expected to lead to increases in both droughts and floods in some regions and cause the sea level to rise about 50 centimeters by 2100. The report concludes that "the balance of evidence suggests a discernible human influence on global climate."[17] However, some scientists refute the theory of global warming, claiming that no solid evidence yet exists to support a human influence on global climate change. The debate will continue. However, we need only look at the smog that hangs over many major cities of the world to know that air pollution is a problem that businesses, consumers, and governments must address together.

Experts worry about airborne toxins that are emitted during some manufacturing processes. Large and small companies together release millions of pounds of chemical wastes into the air each year. Although the effects of many of these substances are unknown, some are known to be carcinogenic (cancer causing). Of special concern in recent years are microscopic particulates in the air that may be responsible for more than 150,000 deaths each year.[18]

Water Pollution Our air is not the only part of our environment to suffer. Water pollution has damaged many U.S. lakes, rivers, streams, harbors, and coastal waters. This pollution comes from a variety of sources: manufacturing facilities, mining and construction sites, farms, and city sewage systems. Although dramatic accidents like the *Exxon Valdez* oil spill in Alaskan waters are widely publicized, the main threat is the careless day-to-day disposal of wastes from thousands of individual sources.

Land Pollution Even if all wastewater were purified before being discharged, our groundwater would still be endangered by leakage from the millions of tons of hazardous substances that have been buried underground or dumped in improper storage sites. Much of this pollution was created years ago by companies that carelessly—but legally—disposed of substances now known to be unhealthy. Cleaning up these wastes is extremely difficult and expensive.

In addition, companies and individuals generate enormous amounts of solid waste—over 200 million tons in the United States each year. Much of this waste ends up in landfills. A large part of the problem is consumer demands for convenience and fashion. These demands lead to creating disposable items, manufacturing products with excess packaging, and discarding useful items that are no longer the hot style or color. Fortunately, recent efforts to conserve and recycle resources are helping to combat the land pollution problem.[19]

Government, Public, and Industry Response

Today, over 80 percent of people in the United States consider themselves environmentalists, and many are willing to pay higher prices in order to reduce pollution. Clearly, the environmental movement has shifted from the fringe to the mainstream.[20] Politicians and businesspeople are aware of the change in the public's concern for the environment, and they're responding accordingly.

ecology
Study of the relationships between living things in the water, air, and soil, their environments, and the nutrients that support them

Widespread concern for the environment has been growing since the 1960s, when **ecology,** or the study of the balance of nature, became a popular cause. In 1963 federal, state, and local governments began enacting laws and regulations to reduce pollution. (See Exhibit 3.3 for a brief summary of major federal legislation.) In December 1970 the Environmental Protection Agency (EPA) was established to regulate air and water pollution by manufacturers and utilities, supervise auto-pollution control, license pesticides, control toxic substances, and safeguard the purity of drinking water. Congress is currently attempting to reform the EPA, because critics contend that the agency's tough restrictions actually prohibit companies from finding the most cost-effective ways to reduce pollution.

One innovative approach to reducing pollution is based on free-market principles. In certain cities, companies can buy and sell pollution rights. Each company is given an allowable "pollution quota" based on such factors as its size and industry. If a company voluntarily reduces pollution below its limit, it can sell its "credits" to another company. This provides an incentive for companies to find efficient ways of reducing pollution. Evidence so far suggests that the plan is effective in reducing overall levels of pollutants such as sulfur dioxide, and the strategy was recently discussed as a possible way to reduce air pollution worldwide at the 150-nation talks on world climate change in Kyoto, Japan. If adopted, businesses in different countries would be able to trade pollution rights in the same way that they now trade other goods and services. However, debate still continues about what constitutes acceptable levels of pollution and whether or not companies should be allowed to regulate themselves.[21]

Although many companies do a good job of regulating themselves, it is often public and government pressure that cause businesses to clean up their acts. Companies that pollute excessively not only risk being charged with violating federal laws but also risk being sued by private citizens. For example, Weyerhaeuser, a major forest products company, was sued for $1 billion by landowners who accused the company of releasing dioxin, a suspected carcinogenic chemical, into waterways around its plant in Columbus, Mississippi. This and other lawsuits prompted a government crackdown on the paper industry, forcing it to invest up to $20 million per paper mill to reduce toxic discharges.[22]

Of course, such costs are ultimately passed on to consumers. Therefore, society as a whole benefits most when companies take it upon themselves to find cost-effective ways of reducing pollution. A promising new approach emphasizes prevention as opposed to correction. Pioneering companies are reducing the flow of pollutants into the environment—and lowering their cleanup bills—by using alternative materials, changing production techniques, redesigning products, and recycling wastes. For example, Weyerhaeuser has dramatically reduced its toxic emissions by developing manufacturing techniques that recycle most of the water used in production and by using safer chemicals. Moreover, the company is searching for ways to completely eliminate water discharge from its production process.[23] Companies like Weyerhaeuser are discovering that expenditures on prevention can end up saving them more money down the road by reducing cleanup costs, litigation expense, and production costs. Prevention also benefits taxpayers because it reduces the costs of enforcing environmental protection laws as well as the costs of tying up the justice system with private litigation.

Progress Toward a Cleaner Environment

Our air, water, and land are gradually becoming cleaner, thanks to government standards, public pressure, and industry's efforts to comply. Annual combined federal, state, and local expenditures to abate and control pollution now top $100 billion. Since 1970, emissions of lead have decreased 98 percent, and emissions of other major pollutants have decreased by over 25 percent.[24] In addition, an agreement among 24 nations to limit the production of chlorofluorocarbons is helping reduce the threat to the ozone layer. Also, Congress has passed a series of tough amendments to the 1970 Clean Air Act that call for cuts in smog, acid rain, toxic emissions, and ozone-depleting chemicals by phasing in improvements through 2005.[25]

Is It True?

A U.S. factory can legally emit four times the amount of air pollution that a German plant can.

Individual states have passed their own tough clean air laws. For example, California requires that 10 percent of all new vehicles sold in the state be pollution free by 2003. In response, both large and small car manufacturers are working to produce electric vehicles. General Motors and Honda have already begun selling their first models.[26]

Progress has also been made in reducing water pollution. The percentage of U.S. rivers and lakes that have become fishable and swimmable has almost doubled since 1970. In

EXHIBIT 3.3

Major Federal Environmental Legislation

Since the early 1960s, major federal legislation aimed at the environment has focused on providing cleaner air and water and reducing toxic waste.

LEGISLATION	DATE	EFFECT
National Environmental Policy Act	1969	Establishes a structure for coordinating all federal environmental programs.
Order of Administrative Organization	1970	Establishes Council on Environmental Quality to advise president on environmental policy and to review environmental impact statements. Leads to formation of Environmental Protection Agency.
		Air pollution
Clear Air Act and amendments	1965, 1963, 1970, 1977, 1990	Assists states and localities in formulating control programs. Sets federal standards for auto-exhaust emissions. Sets maximum permissible pollution levels. Authorizes nationwide air-pollution standards and limitations to pollutant discharge. Requires scrubbers in new coal-fired power plants. Directs EPA to prevent deterioration of air quality in clean areas. Sets schedule and standards for cutting smog, acid rain, hazardous factory fumes, and ozone-depleting chemicals.
		Solid-waste pollution
Solid Waste Disposal Act and amendments	1965, 1984	Authorizes research and assistance to state and local control programs. Regulates treatment, storage, transportation, and disposal of hazardous waste.
Resource Recovery Act	1970	Subsidizes pilot recycling plants. Authorizes nationwide control programs.
Resource Conservation and Recovery Act	1976	Directs EPA to regulate hazardous-waste management.
Surface Mining and Reclamation Act	1976	Controls strip mining and restoration of reclaimed land.
		Water pollution
Federal Water Pollution Control Act and amendments	1972	Authorizes grants to states for water-pollution control. Gives federal government limited authority to correct pollution problems. Authorizes EPA to set and enforce water-quality standards.

addition, major waterways like the Cuyahoga and Potomac rivers, Delaware Bay, and Boston Harbor (all of which were once open sewers) have been cleaned up.[27] This is largely because many companies like Weyerhaeuser have made major investments in treating and reusing wastewater. The government has also made major expenditures to upgrade sewage systems to handle the waste from homes and businesses so that it no longer runs directly into waterways.[28]

Unfortunately, the war on toxic waste has not been quite as successful. For years, many industrial wastes were routinely dumped in landfills, where few (if any) protective barriers could be counted on to prevent dangerous chemicals from leaking into the soil and the water supply. Government attempts to force businesses to clean up these sites have yielded many lawsuits and much expense but with disappointing results. At some sites, the groundwater may never be restored to drinking water purity.

However, today's managers are learning from the mistakes of their predecessors, and they are taking steps to reduce and prevent toxic waste pollution. Some use high-temperature incineration to destroy hazardous wastes, some recycle wastes, some give their wastes to other companies that can use them, some neutralize wastes biologically, and some have redesigned their manufacturing processes so that they don't produce the wastes in the first place. In Kahlundborg, Denmark, a group of companies are practicing what they call

LEGISLATION	DATE	EFFECT
Water Quality Act	1965	Requires states to adopt water-quality standards, subject to federal approval.
Water Quality Improvement Act	1970	Strengthens federal authority over water pollution. Provides for federal cleanup of oil spills.
Safe Drinking Water Act	1974	Sets standards for drinking-water quality.
Clean Water Act	1977	Orders control of toxic pollutants by 1984 using best available, economically feasible technology.
Water Quality Act	1987	Extends grants for sewage-treatment projects. Requires states to control pollution due to rainfall runoff from farm and urban areas, forestry, and mining sites.
Safe Drinking Water Act	1996	Requires municipal water systems to report on contaminant levels; establishes funding to upgrade water systems.
		Other pollutants
Federal Insecticide, Fungicide and Rodenticide Act and amendments	1947, 1967, 1972	Outlaws fraudulent sales claims to protect farmers. Requires registration of poisonous products. Provides authority to license users of pesticides.
Pesticide Control Act and amendments	1972, 1975	Requires pesticides shipped across state lines to be certified effective and harmless to crops, animal feed, animals, and humans. Sets deadline for registration, classification, and licensing of many pesticides.
Noise Control Act	1972	Requires EPA to set standards for major sources of noise and to advise Federal Aviation Administration on standards for airplane noise.
Toxic Substances Control Act	1976	Requires chemicals testing. Authorizes EPA to restrict the use of harmful sub stances.
Comprehensive Environmental Response, Compensation, and Liability Act	1980	"Superfund Act" creates trust fund to clean up hazardous-waste sites. Sets schedules and preferences for cleanup activities
Oil Pollution Act	1990	Sets up liability trust fund. Extends operations for preventing and containing oil pollution.

industrial symbiosis, which means that they work together in a mutually advantageous relationship. Manufacturers as diverse as a pharmaceutical company, an oil refinery, a farm, a building materials company, and a power plant are linked via pipes and ground transportation systems so that each can use the waste products from the others as fuel and raw materials for themselves. The idea started among the managers of the companies as a way to lower costs and boost profits. But the reduction of waste and pollution has been so substantial that the EPA has taken notice. It is now supporting the development of eco-industrial parks in the United States.[29]

Many companies are also reducing the amount of solid waste they send to landfills by implementing companywide recycling programs. The EPA reports that over 20 percent of the solid waste generated in the United States is now recycled.[30] In addition, hundreds of thousands of tons of waste have been eliminated through conservation and more efficient production.[31] Nestlé is one company that takes a proactive approach to reducing waste worldwide. In three years, the company reduced its use of packaging materials by 40,000 tons. This reduction not only saved resources but also saved Nestlé a lot of money. Moreover, Nestlé is a founding member of the European Recovery and Recycling Association (ERRA) whose mission is to help organize packaging recovery and recycling in

Europe.[32] These activities are a part of the *green marketing* movement, in which companies distinguish themselves by using less, recycling more, and developing new products that are easier on the environment.

Business and Consumers

consumerism
Movement that pressures businesses to consider consumer needs and interests

The 1960s activism that awakened business to its environmental responsibilities also gave rise to **consumerism,** a movement that put pressure on businesses to consider consumer needs and interests. Consumerism prompted many businesses to create consumer-affairs departments to handle customer complaints. It also prompted state and local agencies to set up bureaus to offer consumer information and assistance. At the federal level, President John F. Kennedy announced a "bill of rights" for consumers, laying the foundation for a wave of consumer-oriented legislation (see Exhibit 3.4). These rights include the right to safety, the right to be informed, the right to choose, and the right to be heard.

EXHIBIT 3.4

Major Federal Consumer Legislation

Major federal legislation aimed at consumer protection has focused on food and drugs, false advertising, sales practices, product safety, and credit protection.

LEGISLATION	DATE	EFFECT
		Food and drugs
Federal Food, Drug, and Cosmetic Act	1938	Puts cosmetics and therapeutic products under Food and Drug Administration's jurisdiction. Outlaws false and misleading labeling.
Delaney Amendment to the Food, Drug, and Cosmetic Act	1958	Bans chemicals found to induce cancer from use as food additives.
Color Additives Amendment	1960	Mandates disclosure of coloring added to foods.
Kefauver-Harris Drug Amendments to the Food, Drug, and Cosmetic Act	1962	Requires manufacturers to test safety and effectiveness before marketing drugs and to show common or generic drug name on label.
Wholesome Meat Act	1967	Strengthens inspection standards for slaughterhouses of red-meat animals.
Orphan Drug Act and amendments	1983, 1985	Sets incentives and granted exclusive marketing right to promote the development of drugs for rare diseases and conditions.
Drug Price Competition/ Patent Term Restoration Act	1984	Shortens application process for approval of generic versions of certain drugs.
Nutrition Education and Labeling Act	1990	Requires specific, uniform product labels detailing nutritional information. Outlaws certain claims when key information is not shown.
Food, Agriculture, Conservation, and Trade Act	1990	Prevents pesticides banned in United States from being exported to other countries.
		Misbranding and false or harmful advertising
Wool Products Labeling Act	1939	Requires manufacturers to identify the type and percentage of wool content in products.
Automobile Information Disclosure Act	1958	Prohibits car dealers from inflating factory invoice prices of new cars.
Federal Hazardous Substances Act	1960	Requires warning labels on items with dangerous chemicals.
Cigarette Labeling Act	1965	Mandates warnings on cigarette packages and in ads.
Fair Packaging and Labeling Act	1966, 1972	Requires honest, informative package labeling. Labels must show origin of product, quantity of contents, uses or applications.
Public Health Cigarette Smoking Act	1970	Bans radio and TV cigarette ads. Strengthens required warning on packaging.

Go for the Green

BEST OF THE WEB

Maybe you want to lead more of a green lifestyle, but you're not sure where to begin. The Sustainable Business Network (SBN) is a good place to start. The SBN has valuable information on environmental business issues ranging "from recycling to green building, from renewable energy to organic products, from social investing to certified forestry." At the SBN site, you can access databases of information on environmentally conscious companies, locate green business opportunities, and find jobs that let you put your business skills to work to help the environment, just for starters. In addition, you can follow the link to the *EnviroLink Network* for a wealth of additional information on environmental issues.
http://envirolink.org/sbn

LEGISLATION	DATE	EFFECT
Country of Origin Labeling Act	1985	Requires clothing to be labeled with country of origin.
Children's Television Act	1990	Restricts television commercials during children's programming to 10.5 minutes per hour on weekends and 12 minutes per hour on weekdays.
American Automobile Labeling Act	1992	Requires carmakers to identify where cars are assembled and where their individual components are manufactured.
		Sales practices
Land Sales Disclosure Act	1968	Protects consumers from unfair practices in sales of land conducted across state lines.
Trade Regulation Rule	1972	Sets a 72-hour cooling-off period to allow consumers to cancel sales made door-to-door.
Magnuson-Moss Warranty Act	1975	Requires complete written warranties in ordinary language. Required warranties to be available before purchase.
		Product safety
Flammable Fabrics Act	1953, 1967	Prohibits interstate shipment of apparel or fabric made of flammable materials. Sets stronger standards for clothing flammability.
National Traffic Safety Act	1958	Establishes safety standards for cars and tires.
Child Protection Act	1966	Prohibits the sale of hazardous toys; amended in 1969 to include products that pose electrical, mechanical, or thermal hazards.
Consumer Product Safety Act	1972	Creates Consumer Product Safety Commission.
		Credit protection
Truth-in-Lending Act (Consumer Protection Credit Act)	1968	Requires creditors to disclose finance charge and annual percentage rate. Limits cardholder liability for unaruthorized use.
Fair Credit Reporting Act	1970	Requires credit-reporting agencies to set process for assuring accuracy. Requires creditors who deny credit to tell consumers the source of information.
Equal Credit Opportunity Act and amendment	1974, 1978	Prohibits discrimination in granting credit on the basis of gender, marital status, race, color, religion, age, and source of income.
Fair Credit Billing Act	1974	Sets process for disputing credit billing errors.
Fair Debt Collection Practices Act	1978	Outlaws deceptive, unfair collection practices.

The Right to Safety

The U.S. government imposes many safety standards that are enforced by the Consumer Product Safety Commission (CPSC) as well as other federal and state agencies. Theoretically, companies that don't comply with these rules are forced to take corrective action. However, many consumer advocates complain that some unsafe products slip through the cracks because regulatory agencies lack the resources to do an effective job. But even without government action, the threat of product-liability suits and declining sales motivates many companies to meet safety standards. After all, a poor safety record can damage a company's reputation.

Perhaps the most visible example of consumer pressure to eliminate unsafe products is the war on tobacco companies in the United States. Scientists determined long ago that the tar and nicotine in tobacco are both harmful and addictive. In 1965 the Federal Cigarette Labeling and Advertising Act was passed, requiring all cigarette packs to carry the now famous Surgeon General's warnings. And over the years, tobacco companies have spent billions of dollars to defend themselves in lawsuits by smokers suffering from cancer and respiratory diseases. Nonetheless, the tobacco industry has continually denied the harmful effects of cigarettes. It has also denied charges that tobacco companies specifically target children and teenagers with their advertising campaigns. However, in 1996 the Liggett Group, a major U.S. tobacco company, admitted publicly that cigarettes cause cancer, are addictive, and have been promoted to encourage smoking among minors. In 1997 the tobacco industry agreed to pay $368.5 billion over 25 years and an additional $15 billion per year after that to settle lawsuits brought by smoking victims and 40 state governments. Meanwhile, the tobacco industry is facing continued attacks worldwide. Even so, RJR Nabisco chairman Steve Goldstone said recently that "behind all the allegations . . . is the simple truth that we sell a legal product."[33] Does the fact that a product is legal, even when it is proven to be dangerous, justify its sale? Should the government take measures to make the product illegal, or should consumers be allowed to decide for themselves what they will buy?

The Right to Be Informed

Regardless of whether a product is harmful, consumers have a right to know what is in it and how to use it. At the same time, they have a right to know the costs of goods or services and the details of any purchase contracts. The Food and Drug Administration, the Federal Trade Commission, and the Agriculture Department are the federal agencies responsible for regulating product labels to make sure no false claims are made. These agencies are concerned not only with safety but also with accurate information. Research shows that nearly three-quarters of shoppers read labels when deciding whether to buy a food product the first time, so labels are an important element in informing consumers.[34] If a product is sufficiently dangerous, a warning label is required by law, as in the case of cigarettes. However, warning labels can be a mixed blessing for consumers. To some extent, the presence of a warning protects the manufacturer from product liability suits, but the label may not deter people from using the product. The billions of dollars a year still spent on cigarettes in the United States emphasizes this point.

As the world economy becomes more and more service-oriented, consumers are making purchases that don't necessarily carry a label. Therefore, consumers must take it upon themselves to ensure that they are getting what they pay for. Businesses can help by demonstrating ethical behavior. For example, stock brokerage firms have come under fire recently for pushing customers to buy investments that don't really meet their needs but that generate large profits for the brokerage firms. To help reassure customers, a group of 15 discount brokers recently formed the Discount Brokers Association (DBA), which has adopted a code of ethics designed to inform consumers about what they can expect when they buy brokerage services.[35]

The Right to Choose

Business responds very well to the right to choose: The number of products available to consumers is truly amazing. But how far should this right extend? Are we entitled to choose products that can be harmful—liquor, for example? Or sugar-coated cereal? To what extent are we entitled to learn about these products? Should beer and wine ads be eliminated from television, just as ads for other types of alcoholic beverages have been? Should advertising aimed at children be banned altogether?

Consumer groups are concerned about these questions, but no clear answers have been found. Generally speaking, however, business is sensitive to these issues. Recent public concern about drunk driving, for example, has led the liquor industry to encourage responsible drinking. For example, Coors runs advertisements designed to discourage underage drinking and drinking on the job.[36] Similarly, several major broadcast television networks have implemented a rating system to help the public gauge whether a show is appropriate for a particular audience. Most U.S. businesspeople would rather help consumers make informed choices than be told what choices they can offer.

The Right to Be Heard

A final consumer right is the right to be heard. Again, most businesses are extremely responsive to this issue. Many companies have established toll-free consumer information and feedback numbers that are printed on product packages. In addition, more and more companies are now establishing World Wide Web sites to provide product information and gain customer feedback.

Businesses benefit from getting as much information about their customers as possible because it allows them to make informed decisions about changing existing products and offering new ones. It also allows companies to make better use of their advertising budgets by targeting narrower, more focused market segments. However, the pursuit of information has given rise to a new ethical concern—maintaining customer privacy. Credit-card companies have a lot of information about where individual consumers spend their money and how much they spend. These companies are not generally restricted from revealing this information. Similarly, insurance companies aren't restricted from revealing information about their policyholders. And only recently has the government passed legislation to restrict phone companies from using customer information, such as billing records and calling patterns, for marketing purposes. Many companies gather consumer information in the course of doing business, and some consumers are angered when companies sell or share this information. As Internet commerce increases, the issue of consumer privacy will become even more important.[37] Even so, consumer advocacy groups can have an influence over business and public policy. For example, after privacy advocates protested, America Online recently backed out of a plan to make its customers' home telephone numbers available to telemarketing companies.[38]

The right to be heard also covers a broad range of complaints about discrimination against customers. More than 4,000 African American customers complained to the U.S. Justice Department about racial discrimination by some Denny's restaurants. Among their complaints: They were asked to pay for meals in advance (although other customers weren't asked to do this), and they received slower service than other customers. Flagstar, the chain's owner, responded by making a public apology and paying $46 million to settle the claims. In addition, the number of African American–owned Denny's franchisees has risen from 1 to 27 in 3 years, and 12 percent of the company's supplies are now purchased from minority-owned vendors. Some say Denny's still has a long way to go, but the company is clearly committed to change. Flagstar's new CEO, Jim Adamson, tells his employees, "I will fire you if you discriminate."[39]

Business and Workers

Over the past 30 years, dramatic changes have occurred in the attitudes and composition of the work force. These changes have forced businesses to modify their recruiting, training, and promotion practices, as well as their overall corporate values and behaviors.

The Push for Equality in Employment

discrimination
In a social and economic sense, denial of opportunities to individuals on the basis of some characteristic that has no bearing on their ability to perform in a job

minorities
In a social and economic sense, categories of people that society at large singles out for discriminatory, selective, or unfavorable treatment

The United States has always stood for economic freedom and the individual's right to pursue opportunity. Unfortunately, until the past few decades many people were targets of economic **discrimination,** relegated to low-paying, menial jobs and prevented from taking advantage of many opportunities solely on the basis of their race, gender, age, disability, or religion. Examples like Denny's demonstrate that discrimination has not yet been defeated in our society.

The burden of discrimination has fallen on **minorities,** groups such as African Americans, Hispanics, Asian Americans, immigrants, people with disabilities, and elderly people. In a social and economic sense, women and homosexuals are also minorities.

Job discrimination, in particular, has been a vicious cycle. Because they could not hope for better jobs, many minority-group members have had little incentive to seek an education. Because they have not been adequately educated, many have not been able to qualify for those jobs that might otherwise have been available to them. Exhibit 3.5 shows how discrimination has affected the job opportunities of certain minorities.

Government Action The Civil Rights Act of 1964 established the Equal Employment Opportunity Commission (EEOC)—the regulatory agency that battles job discrimination. The EEOC is responsible for monitoring the hiring practices of companies and for investigating complaints of job-related discrimination. It has the power to file legal charges against companies that discriminate and to force them to compensate individuals or groups who have been victimized by unfair practices. The Civil Rights Act of 1991 extended the original act by allowing workers to sue companies for discrimination and by granting women powerful legal tools against job bias.

affirmative action
Activities undertaken by businesses to recruit and promote women and minorities, based on an analysis of the work force and the available labor pool

In the 1960s, **affirmative action** programs were developed to encourage organizations to recruit and promote members of minority groups. Proponents of the programs believe that minorities deserve and require preferential treatment to boost opportunities and to make up for years of discrimination. Opponents of affirmative action believe that creating special opportunities for women and minorities creates a double standard that infringes on the rights of other workers and forces companies to hire, promote, and retain people who are not necessarily the best choice from a business standpoint. Some opponents are members of minority groups who feel that affirmative action programs trivialize their ability to succeed on their own merits. Regardless, any company that does business with the federal government must have an affirmative action program.

Business's Response Since the 1960s, most businesses have taken an active role in setting up affirmative action programs. And in cases where companies have discriminated against minorities, federal courts have imposed rigid numerical hiring and promotion quotas for minorities. In recent years, however, the debate over the effectiveness of affirmative action has been heating up. In 1996 California voters passed the California Civil Rights Initiative

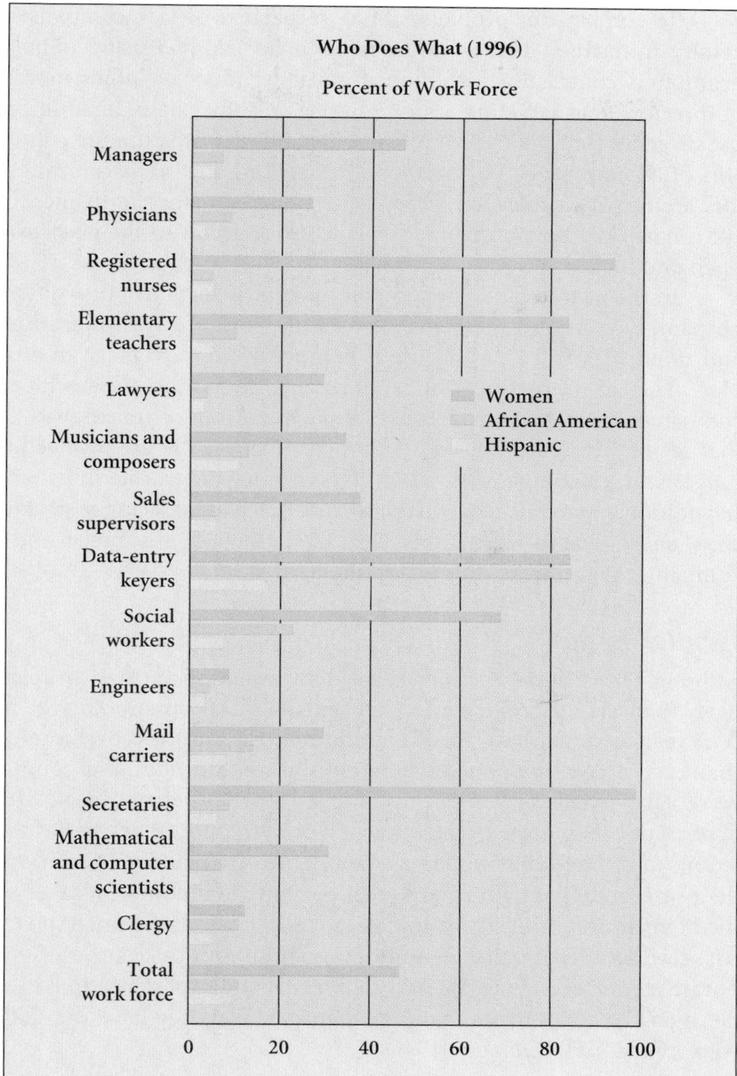

EXHIBIT 3.5

How Discrimination Has Affected Employment of Minorities

Discrimination has resulted in continuing low levels of employment for minorities and has narrowed their choice of career.

(CCRI), which prohibits consideration of race, gender, or ethnicity in the state's public employment, education, and contracting systems. The CCRI was subsequently challenged for conflicting with federal civil rights laws, but the challenge was ultimately rejected by the U.S. Supreme Court. Other states are expected to pass similar laws in the future.[40]

The major reason that affirmative action has not been entirely successful is that efforts to hire more minorities do not necessarily change negative attitudes about differences among individuals. Recently, nearly 1,400 black managers and professionals at Texaco filed a class-action lawsuit against the company, charging that they were denied promotions because of their race. Secretly recorded tapes of a group of senior Texaco executives who had met to discuss the case revealed the use of racial slurs, the mocking of the African American holiday Kwanzaa, and a plot to destroy documents demanded by the prosecution in the suit.[41] The Texaco case illustrates that attitudes and lack of understanding are among the largest barriers to minority advancement.

diversity initiatives
Company policies designed to enhance opportunities for minorities and promote understanding of diverse cultures, customs, and talents

To combat this problem, about 75 percent of U.S. companies have established **diversity initiatives.** These initiatives often involve increasing minority employment and promotion, contracting with more minority vendors, including more minorities on boards of directors, and targeting a more diverse customer base. In addition, diversity initiatives use diversity training to promote understanding of the unique cultures, customs, and talents of all employees. Furthermore, recognizing that an organization's values and behaviors are heavily influenced by top-level policies, many companies, including Texaco and IBM, now tie a portion of managers' compensation to their performance in creating an open and inclusive work environment.[42]

In the next decade, over 85 percent of new hires will be women, African Americans, Hispanics, or Asian Americans. As a result, employers who discriminate against women and minorities will be at a serious competitive disadvantage in attracting talented people.[43] The U.S. Department of Labor recently found that the stock performance of the 100 companies rated highest in equal employment opportunities was 2.5 times higher than that of the firms rated lowest. Although other factors are involved as well, this evidence suggests that a company's level of diversity may play a role in its economic performance. In addition, companies that discriminate often end up facing costly lawsuits, customer boycotts, and damaged reputations. Texaco, Nationwide Insurance, and Avis are examples of companies that learned this lesson the hard way.[44]

Gender Issues

sexism
Discriminating against a person on the basis of gender

Although men do face some sexual discrimination in the workplace, women are more likely than men to feel the effects of **sexism,** discrimination on the basis of gender. In recent years, women have made significant strides toward overcoming sexism on the job, thanks to a combination of changing societal attitudes and company commitments to workplace diversity. Women now account for 35 percent of all MBAs awarded, and 43 percent of U.S. managers are women. However, only 10 percent of the top managerial positions at the nation's 500 largest companies are held by women. At levels of vice president or higher, the figure is only 2.4 percent.[45] Of course, it takes time to develop qualified female and minority candidates for top-level management positions, and only in the past few decades have large numbers of both groups begun the slow climb up the corporate ladder, acquiring the necessary skills and experience to be a vice president, president, or CEO. Nevertheless, many managers feel they have the skills but are being held back by the *glass ceiling.*

glass ceiling
Invisible barrier of subtle discrimination that keeps women out of the top positions in business

The Glass Ceiling The **glass ceiling** is an invisible barrier that keeps women and minorities from reaching the highest-level positions. One theory about the glass ceiling suggests that top management has long been dominated by white males who tend to hire and promote employees who look, act, and think like them. Another theory states that stereotyping by male middle managers leads them to believe that family life will interfere with a woman's work. As a result, women are relegated to less visible assignments in the company, so their work goes unnoticed by top executives and their careers stagnate.[46]

Nevertheless, diversity initiatives are helping shatter the glass ceiling. Such initiatives include long-term commitments to hiring more women, company-sponsored networking and career planning for women, diversity training and workshops, and mentoring programs designed to help female employees move more quickly through the ranks. Pitney Bowes's long-term commitment to diversity has resulted in women holding 5 of the top 11 jobs at the company. Mattel recently named Jill Elikann Barad to be the company's president and chief operating officer. And Patagonia boasts that women hold more than half of the company's top-paying jobs and almost 60 percent of managerial jobs.[47]

Unequal Compensation As women move into higher-paying occupations, the gap between their earnings and men's earnings continues to narrow. Today women earn about 75 percent of what men earn, up from 64 percent in 1980.[48] Despite their progress, however, women continue to earn significantly less than men, even when they compete in the same occupations (see Exhibit 3.6).

The gap between women's and men's wages is wide throughout the world and is getting even wider in some countries. Women also have fewer opportunities than men worldwide.[49] However, in many countries the belief in male superiority over women is much more deeply rooted than in the United States, so it is likely to take a long time before the situation is reversed.

Is It True?

Most women would prefer not to work overseas.

Sexual Harassment Another sensitive issue that women often face in the workplace is sexual harassment. As defined by the EEOC, **sexual harassment** takes two forms: the obvious request for sexual favors with an implicit reward or punishment related to work, and the more subtle creation of a sexist environment in which employees are made to feel uncomfortable by off-color jokes, lewd remarks, and posturing. Recent court cases involving women use the "reasonable woman" standard in deciding whether sexual harassment has occurred. If a reasonable woman would find a situation objectionable, the court deems it sexual harassment.

sexual harassment
Unwelcome sexual advance, request for sexual favors, or other verbal or physical conduct of a sexual nature within the workplace

Research shows that 50 to 85 percent of all working women experience some sexual harassment during their careers, and 90 percent of the top 500 U.S. firms have received complaints of sexual harassment. Moreover, 5 out of 10 men say they've done or said something at work that could be considered sexual harassment by a female colleague.[50] Male employees may also be targets of sexual harassment, and both male and female employees alike may experience same-sex harassment. However, sexual harassment of female employees by male colleagues continues to make up the majority of reported cases.

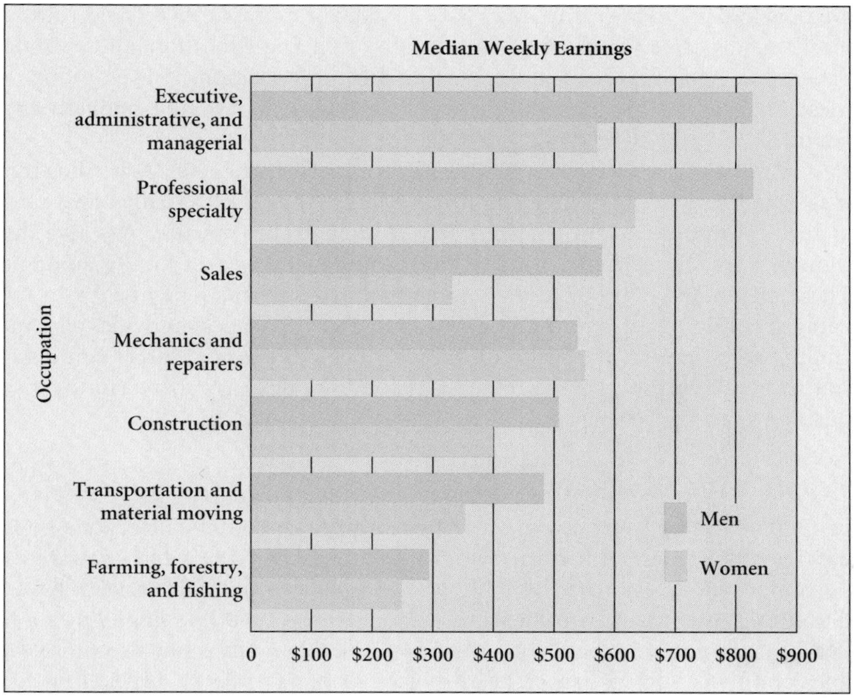

EXHIBIT 3.6

Women's Earnings versus Men's Earnings

Despite more than 30 years of fighting for equal opportunity, women still earn less than men in almost every field.

Patagonia's chief operating officer, Karyn O. Barsa, is proud to work at a company where 60 percent of managers are women.

Mitsubishi Motor Manufacturing of America was recently hit with the largest sexual harassment suit ever filed by the EEOC. After numerous complaints from current and former female employees, as well as a lengthy investigation, the commission charged Mitsubishi with creating a hostile and abusive work environment, failing to respond to complaints, and retaliating against women who complained. The suit could apply to more than 500 past and present female employees of the company, and each could be awarded over $300,000. This is in addition to a private civil suit brought by 29 of the women who say they were harassed and abused. Mitsubishi has since hired former secretary of labor Lynn Martin to help address the problem. She made 34 recommendations in all, including improving training for managers, making sexual harassment workshops mandatory for all employees, and overhauling the company's human resources department.[51] However, if Mitsubishi had acted with concern and sympathy when employees first complained of sexual harassment, the company could have saved a lot in litigation costs, employee turnover, lost productivity, and public image.

Job Security and Benefits

What do businesses owe to their employees? This question has no easy answer, yet the question is raised more and more frequently in the United States today. In the first 25 years following World War II, U.S. companies enjoyed new levels of prosperity, and workers enjoyed high wages, good benefits, and job security. But in recent years, global competition and the threat of hostile takeovers have forced many companies to lay off workers and reduce wages and benefits. AT&T alone laid off over 123,000 employees in the 1990s. In addition, more than a quarter of the U.S. work force now falls below the $15,000-a-year poverty line.[52]

Of course, it is sometimes necessary for companies to restructure if they are to remain competitive, as Bob Haas discovered when he took over Levi's. A company cannot operate efficiently with unnecessary employees on its payroll. However, some companies are now looking to help employees they lay off. For example, AT&T and IBM provide services such as career counseling, money for continuing education, and extended pay and benefits as employees make the transition into new positions.[53] Even though companies incur financial costs to maintain these policies, they gain favorable publicity and customer goodwill.

Another issue facing U.S. businesses today involves benefits. A growing trend in business is to hire more part-time employees because they don't usually receive benefits such as medical insurance and pension plans. Although this practice may save the company money, many argue that it leads to lower morale and weaker loyalty among employees. These conditions can lead to high employee turnover and subsequently to more money being spent on hiring and training new employees. Starbucks provides all employees, including part-timers, with health insurance, stock options, and career counseling. As a result, employee turnover is less than 60 percent annually, compared to the restaurant industry average of 140 percent.[54]

People with Disabilities

In 1990 people with a wide range of physical and mental difficulties got a boost from the passage of the federal Americans with Disabilities Act (ADA), which guarantees equal opportunities for an estimated 50 million to 75 million people who have or have had a condition that might handicap them. As defined by the 1990 law, *disability* is a broad term that protects not only those with obvious physical handicaps but also those with less visible conditions, such as cancer, heart disease, diabetes, epilepsy, AIDS, drug addiction, alcoholism, and emotional illness. In most situations, employers cannot legally require job applicants to pass a physical examination as a condition of employment. The law also forbids firing people who have serious drinking or drug problems unless their chemical dependency prevents them from performing their essential job functions.

Businesses serving the public are required to make their services and facilities accessible to people with disabilities. This requirement means that restaurants, hotels, stores, airports, buses, taxis, banks, sports stadiums, and so forth must try to accommodate people who have disabilities. A hotel, for example, must equip 5 percent of its rooms with flashing lights or other "visual alarms" for people with hearing impairments.[55]

Occupational Safety and Health

Thousands of workers are injured on the job every day. The most current statistics report that the annual cost of all work-related injuries totals $119.4 billion—equal to 53 cents of every dollar of corporate dividends paid to stockholders. What's worse, each year approximately 6,500 work injuries are fatal.[56] Obviously, some jobs are more dangerous than others (see Exhibit 3.7). Concern about workplace hazards mounted during the activist 1960s, resulting in passage of the Occupational Safety and Health Act of 1970, which set mandatory standards for safety and health and which established the Occupational Safety and Health Administration (OSHA) to enforce them.

Even without government supervision, many companies are working to improve the health and safety of their employees, motivated both by genuine concern and by costly workers' compensation claims. Many companies have hired specialists to design work areas that minimize physical strain on employees ranging from assembly workers to accountants. Another way companies contribute to the health and safety of their employees is by offering courses on stress management. Scoville Press, a printing company in Minnesota, has reduced its annual workers' compensation claims by as much as $140,000 through such initiatives.[57]

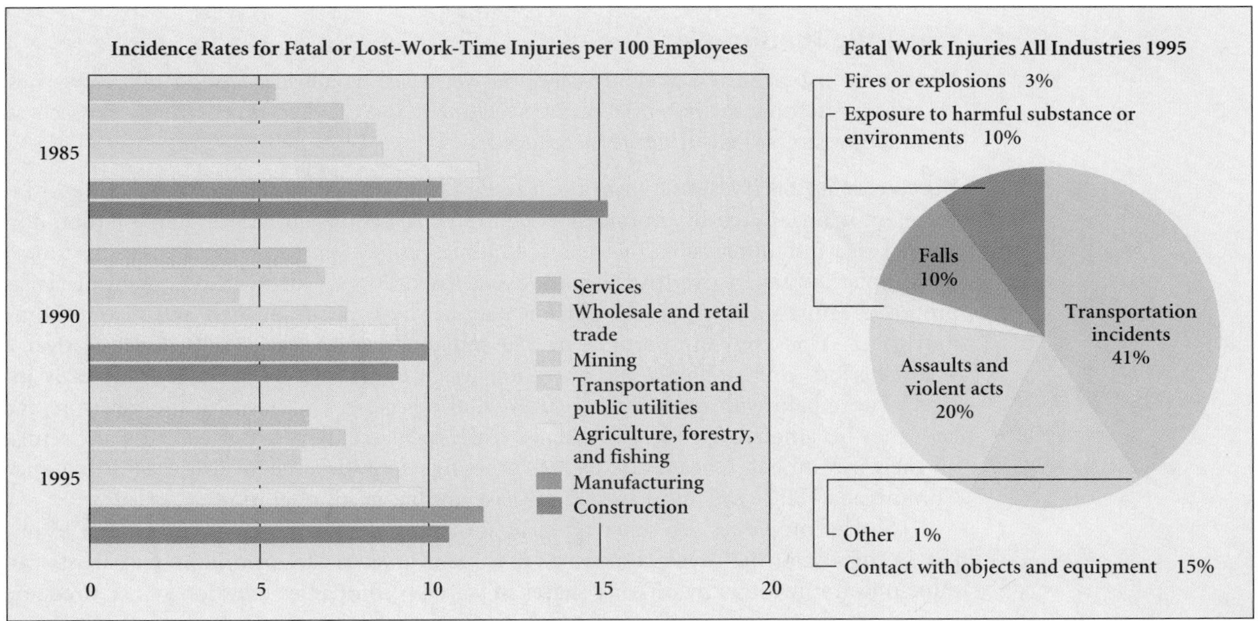

EXHIBIT 3.7

Injuries and Fatalities on the Job

As the first graph shows, construction and manufacturing jobs are the most dangerous, and service workers are the least likely to be injured at work. The second graph shows the causes of work-related fatalities.

New concerns for employee safety have been raised by the international expansion of businesses. Many U.S. companies subcontract production to companies in foreign countries, making it more difficult to maintain proper standards of safety and compensation. For example, when a local labor advocacy group inspected a Nike factory in Vietnam, members discovered violations of minimum wage and overtime laws, as well as physical abuse of workers. Nike has been criticized in recent years for similar conditions in its other Southeast Asian and Chinese factories. Many other companies including The Gap, Guess, and The Body Shop have come under similar criticism. In 1997 a presidential task force composed of apparel industry representatives, labor unions, and human rights groups drafted a code of conduct to uphold the rights of foreign workers of U.S. manufacturing companies. Among the provisions of the code are minimum wage requirements and limits on the number of hours employees work in a week.[58]

BUSINESS AND INVESTORS

In addition to their other responsibilities, businesses are also responsible to those who have invested in the company. Historically, investors have been primarily interested in a company's financial performance. But today a growing number of investors are also concerned about the ethics of the companies in which they invest. One study found that 26 percent of investors consider social responsibility to be extremely important.[59]

Nonetheless, few would argue that a company's major responsibility to investors is to make money on their behalf. Any action that cheats the investors out of their rightful profits is unethical. At the same time, a business can fail in its responsibilities to shareholders by being too concerned about profits.

Cheating the Investor

Investors can be cheated in many ways, but most scams fall into one of two categories: (1) misrepresenting the potential of the investment and (2) diverting earnings or assets so that the investor's rightful return is reduced.

Misrepresenting the Investment Every year tens of thousands of people are the victims of investment scams. Lured by promises of high returns, people sink more than a billion dollars per year into nonexistent oil wells, gold mines, and other fraudulent operations touted by complete strangers over the telephone and the Internet. Fairfield Investment of Dallas promised returns as high as 160 percent per year by investing in first and second home mortgages. The company brought in $56 million from at least 3,500 investors over a 4-year period. Unfortunately, the operation was a Ponzi scheme, meaning that early investors were paid with money raised from later investors. Unknown to the investors, the later they became involved in the scheme, the less chance they had of realizing any return on their investment. Once aware of the company's activities, the Securities and Exchange Commission (SEC) ordered Fairfield to cease and desist all operations.[60]

Shady companies use other types of scams to take people's money, too. For example, in this era of high-tech companies that seem to skyrocket overnight, con artists can dupe unwary investors by offering shares in start-up companies that don't exist. Investors should be especially careful of opportunities advertised over the Internet because it's so difficult for regulators to control online scams.[61]

Many schemes are clearly illegal, but other ways of misrepresenting the potential of an investment fall within the law. With a little "creative accounting," a business that is in

Surf Safely

BEST OF THE WEB

Have you ever gotten a telephone solicitation from a fly-by-night company? Have you ever been the victim of an Internet scam? Although the majority of telemarketing and online businesses are legitimate, fraudulent businesses bilk consumers out of billions of dollars every year. Fortunately, the National Fraud Information Center (NFIC) is helping consumers fight back. The center was established by the National Consumers League (NCL) to safeguard consumers against telemarketing and Internet fraud. Resources on the center's Web site include reports about current online and telephone scams, tips for staying safe online, advice on how to file a fraud report, statistics on the types and frequency of telemarketing fraud, and special advice for elderly persons. Even if you consider yourself a savvy consumer, the site contains a lot of valuable information to help you avoid being ripped off in the future.
http://www.fraud.org

financial trouble can be made to look reasonably good to all but the most astute investors. Companies have some latitude in their reports to shareholders, and some firms are more conscientious than others in representing their financial performance.

Diverting Earnings or Assets Business executives may also take advantage of the investor by using the company's earnings or resources for personal gain. Managers have many opportunities to indirectly take money that rightfully belongs to the shareholders. Perhaps the most common approach is to cheat on expense accounts. Padding invoices and then splitting the overcharge with the supplier is another common ploy. Other tactics include selling company secrets to competitors or using inside information to play the stock market.

Using nonpublic knowledge gained from one's position in a company to benefit from fluctuations in stock prices is **insider trading,** and such incidents have been widely publicized in recent years. Although insider trading is illegal, it is difficult to police. Say you're an accountant for a major corporation. You know the company is about to report a large, unexpected loss. When the news breaks, the price of the stock will undoubtedly fall. You could protect yourself by selling the stock you own before the word gets out. Who would know the difference? Who would care? Consider the people who might buy your shares; chances are *they* would care. Consider the other shareholders, the investors who actually own the company even though they have no day-to-day involvement with it. Would it be fair for you to profit when they did not?

insider trading
Employee's or manager's use of unpublicized information gained in the course of his or her job to benefit from fluctuations in the stock market

Overdoing the Quest for Profits

Most executives would agree that insider trading is damaging to shareholders—but what about trying to maximize profits? How can that be bad? Even though few companies knowingly break laws in an attempt to gain a competitive advantage, many companies have taken questionable steps in their zeal to maximize profits. A recent case involved Sears. The company was concerned about losing money because 132,000 Sears credit-card holders filed for bankruptcy over a period of several years. To protect its earnings, Sears used questionable methods to get bankrupt customers to sign repayment agreements. The company then failed to file the agreements with the federal bankruptcy court, violating federal law. Sears has to pay millions in penalties and restitution, and as a result, its stock price slid almost 4 points. Clearly, this did not benefit Sears shareholders.[62]

Another questionable tactic is corporate spying. Today's competitive environment

EXPLORING GLOBAL BUSINESS

Gift versus Bribe: When a Friendly Exchange Turns into Risky Business

Your company has sent you to an African country to conduct business. You think you've clinched the deal, but then your contact asks you for a "gift" of money to ensure that the deal goes through. Deciding how to handle such situations requires knowing the customs of the country you're doing business in.

Most non-Western countries, especially those in Africa and Asia, have three traditions built around exchanges of gifts: the inner circle, the future-favors system, and the gift exchange. The savvy businessperson who can tap into these traditions will not only clinch today's deal but also establish long-term business relationships—without compromising integrity.

In many non-Western cultures, people see themselves as belonging to an inner circle that consists of relatives, friends, and close colleagues. Members of the inner circle are devoted to mutual protection and prosperity; everyone else is an outsider. Obviously, people prefer to conduct business with insiders, people they know and trust.

In a system of future favors, a gift or service obligates the recipient to return the favor in the future—with interest. Once the favor is returned, the original giver becomes obligated to repay this greater favor. This system of obligations becomes a lifelong relationship, one that can provide access to the inner circle and that can serve as the basis of business dealings.

A third tradition is the practice of giving and receiving gifts to fuel a long-term sequence of gift exchanges. As expert Jeffrey A. Fadiman noted: "The gifts are simply catalysts. Under ideal circumstances the process should be unending, with visits, gifts, gestures, and services flowing back and forth among participants throughout their lives."

By participating in the traditional exchange of gifts and favors and becoming part of an inner circle, Western businesspeople can build trust, gain access to local markets, and minimize risk in a foreign environment. However, it's important to distinguish gifts from bribes. One clue is the size of the request—the smaller the amount, the less likely it is to be a bribe. Another clue is the person the money is to be paid to. If it is supposed to go to a third party—especially someone in power—it is more likely to be a bribe.

Many large U.S. corporations have developed clever and legal strategies for handling requests for payoffs. Instead of making private payments to individuals, they offer donations to build hospitals and schools, they provide engineering or other expert services for public works, or they donate jobs—all with the goal of creating goodwill in the host nation. In the process, they gain a reputation for providing social services instead of paying bribes, and the foreign officials who arrange the donations increase their prestige.

QUESTIONS FOR CRITICAL THINKING

1. What can top managers do to encourage their employees not to offer or accept bribes when dealing with foreign companies?
2. What other ways might a company gain access to the "inner circle" without paying for gifts or bribes?

requires companies to gather as much strategic information as they can. The vast majority of this intelligence gathering is legitimate. But when does legitimate research become unethical or illegal? Stealing patents, searching rivals' trash bins for sensitive information, accessing telephone records, hiring employees from competitors to gain trade secrets, and electronically eavesdropping are examples of unethical behavior that companies sometimes engage in. Such behavior can get a company into hot water. For instance, not long ago

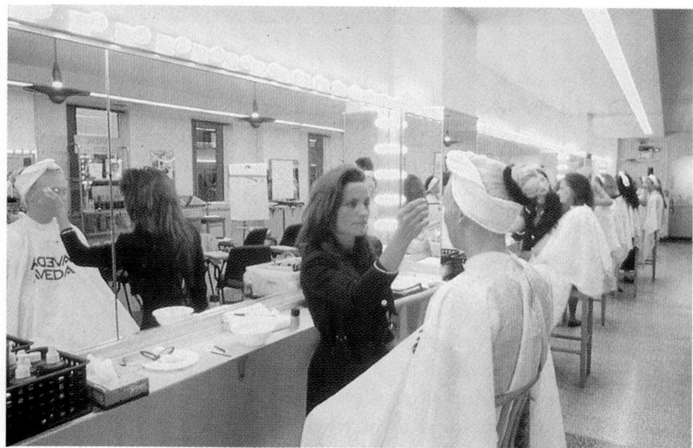

Top managers at Aveda cosmetics believe strongly in setting an ethical example for employees and other companies alike. Aveda's corporate principles state that the company can make a profit and behave responsibly at the same time.

MC Communications, a switch maker for the telecommunications industry, sued a small competitor for stealing 10,000 pages of documents containing trade secrets from MC trash bins.[63] Savvy managers recognize that this kind of unethical behavior can greatly damage a company's reputation and financial position.

The Effort to Become More Ethical

Most companies are concerned about ethical issues, and many are trying to develop approaches for improving their ethics. More than 80 percent of large companies have adopted a written **code of ethics,** which defines the values and principles that should be used to guide decisions. By itself, however, a code of ethics cannot accomplish much. It must be supported by employee communications efforts, a formal training program, and a system through which employees can get help with ethically difficult situations. Ethical behavior starts at the top, where a strong leadership position by the CEO and other senior managers sets the tone for people throughout the company. "At Aveda, our mission is to bring about positive effects through responsible business methods. We do this, quite frankly, out of self-preservation. We want to sustain ourselves," says Horst Rechebacher, founder and chair.

code of ethics
Written statement setting forth the principles that should guide an organization's decisions

Another way companies support ethical behavior is by establishing ethics hot lines that encourage *whistle-blowing*—an employee's disclosure of illegal, unethical, wasteful, or harmful practices by the company. Whistle-blowing can bring with it high costs: Public accusation of wrongdoing hurts the business's reputation, requires attention from managers who must investigate, and damages employee morale. Whistle-blowers also risk being fired or demoted for reporting unethical behavior, and they often suffer career setbacks, financial strain, and emotional stress. The fear of such negative repercussions allows many unethical or illegal practices to go unreported. However, companies that are sincerely interested in operating ethically do work hard to respond appropriately to whistle-blowing. One way to encourage employees to speak up is to allow the whistle-blower to remain anonymous. As Daniel P. Westman, a lawyer and expert on whistle-blowing, says: "Any rational company that has something bad going on within it is going to want to know."[64]

Summary of Learning Objectives

1. **Explain the difference between ethical dilemmas and ethical lapses.**
   An ethical dilemma is an issue with two conflicting but arguably valid sides. An ethical lapse occurs when an individual makes an unethical decision.
2. **List and explain four philosophical approaches to resolving ethical questions in business.**
   When resolving ethical questions, companies may apply standards based on religious teachings, the principles of utilitarianism (the greatest good for the greatest number of people), individual rights (respect for rights guaranteed by legal systems or moral norms and principles), and justice (fair distribution of society's benefits and burdens).
3. **Identify four stakeholder groups to which business has a responsibility.**
   Companies have a responsibility to society, to consumers, to employees, and to investors.
4. **Name three kinds of pollution, and outline actions to control them.**
   Air, water, and land pollution are all significant problems. The government passed the National Environmental Policy Act of 1969 and set up the Environmental Protection Agency to regulate the disposal of hazardous wastes and to clean up polluted areas. Also, many companies have acted to reduce the pollution they produce, to recycle waste materials, and to safely dispose of hazardous wastes.
5. **List the four rights of consumers.**
   Consumers have the right to safety, the right to be informed, the right to choose, and the right to be heard.
6. **Discuss the problem of discrimination, and explain how government and business are working to end it.**
   Discrimination is the practice of restricting an individual's right to pursue opportunity. People are often discriminated against because of their ethnic background, race, gender, age, religion, or physical ability. Government and business have encouraged affirmative action to combat discrimination since the 1960s. Today, many companies are implementing diversity initiatives designed to encourage understanding of the cultures and talents of all individuals.
7. **Discuss two general ways that businesses may cheat investors.**
   Investors are cheated (1) when companies or individuals misrepresent the value of an investment and (2) when companies divert earnings or assets for their personal use, thus reducing the amount available to investors.
8. **Identify steps that businesses are taking to encourage socially responsible and ethical behavior.**
   Businesses are adopting codes of ethics, appointing ethics officers, providing ethics training, developing systems to help employees deal with ethical dilemmas, and establishing ethics hot lines to encourage whistle-blowing.

On the Job: Meeting Business Challenges at Levi Strauss

Bob Haas knew that Levi Strauss & Company faced an uphill battle. The company had uncovered violations of its ethical standards among its Asian suppliers. Meanwhile, consumer tastes had shifted while Levi's looked the other way, and competitors were beating Levi's on price and service. But Haas determined to tackle these problems by refocusing on the original company strengths: strong commercial instincts and a commitment to social values and to the work force.

In the early 1990s, Haas developed global guidelines addressing specific workplace issues, such as length of work periods, fair wages, respect for the environment, and prohibitions against child labor. To add muscle to these guidelines, the company began sending inspectors around the world on surprise visits to look for violations. It was during one of these global audits that Haas discovered some manufacturing contractors in Asia employed underage workers, a clear violation of the guidelines. However, most of the children were significant contributors to family incomes, and losing their jobs would force them into more inhumane ways of earning money. Wanting to retain Levi Strauss as their customer, the factory owners asked Levi's management what to do. Some companies with strong values confronting this issue might simply instruct contractors to discharge underage workers. But Levi Strauss devised a unique solution with positive benefits for everyone.

The contractors agreed to suspend underage workers but still pay their salaries and benefits. For its part, Levi Strauss paid for school tuition and other education-related expenses with no obligations. When the children reached working age, they were all offered full-time jobs in the manufacturing plants. Everyone gained. The children were able to continue both their education and their family income contributions, the contractors kept their good customer, and Levi Strauss retained its quality contractors while protecting company values.

Levi's faced more ethical problems in China, where widespread abuses of human rights clashed directly with the company's ethical principles. So Haas decided to phase out most of Levi's operations in that country over a period of several years. Although some critics argued that the move was just a public relations stunt, and that losing its $50 million annual business in China was small compared to the favorable publicity the company would receive, Levi's maintained that its only objective was to uphold its own ethical standards. "Our hope is that conditions will change and improve so that we can revisit our decision at some time in the future," stated one Levi's executive.

The company could turn to its established ethical guidelines to handle the challenges it faced in Asia, but the another challenge would be harder to deal with. Demand for Levi's products was sagging, so the company had far more manufacturing capacity than it needed. The problem had several causes: (1) The company had failed to notice certain fashion trends that competitors recognized early (such as teenagers' preferences for extra-baggy jeans), (2) the company had no consistent marketing message (which resulted in its blue jeans being perceived as "preppy" or for older generations), (3) the company's slow product-delivery and restrictive pricing policies angered many retailers and prompted some to carry more competing brands, and (4) many competitors produced the majority of their products overseas using more advanced production technology and thus requiring fewer employees, which enabled them to undercut Levi's prices.

To overcome these threats, Haas began a new campaign to listen to the needs of consumers, cut production costs, improve relations with retailers, and refocus its marketing message. Unfortunately, the situation required Haas once again to face the difficult task of laying off large numbers of workers. In early 1997 the company laid off 1,000 management and clerical employees to save $80 million in costs. Nine months later the announcement was made that Levi's would close 11 U.S. plants and lay off nearly 6,400 production workers, a full one-third of its U.S. work force. The decision was not an easy one, but Haas and the rest of Levi's senior managers saw it as necessary in order to keep the company profitable in the years ahead. Nevertheless, Haas was not about to let employees just walk out into an uncertain future. Some had been with Levi's for many years. So, true to the company's high standards for social responsibility, Levi's spent $200 million on severance pay and additional benefits.

Under the generous plan, each laid-off worker received 8 months' paid notice before the job cuts took effect; up to 3 weeks of additional pay for every year of service with the company; a $500 bonus upon finding a new job; paid health benefits for 18 months; and a $6,000 allowance for relocating, retraining, or starting a new business. In addition, Levi's provided career counseling to employees for up to 6 months, and the Levi Strauss Foundation gave $8 million in grants to assist communities affected by the plant closings.

Conventional wisdom holds that the costs of these progressive solutions placed Levi Strauss at a competitive disadvantage. But Bob Haas believes that decisions emphasizing costs alone do not serve a company's best interests. And Haas has taken action on this belief time and again.

Your Mission: As a consultant working for the Consistent Values Group at Levi Strauss, you are responsible for recommending solutions that support company guidelines and principles. Using your knowledge of social responsibility concepts, help Levi Strauss pursue its values. Consider the following dilemmas and recommend the most appropriate action:

1. Levi Strauss wants to enter several developing nations to market products and produce its goods. The guidelines task force has found evidence of human rights violations similar to those found in China. However, changes are under way in some nations that would end the violations and restore political and social stability. With limited resources and the need to focus on current opportunities, Levi wants an appropriate strategy for these markets. What would you recommend and why?
   a. Ignore these markets until political and social stability are clearly established. The company should focus its business on other promising markets where company values are supported.
   b. The new markets are too rich to ignore. Commit marketing and operations resources now to develop plans for market entry once the Levi guidelines have been fully met.
   c. Unlike the situation in China, the direction for these nations is clear. Establish contractor relationships quickly, and enter the market immediately in order to sew up market leadership.
2. Firms that produce goods and market them globally are often faced with difficult choices. For example, for consumers in the U.S. Southwest, Mexico, and Central America, goods can be made (1) in the United States where wages are higher or (2) in countries south of the border where wages are lower. To reduce labor costs, the finance and operations departments have proposed to close a factory in Texas and relocate production to Costa Rica. Given Levi's strong commitment to its work force, how would you respond?

   a. Agree to close the plant in Texas, but provide assistance to factory workers. Given the pressures to reduce operating expenses and increase profits, closing a plant in Texas and relocating to Costa Rica can be justified, provided that displaced U.S. workers receive retraining and educational benefits.
   b. Prepare a case for keeping the plant open in Texas, despite the costs. It would be inconsistent with company values to close the plant in favor of a lower-cost alternative.
   c. Propose a compromise. Reduce the Texas operation to manufacturing goods for the U.S. Southwest, and offer any displaced workers opportunities in other parts of the company. Build a new facility in Central America devoted to goods for the Mexican and Central American markets. Allow the two plants to compete for future manufacturing needs in the region, based on the economic benefits of the respective operations.
3. A group of women and minority managers asked for a private meeting with Bob Haas. Despite Levi's excellent record for providing employment opportunities, the managers sensed invisible barriers keeping women and minorities from advancing in the organization. What course would you recommend to ensure employment opportunities for all?
   a. Implement a formal assessment program that evaluates and rewards employees based on individual achievements regardless of heritage or gender.
   b. Adopt a formal diversity program that promotes the inclusion of women and minorities in senior management roles and on key committees.
   c. To the extent possible, implement formal quotas for women and minorities in all areas, including key senior- and middle-management positions.
4. Levi Strauss has an environmental policy that calls for monitoring all chemicals used by suppliers to uncover any *potential* for harm to the environment. Although the government has established standards for acceptable levels of formaldehyde, a preservative solution used to finish Levi's Sta-Prest pants, there is some question among the group about whether these standards are safe enough. However, reducing formaldehyde levels even further could cost Levi's millions of dollars. What should the company do in this situation?
   a. Stick to the government guidelines. If it they are good enough for Uncle Sam, they are good enough for Levi Strauss.
   b. Adopt a wait-and-see attitude. If current government standards prove to be harmful, spend the money necessary to reduce formaldehyde levels further.
   c. If any potential for harm exists, Levi's must spend the money to reduce its formaldehyde levels now. Consistently adhering to its core values will benefit the company more in the long run than saving a few dollars now.

Key Terms

affirmative action (80)
code of ethics (89)
consumerism (76)
discrimination (80)
diversity initiatives (82)
ecology (72)
ethical dilemma (64)
ethical lapse (65)
ethics (64)
glass ceiling (82)
individual rights (65)
insider trading (87)
justice (65)
minorities (80)
pollution (71)
sexism (82)
sexual harassment (83)
social audit (67)
social responsibility (64)
stakeholders (66)
utilitarianism (65)

Questions

For Review

1. How has business's sense of social responsibility evolved since the turn of the century?
2. What are some of the things business is doing to protect the environment from the dangers of pollution?
3. What can a company do to assure customers that its products are safe?
4. What is insider trading, and how does it harm an investor in a company?
5. What is whistle-blowing, and how can companies learn from it?

For Analysis

6. How might the consumer movement actually benefit business?
7. How do diversity initiatives differ from affirmative action programs?
8. What could Mitsubishi have done to keep its sexual ha-

rassment and discrimination problem from progressing into such a large and costly lawsuit?

9. Many companies now have corporate ethics programs as well as ethics departments, yet the news is still full of companies that are experiencing ethical dilemmas and ethical lapses. Why?
10. How do individuals employ philosophical principles in making ethical business decisions?

For Application

11. Imagine you have been hired as the first corporate ethics officer for an up-and-coming computer software company. You are expected to develop a comprehensive corporate ethics program. Where do you begin? What issues do you need to consider? What goals do you set? How will you measure performance?
12. Assume you are the manager of an independent bookstore with about ten employees. Two female employees have complained to you of sexual harassment by a male assistant manager. How do you approach this problem?

A Case for Critical Thinking ■ Dialing Up Social Responsibility

Working Assets is a telephone service with a conscience. No other telephone service offers customers the opportunity to pay less for long-distance calls and simultaneously show support for social causes. No other telephone service is endorsed by Ralph Nader, prints its bills on completely recycled paper with soy-based ink, or plants 17 trees for each ton of paper it uses. And no other service offers free calls to lawmakers in Washington as well as Citizen Action Letters (monthly letters sent to government officials and corporate executives).

More than 250,000 customers use the services of Working Assets, which was founded by Laura S. Scher and Peter Barnes in 1988. Working Assets is a long-distance reseller, buying phone time at budget rates from bigger telephone companies and then reselling it to customers. In addition to offering low rates for all long-distance calls, the company offers a 25 percent discount when customers place calls to fellow customers.

Although the ability to save on long-distance calls is one reason customers sign up, what sets Working Assets apart from AT&T, MCI, and Sprint is its agenda of social responsibility. The company donates 1 percent of its revenues to nonprofit causes such as civil rights and environmental groups. Every year customers are asked to vote on which causes to support in the coming year.

Working Assets uses its monthly billing statement to communicate with its customers. "No one else thinks of the bill as a product," explains CEO Scher. "They think of the bill as a transaction. This is the crux of our whole operation, and this is where we have fun." The bill gives customers the chance to support social causes by rounding up what they owe in any month. For example, if a bill is $26.85, the customer can choose to pay $30 (or any amount higher than what's being billed). "It's like the penny jar next to the cash register," Scher says. Just as grocery-store customers can drop coins into charity canisters at the checkout, Working Assets customers can add something to their monthly bills, knowing this extra amount will go to a good cause and is deductible on their income taxes as a charitable contribution. Thousands of dollars are raised every month through such contributions.

The bill also invites customers to urge action on a particular issue by calling a government figure or business executive (up to two 5-minute calls per day) or by authorizing the company to send a letter (for a $3 charge). Customers can even send letters online through the company's Web site. Thousands of Working Assets customers participate in any given month. Recent campaigns have sent messages to U.S. senators and representatives supporting national forest protection, hand-gun control, child health care, and tighter EPA controls on pollution. With Citizen Action Letters, Working Assets is a lobbying tool as well as a fund-raising tool.

The company donates millions of dollars to dozens of causes each year. Scher and company president Michael Kieschnick are moving aggressively to expand their customer base and their service offerings so that they can tackle more issues more effectively. The success of the company's long-distance service has led to a Working Assets credit card and pilot programs to sell electric power generated from clean and renewable sources. "The more customers we get, the more money we give to nonprofit groups and the more political clout we get," says Barnes. However, being socially aware doesn't mean giving up the profit focus of a well-managed business. Says Scher, "In some ways we've created an ideal company—one that is able to meet both a financial and a social bottom line."

1. Which of the four basic consumer rights does Working Assets appear to be promoting with its Citizen Letters and Free Speech Day offers? Do you agree with this approach? Why or why not?
2. Is Working Assets acting responsibly by encouraging customers to round up their bills and pay more so that the

company can donate money to social causes? Explain.

3. Working Assets is a private company, which means that management need not be concerned about pleasing shareholders. Why might a public company (one with publicly traded stock held by shareholders) have a more difficult time pursuing social and environmental causes as aggressively as Working Assets does?
4. Go to the Working Assets Web site at <http://www.wald.com>, and follow the links to recent Citizen Action campaigns. Note the diversity of causes Working Assets supports. Are there any initiatives listed that you would not want to support? What do you think customers should do when they disagree with a particular Working Assets campaign? Does the company have a responsibility to stop campaigns that may offend certain customers? What do you think customers should do when they don't support the monthly cause that Working Assets features in its billing statement?

Building Your Business Skills

As directed by your instructor, call or write a local business or franchise operation and request a copy of its code of ethics. As an alternative, visit the periodical section of your library and locate such a code in a business magazine or professional journal article dealing with business ethics. With a group of three other students, evaluate the code. Consider what the code says about the rights of workers, shareholders, and consumers. Who is protected by this code? How does the company balance its obligations to stakeholders with its goals of making products and generating profits? Write a brief (one-page) summary of your evaluation.

Keeping Current Using *The Wall Street Journal*

From recent issues, find a *Wall Street Journal* article related to one or more of the following ethics and social responsibility challenges faced by businesses:

- Environmental issues, such as air and water pollution, acid rain, and hazardous-waste disposal
- Employee or consumer safety measures
- Consumer information or education
- Employment discrimination or diversity initiatives
- Investment ethics
- Industrial spying and theft of trade secrets
- Fraud, bribery, and overcharging
- Company codes of ethics

1. What was the nature of the ethical challenge or social responsibility issue presented in the article?
2. What stakeholder group(s) are affected? What lasting effects will be felt by (a) the company and (b) these stakeholder group(s)?
3. Does the article report any wrongdoing by a company or agency official? Was the action illegal, unethical, or questionable? What course of action would you recommend the company or agency take to correct or improve matters now?
4. Texas Instruments is a recognized leader in corporate ethics and social responsibility. Go to TI's Web site at <www.ti.com>. Click on *Company Info.*, then on *Corporate Citizenship*, and then on *Ethics at TI*. Compare the ethical performance of one of the companies you are reviewing

against TI's policies. Would you say that the company's sense of ethics is as strong as TI's? If not, where do you think the company can improve? Based on the information TI provides about its own ethical standards and policies, what recommendations would you make to the management team of your company for changing or increasing the company's ethical performance in the future?

Exploring the Best of the Web

Build a Better Business, page 71

The Better Business Bureau Web site has a lot of useful information for businesses and consumers alike. Go to the bureau's main page <http://www.bbb.org> and click on the links to answer the following questions.

1. Click on *About the BBB.* What are "BBB Reliability Reports"? What does it mean when the BBB does not have a report on a particular company? How do these reports relate to the consumer's right to be informed?
2. Follow the link to *Programs and Services of the Better Business Bureau.* What is BBB Auto Line? What kind of disputes are handled by the program? What right does a consumer forfeit when accepting the decision of an Auto Line arbitrator? As a consumer, what primary benefits would you expect from this program?
3. From the main page, click on *Advertising Review Programs* and then on *BBB Advertising Guidelines* to access the Code of Advertising. According to the code, when is it acceptable for BBB members to use the word *sale* in advertising? How should BBB members handle "extra charges" in their advertising? On what evidence should claims of particular results be based? Why is it in the best interest of advertisers to comply with the ethical principles of the BBB's guidelines, even if they are not BBB members?

Go for the Green, page 77

The Sustainable Business Network makes it easier for businesses and consumers to find the information that will enable them to make environmentally responsible choices. Visit the network's Web site <http://envirolink.org/sbn> to answer the following questions.

1. Click on *The Library,* then on *Organizations,* and find the link to *Business for Social Responsibility* (BSR). What is this organization's mission? What products and services does BSR provide its members? As a future business person, do you support the goals of BSR? Would you want to work for a company that supports those goals? Why or why not?
2. Follow the links to *Organizations* again and click on *Green Seal.* What is Green Seal and how does it help protect the environment? Why would a business want to have the Green Seal label on its products? Why might a business not want to be associated with Green Seal?
3. From the SBN main page, click on *Green Dream Jobs* and then on *Internships and Fellowships.* Browse through the list and look for any internships that interest you. What skills or experience would help you obtain these positions? What can you do to develop such skills while you are a student?

Surf Safely, page 87

The National Fraud Information Center (NFIC) is a service of the National Consumers League (NCL), the oldest nonprofit consumer organization in the United States. Visit the NFIC's Web site <http://www.fraud.org> to learn how to protect yourself from telephone and Internet con artists. Answer the following questions by navigating the links on the site.

1. Click on *Telemarketing Fraud.* What percentage of U.S. adults have reported receiving fraudulent telephone offers? According to FBI estimates, how many illegal telephone sales companies are operating in the United States? Why should legitimate businesses be concerned about these high rates of telephone fraud?
2. Find *Basic Internet Tips* under *Internet Fraud Watch.* What do you think are the three most important tips for staying safe in cyberspace? Given the recent increase in the number of Internet businesses, how easy or difficult is it for consumers to adhere to these guidelines when they are using the Internet to protect consumers? Why or why not?
3. Click on *How to Report Fraud and Ask Questions.* What two ways can you report fraud to the NFIC? What information should you supply in your report? What results can you expect to receive after filing a report? How does the government benefit from consumers taking action against fraudulent businesses? How does this action indirectly affect all consumers?

Part I: Mastering the Geography of Business ■ The Influence of Immigration on Business

The United States is a country of immigrants, from the early wanderers who came across the Bering Strait into what is now Alaska to the people who are fleeing Hong Kong following China's recovery of the once-British colony. Patterns of immigration have changed over time, often affected by geography and sometimes resulting from events in other parts of the world or from changes in U.S. immigration laws.

Immigration has produced distinct concentrations of ethnic and racial groups across the United States. For instance, the seven states with the highest concentration of African Americans are all in the South, whereas 65 percent of all Hispanic Americans live in states located in three corners of the country: California, Florida, and New York.[61] Geography is a major cause of the Hispanic migration into California and Florida, whereas other factors are probably responsible for the settlement of Hispanic Americans in New York.

The ethnic and racial makeup of a city or state can have a profound effect on business, from the employment opportunities an area offers to the types of products businesses can successfully sell. Consider the makeup of the city or town you're living in, and answer the following questions. You may need to visit the library to conduct some research.

1. What role do you think geography played in creating the ethnic and racial composition of your city? Is the geographic connection direct and obvious (such as people from Asia moving to Hawaii and the West Coast), or is the influence of geography less direct (such as Hispanic populations settling in Idaho and Washington State)?
2. How are businesses in your city affected by ethnic and racial composition? Consider investigating businesses such as restaurants and clothing stores. You might also examine employment patterns in your area.
3. On a map of the world, identify the main countries that produced your city's population. If you can't narrow your city's population to specific countries, identify regions or continents.
4. Use the Internet to get some actual data by visiting the Web site of the U.S. Census Bureau <http://www.census.gov/>, and follow these instructions:

   - Click on the blue button *Search* and then click on words *Place Search.*
   - Enter the name of your city and state (ZIP code is optional—you can use it to narrow your search to a particular section of your city). Click the *Search* button.

- Find your city and click on the *STF3A tables* hot link listed within your city information.
- In the Table (matrix) list that appears, place a check mark in boxes P9 (Race-25) and P35 (Ancestry-37) by clicking on them. Then scroll up and click on the *Submit* button to generate your information request. (Be sure to accept the default HTML format.)
- You should generate two tables of information.

Using the tables generated above, identify the top five countries or origin groups populating your city. How many residents reported multiple ancestry? Using the race and ancestry table, what percentage of your population is black? Asian? Hispanic? (See ancestry—Hispanic origin groups.)

Answers to "Is It True?"

Page 68. False. According to the National Child Labor Committee (NCLC), some 250,000 children work illegally on U.S. farms, many of them migrant workers. In addition, almost every city with a significant population of poor immigrants has sweatshops (factories where employees work long hours for little pay and under unhealthy conditions). Many violations also occur in small manufacturing companies, subcontractors, and restaurants.

Page 73. True.

Page 83. False. In a recent study of Canadian and U.S. firms that sent managers abroad, only 3 percent were female. However, in a study of 1,129 females graduating with MBAs from 7 management schools in the United States, about 84 percent said they would like an international assignment at some point in their careers.

■ PART II

Starting the Business

CHAPTER 4

FORMS OF BUSINESS OWNERSHIP

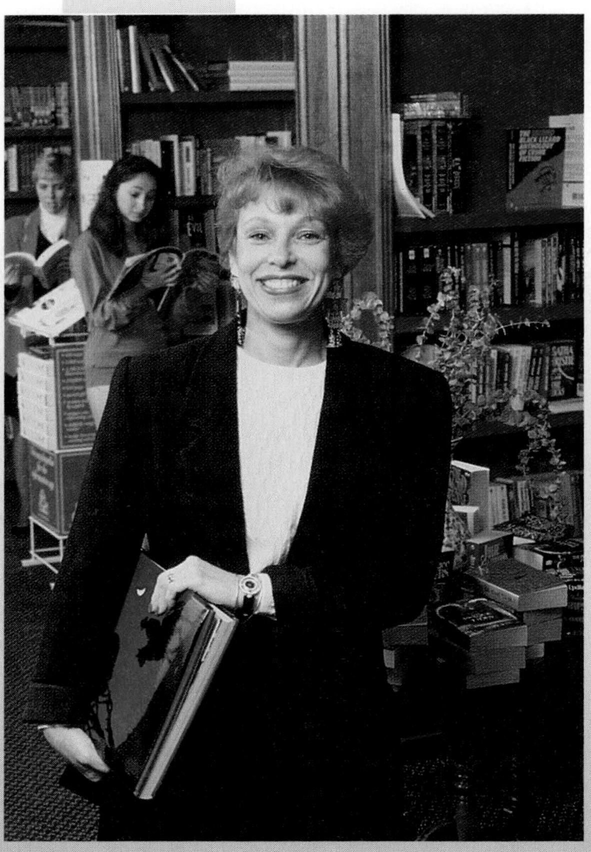

OBJECTIVES

After studying this chapter, you will be able to

1 Identify the two broad sectors of the U.S. economy and its eight subsectors

2 Name five factors that have contributed to the growth of the service sector

3 Discuss the three basic forms of business ownership

4 List five advantages and four disadvantages of forming a sole proprietorship

5 Explain the difference between a general and a limited partnership

6 Delineate the three groups that govern a corporation and describe the role of each

7 Cite four advantages of corporations

8 Describe the five waves of merger activity

ON THE JOB: FACING BUSINESS CHALLENGES AT AJ WRAPS

Wrapping Up a Business—To Go

Alice Thomson and Judith Nantook are identical twin sisters whose passion for food led them into a gutsy decision: opening a chain of fast-food restaurants—starting with one, of course.

AJ Wraps "probably began when we were teenagers working in fast-food restaurants," says Alice. "Then our parents gave us a trip to Paris as a graduation present," adds her twin Judith. "We fell in love with gourmet French cuisine." They had wanted to stay and study with the masters of French cooking, but it just wasn't feasible. So they went home to Illinois to finish college (Alice majored in psychology, Judith in premed zoology). Then Judith met and married Jeff Nantook, following him to San Francisco where he worked as a CPA and tax adviser.

Before long, Judith was begging Alice to move to San Francisco and attend the California Culinary Academy with her. During the week they were learning about sauces and soufflés, and on weekends they were tasting and sampling the city's gourmet offerings while endlessly discussing the restaurant they planned to open after graduation. They were fascinated by the local trend toward multiethnic combinations—and by a "new" eating invention called the wrap. Some say it evolved from a Mexican burrito filled with unexpected ingredients. Others say the idea of a meal wrapped in an easy bundle shows up in every culture sooner or later.

Whatever its origin, the twins saw gold. They started planning a fast-food restaurant that would sell multiethnic, gourmet "wraps" containing exotic, fresh "fusion" (hot and cold) cuisine. They imagined a flavored red tortilla filled with Thai chicken, jasmine-lime rice, and fresh snap peas—or a green one filled with blackened red snapper, Spanish rice, Napa cabbage, and lime-horseradish sour cream. They even started making samples in Judith's home kitchen, much to Jeff's delight.

The twins knew wraps appealed to anyone with a hectic lifestyle—and who doesn't fall into that category at least occasionally? Commuters want to eat behind the wheel, parents want to pick up dinner on the way home, and single people are looking for fresh, healthy, inexpensive meals. Wraps could satisfy all these needs, the twins believed. A National Restaurant Association survey on ethnic cuisine showed that consumers were eager to try more ethnic foods; moreover, a look at the Internet Food Channel's "Ultra Trend Tracker" showed them that the wrap was leading the sandwich category, where focaccia was fading. From coast to coast, newspaper reviews were hailing wraps as the best new fast-food discovery.

Now Judith and Alice face some hard business decisions. Jeff has agreed to share his expertise as financial adviser, but who will manage the food and who will handle the books? How will they share ownership, pay taxes, and compensate themselves? What will they offer financial backers? How will the business grow? Alice and Judith have absolute confidence in their teamwork and their culinary expertise. But they also know that if they don't set the business on the right structural foundation, it could fail overnight—as a lot of well-meaning friends keep pointing out.

How to Categorize Companies by Industry Sector

What do you know about small companies like AJ Wraps or large companies like Exxon? Are they the kind of company you respect? Would you like to work for them? Would you invest your money in them? Would you feel comfortable buying their products or services? To answer these questions, you need to understand what kind of companies they are and what their motivations are. A good place to begin is by categorizing the companies.

service businesses Businesses that provide intangible products or perform useful labor on behalf of another

goods-producing businesses Businesses that produce tangible products

Most companies can be categorized by industry sector. As Exhibit 4.1 illustrates, **service businesses** include finance and insurance, transportation and utilities, wholesale and retail trade, and other services like banking. **Goods-producing businesses** include manufacturing, construction, mining, and agriculture. Broadly speaking, companies in these two major sectors of the economy differ in their growth rate, cycle of business, cost structure, company size, and geographic focus.

The relationship between services and the production of goods is not a battle for dominance. The two sectors are complementary parts of a whole, each dependent on the other. Producers need service businesses to buy and distribute products, and service businesses depend on the production of goods for survival. What would a clothing manufacturer do without department stores? How could AJ Wraps serve up its unique wraps without tortillas, fresh veggies, and spices?

In fact, the line between services and producers has blurred somewhat. Consider IBM. You may think of it as a company that manufactures computers and other business machines. However, at least one-third of IBM's sales come from computer-related services. The company even has a division devoted to providing services worldwide. Many IBM employees perform service tasks such as helping clients come up with innovative solutions to their problems, designing systems for them, offering financial services, and providing product support after the sale. IBM products would be far less attractive to consumers without the services that accompany those products.[1]

Growth of the Service Sector

Services have always played an important part in the U.S. economy, accounting for half of all employment as long ago as 1940. However, in the last two decades, services have be-

EXHIBIT 4.1

Sectors of the U.S. Economy

The service sector provides more than 70 percent of the revenues produced in the United States.

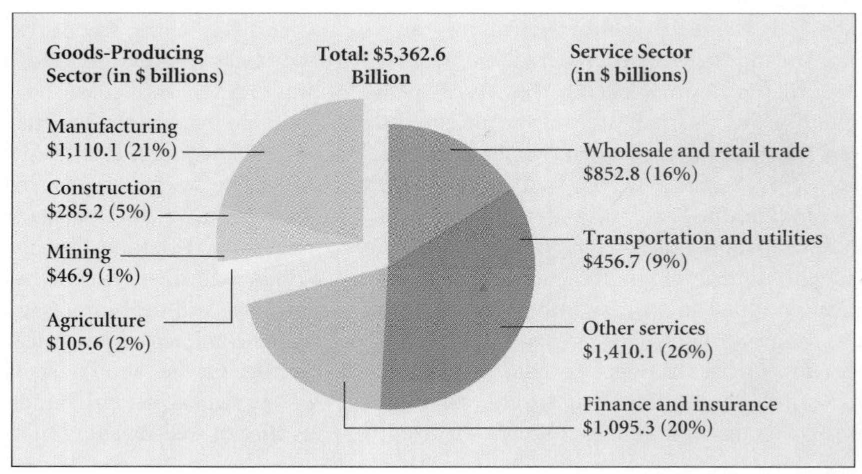

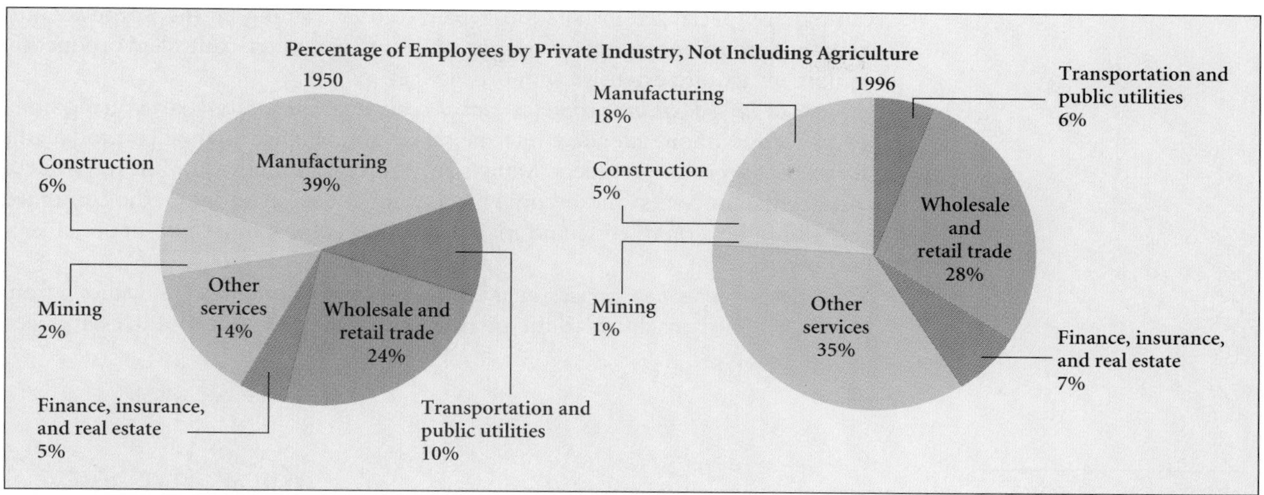

EXHIBIT 4.2

Shifts in Employment by Industry Sector

Since the end of World War II, the service sector has been responsible for creating virtually all job growth in the U.S. economy.

come an increasingly vital force. Service occupations now account for 54 percent of the U.S. GDP, and they employ roughly 70 percent of the 130 million or so people at work in the United States (see Exhibit 4.2). The service sector has created more than 40 million jobs in the last three decades, and more than 20 million more are expected by the year 2005. In contrast, the goods-producing sector has created fewer than 3 million jobs since 1970.

A frequent complaint about service jobs is that they often don't pay as well as manufacturing jobs and don't provide as much room for personal or professional growth. The average hourly wage for service employees has been about $1.70 less than the average wage for employees in the goods-producing sector over the past decade.[2] Nevertheless, many service industries pay well. Advertising, business consulting, legal services, and health care are well-paying service industries that are lumped together in the service sector with typically lower-paying industries such as retail, food services, education, and social services. Many of the higher-paying services are expected to grow at faster rates than the lower-paying services in the coming years.[3]

Factors in Service Sector Growth There are several reasons for the large growth of the service industry in recent years:

- *Economic prosperity increases the demand for services.* The 76 million baby boomers in the United States (people born between 1946 and 1964) are in their peak earning years. These consumers find themselves with more disposable income and look for services to help them invest, travel, relax, and stay fit.
- *Demographic patterns in the United States continue to change.* The United States has more elderly people, more single people living alone, more two-career households, and more single parents than ever before. These trends create opportunities for service companies that can help people with all the tasks they no longer have time for, including home maintenance, food service, and child care.[4]
- *The number and complexity of goods needing service are increasing.* Computers, CD players, recreational vehicles, and security systems are examples of products that

can require specialized installation, repair, or user training. In the workplace, automation products ranging from laser printers to computer-controlled production equipment require extensive support services.
- *Businesses need help in a complex global economy.* Corporate restructuring often leaves firms without adequate internal services. Therefore, many firms today utilize external service providers. Many also turn to consultants to find ways to cut costs, refine processes, and become more competitive. In addition, the continued growth of global marketing and manufacturing requires more international support services.[5]
- *Technology creates new service opportunities.* Many technological advances, from automated teller machines to the Internet, create services that couldn't have been offered before.

BEST OF THE WEB

Know Your Stats!

Quick! What are the total annual sales of all U.S. multinational companies in the service sector? Don't know? Well it's easy to find out. Just check out the *Statistical Abstract of the United States* online. The U.S. Department of the Census has been publishing massive amounts of statistics in this book for years, and now it has made the book available on the Internet. By clicking on the index, you will see that the abstract covers everything from the cost of raising children to the U.S. balance of trade, and from computer programmer salaries to the number of households with VCRs. With almost 1,000 pages of useful data, the *Statistical Abstract* can be a valuable resource for doing market research, for writing term papers, or for just satisfying your curiosity.
http://www.census.gov/prod/www/abs/cc97stab.html (*Note:* the number in this address will change, depending on the year of publication.)

Service Sector Segments The service sector is a rich and varied part of the economy that can be broken down into related segments: retailing and wholesaling, finance and insurance, transportation and utilities, and a final group that contains all other service businesses.

- *Retailing and wholesaling.* In this category, you find many small, family-run retail businesses like AJ Wraps and the neighborhood boutique, as well as large retail corporations like Safeway and Federated Department Stores. You also find wholesale companies that serve as intermediaries between producers and retailers. This is discussed in more detail in Chapter 14.
- *Finance and insurance.* The financial-services sector contains a mix of large and small businesses. For example, giant insurance companies and banks have operations around the world, whereas independent insurance agents, real estate brokers, and local banks operate within well-defined regions.
- *Transportation and utilities.* This sector includes companies like United Parcel Service, American Airlines, and Santa Fe Pacific that move people and packages around the world. Also included are phone companies like GTE, AT&T, and the regional telephone companies, as well as electricity, water, and natural gas suppliers. The companies in this segment of the service sector are usually large. Airlines, electric utilities, and telecommunications companies are **capital-intensive businesses,** meaning that significant amounts of capital are needed to start and operate them.

capital-intensive businesses
Businesses that require large investments in capital assets

It takes a great deal of money to buy airplanes, build power plants, or construct nationwide telephone networks, and small businesses simply lack the funds.

- *Other services.* The last sector includes such diverse businesses as beauty parlors, repair shops, private schools, hospitals, hotels, amusement parks, theaters, and professional consulting companies. Employment in these businesses has more than doubled since 1970.[6] Although hotels, hospitals, and amusement parks all require large amounts of money to operate, many of the services in the "other" category are **labor-intensive businesses**—those that rely to a significant degree on human effort or skill. A law office, for example, is dependent on the knowledge and skills of its lawyers. Similarly, a car-repair shop is dependent on the abilities of its mechanics. In many labor-intensive businesses, the **barriers to entry** are relatively low. In other words, with a little bit of money and some basic skills, almost anyone can enter the business. Coffee stands and dry cleaners are good examples. Because of low barriers to entry, you see many small firms in the "other services" segment.

labor-intensive businesses
Businesses in which labor costs are more significant than capital costs

barriers to entry
Factors that make it difficult to launch a business in a particular industry

Is It True?

American manufacturing employees work less than their foreign counterparts.

Production's Revival

In the early 1980s, the goods-producing sector was plagued by recession, unfavorable exchange rates between the dollar and foreign currencies, tough international competition, and relatively lackluster productivity. However, producers regained much of their momentum by the early 1990s, largely as a result of better management and advances in computer and communication technology. This trend continues today. Across many industries, technology and corporate restructuring are helping lower costs, improve product quality and customer service, and increase worker output. For example, Owens Corning, a major producer of glass products, spent $175 million to revamp its computer systems and link its 150 operating locations. Sales and earnings have already increased as a result, and the company expects a 10 percent increase in productivity. Whirlpool's new equipment and design improvements have raised profits by enabling the company to produce larger volumes more quickly while using fewer parts.[7]

- *Manufacturing.* Large companies dominate the manufacturing sector because large-scale production is more cost effective than small-scale production. Nevertheless, small businesses play an important role in the manufacturing sector, both as suppliers to large manufacturers and as pioneers of new technology. Many of the most exciting scientific developments of recent years have come from small high-tech companies in such fields as biotechnology, computers, robotics, and lasers. Consider Tecnico, a small but growing company that finds commercial uses for space technology. One of its innovations reduced the weight of a Navy submarine component from 200 pounds to less than 22 pounds. The company now fabricates components for several defense contractors, and its revenues are skyrocketing.[8]
- *Construction.* Construction is one of the most *cyclical* businesses in the economy. When interest rates are low, people are more likely to borrow money and build new homes or buildings. Conversely, when interest rates are high, the cost of borrowing money to build and buy property increases, so construction declines. Construction in the United States climbed slowly but steadily throughout the 1990s, and the trend is expected to continue in the next decade.[9]
- *Mining.* Mining is another volatile business, subject to big swings in profitability depending on global economic conditions and on supply-and-demand relation-

The U.S. manufacturing sector has rebounded in recent years by abandoning old factories or upgrading them with new technology that emphasizes quality and productivity.

commodity business
Business in which products are undifferentiated and price becomes the chief competitive weapon; usually applied to basic goods such as minerals and agricultural products

ships. One reason for this volatility is that mining is a **commodity business,** which means that little distinction exists between one unit of production and another, so companies are forced to compete on price. Regardless of who produces it, oil is oil, gold is gold, and copper is copper, and companies cannot do much to differentiate their products. When the supply of commodity products exceeds demand, the producers all cut their prices, and profits fall throughout the industry. For example, in recent years the global supply of many minerals has increased because developing nations have expanded their mining capacity in order to build an export base. This expansion has depressed profits for the mining sector as a whole.

- *Agriculture.* Like mining, agriculture is a commodity business, so profitability hinges on supply-and-demand relationships. More and more developing nations are becoming increasingly self-sufficient in food production. However, global trade of agricultural products remains strong, and U.S. exports of agricultural goods have continued to rise since 1990.[10] The pressure for profits has forced many of the less successful farmers to sell out to larger concerns in recent years. Further consolidation is encouraged by a new farm law passed in 1996 to deregulate commercial farms and reduce government subsidies to farmers over the next several years.[11] Although farm employment represents only a small fraction of total employment in the United States, the health of the nation's farms ripples throughout the economy, affecting equipment makers, banks, and rural retailers.

How to Categorize Companies by Form of Ownership

Figuring out which industry sector a company operates in gives you a general idea of its characteristics. Another way to get a feel for what makes a company tick is to look at its form of ownership. The three most common forms of business ownership are sole proprietorship, partnership, and corporation. As Exhibit 4.3 illustrates, corporations tend to be larger-scale operations, accounting for the lion's share of total receipts in all eight of the economy's industrial subsectors. However, sole proprietorships are more numerous, particularly in the service sector.

Each form of business ownership has its own characteristic internal structure, legal status, size, and field to which it is best suited. Each has key advantages and disadvantages for the owners, and each offers employees a distinctive working environment with its own risks and rewards. Exhibit 4.4 on p. 106 contrasts the characteristics of the three forms of business.

Sole Proprietorships

sole proprietorship
Business owned by a single individual

A **sole proprietorship** is a business owned by one person (although it may have many employees), and it is the easiest and least expensive form of business to start. Many farms, retail establishments, and small service businesses are sole proprietorships, as are many home-based businesses (such as caterers and housekeeping services). The U.S. Census Bureau reports that the number of businesses owned by Native Americans, Asians, and Pacific Islanders has increased by over 60 percent in recent years, and of those, 83 percent are sole proprietorships.[12] However, most sole proprietorships don't make a lot of money. In fact, about two-thirds of them earn less than $25,000 per year.[13]

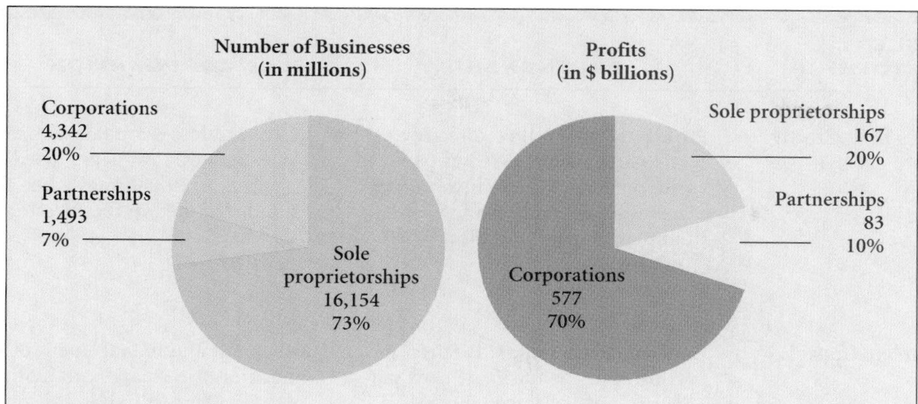

EXHIBIT 4.3

Prevalence and Profits of the Three Forms of Business Ownership

Sole proprietorships are the most common type of business in the United States, accounting for 73 percent of all enterprises. However, corporations account for 70 percent of the profits earned by U.S. businesses.

Advantages of Sole Proprietorships Sole proprietorship has a number of advantages. One is ease of establishment. All you have to do to launch a sole proprietorship is to obtain any necessary licenses, start a checking account for the business, and open your doors. As a sole proprietor, you have the satisfaction of working for yourself. You can make your own decisions, such as which hours to work, whom to hire, what prices to charge, whether to expand, and whether to shut down. Best of all, you can keep all the profits, which are taxed once at your personal income rate tax and not the higher corporate rate.

As a sole proprietor, you also have the advantage of privacy; you do not have to reveal your performance or plans to anyone. Although you may need to provide financial information to a banker if you need a loan, and you must provide certain financial information when you file tax returns, you do not have to prepare any reports for outsiders as you would if you owned a corporation.

Disadvantages of Sole Proprietorships The small scale of most sole proprietorships reflects their limited financial resources. A single person starting a company generally has less capital than a group of people, and she or he may also have more difficulty getting a loan. Furthermore, a sole proprietor may have to pay more for credit because lending institutions are likely to charge higher interest rates to small companies than to large corporations.

However, the major disadvantage of a sole proprietorship is the proprietor's **unlimited liability.** From a legal standpoint, the owner and the business are one and the same. Any legal damages or debts incurred by the business are the owner's responsibility. As a sole proprietor, you might have to sell personal assets, such as your family's home, to satisfy a business debt. And if someone sues you over a business matter, you might lose everything you own.

unlimited liability
Legal condition under which any damages or debts attributable to the business can also be attached to the owner because the two have no separate legal existence

In some cases, the sole proprietor's independence can also be a drawback because it means that the business depends on the talents and managerial skills of one person. If problems crop up, the sole proprietor may not recognize them or may be too proud to seek help, especially given the high cost of hiring experienced managers and professional consultants. A final disadvantage is that sole proprietorships often have a limited life. Although some sole proprietors pass their business on to their heirs as part of their estate, the owner's death may mean the demise of the business. And even if the business does transfer to an heir, the owner's unique skills may be crucial to the successful operation of the business.

ASPECT	SOLE PROPRIETORSHIP	PARTNERSHIP	CORPORATION
Tax treatment	Profits and losses flow directly to the owners, are taxed at personal rates.	Profits and losses flow directly to the partners, are taxed at personal rates. Partners share income and losses equally unless the partnership agreement specifies otherwise.	Profits and losses are taxed at corporate rates. Profits are taxed again at personal rates when they are distributed to the investors as dividends.
Owner's control	Owner has complete control.	**General partnerships:** Partners have control of the business; each partner is entitled to equal control unless the partnership agreement specifies otherwise. **Limited partnerships:** The general partner controls the business; limited partners don't participate in the management.	Ownership and management of the business are separate. Individual shareholders in public corporations are not involved in daily management decisions; in private or closely held corporations, owners are more likely to participate in managing the business.
Owner's liability	Owner assumes unlimited personal liability for the business.	**General partnerships:** Partners assume unlimited liability for the business. **Limited partnerships:** Partners are liable only for the amount of their investment.	Investors' liability is limited to the amount of their investment.
Liquidity of owner's investment	Owner must generally sell the business to get his or her investment out of it.	Partners must generally sell their share in the business to recoup their investment.	Shareholders in public corporations may trade their shares on the open market; shareholders in private corporations must find a buyer for their shares to recoup their investment.
Ease of formation	No expenses or formalities apart from obtaining necessary business licenses.	No formalities or expenses needed apart from obtaining necessary licenses; however, advisable to have an attorney develop a written partnership agreement.	Must follow procedures established by the state in which the business is incorporated; expense and complexity of incorporation vary from state to state. Public corporations must also comply with requirements of their stock exchanges.
Life span of the business	May be limited to the life span of the owner.	Depends on the terms of partnership agreement.	Unlimited.

EXHIBIT 4.4

Characteristics of the Forms of Business Ownership

The "best" form of ownership depends on the objectives of the people involved in the business.

Partnerships

If starting a business on your own seems a little intimidating, you might decide to share the risks and rewards by going into business with a partner. In that case, you would form a **partnership**—a legal association of two or more people as co-owners of a business for profit. You and your partners would share the profits and losses of the business and perhaps the management responsibilities as well. Your partnership might remain a small, two-person operation, or it might grow into an international business with thousands of employees. However, less than 25 percent of all U.S. partnerships earn $100,000 or more per year.[14]

partnership
Unincorporated business owned and operated by two or more persons under a voluntary legal association

Partnerships are of three basic types. In a **general partnership,** all partners are considered equal by law, and all are liable for the business's debts. However, in a **limited partnership,** one or more people act as general partners who run the business, while the remaining partners are passive investors (that is, they are not involved in managing the business). These partners are called limited partners because their liability is limited to the amount of their capital contribution. Therefore, they cannot be sued for more money than they invested in the business. In a **master limited partnership (MLP),** firms act like corporations, selling partner units on a recognized stock exchange. MLPs have advantages similar to those of corporations—limited liability, unlimited life, and transferable ownership. Moreover, if 90 percent of their gross income is passive—such as rental income or other income not requiring the physical efforts of the owners—they pay no corporate taxes. This is because profits are paid to stockholders who pay taxes at individual rates.

general partnership
Partnership in which all partners have the right to participate as co-owners and are individually liable for the business's debts

limited partnership
Partnership composed of one or more general partners and one or more partners whose liability is usually limited to the amount of their capital investment

master limited partnership (MLP)
Business partnership that acts like a corporation, trading partnership units on listed stock exchanges; if 90 percent of income is passive, MLPs are taxed at individual rates

Advantages of Partnerships Proprietorships and partnerships have some of the same advantages. Like proprietorships, partnerships are easy to form, although it's always wise to get a lawyer's advice on the partnership agreement—the legal document that spells out the partners' rights and responsibilities. A key element of this document is the buy/sell agreement, which defines what will happen if one of the partners dies. Partnerships also provide the same tax advantages as proprietorships, because profits are taxed at personal income-tax rates rather than corporate rates.

However, in a couple of respects, partnerships are superior to sole proprietorships, largely because there's strength in numbers. When you have several people putting up their money, you can start a more ambitious enterprise. In addition, the diversity of skills that

Tom and Kate Chappell are partners in their business, Tom's of Maine, a manufacturer of all-natural health and beauty products.

Is It True?

Most people who become self-employed begin with a small amount of capital.

good partners brings to an organization leads to innovation in products, services, and processes, which improves your chances of success.[15] As a partner, you may also have better luck than a sole proprietor in obtaining financing, because you and your partners are all legally responsible for paying off the debts of the group. Finally, by forming a partnership you increase the chances that the organization will endure because new partners can be drawn into the business to replace those who die or retire. For example, the accounting firm KPMG Peat Marwick was founded in 1897, and the original partners died many years ago, but their company continues. Provisions for handling the departure and addition of partners are usually covered in the partnership agreement.

Disadvantages of Partnerships A fundamental drawback of a general partnership arrangement is the unlimited liability of the active partners. If one of your partners makes a serious business or professional mistake and is sued by a disgruntled client, you are financially accountable and stand to lose everything you own. At the same time, you are responsible for any debts incurred by the partnership. Even though malpractice insurance or business-risk insurance offers some financial protection, you pay a premium for your peace of mind.

Another disadvantage of partnerships is the potential for interpersonal problems. Difficulties often arise because each partner wants to be responsible for managing the organization. Electing a managing partner to lead the organization may diminish the conflicts, but disagreements are still likely to arise. Moreover, the partnership may have to face the question of what to do with unproductive partners. And if a partner wants to leave the firm, conflicts can arise over claims on the firm's profits and on capital the partner invested. If the partner goes to a work for a competitor, there is a concern among the other partners that she will take proprietary information with her. As a result, increasing numbers of partnerships are requiring their partners to sign covenants that restrict their claims on the firm's capital when they leave and that make it difficult for them to join competitors.[16] Finally, in the ranks of the aspiring partners, competition is often fierce. The junior employees are vying for a limited number of partnership slots, and they view each other as rivals. This situation may lead to political maneuvering or create a pressure-cooker environment in which everyone is working 80-hour weeks in hopes of looking good.

Strategic Business Partnerships Existing businesses can also form partnerships to accomplish specific purposes. In a joint venture, two or more organizations combine forces to develop, produce, or sell products. Texas Instruments and Hitachi have been partners in building memory chips since 1988. The two companies are actually competitors. However, like a growing number of companies, they have realized that competing in the global economy can be made easier by teaming up with competitors to share technology, finances, and human resources as well as to gain access to global markets.[17]

consortium
Group of companies working jointly to promote a common objective or engage in a project of benefit to all members

cooperatives
Associations of people or small companies with similar interests, formed to obtain greater bargaining power and other economies of scale

A **consortium** is similar to a joint venture, but it involves the combined efforts of several companies. For instance, the David Sarnoff Research Center, General Electric's NBC, France's Thomson S. A., and the Netherlands' Philips Electronics formed an international consortium to design a system for high-definition television (HDTV). Their aim was to offer consumers razor-sharp television pictures.[18]

Cooperatives also serve as a vehicle for joint activities. In a cooperative, a group of people or small companies with common goals work collectively to obtain greater bargaining power and to benefit from economies of scale. Like large companies, these co-ops can buy and sell things in quantity. But instead of distributing a share of the profits to

Understanding Internet Business

BEST OF THE WEB

Do you have an idea for an Internet-based business? How do you know whether your idea will take off? As with any business venture, thoroughly researching your market will improve your chances of success. Many questions need to be asked: How large is the base of potential customers? What types of goods and services are Internet shoppers buying, and which ones are they expected to buy more of in the future? How many competitors are in the market? What percentage of Internet businesses fail? Answers to these and many other questions can be found at *Computerworld's* "emmerce" page—a clearinghouse for current Internet statistics. By analyzing the information on this page, you can get a better feel for the opportunities and obstacles facing Internet-based businesses. It's a great place to start when you're thinking of setting up shop on the Net.
http://'www.computerworld.com/emmerce

stockholders, co-ops divide profits among their members. This type of partnership is common in the agriculture sector. For example, Sunkist Growers and Blue Diamond Growers are cooperatives of smaller growers that have joined forces to become strong competitors and well-known brand names in the citrus and almond industries.[19]

Corporations

A **corporation** is a legal entity with the power to own property and conduct business. Unlike sole proprietorships and partnerships, a corporation's legal status and obligations exist independently of its owners. The modern corporation evolved in the nineteenth century when large sums of capital were needed to build railroads, coal mines, and steel mills. Such endeavors required so much money that no single individual or group of partners could hope to raise it all. The solution was to sell shares in the business to numerous investors, who would get a cut of the profits in exchange for their money. These investors got a chance to vote on certain issues that might affect the value of their investment, but they were not involved in managing day-to-day operations. To protect the investors from the risks associated with such large undertakings, their liability was limited to the amount of their investment.

corporation
Legally chartered enterprise having most of the legal rights of a person, including the right to conduct business, to own and sell property, to borrow money, and to sue or be sued; owners of the corporation enjoy limited liability

It was a good solution, and the corporation quickly became a vital force in the nation's economy. As rules and regulations developed to define what corporations could and could not do, corporations acquired the legal attributes of people. Like you, a corporation can receive, own, and transfer property; make contracts; sue and be sued.

The relationship between a corporation and its **shareholders,** or owners, is a source of enormous strength. Because ownership and management are separate, the owners may get rid of the managers (in theory, at least), if the owners vote to do so. Conversely, because shares of the company, known as **stock,** may be bequeathed or sold to someone else, the company's ownership may change drastically over time while the company and its management remain intact (as long as the company is economically sound). The corporation's unlimited life span, combined with its ability to raise capital, gives it the potential for significant growth, which is often instrumental in achieving economies of scale.

shareholders
Owners of a corporation

stock
Shares of ownership in a corporation

A company need not be large to incorporate. Most corporations, like most businesses, are relatively small, and most small corporations are privately held, which means that the company's stock is not traded publicly. The big ones, however, are *really* big. The 500 largest corporations in the United States, as listed by *Fortune* magazine, have combined sales of over $5 trillion and employ well over 10 million people. Wal-Mart stores alone employ 675,000 people, which is roughly equivalent to the population of Jacksonville, Florida.[20]

Advantages of Corporations No other form of business ownership can match the success of the corporation in bringing together money, resources, and talent; in accumulating assets; and in creating wealth. As it grows, a corporation gains from a diverse labor pool, greater financing options, expanded research-and-development capabilities, and economies of scale. The corporation has certain inherent qualities that make it the best vehicle for reaching these objectives. One of these qualities is limited liability. Although a corporate entity can assume tremendous liabilities, it is the corporation that is liable and not the private shareholders. Take Johannes Schwartlander, who ran his San Fransisco marble and granite business as a sole proprietorship for seven years. When the company began to grow, Mr. Schwartlander decided to incorporate to protect himself. "When we had so many employees and started installing marble panels ten stories up, I realized that if five years later something fell down, I would be responsible," he says. Mr. Schwartlander chose to form an S corporation, primarily for the tax advantages.[21] Incorporation also protects him from personal liability should his business go bankrupt.

liquidity
The level of ease with which an asset can be converted to cash

In addition to limited liability, private corporations have the advantage of **liquidity,** which means that investors can easily convert their stock into cash by selling it on the open market. This option makes buying stock in a private corporation attractive to many investors. In contrast, liquidating the assets of a sole proprietorship or a partnership can be difficult.

Corporations are also often in a better position to make long-term plans as a result of their unlimited life span and the funding available through the sale of stock. As they grow, corporations can benefit from the diverse talents and experience of a large pool of employees and managers. Moreover, large corporations are often able to produce goods more efficiently, reach more customers, and finance projects internally.

Disadvantages of Corporations Corporations are not without some disadvantages. For one thing, publicly owned companies are required by the government to follow certain rules and to publish information about their finances and operations. These reporting requirements increase the pressure on corporate managers to achieve short-term growth and earnings targets in order to satisfy shareholders and attract potential investors. In addition, having to disclose financial information increases the company's vulnerability to competitors and to those who might want to take over the company. The paperwork and costs associated with incorporation can also be burdensome, particularly if you plan to sell stock. The complexity varies from state to state, but regardless of where you live, it is wise to consult an attorney and an accountant before incorporating. In addition, individual shareholders must pay income taxes on their share of the company's profits received as *dividends* (payments to shareholders from the company's profits). Thus corporate profits are taxed twice, whereas the profits in a sole proprietorship or partnership are taxed only once.

government-owned corporations
Corporations formed and owned by a government body for a specific public purpose

Types of Public Corporations Corporations have evolved into various types. The first distinction is whether a company is public or private. Public companies are of two types: government-owned and quasi-government corporations. **Government-owned corporations** (also called *public-owned*) are formed by federal or state governments for a specific public purpose, such as running local school districts, making student loans, or developing major land areas—like the Tennessee Valley Authority's building an extensive dam system in the Tennessee River Valley.

Government-owned companies are more common in many foreign countries, especially those that have or have had communist or socialist governments. For example, even though Russia, a formerly communist state, is converting to a free-market economy and a democratic political system, 40 percent of Russian companies are still owned by the government. The figure is similar in China, which still has a communist government. Even in democratic Europe, governments have only recently begun to privatize ownership of industries such as telecommunications and airlines. In the United States, many state governments are now beginning to turn services such as prisons, motor vehicle registration, and delinquent tax collection over to private companies. This trend toward privatization is based on the belief that free markets lead to more competitive industries and more efficient distribution of services.[22]

Electricity is a product offered in some parts of the country by quasi-government corporations and in other parts by private companies, such as Pacific Gas & Electric in California.

Quasi-government corporations are public utilities having a government-granted monopoly to provide electricity, local phone service, water, and natural gas. However, many of these types of corporations are also beginning to experience competition in the United States as federal and state governments move to deregulate them. In California, for example, the market has been opened for competitive pricing of electricity. This means that a city like Palm Springs can shop among electricity suppliers to find the best overall price for its residents.[23]

Types of Private Corporations The companies on the Fortune 500 list are almost all **private corporations**—companies owned by private individuals or companies. These investors buy stock on the open market, which gives private corporations access to large amounts of capital. In return, the shareholders receive the chance to share in the profits if the corporation succeeds. Not-for-profit organizations can also be private corporations. However, instead of earning money for shareholders, not-for-profit corporations pursue noneconomic goals, such as those targeted by charitable, educational, and fraternal organizations like the Corporation for Public Broadcasting, the American Heart Association, and Harvard University. Although they don't sell stock, not-for-profit corporations may buy stock in for-profit corporations.

quasi-government corporations
Public utilities having a monopoly to provide basic services

private corporations
Companies owned by private individuals or companies

Corporations that are **publicly traded** are called *open corporations* because they actively sell stock on the open market. Both private and quasi-government corporations may be publicly traded, such as Ford and Commonwealth Edison, which supplies power to the Chicago area. Corporations that are **not publicly traded** are called *closed corporations* because they withhold their stock from public sale, preferring to finance any expansion out of their own earnings or to borrow from other sources. By withholding their stock from public sale, the owners retain complete control over their operations and protect their businesses from unwelcome takeover attempts. Such famous companies as Hallmark, United Parcel Service, and Hyatt Hotels have opted to remain closed corporations. Sometimes a group of investors is able to take a publicly traded company off the open market by purchasing all of the company's stock. For example, descendants of Levi Strauss borrowed $3 billion to buy back all the shares of Levi's stock so that the family could maintain control of the company.[24] This is also known as "taking the company private."

publicly traded corporations
Corporations that actively sell stock on the open market; also called open corporations

not publicly traded corporations
Corporations that withhold their stock from public sale; also called closed corporations

Another type of corporation, known as the **S corporation** (or subchapter S corporation), is a cross between a partnership and a corporation. S corporations can be attractive to business owners who plan to sell stock to a limited number of investors; the owners receive the tax advantages of a partnership while they raise money through the sale of stock. In addition, income and tax deductions from the business flow directly to the owners, who are taxed at personal income-tax rates, just as they are in a partnership. More-

S corporation
Corporations with no more than 75 shareholders that may be taxed as a partnership; also known as a subchapter S corporation

over, the shareholders in an S corporation, like the shareholders in a regular corporation, have limited liability. Under the Small Business Job Protection Act of 1996 the maximum number of shareholders allowed in an S corporation increased from 35 to 75; the maximum percentage of stock that an S corporation can own in another corporation increased from 80 percent to 100 percent (provided the other corporation is not an S corporation); and S corporations can now have wholly owned subsidiaries, whereas before they could not. These changes give S corporations more flexibility when seeking additional capital and when investing in other business.[25]

limited liability companies (LLCs)
Organizations that combine the benefits of S corporations and limited partnerships without the drawbacks of either

Companies can also combine the advantages of S corporations and limited partnerships without having to abide by the restrictions of either. **Limited liability companies (LLCs)** allow firms to pay taxes like partnerships while protecting shareholders from personal liability beyond their investments. In addition, LLCs are not restricted in the number of shareholders they can have. Furthermore, members' participation in management is not restricted as it is in limited partnerships. However, unlike a corporation, an LLC's existence is restricted to 30 years.[26]

subsidiary corporations
Corporations whose stock is owned entirely or almost entirely by another corporation

parent company
Company that owns most, if not all, of another company's stock and that takes an active part in managing that other company

holding company
Company that owns most, if not all, of another company's stock but that does not actively participate in the management of that other company

So far this discussion has covered various types of independent corporations. However, not all corporations are independent entities. **Subsidiary corporations** are partially or wholly owned by another corporation known as a **parent company,** which supervises the operations of the subsidiary. A **holding company** is a special type of parent company that owns other companies for investment reasons and usually exercises little operating control over these subsidiaries. Exhibit 4.5 summarizes some of these distinctions.

Corporations can also be classified according to where they do business. An *alien corporation* operates in the United States but is incorporated in another country. A *foreign corporation,* sometimes called an *out-of-state corporation,* is incorporated in one state (frequently the state of Delaware, where incorporation laws are lenient) but does business in several other states where it is registered. And a *domestic corporation* does business only in the state where it is chartered (incorporated).

Corporate Structure and Governance Although a corporation's shareholders own the business, they are rarely involved in managing it, particularly if the corporation is publicly traded. Instead, they elect a board of directors to represent them. The directors, in turn, select and monitor the top officers, who actually run the company (see Exhibit 4.6).

SHAREHOLDERS Theoretically, the shareholders—who can be individuals, other companies, not-for-profit organizations, pension funds, and mutual funds—are the ultimate governing body of the corporation. In practice, most individual shareholders in large corporations—where the shareholders may number in the millions—accept the recommendations of management. However, sometimes the employees of the corporation are major shareholders, as with Avis and United Airlines. Employee stock ownership is one way the shareholders are able to have a more direct influence on the value of their investment.

Typically, the more shareholders a company has, the less tangible the influence each shareholder has on the corporation. However, some shareholders have more influence than others, because different types of stock carry different privileges. *Preferred stock* does not usually carry voting rights; however, it gives stockholders the right of first claim on the corporation's assets (in the form of dividends) after its debts have been paid. *Common stock* carries voting rights, but it gives the stockholder the right of claim on the corporation's assets only after all preferred stockholders have been paid. In other words, preferred stock pays more dependable dividends than common stock, but common stock typically gives the shareholder a greater say in how the company is run. In neither case are dividend payments guaranteed. Chapter 19 covers the types of stock in greater detail.

Some people (or organizations) own more shares with voting rights than others do; a person with 1,000 voting shares, for example, has 1,000 votes and 10 times the impact

TYPE	DEFINITION	EXAMPLE
Government-owned corporation	Business formed by federal or state government for a specific purpose	TVA
Quasi-government corporation	Public utility with a monopoly on providing basic public services	Commonwealth Edison
Private corporation	Business owned by private individuals or companies	General Motors
Not-for-profit corporation	Service or arts institution in which no stockholder or trustee shares in the profits or losses and which is exempt from corporate income taxes	Harvard University
For-profit corporation	Company in business to make a profit	IBM
S corporation	Corporation with no more than 75 owners, whose profits are taxed at personal income-tax rates rather than at corporate income-tax rates	Inland Asphalt
Limited liability company	Business that reaps the benefits of S corporations and limited partnerships without the drawbacks	Realatech
Parent company	Operating company that owns or controls subsidiaries through the ownership of voting stock	General Electric; 27 subsidiaries include NBC, GE Spacenet, and GE Capital Services
Holding company	Corporation organized for the purpose of owning stock in and managing one or more corporations; differs from a parent company in that it generally does not conduct operations of its own	Intermark
Subsidiary corporation	Corporation that is entirely, or almost entirely, owned by another corporation, known as a parent company or holding company	Taco Bell, a subsidiary of PepsiCo

EXHIBIT 4.5

Major Types of Corporations

The most visible corporations are the large, private ones, such as General Motors, IBM, and Coca-Cola, but other types are also common.

of a person with only 100 voting shares. However, some corporations allow cumulative voting to give small shareholders more power. For example, if there are 4 positions open on the board of directors, a shareholder with 100 shares may cast 400 votes (100 x 4) for one candidate rather than 100 votes for each of the 4 open positions. Thus, the smaller shareholders as a group can have more influence on the election of directors.[27]

At least once a year, all the owners of voting shares are invited to a meeting to choose directors, select an independent accountant to audit the company's financial statements, and attend to other business. However, some states limit the types of issues on which shareholders may vote, thereby preventing the shareholders from having much of a voice in management. Shareholders who cannot attend the annual meeting in person vote by **proxy,** signing and returning a slip of paper that authorizes management to vote on their behalf.

In recent years, *institutional investors,* such as pension funds, insurance companies, mutual funds, and college endowment funds, have accumulated an increasing share of stock in U.S. corporations. Forty years ago, institutional investors owned less than 10 percent of U.S. corporate stock; today they own over 50 percent. Moreover, the assets of institutional investors have increased from $672 billion to over $8 trillion in the past two decades alone. These large institutional investors are playing a more powerful role in governing the corporations in which they own shares, especially with regard to boards of directors.[28]

proxy
Document authorizing another person to vote on behalf of a shareholder in a corporation

BOARD OF DIRECTORS Supposedly representing the shareholders, the **board of directors** is responsible for guiding corporate affairs and selecting corporate officers. The board has the power to vote on major management decisions, such as building a new factory, hiring a new president, or buying a new subsidiary. Depending on the size of the com-

board of directors
Group of people, elected by the shareholders, who have the ultimate authority in guiding the affairs of a corporation

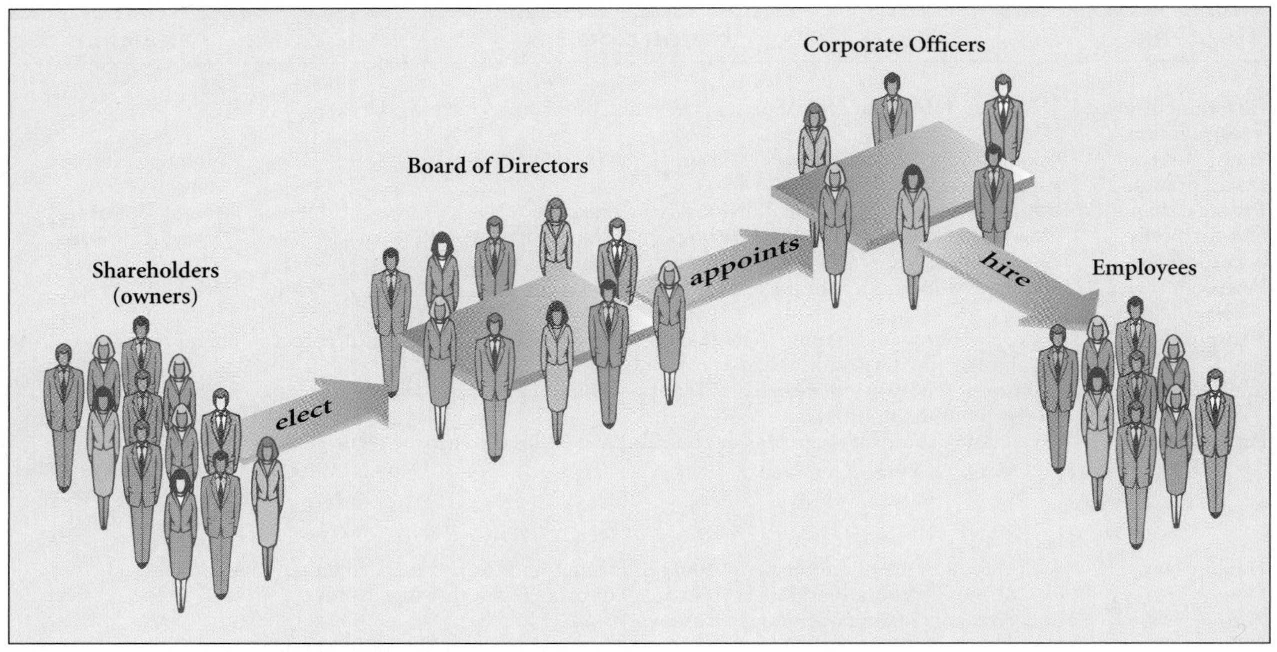

EXHIBIT 4.6

The Corporate Framework

Theoretically, the corporate framework resembles a democracy in which shareholders vote to elect representatives (members of the board of directors) who will establish corporate policy and select competent managers to direct the employees. Actually, the real power in a corporation often lies with the top executives, who suggest a roster of board members for shareholder approval.

pany, the board might have anywhere from 3 to 35 directors, although 15 to 25 is the typical range. In some corporations, several of the directors may be inside directors, people who are also employees of the company. Outside directors are often large shareholders, and many are on the boards of several companies.

The board's actual involvement in running a corporation varies from one company to another. Some boards are strong and independent and serve as a check on the company's management. Others act as a "rubber stamp," simply approving management's recommendations. Assertive boards are becoming far more common these days, mainly because of pressure from institutional investors who want the value of their stock to increase. Today's directors are expected to be involved in corporate strategy, management succession, evaluation of executive performance, and other issues that are crucial to the company's success. To accomplish such involvement, many companies are seeking more outside directors who own large shares in the company. In addition, more companies are compensating directors with company stock instead of salaries and pension plans. In this way, the directors' interests are aligned with the interests of other shareholders. Companies today are also seeking directors who are experienced in corporate management, such as chief executives of other firms. Evidence shows that companies in which directors own large amounts of stock and take an active role in guiding the company usually outperform those with more passive boards consisting of company insiders. The value of Time Warner's stock immediately increased when it announced that its two new board nominees were the chief executives of Hilton Hotels and UAL.[29]

Companies around the world are also looking for foreign directors to bring international perspectives into the board room. One example is former Chrysler president Robert Lutz, who is a director at Ascom, a Swiss telecommunications equipment firm. A

FOCUSING ON CULTURAL DIVERSITY

Can Universal Appeal Overcome Cultural Differences?

As one of the most culturally diverse—and culturally tolerant—nations on earth, the United States is a good training ground for managers who need to lead a multicultural work force. However, even this wonderful learning opportunity doesn't always prepare managers for international assignments. So the question arises: Who should lead a U.S. company's business units in other countries? It actually breaks down to two questions for most U.S. multinationals: Who should be in charge in each country, and who should be in charge of multiple-country regions, such as Europe or Southeast Asia?

Most U.S. companies no longer routinely move U.S. executives to overseas posts; most now send executives overseas only when their specific technical skills can't be found in the country in question. In fact, U.S. citizens now account for less than 2 percent of the people employed outside of the United States by U.S. companies. Most companies prefer to hire locally so that they can benefit from people who are more in tune with local markets, closer to customers, and more readily accepted by the local business community. Another factor that companies have to consider is the expense of temporarily moving U.S. managers to overseas posts. For instance, it costs four times as much to move a U.S. manager to Egypt than to hire an Egyptian locally.

Another key question raises some sticky issues: Who should be put in charge of multiple-country regions? Although we might tend to view Europeans as fairly similar from a cultural standpoint, the reality is often far different. French businesspeople tend to have little patience for the Swedish style of consensus management (in which everybody gets to have a say and must agree on a plan before the company moves forward). Likewise, British employees aren't wild about working for a German boss. So who should be in charge of a region that covers these four countries, and possibly many others? One solution is to pick a manager from Holland or Switzerland, who might be viewed as more neutral, or to pick somebody from the United States.

By the way, are you looking for a career in international management? Many multinational companies are hiring graduates from specialized business schools such as the American Graduate School of International Management in Arizona, the University of South Carolina's International Business Program, and France's INSEAD. If you possess a skill that U.S. companies need overseas (particularly marketing and production), if you speak a foreign language, and if you have an internationally oriented education, you stand a much better chance of getting that dream job.

QUESTIONS FOR CRITICAL THINKING

1. What issues should a company consider when evaluating whether to hire a local manager for its foreign operations or whether to move a U.S. manager to the overseas post?
2. To what degree should a corporation attempt to transplant its corporate culture into a newly acquired foreign subsidiary?

recent study found that about 20 percent of U.S. firms now have at least one non-U.S. citizen on their board.[30]

OFFICERS The center of power in a corporation often lies with the **chief executive officer, or CEO.** Together with the chief financial officer (CFO) and the chief operating officer (COO), the CEO is responsible for establishing company policies, managing corporate direction, and making the big decisions that will affect the company's growth and competitive position. The chief executive officer may also be the chairman of the board, the president of the corporation, or both. As mentioned previously, the CEO may also serve on the board of other corporations. For instance, Gillette CEO Alfred M. Zeien is a director at seven other companies, including Bank of Boston and Polaroid. However, some companies are limiting the number of boards their CEOs can serve on because of the time commitment involved. For example, General Electric chairman Jack Welch insists that all of G.E.'s senior executives refuse all invitations to serve on other company boards.[31]

chief executive officer (CEO) Person appointed by a corporation's board of directors to carry out the board's policies and supervise the activities of the corporation

Mergers and Acquisitions

Regardless of what form a business takes—sole proprietorship, partnership, or corporation—the chances are reasonably good that its form will evolve over time. This evolution may involve acquiring new businesses, selling off old ones, or merging with existing businesses to form new companies. Almost 40 percent of the corporations listed at the start of the 1980s merged with or were acquired by other firms. In that decade, "corporate raiders" realized large short-term gains by buying undervalued companies and selling them off in pieces. Today, many mergers and acquisitions are designed more with long-term financial performance in mind.

merger
Combination of two or more companies in which the old companies cease to exist and a new enterprise is created

acquisition
Combination of two companies in which one company purchases the other and assumes control of its property and liabilities

divestiture
Sale of part of a company

Types of Mergers

The difference between a merger and an acquisition is fairly technical, having to do with how the financial transaction is structured. Basically, in a **merger,** two or more companies combine to create a new company by pooling their interests. In an **acquisition,** one company buys another company, or parts of another company, and emerges as the controlling corporation. The acquiring company also assumes all the debts and contractual obligations of the company it acquires. The flip side of an acquisition is a **divestiture,** in which one company sells a portion of its business to another company.

THINKING ABOUT ETHICS

Do Mergers Threaten Management's Responsibility to Shareholders?

For over a century, mergers and acquisitions have continually changed the face of business in the United States. Today a wave of strategic mergers is changing it all over again as corporations merge to create more competitive organizations that will increase shareholder value. But do shareholders really benefit from mergers? Strong evidence suggests that they often do not.

Steven N. Kaplan, professor of finance at the University of Chicago, says that 49 percent of acquisitions made between 1971 and 1982 were divested, often because the companies had difficulty working together. A more recent study tracked merger performance for up to 3 years after the deals were complete and found that out of 150 mergers and acquisitions valued at $500 million or more in the 1990s, half resulted in decreased returns to shareholders—30 percent resulted in substantial decreases.

Why do such a high percentage of mergers and acquisitions fail? No one answer applies to every situation. However, some common mistakes are made:

- Companies often rush into deals in search of synergies that don't really exist or that quickly change. For example, three major pharmaceutical companies each recently acquired separate distributors with the hope of pushing their medicines to health-care providers while excluding competitors. But the Federal Trade Commission, concerned about anticompetitive practices, ruled that the distributors had to carry all competitors' drugs and that they could not share data about competitors' prices and marketing strategies with their parent companies. As a result, the drug manufacturers are realizing little or no gain from their acquisitions.
- Companies pay excessively high premiums for the companies they acquire. Professor Mark Sirower of New York University's Stern School of Business says that any time an acquiring company pays a premium of 25 percent or more over the trading price of the acquired company's stock, the acquiring company is exposing itself and its shareholders to substantial risk. Paying such high prices means either that acquisitions have to perform extremely well in

Companies have been combining in various configurations since the early days of business in the United States. Mergers tend to happen in waves, in response to changes in the economy. One of the biggest waves of merger activity occurred between 1881 and 1911, when capitalists created giant monopolistic **trusts,** buying enough stock of competing companies in basic industries like oil and steel to control the market. These trusts were **horizontal mergers,** or combinations of competing companies performing the same function. The purpose of a horizontal merger is to achieve the benefits of economies of scale and to fend off competition. The rise of a government antitrust movement and the dissolution of Standard Oil in 1911 marked the end of this wave.

A second great wave occurred in the boom decade of the 1920s. This era was marked by the emergence of **vertical mergers,** in which a company involved in one phase of an industry absorbs or joins a company involved in another phase of the same industry. The aim of a vertical merger is often to guarantee access to supplies or to markets. For example, until fairly recently, both Ford and General Motors owned the companies that supplied most of the parts for their cars.

A third wave of mergers occurred in the late 1960s and early 1970s, when corporations acquired strings of unrelated businesses, often in an attempt to moderate the risks of a volatile economy. These **conglomerate mergers** were designed to augment a company's growth and diversify its risks. Theoretically, when one business was down, another would be up, thus creating a balanced performance picture for the company as a whole.

trusts
Monopolistic arrangements established when one company buys a controlling share of the stock of competing companies in the same industry

horizontal mergers
Combinations of companies that are direct competitors in the same industry

vertical mergers
Combinations of companies that participate in different phases of the same industry (i.e., materials, production, distribution)

conglomerate mergers
Combinations of companies that are in unrelated businesses, designed to augment a company's growth and diversify risk

the short term or that investors must be willing to wait a long time before they receive any benefit.

- Companies are unable to reconcile differences in corporate cultures. When Homedco Group and Abbey Healthcare merged in 1995, executives of both companies thought that the size and geographic reach of their new company, Apria Healthcare, would make them unstoppable. However, Apria's stock price has fallen almost 50 percent, and revenues are much lower than the two companies enjoyed before they merged. Part of the reason is that Homedco was "by-the-book" and hierarchical, whereas Abbey was entrepreneurial and gave greater autonomy to its lower-level employees. The mix was confusing to employees and customers alike. In addition, Homedco executives treated many of Abbey's top people poorly, so they left to work for competitors.

Without question, some mergers and acquisitions are beneficial to companies and shareholders in both the short term and the long term. Synergies can be realized, as was the case when Chemical Bank merged with Manufacturer's Hannover. However, managers need to approach mergers and acquisitions with caution. Will the regulatory environment change? How will competitors respond? Do the expected gains justify the up-front costs? Will the cultures of the two companies blend well? Without carefully seeking honest answers to such questions, management may find it difficult to fulfill its obligation to the company's shareholders.

Questions for Critical Thinking

1. If you were on the board of directors at a company and the CEO announced plans to merge with a competitor, what types of questions would you want answered before you gave your approval?
2. If a CEO has the opportunity to merge with or acquire another company and is reasonably certain that the transaction will benefit shareholders, is the CEO obligated to pursue the deal? Why or why not?

Some of these conglomerates had hundreds of companies at their peaks. Since the late 1960s, many of the superconglomerates have been dismantled or slimmed down to streamline operations, to build up capital for other endeavors, or to get rid of unprofitable subsidiaries. Consider ITT Corporation, which began its life as International Telephone and Telegraph in 1920. Not long ago the company owned businesses as diverse as antilock brake manufacturing, casinos, insurance, and the New York Knicks basketball team. However, the huge size of ITT proved to be a disadvantage, and the company divided into several companies in the mid-1990s; each could now focus more on its core business.[32]

In the 1980s, many companies were actually worth more than the combined value of all their stock, making them attractive takeover targets. During this decade over $3.7 trillion was spent on mergers and acquisitions. Many of these were *leveraged buyouts (LBOs),* in which one or more individuals purchased the company or a division of the company, using borrowed funds guaranteed by the assets of the company they were buying. Although many of these deals were made to improve the operations of the companies involved, the chance to make a quick profit was the motive in some cases.[33] Leveraged buyouts will be discussed in detail in Chapter 18.

In 1996 the value of U.S. mergers grew to almost twice the value of those in 1988 (see Exhibit 4.7). However, unlike the LBOs of the 1980s, today more companies are paying for their acquisitions with stock. Stockholders in the acquired company are given shares in the acquiring company or in the new company formed by the merger. This may dilute the overall value of the company's stock in the short run, but it is less risky than an LBO in the long run because it does not expose the company to huge debt payments.[34]

How Mergers Occur

About 95 percent of all mergers and acquisitions are friendly deals.[35] However, the ones that make the headlines are usually the **hostile takeovers,** where one party fights to gain control of a company against the wishes of the existing management. If the "raider" succeeds in taking over the target company, the existing managers are generally dismissed. Needless to say, they fight tooth and nail to stave off their attacker. However, the companies making the takeover bids often make such attractive offers that it is difficult for managers to justify resistance. For example, American Home Products, the maker

hostile takeovers
Situations in which an outside party buys enough stock in a corporation to take control against the wishes of the board of directors and corporate officers

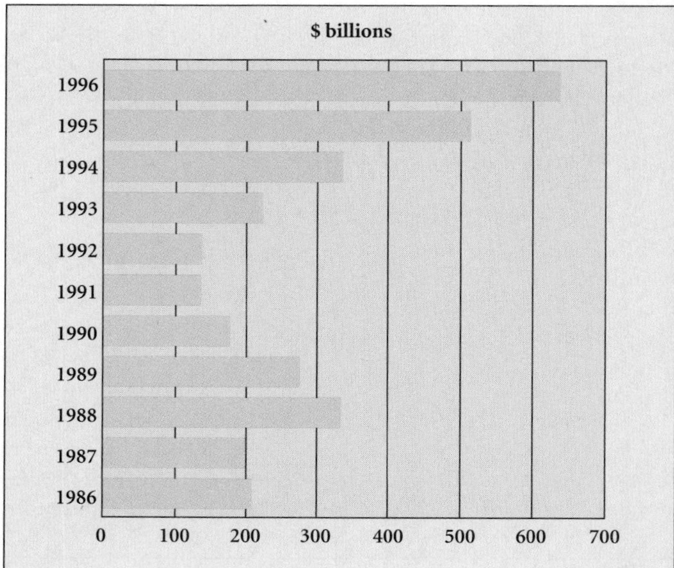

EXHIBIT 4.7

Merger and Acquisition Activity in Recent Years

The volume of merger activity in 1996 almost doubled 1988's peak volume.

of such brand-name products as Anacin and Chef Boyardee, offered $95 a share to acquire pharmaceutical maker American Cyanamid. That price was $32 a share more than Cyanamid's trading price. Clearly, shareholders were pleased with the deal, even if management wasn't.[36]

A hostile takeover can be launched in two ways: by tender offer and by proxy fight. In a **tender offer,** the raider offers to buy a certain number of shares of stock in the corporation at a specific price. The price offered is generally more than the current stock price so that shareholders are motivated to sell. The raider hopes to get enough shares to take control of the corporation and replace the existing board of directors and management. In a **proxy fight,** the raider launches a public relations battle for shareholder votes, hoping to enlist enough votes to oust the board and management. Proxy fights sound easy enough, but they are tough to win. The insiders have certain advantages: They can get in touch with shareholders and use money from the corporate treasury in their campaign.

tender offer
Invitation made directly to shareholders by an outside party who wishes to buy a company's stock at a price above the current market price

proxy fight
Attempt to gain control of a takeover target by urging shareholders to vote for directors favored by the acquiring party

Even friendly mergers and takeovers can be risky. Joining two companies is a complex process involving every aspect of both companies. Executives have to agree on how the merger will be financed and how power will be transferred and shared. Marketing departments often need to figure out how to blend advertising campaigns and sales forces. Mergers in particular often entail layoffs, transfers, and changes in job titles and work assignments. In addition, it is sometimes difficult to blend different corporate cultures. And even the egos of the CEOs who engineer the merger can influence the success of the deal. Recently, an ambitious merger between conservative Bell Atlantic and the entrepreneurial cable giant Tele-Communications Inc. (TCI) fell through, largely because the CEOs of the two companies were accustomed to different ways of conducting their businesses and neither was willing to budge in negotiations.[37]

Find the Right Path

BEST OF THE WEB

What are the top ten companies on the Fortune 500? Who's the latest big name in Hollywood? Did your favorite team win the game last night? It used to be that you had to pick up a newspaper or magazine, watch television, or listen to the radio to get this kind of information. But now all of this and more is available on the Internet, and Time Warner's <Pathfinder.com> is one of the best places to find it. By combining news and features from CNN, *Time, Fortune, People, Entertainment Weekly,* and other Time Warner publications and services, <Pathfinder.com> keeps you current on news in almost every category. You can even discuss current topics with other readers in online chat forums and bulletin boards. With the Internet, staying on top of the news just keeps getting easier and easier.
http://www.pathfinder.com

Current Trends in Mergers and Acquisitions

A new wave of mergers and acquisitions began in the 1990s, often motivated by long-term strategy. Today instead of using debt to take over and dismantle a company for a quick profit, corporate buyers are using cash and stock to selectively acquire businesses that will enhance their position in the marketplace. For example, WorldCom, a global telecommunications company, recently merged with MCI, a pioneer in bringing competition to long-distance telephone communications. MCI shareholders received $51 of WorldCom common stock for each MCI share they owned. The resulting company, MCI WorldCom, is one of the largest providers of Internet services in the world, and the second largest long-distance telephone company in the United States. The new company expects to save billions in operating expenses by combining activities and to increase profits by expanding its access to worldwide markets.[38]

Companies like WorldCom and MCI seek *synergies* in their mergers and acquisitions—that is, they expect the benefits of working together to be greater than if each company acted independently. For instance, MCI WorldCom expects to gain competitive advantages that were not available to either of the individual companies before the merger. Disney also looked for such synergies when it took over ABC television. Disney envisioned using ABC to promote Disney's entertainment businesses, while at the same time enhancing the programming ABC viewers received by broadcasting Disney productions. However, Disney is still struggling to find the right balance of joint activity between the two companies.[39] Disney's purchase of ABC is in many ways a vertical merger because Disney is able to use ABC as a medium to distribute its movies and television programs as well as to advertise its theme parks, stores, movies, and other products. This kind of control over distribution channels is a common motivation for vertical mergers in the 1990s.[40]

Also common today is a return to horizontal mergers. Consolidation is occurring in many industries and among both large and small companies. Fierce global competition has created an environment in which companies must grow significantly in order to be successful. Unlike the environment in the early part of this century, large domestic companies must now vie with foreign competitors even in their home markets. These conditions have led the U.S. government to be more lenient about regulating the growth of companies. Rather than opposing any merger that might allow a company to develop a dominant position in the market, the Federal Trade Commission and the Anti-Trust Division of the Justice Department are seeking new ways to ensure that industries remain open to new competitors.

For instance, by sweeping away decades of regulations, the government hoped to unleash the benefits of telecommunications competition—more choice for phone service and lower rates. Instead, the move fueled a new wave of acquisitions.

That's why when SBC Company (which encompasses the old Southwestern Bell) announced its $56 billion bid to buy Ameritech, many frustrated lawmakers and regulators reignited the debate over where to draw the line with big mergers. Many saw the proposed consolidation as nothing more than a reassembly of the Ma Bell monopoly splintered by the Justice Department in 1984. As one naysayer put it: "First there were seven Baby Bells, then six, then five, and now four. Soon there may be just one, and it won't be a baby."[41] Many expect this mega-merger trend to continue. In fact, mergers that looked like earthquakes in the past, may only look like tremors years from now.[42]

Consider Daimler-Benz and Chrysler. Not only is this $36 billion combination the largest merger in automotive history, but it is also the biggest acquisition of any U.S. company by a foreign buyer—one that will transform the way the auto industry operates worldwide. What's the attraction between two companies whose products and culture are so fundamentally different? Globalization. There is no overlap in products, both are the world's richest automakers, and each company is strong in markets where the other is weak. By combining their product and sales networks, DaimlerChrysler has set the pace for the global car wars to come. As one economist put it, "If you don't play the game as a global company, you're going to wind up a niche player."[43]

The Debate over Mergers and Acquisitions

The rash of mergers and acquisitions that occurred in the 1980s kindled a heated debate that continues even with the new style of deals in the 1990s. Opponents argue that mergers create an immense burden of high-risk corporate debt and divert investment from productive assets. Instead of building new plants or developing new products, say critics, companies borrow huge sums to finance an endless game of "musical ownership."

In many cases, the critics' warnings have proven to be well-founded. A number of companies that took on heavy loads of debt to finance acquisitions in the 1980s subsequently went under or faced severe financial hardships. Some of the prominent companies in this group include the Campeau retailing empire (Allied Stores and Federated Department Stores, which included Bloomingdale's, Stern's, and Jordan Marsh), Borden, Burlington Industries, Goodyear, and Marriott. In fact, at one point in the early 1990s, Goodyear was paying over $1 million *per day* in interest. Fortunately, the company has since rebounded.[44]

Critics also point out that mergers and acquisitions entail high costs for individuals and communities. Even in friendly deals, there are bound to be losers: executives whose careers come to a crashing halt, workers who are laid off through no fault of their own, communities that suddenly find themselves with empty factories because operations are consolidated elsewhere, and consumers who face higher prices when competition diminishes. Another particularly bitter issue is the amount of money that raiders have made on deals that resulted in layoffs and other hardships for thousands of people.

Is It True?

About half of all senior managers either quit or are laid off within one year after their firm is acquired by another firm.

Apart from the deal makers, few people lamented the transition from the finance-driven deals of the 1980s to the strategy-driven deals of the 1990s. However, the mergers of the 1980s had their good points. Shareholders benefited from all the merger activity, which boosted stock prices and fueled big increases in the market value of takeover targets. In addition, the fear of becoming takeover targets forced many companies to become more efficient.

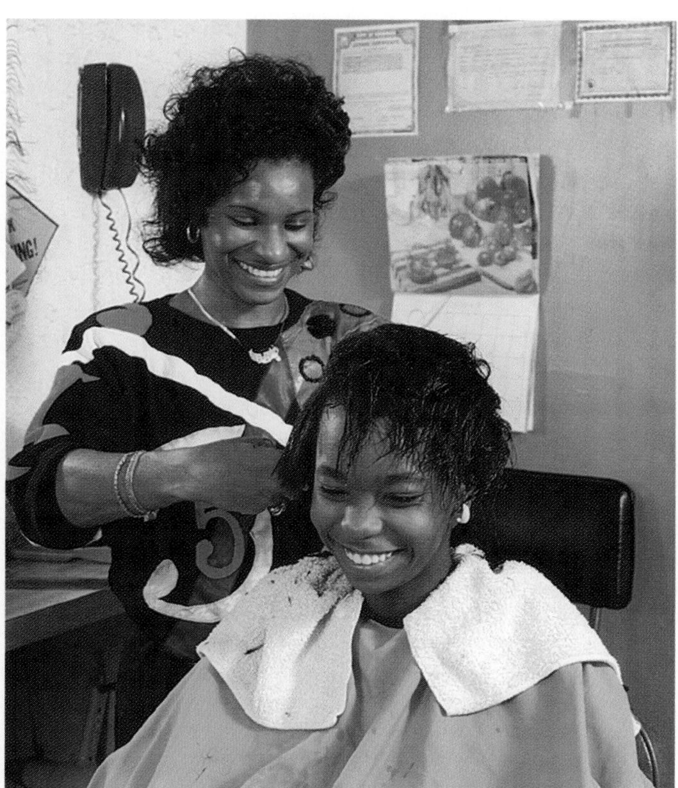

Some people who are displaced by corporate mergers and acquisitions see it as an opportunity to start their own small businesses.

Merger-and-Acquisition Defenses

During the 1980s wave of mergers, when many takeovers were uninvited and even openly hostile, corporate boards and executives devised a number of schemes to defend themselves against unwanted takeovers. Every corporation that sells stock to the general public is potentially vulnerable to takeover by any individual or company that buys enough shares to gain a controlling interest. The ultimate takeover defense is to take the company private. Of course, this radical action requires that holders of your stock are willing to sell and that you either have enough cash on hand to buy all the stock back or are willing to engage in a leveraged buyout. It also means that you've cut off the stock market as a future means of generating cash, so it's not a move that many corporations make.

poison pill
Defense against hostile takeovers that makes the company less attractive in some way to the potential raider

Companies that want or need to remain publicly traded can take several measures to discourage takeovers. Perhaps the most dramatic method is the **poison pill,** a plan to make the company less valuable in some way to the potential raider. Over 1,800 U.S. public corporations now use this defense strategy. Poison pills are set up to be triggered by a takeover attempt; the idea is to discourage the takeover from actually happening. A good example is a special sale of newly issued stock to current stockholders, only at prices below the stock's current market price. Such action increases the number of shares the raider has to buy, making the deal more expensive. Many shareholders believe that poison pills are bad for a company because they can entrench weak management and discourage takeover attempts that would improve company value.[45]

golden parachute
Generous compensation packages guaranteed to executives in the event that they lose their jobs after a takeover

The **golden parachute** method is designed to benefit a company's top executives by guaranteeing them generous compensation packages if they ever leave or are forced out after a takeover. These packages often total many millions of dollars per executive, and therefore make the takeover much more expensive for the acquiring company. In this way, a golden parachute has a similar effect as a poison pill.

shark repellent
Direct takeover defense in which the company's board requires a large majority of voting shares to approve any takeover attempt

The **shark repellent** tactic is more direct; it is simply a requirement that stockholders representing a large majority of shares must approve of any takeover attempt. Of course, such a plan is viable only if the management team has the support of the majority of shareholders.

white knight
Friendly buyer who agrees to take over a company to prevent a raider from taking it over

Finally, if a company feels it is unable to fight off a takeover on its own, it can try to convince a **white knight**—a friendly buyer—to take it over before a raider can. White knights usually agree to leave the current management team in place and to let the company continue to operate in an independent fashion. Starwood Lodging Trust, a large hotel investment firm, recently played the white knight to ITT by offering to purchase the company. The move thwarted a hostile takeover attempt of ITT by Hilton Hotels.[46]

Summary of Learning Objectives

1. **Identify the two broad sectors of the U.S. economy and the eight subsectors.**
The economy consists of (1) the service sector, which includes wholesale and retail trade, finance and insurance, transportation and utilities, and other services; and (2) the goods-producing sector, which includes manufacturing, construction, mining, and agriculture.
2. **Name five factors that have contributed to the growth of the service sector.**
In recent years, the service sector has expanded because economic prosperity has increased the demand for services, demographic patterns in the United States continue to change, the number and complexity of goods needing service are increasing, businesses find themselves needing more services to help them deal with a complex global economy, and technology keeps creating new service opportunities.
3. **Discuss the three basic forms of business ownership.**
A sole proprietorship is a business owned by a single person. A partnership is an association of two or more people who share in the ownership of an enterprise. The dominant form of business is the corporation, a legally

chartered entity having many of the same rights and duties as a person.

4. **List five advantages and four disadvantages of forming a sole proprietorship.**
Sole proprietorships have five advantages: (1) They are easy to establish, (2) they provide the owner with control and independence, (3) the owner reaps all the profits, (4) income is taxed at personal rates, and (5) the company's plans and financial performance remain private. The four main disadvantages of a sole proprietorship are (1) the company's financial resources are usually limited, (2) management talent may be thin, (3) the owner is liable for the debts and damages incurred by the business, and (4) the business may cease when the owner dies.

5. **Explain the difference between a general and a limited partnership.**
A general partnership is owned by general partners who are equally liable for the business's debts. A limited partnership is owned by at least one general partner who runs the business, and limited partners who are passive investors and generally liable for no more than the amount of their investment.

6. **Delineate the three groups that govern a corporation and describe the role of each.**
Shareholders are the basis of the corporate structure. They elect the board of directors, who in turn elect the officers of the corporation. The corporate officers carry out the policies and decisions of the board. In practice, the shareholders and board members have often followed the lead of the chief executive officer. However, board members are becoming increasingly active in corporate governance.

7. **Cite four advantages of corporations.**
Corporations have the power to raise large sums of capital, they offer the shareholders protection from liability, they provide liquidity for investors, and they have an unlimited life span.

8. **Describe the five waves of merger activity.**
The earliest mergers, occurring from 1881 to 1911, were horizontal mergers, combining two companies that compete in the same industry. A second wave of mergers occurred in the 1920s and were vertical mergers, combining two companies that participate in different phases of the same industry. The 1960s and 1970s introduced a third wave of mergers known as conglomerate mergers, combining unrelated companies. The mergers of the 1980s focused on the purchase of undervalued companies, which were then dismantled and sold off piece by piece. The most recent wave of mergers, occurring in the 1990s, can be described as strategic, with large corporations acquiring businesses that will enhance their market position.

On the Job: Meeting Business Challenges at AJ Wraps

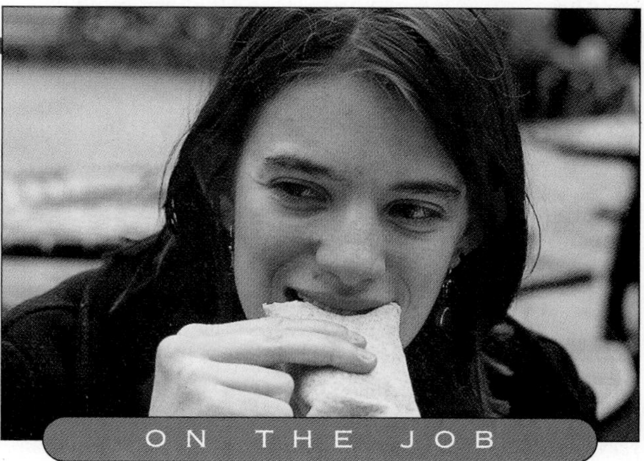

For a time, Alice Thomson and Judith Nantook thought their plans to open AJ Wraps were falling through. Judith's husband Jeff was offered a partnership in a large accounting firm—the catch was, he'd have to move to Los Angeles. However, with a little more research, the twins' enthusiasm was restored. They read about a company partly owned by actor Woody Harrelson: Yoganics, an organic food-delivery service, was apparently reaping tax benefits from a location in South-Central Los Angeles. A 1992 racial uprising left a scarred community that needed to rebuild itself, and the area was designated a "revitalization zone." State officials were offering tax incentives to spur businesses into the area. It was working beautifully, creating new jobs and a positive, thriving atmosphere.

Alice and Judith loved this idea. As financial adviser, Jeff thought the tax savings would help them get rolling, and an eager work force couldn't hurt. Reassured, the twins revised their plans. Their headquarters would be in South-Central Los Angeles, with the first two restaurants nearby. The third they'd open farther south, in bustling, middle-class Orange County. After three AJ Wraps were running successfully, Judith, Alice, and Jeff would sit down and prepare a plan for selling franchises. When it reached that stage, they'd probably want to incorporate, but in the meantime, the business would function as a partnership. Now they had to decide how to divide the responsibilities—and the compensation.

At first, they considered including Jeff as a third partner—after all, his input during the planning stages had been invaluable. But in private meetings Judith and Alice decided that giving Jeff equal management control could eventually interfere in the long-practiced, twin-bonded, team tactics that worked so well between the two of them. They were so attuned to each other's way of thinking and doing that they had always been able to make decisions in a snap.

For a while, they toyed with the idea of offering Jeff a limited partnership (eliminating his management responsibilities and limiting his liability) but realized they frequently needed his advice to make management decisions. As a limited partner, he wouldn't be compensated for that weekly time investment. They also considered writing a general partnership agreement that limited Jeff's management participation, but that approach could lead to some uncomfortable situations (such as having to tell him when to back off and when he was needed). Finally, the twins decided the best option was the simplest one: Alice and Judith would share the business as general partners, hiring Jeff as a consultant and paying him hourly for his expertise. Besides, as Judith pointed out, he'd be sharing in the restaurants' profits anyway as her husband. (At first Jeff's feelings were a little hurt when they told him he wouldn't be a partner. But then he saw the wisdom of it—not to mention the lack of pressure and the easy income. He agreed wholeheartedly.)

Next, Alice and Judith decided that their financial backers (their aunt and uncle, at this stage) would be offered a limited partnership. When and if AJ Wraps incorporated, their backers would be given the option of selling their partnership back to the company or investing further as shareholders in the closed corporation. This would all depend on the company's success, the twins realized, and they knew they could only plan so far ahead; first, their wraps must become a big hit in the new neighborhood.

One of the twins' early planning discussions was about the nature of their business: Were they a service provider or a goods producer? They decided they were both: When interacting with customers, they would provide attentive service with a meal that was fast, inexpensive, and healthful. When working in the kitchen, they'd use all their culinary arts to "manufacture" the best wraps in Los Angeles—or the West!

Your Mission: Three years have passed and you are working as manager for Alice and Judith's third AJ Wraps, located in Orange County's Huntington Beach. The first two restaurants are thriving, especially with identical twin managers. (Suppliers are baffled over that woman who seems to be in two places at once, but the twins refuse to enlighten them and spoil the fun.) Your task is that much harder because you're the new link in a chain that was holding fine without you. But even twins can't manage three restaurants at once without help.

1. The communication between you, the twins, and Jeff has soured. First, you are farther from headquarters than the other restaurants. Second, the twins forget you can't read their minds like they seem to do with each other. And third, Jeff's role as consultant has always left you confused about whether you're his boss or he's yours. What can you do to improve the situation?
   a. Write a memo to the twins explaining your frustrations and asking them to treat you with more respect and equality, and to clarify your relationship with Jeff.
   b. Suggest a meeting among the four of you, choosing a time when your assistants can handle your absence. During the meeting, propose several ways to improve communication—such as using e-mail to shrink the distance between you and avoid phone tag.
   c. Don't say anything. Realize that, in addition to doing the same job as you, Alice and Judith are also general partners who must oversee the entire business. They can't be expected to remember everything. The burden is on you to understand the business structure, and have patience.
2. Are you more of a service provider than a goods producer? Lately, some suppliers have been routinely late, requiring last-minute adjustments in Alice and Judith's recipes. So what's more important: getting the food to the customers on time any way you can, or making sure the wraps are gourmet delicious?
   a. Most of your customers are interested in the "fast" aspect of the food and will probably not notice some small substitutions, or some items missing from the menu on any given day.
   b. Alice and Judith's success is largely based on their unique recipes and the quality of their wraps (and they have a lot of competition). The quality of your product is of utmost importance; it's your edge in the marketplace. Don't serve anything that doesn't meet the twins' original standards.
   c. Both service and product are important—you'll have to make your decisions on a case-by-case basis. Do the substitutions result in a quality product? Can you get the wraps out in sufficient quantity without delays or menu omissions that would irritate your regular customers? Meanwhile, do what you can to improve delivery schedules.
3. You've done well in Huntington Beach, despite the heavy competition, so the twins are moving forward with their franchising plans. You're concerned—what about your future? Will you be demoted beneath a new franchise owner? You want to get a word in before the decisions are made. Which of the following will you suggest?
   a. The twins should keep the third store in the same position as the original two—under their full ownership as a business flagship. You will remain as manager.
   b. You should be promoted to a position on the corporate board and made head of the training program for new franchise owners.
   c. You should buy the franchise for the third store.
4. Your employees have heard rumors about the franchising plans and they're nervous. Keeping good workers on board is important, whatever decision the twins make about the Huntington Beach operation. What should you do?
   a. Try to diminish rumors and quiet the talk about company changes. If employees ask, give vague answers.

However, let it be known that if changes do occur, hard workers will stay, and laggards will not.

b. As employees ask you questions, be honest and direct with everything you know about the franchise plans—including uncertainties about the Huntington Beach operation. Then praise them for their hard work, encourage their loyalty, and voice high expectations for the restaurant's continued success, despite changes.

c. Call in all employees after closing for a major meeting about company plans, even though they are not yet finalized. Allow questions and discussion. Admit what you don't know.

Key Terms

acquisition (116)
barriers to entry (103)
board of directors (113)
capital-intensive businesses (102)
chief executive officer (CEO) (115)
commodity business (104)
conglomerate mergers (117)
consortium (108)
cooperatives (108)
corporation (109)
divestiture (116)
general partnership (107)
golden parachute (122)
goods-producing businesses (100)
government-owned corporations (110)
holding company (112)
horizontal mergers (117)
hostile takeovers (118)
labor-intensive businesses (103)
limited liability companies (LLCs) (112)
limited partnership (107)
liquidity (110)
master limited partnership (MLP) (107)
merger (116)
not publicly traded corporations (111)
parent company (112)
partnership (107)
poison pill (122)
private corporations (111)
proxy (113)
proxy fight (119)
publicly traded corporations (111)
quasi-government corporations (111)
S corporation (111)
service businesses (100)
shareholders (109)
shark repellent (122)
sole proprietorship (104)
stock (109)
subsidiary corporations (112)
tender offer (119)
trusts (117)
unlimited liability (105)
vertical mergers (117)
white knight (122)

Questions

For Review

1. What factors have contributed to the revival of the manufacturing sector?
2. What is a sole proprietorship? Why is it the most common type of business in the United States?
3. Why might two competing corporations want to establish a joint venture and how does this differ from a merger?
4. Describe the two techniques used to conduct a hostile takeover.
5. What are the four main types of merger-and-acquisition defense and how do they work?

For Analysis

6. Discuss the advantages and disadvantages of partnerships.
7. To what extent do shareholders control the activities of a corporation?
8. With all of the deregulation going on in public utilities, is there really any difference between a private and a quasi-government corporation? Explain your answer.
9. How might a company benefit from having a diverse board of directors that includes representatives of several industries, countries, and cultures?
10. Leveraged buyouts can be risky transactions. Apart from hostile takeovers, in what situations do you think companies or individuals might want to pursue this acquisition strategy?

For Application

11. Suppose you and some friends want to start a business to take tourists on wilderness backpacking expeditions. None of you has much extra money, so your plan is to start small. However, if you are successful, you would like to expand into other types of outdoor tours and perhaps even open up branches in other locations. What form of ownership should your new enterprise take and why?
12. Carco, the leading automobile parts manufacturer, is considering acquiring Parts Plus, the nation's third largest automobile parts retailer. Both companies are financially solid, and both have dedicated employees, strong management, and good reputations in their industries. Carco expects to offer Parts Plus shareholders a 20 to 25 percent premium over the company's current stock price. What do you think the chances of success would be if the acquisition went through? What issues might arise that could limit the transaction's success?

A Case for Critical Thinking ■ Shareholder Protection or Legal Opportunism?

Reporting financial results is getting to be a nerve-racking task for many U.S. corporations. If quarterly or annual revenues and profits don't meet expectations—and stock prices drop as a result—corporations stand a good chance of being hit by lawsuits from shareholders. The idea behind these lawsuits is that if shareholders had known the company wasn't performing as well as they thought it was, they could have sold their shares earlier, before the price dropped.

The issue stems from the corporation's responsibility to communicate with its shareholders. Some of this communication is done directly, through quarterly and annual reports. In other cases, the communication is indirect, as when corporate officers talk to groups of financial analysts. These analysts (who usually work for banks, mutual fund companies, or stockbrokers) study what the corporations have to say and then issue recommendations and projections for the stock. If the future seems rosy, analysts will tell people (through newsletters, advice to stockbrokers, appearances on financial television shows, and other avenues) that the stock price is likely to go up as the company's fortunes improve. On the other hand, if analysts question the company's prospects, they may tell people to sell the stock now because it's probably headed downhill. In any case, shareholder expectations are influenced by the perceptions they develop about the stocks they own. If they buy stock with the idea that it will go up, they naturally expect it to go up.

This communication process places a heavy responsibility on corporate executives. To avoid creating false impressions (either positive or negative), they have to be careful about what they tell shareholders and analysts. Naturally, they want to share good news with the world because this helps drive up the price of their company's stock. On the other hand, they have to be honest about bad news or potentially bad news to avoid misleading people. Similarly, if analysts and the public get *too* excited about a company's prospects, the excitement is likely to drive the price higher than it really should be. Sooner or later, it will come crashing down to where it should have been in the first place. You can see that the challenge is to keep the public's perception of the stock's value in line with its real value, based on the company's performance.

When perceptions are out of line with reality, people look for somebody to blame. Did the company mislead investors by hiding bad news? Did analysts overstate growth estimates? Did investors simply jump on a hot stock and mindlessly drive it too high? Increasingly, blame is being pinned on the corporation, as shareholders take them to court. For example, Software developer Legent Computer was sued within hours of announcing quarterly earnings that were below expectations. A federal judge eventually threw the case out for lack of evidence, but not before it took a heavy toll on the company. Legent staffers had to provide 290,000 pages of documents, top executives had to spend much of their time preparing for trial instead of running the business, and the whole affair cost the company several million dollars.

Even though these lawsuits might sound like angry shareholders fighting back after losing money in the stock market, that sour-grape theory isn't always the case. Several law firms across the country scan newspapers, looking for company announcements that don't meet projections. The lawyers then run ads trying to alert all shareholders in the company of a pending *class-action lawsuit* (a suit filed against a company on behalf of more than one person). In other words, the problem doesn't stem from angry shareholders looking for lawyers but from lawyers looking for shareholders. As many as 40 percent of these lawsuits, known as "strike suits," are thrown out of court, as Legent's case was. In many other instances, corporations settle out of court, even when they claim to be innocent, simply to avoid the years of distracting and expensive litigation. The settlements average over $8 million a piece, and the law firms' average cut of the money is about one-third of the settlement, so it's easy to see why some lawyers are eager to find these cases.

In 1995 the Private Securities Litigation Reform Act was passed to protect companies from such frivolous lawsuits. The law provides protection for company executives making projections on earnings and markets, limits how many class-action suits can be filed by the same person in a three-year period, and encourages judges to penalize plaintiffs that bring meritless cases. However, since the law's passage, more lawsuits have simply been filed in state courts when the facts of the case are not sufficient to satisfy the requirements of the new federal law. As a result, California—where the majority of cases are filed—has established state rules to restrict strike suits. Moreover, a group of CEOs from 181 high-tech companies (the most common targets of strike suits), are lobbying Congress for a federal law that would extend the reach of the 1995 law to state courts.

1. What steps can corporations take to reduce the chances of attracting shareholder lawsuits?
2. Why don't shareholders just vote management out of their jobs if they're not happy with the corporation's financial results?
3. Do you think investors should be allowed by law to sue corporations when stock performance does not meet their expectations? Why or why not? What problems might result if investors had no legal recourse when they felt they were misled by management?
4. The Stanford Law School has built a World Wide Web site that lists comprehensive information about all securities fraud class-action lawsuits—including the charges, the

proceedings, and the courts' decisions. Visit the site at <http://securities.stanford.edu>, and select a case to review. Cases may be challenging to read because of the legal language used, but see whether you can determine who the plaintiffs are, what charges they are bringing against the company, and why they believe fraud has occurred. Do you think that your selection is a frivolous case? If the case has been resolved, how did the court rule?

Building Your Business Skills

Some critics believe that growth in the service sector will continue to reduce the number of decent-paying jobs for lower-skilled workers in the United States. During class, divide into groups of three or four. Using the text, the resources in your library, the Internet, and reports in your local newspaper, identify the prevalence of service and goods-producing industries in your area. Which sector contributes the most to the local economy? Within each sector, which categories provide the most jobs? How does this affect local wages? What is the outlook for the future of each industry? What opportunities does this outlook provide for workers with a high school diploma? A two-year degree? A four-year degree? A graduate degree?

- Discuss your findings as a group. Prepare a brief report for your class that summarizes your analysis and predictions.
- Present your findings to the rest of your class. After each group has presented, debate any differences that resulted.
- What does the information presented mean to you as a student?

Keeping Current Using *The Wall Street Journal*

In recent issues of *The Wall Street Journal,* find an article or series of articles illustrating one of the following business developments:

- Merger
- Acquisition
- Divestiture
- Hostile takeover
- Leveraged buyout
- Consortium or joint venture

1. Explain in your own words what steps or events led to this development.
2. What results do you expect this development to have on (a) the company itself, (b) consumers, (c) the industry the company is part of? Write down and date your answers.
3. Follow your story in *The Wall Street Journal* over the next month (or longer, as your instructor requests). What problems, opportunities, or other results are reported? Were these developments anticipated at the time of the initial story, or did they seem to catch industry analysts by surprise? How well did your answers to question 2 predict the results?
4. Periodically visit the Web sites of the companies involved as you track the story (especially look for press releases). Do they mention any news of the deal? Do the companies' perspectives on the benefits and costs of the deal differ in any way from those offered in *The Wall Street Journal?* Based on both the *Journal* information and on the Web site information, do you think that the deal was a wise one for the companies involved in the long run? Why or why not?

Exploring the Best of the Web

Know Your Stats! page 102

If you need meaningful statistics on U.S. industries, demographics (population size, distribution, and characteristics), jobs, products, or other subjects, you have a good chance of finding them in the *Statistical Abstract of the United States* (http://www.census.gov/prod/www/abs/cc97stab.html). Scroll down to the bottom of the main page and click on the index. Browse the index topics to find the appropriate table numbers for answers to the following questions. Return to the main page, and click on the appropriate links to find the tables you're looking for.

1. What was the total number of mergers and acquisitions among U.S. firms last year? Compare this to the number of mergers and acquisitions in 1990 and explain why it has increased.
2. What percentage of college freshmen listed business as their probable field of study last year? How does this compare to the number of business majors in 1985? What factors may have contributed to the decline of business majors in the late 1980s and early 1990s?
3. How much money (in current dollars) did U.S. industries spend on research and development last year? (Use table titled "R&D, Source of Funds and Performance Sector")? How much did the federal government spend? Has R&D spending by industry and government increased or decreased since the mid-1980s? What factors do you think have contributed to these changes (see also table titled "R&D Expenditures")?

Understanding Internet Business, page 109

Computerworld's "emmerce" page combines a large amount of Internet commerce statistics in one convenient location. If you are thinking about starting an Internet business, "emmerce" is an excellent place to begin your research. After you have explored the information available at <http://www.computerworld.com/emmerce>, answer the following questions.

1. What percentage of Internet purchases is made by consumers? What percentage is made by other businesses? What percentage of business-to-business companies has Web sites? What percentage of business-to-consumer companies has them? What do these statistics say about the types of products and services that have the most potential for sales on the Internet?
2. What categories of products are expected to have the highest revenue growth as a result of Internet sales in the coming years? Are these products purchased by consumers, businesses, or both? Which one do you think has the most potential for the consumer market? Why?
3. According to the most recent statistics, how many pages are currently available on the Web? How rapidly is the Web growing? How is the number of U.S. Web users expected to change in the next 3 or 4 years? Is the average number of hours spent online increasing or decreasing? What are the implications for businesses that are thinking about going online?

Find the Right Path, page 119

Explore <Pathfinder.com> for recent articles about business, sports, entertainment, or other areas of interest to you. Try the various links to find out what each online publication has to offer. After you have become familiar with the site, answer the following questions.

1. How might you use this site in research for your classes? How might a businessperson make use of it?
2. Is a service like <Pathfinder.com> an adequate replacement for library research? Why or why not?
3. Overall, how would you rate the way that this site is laid out? If you were the site's designer, how would you change the site to make it easier to navigate or more attractive?

Answers to "Is It True?"

Page 103. False. It is true that Japanese manufacturing employees put in 6 weeks more every year than their U.S. counterparts, typically by working 16-hour days and skipping most vacation time. However, the average U.S employee labors 8 weeks longer than the average German every year. In addition, the average U.S. worker now puts in 163 more hours each year than in 1970.

Page 108. False. Studies show that wealthy people are the ones most likely to become self-employed. Wage workers who enter self-employment tend to be white, older, and married, and to have relatively high levels of education.

Page 121. True.

CHAPTER 5

SMALL BUSINESSES, NEW VENTURES, AND FRANCHISES

OBJECTIVES

After studying this chapter, you will be able to

1. Differentiate between lifestyle businesses and high-growth ventures
2. Identify three characteristics (other than size) that differentiate small companies from larger ones
3. List four important functions of small businesses in the economy
4. Identify three factors contributing to the increase in the number of small businesses
5. Enumerate three ways of getting into business for yourself
6. Outline the pros and cons of owning a franchise
7. Name 12 topics that should be covered in a formal business plan
8. Explain how small businesses can benefit from using the Internet

ON THE JOB

On the Job On the Job

ON THE JOB: FACING BUSINESS CHALLENGES AT TOP OF THE TREE BAKING COMPANY

Baking Up Millions

You can use a lot of words to describe Gordon Weinberger, the founder of Top of the Tree Baking Company. Verbose. Determined. And, of course, tall—6 feet 9 inches. Another man might have shrunk from the task that Weinberger had set for himself a couple of years ago, but Weinberger didn't. For two straight weeks, he would rush home from his day job in Boston, throw back some dinner, and then head upstairs to his study to work the phones from 6 P.M. to 11 P.M.

He worked from a list of more than 70 prospective investors: cousins, aunts, uncles, in-laws, colleagues of his father, and friends of the family—many of whom he hadn't talked to in years. This meant he had a lot of catching up to do before he could even begin to tell them about the new company he hoped to start. Even for Gordon Weinberger, a man with an extraordinary gift of gab, convincing them to invest in his idea might be hard work.

But Weinberger needed money—$100,000 to be exact. In the previous 4 months, he had honed his pie recipe, drawn up a detailed business plan, and sounded out the buyers from area supermarket chains. Almost everywhere he went, the feedback was positive. But without money, he knew his pies weren't going to get much farther than the local county fair.

Each time Weinberger reached for the phone, he drew in a deep breath. Then when the moment arrived, he did what he does best. He told his story. "Hi, this is Gordon. How are you doing? Hey, I'm starting this new company, and I was wondering . . . " By the end of the night, his ear would be sore and his vocal chords scratchy. But it was worth the trouble.

Though it took a few months and a few more phone calls before the money began to roll in, he "sold" his idea to 11 investors, each of whom contributed about $10,000. The structure of the private stock offering was quite simple. The investors agreed that they would have no direct control or say in the affairs of Top of the Tree. In exchange, they were promised double their money back in 5 years.

Although entrepreneurs are often strong on developing their ideas, many stumble when it comes to raising money. Weinberger had little financial experience beyond negotiating a home mortgage. So the question is: How did Weinberger succeed where so many others had failed? If you were Gordon Weinberger, how would you prepare to market your small-business idea to investors? Where might you go for financing? How hard would you be willing to work to turn your vision into reality? What would you include in your business plan?[1]

UNDERSTANDING THE WORLD OF SMALL BUSINESS

Small businesses are the cornerstone of the U.S. economic system. The country was originally founded by people involved in small businesses—the family farmer, the shopkeeper, the craftsperson. Successive waves of immigrants carried on the tradition, launching restaurants and laundries, driving taxicabs, and opening newsstands and bakeries.

This trend continued for many years until improvements in transportation and communication enabled large producers to manufacture goods at lower costs and charge lower prices. As a result, the small, independent businesses could not compete. Scores of them closed their doors, and big business emerged as the primary economic force.

In the last couple of years, however, the trend toward big-ness has reversed. A quick look up and down a typical commercial street or at a strip shopping center is enough to tell you that small businesses are an important element in the U.S. economy today. Even so, determining just *how* important small business is to the economy is surprisingly tricky because *small* is a relative term. For example, a manufacturing firm with 500 employees might be considered small if it competes against much larger companies, but a retail establishment with 500 employees might be classified as big compared with its competitors.

One reliable source of information for small businesses is the Small Business Administration (SBA). This government agency serves as a resource and advocate for small firms—providing them with financial assistance, training, and a variety of helpful programs. The SBA defines a **small business** as a firm that is independently owned and operated, not dominant in its field, relatively small in terms of annual sales, and with fewer than 500 employees. In fact, according to SBA figures, 80 percent of all U.S. companies have fewer than 7 employees.[2]

small business
Company that is independently owned and operated, is not dominant in its field, and meets certain criteria for the number of employees and annual sales revenue

Characteristics of Small Businesses

Small businesses are of two distinct types: Roughly 80 to 90 percent are modest operations with little growth potential (although some have attractive income potential for the solo businessperson). The self-employed consultant working part-time from a home office, the corner florist, and the neighborhood pizza parlor fall into the category of **lifestyle businesses**—firms built around the personal and financial needs of an individual or a family.[3] Lifestyle businesses aren't designed to grow into large enterprises.

lifestyle businesses
Small businesses intended to provide the owner with a comfortable livelihood

In contrast to lifestyle businesses, some small firms are small simply because they are new. Many companies—such as FedEx, Microsoft, and Intel—start out as small entrepreneurial firms but quickly outgrow their small-business status. These **high-growth ventures** are usually run by a team rather than by one individual, and they expand rapidly by obtaining a sizable supply of investment capital and introducing new products or services to a large market. But expanding from a small firm into a large one is not for everyone. That's because there's a world of difference between the two.

high-growth ventures
Small businesses intended to achieve rapid growth and high profits on investment

Innovation Smaller companies can make decisions quickly, partly because company owners are more accessible and partly because these companies offer more opportunity for individual expression. Putting an idea into action in big companies means filing formal proposals, preparing research reports, and attending too many meetings. A good idea could die before it has a chance to take off. According to one expert, the attitude in big companies is to say *no* more often than *yes*, whereas the attitude in smaller companies tends to be, "let's try it."[4]

Is It True?

Gaining work experience in a small business is one way of launching your career with a large corporation.

This innovative spirit frequently gives small businesses a competitive advantage. Consequently, big companies are now trying to stimulate innovation by acting like smaller firms. Some are dividing their companies into smaller work units. Others, like AT&T, du Pont, Motorola, and Hewlett-Packard, are nurturing *intrapreneurs*—people who create innovation of any kind *within* an organization (not to be confused with entrepreneur—a risk taker in the private enterprise system). Of course, corporate intrapreneurs often face giant stumbling blocks within these large organizations. Burdened by traditional corporate cultures, their innovative spirit is soon smothered by strict reporting requirements and formal procedures.[5] In spite of these drawbacks, some people would rather work for large companies because they prefer a more structured environment. The employee benefits at big firms aren't bad either.

Small businesses, such as these retail shops in Dexter, Maine, provide nearly half of all private sector jobs in the United States.

Limited Resources and Hard Work Because small companies generally have limited resources, many owners and employees must learn how to do more with less. This means that they must wear a variety of job hats in order to get the work done. However, this jack-of-all-trades mentality is not for everyone (see Exhibit 5.1). Unfortunately, some people find this out the hard way. They discover that running a small business takes a lot of hard work and that being a successful corporate employee doesn't necessarily translate into being a successful small-business owner.

When Bob Hammer and Sue Crowe purchased Blue Jacket Ship Crafters, a mail-order model-ship-kit manufacturer, they quickly learned that running a small company was not like running Motorola, where the two had been senior managers for the better part of their careers. Blue Jacket was a long way from running on automatic pilot. It took a lot more work and time than they had imagined. Even Crowe admits, "you will put in more money than you thought you would, you will take out a lot less, and you will work harder than you did when you were making a six-figure salary at your large corporation."[6] In fact, three out of four people who start their own company spend at least 50 hours a week on the job; a quarter of them put in 70 hours or more.[7]

On the other hand, Carlos Montero knew exactly what he was getting into when he used $300,000 in savings to buy three Burger Kings 10 years ago. After attending rigorous training sessions to learn everything from cooking burgers to cleaning windows, Montero worked almost 21 hours a day for many, many weeks. Today he owns 22 restaurants with annual revenues approaching $18 million.[8]

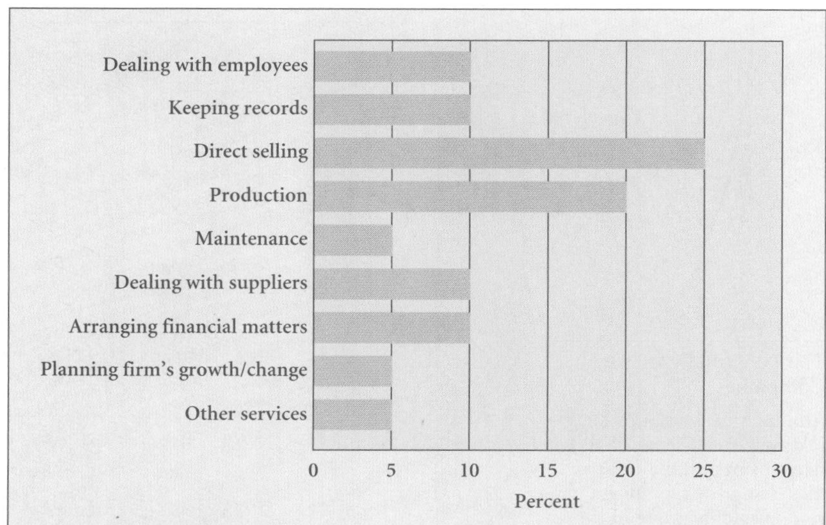

EXHIBIT 5.1

How Entrepreneurs Spend Their Time

The men and women who start their own companies are jacks-of-all-trades, but their top priorities are selling and producing the product.

The Economic Role of Small Businesses

Today large corporations are paying serious attention to small business. They no longer view smaller companies as firms that eat whatever crumbs fall from the corporate table. Perhaps that's because many big companies have been brought to their knees by once small entrepreneurial organizations like Netscape and Intel. As a result, small companies are getting the respect they deserve for performing a number of important roles in our economy:

- *Providing jobs.* Small businesses are a principal source of new jobs. Some 22 million small businesses employ almost half of the private U.S. work force, and these small businesses generate more than half of the U.S. gross domestic product. As Exhibit 5.2 illustrates, most new jobs come from high-growth ventures.[9]
- *Introducing new products.* The National Science Foundation estimates that 98 percent of the nation's "radical" new-product developments spring from small firms, a staggering percentage given the fact that small companies spend less than 5 percent of the nation's research-and-development money.[10]
- *Supplying the needs of large corporations.* Many small businesses act as distributors, servicing agents, and suppliers to large corporations. Consider Parallax. This 160-employee firm inspects nuclear power plants, implements safety procedures, and cleans up hazardous and nuclear waste at power plants and weapons complexes across the nation. Seventy percent of Parallax's business comes from large corporations like Westinghouse and Lockheed Martin. Not bad for a company launched out of the founder's home with $10,000 in personal savings.[11]
- *Providing specialized goods and services.* Cross Colours has taken the clothing industry by storm in the last several years by offering street-inspired garments not readily available from other sources, many with African color schemes and designs. The company started out targeting African Americans but has grown by leaps and bounds and is now one of the most respected firms in the entire industry.[12]

EXHIBIT 5.2

The Role of High-Growth Companies

Although they account for a relatively small share of all new businesses, the companies that grow rapidly are responsible for more of the newly created jobs, sales, and exports.

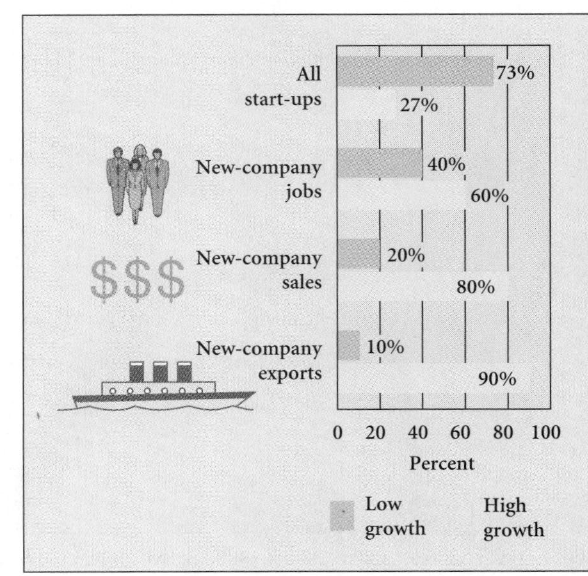

Factors Contributing to the Increase in Small Businesses

A variety of factors is contributing to the increase in the number of small businesses today: technological advances, an increase in the number of minority business owners, and corporate downsizing and outsourcing—to name just a few. Some people find it more satisfying and exciting to work for a small business; others find it is their only option. Regardless of the reason, small businesses are the fastest-growing sector of almost any pie chart these days.

Technology As technology gets cheaper and more advanced, small companies compete on a level playing field with larger companies. In fact, today's new companies may even have a technological advantage; they are unencumbered by the clunky technology of the past.

Look at Isis, a small pharmaceutical company. Being first to introduce a new drug in the market is critical in the pharmaceutical industry. In the past you had to spend millions of dollars on data-crunching systems. But today, less expensive versions of these sophisticated systems are available, enabling smaller firms like Isis to compete. In 1995, Isis invested $300,000 in computer equipment, and today the company files its 40,000-page reports with the U.S. Food and Drug Administration in one-third the time by compressing the information onto one CD-ROM.[13]

Likewise, the advent of computer-aided manufacturing equipment has enabled small manufacturing plants to customize their products and deliver them as efficiently as their larger rivals. In addition, the Internet provides a wealth of information to service-based businesses, that was previously available only to larger firms. With online resources like Lexis-Nexis, Dun & Bradstreet, Electric Library, and Commerce Clearing House's Business Owners' Toolkit, doctors, accountants, writers, and consultants no longer need to purchase their own reference books or resource materials.

Of course, technology also makes it easier to work at home these days (see Exhibit 5.3). Although no one knows with certainty how many people are running businesses from their homes, estimates range from 5.6 million to 30.7 million. Some predict that as much as half the work force may be involved in full- or part-time home-based businesses by 2003.[14]

TYPE OF BUSINESS	NUMBER OF START-UPS, 1996
Construction	19,194
Cleaning services (residential, commercial)	14,238
Retail store	13,707
Consultant	11,078
Designer	9,279
Computer services and repair	7,899
Real estate	7,749
Painter	6,600
Lawn maintenance	6,320
Arts and crafts	6,139
Landscape contractor	6,136
Automotive services and repair	5,173
Building contractor (remodeling, repairing)	5,167
Management and business consulting	5,117
Marketing programs and services	5,090
Trucking	5,043
Wholesale trade, nondurable goods	4,956
Communications consultant	4,949
Restaurant	4,801
Audiovisual production services	4,792

EXHIBIT 5.3

Start-At-Home Businesses

Some 44 percent of the new businesses started in the United States in 1996 were home based. Here's a rundown of the most popular ones.

Winners of the Hispanic Business Entrepreneurs of the Year Award for 1995, the Quintana sisters built a $13 million computer consulting company on a simple premise: Work smart.

Minority Business Owners Studies show that roughly 36 percent of U.S. small companies (7.9 million firms) are owned by women; these firms employ about one in four U.S. workers and ring up more than $2.28 trillion in annual sales. Similar advances are also showing up in other minority segments of the population. From 1979 to 1994, the number of businesses owned by Hispanic Americans doubled, from 225,000 to more than 500,000.[15]

According to the SBA, women entrepreneurs make up one of the fastest-growing segments in the small-business economy. Estimates from the National Foundation for Women Business Owners show that between 1987 and 1996, business start-ups with African American, Hispanic, or Asian women at the helm have grown 153 percent—more than triple the 47 percent rate of U.S. businesses overall. In addition, the number of businesses owned by minority women rose to 1.1 million in 1996 from 342,000 in 1987.[16] Look at Annette and Victoria Quintana. They started Excel Professional Services to provide corporations with software consultants on a project-by-project basis. Since starting up in 1990, Excel's annual revenues have climbed from $250,000 to over $13 million, earning the partners the 1995 Hispanic Business Entrepreneurs of the Year Award.[17]

Corporate Downsizing and Outsourcing Corporate layoffs are also fueling the growth in small businesses. Approximately 160 small high-tech companies were born when IBM, Northern Telecom, and Glaxo Wellcome collectively shed some 4,000 research jobs in the North Carolina area known as the Research Triangle. Many of the newly unemployed scientists admit that they would not have started their own businesses voluntarily, but an abundant supply of financing and a desire to remain in the area motivated them to uncover their hidden entrepreneurial talents.[18]

Still, many people leave the corporate world voluntarily, and some like Annette Quintana are even taking along their former employers as customers. Of course, nailing your former employer as a client can be a classy way to leave a company and start a business at the same time. Everyone wins with this arrangement. After working several years as Coca-Cola's manager of media relations in Atlanta, Harold Jackson broke out on his own and started JacksonHeath Public Relations International, taking Coke with him as his most valuable client.[19]

outsourcing
Subcontracting work to outside companies

Today more and more firms are **outsourcing** or subcontracting special projects and secondary business functions to smaller companies. This trend is especially prevalent in the field of information technology, where numerous small companies are making a living off corporations—no less than $25 billion a year. In 1996 alone, business for small information technology firms increased by more than 25 percent.[20]

BUILDING A SMALL BUSINESS

Could you or should you join the thousands of men and women like Gordon Weinberger who start new businesses every year? It's not for everyone. Laid-off executives who are used to running multibillion-dollar enterprises sometimes have trouble adjusting to the unglamorous details of daily life in a small business. Many miss the support services they enjoyed in large corporations. Perhaps the biggest hurdle for the majority of new small-business owners is the constant challenge to sell, sell, sell.[21]

Suppose you decide to join the ranks of small-business owners like Annette Quintana or Harold Jackson. What are your chances of success? You may have heard some depressing statistics about the number of new businesses that fail. Some reports say your chances of success are only one in three; others claim that the odds are even worse, stating that 85 percent of all new business ventures fail within 10 years.

Dun & Bradstreet (D&B) specializes in analyzing the business environment, and its analyses show that the true failure rate is much lower if you remove those operations that

D&B doesn't consider "genuine businesses." For instance, a freelancer who writes one article for a magazine and then stops writing would be counted as a failed business under the traditional measurement (which is based on tax returns).[22] Regardless of the failure rate, the number one reason why people start small businesses today is to be their own boss. Surprisingly, they cite making money as a secondary reason.[23]

Is It True?

Less than 50 percent of new small businesses survive for the first five years.

Finding Entrepreneurs

For the most part, few of those who take the entrepreneurial plunge today are glamorous adventurers; most are ordinary people like Gordon Weinberger. Yet studies show that entrepreneurs often possess many common qualities: They prefer excitement, are highly disciplined, like to control their destiny, listen to their intuitive sense, relate well to others, are eager to learn whatever skills are necessary to reach their goal, learn from their mistakes, stay abreast of market changes, are willing to exploit new opportunities, seldom follow trends (rather they spot and interpret trends), are driven by ambition, and prefer the excitement and potential rewards of risk taking over security.[24] Exhibit 5.4 lists some recent successful entrepreneurs and the key factor contributing to their success.

BEST OF THE WEB

Increase Your Chances for Success

Starting a new business can be tough. It's not for everyone. Find out whether you have the "right stuff" to be a successful entrepreneur. Learn the nine important ways to increase your chances for success. Hear what the big corporations have to say. Do you know how to network effectively? Better find out. While you're at it, check out *Biz FAQ's* and find the answers to some of the most frequently asked questions by small-business owners. Explore the world of small business now by visiting the *Small Business Advisor*. Select Destination: *The Advisor* and scroll down to click on *Start-Up Topics*.
http:/www.isquare.com

Many entrepreneurs start with relatively small sums of money and operate informally from their homes, at least for a while.[25] These people have diverse backgrounds in terms of education and business experience. Some come from companies unlike the ones they start. Others use their prior knowledge and skills such as editing, telemarketing, public relations, or selling to start their own businesses. Many have less experience but an innovative idea or a better way of doing something that other companies are already doing (see Exhibit 5.5). They find an overlooked corner of the market, exploit an unnoticed demographic trend, or meet an unsatisfied consumer need through better service or a higher-quality product. Moreover, they frequently develop their product quickly, while the rest of the business world ponders whether a market for the product exists.

Starting a New Business

People in the United States are starting new businesses at dizzying rates. A study by the Entrepreneurial Research Consortium shows that more than 35 million U.S. households—roughly one in three—"have had an intimate involvement in a new or small business."[26]

Still, starting and managing a business takes motivation, desire, and talent. It also takes research and planning. Some of the most common reasons for starting a business are wanting to be your own boss, wanting financial independence, wanting creative

EXHIBIT 5.4

Entrepreneurial Success

If you like a product, chances are an entrepreneurial company is behind it.

KEY SUCCESS FACTOR	COMPANY
Persistence	*Breed Technologies:* It took Allen Breed over 10 years to convince carmakers that air bags could save several thousand lives a year. Today Breed Technologies is one of the most profitable suppliers in the automotive industry—his company makes the sensors that trigger the air-bag system. With more than 5,000 employees and branches in eight countries, this company's sales went from zero to nearly half a billion dollars in less than a decade.
Skill	*La Tempesta:* Using Aunt Isa's recipe for biscotti (a twice-baked Italian cookie), Bonnie Tempesta baked them and sold them at a fancy San Francisco chocolate shop. While attending a fancy foods trade show one day, she noticed that she was the only one there with biscotti. Today she sells over $9 million worth through 65 separate regional distributors to 5,000 stores, including Starbucks, Nordstrom, and Neiman Marcus.
Passion	*Transmissions by Lucille:* Lucille Treganowan didn't grow up yearning to repair cars. In fact, she didn't know a transmission from a turnip. So she began asking mechanics questions, reading, and working on cars. In 1973 she started her business. Today, transmissions are more than a business; they are a passion.
Hobby	*Rusty Cos:* Russell Preisendorfer is an avid surfer. To support his habit he began shaping surfboards. Last year his privately owned Rusty Cos grossed $57 million from sales of surfboards and royalties from a line of surfing apparel he helps design.
Common sense	*Auntie Anne's:* To bring in some extra cash, Anne Beiler managed a food stand at a farmer's market in Maryland. She noticed that the fastest-selling items at the stand were hand-rolled pretzels that sold for 55 cents each. Not bad for 7 cents worth of ingredients. So Beiler decided to try the pretzel business herself. Today Beiler's mini empire consists of over 300 franchised pretzel shops in about 35 states.
Talent	*Anthony Mark Hankins Ltd:* When Anthony Hankins was only 7 years old, he sat down at a sewing machine and made a suit for his mother to wear to a wedding. Today, at 27, he is still making clothes for his mother—and millions of other women. After just one year in business, Hankins has seen total retail sales for his clothing collections reach $40 million.

freedom, and wanting to fully use your skills and knowledge. If you decide to take the risk, you can get into business for yourself in three ways: Start from scratch, buy an existing operation, or obtain a franchise.

start-up companies New ventures

Roughly two thirds of new business founders begin **start-up companies;** that is, they start from scratch rather than buying an existing operation or inheriting the family business. Although starting from scratch is the most common route, it's probably the most difficult as well. Exhibit 5.6 is a checklist of some of the many tasks involved in starting a new business. Most of the people who succeed do so because they have enough experience to minimize the risks. They start with something they know how to do and capitalize on an existing network of professional or industry contacts. Hillary Sterba and Nancy Novinc started their tool-engineering company, S&N Engineering, with a combined 26 years of experience in that industry and even more years of business experience in general.[27]

EXHIBIT 5.5

How to Get Good Ideas for New Businesses

When looking for ideas for new companies, think in terms of what people want but can't get. According to the experts, "inventing a fancy gizmo first and then finding out later that no one wants it is a waste of time."

CONCEPT	EXPLANATION	EXAMPLE
Upgrade	Take a basic product and enhance it.	Designer blue jeans, gourmet cookies
Downgrade	Take a quality product and reduce its cost and price.	No-frills motels, budget rental cars
Bundle	Combine products to provide double benefits.	Laundromats that sell food or beverages
Unbundle	Take a product that has multiple features and offer only one of those features independently.	Term life insurance that has no savings value
Transport	Move a product that sells well in one area to another area.	Ethnic restaurants
Mass-market	Take a product that has been used for a specific purpose and find a larger audience for it.	Industrial cleaners repackaged for consumer markets
Narrowcast	Aim for a narrow portion of a large market.	Cable TV service for rural markets
Think big	Offer the broadest possible selection of a general category of goods	Electronics "supermarkets"
Think small	Offer a complete selection of a specific type of product.	Bookstore that sells only mystery novels
Compete on price	Offer more value for the same price, the same value for a lower price, or lower quality at a far lower price.	Warehouse stores

EXHIBIT 5.6

Business Start-Up Checklist

There are many tasks to perform before you start your business. Here are just a few.

- ☑ Choose a business name, verify the right to use it, and register it.
- ☑ Reserve a corporate name if you will be incorporating.
- ☑ Register or reserve state or federal trademarks.
- ☑ Apply for a patent if you will be marketing an invention.
- ☑ Write a business plan.
- ☑ Choose a location for the business.
- ☑ File partnership or corporate papers.
- ☑ Get any required business licenses or permits.
- ☑ Have business phone lines installed.
- ☑ Check into business insurance needs.
- ☑ Apply for sales tax number.
- ☑ Apply for employee identification number if you will have employees.
- ☑ Open business bank account(s).
- ☑ Have business cards and stationery printed.
- ☑ Purchase equipment and supplies.
- ☑ Order inventory.
- ☑ Order signage.
- ☑ Order fixtures.
- ☑ Print brochures and other sales literature.
- ☑ Send out publicity releases.
- ☑ Call everyone you know and tell them you are in business.

GAINING THE COMPETITIVE EDGE

Fattening Up the Mates—The Key to Sizzling Sales

For years, going to a steakhouse meant either putting on the ritz or romping at the ranch. There was no middle ground. Top-end steak houses were flourishing, as were budget eateries. But with casualness creeping back into restaurants, there was an opening for a middle player. With over 16 years of restaurant experience each, Chris Sullivan, Robert Basham, and Timothy Gannon knew how to recognize a "bloomin'" opportunity when they saw one. After all, Sullivan and Basham were partially responsible for steering the Bennigan's restaurant chain from 32 to 140 units, and Gannon knew how to cook steaks to a perfect medium rare.

On the other hand, they also knew that the restaurant business was risky. Restaurants open, shine briefly, and expire regularly as low-wage staffers tune out and take off, as costs spiral, and as popularity and prices sag. In addition, the people who run restaurants on a daily basis work their hides off but seldom get a stake in the ownership. So when the three founders decided to open the Outback Steakhouse, they adopted a highly unconventional management strategy: They took care of their mates.

MANAGEMENT MADNESS

All Outback Steakhouse managers are treated like entrepreneurs. Each manager invests $25,000 in the restaurant he or she runs and earns a base salary plus a bonus of 10 percent of the restaurant's cash intake (bonuses can range from $15,000 to $40,000 and upward). Moreover, each manager receives options to purchase about 4,000 shares of company stock. Any manager choosing to leave after 5 years can cash in on these company stock options and receive a generous payout as well (sometimes exceeding $300,000). Of course, the departing manager's name must be removed from the front door—an indication of who really runs the joint. With a cadre of self-motivated owner-managers running the restaurants, Sullivan,

---

Another way to go into business for yourself is to buy an existing business. This approach tends to reduce the risks—provided, of course, that you check the company out carefully. When you buy a business, you instantly acquire a known product or service and a system for producing it. You don't have to go through the painful period of building a reputation, establishing a clientele, and hiring and training employees. Also financing an existing business is often much easier; lenders are reassured by the company's history and existing assets and customer base. With these major details already settled, you can concentrate on making improvements.

franchise
Business arrangement in which a small business obtains rights to sell the goods or services of the supplier (franchisor)

franchisee
Small-business owner who contracts for the right to sell goods or services of the supplier (franchisor) in exchange for some payment

franchisor
Supplier that grants a franchise to an individual or group (franchisee) in exchange for payments

An alternative to buying an existing business is buying a **franchise** in somebody else's business. This approach enables you to use a larger company's trade name and sell its products or services in a specific territory. In exchange for this right, the **franchisee** (the small-business owner who contracts to sell the goods or services) pays the **franchisor** (the supplier) an initial fee (and often monthly royalties as well). However, owning a franchise is no guarantee that your business will succeed. According to one study, your chances are no better with a franchise operation than with a start-up.[28]

Franchising

When Mario Sbarro brought his family recipe for Italian pizza to the United States over 32 years ago, he had no idea that one day he would be looking at airports, sports stadiums, college campuses, and hospitals to expand his business.[29] About every 6 minutes of every business day, a new franchise opens somewhere in the United States. Franchising now accounts for roughly $900 million, or 40 percent of all U.S. retail sales, and that

Basham, and Gannon can focus on making the company grow—and they can move quickly.

TRIMMING THE FAT

There is no human resources department at Outback. The owners hire the key executives who hire the partners, who in turn hire the managers, who then hire the 75 to 80 people who staff each restaurant. As a result, Outback's command post in Tampa is informal and compact. Its just 55 people—mostly accountants—and their neckties are nowhere in sight. In addition to a lean headquarters, Outback keeps its costs low by serving dinner only and by locating its restaurants in the suburbs—where the people are at night. When you have to prepare for only one shift, you can be economical and flawless. In fact, the average steak dinner at Outback is quite reasonable. Customers can walk out the door with change from a $20 bill. That's one reason customers are patient while they wait at the front door—sometimes more than 2 hours—at all 330 restaurants.

LEADING THE STAMPEDE

Since the first Outback Steakhouse opened in 1988, there has been a stampede of competitors, but Outback still leads the pack. Even so, the three founders aren't resting on their laurels. They're working on a new concept, entering into a joint venture with Carrbabba's Italian Grill. And after that? "I'm sure there will be something else after that," notes Sullivan. "Besides we haven't even touched on our international potential."

QUESTIONS FOR CRITICAL THINKING

1. Should Outback franchise its restaurants? Why or why not?
2. Identify the key entrepreneurial qualities and concepts contributing to Outback's success.

number is expected to reach $1 trillion by the next decade. In our economy, franchises are a factor of rising importance, as Exhibit 5.7 suggests.

Franchises are of three basic types. A *product franchise* gives you the right to sell trademarked goods, which are purchased from the franchisor and resold by the franchisee. Car dealers and gasoline stations fall into this category. A *manufacturing franchise,* such as a soft-drink bottling plant, gives you the right to produce and distribute its products, using supplies purchased from the franchisor. A *business-format franchise* gives you the right to open a business using a franchisor's name and format for doing business. The fast-food chains like McDonald's, Wendy's, and Pizza Hut typify this form of franchising, and they are popping up all over the country—at military bases, college campuses, supermarkets, hospitals, airports, zoos, sports arenas, theme parks, and shopping malls.

Franchised businesses employ more than 8 million people; their suppliers employ another 2.4 million.[30] Corporate downsizing and early retirees have yielded a rich crop of qualified franchisee prospects in recent years. Over 30 percent of all new franchisees are ex-employees of big companies—many equipped with MBAs—and they're fueling a new generation of sophisticated franchisees. Many immigrants, with their unmatched entrepreneurial spirit and their drive to succeed, turn to franchising as a way of starting their own business.[31]

Advantages of Franchising Why is franchising so popular? When you invest in a franchise, you know that you are getting a viable business, one that has "worked" many times before. If the franchise is well-established, you get the added benefit of instant name recognition. Besides,

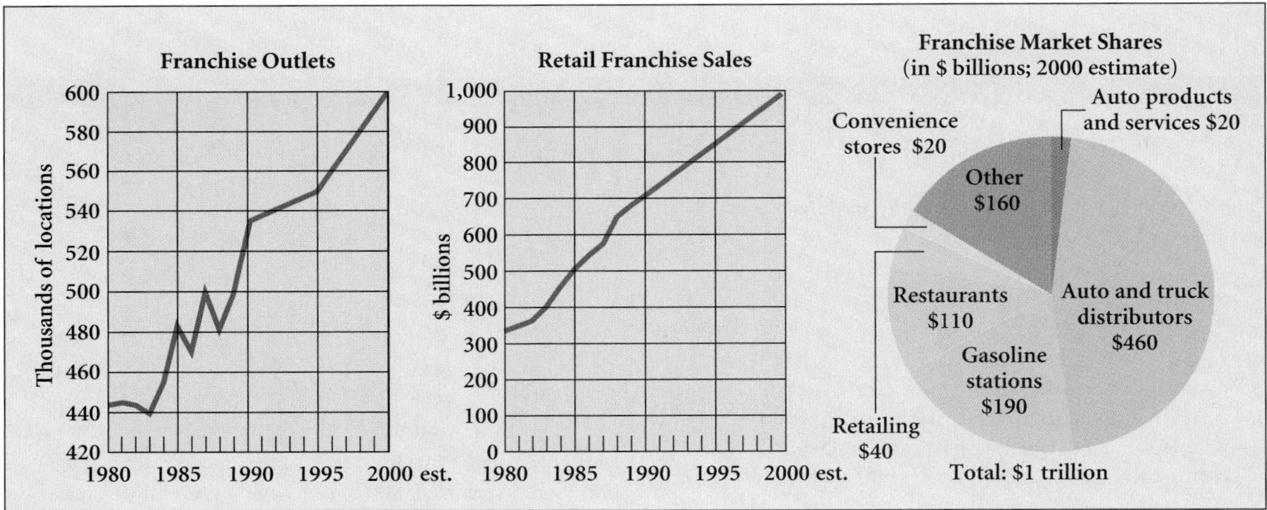

EXHIBIT 5.7

The Growth of Franchising

Both the number and revenue of franchises have increased dramatically over the past two decades.

when it comes to marketing and advertising—the things that most businesses don't have time for—the franchise company does that for you. An independent hamburger stand can't afford a national TV advertising campaign, but McDonald's, Burger King, and Wendy's can.

In addition to giving you a proven formula, buying a franchise gives you instant access to a support network along with a ready-made blueprint for building a business. For an initial investment (from a few thousand dollars to upward of a million, depending on the franchise), you get services such as site-location studies, market research, training, and technical assistance, as well as assistance with building or leasing your structure, decorating the building, purchasing supplies, and operating the business for 6 to 12 months. Few franchisees are able to write a check for the amount of the total investment. Most obtain a loan to cover at least part of the cost. In some cases, the lender is actually the franchisor. Approximately one-quarter of *Entrepreneur Magazine*'s top 500 franchisors offer some sort of financial assistance to their franchisees.[32]

Disadvantages of Franchising Although franchising offers many advantages, it is not the ideal vehicle for everyone. For one thing, owning a franchise is no guarantee of wealth. Even though it may be a relatively easy way to get into business, it isn't necessarily the cheapest. According to some analysts, it costs 10 to 30 percent more to buy a franchise than to open a business independently.[33] In addition, not all franchises are hugely profitable operations. Some franchisees barely survive, in fact.

One of the biggest disadvantages of franchising is the monthly payment, or royalty, that must be turned over to the franchisor. The fees vary widely, from nothing at all to 20 percent of sales. High royalties are not necessarily bad—if the franchisee gets ongoing assistance in return.

Another drawback of franchises is that many allow individual operators very little independence. Franchisors can prescribe virtually every aspect of the business, down to the details of employee uniforms and the color of the walls. Franchisees may be required to buy the products they sell directly from the franchisor at whatever price the franchisor wants to charge. Franchisors may also make important decisions without consulting franchisees. However, the days of franchisors exercising such control are ending.

Current Issues in Franchising When Meineke Discount Muffler Shops used to hit up franchisee Mark Zuckerman for 10 percent of his sales to help pay for advertising, Zuckerman expected to see top-notch ads. But he didn't. So along with other Meineke franchisees, he sued the parent company, and eventually all the chain's franchisees were awarded $347 million for damages sustained—one of the biggest verdicts in the history of franchising. Of course Meineke plans to appeal. But the lawsuit and years of hard-fought battles to ease the imbalance of power between franchisors and franchisees have paid off. Although the laws are still skewed in favor of the franchisor, the pendulum is beginning to swing somewhat in the direction of the franchisees.[34]

Today, the relationship between franchisor and franchisee is becoming more of a joint venture. Some franchisors, like AlphaGraphics and Taco Johns, are tired of complaints from their franchise outlets, so they've scrapped their conventional contracts. "They are rewriting them to become less of a dictatorship," says the CEO of U.S. Franchise Systems. Newer contracts offer stock options, automatic contract renewals, and empowerment through franchise advisory boards. Some are adding "give and take" clauses. Others are even giving franchisees more of a say in issues such as how territories are protected and how advertising funds are handled.

For instance, AlphaGraphics can no longer decide how every penny of royalties will be used. Instead, 25 percent of royalty fees are set aside to pay for services of each franchisee's choosing. In addition, AlphaGraphics franchisees can now pay for what amounts to a no-fault divorce. By paying no more than three years' royalties, divorced franchisees are free to keep their customers and even compete with the parent company.[35]

Some franchisees, such as Jiffy Lube dealers, are forming independent groups to gain more bargaining power against franchisors. Others are relying on legislation to do it for them.[36] Legislative proposals are being considered that would require franchisors to meet certain criteria (something like an accreditation) before they can sell a franchise in the United States.[37]

Due Diligence How do you protect yourself from a poor franchise investment? The best way is to study the opportunity very carefully before you commit. Since 1978 the Federal Trade Commission has required franchisors to disclose information about their operations to prospective franchisees. By studying this information, you can determine the financial condition of the franchisor and ascertain whether the company has been involved in lawsuits with franchisees. Before signing a franchise agreement, it's also wise to consult an

Because franchise outlets tend to be well defined and operator-ready, they draw people from all walks of life—from recent college graduates to downsized professionals.

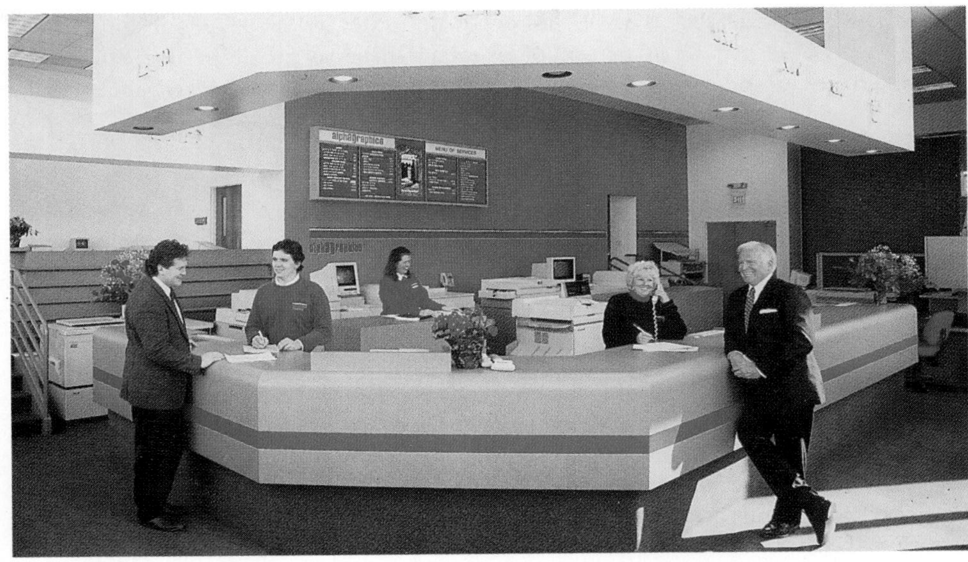

Like other franchisers, AlphaGraphics licenses out its name and business format in return for fees and royalties.

attorney. Exhibit 5.8 suggests some points to consider as you study the package of information on the franchise.

Nevertheless, some people find out too late that franchising isn't the best choice for them. They make a mistake that is common among prospective franchisees—buying without really understanding the day-to-day business. Often, prospects simply don't get beyond the allure of the successful name or concept—or the mistaken notion that a franchise brings instant success. "People go into a sub shop at the noon hour and see the cash register opening and closing," says the president of Franchise Solutions. "What they don't see is having to get there at 4 A.M. to bake the bread." Buying a franchise is much like buying any other business: It requires finding capital, choosing a site, hiring employees, and buying equipment. The process also includes an element not found in other businesses—evaluating the franchisor.[38]

EXHIBIT 5.8

Ten Questions to Ask Before Signing a Franchise Agreement

A franchise agreement is a legally binding contract that defines the relationship between the franchisee and the franchisor. Because the agreement is drawn up by the franchisor, the terms and conditions generally favor the franchisor. Before signing the franchise agreement, be sure to consult an attorney.

1. Are your legal responsibilities as a franchisee clear? Are your family members similarly obligated?
2. Who is responsible for selecting the location of your business?
3. Is the name or trademark of your franchise legally protected? Can the franchisor change or modify the trademark without consulting you?
4. Has the franchisor made any oral promises that are not reflected in the written franchise agreement?
5. What are your renewal rights? What conditions must you meet to renew your agreement?
6. Do you have exclusive rights to a given territory, or could the franchisor sell to additional franchisees who would become your competitors?
7. Under what terms are you allowed or required to terminate the franchise agreement? What becomes of the lease and assets if the agreement is terminated? Are you barred from opening a similar business?
8. Under what terms and conditions are you permitted or required to sell some or all of your interests in the franchise?
9. Are you required to buy supplies from the franchisor or other specified suppliers? Under what circumstances can you choose your own suppliers?
10. Has your attorney studied the written franchise agreement? Does it conform to the requirements of the Federal Trade Commission?

One of the best ways to evaluate a prospective franchisor is by talking to other franchisees. You might even want to spend a few months working for someone who already owns a franchise you're interested in. At a minimum, you should find out what other franchisees think of the opportunity. If they had it to do over again, would they still invest?

Get Smart

BEST OF THE WEB

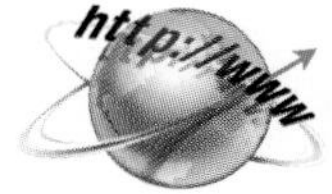

It seems like one-stop shopping is the way to go these days—everything under one roof, or on one page if you're on the Net. Smartbiz puts the world of business resources at your fingertips with business articles, resources, hot tips, franchise information, home office ideas, Internet links, and more. Thinking about buying an existing franchise? Better check out the franchisor first. Perhaps starting a home business sounds more appealing. Where should you begin? What are some of the advantages or disadvantages? Be sure to *Browse SBS* for some answers. Do you have a Web site? Why not build a home page right now. It takes only five minutes. Find out how by visiting Smartbiz, click *Business on the Net,* and scroll down to the hot link *The Home Page Maker.* Don't forget to e-mail us your URL.
http://www.smartbiz.com

Obtaining Financing and Special Assistance

Once you've decided whether you will build a business from scratch, buy an existing business, or invest in a franchise, you will probably need some money to get started. How much money will you need, and where should you turn first for capital? The answer depends on the size and type of business you want to launch. Retail and service businesses generally require less start-up cash than manufacturing companies or hi-tech research-and-development ventures. On average, though, nearly half of small businesses are launched with less that $20,000.[39] Chapter 18 discusses in detail the many sources for financing a new enterprise. One increasingly popular source for small-business financing is the SBA.

State and Local Government Programs Hoping to boost their economies and create jobs, state and local governments have launched hundreds of programs to help small businesses. Most now have some sort of small-company financing, and more than half offer venture-capital funds (financing for business start-ups) as well as research-and-development grants.[40]

If you apply to several banks and are turned down by all of them, you may be able to qualify for a loan backed by the SBA. To get an SBA-backed loan, you apply to a regular bank, which actually provides the money; the SBA guarantees to repay 85 to 90 percent of the loan if you fail to do so. The average SBA-backed loan is about $100,000; the upper limit is $750,000. Guaranteed loans provided by the SBA launched FedEx, Intel, and Apple Computer. These three now pay more annual taxes to the federal government than the entire yearly cost of running the SBA.[41] In addition to operating its loan guarantee program, the SBA provides a limited number of direct loans to minorities, women, and veterans.[42]

From the businessperson's standpoint, SBA-backed loans are especially attractive because they generally have longer repayment terms than conventional bank loans—9 years as opposed to 2 or 3. A longer repayment term translates into lower monthly payments. Unfortunately, demand for SBA loans vastly outstrips the agency's supply of capital.

Aspiring entrepreneurs like Karla Brown, who might not qualify for regular bank loans, can apply for SBA microloans to make their dreams come true.

Consequently, getting an SBA loan is difficult. In a typical year, only about 17,000 businesses are lucky enough to qualify.[43]

Karla Brown is one of the lucky ones. With plenty of perseverance and a $19,000 microloan from the SBA, Brown started her business, Ashmont Flowers Plus. The SBA microloan program was begun in 1992 to help people realize the American dream—to own a business and be self-sufficient. Microloans range from $100 to $25,000 with the average loan of $10,000 paid back over 4 years. So far, 42 percent of microloans have been granted to women and 39 percent to minorities.[44]

Mentors and Incubators Another excellent government resource for small business is the **Service Corps of Retired Executives (SCORE),** a resource partner of the SBA. SCORE volunteers are working and retired executives and small-business owners who offer advice and one-to-one counseling sessions on topics such as developing a business plan, securing financing, and managing business growth. To date, more than 3.5 million clients like New York Bagel have been served by SCORE counselors.[45]

Service Corps of Retired Executives (SCORE)
SBA program in which retired executives volunteer as consultants to assist small businesses

Whether you use a SCORE counselor or find a private mentor, having someone to bounce an idea off of or help you create a five-year financial forecast can increase the chances of your business surviving. That's because mentors know the hazards of business and can help you avoid them.[46]

Many state and local economic development offices and universities are forming *incubator* facilities to nurture fledgling businesses. **Incubators** are centers that provide "newborn" businesses with low-cost offices and basic business services. Create-A-Saurus, based in Oakland, California, produces a line of playground equipment assembled from recycled and reconditioned tires. The company got its start in the Oakland Small Business Growth Center, one of the 550 business incubators in the United States and Canada. In a typical incubator, new companies can lease space at bargain rates and share secretaries, recep-

incubators
Facilities that house small businesses during their early growth phase

tionists, telephone equipment, financial and accounting advice, marketing support, and credit-checking services.

Recent studies show that incubator companies are much more likely to grow into viable job-creating businesses than firms without such support. In fact, these studies show that 8 out of 10 businesses nurtured in incubators succeed.[47] Some incubators are open to businesses of all types, and many specialize. For example, the Spokane Business Incubation Center operates the Kitchen Center, where small food-processing companies can share a commercial kitchen.[48]

Planning and Managing a Small Business

You can find plenty of successful entrepreneurs who claim to have done very little formal planning, but even the most intuitive of them have *some* idea of what they're trying to accomplish and how they hope to do it. Before you rush in to supply a product, you need to be sure that a market exists. No amount of hard work can make a bad idea into a profitable one: The health-food store in a meat-and-potatoes neighborhood and the child-care center in a retirement community are probably doomed from the beginning.

You must also try to foresee some of the problems that might arise and figure out how to cope with them. What will you do if one of your suppliers suddenly goes out of business? Can you locate another supplier quickly? What if the neighborhood suddenly starts to change—even for the better? An influx of wealthier neighbors may cause such a steep increase in rent that your business must move. Also, tough competition may move into the neighborhood along with the fatter pocketbooks. Do you have an alternative location staked out? What if fashions suddenly change? Can you switch quickly from, say, hand-painted T-shirts to some other kind of shirt?

Preparing a Business Plan

One of the first steps you should take toward starting a new business is to develop a **business plan,** a written document that communicates a company's goals and how it intends to achieve goals. Preparing a business plan will help you decide how to turn your idea into reality, and if you need outside financing, the plan will also help you persuade lenders and investors to back your business. In fact, without a business plan many investors won't even grant you an interview.

business plan
A written document that provides an orderly statement of a company's goals and how it intends to achieve those goals

If you are starting out on a small scale and using your own money, your business plan may be relatively informal. But at a minimum, you should describe the basic concept of the business and outline specific goals, objectives, and resource requirements. Although the business plan has a simple, straightforward purpose, it still requires a great deal of thought. For example, before you even open your doors, you have to make important decisions about personnel, marketing, facilities, suppliers, and distribution. And a written business plan forces you to think about these issues and develop programs that will help you succeed.

A formal plan, suitable for use with banks or investors, should cover the following points (keep in mind that your audience wants short, concise information, not lengthy volumes):[49]

- *Summary.* In one or two pages, describe your product or service and its market potential. Describe your company and its principles, highlighting those things that will distinguish your firm from the competitors. Summarize your financial projections and the amount of money investors can expect to make on their investment. Also indicate how much money you will need and for what purpose.

- *Company and industry.* Give full background information on the origins and structure of your venture and the characteristics of its industry.
- *Products or services.* Give a complete but concise description, focusing on the unique attributes of your products or services. Tell how customers will benefit from using your products or services instead of those of your competitors.
- *Market.* Provide data that will persuade the investor that you understand your market and can achieve your sales goals. Be sure to identify the strengths and weaknesses of your competition.
- *Management.* Summarize the background and qualifications of the principals, directors, and key management personnel in your company. Include résumés in the appendix.
- *Marketing strategy.* Provide projections of sales and market share, and outline a strategy for identifying and contacting customers, setting prices, servicing customers, advertising, and so forth. Whenever possible, include evidence of customer acceptance, such as advance product orders.
- *Design and development plans.* If your product requires design or development, describe the nature and extent of what needs to be done, including costs and possible problems.
- *Operations plan.* Provide information on the facilities, equipment, and labor needed.
- *Overall schedule.* Show development of the company in terms of completion dates for major aspects of the business plan.
- *Critical risks and problems.* Identify all negative factors and discuss them honestly.
- *Financial information.* Include a detailed budget of start-up and operating costs, as well as projections for income, expenses, and cash flow for the first three years of business.
- *Exit strategy.* Explain how investors will be able to cash out or sell their investment, such as through a public stock offering, sale of the company, or a buyback of the investors' interest.

What distinguishes a winning business plan from others? According to the MIT Enterprise Forum, a national clinic providing assistance to emerging growth companies, a winning plan must explain what the company expects to accomplish in three to seven years in the future, show how the user will benefit from the company's products or services, present hard evidence of the demand for the company's products or services, portray the partners as a team of experienced managers with complementary business skills, and show how investors can earn (relatively quickly) a substantial profit. In addition to the above, a winning business plan must present both the company's strengths and anticipated weaknesses. Finally, it must be realistic in its projections for growth.[50]

Expanding a Business

Growing from an entrepreneurial business into a professionally managed company is not an easy task. Many small businesses experience a similar pattern: An entrepreneur has a good idea, turns it into a successful company, and expands it—perhaps to many locations. For some, this pattern is appealing. For others, it can mean losing what you like most about being small—the ability to work closely with your employees in a hands-on environment.

Although some entrepreneurs are good at launching companies, sometimes they lack the skills needed to manage them over the long term. The person who excels during the start-up phase may not be able to delegate work well or may have problems figuring out how to expand the business. Even if the person is flexible enough to adjust to changing conditions, there is a lot to learn as a company grows. Arranging additional financing, hiring new people, adding new products, computerizing the record keeping—all these activities are demanding. And nothing can kill a successful business faster than expanding too soon or sometimes not expanding fast enough.

Managing Growth and Product Demand One of the most difficult problems you may face as the owner of a new business is success. Some companies are so successful in marketing their products or services that they are not able to satisfy customer demand. Take Grandmother Calendar. When Harvey Harris started selling elaborate cut-rate personalized calendars, he anticipated strong demand, but Harris never dreamed that this demand would someday cause his demise. Using photos and personal memorabilia sent in by customers, the company scanned them into a computer and created personalized photo calendars. When orders came in much faster than the company could fill them, Harris rushed production and quality suffered. Still, he kept on marketing the product nationally. Eventually the backlog caught up with him, so he notified his customers that their orders would not be filled on time—for Christmas presents that is. As a result, customers canceled their orders and took their business elsewhere, and Harris closed up shop. Grandmother Calendar was just a small company trying to satisfy a nation of calendar buyers.[51]

Franchising Your Business to Others One way companies expand their business is by franchising their concept to others. Why consider franchising? Aside from allowing you to grow more quickly than you could otherwise, franchisees often represent a ready source of capital. In addition, although it's difficult to find motivated managers and employees to run company-owned stores, franchisees are often more motivated because they are owners themselves. According to the president of the International Franchise Association, franchising has triple benefits: "The franchisor wins because he builds a strong foundation for his company. The franchisee wins because he can take advantage of the franchisor's proven business system. And the general public benefits from the consistency of the product or service."[52]

But building a franchise organization requires different skills. Franchising is like starting an additional business. If you're in the dry-cleaning business and you start franchising, you're no longer a dry cleaner—you're a franchisor. And your customers are no longer

Is It True?

One dollar out of every three spent for U.S. goods and services is spent in a franchised business.

Grow Your Business

BEST OF THE WEB

Thinking about starting your own small business? The U.S. government has an office you might want to visit. The Small Business Administration (SBA) online puts you in touch with a host of government agencies willing to assist you in your start-up. Perhaps you would like some professional business counseling, financial assistance, or advice on expanding your business overseas. Even if you go global, you'll still need to learn about the rules and regulations of the workplace. After all, as a small-business owner you're responsible for the well-being of your employees. Understanding what constitutes racial, ethnic, and sexual harassment is often the first step in prevention. So log on to the SBA, click on *Legislation,* and check out the *EEOC.* You might also want to learn about some *Substantive Issues of Concern to Small Businesses.*
http:/www.sbaonline.sba.gov

UNDERSTANDING THE HIGH-TECH REVOLUTION

Creating a Winning Web Site

Which is a more effective way of enticing consumers to buy your custom-designed area rugs: a mailer describing your product with a photo of your latest creations, or a virtual store that allows consumers to browse your creations and click on the ones they want to see in detail? Many small businesses today are going virtual and creating Web sites on the Internet to display their products. Some are very creative. Others are quite informative. So if you're considering the possibility of creating a winning Web site for your company—whether you build it yourself or hire a consultant to design it for you—here are a few tips for you to consider.

PRESENT A PROFESSIONAL CORPORATE IMAGE

One of the best ways of deciding what to include in your company Web site is to visit your competitors' sites. See what they are up to. How do they present their company image? What types of information do they include? What's missing? How easy is it to navigate around the site?

Be sure to provide a corporate profile that tells people a little bit about your company. Include news releases or articles about your business so that customers can see how well known or dynamic you are in the industry. Make sure your material is accurate. Remember, successful sites provide information that is both interesting and related to your products. So make sure you identify the key benefits of your product. Include product details on a second page.

MAKE YOUR WEB SITE EASY TO USE

Sites that take forever to load are a major source of user irritation. Keep large graphics to a minimum. Long-winded sites will be quickly passed over as users sit, fidget, and finally give up waiting for long file transfers to complete. If you're planning to include any large, embedded graphics or photos, provide an option for users to select a text-only interface, or provide small images of photos (called thumbnails) for users to select if they want to view a larger, more detailed photo. Always provide hot links at the bottom of each page to allow users to navigate your Web site by moving backward and forward through a multipage site.

ANTICIPATE YOUR CUSTOMERS' QUESTIONS

Plan ahead. Provide enough customer information by asking your sales or service personnel to generate a list of

the people who come in the door with dirty clothes, but the franchisees who have invested their life savings in your concept. How can you determine whether your business concept is franchisable? Experts agree that it must have the following characteristics: The business works anywhere, and it's teachable, profitable, affordable, and marketable.[53]

Expanding Globally Larry Flax and Rick Rosenfield didn't want to open just another pizza shop. When the two defense attorneys exchanged their legal pads for pizza cutters in 1985, their goal was to give a new spin to the traditional pizza and then serve it quickly in a pleasant dining room. Twelve years later, their California Pizza Kitchen (CPK) chain is now in 80 U.S. cities, and the partners are planning to take their restaurants overseas.[54]

But Flax and Rosenfield know that taking your products overseas requires careful planning. For example, you must understand the culture, customer preferences, regulations, and commercial laws of the countries where you plan to do business. Consequently, venturing abroad can be a wrenching experience—especially if you're a small company. That's because a big firm can acquire the expertise and assistance it needs to go global by hiring

frequently asked questions. Then include this list of questions and answers on your Web site. Chances are you'll cover about 90 percent of your customers' concerns. Be sure to provide an active customer feedback mechanism. Incorporating e-mail into your site is one way to accomplish this. Another way is to provide open feedback forms, structured survey forms, or even a simple telephone or fax number. Remember, users tend to provide both frank and useful input, but only if you ask them for it.

Promote Your Web Site

Be sure to list with numerous Web search engines—giant indexes where Web users go to find information by entering key words. Most of these listings are free. Maximize the number of times your site will be listed by jamming in as many words as you can that best describe your site. And don't forget about the more traditional approach. Take out an ad in the newspaper or submit a press release announcing your site and listing the site's address, or URL (uniform resource locator). Join newsgroups, and list your company in the Internet yellow pages. And remember, don't just sit back and expect the Web site to perform magic. Use it to find out as much as possible about your customers. Keep asking yourself how your company can benefit from all this information.

Questions for Critical Thinking

1. When building a Web site, what information should you include about your company?
2. List some of the ways companies can benefit from having a Web site on the Internet.

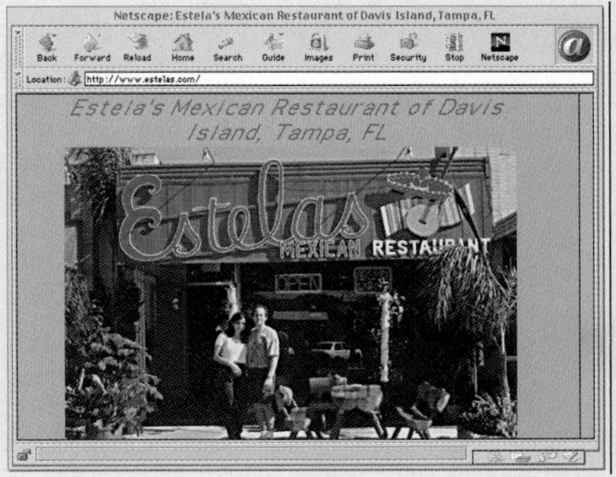

the best experts available. In fact, if a big firm spots an opportunity anywhere in the world, it has the means to explore it and, if it chooses, develop it.[55] But smaller companies don't have the deep pockets to staff specialists on everything from international law to cultural differences like the giants do. And without experienced lawyers, small businesspeople can easily run into trouble with labor or copyright laws. Plus without researchers or advisers, they can miss out on the subtleties of foreign cultures, such as the fact that in countries like Japan consumers rely more heavily on direct mail instead of newspaper advertising.

One way to overcome these obstacles is by using an *export management company,* a domestic firm specializing in performing international marketing services on a commission basis, or an *export trading company,* a general trading firm that will buy your products for resale overseas as well as perform a variety of importing, exporting, and manufacturing functions. Still another alternative is to use a foreign distributor. Valuable services and expertise offered by these parties include knowledge of the foreign market, connections, and understanding what product modifications might be necessary for success in that market.[56]

Today economic expansion is available to large and small players alike. The affordability of advanced telecommunications is quickly linking the entire world electronically and empowering individuals and small firms as never before. By using the Internet, small and microsized firms can conduct business from any location, at any time, and all over the globe.

Doing Business on the Internet

Scores of big and small companies are setting up shop on the Internet by creating a Web site, or home page. It's estimated that over 13 percent of small businesses have a home page, and this number is expected to increase to 30 percent in the near future.[57] Many businesses today are using Web sites to seek assistance and find resources, market and distribute their products, and communicate with their customers. Of course, because no one knows how big you are when you're on the Internet, small companies can compete on a par with larger ones.

Using the Internet as a Resource Sometimes the key to unlocking valuable advice, business leads, or other small business assistance is right at your fingertips. Sonja Edmond, owner of Heavenly Bounty Giftbaskets, a hand-crafted gift-basket business, had to look no farther than her keyboard when she needed help. Although she enjoyed making gift baskets as a hobby, she wasn't sure there was a viable market to support a home-based business. So she posted a price-setting question on CompuServe's Working from Home and Handcrafts forum. Within 24 hours, her e-mail box was flooded with answers from subscribers, who "convinced me I could do this," she says. Edmond struck a mentoring gold mine: Not only did she find the encouragement she needed to plunge into entrepreneurship, she also got valuable business leads and advice on licensing her product.[58]

Using the Internet to Market Your Products The Dallas Art Museum uses the Internet to gain members and advertise its exhibits and events. Winn Dixie supermarkets in Atlanta allows customers to order their groceries online. And Faucet Outlet has increased its business by establishing an Internet site to display its merchandise to potential customers. "It costs just pennies for me to get leads on the Internet," notes Dan Sullivan, the owner, "and I can show so much more with an Internet catalog than a paper catalog."[59]

Marketing your products and services on the Internet can take many forms. Some of the most popular ways include listing product announcements, pricing information, electronic catalogs, electronic publications, company contacts, and company events. In addition, companies can provide product demonstrations, free samples, customer support, documentation and manuals, customer surveys, service evaluations, employee recruitment, and even dialogue with customers. Keep in mind, however, that establishing a Web site does not necessarily increase your sales. Although customers may stop by and visit, they'll buy only if you offer something of value.

Summary of Learning Objectives

1. **Differentiate between lifestyle businesses and high-growth ventures.**
   Most small businesses are lifestyle businesses, intended to provide the owner with a comfortable living. High-growth ventures, on the other hand, are businesses with ambitious sales, profit, and growth objectives.

2. **Identify three characteristics (other than size) that differentiate small companies from larger ones.**
   They tend to be more innovative, have limited resources, and their owners perform a variety of job functions.

3. **List four important functions of small businesses in the economy.**
   Small businesses provide jobs, introduce new goods and services, supply the needs of large corporations, and provide specialized goods and services.
4. **Identify three factors contributing to the increase in the number of small businesses.**
   The affordability and advancement of technology, an increase in the number of minority entrepreneurs entering the work force, and corporate downsizing and outsourcing are three factors contributing to the growth in the number of small businesses today.
5. **Enumerate three ways of getting into business for yourself.**
   You can start a new company from scratch, buy a going concern, or invest in a franchise.
6. **Outline the pros and cons of owning a franchise.**
   A franchisee has the advantages of wide name recognition, mass advertising, financial help, training, and support, but owning a franchise involves considerable start-up expense, monthly royalty payments to the franchisor, and constraints on the franchisee's independence.
7. **Name 12 topics that should be covered in a formal business plan.**
   A formal business plan should (1) summarize your business concept, (2) describe the company and its industry, (3) explain the product, (4) analyze the market, (5) summarize the background and qualifications of management, (6) describe your marketing strategy, (7) discuss design and development plans, (8) explain your operations plan, (9) provide an overall schedule, (10) identify risks and potential problems, (11) provide detailed financial information, and (12) explain how investors will cash out on their investment.
8. **Explain how small businesses can benefit from using the Internet.**
   Small companies can market and distribute their products globally, seek assistance and find resources to help them do a better job, establish two-way communication with customers, and test to see whether a market exists for their product or service.

On the Job: Meeting Business Challenges at Top of the Tree Baking Company

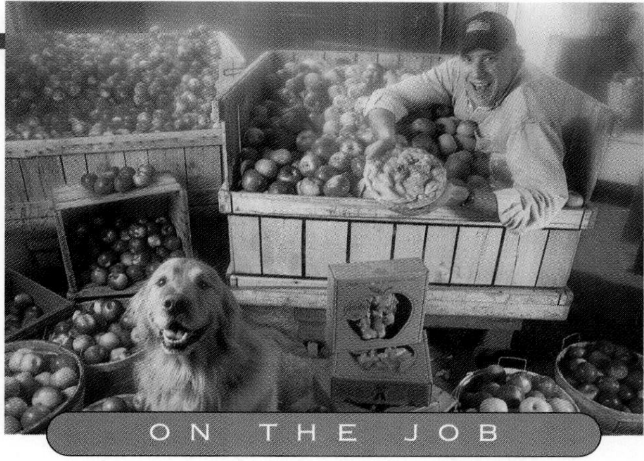

Gordon Weinberger knew he had his work cut out for him. After all, the pie industry was very competitive indeed. Behemoths like Mrs. Smith's and Entenmann's dominated the price-sensitive end of the spectrum, and anyone who wanted something akin to what grandma used to make headed for the bakery department.

In his informal research of the bakery pies, Weinberger learned two things: First, appearances aside, pies were rarely baked on premises. Second, in his view, they didn't taste half as good as his pies. Taking a cue from Ben & Jerry's Homemade ice cream, Weinberger believed there was room in the market for a relatively expensive, fresh apple pie. And apparently, some people agreed—including Jerry Weissman, a businessman and friend of the family.

Weissman took Weinberger's business plan to a few friends who were enthralled. The plan had short-term goals, long-term goals, and a ladder-type path to reach those goals. And Weissman liked something else, something far less tangible than Weinberger's well-thought-out plan. Weissman sensed that Weinberger had the character and commitment to carry out the plan—and he was right.

Weinberger's entrepreneurial pie odyssey began at a 1992 Old Home Day fair in Londonderry, New Hampshire, where he won the apple pie baking contest with his great-grandmother Anne's family pie recipe. After twice repeating his victory, he began to think he might have a recipe for success, not to mention a way to leave his job running the public relations division for a Boston advertising agency.

To develop interest in his pies, Weinberger approached individual branches of supermarkets, Shop & Save in New Hampshire and Star Marketing in Boston, conducting in-store tastings and parking lot pie-eating contests. For meetings with supermarket buyers, Weinberger spread checkered tablecloths on the executives' desks, played a tape-recorded jingle, and served up warm pie and cold milk.

During their first summer, a period when pie sales notoriously are in the doldrums, Weinberger and company hitched an 11-foot-tall fiberglass apple to the back of their truck for a tour through Boston and four other New England cities. Once they arrived, they threw open the doors and began handing out thousands of free pies and pints of frozen yogurt. It was a public relations coup, earning Weinberger spots on the evening news and attention in local newspapers.

By the end of 1995, his first year in business, Top of the Tree was churning out 3-pound pies at the rate of 6,000 a week and had racked up about $1 million in sales. The figures were almost exactly what Weinberger projected in his business plan, even though the route wasn't exactly as he had envisioned. That's because his sales got an unexpected boost from a stint selling his pies on the QVC home shopping network. During the original segment, which has since turned into a monthly event, he sold 2,700 pies in less than 2 minutes!

To raise funds for branching out and automating his pie works, Weinberger undertook some unusual methods to market his pies. For example, to increase awareness and get people excited about his pies, Weinberger and his pie staff toured the United States in a refurbished school bus, serving up apple pie to would-be consumers. Not only was it an effective marketing tool, but the bus became a mobile fund-raiser. In the "Find the Dough Campaign," headed by pie specialist Scott Mayo, the bus was used to seek out more capital. By using valet parking outside swank restaurants and hotels, the pie staff had ready access to potential investors.

One recent weekend the pie staff embarked on a tour of Boston, where they picked people up, fed them pie, and dropped them off at their destinations—just like Mass Transit, only with dessert. Afterward they parked outside of the Ritz Carlton, where Weinberger and his pie staff provided information on Top of the Tree. "It's incredible," says Weinberger. "We are touching people in ways that they never envisioned."

To date, Weinberger has secured $1 million in additional capital with his unusual marketing tactics, and he's intent on raising more money without giving up a significant amount of control of the company. "I don't want to give up half the company for $2 million," says Weinberger. The perfect investors, according to Weinberger, would have a lot of money in their wallet but be willing to step back and let him run the company.

From its fledgling roots, Top of the Tree has blossomed, almost tripling its sales during its second year of operation. There is no doubt that Weinberger's dynamic marketing strategies will see him through to his goal: to become a $20 million company within the next 3 or 4 years.

Your Mission: You are a new recruit on Weinberger's management team. In addition to learning the pie business from the ground up, you will handle special projects for Weinberger. And you'll have to wear many different hats—a characteristic of small-business managers. Here's your first set of projects:

1. Weinberger needs money—about $1 million—to expand the company's baking facility. Which of the following courses of action sounds like the best alternative?
   a. Revise the business plan and go to the banks. Even though the company has only been in business for a few years, Weinberger knows his pies.
   b. Get out the bus and find the dough. These unusual fund-raising methods worked well in the past. And call the relatives. See if they want to double their investments.
   c. Seek assistance from the SBA. The repayment terms are generally more attractive, and Top of the Tree Baking would certainly meet its qualifications.
2. Weinberger is working 80 hours a week. "It's time to add another manager," he says. Weinberger has narrowed it down to three candidates. Which one do you think would be the best for Top of the Tree Baking for the long term?
   a. Candidate A—An MBA from one of the top business schools. Ten years work experience as the director of marketing for Entenmann's (a national baked-goods provider). Knows the industry quite well. Has good business connections.
   b. Candidate B—A self-starter. Ran a small marketing business for ten years. Very creative. He's even got some better ideas than Weinberger. One of his clients was a large supermarket chain. He knows the challenges of getting new products into the store.
   c. Candidate C—A number-cruncher. Bright CPA. Great with computers. Worked for a large accounting practice for ten years. Handled both large and small company clients. Some were start-ups. Has no industry experience, but is willing to learn.
3. Unusually bad weather in the Northeast will affect this year's apple harvest. It's expected that the price per pound will double. Weinberger seeks your advice. Which alternative will you recommend?
   a. Purchase as much of last year's bumper crop as you can. Bake the pies in advance and freeze them. Mrs. Smith's (a leading competitor) does this all the time.
   b. Raise the price of this year's pies to cover any increased costs. Customers will understand.
   c. Keep the price the same and eat the price difference. It's only for one year. This way the company won't risk losing any customers. In fact, we'll get many more.
4. Weinberger is looking for the best way to grow the business. He has several options. Which one will you recommend?
   a. Franchise Top of the Tree Baking to other businesses. They'll get the recipes, special equipment, marketing, and Weinberger's experience—not to mention the Top of the Tree Baking name.
   b. Outback Steakhouse (a national restaurant chain) is looking for an exclusive pie supplier. Current figures show that the restaurants use about 150,000 pies annually.
   c. Fruit of the Month Club is interested in expanding its successful business to include fruit pies. They are also looking for an exclusive pie supplier. They project that pie orders will range from 15,000 to 25,000 a month, depending on the time of the year.[60]

Key Terms

business plan (147)
franchise (140)
franchisee (140)
franchisor (140)
high-growth ventures (132)
incubators (146)
lifestyle businesses (132)
outsourcing (136)
Service Corps of Retired Executives (SCORE) (146)
small business (132)
start-up companies (138)

Questions

For Review

1. What qualities usually characterize the people who run successful small businesses?
2. What are some of the most common reasons for starting a business of your own?
3. What is a business incubator?
4. What distinguishes a winning business plan from others?
5. What are the advantages and disadvantages of franchising your business to others?

For Analysis

6. How is technology leveling the playing field between small and big companies?
7. How is the pendulum swinging in favor of the franchisee today and why?
8. What are some of the things you should learn about a franchisor before signing a franchise agreement?
9. What are SCORE volunteers, and how do they assist small businesses?
10. Why is writing a business plan an important step in starting a new business?

For Application

11. Why is franchising becoming increasingly popular today? Discuss this issue from the perspective of both the franchisor and franchisee.
12. Why is it more difficult for small businesses to sell their products in the global market? What steps can they take to minimize their risk?

A Case for Critical Thinking ■ Growing Pains

It used to be that if you ran a small business, you ran your life, controlled your destiny, and in the process made a good living. Even though running a small business in earlier times was hard, it was not necessarily complex. But that's not the case anymore. Look at Kiva Container.

Run by the Stafford family for three generations, Kiva makes corrugated paper boxes and corrugated plastic containers for local and regional manufacturers of consumer goods. Ruth Stafford, her husband Ron, and their son Tom run the company now. Most of the time they work ten-hour days at the office. Then they take their work home at night. Here's why.

COMPETITION IS TOUGHER

Competition is chipping away at Kiva's $10 million annual sales. For instance, there used to be a clear separation of markets between the big suppliers and the smaller ones—the big guys would ship by the trailer load to the large national and international accounts, and the smaller ones like Kiva would concentrate on local or regional markets. But now the billion-dollar multinational companies like Stone Container and Packaging Corporation of America are flooding local markets. They're shipping smaller orders—500 pieces at a time. And some regional manufacturers are willing to sell the boxes at cost during bad seasons—just to keep their plants running. Meanwhile the number of small packaging companies competing in Kiva's market has tripled in the past decade.

CUSTOMERS ARE MORE DEMANDING

Five years ago Kiva made four basic products and variations thereof. But customers today want more. So Kiva expanded its product line by 1,000 percent, enticing efficiency-minded customers with the promise of one-stop, one-invoice shopping. In addition, the company began producing more customized products—like custom corrugated plastic containers that can last 40 times longer than corrugated cardboard plastic containers. Kiva even invested $50,000 in a CAD/CAM computer system to generate new container designs quickly. However, the Staffords soon learned that sophisticated computer technology creates additional customer expectations. Moreover, product innovation requires a lot of preliminary design and development work with no guarantee that it will yield a contract. In one year Kiva spent $50,000 on product proposals that resulted in zero sales.

CUSTOMERS ARE EXPENSIVE

Not only do Kiva's customers want more but their requests are expensive. They want ever-improving quality, increasing innovation, better pricing, and just-in-time delivery—forcing Kiva to warehouse more product. The company used to send out one full delivery truck a week. Now it sends out one truck a day, often carrying only a few orders. In addition, larger customers now insist that Kiva manufacture according to ISO 9000 (the highest quality) standards—which for a box maker is overkill. The manual for the purchasing agent alone is two inches thick. Kiva's manufacturing costs have skyrocketed.

CUSTOMERS AREN'T LOYAL

Customer loyalty is disintegrating. In fact, sometimes customers come in, look at Kiva's ideas, and go elsewhere to have them executed. Kiva used to feel comfortable with the smaller accounts, but now they jump around a lot. Four years ago Kiva's largest customer (representing 15 percent of the company's business) suddenly canceled the last year of a three-year contract. Kiva lost $2.5 million in business overnight. Then a major customer falsified financial information, declared bankruptcy, and left Kiva with $180,000 in unpaid bills.

RED TAPE IS EVERYWHERE

You can barely move in Kiva's plant without running into something touched by the government. The Occupational Safety and Health Administration inspects the equipment, the Department of Commerce reviews shipping records, the Environmental Protection Agency regulates chemicals, and the Department of Transportation oversees the labels on packaging. When Kiva removed two underground fuel storage tanks, one tank was discovered to be leaking. The site was declared hazardous by the Environmental Protection Agency. All the contaminated soil had to be removed. Three sets of government lawyers got involved in the case, and each time Kiva found an attorney astute enough in environmental law, he quit. By the time the dirt was disposed of, it had cost the company over $100,000.

COSTS ARE RISING

Legal fees aren't the only rising costs. Attending trade shows has become an important source for new business. But a large regional show can cost Kiva $25,000 to $30,000, and the number of shows has increased exponentially—all to meet the market's expectations. Moreover, health-care costs are up 150 percent, state sales tax has doubled in the past 14 years, and property taxes have quadrupled in 10 years.

FAMILY TIES ARE UNRAVELING

Tom Stafford has reviewed the statistics for family-run businesses. The chances of a family-run company being passed intact from the first generation to the next are fewer than one in three. In an average week the phone rings twice at Kiva with someone inquiring whether the business is for sale. In spite of Kiva's problems, the company still operates profitably. In fact Ruth and Ron Stafford could sell the company tomorrow, but then there would be nothing to pass on to their son Tom or to his 6-year-old son Chad. On the other hand, they worry that if things don't improve, they might not have much of a company left to pass on anyway.

1. What steps could Kiva take to help control its skyrocketing costs?
2. How might Kiva benefit from preparing a business plan?
3. Is it wise to keep this business "all in the family"? What factors should the Staffords consider before deciding whether or not to sell the business?
4. Visit the Family Business Net Center at <http://www.nmq.com/> to help Tom find some data on the challenges of passing family businesses to successive generations. Type in the word *succession* in the designated Internet Search Field, hit *enter*, then scroll down (just past the halfway point of the page) to the *Arthur Andersen/Mass Mutual American Family Business Survey '97*. Answer the following:
   a. How many family businesses have written strategic plans for succession?
   b. Of CEOs age 56 to 60 and expecting to retire within 5 years, what percentage have yet to name a successor?

Before leaving be sure to check out Kiva's Web site <http://www.kiva-intl.com/>.

Building Your Business Skills

As directed by your instructor, select a local franchise operation that interests you. Call or write the manager of the franchise requesting a short telephone interview. Using the information discussed in this chapter, prepare a list of about ten questions that will help you gain a better understanding of franchise operations. For example, some of the questions you might want to ask are:

- Is the franchise required to pay royalty fees? How are these fees calculated?
- What types of support does the franchisor offer?
- Is the franchise required to buy all its products from the franchisor?
- How was the location for this franchise selected?

Learn as much as you can by preparing your questions in advance. Following the interview, review and edit your notes. Be prepared to give a short oral report of your findings to your class.

Keeping Current Using *The Wall Street Journal*

Scan issues of *The Wall Street Journal* for articles describing problems or successes faced by small businesses in the United States. Clip or copy three or more articles that interest you and then answer the following questions.

1. What problem or opportunity does each article present? Is it an issue that faces many businesses, or is it specific to one industry or region?
2. What could a potential small-business owner learn about the risks and rewards of business ownership from reading these articles?
3. Have you ever considered starting a business? What impact did these articles have on your interest? Why?
4. Before starting your business, you'll need to prepare a business plan. Visit the Small Business Exchange <http://www.americanexpress.com/smallbusiness/> and click on the link to *Business Planning and Resources.* Click on *Starting Your Business* and then scroll down and click on *Create an Effective Business Plan.* Be sure to *Try It Yourself* for some actual practice on someone else's business. Browse the site. What other information does this site contain that is helpful to small-business owners?

Exploring the Best of the Web

Increase Your Chances for Success, page 137

Many Web sites publish answers to their most frequently asked questions (FAQs). Check out the *Biz FAQs* under the *Contents* section of the Small Business Adviser <http://www.isquare.com> to find the answers to these questions.

1. If you are a sole proprietor without employees, do you need to get a Employer Identification Number from the IRS?
2. What is a DBA?
3. What is the minimum hourly wage for your state? Name three states that do not have a minimum wage law.

Get Smart, page 145

Buying a franchise in somebody else's business is sometimes easier than starting from scratch, provided of course, that you understand what you're getting into. Use this Web site to help in your investigation. Go to Smartbiz <http://www.smartbiz.com>, click on the *Browse SBS* icon, highlight the category *franchising,* and click *Go To Selected Topics.*

1. Find the *Checklist for Evaluating Your Suitability as a Franchisee.* Explain why the following items appear on this checklist: (a) Are you prepared to give up some independence of action in exchange for the advantages the franchise offers you? (b) Is it possible for either you or your spouse to become employed in the type of business you seek to buy before any purchase?
2. Find the *Checklist of Information to Secure from a Franchisor.* Why is it important to know whether you will have the right of first refusal to adjacent areas?
3. Visit a related Web site, Fran Info, by entering the following URL: <http:\\www.franinfo.com>. Take the Self Test #1 to determine whether you are suited to become a franchise owner.

Grow Your Business, page 149

Selling your product overseas is one way to expand your business. But this requires careful planning. Follow this path to explore the potential of selling your products in India. Go to SBA online <http://www.sbaonline.sba.gov>, click on *Expanding,* click on *Outside Resources,* and find *India Market Place.* Begin your journey here.

1. Click on *All About India,* then scroll down to *Contents* and click on *The Consumer Market.* Check out the market potential for packaged goods. What is the estimated growth rate for expenditures on packaged goods in the *rural* market?
2. Go Back to *All About India—Contents.* Check out the *Infrastructure.* What is the best way to transport your products in India, by roads or by railway?
3. Go Back to *All About India—Contents.* Check out the *27 States—Diverse Opportunity.* What are the three most important parameters in choosing a marketing location in India? Where should you sell your products, Andhra Pradesh or Tamil Nadu? Explain. (*Hint:* Click on the state hot key to find your answer.)

Part II: Mastering the Geography of Business ■ Communicating with International Suppliers

With 95 percent of the world's population living outside the United States, more and more U.S. businesses today are purchasing and selling their products globally. Chances are, even if you own a small business in a strip mall, you're purchasing merchandise or supplies from somewhere else in the world.

Take a moment to think about just how international your own daily life is becoming. Look at your clothes, your car, the food you eat, the movies you see, the materials that built and decorated your home. How many of these items came, in whole or in part, from another country? As a new business owner, you will be communicating with many international businesses and customers. In preparation, visit several local small stores and learn how they do business in the global marketplace.

1. Look around the stores. How many products can you easily identify as coming from outside the United States?
2. Arrange to meet with the stores' owners or managers. Find out how they order these international products. Do they submit their orders by mail? telephone? fax machine? Internet? Find out whether these local stores sell any of their products overseas. How do their international customers purchase products from them? Do they have a Web site? Do they send out international mailings or catalogs?
3. Although it's easier today, doing business around the globe increases your need to understand world geography. Consider time differences, for example. Your U.S. business hours certainly won't coincide with the store hours of your suppliers in Europe or Asia. How will you adjust for these

differences? E-mail and faxes of course, are one way. But what if you really need to talk to the store manager? When should you place the call? Visit your local library or use resources such as the *World Almanac* to learn more about international time.

a. How many time zones are there in the United States (including possessions)?
b. If it's 12:00 noon in New York City, what time is it in Cape Town, South Africa? Copenhagen, Denmark? Sydney, Australia? Tokyo, Japan? Athens, Greece? Honolulu, Hawaii? Moscow, Russia?

4. As a new business owner, you will be communicating with people who speak many different languages. Visit the Online Dictionaries and Translators Web site at <http://rivendel.com/~ric/resources/dictionary.html>. Click on *Current Dictionary Languages.* How do you say "inventory" in Hawaiian? Portuguese? German? French? Norwegian?

Answers to "Is It True?"

Page 132. False. It's common knowledge that many large businesses will think twice before seriously considering a job candidate from a small business. Corporations and small businesses fundamentally differ in how they do business and in entrepreneurial spirit. In the highly political and hierarchical world of corporations, these differences are often viewed negatively.

Page 137. False. A study of 812,000 small, young companies indicates that well over half of these new businesses survived at least 8 years. In fact 33 percent survived more than 10 years.

Page 149. True.

■ PART III

Managing the Business

CHAPTER 6

MANAGEMENT FUNDAMENTALS

OBJECTIVES

After studying this chapter, you will be able to

1. Explain the role that goals and objectives play in management
2. Describe the three levels of management
3. Identify and explain the three types of managerial skills
4. Clarify how total quality management (TQM) is changing the way organizations are managed
5. Define the four management functions
6. Discuss how strategic, tactical, and operational plans are developed and used
7. Cite three leadership styles and explain why no one style is best
8. Describe six measures that companies can take to better manage crises

ON THE JOB: FACING BUSINESS CHALLENGES AT MICROSOFT

Struggling to Survive Success

Shrewd business deals and sheer luck propelled the pioneering software company into a leading role at the center of the ever-changing, hotly competitive computer industry. However, Microsoft's success brought its own management problems. Spectacular 50 percent annual growth left the company unwieldy and disorganized, even as software companies such as Lotus and Novell were taking aim at its market share. Computer technology continued to evolve at a rapid pace, consumers grew more demanding, and rival programmers worked around the clock to create new and better applications. For founder and chief executive officer Bill Gates, managing Microsoft required heroic effort.

Visionary leadership played a large role in Microsoft's wild success. When Gates dropped out of Harvard to found the company in 1975, personal computers were toys for the "hard-core technoid," as he once described himself. Nevertheless, Gates envisioned a computer in every home and in every office, with Microsoft software in every computer. He made an early alliance with computer giant IBM, putting Microsoft's basic operating program into 80 percent of the United States's 50 million personal computers. He also led Microsoft boldly into Europe and Asia. His energy and technical knowledge motivated Microsoft employees to continually improve the company's products and to develop new software offerings for the home and office.

As the company grew, however, good ideas were no longer enough. Gates found he was so busy that he could hardly handle day-to-day operational details, much less develop the vision he needed to stay ahead of the competition in the twenty-first century. Organization was lacking, and planning became increasingly difficult. Time after time, his company targeted a new market only to introduce a mediocre product the first time out. Gates personally took charge of five important product lines but then couldn't find the time to tailor them to customer needs. Projects died, and customers got angry.

Gates also worried about a threat to his leadership: He feared losing touch with his employees, the people who put his vision into action. In the relaxed atmosphere of Microsoft, talking shop with the CEO was an important morale booster as well as a way to introduce employees to company values. Gates relished personal contact with employees, but their number had grown into the thousands, and they were spread around the world.

Although Gates had always made the big decisions at Microsoft, more decisions were needed, and he was already working in excess of 65 hours a week. How could he plan for the long term and still manage daily affairs effectively? What could he do to reach the staff and spread his vision? How could he ensure Microsoft's success in the twenty-first century?[1]

THE SCOPE OF MANAGEMENT

management
Process of coordinating resources to meet organizational goals

quality
A measure of how closely a product conforms to predetermined standards and customer expectations

Microsoft's Bill Gates would be the first to admit that management is needed in every type of organization. An auto plant, a city government, a baseball team, an army, and a church committee all require management. Every organization has goals. **Management** entails planning, organizing, leading, and controlling resources (land, labor, capital, and information) to efficiently reach those goals.[2] The challenges of management include maintaining an organizational structure, developing both long- and short-term plans, motivating employees, and maintaining **quality**—a measure of how closely goods or services conform to predetermined standards and customer expectations. To meet these challenges, managers must possess certain skills that enable them to fulfill specific roles. As Gates has demonstrated, when managers possess the right combination of vision, skill, experience, and determination, they can lead an organization to success.

Managerial Goals

vision
A viable view of the future that is rooted in but improves on the present

mission statement
A statement of the organization's purpose

Why do organizations like Microsoft, Ford, and the United Way exist? Like most organizations, they were formed in order to realize a **vision,** a realistic, credible, and attractive view of the future that grows out of and improves upon the present.[3] Henry Ford envisioned making affordable transportation available to every person. Bill Gates envisioned making the computer a useful household and business tool. Without such visionary managers, who knows how the world would be different. In today's innovative and competitive business environment, companies that strive to envision and define the future often have an advantage over those that simply react to the present.

Of course, having a vision is no guarantee of success. In order to transform vision into reality, managers must define specific organizational goals and objectives. A starting point is to write a **mission statement** that defines why the organization exists and what it seeks to accomplish. A mission statement often focuses on the market and customers that the company serves. A statement may also describe the company's products and services

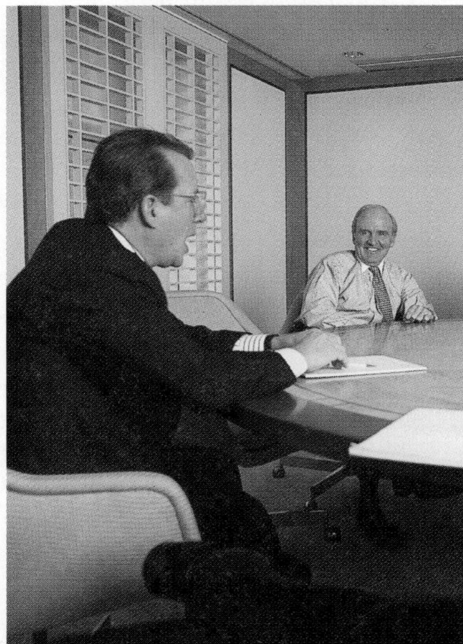

Jack Welch, Chairman and CEO of General Electric, (right) is known for being an excellent leader and manager. General Electric executives have commented that Welch's vision and energy continually motivate them to higher levels of performance.

as well as its values and culture (including ethics and social responsibility). Regardless, it should be both focused enough to be attainable and broad enough to allow the company to evolve. It should also inspire and guide management and employees alike. As the company grows, management can refer to the mission statement as a means of evaluating whether proposed actions are in line with the company's stated purpose and values. Consider Edge Learning Institute, an employee-training firm based in Tempe, Arizona. Edge executives were considering mass-marketing their training videos through television "infomercials." However, they realized that this was contrary to the company's mission of using "the human touch when providing individuals and organizations with information." So they decided instead to expand Edge's reach by developing a network of franchises that follow the company's training methods. Edge now has four successful franchises and eight more in the works.[4]

As managers at Edge Learning Institute know, a company's mission is realized by establishing goals and objectives. Although these terms are often used interchangeably, a **goal** is a broad, long-range target of the organization, and an **objective** is a specific, short-range target. For Edge, a goal might be to become the West Coast leader in employee training, and an objective might be to open ten franchises in its first year of expansion. The best organizational goals are specific, measurable, relevant, challenging, attainable, and time limited. Moreover, goals are often designed to give the company a competitive edge through at least one of three methods:

goal
Broad, long-range target or aim

objective
Specific, short-range target or aim

- *Differentiation.* A company using differentiation develops a level of service, a product image, unique product features (including quality), or new technologies that distinguish its product from competitors' products.
- *Cost leadership.* With cost leadership, the organization seeks to produce products more efficiently than competitors, thereby offering lower prices or increasing profits.
- *Focus.* When using a focus strategy, companies concentrate on a specific regional market or consumer group, such as the Southwest United States or economy car drivers. This type of strategy enables organizations to develop a better understanding of their customers and to tailor their products specifically to customer needs.[5]

Setting appropriate goals increases employee motivation, establishes standards for measuring individual and group performance, guides employee activity, and clarifies management's expectations.

Catch the Buzz!

BEST OF THE WEB

Buzzwords. You may already hear them often in your business classes, but they will come at you from all sides when you enter the business world. How can you stay on top of all of these management terms? You can look them up in the *Management and Technology Dictionary.* This online dictionary of management terms includes definitions of established terms and trendy buzzwords alike. The site classifies each word as either a management term or a technology term, and it also includes descriptions of leading-edge companies. In addition, unlike a standard dictionary, this online dictionary invites you to interact with the authors by sending your comments on a particular definition or on the site in general.
http://www.euro.net/innovation/Management_Base/Mantec.Dictionary.html

Managerial Structure

management pyramid
Organizational structure comprising top, middle, and lower management

top managers
Those at the highest level of the organization's management hierarchy; they are responsible for setting strategic goals, and they have the most power and responsibility in the organization

strategic goals
Goals that focus on broad organizational issues and aim to improve performance

In order to distinguish among the various types of goals that managers set, you must first understand how management is structured. In all but the smallest organizations, more than one manager is necessary to guide the organization's activities. That's why most companies form a **management pyramid** with top, middle, and bottom management levels. More managers are at the bottom level than at the top, as illustrated in Exhibit 6.1. However, in many of today's leaner companies, fewer levels separate managers at the top and bottom. Computer Associates is a software company with over 10,000 employees and a reputation for being a tough competitor. The company has just four management layers between the lowest-level employees and the top brass. To put this into perspective, even notoriously lean Toyota had seven layers of management until it recently reorganized.[6]

Top managers are the upper-level managers who have the most power and who take overall responsibility for the organization. An example is the chief executive officer (CEO). Top managers set **strategic goals,** which focus on broad issues, apply to the company as a whole, and aim to enhance the company's performance. These goals encompass eight ma-

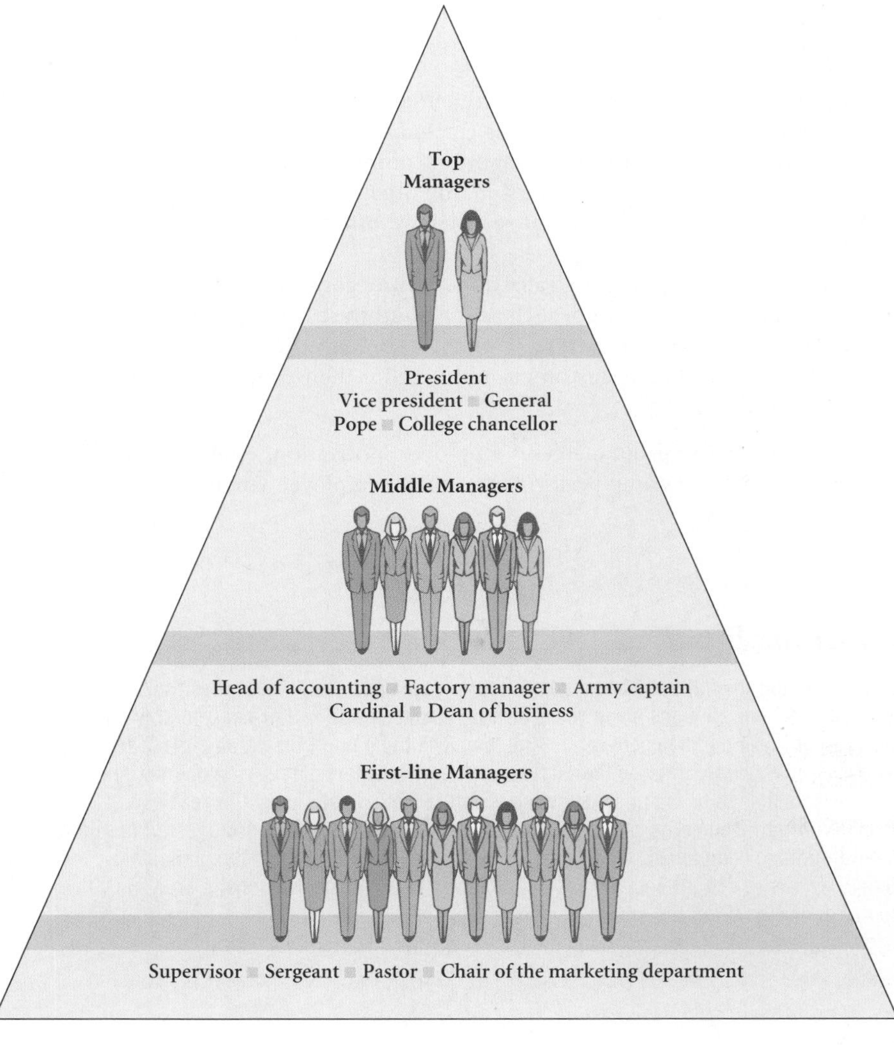

EXHIBIT 6.1

The Management Pyramid

Separate job titles are used to designate the three basic levels in the management pyramid.

jor areas of concern: market standing, innovation, human resources, financial resources, physical resources, productivity, social responsibility, and financial performance.[7] Top managers also make long-range plans, establish major policies, and represent the company to the outside world at official functions and fund-raisers.

Middle managers report to top-level managers. They develop plans for implementing the broad goals set by top managers, and they coordinate the work of first-line managers. To accomplish this, middle managers set **tactical objectives,** which focus on departmental issues and define the results necessary to achieve the organization's strategic goals. At the middle level are plant managers, division managers, branch managers, and other similar positions.

At the bottom of the management pyramid are **first-line managers** (or *supervisory managers*). These managers oversee the work of operating employees, and they put into action the plans developed at higher levels. First-line managers set **operational objectives,** which focus on short-term issues and define the results necessary to achieve both the tactical objectives and the strategic goals. Positions at this level include supervisor, department head, and office manager.[8]

middle managers
Those in the middle of the management hierarchy; they develop plans to implement the goals of top managers and coordinate the work of first-line managers

tactical objectives
Objectives that focus on departmental issues and describe the results necessary to achieve the organization's strategic goals

first-line managers
Those at the lowest level of the management hierarchy, who supervise the operating employees and implement the plans set at the higher management levels; also called supervisory managers

operational objectives
Objectives that focus on short-term issues and describe the results needed to achieve tactical objectives and strategic goals

roles
Behavioral patterns associated with certain positions

Managerial Roles

Managers perform a number of duties as they coordinate the organization's work. They also build a network of relationships with bosses, peers, and employees. These duties and relationships can be described as **roles,** or behavioral patterns, and they fall into three categories:

- *Interpersonal roles.* Managers perform ceremonial obligations, provide leadership to employees, and act as liaison to groups and individuals both inside and outside the company (such as suppliers, competitors, government agencies, consumers, special-interest groups, and interrelated work groups).
- *Informational roles.* Managers spend a fair amount of time gathering information by questioning people both inside and outside the organization. They also distribute information to employees, other managers, and outsiders.
- *Decisional roles.* Managers use the information they gather to encourage innovation, to resolve unexpected problems that threaten organizational goals (such as reacting to an economic crisis), and to decide how organizational resources will be used to meet planned objectives. They also negotiate with many individuals and groups, including suppliers, employees, and unions.[9]

Certain managerial roles may be emphasized more than others, depending on a manager's organizational level. However, being able to move easily between these roles is a skill that serves managers well throughout their career.

Is It True?

Top managers communicate often with their employees.

Managerial Skills

In addition to setting goals and assuming various roles, managers also employ skills that fall into three basic categories: *interpersonal, technical,* and *conceptual* skills. As managers rise through the hierarchy, they may need to strengthen their abilities in one or more of these skills; fortunately, managerial skills can usually be learned.[10]

Interpersonal Skills All the skills required to communicate with other people, work effectively with them, motivate them, and lead them are **interpersonal skills.** Because they mainly get things done through people, managers at all levels of the organization use interpersonal skills in countless situations. Encouraging employees to work together toward common goals, interacting with employees and other managers, negotiating with partners and suppliers, developing employee trust and loyalty, and fostering innovation—all these activities require interpersonal skills.

interpersonal skills
Skills required to understand other people and to interact effectively with them

TLC Beatrice CEO Loida Lewis is recognized by her staff as being an open and effective communicator.

Communication, or exchanging information, is the most important and pervasive interpersonal skill that managers use. Your ability to communicate increases your own productivity as well as the organization's. It shapes the impressions you make on your colleagues, employees, supervisors, investors, and customers. Communication allows you to perceive the needs of these stakeholders (your first step toward satisfying them), and it helps you respond to those needs.[11] All businesses are built on relationships, as Microsoft's early alliance with IBM illustrates, and all relationships flourish with good communication. Loida Lewis, CEO of global food company TLC Beatrice, is known for being a great communicator. Her ability to ask probing questions in a sensitive way and then listen intently to the answers has earned her the respect and dedication of her executive team.[12]

technical skills
Ability and knowledge to perform the mechanics of a particular job

administrative skills
Technical skills in information gathering, data analysis, planning, organizing, and other aspects of managerial work

Technical Skills A person who knows how to operate a machine, prepare a financial statement, program a computer, or pass a football has **technical skills**; that is, he or she has the knowledge and ability to perform the mechanics of a particular job. Technical skills are most important at lower organizational levels. First-line managers need particularly strong technical skills because they work directly with the tools and techniques of a particular specialty, such as automotive assembly or computer programming, and because they manage other technical employees. However, managers at all levels use **administrative skills,** which are the technical skills necessary to manage an organization. Administrative skills include the ability to make schedules, gather information, analyze data, plan, and organize. Managers often develop such skills through education and then improve them by working in one or more functional areas of an organization, such as accounting or marketing.[13]

conceptual skills
Ability to understand the relationship of parts to the whole

Conceptual Skills Managers need **conceptual skills** to see the organization as a whole, in the context of its environment, and to understand how the various parts interrelate. Conceptual skills are especially important to top managers. These managers are the strategists who develop the plans that guide the organization toward its goals. Managers like Microsoft's Bill Gates use their conceptual skills to acquire and analyze information, identify both problems and opportunities, understand the competitive environment in which their companies operate, develop strategies, and make decisions.

decision making
Process of identifying a decision situation, analyzing the problem, weighing the alternatives, choosing and implementing an alternative, and evaluating the results

DECISION MAKING A key managerial activity requiring conceptual skills is **decision making,** which has five distinct steps: recognizing the need for a decision, analyzing and defining the problem or opportunity, developing alternatives, selecting and implementing the chosen alternative, and evaluating the results. Managers monitor the results of decisions over time to see whether the chosen alternative works, whether any new problem or opportunity arises because of the decision, and whether a new decision must be made.[14]

There are two types of management decisions. *Programmed decisions* are routine, recurring decisions made according to a predetermined system of decision rules. In contrast, *nonprogrammed decisions* are unique and nonroutine. As a result, they generally cannot be made according to any set procedures or rules, although analogies, similar past experiences, or common sense may offer some guidance. Managers make both types of decisions based on varying amounts of information, which means their decisions have varying degrees of possible success or failure. Generally speaking, nonprogrammed decisions are riskier than programmed decisions because they carry a stronger element of the unknown. The less information a manager has, the larger the risk. However, great organizations like Microsoft are built by managers who aren't afraid to take calculated risks. After all, between the current situation and a vision of the future are a lot of unknown factors. Exhibit 6.2 illustrates the possible environments in which managers make decisions and the level of risk involved with each.

Trends Affecting Decision Making As companies change the way they are managed, they also change the way decisions are made. Today's flatter organizations use fewer middle managers. In addition, computerized information systems allow information to flow more freely between all levels of the organization. As a result, many of the decisions that middle managers would have made are either being made by top managers or being pushed down to lower organizational levels. At the same time, organizations are leaning toward empowering operating employees and teams with increasing discretion over work-related decisions.[15] These changes in decision making can make an organization much more flexible. Consider Sears. Less than a decade ago, the formidable retailer was almost dead. Today Sears is back in good health, thanks in part to changes in its operating structure that are designed to place decision making closer to the customer.[16]

The Process of Management

A managerial structure, specific goals, and skilled managers are key ingredients in any successful organization. However, these factors are not all that is required. Achieving a vision also depends on policies and processes that allow managers to make the most of both their talents and the resources available to them within the organization. In this way, they can perform the four basic functions necessary for the organization's success: (1) planning, (2) organizing, (3) leading, and (4) controlling. One way that managers are able to perform these four functions effectively is through total quality management (TQM). The

Much Information →			Little Information
Certainty: Managers have all necessary information and are confident about the success of their decisions.	Risk: Managers are lacking some information and are less confident about the success of their decisions.	Uncertainty: Managers are required to make many assumptions that might be wrong.	Ambiguity: Managers have unclear objectives and poorly defined alternatives.
Low Risk →			High Risk

Exhibit 6.2

Managerial Decision Environments

Managers make decisions within several environments that involve varying amounts of information and that carry varying levels of risk.

THINKING ABOUT ETHICS

When Decisions Are More Than Right or Wrong

Decision making is one of the primary responsibilities of a manager. Many of these managerial decisions appear to carry no ethical implications because the manager has all the facts, the information is clear-cut, and the choice is either right or wrong. However, situations can be clouded by conflicting responsibilities, incomplete information, and multiple points of view. Sometimes a decision that seems relatively easy can carry serious ethical implications.

For example, ethical problems arise when a brokerage firm pays huge bonuses to top managers just before declaring bankruptcy, when a government contractor hides true costs from customers, and when a lawyer trades on inside information. Less newsworthy issues include a boss who lies at an employee's expense, a worker who pads her expense account, or a supervisor who uses the company's phone for personal calls. The way you handle such everyday ethical decisions shapes the overall ethics of your company, and handling them ethically may help you avoid the sort of scandals that frequently make the front page. That's why it's so important for organizations to address ethical issues and encourage ethical decision making by all of their managers and employees.

Assume you're leaving your employer to start your own company. Is it ethical to take one or two co-workers with you? Is it ethical to take your employer's customers with you? If you need to borrow money to make a go of your new business, is it ethical to withhold information from your banker? Three businesspeople faced these questions and made their own decisions.

- Andy Friesch founded Heartland Adhesives & Coatings in Germantown, Wisconsin. Before starting his own business, he was still a top sales producer for a very large company in the industrial adhesives indus-

next section explores some of the fundamentals of TQM. Then following sections discuss each of the management functions in detail and examine how TQM influences the managers performing each function.

Total Quality Management

total quality management (TQM)
Comprehensive, strategic management approach that builds quality into every organizational process as a way of improving customer satisfaction

Total quality management (TQM) is both a management philosophy and a strategic management process that focuses on delivering the optimal level of quality to customers by building quality into every organizational activity (see Exhibit 6.3). Although it has only recently been adopted by U.S. companies, TQM has been popular in Japan since the 1950s, when Japanese businesses turned to the quality teachings of W. Edwards Deming and J. M. Juran to rebuild their industrial strength. TQM redirects management to focus on four key elements: employee involvement, customer focus, benchmarking, and continuous improvement.[17]

Employee Involvement TQM involves every employee in quality assurance. Workers are trained in quality methods, and they are empowered to stop a work process if they feel that products or services are not meeting quality standards. It also means that managers encourage employees to speak up when employees think of better ways of doing things. At Landis, a machine-tool manufacturer, every employee undergoes at least 25 hours of quality training. In addition, Landis management has changed its rigidly hierarchical management structure in order to empower employees. Landis general manager C. L. Hartle encourages employees to run their own departments, and he strives to give workers on the plant floor greater decision-making power. At the same time, Landis managers share all of the information they can with all employees and supervisors.[18] Landis's new approach to managing the company exemplifies a **participative management** style. This sharing of information at all levels of the organization is also known as *open-book management.*

participative management
Sharing information with employees and involving them in decision making

try. He believed that two co-workers would be assets to his own firm, so he asked them to join him in his new enterprise. Says Friesch: "When it comes to corporate America, individuals have to do what's in their own best interest. Corporations look out for themselves first and employees second." As it turned out, Friesch's co-workers did not go with him.

- John G. McCurdy founded Sunny States Seafood in Oxford, Mississippi. He was still working for another Mississippi seafood distributor when several of his employer's customers asked to go with him. He believed taking his employer's customers was unethical, so he refused. McCurdy observes: "I'm only 24 years old, I've got another 40 years left in business, and if I do somebody like that, somebody's going to do me like that."
- W. Mark Baty Jr. founded Accredited Business Services, a metals-recycling business in Cleveland, Ohio. He needed to purchase a $60,000 specialized truck to service a big account. He asked his bank for a loan, knowing that his finances were a little shaky. He did not lie to the bank, but neither did he reveal the amount of money he owed to relatives and on credit cards. He got the loan. Says Baty: "You don't lie to a bank—but I certainly don't believe in offering them more information than they ask for." Baty paid off his loan, and his banker never learned of his overextended finances.

QUESTIONS FOR CRITICAL THINKING

1. Do employees have an obligation to make ethical decisions even if those decisions result in higher costs or missed opportunities?
2. Do companies have an obligation to encourage ethical decision making by their employees?

EXHIBIT 6.3

The 14 Points of Total Quality Management

These 14 points, based on the work of W. Edwards Deming, can help managers improve their goods and services through total quality management.

1. **Create constancy of purpose for the improvement of goods and services.** The organization should constantly strive to improve quality, productivity, and customer satisfaction to improve performance today and tomorrow.
2. **Adopt a new philosophy to reject mistakes and negativism.** Customers, managers, and employees all need to change their attitudes toward unacceptable work quality and sullen service.
3. **Cease dependence on mass inspection.** Instead of inspecting products after production to weed out bad quality, improve the process to build in good quality.
4. **End the practice of awarding business on price alone.** Create long-term relationships with suppliers who can deliver the best quality.
5. **Improve constantly and forever the system of production and service.** Improvement is not a one-time effort; managers must lead the way to continuous improvement of quality, productivity, and customer satisfaction.
6. **Institute training.** Train all organization members to do their jobs consistently well.
7. **Institute leadership.** Managers must provide the leadership to help employees do a better job.
8. **Drive out fear.** Create an atmosphere in which employees are not afraid to ask questions or to point out problems.
9. **Break down barriers between units.** Ensure that people in organizational departments or units do not have conflicting goals and are able to work as a team to achieve overall goals.
10. **Eliminate slogans, exhortations, and targets for the work force.** These alone cannot help anyone do a better job, and they imply that employees could do better if they tried harder; instead, management should provide methods for improvement.
11. **Eliminate numerical quotas.** Quotas count only finished units, not quality or methods, and they generally lead to defective goods, wasted resources, and demoralized employees.
12. **Remove barriers to pride in work.** Most people want to do a good job but are prevented from doing so by misguided management, poor communication, faulty equipment, defective materials, and other barriers that managers must remove to improve quality.
13. **Institute a vigorous program of education and retraining.** Both managers and employees have to be educated in the new quality methods.
14. **Take action to accomplish the transformation.** With top-management commitment, have the courage to make the changes throughout the organization that will improve quality.

Customer Focus Focusing on the customer simply means finding out what customers really want and then providing them with it. This requires casting aside assumptions about customers and relying instead on accurate research.[19] At Honeywell, CEO Michael Bonsignore looks to customers for input about how Honeywell can improve its products and service. Customer-feedback systems encourage an ongoing dialogue between the company and its customers. "Our customer-feedback mechanisms not only tell us whether they are satisfied but also why they are satisfied or dissatisfied and what we can do differently," says Bonsignore.[20] Customer feedback has even led to new products and processes at Ames Rubber Corporation. Vice president of sales and marketing Robert G. Dondero says that dialogue with customers "solved some key technology problems" and enabled the company to reduce costs, cycle time (the steps required to complete a process), and scrap (waste).[21]

Is It True?

The majority of quality problems are caused by employees' poor work habits and poor attitudes.

Benchmarking *Benchmarking* is comparing your company's processes and products to the standards of the world's best companies and then working to match or exceed those standards. This means rating the manufacturing process, product development, distribution, and other key functions against those of acknowledged leaders; analyzing how these role models achieve their outstanding results; and then applying that knowledge to make quality improvements. Among the world-class organizations frequently cited as benchmarks for production are Toyota, IBM, and Hewlett-Packard; for distribution are L. L. Bean and FedEx; and for customer service are American Express and Nordstrom. Xerox is frequently cited for the benchmarking programs themselves.[22]

Continuous Improvement Total quality management can work only when companies are committed to continuously improving their goods, services, and processes. This requires an ongoing effort to reduce defects, cut costs, slash production and delivery times, and offer customers innovative products. Improvements are often small, incremental changes that add up to greater competitiveness over the long run. Responsibility for such improvements often falls on employees, so management must provide incentives for them to want to improve. Geon, a manufacturer of polyvinyl chloride (PVC) resins, motivates its employees through two programs. The first links employee bonuses to improvements in productivity, quality, and manufacturing. In recent years, employees have received an average bonus of 11 percent of their annual salaries through the program. The second program is a success-sharing plan tied to sales gains and stock price. This plan pays out millions of dollars in stock each year. Both initiatives have helped Geon produce 20 percent more PVC resin with 25 percent less manufacturing capacity, putting the company in a much better financial position.[23]

L. L. Bean's distribution employees, like the one pictured here, recently traded jobs with stockers in retail stores to learn how to serve each other better.

Although many U.S. companies are enjoying greater success as a result of total quality initiatives, a recent study of Fortune 500 companies indicates that such initiatives have fallen short of expectations in a large number of companies. However, the fact that total quality principles played a significant role in propelling Japanese businesses from postwar ruins to pillars of innovation and productivity suggests that much can be gained from the process. What may be lacking in the United States is a firm commitment to TQM. Many companies have jumped on the TQM bandwagon hoping for a quick boost in performance without really thinking about how to make total quality a part of their long-term strategy. Such companies often fail to provide the necessary managerial and financial support for the programs. In about half of the firms studied, less than 40 percent of workers and less than 80 percent of management teams were sufficiently knowledgeable of TQM philosophy, concepts, and tools.[24] Experts agree that the entire organization—all the way up to the CEO—must be actively and visibly involved in order for TQM to work. Companies that make a halfhearted commitment to the four elements discussed above should not expect dramatic improvements.[25]

At the same time, pursuing TQM is not necessarily a prerequisite for success. Many successful companies do not have TQM programs.[26] However, no business that operates in a competitive environment can expect long-term success unless managers strive to meet customers' needs, improve processes, lower costs, and empower employees in one way or another. Managers should keep this in mind as they pursue the four functions of management.

The Planning Function

Without a doubt, planning is the primary management function, the one on which all others depend. Managers engaged in **planning** establish objectives and goals for the organization and determine the best ways to achieve them. To establish effective goals, managers consider budgets, schedules, data about the industry and the economy, the company's existing resources, and resources that may realistically be obtained. They also carefully evaluate basic assumptions: Just because a business has developed along certain lines in response to previous conditions doesn't mean that another way might not be appropriate given today's conditions. Strong conceptual skills play a key role in making such judgments and in all planning activities.

planning
Establishing objectives and goals for an organization and determining the best ways to accomplish them

Planning Levels An earlier section of this chapter discusses strategic goals, tactical objectives, and operational objectives that managers set to help fulfill the organization's mission. By establishing organizational goals, managers set the stage for the actions needed to achieve those goals. If actions aren't planned, the chances of reaching company goals are slim. Therefore, each level of goals has a corresponding level of plans for how those goals will actually be achieved.[27]

Strategic plans define the actions and the allocation of resources necessary to achieve strategic goals over a period of two to five years. Strategic plans are usually long-term, and they are laid out by top managers, who consult with board members and middle managers. **Tactical plans** lay out the actions and the allocation of resources necessary to achieve tactical objectives and to support strategic plans. Usually developed by middle managers (who consult with first-line managers before committing to top management), tactical plans typically cover a period of one to three years. **Operational plans** designate the actions and resources required to achieve operational objectives and to support tactical plans. Operational plans usually define actions for less than one year. They are developed by first-line managers, who consult with middle managers. Exhibit 6.4 shows the relationships among the three levels of management, the goals and objectives set by each level, and the plans developed by each. Note that as business goals become more closely tied to computer technology and the Internet in many industries, the time frames in which the various levels of plans can be executed are shrinking. Today's rapid pace of change and the competitive threats from small high-tech companies mean that managers in areas like software, biotechnology, and electronics must be willing and able to adapt their plans quickly.

strategic plans
Plans that establish the actions and the resource allocation required to accomplish strategic goals; usually defined for periods of two to five years and developed by top managers

tactical plans
Plans that define the actions and the resource allocation necessary to achieve tactical objectives and to support strategic plans; usually defined for a period of one to three years and developed by middle managers

operational plans
Plans that lay out the actions and the resource allocation needed to achieve operational objectives and to support tactical plans; usually defined for less than one year and developed by first-line managers

Different levels of planning typically correspond to the different managerial levels; however, some companies are discovering that breaking down the hierarchical distinctions can lead to greater success. For example, jam and jelly maker J. M. Smucker recently included a team of 140 employees in a strategy-development exercise. One result of the exercise was a plan to partner with Brach & Brock Confections to produce Smucker's jelly beans. The idea originated in a team that included employees who would otherwise never have been a part of Smucker's strategy formulation.[28]

Forecasting Changes occur all the time in technology, culture, product development, service offerings, competition, government priorities, social values, the environment, and the economy as a whole. Any one of these factors can affect a company's success. Managers attempt to make educated assumptions about future trends and events so that their business is not adversely affected by these external changes and so that they can make plans. This is known as **forecasting**, which helps managers make wise use of the resources necessary to fulfill the organization's mission.

forecasting
Making educated assumptions about future trends and events that will have an impact on the organization

Managers can use any number of published forecasting tools available to them, such as *Industry Week*'s "Trends and Forecasts," *Business Week*'s "Survey of Corporate Performance," and Standard & Poor's *Earnings Forecast.* These publications depend on accurate forecasts for their continued success, so they usually offer some of the best projections available. However, published forecasts may not always include certain key variables specific to an individual company or industry. Moreover, because these forecasts are public documents, competitors have access to them as well. Therefore, managers must also develop their own forecasts. Managerial forecasts fall under two broad categories: *quantitative,* which are typically based on historical data or tests and which involve complex statistical computations; and *qualitative,* which are based on intuitive judgments or consumer research. Statistically analyzing the cycles of economic growth and recession over several decades to predict when the economy will take a downward turn is an example of quantitative forecasting. Making predictions about sales of a new product based on past experience and consumer responses to a survey is an example of qualitative forecasting. Nei-

Is It True?

IBM's original forecast estimated the *total* market for personal computers at 200,000.

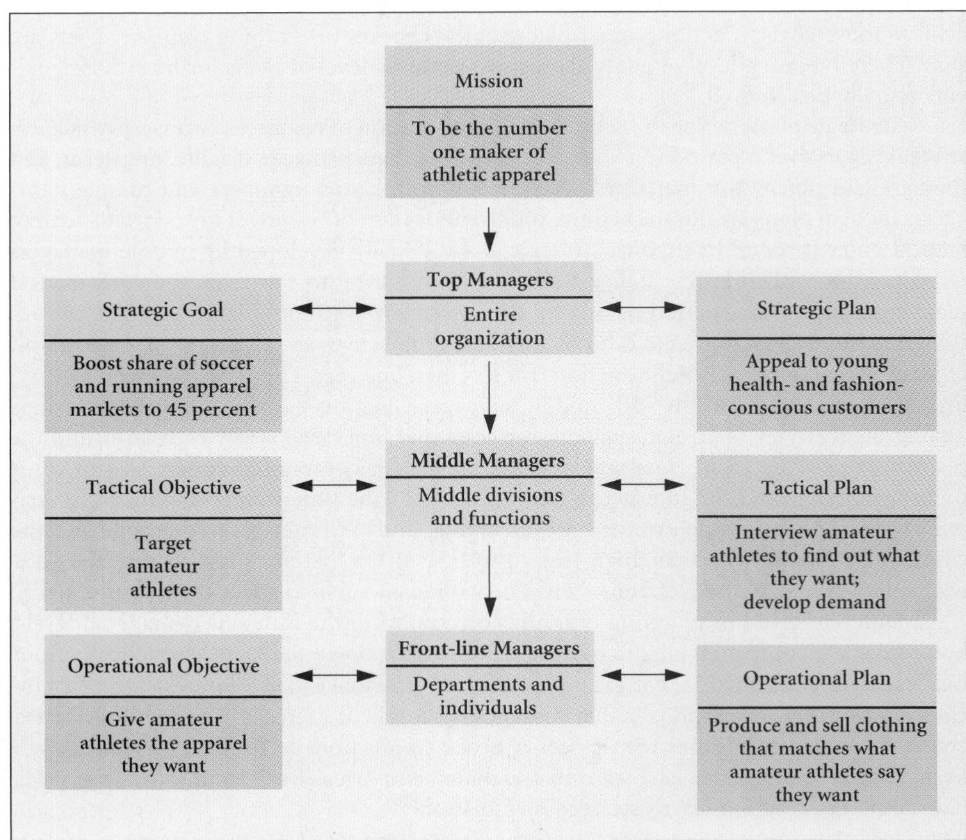

EXHIBIT 6.4

Managerial Planning

Managers set clear goals and objectives and then carefully develop plans to achieve them.

See the Future

BEST OF THE WEB

Managers sometimes wish they had a crystal ball that would allow them to see the future of the business environment. Of course, such a tool doesn't exist, but Dun & Bradstreet online might just be the next best thing. Dun & Bradstreet publishes many helpful forecasts for free on its Web site. For example, the *Economic Outlook* tells managers what trends they can expect in consumer spending, manufacturing production, economic growth, and employment. In addition, managers will find insightful analyses of global economic trends as well as helpful articles that make predictions about the future of specific industries. Perhaps even more important, Dun & Bradstreet explains the methods used to arrive at its predictions. In some ways, this beats the crystal ball because it enables managers to decide for themselves whether the information is solid enough to base future plans on.
http://www.dnb.com

ther method is foolproof, but both are valuable tools, enabling managers to fill in the unknown variables that inevitably crop up in the planning process.

TQM in Planning When planning, managers working in those organizations that practice TQM must take into account employee involvement, customer focus, benchmarking, and continuous improvement. For example, strategic plans set by top managers may involve developing new products that are designed with the help of customer feedback gained through surveys and other quality initiatives. Tactical plans will likely include benchmarking and use continuous improvement methods to ensure that both the product and the manufacturing process meet world-class standards. And as the product goes into production, employee empowerment will play a key role in the operational plans established by front-line managers to ensure minimal defects and cost reductions. Throughout the organization, planning and the commitment to quality go hand in hand.

The Organizing Function

organizing
Process of arranging resources to carry out the organization's plans

Organizing is the process of arranging resources to carry out the organization's plans. During the organizing stage, managers think through all the activities that employees carry out (from programming the organization's computers to mailing its letters), as well as all the facilities and equipment employees need to complete those activities. They also give people the ability to work toward organizational goals by determining who will have the authority to make decisions, to perform or supervise activities, and to distribute resources. Like the planning function, the organizing function requires a manager to have strong conceptual skills.

Generally, top managers establish the structure for the organization as a whole, and they select the people who fill the upper-level positions. Middle managers have similar responsibilities, but usually for just one division or unit. First-line managers seldom set up the organization structure, but they typically play an important role in the organizing function by hiring and training operational employees.

Organizing and Change Organizing is particularly challenging because any organization is likely to undergo constant change. Long-time employees leave, and new employees arrive. Equipment breaks down or becomes obsolete, and replacements are needed. The public's tastes and interests change, and the organization has to reevaluate its plans and activities. Shifting political and economic trends can lead to employee cutbacks—or perhaps expansion. Long-time competitors take unexpected actions, and new competitors enter the market. Every week the organization faces new situations, so management's organizing tasks are never finished.

TQM in Organizing Many companies pursuing TQM initiatives attempt to become more competitive by replacing individuals with teams as the building blocks of organizations. Teams may be formed at any level of the organization or even across levels. By directly involving employees in decision making, teams increase the power of employees in an organization and improve the flow of information between employees and managers. Therefore, teams can increase employee satisfaction, organizational productivity, and product quality. In addition, the broadening of employee tasks makes the organization more flexible. For example, Mattel used a team of toy designers, computer experts, artists, and car designers to create a new line of toy cars in only 5 months, whereas the traditional toy design process took a full 18 months to complete.[29] Teams are discussed in greater detail in Chapter 7.

The Leading Function

Into the positions and relationships determined by the organizing process come individuals from differing backgrounds, each with unique interests, ambitions, and personal goals. To meld all the people in the organization into a productive work team, managers apply the third major management function, **leading**—the process of influencing and motivating people to work effectively and willingly toward company goals. Managers who possess good leadership skills have the ability to influence the attitudes and actions of others, both through the demonstration of specific tasks and through the manager's own behavior and spirit. Effective leaders are good at **motivating,** giving employees a reason to do the job and to put forth their best performance (see chapter 9). As you can see, leading requires strong interpersonal skills.

leading
Process of guiding and motivating people to work toward organizational goals

motivating
Instilling employees with a desire to do the job and to perform at their peak

Leadership Traits When early researchers studied leadership, they looked for specific characteristics, or *traits,* common to all good leaders. At the time, they were unable to prove any link between particular traits and leadership ability. Later researchers found that leaders who have specific traits, such as decisiveness and self-confidence, are likely to be more effective.[30] Nevertheless, traits alone do not define a leader. Different leadership traits are appropriate under different leadership situations.[31]

Leadership Styles *Leadership style* is the way authority is used by a manager to lead others. Every manager, from the baseball coach to the university chancellor, has a definite style. The three broad categories of leadership style are *autocratic, democratic,* and *laissez-faire.* **Autocratic leaders** make decisions without consulting others. "My way or the highway" summarizes this style, which tends to go more with traditional, hierarchical organizational structures. Although autocratic leadership can be highly effective when quick decisions are necessary, it doesn't do much to empower employees or encourage innovation.

autocratic leaders
Leaders who do not involve others in decision making

In contrast, **democratic leaders** delegate authority and involve employees in decision making. Even though this approach can lead to slower decisions, soliciting input from people familiar with particular situations or issues may result in better decisions. As more companies adopt the principles of TQM and teamwork, democratic leadership continues to gain in popularity. For example, managers at Rhone-Poulenc, the U.S. subsidiary of France's leading chemical and pharmaceutical manufacturer, gradually made the transition from autocratic to democratic leadership as the organization moved from a hierarchical structure to a team-based environment. CEO Peter Neff says, "I don't look over people's shoulders anymore . . . My role now is to enable people to do the best they know how to do." For Neff, this means acting as an opportunity seeker, coach, facilitator, motivator, and mentor rather than as a controller or problem solver.[32]

democratic leaders
Leaders who delegate authority and involve employees in decision making

A third leadership style is laissez-faire, which is sometimes also referred to as free-rein leadership. The French term *laissez faire* can be translated as "leave it alone" or more roughly as "hands off." **Laissez-faire leaders** take the role of consultant, encouraging employees' ideas and offering insights or opinions when asked. The laissez-faire style may fail if the group pursues goals that do not match the organization's. However, the style has proven effective in some situations. Managers at Hewlett-Packard's North American distribution organization adopted a laissez-faire style when they were given nine months to reorganize their order-fulfillment process. The managers eliminated all titles, supervision, job descriptions, and plans, and they made employees entirely responsible for the project. At first there was chaos. However, employees soon began to try new things, make mistakes, and learn as they went. In the end, the team finished the reorganization ahead of schedule, reduced product delivery times from 26 days to 8 days, and cut inventory by 20 percent. Moreover, the employees experienced a renewed sense of challenge, commitment, and enjoyment in their work.[33]

laissez-faire leaders
Leaders who lead by leaving the actual decision making up to employees

More and more businesses are adopting democratic and laissez-faire leadership as they reduce management layers and increase teamwork. However, experienced managers know that no one leadership style works every time. In fact, a recent study found that in the most successful companies, the CEO adapts his or her leadership approach to match the requirements of the particular situation.[34] The best approach depends on the leader's personality, the employees' skills and backgrounds, and the situations the company is facing. Adapting leadership style to current business circumstances is called **contingency leadership.** You can think of leadership styles existing along a continuum of possible leadership behaviors, as suggested by Exhibit 6.5.

contingency leadership
Adapting the leadership style to what is most appropriate, given current business conditions

Leadership versus Management In recent years, a hot topic of discussion has been about the difference between leadership and management. Both are important to organizations. However, not all managers are good leaders, and not every leader can manage effectively. Management power comes from the structure of the organization, and it focuses on building stability, order, and problem-solving mechanisms. Those who excel at management functions are known as **transactional leaders,** and they are usually focused on keeping things running smoothly and efficiently. In contrast to management power, leadership power comes from personal qualities, such as personality traits and special knowledge that the leader possesses. This type of power promotes vision, creativity, and change. Leaders who possess these leadership skills are known as **transformational leaders.**[35] A transactional leader may be very good at devising methods for completing a task and motivating employees to get the job done. However, it takes a transformational leader to inspire employees to exceed performance expectations on a long-term basis. Charisma, character, integrity, and respect for employees are key attributes in leaders that are able to inspire such commitment.[36]

transactional leaders
Leaders who excel at creating an efficient organization and motivating employees to meet expectations

transformational leaders
Leaders who possess the ability to inspire long-term vision, creativity, and change in their employees

Dr. Armand Feigenbaum, a noted authority on total quality systems, uses a Chinese proverb to explain the qualities of a superior leader: "A bad leader is somebody from whom the people turn away. A good leader is somebody whom the people turn toward. A great leader is someone of whom the people say, 'We did it ourselves.' "[37] Executives and employees at Rodel would agree. The company is a major manufacturer of products used in the production of silicone wafers and microchips. It strives to empower and motivate its employees through a program it calls "Leadership Intensive Training." Program architect Lloyd Fickett sees leadership as a fluid process in which "one person might provide leadership at one moment, and someone else might provide it at another." Rodel has found that training employees in leadership skills and encouraging leadership behavior promotes commitment at all levels of the organization. As a result, the company has become much more competitive in recent years.[38]

Boss-centered Leadership ← → Employee-centered Leadership

Use of authority by the manager

Area of freedom for workers

Manager makes decision, announces it.	Manager "sells" decision.	Manager presents ideas, invites questions.	Manager presents tentative decision subject to change.	Manager presents problems, gets suggestions, makes decisions.	Manager defines limits, asks group to make decision.	Manager permits workers to function within defined limits.

EXHIBIT 6.5

Continuum of Leadership Behavior

Leadership style is a continuum, ranging from boss-centered to employee-centered. Situations that require managers to exercise greater authority fall toward the boss-centered end of the continuum. Other situations call for a manager to give workers leeway to function more independently.

coaching
Helping employees reach their highest potential by meeting with them, discussing problems that hinder their ability to work effectively, and offering suggestions and encouragement to overcome these problems

Coaching and Mentoring Managers can provide effective leadership in two ways: by coaching and by mentoring their employees. On a winning sports team, the coach focuses on helping all team members to perform at their highest potential. In a similar way, *coaching* managers strive to bring out the best in their employees. **Coaching** involves taking the time to meet with employees, discuss any problems that may hinder their ability to work effectively, and offer suggestions and encouragement to help employees work through these difficulties. This process requires keen powers of observation, sensible judgment, and both a willingness and an ability to take appropriate action. However, just as a sports coach can-

Lou Gerstner's transformational leadership has changed IBM from a slow-moving "dinosaur" to a cutting-edge company once again. This employee's casual dress looks nothing like the IBM of a decade ago, and neither does the product he is working on.

not play the game for team members, a coaching manager must step back and let employees perform when it's "game time." Coaching managers develop a solid game plan and empower their team to carry it out. If the team gets behind, the manager offers encouragement to boost morale. And when team members are victorious, the manager recognizes and praises their outstanding achievement.[39]

Linking to Management Resources

BEST OF THE WEB

Some of the best sites on the World Wide Web don't contain much original content of their own. Instead, they contain links that will carry you to a vast array of other sites. One such site is the Institute of Management and Administration (IOMA) *Business Directory,* which has a comprehensive collection of links for managers. At this site you will find links to a huge number of informative sites under topics such as corporate and financial management, customer service, exports and imports, law, sales and marketing, small business, and many others. You can also access current business news from sources such as the Dow Jones Business Directory, the CNN Financial Network, and *The New York Times.* You may hit a few dead ends before you find what you're looking for, but with so many options, IOMA is bound to have what you need. http://www.ioma.com

Acting as a mentor is similar to coaching, but mentoring also emphasizes helping employees understand how the organization works. A **mentor** is usually an experienced manager or employee who can help guide other employees through the corporate maze. Mentors have a deep knowledge of the business and a useful network of industry colleagues. In addition, they can explain office politics, serve as a role model for appropriate business behavior, and provide valuable advice about how to succeed within the organization.

mentor
Experienced manager or employee with a wide network of industry colleagues who can explain office politics, serve as a role model for appropriate business behavior, and help other employees negotiate the corporate structure

Your mentor won't always be your boss. Relationships with mentors often develop informally between the individuals involved. However, some companies have formal mentoring programs. In a formal program at Xerox, women employees can spend a few hours every month discussing work or career issues with any of the women executives participating in the program.[40] The less experienced employees gain from their mentors' advice and ideas; the mentors gain new contacts for their networks, as well as personal satisfaction.

Building an Organizational Culture Strong leadership is a key element in establishing a productive **organizational culture,** the set of underlying values and norms shared by members of an organization that form the foundation of the management system and of management and employee practices. In corporations, this force is often referred to as *corporate culture.* The shared values of organizational culture call attention to what is important, shaping the patterns of behavior that become norms and guide the way things are done in a particular organization.

organizational culture
A set of shared values and norms that support the management system and that guide management and employee behavior

Consider Medtronic, a medical products company in Minneapolis. Earl Bakken and his brother-in-law founded the company with passionate hopes of applying technology to help humanity. From this idealistic beginning grew a paternalistic company with an emphasis on home-grown scientific ingenuity. As the company expanded, it ran into competition, developed profitability problems, and needed a more consistent method of product development. To meet these challenges, management began to emphasize profits and performance, both personal and organizational. At the same time, management pursued a course of controlled but steady growth using diversification. Now the organizational culture stresses profitability as well as the founders' passion for improving human welfare.[41]

The Controlling Function

controlling
Process of measuring progress against goals and objectives and correcting deviations if results are not as expected

In management, **controlling** means monitoring progress toward organizational goals, resetting the course if goals or objectives change in response to shifting conditions, and correcting deviations if goals or objectives are not being attained. Managers use their technical skills for the controlling function, comparing where they are with where they should be. If everything is operating smoothly, controls permit managers to repeat acceptable performance. If results are below expectations, controls help managers take any necessary action. This section discusses the relationship between management and controlling. Control methods are examined in greater detail in Chapter 8.

standards
Criteria against which performance may be measured

TQM in Controlling The controlling function is an important part of total quality management, which is sometimes referred to as *total quality control.* In the past, many companies inspected finished products and reworked or discarded items that didn't meet quality standards. Today many firms control for quality through a four-step cycle that involves all levels of management and all employees (see Exhibit 6.6). In the first step, top managers set **standards,** criteria for measuring the performance of the organization as a whole. At the same time, middle and first-line managers set departmental quality standards so they can meet or exceed company standards. Establishing control standards is closely tied to the planning function and depends on information supplied by employees, customers, and other external sources such as benchmarks. Examples of specific standards include:

- Increase the profit margin from 17 to 20 percent
- Produce 1,500 circuit boards monthly with less than 1 percent failures

FOCUSING ON CULTURAL DIVERSITY

How Successful Companies Promote Diversity in Organizational Cultures

Managers have a tremendous influence on an organization's culture. Because employees look to management for leadership, management's words and actions set the standard for the way employees think, speak, and behave within the organization. Effective managers strive to set examples that promote a harmonious, innovative, and productive corporate culture. Part of achieving such a culture is a commitment to diversity.

One way managers can promote a corporate culture committed to diversity is by encouraging respect for diversity among employees. By embracing a work environment that hires and promotes qualified people, regardless of race, gender, age, ethnic origin, or sexual orientation, the company demonstrates that all employees are valued. At the same time, the company benefits from the broad range of ideas, talents, and skills that a diverse work force possesses.

However, experts say that in some companies hiring and promoting a diverse work force is not sufficient. R. Roosevelt Thomas, a leading authority on corporate diversity, suggests that a company's diversity program is often only a plan on paper and not truly valued by the organization. These paper plans exist because managers are rarely evaluated or compensated for how they deal with interpersonal issues. Roosevelt found that a *cultural audit* can help a company understand whether it truly values diversity or only pays lip service to the idea. "Building relationships and mutual adaptation," he says, "are the only actions that embrace diversity." And as effective managers know, a company's culture can either promote or restrict the development of productive relationships.

Microsoft is one company that is especially progressive when it comes to promoting diversity in its corporate culture. In fact, one of Microsoft's objectives for

- Make 20 sales calls each week
- Fulfill each customer order in 24 hours or less

In the second step of the control cycle, managers assess performance, using both quantitative (specific, numerical) and qualitative (subjective) performance measures. In the third step, managers compare performance with the established standards and search for the cause of any discrepancies. If the performance falls short of standards, the fourth step is to take corrective action, which may be done either by adjusting performance or by reevaluating the standards. If performance meets or exceeds standards, no corrective action is taken.

The control cycle enables managers and employees alike to identify problems and design ways of continuously improving the quality of the company's goods and services. Consider how Granite Rock of Watsonville, California, used the control cycle to help improve its delivery service. Granite management learned through surveys that on-time delivery is the customers' highest priority. Because it couldn't find another noncompeting concrete company that had delivery standards worthy of using as a benchmark, Granite used Domino's Pizza's 30 minute guarantee as its standard. The company then began to measure the delivery time of each load and carefully track the results. The information that Granite gained from this control process led the company to change the way it delivers its products. Now customers just drive up with a truck, insert a card into a machine, and punch in the material and amount needed. The truck is loaded automatically, and a bill is sent later.[42]

achieving success is promoting a diverse work environment. To meet this objective, the company sponsors scholarships, promotes diversity activities within the company, maintains ties with organizations committed to diversity and equality, and sends managers to conferences throughout the United States to find new, diverse candidates for the Microsoft work pool. In addition, Microsoft supports many diverse groups within the company through the Microsoft Diversity Advisory Council. Such groups include blacks at Microsoft; gay, lesbian, and bisexual employees at Microsoft; Microsoft Women's Group; and Native Americans at Microsoft. These and other groups provide support and advocacy for their members, and they promote understanding among all Microsoft employees and managers.

Two other companies that strive to make diversity a part of their corporate culture are Sara Lee and Procter & Gamble. Both companies were recently honored for their efforts by the National Association for the Advancement of Colored Persons (NAACP). Procter & Gamble CEO John Pepper was praised for demonstrating a personal commitment to diversity. When he took over as CEO in 1995, one of the first memos he sent to his staff dealt with the company's diversity policy. Such action by top managers goes a long way toward encouraging a commitment to and respect for diversity among employees at all levels of an organization.

Questions for Critical Thinking

1. What specific actions can managers take to establish a culture that values diversity?
2. Should management compensation be based in part on the type of corporate culture they promote? Why or why not?

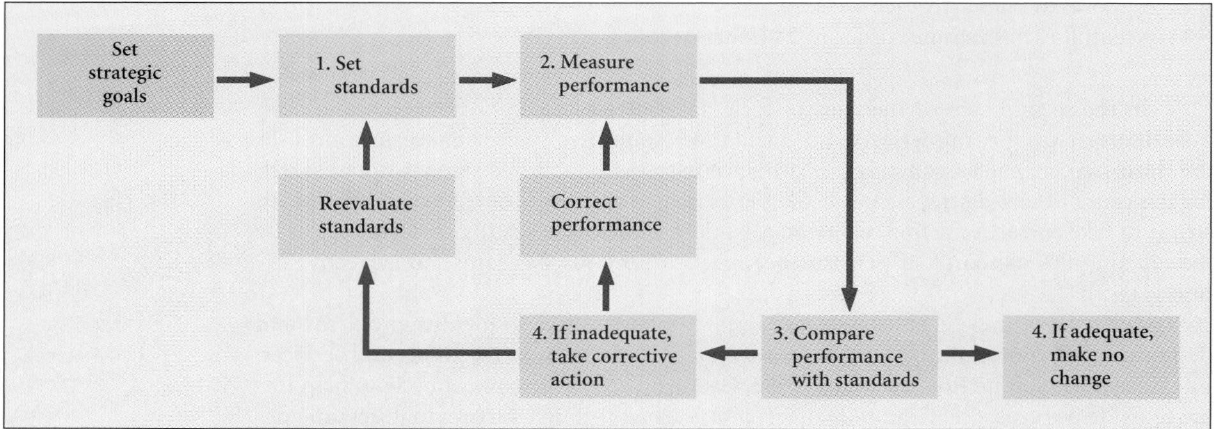

EXHIBIT 6.6

The Control Cycle

The control cycle has four basic steps: (1) Based on strategic goals, top managers set the standards by which the organization's overall performance will be measured; (2) managers at all levels measure performance; (3) actual performance is compared with the standards; (4) appropriate corrective action is taken (if performance meets standards, nothing other than encouragement is needed; if performance falls below standards, corrective action may include improving performance, establishing new standards, changing plans, reorganizing, or redirecting efforts).

management by objectives (MBO)
A motivational tool whereby managers and employees work together to structure personal goals and objectives for every individual, department, and project to mesh with the organization's goals

Management by Objectives Another well-known method of controlling performance is **management by objectives (MBO),** a companywide process in which managers and employees jointly define their goals, the responsibility for achieving these goals, and the means of evaluating individual and group performance. MBO provides a systematic method of setting goals for work groups and for individuals so that all their activities are directly linked to achieving organizational goals. The MBO process consists of four steps: setting goals, planning action, implementing plans, and reviewing performance.[43] This process is explained in Exhibit 6.7.

Many organizations, including Xerox, Intel, and du Pont, use MBO to improve performance at all company levels. Because this process ties the goals of each manager to those of managers at levels above and below, MBO acts as a coordinating system that facilitates teamwork throughout the organization, improves communication, encourages participation, and motivates employees through a sense of shared responsibility. However, MBO must have the involvement and commitment of top management to succeed. In addition, problems can result if employees or managers focus too narrowly on their own operational objectives at the expense of the company's strategic goals or the objectives of other departments. Also, if too much paperwork is required for goal setting, performance standards, and reviews, employees may lose their enthusiasm for meeting their objectives. Finally, if the MBO process is administered too rigidly, managers may lose the flexibility to respond to change effectively.[44]

CRISIS MANAGEMENT

No matter how well a company is managed on a daily basis, any number of problems can arise to threaten its very existence. An ugly fight for control of a company, a product fail-

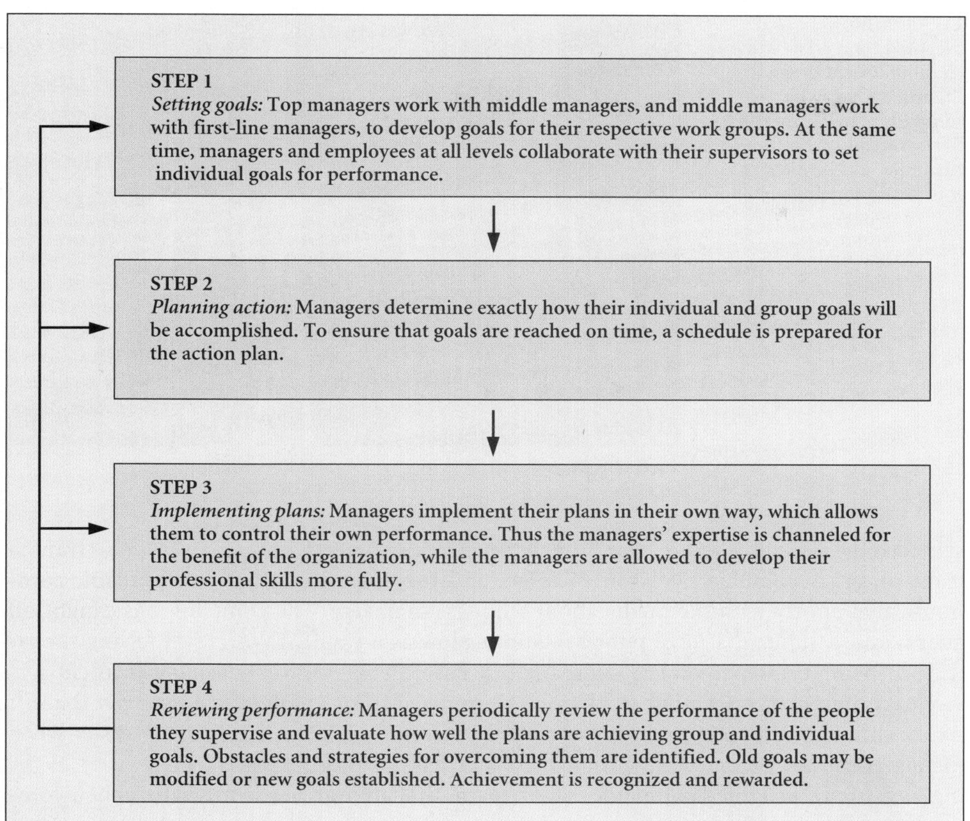

STEP 1
Setting goals: Top managers work with middle managers, and middle managers work with first-line managers, to develop goals for their respective work groups. At the same time, managers and employees at all levels collaborate with their supervisors to set individual goals for performance.
STEP 2
Planning action: Managers determine exactly how their individual and group goals will be accomplished. To ensure that goals are reached on time, a schedule is prepared for the action plan.
STEP 3
Implementing plans: Managers implement their plans in their own way, which allows them to control their own performance. Thus the managers' expertise is channeled for the benefit of the organization, while the managers are allowed to develop their professional skills more fully.
STEP 4
Reviewing performance: Managers periodically review the performance of the people they supervise and evaluate how well the plans are achieving group and individual goals. Obstacles and strategies for overcoming them are identified. Old goals may be modified or new goals established. Achievement is recognized and rewarded.

EXHIBIT 6.7

Management by Objectives

The MBO system has four steps. This cycle is refined and repeated as managers and employees at all levels work toward their established goals and objectives, thereby accomplishing the organization's strategic goals.

ure, a breakdown in routine operations (as a result of fire, for example), or an environmental accident could develop into a serious and crippling crisis. Managers can help a company survive these setbacks through **crisis management,** the handling of such unusual and serious problems.

crisis management
System for minimizing the harm that might result from some unusually threatening situations

Managing a crisis effectively requires speedy, open communication. The company should make every effort to share its information with employees and the public. NBC senior vice president for corporate communications Judy Smith suggests selecting in advance a communications team and a knowledgeable spokesperson to handle the many requests for information that arise during a crisis. The individuals selected should be able to remain honest and calm when a crisis hits.[45] Other experts add that the company's top managers should be visible in the hours immediately following the crisis to demonstrate that the company will do whatever is necessary to control the situation as best it can, find the cause, and prevent a future occurrence.

TWA was criticized for not taking either of these actions when Flight 800 crashed off the coast of Long Island in July of 1996, killing 230 people. Critics accused TWA of taking too long to release the names of people onboard the airplane and criticized the company for being unresponsive to the media. Furthermore, many felt that CEO Jeffrey Erickson waited too long before addressing the public about the crash. TWA was simply not prepared for the crisis: Erickson was in London at the time of the crash, two of his top executives who might have been able to handle the situation in his absence had re-

TWA was not very well prepared for a crisis when Flight 800 went down in the Atlantic Ocean. The company's slow response to the crisis caused both customer and investor confidence to plummet.

signed only a month before, the human resources executive who heads TWA's "trauma team" of crisis volunteers was on vacation, and the executives who were available communicated poorly with the media about who was in charge. The company was caught off guard, and it suffered a huge public relations blow as a result. TWA is still feeling the effects of being unprepared. The company lost customers, eventually forcing it to cut service to certain markets, and its stock price plummeted from a high of $23 to $6 per share.[46]

Although not every crisis is preventable, responding to a crisis is much easier when management has prepared for problems by actively looking for signs of a disaster in the making. Many farsighted companies set up teams that attempt to identify where their companies are vulnerable, generally by studying past mistakes committed by their own companies and others. Next these teams prepare **contingency plans,** actions the company can take to cope with unexpected or unpredictable events. Created with the company's strategic goals in mind, these plans outline steps that can prevent or counter the most serious threats and help the company recover quickly. Once developed, contingency plans should be reviewed and updated from time to time. Consider Inland Steel Industries, one of the largest U.S. steelmakers. Inland has a crisis response plan and a list of media contacts that it reviews and updates periodically. The company also runs periodic drills to simulate a crisis, and employees must respond as though it were a real situation. Should a real crisis ever occur, Inland believes it will be ready.[47]

contingency plans
A blueprint for actions the company can take to cope with unforeseen events

Summary of Learning Objectives

1. **Explain the role that goals and objectives play in management.**
Goals and objectives establish long- and short-range targets that help managers fulfill the company's mission. Setting appropriate goals increases employee motivation, establishes standards by which individual and group performance can be measured, guides employee activity, and clarifies management's expectations. In addition, goals are often designed to give the company a competitive edge by using differentiation, cost leadership, or focus strategies.

2. **Describe the three levels of management.**
Top managers take overall responsibility for the organization and set strategic goals. Middle managers have the task of implementing the broad goals set by top management as well as setting tactical objectives and coordinating the work of first-line managers. First-line managers establish operational objectives and supervise the work of operating employees.

3. **Identify and explain the three types of managerial skills.**

Managers use (1) interpersonal skills to communicate with other people, work effectively with them, and lead them, (2) technical skills to perform the mechanics of a particular job, and (3) conceptual skills (including decision making) to see the organization as a whole, to see it in the context of its environment, and to understand how the various parts interrelate.

4. **Clarify how total quality management (TQM) is changing the way organizations are managed.**
Total quality management is both a management philosophy and a management process that focuses on delivering quality to customers. TQM redirects management to focus on four key elements: Employee involvement includes team building and soliciting employee input on decisions. Customer focus involves gathering customer feedback and then acting on that feedback to better serve customers. Benchmarking involves measuring the company's standards against the standards of industry leaders. Continuous improvement requires an ongoing commitment to reducing defects, cutting costs, slashing production and delivery times, and offering customers innovative products.
5. **Define the four management functions.**
The four management functions are (1) planning—establishing objectives and goals for the organization and determining the best ways to achieve them; (2) organizing—arranging resources to carry out the organization's plans; (3) leading—influencing and motivating people to work effectively and willingly toward company goals; and (4) controlling—monitoring progress toward organizational goals, resetting the course if goals or objectives change in response to shifting conditions, and correcting deviations if goals or objectives are not being attained.
6. **Discuss how strategic, tactical, and operational plans are developed and used.**
Strategic plans usually cover two to five years and are designed by top managers to achieve strategic goals. Tactical plans are then laid out to achieve tactical objectives and to support strategic plans. They usually cover one to three years and are designed by middle managers who consult with first-line managers before reporting to top management. Operational plans are laid out to achieve operational objectives and to support tactical plans. They cover less than one year and are designed by first-line managers, who consult with middle managers.
7. **Cite three leadership styles, and explain why no one style is best.**
Three leadership styles are autocratic, democratic, and laissez-faire (also called free-rein). Each may work best in a different situation: autocratic when quick decisions are needed, democratic when employee participation in decision making is desirable, and laissez-faire when fostering creativity is a priority. Good leaders are flexible enough to respond with the best approach for the situation.
8. **Describe six measures that companies can take to better manage crises.**
During a crisis, an organization can (1) move quickly to explain the problem to the public and to its employees, (2) make senior managers available to the media and the public to demonstrate concern and commitment, and (3) make every effort to control the situation. Before the crisis occurs, an organization may (4) set up a crisis team of people who react well under stress and who can communicate effectively, (5) prepare contingency plans to deal with the most serious threats, and (6) hold drills under simulated crisis conditions.

On the Job: Meeting Business Challenges at Microsoft

As projects slipped behind schedule and competitors stepped up their attacks, Microsoft chief executive officer Bill Gates knew he had to take himself out of day-to-day operations. Microsoft had great ideas, but it was failing to plan and implement effectively. Now the company's reputation was on the line.

So Gates got help. He turned over daily operations to a three-person office of the president, which freed Gates for more creative work: envisioning products for the twenty-first century and planning for the company's long-term future. Then he reorganized the company into three major groups: products, sales and support, and operations. This new organization was designed to increase the company's efficiency and its responsiveness to customer needs. However, Gates didn't want to lose the entrepreneurial spirit that characterized the company's early years. The organization's structure was planned around small, self-sufficient working groups that encouraged individual employees to feel greater responsibility for their work.

Even though Gates could now effectively lead his managers, he was still concerned that his growing staff might lose touch with him and his strategic goals. He didn't have to look far for the solution: Microsoft established an electronic network that now links over 20,000 employees around the world. This network includes an electronic-mail system that lets virtually any employee communicate directly with the CEO. Dozens do so daily, and Gates tries to respond the same day he receives a message. Employees feel they have direct access to the top. They say Gates's messages are blunt and sometimes sarcastic—but always entertaining. By staying in touch with every level and every employee at Microsoft, Gates ensures that his vision is acknowledged and understood by everyone at Microsoft.

Gates's vision and drive have helped Microsoft achieve a commanding lead in the race for a piece of the software market. As much as 85 percent of all personal computers now run on Microsoft operating programs. Also, Gates is boldly moving the company into new frontiers. In recent years, Microsoft has acquired several start-up companies that possess cutting-edge Internet technologies. The company is integrating Internet features into many of its popular home and business programs. Gates is also looking at ways of marrying the computer and the television set to create a combination entertainment-information device. A major step was the launch of MSNBC, a cable news channel and companion Web site that the company developed with NBC. More recently, Microsoft purchased WebTV Networks, a company whose products allow you to surf the Internet on your television while watching your favorite programs.

Although Microsoft's future growth will not be as explosive as it was in the early years, Gates knows that effective management on all levels is what will keep the company on top.

Your Mission: You work in the Microsoft unit that's developing complex software to let companies tie all their computers together into one network. Although you started as a programmer, you have been a manager for several years and are no longer an expert on the latest technical developments. In the following situations, choose the best responses.

1. You're nearing a critical deadline and an employee keeps missing his objectives. He promises to do too much and then winds up pleading for more time and resources. He's a recent college graduate with lots of theory but little practical experience. How do you react?
   a. You have already sent a memo stressing the importance of deadlines. You should privately reprimand this employee and inspire better performance.
   b. The employee is clearly enthusiastic and has the necessary technical skills, but he may lack the conceptual skills needed in this situation. You can help by talking with him and sharing your experience and perspective.
   c. Ask the employee to explain the hours and resources he has spent on the project and the methods he is using. Then have him pinpoint his least effective and least efficient areas so that he can work on these problems.
2. Gates has just left a meeting with your programmers and seems more agitated than usual. During the meeting, one programmer flipped a football, another nonchalantly paged through a magazine, and a third directly answered the CEO's criticism with little show of respect. In response, Gates called parts of one program "stupid." You're already behind schedule, and you don't need the CEO breathing down your neck. What should you do?
   a. You were intimidated at the meeting because you didn't understand all the technical talk. Put in some time studying programming again so that you can follow the technical discussion and be able to defend your people.
   b. Try to persuade Gates to go through you instead of going straight to your programmers. This approach would give you more control.
   c. Gates encourages employees to speak up, and so should you. Talk with your programmers about what they thought of the meeting.
3. In the past five years, Oracle (a major networking software company) has consistently beaten your group to market with competing products. Although the functionality of the products is usually similar to Microsoft's, Oracle has established a competitive advantage in speed and efficiency of product development. What can you do about this?
   a. Pay no attention to Oracle. They may be the first to market, but you know that Microsoft makes better products. Microsoft didn't get where it is today by playing follow-the-leader.
   b. Build even more functionality into your products. It might mean delaying product releases a few more months, but customers will wait because they know they will get a better product down the road.
   c. Use Oracle's product-development process as a benchmark. Find out all you can about how the company consistently develops its products more efficiently, and then design changes into your own processes that will enable you to achieve similar results.
4. Some of Microsoft's software has come under criticism lately for having too many "bugs" or flaws that can cause problems for the people who use it. Gates has announced a company-wide effort to eliminate 99 percent of bugs before the software is shipped to consumers. He is allowing the manager of each software development group to formulate a strategy that will enable them to meet this goal most effectively. Of the following choices, which one will be the most important element of the strategy you develop?
   a. Drafting a set of procedures that software developers must follow to make sure that their work is free of defects.

b. Giving the employees in your group the power and incentive to test their work as they go, stop the development process when a bug is found, and bring it to the attention of the rest of the group so that it can be fixed.

c. Making sure that your beta version (the version of the software that is released to testers before the final version is developed) is available to a greater number of software testers so that more flaws are uncovered.[48]

Key Terms

administrative skills (166)
autocratic leaders (174)
coaching (176)
conceptual skills (166)
contingency leadership (175)
contingency plans (182)
controlling (178)
crisis management (181)
decision making (166)
democratic leaders (174)
first-line managers (165)
forecasting (172)
goal (163)
interpersonal skills (165)
laissez-faire leaders (175)
leading (174)
management (162)
management by objectives (MBO) (180)
management pyramid (164)
mentor (177)
middle managers (165)
mission statement (162)
motivating (174)
objective (163)
operational objectives (165)
operational plans (171)
organizational culture (177)
organizing (173)
participative management (168)
planning (171)
quality (162)
roles (165)
standards (178)
strategic goals (164)
strategic plans (171)
tactical objectives (165)
tactical plans (171)
technical skills (166)
top managers (164)
total quality management (TQM) (168)
transactional leaders (175)
transformational leaders (175)
vision (162)

Questions

For Review

1. What is management? Why is it so important?
2. Why are interpersonal skills important to managers at all levels?
3. What are the two categories of managerial decisions and how do they differ?
4. What is forecasting and how does it relate to the planning function?
5. What is the goal of crisis management?

For Analysis

6. Explain whether the following statement is an example of a strategic goal, a tactical objective, or an operational objective: "To become the number one retailer of computers and computer accessories in terms of revenue, growth, and customer satisfaction."
7. How do the four main elements of total quality management relate to the goal of delivering quality to customers?
8. What types of skills and planning are necessary for middle managers to reach their tactical objectives?
9. How can the use of teams enhance a company's competitive position?
10. How can managers incorporate the control cycle into the planning function?

For Application

11. If you were the manager of a small service company or retailer, such as a restaurant, bookstore, or gas station, what elements would you include in your mission statement?
12. Pretend you are a middle manager at a manufacturing company. Top management has asked you to organize a team to redesign the process of transferring finished goods from the warehouse to the customer. Your objectives are to reduce delivery times and inventory levels, and you have only three months to complete the task. What leadership style do you think would work best to motivate your team and meet the stated objectives?

A Case for Critical Thinking ■ New Management Techniques for Electrifying Performance at GE

Aircraft engines, major appliances, broadcasting, financial services, medical systems—in these areas and many others, General Electric businesses held first or second place in worldwide market share. The huge firm employed more than 200,000 people, and its revenues topped $50 billion. Some units were struggling, but overall profits rose year after year. In short, GE looked for all the world like a highly successful business.

But despite GE's achievements, chief executive officer John F. (Jack) Welch Jr. believed that a new management approach was needed. For years, managers had simply handed down orders without inviting employee comment. As long as company goals were met, such autocratic methods weren't questioned, even when they discouraged employees from contributing their ideas. Looking at the challenges ahead, Welch reasoned that continuing GE's success into the twenty-first century would require the creativity and the talents of every person who worked at GE—managers and employees alike.

However, moving toward participative management would require a major change in the company's management style. Instead of giving orders, GE managers would have to be more democratic. They would need to learn how to coach and how to energize their employees. Moreover, to tap the ideas of people from the top to the bottom of the company, the managers would also have to find ways of including employees in the decision-making process at every level.

As Welch thought about what the GE of the future would look like, he decided to encourage, in his own words, "speed, simplicity, and self-confidence" and to give every person in every department "the freedom to be creative." He felt that the way to improve productivity was by "getting people involved and excited about their jobs." At the same time, he realized that this approach would fail if GE employees didn't change their thinking.

Some employees had become so used to the autocratic management style of the past that they lacked the self-confidence to speak up or to question their managers. Others had simply stopped offering ideas when they saw that their managers didn't react well to employee initiative. In Welch's eyes, GE employees needed more fire and zest to propel GE toward higher revenues, productivity, and profits.

To encourage a more productive employee-management relationship, Welch introduced the Workout program. Several times a year, the heads of each GE facility meet with up to 100 people drawn from various levels and functions. The facility's top manager outlines several challenges to be addressed, and the group works on its own to develop plans for meeting those challenges. Although the top manager must approve all ideas before they are implemented, most are innovative and cost efficient, and few ideas are rejected.

Welch also encourages employees to question any unnecessary practices that might hold the company back from peak performance. By challenging their bosses, employees are able to expose and clear away outdated methods of doing things. In addition, encouraging employees to speak up and be heard increases the employees' self-confidence.

Finally, Welch provided extensive leadership training to help GE managers learn and practice new leadership skills and approaches. He also changed the standards by which managers are evaluated, to reflect the new emphasis. Promotions now go to managers who achieve company goals by sharing ideas with and from employees, by having the self-confidence to delegate work, by being honest in their communications, and by making and implementing decisions more quickly. Managers who achieve company goals by forcing performance out of their employees are not promoted.

Transforming GE managers into more participative leaders has not been an overnight process. However, after several years of the Workout program, most managers have realized significant benefits. Workouts now take place naturally and regularly within most GE businesses. At the same time, Welch has introduced the "change acceleration process (CAP)," which is a training program designed to help managers consistently manage the changes occurring in the global business environment. Welch wants his managers to view change as an opportunity, rather than a threat.

Welch's visionary leadership and groundbreaking management initiatives have led to a change in spirit among people at all levels. The company has enjoyed a significant rise in productivity as well. Armed with this new management style—and renewed employee enthusiasm—GE is well positioned to meet the challenges ahead.

1. How does the Workout program encourage a nondirective management approach?
2. How does the Workout program encourage a total quality approach to the four functions of management?
3. Can you think of any problems that might result from encouraging employees to challenge managers on the way they do things? Do the benefits outweigh the costs? What kinds of managerial skills are most important to make such a policy work?
4. Go to GE's Internet site at <http://www.ge.com>, and click on the link to the company's annual report. Next, click on *The GE Growth Model.* Use the information on this page to answer the following questions: (a) What are the qualities GE expects of its leaders, and what type of leadership (transactional or transformational) does this require? (b) What is GE's "core belief"? (c) Given this belief, what do you think GE's primary global strategy is? (d) Does GE view itself as a visionary company?

Building Your Business Skills

Research at least two companies that have restructured their management pyramids in recent years to create flatter, less hierarchical organizations. Either locate articles that describe the change or interview members of the companies' management teams.

- Consider how the restructuring has affected managers at all levels of the organizations, specifically with regard to (1) their roles (interpersonal and informational) within the structure of the organizations and (2) the skills (technical, interpersonal, conceptual) required for the positions they hold.
- Examine how the functions of planning, organizing, leading, and controlling have changed. Has responsibility for any of the functions shifted? Has the change led to higher-quality processes in any of these functions?
- Prepare a brief presentation describing the changes in the companies you researched. Compare your findings with those of other members of your class. What conclusions can you draw as a class?

Keeping Current Using *The Wall Street Journal*

Find two articles in *The Wall Street Journal* that profile two senior managers who lead business or nonprofit organizations.

1. What experience, skills, and business background do the two leaders have? Do you see any striking differences in their backgrounds or leadership strengths?
2. What kinds of business challenges have these two leaders faced? What actions did they take to deal with those challenges?
3. Describe the leadership strengths of each person as they are presented in the articles you selected. Is either leader known for his or her ability as a team builder? Long-term strategist? Shrewd negotiator? What are their greatest areas of strength? Financial planning and control? Marketing strategy? Motivating and communicating the company's mission to employees? Some other aspect of the management process?
4. Visit the Web site of one of the companies whose leader you are investigating and read the company's mission statement. If the mission statement is not available on the site, or if the company has no Web site, search the resources in your library (usually the company's mission is explained in its annual report). Based on what you know about the manager's leadership style and abilities, do you feel that he strives to meet the ideals expressed in the mission statement? Why or why not? What affect does this appear to have on the company?

Exploring the Best of the Web

Catch the Buzz!, page 0163

The online *Management and Technology Dictionary* can help you identify business terms that are unfamiliar to you and can keep you up to date on current management buzzwords. Explore the dictionary <http://www.euro.net/innovation/Management_Base/Mantec.Dictionary.html> to answer the following questions.

1. What is the definition of *dependent demand?* Give an example.
2. What are *knowledge workers,* and what challenges do they present to managers?
3. Explain what a *learning organization* is and how it relates to the concept of total quality management.

See the Future, page 173

Managers rely on solid information to help them forecast future trends during the planning function. Dun & Bradstreet online is one of the many Internet tools managers can access at their desks. From Dun & Bradstreet's main Web page <http://www.dbn.com> follow the links to *Industry Focus* and *News, Views, and Trends* to answer these questions.

1. Choose a link under *Economic Outlook* and read the summaries and forecasts about the current and future state of the U.S. economy. In your own words, summarize a current trend or prediction about the future and explain the methodology used by Dun & Bradstreet to obtain this information.
2. Scroll down the *News, Views, and Trends* page to the heading *Global Trends.* Select an article to review. Briefly summarize the article and explain how the manager of a global company or of a company that is considering international expansion could use this information in the planning stage.
3. Scroll down further to *Trends—some brief observations of our marketplace.* Choose a topic of interest to you from the menu. In a few sentences, summarize the trend described here. Do you think this trend will be of more interest to top, middle, or first-line managers? Explain.

Linking to Management Resources, page 177

With so many pages on the World Wide Web, sometimes finding the information you need can be a frustrating experience. The Institute of Management and Administration (IOMA) makes it easier by grouping hundreds of links to business resources under various functional headings. Go to IOMA's Web site <http://www.ioma.com> and click on *Business Directory.* After exploring the site and some of the links, answer the evaluative questions below.

1. Do you think that IOMA has grouped its links in a logical and easy-to-use way? Why or why not?
2. If you were IOMA's Web site designer, what would you do differently to make the site more attractive or easier to navigate?

3. Choose a topic that you would like to find some information about, such as the qualities of an effective leader or how to manage a small business. Test some of the links to find answers to your question. How many links did you have to follow to find what you wanted? Now scroll down to the bottom of the page and search the IOMA archives for your topic. Which strategy worked best?

Answers to "Is It True?"

Page 165. False. Of the CEOs surveyed by management consulting firm Foster Higgins, 97 percent said communicating with employees has a positive effect on job satisfaction, and 79 percent think it helps the company's financial performance, but only 22 percent actually do it weekly.

Page 170. False. According to quality gurus W. Edwards Deming and J. M. Juran, 85 percent of quality problems are the result of management decisions or inertia, such as not upgrading machines.

Page 173. True.

CHAPTER 7

ORGANIZATION, TEAMWORK, AND COMMUNICATION

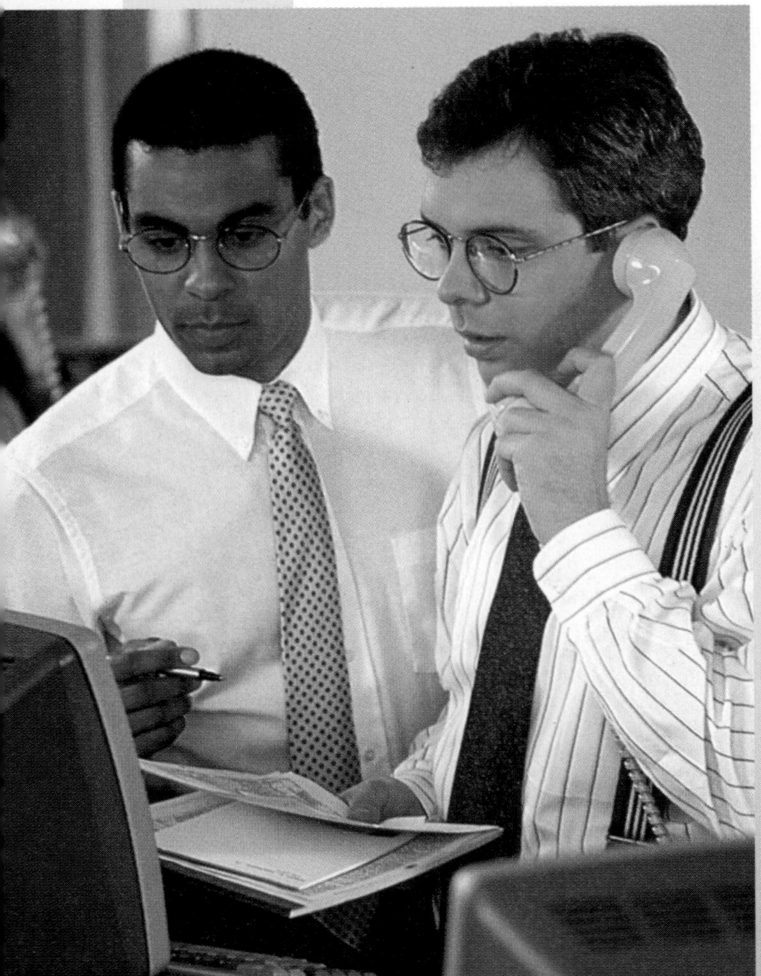

OBJECTIVES

After studying this chapter, you will be able to

1. Describe the three ways to design a company's formal organization structure
2. Explain the concepts of authority, accountability, responsibility, delegation, and span of management
3. Define four types of departmentalization
4. Clarify how vertical organization differs from horizontal coordination
5. Describe the four primary types of teams
6. Review the five stages of team development
7. Explain how companies use internal and external communication networks
8. List some of the barriers to effective communication and explain how to overcome them

ON THE JOB: FACING BUSINESS CHALLENGES AT LEXMARK INTERNATIONAL

From IBM to Independence

How do you build a new, independent organization after years of control by a gigantic, global parent? That was the challenge facing top executives at Lexmark International. The original factory in Lexington, Kentucky, was a division of IBM, manufacturing electric typewriters renowned for their durability and useful features. In later years, after IBM introduced the personal computer, the division also made keyboards and printers. Then IBM decided to get out of the typewriter and printer business. An investment firm bought the division in 1991, along with the right to use the IBM name on its products until 1996.

The new company was called Lexmark, a combination of *lex* (derived from *lexicon,* a dictionary or a particular vocabulary) and *mark* (from the idea of making a mark on paper, like a printer). A 32-year veteran of IBM, Marvin L. Mann was appointed CEO. In turn, he recruited other IBM executives to head production, research and development, human resources, and sales and marketing. Together, they were responsible for planning the transition from operating as one of many IBM divisions to operating as an independent company making $1.8 billion in sales to customers all over the world.

Lexmark started life with more than 5,000 employees but soon slimmed down to 4,100 by offering payouts to people who agreed to leave the company voluntarily. The company inherited a well-trained and motivated work force from parent IBM, and it shared IBM's commitment to high quality and strict ethical standards. However, Mann wanted some things at Lexmark to be different from the way they were under IBM. He was concerned that the new company would have a hard time putting creative ideas in motion if employees on the shop floor had to go through layers of management to talk with decision makers at the top. He also wanted to speed up decision making by avoiding the delays IBM experienced when managers from different departments challenged each other's proposals. Finally, he wanted Lexmark employees to risk trying new things without fearing that they would be punished for failures.

Mann and his management team knew well that these changes wouldn't be easy—altering the way employees work together and even modifying the way ideas flow upward and downward. If the new company was to thrive on its own, managers and employees alike would have to forget the IBM way and build an entirely new organization. How could Mann set up a structure that would unleash his employees' creativity and entrepreneurial spirit? In what way could he arrange work tasks to manufacture printers more efficiently? How could he streamline Lexmark to allow the company to respond quickly to changes in customer needs and shifts in competitive pressures?[1]

ORGANIZATION

organization structure
Framework enabling managers to divide responsibilities, ensure employee accountability, and distribute decision-making authority

organization chart
Diagram showing how employees and tasks are grouped and where the lines of communication and authority flow

As Marvin Mann can tell you, a company's strategy is supported by its organization. Strategic planning defines a company's goals and how it will accomplish them; **organization structure** helps the company achieve its goals by providing a framework through which managers can divide responsibilities, hold employees accountable for their work, and effectively distribute the authority to make decisions. When managers design the organization's structure, they use an **organization chart** to provide a visual representation of how employees and tasks are grouped and how the lines of communication and authority flow. Exhibit 7.1 shows the organization chart for a large consumer-products company.

Small companies also depend on organizational structures. Of course, the structure of a small company is usually much simpler than that of a huge corporation like Boeing or Safeway, and employees may be called on to perform a broader range of functions within smaller organizations. However, the organizational charts of small companies usually follow designs similar to those of large companies, with at least one manager at the top who is supported by various other managers and workers below. Exhibit 7.2 shows the organization chart for a small but growing Web page design company.

An organization chart depicts the official design for accomplishing tasks that lead to achieving the organization's goals, a framework known as the *formal organization.* Every

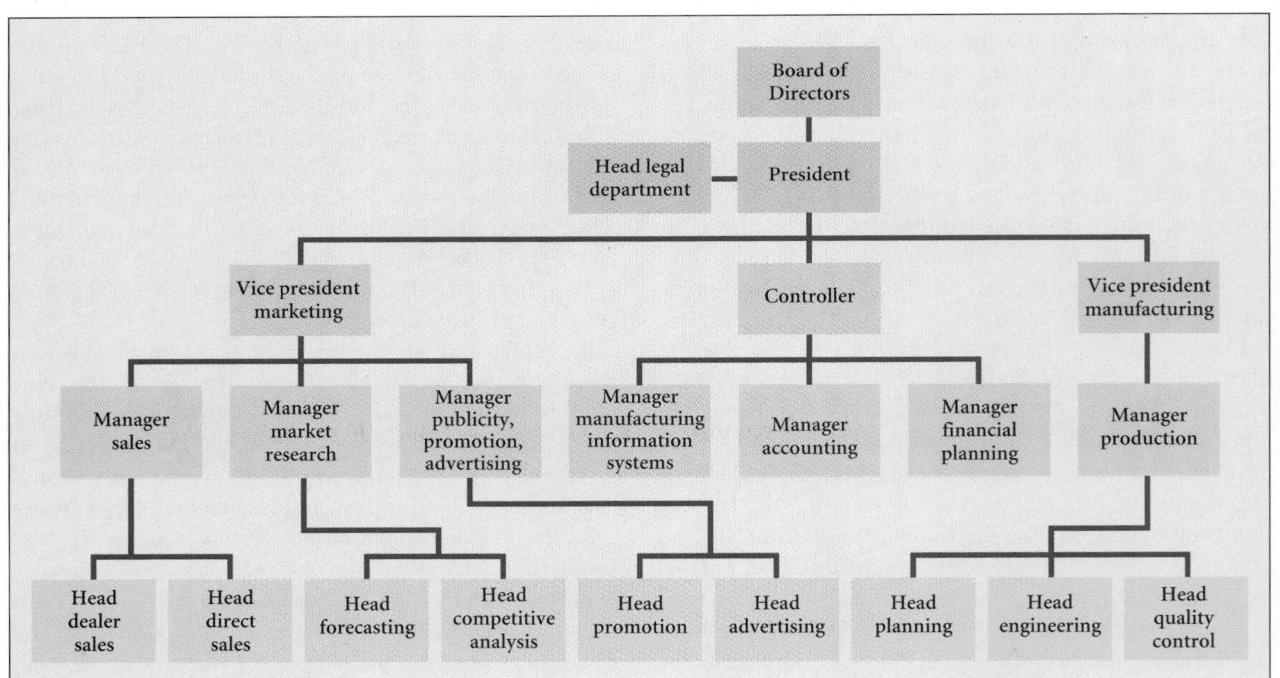

EXHIBIT 7.1

Organization Chart for a Large Consumer-Products Company

At first look, organization charts may appear very similar. In fact, the traditional model of an organization is a pyramid in which numerous boxes form the base and lead up to fewer and fewer boxes on higher levels, ultimately arriving at one box at the top. A glance at a company's organization chart reveals who has authority over whom, who is responsible for whose work, and who is accountable to whom.

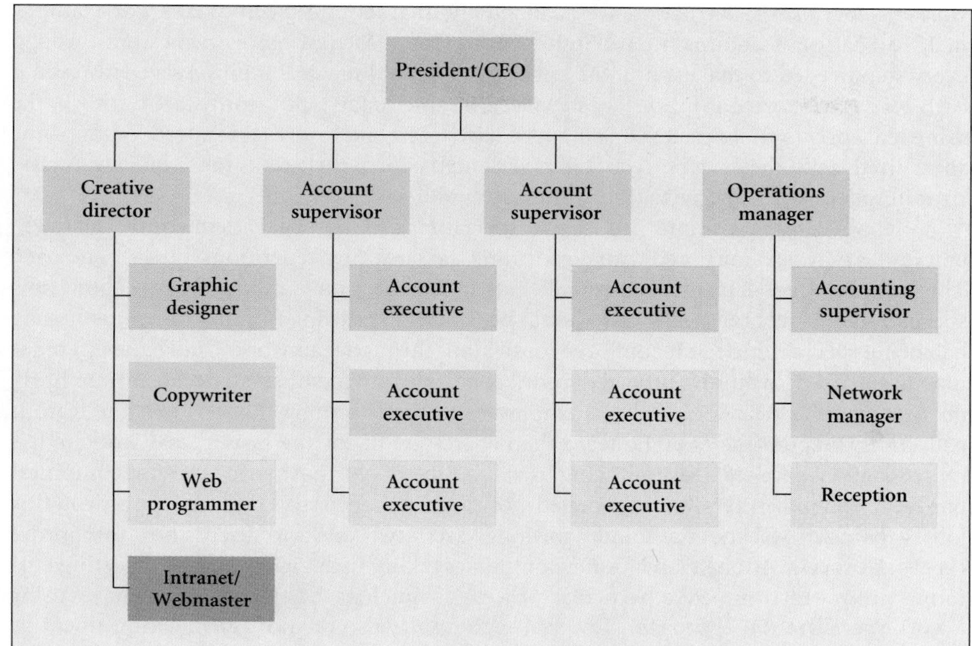

EXHIBIT 7.2

Organization Chart for Web Creations

Although employees in a small company may be called on to fulfill a broader range of roles than their counterparts in larger firms, the organization charts of both small and large companies follow a similar pattern.

company also has an **informal organization**—the network of interactions that develop on a personal level among workers. Sometimes the interactions among people in the informal organization parallel their relationships in the formal organization, but interactions often transcend formal boundaries. Crossing formal boundaries can help establish a more pleasant work environment, but it can also undermine formal work processes and hinder a company's ability to get things done.[2]

informal organization
Network of informal employee interactions that are not defined by the formal structure

Managers rely on a formal organization structure to coordinate and control the organization's work. In some organizations, this structure is a relatively rigid, vertical hierarchy like the management pyramid described in Chapter 6. In other organizations, teams of employees and managers from across levels and functions work together to make decisions and achieve the organization's goals.[3] To design a company's formal organization structure, managers have traditionally considered three phases: (1) vertical organization—defining individual jobs to complete the tasks necessary to achieve company goals; (2) departmentalization—grouping jobs into departments and larger units; and (3) horizontal coordination—aligning all tasks across departments and divisions. All three elements are needed for a company to achieve its goals.

Vertical Organization

Vertical organization links the activities at the top of the organization with those at the middle and lower levels.[4] After top managers set the mission and organizational goals, they define the tasks and hire the people necessary to achieve those goals.

vertical organization
Structure linking activities at the top of the organization with those at the middle and lower levels

Work Specialization Because businesses perform a wide variety of tasks, work can be completed more efficiently if employees are allowed to specialize. **Work specialization,** also referred to as *division of labor,* is the degree to which organizational tasks are broken down into separate jobs.[5] Few employees have the skills to perform every task a company needs. Therefore, work specialization can improve organizational efficiency by enabling each

work specialization
Specialization in or responsibility for some portion of an organization's overall work tasks; also called division of labor

worker to perform tasks that are well defined and that require specific skills. For example, in 1776 Scottish economist Adam Smith found that if each of ten workers went through every step needed to make a pin, the entire group could make 200 pins a day. However, if each worker performed only a few steps and no one made a pin from start to finish, the same ten workers could make 48,000 pins a day. When employees concentrate on the same specialized tasks, they can perfect their skills and perform their tasks more quickly. A classic example of work specialization is the automobile assembly line.

However, organizations can overdo specialization. If a task is defined too narrowly, employees may become bored with performing the same tiny, repetitious job over and over. They may also feel unchallenged and alienated. Managers must think carefully about how specialized or how broad each task should be. In fact, a growing number of companies are balancing specialization and employee motivation through teamwork. Unlike the pin manufacturers of Adam Smith's time, teamwork enables group members to decide how to break down a complex task, and it allows employees to rotate among the jobs that the team is collectively responsible for. The team then shares credit for the results, and workers feel more like they have created something of value. One of North America's largest computer-hardware manufacturers has eliminated position boundaries by creating teams, rotating job assignments weekly, and holding meetings every two weeks to discuss how to improve the work process. As one study found, companies taking such an approach to meeting customer needs can complete a particular process as much as 7.4 times faster than by using a work specialization approach. However, such results also require a firm commitment by management to create a collaborative corporate culture.[6] The team approach to organization is discussed in more depth later in this chapter.

Is It True?

Three out of four Fortune 1000 executives surveyed would give up their private offices if they knew it would improve productivity at their companies.

responsibility
Obligation to perform the duties and achieve the goals and objectives associated with a particular position

accountability
Obligation to report results to supervisors or team members and justify outcomes that fall below expectations

authority
Power granted by the organization to make decisions, take actions, and allocate resources to accomplish goals

Authority, Accountability, Responsibility, and Delegation Regardless of how an organization divides its tasks, it will function more smoothly if employees are clear about two things: who is responsible for each task, and who has the authority to make official decisions. All employees have a certain amount of **responsibility**—the obligation to perform the duties and achieve the goals and objectives associated with their jobs. As they work toward the organization's goals, employees must also maintain their **accountability,** the obligation both to report the results of their work to supervisors or team members and to justify any outcomes that fall below expectations. Managers ensure that tasks are accomplished by exercising **authority,** the power to make decisions, issue orders, carry out actions, and allocate resources to achieve the organization's goals. Authority is vested in the positions that managers hold, and it flows down through the management pyramid. Thus vertical structure helps managers delegate author-

BEST OF THE WEB

Learn How to Make It "Small-Time"

So you want to be your own boss? You're not alone. Many people who have grown tired of working for large organizations are now striking out on their own to start small businesses. It's an exciting prospect but also a little bit scary. Suddenly you're at the top of the organization chart, and others are depending on you to set goals, define priorities, and delegate tasks. Fortunately, help is available in the form of The American Express Small Business Exchange. This easy-to-use site provides a vast amount of information on topics of interest to small-business owners: how to get started, where to find financing, how to manage your employees, and how to stay organized. You will also find resources for promoting your business, expanding internationally, managing growth, and more. And if you have a specific question, you can e-mail it to American Express for expert advice.
http://americanexpress.com/smallbusiness

ity to positions throughout the organization's hierarchy. **Delegation** is the assignment of work and the transfer of authority and responsibility to complete that work.[7]

delegation
Assignment of work and the authority and responsibility required to complete it

Look again at Exhibit 7.1. The sales manager delegates responsibilities to both the head of dealer sales and the head of direct sales. These department heads have the authority to make certain decisions necessary to fulfill their roles, and they are accountable to the sales manager for the performance of their respective divisions. In turn, the sales manager is responsible for total sales performance and is accountable to the vice president of marketing.

Of course, department heads and lower-level managers sometimes face decisions that are broader than their scope of authority. At such times, they may push decisions up the **chain of command**—the unbroken line of authority that connects each level of management. So the head of dealer sales may pass the decision on to the sales manager, the vice president of marketing, or even the president.

chain of command
Pathway for the flow of authority from one management level to the next

The simplest and most common chain-of-command system is known as **line organization** because it establishes a clear line of authority flowing from the top down. Everyone knows who is accountable to whom, as well as which tasks and decisions they are responsible for. The chart in Exhibit 7.1 is a line organization. However, line organization sometimes falls short because the technical complexity of a firm's activities may require specialized knowledge that individual managers don't have and can't easily acquire. A more elaborate system called **line-and-staff organization** was developed out of the need to combine specialization with management control. In such an organization, managers in the chain of command are supplemented by functional groupings of people known as *staff,* who provide advice and specialized services but who are not in the line organization's chain of command (see Exhibit 7.3).

line organization
Chain-of-command system that establishes a clear line of authority flowing from the top down

line-and-staff organization
Organization system that has a clear chain of command but that also includes functional groups of people who provide advice and specialized services

Span of Management The number of people a manager directly supervises is called the **span of management** or *span of control.* When a large number of people report directly to one person, that person has a wide span of management. This is common in **flat organizations** that have relatively few levels in the management hierarchy. Sun Microsystems, Visa,

span of management
Number of people under one manager's control; also known as span of control

flat organizations
Organizations having a wide span of management and few hierarchical levels

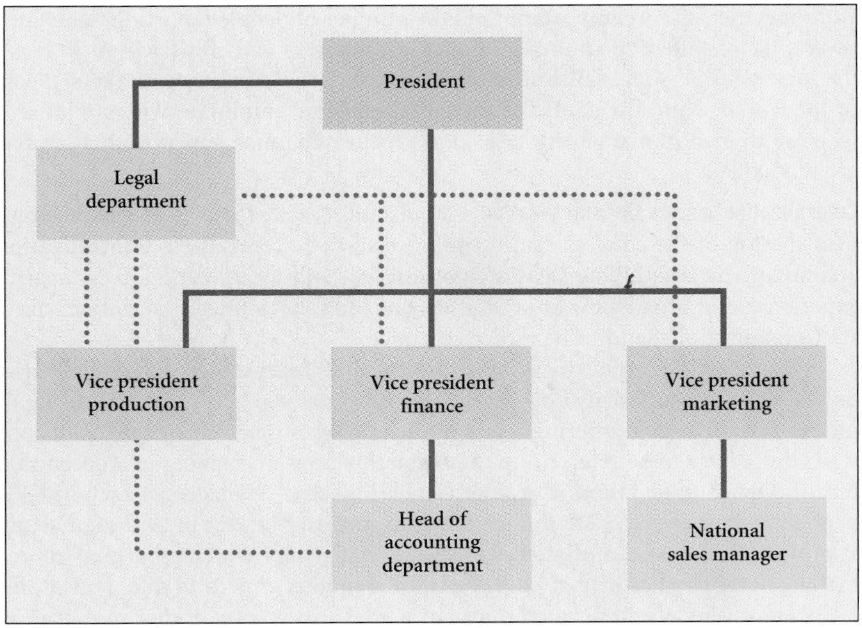

EXHIBIT 7.3

Simplified Line-and-Staff Structure

A line-and-staff organization divides employees into those who are in the direct line of command (from the top level of the hierarchy to the bottom) and those who provide staff (or support) services to line managers at various levels. Staff reports directly to top management.

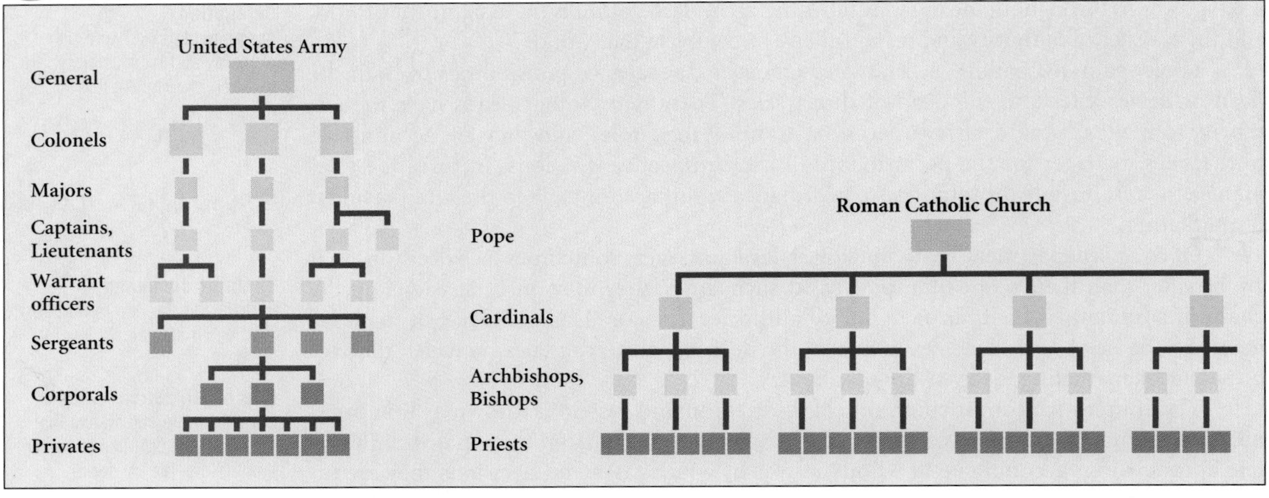

EXHIBIT 7.4

Tall versus Flat Organizations

A tall organization has many levels with a narrow span of management at each level so that relatively few people report to each manager on the level above them. In contrast, a flat organization has relatively few levels with a wide span of management so that more people report to each manager.

tall organizations
Organizations having a narrow span of management and many hierarchical levels

centralization
Concentration of decision-making authority at the top of the organization

decentralization
Delegation of decision-making authority to employees in lower-level positions

and Oticon (a hearing-aid manufacturer in Denmark) are all companies that have flat organizations. In contrast, **tall organizations** have many hierarchical levels, usually with only a few people reporting to each manager. In such cases, the span of management is narrow (see Exhibit 7.4). General Motors has traditionally had a tall organizational structure with as many as 22 layers of management. However, like many companies, GM is trying to flatten its organization structure by delegating some middle management responsibilities to work teams.[8]

No formula exists for determining the ideal span of management. How well people work together is more important than the number of people reporting to one person. Still, several factors affect the number of people a manager can effectively supervise, including the manager's personal skill and leadership ability, the skill of the workers, the motivation of the workers, and the nature of the job. In general, employees who are highly skilled or who are trained in many work tasks don't require as much supervision as employees who are less skilled.

Sun Microsystems CEO Scott G. McNealy has built a very successful company with a flat organizational structure.

Centralization versus Decentralization Organizations that focus decision-making authority near the top of the chain of command are said to be centralized. **Centralization** benefits a company by simplifying vertical coordination and by utilizing top management's rich experience and broad view of organizational goals. Both line organizations and line-and-staff organizations tend to be rather centralized.

However, the trend in business today is to decentralize. **Decentralization** pushes decision-making authority down to lower organizational levels, thereby easing the burden on top executives and offering lower-level employees more challenge. Also, because decisions don't have to be referred up the hierarchy, decision making in a decentralized organization tends to be faster.[9] Consider General Electric. Managers at each of GE's 13 independent businesses have $25 million they can spend as they see fit, without having to get the approval of the board of directors or the CEO. Giving each core business more decision-making authority has helped GE achieve tremendous growth in sales and profits.[10]

However, decentralization does not work in every situation or in every company. In times of crisis, strong authority from the top of the chain of command may be needed to keep the organization focused on immediate goals. Managers should select the level of decision making that will most effectively serve the organization's needs given the individual circumstances.[11]

Departmentalization

Whereas an organization uses vertical structure to define formal relationships and the division of tasks among employees and managers, that organization must also define specific jobs and activities across vertical levels. For vertical organization, managers use **departmentalization**—the arrangement of activities into logical groups that are then clustered into larger departments and units that form the total organization.[12] Four common ways of departmentalizing are by function, division, matrix, and network. An organization may use more than one method of departmentalization, depending on its particular needs.

departmentalization
Grouping people within an organization according to function, division, matrix, or network

Function **Departmentalization by function** groups employees according to their skills, resource use, and expertise. Common functional departments include operations, marketing, human resources, finance, research and development, and accounting, with each department working independently of the others.[13] Functional departmentalization is highly centralized and offers several advantages: (1) Grouping employees by specialization allows for the efficient use of resources and encourages the development of in-depth skills. (2) Centralized decision-making enables unified direction by top management. (3) Centralized operations enhance communication and the coordination of activities within departments. However, functional departmentalization can allow barriers and conflicts to develop between departments, thereby slowing response to environmental change, hindering effective planning for products and markets, and overemphasizing work specialization (which alienates employees),[14] which is why most large companies have abandoned the functional structure in the past decade or so. One company that still uses a functional design, however, is Food Lion, a grocery store chain based in Salisbury, North Carolina (see Exhibit 7.5).[15]

departmentalization by function
Grouping workers according to their similar skills, resource use, and expertise

Division **Departmentalization by division** establishes self-contained departments that encompass all the major functional resources required to achieve their goals—such as research and design, manufacturing, finance, and marketing. These departments are typically formed according to similarities in product, process, customer, or geography. Time Warner uses a structure based on **product divisions**—grouping companies that make similar products into appropriate divisions such as Publishing (magazines and books), Time Warner Entertainment Group (films, television, and theme parks), and Warner Music Group (recorded music) (see Exhibit 7.6). Other companies that use product divisions include General Motors, du Pont, and Procter & Gamble.[16]

departmentalization by division
Grouping departments according to similarities in product, process, customer, or geography

product divisions
Divisional structure based on products

In contrast, **process divisions,** also called *process-complete* departments, are based on the major steps of a production process. For example, a table-manufacturing company might have three divisions, one for each phase of manufacturing a table (see Exhibit 7.7). Astra/Merck, a company that markets anti-ulcer and high-blood-pressure drugs, is organized around six process divisions, including drug development and distribution.[17]

process divisions
Divisional structure based on the major steps of a production process

The third approach, **customer divisions,** concentrates activities on satisfying specific groups of customers. For example, Johnson & Johnson devotes a separate division to each of its three main types of customers for health-care products: (1) consumer, (2) professional, and (3) pharmaceutical markets (see Exhibit 7.8).

customer divisions
Divisional structure that focuses on customers or clients

Finally, **geographic divisions** enable companies that are spread over a national or an international area to respond more easily to local customs, styles, and product preferences.

geographic divisions
Divisional structure based on location of operations

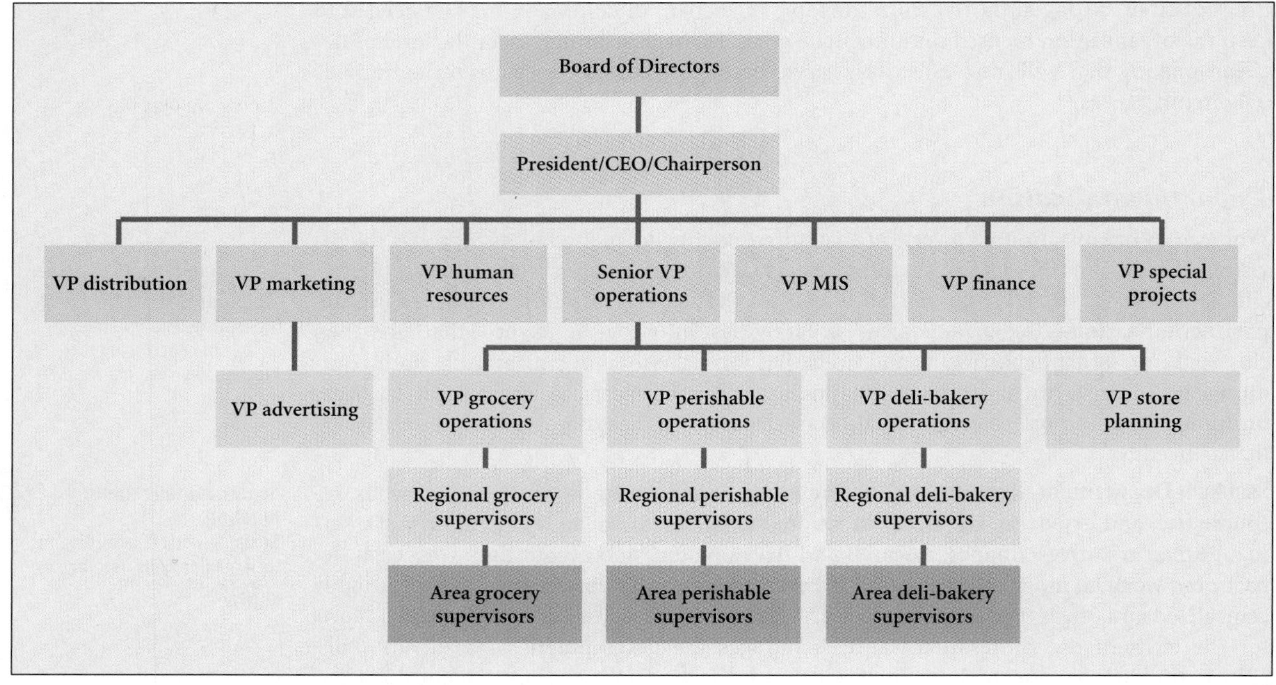

EXHIBIT 7.5

Departmentalization by Function

Departmentalization by function divides employees into groups according to their job functions, allowing specialists to have direct authority in their area of expertise. The Food Lion grocery store chain is organized according to seven primary functional areas.

For example, Quaker Oats has two main geographic divisions: (1) U.S. and Canadian Grocery Products and (2) International Grocery Products. Each division is further subdivided to allow the company to focus on the needs of customers in specific regions (see Exhibit 7.9).

Divisional departmentalization offers both advantages and disadvantages. First, because they are self-contained, divisions can react quickly to change, thus making the organization more flexible. In addition, because each division focuses on a limited number

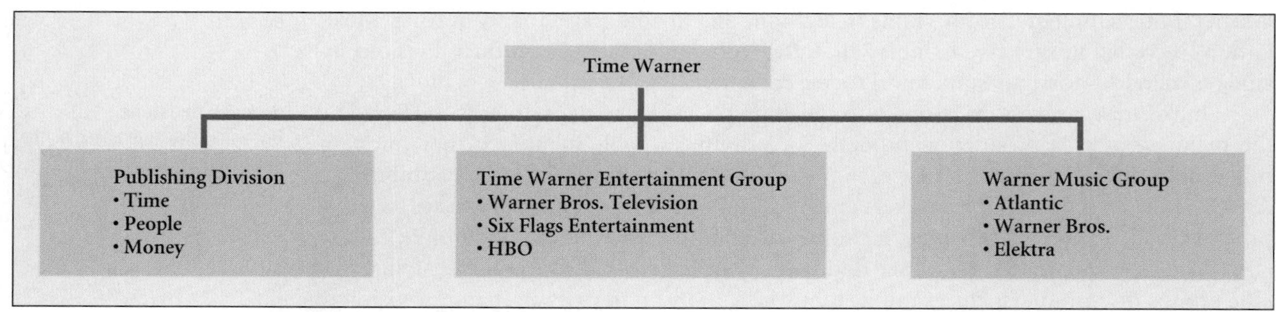

EXHIBIT 7.6

Product Divisions

Time Warner employees are grouped according to what they produce, which brings together people of diverse skills.

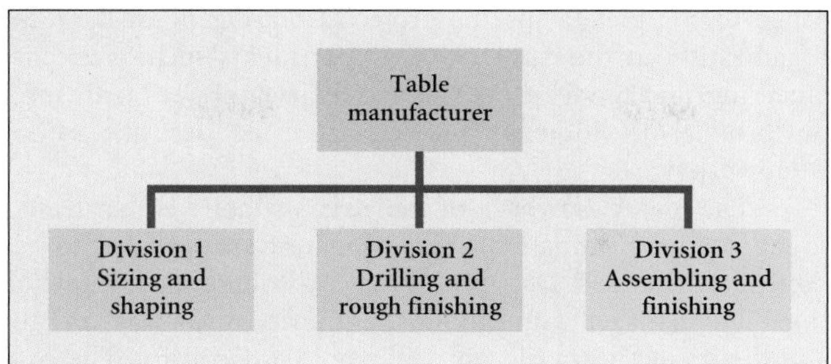

EXHIBIT 7.7

Process Divisions

Because process divisions allow employees to specialize in particular tasks, the production overall is more efficient.

of products, processes, customers, or locations, divisions can offer better service to customers. Moreover, top managers can focus on problem areas more easily, and managers can gain valuable experience by dealing with the various functions in their divisions. However, divisional departmentalization can also increase costs by duplicating the use of resources such as facilities and personnel. Furthermore, poor coordination between divisions may cause them to focus too narrowly on divisional goals and neglect the organization's overall goals. Finally, divisions may compete with one another for employees, money, and other resources, causing rivalries that hurt the organization as a whole.[18]

departmentalization by matrix
Assigning employees to both a functional group and a project team (thus using functional and divisional patterns simultaneously)

Matrix **Departmentalization by matrix** is a structural design in which employees from functional departments form teams to combine their specialized skills. This structure allows the company to pool and share resources across divisions and functional groups. The matrix may be a permanent feature of the organization's design, or it may be estab-

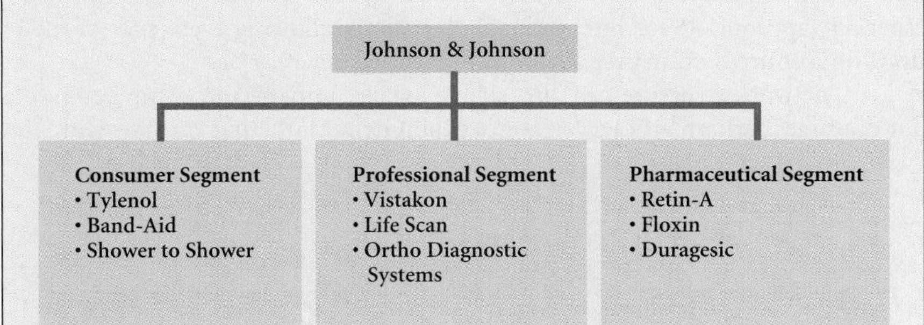

EXHIBIT 7.8

Customer Divisions

Customer divisions lead employees to focus on customer needs and customer service.

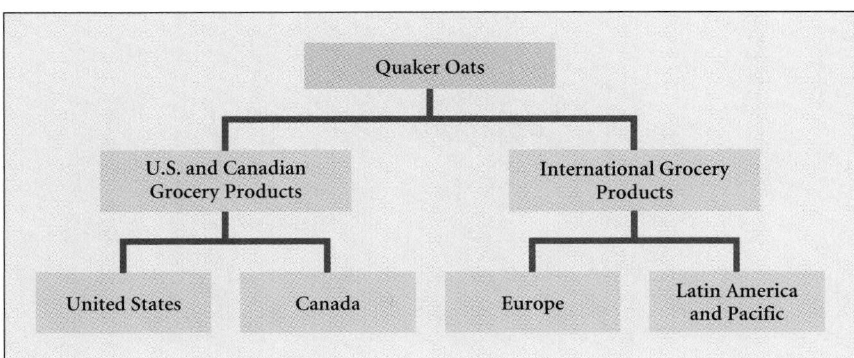

EXHIBIT 7.9

Geographic Divisions

Geographic divisions, such as those established by Quaker Oats, allow employees to concern themselves with local and regional issues.

lished to complete a specific project. Consider Black & Decker, which formed a matrix organization in the early 1990s. Departments such as mechanical design, electrical engineering, and model shop assigned their employees with specific technical skills to work on product-development projects in categories like saws, cordless appliances, and woodworking.[19]

The major drawback of a matrix structure is that team members usually continue to report to their functional department heads as well as to a project team leader (see Exhibit 7.10). Black & Decker realized this soon after it implemented the matrix organization. The manager with the most authority was always the functional department head, and the project team did not really hold any control. The company has since redesigned its organizational structure, which is now based on product divisions that employ teams of people from many functional areas.[20]

In a matrix organization, excellent communication and coordination are necessary to avoid potential conflicts that may arise. In addition, companies may find it difficult to coordinate the tasks of diverse functional specialists so that projects are completed efficiently.[21] However, because it facilitates the pooling of resources across departments, a matrix organization can also enable a company to respond better to changes in the business environment.

departmentalization by network
Electronically connecting separate companies that perform selected tasks for a small headquarters organization

Network **Departmentalization by network** is a method of electronically connecting separate companies that perform selected tasks for a headquarters organization. Also called a *virtual organization*, the network organization *outsources* engineering, marketing, research, accounting, production, distribution, or other functions. This means that the organization hires other organizations under contracts to handle one or more of these functions. In fact, companies like Nike, Liz Claiborne, and Dell Computer sell hundreds of millions of dollars' worth of products, even though they don't own manufacturing facilities—they all outsource manufacturing. As these companies have learned, the network approach is especially appropriate for international operations, allowing every part of the business to draw on resources no matter where in the world they may be.[22]

A network structure can also enable small companies to compete on a large scale. For example, Barbara Schrager operates Attainment Marketing Partners with only one em-

EXHIBIT 7.10

Departmentalization by Matrix

In a matrix structure, each employee is assigned to both a functional group (with a defined set of basic functions, such as production manager) and a project team (which consists of members of various functional groups working together on a project, such as bringing out a new consumer product).

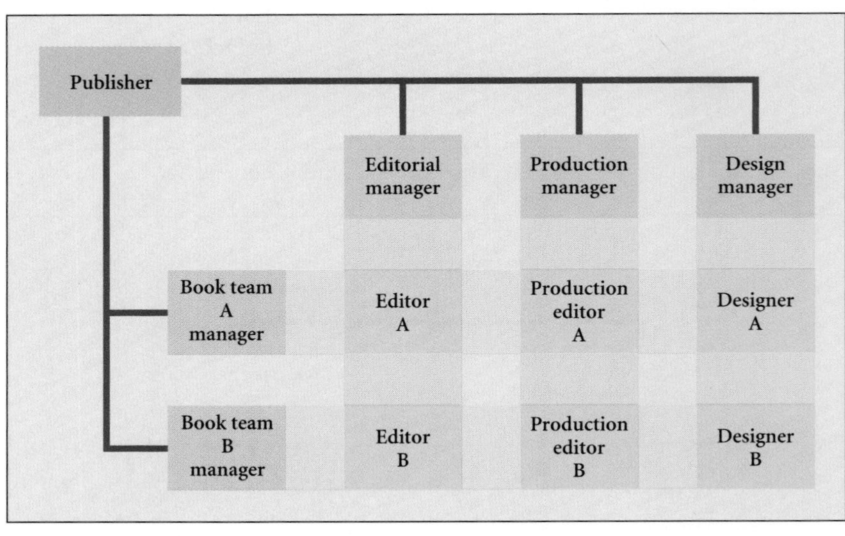

ployee. By using a virtual staff of designers and copywriters who work for her under contract on specific projects, she is able to create marketing, advertising, and public relations campaigns for major clients in New York.[23]

As Barbara Schrager knows, a network structure is extremely flexible because it gives companies the ability to hire whatever services are needed and then change them after a short time. In addition, the limited hierarchy required to manage a network organization permits the company to make decisions and react to change quickly. The organization can also continually redefine itself, and a lean structure usually means employees have greater job variety and satisfaction. However, the network approach lacks hands-on control, because the functions are not in one location or company. Also, if one company in the network goes out of business or fails to deliver, the headquarters organization could suffer or even go out of business. Finally, strong employee loyalty and team spirit are less likely to develop because there is a much weaker emotional connection between the employee and the organization.[24]

Horizontal Coordination

Regardless of whether it uses a functional, divisional, matrix, or network structure, every organization must coordinate activities and communication among its different departments. **Horizontal coordination** facilitates communication across departments without the need to go up and down the vertical chain of command. Horizontal coordination also gives employees the opportunity to share their views, which strengthens their willingness to understand, support, and implement innovative ideas. Without horizontal coordination, departments would be isolated from one another, and they would be unable to align their objectives. As a result, the company would be inefficient.[25]

horizontal coordination
Coordinating communication and activities across departments

One way organizations achieve horizontal coordination is by sharing information, processing data, and communicating ideas through information systems. These information systems include internal written communications, such as reports, bulletins, and memos, as well as electronic communication devices, such as computers, electronic mail, and teleconferences. Another means of achieving horizontal coordination is to use a **managerial integrator** who coordinates the activities of several functional departments, usually in relation to a specific project, without officially being a member of any particular department. These managers often have titles such as project manager, product manager, brand manager, program manager, or branch manager. However, even though integrating managers have authority over the project, product, brand, program, or branch, they have no authority over the employees working on it because functional department managers retain line authority over their employees. Nevertheless, when integrating managers use their human relations skills to resolve problems that arise between departments, they improve the horizontal coordination of their projects.[26] Janine Coleman has been a project manager for AT&T's global business communications systems for over a decade. Although Coleman is responsible for the outcomes of the projects she controls, she doesn't have a budget or a staff. Both of these resources come from other departments, and they change from project to project. So Coleman must work hard to coordinate resources between departments. "If a (vice president) won't go along," she says, "it's up to the project manager to get him to."[27]

managerial integrator
Manager who coordinates activities of several functional departments but belongs to none

A company's character is defined by the degrees of vertical and horizontal organization it has. An organization that emphasizes vertical structure maintains tight control over hierarchical levels, defines jobs rigidly, sets up many specific rules, centralizes authority, and communicates through the vertical hierarchy. However, an organization that emphasizes horizontal coordination loosens the control, allows tasks to be redefined to fit employee or environmental needs, decentralizes authority and decision making, and encourages communication. Many organizations try to strike a balance between vertical and horizontal structures so that they can benefit from the best features of both.[28] One way to accomplish this is through teamwork.

TEAMWORK

Even though the vertical chain of command is a tried-and-true method of organizing for business, it is limited by the fact that decision-making authority is often located too high up the management hierarchy. As a result, companies may become slow to react to change, and high-level managers may overlook many great ideas for improvement that originate in the lower levels of the organization. Many studies of individual industries show that companies using teamwork to organize, plan, and control activities enjoy greater productivity, increased profits, fewer defects, lower employee turnover, less waste, and even increased market value.[29] Teamwork enables managers to delegate more authority and responsibility to lower-level employees, which inspires greater commitment and innovation in workers. At Westinghouse Hanford, an electric power company, one team member notes that through teamwork "we come up with better ideas, work more cohesively and find better ways to solve problems." All of these factors help companies become more flexible and respond more quickly to the challenges of the competitive global environment.[30]

In a recent survey of Fortune 1000 executives, 83 percent said their firms are working in teams or moving in that direction.[31] Even though this sounds promising, achieving results may require a fundamental shift in the organization's culture. Management must

GAINING THE COMPETITIVE EDGE

The Challenge of Managing the Changing Organization

Unprecedented change is challenging U.S. businesses. Companies are trying to adapt to deregulation, rapid technological progress, takeover threats, and intense competition from abroad. On the other hand, change is itself being sought by some companies as a way to compete. Whether reacting to change or seeking it out, companies can use several organizational techniques to manage it. Among the most common are restructuring and downsizing, but managers are also using intrapreneurs, financial incentives, and corporate culture to manage change.

RESTRUCTURING

Rather than just rearranging boxes on the organization chart or changing individual work tasks, more companies are restructuring entire work processes. In this fundamental restructuring, known as *reengineering,* the organization rethinks a group of tasks that has become irrelevant and creates a new, more productive process that works better for the company and its customers.

One example is Digital Equipment Corporation (DEC). In order to consolidate its operations, DEC formed cross-functional, multicultural teams that encompass such areas as marketing, manufacturing, design engineering, product development, customer support, sales, and distribution. Since their implementation, the teams have reduced the time needed to develop new products from between one and three years to only six months.

DOWNSIZING

To reduce costs and become nimble enough to manage rapid change, companies are also reducing the number of people they employ. However, downsizing without restructuring work processes can lead to an organization so nervous about who will be laid off next that employees begin to think only of themselves and become unwilling to take risks that might benefit the firm. In addition, downsizing can cripple a company's long-term ability to meet customer needs. Eastman Kodak, Kohlberg Kravis Roberts, and Nynex are just a few of the many companies show strong support for team concepts by empowering teams to make important decisions about the work they do. Teams must also have clear goals that are tied to the company's strategic goals, and their outcomes need to be measured. In addition, employees must be motivated to work together in teams, which often involves extensive training and a compensation system that is based, at least in part, on team performance. This is sometimes accomplished though the use of stock options, profit sharing, and performance bonuses. Companies like Hewlett-Packard, Whole Foods Markets, and General Electric even base managers' salaries in part on the performance of teams.[32]

Is It True?

The majority of team failures are the result of employees not being compensated as a team.

Teams Defined

A **team** is a unit of two or more people who work together to achieve a goal. Unlike other groups of people, team members have a shared mission and are collectively responsible for their work. By coordinating their efforts, team members achieve performance levels that exceed what would be accomplished if they had worked individually.[33] At Microsoft, almost all work is completed in teams. Two factors that have made Microsoft teams so successful are clear goals and strong leadership.[34] Although the team's goals may be set either by the team or by upper management, it is the job of the team leader to make sure the team stays on track to achieve those goals. Team leaders are often appointed by senior managers, but sometimes they emerge naturally as the team develops.

team
A unit of two or more people who share a mission and collective responsibility as they work together to achieve a goal

The type, structure, and composition of individual teams within an organization all depend on the organization's strategic goals. This might mean creating a *formal team* that becomes part of the organization's structure, or it may involve establishing an *informal*

that lost sales or increased costs after downsizing. Before launching into a downsizing campaign, it is important for a company to consider how reducing costs will affect the level of benefits offered to customers. Building a leaner, more efficient organization is desirable, but it should not come at the expense of quality.

OTHER APPROACHES

Companies can encourage change and innovation by supporting intrapreneurs, entrepreneurs within the organization. Intrapreneurs use corporate resources to start their own product line under the corporate umbrella. For example, S. C. Johnson & Son (maker of Johnson Wax and Raid bug spray) has set up a $250,000 seed fund available to anyone at the company with a promising idea for a new product.

Organizations can also encourage change and innovation through financial incentives and recognition. For instance, the California state government pays employees 10 percent of any cost savings generated by their ideas. The program recently paid one man $109,000. And Callaway Golf uses high salaries, stock options, bonuses, praise, and public recognition to encourage employee innovation. Company founder Ely Callaway says that product innovation is his number one priority, and that "sprinkling gold dust on the employees always helps the bottom line."

Finally, many companies are encouraging innovative change by giving their employees more freedom. Hewlett-Packard, for example, allows its engineers access to company labs around the clock. In addition, it allows researchers to devote 10 percent of company time to exploring their own ideas, without fear of penalty for failure. Using these methods and more, the most successful companies these days are those that successfully manage change.

QUESTIONS FOR CRITICAL THINKING

1. Besides downsizing, how can companies reduce costs and increase their ability to respond to change?
2. What new challenges do you think a company may face as a result of downsizing or restructuring?

team that is designed to encourage employee participation but which is not part of the formal organization. Formal teams typically fall into three categories: vertical teams, horizontal teams, and special-purpose teams. The most common type of informal team is the problem-solving team.

problem-solving teams
Informal teams of 5 to 12 employees from the same department who meet voluntarily to find ways of improving quality, efficiency, and the work environment

Problem-Solving Teams Employees are often introduced to teamwork through **problem-solving teams.** These informal teams usually include 5 to 12 employees from the same department who meet voluntarily to find ways of improving quality, efficiency, and the work environment. Any recommendations they come up with are then submitted to management for approval.[35] Such teams are sometimes referred to as *quality circles.* Land Rover, a manufacturer of luxury sport-utility vehicles, was able to save millions of dollars, improve productivity, and sell more vehicles by using this type of team.[36] If the problem-solving teams are able to successfully contribute to the organization, as Land Rover's were, they may evolve into formal teams, which represents a fundamental shift in the way the organization is structured.

functional teams
Teams whose members come from a single functional department and that are based on the organization's vertical structure

Vertical Teams Vertical teams are organized along the lines of the organization's vertical structure. Usually referred to as **functional teams** or *command teams,* they are composed of managers and employees within a single functional department. For example, look again at Exhibit 7.4. Functional teams could be formed in Food Lion's marketing, human resources, and finance departments. The structure of a vertical team typically follows the formal chain of command. In some cases, the team may include several levels of the organizational hierarchy within the same functional department.[37]

cross-functional teams
Teams that draw together employees from different functional areas

Horizontal Teams In contrast to vertical teams, horizontal teams are composed of employees from about the same level of the hierarchy but from different functional areas. These teams are often called **cross-functional teams** because they draw together employees with different areas of expertise. For example, Boeing used hundreds of "design-build" teams that integrated design engineers and production workers to develop its new 777 airplane. In the past, the two groups worked independently, and engineers often came up with designs that production workers thought were either too costly or unbuildable. But now, says CEO Phillip Condit, Boeing is trying to "destroy all the old functional hierarchies."[38]

Cross-functional teams contribute in several ways to the organization's horizontal structure: (1) They facilitate the exchange of information between employees, (2) they generate ideas for how to best coordinate the organizational units that are represented, (3) they encourage new solutions for organizational problems, and (4) they aid the development of new organizational policies and procedures.[39] In many cross-functional teams, employees are cross-trained to perform a variety of tasks. At Pillsbury, the most experienced workers can handle 23 different jobs. Vice president of human resources David Ahlers believes that the more employees understand their roles in the entire process and how those roles affect others in the company, the more efficient each employee will be.[40] Cross-functional teams like Pillsbury's may report to a manager within the vertical hierarchy, or they may by completely self-directed.

self-directed teams
Teams in which members are responsible for an entire process or operation

Self-Directed Teams In addition to cross-training all team members, a **self-directed team** must obtain all the information, equipment, and supplies necessary to perform its assigned tasks. Furthermore, the team has the authority to make decisions such as whether to spend money, whom to hire, and what plans to make for the future. When Solectron implemented self-directed teams, the manufacturer of circuit boards and electronic components increased productivity almost 20 percent, as well as increasing quality substantially.[41]

As the name implies, self-directed teams manage their own activities and require minimum supervision. As you might imagine, many managers are reluctant to embrace this approach to goal achievement because it means they must give up much of the control they have grown accustomed to. For example, GM aspires to incorporate self-directed teams into its organization structure, as Ford and Chrysler have done. However, Oldsmobile general manager John Rock notes that many of the company's middle managers are unwilling to turn over their traditional areas of power.[42]

TASK FORCES A **task force** is a type of cross-functional team formed to work on a specific activity with a completion point. Several departments are usually involved so that all parties who have a stake in the outcome of the task are able to provide input. However, once the goal has been accomplished, the task force is disbanded.[43] Saint Francis Hospital in Tulsa, Oklahoma, established a task force to find ways to reduce the cost of supplies. The team members came from many departments, including surgery, laboratory, nursing, financial planning, administration, and food service. The team not only helped the hospital save money by curbing supply waste but also generated excitement among hospital employees about working together for common goals.[44]

COMMITTEES In contrast to a task force, a **committee** usually has a long life span and may become a permanent part of the organization structure. Committee members are usually selected based on their titles or positions rather than their personal expertise. This is because committees often require official representation in order to achieve their goals, which typically involve dealing with regularly recurring tasks. For example, a grievance committee may be formed as a permanent resource for handling employee complaints and concerns.

VIRTUAL TEAMS As a result of both globalization and advances in technology, another type of cross-functional team, the **virtual team,** has emerged as a way of bringing together geographically distant employees to accomplish goals. A company may have plants and offices around the world, but it can use computer networks, teleconferencing, e-mail, and global transportation to build teams that are as effective as those in organizations functioning under a single roof. As the leading provider of credit-card authorization equipment and networks, VeriFone has developed a competitive advantage by using a corporate computer network to link its employees in 30 locations around the world. All new VeriFone employees receive a laptop computer before even getting a desk, and they are encouraged to share information by accessing the network continually when they travel. The company's CEO boasts that VeriFone has "marketing tentacles everywhere," and that there is "no opportunity we don't find out about before our competitors do."[45]

At *La Opinion,* a Los Angeles newspaper directed to the Hispanic community, reporters, designers, and computer operators work in teams to share information and coordinate their activities.

task force
Team of people from several departments who are temporarily brought together to address a specific issue

committee
Team that may become a permanent part of the organization and is designed to deal with regularly recurring tasks

virtual teams
Teams that use communication technology to bring geographically distant employees together to achieve goals

Building Teams in the Cyber Age

BEST OF THE WEB

So you want to learn more about building effective teams? Many excellent books are available to help you. But you might be surprised by just how much information about team building you can find on the Internet. You can begin by accessing the Self Directed Work Teams Page (SDWT). This site's designers are passionate about teamwork, and they want to make it easier for others to work effectively in teams. Therefore, they have compiled many links to teamwork-related sites. Read the *Frequently Asked Questions* (FAQ) to better understand the site's mission, and then explore some of the links to discover more about how to work effectively in teams.
http://users.ids.net/7Ebrim/sdwth.html#ONE

special-purpose teams
Temporary teams that exist outside the formal organization hierarchy and are created to achieve a specific goal

Special-Purpose Teams **Special-purpose teams,** like task forces, are created as temporary entities to achieve specific goals. However, special-purpose teams are different because they exist outside the formal organization hierarchy. Such teams remain a part of the organization, but they have their own reporting structures, and members view themselves as separate from the normal functions of the organization. A special-purpose team might be used to develop a new product when complete creative freedom is needed. By operating outside the formal organization, the team would be able to test new ideas and new ways of accomplishing tasks.[46]

Team Characteristics

When developing teams of any type, managers must consider certain team characteristics, such as size and member roles. The optimal size for teams is generally thought to be between 5 and 12 members. Teams smaller than 5 may be lacking in skill diversity and may therefore be less effective at solving problems. Teams of more than 12 may be too large for group members to bond properly and may discourage some members from sharing their ideas. Larger groups are also prone to disagreements and factionalism because so many opinions must be considered, which makes the team leader's job more difficult. Moreover, studies have shown that turnover and absenteeism are higher in larger teams because members tend to feel that their presence makes less of a difference.

For a team to be successful over time, it must be structured to accomplish its task and also to meet its members' social well-being. Effective teams usually fulfill both of these requirements with a combination of members who assume one of four roles: task specialist, socioemotional, dual, or nonparticipator. People who assume the *task-specialist* role focus on helping the team reach its goals. In contrast, members who take on the *socioemotional role* focus on supporting the team's emotional needs and strengthening the team's social unity. Some team members are able to assume *dual roles,* contributing to the task and still meeting members' emotional needs. These members often make effective team leaders. At the other end of the spectrum are members who assume the *nonparticipator role,* contributing little either to reaching the team's goals or to meeting members' emotional needs. Exhibit 7.11 outlines the behavior patterns associated with each of these roles.

EXHIBIT 7.11

Team Members Roles
Team members assume one of these four roles. Members who assume a dual role often make effective team leaders.

Member Task Behavior	Low Member Social Behavior	High Member Social Behavior
High	**Task Specialist Role** Focuses on task accomplishment over human needs Important role, but if adopted by everyone, team's social needs won't be met	**Dual Role** Focuses on task and people May be a team leader Important role, but not essential if members adopt task specialist and socioemotional roles
Low	**Nonparticipator Role** Contributes little to either task or people needs of team Not an important role—if adopted by too many members, team will disband	**Socioemotional Role** Focuses on people needs of team over task Important role, but if adopted by everyone, team's tasks won't be accomplished

Team Development

Like the members who form them, teams grow and change as time goes by. You may think that each team evolves in its own way. However, research shows that teams typically go through five definitive stages of development: forming, storming, norming, performing, and adjourning.[47] The *forming stage* is a period of orientation and breaking the ice. Members get to know each other, determine what types of behavior are appropriate within the group, identify what is expected of them, and become acquainted with each other's task orientation. In the *storming stage,* members show more of their personalities, and they become more assertive in establishing their roles. Conflict and disagreement often arise during the storming stage as members may jockey for position or form coalitions to push their own perceptions of the group's mission. During the *norming stage,* these conflicts are resolved, and team harmony develops. Members come to understand and accept one another, they reach a consensus about who the leader is, and they reach agreement on what each member's roles are. In the *performing stage,* members are really committed to the team's goals. Problems are solved, and disagreements are handled with maturity in the interest of task accomplishment. Finally, if the team has a limited task to perform, it goes through the *adjourning stage* after the task is complete. In this stage, issues are wrapped up and the team is dissolved.

As the team moves through the various stages of development, two things happen. First, the team develops a certain level of **cohesiveness,** a measure of how committed the members are to the team's goals. The team's cohesiveness is reflected in meeting attendance, team interaction, work quality, and goal achievement. Cohesiveness is influenced by many factors. Two primary factors are competition and evaluation. If a team is in competition with other teams, cohesiveness increases as the team strives to win. In addition, if a team's efforts and accomplishments are recognized by the organization, members tend to be more committed to the team's goals. Strong team cohesiveness generally results in high morale. Moreover, when cohesiveness is coupled with strong management support for team objectives, teams tend to be more productive.

cohesiveness
A measure of how committed the team members are to their team's goals

The second thing that happens as teams develop is the emergence of **norms**—informal standards of conduct that members share and that guide their behavior. Norms define what is acceptable behavior. They also set limits, identify values, clarify what is expected of members, and facilitate team survival. Norms can be established in various ways: from early behaviors that set precedents for future actions, from significant events in the team's history, from behaviors that come to the team through outside influences, and from a leader's or member's explicit statements that have an impact on other members.[48]

norms
Informal standards of conduct that guide team behavior

Team Conflict

Managing a team requires many skills. However, none is more important than the ability to handle *conflict*—the antagonistic interactions resulting from differences in ideas, opinions, goals, or ways of doing things. Conflict can arise between team members or between different teams. Conflict interferes with the productive exchange of information and can destroy a team's cohesiveness.

Causes of Conflict Team conflicts can arise for a number of reasons. First, teams and individuals may feel they are in competition for scarce or declining resources, such as money, information, and supplies. Second, people may disagree about who is responsible for a specific task, which is usually the result of poorly defined responsibilities and job boundaries. Third, poor communication can lead to misunderstandings and misperceptions about other team members or other teams. In addition, intentionally withholding information can undermine trust among members. Fourth, basic differences in values, attitudes, and personalities may lead to clashes. Fifth, power struggles may result when one party questions the authority of another or when people or teams with limited authority attempt to increase their power or exert more influence. Sixth, conflicts can arise because individuals or teams are pursuing different goals.[49] For example, a British cardboard-manufacturing company switched from a hierarchical, functionally oriented organization to a team-based structure with the hope of empowering employees and reducing scrap. However, once they got started, the teams realized that the company had many problems to solve. Conflicts resulted when team members couldn't agree on which problems to tackle first.[50]

Conflict Resolution Each team member has a different style of dealing with conflict. These styles are primarily based on how competitive or cooperative team members are when a conflict arises. Depending on the particular situation, the same individual may use one of several styles, which include avoidance, defusion, and confrontation.[51] Avoidance may involve ignoring the conflict in the hope that it will subside on its own, or it may even involve physically separating the conflicting parties. Defusion may involve several actions, including downplaying differences and focusing on similarities between team members or teams, compromising on the disputed issue, taking a vote, appealing to a neutral party or higher authority, or redesigning the team. Confrontation is an attempt to work through the conflict by getting it out in the open, which may be accomplished by organizing a meeting between the conflicting parties.

These three styles of conflict resolution come into play after a conflict has developed. In the example of the British cardboard manufacturer, the team members defused the conflict by taking a vote. Each member nominated problems that they most wanted to fix, and those problems that had team consensus were addressed first.

Teams and team leaders can also take several steps to stop conflicts before they start. First, by establishing clear goals that require the efforts of every member, the team reduces the chance that members will battle over their objectives or roles. Second, by developing well-defined tasks for each member, the team leader ensures that all parties are aware of their responsibilities and the limits of their authority. And finally, by facilitating open communication, the team leader can ensure that all members understand their own tasks and objectives, as well as those of their teammates. Communication builds respect and tolerance, and it provides a forum for bringing misunderstandings into the open before they turn into full-blown conflicts.

Team Benefits and Costs

Even though teams can play a vital role in helping an organization reach its goals, they are not appropriate for every situation. Managers must weigh both the benefits and the costs of teams when deciding whether to use them.[52]

Benefits Teams have the potential to unleash vast amounts of creativity and energy in workers. Motivation and performance are often increased as workers share a sense of purpose and mutual accountability. Teams can also fill the need to belong to a group. In this way, they can reduce boredom, increase feelings of dignity and self-worth, and reduce stress and tension between workers. In addition, teams empower employees to bring more knowledge and skill to the tasks they perform, which often leads to greater efficiency and cost reduction. Finally, when employees work together in teams and are able to exchange jobs, the organization becomes more flexible. Workers can be reallocated as needed, and the company can meet changing customer needs more effectively. All of this can add up to more satisfied employees performing higher-quality work that helps the organization achieve its goals. Consider Kodak. Using teams has allowed it to cut in half the amount of time it takes to move a new product from the drawing board to store shelves. Tennessee Eastman, a division of Eastman

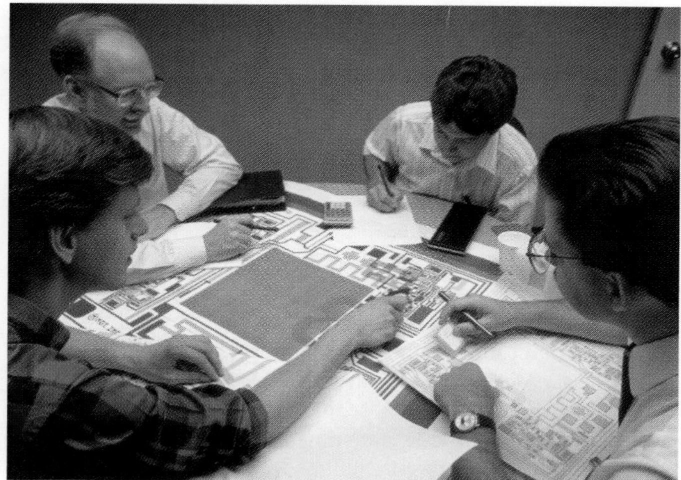

At Motorola in Phoenix, Arizona, this micromechanics design team meets frequently to make sure everyone's efforts are focused toward the same goal. As in any meeting, their understanding of the dynamics of their group helps them accomplish their objectives.

Chemical, increased labor productivity by 70 percent, Texas Instruments increased revenues per employee by over 50 percent, and Ritz-Carlton Hotels jumped to the top of the J. D. Power and Associates consumer survey of luxury hotels—all as a result of teamwork.[53]

Costs Although teamwork has many advantages, it also has a number of potential costs. For one thing, power within the organization becomes realigned with teams. Successful teams mean that fewer supervisors are needed—usually fewer middle and front-line managers. Adjusting to their changing job roles, or even to the loss of their jobs, is understandably difficult for many people. Another potential cost involves **free riders,** team members who don't contribute their fair share to the group's activities because they aren't being held individually accountable for their work. This attitude can lead to certain tasks going unfulfilled. A third drawback to teamwork is the high cost of coordinating group activities. Aligning schedules, arranging meetings, and coordinating individual parts of a project can eat up a lot of time and money. So members sometimes feel they are wasting time that could otherwise be spent completing their tasks. Fourth, a team may develop *groupthink,* a situation in which pressures to conform to the norms of the group cause members to withhold contrary or unpopular opinions. Groupthink can lead to less effective decision making because some possibilities will be overlooked.[54] Finally, creating teams can raise legal concerns in unionized organizations. Unions have a lot of power over how work will be structured in many companies. Although some unions embrace teamwork, others fear it as a tactic to crush union power. The Wagner Act of 1935 prevents companies from forming groups to undermine legitimate unions, but so far the courts have been vague as to whether or not work teams constitute such groups.[55]

free rider
Team member who doesn't contribute sufficiently to the group's activities because members are not being held individually accountable for their work

ORGANIZATIONAL COMMUNICATION

Whether an organization has a tall, vertical structure or is made up of cross-functional teams, communication provides the crucial link between individuals, teams, departments, and divisions. The sharing of information among the parts of an organization, as well as between the organization and the outside world, is the glue that binds the organization together.

Regardless of the field you're in or the career you choose, your chances of being hired by an organization are better if you possess strong communication skills. That's because every member of an organization is a link in the information chain. Whether you're a top man-

UNDERSTANDING THE HIGH-TECH REVOLUTION

How Computer Networks Are Changing the Way We Work

In the eighteenth century, the steam engine ignited the Industrial Revolution and would come to change the way people around the world work and live. In the late twentieth century, computers are having a similar effect. Network computing in particular has radically altered the way individuals communicate within organizations as well as how organizations communicate with one another.

For one thing, network communication can flatten an organization structure even when the organization chart is left intact. Historically, management passed decisions down through organizational layers; today, managers and employees can communicate instantaneously throughout the organization without always having to go through formal channels. This wider distribution of authority enables employees to integrate their work tasks and upgrade their work skills more easily. For example, using an advanced telecommunication system, the 1,200 employees of Buckman Labs are able to share information on projects at any of the company's 20 locations around the world.

Another way networks have changed the workplace is by making *telecommuting* possible. Telecommuters perform at least some of their work at home or on the road, communicating with other employees via e-mail, telephone, voice mail, and teleconferencing. Studies indicate that around 10 million people in the United States now telecommute at least part-time, and that number is expected to grow to 14 million over the next few years. KPMG Peat Marwick has even launched a practice to provide management consulting services to help companies design, implement, and manage telecommuting programs. When this giant of the consulting world goes into the business, you know the trend is more than a fad.

Of course, some jobs are clearly not designed for telecommuting. Production workers, researchers, and designers who require highly technical equipment; customer-

ager or an entry-level employee, you have information that others need to perform their jobs. At the same time others have information that is crucial to you. Your ability to receive, evaluate, use, and pass on information affects your company's success, as well as your own. Companies rely on employees who are skilled in both internal and external communication.

Internal Communication

internal communication
Communication among employees within an organization

Internal communication refers to the exchange of information and ideas within an organization. In a small business with only five or six employees, much information can be exchanged casually and directly. In a large organization, transmitting the right information to the right people at the right time is a real challenge. To meet this challenge, organizations depend on both formal and informal communication channels.

formal communication network
Communication network that follows the official structure of the organization

Formal Communication Channels The **formal communication network** is aligned with the official structure of the organization. As we have seen, this structure is illustrated by an organization chart like the one in Exhibit 7.1. Each box in the chart represents a link in the chain of command, and each line represents a formal channel for the transmission of official messages. Information may travel down, up, and across channels in the organization's formal hierarchy.

distortion
Misunderstanding that results from a message passing through too many links in the organization

When managers depend too heavily on formal channels for communicating, they risk encountering **distortion,** or misunderstanding. Every link in the communication chain opens up a chance for error. So by the time a message makes its way all the way up or down the chain, it may bear little resemblance to the original idea. As a consequence, people at lower levels may have only a vague idea of what top management expects of them, and executives may get an imperfect picture of what's happening lower down the chain. This is less of a problem in flat organizations than it is in tall organizations, as fewer levels means fewer links in the communication chain.

service employees; and managers who must meet continually with co-workers clearly need to work in a company facility. However, some jobs can actually be performed more effectively when employees are out of the office. Sales, writing, and research analysis are often perfect fits. Travelers Insurance actually encourages its account executives to spend as much time away from the office as they can. The company supplies them with powerful laptop computers and a corporate network that enables remote access to company records from almost any location. Account executives can now perform insurance audits from a customer's office, a hotel room, or a parking lot. Time that used to be spent traveling back and forth to the office can now be spent calling on customers. Moreover, audit processing time has been cut from 40 days to 24 hours.

In addition to providing employees with greater flexibility in their lives, telecommuting can also save a company money. For example, IBM used to have more offices than it had employees. However, now the company has embraced telecommuting as a way of reducing corporate overhead. "Hoteling" (assigning an open desk via a reservations system) and "hot desking" (assigning several people to the same desk at different times) are used to provide telecommuters with temporary work space when they need to come into the office.

Of course, telecommuting isn't for everyone. Some people simply perform better in a traditional work environment. But if your job description and personality enable you to work away from the office, you may just find yourself on the leading edge of a business revolution.

QUESTIONS FOR CRITICAL THINKING

1. What types of skills do you think a person needs to be a successful telecommuter?
2. What can telecommuters do to make sure their presence is still felt and valued within the organization?

DOWNWARD INFORMATION FLOW In most organizations, decisions are made at the top and then flow down to the people who will carry them out.[56] Downward messages might be transmitted verbally in a casual conversation, in a formal meeting, in a workshop, on videotape, or through voice mail. Messages might also be written in a memo, a training manual, a newsletter, a bulletin-board announcement, a policy directive, or an e-mail message. Most of what filters downward is geared toward helping employees do their jobs. Typical messages include briefings on the organization's mission and strategies, job instructions, explanations of policies and procedures, feedback on employee performance, and motivational pep talks. In hard times, downward communication is especially important because it lets employees know where the organization stands. American Airlines communications director Tim Doke doesn't want employees to "hear news about the company driving to work in the morning," so he uses a sophisticated, electronic communications system to disseminate crucial information in a timely manner.[57]

UPWARD INFORMATION FLOW Upward communication is just as vital as downward communication. To solve problems and make intelligent decisions, managers must learn what's going on in the organization. Because they can't be everywhere at once, executives depend on lower-level employees to furnish them with accurate, timely reports on problems, emerging trends, opportunities for improvement, grievances, and performance. For example, Southwest Airlines considers its 14,000 employees to be its major marketing research unit because they are in daily contact with customers and they report back to management what customers tell them.[58]

The danger, of course, is that employees will report only the good news. People are often afraid to admit their own mistakes or to report information that suggests their boss was wrong. Companies try to guard against the "rose-colored glasses" syndrome by creating reporting systems that require employees to furnish vital information on a routine basis. As CEO of a packaging-machinery manufacturer called Lantech, Pat Lancaster requires his managers to fill out a report at the end of every week to keep him aware of their problems and successes. Lancaster says it saves valuable time that used to be wasted trying to find answers to his questions.[59] Other methods for channeling information upward include group meetings, "exit interviews" with employees who are leaving the company, and formal procedures to resolve grievances.

Horizontal Information Flow In the formal communication network, horizontal communication flows from one department to another, either laterally or diagonally. This flow of information helps employees coordinate tasks and is especially useful for solving complex problems.[60] For example, in Exhibit 7.1, the sales manager might write a memo to the controller, outlining sales forecasts for the coming period; or the manager of production might phone the manager of advertising and promotion to discuss changes in the production schedule.

Companies that encourage horizontal communication report dramatic increases in productivity, largely because cooperation between employees from various departments breaks down the bureaucratic barriers that inhibit innovation and camouflage problems. At softwaremaker Oracle, where problems used to be taken to senior managers to be solved, horizontal communication has now become the norm. A program called "Vision and Values" requires employees to discuss issues first with peers before taking them to the next step in the formal chain of command.[61]

Informal Communication Channels Formal organization charts illustrate how information is supposed to flow. In actual practice, however, lines and boxes on a piece of paper cannot prevent people from developing other communication channels. As discussed earlier in this chapter, every company develops an informal organization in which the boundaries associated with official positions don't have the same meaning that they have in the formal organization. Within the informal organization is an informal communication network, or **grapevine,** that supplements official channels. As people go about their work, they have casual conversations with their friends in the office that deal with both business and nonbusiness matters. Sometimes these conversations spread rumors or gossip. Regardless, much useful information is also communicated through the grapevine. Exhibit 7.12 illustrates a typical informal communication network, which is often a very powerful structure within the company.

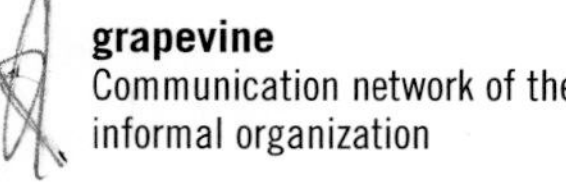

grapevine
Communication network of the informal organization

Some executives are wary of the informal communication network, possibly because it threatens their power to control the flow of information. However, rather than trying to eliminate the grapevine, savvy managers tap into it to spread and receive informal information. Managers can learn much about employee attitudes and perceptions of the company by staying linked to the grapevine. In fact, a technique called *management by walking around (MBWA)* encourages managers to interact with employees and become interested in their personal lives as well as their work lives. In addition to increasing a positive team spirit, MBWA, if done naturally and honestly, keeps managers tied into the informal communication network. However managers should not use informal communication channels for distributing official information.

networking
Making and using contacts both inside and outside the organization

Yet another form of information communication is **networking,** the art of making and using contacts both inside and outside the organization. Networking involves meeting many people, making your skills and talents known, and creating a positive impression of yourself as you interact with others. The more influential people you get to know, the broader your network is. Many managers move ahead quickly in their careers because of the relationships they've built through networking.[62]

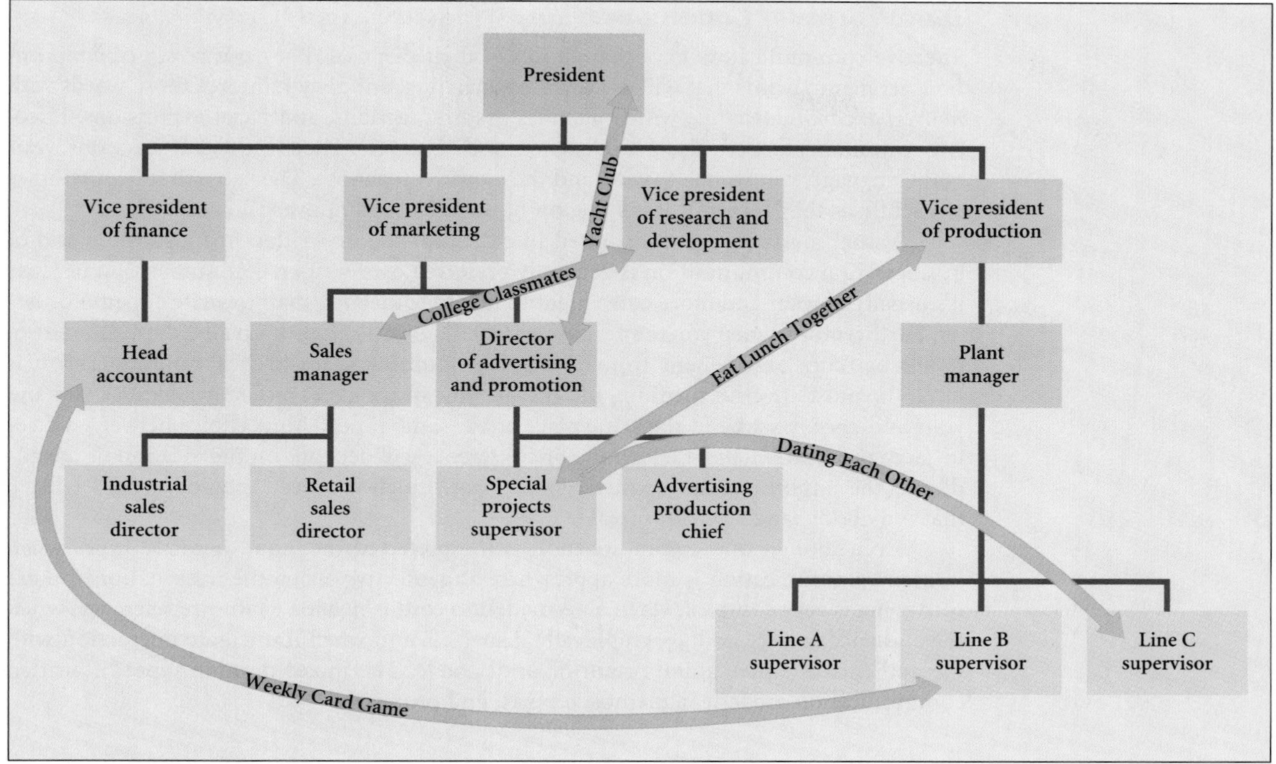

EXHIBIT 7.12

Informal Communication Network

In addition to its formal channels of communication, every company has an informal communication network. This network of social connections is often formed without regard for hierarchy or departmentalization.

External Communication

external communication network
Communication channels that carry information in and out of the organization

Just as the internal communication network carries information up, down, and across the organization, the **external communication network** carries information in and out. Companies constantly exchange messages with customers, vendors, distributors, competitors, investors, journalists, and government and community representatives. Most organizations attempt to control this external flow of information, and the marketing and public relations departments usually play major roles in such efforts.

However, not all external communications pass through formal channels. Every employee also acts as an informal channel of communication with the outside world. In the course of their daily activities, employees unconsciously absorb bits and pieces of information that add to the collective knowledge pool of the company. What's more, every time they speak for or about their company, employees send a message. In fact, those who have public-contact jobs don't even have to say anything. They create impressions about their company through their tone of voice, facial expressions, and general appearance.

Top managers rely on informal contacts with outsiders to exchange information useful to their companies. Just as employees and managers network within organizations, networking with customers, competitors, suppliers, and representatives of unrelated companies and industries eases the exchange of information that leads to better products and processes.

Basic Forms of Communication

Effective communicators have many tools at their disposal. They use *verbal communication,* arranging words that will convey their meaning, and they reinforce those words with *nonverbal communication,* which includes gestures, actions, and facial expressions. Effective communicators are also good listeners and observers. They study your reactions, your body language, your tone of voice, and the words you choose. They absorb information as efficiently as they transmit it, relying on both verbal and nonverbal cues.

Verbal messages are transmitted in either spoken or written form. In the world of business, oral communication is generally preferred over written communication because it's usually quicker and more convenient to talk to somebody than to write a memo or letter. Furthermore, when you're speaking or listening, you can pick up added meaning from nonverbal cues and benefit from immediate feedback. Face-to-face communication is often the most effective medium, but it's also one of the most restrictive because you and your audience must be in the same place at the same time.[63] Your choice between a face-to-face conversation and a telephone or conference call depends on the location of the audience, the importance of the message, and how much you need the nonverbal feedback that only body language can reveal.

Even though oral communication is the preferred medium, there are times when written communication is more appropriate and effective: when the information you are conveying is very complex, when a permanent record is needed for future reference, when the audience is large and geographically dispersed, and when immediate interaction with the audience is either unimportant or undesirable. The most common types of written communication are letters, memos, reports, and proposals.

Technology and Communication

Over the past few decades, technological advances have led to the development of *electronic communication.* Voice mail, teleconferencing, e-mail, and computer networks have revolutionized both oral and written communication and have become vital elements in achieving organizational goals. However, each form of communication also has limitations. Protocols must be followed; individuals must learn the appropriateness of each form.

electronic mail (e-mail)
Communication system that enables computers to transmit and receive written messages over telephone lines or other electronic networks

E-mail and Networks **Electronic mail,** or **e-mail,** transmits and receives written messages between computers via phone lines or other networks. *Intranets* connect employees within organizations, and the Internet links individuals and organizations around the world. These connections allow people to share ideas and information—people who might otherwise have no contact with each other.

E-mail has several advantages. For one thing, it can help break down barriers between organization levels because anybody can send a message to almost anybody else in the company. At the same time, e-mail is less formal than other forms of written communication, allowing you to get your point across as quickly as possible. E-mail can also reach a wide audience instantly, which reduces the cost and labor of distributing information.

However, e-mail also has drawbacks. One major disadvantage of e-mail is that employees can come to rely on it too much. As a result, issues that really should be discussed in a face-to-face meeting or on the phone are taken care of over the network—especially when the message deals with a controversial or confrontational issue. In addition, employees can experience *information overload* and become bogged down with too many irrelevant messages. A recent Pitney Bowes study reported that the average worker at a Fortune 1000 company sends and receives 178 messages each day.[64] And in a study conducted by the consulting firm Ernst & Young, some managers reported getting over 500 messages each day. "These executives spend so much time processing marginally relevant information," says study director David DeLong, "that they, by necessity, are less responsive to the things that really matter."[65]

Another drawback is that confidential information is more likely to be leaked when it's transmitted over e-mail. To help avoid such problems, some organizations, including the Children's Television Workshop (CTW), have created guidelines to help employees determine when e-mail is the correct medium for their communications. The CTW guidelines address issues like proper e-mail use, confidentiality, obtaining approval for widely distributed messages, and e-mail etiquette. CTW believes that clarity, accuracy, and speed should be the objective of every e-mail message.[66]

Is It True?

Over 3 trillion e-mail messages move through U.S.-based computer networks every day.

Mind Your Manners While Online

BEST OF THE WEB

Did you know that writing an e-mail in all capital letters is the equivalent of shouting in cyberspace? Are you aware that you can lose your Internet access if you send unsolicited e-mail advertisements (known as "spamming")? Did you know that messages you send can be viewed by people other than yourself and your recipient? Although e-mail is making communication easier for businesses and individuals alike, it carries with it a whole new set of communication protocols that must be observed. You can learn more about proper "Netiquette" at *The Net: User Guidelines and Netiquette.* This handy online guide tells you about the responsibilities of e-mail users and explains the etiquette of communicating electronically.
http://fau.edu/rinaldi/net/index.htm

Voice Mail *Voice mail* is similar to e-mail in concept, except that it doesn't require each user to have a computer, and it enables users to send, store, and retrieve spoken, rather than written, messages. Accessed via telephone, voice mail allows much longer messages than traditional answering machines, and it enables the sender to review a message before hanging up. The receiver can then save, erase, or forward messages as needed. Voice mail also helps overcome time-zone differences, and it can reduce interoffice paperwork.[67] However, voice mail can also lead to *information overload* problems similar to those caused by too many e-mail messages. In addition, when customers call, they usually prefer to reach a live person rather than a recorded voice.[68] Moreover, voice mail does not allow the user to print out messages the way e-mail does.

Teleconferencing Technology can also lend a hand when people need to communicate in groups. Group communication used to take place in person, with everyone in the same room, but teleconferencing has changed that. *Teleconferencing* uses phone lines and satel-

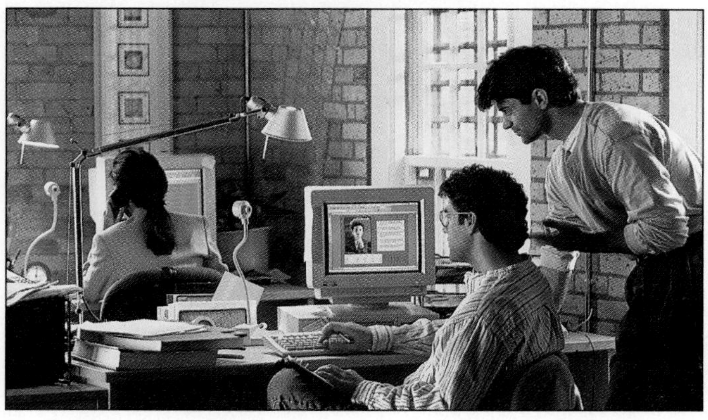

Avalon Productions, a television commercial production company, uses videoconferencing technology to expand its talent pool. Video cameras and multimedia software enable the company to screen models at a New York talent agency from Avalon's offices in Santa Monica, California.

lites to connect people in different geographical areas through audio and video transmissions.[69] For example, managers in different regions can hold an audioconference to discuss strategy. Although they are located in different offices or hotels that are miles apart, they can all hear each other and interact verbally as though they were seated around the same table. If they use videoconferencing, they can view each other on monitors as well. In this way, a manager could show his or her colleagues a chart depicting profit projections for the coming year. This type of technology is especially important in helping virtual teams work together effectively. For example, Ford uses teleconferencing to link car-design teams from around the world into a single, unified group.[70]

Barriers to Communication

Many individual and organizational barriers to effective communication exist within organizations.[71] Perhaps the most common barrier is simply a lack of attention on the receiver's part. We all let our minds wander now and then, regardless of how hard we try to concentrate. This is especially true if we are tired, or if we feel that the information is too difficult or unimportant. Communication can also break down if either the sender or the receiver has strong emotions about a subject.

Another pervasive barrier to effective communication is perceptual differences. To understand each other, you and the person you are communicating with must share similar meanings for words, gestures, tone of voice, and other symbols; that is, you must perceive these things in a similar way. Often perceptual differences are affected by a person's background, including age, culture, education, gender, economic position, religion, or political views. To overcome these differences, try to predict how your message will be received, anticipate your receiver's reactions, and shape the message accordingly—constantly adjusting to correct any misunderstanding. In addition, try not to apply the same solution to every problem, and frame messages in terms that have meaning for your audience.

Still another barrier is incorrect filtering—the screening out or abbreviation of information before a message is passed on to someone else. In business, secretaries, assistants, associates, and voice mail are just a few of the filters that exist between you and your receiver. To overcome filtering barriers, try to establish more than one communication channel so that information can be verified through multiple sources. Also, try to condense message information to the bare essentials to reduce the chances of your message becoming distorted.

Language may also present a problem, even among people of the same culture. If you have ever tried to read a legal contract, you know the problem. Lawyers, doctors, ac-

Carolyn Fushima, a supervisor at Home Depot, knows that effective employee communication requires sensitivity to differences in culture, religion, age, gender, and ethnic background.

countants, and computer programmers all use different vocabularies, which affects their ability to communicate ideas. Language barriers can be overcome by using the most specific and accurate words possible. Stick to using language that describes rather than evaluates, and try to present observable facts, events, and circumstances.

Additional organizational barriers to communication include lack of trust between employees; steep hierarchical boundaries; improper choice of communication medium by the sender; authoritarian leadership; poor ethical standards (which undermines the credibility of communications); and physical distractions such as bad connections, poor acoustics, noise, and illegible copy. Obviously, many factors can distort both the messages you send and those you receive in an organization. However, through a conscious commitment to quality communication, almost any barrier can be overcome.

As you learn how to overcome communication barriers, you become more successful as a business communicator. Think about the people you know. Which of them are successful communicators? What do these people have in common? Chances are they share five traits:

- *Perception.* They are able to predict how you will receive their message. They anticipate your reaction and shape the message accordingly. They read your response correctly and constantly adjust to correct any misunderstanding.
- *Precision.* They create a "meeting of the minds." When they finish expressing themselves, you share the same mental picture.
- *Credibility.* They are believable. You have faith in the substance of their message. You trust their information and their intentions.
- *Control.* They shape your response. Depending on their purpose, they can make you laugh or cry, calm down, change your mind, or take action.
- *Congeniality.* They maintain friendly, pleasant relations with you. Regardless of whether you agree with them, good communicators command your respect and goodwill. You are willing to work with them again, despite your differences.

Effective communicators overcome the main barriers to communication by creating their messages carefully, thinking about which medium is the most appropriate to convey their message, minimizing *noise* (any interference in the transmission process), and facilitating feedback. Of course, certain organizational barriers may remain. However, communicators who embody these five traits will usually find a way to make their message heard.

Summary of Learning Objectives

1. **Describe the three ways to design a company's formal organization structure.**
Three ways to design a formal organization structure include (1) vertical organization—defining individual jobs to complete the tasks necessary to achieve company goals; (2) departmentalization—grouping jobs into departments and larger units; and (3) horizontal coordination—aligning all tasks across departments and divisions.
2. **Explain the concepts of authority, accountability, responsibility, delegation, and span of management.**
Authority is the power to make decisions, issue orders, carry out actions, and allocate resources to achieve the organization's goals. Accountability is the obligation to report work results to supervisors or team members and to justify any outcomes that fall below expectations. Responsibility is the employee's obligation to perform the duties and achieve the goals and objectives associated with a job. Delegation is the assignment of work and the transfer of authority and responsibility to complete that work. Span of management refers to the number of employees that a manager directly supervises (a manager who oversees many employees has a wide span of management, and one who oversees relatively few employees has a narrow span of management).
3. **Define four types of departmentalization.**
Companies may departmentalize in any combination of four ways: (1) by function, which groups employees according to their skills, resource use, and expertise; (2) by

division, which establishes self-contained departments formed according to similarities in product, process, customer, or geography; (3) by matrix, which assigns employees from functional departments to interdisciplinary project teams and requires them to report to both a department head and a team leader; and (4) by network, which connects separate companies that perform selected tasks for a headquarters organization.

4. **Clarify how vertical organization differs from horizontal coordination.**
Vertical organization links the activities of top, middle, and lower organizational levels, whereas horizontal coordination links the activities of and facilitates the communication between departments without having to involve the vertical chain of command.

5. **Describe the four primary types of teams.**
The four primary types of teams are (1) vertical teams, which are organized along the lines of the organization's vertical structure and are limited to a single functional area; (2) horizontal teams, which are composed of employees from similar levels of the organization and draw together people with different areas of expertise; (3) special-purpose teams, which are temporary entities created to achieve a specific goal and which stand apart from the normal functions of the organization; and (4) self-directed teams, which are composed of cross-trained employees and are empowered to manage their own activities.

6. **Review the five stages of team development.**
Teams typically go through five stages of development. In the forming stage, team members become acquainted with each other and with the group's purpose. In the storming stage, conflict often arises as coalitions and power struggles develop. In the norming stage, conflicts are resolved and harmony develops. In the performing stage, members focus on achieving the team's goals. In the adjourning stage, the team dissolves upon completion of its task.

7. **Explain how companies use internal and external communication networks.**
Companies use internal communication networks to exchange information and ideas within the organization. Internal communication involves both formal communication channels (which follow the official organization chart and transmit communication up, down, and across the hierarchical levels) and informal communication channels (which develop from the personal relationships people form within the organization). In contrast, external communication is used to send and receive information between the organization and outside entities such as customers, vendors, suppliers, competitors, and community representatives.

8. **List some of the barriers to effective communication, and explain how to overcome them.**
The barriers to effective communication include perceptual differences, filtering, cultural differences, language, lack of attention, information overload, lack of trust, steep hierarchies, physical distractions, and improper medium selection. Effective communicators overcome these barriers by crafting their messages carefully, thinking about which communication medium is the most appropriate for their message, minimizing noise, and facilitating recipient feedback.

On the Job: Meeting Business Challenges at Lexmark International

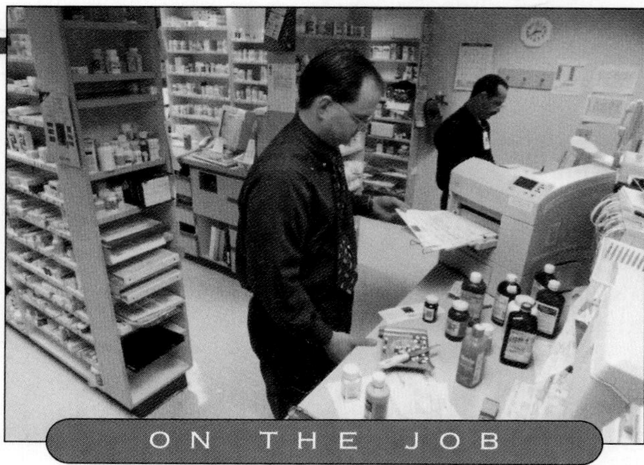
ON THE JOB

Marvin Mann knew that Lexmark's move from IBM to independence would require an entirely new organization structure. Under the IBM system, eight layers of management had separated assembly-line workers from top managers, and employees had to approach manager after manager to get the necessary approvals for changes or new projects. In addition, coming up with new products took 2 or 3 years from the time an idea was proposed (say, for a new printer) until the first printer rolled off the assembly line. Meanwhile, aggressive competitors like Hewlett-Packard, Apple, Canon, and Epson were moving quickly to bring out new printers packed with clever features that customers desired.

Mann started by reorganizing Lexmark according to product, creating four groups that each focused on a set of related products. Next, Mann cut the number of management layers from eight to four. This action helped speed up communication and decision making throughout the company. Mann also abandoned the IBM method of studying and debating proposals for months before making decisions, giving more power to managers and employees at every level. "Our people have a lot more freedom to get things done than before," he observes.

Instead of a rigid hierarchical structure, Mann formed teams to tackle routine problems as well as special situations. For example, a team of assembly-line workers assumed complete responsibility for designing a more efficient production process for laser printers. When all members of the team were satisfied that the new process would work, they signed their names to the proposal—and were given the authority to implement the change.

Similarly, teams of people from manufacturing, finance, marketing, and other departments are totally responsible for designing and producing new products. Because the departments coordinate their efforts from the start, they can get a new product to market in about half the time they needed under the IBM system. What's more, they've been able to double the number of products under development without adding more designers.

With these organizational changes in place, Lexmark was able to introduce an ambitious new-product program only months after leaving the IBM family. The company revamped its existing printers and came up with a new line of laser printers, which were praised by computer magazines for their simplicity, reliability, and print quality. In addition, Lexmark recently became the first company to offer ink-jet printers with 1,200 dots-per-inch print quality. The new line of printers offers photographic quality printouts with 38 percent higher print density than the nearest competitor. Furthermore Lexmark workers (not managers) set and then achieved a goal of 100 percent accuracy in making and shipping the millions of items Lexmark produces every year. As a result of these and many other initiatives, sales are strong, profit margins are increasing, manufacturing costs are down, and quality is up.

Lexmark has established itself as a technology leader on solid financial ground. The U.S. Environmental Protection Agency even named the company its 1996 "Office Equipment Printer Partner of the Year." No wonder Mann sees the "printing on the wall" for a bright future.

Your Mission: You are a consultant specializing in organizational structure, teamwork, and communication. Marvin Mann has asked you to offer suggestions that will help Lexmark organize and work more effectively. Select the best solution for each of the following situations.

1. Mann asks you about the span of management in an experienced production unit that will be manufacturing a new portable laser printer. He wants your opinion on whether the assembly-line workers in this unit should be supervised using a wide or narrow span of management. What advice would you offer?
   a. Use a narrow span of management to allow managers to keep a close watch on the manufacturing process. After all, when making a new product, the company has to be able to catch and correct problems quickly.
   b. Use a wide span of management to allow workers the same degree of responsibility and accountability as in other Lexmark units. The workers are experienced and are just as concerned as the managers about the quality of the new products.
   c. Start with a narrow span of management to maintain tight control when the unit begins making the new product. Later, after the managers have solved any initial problems, switch to a wider span of management.
2. The head of human resources comes to you for ideas about how to handle a newly hired manager who has difficulty delegating responsibility to her workers. This work group has done well in the past, but the new manager is afraid that any problems will make her look bad. To avoid mistakes, she tries to control everything her workers do. What's the best advice you can offer?
   a. Until the new manager sees the kind of work her employees are capable of, she won't trust them to do their jobs without close supervision. Intervening now won't help; time is the best solution for this problem.
   b. Let this manager's boss suggest that she start delegating responsibility by defining the tasks to complete, setting performance goals, monitoring progress toward the goals, and coaching when workers need her support. Then she'll see how well her workers handle their tasks without close supervision.
   c. Let this manager's boss stress that delegation is the only way to get things done in a large organization. He should explain that he has to delegate to the people below him, because he can't do everybody's work, and she has to delegate to the people below her if anything is to be accomplished.
3. A special cross-functional team consisting of 11 employees has been set up to design the next generation of ink-jet printers. Whereas the team was productive in the early weeks of its existence, it has now begun to storm heavily. According to the group leader, at least one member appears to be free riding, another tries to dominate every meeting, and two others have disagreed with every idea proposed so far. What course of action do you recommend?
   a. Explain to the leader that every team goes through a period of storming and that once the storm is over, the team will move into the performing stage.
   b. Suggest that the team hold a special meeting in which the members specifically address some of the concerns mentioned. Tell the team leader not to accuse anyone, but to let each person communicate how he or she feels about the group's performance. Recommend that the team examine its goals to make sure everyone understands them, as well as the tasks that each member must fulfill to achieve those goals.

c. Offer to speak individually with the difficult team members. That way you can uncover the true causes of the problems and report them back to the team leader. The leader will then be better able to develop a strategy for fixing the problems.

4. For the past few days, a rumor about layoffs has been spreading through the Lexmark grapevine. Even though the rumor is untrue, many employees are beginning to worry about their jobs. What do you suggest Mann do?
   a. Mann should prepare a straightforward message about the facts of the situation. Next, he should use every available method to communicate with all employees, including memos, face-to-face meetings, and so on.
   b. Mann should prepare a brief memo that denies the rumored layoffs and wastes no time with muddying details. A reassuring word from the CEO is all that's needed to stop a false rumor.
   c. Tell Mann to ignore the rumor. No matter what he says, employees will believe that the rumor must have some basis in fact. Because the threat of layoffs is unfounded, talk will eventually die down.[72]

Key Terms

accountability (194)
authority (194)
centralization (196)
chain of command (195)
cohesiveness (207)
committee (205)
cross-functional teams (204)
customer divisions (197)
decentralization (196)
delegation (195)
departmentalization (197)
departmentalization by division (197)
departmentalization by function (197)
departmentalization by matrix (199)
departmentalization by network (200)
distortion (210)
electronic mail (e-mail) (214)
external communication network (213)
flat organizations (195)
formal communication network (210)
free rider (209)
functional teams (204)
geographic divisions (197)
grapevine (212)
horizontal coordination (201)
informal organization (193)
internal communication (210)
line organization (195)
line-and-staff organization (195)
managerial integrator (201)
networking (212)
norms (207)
organization chart (192)
organization structure (192)
problem-solving teams (204)
process divisions (197)
product divisions (197)
responsibility (194)
self-directed teams (204)
span of management (195)
special-purpose teams (206)
tall organizations (196)
task force (205)
team (203)
vertical organization (193)
virtual teams (205)
work specialization (193)

Questions

For Review

1. Why is organization structure important?
2. What are the characteristics of tall organizations and flat organizations? Is the U.S. Navy a tall organization or a flat one? How do you know?
3. What can managers do to help teams work more effectively?
4. How can using the informal communication network help a manager be more effective?
5. Which form of verbal communication is usually preferred in business? Why?

For Analysis

6. Why would you expect a manager of a group of nuclear physicists to have a wide span of management?
7. How does horizontal coordination promote innovation?
8. How does a task force differ from a committee?
9. How can companies benefit from using virtual teams?
10. How is technology changing the way organizations communicate?

For Application

11. You are the leader of a cross-functional work team whose goal is to find ways of lowering production costs. Your team of eight employees has become mired in the storming stage. They disagree on how to approach the task, and they are starting to splinter into factions. What can you do to help the team move forward?
12. Your team has come up with several ideas for lowering production costs. It is your job as team leader to communicate the team's suggestions to the production manager. What communication channel do you choose? Why?

A Case for Critical Thinking ■ Revving Up a New Organization at Chrysler

There was a time in U.S. business when vertical integration was seen as one of the best ways to build a competitive advantage. Companies that could control the supply of all the components necessary to build their products were less vulnerable to changes in the marketplace. General Motors and Ford built their names this way in the 1920s and 1930s, building tall organization structures with very steep and centralized management hierarchies to tightly control every step in the production process.

Although this system worked well in the past, today's fast-moving, technology-driven world has rendered it obsolete. Today's companies are competing by developing network organizations that are flatter, decentralized, team-based, and more focused on their core businesses. One of the most successful companies performing under this model is Chrysler.

Chrysler has never been as vertically integrated as Ford and GM, and that is turning out to be a good thing. Whereas the other companies are trying to shed excess operations in the hopes of becoming more flexible, Chrysler already enjoys lower production costs by outsourcing much of the work to suppliers. It costs almost $50 an hour to employ an autoworker, but some tasks can be performed more effectively and up to four times less expensively by suppliers. Whereas other carmakers are busy turning the screws on their parts suppliers, attempting to get the lowest price possible, Chrysler brings suppliers onto its teams early in the design process. For example, on the Dodge Viper, suppliers worked with Chrysler employees to design and build an adjustable pedal system and an electric door-opening system. Overall, outsourcing production and fostering teamwork enables Chrysler to develop products for as little as half the cost of Ford and GM.

Another key factor in Chrysler's success is teamwork. In the old days, different functional departments performed a task on a vehicle and then passed it on to the next department. But today, Chrysler uses "platform teams" composed of engineers, designers, suppliers, and factory workers that work simultaneously on individual vehicle platforms. In addition, the company has eliminated time clocks on the production floor, supervisors are called in only if there is an emergency, and assembly-line workers have a say in the way the cars are made. Because of this teamwork, Chrysler is able to produce vehicles faster and at a lower cost. For example, the new Durango utility vehicle took only 24 months to design and produce. This is about as short a time as any car manufacturer in the world can get a product to market. General Motors usually takes five years. Chrysler's teamwork approach also enables the company to build its midsize cars on the same assembly line as its larger models. Vice chairman Bob Lutz estimates that this gives the company a cost advantage of $1,000 to $1,500 per vehicle over Ford.

Networking with suppliers has generated even more ideas for saving money and improving quality. Over 70 percent of the parts used to build a Chrysler vehicle are purchased from outside suppliers. A few years ago Chrysler offered suppliers a percentage of any cost savings they could achieve. Known as Supplier Cost Reduction Effort (SCORE), the system was soon expanded by offering incentives to motivate suppliers to suggest products that would help Chrysler reduce its costs. Now SCORE saves the company more than a billion dollars a year. In addition, the system has been put online to make it even easier for suppliers to communicate with Chrysler. The suggestions now roll in at an average of 165 per week, and the company expects to save $2 billion a year in the next few years.

The results of Chrysler's new approach to organizing its operation are very apparent. The company went from a net loss $3.5 billion in 1993 to become the most profitable of the Big Three U.S. carmakers. In addition, while the other companies are building new facilities to expand production, Chrysler keeps finding new ways to squeeze more productive capacity out of its existing plants. In fact, by merging operations with Daimler-Benz, analysts predict that the new DaimlerChrysler will realize a $3 billion annual cost savings from sharing parts and components. Plus the new company will be able to plunge into global markets that neither could attempt alone. That's a pretty classy turn of events for a company that lurched from one crisis to another in the 1970s, nearly collapsed, was rescued by the government, and reemerged as a low-cost provider that invented the mini-van. Stay tuned. DaimlerChrysler promises to rock the global auto industry.

1. How does using a network organization give Chrysler a competitive advantage over GM and Ford?
2. How would you characterize Chrysler's teams? Are they functional or cross-functional? Are they self-directed?
3. Does the SCORE program make use of the internal communication network, the external communication network, or both? Do you think upward communication flow or downward communication flow is more important to the program's success? Explain your answers.
4. Visit the Chrysler Web page at <http://www.chryslercorp.com>. You will find the story of the minivan by following the links to *Service Center, Uncommon Approach,* and *Industry Solutions.* Based on the information provided, what would you say were the platform team's strategic goals when it redesigned the Chrysler minivan?

Building Your Business Skills

Either as an individual or with a classmate, examine the formal organizational structure of a business or an institution (such as a hospital, college, or public service agency). If you are unable to obtain an organization chart for this business or institution, you might find it useful to create one using the information you can gather by observing operations or talking with managers.

- Using information from the text, determine the level of work specialization, the form of departmentalization, the degree of centralization, and the prevalence of teamwork in your chosen business or institution.
- Describe the organization in a written or an oral presentation. Compare the structure with that of businesses or organizations examined by other class members. Is any organization taking an innovative approach to organizing work? If so, is this approach effective?

Keeping Current Using *The Wall Street Journal*

Choose an article from *The Wall Street Journal* describing a company that uses teamwork to achieve its goals.

1. What types of teams (vertical, horizontal, or self-directed) are being used? What changes were necessary in the company's organization structure or corporate culture for the teams to be formed?
2. What problems did the company encounter as it implemented the teams? How did the company overcome these problems?
3. Have the teams been successful from management's perspective? From the employees' perspective? What effects has teamwork had on the company, its customers, and its products?
4. *Fast Company* is an online business magazine with a growing archive of stories on effective management. The article "Four Rules for Fast Teams" describes how software developer Cambridge Technology Partners (CTP) used teamwork to deliver a customized product to AT&T in a very short time. Read the article (http://www.fastcompany.com/04/speed3.html), and compare and contrast CTP's experience with that of the company you are reviewing. What can the company learn from CTP's experience? Do CTP's rules apply to every business team? Why or why not?

Exploring the Best of the Web

Learn How to Make It "Small-Time," page 194

The American Express Small Business Exchange can take some of the uncertainty out of starting your own small business. Explore the site at <http://americanexpress.com/smallbusiness> to learn about starting and running a small business. Then answer the questions below.

1. From the main page, click on *Business Planning and Resources,* then on *Managing Your Business,* and scroll down to *Learning to Delegate.* What are the three key reasons why small business owners have a hard time delegating, and how can they overcome these obstacles? Do these same factors apply to managers in large organizations? List some additional factors that might apply, and suggest some strategies for dealing with them.
2. From the main page, click on *Business Planning and Resources,* then on *Starting Your Business,* and scroll down to *Choosing a Board of Directors.* What types of small businesses must have a board of directors, and what types should consider forming advisory boards? How do the two types of boards differ? What kinds of skills should a small-business owner seek in board members?

3. Go back to the *Managing Your Business* page and scroll down to *Setting Goals for Your Business.* What are the qualities of good small-business goals? Based on this information as well as on what you have already learned about setting goals and organizing for business, identify some of the advantages small businesses have over large businesses in setting and reaching their goals. What are some of the disadvantages?

Building Teams in the Cyber Age, page 205

The wealth of information on the Internet makes it easier to learn more about almost any topic, and teamwork is no exception. Visit the Self Directed Work Teams (SDWT) page (http://users.ids.net/7Ebrim/sdwth.html#ONE) and explore the links to get a better feel for the many resources available. Then answer the following questions.

1. From the main page, click on *Sites on Team Basics* and then on *Ideas on Teams and Teamwork.* According to IBM Canada, what are the 10 key elements of high-performing teams? Drawing on what you have learned about team dynamics, identify at least one strategy that teams can pursue to achieve high levels of performance for each of the ten elements.
2. From the *Sites on Team Basics* page, click on *Essential Questions—Poynter.* Read through the Poynter Institute's list of the major issues facing teams. How might the importance of each issue vary among different types of teams? Which three issues are most important to the assigned in-class teams you've been part of? Which three do you think are most important to a team of production workers looking for ways to reduce costs and production time?
3. From the main page, click on *Sites on Skills/Steps* and then on *Tips for Teams.* According to consultant Richard Wellins, what types of problems do teams often encounter in their first 6 months to 2 years of existence? What factors might contribute to the development of leader dependency in corporate teams? Identify at least one strategy to overcome each factor.

Mind Your Manners While Online, page 215

"Netiquette" refers to the general protocols that people are expected to follow when they communicate via e-mail and when they surf the World Wide Web. Because standards are different for e-mail than for any other business communication medium, it is best to learn the dos and don'ts before going online. Read the introduction to *The Net: User Guidelines and Netiquette* (http://www.fau.edu/rinaldi/net/index.htm) and explore various links to learn more. Then answer the questions below.

1. Follow the link to *Electronic Communications.* Why is it important to include a title in your e-mail messages? What standards should you use when deciding whether to send an e-mail to someone higher up the chain of command?
2. From the main index, click on *Electronic Mail and Files—User Responsibility.* What is the recommended standard for judging whether or not the content of your e-mail is acceptable? Should this standard also be applied to other forms of written business communication? Why should companies be especially concerned about the content of e-mail messages that are sent through the external communication network?
3. Follow the links to *Discussion Groups,* and recall what you read in the *Introduction.* In addition to the standard e-mail and discussion group protocols, what other guidelines should you be aware of when using individual discussion groups? What consequences may result from sending inflammatory messages? Why is it important to guard your user name and password?

Answers to Is It True?

Page 194. True.

Page 203. False. Only 30 percent of teams fail as a result of team-based pay issues. Over half of team failures are caused by unclear goals, changing objectives, or lack of accountability.

Page 215. True.

CHAPTER 8

PRODUCTION OF QUALITY GOODS AND SERVICES

OBJECTIVES

After studying this chapter, you will be able to

1. Explain the strategic importance of production and operations management
2. Describe the evolution of production efficiency
3. Discuss the role of computers and automation technology in production
4. Identify the key issues managers must consider when designing operations
5. Explain the strategic importance of managing inventory and review the management systems used to control it
6. Describe the advantages and disadvantages of just-in-time (JIT) systems in production planning
7. Discuss the differences between quality control and quality assurance
8. Define the five basic steps in production control

ON THE JOB

ON THE JOB: FACING BUSINESS CHALLENGES AT HARLEY-DAVIDSON

Staying on the Road to Higher Sales

When Japanese manufacturers began selling heavyweight motorcycles in the United States during the early 1970s, Harley-Davidson remained calm. The Milwaukee company controlled 99.7 percent of the market and saw no reason to panic. After all, if your customers love your product so much that they tattoo your logo on their chests, can't you count on their loyalty?

The company was mistaken. The Harley was no longer the superb machine it once had been. It leaked oil, vibrated wildly, and broke down frequently. Harley's older customers patiently rebuilt their motorcycles, but younger riders were not so forgiving. Increasing numbers of them chose the trouble-free, smooth-riding imports, and Harley's U.S. market share eventually tumbled to 23 percent.

During the 1980s, Harley decided to open the throttle on quality production. The company changed its design and manufacturing systems to stress quality and reliability, and it carefully controlled the number of motorcycles produced so that their quality could be maintained. This turnaround reestablished Harley's worldwide reputation for superior quality. Customers liked the new motorcycles, and sales began to climb.

By the early 1990s, market share had returned to 64 percent, a number that could have been higher if the company hadn't presold its entire output by the middle of every year. With $1.2 billion in sales, Harley's biggest problem now was to make enough motorcycles to keep up with soaring demand in the United States and abroad. Dealers were frustrated because they couldn't give customers what they wanted. As dealer Debra Meyers put it: "People don't understand. Not only can't they have the color they want, they can't have the bike. Period."

The last thing Harley CEO Richard F. Teerlink wanted was to frustrate dealers and customers. Although he recognized that higher production would lead to higher sales and profits, he refused to increase output at the risk of damaging the company's new reputation for quality. Faced with a sea of clamoring customers and anxious dealers, how could Teerlink boost Harley's production while keeping a firm grip on the quality that had brought the company back to its dominant position in the motorcycle industry? What could the CEO do to monitor the production process and keep it on track and on time? How could he make Harley flexible enough to handle the constant change needed to compete with rivals all over the globe?[1]

Developing Quality and Competitiveness

The managers at Harley-Davidson faced the same situation that managers around the world are facing today: The extremely competitive nature of the global business environment requires companies to produce high-quality goods in the most efficient way possible or else be shredded by the competition. In almost every industry you can name, this global challenge has caused companies to reexamine their definition of quality. High efficiency, few defects, fast production, low costs, excellent customer service, broad market reach, innovative products and processes, less waste, and high flexibility are all objectives that improve quality by adding value to the good or service being produced. Companies pursue these objectives in order to maintain a competitive advantage. And as Harley-Davidson's managers learned, the level of quality that a company aspires to is a strategic decision that affects the production process.[2]

production
Transformation of resources into goods or services that people need or want

Production is the transformation of resources into goods or services that people need or want. At the core of production is the *conversion process,* the sequence of events that convert resources into products. The conversion process can be diagrammed simply (see Exhibit 8.1):

$$Input \rightarrow transformation \rightarrow output$$

This formula applies to both intangible services and tangible goods. For example, for a taxi cab company to serve its customers, tangible and intangible resources—the cab, the driver's skill, the fuel, and a passenger—are transformed into the intangible service of transporting the customer to the destination. For a shirt maker to produce a shirt, the resources that are converted—cloth, thread, and buttons—are tangible and so is the output—the shirt.

analytic system
Production process that breaks incoming materials into various component products

synthetic system
Production process that combines two or more materials or components to create finished products; the reverse of an analytic system

Conversion is of two basic types. An **analytic system** breaks raw materials into one or more distinct products, which may or may not resemble the original material in form and function. In meatpacking, for example, a steer is divided into hide, bone, steaks, and so on. A **synthetic system** combines two or more materials to form a single product. For example, in steel manufacturing, iron is combined with small quantities of other minerals at high temperatures to make steel.

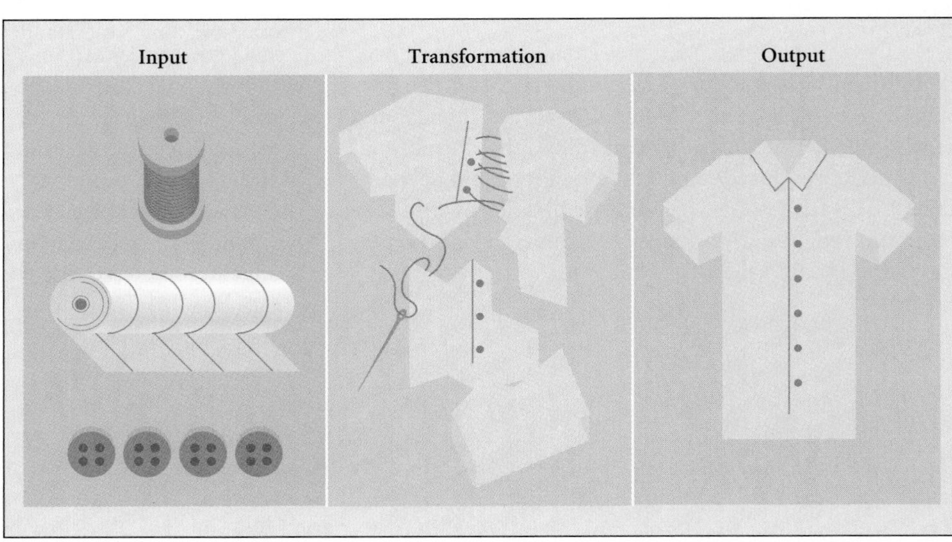

Exhibit 8.1

The Conversion Process

Production of goods or services is basically a process of conversion. Input (the basic ingredients or skills) is transformed (by the application of labor, equipment, and capital) into output (the desired product).

Production and operations management (POM) is the coordination of an organization's resources for manufacturing goods or producing services. Like other types of management, POM involves the basic functions of planning, organizing, leading, and controlling. It also requires careful consideration of the company's goals, the strategies for attaining those goals, and the standards against which results will be measured.

production and operations management (POM)
Coordination of an organization's resources for the manufacture of goods or the delivery of services

POM is growing as one of the business world's most dynamic areas of specialization. For one thing, it is becoming the focus of many companies' efforts to improve quality and competitiveness. The field is challenging because (1) it is undergoing rapid change; (2) it involves many activities, from interpreting market research (determining what kinds of goods and services should be produced) to production planning and control of the production process; and (3) it applies to all kinds of companies, regardless of size or product. As a result, POM is enjoying a surge in popularity as a business career track.

Understanding the Evolution of Production

Throughout most of human history, people have sought ways of improving **production efficiency**—lowering costs by optimizing output from each resource used in the production process. Consider the feudal system, the political and economic system of medieval Europe in which lords rented land and gave protection to their tenant farmers in exchange for a portion of their output. Production under the feudal system provided a more efficient division of labor than nomadic life or small tribal settlements.

production efficiency
Minimizing cost by maximizing the level of output from each resource

Later, a series of technological advances in eighteenth-century England brought about even more efficient production and ushered in a period known as the Industrial Revolution. The first of these technological advances was **mechanization,** the use of machines to do work previously done by people. Adding to mechanization's efficiency was **standardization,** or the production of uniform, interchangeable parts. This development eliminated the need to craft products one at a time, and it reduced the level of skill that workers needed to produce many goods.

mechanization
Use of machines to do work previously done by people

standardization
Uniformity in goods or parts, making them interchangeable

In the early twentieth century, Henry Ford was a big fan of standardization. He once commented that customers could have any color car they wanted as long as it was black.[3] Ford also introduced the technological advance with the most wide-ranging influence, the **assembly line,** which involves putting a product together as it progresses past a number of workstations where each employee performs a specific task.

assembly line
Series of workstations at which each employee performs a specific task in the production process

As manufacturers became more adept at integrating mechanization, standardization, and the assembly line into the production process, they turned their attention toward eliminating as much costly manual labor as possible through **automation,** the process of performing a mechanical operation with the absolute minimum of human intervention. In automated production, people put the machines into operation, monitor or regulate them, and inspect their output. Beyond that, the machines do the work. These four advances in production efficiency allowed for the development of **mass production**—manufacturing uniform goods in great quantities. Mass production reduces production costs and makes products available to more people. Some service companies also use mass production techniques. For example, fast-food chains, hotels, accounting firms, car-rental agencies, and even some real estate firms mass-produce their services through standardized and automated procedures.

automation
Process of performing a mechanical operation with the absolute minimum of human intervention

mass production
Manufacture of uniform products in great quantities

Even though mass production has several advantages, the competitive pressures of the global economy often require production techniques that are more flexible, customer focused, and quality-oriented. Sometimes these techniques replace traditional mass production, and sometimes they simply improve on it. Consider Andersen Windows. Throughout its long history, Andersen made a range of standard windows in large batches. However, in the early 1990s customer demands and an increasing error rate caused Andersen to rethink the way it builds windows. To better meet customer needs, the company developed an interactive computer catalog that allows customers to add, change, and remove features of Andersen's standard windows until they've designed the windows they want. The computer then automatically generates a price quote and sends the order to the factory, where standardized parts are tailored to customer specifications. The company now offers close to 200,000 different products and is virtually error free. Andersen's new production system is known as **mass customization**—using mass production techniques to produce customized goods. The company's next goal is to use *batch-of-one manufacturing*, in which every product is made to order from scratch and virtually no standard inventory is kept on hand. Andersen is already achieving this in one factory that makes customized replacement windows.[4]

mass customization
Producing customized goods and services through mass production techniques

Is It True?

The cost to most companies of poor-quality products and services is less than 10 percent of sales.

Improving Production Through Technology

Managers at Andersen Windows strive for quality production. They are able to achieve their goals for flexibility and customer service partly as a result of recent advances in production technology. In fact, together with innovative management, technology is making production a strategic weapon in gaining a competitive advantage.

Today more and more U.S. companies are refitting and reorganizing their factories to improve efficiency and productivity. The most visible advances in production technology are computers and **robots**—programmable machines that work with tools and materials to perform various tasks. Although industrial robots may seem exotic, like some science fiction creation, they are quite common and are really nothing more than smart tools. Industrial robots can easily perform precision functions as well as repetitive, strenuous, or hazardous tasks.[5] For instance, Toyota uses robots to handle jobs that are dirty and noisy (such as sanding car bodies) as well as delicate tasks (such as aligning car hoods with engine compartments).[6] In fact, more than any other industry, car companies use robots for painting, welding, and moving objects from one specific place to another nearby (known as *pick and place* functions). Other uses for robots include testing electronics and even assisting with surgery.

robots
Programmable machines that can complete a variety of tasks by working with tools and materials

Another type of robot is the automated guided vehicle (AGV)—a driverless, computer-controlled vehicle that moves materials from any location on the factory floor to any other location. Although an AGV's movements must be preprogrammed, some robots are being given limited *artificial intelligence* that enables them to make certain decisions. AGVs will probably lead to robots with *navigational capabilities,* which will enable them to move under their own power of direction. Hospitals, security companies, hazardous-material-disposal companies, and the military are all currently using mobile-robot technology.[7]

Computer-Aided Design and Engineering The starting point for all production is product design. Widely used today is **computer-aided design (CAD),** the application of computer graphics and mathematical modeling in the design of products. A related process is **computer-aided engineering (CAE),** the use of computer-generated three-dimensional images and computerized calculations that allow engineers to test products. With CAE, engineers can subject proposed products to changing temperatures, various stresses, and even simulated accidents, without ever building preliminary models. Moreover, the *virtual reality* capability of today's computers even allows designers to see and feel how finished products will look and operate before physical prototypes are built. Virtual reality is discussed in more detail in Chapter 16.

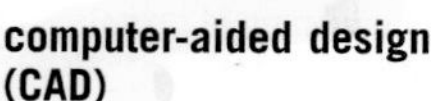

computer-aided design (CAD)
Use of computer graphics and mathematical modeling in the development of products

computer-aided engineering (CAE)
Use of computers to test products without building an actual model

Using computers to aid design and engineering saves time and money because revising computer designs is much faster than revising hand-drafted designs and building physical models. In addition, designs can be adapted more easily to other products. All of this leads to better overall product quality. For example, when Boeing engineers designed the new

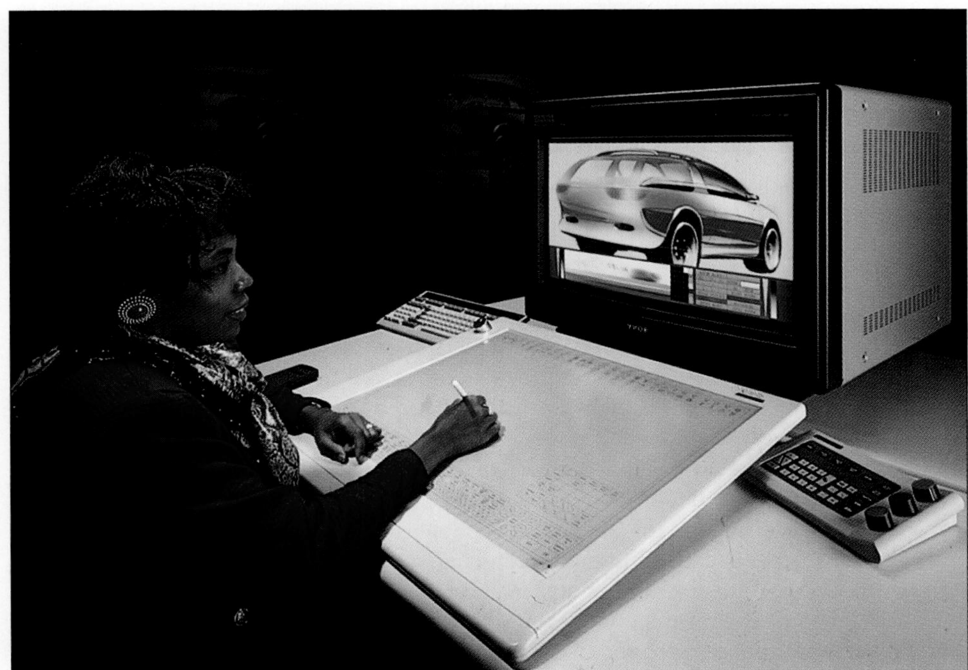

Designers at Ford use computer-aided design systems to plan new-car models in great detail.

777 airplane, they corrected problems and tried out new ideas entirely on their computer screens. Digitally pre-assembling the 3 million parts of the 777 allowed Boeing to exceed its goals for reducing errors, changes, and rework.[8] Thanks to computers and other technology, a product can now be perfected—or a bad idea abandoned—before production even begins.

Computer-Aided Manufacturing The use of computers to control production equipment is called **computer-aided manufacturing (CAM).** In a CAD/CAM system, computer-aided design data are converted automatically into processing instructions for production equipment to manufacture the part. This integration of design and production can increase the output, speed, and precision of assembly lines, as well as making customized production much easier.[9] In addition, the latest CAD/CAM software allows company departments to share designs and data over intranets and the Internet, enabling geographically dispersed departments to work together on complex projects.[10]

computer-aided manufacturing (CAM)
Use of computers to control production equipment

Computer-aided systems are improving the quality of production in all sorts of companies. For example, Ford uses a CAD/CAM/CAE system it calls C3P to develop new vehicle prototypes. It used to take 2 to 3 months to build, assemble, and test a car chassis prototype, but C3P enables the company to complete the entire process in less than 2 weeks. Although the program is still quite new, Ford expects it to improve engineering efficiency by 35 percent and reduce prototype costs by up to 40 percent.[11]

Computer-Integrated Manufacturing The highest level of computerization in operations management is **computer-integrated manufacturing (CIM),** in which all the elements of design, engineering, testing, production, inspection, and materials handling are integrated by computer networks linked across departments. CIM is not a specific technology, but rather a strategy that uses technology for organizing and controlling a factory. Its role is to link the people, machines, databases, and decisions involved in each step of producing a good.[12]

computer-integrated manufacturing (CIM)
Computer-based systems that coordinate and control all the elements of design and production, including CAD and CAM

Around the world, CIM is helping companies become more competitive. For example, the Taiwanese government is working closely with Digital Equipment Corporation to develop new CIM techniques that will boost the country's domestic information and electronics industries. In the Malaysian province of Penang, the Skills Development Center has a brand-new CIM lab to train workers in the use of integrating technologies so that they remain competitive. And in Canada many small manufacturers are using CIM to produce parts for larger firms, including the Big Three U.S. automakers.[13]

Flexible Manufacturing System (FMS) Advances in design technology have been accompanied by changes in the way the production process is organized. Traditional automated manufacturing equipment is *fixed* or *hard wired,* meaning it is capable of handling only one specific task. Although fixed automation is efficient when one type or model of good is mass produced, a change in product design requires extensive equipment changes. Such adjustments may involve high **setup costs,** the expenses incurred each time a manufacturer begins a production run of a different type of item. In addition, the initial investment for fixed automation equipment is high because specialized equipment is required for each of the operations involved in making a single item. Only after much production on a massive scale can a company recoup the cost of that specialized equipment. For example, Harley-Davidson invested $4.8 million in fixed manufacturing to make a particular motorcycle—only to dismantle the operation when demand for that product faded.[14]

setup costs
Expenses incurred each time a producer organizes resources to begin producing goods or services

An alternative is a **flexible manufacturing system (FMS),** which links numerous programmable machine tools by an automated material handling system of conveyors or AGVs. The system is controlled by a central computer network. With flexible manufacturing, changing from one product design to another requires only a few signals from the computer. Each machine changes tools automatically, making appropriate selections from built-in storage carousels that can hold more than 100 tools. In addition, the sequence of events involved in building an item can be completely rearranged.[15] This flexibility saves both time and setup costs. Moreover, producers can outmaneuver less agile competitors by moving swiftly into profitable new fields. Flexible manufacturing also allows producers to adapt their products quickly to changing customer needs.[16] Exhibit 8.2 diagrams the FMS at Ingersol Rand, a manufacturer of industrial machinery.

flexible manufacturing system (FMS)
Production system using computer-controlled machines that can adapt to various versions of the same operation

As a $10 million manufacturer of precision metal parts, Cook Specialty is one small company that is able to compete with larger manufacturers through flexible manufacturing. Cook used to make only certain products, such as basketball hoops and display racks. However, the company has transformed its production facilities so that it is now capable of manufacturing custom-engineered medical instruments and precision parts for high-tech equipment. Technical innovations for these devices advance rapidly, but Cook is able to adapt its production facilities to keep up with the changes. In fact, almost one-third of the products Cook manufactures each year are new. Multifunctional teams of people and

BEST OF THE WEB

Setting Standards

The National Institute of Standards and Technology is a U.S. government agency that works "to assist industry in the development of technology . . . needed to improve product quality, to modernize manufacturing processes, to ensure product reliability . . . and to facilitate rapid commercialization . . . of products based on new scientific discoveries." That's a pretty big charter. But the institute accomplishes the task by partnering with business to conduct research, develop technology standards, provide technical assistance, share costs, and reward success. Visit the NIST Web site to learn more about how the government is working with private industry to meet production challenges head-on.
http://nist.gov/public_affairs/guide/

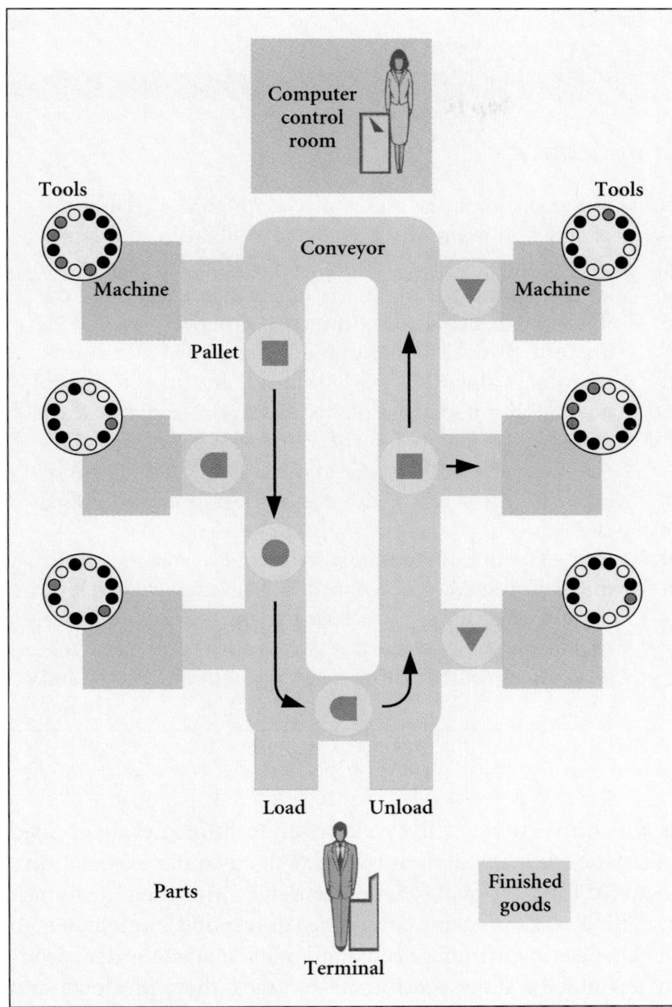

EXHIBIT 8.2

Flexible Manufacturing System

Ingersol Rand's flexible manufacturing system uses AGVs to move materials to various stages on the production line where automated machines process components and assemble them into finished goods. The system is controlled by computers, and managers track daily output data by consulting remote terminals.

arrangements of equipment are quickly reconfigured as needed. In addition, the company works with its customers to custom design new products that meet customers' precise standards. "We don't really have a product line," says president Tom Panzarella. "What we have is expertise in engineering and manufacturing."[17]

Flexible manufacturing systems are particularly desirable for *job shops,* which make dissimilar items or produce at so irregular a rate that repetitive operations won't help. Most small machine shops are examples. Many job shops are becoming even more flexible by partnering with other shops to share ideas, resources, and suppliers.[18] For example, in Pennsylvania a group of 19 small companies that represent a wide range of functional areas have come together in what they call the Agile Web. When a customer firm wants to outsource the design and manufacture of a complex component, it calls the Web's CEO, Ted Nickel. Nickel then notifies Web members who have expertise in designing or building the component the customer needs. A team can be assembled in 24 hours to meet with the customer, come up with a plan, and provide price quotes. By working together in a virtual organization, the Web companies are able to do more in less time. And by focusing on customization and quick response, they are able to serve customer needs better than many large companies can.[19]

UNDERSTANDING THE HIGH-TECH REVOLUTION

Smart Factories and the Revival of U.S. Manufacturing

Say that you need a pager to keep in touch with your home or office. However, you don't want just any pager—you want the right color (after all, you do have to wear it), and you want it to play a discrete musical sequence when a call arrives. In short, you want a product created for your unique needs. Where can you find somebody to make just the pager you want? Pagers are mass-produced gadgets that roll off production lines by the thousands. You can't expect anybody to customize one for you, at least not without waiting for weeks and spending hundreds or thousands of dollars for it—can you?

For your customized pager, you can call Motorola's pager factory in Boynton Beach, Florida. How long will it take? Motorola can usually have your pager built within an hour and a half. (If you think that's fast, the plant's director of manufacturing, Sherita Ceasar, says the company is close to building a custom pager while the customer is still on the phone placing the order!) Then, depending on where you live, the unit will be in your hands the same day, or the next day at the latest.

Manufacturing that is this fast and still this flexible is no small accomplishment. Moreover, it provides a strong dose of hope for the future of U.S. industry. Motorola's Boynton Beach facility joins an elite group of U.S. manufacturing plants that are racing past their global rivals (including the vaunted Japanese automation marvels) in the quest to deliver high-quality products in a hurry, often with customization for individual clients.

The force behind this industrial renaissance is the microprocessor, the computer-on-a-chip device that controls just about everything from toasters to automobile engines. In factories such as Motorola's, microprocessors route customer orders, direct robots, and

Electronic Information Systems Of course, none of the production technologies mentioned above will increase profits unless the company designs products to customer expectations. Today, many companies recognized for their quality link themselves with their customers through information systems. These systems enable companies to respond immediately to customer issues, support rapid changes in customer needs, and offer "made to order" products. Moreover, information technology allows customers to track their products and obtain status reports throughout the production cycle. It can also promote better communication within the company, thereby increasing the efficiency of employees and machines alike. In fact, many companies now rely on information systems to help establish a competitive advantage. For example, Siemens, a global producer of goods and services in industries ranging from communications to health care, cites its use of information technology as the key to its rapid growth in productivity.[20]

electronic data interchange (EDI)
Information systems that transmit documents such as invoices and purchase orders between computers, thereby lowering ordering costs and paperwork

One important type of information technology is **electronic data interchange (EDI).** EDI systems transmit specially formatted documents (such as invoices and purchase orders) from one company's computers to another's. This can greatly reduce the time, paperwork, and cost associated with placing and processing orders, thereby making it easier and more profitable for a customer to do business with the company.

Wise Use of Technology Even though robots, automation, and information systems can greatly improve the way a company designs, manufactures, and delivers goods, one of the worst mistakes the company can make is to automate a series of tasks without first examining the underlying process. If the basic process creates the wrong products or involves needless steps, nothing is gained by automating it without first cleaning it up. Otherwise you run the risk of simply doing the wrong things faster. Problems can also result from using production technology without properly preparing the work force to implement and use the technology.

control the flow along assembly lines. However, this isn't the hands-off, robotic automation often associated with flexible manufacturing systems (FMS). Humans play the central role here, making split-second decisions and performing precision assembly work that robots stumble over.

Motorola's plant and others like it are built around teams of highly trained employees and agile computer systems. The idea is not to produce thousands of identical products one after the other, but to customize products as much as possible for every customer. Because information flow is so vital when you're building in small batches or even individual units, software has become more important than machinery in these factories.

An IBM manufacturing manager calls the microprocessor "America's secret weapon" in the global marketplace. In fact, some of Japan's massive automated factories that inspired awe and even fear just a few years ago are now starting to look like a disadvantage. Not only does their complexity create all kinds of operating problems, but they have trouble responding to the growing demand for customized products. The best sign of how well U.S. manufacturers are doing these days is the number of overseas visitors trooping through U.S. factories to see what this secret weapon is all about.

QUESTIONS FOR CRITICAL THINKING

1. What sort of competitive advantage does Motorola establish by being able to build customized pagers in such a short time?
2. How can building pagers only after they have been ordered help Motorola reduce costs?

TRW is a global manufacturing and service company that targets the automotive, space, and defense industries. TRW regularly and carefully checks its automated production systems to make sure it's improving the production process without wasting capital. One employee focuses full-time on auditing machines for output mistakes, developing strategies for error reduction, and training other employees. Rather than automating for speed, the company focuses its efforts on designing "mistake-proofing" technology into its equipment, ensuring that it uses technology to work smarter as well as faster.[21]

DESIGNING OPERATIONS

In addition to designing goods and services, managers must design the operations that will produce them. When Richard Teerlink and his management team at Harley-Davidson set out to return Harley to a competitive position, they learned that the way an organization designs its operations can have a dramatic impact on its ability to deliver quality products. When designing operations, managers consider factors such as capacity planning, facility location, and facility layout.

Capacity Planning

Once products have been designed, organizations must address their ability to produce the goods or services. The term *capacity* refers to the volume of manufacturing or service capability that an organization possesses. **Capacity planning** is a long-term strategic decision that establishes the overall level of resources an organization has to meet customer demand.[22] The neighborhood convenience store needs to consider traffic volume throughout the day and night in order to plan staffing levels appropriately. At the other extreme

capacity planning
A long-term strategic decision that determines the level of resources available to an organization to meet customer demand

of complexity, when planning for the production of an airliner, Boeing has to consider not only the staffing of thousands of people but also factory floor space, material flows from hundreds of suppliers, internal deliveries, cash flow, tools and equipment, and dozens of other factors. Because of the potential impact on finances, customers, and employees, capacity planning involves some of the most difficult decisions that managers have to make.

Top management uses long-term capacity planning to make significant decisions about an organization's ability to produce goods and services, such as expanding existing facilities, constructing new facilities, or phasing out unneeded ones. Such decisions involve a great deal of risk for two reasons: (1) Large shifts in demand are difficult to predict accurately, and (2) long-term capacity decisions can be difficult to undo. For example, if a new facility is built on order to produce a new product that fails, or if demand for a popular product suddenly declines, the company will find itself with expensive excess capacity. Managers must then decide whether or not to eliminate this excess capacity. If they eliminate it and demand picks up again, the company will have to forego profits because it is unable to meet customer demand.[23]

BEST OF THE WEB

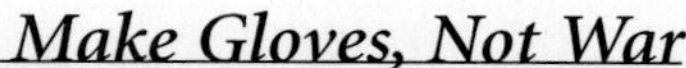

The problem of having too much manufacturing capacity is probably most apparent in the defense industries. When the nation is at war, factories may have to run at full speed, 24 hours a day just to keep up with the demand for weapons and ammunition. However, soon after the war ends, factories sit idle because producing in such quantities is no longer needed. But the U.S. Army has figured out a way to get those facilities moving again. The Armament Retooling Manufacturing Support (ARMS) program encourages businesses to move in and use idle military facilities to manufacture their own peace-time products. To encourage participation, the U.S. government offers assistance with marketing; using of land, buildings, and equipment; obtaining state and federal permits; guaranteeing loans; and planning grants. For a company looking to expand capacity, this could be just the ticket.
http://www.openterprise.com

Facility Location

One long-term issue that management must resolve early is the location of production facilities. The best locations minimize costs in three categories: (1) regional costs—including the cost of land, construction, labor, local taxes, leasing, and energy; (2) transportation costs; and (3) raw materials costs.[24] When choosing a location, companies must consider regional costs, including local living standards; the local government's position on offering tax incentives for relocating companies; and the type, availability, and cost of local energy. In addition, managers must consider whether the local labor pool has the skills that the firm needs. For example, firms that need highly trained accountants, engineers, or computer scientists often locate near university communities such as Boston. On the other hand, if most of the jobs can be filled by unskilled or semiskilled employees, firms can choose locations where such labor is available at a relatively low cost. The search for low-cost labor has led many U.S. companies to locate their manufacturing operations in countries such as Mexico, China, and Indonesia, where wages are much lower. However, companies that fail to compensate foreign workers fairly are risking strong consumer backlash in the United States.

Also affecting location are transportation costs, which cover the shipping of finished goods. Almost every company needs easy, low-cost access to ground transportation such as highways and rail lines. Moreover, companies that sell a lot of products overseas must be able to arrange for efficient air or water transportation.

Finally, companies must consider raw materials costs. For example, the location of a coal-based power plant must be chosen to minimize the cost of distributing electric power to its customers and to minimize the cost and *lead time* of shipping coal to the plant.

Location considerations may be different for some service organizations. Although they may also take regional costs into consideration, the main objective for many service firms is to locate where profit potential is greatest. Because they often require one-on-one contact with customers, service organizations such as gas stations, restaurants, department stores, and charities must locate where their target market is large and sustainable. Therefore, market research often plays a central role in site selection.[25] However, for service companies that reach customers primarily by telephone, mail, or the Internet, proximity to customers is less of a consideration.

Facility Layout

After the site has been selected for a facility, managers must turn their attention to *facility layout,* the arrangement of production work centers and other elements (such as material, equipment, and support departments) needed to process goods and services. Facility layout affects the amount of on-hand inventory, the efficiency of materials handling, the utilization of equipment, and the productivity and morale of employees. In goods manufacturing, the primary concern is the efficient movement of resources and inventory. In the production of services, facility layout controls the flow of customers through the system and influences the customer's satisfaction with the service.[26] Four typical facility layouts include *process layout, product layout, cellular layout,* and *fixed-position layout* (see Exhibit 8.3).[27]

A **process layout** is also called a *functional layout* because it concentrates in one place everything needed to complete one phase of the production process. Specific functions, such as drilling or welding are performed in one location for different products or customers (see Exhibit 8.3A). Process layout is frequently used in machine shops as well as in service industries. For example, a medical clinic might dedicate one room to x-rays, another room for routine examinations, and still another for outpatient surgery.

process layout
Method of arranging a facility so that production tasks are carried out in separate departments containing specialized equipment and personnel

An alternative to the process layout is the **product layout,** also called the assembly-line layout, in which the main production process occurs along a line, and products in progress move from one workstation to the next. Materials and subassemblies of component parts may feed into the main line at several points, but the flow of production is continuous. Electronics and personal-computer manufacturers are just two of many industries that typically use this layout (see Exhibit 8.3B).

product layout
Method of arranging a facility so that production proceeds along a line of workstations

Some production of services is also organized by product. For example, when you go to your local department of motor vehicles to get a driver's license, you usually go through a series of steps that are administered by several different people: registering, taking a written or computerized test, having an eye exam, and getting your picture taken. You emerge from this system a licensed driver, unless of course you fail one of the tests.

The **cellular layout** groups together dissimilar machines into work centers (or cells) to process parts that have similar shapes or processing requirements (see Exhibit 8.3C). Arranging work flow by cells can improve the efficiency of a process layout while maintaining its flexibility. At the same time, grouping smaller numbers of workers in cells facilitates teamwork and joint problem solving. Employees are also able to work on a product from start to finish, and they can move between machines within their cells, thus increasing the flexibility of the cell's team. Cellular layouts are commonly used in computer chip manufacture and metal fabricating.[28]

cellular layout
Method of arranging a facility so that parts with similar shapes or processing requirements are processed together in work centers

Finally, the **fixed-position layout** is a facility layout in which labor, materials, and equipment are brought to the location where the good is being produced or the customer

fixed-position layout
Method of arranging a facility so that the product is stationary and equipment and personnel come to it

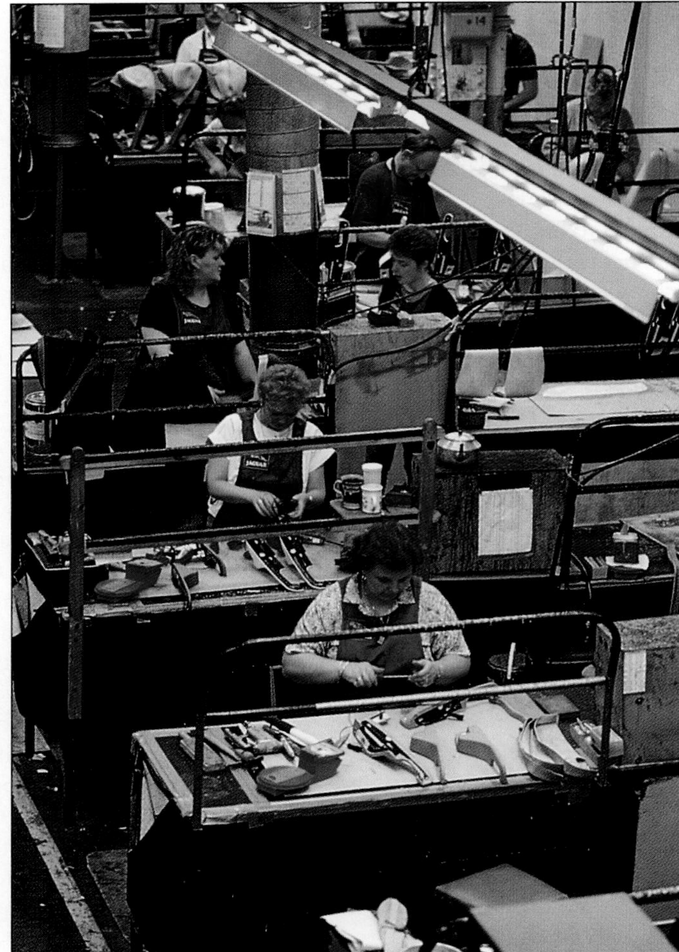

The Jaguar plant in Brownslane, England, uses a process layout to locate in one place all of the operations and materials needed for each step in the production process. The employees in this section of the plant all use the same parts and operations to assemble components for car door panels.

is being served. Building, road, bridge, airplane, and ship construction are typical examples of a fixed-position layout (see Exhibit 8.3D). Service companies often use fixed-position layouts as well: A plumber, for example, goes to a job site bringing the tools, material, and expertise needed to repair a broken pipe.

Managing Operations

In addition to designing the production facilities and strategy, organizations must also design operations systems to manage the production process. Specific areas of concern include purchasing management, inventory management, quality assurance, and production control. These systems must be able to meet the ongoing needs of the organization. Moreover, as the organization's needs change (for instance, when products or existing production equipment becomes obsolete), operations systems must often be redesigned.

Purchasing

purchasing
Acquiring the raw materials, parts, components, supplies, and finished products needed to produce goods and services

Purchasing is the acquisition of the raw materials, parts, components, supplies, and finished products required to produce goods and services. The goal of purchasing is to make sure that

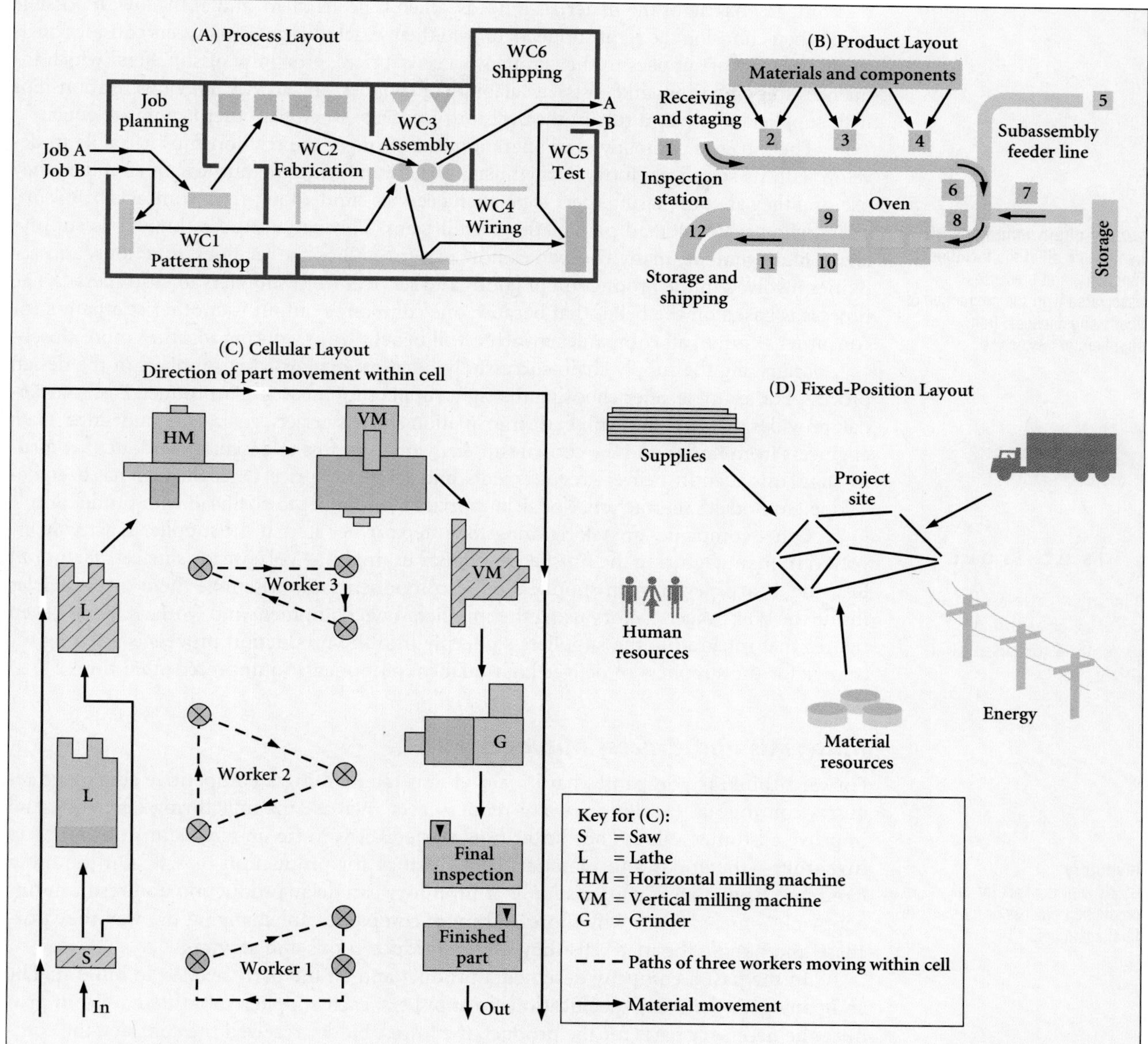

EXHIBIT 8.3

Types of Facility Layouts

Facility layout is often determined by the type of product an organization is producing. Typically, a process layout is used for an organization producing made-to-order products. A product layout is used when an organization is producing large quantities of just a few products. A cellular layout works well in organizations that practice mass-customization. And a fixed-position layout is used when the product is too large to move.

(A) A process layout is arranged according to the specialized employees and materials involved in various phases of the production process.

(B) In a product or assembly-line layout, the developing product moves in a continuous sequence from one workstation to the next.

(C) In a cellular layout, parts with similar shapes or processing requirements are processed together in work centers, which facilitates teamwork and flexibility.

(D) A fixed-position layout requires employees and materials to be brought to the product.

the company has all of the materials it needs, when it needs them, and at the lowest possible cost. When choosing the right suppliers to help them reach this goal, managers consider quality, conformity of supplies to the company's needs, prices, proximity of suppliers (which influences shipping times and costs), availability of supplies, and service. Previous relationships with suppliers also play a role in the decision, especially when the other factors are equal.

The longer a company is in operation, the stronger the relationships it is able to develop with its suppliers. Today many businesses are reducing the number of suppliers they use, and they are purchasing specific parts and services under long-term contracts from suppliers who are considered part of the overall team. Through a process known as **supply-chain management,** many companies now integrate all of the facilities, functions, and activities involved in the production of goods and services from suppliers to customers.[29] The process is based on the belief that because one company's output is another company's (or consumer's) input, all companies involved will benefit from working together more closely.

supply-chain management
Integrating all of the facilities, functions, and processes associated with the production of goods and services, from suppliers to customers

Managing the supply chain successfully often means involving suppliers in the design process. For example, after choosing the right supplier for a particular product, Eastman Kodak provides that supplier with basic information such as targets, goals, and guidelines. Then engineers from Kodak and the chosen supplier work in teams to design the product, set quality standards, identify delivery requirements, and agree on a price. Once the plan has been developed to Kodak's satisfaction, Kodak authorizes the supplier to go ahead with production.[30]

Other companies are taking things one step further so that the supplier is actually involved in manufacturing the finished good. For example, at Volkswagen's newest factory in Resende, Brazil, seven main suppliers build components and assemble them onto vehicles inside the Volkswagen factory using the suppliers' own equipment and workers. Volkswagen figures that integrating the suppliers so deeply into the production process is a strong incentive for the suppliers to deliver high-quality components in unprecedented times.[31]

Is It True?

Making a Coca-Cola can costs twice as much as making the drink that fills it.

Materials and Process Management

Forward-thinking companies have realized that maintaining a competitive advantage requires continuously seeking ways to reduce costs, increase manufacturing efficiency, and improve customer value. They know how wasteful it is to tie up large sums of money in **inventory**—the goods and materials kept in stock for production or sale. On the other hand, not having an adequate supply of inventory can delay production and result in unhappy customers. That's why more and more companies are changing the way they purchase and handle the materials they use to produce goods and services.

inventory
Goods kept in stock for the production process or for sales to final customers

In the past a company designed a product and all the parts needed to build it: The company gave the parts specifications to suppliers, each supplier submitted a bid to produce the necessary parts for the product, the lowest bidder received the contract, the company bought a large enough inventory to make sure it would not run out during peak production times, and new parts were ordered when inventory levels dropped to a predetermined level. Many companies continue to operate this way, which does offer certain benefits. For example, companies typically get a better price when they buy inventory in bulk, and having a large supply on hand enables them to meet customer demand quickly. Unfortunately, carrying a large inventory also ties up the company's money and increases the risk of products becoming obsolete. Moreover, maintaining distant relationships with suppliers can lead to poor-quality components and delayed deliveries.

So many companies today are seeking new ways of managing inventory. One of their goals is to shorten and stabilize the **lead time**—the period that elapses between placing the supply order and receiving the materials. Another goal is to establish a system of **inventory control**—some way of (1) determining the right quantities of supplies and products to have on hand and (2) tracking where those items are. Two methods that compa-

lead time
Period that elapses between the ordering of materials and their arrival from the supplier

inventory control
System for determining the right quantity of various items to have on hand and keeping track of their location, use, and condition

nies use to control inventory and manage the production process are *materials requirement planning* and *manufacturing resource planning.*

Materials Requirement Planning **Material requirements planning** (MRP) is an inventory-control technique that helps a manufacturer get the correct materials where they are needed, when they are needed, and without unnecessary stockpiling. Managers use computer programs to calculate when certain materials are needed, when they should be ordered, and when they should be delivered so that they won't cost too much to store. MRP systems are so effective at reducing inventory levels that they are used almost universally in both large and small manufacturing firms.[32]

material requirements planning (MRP)
Method of getting the correct materials where they are needed, on time, and without carrying unnecessary inventory

MRP systems are especially powerful when combined with electronic data interchange technology. Consider XEL Communications, which makes electronic products for the telecommunications industry. The company transmits its MRP information to key suppliers via a computer network, thereby giving suppliers advance information about what the company will need in the future. XEL's production team says that the system has reduced lead and cycle times and has decreased the number of purchase orders and other paperwork necessary to manage materials efficiently.[33]

A more automated form of materials requirement planning is the **perpetual inventory** system in which computers monitor inventory levels and automatically generate purchase orders when supplies fall below a certain point. The price scanners found at the checkout counters of many stores are part of perpetual inventory systems. Every time a product is purchased, the scanner deletes that particular item from the computer system's inventory data. When inventory of the product reaches a predetermined level, the system generates an order for more. Often the store's system is linked to the supplier's own computer system, which enables the order to be placed with virtually no human involvement.

perpetual inventory
System that uses computers to monitor inventory levels and automatically generate purchase orders when supplies are needed

Manufacturing Resource Planning The MRP systems on the market today are made up of various modules, including inventory control, purchasing, customer order entry, production planning, shop-floor control, accounting, and others. With the addition of more and more modules that focus on capacity planning, marketing, and finance, the MRP system evolves into a **manufacturing resource planning** (**MRP II**) system.

manufacturing resource planning (MRP II)
Computer-based system that integrates data from all departments to manage inventory and production planning and control

Because it draws together all departments, an MRP II system produces a company-wide game plan that allows everyone to work with the same numbers (see Exhibit 8.4). People on the factory floor can even draw on data once reserved for top executives, such as inventory levels, back orders, and unpaid bills. Moreover, the system can track each step

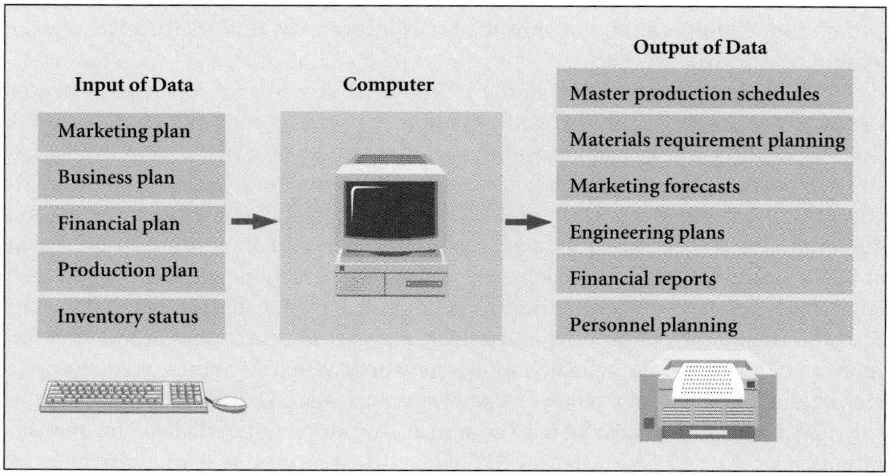

EXHIBIT 8.4

MRP II

An MRP II computer system gives managers and workers in every department easy access to data from all other departments, which in turn makes it easier to generate—and adhere to—the organization's overall plans, forecasts, and schedules.

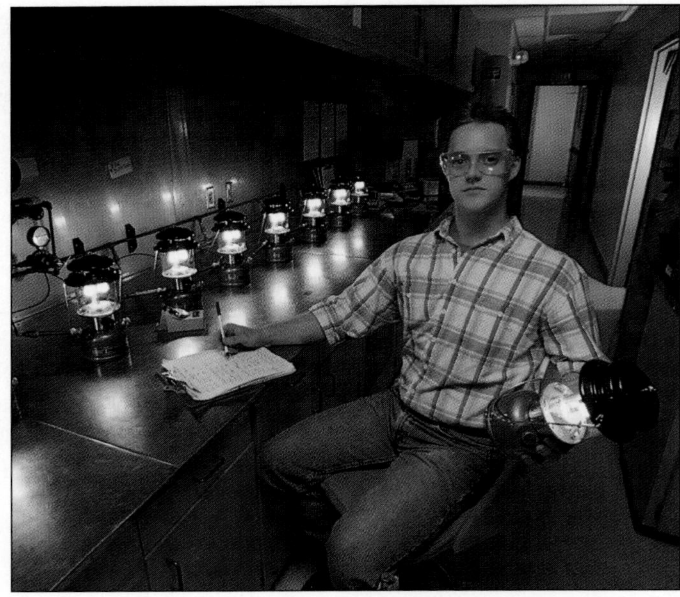

Coleman, which makes lanterns, coolers, and camping stoves, adopted a just-in-time system as a way of reducing inventory costs and the need for storing work in progress. Paul Grimes works in the Wichita, Kansas, plant, which uses JIT to turn out more products without more employees.

of production, allowing managers throughout the company to consult other managers' inventories, schedules, and plans. In addition, MRP II systems are capable of running simulations (models of possible operations systems) that enable managers to plan and test alternative strategies.[34] And thanks to the Internet and some highly complex software, even geographically distant facilities can now be integrated into the planning system as though they were all under one roof.[35]

just-in-time (JIT) system
Continuous system that pulls materials through the production process, making sure that all materials arrive just when they are needed with minimal inventory and waste

Just-in-Time Systems An increasingly popular method of managing operations, including inventory control and production planning, is the **just-in-time (JIT) system.** Like MRP, just-in-time systems aim to have only the right amounts of materials arrive at precisely the times they are needed. A manufacturer produces only enough to fill orders when they are due, thus eliminating finished-goods inventory. Workers on the production line take only those parts or materials from the previous station that they can process immediately, thus *pulling* the work through the system rather than pushing it through the way mass production does. And the manufacturer orders supplies to arrive just as they are needed, and no sooner, thus eliminating raw materials inventories. As a result, waste is reduced and quality is improved.

JIT evolved in Japan during the 1950s when demand for Japanese automobiles was so low that no manufacturer was able to apply the principles of mass production. Japanese firms were also short on capital and storage space following World War II. Therefore, they strove to reduce inventory, which soaks up both capital and storage space. Eiji Toyoda of Toyota told his employees to eliminate all waste, which he defined as anything more than the minimum amount of equipment, materials, parts, space, and time absolutely necessary to add value to the product. The result of Toyoda's directives was the JIT production system, which is characterized by multifunctional teamwork, flexible manufacturing, small-batch production, strict production control, quick setups, consistent production levels, preventive maintenance, and reliable supplier networks. When all of these factors work together in sync, the manufacturer achieves *lean production*—that is, it can do more with less.[36]

JIT concepts can also be used to reduce inventory and cycle time for service organizations. Consider Koley's Medical Supply, which manages inventory for hospitals using what it calls "stockless distribution." Rather than making large, general deliveries to the stockroom, the company delivers specific items in just the right quantities to the various floors and rooms in the hospital. This isn't always easy: At one hospital, Koley's has to make deliveries to 168 individual receiving points. But the system creates value for Koley's customers. For example, in Omaha, Nebraska, Bishop Clarkson Memorial Hospital reduced its annual inventory costs from $500,000 to just $7,000. Clarkson has also reduced its administrative costs associated with supplies. Through such innovative programs, Koley's is able to serve its customers better and increase its own profits.

A JIT system requires careful planning, which has some indirect benefits. For instance, reducing stocks of parts to practically nothing ("zero inventory") encourages factories to keep production flowing smoothly, from beginning to end, without any holdups. And a constant flow requires good teamwork. On the other hand, JIT exposes a company to greater risks, as a disruption in the flow of raw materials from suppliers can slow or stop the production process. JIT also places a heavy burden on suppliers, such as the steel companies that supply a car factory, because they must be able to meet the production schedules of their customers. However, the conversion of a major customer to a JIT system can provide an incentive for suppliers to adopt the system as well.

Because of the inability of manufacturers and suppliers to coordinate their schedules, JIT doesn't always work. For example, shoemaker Allen-Edmonds cannot get its principal raw material whenever it wants because calfskin hides come on the market only at certain times each year.[37] Similarly, Dell Computer's ability to quickly assemble made-to-order computers is sometimes constrained by suppliers' long lead times.[38] Additional factors can also affect JIT: whether a product is seasonal or promotional or perishable; whether it has unusual handling characteristics; its size; its weight; and the volatility of the sales cycle.[39]

Quality Assurance

As we have seen so far, companies today are more focused on quality than ever before. Like Harley-Davidson, many U.S. companies have been forced to examine the quality of their goods, services, and processes largely as a result of tough foreign competition. And just as Harley-Davidson was able to reestablish itself as the worldwide quality leader, today many U.S. companies are setting new standards for quality.

The traditional means of maintaining quality is called **quality control**—measuring quality against established standards after the good or service has been produced and weeding out any defects. A more comprehensive approach is **quality assurance,** a system of companywide policies, practices, and procedures to ensure that every product meets

quality control
Routine checking and testing of a finished product for quality against an established standard

quality assurance
System of policies, practices, and procedures implemented throughout the company to create and produce quality goods and services

Making Quality Count

BEST OF THE WEB

In today's competitive business environment, companies have to be concerned about the quality of their goods and services. As a future businessperson, the more you know about this important topic, the better prepared you will be to meet the competitive challenges of the future. And once again, the Internet makes it easy for you. The American Society for Quality (ASQ) maintains a Web site containing information about all things quality. You can find out who won the latest Malcolm Baldrige awards, learn more about ISO 9000 and other quality standards, search an online glossary of quality-related terms, and browse a bibliography of books and software on topics like supplier management, teams, benchmarking, and customer satisfaction. At the ASQ, quality is only a click away.
http://www.asqc.org

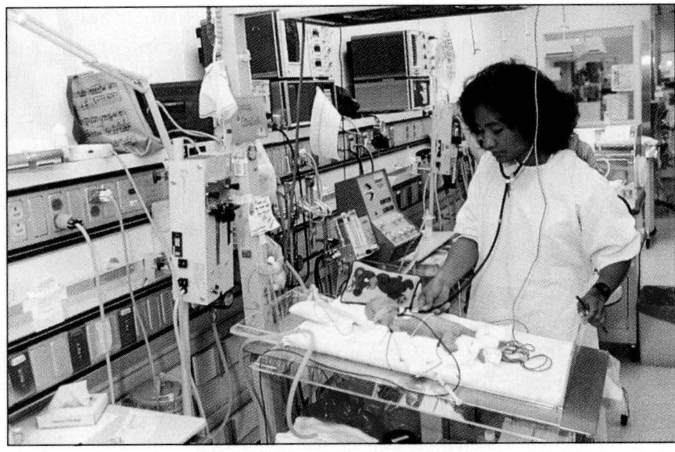

Computerized infant-monitoring equipment has improved productivity and the quality of health care at Stanford Hospital's newborn intensive care unit. The sensors automatically detect any changes in the infants' vital signs and alert nurses so that they can respond.

preset quality standards. Quality assurance includes quality control as well as doing the job right the first time by designing tools and machinery properly, demanding quality parts from suppliers, encouraging customer feedback, training employees better, empowering employees, and encouraging them to take pride in their work. A pioneer of the quality movement, Armand Feigenbaum says that the goal of quality assurance is to reduce the costs of failing to do things right. By eliminating only one inefficiency, such as a defect or an excessively complex process, you reduce total product costs because less money is spent on inspection, complaints, and product service. In addition, as you reduce failure costs, which Feigenbaum estimates average 25 percent of gross sales in most large U.S. firms, "by definition you improve customer satisfaction."[40]

Companies approach quality assurance in various ways. As a builder of sheet-metal components and electromechanical assemblies, Trident Precision Manufacturing empowers workers to make decisions on the shop floor, and it spends 4.7 percent of payroll on employee training.[41] High-end computer maker Sequent Computer Systems has a "customer process engineering manager" whose primary responsibility is to continually communicate with customers and identify any recurring problems. Throughout the day, MBNA America Bank posts customer service performance measurements on scoreboards set up in its offices, keeping employees tuned in to quality goals.[42] In service organizations like MBNA where no tangible product is manufactured, taking regular measurements of customer satisfaction is especially important to maintaining quality standards.

Is It True?

Attaining a 99 percent defect-free rate is an exceptional level of service for any business.

Statistical Quality Control Quality assurance also includes the now widely used concept of **statistical quality control (SQC),** in which all aspects of the production process are monitored so that managers can see whether the process is operating as it should. The primary tool of SQC is called **statistical process control (SPC),** which involves taking samples from the process periodically and plotting observations of the samples on a *control chart* (see Exhibit 8.5). A sample provides a reasonable estimate of the entire process. By observing the random fluctuations in the process that are graphed on the chart, managers and workers can identify whether such changes are normal or whether they indicate that some corrective action is required. In this way SPC can prevent poor quality before it occurs.[43]

statistical quality control (SQC)
Monitoring all aspects of the production process to see whether the process is operating as it should

statistical process control (SPC)
Use of random sampling and control charts to monitor the production process

As one of the fundamental teachings of quality guru W. Edwards Deming, statistical quality control is not limited to goods-producing industries. For example, financial services provider G.E. Capital uses statistical control methods to make sure the bills it sends to customers are correct. This lowers the cost of making adjustments while improving customer satisfaction.[44]

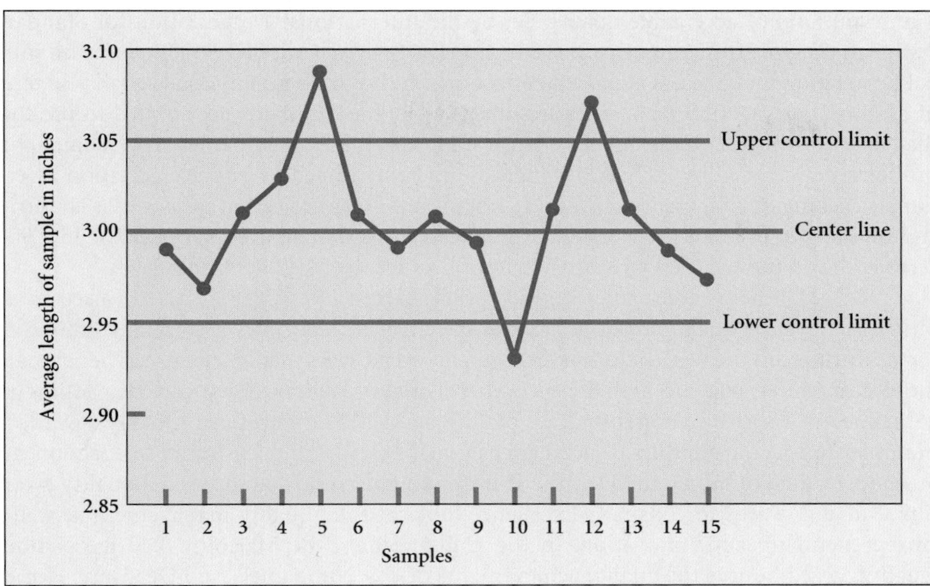

EXHIBIT 8.5

Statistical Process Control Chart

In this example of a control chart, the acceptable length of a bolt being manufactured ranges from 2.95 to 3.05 inches. The chart shows that two samples were unacceptably long, one sample was too short, and the rest were clustered around the center line of 3.00 inches.

Continuous Improvement In addition to using statistical quality control, companies can empower each employee to continuously improve the quality of goods production or service delivery. The Japanese word for continuous improvement is *kaizen*. Japanese manufacturers learned long before many U.S. manufacturers did that continuous improvement is not something that can be delegated to one or a few people. Instead it requires the full participation of every employee. This means encouraging all workers to spot quality problems, halt production when necessary, generate ideas for improvement, and adjust work routines as needed.[45]

ISO 9000
Global standards set by the International Organization for Standardization establishing a minimum level of acceptable quality

Global Quality Standards and Awards Companies that do business in Europe have to leap an extra quality hurdle. Many manufacturers and service providers in Europe require their suppliers to comply with **ISO 9000,** a set of international quality standards that establishes a

High costs and inefficient production brought Porsche to the brink of bankruptcy in the early 1990s. But thanks to a lot of coaching in quality production methods from Japanese managers, the sports-car company is back in the pink again.

minimum level of acceptable quality. Set by the International Organization for Standardization, a nongovernment entity based in Geneva, Switzerland, ISO 9000 focuses on internal production and process issues that affect quality, but it doesn't measure quality in terms of customer satisfaction or business results. Usually the standards are applied to products that have health-and safety-related features. However, even companies that manufacture products not covered by ISO 9000 standards are being forced to gain accreditation by customers seeking quality assurance. The standards are now recognized in over 100 countries, and one-fourth of all of the world's corporations insist that all their suppliers be ISO 9000 certified. Even the U.S. Navy requires its suppliers to meet ISO 9000 standards.[46]

ISO 9000 helps companies develop *world-class manufacturing,* a term used to describe the level of quality and operational effectiveness that puts a company among the top performers in the world. Companies seeking world-class quality can use as benchmarks those companies that are globally recognized quality leaders. They can also follow the guidelines of various national or state quality awards. The European Quality Award, for example, honors outstanding performance in quality leadership, customer satisfaction, and business results. In Japan, the Deming Prize is a highly regarded industrial quality award. The Canada Awards for Business Excellence looks at total quality management as well as entrepreneurship and innovation. In the United States, the Malcolm Baldrige National Quality Award honors the quality achievements of U.S. companies. And Delaware, Florida, Maine, New York, and Wyoming are just some of the states that have instituted quality awards to encourage higher quality levels.[47]

Custom Research of Minneapolis recently became only the second service company to win the Baldrige award for small businesses. For one thing, Custom Research interviewed customers to find out how to better serve them, which enabled the company to significantly increase customer satisfaction. "We're really proud that we're able to apply Baldrige criteria to a service company and measure things that have not been measured before," says co-owner Judy Carson.[48] Of course, even if an organization doesn't want to actually apply for an award, quality can be improved by measuring performance against the award's standards and working to overcome any problems uncovered by this process (see Exhibit 8.6).

Production Forecasting and Control

In order to oversee creation of the product, production and operations managers must be able to estimate future demand, foresee possible product changes, and gather the resources

EXHIBIT 8.6

Criteria for the Malcolm Baldrige National Quality Award

The Malcolm Baldrige National Quality Award is given annually to companies that demonstrate an outstanding commitment to quality. Named after former Secretary of Commerce Malcolm Baldrige, the awards are given to companies in each of four categories: manufacturing, services, small businesses, and universities and hospitals. This chart lists the criteria on which companies are judged for the award.

- *Leadership.* Have senior leaders clearly defined the company's values, goals, and ways to achieve the goals? Is the company a model "corporate citizen"?
- *Information and analysis.* Does the company effectively use data and information to support customer-driven performance excellence and marketplace success?
- *Strategic planning.* How does the company develop strategies and business plans to strengthen its performance and competitive position?
- *Human resources development and management.* How does the company develop the full potential of its work force? How are its human resource capabilities and work systems aligned with its strategic and business plans?
- *Process management.* How does the company design, manage, and improve key processes, such as customer-focused design and product and service delivery?
- *Business results.* How does the company address performance and improvement in key business areas—product and service quality, productivity and operational effectiveness, supply quality, and financial performance indicators linked to these areas?
- *Customer focus and satisfaction.* How does the company determine requirements, expectations, and preferences of customers? What are its customer satisfaction results?

needed to respond to customer or competitor shifts. To do so, they start with **production forecasting,** which deals specifically with the question of how much to produce in a certain time span. Using customer feedback, market research, past sales figures, industry analyses, and educated guesses about the future behavior of the economy and competitors, managers estimate future demand for the company's products. These estimates are used to plan, budget, and schedule the use of resources.

production forecasting
Estimating how much of a company's goods and services must be produced in order to meet future demand

However, remember that forecasts are never 100 percent accurate. Many factors cause variances between the estimates and actual demand.[49] And the more a company uses JIT production methods, the more it can base production on customer orders rather than on forecasts.

To oversee the actual process of production, POM managers use **production control**—a set of steps leading to the efficient production of a high-quality product. The manufacture of complex goods is not simply a matter of adding part A to part B to part C and

production control
Planning, routing, scheduling, dispatching, and following up on production so as to achieve efficiency and high quality

EXPLORING GLOBAL BUSINESS

Merging Hand-Made Craftsmanship and World-Class Manufacturing

Can advanced technology share a factory with old-fashioned craftsmanship? Rolls-Royce has proven that the answer is yes. The legendary British company is renowned for its luxurious Rolls-Royce and Bentley cars and limousines. At its peak, the company was selling more than 3,000 vehicles a year in Great Britain and international markets, with the lowest-priced car costing well over $100,000.

However, like General Motors, Ford, Chrysler, and Toyota, Rolls-Royce saw its car sales stall when the world economy faltered in the early 1990s. To remain competitive, Michael J. Donovan, one of Rolls-Royce's managing directors, realized that the company had to cut production costs and improve productivity. Donovan and other top managers came up with a plan to combine the two factories into one and cut time out of the 50 days needed to manufacture each car. Using cross-functional teamwork and benchmarking, they also set out to meet or exceed the highest international standards of automobile manufacturing.

Top executives slashed the number of management layers in the factory from seven to four and reduced the work force from 5,700 to 2,400 through voluntary retirements and buyouts. Next, they redesigned the factory to create 16 manufacturing zones. Every zone operated as a "factory within a factory" to manufacture its part of the product on time and within budget. Each of the 10 or so teams in each zone was composed of production employees, engineers, and any other employees needed to accomplish the team's tasks. Teams were given freedom to complete their work as they saw fit, and they quickly found ways of speeding up production while boosting quality beyond the already high levels.

The new arrangement pleases Paul Simm, who used to sit at one of the workstations on the assembly line and handle the same task over and over. Now Simm is a member of a team that assembles V-8 engines, and he puts together much of each engine he touches. "It's more interesting; I've got more responsibility, and in the end you've got something with your name on it," Simm says. "That certainly helps improve quality. If there's a problem, it's going to come back to you."

Despite the streamlined production methods, hand-crafted quality has not disappeared from the Rolls-Royce factory. Metalworkers still craft each stainless steel front grille and hood ornament by hand. And at a customer's request, the woodworking shop will make a dashboard in any type of wood. Even with the hand crafting, Rolls-Royce has been able to reduce production time to 30 days and retain the painstaking attention to detail and quality that made the company famous.

QUESTIONS FOR CRITICAL THINKING

1. What else is Rolls-Royce selling its customers besides an automobile?
2. What do you think is the most important dimension of quality at Rolls-Royce?

so forth until a product emerges ready to ship. For example, the new Mercedes M-Class sport-utility vehicle is assembled from subunits built by 65 major suppliers and many other smaller ones.[50] Making sure that all the pieces are put together in the proper sequence and at the proper time requires large-scale planning and scheduling. The same is true for the production of complex services.

Production-control procedures vary from company to company. However, most manufacturing processes have five steps: planning, routing, scheduling, dispatching, and following up. To get a feel for the complexities involved, follow the five steps taken by an imaginary small company as it makes a simple product—wooden tables. The company has just received a rush order for 500 white and 500 unpainted tables.

bill of materials
List of all parts and materials in a product that are to be made or purchased

Step 1: Production Planning From industrial and design teams, the production manager receives lists of all the labor, machinery, and materials needed to make the 1,000 tables that have been ordered. A **bill of materials** lists all the required parts and materials and specifies whether they are to be made or purchased:

MAKE	PURCHASE
1,000 tabletops	4,000 dowels (one to fasten each leg)
4,000 table legs	50 gallons of white paint

The production manager must determine the quantity of these materials already on hand. A report from the MRP system reveals that the company has enough wood and paint but only 2,000 dowels. So an additional 2,000 dowels are ordered via EDI from a trusted supplier who can deliver on time.

routing
Specifying the sequence of operations and the path the work will take through the production facility

Step 2: Routing **Routing** is the task of specifying the sequence of operations and the path through the facility that the work will take. The way production is routed depends on the type of product and the layout of the plant.

The table-manufacturing company uses a process layout because it has three departments, each handling a different phase of the table's manufacture and each equipped with specialized tools, machines, and employees. Department 1 cuts wood into tabletops and legs. These pieces are then sent to department 2, where holes are drilled and rough finishing is done. Finally, the individual pieces are routed to department 3, where the tables are assembled and painted. The dowels and paint are routed directly to department 3 from inventory.

scheduling
Process of determining how long each production operation takes and then setting a starting and ending time for each

Step 3: Scheduling In any production process, managers must use **scheduling**—determining how long each operation takes and setting a starting and ending time for each. This is not easy, even in a business as simple as our hypothetical table company. Here is what the table manufacturer's production manager has to consider in order to construct a schedule: If department 2 can drill 4,000 dowel holes in a day, then all 4,000 legs and all 1,000 tabletops should arrive in department 2 on the same day. If department 1 can make 1,000 tabletops and 1,000 legs a week, it should start on the legs 3 weeks before it starts to cut the tops, or not all of the parts will be ready for departments 2 and 3 at the same time. If the entire order is to be shipped at the same time and as soon as possible, department 3 should paint the first 500 tables as they are assembled and finished so that the paint will be dry by the time the last 500 are completed. The schedule must also show how much time will elapse before the job reaches department 3—that is, how much time department 3 has available to work on other jobs before this one arrives.

Gantt chart
Bar chart used to control schedules by showing how long each part of a production process should take and when it should take place

When a job has relatively few activities and relationships, like our table example, many production managers keep the process on schedule with a **Gantt chart.** Developed

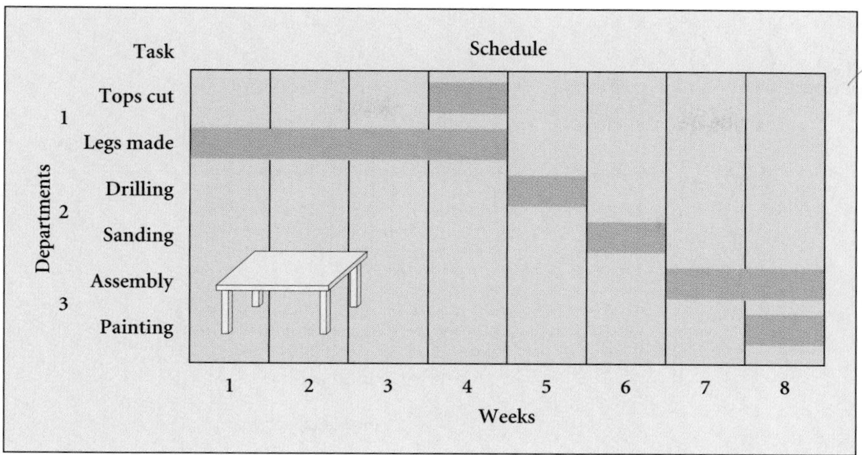

EXHIBIT 8.7

A Gantt Chart: Scheduling a Table Order

A chart like this enables a production manager to see immediately the dates on which production steps must be started and completed if goods are to be delivered on schedule. Some steps may overlap to save time. For instance, after three weeks of cutting table legs, cutting tabletops begins. This overlap ensures that the necessary legs and tops are completed at the same time and can move on together to the next stage in the manufacturing process.

by Henry L. Gantt earlier this century, the Gantt chart is a bar chart showing the amount of time required to accomplish each part of a manufacturing process. It allows managers to see at a glance whether the process is in line with the schedule they had planned (see Exhibit 8.7).

For more complex jobs, the **program evaluation and review technique (PERT)** is helpful. PERT is a planning tool that helps managers identify the optimal sequencing of activities, the expected time for project completion, and the best use of resources within a complex project. It was originally developed in 1957, when the U.S. Navy was grappling with the enormous task of coordinating the thousands of suppliers and activities needed to build the Polaris submarine fleet. Today it is used by businesses to schedule production tasks.

program evaluation and review technique (PERT)
Planning tool that managers of complex projects use to determine the optimal order of activities, the expected time for project completion, and the best use of resources

To use PERT, the manager must (1) identify the activities to be performed, (2) determine the sequence of activities, (3) establish the time needed to complete each activity, (4) diagram the network of activities, (5) calculate the longest path through the network that leads to project completion, and (6) refine the network's timing or use of resources as activities are completed. The longest path through the network is known as the **critical path** because it represents the minimum amount of time needed to complete the project.

critical path
In a PERT network diagram, the sequence of operations that requires the longest time to complete.

In place of a single time projection for each task, PERT uses four figures: an *optimistic* estimate (if things go well), a *pessimistic* estimate (if they don't go well), a *most likely* estimate (how long the task usually takes), and an *expected* time estimate, an average of the other three estimates.[51] The expected time is used to diagram the network of activities and determine the length of the critical path.

Consider the manufacture of shoes in Exhibit 8.8. At the beginning of the process, three parallel paths deal with heels, soles, and tops. All three processes must be finished before the next phase (sewing tops to soles and heels) can be started. However, one of the three paths—the tops—takes 33 days, whereas the other two take only 18 and 12 days. The shoe tops, then, are on the critical path because they will delay the entire operation if they fall behind schedule. In contrast, soles can be started up to 21 days after starting the tops without slowing down production. This free time in the soles schedule is called *slack time* because managers can choose to produce the soles anytime during the 33-day period required by the tops.

Step 4: Dispatching **Dispatching** is issuing work orders to department supervisors. These orders specify the work to be done and the schedule for its completion. In the case of the table manufacturer, the production manager would dispatch orders to the storeroom, re-

dispatching
Issuing work orders and schedules to department heads and supervisors

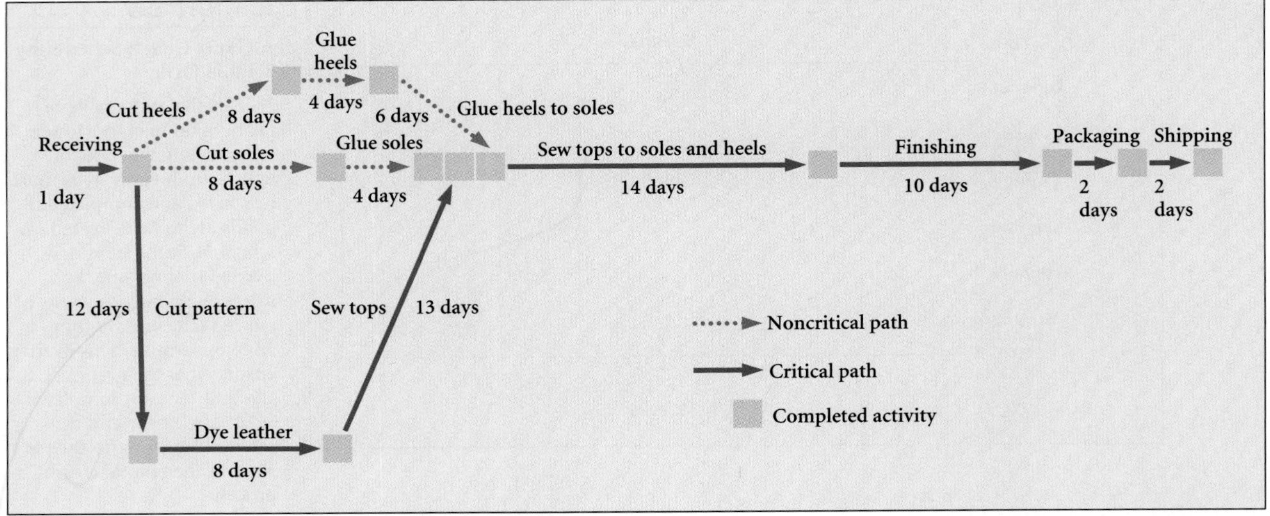

EXHIBIT 8.8

PERT Diagram for Manufacturing Shoes

In the manufacture of shoes, the critical path involves receiving, cutting the pattern, dyeing the leather, sewing the tops, sewing the tops to soles and heels, finishing, packaging, and shipping—a total of 62 time units.

questing delivery of the needed materials (wood, dowels, paint) to the appropriate departments and machines before the scheduled starting time (although if the company were utilizing a JIT system, these items would come directly from suppliers). The work orders also inform department supervisors of their operational priorities and the schedule they must maintain.

Step 5: Following Up Once the schedule has been set and the orders dispatched, a production manager cannot just sit back and assume that the work will get done correctly and on time. Even the best scheduler may misjudge the time needed to complete an operation, and production may be delayed by accidents, mechanical breakdowns, or supplier problems. Therefore, the production manager needs a system for handling delays and preventing a minor disruption from growing into chaos. A successful system is based on good communication between the employees and the production manager.

Suppose a machine breakdown causes department 2 of the table company to lose half a day of drilling time. If the schedule is not altered to direct other work to department 3, the employees and equipment in department 3 will sit idle for some time. However, if department 2 informs the production manager of its machine problem right away, the production manager can immediately reschedule some fill-in work for department 3.

In addition to such a follow-up system, production managers must make sure products meet quality standards. As discussed earlier in this chapter, managers may use a variety of quality assurance measures. However, it is most important to give all employees responsibility for maintaining the quality of their work, to empower them to stop the production process if quality is suffering, and to motivate them to continuously improve the quality of the company's products and services.

Summary of Learning Objectives

1. **Explain the strategic importance of production and operations management.**
Production and operations management (POM) is the coordination of an organization's resources for manufacturing goods or producing services, using the basic functions of planning, organizing, leading, and controlling. Companies are using POM to improve quality and competitiveness by focusing on high efficiency, few defects, fast production, low costs, excellent customer service, broad market reach, innovative products and processes, less waste, and high flexibility.
2. **Describe the evolution of production efficiency.**
Since the Industrial Revolution 200 years ago, a series of technological advances have made production more efficient. The first was mechanization—the use of machines to perform tasks. This led to standardization—the production of uniform, interchangeable parts. Henry Ford introduced the assembly line, where an item is put together as it progresses past a number of workstations. Eventually, many areas achieved automation—the process of performing a mechanical operation with the absolute minimum of human intervention. As technology advanced, so did mass production.
3. **Discuss the role of computers and automation technology in production.**
Computers and automation technology improve the production process in several ways: (1) Robots perform repetitive or mundane tasks quickly and with great precision; (2) AGVs move materials easily around factory floors; (3) CAD and CAE systems allow engineers to design and test virtual models of products; (4) CAM systems easily translate CAD data into production instructions; (5) CIM systems link the people, machines, databases, and decisions involved in each step of producing a good; (6) flexible manufacturing systems (FMS) reduce setup costs and time by linking programmable, multifunctional machine tools through a computer network and an automated material handling system; and (7) EDI systems make ordering supplies faster and easier.
4. **Identify the key issues managers must consider when designing operations.**
Managers must first consider capacity, which is the volume of manufacturing or service delivery that an organization possesses. Second, they must find a facility location that minimizes regional costs (the cost of land, construction, labor, local taxes, leasing, and energy), transportation costs, and raw materials costs. Finally, managers need to consider facility layout, the arrangement of production work centers and other facilities (such as material, equipment, and support departments) needed for the processing of goods and services. The four possible layouts include the process layout, the product layout, the cellular layout, and the fixed-position layout.
5. **Explain the strategic importance of managing inventory, and review the management systems used to control it.**
The goods and materials kept in stock for production or sale make up inventory, which must be managed to minimize costs and ensure that the right supplies are in the right place at the right time. Many companies use material requirements planning (MRP) and perpetual inventory systems to determine when materials are needed, when they should be ordered, and when they should be delivered. A more advanced system is manufacturing resource planning (MRP II), which brings together data from all parts of a company (including financial, design, and engineering departments) to better manage inventory and production planning and control.
6. **Describe the advantages and disadvantages of just-in-time (JIT) systems in production planning.**
Just-in-time (JIT) systems reduce waste and improve quality in the following ways: (1) The manufacturer produces only enough to fill orders when they are due, thus eliminating finished-goods inventory; (2) workers on the production line take from the previous station only those parts or materials that they can process immediately, thus *pulling* the work through the system rather than pushing it through; and (3) the manufacturer orders supplies only when they are needed, thus eliminating raw materials inventories. This system encourages efficiency and teamwork. However, JIT systems are more susceptible to disruptions in the flow of raw materials, and they can place a heavy burden on suppliers.
7. **Discuss the differences between quality control and quality assurance.**
Quality control focuses on measuring finished products against a preset standard and weeding out any defects. On the other hand, quality assurance is a system of company-wide policies, practices, and procedures that build quality into a product and assure that each product meets quality standards.
8. **Define the five basic steps in production control.**
(1) Planning is the analysis of what to produce and how much to produce, as well as where and how to produce it. (2) Routing is figuring out how production will proceed. (3) Scheduling establishes the time frame for the production process. (4) Dispatching is sending production orders. (5) Following up is making sure that everything proceeds according to plan and figuring out how to cope with problems as they arise.

On the Job: Meeting Business Challenges at Harley-Davidson

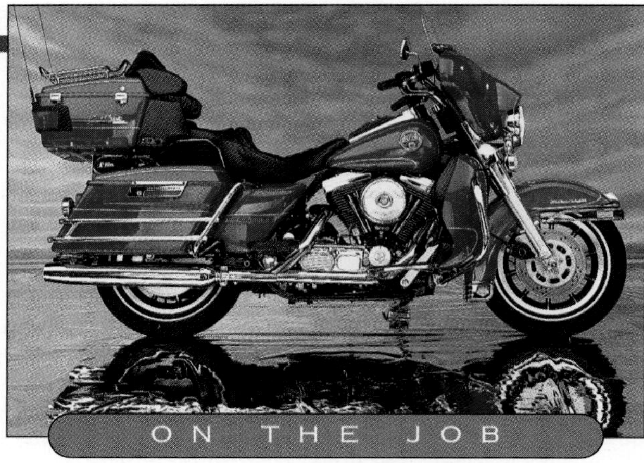

Even though Harley-Davidson had regained its reputation for building dependable motorcycles, higher demand created a new dilemma for CEO Richard Teerlink: how to increase production and boost sales without sacrificing quality. Even though motorcycle enthusiasts in Europe, Japan, and Australia were eager to buy, Harley agreed to limit international exports to 30 percent of all sales until production caught up with demand in North America. Now Teerlink turned his attention to production and operations, the areas that had fueled Harley's return to prominence in the late 1980s.

Following Honda's lead, Harley installed the JIT system of inventory management. Among other things, JIT lowered the number of parts and supplies held in waiting, so Harley could spend more on research to improve quality and to speed up the manufacturing process. Harley adapted to JIT by changing everything from its purchasing practices to the layout of its factories. It also forged closer relationships with a smaller group of suppliers who could deliver high-quality parts on time. Because Harley was using fewer suppliers, it was able to place larger orders and qualify for bulk discounts.

In addition, Harley redesigned its production machinery and created more standardized parts for multiple bike models. With this approach, the company could build individual models in smaller batches, which allowed for more frequent product upgrades. The smaller batches also cut down on the number of defective parts.

Now Teerlink decided that Harley had to do more. He appointed a vice president of continuous improvement to oversee further reductions in waste, defects, and variability. He also moved Harley deeper into flexible manufacturing, and he set up a create-demand team, a production team, and a product support team to tap the knowledge of people who had experience in a variety of functions.

This emphasis on quality and world-class manufacturing has kept Harley well ahead of second-place Honda. Revamping its production and operations processes has even positioned Harley to turn the tables on Japanese companies: Harley-Davidson is now the best-selling imported motorcycle in Japan.

Your Mission: Teerlink has hired you as an operations consultant to evaluate Harley's manufacturing systems and to help plot its strategy for the future. For each of the following situations, choose the best response:

1. Harley doesn't automate any part of its operations without evaluating the underlying processes, fixing any problems, and then deciding whether automation makes sense. At a recent meeting with production staff, you ask for ideas about automating tasks that are still done manually. Which one of the following areas would you recommend that Harley automate?
   a. A machining area where employees make a wide variety of unique tools and fixtures for use on the production line
   b. The assembly area where gas tanks are attached to the cycle frames and where employees are complaining that they have to do the same simple job over and over again
   c. The department where incoming parts (some of which are quite heavy and hard to handle) are unpacked and directed to the appropriate locations on the production line

2. The company's employees continually offer suggestions on improving quality, but you want to implement only those related to quality assurance rather than quality control. Which one of the following suggestions should you accept?
   a. Have an inspector measure the time it takes to start the engines on finished motorcycles when the bikes are driven off the assembly line.
   b. Find out why the stitching in some seat covers is breaking after a few months of use; then ask the manufacturer concerned to fix the problem.
   c. Survey dealers to find out how often the factory ships the wrong owner's manual with a motorcycle; ask if this error rate is acceptable.

3. Harley's managers are well aware of the impact that employee attitudes and motivation have on quality and productivity. When studying several other manufacturing firms, managers have uncovered a number of approaches to getting employees involved and making sure they are satisfied with their work. Considering both cost and effectiveness, which of the following involvement/motivation programs do you think Harley should adopt?
   a. Rotate employees through all the factory jobs, from engineering and design all the way through shipping, cler-

ical work, and even janitorial work. Employees will better appreciate the challenges each job entails, and the result will be a more cohesive work force with a greater sense of teamwork.

b. Encourage employees to start problem-solving teams throughout the plant, and make sure they link their efforts to the company procedures for statistical quality control.

c. Adapt (b) so that employees start problem-solving teams, but do not require the statistical reporting element; too much attention to tracking and monitoring will demoralize employees who feel that their every move is being watched and criticized.

4. One phase of the motorcycle assembly process is split into three parallel task groups, each taking care of one general area of the motorcycle. The assembly line continues in a single line after the three parallel tasks are done (similar to the three parallel task groups in Exhibit 8.8). Considering the individual task times and critical path analysis, where should you assign several people whose old jobs in another factory have been eliminated?

TASK	TIME REQUIRED
Preparing stereo	15 minutes
Preparing saddle bags	5 minutes
Preparing mirrors	6 minutes
Preparing fog lights	10 minutes
Inspecting paint-job quality	45 minutes
Cutting wires to length	9 minutes
Installing connectors	18 minutes
Testing for continuity	10 minutes

a. Task group 1: Preparing accessories, which includes the stereo, the saddle bags, the mirrors, and the fog lights

b. Task group 2: Inspecting paint, which is done entirely by an automated electro-optical inspection robot

c. Task group 3: Assembling the electrical harness, which includes cutting wires to length, installing connectors, and testing for continuity[52]

Key Terms

analytic system (226)
assembly line (227)
automation (227)
bill of materials (246)
capacity planning (233)
cellular layout (235)
computer-aided design (CAD) (228)
computer-aided engineering (CAE) (228)
computer-aided manufacturing (CAM) (229)
computer-integrated manufacturing (CIM) (229)
critical path (247)
dispatching (247)
electronic data interchange (EDI) (232)
fixed-position layout (235)
flexible manufacturing system (FMS) (230)
Gantt chart (246)
inventory (238)
inventory control (238)
ISO 9000 (243)
just-in-time (JIT) system (240)
lead time (238)
manufacturing resource planning (MRP II) (239)
mass customization (228)
mass production (227)
material requirements planning (MRP) (239)
mechanization (227)
perpetual inventory (239)
process layout (235)
product layout (235)
production (226)
production and operations management (POM) (227)
production control (245)
production efficiency (227)
production forecasting (245)
program evaluation and review technique (PERT) (247)
purchasing (236)
quality assurance (241)
quality control (241)
robots (228)
routing (246)
scheduling (246)
setup costs (230)
standardization (227)
statistical process control (SPC) (242)
statistical quality control (SQC) (242)
supply-chain management (238)
synthetic system (226)

Questions

For Review

1. Explain the conversion process and distinguish between analytic and synthetic systems.
2. Why is production and operations management particularly important today?
3. What is mass customization?
4. What factors need to be considered when selecting a site for a production facility?
5. Why is an effective system of inventory control important to every manufacturer?

For Analysis

6. Why is capacity planning an important part of designing operations?
7. How does material requirements planning (MRP) differ from manufacturing resource planning (MRP II)?
8. Explain how JIT systems go beyond simply controlling inventory.
9. Why have companies moved beyond quality control to quality assurance?
10. How can supply-chain management help a company establish a competitive advantage?

For Application

11. Assume you are the production manager for a small machine shop that manufactures precision parts for industrial equipment. How can you use CAD, CAE, CAM, CIM, FMS, and EDI to manufacture better products more easily?
12. If your final product requires several unique subunits that are all produced with different machinery and in differing lengths of time, what facility layout would you choose and why?

A Case for Critical Thinking ■ Companies Compete on Customer Service

It would be difficult to find a company today that doesn't have some sort of quality assurance program. As the competitive pressures of the global business environment become stronger, manufacturers and service companies alike are seeking new ways to distinguish themselves as quality leaders. Of course, when everyone is doing it, offering quality products becomes less of a distinguishing characteristic. So how does a company get customers to recognize that its quality surpasses everybody else's? Many companies are finding the answer in customer service.

Consider Fanuc Robotics. Company president and CEO Eric Mittelstadt says: "Everyone has become better at developing products. In robotics, the robot itself has become sort of a commodity. The one place you can differentiate yourself is in the service you provide." Therefore, Fanuc has transformed itself from a robot producer into a designer and installer of customized manufacturing systems, which requires designing systems that meet the specific needs of individual customers.

Throughout the United States, companies in almost every industry are discovering that they can add value to their products by improving the quality of their service—even if their main product *is* a service. Progressive is an insurance company that specializes in high-risk drivers, but it doesn't settle its customers' claims by making them wade through a long stream of paperwork. The company now offers its customers settlements on-the-spot in the comfort of an air-conditioned van equipped with chairs, a desk, and cellular phones. Representatives also advise accident victims on medical care, repair shops, police reports, and legal procedures. Progressive now sees itself more as a mediator of human trauma than as an insurance company.

Quality customer service can also help lessen the impact of defective products. For example, a month after Saturn launched its first cars, the company found a defect in the front-seat recliner mechanisms. Determined not to let any problem tarnish the reputation that it sought to build, Saturn voluntarily recalled 1,480 cars. The company immediately briefed dealers on the recall via closed-circuit television, and then it sent overnight letters to all customers, letting them know whether or not their car was defective. Saturn even shipped a replacement seat by air to a customer in Alaska (because the company had no dealer there yet). In the end, the recall went so smoothly that it actually contributed to Saturn's reputation for quality.

Other companies are finding that customer service can even increase product sales in mature markets. For example, printer manufacturer Okidata offers toll-free customer service and around-the-clock technical support. "We are the only printer manufacturer offering this depth of service to customers," says Joe Mangiaracina, general manager for customer service and support. "Our goal is to keep customers loyal to Okidata and to impress upon new buyers that we have superior service."

Of course, as with all other dimensions of quality, achieving superior customer service requires a devoted, companywide effort. Many companies say they have this commitment, but not all of them really do. In fact, a recent study found that 85 percent of Fortune 500 firms include the words *customer relationships* in their mission statements, but a mere 18 percent have established a system for measuring how strong those relationships are. As principal consultant in KPMG Peat Marwick's Global Supply Chain Unit, Brian Scholey believes that attitudes are changing, "but there is still a long way to go." He adds that "suppliers and customers who are complacent with their level of customer service will not succeed in the long term."

1. How can a company build customer service into its quality assurance program?
2. How can information technology help companies improve customer service?
3. What factors constrain a company's ability to compete on customer service?
4. Explore Saturn's Web site at <http://www.saturncars.com>. How would you rate the site in terms of customer service? Does it enhance Saturn's ability to serve its customers, or is it just another site on the World Wide Web? Consider issues such as the information that the site provides, whether it facilitates two-way communication (between Saturn and customers), and whether it encourages good feelings about the company.

Building Your Business Skills

Many phases of production, from design to inspection, have become automated or computerized. With your class, or in small groups of three or four students, discuss the personnel issues that you believe have arisen as a result of this technological revolution in business. You might draw a chart that depicts the positive and negative results of technology on human resource management. Develop a consensus opinion (or a written summary) regarding the various issues discussed.

- How has technology affected the job market? Are jobs being enhanced or replaced by computers? What does this mean to you as a student?
- Consider pride in process. Has computerized production created a feeling of distance from the end product for some employees? What are the implications for product quality?
- How have companies engaged employees in an effort to improve morale and make them feel more involved in light of technological advances?

Keeping Current Using *The Wall Street Journal*

Find an article in *The Wall Street Journal* that describes how a company improved its performance by focusing on quality in the production of its goods or services. As you read, consider the following issues:

- Technology in manufacturing
- Supplier relationships
- Employee involvement
- Inventory control
- Quality assurance techniques

1. What problems led the company to rethink its production process? What changes did it make in response to these problems?
2. What costs did the company incur when it implemented the changes? Were all of these costs justified?
3. How has customer satisfaction improved since the changes were implemented? How has employee satisfaction improved? How has the company's financial performance improved?
4. Visit the American Customer Satisfaction Index (ACSI) Web site at <http://www.acsi.asq.org>, and click on the link to the most recent results. According to ACSI, how do the company's competitors rate in customer satisfaction? Have their ratings increased or decreased in recent years? What implications does this have for the company you are investigating?

Exploring the Best of the Web

Setting Standards, page 230

The National Institute of Standards and Technology (NIST) works with private industry to develop standards for emerging industries and to improve U.S. competitiveness in mature industries. Explore the NIST Web site at <http://nist.gov/public_affairs/guide/> and answer the questions below.

1. From the main page, click on *Advanced Technology Program* and then on *Overview.* What is the goal of the Advanced Technology Program? Why does the federal government have an interest in promoting the development of advanced technologies?

2. Click on the *ATP Project Sampler* to learn about some of the advanced technology projects the NIST sponsors. As you can see, developing these technologies is a long and costly process. Why might investors be reluctant to fund the development of such technologies? On the other hand, why might investors want to have a stake in developing them?
3. From the main page, follow the link to *Measurement and Standards Laboratories.* What benefits do NIST's Measurement and Standards Laboratories provide to businesses, industries, and the scientific community? Why do you think it is important that common languages and standards are developed among all users of a particular technology?

Make Gloves, Not War, page 234

The Armament Retooling Manufacturing Support (ARMS) program helps manufacturers to solve their capacity problems by using idle ammunition factories. Visit the Operation Enterprise Web site at <http://www.openterprise.com>, and read more about this innovative partnership between the government and private industry. Then answer the following questions.

1. Read about ARMS by following the links to *The ARMS Program: An Overview.* Who owns the facilities operated under ARMS? What kinds of businesses or industries do you think would be particularly attracted to this program?
2. From the main page, click on *The ARMS Program: Performance Report,* and navigate the various links to read through the report. Why do many businesses that operate under the ARMS program have access to a supply of skilled labor? What do you see as the primary long-term drawback to operating in an ARMS facility?
3. The U.S. government has made the ARMS program attractive by minimizing regional costs such as land, construction, labor, local taxes, leasing, and energy. What other costs must businesses consider when they evaluate facility locations? What types of service industries can you think of that would be candidates for the ARMS program?

Making Quality Count, page 241

The American Society for Quality (ASQ) is dedicated to improving quality in U.S. goods and services. Visit the ASQ's Web site at <http://www.asqc.org> to learn more about its mission and programs. Then answer the questions below.

1. Click on the link to *About ASQ* and then on *Mission and Ethics* to read the society's code of ethics. How do you think an individual employee's attitude toward ethics can affect the overall level of quality in an organization? How do the society's ethical principles relate to the principles of effective teamwork?
2. From the main page, click on *About Quality* and follow the links to the Malcolm Baldrige National Quality Award page. Click on the list of the most recent recipients of this prestigious award and read their success stories. What values do these companies share in their pursuit of quality goods and services? Have they adopted similar policies and processes? How do their approaches to quality differ?
3. From the main page, click on the link to *ISO 14000.* What is ISO 14000? What are its anticipated benefits? Can a company be considered a quality producer if it has a reputation for producing excellent goods or services but also has a spotty environmental record? Why or why not?

Part III: Mastering the Geography of Business ■ Why Is the Silicon Valley in California Rather than Colorado or Kentucky?

Comparing geographic information about companies and industries can lead to some interesting questions. For instance, why are so many high-tech companies located in California's Silicon Valley (an area encompassing San Jose, Santa Clara, Palo Alto, and surrounding cities south of San Francisco)? For some industries, patterns of location and development seem fairly obvious. Florida has an ideal climate for citrus trees. Various cities along the East, West, and Gulf coasts have excellent natural harbors, which aided the development of a healthy shipping industry in those areas. Sometimes studying physical geography leads you to answers fairly quickly.

In other industries, however, the geographic connection seems weaker. For instance, why is so much of the insurance industry centered in Hartford, Connecticut? Why is Washington's manufacturing output (measured in dollar value) more than twice as high as Maryland's even though the two states have similar populations?[53] Why are the three largest U.S. steel producers headquartered in Ohio and Pennsylvania when most iron ore (source of the primary ingredient in steel) is mined in Minnesota, Michigan, Utah, and Missouri?

Exploring these geographic patterns helps you understand how industries develop and how they affect local and regional economies and societies. Choose one of the following five industries.

- Computer software
- Automobiles
- Carpeting
- Commercial passenger aircraft
- Poultry processing

Using the research tools in your library and on the Internet, answer the questions that follow.

1. Where did the industry start in the United States?
2. Who are the biggest competitors today?
3. Where are they located?
4. What influence has geography had on the industry's growth?
5. How strong is the influence of physical geography compared with the influence of other factors (such as where an industry pioneer happened to be living or where the cost for labor happened to be less expensive)?
6. Search the World Wide Web for specific companies in the industry you are researching. Visit the companies' Web sites, and find out in how many different geographic locations each company now operates. Based on your research and on what you have learned from the text, what are some of the factors that have influenced the geographic expansion of these particular companies?

Answers to "Is It True?"

Page 228. False. Studies show that the average cost of poor-quality products and services is close to 25 percent.

Page 238. True.

Page 242. False. Consider the following examples of a 1 percent defect level in certain industries: at least 20,000 wrong drug prescriptions each year; unsafe drinking water for almost one hour each month; two short or long landings each day at airports in Chicago, New York, Los Angeles, and Atlanta; and nearly 500 incorrect surgical operations each week.

■ PART IV

Managing Human Resources

CHAPTER 9

HUMAN RELATIONS, MOTIVATION, AND PERFORMANCE

OBJECTIVES

After studying this chapter, you will be able to

1 List the three main components of good human relations within an organization

2 Explain how the five levels in Maslow's hierarchy of needs relate to employee motivation

3 Identify the two factors affecting employee motivation in Herzberg's two-factor theory

4 Describe how Theory X, Theory Y, and Theory Z link employee motivation and management style

5 Explain how changes in work-force demographics have complicated the challenge of motivating employees

6 Explain how changes in the economy create barriers to employee motivation

7 Describe how corporate cultures must change in order to keep employees motivated

8 Discuss the use of goal setting, behavior modification, investing in employees, and improved quality of work life as motivational techniques

ON THE JOB: FACING BUSINESS CHALLENGES AT HALLMARK CARDS

Sending the Right Message to Employees

One of Hallmark's sympathy cards reads "Please remember that winter's darkness emerges into spring." Given the troubles at Hallmark Cards, it's just the kind of message that Human Resources vice president Ralph Christenson wants to send to employees.

From the early- to mid-1990s the privately held greeting card firm saw its market share slip from well over 50 percent to about 45 percent, as new players in the market made cards that were more attractive and up to date. Even though Hallmark sales remained strong at about $4 billion annually, many profit measures slipped dramatically. It's hard to say just how bad things were because Hallmark profits are kept secret, even from the 20,000 employees who own part of the company. But it wasn't good news when Hallmark's profit-sharing contributions slipped from 10 percent of salaries to about 5 percent. Newly arrived in the Human Relations department, Christenson needed to find ways of keeping company employees happy. After all, the company's core mission is to communicate affection, love, and friendship through the warm messages that employees dream up.

Hallmark started out in 1910 as a family-run business, and the Hall family's leadership continues today. Based in Kansas City, Missouri, the company has always attracted talented and creative people through its friendly and family-oriented atmosphere. Because Hallmark products are based on enhancing relationships, it stands to reason that the company would focus on keeping employees happy. For example, back in the 1950s, the Hall family set up one of the first profit-sharing arrangements for employees. Today, employees own about one-third of the company. In addition, the tuition-reimbursement program pays 100 percent of education expenses for full-time staff. Other initiatives focus on child care and alternative work arrangements such as work sharing and job sharing. And the company's policies are flexible to meet employees' special needs, such as allowing time off to care for aging parents. Overall, the company has always done such a good job helping its employees that Hallmark consistently ranks among the best companies to work for in the United States.

But in the mid-1990s Hallmark faced declining market share and shrinking profit. Consultants suggested major cost-cutting efforts, including a merger of the administrative, marketing, and product-development functions for the various card brands. To save money, Hallmark threw out its old organization and the ways that employees had been doing their jobs. With the new focus on finances, employees were concerned that their family-oriented benefits would disappear. Moreover, many employees feared that their jobs would be changed dramatically or eliminated altogether. The organization was in turmoil.

Christenson had come to Hallmark because he believed the company cared deeply about its employees as people. Because of management's recent sharp focus on corporate profits, Christenson worried that Hallmark wouldn't be able to keep up its long tradition of caring for employees and their families. For the company to see its way through the current crisis, he had to inspire the employees who create and produce Hallmark products. Christenson needed new ways to strengthen the family-oriented programs and shore up morale.

If you were Ralph Christenson, what motivational techniques would you employ to keep Hallmark operating at peak levels? During times of massive organizational change, what would you recommend to reassure employees and help them deal with stress? How could you improve the company's communication with employees? What steps would you recommend for maintaining Hallmark's traditional focus on employee needs?[1]

Human Relations Within an Organization

The challenges faced by Ralph Christenson are the same ones faced by managers in all organizations. Keeping the organization operating at peak levels requires motivating employees to work effectively and efficiently toward achieving the organization's goals. All the same, managers must recognize that employees have interests and obligations outside of work, such as family, volunteer activities, and hobbies, which can affect their performance. And every employee, by human nature, needs to feel valued, challenged, and respected. In organizations, the goal of **human relations**—interactions among people within the organization—is to balance these diverse needs. This chapter looks at the ways in which organizational culture and management practices, as well as other more general forces, affect human relations and employee performance.

human relations
Interaction among people within an organization for the purpose of achieving organizational and personal goals

The way people behave towards others

The Roles of the Organization and Management

Most organizations and their managers realize the importance of maintaining good human relations. A climate of openness and trust encourages better performance and more loyalty from employees. For example, Bob Shapiro, CEO of biotechnology company Monsanto, is connected by e-mail to most of the company's 30,000 employees. "I tell them that if you come up with a good entrepreneurial idea and you can't convince anybody in the organization that it's worthwhile, just drop me an e-mail," Shapiro says. And he vows to pursue all promising ideas, whether it's for a new product or for a better way of designing work processes.[2] This kind of open and empowering atmosphere can only have a positive effect on human relations. And when employees are satisfied with the interpersonal component of their jobs, productivity usually improves.

Is It True?

The typical *U.S. leading-edge* company receives only six employee suggestions per year.

The Components of Good Human Relations

Three components are particularly important to good human relations: leadership, motivation, and communication. As discussed in Chapter 6, leadership is the ability to influence and motivate people to work effectively and willingly toward the organization's goals. A leader's approach is determined by the demands of the situation, by the needs and personalities of his or her employees, and by the culture of the organization. Managers need to distinguish between authority—the ability to *make* someone do something—and leadership—the ability to *inspire* someone to do something. The manager who inspires enthusiasm and who works hard alongside employees is usually more effective than the boss who invokes authority and takes credit for the group's accomplishments.

motivation
Force that moves someone to take action

Motivation is the force that moves individuals to take action. In some cases, fear of management or of losing a job may move someone to take action, but such negative motivation is much less effective than encouraging an employee's own sense of direction, creativity, and pride in doing a good job. Effective managers take into account employees' individual needs and show them how those needs can be satisfied within the organization's framework (see Exhibit 9.1).

Effective leadership and motivation depend heavily on communication. Through listening, speaking, writing, and reading, managers and employees not only share crucial job-related information but also build interpersonal networks and patterns of interaction. Effective business communication is clear, and at the same time, it embodies courtesy and respect.

morale
Attitude an individual has toward his or her job and employer

Leadership, motivation, and communication all affect **morale,** a person's attitude toward both the job and the organization. In turn, a person's morale has a large impact on work performance. Traditionally, managers believed that performance was determined by real conditions, such as sufficient resources, competent employees, efficient systems, and clear organizational goals. Today, managers realize that performance is also significantly affected by *perceived* conditions—fairness in rewards, clarity of personal and work-group goals, demonstrated appreciation for employees, responsiveness to employee needs and concerns, and employee empowerment. Employees perform better when they feel positive about perceived conditions.[3] Consider Illinois Trade Association. This media and travel company hasn't lost an employee in five years other than for reasons of pregnancy or a spouse's relocation. The company's secret is simply demonstrating to workers that the organization respects them and wants to enrich their lives. CEO Jack Schacht makes an effort to know what his employees' talents are outside of work, and then he looks for ways to integrate those talents into the workplace. Schacht believes that people gain a sense of meaning by being able to express themselves. In addition, the company benefits by retaining productive employees, which reduces the high costs of hiring and training new employees.[4]

An employee with high morale is more likely to be cheerful, enthusiastic, loyal, and productive. However, morale is only one element of good human relations. To better understand the specific challenges of motivating today's work force, consider the following theories of motivation.

MOTIVATION THEORY

Motivation has been a topic of interest to managers for more than a hundred years. One of the earliest managers to think about the link between employee morale and motivation was Robert Owen, a nineteenth-century Scottish industrialist. He reduced working hours, provided meal facilities, improved employee housing, and introduced other innovations

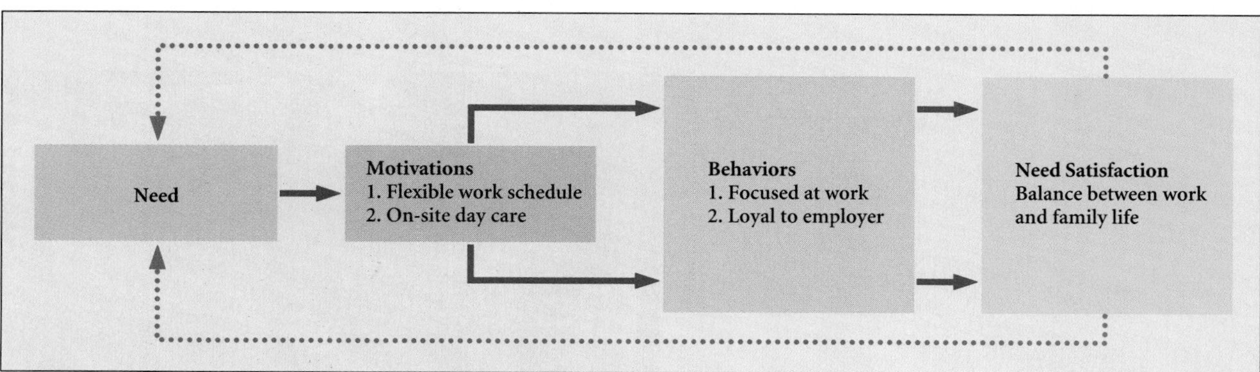

EXHIBIT 9.1

The Motivation Process

The key to effective motivation is to demonstrate to employees that their individual needs dovetail with the needs of the organization.

at his textile mill in New Lanark, Scotland. Although Owen's factory became a showplace of productivity, his methods weren't widely copied by other managers; not until the turn of the century did business owners begin thinking about methods for motivating rather than driving employees to produce.[5]

Scientific Management

scientific management
Management approach designed to improve employees' efficiency by scientifically studying their work

piecework system
Compensation system that pays employees a certain amount for each unit produced

Frederick W. Taylor was a machinist and engineer from Philadelphia who became interested in employee efficiency and motivation late in the nineteenth century, when he worked for Midvale Steel. Taylor developed **scientific management,** a management approach that seeks to improve employee efficiency through the scientific study of work. In Taylor's view, people were motivated almost exclusively by money, so he set up pay systems that rewarded employees when they were productive.

Under Taylor's **piecework system,** employees who just met or fell short of the quota were paid a certain amount for each unit produced. Those who produced more were paid at a higher rate for *all* units produced, not just for those that exceeded the quota; this pay system gave employees a strong incentive to boost productivity. When Taylor went on to introduce his system of scientific management at Bethlehem Steel, the results were profitable for everyone. The average steel handler's wage rose from $1.15 to $1.85 a day, and productivity increased so sharply that handling costs were cut by more than half.

Money has always been a powerful motivator, and it continues to spur employees to give their all for an organization. In fact, one autoworker recently earned over $100,000 for 2 years in a row by working long overtime hours to help Chrysler meet customer demand.[6] However, scientific management's concentration on money as the prime motivator fails to take into account other motivational elements, such as opportunities for personal satisfaction or individual initiative. As a result, scientific management can't explain why a person still wants to work even though his or her spouse already makes a good living or why a Wall Street lawyer will take a hefty pay cut to serve in government. Therefore, other researchers have looked beyond money to discover what else motivates people.

Maslow's Hierarchy of Needs

In 1943 psychologist Abraham Maslow proposed the theory that behavior is determined by a variety of needs. He organized these needs into five categories and then arranged the categories in a hierarchy (see Exhibit 9.2). The most basic needs were at the bottom of this hierarchy, and the more advanced needs were toward the top. A human being, according

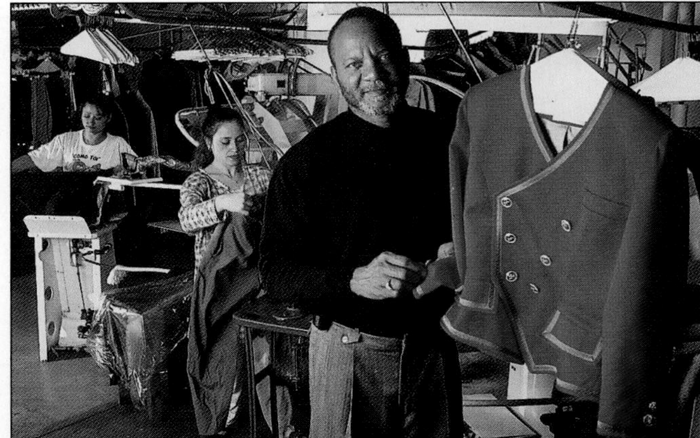

Willis T. White, Jr. motivates employees of his commercial dry cleaning and laundry service by being sensitive to their emotional needs.

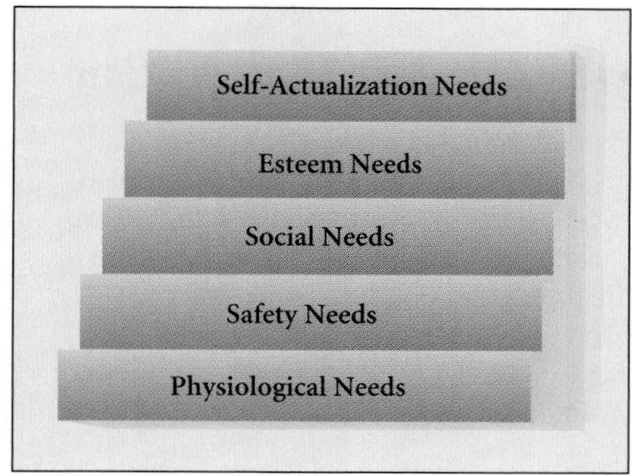

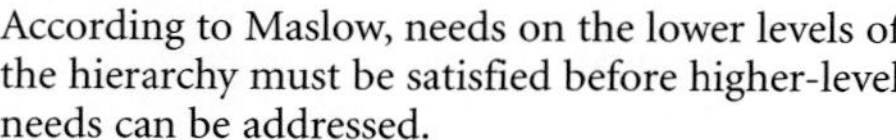

EXHIBIT 9.2

Maslow's Hierarchy of Needs

According to Maslow, needs on the lower levels of the hierarchy must be satisfied before higher-level needs can be addressed.

to Maslow, is a "perpetually wanting animal." When lower-level needs have been satisfied, at least in part, a person tries to satisfy needs on the next level.[7]

In Maslow's hierarchy, all of the requirements for basic survival—food, clothing, shelter, and so on—fall into the category of *physiological needs.* These basic needs must be satisfied before the person can consider other needs. Today, physiological needs are so readily fulfilled by most wage earners that advanced needs tend to be more motivating. For example, when the bare essentials have been taken care of, a person is motivated to fulfill the need for security. Such *safety needs* may be satisfied through health insurance, pension plans, job security, and safe working conditions. S. C. Johnson & Son has a unique way to meet employees' safety needs: The maker of home-cleaning products subsidizes massages to help employees reduce stress.[8]

Beyond safety needs, human beings have a powerful need to associate with others, to give and receive love, and to feel a sense of belonging. These *social needs* have a definite influence on actions. In fact, one of the reasons teamwork has been so successful in many organizations is that it fulfills employees' social needs.

People also have *esteem needs*—the need for a sense of personal worth and integrity. Moreover, people need the respect of others, a respect based on competence and achievement. These needs are closely related to the idea of status, which is one's rank or importance in the eyes of others. The opportunity to fulfill these needs can be a powerful motivator. In fact, one recent study found that accomplishment and recognition are more important to working women than money, career advancement, or benefits.[9] And head of product design for Sony's U.S division, Kei Totsuka says that the company's designers don't care about monetary rewards: "The most important thing we could receive is recognition from top management."[10]

At the top of Maslow's hierarchy is *self-actualization*—the need to become everything one is capable of. This need is also the most difficult to fulfill. Employees who reach this point work not only to make money or to impress others but also because they feel their work is worthwhile and satisfying in itself. Such needs partially explain why some businesspeople make radical career changes or strike out on their own as entrepreneurs.

Although Maslow's hierarchy is a convenient way to classify human needs, it would be a mistake to view it as a rigid sequence. A person need not completely satisfy each level of needs before being motivated by a higher need. Indeed, at any one time, most people are motivated by a combination of needs.

Two-Factor Theory

In the 1960s, Frederick Herzberg and his associates undertook their own study of human needs. They asked accountants and engineers to describe specific aspects of their jobs that made them feel satisfied or dissatisfied. Upon analyzing the results, they found that two

BEST OF THE WEB

Measuring Employee Satisfaction

Motivating employees to perform at their highest potential is one of the many challenges managers face on a daily basis. However, it is often difficult to judge just how satisfied and motivated employees are at work, especially for managers who oversee large numbers of workers. Therefore, many managers find out about their employees' true feelings through surveys. Employees are asked how they feel about their responsibilities, work objectives, management support, communication with co-workers, level of control over their work, and other pertinent questions. Responses are scored and analyzed to provide managers with an overall view of employee satisfaction and morale. You can view an employee satisfaction survey on the Internet and even take the survey yourself to better understand what factors can affect employee morale.
http://www.fdgroup.co.uk/neo/djassoc/dj_jdq.html

hygiene factors
Aspects of the work environment that are associated with dissatisfaction

motivators
Factors of human relations in business that may increase motivation

entirely different sets of factors were associated with satisfying and dissatisfying work experiences (see Exhibit 9.3). What Herzberg called **hygiene factors** were associated with dissatisfying experiences. These potential sources of dissatisfaction include working conditions, company policies, and job security.

Management may lessen dissatisfaction by improving hygiene factors that concern employees, but such improvements won't influence satisfaction. On the other hand, managers can help employees feel more motivated and, ultimately, more satisfied, by paying attention to **motivators** such as achievement, recognition, responsibility, and other personally rewarding factors. Herzberg's theory is related to Maslow's hierarchy of needs: The motivators closely resemble the higher-level needs, and the hygiene factors resemble the lower-level needs.

EXHIBIT 9.3

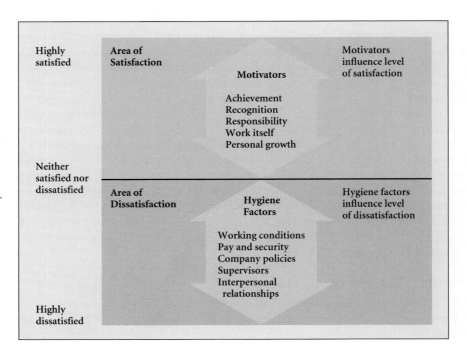

Two-Factor Theory

Hygiene factors such as working conditions and company policies can influence employee dissatisfaction. On the other hand, motivators such as opportunities for achievement and recognition can influence employee satisfaction.

Highly satisfied	**Area of Satisfaction**	**Motivators** Achievement Recognition Responsibility Work itself Personal growth	Motivators influence level of satisfaction
Neither satisfied nor dissatisfied			
	Area of Dissatisfaction	**Hygiene Factors** Working conditions Pay and security Company policies Supervisors Interpersonal relationships	Hygiene factors influence level of dissatisfaction
Highly dissatisfied			

Should managers such as Hallmark's Christenson concentrate on motivators or on hygiene factors? It depends. A skilled, well-paid, middle-class, middle-aged employee may be motivated to perform better if motivators are supplied. However, a young, unskilled employee who earns low wages, or an employee who is insecure, will probably still need the support of strong hygiene factors to reduce dissatisfaction before the motivators can be effective.[11]

Motivation and Management Style

Employee motivation is highly influenced by the attitudes of managers. Over the years, a number of management styles have come into and gone out of vogue.

Theory X and Theory Y In the 1960s, psychologist Douglas McGregor identified a certain set of assumptions as underlying most management thinking. He labeled this set of assumptions **Theory X:**

Theory X
Managerial assumption that employees are irresponsible, unambitious, and distasteful of work and that managers must use force, control, or threats to motivate them

- The average person dislikes work and will avoid it if possible.
- Because of the dislike for work, the average person must be forced, controlled, directed, or threatened with punishment in order to be motivated to work toward achieving organizational goals.
- The average person prefers to be directed, wishes to avoid responsibility, has relatively little ambition, and wants security.

According to McGregor, Theory X–oriented managers believe that employees can be motivated only by the fear of losing their jobs or by *extrinsic rewards* such as money, promotions, and tenure. This management style emphasizes physiological and safety needs and tends to ignore the higher-level needs in Maslow's hierarchy.

To counteract this management focus on lower-level needs, McGregor proposed another set of assumptions for managers. He based these assumptions, called **Theory Y,** on Maslow's higher-level needs:

Theory Y
Managerial assumption that employees like work, are naturally committed to certain goals, are capable of creativity, and seek out responsibility under the right conditions

- The average person does not dislike work; it is as natural as play or rest.
- External control and the threat of punishment are not the only ways to motivate people to meet organizational goals; on average, people naturally work toward goals they are committed to.
- How deeply a person is committed to an organization's objectives depends on the rewards earned for achieving them.
- Under favorable conditions, the average person learns not only to accept responsibility but also to seek it.
- Many people are capable of using imagination, cleverness, and creativity to solve problems that arise within an organization.
- Especially in modern industrial life, the average person's intellectual potential is only partially realized.

Theory Y–oriented managers believe that employees can be motivated by the opportunity to be creative, to work hard for a cause they believe in, and to satisfy needs beyond the basic need to pay the rent. Thus they seek to motivate employees through *intrinsic rewards.*

The assumptions behind Theory X emphasize authority; the assumptions behind Theory Y emphasize growth and self-direction. It was McGregor's belief that although some employees need the strong direction demanded by Theory X, those who are ready to realize their social, esteem, and self-actualization needs will not work well under Theory X assumptions.[12]

Theory Z
Human relations approach that emphasizes involving employees at all levels and treating them like family

Theory Z Another perspective on motivation was developed by William Ouchi, who studied management practices in Japan and the United States. Ouchi's **Theory Z** assumes that

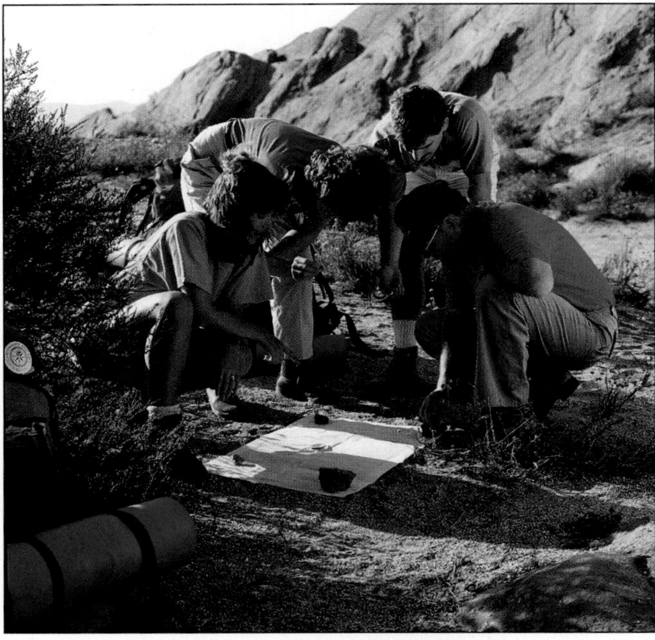

General Electric applies Theory Y in its global operations. Here, GE managers in an Outward Bound workshop practice team-building skills to achieve a common goal.

the best management involves employees at all levels of the organization and treats employees like family. This theory combines elements of both U.S. and Japanese management techniques. Specific attributes of Theory Z management include long-term employment, group decision making, personal responsibility, slow evaluation and promotion, less specialized career paths, informal control, and concern for the individual that transcends work-related issues.[13]

Theory Z satisfies the lower-level needs in Maslow's hierarchy by looking after employee welfare. It also satisfies middle-level needs by using the group process to make decisions. In addition, it satisfies higher-level needs by inviting employees to take individual responsibility. Managers who adopt Theory Z believe that employees with a sense of identity and belonging are more likely to perform their jobs conscientiously and will try more enthusiastically to achieve company goals.

Can people in the United States be effectively motivated by management techniques that are based on Japanese practices? In many Japanese firms, everyone participates in decision making, and duties are rotated to avoid boredom, extreme specialization, and rigidity. To survive in a small, densely populated land with few resources, people in Japan have come to rely on teamwork and compromise. On the other hand, people and businesses in the United States have always valued individualism and self-reliance. The two traditions seem incompatible. Even so, Theory Z thinking has become much more influential in the United States in recent years. Chapters 6 through 8 show how many firms are boosting productivity and innovation by emphasizing teamwork and by delegating decision-making authority to employees throughout the organizational hierarchy. In addition, many companies are showing more concern for employees by offering flexible work schedules, telecommuting, on-site child care, and other benefits that help them lead more balanced lives. At Merck one senior analyst was torn between work and family when her daughter needed tonsil surgery during the year-end business rush. Not expecting to get time off, she was surprised when her boss just looked and her and said, "Your daughter comes first."[14]

THE CHALLENGE OF MOTIVATING EMPLOYEES

Hallmark's Ralph Christenson isn't the only one concerned with employee motivation. Managers everywhere face a number of challenges that make motivating employees especially difficult. These challenges stem from changes in the work force, the economy, and organizational cultures.

Demographic Changes Affecting the Work Force

The work force in North America is undergoing significant demographic changes that will require major alterations in how managers keep employees happy and productive in the twenty-first century. Some of the most significant trends include the aging of the population, the changing nature of families, and the increasing cultural diversity in the work force.

The Aging of the Population The population in the United States is aging (see Exhibit 9.4). This creates new challenges and concerns for employers and employees alike. You often hear about the baby boomers—people born between 1946 and 1964. When these 76 million people began entering the work force, the average age of U.S. employees fell. Now that they are approaching mid-career, the average age is again rising. The general aging of the population and the declining number of young people entering the work force is largely due to baby boomers' decisions to marry later, to postpone or forgo starting a family, and to have fewer children.

Because many older workers have been with their companies for years and are often paid high wages, companies today have more difficulty offering good wages and benefits to younger people just entering the work force. This situation is complicated by the fact that many older workers in the United States are working longer. In fact, some experts predict that because of inadequate pensions, high medical costs, and a general desire to stay active, baby boomers will put off retirement until they are in their 70s. As a result, today's younger employees are finding fewer opportunities for advancement, which means they have difficulty developing new skills fast enough to keep pace with the changing work

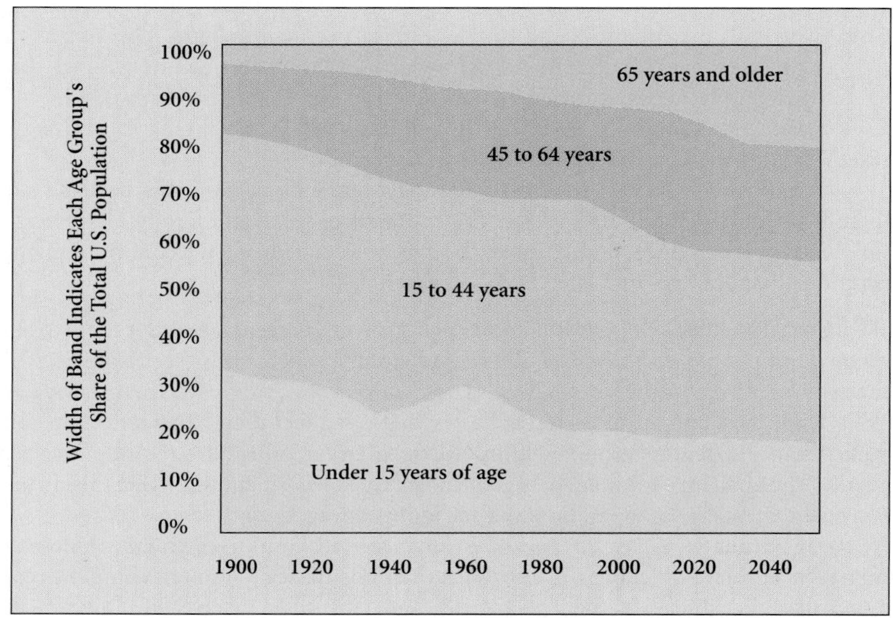

EXHIBIT 9.4

The Aging of the Population

As the baby boomers grow older, the overall age of the U.S. population goes up as well.

environment. Such restricted advancement also means that employers are hiring more low-paid, temporary employees. The U.S. Department of Labor reports that the use of temporary workers has risen 400 percent since 1982.[15] Consider Cummins Engine, the world's biggest maker of large diesel engines. The company's plant in Columbus, Indiana, hasn't hired a permanent full-time employee since 1978. In addition, all the plant's hourly workers will be at least 65 within the next decade. Most of the younger employees in the plant are temporary, work at low-skill jobs, and earn at least $10 an hour less than their full-time co-workers.[16]

Even though this gap between older and younger employees is widening, many boomers (who are between their mid-thirties and mid-fifties) still need the same things from their jobs as the 38 million twenty-somethings now entering the work force. Today's employees want more than a good paycheck and satisfying work. They are trying to balance their careers and their family lives, so they want flexible work schedules and a choice of career paths to help them in this balancing act. "This is the most difficult generation ever to manage," says Marilyn Moats Kennedy, a career consultant. "The traditional appeals—money, prestige—have no appeal. They are much less easily motivated than people motivated by money. They want to do their job, get home, and have a life."[17]

Another effect of the aging population is that more people are now caring for elderly parents. Today 28 percent of employees over the age of 30 spend an average of 10 hours a week providing care to an older relative. For many the time commitment is much greater. In addition, 12 percent of workers who take care of elderly relatives must quit their jobs to do so. As the baby boomers continue to age, more employers are seeking ways to help them. Assistance programs range from information and referral services to specialized care insurance. As always, managers are challenged to balance the needs of employees with the needs of the organization.[18]

Is It True?

More men than women in the United States are taking on second jobs.

The Changing Nature of Families Today approximately 64 percent of all married women with children under 6 years of age have jobs, compared to 18.6 percent in 1960 and 53.4 percent in 1985 (see Exhibit 9.5).[19] Because of the growing number of two-career households, transferring an employee to another part of the country is no longer easy. At the same time, the number of single-parent households has been rising and is expected to grow by another 11 percent by the year 2010.[20] Employees are demanding more control over their time to be with their families and to take care of personal matters. This means that employers can no longer assume that employees of either gender will be willing—or able—to sacrifice family needs in order to work overtime. Even Brenda Barnes, CEO of Pepsi-Cola North America and one of the United States's highest ranking executives, recently resigned in order to spend more time with her family.[21]

Employment decisions today increasingly take into account the needs of *all* family members. To help employees balance the demands of work and family, businesses can offer child-care assistance, family leave, flexible work schedules, telecommuting, and other solutions that are explored later in this chapter.

The Continuing Influence of Cultural Diversity A growing percentage of the U.S. work force is made up of people with diverse cultural and ethnic backgrounds (see Exhibit 9.6), a trend that will continue in the years ahead. These employees bring with them a wide range of skills, traditions, and attitudes toward work that can affect their behavior on the job. Some come from indigenous groups within North America; others are recently arrived immigrants. The challenge for managers is to communicate with and motivate this diverse work force while fostering cooperation and harmony among employees.

Unfortunately, some managers do not treat all employees equally. However, those managers will have to change if they want their businesses to remain competitive. Experts agree that the ability to manage racially and ethnically diverse employees will be an

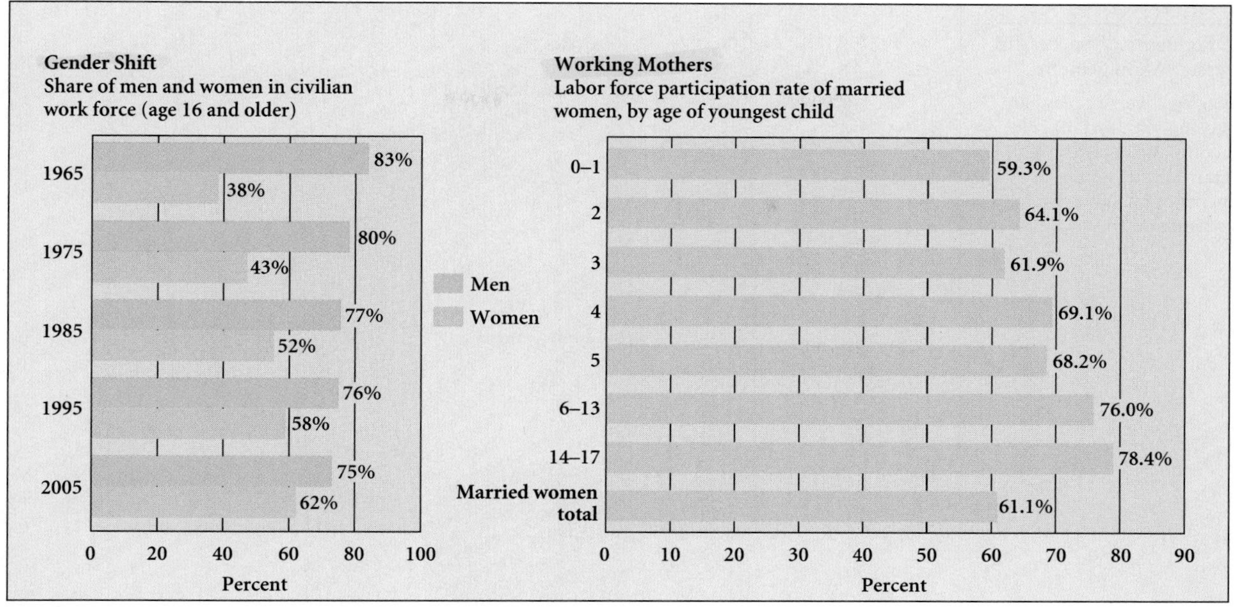

EXHIBIT 9.5

Women and Mothers in the Work Force

The participation of women in the work force is expected to reach 62 percent by 2005, and an increasing percentage of those women will be mothers with children at home.

increasingly important skill as these employees enter more industries and continue to move up the organizational hierarchy (see Exhibit 9.7).[22] According to Paul J. Giddens of paper manufacturer Georgia-Pacific, managers who develop diversity skills will gain a source of ideas that can be "the key to innovative survival in the years to come."[23]

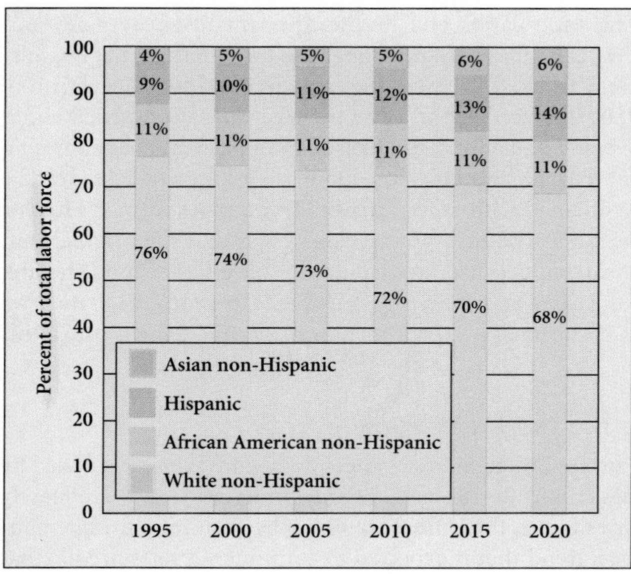

EXHIBIT 9.6

Ethnic Composition of the U.S. Work Force

African American, Hispanic, and Asian American employees are making up a greater proportion of the U.S. work force.

EXHIBIT 9.7

The Elements of Successful Diversity Management

Managing diversity plays an increasingly important role in a company's success. This diagram illustrates the elements of effective diversity management.

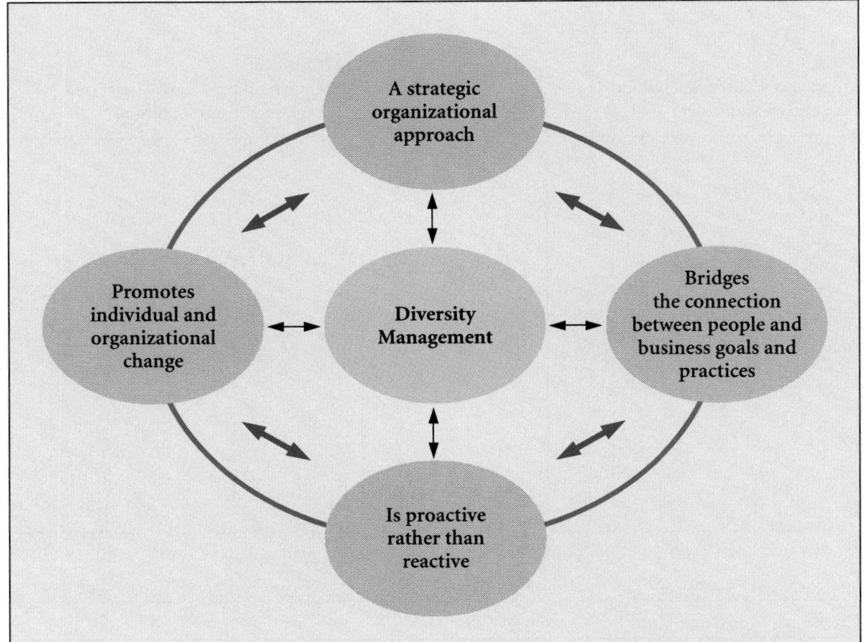

Many companies are recognizing the importance of diversity awareness and promotion by instituting diversity-training programs. At the Marriott Marquis Hotel in New York, mandatory diversity-training classes teach managers how to avoid defining problems in terms of gender, culture, or race. These classes also discuss cross-cultural norms (such as body language, eye contact, touching behavior, and religious customs) that help managers become more sensitive to the behavior and communication patterns of employees with diverse backgrounds.

However, even though encouraging sensitivity to employee differences is important, a company stands to benefit most when it incorporates its employees' diverse perspectives into the organization's work. This assimilation enables the company to uncover new opportunities by rethinking primary tasks and redefining markets, products, strategies, missions, business practices, and even cultures. Consider the small public-interest law firm of Dewey & Levin. In the mid-1980s the firm had an all-white legal staff. Concerned about its ability to serve ethnically diverse populations, the firm hired a Hispanic woman as an attorney. She introduced Dewey & Levin to new ideas about what kinds of cases to take on, and many of her ideas were pursued with great success. Hiring more women of color brought even more fresh perspectives. The firm now pursues cases that the original staff members would never have considered because they would not have understood the link between the issues involved in the cases and the firm's mission.[24] In short, diversity is an asset, and one of the challenges of corporate human relations is to make the most of this asset.

Economic Changes Affecting the Work Force

The way business is conducted in the United States changes daily. This change is fueled by the evolution of both the domestic and the global economy. Indeed, the two are closely linked in the modern world. For example, the United States has been shifting from a manufacturing to a service economy, a trend that is expected to continue. Experts predict that

FOCUSING ON CULTURAL DIVERSITY

Organizations Learn the Value of Diversity

Successful organizations believe that work-force diversity presents an opportunity to expand the pool of people who can contribute to the organization. In fact, recent studies confirm that culturally diverse work groups come up with more innovative and effective solutions to business problems than do groups lacking such diversity. These results are encouraging more companies to go beyond what is required by law and to take steps that will promote a culturally diverse work force.

However, despite the benefits of cultural diversity, managing such a work force sometimes requires managers to take extra steps. Training in cultural diversity (used by a growing number of organizations) is accomplished through seminars, videotapes, workshops, even games. Burger King is just one of the many companies that have used a board game called *The Diversity Game* to raise managers' awareness of diversity issues.

Improving cultural diversity in the work force has become such an important goal that some companies measure results and hold managers accountable for the success of diversity initiatives. Gannett, the parent of *USA Today*, requires managers to set specific goals for achieving work-force diversity, such as buying from minority suppliers and other targets. At Mobil Oil, the presidents of each subsidiary meet with the company chairman once a year to explain their plans for improving diversity; progress is monitored by the vice president of employee relations.

Even successful companies can benefit from work-force diversity. Consider the situation found by Nadia Ali when she was hired as U.S. southwest district manager for the gift and engraving retail chain Things Remembered. Half of her local customers spoke Spanish, but many of the employees in the southwest stores spoke only English, so they couldn't communicate with their Spanish-speaking customers. Ali decided that the employees and managers she hired in the future would have to be able to speak conversational Spanish. She also arranged for current employees to take Spanish lessons, a program paid for by headquarters.

By increasing the work-force diversity in her district, Ali was able to better serve her customers and in turn boost district sales. Employees got more out of their jobs and didn't leave as quickly as in the past. What had been a frustrating situation for both customers and employees was transformed into a situation that benefited everybody. As more organizations expand their operations to other areas or pursue customers in other lands, cultural diversity in the work force will be recognized as a vital prerequisite for doing business in today's global business environment.

QUESTIONS FOR CRITICAL THINKING

1. Which type of company do you think has a harder time establishing an effective diversity program: a large company with many employees or a small company with relatively few employees? Why?
2. What do you think is the most important factor to the success of a diversity training program? Why?

83 percent of the U.S. work force will be in the service sector by the year 2025. One reason for this shift is that the aging of the U.S. population creates a greater demand for the many services that people need as they get older. However, an equally important reason is that lower labor costs in the emerging economies of Asia and Latin America have given those countries a comparative advantage in the production of many consumer goods made by low-skilled workers. As a result, production of many goods is shifting abroad, and low-skilled U.S. manufacturing workers are finding themselves out of jobs. These losses are typically offset by the creation of service sector jobs, but many of the new jobs require higher-skilled employees. For example, the manufacture of computers has shifted abroad, but their expanded role at work and at home creates the need for people who can offer maintenance, training, and consulting services to all those computer users.[25]

Another economic trend is technology's increasingly important role in the workplace. Companies are installing more sophisticated equipment, which in turn requires more skilled operators. This technological change makes it difficult for former production employees and less skilled employees to qualify for jobs in upgraded factories unless they receive special training. In some industries, such as agriculture, technology simply replaces many of the workers needed to perform a task. Although many of these displaced employees find work in the growing service sector, many of them must accept lower wages or find training to adequately upgrade their skills.

Economic and technological evolution are having a strong impact on U.S. workers. Two significant effects are apparent in the United States today: (1) downsizing and restructuring and (2) a growing gap between highly skilled and low-skilled workers.

The Challenges of Downsizing and Restructuring In the past, hardworking, loyal employees could expect job security and the chance to move up the organizational hierarchy. But throughout the 1990s, advances in technology, global competition, and the pursuit of short-term financial gains have led to intense corporate downsizing in the form of layoffs and employee buyouts. AT&T eliminated 40,000 jobs and IBM 35,000, just to name two. Moreover, a recent survey of Fortune 1000 companies found that 60 percent planned on cutting employees in the future.[26] These figures are unprecedented in the history of U.S. business, and they have many employees fearing for their futures. The percentage of employees who frequently worry about being laid off has more than doubled in recent years to 46 percent. In addition, 55 percent worry about the future of their company, and only 50 percent feel their job is secure if they perform well.[27] An important side effect of this downsizing trend is that employees are less loyal now than they were just a few years ago. One manufacturing manager sums up the situation this way: "Loyalty will return only when management discovers that employees are a valuable resource—more valuable than capital equipment—and begins to treat employees accordingly."[28]

Restructuring brought on by mergers, acquisitions, and divestitures can cause similar motivation problems. When Chase Manhattan Bank was taken over recently by Chemical Bank, many employees were downsized, and surviving employees didn't know from one week to the next whether they would still have jobs. As a result, workers felt forlorn and even hostile. One Chase manager says that employees are now "a lot less amenable to being absorbed into the work culture. It's pay me, don't play with me . . . And they're more suspicious of management."[29] Managers have great difficulty motivating employees who are in such a state of mind. In fact, a recent *Wall Street Journal* study reported that employees trust management less after a restructuring. Even worse, a separate study revealed that 64 percent of employees believe that management often lies to them.[30]

Another result of downsizing and restructuring is that many employees find they must carry a heavier workload than in the past, and they are working longer hours just to keep up. For instance, when 3M spun off its data storage and medical imaging divisions, some employees began putting in 80 hour weeks. One 3M customer service consultant summed up the feelings of many employees when he said, "I always perceived work to be a means to an end, but not *the* end."[31] Such long hours can lead to employee *burnout,* which is characterized by emotional exhaustion, depersonalization, and lower levels of achievement. Severe burnout may even lead to depression.[32]

The point is not that firms should never downsize. It is always unfortunate when an employee loses a job, but it is sometimes impossible for a company to compete in today's global economy without cutting the size of its labor force. The objective of this discussion is to show that today's business leaders face the challenge of motivating employees who are sometimes frightened, cynical, and overworked. Some companies are finding they can help laid-off employees by providing job-locating assistance and training programs. Many are helping their employees reduce stress and achieve a better balance between work and the demands of their personal lives. For example, some companies now have staff that will run errands and do laundry for their employees. Others even build schools on company property so that parents can visit their children at lunch time. Such programs not only make employees' lives easier but also encourage loyalty. These programs are examined in more detail later in the chapter.

Working Hard on the Web

BEST OF THE WEB

Frustrated workers and managers now have a place to go to voice their opinions, commiserate with others who share their woes, and get advice on how to motivate employees. The place is Hard@Work, a Web site with a mission "to reduce the oversupply of fear and alienation in the workplace by meeting the pent-up demand for constructive communication about what's happening on the job." Visitors can hang out at the "Water Cooler" to chat with others about their work and careers in general; play a game of "Stump the Mentor," which offers suggestions for dealing with difficult work situations; or dig into the "Rock Pile," which offers case studies on contemporary career issues. The site also contains suggestions for successful interviews and salary negotiations. With so much free information, Hard@Work offers something for workers and work seekers alike. http://www.hardatwork.com

The Gap in Employee Skill Levels Even as some companies cut employees, others seem unable to find enough. As already mentioned, many companies are investing more in businesses and technologies that demand employees with advanced skills. At the same time, the shift from a manufacturing economy to a service economy has displaced many production employees. The result is a surplus of low-skilled employees and a shortage of highly skilled employees. "There aren't enough people in the world to do all the work we have right now," says Ralph Miller, president of the design and engineering company MSX International.[33] The same is true in many

Hewlett-Packard employees enjoy greater job satisfaction and opportunities for advancement through company-sponsored training. In addition, the company benefits from greater employee loyalty and versatility on the job.

other high-tech fields such as computers and biotechnology. That's why companies are wooing top applicants with hiring bonuses, flexible work schedules, job training, and other incentives. Managers in these industries are scrambling to offer incentives that will encourage loyalty so that employees will not be enticed away by other firms.

Businesses can sometimes help low-skilled employees upgrade their skills so that they are more competitive job candidates. Retraining employees to meet the needs of the changing workplace may even help a company avoid layoffs altogether. For example, FedEx cross-trains all of its employees so that they are able to take on other responsibilities when their jobs are affected by changing economic and competitive conditions. A pleasant side effect is that employees are less fearful of automation or other causes of displacement, so the company can count on morale remaining high during hard times.[34]

Organizations are starting to realize that investing in human capital can make a company more flexible while providing a valuable source of creative potential. However, as smart investors know, most investments take a while to appreciate. Similarly, although the immediate results of retraining employees may be small, adopting a long-term approach can lead to much greater success down the road.

Changes in Organizational Culture

In addition to the changes in work force demographics and the economy, corporate cultures are changing as well. When promotions are fewer and slower in coming, managers have to downplay the importance of job advancement as the main source of job satisfaction. Otherwise, turnover will become an even more crucial problem as employees change

THINKING ABOUT ETHICS

Should Corporate Cultures Stress Only English on the Job?

When Frances Arreola read the memo announcing that employees should speak only English on the job, she was outraged. Arreola is a lens inspector for Signet Amoralite, a lens-manufacturing firm in southern California, and she remembers being punished and humiliated by elementary school teachers for speaking her native Spanish. She is now fluent in both English and Spanish but feels that the English-only rules stressed in some corporate cultures constitute discrimination.

Over half of Signet Amoralite's 900 employees are Asian, Filipino, or Hispanic. The company defends its English-only rule on the grounds that "speaking in another language that friends and associates cannot fully understand can lead to misunderstandings, is impolite, and can even be unsafe." The company claims that the English-only requirement is not written policy, just a guideline, and that violating it carries no punishment.

Nevertheless, this policy—and ones like it at hundreds of companies throughout the United States—is incorporated into the company's culture, and it is considered by critics to violate federal laws against discrimination on the basis of national origin. According to Equal Employment Opportunity Commission rules, employers can establish language restrictions only when such restrictions are required by valid business necessities.

A similar situation occurred at the Allied Insurance Agency in Amarillo, Texas. Two clerks at the agency, Rosa Gonzales and Ester Hernandez, were hired partly because they are fluent in Spanish and therefore able to communicate with Spanish-speaking customers. However, the agency's owners became irritated when the two women chatted with each other in Spanish during the workday. Both women were subsequently let go after they refused to sign a pledge that would make Allied "an English speaking office except when we have customers who can't speak our language." Since then, the agency has been boycotted by two Hispanic groups and has been threatened with lawsuits.

Managers are caught in the middle. On one side are employees who are disturbed by co-workers speaking to each other in a language they don't understand—an act they consider rude. According to Allied

jobs in a continuing effort to climb to the top. One way organizational culture is changing is by offering a career path that combines horizontal as well as vertical advancement. "Employees shouldn't think just in terms of moving up all the time, but should consider lateral moves to improve skills and knowledge of the company," says Frank Spaulding, vice president of Household International, a financial-services giant.[35]

Organizational cultures are becoming more open. For example, honest communication during restructuring keeps rumors from getting out of control, improves morale, and allows employees to concentrate on performance. If employees are too concerned about job security, they are less willing to think creatively and to take risks. As a business analyst at Chase says about his company's recent merger, it "has eliminated for me a certain motivation and all risk-taking."[36] The best way to overcome such barriers is to communicate openly with employees, showing empathy and concern and demonstrating integrity through actions and words. "People don't think CEOs have feelings," says management consultant Lynne Doll. "You have to put a human face on decisions like layoffs or you become a part of the corporate machinery."[37]

Some companies are promoting a culture that makes it enjoyable to come to work. "You can't get too uptight," says Joel Slutzky, CEO of Odetics, a maker of robots and spacecraft flight equipment. Slutzky once came to work dressed as a leprechaun on St. Patrick's Day. In Arlington, Virginia, AES is a power-generation company that lists fun among its core values. "Creating a fun workplace environment requires a positive view of humanity that begins with the people who work in the corporation," says the company's CEO. "We regard our people as creative, thinking, capable, trustworthy, responsible, unique, and, yes,

Insurance's owners, the women's chatting in Spanish was "almost like they were whispering behind our backs." On the other side are employees who feel they have a right to speak in a more familiar language as long as it doesn't affect their work. "I'm not doing it to offend anybody. It just feels comfortable," says Gonzales. What is a manager to do?

The best solution, according to experts, is to offer cultural-sensitivity training that will eliminate misconceptions on both sides and create a more open corporate culture. Native English speakers often assume that nonnative speakers don't want to make the effort to learn and use English. More commonly, however, nonnative speakers are highly motivated to learn English because they believe it will improve their chances for advancing in the work world. "They tend to speak English as often as they can," says Michael Adams, who helps run cultural-sensitivity programs for employees at the University of California at San Francisco. "When they speak another language, it's done in order to help a fellow employee understand something."

Colleagues may empathize if they step into the nonnative speaker's shoes. They can be asked to imagine traveling overseas and encountering someone from their home country. What language would they converse in? Would that be rude, or would it simply be more comfortable? An increasing number of companies have found that training can help improve understanding and reduce tensions between culturally diverse employees in a single corporate culture.

QUESTIONS FOR CRITICAL THINKING

1. If a company hires an employee knowing that she is not fluent in English, should the company have a right to establish a policy like Amoralite's? Why or why not?
2. If you took a job in a country where you weren't fluent in the native language, would you feel compelled to learn the language even if your employer did not require you to? If your employer did suddenly decide to implement a one-language policy at work, how do you think you would react?

fallible."[38] Such an attitude can go a long way toward inspiring productivity, commitment, and loyalty.

The changing work force, the changing economy, and the changing corporate culture all influence employee motivation and morale. But what is the best way to motivate employees given all of these variables? The next section examines some specific motivation techniques that have been developed through the years.

MOTIVATIONAL TECHNIQUES

Humans are motivated by many factors. The challenge for managers is to select motivators that will inspire employees to achieve organizational goals. When asked which motivators were most important, employees identified the techniques shown in Exhibit 9.8. As you can see, today's employees are motivated by more than just good pay; satisfaction of higher-level needs is equally important. To motivate people, employers must go beyond traditional incentives. Many now boost motivation and morale through goal setting, behavior modification, investment in employees, better quality of work life, flexible schedules, telecommuting, and work and job sharing.

Goal Setting

Some employees are highly motivated by clear and challenging—but achievable—goals. At AptarGroup, a manufacturer of aerosol valves, finger pumps, and other caps for bottles, employee work teams set their own goals and report on their progress to senior management. This sort of responsibility can be intimidating for some employees, but it can also motivate them by creating a desire to follow through on what they said they would accomplish. Rob Revak, director of human resources at one of Aptar's divisions, says that setting their own goals has helped motivate employees. He finds that they strive hard to reach their goals and are very proud when they can present their accomplishments to top management.[39]

Many companies today are also involving employees in the process of setting organizational goals, which establishes a better dialog between management and employees. Furthermore, effective goal-setting programs allow employees to find out firsthand whether they are in fact meeting their goals. This is the essence of management by objectives, discussed in Chapter 6. However, if goals are simply imposed from above, the advantage of

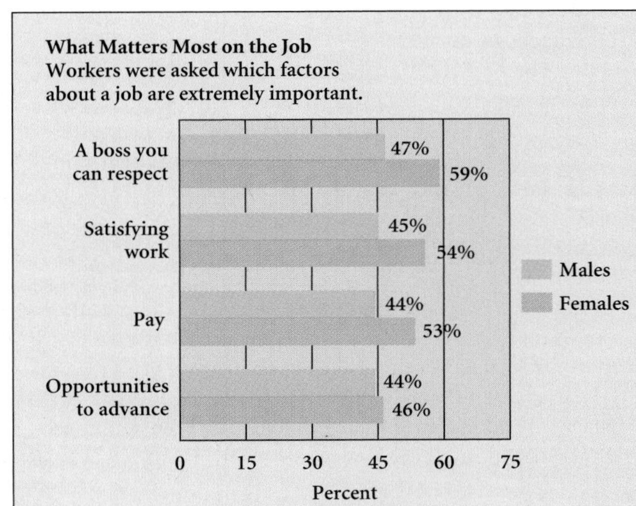

EXHIBIT 9.8

Motivating Forces for Today's Employees

This graph shows the results of a survey of employees who were asked to identify the motivators that were most important to them.

bringing the employees' higher-level needs into play will be lost, and employees will feel manipulated.

Behavior Modification

behavior modification
Systematic use of rewards and punishments to change human behavior

The idea behind **behavior modification** is simple: Change employee actions by systematically encouraging those actions that are desirable and discouraging those that are not. Managers start by determining which actions are desirable and which they want to change. Then they use the appropriate method of reinforcement to encourage employees to make the change. Studies have found that offering praise and recognition (positive reinforcement) for an employee's efforts is more effective than offering reprimand, ridicule, or sarcasm (negative reinforcement) for undesirable actions. In fact, a recent national survey listed "limited praise and recognition" as the number one reason why employees leave their jobs today.[40]

Praise as a means of behavior modification has been used successfully by many companies. At Eastern Connection, an overnight courier business with geographically scattered operations, employees have even developed a plan to offer praise to each other. Under the "Shoot for the Stars" program, employees can send stars to other employees who have performed exceptionally well on the job. Management is kept aware of who receives stars and what they did to deserve them. Thus employees get to thank each other in ways that promote recognition in the company. The program "has really built a strong team environment, which we feel we have to have to succeed," says company president Jim Berluti.[41]

Companies also use various kinds of rewards to reinforce the behavior of hardworking employees. These rewards include gifts, certificates, medals, dinners, trips, and so forth. After Glen Quinn's Exxon shop won the company's coveted Commitment to Excellence Award, Quinn hosted a barbecue for employees and their families at his home. "*Everybody* felt like winners," he says. Quinn also rewards individual employees with weekend getaways for their hard work.[42] Exhibit 9.9 offers some tips on how to make sure such rewards are effective.

Investing in Employees

The insecurity that many employees feel over the threat of losing their jobs can lead to lower motivation and can threaten organizational productivity. Job worries may also lead

- ☑ Reward employees when they meet goals.
- ☑ Give rewards soon after employees have acted to make the positive reinforcement even stronger.
- ☑ Offer rewards that people will appreciate.
- ☑ Be specific in explaining what the employee did well.
- ☑ Reward employees with greater autonomy and responsibility when they demonstrate initiative and ability.

EXHIBIT 9.9

Tips for Effective Employee Reward

to personal problems that can interfere with an individual's work performance. One way to motivate anxious employees is to sponsor training that will sharpen skills or to offer retraining that will give employees entirely new skills. Manufacturing employees may learn to operate robots and other automated equipment instead of tightening bolts; service employees may learn to manage instead of sell. At carpet manufacturer Collins & Aikman, classes were offered so that employees could learn math and other skills needed to operate computerized weaving equipment.[43] Southwest Airlines offers continuing training through its "University for People," and the company has remained consistently profitable while other airlines struggle. Employees are able to choose courses that will help them to do their jobs more effectively and be more flexible in the tasks they can perform.[44]

Although some people may not adjust easily to training or retraining, most appreciate the opportunity to become more useful to their companies or to the economy as a whole. In fact, linking advanced training with other incentives can even motivate highly skilled employees to develop more loyalty. Consider Grant St. John, a network integrating company in Columbus, Ohio. It pays employees based on the amount of training they receive. The promise of higher pay encourages employees to stay with the company and continue training. Moreover, the company benefits from advanced employee skills.[45]

Is It True?

In the United States, most on-the-job training and development is focused on white-collar and technical employees, rather than on production and service personnel.

Another company that invests heavily in its employees is software maker Autodesk. The company has an elaborate development and leadership program for employees that includes personal coaching, continuous feedback, and team building. Vice president of human resources Steve McMahon says that employees "appreciate the investment that's being made in them, and they also like the fact that they don't have to pretend to do everything perfectly." As a result, Autodesk maintains an environment of trust, and the company is able to retain many of its best employees—an important accomplishment in the highly competitive software industry.[46]

Better Quality of Work Life

Although dividing work into tiny specialized tasks helped managers deal with uneducated employees early in this century, that approach doesn't make as much sense today. Highly specialized jobs rarely satisfy today's better-educated and more sophisticated employees, some of whom know more about the technical aspects of their work than their supervisors do. As a result, many organizations are working to improve the **quality of work life (QWL),** the environment created by work and job conditions.[47] An improved QWL benefits both the individual and the organization: Employees gain the chance to use their special abilities, improve their skills, and balance their lives. The organization gains a more motivated employee.

quality of work life (QWL)
Overall environment that results from job and work conditions

job enrichment
Reducing work specialization and making work more meaningful by adding to the responsibilities of each job

A common way of improving QWL is through **job enrichment,** which reduces specialization and makes work more meaningful by expanding each job's responsibilities. For example, truck drivers who work for Ryder System not only deliver Xerox copying machines but also set them up, test them, and train customers to use them.[48] In addition, job enrichment includes demonstrating to employees the significance of their work. Consider Textron, a manufacturer of airplane wings. The company threw a party for its employees at an airfield, and as they ate, drank, and listened to music, employees could watch airplanes take off and land. Afterward, the employees had a better understanding of how important each rivet or seam is to airplanes, pilots, and passengers.[49] Other companies demonstrate employee impact through open-book management—sharing as much company information with them as possible. Many companies also include other elements of job enrichment such as greater employee autonomy and being involved in the production of a good or service from start to finish.[50] With the growing emphasis on quality production, teamwork, and empowerment, more and more companies are restructuring their processes and policies to enrich employees' jobs in these areas as well.

The teamwork that Vision Tek employees build on the company's basketball court carries over into their work roles.

Quality of work life can be improved in other ways, too. For example, software maker Open Market allows its employees to bring their dogs to work. Andersen Consulting will send someone to be at an employee's home when the cable guy shows up or to pick up an employee's car from the repair shop. Pepsi has an on-site dry cleaning drop-off at its New York headquarters. And American Banker's Insurance Group, Barnett Banks, and Hewlett-Packard all have sponsored schools at company sites that allow employees to visit their children at lunch and after school. All of these measures can improve employees' lives by freeing up their time and by making work a more enjoyable place to be. Such programs also benefit companies by helping them attract and retain talented employees. "We compete with the IBMs, Microsofts, and Oracles of the world," says Open Market chairman Shikhar Gosh. "So we have to make sure that our work environment allows people to give their best in ways that companies that are much larger than us will find difficult to do."[51]

Flexible Schedules

The changing work force is changing lifestyles and needs. Two-career couples with children must perform miracles of scheduling and routing to make sure that the kids get to school or to the baby-sitter and that the adults get to work on time. Single parents have half the resources and twice the problem. In addition, many employees are going back to school or working at second jobs. No wonder so many people applaud **flextime,** a scheduling system that allows employees to choose their own hours within certain limits. For instance, a company may require everyone to be at work between 10:00 A.M. and 2:00 P.M., but employees may arrive or depart whenever they want as long as they work a total of 8 hours every day. Another popular schedule is to work four 10-hour days each week. Some companies, such as People's Bank, also offer *paid-leave banks,* which group sick days, vacation days, and floating holidays into a single bank that employees can draw on at any

flextime
Scheduling system in which employees are allowed certain options regarding time of arrival and departure

time for whatever reason they choose.[52] The sense of control employees get from arranging their own work schedules is motivating for many people.

Many working adults would prefer to have flexible hours in order to spend more time with their families, even if it means slower career advancement.[53] In response to this employee need, a growing number of companies—66 percent according to one recent survey—are offering flextime.[54] Among the companies nationally recognized for having superior flextime policies are Pillsbury, Deloitte & Touche, and Aetna Life & Casualty. At Bank of Montreal, each employee creates a proposal explaining why flexible work hours would make life easier. Employees present their proposals to management, and a trial period usually ensues. During this time, employees can test whether their new schedules really do enrich their lives and whether they are able to continue to meet the goals of the company. If the schedule is accepted by both employees and management, it is registered with the company's office of Work Place Equality so that management can track and understand what people are doing. Bank executives say that employee initiative is one of the strengths of the program.[55]

Flextime is more widespread in white-collar businesses that do not have to maintain standard customer-service hours. Unfortunately, it is not usually an option for employees on production teams, in retail stores, or in many offices where employees have to be on hand to wait on customers or answer calls. Other possible drawbacks to flextime include (1) supervisors feeling uncomfortable and less in control when employees are coming and going, and (2) co-workers possibly resenting flextimers and assuming they take their jobs less seriously.

In addition, flextime will probably not have its intended effect of increasing employee motivation if the organizational culture does not support it. According to Artemis Management Consultants, managers should examine traditional assumptions about employees and work, such as the belief that an employee who works nights and weekends is inherently more dedicated than an employee who works efficiently and leaves at a reasonable time. Such beliefs provide a disincentive for employees to make effective use of flextime programs. On the other hand, many companies that are truly supportive of flextime have found that it reduces turnover, enables the company to adapt to business cycles, allows operation of a round-the-clock business, and helps maintain morale and performance after reengineering or downsizing.[56]

BEST OF THE WEB

Sticking to Business at Home

Telecommuting is an effective way for companies to meet the flexible scheduling requirements of some employees. Taking the work to the worker instead of bringing the worker to work can also lower the company's facilities costs. But how does a company go about setting up a telecommuting program? What sort of technologies and costs are involved? And how can the company ensure that employees will be motivated to work effectively at home? The Pacific Bell Network has some good answers to these and other questions about telecommuting on its Web site. Of course, PacBell has an interest in increasing the number of telecommuters, because it sells many of the products and services that make telecommuting possible. Visit the company's Web site to learn more about this growing business trend, and consider whether telecommuting is right for you.
http://www.pacbell.com/products/business/general/telecommuting

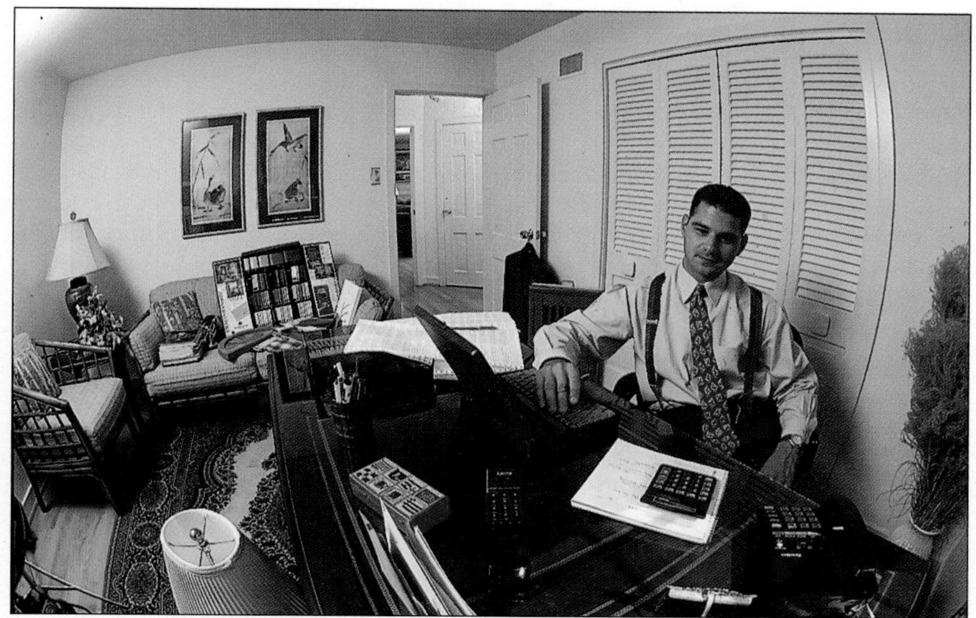

Some jobs, and some people, are better suited to telecommuting than others are. Marc Accristo, owner of Marc Accristo Interior Designs, can arrange client meetings, coordinate projects, and order materials easily from his home office.

Telecommuting

Related to flexible schedules is **telecommuting**—working from home using computers and telecommunications equipment to stay in touch with the employer's offices. Many companies are discovering that allowing their employees to perform at least some of their work tasks at home helps meet employee needs for flexibility while boosting their productivity as much as 20 percent. In addition, telecommuting can save the company money in equipment and space costs. Moreover, it can enable a company to hire talented people in distant areas without requiring them to relocate. This expands the company's pool of potential job candidates while benefiting employees who have a spouse with a job, children in school, or elderly parents to care for.[57] Employees also like telecommuting because they can set their own hours, reduce job-related expenses such as commuting costs, and spend more time with their families.

telecommuting
Working from home and communicating with the company's main office via computer and communication devices

Of course, telecommuting does have its limitations. For example, a printer who runs giant color presses can't run the presses from home. In addition, some home-based workers find they miss interacting with colleagues. When Apple Computer started a telecommuting program, it expected, but didn't get, a large response. Many people simply didn't want to work at home, and others were reluctant to give up the social environment of the office.[58] Furthermore, some telecommuters have found that they actually put in longer hours or that they encounter too many distractions, such as young children requiring attention. However, many telecommuters also find that the benefits outweigh the drawbacks.

Work Sharing and Job Sharing

When there is a mismatch between the amount of work available and the amount of work desired by an employee, two techniques can be used to improve morale. **Work sharing,** which is more common in economic downturns, distributes the hardships among a company's entire work force by slicing a few hours off everybody's workweek and cutting pay. **Job sharing** lets two employees share a single full-time job and split the salary and benefits.

work sharing
Slicing a few hours off everybody's workweek and cutting pay to minimize layoffs

job sharing
Splitting a single full-time job between two employees for their convenience

When a company adopts work sharing instead of laying people off, nearly everyone stands to gain. Employees are less anxious about being unemployed and are thus willing to spend more money, which helps local merchants stay in business. Because most employees keep their jobs rather than being "bumped" from one job to another by those employees with seniority, quality remains high. And when business surges forward again, companies that have instituted work sharing are better equipped to meet the stepped-up demand because they do not have to call back old employees or train new ones. Consider J. W. Pepper & Son, a sheet-music distributor that ships more product in the fall than at any other time during the year. In order to keep employees for the busy times, all employees work four 7.5 hour days but get paid for five during the 29 slowest weeks of the year. In exchange, employees get no paid sick leave. The policy motivates employees to work harder and has almost eliminated absenteeism.[59] Employees like those at Pepper are also more willing to put in long hours for a firm that helps them through a tough spell.

In contrast, job sharing is a voluntary solution to the needs of working parents, employees going back to school, and the like. It is usually offered to people who already work for the company but need to cut back their hours. Rather than lose a good employee or have to find and train someone new, the company finds a way to split responsibilities.

Other Motivational Techniques

As discussed earlier, employee empowerment can be a powerful motivational tool because it gives employees more say in the actual workings of the company, usually by offering them greater decision-making power. At the same time, empowerment places more value on employee ideas, which gives employees greater responsibility and greater accountability for the company's performance. This type of involvement leads to a deeper sense of satisfaction when employees' ideas and work contributions help achieve the company's goals, an especially important consideration when a company must continually improve its products and processes. And when managers make an effort to solicit employee ideas and opinions, they can further enhance motivation by providing feedback. Creating a continuous dialog between management and employees can go a long way toward developing trust and a sense of shared commitment.

Another powerful motivator is teamwork. As teamwork becomes more the norm in businesses worldwide, increasing numbers of companies are realizing productivity and quality gains even as costs decrease. Once teamwork becomes embedded in the organization's culture, managers find that motivating employees is easier because they are more committed to the goals of the organization. Furthermore, when team members are dependent on each other to complete a project, they are more likely to benefit from each other's energy and inspire each other. This reduces the burden on management to find ways of motivating employees. However, team-oriented companies that continue to compensate employees individually may actually be sending them mixed signals that can counteract the effects of teamwork. This subject is examined in more detail in Chapter 10, which also discusses how employee stock options can motivate employees by establishing a connection between companywide performance and personal financial reward.

Summary of Learning Objectives

1. **List the three main components of good human relations within an organization.**
Leadership, motivation, and communication are the major elements that contribute to good human relations.

2. **Explain how the five levels in Maslow's hierarchy of needs relate to employee motivation.**
Physiological needs, the most basic requirements for human life, are seldom strong motivators for modern wage

earners. Safety (or security) needs can be met through job security and pension plans. Social needs, which drive people to seek membership in informal groups, may be more important than financial considerations. Esteem needs, which relate to feelings of self-worth and respect from others, are met by motivational techniques of recognition. Self-actualization needs may be met by giving employees the opportunity to expand their skills and take on additional responsibility.

3. **Identify the two factors affecting employee motivation in Herzberg's two-factor theory.**
   Hygiene factors—such as working conditions, company policies, and job security—have a bad effect on motivation only if they are deficient. Motivators—achievement, recognition, and responsibility—are related positively to increases in productivity.
4. **Describe how Theory X, Theory Y, and Theory Z link employee motivation and management style.**
   Theory X and Theory Y describe two opposite sets of assumptions about employees' motives for working; Theory X emphasizes management authority, and Theory Y emphasizes employee growth and self-direction. Theory Z, which describes human relations within U.S. companies that have adopted certain Japanese management techniques, assumes that employees are part of a family and that their needs therefore deserve consideration.
5. **Explain how changes in work-force demographics have complicated the challenge of motivating employees.**
   Because of changes in work force demographics, managers need to find new ways of keeping employees happy and productive on the job. Older employees are holding on to high-paying positions longer. Baby boomers and younger employees find it harder to advance, and they want more participation in work decisions and a balance between work and home life. And increasing cultural diversity brings a wider range of work skills, traditions, and attitudes to the workplace, which can affect behavior on the job.
6. **Explain how changes in the economy create barriers to employee motivation.**
   Because of global competition, work-saving technologies, and the pursuit of short-term profit, businesses require many highly skilled employees to work longer hours, which can lead to low morale and burnout. At the other end of the spectrum, low-skilled employees are increasingly taking jobs in the service sector that offer little security and opportunity for advancement. Both situations make it difficult for managers to motivate employees.
7. **Describe how corporate cultures must change in order to keep employees motivated.**
   To reduce turnover, corporate cultures have to downplay job advancement as the primary source of job satisfaction. At the same time, corporate cultures must become more open in order to control rumors, improve morale, allow employees to concentrate on performance, and encourage employees to take risks. Management can also improve morale by showing more empathy for employees and by finding ways to make work more enjoyable.
8. **Discuss the use of goal setting, behavior modification, investing in employees, and an improved quality of work life as motivational techniques.**
   Some companies motivate their employees by allowing them to set clear and challenging personal goals that support organizational goals. With behavioral modification, managers seek to change employee behavior by systematically encouraging actions that are desirable and discouraging those that are not. To motivate employees who are worried about job security, employers can sponsor training that will sharpen employee skills. Improving the quality of work life leads to better work conditions, which give employees the chance to use their special abilities and build their skills.

On the Job: Meeting Business Challenges at Hallmark Cards

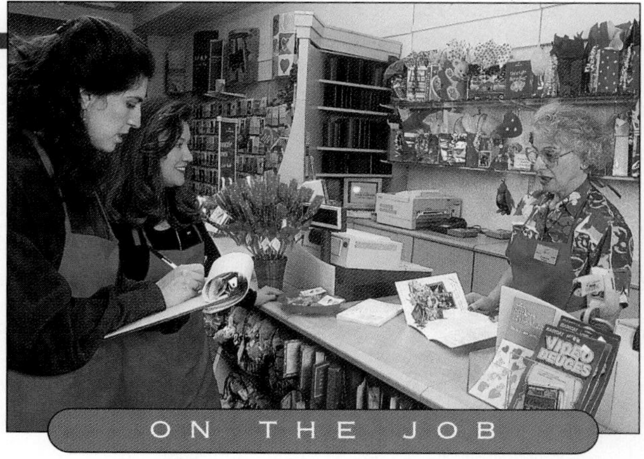

As the new vice president of Human Relations, Ralph Christenson was facing restructuring and disruption at Hallmark. Rumors of layoffs or massive job change and loss of benefits echoed along the corridors of Hallmark's Kansas City headquarters. Employees worried that profit sharing might be cut and that other important benefits such as child-care help, tuition reimbursement, and work sharing would be lost. Always known for its family-oriented atmosphere, the company had consistently ranked among the best places to work in America. But now employees' faith in Hallmark wavered, and Christenson needed to reassure company employees that things would work out.

Although Hallmark Cards was a healthy company, management knew the underlying cost structure was too high. Moreover, the time it took to deliver new products to market was as much as three years, far too long when customer tastes can change rapidly and the competition can react more quickly. So with the help of outside consultants, Hallmark's management developed several strategies to reduce costs and introduce products with greater speed.

During this time of change, preserving employee jobs and improving morale were Christenson's primary concerns. So he developed a creative solution for containing costs by looking beyond what people were originally hired to do. To retain employees displaced by the merger of three divisions, Christenson developed a program for retraining factory workers to handle office jobs. Yet another group of factory employees helped paint an operating plant while receiving their standard wages. When factory work is slow, employees can even choose to volunteer for community work while drawing their usual paychecks. And no employee with more than two years with the company can be let go without a case review by company executives. So with Christenson's help, Hallmark was able to perpetuate its special caring for employees and its history of no layoffs.

Then to speed up the time it takes to develop and introduce new card products, Christenson helped Hallmark create cross-functional teams. Before these changes, Hallmark artists, designers, printers, and financial staff were working as much as a city block apart even though some of them were working on the same card design. With the new team concept, these employees have been brought together into one room to create, develop, cost-justify, and produce new cards. This approach cut the overall time to market from three years to about one year and helped Hallmark compete more effectively in the rapidly changing greeting card business. Employees quickly adapted to the idea of working together in teams, and they embraced the opportunity to learn more about the company's overall operations.

Next, Christenson addressed employee benefits. Although workers were generally happy with the existing benefits package, Christenson wanted to offer even more solutions to keep Hallmark employees satisfied. He needed to build a two-way communication channel that allowed him to hear employee concerns firsthand; he set up a series of feedback sessions in which employees could tell him what was on their mind. As a result, Christenson reorganized the human relations department to focus on a number of themes important to employees.

Your Mission: You've joined Ralph Christenson's team to develop cost-effective recommendations for retaining employees, improving overall morale, and enhancing productivity. Select the best solution for the following problems, and be prepared to explain your choices.

1. Of the three primary components of human relations programs (leadership, motivation, and communication) which could help Hallmark the most?
   a. The strength of the Hallmark Company lies in its long tradition of family leadership. Generations of Hallmark employees have enjoyed the benefits of the benevolent family-oriented style. Using a new internal communications program, Christenson should put the leadership of the Hall family and other company executives at the forefront so that employees are assured that company management fully supports them.
   b. During periods of companywide stress, increased quality communication with employees is the best way to separate facts from rumors. Even though Hallmark has already introduced a number of communication channels (such as the feedback sessions to the Human Relations department), Christenson should offer opportunities for staff to communicate directly with company executives.
   c. Employees perform at top levels when they are motivated. Christenson should spend more time now on developing programs to increase compensation, provide recognition for individual and team contributions, and fine-tune the benefits package.
2. Although they don't mean to, companies occasionally create periods of stress for employees. In times of cost cutting, what steps would you take to reassure employees that you are looking out for their best interests as well as the company's?
   a. To keep Hallmark's strong leadership at the forefront, Christenson should sponsor a daylong company retreat that provides open discussion with management, along with entertainment and fine cuisine. It's always best to speak openly about company problems, and employees appreciate the message more when it's delivered honestly and in a friendly setting.
   b. Periodic open forums with company decision makers will keep employees up to date on company news and benefits issues.
   c. The strongest support for employees comes in the company's commitment to the benefit package. Now is the time to reaffirm the Hallmark commitment to employee well-being.
3. A good communication program is important to keep employees up to date with company matters. But too many communication vehicles can be expensive. What communication project should Christenson focus on?
   a. The company should continue to deal with employee information needs by improving the companywide newsletter. Include financial results and news about competitors and their products. The more employees know about the environment that affects their company, the more they can dedicate themselves to the company's activities.
   b. The company's midlevel management plays an important role in Hallmark's success. The company should expand communications by targeting managers and supervisors.

c. Nothing provides greater satisfaction than a face-to-face exchange. Christenson should investigate ways of making Hallmark executives accessible to employees through periodic meetings.

4. Talented people want to join Hallmark because of the company's record for providing employee benefits. What kind of benefit program would you recommend to Christenson for Hallmark employees? Remember that company costs must be kept down.

   a. Many Hallmark employees expressed interest in expanded child-care programs. For example, parents would like to take sick children from school to a day-care place where they can have a nurse's attention.

   b. Hallmark should sponsor a lunchtime seminar series covering such issues as caring for children and aging parents, work sharing and job sharing options, and telecommuting opportunities. The company could even add a special monthly seminar in the evening so that spouses and other family members could also attend.

   c. Many large companies have adopted a flexible "cafeteria" approach to employee benefits, setting up benefit accounts and allowing employees to select individual benefit choices up to specific dollar amounts. Some employees could spend all their account dollars on dental care, for example, whereas other employees could spend their benefits on child-care assistance.

Key Terms

behavior modification (275)
flextime (277)
human relations (258)
hygiene factors (262)
job enrichment (276)
job sharing (279)
morale (259)
motivation (258)
motivators (262)
piecework system (260)
quality of work life (QWL) (276)
scientific management (260)
telecommuting (279)
Theory X (263)
Theory Y (263)
Theory Z (263)
work sharing (279)

Questions

For Review

1. What challenges do companies face when managing a diverse work force?
2. What is morale, and how does it relate to motivation?
3. Why do managers often find it difficult to motivate employees who remain after downsizing?
4. What is quality of work life, and how does it influence employee motivation?
5. What is the most effective form of behavior modification and how is it best used?

For Analysis

6. What are the practical implications of Maslow's hierarchy? What are its limitations?
7. How do Theories X and Y relate to Theory Z?
8. Is work sharing a Theory X, Theory Y, or Theory Z motivation technique? Explain your answer.
9. How might motivation techniques such as flextime and telecommuting alter the group norms that develop among employees in an organization?
10. Given the demographic and economic changes taking place, what is the highest priority for new employees today in order to ensure opportunities for advancement in the future?

For Application

11. Assume you are a manager who supervises several employees in a customer sales and service department. Most of your staff spend a lot of time making follow-up phone calls to customers to solicit their feedback on your company's product. One of your better employees seems unusually stressed lately. He has been coming in late a lot and sometimes has a short fuse with customers. You know that he has two small children and that his wife also works full-time. What can you do to motivate this employee?
12. Another talented and hard-working employee comes to you one day and says she does not feel challenged. When she took the job a year ago, she expected to be able to diversify her skills more and take on greater responsibility than she now has. How do you respond?

A Case for Critical Thinking ■ Flying High on Employee Morale

If you've ever flown on Southwest Airlines, you've probably noticed that it does things a little bit differently than the other major airlines. For one thing, you won't get anything more than a bag of peanuts on this no-frills carrier. But what you will get is a travel experience unlike any in the airline industry. Your flight attendants might sing the safety instructions, pilots may tell jokes over the P.A. system, and you could find yourself scrambling to win an impromptu game of "who has the biggest hole in his sock?" Such occurrences may seem a little nutty, but that's just the way CEO Herb Kelleher wants it. "We look for attitudes; people with a sense of humor who don't take themselves too seriously," he says. Kelleher himself once showed up to the company's annual meeting in a straitjacket.

Southwest's recruitment and hiring procedures are based on the idea that humor motivates people to thrive during times of change, remain creative when they are under stress, perform their jobs more effectively, play more enthusiastically, and remain in better health. The airline also encourages employees to take risks, and it empowers them to make decisions on their own. "If one of our employees commits Southwest Airlines to doing something," Kelleher says, "we stand behind that commitment—even if it's a bad business decision." For example, once the company's new manager of properties committed to a deal with the city of Austin that was soon revealed to be a $400,000 mistake. Although the deal had not been signed, the manager had promised that Southwest would do so. Kelleher's main concerns were that the company follow through on its promise, and that the manager learn from his mistake.

You might think that any company with such a supportive attitude toward its employees probably doesn't make much money. Think again. Whereas American, Delta, and United racked up billion-dollar losses in the early 1990s, Southwest remained consistently profitable. And for four consecutive years, the company had the fewest complaints, delays, and mishandled bags, according to the U.S. Department of Transportation. What's more, Southwest has never laid off an employee. "We won't staff up for peak and then furlough people once the peak season is over," says director of corporate employment Sherry Phelps.

Southwest treats its employees like family and invests heavily in their success. At the company's "University for People," employees can take classes that add to their flexibility and enhance their career opportunities. Employees also share in the wealth of the company through a profit-sharing plan. As a result of such incentives, employees think nothing of assuming multiple roles if they believe it will help the airline succeed. For example, you may see a flight attendant or pilot picking up litter in the passenger waiting area.

An important reason for the commitment of Southwest employees is the culture that Kelleher strives to create. Kelleher and executive vice president for customers Colleen Barrett send cards to employees on their birthdays and anniversaries to thank them for a job well done. Furthermore, letters from customers are often delivered to employees with a note from Herb and Colleen saying, "Keep up the good job." Southwest is also sensitive to the personal and family lives of its employees. For example, people can swap jobs and shifts if they need time off for any reason. And management makes a point of providing employees with access to the information they need to do their jobs most effectively. Management believes that when employees have the critical information they need, they solve problems quicker.

Southwest seems to be doing all the right things to motivate employees and keep morale high. It may be hard to believe that such a company exists in the world today, but perhaps Kelleher's philosophy of company-employee relations helps explain: "I feel that you have to be with your employees through all their difficulties, that you have to be interested in them personally. They may be disappointed in their country. Even their family might not be working out the way they wish it would. But I want them to know that Southwest will always be there for them."

1. Southwest Airlines receives about 140,000 unsolicited job applications per year, even though the company often pays less than other airlines. In terms of Maslow's hierarchy, what employee needs does Southwest meet so well that such large numbers of people are hoping to get jobs with the company?
2. Citing examples from the case to support your answer, explain whether Southwest Airlines manages employees under Theory X, Theory Y, or Theory Z assumptions.
3. Many managers would say that Southwest's policies, which place so much value on keeping employees happy, are not feasible in the long run. However, the company has been profitable for 25 years. How do you explain this?
4. Visit the Southwest Airlines Web site at <http://www.iflyswa.com> and read the brief message from Herb Kelleher. How do you think Southwest's corporate culture enables Kelleher to implement his strategy for increasing revenue and offering lower fares?

Building Your Business Skills

With a small group of three or four students (preferably students you don't know well), select a ready-made assembly project that can be completed in one or two hours. This can be a jigsaw puzzle, a plastic model, or some other similar craft project. As you work, consider the process that your group goes through to complete the project. How did you decide on the project? Did your group select a leader, or was leadership a shared responsibility? How did you delegate responsibilities in the project? After you complete the project, write a brief summary of the activities of your group as they relate to the following factors: human relations, leadership, communication, motivation, and morale. Which factors (if any) created barriers to completing the project efficiently? Which factors seemed to work well? How could the process have been improved? As a class, share and discuss the experiences of each group.

Keeping Current Using *The Wall Street Journal*

Select one or two articles from recent issues of *The Wall Street Journal* that relate to employee motivation or morale.

1. What is the problem, solution, or trend described in the article(s), and how does it influence employee attitudes or motivation?
2. Does this problem relate to just one company's experience, or does it have broader implications? Who is affected by it now, and who do you think might be affected by it in the future?
3. What challenges and opportunities does this development offer management in this company or industry? The employees?
4. Search for more information about this particular problem, solution, or trend on the Internet by entering key words that pertain to the issue in one of the many search engines available. Read the search engine's "tips" page first to make your search more efficient. Can you identify some strategies for handling the issue that differ from those followed by the company(s) in your article(s)? Are there certain businesses that offer training or consulting services to deal with this particular situation? What do you think are some of the costs and benefits of hiring a consultant as opposed to dealing with the situation internally?

Exploring the Best of the Web

Measuring Employee Satisfaction, page 262

Managers use surveys to gain a better understanding of how satisfied and motivated employees are at work. One survey has been designed to understand the patterns of job satisfaction among employees who use an information technology (IT) system, and it is available on the Internet at

<http://www.fdgroup.co.uk/neo/djassoc/dj_jdq.html>. Read the survey, as well as the explanatory information that precedes it, and then answer the following questions.

1. According to the opening explanatory information, how will this survey be most useful? Why do you think it is important for survey participants to discuss the results as a group with management? Why is it important for respondents to remain anonymous?
2. Which needs in Maslow's hierarchy do the questions in this survey appeal to? Explain your answer. What steps should managers take after evaluating the surveys and discussing them with employees to ensure that those needs are met?
3. What are this survey's biggest strengths and weaknesses? Think about your satisfaction in your present job, a previous job, or in class. Are there any particular issues this survey doesn't address? If so, formulate your own questions to address them.

Working Hard on the Web, page 271

Visitors of the Hard @ Work Web site at <http://www.hardatwork.com> can get help with difficult work scenarios, improve their career development skills, or chat with others about work and careers. Read *HQ Country* first to learn about the site's creators, then check out what else the site has to offer and answer the questions below.

1. Follow the link to the *Rock Pile,* and select a case study to review. Formulate a response to deal with the situation presented. Then get together with one or more other students in your class and discuss your responses. Do your responses differ? What does this say about the challenges of managing and motivating different employees?
2. Follow the link to *Stump the Mentor.* Write a message describing a difficult situation you are currently facing at work or have faced in the past. Print out both your question and the Mentor's response. Do you agree with the response you received? Why or why not? If your situation has been resolved, what action did you take and why? If it has not been resolved, how do you plan to handle the situation in the future?
3. After exploring some of the other links on the site, write a paragraph or two that evaluates its content and presentation. Who would benefit most from this site: human resources professionals, managers, workers, or job seekers? Do you find the information to be valuable? Is the information presented logically? Is this a site you would come back to in the future? Why or why not?

Sticking to Business at Home, page 278

The Pacific Bell Network's Web site offers guidelines for companies that are considering implementing a telecommuting program, as well as helpful advice for telecommuters about how to stay focused and motivated while working at home. Explore the site at <http://www.pacbell.com/products/business/general/telecommuting> to learn more about this hot business trend, and then answer the questions below.

1. Follow the link to the *Telecommuting Guide,* and click on *Start-up.* In terms of motivation, what qualities should an employee have in order to work effectively at home? Based on what you have learned in this chapter, list some strategies that managers can use to help keep their telecommuting employees focused and productive.
2. From the index, click on *Management* and read about the considerations of managing telecommuters. Based on this information and what you have learned in the text, list some strategies that managers can use to encourage a sense of shared purpose and teamwork between telecommuters and traditional employees.

3. Assess your own skills, work habits, and personality to decide whether you would make an effective telecommuter. Consider the issues you raised on the PacBell Web site. What kind of work environment do you thrive in? Do you enjoy close contact with others, or do you work best on your own? Are you easily distracted? Do you require co-workers nearby to help you stay focused and motivated? Are you able to meet deadlines? Write a brief summary of your assessment and explain why you would or would not like to participate in a telecommuting program.

Answers to "Is It True?"

Page 258. False. The correct number is actually lower: 2.3 suggestions per employee per year.

Page 266. False. Since 1970 the number of men in the United States working more than one job rose only 1 percent, while the number of women doing so rose 390 percent.

Page 276. True.

CHAPTER 10

HUMAN RESOURCES MANAGEMENT

OBJECTIVES

After studying this chapter, you will be able to

1 List the six main functions of human resources departments

2 Identify the six stages in the hiring process

3 Explain why companies use training and development programs

4 State two general methods for compensating employees

5 Describe the main components of employee pay

6 Explain five employee benefits

7 Describe five ways an employee's status may change

8 Identify the two reasons that employers may terminate employment

ON THE JOB

On the Job On the Job

ON THE JOB: FACING BUSINESS CHALLENGES AT JOHNSON & JOHNSON

Keeping Employees in the Pink and the Company in the Black

Does a healthier work force translate into healthier profits? This was one of the key issues facing Johnson & Johnson CEO Ralph S. Larsen and his predecessor, James E. Burke, as they considered the challenge of managing the company's human resources and keeping employees satisfied and productive. Johnson & Johnson operates throughout the world, employing more than 70,000 people to research, manufacture, and market health-care products in dozens of countries.

Employee health was a major concern for several reasons. Company studies showed that over 30 percent of Johnson & Johnson's employees were smokers, and one internal report revealed that smokers had a 45 percent greater rate of absenteeism than nonsmokers. Smokers also contributed disproportionately to the company's medical expenses (30 percent higher than nonsmokers), an ominous statistic at a time when health-care costs were rising at nearly twice the rate of inflation.

Another problem confronting J&J was how changing demographics were affecting employees. Employees increasingly fell into one of three groups: They were part of two-career couples with children; they were responsible for an aging parent; or they were single mothers or fathers. A survey of 10,000 J&J employees revealed that they were frustrated by their inability to meet all their obligations, both to their families and to their employer. Many stated that they had difficulty finding day care, especially sick-child care and infant care, and almost 20 percent responded that they could not afford day care even if they could locate a suitable provider.

Although these employees felt torn between family pressures and employment roles, they found little help at work. Most stated that their managers were unsympathetic about the dilemma. Balancing their work and family obligations took its toll on employees, who reported higher levels of stress, greater absenteeism, and lower job satisfaction.

For guidance on these issues, the CEOs turned to Johnson & Johnson's operating document, the corporate credo written by Robert Wood Johnson, son of a founding Johnson brother and chairman of the company for 25 years. Johnson ranked the company's obligation to its employees ahead of its responsibility to its shareholders and second only to its commitment to its customers. This credo would serve as a blueprint for successful human resources management.

So how could J&J top managers promote health in the workplace? How could they help J&J employees balance family and career obligations? What programs could be established to meet the personal and professional needs of their employees more effectively? What effect would such programs have on the company's bottom line?[1]

THE PROCESS OF HUMAN RESOURCES MANAGEMENT

As Johnson & Johnson's managers know, employees are an important component of every business. In fact, more and more companies consider employees their most valuable asset. Such attitudes have fueled the rising emphasis on hiring the right people to help a company reach its goals and then overseeing their training and development, motivation, evaluation, and compensation. This specialized function, formerly referred to as *personnel management,* is now termed **human resources management (HRM)** to reflect the importance of a well-chosen and well-managed work force in achieving company goals. Because of the accelerating rate at which the work force, the economy, and corporate culture are being transformed, the role of HRM is increasingly viewed as a strategic one.

human resources management (HRM)
Specialized function of planning how to obtain employees, oversee their training, evaluate them, and compensate them

Human resources (HR) managers must figure out how to attract qualified employees from a shrinking pool of entry-level candidates; how to train less educated, poorly skilled employees; how to keep experienced employees when they have fewer opportunities for advancement; and how to lay off employees equitably when downsizing is necessary. They must also retrain employees to enable them to cope with increasing automation and computerization, manage increasingly complex (and expensive) employee benefits programs, shape workplace policies to changing work-force demographics and employee needs, and cope with the challenge of meeting government regulations in hiring practices and equal opportunity employment.

BEST OF THE WEB

Staying on Top of the HR World

As in all areas of business, the world of human resources changes quickly. HR managers need to be well informed about trends in recruiting, compensation, benefits, and employee satisfaction, just to name a few. In the past, this required a lot of reading and networking with colleagues. However, today networking of a different kind makes it easy to find information on hot HR issues. HR Live is an online resource that provides HR professionals with information about growing recruitment markets, recent layoffs by other companies, important HR news topics, current statistics, and more. Even if you are not in the HR field, a lot of valuable information at HR Live will interest you.
http://www.hrlive.com

In addition, personnel strategy has become a major challenge in global business, and human resources executives are increasingly required to take an international perspective. Just a few of the global issues that human resource professionals must tackle include international health care, employment-taxation problems, legal systems, performance measurement, and the relocation of *expatriates* (employees who live and work in a foreign country).[2] Given the growing importance and complexity of human resources problems, it's not surprising that all but the smallest businesses either employ an HR staff or outsource to HR professionals to deal with those problems.

What exactly do human resources departments do? Human resources staff members plan how to meet a company's human resources needs, recruit and select employees, train and develop employees and managers, and appraise employee performance. The staff also administers pay and employee benefits and oversees changes in employment status (promotion, reassignment, termination or resignation, and retirement). Overall, the human resources department keeps the organization running smoothly at every level, easing the integration of people from a variety of cultures and backgrounds so that everyone works cooperatively toward the common goals.[3] This chapter explores each of these human resources responsibilities, beginning with planning.

Human Resources Planning

The first step in staffing business organizations, as in any other management endeavor, is to plan (see Exhibit 10.1). Planning is crucial because a miscalculation could leave a company without enough employees to keep up with demand, resulting in customer dissatisfaction and lost business. Yet if a company expands its staff too rapidly, profits may be eaten up by payroll, or the firm may have to lay off people who were just recruited and trained at considerable expense. That's why forecasting future staffing needs is a key part of human resources planning.

Forecasting Supply and demand are factors in human resources planning, just as they are in more general business planning. Forecasting begins with estimates of *demand,* the numbers and kinds of employees that will be needed at various times. For example, a shoe chain that is planning to open another store within six months would estimate that it needs an additional store manager and an assistant manager as well as part-time salespeople. Although the chain might start looking immediately for someone as highly placed as the manager, hiring salespeople might be postponed until just before the store opens.

The next task is to estimate the *supply* of available employees. In many cases, that supply is within the company already—perhaps just needing training to fill future requirements. The shoe chain may well find that the assistant manager at an existing store can be promoted to manage the new store, and one of the current salespeople can be named assistant manager. If existing employees cannot be tapped for new positions, the human resources manager must determine how to find people outside the company who have the necessary skills.

THE CHANGING LABOR MARKET Every business needs to know whether enough people with the required skills are available in the general work force. Keeping track of the labor market is not easy, because it is undergoing substantial change. Fewer jobs are available today for low-skilled factory employees in traditional "smokestack" industries such as steel manufacturing. However, many of these workers are finding jobs in the booming

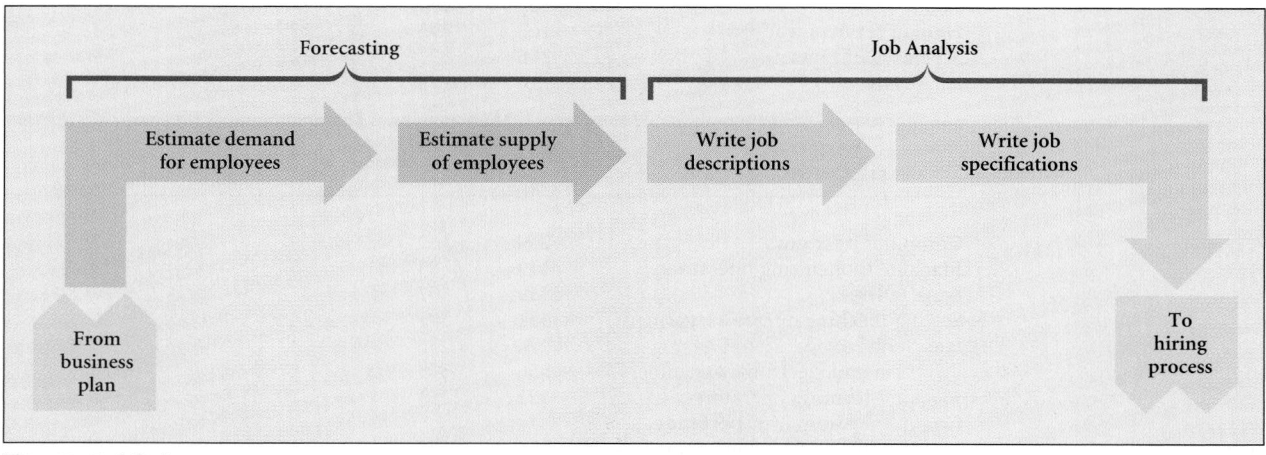

EXHIBIT 10.1

Steps in Human Resources Planning

Careful attention to each phase of this sequence helps ensure that a company will have the right human resources when it needs them.

service sector—although sometimes at lower wages. In addition, the demand for people with engineering, computer, and other technical skills is mushrooming. At the same time, outsourcing by large companies has led to a shortage of workers in many of the smaller companies they contract with. The result is that the U.S. rate of unemployment is hovering at around 5 percent, which most economists consider to be full employment.[4]

Many jobs are expected to experience rapid growth between now and 2005, including home health aides, systems analysts, computer engineers, and special education teachers. Exhibit 10.2 lists the ten fastest growing occupations and the ten fastest shrinking occupations. Note that many of the growing occupations are service-oriented and require specialized skills or training, whereas the shrinking occupations involve activities that require fewer skills or that are increasingly being automated.[5]

The gap is widening between what employers will require of new employees in the years ahead and the actual skills of these employees. Productivity in the United States could suffer if the education and skill levels of the work force are not upgraded (see Exhibit 10.3).[6] As more organizations expand into global markets, they need managers and employees with technical skills, as well as the ability to adapt to other cultures and the foresight to spot local, national, and international trends.[7] At the same time, workplace technologies require front-line production employees to have more mathematics, reading, and writing skills than many do today. Dudley Kell, 52-year-old team leader for forest products company Weyerhaeuser, says, "If you can't read today, you probably won't make it in

EXHIBIT 10.2

Fastest Growing and Fastest Shrinking Occupations

GROWING OCCUPATIONS*	EMPLOYMENT 1994	EMPLOYMENT 2005	NET JOB GROWTH (1,000S)	% CHANGE IN EMPLOYMENT
Personal and home care aides	179	391	212	118
Home health aides	420	848	428	102
Systems analysts	483	928	445	92
Computer engineers	195	372	177	91
All other computer scientists	149	283	134	90
Physical therapists	102	183	81	79
Residential counselors	165	290	125	76
Human services workers	168	293	125	74
Medical assistants	206	327	121	59
Paralegals	110	175	65	59
SHRINKING OCCUPATIONS*				
Computer operators	259	162	−97	−37
Machine tool cutting operators	119	85	−34	−29
Bank tellers	559	407	−152	−27
Sewing machine operators, garment	531	391	−140	−26
File clerks	278	236	−42	−15
Electrical and electronic assemblers	356	309	−47	−13
Machine-forming operators	171	151	−20	−12
Communication, transportation, and utilities operations managers	154	135	−19	−12
Tool and die makers	142	127	−15	−11
Service station attendants	167	148	−19	−11

*Only occupations with at least 100,000 employees in 1994 are included.

a sawmill." Kell was able to boost his own reading skills by about five grade levels in Weyerhaeuser's Read Right program.[8]

STRATEGIC STAFFING TECHNIQUES Human resources planners must also take into account today's fluid business conditions. To avoid drastic overstaffing or understaffing, companies use a variety of strategic staffing techniques. For example, more and more businesses trying to save money and increase flexibility have built their work forces around part-time employees, whose schedules can be rearranged to suit the company's needs. As a result, the part-time labor force has increased by leaps and bounds in recent years,

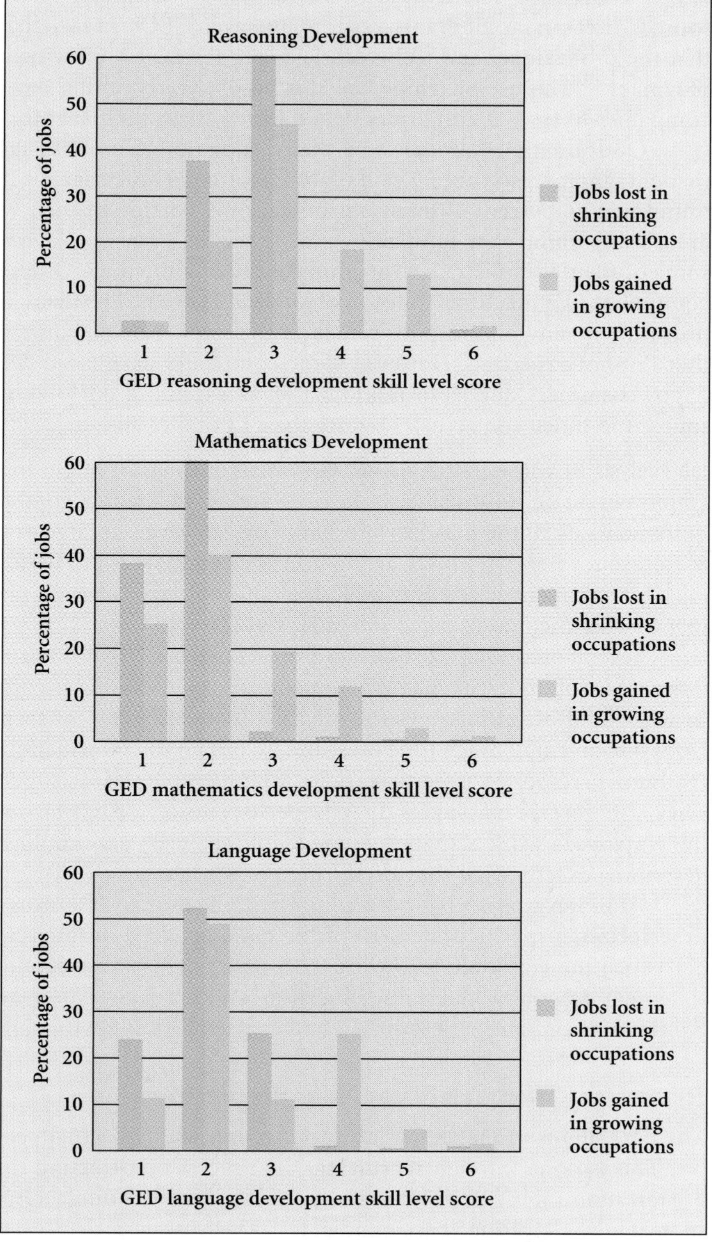

EXHIBIT 10.3

Skill Levels Required for Growing and Shrinking Occupations

The U.S. Department of Labor divides cognitive skills needed by workers into three "General Education Development" (GED) components: reasoning development, mathematics development, and language development. The three components are categorized into six different levels, with level 1 being the most elementary and level 6 being the most advanced. These graphs show that jobs gained in growing occupations require higher levels of all three skills components than jobs lost in shrinking occupations.

particularly the segment made up of "involuntary" part-timers. These are people who want full-time jobs but who are forced to settle for part-time. Between 1970 and 1990, the number of such involuntary part-timers grew by 121 percent, and they continue to make up a growing percentage of the more than 30 million part-time U.S. workers.[9]

A large percentage of the work force is also made up of temporary employees. In 1983 there were 619,000 temporary jobs in the United States. By 1994 that number had more than tripled to 2.25 million, and the U.S. Department of Labor projects it will grow another 60 percent by 2005. Currently, about 3 percent of all jobs are held by temporary workers, but some 85 percent of U.S. firms use "temps" to handle a variety of jobs at all levels of the organization. Moreover, two-thirds of executives surveyed expect their use of temps to increase. The temporary ranks include computer systems analysts, human resources directors, accountants, doctors, and even CEOs. In fact, the Labor Department says that the professional and technical fields are the fastest-growing areas of temporary employment.[10] The use of temps has also become a recruiting technique because it allows companies to try out employees before hiring them permanently.

Outsourcing is another way that companies accomplish tasks without hiring permanent employees. A recent poll of 26 major companies like du Pont, Exxon, and Honda found that 86 percent of them outsource some portion of their work. In addition, a separate study found that companies with fewer than 100 employees are likely to outsource some of their administrative functions to other companies. One such company is medical equipment manufacturer Innovative Medical Systems. President Tom Asacker says, "I improve my quality and responsiveness to the market by outsourcing to experts the things that I'm not expert at." However, some companies have faced delays, loss of quality, unhappy customers, and labor union battles as a result of outsourcing. Companies that outsource too much can actually reduce their flexibility and creativity.[11]

Job Analysis If you were the owner of a small business, it might make sense for you to hire employees on an informal basis, because you would be in a good position to know the requirements of all the jobs in your company. However, in large organizations like Johnson & Johnson, where hundreds or thousands of employees are performing a wide variety of jobs, management needs a more formal and objective method of evaluating job requirements. That method is called **job analysis.**

job analysis
Process by which jobs are studied to determine the tasks and dynamics involved in performing them

Several questions must be asked in job analysis: What is the purpose of the job? What tasks are involved in the job? What qualifications and skills are needed to do it effectively? In what kind of setting does the job take place? Is there much public contact involved? Does the job entail much time pressure? To obtain the information needed for a job analysis, human resources experts start by asking employees or supervisors for information. They also observe employees directly, perhaps using a stopwatch or videotape to monitor the employee's work activities. Some employers even ask employees to keep daily diaries describing exactly what they do during the workday.

job description
Statement of the tasks involved in a given job and the conditions under which the holder of the job will work

job specification
Statement describing the kind of person who would be best for a given job—including the skills, education, and previous experience that the job requires

After job analysis has been completed, the human resources manager develops a **job description,** a specific statement of the tasks involved in the job and the conditions under which the employee will work. The manager may also develop a **job specification,** a statement describing the skills, education, and previous experience that the job requires. Exhibit 10.4 presents a description and a specification for the same job.

Recruiting and Selecting New Employees

recruiting
Process of attracting appropriate applicants for an organization's jobs

The next step is to match the job specification with an actual person or selection of people. This is done through **recruiting,** the process of attracting suitable candidates for an organization's jobs. Recruiters are specialists on the human resources staff who are responsible for locating these candidates. They use a variety of methods and resources,

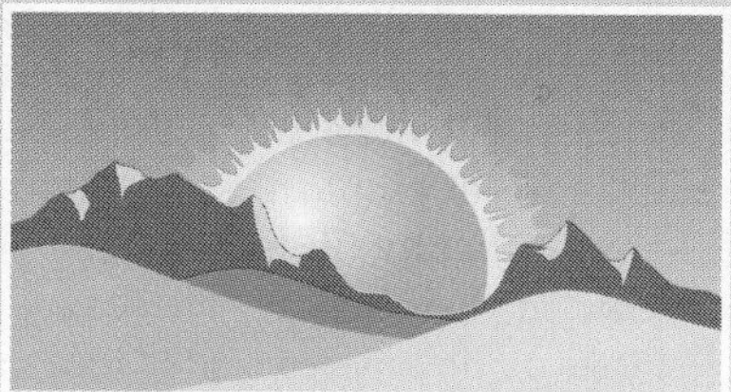

SUNNYVALE GENERAL HOSPITAL

Job Description and Specifications

Job Title: Job Analyst

Job Code: 166.088

Date: September 1, 1999

Job Location: Human Resources Department

Supervisor: Anitra Jacobson

Job Description:

Job Summary
Collects and develops job analysis information through interviews, questionnaires, observation, or other means. Provides other human resources specialists with needed information.

Job Duties
Designs job analysis schedules and questionnaires. Collects job information. Writes job descriptions and job specifications. Performs other duties as assigned by supervisors.

Working Conditions
Works mostly in an office setting. Travels to hospital clinics in county from one to three days per month. Travels around each work site collecting job information.

Job Specifications:

Skill Factors
Education: College degree required.

Experience: At least one year as job analyst trainee, recruiter, or other professional assignment in personnel area.

Communication: Oral and written skills should demonstrate ability to summarize job data succinctly.

Effort Factors
Physical Demands: Limited to those normally associated with clerical jobs: sitting, standing, and walking.

Mental Demands: Extended visual attention is needed to observe jobs. Initiative and ingenuity are mandatory since job receives only general supervision. Ability to analyze and synthesize large amounts of abstract information into job descriptions, job specifications, and job standards is essential.

EXHIBIT 10.4

Sample Job Description and Job Specification

A job description lists the tasks the job involves and the conditions under which those tasks are performed. A job specification spells out the characteristics—skills, education, and experience,—of the ideal candidate for the job.

including internal candidates, newspaper advertising, public and private employment agencies, union hiring halls, college campuses and career offices, trade shows, corporate "headhunters" who try to attract people at other companies, and referrals from employees or colleagues in the industry. Although Microsoft has a recruiting staff of some 80 people, human resources director Dave Pritchart says that about 30 percent of all new software developers are referred by current employees.[12]

When recruiters have difficulty finding qualified candidates in the immediate area, they become more creative in their efforts. They may advertise in areas where a similar business has recently closed or downsized, enter into cooperative arrangements with vocational schools that offer training in desired skills, look abroad for people with the needed skills, or rehire previous employees. They may even offer a bounty. For example, BBI Professional Placement Group in Dallas will pay $2,000 to anyone who brings the company a qualified individual who ends up taking a permanent position with one of BBI's clients. Deloitte & Touche pays up to $5,000.[13] Such is the demand for highly skilled workers today. The shortage is even causing some small companies to turn away business, thereby limiting their ability to grow.[14]

One of the fastest-growing recruitment resources for both large and small businesses is the Internet. Today over 5,800 companies recruit online through their Web sites, as well as through some 3,500 online recruiting services. National Data Corporation estimates that its online recruiting effort reduces average recruiting costs by as much as one-half because it allows the company to use less paid advertising and fewer corporate headhunters. Software maker Oracle even staged an online career fair at its Web site to attract a large number of candidates to support the company's rapid growth. These companies and many others believe that online recruiting allows them to access a broader selection of applicants, target specific types of applicants more easily, reach highly skilled applicants more efficiently, and give applicants quicker responses to their queries. However, there are also drawbacks. The biggest complaint is that companies must process more applications than ever before. Another is that not everyone has Internet access, making it especially difficult to reach nontechnical people.[15]

The Hiring Process After exploring at least one—but usually more—of the available recruitment channels to assemble a pool of applicants, the human resources department may spend weeks and sometimes months on the hiring process. Most companies go through

Like most other department stores, Filene's hires part-time temporary employees to help out during the winter holidays, when business is brisk. When business slows down again, these employees are usually laid off or scheduled to work fewer hours.

the same basic stages in the hiring process as they sift through applications to come up with the person or people they want.

The first stage is to select a small number of qualified candidates from all of the applications received. A person may be chosen on the basis of a standard application form that all candidates fill out, or on the basis of a **résumé**—a summary of education, experience, and personal data compiled by the applicant. Sometimes both sources of information are used. Many organizations now use computer scanners to help them quickly sort through résumés and weed out those that don't match the requirements of the job.

résumé
Brief description of education, experience, and personal data compiled by a job applicant

The second stage in the hiring process is to interview each candidate to clarify qualifications and to fill in any missing information. Another goal of the interview is to get an idea of the applicant's personality and ability to work well with others. Depending on the type of job at stake, candidates may also be asked to move to a third stage, taking a test or a series of tests.

Is It True?

Half of all workers hired in the past decade are minorities.

After the initial interviews comes the third stage, when the best candidates may be asked to meet with someone in the human resources department who will conduct a more probing interview. For higher-level positions, candidates may go through a series of interviews with managers, co-workers, and the employees who will make up the successful candidate's staff. In the fourth step, the employee's supervisor evaluates the candidates, sometimes in consultation with a higher-level manager, the human resources department, and staff. During the fifth stage, the employer checks the references of the top few candidates. The employer may also check the candidates' education, previous employment, criminal records, or motor vehicle records. A growing number of employers are also checking candidates' credit histories, a practice that is drawing criticism as a violation of privacy.[16] In the sixth stage, the supervisor selects the most suitable person for the job. Now the search is over—provided the candidate accepts the offer.

Two of the stages in the hiring process, interviewing and testing, can both play a crucial role in hiring decisions, as discussed in the following sections. You will also glimpse the legal land mines that human resources managers must avoid in the course of screening job applicants and making hiring decisions.

Interviewing Useful interviews follow established, standardized procedures tailored to the company's needs. If you were a member of the human resources department preparing to interview a candidate, you would provide a comfortable, private environment for the meeting, allow sufficient time, and develop a set of questions that are based on the candidate's résumé and application as well as on your job analysis. Thorough preparation helps you set the stage for a productive interview.

During the course of the interview, keep the conversation focused on job-related issues in order to determine whether the person is right for the job and whether the job is right for the person. Ask about the applicant's background and work experience, professional goals, and related skills and interests. Although it is important to ask each candidate standard questions so that all can be evaluated on the same basis, good interviewers are also adept at following up with questions that probe specific areas in more depth. The questions in Exhibit 10.5 are typical. Also leave time for the candidate to ask you questions. Listening, building trust, and encouraging communication can help interviewers gather the important information needed for hiring decisions as well as helping the candidate evaluate whether the job is right for him.

Testing One much-debated aspect of the hiring process is testing—not just the tests that prospective employers give job applicants, but any devices that they may use to evaluate employees when making job decisions. Tests are used to gauge abilities, intelligence, interests, and sometimes even physical condition and personality.

EXHIBIT 10.5

Interview Questions

These are some of the most important questions that should be asked during a job interview.

EMPLOYMENT HISTORY

- Why do you wish to change employment?
- What do you like the least about your current position?
- What goals do you expect to achieve in your current job that you have not already accomplished?

THE NEW POSITION

- What are your expectations of this position?
- What do you anticipate being the most challenging aspects of this job?
- What can you contribute to this position?
- What would be your first goal in this position?
- How would you handle a 10 percent budget cut in your area of responsibility?

CAREER GOALS

- What are your long-term goals?
- How have you moved from each stage in your career to the next?
- What factors are most important to you in terms of job satisfaction?
- When do you anticipate a promotion?

COMPANY "FIT"

- Are you a team player or are you more satisfied working alone?
- Do you praise the contributions of others?
- What characteristics do you believe an outstanding employee should possess? A peer? A supervisor?
- How would you handle a "problem" employee?
- How would you deal with a colleague who has competed with you for a position, feels better qualified than you, and now works for you?

Many companies rely on preemployment testing to determine whether applicants are suited to the job and whether they'll be worth the expense of hiring and training. Companies use three main procedures: job-skills testing, psychological testing, and drug testing. Job-skills tests are the most common type, designed to assess competency or specific abilities needed to perform a job. For example, the three big U.S. carmakers contract with HR Strategies to test production applicants on reading and math skills, manual dexterity, understanding of spatial relations, and ability to work in teams.[17] Other companies use *assessment centers* to simulate work assignments in an officelike setting and test management candidates on such elements as decision making and interpersonal skills.

Psychological tests usually take the form of questionnaires filled out by job applicants. These tests can be used to assess overall intellectual ability, attitudes toward work, interests, managerial potential, or personality characteristics—including dependability, commitment, and motivation. People who favor psychological testing say that it can predict how well employees will actually perform on the job. For example, Spirit Rent-A-Car uses a combination of personality and aptitude tests to give the company a better idea of whether a candidate is outgoing and likes meeting people—both crucial traits for effective salespeople.[18] However, critics say that such tests are ineffective and potentially discriminatory. Human resources managers who use preemployment tests must administer them to all candidates for the same position, make sure that results accurately measure qualities related to job performance, and never rely only on test results in hiring decisions.

To avoid the increased costs and reduced productivity associated with drug abuse in the workplace (estimated to cost industry some $100 billion a year), some employers also require applicants to be tested for drug use. Studies have shown that drug users have greater absenteeism rates, are involved in significantly more on-the-job accidents, and incur much higher medical costs than employees who do not use drugs. According to the U.S. Department of Labor, about 62 percent of all employees of large companies work for firms that use drug testing. The figures are somewhat lower for employees of smaller firms.[19] A separate study by the American Management Association found that 96 percent of firms that test for drug use will not hire applicants who test positive.[20]

The legal aspects of drug testing vary from state to state, and they continue to change. Some states prohibit drug testing by private employers, whereas others severely limit the situations in which testing can be used. On the other hand, the U.S. government mandates that certain government employees and employees of federal contractors undergo drug screening. In any case, it is important to make sure that applicants sign a waiver consenting to the testing, that the testing be conducted reliably and accurately, and that the results be kept confidential. Furthermore, those who test positive should be given an opportunity for a retest.

Hiring and the Law Federal and state laws and regulations govern many aspects of the hiring process. In particular, employers must be careful to avoid discrimination in the wording of their application forms, in interviewing, and in testing. They must also obtain sufficient information about employees to avoid becoming the target of a negligent-hiring lawsuit. For example, a trucking company would check applicants' driving records to avoid hiring a new trucker with poor driving skills. As we will see, striking the right balance can be quite a challenge.

SCREENING EMPLOYEES Application forms typically include questions about a person's job experience and may also include questions about matters that are not strictly job related (outside activities and so on). Questions about unrelated factors such as marital status, age, and religion violate the Equal Employment Opportunity Commission's regulations because they may lead to discrimination. In addition, questions about whether the person is married or has children, whether he or she owns or rents a home, what caused a physical disability, whether the person belongs to a union, whether he or she has ever been arrested, and when the person attended school are not allowed. The exception is when such information relates to a bona fide occupational qualification for the specific job.

Since the Immigration Reform and Control Act was passed in 1986, employers must also be wary of asking too few questions. Almost all U.S. companies are forbidden to hire illegal aliens and must verify that the newly hired are legally eligible to work. However, the act also prohibits discrimination in hiring on the basis of national origin or citizenship status, resulting in a sticky situation for many employers trying to determine their applicants' citizenship. Consider Monfort, a Colorado beefpacking company. After being charged with employing over 300 illegal aliens, the company launched an investigation into whether any remaining employees had false citizenship papers. Monfort was then fined $45,576 for asking employees overly intrusive questions. To combat such problems, the Immigration and Naturalization Service (INS) now helps employers check workers' papers via computer, and it assists with finding legal workers to replace illegal ones.[21]

NEGLIGENT HIRING Violence in the workplace is an increasing threat that can harm employees and customers, hurt productivity, and lead to expensive lawsuits and higher health-care costs. More than 1 million physical assaults and thousands of homicides occur at work each year. If an employer fails to prevent "preventable violences," that employer will likely be found liable. This means that companies need to be especially careful about negligent hiring.[22] In one case, Saks Fifth Avenue hired an undercover security officer at its flagship store in New York without adequately checking the man's background. After he raped a young woman executive twice in her office, it was discovered that the security officer had been convicted of sexually abusing an 11-year-old girl in Kentucky.[23]

This and similar cases emphasize the need for employers to conduct thorough background checks on job applicants, including verifying all educational credentials and previous jobs, accounting for any large time gaps between jobs, and checking references. Background checks are particularly important for jobs in which employees are in a position to possibly harm others. In these situations, the human resources department has to weigh the need for uncovering information against a respect for the privacy of applicants.

Training and Development

orientation
Session or procedure for acclimating a new employee to the organization

In one way or another, every new employee needs training. Each company has its own way of doing even routine procedures. To make sure that all new employees understand the company's goals, policies, and procedures, most large organizations and many small ones have well-defined **orientation** programs. Although they vary, such programs usually include information about company background and structure, equal opportunity practices, safety regulations, standards of employee conduct, employee compensation and benefit

THINKING ABOUT ETHICS

Employee Privacy versus Company Security

Companies have the right—and, to some extent, the obligation—to protect themselves against lawsuits, theft, and high costs; to protect their employees against unsafe conditions; and to protect their customers against unhealthy and faulty products. However, some people have criticized the methods companies use to uphold these rights. Of particular concern is preemployment testing.

Should employers be allowed to test job applicants and employees to ensure that they won't expose companies to undue risk? Many employers think so. Some companies are concerned about employee abuse of drugs and alcohol, which can impair productivity and pose a safety hazard to others. Although some states have laws restricting drug testing, firms frequently try to screen out substance abusers by testing prospective (and sometimes current) employees. However, critics charge that a company's right to know is offset by an employee's "right to be let alone," in the now historic words of U.S. Supreme Court Justice Louis D. Brandeis. Such testing, say the critics, invades employee privacy, especially because it relates to what employees do when they're not on the job.

Another debated issue is the use of personality tests. Currently, approximately 18 percent of companies administer such tests to hourly workers and 22 percent test managers. Popular tests include the Minnesota Multiphasic Personality Inventory (MMPI), the Myer's-Briggs Personality Type Indicator, and the Enneagram. Most personality tests categorize applicants by significant personality traits according to their answers to a series of questions. Managers then use these results to help them decide whether the applicant's traits match the job requirements.

Handwriting analysis, or *graphoanalysis,* uses a very different method to achieve the same end. By studying applicant handwriting samples, experts say they can identify traits that can either help or hinder an applicant's ability to succeed in a particular job. At least 6,000 U.S. companies now use graphoanalysis, and the technique is widely used in Europe.

Advocates of such tests say that today's competitive business environment means that businesses need to be as certain as they can that they are hiring the right person for the job. Personality tests, they contend, help plans, work times, and other topics that newly hired employees might have questions about.[24] Orientation programs help new employees understand their role in the organization and feel more comfortable.

Most companies also offer training (and retraining), because employee competence has a direct effect on productivity and profits. At Wal-Mart, senior vice president of human resources Coleman Peterson believes that training is the most important part of human resources management. "Wal-Mart is in the business of keeping and growing talent," he says.[25] In most companies, training may take place at the work site, where an experienced employee oversees the trainee's on-the-job efforts, or in a classroom, where an expert lectures groups of employees. Northeast Tool & Manufacturing is one of a growing number of companies that invests heavily in employee training to become more competitive. Some of its employees are sent to a community college, others take remote courses in the plant via computers, and still others attend classes by professors who are brought into the plant. "I want these guys to be managing the business from the shop floor," says one Northeast Tool plant manager.[26]

Employee training may also involve a self-study component using training manuals and tests. For example, Fred Meyer discount stores use Computer Based Learning (CBL) in which employees access a series of multimedia training modules on CD-ROM at computer terminals.[27] Other companies are now distributing training and orientation materials via their intranets. For instance, Silicone Graphics publishes training documents such as product directions, diversity information, and sales tips in electronic formats that can be accessed by employees whenever they want. Electronic formatting also makes it much

employers make more informed decisions. However, some tests have gotten companies into legal disputes. Dayton Hudson, the nation's fourth largest retailer, was found to have violated the constitutional right to privacy of applicants for security guard positions when it administered a test containing questions regarding the applicants' religious beliefs and sexual practices. Any test asking questions that are not specifically job related can get an employer in hot water.

Preemployment testing will become even more controversial as more and better genetic tests are developed. Several tests are now available in the medical community that indicate whether a person has a genetic predisposition toward certain diseases like colon or breast cancer. As genetic tests are refined and expanded, more companies may require their use to determine which employees have a greater risk of high medical bills. These companies could then limit employee medical coverage or deny employment altogether. Although at least two bills on genetic privacy issues were introduced in Congress in 1997, so far no action has been taken.

It is difficult to fault companies for trying to make their products safer, their work sites more secure, and their costs less burdensome. However, few companies have adopted formal policies regarding employee privacy, which leaves room for abuse. Many employee-privacy issues have yet to be tested in court, and privacy laws vary from state to state. However, one thing is certain: Drug, personality, and genetic testing will present businesses with significant ethical challenges for years to come.

QUESTIONS FOR CRITICAL THINKING

1. Although many personality tests are widely recognized for their accuracy, how might the use of such tests actually be detrimental to the company's competitive position?
2. Do employees have an ethical obligation to inform their employers of physical or mental health conditions that could prove costly to the company over time?

TRW screens job applicants carefully to hire employees who will help the company fill its mission and achieve its strategic goals.

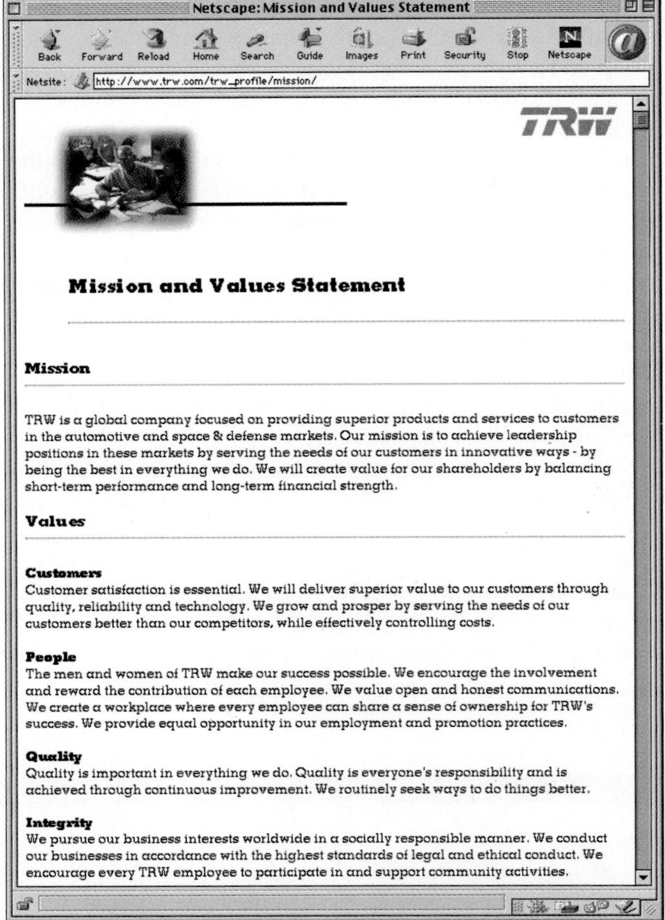

easier for companies to update training materials and reduce distribution costs. Exhibit 10.6 explains additional benefits of intranet training.[28]

A growing number of companies are helping their employees while they help themselves by offering college degree programs. For instance, telecommunications firm Nynex pays for 1,000 employees to attend college courses one day each week. By completing a 4-year program, employees earn an associate degree in telecommunications technology. Their enhanced skills mean better job opportunities, and Nynex believes that the more highly skilled work force boosts its bottom line.[29] American Express, America West Airlines, and Caribbean Hotel Management Services offer similar programs.[30]

Managers, too, must continue learning throughout their professional lives if they are to remain effective in the face of ever-changing management challenges. To address such needs, many organizations arrange for management training and development programs to sharpen their managers' skills. United Parcel Service has taken a unique approach by placing senior managers in not-for-profit organizations for a 4-week period. UPS has found that the program exposes managers to new experiences and situations that help them develop the people skills and caring needed to work with an increasingly diversified work force. At the same time, the not-for-profit agencies benefit from the managers' expertise.[31]

In response to the pressures of globalization and the need for a highly skilled work force, many U.S. businesses, including Kodak and Motorola, are also partnering with

EXHIBIT 10.6

Ten Reasons to Use Intranets for Training

1. *Consistency.* The same training materials can be used by any employee.
2. *Pull versus push approach.* Employees can *pull* only the information they need onto their desktops, rather than the HR department *pushing* information that doesn't apply to them through a large print manual.
3. *Interactivity.* Discussion groups, comprehension tests, and other forms of two-way communication can be incorporated into training manuals.
4. *Ease and low cost of updates.* Online publications can be updated continually, easily, and at much less expense than print publications.
5. *User-friendly interface.* "Point-and-click" navigation enables users to easily find the information they seek, making them more likely to use that information.
6. *Centralization.* Training information can be accessed anytime, from any networked computer, at home, in the office, or on the road.
7. *Simplicity in creation and maintenance.* Most Intranet sites can be created with a minimum of programming expertise, and support staff can easily make changes once a site is developed.
8. *Keeping up with your work force.* Younger employees are becoming more accustomed to receiving information through electronic media, and less willing to receive it through slides or print.
9. *Flexibility.* Once your site is in place, you can continue to build a library of training and reference materials, increasing the value of your site as it evolves.
10. *Potential.* As technology continues to evolve, more features, such as real-time training for geographically scattered employees, will be available.

schools to prepare students at all levels for future jobs. The U.S. subsidiaries of Siemens, a Munich-based producer of high-tech goods and services, spend $3 million to $4 million annually on school-to-work programs, and Chevron spends almost $8 million a year to support education. Many companies with fewer than 100 employees also invest in training and apprenticeships for students because they recognize that the financial commitment will pay off in the future.[32]

Appraising Employee Performance

When should an employee be given a raise in pay? When should someone be promoted, demoted, transferred, or let go? The answers to such questions can be obtained by evaluating the employee's performance—but how should an employee's work be evaluated?

Many companies have developed **performance appraisal** systems to objectively evaluate employees according to set criteria. Such systems promote fairness because their standards are usually job related ("Rhonda turns in weekly reports on time" rather than "Rhonda's always bustling around the office, so she must be doing an efficient job"). When performance appraisals are used, the standards are written down so that both employee and supervisor understand what is expected and are therefore able to determine whether

performance appraisal
Evaluation of an employee's work according to specific criteria

UNDERSTANDING THE HIGH-TECH REVOLUTION

It Sure Would Be Nice to Learn Algebra This Way

Training employees is always necessary and often expensive. Whether the subject is algebra or advertising strategy, people often learn things long before they actually need to apply them. So when it's time to use this information on the job, most people have forgotten much of what they learned. Moreover, managers are concerned about the expense of pulling people off their jobs and sending them to sit in training rooms so that they can learn new information and skills. For example, Hewlett-Packard used to spend $5 million every time it brought its worldwide sales force together to learn about new products.

Now, along with other leading-edge companies, HP is responding to such problems by completely redefining the way it trains employees. Rather than separating training from the actual job, innovators are working to make learning a part of the job. One key to this approach is changing the emphasis from the teaching process to the learning process—and computers are playing an important role.

As the world's largest management-consulting firm, Andersen Consulting believes that its most important asset is the accumulated knowledge of its work force. As the firm's 27,000 consultants work with clients around the world, they add to Andersen's storehouse of experience. However, the company's global reach presents a huge challenge: How can employees in Chicago share their skills with employees in Frankfurt or Tokyo? Andersen Consulting uses The Knowledge Xchange system, a worldwide, computerized learning network that stores the company's accumulated knowledge and skills, letting any Andersen consultant tap into this vast treasure chest. Rather than sitting in classrooms learning about all the various things the company can teach them, the consultants get the information they need when they need it. For instance, an employee needing to learn about a particular manufacturing technology for a client project can quickly identify which other employees have experience in that area and then see what they've already learned about it.

In a similar approach, HP's learning network—dubbed the Hewlett-Packard Interactive Network (HPIN)—brings instructors and learners together for live sessions, even when the participants are located around the globe. In addition to making the learning process more effective, the computer network has cut that $5 million new-product training cost to just $85,000. The salespeople who need to learn about new products spend far less time traveling and sitting in classrooms, so they can spend more time doing what they're supposed to do—selling those new products.

QUESTIONS FOR CRITICAL THINKING

1. What steps can managers take to make sure that computer-based training programs are delivering consistently high-quality training?
2. What other types of industries could benefit from a database like Andersen's Knowledge Xchange?

the work is being done adequately. Most formal systems also require regular, written evaluations of each employee's work (see Exhibit 10.7). These evaluations provide a record of the employee's performance, which may protect the company in cases of disputed *terminations.* Finally, many performance appraisal systems require the employee to be rated by several people (including more than one supervisor and perhaps several co-workers). This practice further promotes fairness by correcting for the possible bias that might influence one person's appraisal.

The biggest problem with appraisal systems is finding a way to measure performance. Productivity is the ultimate criterion, but it's not always easy to measure. In a production job, the person who types the most pages of acceptable copy or who assembles the most defect-free microprocessors in a given amount of time is clearly the most productive. However, how does an employer evaluate the productivity of the registration clerk at a hotel or the middle manager at a large television station? Although the organization's overall productivity can be measured (number of rooms booked per night, number of viewers per hour), often the employer can't directly relate the results to any one employee's efforts.

Name ______ *Title* ______ *Service Date* ______ *Date* ______
Location ______ *Division* ______ *Department* ______
Length of Time in Present Position ______ *Period of Review* *From:* ______ *To:* ______ *Appraised by* ______
Title of Appraisor ______

Area of Performance	*Comment*	*Rating*
Job Knowledge and Skill *Understands responsibilities and uses background for job. Adapts to new methods/techniques. Plans and organizes work. Recognizes errors and problems.*		*5 4 3 2 1*
Volume of Work *Amount of work output. Adherence to standards and schedules. Effective use of time.*		*5 4 3 2 1*
Quality of Work *Degree of accuracy–lack of errors. Thoroughness of work. Ability to exercise good judgment.*		*5 4 3 2 1*
Initiative and Creativity *Self-motivation in seeking responsibility and work that needs to be done. Ability to apply original ideas and concepts.*		*5 4 3 2 1*
Communication *Ability to exchange thoughts or information in a clear, concise manner. Dealing with different organizational levels of clientele.*		*5 4 3 2 1*
Dependability *Ability to follow instructions and directions correctly. Performs under pressure. Reliable work habits.*		*5 4 3 2 1*
Leadership Ability/Potential *Ability to guide others to the successful accomplishment of a given task. Potential for developing subordinate employees.*		*5 4 3 2 1*

5. *Outstanding*	*Employee who consistently exceeds established standards and expectations of the job.*
4. *Above Average*	*Employee who consistently meets established standards and expectations of the job. Often exceeds and rarely falls short of desired results.*
3. *Satisfactory*	*Generally qualified employee who meets job standards and expectations. Sometimes exceeds and may occasionally fall short of desired expectations. Performs duties in a normally expected manner.*
2. *Improvement Needed*	*Not quite meeting standards and expectations. An employee at this level of performance is not quite meeting all the standard job requirements.*
1. *Unsatisfactory*	*Employee who fails to meet the minimum standards and expectations of the job.*

I have had the opportunity to read this performance appraisal.

Signature ______ *Date* ______

How long has this employee been under your supervision? ______

Signature of Supervisor ______ *Date* ______

EXHIBIT 10.7

Sample Performance Appraisal Form

Many companies use forms like this one to ensure performance appraisals are as objective as possible.

Thus, additional criteria, such as customer satisfaction, the ability to meet goals, employee behavior toward co-workers and customers, job knowledge, motivation, and skills, are needed to help judge employee performance. Keep in mind that the ultimate goal of performance appraisals is not to judge employees, but rather to improve business.

THE ROLE OF COMPENSATION

compensation
Money, benefits, and services paid to employees for their work

In return for their services, employees receive **compensation,** a combination of payments, benefits, and employer services. Although it isn't the only factor in motivating employees, proper compensation plays an important role. In fact, many people use compensation as a yardstick for measuring their success in the world of work.

Wage and Salary Administration

On what basis should employees be paid? How much should they be paid? When should they be paid? These questions relate to wage and salary administration, one of the major responsibilities of the human resources department.

wages
Cash payment based on the number of hours the employee has worked or the number of units the employee has produced

Wages versus Salaries Many blue-collar (production) and some white-collar (management and clerical) employees receive compensation in the form of **wages,** which are based on a calculation of the number of hours the employee has worked, the number of units he or she has produced, or a combination of both time and productivity. Wages provide a direct incentive to an employee: The more hours worked or the more pieces completed, the higher the employee's pay. Moreover, employers in the United States must comply with the Fair Labor Standards Act of 1938, which sets a minimum hourly wage for most employees and mandates overtime pay for employees who work longer than 40 hours a week. Most states also have minimum wage laws intended to protect employees not covered by federal laws or to set higher wage floors.[33]

salaries
Fixed weekly, monthly, or yearly cash compensation for work

Employees whose output is not always directly related to the number of hours worked or the number of pieces produced are paid **salaries.** Like wages, salaries base compensation on time, but the unit of time is a week, two weeks, a month, or a year. Salaried employees such as managers normally receive no pay for the extra hours they sometimes put in; overtime is simply part of their obligation. However, they do get a certain amount of leeway in their working time.

comparable worth
Concept of equal pay for jobs that are equal in value to the organization and require similar levels of education, training, and skills

Both wages and salaries are, in principle, based on the contribution of a particular job to the company. Thus, a sales manager, who is responsible for bringing in sales revenue, is paid more than her secretary, who handles administrative tasks but doesn't sell or supervise. However, in recent years, human resources managers have grappled with the concept of comparable worth. **Comparable worth** theory contends that although different jobs may be of equal value to the organization, some jobs, especially those held by women, are paid a lower rate than others.[34] Under a comparable worth system, men and women who perform jobs that entail similar levels of education, training, and skills receive the same pay. Advocates of laws mandating comparable worth want to ensure that wages for jobs traditionally held by women are brought in line with the value they contribute to the organization. However, opponents say that comparable worth laws would increase labor costs and require new, more complex methods of setting compensation.

Is It True?

U.S workers are paid more than workers in other parts of the world.

Pay varies widely by position, industry, and location. For example, a credit manager can command better pay in New York City than in Salt Lake City. Among the best-paid employees in the world are chief executive officers of large U.S. corporations. In 1996 the mean CEO pay at the largest U.S. companies was $2,375,620 (including bonuses, stock options, and other long-term compensation), whereas the average U.S. employee received pay of about $27,000. As Exhibit 10.8 shows, CEO compensation has risen more rapidly than that of other white-collar employees every year since 1991.[35] And during the 1980s, CEO pay grew 212 percent, outpacing growth in earnings per share (company revenue per share of stock) by a wide margin.[36] Employees are baffled and angry that chief executives con-

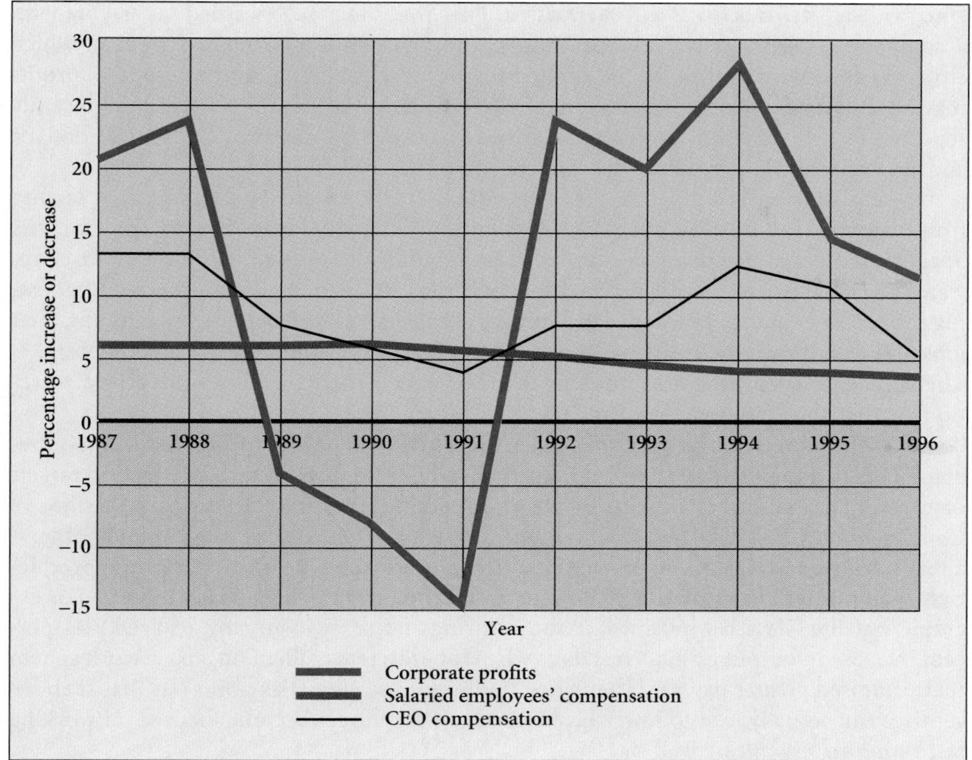

EXHIBIT 10.8

Compensation Differences Between CEOs and Employees

The disparity compensation for CEOs and workers has stirred much debate recently. However, new compensation systems have slowed the growth of CEO pay.

tinue to make big money even as they lay off massive numbers of employees. As a result, more companies are linking executive compensation to overall company performance. For example, the CEO of BankAmerica was awarded stock options that can't be exercised unless the company's stock price increases substantially.[37] Another method is the *value-based pay system,* in which compensation is based in part on whether or not returns to shareholders meet expected targets.[38]

Incentive Programs Johnson & Johnson and many other companies around the world are concerned with productivity. To encourage employees to be more productive, innovative, and committed to their work, companies often provide managers and employees with **incentives,** cash payments that are linked to specific individual, group, and companywide goals; overall productivity; and company success. In other words, achievements, not just activities, are made the basis for payment. Incentives are even more common now that companies are becoming more team-oriented.

incentives
Cash payments to employees who produce at a desired level or whose unit (often the company as a whole) produces at a desired level

BONUSES AND COMMISSIONS For both salaried and wage-earning employees, one type of incentive compensation is the **bonus,** a payment in addition to the regular wage or salary. As an incentive to reduce turnover during the year, some firms pay an annual year-end bonus, amounting to a certain percentage of each employee's wages. Other cash bonuses are tied to company performance. Although such bonuses were once reserved for the executive and management levels, they are becoming increasingly available to employees at other levels as well.[39] In contrast, **commissions** are a form of compensation that pays employees a percentage of sales made. Used mainly for sales staff, they may be either the sole compensation or an incentive payment in addition to a regular salary.

bonus
Cash payment in addition to the regular wage or salary, which serves as a reward for achievement

commissions
Payments to employees equal to a certain percentage of sales made

profit sharing
System for distributing a portion of the company's profits to employees

gain sharing
Plan for rewarding employees not on the basis of overall profits but in relation to achievement of goals such as cost savings from higher productivity

pay for performance
Accepting a lower base pay in exchange for bonuses based on meeting production or other goals

Profit Sharing and Gain Sharing Employees may be rewarded for staying with a company and encouraged to work harder through **profit sharing,** a system in which employees receive a portion of the company's profits. Depending on the company, profits may be distributed quarterly, semiannually, or annually. For example, when Intel recently reported record year-end profits, the company paid out hundreds of millions of dollars, equaling roughly 33 percent of the average employee's base salary.[40]

Gain sharing is similar to profit sharing, but the rewards are tied to cost savings from meeting specific goals such as quality and productivity improvement. For example, Springfield Remanufacturing, a company that rebuilds diesel engines, links employee rewards to goals such as increasing inventory accuracy, diversifying the business, and boosting profits. The financial incentive encourages employees to find better ways of doing their jobs and to improve their own skills, which also makes the company more competitive.[41] The success of such programs often depends on how closely incentives are linked to actions within the employee's control.

One approach to gain sharing, often referred to as **pay for performance,** requires employees to accept a lower base pay, but it rewards them if they reach production targets or other goals. Sandra O'Neal, principal at consulting firm Towers Perrin and author of *Compensation Challenges and Changes,* estimates that 30 percent of U.S. companies have already adopted at least some pay-for-performance measures. Many have realized productivity gains as well as greater flexibility in keeping employees during hard times.[42] For example, Safelite Glass, a windshield manufacturing and repair company, realized a 41 percent increase in output by glass installers when it began to pay them on a piecework system that promised greater pay for faster work.[43] However, some critics point out that such incentives can actually lead to lower quality because employees become focused on working fast rather than working well.

knowledge-based pay
Pay tied to an employee's acquisition of skills; also called skill-based pay

broadbanding
Payment system that uses wide pay grades, enabling the company to give pay raises without promotions

Knowledge-Based Pay and Broadbanding An approach to compensation being explored by such companies as Alcoa, TRW, and Westinghouse is **knowledge-based pay,** or skill-based pay, which is tied to employees' knowledge and abilities rather than to their job per se. Typically, the pay level at which a person is hired is pegged to his or her current level of skills; as the employee acquires new skills, the pay level goes up. Because a single employee can acquire the skills to perform a variety of jobs, knowledge-based pay systems can reduce staffing requirements. At the same time, because employees do not compete with each other to increase their pay through promotions, knowledge-based pay enhances teamwork, flexibility, and motivation.[44]

Broadbanding also allows companies to give pay raises without promoting employees. Instead of having many narrow pay grades, the company has fewer, broader pay grades. For example, instead of a range of $30,000 to $40,000 for a particular job, a broadband range may be $20,000 to $50,000. This approach allows today's flatter organizations to reward employees without having to move them up a hierarchy. It also allows companies to move employees to different positions without being restricted by the pay grades normally associated with specific jobs. Sears implemented a broadband system to encourage employees to consider how a job change could improve their personal development rather than just how much the job paid.

However, companies often find it difficult to change the way workers think about pay. For a long time, businesses have trained their employees to associate higher job grades with status, titles, and eligibility for additional benefits. Moreover, some critics say that broadbanding doesn't benefit employees but is just another way for companies to keep labor costs down. One study by compensation consulting firm William M. Mercer reported that under broadbanding employees' long-term career earnings actually decrease between 10 and 50 percent.[45]

Employee Benefits and Services

employee benefits Compensation other than wages, salaries, and incentive programs

Companies also regularly provide **employee benefits**—financial benefits other than wages, salaries, and incentives. For example, Starbuck's Coffee offers medical and dental insurance, vacation and holiday pay, stock options, discounts on Starbuck's products, and a free pound of Starbuck's coffee every week. The benefits package is available to part-time as well as full-time employees, so Starbuck's attracts and retains good people at every level.[46]

In the following sections, we discuss only the benefits most commonly provided by employers. Be aware, however, that benefits and services are undergoing considerable change to meet the shifting needs of the work force. Today's work force is much less homogeneous than in the past, and a two-career family has far different needs for benefits. Instead of two sets of insurance benefits, for example, a two-career family may prefer one spouse to receive insurance and the other to receive day-care assistance. In addition, a growing number of employers, including IBM, Barnes & Noble, Walt Disney, and the city of Boston, offer health-care coverage for domestic partners of homosexual employees. Some companies extend these partner benefits to unmarried heterosexual employees, as well.[47]

Insurance Although it is entirely optional, insurance is the most popular employee benefit. Many businesses offer substantial compensation in the form of life and health insurance, but dental plans, disability insurance, and long-term-care insurance are also gaining in popularity. Often a company will negotiate a group insurance plan for employees and pay most of the premium costs. However, many managed-care companies have sought premium increases of 4 to 8 percent in the latter part of the 1990s. Combined with a tight job market, many executives and economists expect health-care costs to increase dramatically. Today only about 61 percent of employees are covered by a company health plan. The number is expected to dip even further as costs rise.[48]

Faced with exploding costs, many companies now require employees to pay part of their insurance premiums or more of the actual doctor bills. In addition, more companies are hiring part-time and temporary workers who typically receive very few company benefits. Nonetheless, some companies like Starbuck's provide benefits because it discourages employee turnover. Starbucks CEO Charles Schultz figures that recruiting, interviewing, and training a new employee costs more than two years of medical coverage for an employee who stays with the company.[49]

Retirement Benefits In the past, few people were able to save enough money in the course of their working years for their retirement. The main purpose of the Social Security Act was to provide basic support to those who could not accumulate the retirement money they would need later in life. Nonetheless, nearly everyone who works regularly has become eligible for Social Security payments during retirement. This income is paid for by the Social Security tax, part of which is withheld by the employer from employees'

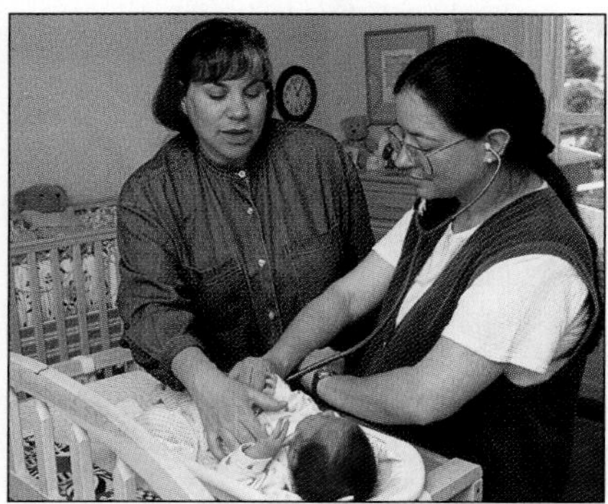

Some companies save costs by helping employees detect potentially serious health problems early on. Here a Registered Pediatric Nurse examines a newborn as part of the Home and Healthy postpartum home visit program that Eddie Bauer offers to all its new parents free of charge.

wages and part of which is paid by the employer. However, by 2011 the amount of Social Security payments to retiring baby boomers is expected to exceed the taxes paid in by a continually increasing amount. As a result, aging workers are likely to put off retirement and remain in the work force longer.[50]

pension plans
Company-sponsored programs for providing retirees with income

A variety of company-sponsored **pension plans** have been developed as a way of providing additional retirement security. However, the cost and complexity of such plans increased so dramatically during the past two decades that some employers began canceling them. As a result, fewer companies offer pension plans today than in the past.[51]

For those employees who do receive pension plans, most are funded by money that is set aside on a regular basis to pay retirement benefits in the future. Under *defined benefit plans,* the payments received upon retirement vary by age and length of service with the company. Such plans are regulated by the Employees' Retirement Income Security Act of 1974 (ERISA), which established a federal agency to insure the assets of pension plans. However, 80 percent of new pension plans are *defined-contribution plans,* in which employers make regular retirement contributions and employees are free to match some portion of that amount—usually 50 percent—by allocating a portion of their paycheck. The money is invested, and the employee receives payments after retirement based on the value of the accumulated funds. A popular plan today is the *401(k) plan,* in which employee contributions of up to $9,240 per year are excluded from federal and state income and Social Security taxes until the employee begins to draw on the account after retirement. Employees who work for very small companies or who are self-employed usually enjoy no such benefits and must bear the entire burden of saving for their retirement.[52]

employee stock-ownership plan (ESOP)
Program enabling employees to become partial owners of a company

Employee Stock-Ownership Plans Another employee benefit being offered by a number of companies is the **employee stock-ownership plan (ESOP),** under which a company places a certain amount of its stock in trust for some or all of its employees, with each employee entitled to a certain share. If the company does well, the ESOP may be a substantial employee benefit. An additional advantage of the ESOP is that it's free to the employee and nearly so to the employer (because companies offering such programs are eligible for a federal tax credit).

BEST OF THE WEB

Understanding Employee Ownership

Employee ownership through ESOPs and stock options has become a popular way for companies to reward and motivate employees in recent years. The National Center for Employee Ownership (NCEO) is a nonprofit organization dedicated to improving awareness of and participation in employee ownership programs. The NCEO's site on the World Wide Web contains useful information about employee ownership in the United States and foreign countries. Although there are pay services on the site, much of the information is free. Explore the site to learn more about the ownership programs covered in this chapter. After you read the brief introduction, follow the *Library* link for a comprehensive list of topics.
http://nceo.org

stock option plan
Program enabling employees to purchase a certain amount of stock at a discount after they have worked for the company a specified length of time or after the company's stock reaches a specific market price

A related method for tying employee compensation to company performance is the **stock option plan.** Stock options grant employees the right to purchase a certain amount of stock at a discount after they have worked at the company for a specified amount of time or after the stock has reached a certain market price. As Exhibit 10.9 shows, the number of companies offering stock to employees has boomed in recent years. Financial services companies Merrill Lynch and Morgan Stanley have each allocated about 40 percent of their stock to such plans.[53]

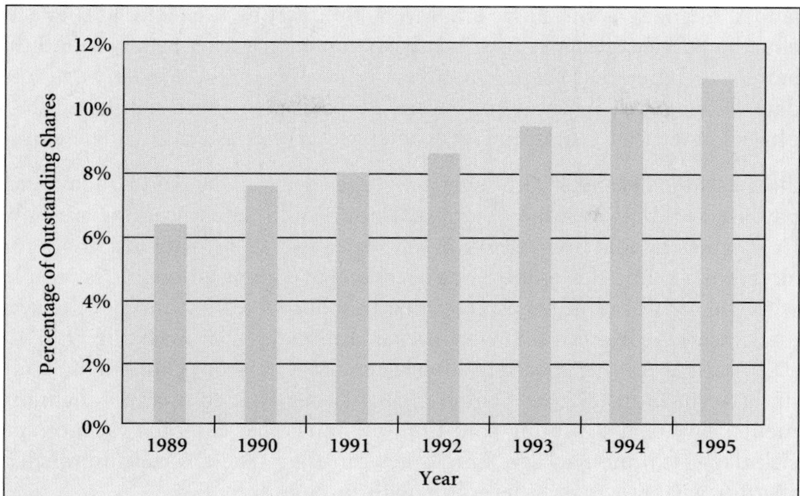

EXHIBIT 10.9

Employee Stock Ownership

The amount of stock allocated to employees through ESOPs and stock options is on the rise. This graph shows the amount allocated as a percentage of shares outstanding at the United States' largest publicly traded industrial and service companies.

However, just as stock ownership can create wealth for employees, it can also lead to financial loss. For example, Wal-Mart's stock took a dive in the mid-1990s, strongly affecting employees who depended on ownership plans and options for a portion of their pay. The stagnant stock price caused morale to sink as well. The number of shareholders who oppose employee stock-ownership plans is rising because many shareholders believe such plans reduce the value of their own stock. Nevertheless, because shareholders often earn from their investments many times the average increase in employee pay and benefits, firms likely will continue to offer their workers stock ownership and options.[54]

Family Benefits The Family Medical and Leave Act (FMLA), signed into law in 1993, requires employers of 50 or more workers to provide them with up to 12 weeks of unpaid leave per year for childbirth; adoption; or the care of oneself, a child, a spouse, or a parent with serious illness.[55] Some companies go even further than the law requires. For example, Johnson & Johnson provides on-site child care at two of its facilities and family-care leave of up to one year. In addition, about one-third of employers now have a paternity-leave program. Such family benefits are proving helpful to companies as well as workers in the form of higher employee morale, greater productivity, and lower absenteeism.[56]

Day care is another important family benefit, especially for two-career couples. Although only 10 percent of companies provide day-care facilities on the premises, 86 percent of companies surveyed by Hewitt & Associates offer child-care assistance. Types of assistance include dependent-care spending accounts and resource and referral (R&R) services, which help employees find suitable child care. Firms estimate that they save anywhere from $2.00 to $6.75 in lost productivity and employee absenteeism for every $1.00 they spend on R&R programs.[57] Moreover, Johnson & Johnson, IBM, Fel-Pro (a family-run automotive products company in Skokie, Illinois), and similar firms have conducted studies clearly showing that supporting employees with family-friendly policies leads to greater employee motivation, productivity, and retention.[58]

A related family issue is care for aging parents. An estimated 77 percent of large corporations offer some form of elder-care assistance, ranging from referral services that help find care providers to dependent-care allowances. Some companies will even agree to move elderly relatives when they transfer an employee to another location. For instance, du Pont moved one employee's in-laws from New York to North Carolina, where the employee was transferred. NationsBank has also moved older relatives of employees transferred.[59]

Although efforts by U.S. business to adopt more family-friendly policies have been lauded by many, some single employees are upset by the fact that they receive fewer benefits than their colleagues with families. Moreover, a recent study found that 81 percent of employees agree that single employees generally carry a heavier work load to accommodate the needs of married employees. Perhaps even more significant, 69 percent of employees agree that U.S. businesses can expect a backlash from single employees.[60]

Other Employee Benefits Although sometimes overlooked, paid holidays, sick pay, premium pay for working overtime or unusual hours, and paid vacations are important benefits. Companies handle holiday pay in various ways. To provide incentives for employee loyalty, most companies grant employees longer paid vacations if the employees have been with the organization for a prescribed number of years, although the average number of paid vacation days for U.S. workers is shrinking. It is now about 11.37 days, down from 12.17 days in 1997.[61] Sick-day allowances also vary from company to company, and from industry to industry (see Exhibit 10.10). Some U.S. companies, including Texas Instruments, have begun offering paid-time-off banks that combine vacation, personal use, and sick days into one package. Employees can then take a certain number of days off each year for whatever reason necessary, with no questions asked.[62]

Among the many other benefits that companies sometimes offer are sabbaticals, tuition loans and reimbursements, personal computers, financial counseling and legal services, assistance with buying a home, and paid expenses for spouses who travel with employees. Since 1994 Eddie Bauer has introduced more than 20 new benefits programs ranging from on-site mammography to emergency child-care services.[63] Xerox employees can even take paid leaves of absence to work for charitable organizations.[64]

EXHIBIT 10.10

Average Number of Sick Days by Industry

The average number of sick days employees are granted varies with the industry they work in, but the average employee does not use all of the sick days granted.

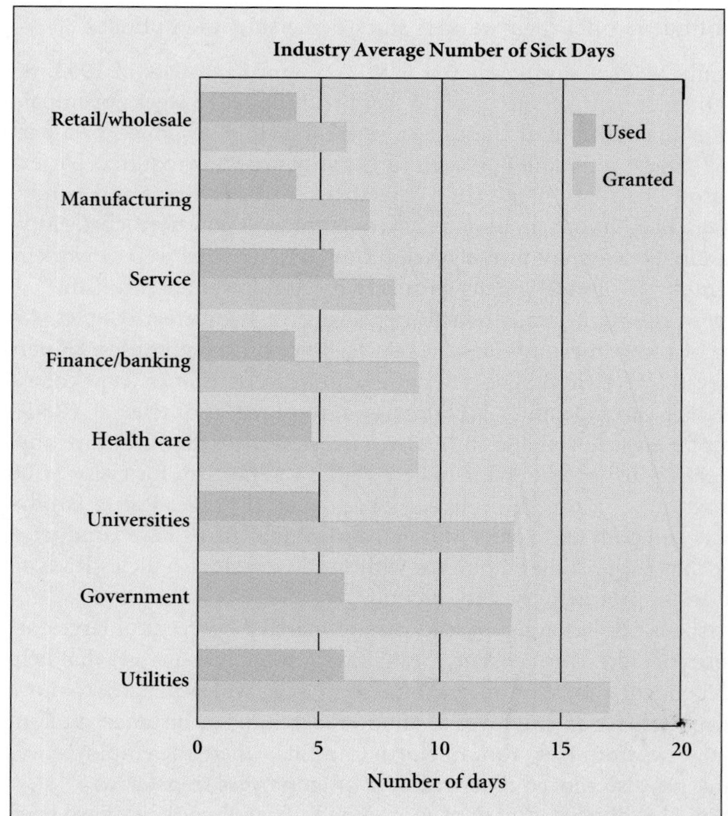

Benefits such as company cars and paid country club memberships are often referred to as perks, or perquisites. Since the 1980s, many U.S. companies have cut back on perks to save money. However, with today's tight job market, perks are being offered more frequently in order to attract and maintain the best managers.[65]

Flexible Benefits Until recently, most employee benefits came as a package with a particular job. Once hired, the employee got whatever insurance, paid holidays, pension plan, and other benefits the company had set up. However, a newer approach allows employees to pick their benefits—up to a certain dollar amount—to meet their particular needs. An employee with a young family might want extra life or health insurance, for example, and might feel no need for a pension plan. A single employee might pass up life insurance and choose a tax-deferred retirement plan. Another employee might "buy" an extra week or two of vacation time by giving up some other benefit. Such plans help smooth out imbalances in benefits received by single employees and workers who have families.[66]

Is It True?

Today $1 of every $9 spent in the United States goes to health care.

Health and Safety Programs

Health and safety programs reduce potential suffering and keep health-related losses to a minimum, which is why they're a major concern for human resources managers. By educating employees in safety procedures, setting and enforcing safety regulations, and redesigning work environments to minimize the potential for death, injury, and illness, businesses can make the workplace safer for employees and, at the same time, cut health-related losses. Many companies have hired specialists that use **ergonomics**—the study of human performance in relation to the tasks performed, the equipment used, and the environment—to design work areas that minimize physical strain on employees ranging from assembly workers to accountants. Another way companies contribute to the health and safety of their employees is by offering courses on stress management. Scoville Press, a printing company in Minnesota, has reduced its annual workers' compensation claims by as much as $140,000 through such initiatives.[67]

ergonomics
Study of how tasks, equipment, and the environment relate to human performance

The Reverend C. Alan Tyson counsels 1,600 workers as the chaplain for Hudson Foods.

In addition, businesses today are taking a more active role in maintaining employee health. For example, Johnson & Johnson has had great success with its Live for Life program. Participants receive an individualized health-risk profile and are encouraged to watch their diets, exercise, and give up smoking. The wellness program includes on-site gyms and healthy foods in the cafeteria.[68] According to the Wellness Councils of America, a not-for-profit group dedicated to promoting healthier lifestyles, over 81 percent of U.S. businesses with 50 or more employees have some form of health promotion program—the most popular being exercise, stop-smoking classes, back-care programs, and stress management.[69]

employee assistance program (EAP)
Company-sponsored counseling or referral plan for employees with personal problems

A number of companies are also instituting an **employee assistance program (EAP)** to help employees with personal problems, especially drug or alcohol dependence, or to refer them to others for help. Such programs have been reported to reduce (on the average) absenteeism by 66 percent, health-care costs by 86 percent, sickness benefits by 33 percent, and work-related accidents by 65 percent.[70] Some companies now even hire chaplains to help counsel employees on issues such as marital problems, depression, and financial difficulties, as well as to provide the kind of personal sympathy that may be difficult for some managers to give.[71]

Changes in Employment Status

Sometimes, despite the most rigorous planning, recruiting, selecting, and training, employees leave the jobs for which they were hired. Employees may decide to retire or may resign voluntarily to pursue a better opportunity. On the other hand, the company may take the initiative in making the change—by reassigning, promoting, or laying off employees. Whatever the reason, losing an employee usually means going to the trouble and expense of finding a replacement, whether from inside or outside the company.

Promoting and Reassigning Employees

When a person leaves the company or is promoted to a position of more responsibility, the company has to find someone else for the open job. Many companies prefer to look within the company for such candidates. In part, this "promote from within" policy allows a company to benefit from the training and experience of its own work force. This policy also rewards employees who have worked hard and demonstrated the ability to handle additional tasks. In addition, morale is usually better when a company promotes from within because employees see that they can advance.

However, a potential pitfall of promotion is that a person may be given a job beyond his or her competence. A common practice is for someone who is good at one kind of job to be made a manager, but the new position requires a completely different set of skills. Someone who consistently racks up the best sales in the company, for example, is not necessarily the person who should be promoted to sales manager. If the promotion is a mistake, the company not only loses its sales leader but also risks losing the employee altogether. People who can't perform well in a new job generally become demoralized and lose confidence in the abilities they do have. At the very least, support and training are needed to help promoted employees perform well.

One big issue these days is *relocation* of promoted and reassigned employees. In the past, companies transferred some employees fairly often, especially those being groomed for higher management positions. Now, however, fewer and fewer employees are willing to accept transfers. The reasons are many: the disruption of a spouse's career; the strong ties to family, friends, and community; the expense of relocating (buying and selling homes, planning around the reduction of a spouse's income, facing a higher cost of living in the new location); the availability of good schools and child care; and the fear that relocating won't be good for the employee's career. A recent survey of relocated employees found that 83 percent felt the move benefited the company, but only 53 percent felt that they personally benefited by it.[72]

To encourage employee relocation, many employers today are providing house-hunting trips, as well as moving, storage, transportation, and temporary living expenses. In addition, many employers are now helping spouses find good jobs in new locations, assisting transferees with home sales, providing school and day-care referral services, and sometimes reimbursing employees for spouses' lost wages or for financial losses resulting from selling and buying houses. Many companies are also reconsidering their transfer policies and asking employees to transfer only when it is absolutely necessary.

Downsizing and flattening organizations have left fewer opportunities for advancement through promotion. At the same time, the demands of family and personal life have made the added responsibility of management positions unattractive to some employees. As a result, some companies are motivating employees through *lateral transfers*—sideways moves from one department to another, such as from electrical engineering to quality control. Others offer employees challenging tasks in unfamiliar areas to broaden their experience. Still other approaches being used to motivate employees who have fewer chances for upward movement include overseas assignments, academic sabbaticals, and career-development programs.[73]

Terminating Employment

A company invests time, effort, and money in each new employee it recruits and trains. This investment is lost when an employee is removed by **termination**—permanently laying the employee off because of cutbacks or firing the employee for poor performance. Many companies facing a downturn in business have avoided large-scale layoffs by cutting administrative costs (curtailing travel, seminars, and so on), freezing wages, postponing new hiring, implementing job-sharing programs, or encouraging early retirement. However, sometimes a company has no alternative but to reduce the size of its work force, leaving the human resources department to handle layoffs and their resulting effects on both the terminated and the remaining employees.

termination
Act of getting rid of an employee through layoffs or firing

Layoffs **Layoffs** are the termination of employees for economic or business reasons unrelated to employee performance. To help ease the pain of layoffs, many companies are now providing laid-off employees with job-hunting assistance. *Outplacement* aids such as résumé-writing courses, career counseling, office space, and secretarial help are offered to laid-off executives and blue-collar employees alike. For example, AT&T has seven career resource centers that help laid-off workers match their qualifications with more than 100,000 job leads from other companies. The centers offer courses and tests to help employees decide what types of jobs are best for them. AT&T also recently offered 4,000 laid-off managers $10,000 each to be used for retraining, relocation, or financing a small business.[74]

layoffs
Termination of employees for economic or business reasons

Some companies have adopted no-layoff, or guaranteed-employment, policies. Employees may still be fired for consistently poor job performance, but in an economic downturn, they may be shifted to other types of jobs, perhaps at reduced pay, or given the chance to participate in work-sharing programs. These no-layoff policies help promote employee loyalty and motivation, which benefits the company over the long run. Rhino Foods realized the benefit of this when the company hit a downturn in the mid-1990s. Employees voluntarily took temporary jobs with other companies, which Rhino helped them find. If the companies paid lower wages than the employees normally received, Rhino made up the difference. Employees also kept their Rhino seniority, benefits, and accrued vacation time. When business picked up again, the employees returned. As a result of the exchange program, Rhino enjoys much higher employee morale, loyalty, and trust than it would had it laid off workers.[75]

employment at will
Employer's right to keep or terminate employees as it wishes

wrongful discharge
Firing an employee with inadequate advance notice or explanation

Firings and Employment at Will It has long been illegal for a U.S. company to fire employees because they are would-be union organizers, have filed a job-safety complaint, or are of a particular race, religion, gender, or age. Beyond these restrictions, the courts have traditionally held that any employee not covered by a contract may be fired "at will." **Employment at will** is the right of the employer to keep or terminate employees as it sees fit. Recently, however, a number of legal decisions have begun to alter this doctrine. The most far-reaching decisions have held that there may be an implied contract between employer and employee requiring that any firing be done "fairly." **Wrongful discharge** suits—lawsuits that contend the employee was fired without adequate advance notice or explanation—have been plentiful in light of the massive layoffs in recent years. Some fired employees have even argued that their being called "permanent" employees by the company should protect them from firing—or at least from unfair firing. To combat this problem, many companies require employees to sign an "employment at will" statement acknowledging that they may be fired at any time at the company's discretion.

Nevertheless, employment at will statements do not protect the company from discrimination lawsuits. In fact, there has been a 2,200 percent increase in the number of discrimination lawsuits filed in the past 20 years. Many of these suits are brought on the basis of racial or sexual discrimination. However, because companies have been laying off a disproportionate number of employees over 40, attorneys say that the largest increase is in suits based on age discrimination. For example, after laying off 12,000 mostly older workers, Westinghouse faced a class-action suit filed on behalf of 250 employees aged 40 or above, in addition to other individual lawsuits. The cost of legal defense in such cases typically ranges from $100,000 to $250,000, and that expense is on top of any damages, back pay, and plaintiff legal fees that the company may have to take care of if it loses the lawsuit.[76]

BEST OF THE WEB

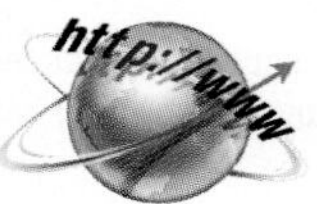

Discover a Gold Mine of Information at the Bureau of Labor Statistics

By now you are probably aware that the U.S government has a different agency for almost every purpose, and that many of these agencies gather facts and statistics on trends in the United States. Some would argue that this is unnecessary. However, when you want information about employment conditions, the Bureau of Labor Statistics (BLS) is a mighty good friend to have. The BLS Web site allows HR professionals, researchers, students, and anyone else who may be interested to access customized reports on workers, wages, employment, prices, and the economy in general. As a student, you may find this information helpful in research for your classes. And as a businessperson, the BLS Web site can help keep you up-to-date on trends in hiring, benefits, compensation, and more.
http://www.bls.gov

Retiring Employees

mandatory retirement
Required dismissal of an employee who reaches a certain age

The U.S. population is aging rapidly. For the business community, an aging population presents two challenges. The first is to give job opportunities to people who are willing and able to work but who happen to be past the traditional retirement age. Many older citizens are concerned about their ability to live comfortably on fixed retirement incomes. Others simply prefer to work. For several decades, many companies and industries had **mandatory retirement** policies that made it necessary for people to quit working as soon as they turned a certain age. Then in 1967 the federal Age Discrimination in Employment

When he was laid off after 30 years as vice president of Investigations and Fraud at Macy's, Jim Pallouras asked psychologist and outplacement specialist Dee Soder to help him assess his strengths and weaknesses. One of Soder's tests is to gauge how clients react to the big fish on her office wall, which she says is an indication of how comfortable they are conversing with strangers.

Act outlawed discrimination against anyone between the ages of 40 and 65. In 1986 Congress amended the act to prohibit mandatory retirement for most employees. As a corollary, employers are also forbidden to stop benefit contributions or accruals because of age.

However, as the baby-boom generation ages, it will be pushing hard for higher-level jobs held by older executives. The second challenge facing the business community is to encourage some older employees to retire early. One method a company may use to trim its work force is simply to offer its employees (often those nearing retirement) financial incentives to resign, such as enhanced retirement benefits or one-time cash payments. Inducing employees to depart by offering them financial incentives is known as a **worker buyout.** This method can be a lot more expensive than firing or laying off employees. For example, the $10,000 incentive included in the buyout packages offered to the 4,000 AT&T managers would cost the company $40,000,000 if they all accepted it. However, the method also has several advantages: The morale of the remaining employees is preserved because they feel less threatened about their own security, younger employees see a rise in their chances for promotion, and the risk of age-discrimination lawsuits is minimized.

worker buyout
Distribution of financial incentives to employees who voluntarily depart, usually undertaken in order to shrink the payroll

MANAGING GLOBAL HUMAN RESOURCES

Managing human resources successfully has become one of the toughest challenges of doing business internationally. When U.S. companies expand their operations in other parts of the world, they cannot expect to simply transplant their domestic HR policies. Rather, they must be prepared to adapt their human resources strategies to each local area. As vice president of HR services at Allied-Signal (a global manufacturer of aerospace, automotive, and machinery materials), Sally Griffith Egan says that when conducting business overseas, you must respect the nuances of the local business culture as you strive for consistency within the overall corporate culture. You must develop unique ways of managing global human resources that mesh with the company's long-term global business strategy.[77]

Many of the issues that HR professionals deal with in the global business environment are the same as those they face in their home country: recruiting qualified employees, going through the hiring process, motivating employees, compensating them, and helping them develop fulfilling and productive careers. However, going international adds an element of the unknown for many HR professionals. Differences in employee attitudes toward work, their expectations for compensation and benefits, their perceptions of power and status, their education and skill levels, the labor laws, the availability of training, and the culture in general demand flexible policies and procedures that can be adapted as needed. Many questions need to be asked: Are performance management systems suited to the needs of different countries and cultures? Are job descriptions common and culturally acceptable, and has the correct language been used? Would an expatriate be best able to fill the position, or should a local applicant be hired? What are the compensation and tax consequences of sending expatriates to international locations? What sort of training is needed? Is adequate health-care coverage available in the host country, and can it be linked with the company's existing health plan? How can the company's global strategy be linked to employee career development? Many other issues must be examined as well.

The key to successful international human resources management is to involve the HR department early on and in every step of international expansion efforts. Asking the right questions up front can help avoid a lot of problems down the road. Benchmarking with other companies that have expanded internationally can be very helpful, because it allows you to learn from the experiences and mistakes of others. In the long run, a well-planned, flexible human resources strategy will help assure the company's success in global markets.[78]

Summary of Learning Objectives

1. **List the six main functions of human resources departments.**
Human resources departments engage in planning, recruiting and selecting new employees, training and developing employees, appraising employee performance, compensating employees, and accommodating changes in employment status.

2. **Identify the six stages in the hiring process.**
The stages in the hiring process are (1) narrowing down the number of qualified candidates, (2) interviewing, (3) administering employment tests (optional), (4) evaluating candidates, (5) conducting reference checks, and (6) selecting the right candidate.

3. **Explain why companies use training and development programs.**
Companies use orientation training to help new employees learn procedures, policies, and goals. They use job-skills training to teach employees how to perform specific work tasks, and they use basic-skills training in mathematics and language to help employees master skills for working with each other and with customers and suppliers. Management-development programs are used to help new and experienced managers sharpen their skills.

4. **State two general methods for compensating employees.**
Employees are compensated through payments, such as wages and salaries, and through benefits and services.

5. **Describe the main components of employee pay.**
Wages (for hourly employees) and salaries (for nonhourly employees) are the most typical components of employee pay. Some employees also receive incentive payments (bonuses, commissions, profit sharing, and gain sharing), which are cash payments tied to employee, group, or company performance in order to encourage higher performance.

6. **Explain five employee benefits.**
The most popular type of benefits are health benefits, which help protect employees and their families when they become ill. Retirement benefits are also popular as a means of helping people save for later years. Employee stock-ownership plans (ESOPs) and stock options are ways for employees to receive or purchase shares of the company's stock, and they give employees a stake in the company. Family-benefit programs include maternity and paternity leave, child-care assistance, and elder-care assistance. Flexible benefit plans allow employees to choose the unique combination of benefits that suit their needs. Health and safety programs (including fitness and wellness programs) help keep employees at peak productivity.

7. **Describe five ways an employee's status may change.**
An employee's status may change through promotion to a higher-level position, through reassignment to a similar or lower-level position, through termination (removal from the company's payroll), through voluntary resignation, or through retirement.

8. **Identify the two reasons that employers may terminate employment.**
Layoffs occur because of a downturn in business or because company strategy requires a leaner work force. Such terminations are not performance related. Firings are permanent removals of employees because of poor performance.

On the Job: Meeting Business Challenges at Johnson & Johnson

Ralph Larsen and James Burke understood that effective human resources management was the key to the satisfied and highly productive work force so necessary to Johnson & Johnson's future success. The first step toward improving productivity was to help employees meet their dual responsibilities to family and job. To start, the company opened child-care centers at its corporate headquarters in New Brunswick, New Jersey, and its nearby Somerset office. Child-care costs at these centers are limited to 10 percent of an employee's disposable income. Then J&J expanded its child-care program to include home care. The company contracts with child-care providers to offer employees reduced rates on home-based child care. It also gives the providers advanced training and access to the resources in its on-site child-care facilities, such as books and toys.

Under its Balancing Work and Family Program, J&J helps employees locate resources and referrals for child care and elder care. It also goes beyond the bare legal minimum, allowing employees to take family-care leave of up to one year after the arrival of a newborn or adopted child and letting employees arrange a flexible work schedule to attend to an ailing family member. Moreover, employees in some locations can set flexible schedules that allow them to better meet their family obligations and still do excellent work.

In addition, Johnson & Johnson managers participated in training to sensitize them to work and family issues. To underscore the company's commitment to family care, human resources managers added a new sentence to the company credo: "We must be mindful of ways to help our employees with their family responsibilities." This commitment to helping employees better manage family pressures boosted productivity by reducing absenteeism, tardiness, and stress. In addition, the company's commitment to work/family policies helped attract and keep qualified employees in a tightening labor market.

Productivity was also enhanced by a wellness program. Live for Life was designed to emphasize steps employees can take to maintain and improve their health. The program sets four goals for employees: They should quit smoking, eat more fruit and fewer fatty foods, exercise regularly, and buckle their seat belts. At J&J headquarters, employees can work out in a gym, select "healthy heart" foods in the cafeteria, and check their weight in rest rooms. To encourage participation, employees are eligible to win prizes for meeting their goals. Over 35 J&J locations now have fitness centers and wellness programs, and 75 percent of the work force participates.

The results have been impressive. Smoking among employees has been reduced to less than 20 percent, a decline of more than one-third. Live for Life costs J&J $225 a year for each employee, but lower absenteeism and reduced health costs have saved $378 per employee.

ON THE JOB

Live for Life was so successful that J&J formed a new company, Johnson & Johnson Health Management, to market the Live for Life program. The new company assists with fitness center design and management, and it orchestrates health-promotion campaigns in such areas as smoking cessation, nutrition, and stress management. Live for Life is available at 60 leading corporations and medical centers that together employ more than 850,000 people.

Johnson and Johnson maintains other progressive benefits policies as well, including medical, dental, and life insurance and a generous 401(k) retirement plan. By making such generous attempts to help employees balance their work and family lives, Ralph Larsen is demonstrating that Johnson & Johnson employees truly are the company's most valuable asset.

Your Mission: Ralph Larsen wants to keep costs low while improving quality. As vice president for human resources, your mission is to create employee programs that reflect Larsen's vision of a leaner, more streamlined Johnson & Johnson by maintaining the loyalty, well-being, and productivity of employees. How would you handle the following situations?

1. One of Larsen's biggest challenges is revitalizing J&J's consumer-goods operations in the United States. To boost sales, J&J introduced new products such as No More Tears Baby Sunblock, Tylenol Chewables, and Johnson's Creamy Baby Oil. Because it is the consumer-products sales team that will ultimately place these items on supermarket shelves, Larsen has asked you to use human resources methods to increase the effectiveness of the sales force. You devise a list of three steps that you should take. Which should you implement first?
   a. Conduct a job analysis of the sales department to ensure that the components needed for a well-coordinated, effective sales effort are in place.
   b. Have all salespeople participate in a one-week training program to refamiliarize them with J&J products and to boost their assertiveness.

c. Review the sales force's employee performance appraisals and conduct new appraisals if necessary. Weed out weak employees and promote those who have demonstrated their ability to sell.

2. Johnson & Johnson's Acuvue disposable contact lenses have become the leading soft contact lens in the United States, so Johnson & Johnson Vision Products is doubling the size of its facility. B. D. Walsh, president of Johnson & Johnson Vision Products, asks for advice on evaluating applicants for new manufacturing positions. Walsh is looking for employees with a high degree of manual dexterity who have experience working on an assembly line. He gives you a list of the three selection methods he intends to use, but he is uncertain about weighting them. Which method should be given highest priority in the employee-selection process?
   a. Job applications
   b. Interviews
   c. Performance tests

3. Walsh is concerned that some assembly-line employees abuse drugs and alcohol, which might lead them to inadvertently jeopardize the health of customers and undermine the reputation of the Acuvue brand. Walsh wants to institute drug testing and asks you for suggestions about how tests might be administered. What do you recommend?
   a. You suggest testing only those employees who are suspected of substance abuse.
   b. You sympathize with people who resent having to take a drug test. You suggest testing only those assembly-line employees who could end up harming the customer if they are careless on the job.
   c. You believe the only fair way to administer a drug test is to test everyone at Johnson & Johnson Vision Products. You suggest that Walsh set an example and volunteer to take the first test.

4. Larsen wants you to review the Live for Life program and the Balancing Work and Family Program to determine where costs can be cut. You draw up a preliminary list of suggestions. After reviewing them, you forward one to Larsen's office. Which one do you choose?
   a. Statistics show that the voluntary Live for Life program saves J&J more than $100 for each person enrolled. Require that all employees participate so that the company can save even more.
   b. Raise the percentage that employees pay for child care to 25 percent of their disposable income.
   c. Offer employees on family-care leave the option of working at least 15 hours a week at home on a flexible schedule.[79]

Key Terms

bonus (307)
broadbanding (308)
commissions (307)
comparable worth (306)
compensation (306)
employee assistance program (EAP) (314)
employee benefits (309)
employee stock-ownership plan (ESOP) (310)
employment at will (316)
ergonomics (313)
gain sharing (308)
human resources management (HRM) (290)
incentives (307)
job analysis (294)
job description (294)
job specification (294)
knowledge-based pay (308)
layoffs (315)
mandatory retirement (316)
orientation (300)
pay for performance (308)
pension plans (310)
performance appraisal (303)
profit sharing (308)
recruiting (294)
résumé (297)
salaries (306)
stock option plan (310)
termination (315)
wages (306)
worker buyout (317)
wrongful discharge (316)

Questions

For Review

1. What are the strategic staffing techniques that organizations are using today to avoid overstaffing and understaffing?
2. What is the purpose of conducting job analysis? What are some of the techniques used for gathering information?
3. Why are more companies offering family benefits and flexible benefits?
4. What are the major legal pitfalls in the hiring process?
5. What are some of the problems facing workers who are nearing retirement?

For Analysis

6. How are computers changing the ways in which companies train their employees?
7. What effect has downsizing had on promotion and reassignment of workers? On termination procedures?
8. Under what conditions would broadbanding be the most effective compensation system?

9. Why do some employers offer comprehensive benefits even though the costs of doing so have risen significantly in recent years?
10. Why might a company choose to hire local managers instead of relocating current managers when the company expands internationally?

For Application

11. If you were on the human resources staff at a large health-care organization that was looking for a new manager of information systems, what recruiting method(s) would you use and why?
12. Assume you are the manager of human resources at a manufacturing company that employs about 500 people. A recent cyclical downturn in your industry has led to financial losses, and top management is talking about laying off workers. Several supervisors have come to you with creative ways of keeping employees on the payroll, such as exchanging workers with other local companies. Why might you want to consider this option?

A Case for Critical Thinking ■ Serving Billions Around the World

Every 3 to 4 hours another McDonald's opens for business. As a result, the chain now has over 23,000 restaurants in more than 90 countries around the world. Not bad for a company that started with just one store in Des Plaines, Illinois, a little more than four decades ago. What's the secret of the golden arches' success? Of course Big Macs and french fries have a lot to do with it. But equally important is the McDonald's approach to human resources management. "We're in the people business," says Stan Stein, senior vice president of human resources. "We're going to win in the competitive marketplace because of the quality of our people and because of how well we manage them, how well we create opportunities for them, and how well we motivate them."

That philosophy is evident in the company's hiring strategies and incentive programs. McDonald's is one of the largest U.S. employers of young people, and half of its employees are students. But if a student's grades start to suffer, often the first answer is to quit working. So to retain their employees, many McDonald's offer extra pay for good grades, reimbursement for schoolbooks, and paid study hours. In addition, the company sponsors the largest school-to-work program in the United States. The four-year program, called McDonald's Youth Apprenticeship, prepares students for business management careers by building basic skills such as reading and math, as well as problem-solving, computer, leadership, and TQM skills.

Another recruiting strategy that gives McDonald's an edge over the competition is the ReHIREment program, which provides part-time jobs for more than 40,000 older workers, many of whom are retired. Older workers have proven to be very loyal, which lowers the company's turnover costs. In addition, many older workers have Social Security benefits and pensions from previous careers, thus reducing their demands on McDonald's to pay for such programs. Flexible scheduling allows previously retired employees to set the number of hours they work each week so that their Social Security benefits are not jeopardized.

McDonald's is also recognized as one of the most progressive companies in employee diversity. Nearly half of McDonald's restaurant managers are minorities, and half are women. Moreover, the combined sales of African American–owned McDonald's franchises make it the largest African American enterprise in the United States today. One of the reasons for this success is the McDonald's Changing Workforce Programs, which help employees work through cultural and gender differences in a series of courses that examine how those differences affect company and employee success.

However, McDonald's commitment to diversity is not limited to its U.S. operations. Around the world, McDonald's restaurants strive for flexibility and sensitivity to local cultural customs and tastes. For example, the company recently opened its first restaurant in India, where the dominant Hindu religion shuns the consumption of beef products. So instead of the traditional "two all beef patties," the Indian restaurant serves "vegiburgers." Cultural sensitivity carries over to the company's international staffing, training, and management strategies as well. Rather than trying to push the U.S. way of doing things, McDonald's takes its best practices from around the world and then adapts them to local practices. "One of our guiding principles is that our restaurants should always be a reflection of the communities they serve—not only the individuals we employ and the culture and ethnicity of those communities, but also the employment practices," says Rita Johnson, an international human resources staff director.

To make certain that the company is in compliance with all local employment laws and customs, McDonald's benchmarks with other companies in the local area to discover what issues and problems they have had to contend with. The human resources staff then digs deeper into crucial HR questions: What are the local labor laws? Can part-time and flexible work schedules be established? Are employees limited to working specific hours? Can the company employ teenagers? Asking these questions at the outset reduces the risk of problems later. For example, in Latvia, Romania, and Poland, all restaurants are required to provide showers and lockers for their employees. Obviously, such issues must be brought forward before the restaurant is even built.

In the quick-service restaurant industry, quality depends not just on the food, but on the people who serve it. According to Rita Johnson, McDonald's restaurants "always employ the most positive people practices and exceed the expectations of our employees." With such a commitment to effective human resources management, it's no wonder the golden arches have become a recognized symbol for quality around the world.

1. Are McDonald's staffing techniques strategic? Why or why not?
2. McDonald's Youth Apprenticeship program provides career opportunities for many young people, but how does it benefit the company in the long run?
3. How does McDonald's policy of adapting its human resource policies to local markets help drive the company's international success?
4. Go to the McDonald's Internet Web site at <http://www.mcdonalds.com>, and follow the links to career information. How does McDonald's train its employees worldwide? What is the primary focus of training efforts at Hamburger University? In terms of establishing a consistent identity for McDonald's worldwide, what is the primary benefit of this training program?

Building Your Business Skills

Use job analysis to evaluate the specific requirements of a position you are interested in. Develop a job description and a job specification for a particular position you would like to hold. With the members of your class, generate a list of items that should be included in the job analysis. To obtain information about the career you've chosen, you might interview a person working in that field, interview a human resources manager with a company that employs people in that field, use reference books that provide information about your desired job and career, and search the Internet—including (1) the Web sites of companies that employ people in the career that interests you and (2) job-oriented sites like E-Span <http://www.espan/>, CareerMosaic <http://www.service.com:80/cm/>, CareerWeb <http://www.cweb.com>, The Monster Board <http://www.monster.com>, and Job World <http://www.job-world.com>.

Keeping Current Using *The Wall Street Journal*

Locate one or more articles in *The Wall Street Journal* that illustrate how a company or industry is adapting to changes in its work force. (Examples include retraining, literacy or basic-skills training, flexible benefits, and benefits aimed at working parents or people who care for aging relatives.)

1. What employee needs or changes in the work force caused the company (or industry) to adapt?
2. Was the company (industry) forced to change for some financial or legal reason, or did it move voluntarily to meet the need or adapt to the change? Why?
3. What other changes in the work force or in employee needs do you think this company or industry is likely to face in the next few years? Explain your reasons for making this prediction.
4. Visit the Web site of the company you are reporting on. If the company has no Web site, or if you are reporting on an industry, visit the Web site of another company within that industry. What can you learn about the company's current ability to adapt to change, based on the information on the Web site and in the article(s) you reviewed. Does the company view itself as forward-thinking? Does this coincide with what you learned in the article(s)? What recommendations would you make to senior management to better prepare the company for future work-force changes?

Exploring the Best of the Web

Staying on Top of the HR World, page 290

HR Live provides free online information about current human resources topics useful to more than just HR professionals. Explore the site at <http://www.hrlive.com>. Answer these questions.

1. Click on the link to *Markets* and browse through some of the top recruiting markets for occupations that interest you. How might an HR manager with a growing company use this

information to attract new employees as the company expands? How might this information figure into senior management's decision about where to locate new facilities?

2. Click on *Layoffs*, and review one of the reports about a company that recently laid off employees. What circumstances led the company to lay off employees? Do the layoffs include management as well as workers? Are the laid-off employees highly skilled or lower skilled? Compare this report with reports about layoffs in other industries. Do you notice any similarities in circumstances between the different industries? What conclusions can you draw?
3. Click on *Reports*, and read the report on employee referral programs. What actions can companies take to ensure the success of employee referral programs? Under what circumstances might an HR manager decide to implement such a program? When would the program be least attractive as a recruitment tool?

Understanding Employee Ownership, page 310

The National Center for Employee Ownership (NCEO) provides valuable information about many types of employee ownership programs. Explore the organization's Web site at <http://nceo.org> to learn more about this growing trend in employee compensation. Then answer the following questions.

1. Read the brief introduction to employee ownership, then follow the *Library* link. Read the *Employee Owner Fact Sheet.* When does a 401(k) plan become a form of employee ownership? Do you think this form would be more or less effective at motivating employees than a stock option plan or an ESOP in the short term? Why?
2. Click on *How ESOPs Work*, and read the information on the page. What are some of the drawbacks to ESOPs? What actions would you recommend a company take in conjunction with establishing an ESOP to ensure that the plan inspires greater productivity in employees?
3. Read the *Employee Stock Options Fact Sheet.* In what kinds of companies do employees stand to gain the most from stock options? Assume you are hired by a large, established company that anticipates slow growth but stable revenues over the next decade. Would you rather receive stock options or an ESOP? Why?

Discover a Gold Mine of Information at the Bureau of Labor Statistics, page 316

The Bureau of Labor Statistics compiles data on workers, wages, employment, prices, and the economy in general. You can generate your own customized reports or follow the links to previously formatted reports. Explore the site at <http://www.bls.gov> and answer the questions below.

1. Click on *Economy at a Glance.* Take a look at the unemployment rate, average hourly earnings, and the consumer price index (which measures inflation) over the past several months. What do these numbers say about the health of the economy?
2. From the main page, click on *Data*, and then on *Selective Access*, and follow the link to *Employee Benefits Survey.* Enter a search for data on a particular employee benefit of interest to you according to the instructions given. Identify the benefit you are researching, and explain whether the number of employees who receive this benefit is rising or declining. How might this information be of use to HR professionals? Are there any limitations to the data you received?
3. From the main page, click on *Keyword Search of BLS Web Pages*, and enter a search for "foreign labor statistics." Scroll to the link to *Foreign Labor Statistics Home Page*, and browse some of the reports available. How might this data be useful to you as a business student?

Answers to "Is It True?"

Page 297. True.

Page 306. False. U.S. hourly labor costs are among the lowest in the industrial world.

Page 313. True.

CHAPTER 11

EMPLOYEE-MANAGEMENT RELATIONS

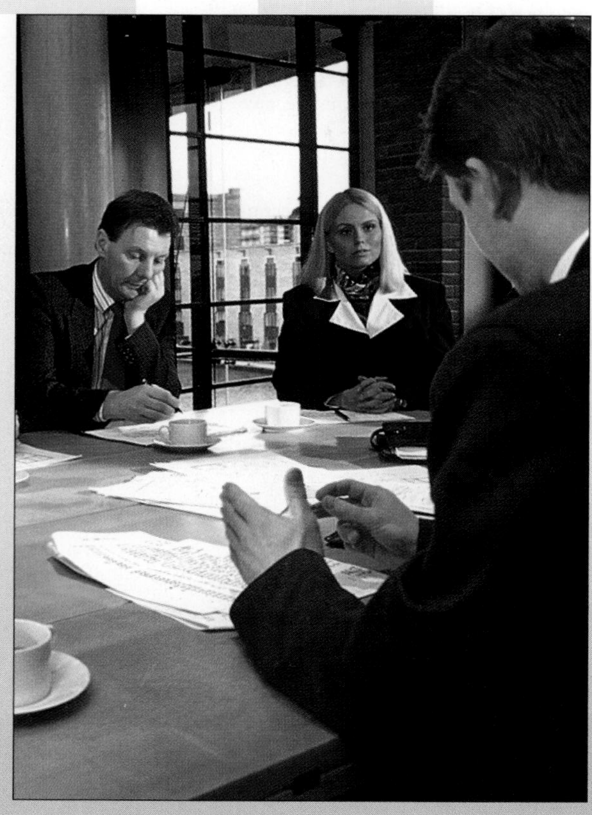

OBJECTIVES

After studying this chapter you will be able to

1. Identify two main types of labor unions
2. Outline the organizational structure of unions
3. Explain the two steps unions take to become the bargaining agent for a group of employees
4. Describe the four stages in collective bargaining
5. List five general issues that may be addressed in a labor contract
6. Discuss four options that unions have when negotiations with management break down
7. Discuss four options that management has when negotiations with the union break down
8. Explain how employee-management relations are changing to meet the challenges of today's business environment

ON THE JOB

ON THE JOB: FACING BUSINESS CHALLENGES AT SATURN

Negotiating a Radically New Contract

Richard LeFauve of General Motors and Donald Ephlin of the United Auto Workers (UAW) had been adversaries for years. LeFauve represented management (white collars, planners, order givers) and Ephlin represented labor (blue collars, strong backs, order takers) as they faced one another from opposite sides of the negotiating table. However, when LeFauve became president of GM's Saturn division, both men agreed that a drastic change was needed in the relationship between management and labor. Facing aggressive Japanese automakers, both men believed that management *and* labor had a lot to lose unless an altogether new relationship could be forged.

LeFauve recognized that GM was battling fierce competition. Honda, Toyota, and Nissan had aggressively entered the U.S. market, reducing GM's share to about 35 percent. Customers believed that buying GM meant they were getting less car for their money, and GM was finding it increasingly difficult to compete on cost alone. For one thing, Japanese companies could build a car in about 100 hours, including suppliers' labor. General Motors took twice as long, and LeFauve saw union work rules as one cause of low productivity. At some plants, union jobs were divided into more than 100 classifications, so an entire assembly line might be shut down while a lone electrician rewired a faulty outlet. Disagreement over employees' seniority rights, job security, and wage increases threatened successive contract negotiations as GM tried in vain to streamline production rules. LeFauve believed that changes were necessary to keep the company competitive.

Yet Ephlin saw union members facing more than the possibility of losing market share. Employees were concerned with personal security: More than 230,000 union jobs had already disappeared because of foreign competition, and at least 83,000 more were expected to vanish as Japanese carmakers stepped up production in nonunion U.S. factories. Pride was also at stake. Auto plants in the United States were averaging 82 defects for every 100 cars, whereas plants in Japan averaged only 65. Union autoworkers blamed the problem on managers who were more interested in production schedules and quotas than in raising employee proficiency. Ephlin noted that Japanese autoworkers received an average of 370 hours of job training, whereas their U.S. counterparts received perhaps 46 hours. Ephlin believed that change was necessary to improve the skills and job security of his union members.

As General Motors planned its Saturn Division, both LeFauve and Ephlin were facing some of the most crucial questions in their long careers. How could management persuade labor to streamline production rules for the good of the company? How could labor persuade management to look beyond purely financial goals? Most important, could management and labor become teammates instead of adversaries?[1]

Labor Organizations in the Global Economy

As LeFauve and Ephlin are well aware, certain unavoidable differences of interest exist between management and employees. On the one hand, owners and managers of businesses have a right to use their resources as they see fit in order to increase productivity and profits. On the other hand, employees have a right to job security, safe and comfortable working conditions, and pay that rewards their contributions to the organization. In the best of times and in the most enlightened companies, these two sets of needs can often be met simultaneously. However, when the economy slows down and competition speeds up, the needs of employees and management often differ. Because of this potential for conflict, employees form **labor unions,** organizations that seek to protect employee interests by negotiating with employers for wages and benefits, working conditions, and job security.

labor unions
Organizations of employees formed to protect and advance their members' interests

Companies sell goods and services, and employees sell their own labor—the services they can perform for the employer. Naturally, both want to get the best possible price. Just as the price that a company charges for a product is affected by the forces of supply and demand, so is the price that employees charge for their services. Unions alter the supply-and-demand equation by representing most or all of the employees—the supply of labor—that the company needs. By using their combined bargaining strength, employees can put more pressure on management than they could as individuals.

Not all employees support labor unions. Many believe that unions stifle individual initiative and are not necessary to ensure fair treatment from employers. Nevertheless, unions are a powerful force in employee-management relations in the United States. To understand how they work, we must first examine how they came to be.

The Origins and Growth of Unions

In 1792 a group of shoemakers held a meeting in Philadelphia to discuss matters of common interest. The result of their modest assembly was the formation of the first known union in the United States. During the next several decades, many other unions were formed. They were chiefly local **craft unions,** made up of skilled artisans belonging to a single profession or craft, such as carpentry. Like today's unions, they bargained with their employers for better wages and working conditions.

craft unions
Unions made up of skilled artisans belonging to a single profession or practicing a single craft

In the 1840s and 1850s, improvements in transportation cut shipping costs, created a national market, and made employees more mobile. At the same time, local craft unions banded together into national craft unions. In 1869 several national craft unions joined forces as the Knights of Labor. Over the next two decades, membership reached 700,000. However, several member unions became dissatisfied with the leadership's emphasis on moral betterment instead of improvements in wages and working conditions. Factions developed, and a split occurred. By 1890 control of the union movement had passed to a rival group, the American Federation of Labor (AFL), founded in 1886. The AFL dominated the labor movement for the next 40 years.

Between the late eighteenth century and early twentieth century, union membership waxed and waned due to changes in the economic and political climate of the United States. Membership declined significantly in times of economic depression, as scarce jobs made employees fearful of jeopardizing their positions, only to rebound when the economy recovered. Then in 1886, a bomb exploded among Chicago police who were trying to break up a labor rally. This incident, known as the Haymarket Riot, turned public opinion against the labor movement. During the four decades that followed, business was often successful in suppressing union activities.

When the Great Depression hit, very few workers were in a position to place demands on management. However, labor unions expanded their membership enormously during the 1930s, especially among unskilled employees, largely as a result of legislation passed during President Franklin D. Roosevelt's four terms in office. (The most significant laws relating to unions, many dating from this era, are described in Exhibit 11.1.) Unions also benefited from the work of an unofficial Committee for Industrial Organization, which was organized by certain members of the AFL in 1935. Its goal was to organize **industrial unions** representing both skilled and unskilled employees from all parts of a particular industry.

industrial unions
Unions representing both skilled and unskilled employees from all phases of a particular industry

This committee successfully organized the auto and steel industries, which eventually became the pillars of organized labor. However, three years later, the AFL formally expelled the committee because the craft unionists who controlled the AFL viewed the industrial unions as a threat. The committee then became a fully independent federation of industrial unions and changed its name to the Congress of Industrial Organizations (CIO).

During World War II, full employment helped unions grow even more. In exchange for

EXHIBIT 11.1

Key Legislation Relating to Unions

Most major labor legislation was enacted in the 1930s and 1940s. However, some more recent legislation has also been passed to protect organized labor.

LEGISLATION	PROVISION
Norris–La Guardia Act of 1932	Limits companies' ability to obtain injunctions against union strikes, picketing, membership drives, and other activities
National Labor Relations Act of 1935 (Wagner Act)	Prohibits employers from interfering with employees' right to form, join, or assist labor organizations; from interfering with labor organizations by dominating them or by making financial contributions to them; from discouraging membership in labor organizations by discriminating against members in employment or by requiring promises not to join union as condition of employment; from refusing to bargain collectively with the labor organization chosen by employees to represent them; from discharging employees because they have testified or filed charges against their employer under this act
Labor-Management Relations Act of 1947 (Taft-Hartley Act)	Amends Wagner Act to restrict unions (declares closed shop illegal, requires 60-day notice before strike or lockout, empowers federal government to issue injunctions to prevent strikes that would endanger national interest); declares jurisdictional strikes (in disputes between unions), featherbedding, refusal to bargain in good faith, and secondary boycotts illegal; requires union officers to certify that they are not communists; requires unions to submit financial reports to secretary of labor; allows unions to sue employers for contract violations; permits employers to petition National Labor Relations Board for elections under certain circumstances
Landrum-Griffin Act of 1959	Aims to control union corruption by penalizing bribery of union officials by employers; closing loopholes in law forbidding secondary boycotts; prohibiting hot-cargo clauses in employment contracts, which give unions the right not to handle goods of a company whose employees are on strike; requiring all unions to file constitutions and bylaws with the secretary of labor; requiring all unions to publish financial records open to inspection by members; making union officials more personally responsible for unions' financial affairs, making embezzlement of union funds a federal offense, and forbidding union loans of more than $2,000 to officers; denying convicted felons the right to hold union office for five years following release from prison; giving every union member an equal right to vote on issues, attend meetings, and speak freely; forbidding unions from raising dues unless a majority of members votes for the increase by secret ballot; giving union members the right to sue unions; requiring that members be formally charged and given fair hearing before being fired, expelled, or punished in any way by the union
Plant-Closing Notification Act of 1988	Requirement that employees and local elected officials receive 60 days' advance notice of plant shutdowns or massive layoffs

a no-strike pledge, unions were able to win many concessions from management. However, after the war, labor's demands for wage increases erupted into a series of severe strikes. In 1947 legislators in Washington responded by enacting the Labor-Management Relations Act (known informally as the Taft-Hartley Act), which restricted some of the organizing practices used by labor, such as making union membership a condition of employment.

In 1955 the AFL and the CIO merged their 16 million members. The intense 18-year competition between the two groups had boosted union membership from almost 9 million in 1939 to 17 million by the time they merged.[2] Although membership numbers would continue to rise, the percentage of U.S. workers belonging to unions peaked in 1946 at 36 percent. In the next few years, disclosures of union corruption and other problems prompted Congress to act to curb such abuses through federal legislation. Since the 1970s, the global economic climate has again caused union membership to slip. However, just as in the past, hard times may be giving rise to yet another rebirth for organized labor.

BEST OF THE WEB

Spreading the Union Message

Of all of the Web sites dedicated to union causes, the AFL-CIO's site offers perhaps the most extensive information on union issues and programs. The site is a strategic marketing tool designed to bring new members into the fold of organized labor while keeping current members informed and excited about union activities. Topics of emphasis include union membership campaigns, issues for working women, and work-related injuries. The AFL-CIO also publishes online directories of members of both the U.S. Senate and the House of Representatives, including their e-mail addresses, and it provides sample letters to encourage letter writing. The site also flexes the muscle of union buying power by providing a comprehensive list of current boycotts with links to information describing why they have been implemented.
http://aflcio.org

The Labor Movement Today

Unions now represent only 14 percent (16.3 million) of workers in the United States (see Exhibit 11.2). The decline in union power has also been felt in many other countries. For example, since 1985 union membership has dropped 25 percent in the United Kingdom, 31 percent in France, 32 percent in Venezuela, 47 percent in New Zealand, and 76 percent in Israel. Although union membership has increased in some countries—127 percent in

EXHIBIT 11.2

Union Membership Among Nonagricultural Employees

The influence of labor unions has declined since they first gained strength in the 1930s and peaked in the 1940s and 1950s. However, recent union efforts to organize government employees, health-care personnel, women, minorities, and other groups may slow or stop the decline in membership.

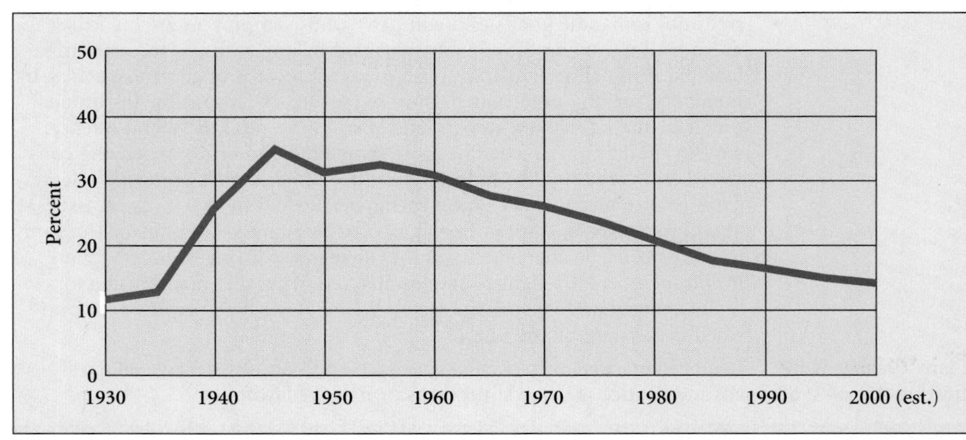

South Africa, 93 percent in Spain, 90 percent in Chile, 50 percent in China, 19 percent in Finland, and 11 percent in Canada—only about 12.5 percent of the world's estimated 1.3 billion workers belong to unions.[3]

One key reason for the decrease in union membership in the more developed nations is a massive shift in industry brought on by the demands of competing in the global economy. Manufacturing industries that employ blue-collar workers are on the decline, many of them either shifting production to developing countries that pay lower wages or eliminating jobs through automation. In contrast, the number of white-collar employees is increasing, but they tend to be less attracted to unions. Another factor is the changing nature of the labor force. Women, young workers, and highly skilled workers have been harder to organize with traditional methods, as have workers in less hierarchical organizations.[4]

In addition, since the late 1970s workers in the United States have become so fearful of losing their jobs to foreign competition, downsizing, and restructuring that fewer and fewer of them have been willing to take on the strong anti-union sentiment among managers in many companies. Many workers also recognize that as companies try to remain competitive, they are having greater difficulty paying high union wages and can no longer guarantee workers lifetime employment. The same is true all over the world. Workers in countries like France, Germany, Italy, and the United Kingdom are now facing large cuts in their historically generous compensation packages and social safety nets. Workers in Japan have also seen their country's system of lifetime employment begin to break down.[5]

Does this mean that unions are dying out? The answer is no. In fact, dynamic labor leaders are beginning to breathe new life into unions. They have recognized that their own inertia is partly to blame for the unions' decline, and they are taking corrective measures. In the United States, AFL-CIO president John Sweeney has beefed up recruiting efforts, especially among low-wage service workers, minorities, and women. In addition, new industries are being targeted, including high technology and health care. (Exhibit 11.3 illustrates current union membership in the United States by industry.) Sweeney has also launched a highly visible public relations campaign, and has begun to target people in smaller businesses and self-employed workers to bring them into the union fold. Some unions have already begun to show increases in membership as a result.[6] In Spain, Italy, Germany, France, and Britain, labor leaders are also challenging unions to shift their focus so that they can flourish again in the twenty-first century.[7]

As more manufacturing jobs move to developing countries, U.S. unions are also expanding their efforts to organize employees globally. For example, the United Electrical Workers lost nearly 20 percent of its membership when some manufacturers shifted production to Mexican plants. But the union followed the jobs and began to support union organizing efforts at General Electric's Mexican factories.[8] "As American companies increasingly expand, we hope to extend our resources, focus, and assistance to those workers who will be employed by those companies in their operations around the world," says Barbara Shailor, director of the AFL-CIO's international affairs department.[9]

Today's unions fight for many of the same rights unions have always sought—good wages, safe conditions, and benefits. But the waves of downsizing that helped to curb union power have also raised some new issues that now serve as the unions' rallying cry, including job security, health-care costs, no-layoff guarantees, labor involvement in decisions, and more job training. In addition, because of their efforts to sign up more women and minorities, unions have begun to focus on issues like child care, affirmative action, and sexual harassment.[10]

Is It True?

The average hourly wages of union workers are 20 percent greater than those of nonunion workers, and their fringe benefits are worth two to four times as much.

Why Employees Join Unions Employees are most likely to support union initiatives if they are deeply dissatisfied with their current job and employment conditions, they believe that unionization can be helpful in improving those job conditions, and they are willing to

EXHIBIT 11.3

U.S. Labor Union Membership by Industry

Union membership is highest among government employees in the United States. However, unions are spending heavily to boost membership in all sectors.

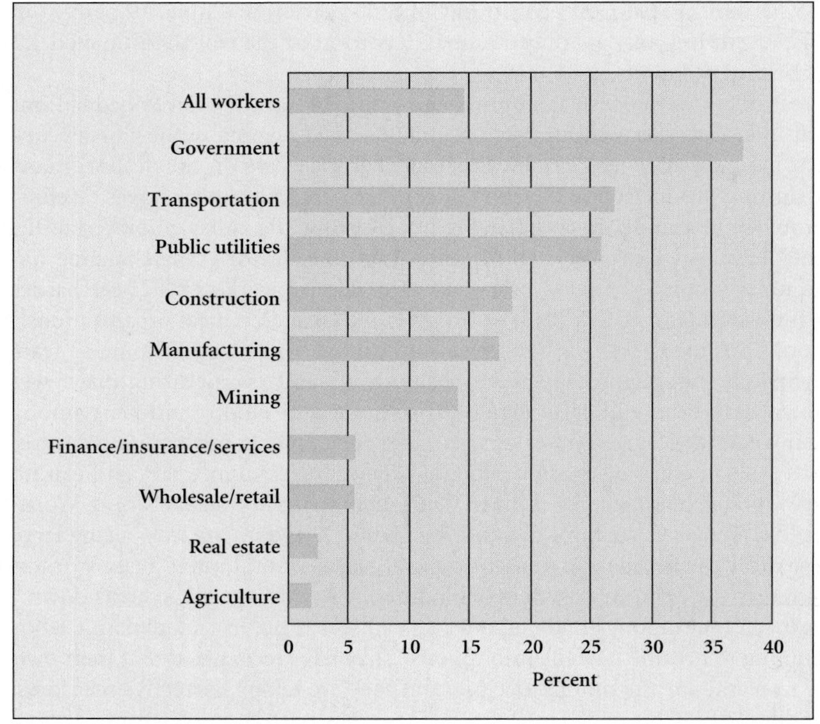

overlook negative stereotypes that have surrounded unions in recent years.[11] Many low-wage health-care workers in West Virginia, Kentucky, and Ohio have expressed such feelings, and their union has grown by 13,000 since 1980.[12]

The companies that have most successfully resisted unionization seem to have adopted participative management styles and an enhanced sense of responsibility toward employees. Nevertheless, even the best working conditions are no guarantee that employees won't seek union representation. For instance, although Starbuck's is renowned for its generous employee benefit programs and supportive work environment, employees of stores in Vancouver, British Columbia, recently organized and successfully bargained for higher wages.[13]

national union
Nationwide organization made up of local unions that represent employees in locations around the country

locals
Relatively small union groups, usually part of a national union or a labor federation, that represent members who work in a single facility or in a certain geographic area

How Unions Are Structured A **national union** is a nationwide organization composed of many local unions that represent employees in specific locations; examples are the United Auto Workers (UAW) of America and the United Steelworkers of America. *International unions* have members in more than one country, such as the Union of Needletrades, Industrial, and Textile Employees (UNITE). **Locals,** or local unions, each represent employees in a specific geographic area or facility; an example is Local 1853, which represents GM's Saturn employees.

A national union is responsible for such activities as organizing new areas or industries, negotiating industrywide contracts, assisting locals with negotiations, administering benefits, lobbying Congress, and lending assistance in the event of a strike. In return, local unions send representatives to the national delegate convention, submit negotiated contracts to the national union for approval, and provide financial support in the form of dues. They have the power to negotiate with individual companies or plants and to undertake their own membership activities.

The AFL-CIO is a **labor federation** consisting of a variety of national unions and of local unions not associated with any other national union. The AFL-CIO's two primary roles are to promote the political objectives of the labor movement and to provide assistance to member unions in their collective-bargaining efforts.[14] In recent years, the AFL-CIO has also become much more active in recruiting new members, organizing new locals, and publicizing unions in general.

labor federation
Umbrella organization of national unions and unaffiliated local unions that undertakes large-scale activities on behalf of their members and that resolves conflicts between unions

Each local union is a hierarchy with a broad base of *rank-and-file* members, the employees the union represents. These members pay an initiation fee, pay regular dues, and vote to elect union officials such as a president. Each department or facility also has or elects a **shop steward,** who works in the facility as a regular employee and serves as a go-between with supervisors when a problem arises. In large locals and in locals that represent employees at several locations, an elected full-time **business agent** visits the various work sites to negotiate with management and enforce the union's agreements with those companies.

shop steward
Union member and employee who is elected to represent other union members and who attempts to resolve employee grievances with management

business agent
Full-time union staffer who negotiates with management and enforces the union's agreements with companies

National unions, international unions, and labor federations have a full complement of officers and often a sizable staff of experts (see Exhibit 11.4). The organizers who go out to set up new locals are an essential element at this level, although recent organization efforts have begun to focus more on mobilizing the rank-and-file members rather than on using professional organizers.[15] In addition to the permanent staff, delegates elected by the locals attend regularly scheduled national conventions to elect the officers and approve changes to the umbrella organization's constitution.

How Unions Organize Union organizers, whether professional or rank and file, generally start by visiting with employees, although dissatisfied employees may also approach the union (see Exhibit 11.5 on page 333). The organizers survey employees by asking questions such as "Have you ever been treated unfairly by your supervisor?" Employees who express interest are sent information about the union along with **authorization cards**—sign-up cards used to designate the union as their bargaining agent. If 30 percent or more of the employees in the group sign the union's authorization cards, the union may ask management to recognize it. Usually, however, unions do not seek to become the group's bargaining agent unless a majority of the employees sign.

authorization cards
Sign-up cards designating a union as the signer's preferred bargaining agent

Often the company's management is unwilling to recognize the union at this stage. The union can then request a **certification** election, the process by which a union becomes the official bargaining agent for a company's employees. This election is supervised by the National Labor Relations Board (NLRB), an independent federal agency created in 1935 to administer and enforce the National Labor Relations Act. If a majority of the affected employees choose to make the union their bargaining agent, the union becomes certified. If not, that union and all other unions have to wait a year before trying again.

certification
Process by which a union is officially recognized by the National Labor Relations Board as the bargaining agent for a group of employees

Why Unions Are Challenged or Removed Once a company becomes aware that a union is seeking a certification election, management may mount an active campaign to point out the disadvantages of unionization. However, a company is not allowed to make specific threats or promises about how it will respond to the outcome of the election, nor is it allowed to change general wages or working conditions until the election has been concluded.

Even when a union wins a certification election, there's no guarantee that it will represent a particular group of employees forever. Sometimes employees become dissatisfied with their union and no longer wish to be represented by it. When this happens, the union members can take a **decertification** vote to take away the union's right to represent them. If the majority votes for decertification, the union is removed as bargaining agent. Decertification elections represent a relatively small percentage of all union elections, but unions lose about three-quarters of them.[16] Since 1980 the UAW has lost over 21,000 members due to decertification votes.[17]

decertification
Process employees use to take away a union's official right to represent them

EXHIBIT 11.4

How Unions Are Structured

This chart illustrates the complex structure of the AFL-CIO.

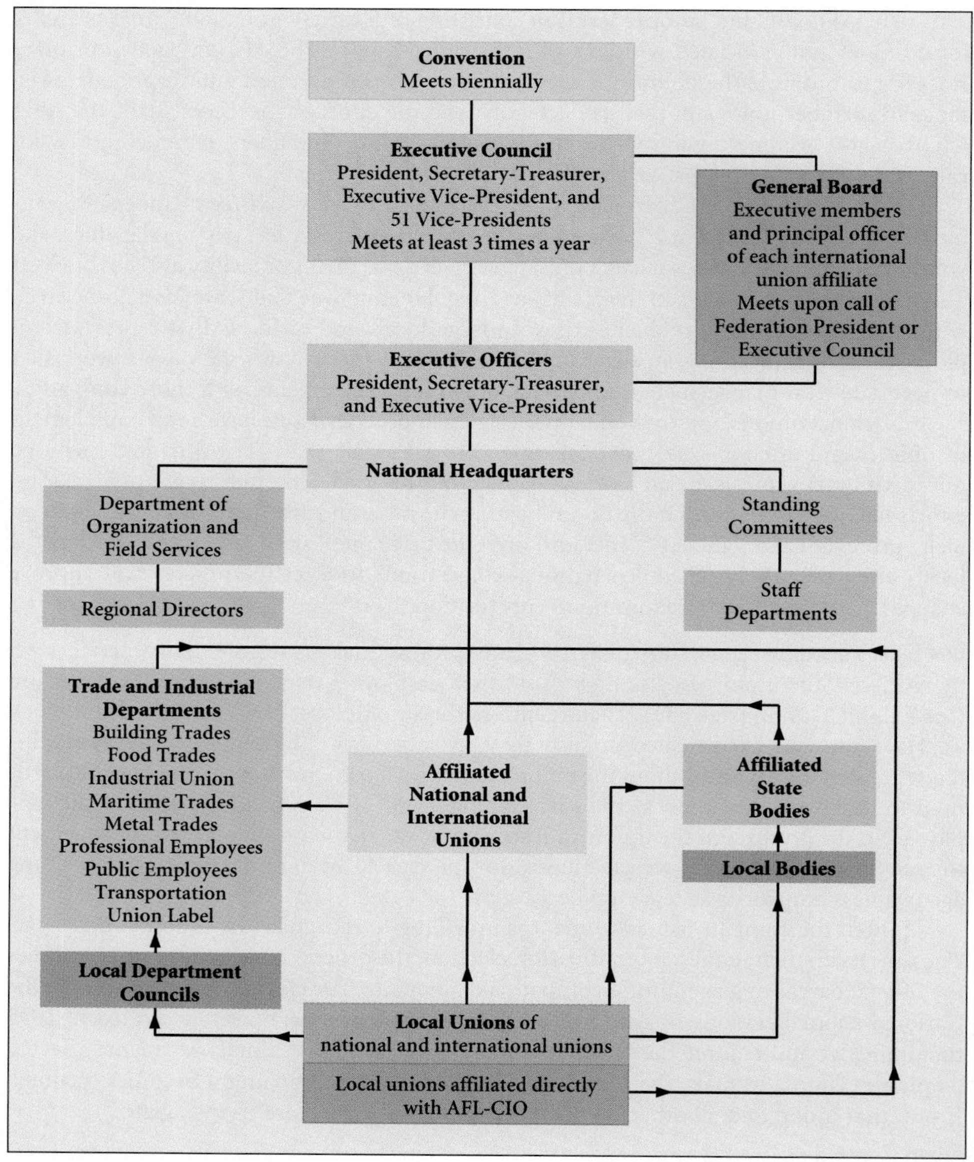

THE COLLECTIVE-BARGAINING PROCESS

collective bargaining
Process used by unions and management to negotiate work contracts

As long as a union has been certified as the bargaining agent for a group of employees, its main job is to negotiate employment contracts with management. In a process known as **collective bargaining,** union and management negotiators work together to forge the human resources policies that will apply to the unionized employees—and other employees covered by the contract—for a certain period, usually three years.

Most labor contracts are a compromise between the desires of union members and those of management. The union pushes for the best possible deal for its members, and management tries to negotiate agreements that are best for the company (and the shareholders, if a corporation is publicly held). Both sides have tools they can use to influence

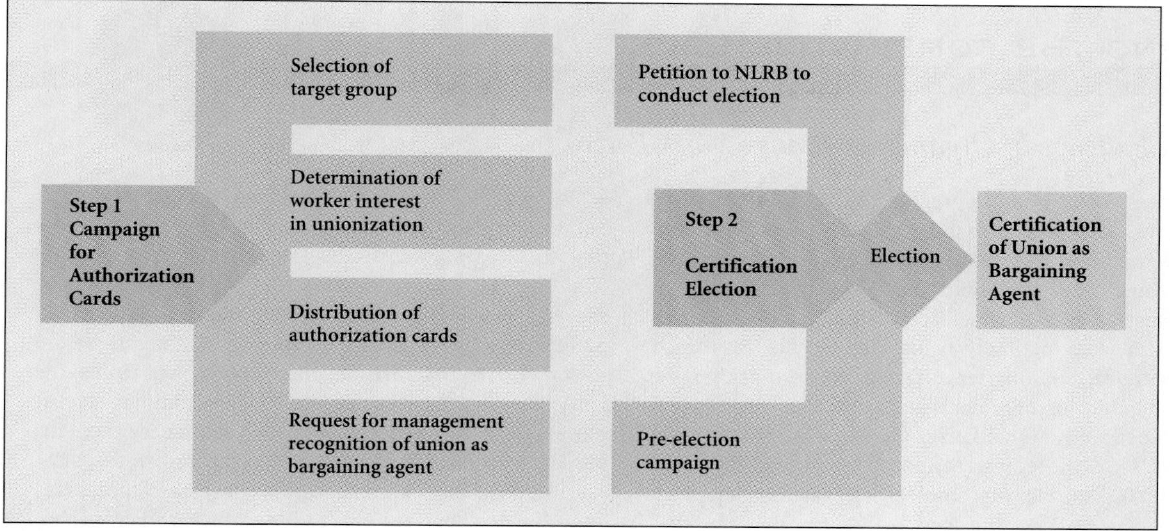

EXHIBIT 11.5

The Union-Organizing Process

This diagram summarizes the steps a labor union takes when organizing a group of employees and becoming certified to represent them in negotiations with management. The certification election is necessary only if management is unwilling to recognize the union.

the other during the collective-bargaining process. Exhibit 11.6 on page 335 illustrates the process described here.

Preparing to Meet

Before meeting with management, the union negotiating team must thoroughly understand the needs of its members as well as the company's situation. Sometimes the union hires investment bankers and consultants to analyze the company's business situation in advance.[18] Meanwhile, the management side tries to anticipate the union's needs and demands and determines what the company is willing to offer. These estimates are often withheld from the other side at the beginning of negotiations, because each side is trying to outguess the other. Both sides may come to the bargaining table with extreme positions from which they can fall back during actual bargaining. For instance, management may offer a contract with no wage gains, and the union may demand an outrageous pay increase. Neither really expects these demands to be met, but both sides gain the room to negotiate an acceptable compromise.

Before or during negotiations, the union may show strength by calling a strike vote. This vote may not actually signal a strike; sometimes it is called merely to demonstrate that the members are solidly behind their negotiating team and to remind management that a strike is possible when the current contract expires. However, if negotiations don't progress to the union's satisfaction, a strike vote can result in employees walking off the job.

Meeting and Reaching an Agreement

When the negotiating teams actually sit down together, management's chief negotiator may be the vice president in charge of industrial relations or someone hired from the outside. The union's chief negotiator may be the local's business agent or a negotiator supplied by national headquarters. Although insiders might be expected to know more about their

GAINING THE COMPETITIVE EDGE

The Challenge of Organizing Today's Work Force

It's not easy being a union organizer these days—not that it ever was. However, with today's diverse work force and declining interest in union membership among employees in some industries, union organizers have to be even more creative when it comes to recruiting members. Some organizers work patiently behind the scenes to attract members over the long term. Others try to quickly rally support before management finds out what's going on.

The International Ladies Garment Workers Union (ILGWU) uses the long-term approach to attract the more than 100,000 immigrants who work in garment shops in Los Angeles, El Paso, and New York City. Such employees speak little English, usually do not understand their legal rights, and are afraid to do anything that might jeopardize their jobs. So ILGWU organizers get involved with community groups where they can patiently counsel employees on their rights under immigration and labor law. They also teach the employees English as a second language. The union then offers "associate membership" with dues often as low as $1 a month. Eventually some of the associate members win formal union representation at their shops.

Organizers for the United Steelworkers, on the other hand, use a different tactic for reaching beyond the union's traditional manufacturing base to work with office employees. Of course, observers note that organizing office employees can be a tough transition for some of the seasoned organizers used to dealing with disgruntled laborers in steel mills. That's exactly why the Steelworkers hired Katie Gohn. One of the union's newest organizers, Gohn is a 41-year-old former secretary with a business degree. She'd never even set foot in a steel mill, but more important to Gohn's success was learning union organizing strategies. To accomplish that, she spent four months at the AFL-CIO's Organizing Institute and served as apprentice on half a dozen organizing campaigns before starting out to organize an office on her own. Unlike the ILGWU's long-term approach to new immigrant employees in the garment industry, Gohn pursues office employees with intense campaigns that last only a few days.

On the job, Gohn surveys employees to find issues appealing to them. She also calls on other women and on ethnic organizers to help reach the diverse work force. Gohn's busy schedule often means putting in 14-hour days and eating in her motel room. During one year with the Steelworkers, Gohn spent only 6 weeks at home, and during some campaigns she has gone without sleep for 3 days at a time. Even so, her 17-year-old daughter and her husband (who's a member of the Teamsters) support her work as an organizer. Winning over today's work force may not be easy, but union organizers are still convinced that the challenge is worthwhile.

QUESTIONS FOR CRITICAL THINKING

1. What qualities do you think are necessary to be a successful union organizer?
2. Do you think the United Steelworkers' strategy of recruiting office workers will be beneficial or detrimental to the union in the long run?

side's needs, outsiders often do a better job in tough negotiations because their nerves are less likely to become frayed in grueling bargaining sessions. Near the end of negotiations, meetings may last 12 to 15 hours—and calm discussion may give way to personal insults. However, labor and management negotiators generally try to remain composed and reasonable.

Once the negotiating teams have assembled, they state their opening positions, and each side discusses them point by point. Labor usually wants additions to the current contract. Management counters with the changes it wants, sometimes including **givebacks,** concessions made by union members to rescind promised increases in wages or benefits that the organization says will hurt its competitive or financial position. For example, Cleveland public school officials recently sought givebacks from teachers in order to erase a $23 million operating deficit.[19]

givebacks
Concessions made by union members to give up promised increases in wages or benefits in order to enhance the company's competitive position

In a cooperative atmosphere, the real issues behind the demands gradually come to light. For example, management may begin by demanding the right to determine the sizes

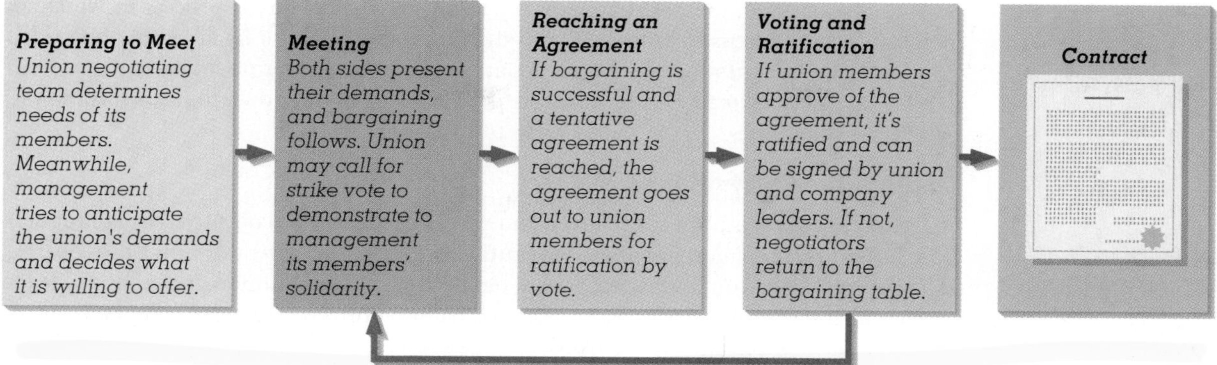

Preparing to Meet
Union negotiating team determines needs of its members. Meanwhile, management tries to anticipate the union's demands and decides what it is willing to offer.
Meeting
Both sides present their demands, and bargaining follows. Union may call for strike vote to demonstrate to management its members' solidarity.
Reaching an Agreement
If bargaining is successful and a tentative agreement is reached, the agreement goes out to union members for ratification by vote.
Voting and Ratification
If union members approve of the agreement, it's ratified and can be signed by union and company leaders. If not, negotiators return to the bargaining table.
Contract

EXHIBIT 11.6

The Collective-Bargaining Process

Contract negotiations go through the four basic steps shown here.

of work crews when all it really wants is smaller crews; the union is unlikely to give up total control over crew sizes, which is a key element of its power, but may agree to certain reductions. After many stages of bargaining, each party presents its package of terms, and any gaps between labor and management demands are then dealt with.

What if one side or the other simply refuses to discuss a point? If one side is unwilling even to talk, the other side can ask the NLRB to rule on whether the topic is a permissive subject or a mandatory subject. **Permissive subjects,** also called *voluntary subjects,* are those that are not required and cannot be insisted upon as a condition of a contract. Examples include health insurance for retired employees and promotion of employees to supervisory positions. **Mandatory subjects** are those that can be categorized as "wages, hours, and other terms and conditions of employment" as defined by the National Labor Relations Act. Both sides are required to address mandatory subjects in good faith.[20]

permissive subjects
Topics that may be omitted from collective bargaining

mandatory subjects
Topics that must be discussed in collective bargaining

If negotiations reach an impasse, outside help may be needed. The most common alternative is **mediation**—bringing in an impartial third party to study the situation and make recommendations for resolution of the differences. Mediators are generally well-respected community leaders whom both sides will listen to. However, the mediator can only offer suggestions, and his or her solutions are not binding. When a legally binding

mediation
Process for resolving a labor-contract dispute in which a neutral third party meets with both sides and attempts to steer them toward a solution

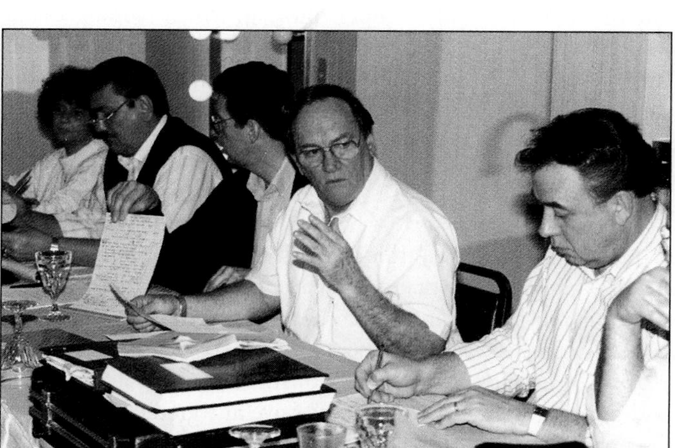

Negotiations over provisions in union contracts generally take time. Navistar International and the United Auto Workers talked for 14 consecutive days before agreeing on a contract that limited layoffs, boosted retirement benefits, increased pay, and improved health-care benefits.

settlement is needed, the negotiators may submit to **arbitration**—a process in which an impartial referee listens to both sides and then makes a judgment by accepting one side's view. In *compulsory arbitration*, the parties are required by a government agency to submit to arbitration; in *voluntary arbitration*, the parties agree on their own to use arbitration to settle their differences.

arbitration
Process for resolving a labor-contract dispute in which an impartial third party studies the issues and makes a binding decision

Voting and Ratifying a Contract

Once the contract has been constructed and agreed to during the collective-bargaining sessions, it goes to the union members for **ratification,** a vote to accept or reject the contract in its entirety. If the contract is accepted, it has been ratified, and union and company leaders sign it. If the contract is rejected, the negotiators return to the bargaining table to try to bring the contract more in line with employee wishes.

ratification
Process by which union members vote on a contract negotiated by union leaders

Ratification procedures vary among unions. Some unions use representatives of different groups of employees with special interests to help secure ratification. When a companywide agreement is negotiated, many unions first send a proposed agreement to a council of lower-level union officers. However, union constitutions usually require that all employees covered by an agreement have an opportunity to approve contract settlements.[21]

Signing a collective-bargaining agreement (or contract) between union and management doesn't mark the end of negotiations. Rather, it lays the groundwork for discussions that will continue throughout the life of the contract to iron out unspecified details of the various contract issues.

As Saturn's LeFauve and the UAW's Ephlin recognize, most labor contracts cover similar issues. Whether a union represents teachers, hospital employees, miners, or assembly workers, the issues of common concern are union security and management rights, compensation, job security, work rules, and employee safety and health.

Union Security and Management Rights Once a union is established, the contracts it negotiates begin with a provision guaranteeing the security of the union. This provision is included because unions want a firm institutional base from which to work.

Ideally, a union would like to have all employees under its jurisdiction, but such a **closed shop,** in which employees are compelled to join the union as a condition of being hired, is illegal under the Taft-Hartley Act. The next best alternative for labor is the **union shop,** which allows an employer to hire new people at will, but after a probationary period—usually 30 days—the employees must join the union. Another alternative is the **agency shop,** which requires nonunion employees who benefit from agreements negotiated by the union to pay the union service fees. Approximately 1.9 million nonunion workers currently benefit from union representation at their workplace, although not all of them pay service fees.[22] The opposite of a closed shop is an **open shop,** in which employees are not required to join the union or pay dues, although they may join voluntarily. Certain states, mostly in the Sunbelt and the West, have passed **right-to-work laws,** which give employees the explicit right to keep a job without joining a union (see Exhibit 11.7).

closed shop
Workplace in which union membership is a condition of employment

union shop
Workplace in which the employer may hire new employees at will, but where the employees are required to join the union after a probationary period

agency shop
Workplace requiring nonunion employees who are covered by agreements negotiated by the union to pay service fees to that union

open shop
Workplace in which union membership is voluntary and employees need not join or pay dues

right-to-work laws
Laws giving employees the explicit right to keep a job without joining a union

Compensation A collective-bargaining agreement addresses several issues relating to employee compensation. The most common issues are wage rates, cost-of-living adjustments, profit sharing, and employee benefits.

WAGE RATES Throughout the past few decades, unions often negotiated similar wages for members working for all companies in a particular industry or at all plants within a particular company. This practice is referred to as **pattern bargaining.** But in the 1980s, many companies, including the major steel companies, railroads, coal companies, and meatpackers, began breaking away from patterns in their industries and negotiating separately with the unions. This allows negotiators to tailor collective agreements to suit the particular economic situation of individual employers, while loosening national union restrictions on employee involvement in team production strategies.[23]

pattern bargaining
Negotiating similar wages and benefits for all companies within a particular industry

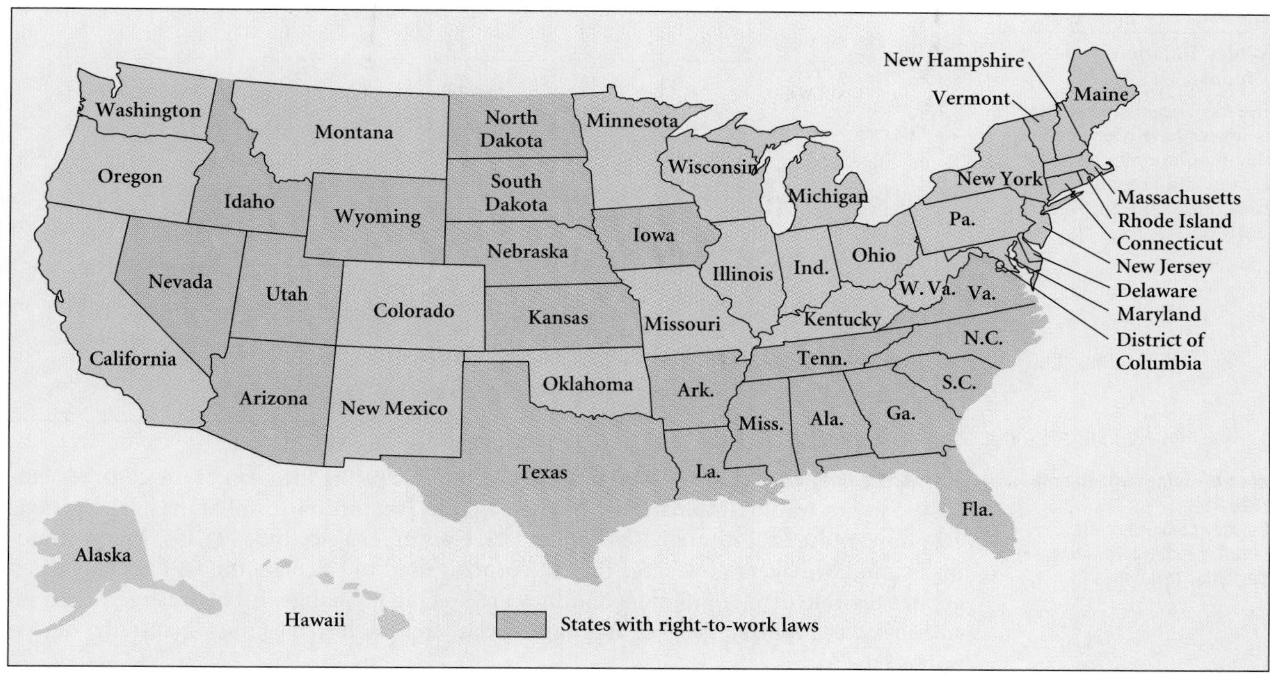

EXHIBIT 11.7

Right-to-Work States

Twenty-one states have laws that give employees the right to get a job without joining a union.

Two primary factors have prompted the recent changes in the way unions negotiate wage rates: economic recessions and tough foreign competition. When the most recent recession slowed the U.S. economy in the early 1990s, many unions agreed to contracts freezing wages at current levels or cutting wages or benefits in return for job security guarantees. The reasoning was that it's better to have a job at a lower wage than to have no job at all. That's what happened at Rubbermaid's plant in Wooster, Ohio, where the Rubber Workers Local 302 accepted givebacks in exchange for some measure of job security. Because of the union's concessions, the company stopped shifting production and jobs to nonunionized plants where costs were lower.[24] However, as the recent wave of downsizing has shown, even wage concessions by employees cannot guarantee long-term employment in today's competitive global economy.

To pay long-time union employees the wages they are accustomed to while still cutting labor costs, companies can use a **two-tier wage plan,** in which the pay scale of new employees is lower than that of senior employees. However, this strategy has come under fire in recent years because of the morale problems it creates for lower-paid newcomers, and some workers have used strikes successfully to overturn such plans. Nonetheless, as recently as 1996, Ford negotiated a two-tier system with the United Auto Workers.[25]

two-tier wage plan
Compensation agreement in which new employees are put on a wage scale lower than that of veteran employees

As a result of such concessions, givebacks, and other small wage increases negotiated over the past decade, union wages have sometimes increased at a slower rate than nonunion wages—and sometimes more slowly than the cost of living (see Exhibit 11.8). Today private sector union wage gains are at the lowest point in the past few decades, although union employees still average 16 percent higher wages than nonunion employees.[26]

COLAs In 1950 the United Auto Workers and General Motors adopted an innovative policy. To guarantee that employees' pay would keep pace with inflation, their contract

EXHIBIT 11.8

Wages, Inflation, and Unions

In recent years, union wage increases have been smaller than nonunion wage increases and in many cases have not even kept pace with inflation.

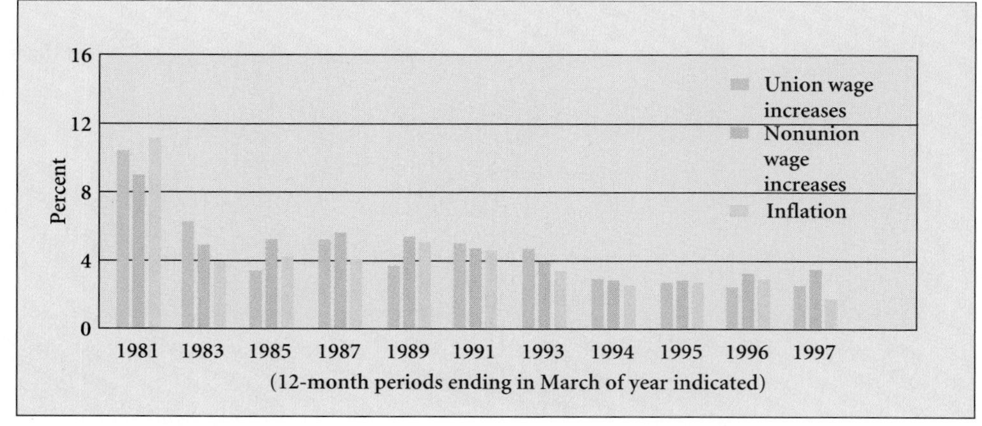

cost-of-living adjustment (COLA)
Clause in a union contract ensuring that wages will rise in proportion to inflation

adopted a **cost-of-living adjustment (COLA)** clause. During the term of the contract, employee wages would automatically be increased in proportion to inflation in the general economy. Most COLAs are based on the U.S. Consumer Price Index (CPI). Many economists and lawmakers now agree that the process used to calculate the CPI actually exaggerates the rate of U.S. inflation, and they are seeking to change it. This change would result in lower reported rates of inflation and, therefore, lower COLAs. Naturally, unions oppose the idea.[27]

About three-fifths of workers covered by major collective-bargaining agreements received COLAs in the late 1970s and early 1980s. However, after the inflation rate was brought under control in the mid-1980s, union workers began to see little or no pay gains from COLAs. As a result, negotiators began to give up COLAs in order to gain concessions on more pressing issues such as health-care benefits, pensions, and job security. In the mid-1990s only 16 percent of employees covered by major labor contracts received COLA increases.[28]

PROFIT SHARING Both management and unions are increasingly looking at profit sharing as a means of reducing wage inflation and increasing productivity. However, labor has some apprehension about the income risks associated with profit sharing. In fact, the AFL-CIO recently advised its affiliates to make profit sharing the smallest part of any total economic package they negotiate.[29] Union negotiators are also developing innovative bargaining strategies to protect employees when profits are down. For example, the United Steelworkers agreed to a wage-cut/profit-sharing arrangement with LTV Steel, in which wage cuts are treated as loans to be repaid from future profits. In addition, just in case future profits turn out to be insufficient to satisfy the debt, the contract requires LTV to issue interest-bearing stock to employees for the unpaid balance.[30]

EMPLOYEE BENEFITS Benefits have become a subject of increasing contention between labor and management in the past two decades. The cost of medical care has escalated so much that many employers are bargaining hard to cap the amount of medical benefits paid to employees or to substitute less expensive medical programs. Likewise, employers are seeking to limit their liability for employee pensions. Of course, unions strongly oppose any reductions in their expected benefit levels. However, employers have made some headway with regard to decreasing the number of paid holidays that employees receive. In addition, with the increasing proportion of women in the work force and on union membership rosters, employer-assisted day care has become an increasingly prominent issue at the bargaining table.[31]

Job Security In the face of continuing corporate cutbacks, deregulation, and competition from importers and nonunionized domestic companies, unions have been stressing job security over wage increases. In fact, job security is *the* issue of the 1990s. Consider the recent strikes by the UAW and the Canadian Auto Workers (CAW) to protest outsourcing by the Big Three U.S. carmakers. Because the vast majority of outside auto parts suppliers are not unionized, these suppliers are able to produce parts at a lower cost than the carmakers themselves. In their desire to control costs, the Big Three have been shifting more work to these suppliers at the expense of union jobs. In protest, workers at GM and Chrysler plants went on strike several times in the mid-1990s. GM alone lost $1.2 billion in net income to these strikes in 1996.[32]

Nevertheless, in spite of outsourcing and tough competition, auto workers at Ford, Chrysler, and GM continue to enjoy relatively strong job security. For example, Ford recently signed a contract that guarantees employment for 95 percent of its workers. Chrysler followed with a similar agreement for workers in its Canadian plants, and then GM offered its blue-collar employees guaranteed jobs for life. This example also demonstrates that pattern bargaining is still strong in the automobile industry, where a labor contract in one company influences contracts in others.[33]

Is It True?

By 1960 U.S. autoworkers made about half the cars in the world; today they make about 40 percent.

Automation can pose another threat to job security. Unions are demanding that management give them advance notice of any attempts to introduce new equipment that would cost their members jobs. In addition, they are demanding that management not lay off employees because of automation. One union acutely aware of the potential of automation to eliminate jobs is the International Longshoremen's and Warehousemen's Union (ILWU). Over the years, advances in shipping and dock equipment, such as containers and cranes, have greatly reduced the number of longshoremen needed to load and unload ships. Expected future changes, including computer-controlled vehicles and bar-coded shipping containers, promise to reduce the number even more. But rather than trying to block progress, the ILWU has allowed automation to increase efficiency and productivity on the docks. In exchange, employers have improved wages and pensions and granted workers a no-layoff policy, choosing instead to reduce excess workers through early retirement and attrition (workers leave on their own and are not replaced).[34]

Work Rules and Job Descriptions High on the list of issues that Saturn's LeFauve and the UAW's Ephlin had to grapple with were traditional work rules and restrictive job classifications, both of which tend to reduce productivity. **Work rules** are definitions of the types of work that covered employees may do and of the working conditions they must have. In the past, unions used narrow work rules to preserve jobs. For example, a union may specify in its contract that 20 employees are needed to complete a particular work task, even though 2

work rules
Policies set during collective bargaining that govern what type of work union members will do and the conditions under which they will work

Outsourcing and automation are two significant threats to job security of production workers today. Nevertheless, strong pattern bargaining has gained guaranteed employment for many auto workers, including those employed at this General Motors plant.

featherbedding
Practice of requiring employees to be kept on the payroll for work they don't do or for work that isn't necessary

workers will sit idle. The practice of requiring employees to be paid for work they don't do or for work that isn't needed is known as **featherbedding.** However, in the past 25 years, both management and unions have realized that in order to remain competitive, such work rules must be eliminated and many job descriptions must be broadened.

Employee Safety and Health Most union contracts contain provisions covering employees' safety and health, although the contracts rarely do more than restate federal regulations already in force. However, the combination of escalating health-care costs and greater awareness of environmental hazards has given rise to important new demands in labor negotiations. Some current issues include concern over injuries due to repetitive motions in typing or assembly activities and exposure to radiation emitted by computer display terminals.[35]

Administering the Agreement

grievances
Employee complaints about management's violating some aspect of a labor contract

due process
System of procedures and mechanisms for ensuring fair treatment on the job

Once a collective-bargaining agreement goes into effect, management and union representatives must make it work. **Grievances** are complaints about management violation of some aspect of the contract. Grievances typically come up when employees feel that they have been passed over for promotion, aren't getting a fair share of overtime, or are being asked to work too much overtime.

A contract's grievance procedures protect the employees' right to **due process,** which is a system of procedures and mechanisms for ensuring equity and justice on the job. Under the Fifth Amendment, "No person shall . . . be deprived of life, liberty, or property, without due process of law." Because most employees covered by a collective-bargaining agreement have a "property interest" in their employment, they can't be disciplined or terminated without an explanation and an opportunity to present their side of the story.

Although grievance procedures vary somewhat from contract to contract, grievances are usually referred first to the union's shop steward, who discusses them with the employee's immediate supervisor. If these discussions fail, the problem may then be discussed by the union's chief steward and the company's department head. The next step in the process brings together the union grievance committee and the company human resources manager. If they fail to solve the grievance, it is then up to the union business agent and the company plant manager to try to resolve the issue.

If the employee's complaint still cannot be satisfied, it goes to an *arbitrator,* whose powers are defined in the contract and whose ruling is usually final. Arbitration is generally considered a last resort because it removes control from both union and management, and it may be complicated and expensive. That's why unions and business have been shifting to *grievance mediation,* in which a neutral third party meets with both sides and attempts to steer them toward a solution.

BEST OF THE WEB

Standing Tall in Cyberspace

Some people say that labor unions are on their way out. Others believe that the union renaissance is just getting started. If union supporters prove to be correct, the Internet may end up playing a major role. LaborNet is one online service that makes it easy for Web surfers to find current news about unions, links to union Web pages, strike information, and job openings. The site also maintains links to labor organizations in foreign countries, and it provides special alerts to union members about threats to organized labor. With resources like LaborNet, it has become much easier for union supporters to share information and stand together for their cause.
http://www.igc.org/igc/labornet/index.html

Although grievance procedures are still an important aspect of contract administration, they are designed to resolve conflicts after the fact. Today's competitive environment has caused labor to focus less on grievances and more on cooperation and teamwork, which seeks to increase harmony and prevent conflicts from occurring. GM's Saturn division is just one example of a team effort between labor and management that minimizes conflicts and promotes cooperation.

When Negotiations Break Down

The vast majority of management-union negotiations are settled quickly, easily, and in a businesslike manner. Nevertheless, sometimes negotiations reach an impasse, and neither side is willing to compromise. Both labor and management are able to draw on many powerful options when negotiations or mediation procedures break down.

Labor's Options

Strikes and picket lines are perhaps labor's best-known tactics, but a number of other options are also used. For example, in a **slowdown,** employees continue to do their jobs, but at a snail's pace. One surprising example involves the Girl Scouts. In the middle of the cookie-selling season, 27 troops in Mount Laurel, New Jersey, demanded a bigger commission from the local Girl Scout council. When their demand was rejected, the scouts initiated a slowdown by selling no more than the 12-box minimum.[36] It's important to note that regular union employees (which excludes the Girl Scouts) who participate in slowdowns are not protected under the National Labor Relations Act and thus may be disciplined by management. Other union tactics include boycotts and the judicious use of financial influence, political influence, and publicity.

slowdown
Decreasing employee productivity to pressure management

Strikes and Picket Lines The most powerful weapon that organized labor can use is the **strike,** a temporary work stoppage aimed at forcing management to accept union demands. The basic idea behind the strike is that, in the long run, it costs management more in lost earnings to resist union demands than to give in. An essential part of the strike is **picketing,** whereby union members positioned at entrances to company premises march back and forth with signs and leaflets, trying to persuade nonstriking employees to join them and to persuade customers and others to stop doing business with the company. One union will often honor another's picket line, so that even a relatively small union can shut down an employer. For example, striking department-store employees can close down a business if union truckers won't cross their picket line to make deliveries. Although it is illegal for federal employees and essential state workers, such as police and firefighters, to strike, they can achieve a similar effect through tactics such as calling in sick repeatedly.[37]

strike
Temporary work stoppage by employees who want management to accept their union's demands

picketing
Strike activity in which union members march before company entrances to persuade nonstriking employees to walk off the job and to persuade customers and others to cease doing business with the company

Since the late 1970s, the number of strikes in the United States involving 1,000 workers or more has dropped dramatically—from 298 in 1977 to 37 in 1996. One reason for this decline is that many companies are able to continue operating throughout a strike, either because they are highly automated or because union jobs can be performed by management and temporary employees. For example, Caterpillar used retirees, engineers, middle managers, secretaries, and up to 5,600 temporary employees to replace 8,700 striking workers in 1995. Highly automated work processes made it much easier for the company to keep production going, and the defeated strikers ended up returning to work before a contract agreement was reached. Many analysts viewed the situation as a devastating blow to organized labor in general.[38]

However, sometimes employees have the upper hand in a strike situation. In 1997 a crippling strike by more than 185,000 unionized employees at United Parcel Service ended after only 16 days, with the union winning sweeping concessions from management. Huge daily losses of revenue and the rapid migration of customers to competitors like the U.S. Postal Service and FedEx prompted management to settle the dispute quickly. The strike focused on improving pay, work conditions, and advancement opportunities for part-time employees and was considered a victory not just for UPS employees but for organized labor in general. Polls during the strike showed that the public supported the striking workers over management by a margin of two to one.[39]

boycott
Union activity in which members and sympathizers refuse to buy or handle the product of a target company

Boycotts A less direct union weapon is the **boycott,** in which union members and sympathizers refuse to buy or handle the product of a target company. Millions of union members form an enormous bloc of purchasing power, which may be able to pressure management into making concessions. One of the best-known boycotts was the grape boycott organized by Cesar Chavez in the early 1970s. In order to pressure California growers into accepting the United Farm Workers (UFW) as the bargaining agent for previously unorganized farm laborers, he and his colleagues persuaded an estimated 17 million people in the United States to stop buying grapes. Eventually, the California legislature passed the country's first law guaranteeing farmworkers the right to hold union elections.[40] More recently, major hotels around the United States have become the targets of boycotts for policies and actions that the Hotel Employees and Restaurant Employees International Union consider to be antiunion.[41]

A 1988 Supreme Court decision paved the way for more aggressive boycotting activities by clarifying the legality of *secondary boycotts,* or boycotts of companies that do business with the targeted union employer. For example, striking garment workers might organize a boycott of retailers that sell the targeted manufacturer's products. However, many experts agree that although boycotts draw public attention to an issue, they rarely hurt a company's bottom line or achieve their desired outcomes.[42]

Financial and Political Influence Many unions have huge financial assets, including more than $6 trillion in their members' pension, savings, and stock-ownership plans, and they can leverage this wealth to help achieve their objectives. For example, moving a union's pension funds and other bank accounts out of banks that are tied to a targeted organization can lead to strained relations between the bank and the organization. Moreover, the AFL-CIO has recently become more active in leveraging members' assets to promote job security and limit the growth of executive pay at companies in which the pension funds are invested. The organization also launched a new unit called the Center for Working Capital to help pension-fund trustees pressure firms to develop long-term goals that aim to stop layoffs and company breakups while still providing good returns to investors.[43]

Unions may also exercise significant political power by endorsing candidates and encouraging union members to vote for them. Unions often raise funds for candidates as well. Founded by the AFL-CIO in 1955, the Committee on Political Education (COPE) solicits funds from union members for distribution to candidates who favor labor's positions. In 1996 the AFL-CIO gave Democratic congressional candidates over $35 million in contributions. Furthermore, in the first half of 1997, the AFL-CIO spent $5 million for TV and radio advertisements designed to acquaint U.S. voters with labor's political agenda and target labor's opponents in Congress. However, the direct participation of union members in the political process may be even more effective. More than a fourth of the delegates to the 1996 Democratic presidential nominating convention were union members.[44] In addition, local and national unions organize political rallies, run phone banks, and launch letter-writing campaigns to lawmakers. One campaign by the United Steelworkers produced 54,000 letters to Congress. Activities like these have helped derail legislation that organized labor views as antiunion.[45]

Recruiting younger workers is one strategy that unions are pursuing to increase membership. Twenty-seven year old Carla Naranjo is organizing Latino garment workers in Texas.

Publicity Increasingly, labor is pressing its case by launching publicity campaigns, often called *corporate campaigns,* against the target company and companies affiliated with it. These campaigns might include sending alerts to investors that question the firm's solvency, staging rallies during peak business hours, sending letters to charitable groups questioning executives' motives, handing out leaflets to customers that allege safety and health-code violations, and stimulating negative stories in the press. Although critics say that such tactics spread lies and promote fears about their targets, union leaders contend that increased antiunion activity by management is forcing organized labor to take stronger measures to publicize its concerns. One veteran labor activist and corporate campaign leader reminds workers, "You have a lot more power than to withhold your labor."[46]

Organized labor can also launch public relations campaigns designed to improve the image of unions. In the late 1990s, the AFL-CIO spent millions for television advertising depicting unions as hardworking and progressive. An increasingly successful tactic is to enlist the support of religious, political, and environmental groups to aid publicity efforts. For example, the AFL-CIO recently teamed up with the Sierra Club, the National Association for the Advancement of Colored People (NAACP), the National Baptist Convention, and political leaders such as Rep. Joseph P. Kennedy II (D-MA) in a campaign to force strawberry farmers to accept the United Farm Workers (UFW) as the representative of 20,000 strawberry pickers. These high-visibility groups help the unions reach greater numbers of people.[47] And the attitude of the public toward unions has been improving as a result of their efforts. A recent *Newsweek* poll found that 62 percent of people in the United States approve of unions, up from 51 percent in 1981. Moreover, the approval rating is 68 percent among people 18 to 29 years old.[48]

Is It True?

The average hourly pay of strawberry pickers in the United States has shrunk from over $9 in 1985 to only $6 today, whereas production has increased by over 50 percent.

Management's Options

As powerful as the union's tactics are, companies are not helpless when it comes to fighting back. Management can use a number of legal methods to pressure unions when negotiations stall.

Strikebreakers When union members walk off their jobs, management can legally replace them with **strikebreakers,** nonunion workers hired to do the jobs of striking workers. (Union members brand them as "scabs.") For example, when over 2,000 union workers struck at the *Detroit News* and *Detroit Free Press* newspapers, management kept the presses rolling by hiring 1,400 replacement workers. Although the strike caused both papers to lose customers, advertisers, and profits, the papers persevered for 19 months until the union gave in. By that time, many temporary replacements had been hired permanently, which management is legally permitted to do if it's necessary to keep a business going.[49] Recently,

strikebreakers
Nonunion workers hired to replace striking workers

a union-supported bill to prohibit the use of permanent replacement workers was introduced in Congress, but it was defeated.[50]

lockouts
Management tactic in which union members are prevented from entering a business during a strike in order to force union acceptance of management's last contract proposal

Lockouts The United States Supreme Court has upheld the use of **lockouts,** in which management prevents union employees from entering the workplace in order to pressure the union to accept a contract proposal. However, a lockout is legal only if the union and management have come to an impasse in negotiations and the employer is defending a legitimate bargaining position. During a lockout, the company may hire temporary replacements as long as it has no antiunion motivation and negotiations have been amicable.[51] One example is the Timex lockout of employees in Dundee, Scotland. The plant had been unprofitable, and labor and management had long battled over wages, benefits, and layoffs. Union employees went on strike, Timex locked them out, and the company finally closed the plant six months later.[52] Another example involves professional basketball players. In the mid-1990s, players were locked out by team owners for two summers in a row in a dispute over players' salaries. Although the lockouts did not affect regular season play, they did disrupt off-season training.[53]

injunction
Court order prohibiting certain actions by striking workers

Injunctions An **injunction** is a court order prohibiting union workers from taking certain actions. Management used this weapon without restriction in the early days of unionism, when companies typically sought injunctions to order striking employees back to work on the grounds that the strikers were interfering with business. Today injunctions are legal only in certain cases. For example, the president of the United States has the right, under the Taft-Hartley Act, to obtain a temporary injunction to halt a strike deemed harmful to the national interest. However, sometimes the president can influence a strike's resolution without an injunction. In 1993 President Clinton persuaded American Airlines management and striking flight attendants to accept binding arbitration to end the strike. Three and a half years later, in 1997, Clinton again intervened in an American Airlines labor dispute—this time with the pilots' union. The president designated a 60-day period during which a specially appointed arbitration panel was to help the two sides reach an agreement. Although the workers were free to strike after 60 days, an agreement was reached, and a strike was avoided.[54]

Industry Pacts and Organizations Some industries have copied the united-front strategy of the AFL-CIO by forging mutual-assistance pacts: They temporarily agree to abandon competition in order to assist a competitor singled out for a strike. Such agreements provide a form of strike insurance to help the company hold out against union demands. Certain industries have also formed national organizations, such as the National Association of Manufacturers and the American Chamber of Commerce, to counterbalance the national union organizations. These organizations try to coordinate industrywide strategy and to keep wage and benefit levels even among companies. They also lobby for legislation to protect management against union demands.

EMPLOYEE-MANAGEMENT RELATIONS IN A CHANGING ENVIRONMENT

Economic pressures have created some serious challenges to the twin goals of maintaining the health of U.S. companies and protecting the rights of employees. To survive tough foreign and domestic competition, employees and management alike are having to change the way they relate to each other. Although the need for flexibility means that employees can no longer expect lifetime employment and ever-expanding compensation packages, the need to attract talented and productive employees requires companies to provide some measure of job security and competitive wages and benefits.

EXPLORING GLOBAL BUSINESS

Workers Unite! Travailleurs Univ! Trabajadores Unir!—Labor Unions Around the World

You now know a lot about organized labor in the United States, but what about labor unions in other countries? They're probably pretty similar, right? Well, yes and no. The one thing they all have in common is that they represent employees for the purpose of improving work conditions and compensation. However, their structures and the regulatory environments they operate under are all unique.

Consider Great Britain. Under the British system, employers are not legally obligated to recognize unions or bargain with their employees. Furthermore, employees have no legally protected rights to organize a union. Any collective agreement between labor and management in Britain is more like a "gentlemen's agreement" and is not a legally binding contract. In spite of this, unions have, in the past, enjoyed considerable strength in Britain. However, legislation passed since 1980 has left British unions considerably weakened.

In Germany, union-management relations have long been guided by the principle of *mitbestimmung,* or *codetermination,* which is based on the belief that workers' interests are best served if employees have a direct say in how the company is managed. Consequently, unions often enjoy seats on corporate boards, and managers are encouraged to consult with unions on major decisions like mergers, plant closings, investments, and reorganizations. German unions also have complete access to company records, and they maintain the right to veto subcontracts. Another unique feature of German unions is that they are highly centralized, with most internal decisions being handed down from the top.

In contrast to German unions, Japanese unions are highly decentralized. Ninety percent of all unions in Japan are enterprise unions, which means they are organized on a company-by-company basis. These unions are then grouped into four industrywide federations that coordinate unified standards. However, the enterprise unions remain largely autonomous, solving many labor-management disputes directly, and passing only 10 percent to 20 percent of members' dues on to the federation. What is perhaps most unique about Japanese unions is that they often represent white-collar employees as well as blue-collar employees. In fact, some of Japan's top executives have been labor leaders in their careers.

Mexico's labor unions are also quite different from those of its northern neighbor. When a union strikes in Mexico, the Mexican Federal Labor Law requires all employees, including management, to leave the plant. If the strike is legal, workers continue to receive their wages throughout its duration.

In France and Italy, the major union federations are closely tied to those countries' communist parties. The Canadian system of unions and labor laws is the most similar to the U.S. system. However, provincial labor laws, rather than federal laws, cover Canadian unions. Moreover, Canadian laws require frequent government intervention before workers are allowed to strike.

As you can see, unionized workers around the world share similar goals and ideas. However, the way they organize to reach those goals and the labor laws that govern them are as different as the countries themselves.

QUESTIONS FOR CRITICAL THINKING

1. Why do you think so many different variations of unions have developed around the world?
2. In what ways are German unions similar to unions in the United States?

How can the needs of both labor and management be met? As we have seen, the traditional model has been for workers and management to relate to each other as adversaries, each trying to win concessions from the other. But the economic and competitive climate of the past few decades is fast rendering this model obsolete. The growing emphasis on quality and efficiency requires a new model that ends the combative relationship between management and employees by building trust and cooperation. This requires a demonstrated respect for and commitment to each other's needs. When adverse conditions arise, such as lost sales or lower profit margins, management and employees must work together to find ways of solving the problems. Rather than blaming each other or trying to squeeze each other for more concessions, they must seek solutions that will be mutually beneficial. This model is already being used in union and nonunion shops alike with great success.

Relations in Nonunion Companies

Consider Marriott International. Because they employ many low-wage workers, such as housekeepers and dishwashers, Marriott and other hospitality companies are attractive targets for union organizers. However, Marriott has recognized that the primary reason employees consider unionizing is because they feel they are not valued or treated well by management. In order to demonstrate to workers that they are valued, Marriott offers a variety of programs such as stock options, social-service referral networks, day care, training classes, and opportunities for advancement. As a result, employee turnover is well below that of most hotel companies, and employee enthusiasm is high. Marriott is thus able to maintain high levels of productivity while meeting many employee needs. Workers and management alike benefit, and the company continues to prosper.[55]

Developing a system to handle employee grievances is also a key element in keeping nonunionized employees happy. According to one study, at least 30 percent of all nonunion employers have established formal grievance procedures to settle disputes between management and employees. For example, a *peer-review system* allows an unhappy employee to appeal to a board of employees and managers. The board listens to both sides, gathers information, and then votes on a final decision.[56]

Recent legislation has also clarified employers' responsibility for pension plans, and the minimum wage law has been steadily expanded to include all employees. Moreover, laws now mandate health and safety standards on the job, and a variety of federal and local laws forbid discrimination on the basis of race, gender, or age. As a result, many nonunionized employees now enjoy rights that early unions had to fight hard to receive.

Relations in Unionized Companies

Even in companies where unions have fought hard to win their rights, workers and managers are beginning to realize the quality of their relationship will affect the company's long-term success. Consider Ford, a heavily unionized company. In the early 1980s, when U.S. carmakers were reeling from the onslaught of Japanese competition, Ford management began to realize that workers' ideas could help the company save money. Management also realized that hourly labor represents only 15 percent of the cost of building a

BEST OF THE WEB

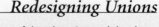

Redesigning Unions

The Teamsters are one of the United States' most powerful and controversial unions. For one thing, the Teamsters are said to have strong ties to organized crime. In addition, because they have organized many U.S. transportation workers, the Teamsters have the power to affect the flow of commerce in the United States and around the globe. This was illustrated when United Parcel Service drivers, who are organized by the Teamsters, struck in 1997. However, like most unions, the Teamsters are trying to create a new image for themselves as a champion of working families in the United States, rather than as a heavy-handed and confrontational organization. The Teamsters Web site offers a wealth of information about the organization, its mission, and its activities. Check out the Web site to catch a glimpse of organized labor's new face. http://www.teamsters.org

vehicle. Management figured that if it got hung up on lowering labor costs, the company would miss opportunities to lower costs and increase efficiency elsewhere. Therefore, Ford management set out to develop a relationship with workers based on trust, honest communication, and the pursuit of mutually beneficial goals. These efforts are paying off. Although GM and Chrysler have been plagued by strikes recently, Ford hasn't had a major shutdown in years. The company also figures it has saved billions by keeping poor relations from affecting quality. In fact Ford contends that its partnership with the UAW is a primary reason for Ford's competitiveness. To maintain this partnership, Ford grants its employees generous contracts and encourages its suppliers to support the UAW in their plants.[57]

Strategies for Building Better Relations

Several strategies are now being used in both unionized and nonunionized companies to bring the goals of labor and management more in line with each other. One strategy is to increase the employees' financial stake in the company. Chapter 10 discusses how stock options, ESOPs, profit sharing, and gain sharing help align employees' goals with those of management and shareholders. The employees of United Airlines learned how successful such strategies can be after they purchased the company through an ESOP valued at $5 billion. Because employees accepted givebacks averaging 15 percent of their pay in exchange for 55 percent of the company and 3 of its 12 board seats, United's stock price has more than doubled. Productivity is rising, and grievances have dropped significantly. Now Northwest Airlines, Delta, and U.S. Air are considering employee ownership as well.[58]

Another strategy for aligning labor and management is to give employees more say in how the company is run. Consider Xerox. To compete with overseas rivals, management needed to cut $3 million from the cost of manufacturing certain photocopier parts. After members of the Amalgamated Clothing and Textile Workers Union came up with ways to save $2.9 million at Xerox's plant in Webster, New York, the company agreed to continue production there rather than shifting it to a company factory in Mexico. Management and union members also worked in teams to determine the best way to complete each production task and to improve quality. The result? "The cost of building the product is competitive with what others can build it for, and we think we've built a better one," says Joe Laymon, Xerox's director of corporate industrial relations.[59]

Even as more companies establish employee-management teams to solve problems or deal with workplace issues, the use of such groups has been brought into question by a recent ruling from the National Labor Relations Board. Electromation is an electronic-

Employee productivity has taken off and grievances have taken a nosedive since United Airlines employees bought a majority stake in the company and took over 3 of its 12 board seats.

component maker in Elkhart, Indiana, that organized committees to study cost-cutting measures that would affect wages and bonuses. The Teamsters Union, which was trying to establish itself at Electromation, protested the company's employee-management committees to the NLRB, arguing that such activities were illegal under the National Labor Relations Act of 1935. Because management set up the committees, told committee members what to study (such as issues that concerned terms of employment), provided meeting space, and gave employees paid time off from their regular duties to participate, the NLRB ruled that Electromation had illegally established a management-dominated labor organization. This ruling applies to all nonunion companies.

In 1996 Congress passed legislation designed to eliminate this barrier to management-employee teams, called the Teamwork for Employees and Managers (TEAM) Act. However, the legislation was vetoed by President Clinton in response to labor's fears that the law would result in company-sponsored "sham unions."[60] However experts say that companies can avoid problems by allowing employee-involvement teams to deal only with subjects such as efficiency and productivity and not with pay practices, working conditions, or other subjects generally covered by collective-bargaining agreements. In addition, management by itself can't determine the size or structure of these teams, set the meeting times and places, or dictate the topics to be examined. Finally, companies can avoid problems by inviting all employees to participate so that employees who take part aren't representing nonparticipating employees.[61]

NEW DIRECTIONS FOR EMPLOYEE-MANAGEMENT RELATIONS

What does the future hold for employee-management relations? It is very difficult to make predictions. Although the leadership of John Sweeney is boosting enthusiasm and political action among union members, as well as generating a new wave of recruiting and organizing, many experts agree that today's global economic conditions severely limit the ability of unions to regain the strength they once had. This is true in the United States as well as in other countries.

Nevertheless, the union promise of better pay, benefits, and working conditions, as well as more equitable treatment by management, has a strong appeal for many downsized workers. And even though unions are sticking to their traditional causes, they are changing to meet the challenges of the twenty-first century. Progressive labor leaders have started to pursue new issues and different employees, and they are doing so in unique ways.

For example, as president of the 500,000-member United Brotherhood of Carpenters, Douglas J. McCarron recently guided his organization through a modernization process that resembled a corporate restructuring. McCarron fired or retired more than one-third of the Brotherhood's headquarters staff of 225, and he slashed some depart-

Although many experts doubt that organized labor will ever recover the strength it once enjoyed, AFL-CIO president John Sweeney is breathing new life into the U.S. labor movement through his visibility, leadership, and charisma.

ments by outsourcing their functions. In addition, 110 of the union's 1,251 councils and locals were eliminated through mergers. McCarron says the leaner structure saves money that can be spent on recruiting while making it easier for contractors to hire union employees. Does this sound like a competitive business? In many ways it is. "People have to understand that we're here to deliver the best possible product for members' money," says McCarron. If his tactics succeed, other unions may follow suit.[62]

Another evolving union is the International Association of Machinists (IAM), which operates a school to train managers in developing labor-management partnerships that spur productivity while protecting jobs. The IAM also sends out its expert consultants—free of charge—to help managers and union leaders create team systems and joint decision-making councils. The union's goal is to help employers figure out how to stay competitive with union wages and then help them achieve it.[63]

Other unions are rising to the challenge as well. For example, the United Steelworkers trains union leaders in business skills so that they can sit on union-management councils, and the Hotel Employees and Restaurant Employees Union in Las Vegas has established cooperative relations with hotel managers by eliminating cumbersome work rules. Said one Hilton Hotel executive of the progressive union employees, "They typify what the labor leaders of tomorrow will be."

Summary of Learning Objectives

1. **Identify two main types of labor unions.**
   Craft unions, which developed first, are composed of people who perform a particular type of skilled work, such as carpentry. Industrial unions organize people who perform different types of work within a single industry, such as the automobile and steel industries.
2. **Outline the organizational structure of unions.**
   National unions are composed of local unions; labor federations are composed of national unions and unaffiliated local unions. Each local has a hierarchy consisting of rank-and-file members, an elected president, elected shop stewards, and perhaps a business agent. National unions and federations consist of delegates elected by the local unions, who in turn elect officers; staff experts and organizers are hired to carry out the unions' programs.
3. **Explain the two steps unions take to become the bargaining agent for a group of employees.**
   First, unions distribute authorization cards to employees, which designate the union as bargaining agent, and if at least 30 percent (but usually a majority) of the target group sign the cards, the union asks management to recognize it. Second, if management is unwilling to do so, the union asks the National Labor Relations Board to sponsor a certification election. If a majority of the employees vote in favor of being represented by the union, the union becomes the official bargaining agent for the employees.
4. **Describe the four stages in collective bargaining.**
   The first stage is preparing to meet, which may involve a strike vote. The second stage is actually negotiating. The third stage is forming a tentative agreement. The fourth stage is ratifying the proposed contract.
5. **List five general issues that may be addressed in a labor contract.**
   Among the issues that may be subject to negotiation are union security and management rights, compensation, job security, work rules, and employee safety and health.
6. **Discuss four options that unions have when negotiations with management break down.**
   Unions can conduct strikes, organize boycotts, exercise financial and political influence, and use publicity to pressure management into complying with union proposals.
7. **Discuss four options that management has when negotiations with the union break down.**
   To pressure a union into accepting its proposals, management may continue running the business with strikebreakers and managers, institute a lockout of union members, seek an injunction against a strike or other union activity, or seek a pact with other companies in the industry.
8. **Explain how employee-management relations are changing to meet the challenges of today's business environment.**
   Employees and managers are becoming more cooperative and less adversarial. Specific actions by management include making more efforts to meet the life needs of employees, establishing employee grievance systems, complying with legislation that protects employee rights, and involving employees more in decision making and daily business operations. Actions by employees include helping management find ways to cut costs and improve efficiency, accepting more flexible compensation systems to help the company weather hard times, and reducing cumbersome work rules.

On the Job: Meeting Business Challenges at Saturn

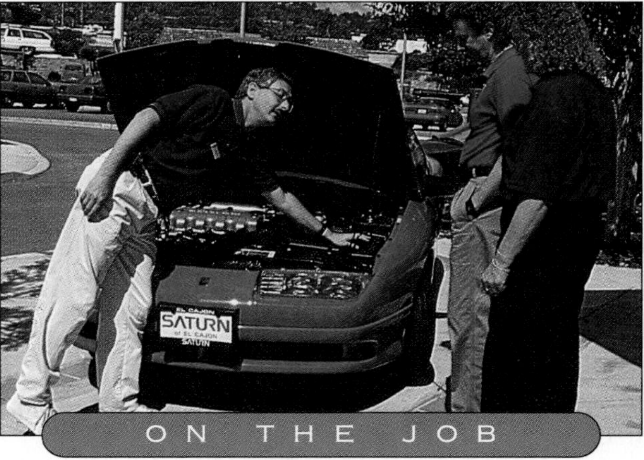

Saturn could be viewed as one of the most expensive and risky experiments in the history of U.S. manufacturing: $5 billion for a mile-long factory to produce a car that, as one dealer said, "drives and feels like a Honda." To Richard LeFauve and Donald Ephlin, it was the beginning of a new relationship between management and labor. Although parts of the agreement between General Motors and the United Auto Workers have been implemented in other industries, Saturn's agreement was the first to combine so many ideas in one pact.

Instead of the traditional boss-worker structure, managers and employees are joined into teams and committees to make decisions by consensus. These groups decide everything about Saturn's operation, including who does what job, who goes on vacation when, how to engineer component parts, how to market the car, and even the company's long-range strategy. For the first time, labor is involved in decisions concerning product, personnel, and profits. Union representatives helped choose an advertising agency and helped select which GM dealers would sell the car. Union employees are paid a salary instead of an hourly wage, and 80 percent of them—determined by seniority—cannot be laid off, except in the case of some catastrophic event. Even then, the joint management-labor committees can reduce the hours of operation or even stop production to prevent layoffs.

For its part, the UAW agreed to streamline the production process. The key change was a reduction in job classifications from more than 100 to a maximum of 6 for production employees and up to 5 for skilled employees. This change, combined with state-of-the-art production processes and equipment, helped boost productivity. The union also agreed to an initial 20 percent cut in compensation in exchange for the salaries and management-style bonuses employees now receive. Future salary levels are decided by consensus of the Strategic Advisory Committee, the highest group of decision makers in the Saturn hierarchy, and these levels are based on the average hourly rates at all U.S. manufacturing plants, including those owned by Japanese companies. Finally, in an effort to tear down the walls between management and labor, all employees park in the same parking lots and eat in the same cafeterias.

In contrast to the 597-page UAW contract covering all other GM operations, which must be renegotiated every three years, the 28-page Saturn agreement is known as a living document, and it never expires. However, it can be altered at any time, as long as both parties agree. Some other plants have been the scene of angry confrontations between labor and management as GM closes some factories, outsources parts production, and takes other steps to cut costs. The Saturn plant, on the other hand, has generally avoided such problems because its contract allows both sides to be flexible in dealing with issues as they arise. When falling demand for smaller cars led to production cutbacks and shrinking employee bonuses at Saturn in early 1998, a large majority of the UAW Local 1853 still voted to keep the unique contract. Shop chairman Mike Bennett said the vote reaffirms that Saturn employees are "committed to the original Saturn idea," and that "The partnership is alive and well in Spring Hill."

Whether the UAW will let GM negotiate a similar contract for future plants is an open question; so far, GM contracts have generally followed the pattern bargaining of the industry. Still, Saturn's success shows that union and management are capable of working together so that both benefit. These days, 6,000 Saturn employees produce about 300,000 cars a year, and the car has earned a reputation for quality. That success has both Chrysler and Ford looking carefully at the model of cooperation that the UAW and GM have established.

Your Mission: You serve as a labor relations consultant to United Auto Workers officials and to Local 1853, which represents Saturn workers. You're familiar with other contracts in the industry, and you are helping the union with long-term planning. How would you handle the following situations?

1. When Saturn's profits are low, employees lose because their pay depends, in part, on company profit. Given these circumstances, what would be the best approach for the UAW when negotiating at other GM plants?
   a. Press for a Saturn-type agreement at all GM plants.
   b. Negotiate a more traditional contract at other GM plants, and wait for the Saturn agreement to prove its viability.
   c. Ignore Saturn; it's an experiment that doesn't relate to GM's other plants, mainly because no other plant incorporates the state-of-the-art design and manufacturing processes found at Saturn.
2. A few of the decisions made by Saturn committees have turned out to be bad ones. Management says that poorly trained union representatives serving on those committees are to blame. Union employees, on the other hand, say that management team members agreed to proposals made by

union members and that all committee decisions were reached by consensus. What should the UAW do?

a. Try to force changes in the consensus process so that union members can't be blamed for poor group decisions.

b. Press for better business management education for all team members so that they will be better able to understand complex business problems.

c. Gain greater union representation on all committees. This approach has been suggested by some UAW members who believe that the poor decisions were a result of the disproportionate influence of managers on the committees.

3. Relations between Saturn managers and the production-line employees have been so smooth that some employees are questioning the union's value. A group has asked for your help in planning a decertification vote. The request leaves you in an uncomfortable position. How should you respond?

a. You don't want the union to think you're undercutting its efforts, so you should tell the group to make plans without your support.

b. Explain that a decertification attempt might jeopardize the cooperative situation at Saturn. Suggest that the group approach union leaders to discuss these concerns, and offer to talk with leaders yourself if the group can't make contact on its own.

c. Tell the group that the union is committed to their success and that they should remain loyal to it.

4. Saturn's daily operations are smooth. However, you know that it's crucial to have a plan in place for emergency situations—fire, flooding, and so on. Which of the following would be the best approach to take?

a. During a crisis, fast, decisive action is absolutely necessary. Consequently, management simply doesn't have the time to get employees or the union leadership involved. Management should have free rein to act according to its own instincts in the event of an emergency.

b. Although there isn't always time to get input from everyone, the union shouldn't be shut out completely. The best idea would be to involve both GM and UAW personnel in planning escape routes and other actions.

c. The union watches out for the safety of employees during normal times, so it should have the responsibility of doing so during a crisis as well. Let union leaders handle any problems that arise.[64]

Key Terms

agency shop (336)
arbitration (336)
authorization cards (331)
boycott (342)
business agent (331)
certification (331)
closed shop (336)
collective bargaining (332)
cost-of-living adjustment (COLA) (338)
craft unions (326)
decertification (331)
due process (340)
featherbedding (340)
givebacks (334)
grievances (340)
industrial unions (327)
injunction (344)
labor federation (331)
labor unions (326)
locals (330)
lockouts (344)
mandatory subjects (335)
mediation (335)
national union (330)
open shop (336)
pattern bargaining (336)
permissive subjects (335)
picketing (341)
ratification (336)
right-to-work laws (336)
shop steward (331)
slowdown (341)
strike (341)
strikebreakers (343)
two-tier wage plan (337)
union shop (336)
work rules (339)

Questions

For Review

1. Why do employees choose to join labor unions? Why do they not join labor unions?
2. What factors have contributed to the current decline in union membership?
3. What employee compensation issues are most commonly addressed by a union contract?
4. How do employee-involvement programs work, and what potential problems do they create?
5. How are unions able to influence politics?

For Analysis

6. How does a closed shop differ from a union shop, an agency shop, and an open shop?

7. Why might a peer review system be more effective than the typical grievance proceedings in a unionized workplace?
8. How do arbitration and mediation differ?
9. How might aggressive corporate campaigns be detrimental to union causes?
10. What are the most important elements in successful employee-management relations and why?

For Application

11. Assume you are the union shop steward at a large plant that manufactures tires for cars and light trucks. Although labor-management relations have always been civil at the company, employees are rarely involved in strategy development or decision making. The plant manager informs you one day that tough foreign competition has caused the company to slash prices to the point where your plant is no longer profitable. Top management is seriously considering closing the plant in the next year and moving manufacturing operations to Southeast Asia. What are your options?
12. Now assume you are the plant manager. Upon hearing about the possible plant closing, the union voted to launch a strike in one week if its demands for job security aren't met. Because of a recent surge in orders, the company is not in a position to close the plant yet. What are your options as you continue to negotiate with union representatives? Which option would you choose and why?

A Case for Critical Thinking ■ Labor and Management Bury the Hatchet

As a government support contractor based in Bridgeville, Pennsylvania, SSI Services won a contract to provide mission support services for the U.S. Air Force Materiel Command's Arnold Engineering Development Center (AEDC), and with the contract came some tough employee relations problems. The AEDC develops, certifies, and tests aircraft, missile, and space guidance systems for the Air Force. SSI's role was to take care of various services on the base (such as facilities maintenance, fire protection, security, logistics), and to operate fabrication and precision machine shops. All of these responsibilities required 1,350 workers, who were represented by 13 different unions. Most of the workers had been employed by the previous base contractor and were rehired by SSI.

Because they had seen contractors come and go, workers had little loyalty to SSI. In addition, a hierarchical organization structure at SSI made employee-management relations difficult. When SSI attempted to change work rules to lower costs and increase productivity, the unions countered with demands for job security, more benefits, and a better overall quality of life for workers. Stalled negotiations led to a 57-day strike. Although both sides eventually made concessions to end the strike, an atmosphere of mistrust and animosity lingered for 3 years.

Finally, both labor and management realized that relations had to improve if the company was to succeed. As a first step, SSI general manager John Stubbs and human resources manager Anthony J. Taylor met with six union leaders to discuss how the strike had damaged trust, teamwork, and morale. Putting their titles and positions aside, team members discussed the problems openly. Over the course of a year, additional meetings included other union representatives, managers, and human resources staff. With the help of a team of skilled consultants, the participants divided into "breakout teams" of about ten people to discuss options for solving specific work problems. Some of the issues they tackled together included reducing health insurance costs, revamping the company's sick-leave policy, and implementing a four-day workweek.

By communicating openly during these meetings, both sides were better able to see the situation from the other's perspective. This improved relations so much that team members decided to "bury the hatchet." In a mock funeral procession, complete with music, team members carried a tiny coffin bearing a real hatchet out to a grassy area on the base and buried it. "We all agreed that we would never, ever again allow the relationship [between labor and management] to deteriorate to the point that we would have another strike," says Taylor.

Because they had worked through many issues in their "breakout teams," both labor and management were able to narrow down to 13 the number of issues to be negotiated in the next round of collective bargaining. "That's really different from the 40 to 50 that people usually have," Taylor says. And if negotiators had trouble agreeing on an issue, a team was assigned to work on it. Some of the solutions they came up with during negotiations included forming total quality teams to give employees more say in the way the organization is run and providing advanced training to craft employees to help them upgrade their skills and add value to the company. Other topics of negotiation included overtime administration, temporary employment guidelines, job-posting procedures, and wages and compensation. As a result of labor-management cooperation, the collective-bargaining process was completed in record time, and a five-year contract was signed.

Today the spirit of ongoing communication, training, and joint problem solving continues at SSI. The human resources manager and chief shop steward co-chair a Labor and Management Relations Committee (LMRC) that meets monthly to tackle issues as they arise. Committee members also receive training in teamwork, quality, and alternate dispute resolution methods. In addition, labor-management problem-solving teams work together to continuously improve the organization. But perhaps the most important benefit of SSI's unique approach to labor-management relations is that the atmosphere of mistrust has disappeared.

1. After taking over the AEDC contract, what could SSI management have done to help avoid the years of labor disputes that erupted? What could the workers have done?
2. Based on the SSI case, what do you think has to happen before an adversarial employee-management relationship can be transformed into a cooperative and productive relationship?
3. Beyond SSI workers and managers, who else benefits from this new relationship?
4. Visit the SSI Services Web page at <http://vanadium.com/ssi.html>, and follow the link to *Facilities Management.* After reading the information provided, describe the company's mission. Then, based on the information in the case, explain how SSI's unique approach to labor-management relations supports that mission.

Building Your Business Skills

Debate the pros and cons of union membership with a small group of three or four students. Consider the relevance of unions at a time when legislation is becoming more protective of employees' rights and companies are having to become leaner in order to compete. Also think about the gap between the salaries and bonuses paid to employees and those paid to senior management. Are unions necessary now that participatory management and employee involvement in decision making are becoming more commonplace? What about the role of unions in occupations considered professional? Are unions more relevant in specific industries or businesses?

- If possible, come to an agreement about the relevance of unions, and draft a brief (one-page) statement outlining your group's position on the issues you discussed.
- Compare the attitudes of your group with those held by other class members. What issues do groups agree on? What do they disagree on?

Keeping Current Using *The Wall Street Journal*

Choose one or two articles from *The Wall Street Journal* illustrating one of the following aspects of labor-management relations:

- Union organizing
- Collective-bargaining negotiations
- Strikebreakers or lockouts
- Employee layoffs and plant closings
- Union givebacks and concessions
- Government-mandated labor practices

1. What are the major issues described in the article?
2. From the information presented in the article, what seem to be the major sources of disagreement between management and labor, the major reasons behind a drive to unionize, or the major issues surrounding the government-mandated labor practices?
3. Are the issues or problems still unresolved, or has some kind of agreement or solution been reached? If so, what are the terms of the agreement? What did each side gain? What did each side concede? If you were a member of the union involved, how would you react to this agreement?
4. Visit the Web sites of the union(s) involved in the issues you are examining. Search for information about the issues. If none is available, search LaborNet's *Headline Archive* at <http://www.igc.org/igc/labornet/hl/index.html>. Does the information offered by these labor organizations provide a different perspective from that found in *The Wall Street Journal?* List the similarities and differences in the way the facts are presented. What conclusions can you draw?

Exploring the Best of the Web

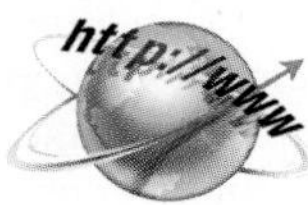

Spreading the Union Message, page 328

The AFL-CIO maintains one of the most comprehensive sites on the Internet pertaining to union activities and issues. More than just a center of information for current union members, the site aims to persuade nonunion workers to join the union fold. Explore the information contained on the site at <http://aflcio.org> before answering the following questions.

1. What is the Union City campaign, what action does it require of local unions, and what incentives does it offer them? Based on what you have learned about the position of U.S. business in the global economy, do you think that the goals of this campaign are viable? Are there ways of achieving these goals besides through union activities? Explain.
2. What appeals does the AFL-CIO make on its Web site in order to increase the attractiveness of union membership? Consider the various employee issues and union benefits it mentions. Do you think the site is effective as a marketing tool? Why or why not?
3. What actions does the AFL-CIO suggest to limit the growth of executive pay? As a student of business, how do you feel about such campaigns? Should employees have a say in how much managers can earn? What are some of the positive and negative effects that might result from union activities on this issue?

Standing Tall in Cyberspace, page 340

LaborNet is a service that brings unions and union members together on the Internet. You can use the site as a starting point to locate other union Web sites, or you can brush up on current news and topics of interest to organized labor. Explore the site at <http://www.igc.org/igc/labornet/index.html> and some of its links; then answer the following questions.

1. How would you rate LaborNet as a tool for the advancement of labor unions? Give examples from the Web site that support your position.
2. In what ways can the Internet strengthen the organized labor movement around the world? What factors limit its impact on union growth?
3. Click on the link to *Index of Labor Organizations on the Internet,* and then on *Stonecutters Union of North America.* What caused the decline of this once strong union? What are the implications for the future survival of labor unions? What strategies can unions borrow from business to remain strong in the face of an ever-changing marketplace?

Redesigning Unions, page 346

Like the AFL-CIO, the Teamsters are working hard to improve their image and boost their membership. However, because of their controversial past, the Teamsters may face more of an uphill battle. Explore the organization's Web site at <http://www.teamsters.org> to find out more about the Teamsters and their current activities. Then answer the following questions.

1. Follow the link to *Teamster Organizing,* and select at least one recent organizing campaign to read about in more depth. What reasons do the involved workers cite for attempting to organize? What tactics are they using to encourage support? Drawing on what you have learned in the text, explain whether you think these tactics will be effective.
2. Click on the link to *Rights on the Job.* What is the Teamsters' position on drug testing in the workplace? What specific rights do some unions have with regard to drug testing? Do you believe such rights should apply to all employees? Explain your answer, and be sure to consider the issue from both management and employee perspectives.
3. After exploring the rest of the Web site, rate its effectiveness in explaining the issues of importance to organized labor. Does the site examine the issues in sufficient detail? Does it leave you wanting more information, or does it just make you want to leave? What suggestions would you make for improving coverage?

Part IV: Mastering the Geography of Business ■ People Are the Same Everywhere, Aren't They?

Companies that expand across national or cultural borders sometimes run into barriers they don't expect in human resources management. For example, Japanese automakers were surprised when they tried to get workers in their new U.S. plants to join in for daily warm-up exercises. Even though the activity is commonplace in Japan, it simply didn't catch on in the United States.

When companies operate across national and cultural borders, understanding cultural expectations and norms is crucial to effective management. Some of the concepts to consider involve personal space, conversational formalities (or lack thereof), friendliness, willingness to "job hop," respect for authority figures, and awareness of social class distinctions.

You can identify a number of potentially important workplace issues by exploring a country's general culture. Egyptians, for instance, address each other by first names only in informal, private settings. When in public, even good friends may add titles when addressing each other. Egyptians tend to be more conscious of social classes than are people in the United States. Moreover, they place great value on visiting friends and relatives.[65]

Assume that you're the president of a financial-services firm based in Indianapolis and that you're ready to expand overseas. To ease your first attempt at international expansion, you're trying to find a country with workplace characteristics most similar to those in the United States. Gather as much relevant information as you can about the four countries that follow. Choose the one with work styles that feel most like those of the United States, and explain your choice. In addition to the resources in your library, explore the information available on the Internet. Possible Internet resources include the *Region and Country Information* of the International Trade Administration at <http://www.ita.doc.gov>, *Background Notes* at <http://www.state.gov/www/background_notes.index.html> published by the U.S. Department of State, the Library of Congress' *Country Studies* at <http://lcweb2.loc.gov/frd/cs/cshome.html>, and the *CIA World Factbook* at <http://odci.gov/cia/publications/nsolo/wfb-all.htm>. (Your instructor may want you to do this as a group exercise.)

- England
- France
- South Korea
- Mexico

Answers to "Is It True?"

Page 329. True.

Page 339. False. The number of cars made by U.S. autoworkers has shrunk to 20 percent.

Page 343. True.

■ PART V

Managing Marketing

CHAPTER 12

MARKETING AND CUSTOMER SATISFACTION

OBJECTIVES

After studying this chapter, you will be able to

1 Explain what marketing is
2 Describe the four utilities created by marketing
3 Clarify how technology is shaping the marketing function
4 List the benefits of delivering quality products and superior customer service
5 Define market segmentation and review the five factors used to identify segments
6 List five factors that influence the buyer's purchase decision
7 Discuss how marketing research helps the marketing effort and highlight its limitations
8 Distinguish between relationship marketing, database marketing, and one-to-one marketing

On the Job On the Job

ON THE JOB: FACING BUSINESS CHALLENGES AT SHE'S FLORISTS

Profiting from a Bunch of Data

With only $500 in their pockets, Helen and Marty Shih (pronounced "she") came to the United States from Taiwan in 1979 to pursue a graduate education. But the brother and sister were sidetracked—instead of using the money Dad had given them to begin their studies, they invested it in flowers. A visionary with a passion for life, Marty Shih believed they had a one-way ticket to a better life. So he and sister Helen set up a flower stand on a Los Angeles street corner.

They worked hard—sometimes 16 and 18 hours a day—and before long they were able to move their business indoors. Neither had a formal education in marketing, but they understood the importance of customer service. They began making notes about who their customers were, where they lived, why they were buying flowers, who they were sending them to, and what types of flowers they liked. The Shihs used this information to send postcards reminding customers that a special day was approaching.

Their customers appreciated being reminded to send flowers, and business grew. Customer by customer, the Shihs expanded beyond their little lobby stand, eventually opening 16 She's Flowers shops in the Los Angeles area. They did more than just sell their blooms. They mass-produced their arrangements on an assembly line, just like McDonald's mass-produces hamburgers. Each shop offered between 15 and 21 designs, which were listed on a menu board. Again, customers appreciated the speed and consistency of these flower arrangements.

However, bouquets weren't the only things blossoming at She's Flowers. Over time, the company's customer information files had grown and were full of valuable names—mostly Asian American immigrants. In fact, the Asian American market became the Shihs' primary focus. Pulling Asian names and addresses out of phone books and recording customers one-by-one, the Shihs eventually gathered so many names (all potential customers) that they decided to spend $200,000 to computerize their database. In 1985 they designed a database program that allowed them to track much more information than they had been able to keep by hand—credit-card numbers, payment dates, personal messages, delivery and vendor services, preferred floral arrangements, and so on. Simple to run, the database was integrated with all the shops' cash registers. In fact, employees could not complete a sales transaction without inputting all customer data, including personal notes like "Mr. Jones never wants the orchid arrangement to be sent to Mrs. Jones."

It wasn't long before Floralfax invited She's Flowers to join a worldwide telemarketing organization that was staffed by American Airlines reservationists during slow travel periods. After joining, the Shihs' annual revenues for the 16 shops doubled—from $2 million to $4 million. Convinced that telemarketing was a garden of opportunity, Marty Shih began exploring the possibility of selling other products to customers.

If you were Marty Shih, how would you profit from a customer information file that contained data on mostly Asian American immigrants? What other products might you market to your customers? How would you continue to build relationships with your customers and keep their business?[1]

THE CHANGING NATURE OF MARKETING

Today's markets are changing at a swift pace. Technological advancements, globalization, increasing consumer demands, giant retailers, and the Internet are all changing the way we buy and sell products—and the turmoil is throwing companies into a state of confusion.

Look at how quickly things are evolving. To reach 10 million customers took the telephone 40 years, the VCR only 8 or 9 years, and Web browsers less than 18 months.[2] No wonder companies today are finding it difficult to keep up with the changing marketplace. Not only are things moving faster, but organizations are finding that many of the successful marketing strategies from the 1980s and early 1990s are less effective today. One reason for such a change is that companies are shifting from the old standardized products, mass marketing, and mass media to the newer mass-customized products (tailor-made goods manufactured for individual buyers by using a single production line). Another reason marketing strategies are changing is that merely selling goods and services effectively is no longer enough. Today's marketers must communicate with customers, build relationships with them, and satisfy their individual needs in order to win customers and keep them.

Marketing Defined

You probably already know quite a bit about marketing. People have been trying to sell you things for years, and you've learned something about their techniques—contests, advertisements, tantalizing displays of merchandise, price markdowns, and product give-aways. However, marketing involves much more than a fancy display of merchandise, a clever commercial, or a special contest. In fact, it takes a lot of planning and execution to develop a new product, set its price, get it into stores, and convince people to buy it.

The same is true for services as well. Suppose you're going to open a restaurant. Think about all the planning and decisions you'll have to make. How many items will you have on your menu? How will they be priced? Where will you locate? How will you get customers? What if another restaurant opens next door? These are a few of the many marketing decisions that companies must make in order to be successful. In fact, marketing is really an orderly and insightful process of thinking and planning for markets. It involves understanding customers and their buying behaviors, analyzing the external forces that affect businesses, developing the best product, finding the most effective way to sell it, creating consumer awareness, and outsmarting competitors.

marketing
Process of planning and executing the conception, pricing, promotion, and distribution of ideas, goods, and services to create and maintain relationships that satisfy individual and organizational objectives

The American Marketing Association (AMA) defines **marketing** as planning and executing the conception, pricing, promotion, and distribution of ideas, goods, and services to create exchanges that satisfy individual and organizational objectives.[3] Marketing involves all decisions related to determining a product's characteristics, price, production specifications, market-entry date, sales, and customer service. In fact, if you set out to handle all a firm's marketing functions, you would be very busy indeed. In smaller companies, it's quite common for only one or two people to be responsible for all the marketing decisions. In larger organizations, however, the trend today is to involve cross-departmental teams of specialists from research to production to advertising—and even include the customers—in strategic marketing planning. As David Packard of Hewlett-Packard put it: "Marketing is too important to be left to the marketing department."[4]

Most people think of marketing in connection with selling tangible products for a profit (the term *product* is used in this text to refer to any "bundle of value" that can be exchanged in a marketing transaction). But marketing applies to services, ideas, and causes as well. Politicians always market themselves. So do places like France or Washington, D.C.

Place marketing describes efforts to market geographic areas ranging from neighborhoods to entire countries. **Cause-related marketing** promotes a cause or social issue—like physical fitness, recycling, or highway safety.

place marketing
Marketing efforts to attract people and organizations to a particular geographic area

cause-related marketing
Identification and marketing of a social issue, cause, or idea to selected target markets

The Role of Marketing in Society

Take another look at the AMA definition of marketing. Notice that marketing involves an exchange between two parties—the buyer and the selling organization—both of whom obtain satisfaction from the transaction. This definition suggests that marketing plays an important role in society by helping people satisfy their needs and wants and by helping organizations determine what to produce.

Needs and Wants To survive, people need food, water, air, shelter, and clothing. A **need** represents a difference between your actual state and your ideal state. You're hungry and you don't want to be hungry; you need to eat. These needs create the motivation to buy products and are therefore at the core of any discussion of marketing.

need
Difference between a person's actual state and his or her ideal state; provides the basic motivation to make a purchase

Your **wants** are based on your needs, but are more specific. Producers do not create needs, but they do shape your wants by exposing you to alternatives. For instance, when you need some food, you may want a Snickers bar or an orange. A fundamental goal of marketing is to direct the customer's basic need for various products into the desire to purchase specific brands. According to Al Ries and Jack Trout, co-authors of *The 22 Immutable Laws of Marketing*, customers' wants are directed by changing people's perception of products.[5] After all, what's the real difference between Viva and Bounty paper towels? Is one actually more absorbent than the other, or do you only perceive it that way?

wants
Things that are desirable in light of a person's experiences, culture, and personality

Exchanges and Transactions When you participate in the **exchange process,** you trade something of value (usually money) for something else of value, whether you're buying dinner, a car, or a college education. When you make a purchase, you cast your vote for that item and encourage the producer of that item to make more of it. In this way, supply and demand are balanced, and society obtains the goods and services that are most satisfying.

When the exchange actually occurs, it takes the form of a **transaction.** Party A gives Party B $1.29 and gets a medium Coke in return. A trade of values takes place. Most transactions in an advanced society involve money, but money is not necessarily required. When you were a child, perhaps you traded your peanut butter sandwich for a friend's bologna and cheese in a barter transaction.

exchange process
Act of obtaining a desired object from another party by offering something of value in return

transaction
Exchange between parties

utility
Power of a good or service to satisfy a human need

The Four Utilities To encourage the exchange process, marketers enhance the appeal of their products and services by adding **utility,** something of value to customers (see Exhibit 12.1). When organizations change raw materials into finished goods, they are creating **form util-**

form utility
Consumer value created by converting raw materials and other inputs into finished goods and services

EXHIBIT 12.1

Examples of the Four Utilities

The utility of a good or service has four aspects, each of which enhances the product's value to the consumer.

TYPES OF UTILITY	EXAMPLE OF UTILITY
Form utility	Sunkist Fun Fruits appeal to youngsters because of their imaginative shapes—numbers, dinosaurs, letters, spooks, animals. The bite-sized fruit snacks are both functionally and psychologically satisfying.
Time utility	LensCrafters has captured a big chunk of the market for eyeglasses by providing on-the-spot, one-hour service.
Place utility	By offering home delivery, Domino's has achieved a major position in the pizza market and prompted competitors to follow suit.
Possession utility	TEST, Inc., a manufacturer of materials-testing equipment for the aerospace industry, allows customers to try its $100,000 machine free of charge on a 90-day trial basis.

ity desired by consumers. For example, when Nike combines leather, glue, and other materials to make athletic shoes, the company is providing form utility. In other cases, marketers try to make their products available when and where customers want to buy them, creating **time utility** and **place utility.** Overnight couriers like Airborne Express create time utility, whereas coffee carts in offices and ATM machines in shopping malls create place utility. The final form of utility is **possession utility**—the satisfaction that buyers get when they actually possess a product, both legally and physically. A mortgage company creates possession utility by allowing you to buy a home you could otherwise not afford.

time utility
Consumer value added by making a product available at a convenient time

place utility
Consumer value added by making a product available in a convenient location

possession utility
Consumer value created when someone takes ownership of a product

The Evolution of Marketing

The marketing function has changed significantly over the years. During the production era (which lasted until the 1930s), manufacturers were generally able to sell all that they produced. They could rely on a good, solid product to sell itself, so they could comfortably limit their marketing efforts to taking orders and shipping goods. The production era had **sellers' markets** in many industries, meaning that demand for products exceeded supply.

sellers' market
Marketplace characterized by a shortage of products

Once new technological advancements increased production capacity, however, the market for manufactured goods became more competitive. To stimulate demand for their products, firms spent more on advertising, but they still focused on selling whatever the company produced. Consequently, this period (1930s to 1950s) was labeled the sales era, and it lasted until companies began facing a new challenge—an overabundance of products or a **buyer's market**; that is, supply exceeded demand.

buyer's market
Marketplace characterized by an abundance of products

Faced with excess product, companies shifted from pushing whatever they produced on all consumers to finding out what buyers wanted and then filling that specific need. They became more customer centered. This shift in focus began the marketing era that continues to develop and expand today.

Although some companies still operate with sales or production-era values, most have adopted the **marketing concept.** They stress customer needs and wants, they concentrate on target markets, they seek long-term profitability, and they integrate the marketing function—that is, they use cross-departmental teams to make marketing decisions. These teams draw from the collective knowledge and experiences of employees working in sales, advertising, product management, market research, and so on (see Exhibit 12.2).[6]

marketing concept
Approach to business management that stresses customer needs and wants, seeks long-term profitability, and integrates marketing with other functional units within the organization

Technology and the Changing Marketplace

One of the most dramatic forces shaping marketing today is technology. Technological advances are responsible for the growth in mass customization, the dawn of electronic commerce, and the shift from one-way broadcast marketing to two-way interactive marketing. Technology is the driving force behind globalization, a critical tool for communication, and an important resource for selling and marketing products.

Consider interactive *kiosks.* These small, free-standing electronic structures not only vend products and services but also provide marketers with the opportunity to find out more about customers' lifestyles, product preferences, and buying habits while introducing new products in dynamic ways.[7] Technological advancements also allow companies to give customers exactly what they want, when, where, and how they want it: Companies can adapt their order entry, product design, production scheduling, manufacturing, inventory management, product delivery, and customer feedback systems to customize large volumes of goods or services for individual customers at relatively low costs. For instance, Levi Strauss mass-customizes blue jeans for women by using a computerized fabric-cutting machine to custom-cut the perfect fit once individual measurements are entered into the computer. Meanwhile, customers pay only a $10 premium for this special service.[8]

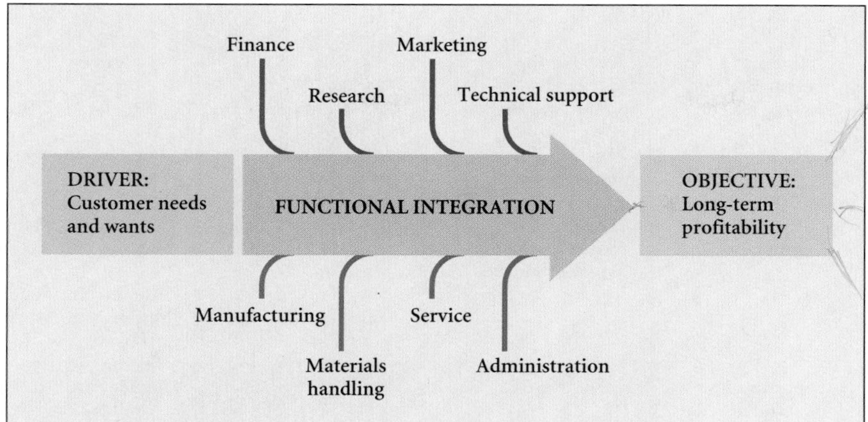

EXHIBIT 12.2

The Marketing Concept

The marketing concept combines functional integration with customer satisfaction and long-term profitability.

Technology is also equalizing the marketplace. Small businesses today are using the Internet to reach millions of potential customers—all over the globe. Like large companies, they are setting up databases on personal computers to remember customers' favorite foods, authors, and clothing designers. Savvy small companies like MiAmore Pizza and Pasta are using marketing databases to track customer purchases. If the regulars haven't stopped by in 60 days, this company's PC-based system sends out a postcard to lure them back with a discount.[9]

Technology and Relationship Marketing How does a company know which products to make? And why do some companies offer a product in 47 different sizes and colors, whereas others stick with only 2 choices? One way companies learn about customer preferences is by developing and maintaining close relationships with their customers—like the Shihs did. In **relationship marketing** you build long-term satisfying relationships with key parties—customers, suppliers, distributors—in order to retain their long-term business. In the past, the relationship between customer and company often ended with the sales transaction. Companies developed products based on information gathered from surveys, research, and *focus groups* (gatherings of 8 to 12 people in one location to discuss a good, service, or organization with a skilled moderator). Then they pushed their products to market quickly and expected marketing departments to create awareness for these new products.

relationship marketing
Focus on developing and maintaining long-term relationships with customers, suppliers, and distributors for mutual benefit

In contrast, many companies today use technology to shift their marketing efforts from one-way broadcast communication to a two-way dialogue with customers. They're using e-mail, Web pages, fax machines, and toll-free telephone numbers to stay in touch with customers long after the sale takes place. Some are even involving their customers in the design and development of new technology products. Consider Intuit, developer of Quicken financial management software. In the company's "follow-me-home" program, company representatives actually follow Quicken buyers home and observe them while they use the software for the first time. The representatives take notes and incorporate users' recommendations in future software releases—making it easier for the next generation of first-time Quicken users.[10]

The Internet According to management consultant Peter Drucker, the most important sources of information for strategic decision making come not from internal data but from the outside world.[11] The Internet is bringing this outside world closer by shrinking the distance between continents to the distance between your fingers and the keyboard. It allows businesses to pursue markets beyond their borders, expand their supplier source, and publish and market to the world. In addition, many companies are using the Internet to

EXHIBIT 12.3

How the Internet Enhances Customer Relations

The Internet is a powerful tool for marketing research, establishing new markets, testing customer interest in emerging products, and conducting a dialogue with customers.

Internet capability →	Marketing and product research	Sales and distribution	Support and customer feedback
Benefits to company →	• Provides data for market research • Establishes consumer response to new products	• Reaches new customers • Provides a low-cost distribution method • Electronic catalogs	• Improves customer access • Puts more staff in contact with customers • Allows immediate response to customer problems
Opportunities →	Increased market share	Lower costs	Enhanced customer satisfaction

Is It True?

Having a Web site makes it easy for customers to find you.

obtain support from vendors, collaborate on projects, provide customer support, test consumer interest in emerging products, sell products online, and conduct a dialogue with customers.

COMMUNICATING WITH CUSTOMERS Exhibit 12.3 shows how the Internet provides an unparalleled opportunity to communicate with customers. Companies like A&a Printers use the Internet to allow their customers to place orders, track the status of their projects, and make project revisions. "Printing and publishing have always been a collaborative function," notes Robert Hu, company president. "We see the Internet as an opportunity to give our customers greater involvement in their print jobs."[12] Like A&a, many companies recognize that the Internet is more than a one-way channel for broadcasting messages and distributing products. The real benefit of the Internet is the ability to draw customers into a conversation with the company. Real-time dialogues with customers can cut through the market chaos and establish binding relationships.

SHOPPING ON THE INTERNET Today's consumer has a variety of shopping alternatives. You can purchase from department stores, specialty shops, superstores, mail-order catalogs, home shopping networks, interactive kiosks, and virtual stores on the Internet. With a click of the mouse, you can get information on products, place orders, and find the best values—anywhere. You can compare model specifications, statistics, and prices, and you can order brochures and videotapes for your dream car. You can preview books, movies, and CDs before buying them. You can even download Dave Matthews Band sound bites before purchasing the group's latest release from CD Universe.[13]

BEST OF THE WEB

Fasten Your Seatbelt

Learn how to be a smart consumer. Fasten you seatbelt and see how technology is changing the way consumers learn about products. Buying a car used to be a consumer nightmare, but going car shopping on the Internet is a breeze. Who needs the auto show. Log on to CarSmart and get smart. Imagine what you'll do with all this information when you enter the dealer's showroom. Will the sales people be ready for you?
http://www.carsmart.com/autoadvr.htm

As more people become linked electronically, there will be less need for people to physically go to stores. Of course mouse clicking won't fully replace tire kicking, but many products will be ordered and delivered to homes by companies like UPS and FedEx. The shopping experience will be captured by virtual reality programs that allow viewers to prescreen homes for sale, watch models exhibit the latest fashions, walk through a mall and into a store, take a product from a grocery shelf, and closely examine it.[14] In spite of these benefits, electronic shopping presents many new challenges to marketers. Selling online shifts the marketing control to users. Getting into the customer's home, reaching customers, and enticing them to click and stay awhile is one of the biggest challenges marketers will face in the future. Understanding customers and responding to their individual needs is another.

THE IMPORTANCE OF UNDERSTANDING CUSTOMERS

According to management consultant Peter Drucker, "The aim of marketing is to know and to understand the customer so well that the product or service fits him and sells itself."[15] This is a challenge because today's customer is sophisticated, demanding, quality driven, and often difficult to understand. Nevertheless, Baxter International is meeting this challenge. The company not only supplies medical equipment to hospitals but in many cases also develops long-term arrangements with hospitals, which allows Baxter to assume complete management of the hospitals' purchasing function and thus to become the sole supplier for medical and other products. Baxter is successful because the company has defined *understanding its customers* to mean "thoroughly understanding hospital operations and their customers' needs."[16]

On the other hand, SkyMall got into trouble because it didn't understand its customers. Company founder Robert Worsley was so focused on providing passengers the best service that he decided to hand-deliver their catalog orders when they landed at airports. Of course, executing this plan was costly. It required large warehouses filled with inventory. But Worsley didn't care, he wanted to please his customers. As it turned out, however, his customers were already burdened with luggage, briefcases, and PCs, and they weren't eager to carry more packages. Although they had plenty of time to browse SkyMall catalogs and order merchandise in flight, they didn't want to pick up merchandise at the airport.[17] Worsley went overboard and almost lost the company because it offered services that customers didn't want.

How do you balance giving customers what they want with keeping company operations under control? For most companies, finding the right balance is a process of trial and error. Look at supermarkets. For years, this $400 billion industry was slowly committing suicide because stores were not responding quickly enough to changing customer lifestyles. Today, however, supermarkets are meeting the challenge. Many are offering freshly made foods, takeout meals, eat-in restaurants, chef demonstrations, photo processing, home delivery, and banking. Still, as more and more customers turn to shopping over the Internet, supermarkets will have to meet different challenges. For example, online shoppers are not being tempted by in-store product tastings or eye-catching displays. Furthermore, they could not care less whether their products are delivered from a warehouse or a fancy grocery store situated on high-priced real estate. In short, today's changes in consumer purchasing habits and lifestyles make it even more important for suppliers and retailers to understand their customers.[18]

Delivering Quality and Customer Service

SkyMall's experience shows that understanding customers is an important part of delivering quality and customer service. Whereas quality is the degree to which a product meets

Responding to customers' changing lifestyles, today's supermarkets offer more food options than ever before. Some are even transforming themselves into take-out caterers.

customer expectations and specifications, customer service encompasses everything a company does to satisfy its customers.[19] Consider Saturn. Buying a car from this company is an almost cult-like experience. New owners are showered with roses and balloons by cheering staff members. Later on, they can participate in barbecues and brunches with other Saturn owners. Or consider Southwest's airport terminals, where passengers waiting for flights may be treated to a quick neck massage by roving massage therapists.[20] Even though delivering such perks may cost you more initially, these companies know that the payoff can be quite handsome. Satisfied customers are the best advertisement for a product. In

UNDERSTANDING THE HIGH-TECH REVOLUTION

Cybershopping for Groceries: From Screen to Table in 30 Minutes

How would you like to do a week's worth of grocery shopping in 10 minutes and never leave your home? At Peapod thousands of busy people are trading their shopping carts for keyboards. Rather than fight the crowds in Chicago, San Francisco, Boston, and other major metropolitan areas, Peapod subscribers go shopping at the virtual grocery store by logging on to a system that lets them interactively shop for grocery items.

HERE'S HOW IT WORKS

Once online, subscribers can:

- Choose from over 20,000 items
- Compare prices instantly to find the best deal
- Create personal shopping lists to save time
- View images of products
- Check out store specials
- View nutritional labels for products
- Sort products by category, item, brand, or nutritional content
- Check their subtotal at any time to stay within budget
- Choose a delivery time that fits their schedule

And that's not all. Peapod's customers shop so effectively in its virtual supermarket that most save money. That's because they use more coupons, do better comparison shopping, and buy fewer impulse items than they would if they shopped at a real supermarket. In addition, they save time because they can shop from home or work whenever they want.

MASS CUSTOMIZATION

Peapod mass-customizes all shopping and delivery processes. When you send your shopping list to Peapod,

addition, firms perceived to offer superior customer service find that they can charge as much as 10 percent more than their competitors.[21]

Customer Satisfaction How do you know whether your customers are satisfied? One of the best ways to measure customer satisfaction is to analyze your customer base. Are you getting new customers? Are good ones leaving? What is your customer retention rate? In other words, are your customers loyal?

Many companies use customer satisfaction surveys to learn how happy their customers are with their products or services. However, if not carefully worded and administered, surveys can be misleading, as well as a poor predictor of future buying behavior. For example, more than 90 percent of car buyers are either "satisfied" or "very satisfied" when they drive away from the dealer's showroom, but less than half of this once happy crowd buy the same car the next time around.[22] In fact, customer repurchase rates in general remain mired in the 30 to 40 percent range, and companies are finding that satisfied customers often don't come back.[23] Plus, research shows that dissatisfied customers may tell as many as 20 other people about their bad experiences.[24]

One problem with customer satisfaction surveys in general is that some survey respondents fill in whatever the salesperson tells them to write; others will write down anything. Another problem with customer satisfaction surveys is that they can sometimes lead to complacency. That's because surveys generally measure the level of service that the company currently provides instead of identifying ways to propel a company beyond its current state of service. Successful companies know these limitations.[25]

Consider FedEx. This company decided that "good" wasn't good enough. So it designed a special Web site to allow its 12,000 daily customers to request package pickups, click and pinpoint the exact location of their parcels, and print electronic invoices.[26] And

an order is transmitted to the nearest partner store. A professional, trained shopper takes your order, grabs a shopping cart, and does your shopping for you. Then the order is taken to a holding area where the cold items are kept cold or frozen until the deliverer picks up a set of orders and takes them to the customer's home. At each stage—ordering, shopping, holding, and delivering—the processes are modularized to provide personalized service at a relatively low cost.

Learning About Customers

Peapod treats each interaction with a customer as an opportunity to learn. Most companies consider a 10 percent response rate to customer-satisfaction surveys to be good, but Peapod gets customer feedback on 35 percent of its orders. And it uses this feedback to improve its customer service—like providing nutritional information, making deliveries within a half-hour window rather than the usual 90-minute window, and accepting detailed requests (such as three ripe and three unripe tomatoes).

Of course, customers are not the only ones benefiting from this service. Peapod has a customer retention rate of more than 80 percent; the supermarkets where Peapod shops have incremental sales volume (about 15 percent of sales are generated from Peapod customers); and customers can have their cake and eat it too—without ever leaving home.

Questions for Critical Thinking

1. What are some of the issues supermarket suppliers (like Kraft or Kellogg) will face as more consumers shop online or over the telephone?
2. Which of the four types of utilities (form, time, place, possession) does online grocery shopping appeal to?

at Intuit, customer satisfaction means that every employee—including the president—spends a few hours each month working the customer-service lines. Intuit worries that customers who are "satisfied" might still find it easy to switch software programs as soon as a better one comes along. Airlines share that concern as well. That's why they initiated frequent-flyer programs. After all, would you really care if you flew American or United if it weren't for the miles? Actually, it takes a lot more than customer satisfaction to keep today's customers loyal (see Exhibit 12.4).

Customer Loyalty Users of Intuit's Quicken program are fiercely loyal. As one marketing consultant put it: "People would rather change their bank than switch from Quicken."[27] Of course customer loyalty like that is an anomaly in today's market. On average, U.S. companies lose half their customers every five years. Why are customers less loyal today? First, they have more choices—more styles, options, services, and products are available to choose from than ever before. Second, customers have more information—brochures, consumer publications, and even the Internet empower buyers and raise expectations. Third, when more and more things start to look the same, nothing stands out for customers to be loyal to. And fourth, time is scarce—if it's easier to buy gas at a different service station each week, customers will.[28]

Is It True?

For every complaint a company receives, 26 other unsatisfied customers do not complain.

So even though winning a new customer can be a difficult task, keeping customers is often a bigger challenge. Consider the benefits: New customers can cost up to five times as much as keeping an existing customer. That's because long-term customers buy more, take less of a company's time, bring in new customers, and are less sensitive to price (see Exhibit 12.5).[29] Still, customer loyalty must be earned every day because customer needs and purchasing patterns are constantly changing. One way to keep customers loyal is by focusing on *customer value disciplines.*

Customer Value Disciplines Why are some companies so much better at serving their customers than others? Why can Wal-Mart continue to offer the absolute lowest prices? Why can Casio sell a calculator that costs less than a box of Kellogg cornflakes? Why can FedEx

EXHIBIT 12.4

Beyond Customer Satisfaction

Satisfying the customer is no longer the ultimate business virtue. More important is that companies must look for ways to increase customer loyalty.

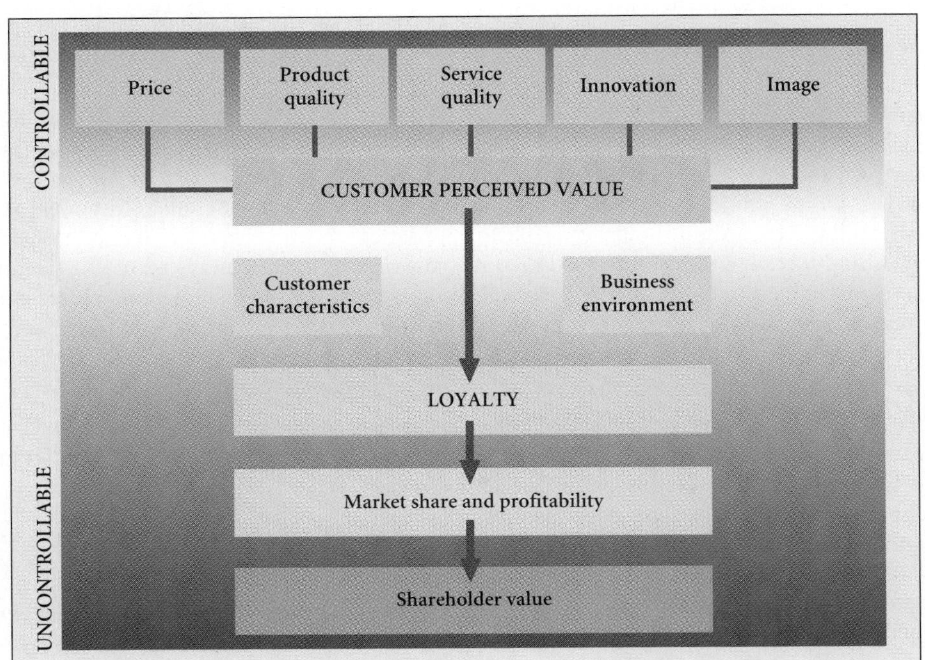

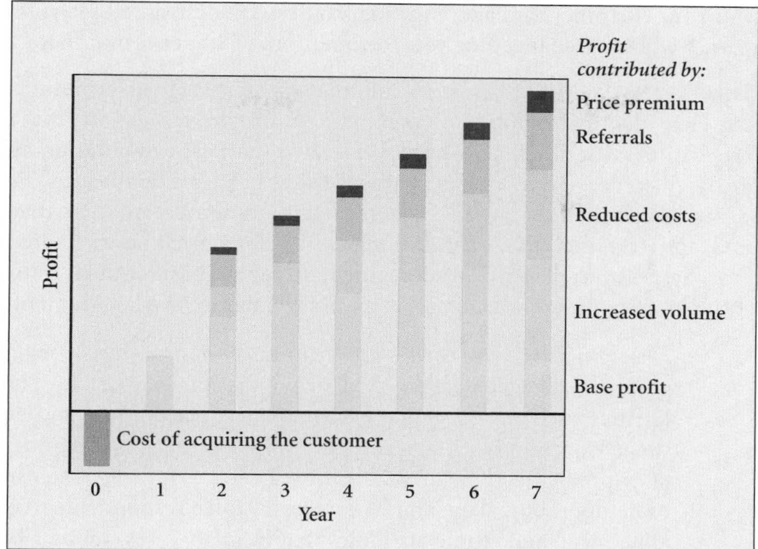

EXHIBIT 12.5

Keeping Customers Pays Off

Repeat customers know your company and service. They advertise your product by word of mouth, and they can be your greatest asset.

"absolutely, positively" deliver a package overnight when Delta, American, and United have trouble keeping your bags on the right plane? Here's why. Market leaders know that they can't be all things to all people. So they choose to focus on or excel in one of three *customer value disciplines.* In other words, they fulfill customer expectations in one of three possible ways: (1) lowest cost or hassle-free service, (2) product leadership, or (3) customer intimacy (developing close customer relationships). You might think that a company doesn't have to choose one value discipline over another, but studies show that companies aiming at all three disciplines are merely mediocre across the board.[30]

For instance, Casio focuses on low cost. So does Wal-Mart. And Hertz makes car rental nearly as hassle-free as taking a cab. On the other hand, Sony and Nike focus on product leadership, and FedEx builds close working relationships with its customers. All of these companies are thriving because they shine in a way their customers care most about. They have honed at least one component of value to a level of excellence that puts all competitors to shame, while still maintaining an appropriate level of customer service in the other values. For example, consider Home Depot. Even though this company goes to great lengths to help customers choose the right hammer (focusing on customer relationships), the company must also carry quality products. After all, if the hammer breaks shortly after it's purchased, all that helpful advice means nothing.[31]

FedEx promises customers to "absolutely, positively" get your package to its destination on time, and it delivers on its promise.

How do companies know which value is most important to their customers? Better still, how do companies determine who their customers should be in the first place? This might sound like an obvious question, but it can be one of the toughest questions a business must answer, primarily because businesses can identify more opportunity than they have the resources to pursue.

Defining Market Segments and Niches

Developing a successful marketing strategy begins with defining and understanding your *market.* A **market** contains all the customers or businesses who might be interested in a product and have the ability to pay for it. Some businesses practice *undifferentiated marketing.* They ignore differences among buyers and produce only one product or product line to satisfy the entire marketplace. This one-size-fits-all approach to marketing is not economical in a world of customization and limited resources. By the time you figure out

market
People or businesses who need or want a product and have the money to buy it

who your customers are and which customers are best suited for your product, either the market will have changed or your competitors will have found them first.

market segmentation
Division of total market into smaller, relatively homogeneous groups

Market Segments Most companies subdivide the market in an economical and feasible manner. They identify homogeneous submarkets, or *market segments,* that are significantly different from each other. This process is called **market segmentation** and its objective is to group customers with similar characteristics, behavior, and needs. Each of these market segments can then be targeted by producing numerous products that are priced, distributed, and promoted to satisfy each segment—a practice known as *differentiated marketing.*

Several varieties of market segmentation have been popular in the past. Here are five of the most popular factors marketers use to identify market segments (see Exhibit 12.6).

demographics
Study of statistical characteristics of a population

- *Demographics.* One of the most common approaches is segmentation by **demographics,** the statistical analysis of population. Markets are subdivided by characteristics such as age, gender, income, race, occupation, and ethnic group. Unfortunately, a number of recent studies have shown that demographic variables are poor predictors of behavior.[32] One reason is that the U.S. Census is the chief source of demographic data, and its categories force respondents to choose between separate racial and ethnic attributes that in many cases can be a blend of possibilities.

geographic segmentation
Categorization of customers according to their geographic location

- *Geographics.* When differences in buying behavior are influenced by where people live, it makes sense to use **geographic segmentation.** Segmenting markets by geography provides a definite direction for advertising. For example, more snow shovels are bought in Detroit than in Miami, and more surfboards are bought in Honolulu than in Manhattan. Campbell Soup Company manufactures two types of nacho cheese sauce—a spicy one for customers in the Southwest and West, and a mild one for everyone else.[33]

psychographics
Classification of customers on the basis of their psychological makeup

- *Psychographics.* Whereas demographic segmentation is the study of people from the outside, **psychographics** is the analysis of people from the inside, focusing on consumers' psychological makeup, including social roles, activities, attitudes, interests, opinions, and lifestyle. Psychographic analysis focuses on why people be-

EXHIBIT 12.6

Common Bases for Segmenting Markets

The purpose of segmenting a market is to identify a group of customers who are likely to value the same things in a particular product or service. (Note: Geodemographic segmentation combines demographic and geographic data.)

CATEGORY	SEGMENTATION VARIABLE	
Demographic	Age Gender Buying power Occupation	Education Race and nationality Family life cycle
Geographic	Global regions Nations National regions States Counties Cities Neighborhoods	Climate Terrain Population density Market density
Psychographic	Social class Personality Lifestyle	
Behavioral	Amount of usage Type of usage Brand loyalty Benefits sought	

have the way they do by examining such issues as brand preferences, radio and TV preferences, reading habits, values, and self-concept. Whereas demographics can define such segments as "women 18 to 34 years old," psychographics defines segments with names like "adventurers" or "self-actualizers."

- *Geodemographics.* Do you ever wonder why cashiers ask you for your ZIP code? Think about your neighborhood: Does it have a distinct character, with people of fairly similar income levels, lifestyles, and other characteristics? In most cases, the answer is yes. Segmenting the country by neighborhoods is the goal of **geodemographics,** combining geographic data with demographic data. The pioneering geodemographic system, developed by Claritas Corporation, divides the United States into 40 neighborhood types, with labels such as "Blue Blood Estates" and "Old Yankee Rows." This system uses postal ZIP codes for the geographic segmentation part, making it easy to reach individual neighborhoods with specialized marketing programs.[34]

geodemographics
Method of combining geographic data with demographic data to develop profiles of neighborhood segments

- *Behavior.* Another way to segment a market is to classify customers on the basis of their knowledge of, attitude toward, use of, or response to products or product characteristics. This approach is known as **behavioral segmentation.** Imagine that you are in the hotel business. You might classify potential customers according to when and why they stay in hotels, making a distinction between business travelers and vacationers. The business traveler might be attracted by ads in *The Wall Street Journal,* whereas the tourist might respond to ads in a travel magazine.

behavioral segmentation
Categorization of customers according to their relationship with products or response to product characteristics

Place These Data in Your Marketing Toolbox

BEST OF THE WEB

How much does the typical family spend on food away from home? Entertainment? Laundry and cleaning supplies? Are these consumer expenditures increasing each year? Find out by visiting The American Demographics Marketing Tools Web site and explore its toolbox of useful information. Read some of the current marketing articles. Take its link to the Bureau of Labor Statistics (BLS) Web site. With all these data, no wonder marketers can better understand their customers today.
http://www.marketingtools.com

Once you segment your market, you are likely to end up with several consumer segments, each representing a potentially productive focal point for marketing efforts. However, keep in mind that a single segment can have customers with a variety of needs. For example, people from the same neighborhood may purchase Colgate toothpaste, but some will buy it for its flavor, others because it prevents decay, and others because it has a peroxide whitener. One way to recognize these needs is to segment your market into *niches.*[35]

Market Niches *Niche marketing* simply takes segmentation one step further by dividing a market segment into microsegments. For example, producing an all-purpose athletic shoe is an example of servicing a market segment, whereas producing different kinds of athletic shoes—running, walking, tennis, aerobics, bicycling, cross-training, and so on—is an example of niche marketing. How do you define these niches? One way is to approach your market from the bottom up. First you identify an unfilled need in the market and then you gradually build a customer base by marketing to customers with similar needs and consumption patterns. In addition, some companies like Nike direct their marketing efforts to servicing several target segments; others like Gymboree focus on a single segment—a practice known as *concentrated marketing.* Gymboree has built a multimillion-dollar chain by targeting only the toddler segment of the clothing market.[36]

Throughout the 1980s, bottled water had an ultra chic appeal. Today, its popularity has moved beyond trendiness, appealing to an increasingly health-conscious consumer.

One-to-One Marketing *One-to-one marketing* reduces market segmentation and niches to the tiniest segment—the individual. It requires a thorough understanding of each customer's personal preferences and the maintenance of a detailed record of each customer's interactions with the company. For example, in Panama City, Florida, Speedy Car Wash keeps a computerized record of each customer's visit. Whenever customers come in for service, the attendant enters their license plate number into the computer and reviews their customer information file to see whether they like the trunk vacuumed or are due a discount or a waxing. Likewise, at its virtual grocery store, Peapod keeps a computerized record of your previous orders so that you don't have to indicate your favorite brand of peanut butter or laundry detergent each time you shop online. At the Custom Foot, customers select a shoe style, pick a color, and then get their feet measured. Everything is available at this store because your feet are measured with a computerized scanner, and shoes are custom-made to fit your feet perfectly—even if one foot is larger than the other.[37]

These companies know that treating customers as individuals is one way of keeping customers loyal. That's because the more time and energy a customer spends in teaching a firm how to customize to his or her own tastes, the more trouble it will be for the customer to obtain the same level of customized service from a competitor. After all, when a customer spends time teaching your firm about his or her preferences, the customer develops a stake in the learning process. And this cements customer loyalty.[38]

Analyzing Consumer Buying Behavior

consumer buying behavior
Behavior exhibited by consumers as they consider and purchase various products

How do customers make a purchase decision? What factors influence that decision? Marketers study **consumer buying behavior** to understand what induces individuals to buy products. For example, the city of Houston wants to know why "people love to drink water out of plastic bottles." In fact, it is even considering bottling its own tap water for sale.[39] Sega wants to know why teens select one video game and reject another. Likewise Nintendo, The Gap, Abercrombie and Fitch, The Limited, and other stores are trying to figure out what makes you buy and why you select one product over another. Armed with this information, companies can tailor their marketing efforts to appeal to your needs and wants.

The Buyer's Decision Process Suppose you want to buy a car. Do you rush to the store, plunk down several thousand dollars, and purchase the first thing you see? Of course not. Like most buyers, you go through a decision process that begins with identifying a problem, which in this case is the need for a car. Once you've identified this problem, your next step is to look for a solution. Possibilities occur to you on the basis of your past experience (perhaps your prior use of certain car) and on your exposure to marketing messages. If none of the obvious solutions seems satisfying, you gather additional information. The more complex the problem, the more information you are likely to seek. For example, you may turn to friends or relatives for advice, read articles in magazines, talk with salespeople, compare products and prices in stores, and study sales literature and advertisements.

Once you have satisfied your information needs, you are ready to make a choice. You may select one of the alternatives, like a new Chevy Blazer or a Ford Explorer. You might even postpone the decision or decide against making any purchase at all, depending on the magnitude of your desire, the outside pressure to buy, and your financial resources. If you decide to make a purchase, you will evaluate the wisdom of your choice (see Exhibit 12.7). If the item you bought is satisfying, you might buy the same product again under similar circumstances, thus developing a loyalty to the brand. If not, you will probably not repeat the purchase. Often, if the purchase was a major one, you will suffer from **cognitive dissonance,** commonly known as buyer's remorse. You will think about all the alternatives you rejected and wonder whether one of them might have been a better choice. At this stage, you're likely to seek reassurance that you have done the right thing. Realizing

cognitive dissonance
Anxiety following a purchase that prompts buyers to seek reassurance about the purchase; commonly known as *buyer's remorse*

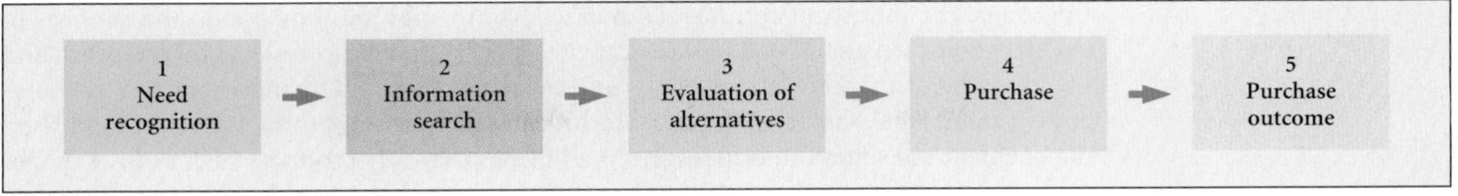

EXHIBIT 12.7

The Consumer Decision Process

Consumers go through a decision-making process that can include up to five steps.

this tendency, many marketers try to reinforce their sales with guarantees, phone calls to check on the customer's satisfaction, user hot lines, follow-up letters, and so on. Such efforts help pave the way for repeat business.

Factors That Influence Buying Behavior Throughout the buying process, various factors may influence a buyer's purchase decision. An awareness of these factors and consumer preferences enables companies to appeal to the group most likely to respond to its products and services. Some of these factors include the following:

- *Culture.* The cultures and subcultures we belong to shape our values, attitudes, and beliefs, and they influence the way we respond to the world around us. Understanding culture is therefore an increasingly important step in international business and in marketing in diverse countries such as the United States.
- *Social class.* In addition to being members of a particular culture, we also belong to a certain social class—be it upper, middle, lower, or somewhere in between. In general, members of various classes enjoy different activities, buy different goods, shop in different places, and react to different media.
- *Reference groups.* A reference group consists of people who have a good deal in common—family members, friends, co-workers, fellow students, teenagers, sports enthusiasts, music lovers, computer buffs. We are all members of many such reference groups, and we use the opinions of the appropriate group as a benchmark when we buy certain types of products or services. For example, shopping malls are today losing what has long been their most faithful audience—teens. That's because Generation Xers (those born between 1965 and 1978) think that malls are for parents and that malls have too many rules. So some retailers like Urban Outfitters and Tower Records refuse to open stores in most malls.[40]
- *Self-image.* The tendency to believe that "you are what you buy" is especially prevalent among young people. Marketers capitalize on our need to express our identity through our purchases by emphasizing the image value of products and services. That's why professional athletes and musicians are frequently used as product endorsers—so that we incorporate part of their public image into our own self-image. After all, doesn't everyone want to "be like Mike" Jordan?
- *Situational factors.* These factors include events or circumstances occurring in our lives that are more circumstantial in nature. For example, you have a coupon, you're in a hurry, it's Valentine's Day, it's your birthday, you're in a bad mood, and so on. Situational factors influence our buying patterns.

Organizational versus Consumer Buyers Another factor that companies must take into consideration when designing their marketing programs is the different buying behaviors of *organizational* and *consumer markets.* The **organizational market** is made up of three main

organizational market
Customers who buy goods or services for resale or for use in conducting their own operations

subgroups: the industrial/commercial market (companies that buy goods and services to produce their own goods and services), the reseller market (wholesalers and retailers), and the government market (federal, state, and local agencies).[41] Organizations buy raw materials (grain, steel, fabric) and highly technical and complex products (printing presses, management consultation, buildings). In addition, they buy products such as food, paper products, cleaning supplies, and landscaping services. Even though consumers also buy many of these products, the quantities purchased and the buying processes are different in organizational markets than in **consumer markets**—which consist of individuals or households that purchase goods and services for personal use.

consumer markets
Individuals or households that buy goods or services for personal use

Organizational purchases tend to be larger (like blast furnaces or skyscrapers) and are often more complex. Also, the buying process can stretch out over several years, and the motivations behind consumer and organizational purchases are different. As a consumer, you purchase airline tickets to visit relatives or to escape to the beach during spring break. But as a businessperson, you purchase airline tickets so that you can make sales calls, service equipment, or negotiate with suppliers. Finally, many organizational purchases entail much greater risks to the buyer than consumer purchases do. Choosing the wrong equipment or suppliers can cripple a business. If you choose United Airlines for your vacation travel and your flight turns out to be late, the consequences aren't usually disastrous. However, if United chooses the wrong computers for its reservations and ticketing system, it could lose millions of dollars. Because of this risk, organizational buyers make more of a commitment to the important products and suppliers they select.[42]

Marketing Research and Databases

So far this chapter has discussed the many changes occurring in marketing today and the importance of understanding customers. It has also discussed how marketing is a series of strategic steps that involves defining market segments and niches, analyzing consumer buying behavior, and choosing customer value disciplines. This section discusses how the quality of every marketing decision depends to a large degree on the quality of the information a company has when making that decision. Companies lacking the information and the flexibility to reach the micromarket level will find that products designed for everyone may actually appeal to no one.

How do companies learn about changing customer preferences, changing market trends, and new competitor products? Where do they get that information? Today's marketing managers and sales reps have immediate access to information about their prospects and customers by accessing customer databases, developing long-term relationships with their customers, and utilizing a variety of marketing research techniques.

How Research Can Help the Marketing Effort

marketing research
Collection and use of information for marketing decision making

Marketing research is the process of gathering data about marketing issues and transforming that raw data into meaningful information that can improve the quality of marketing decisions and reduce the risks inherent in every marketing action. Companies rely on research when they set product goals, develop new products, segment markets, and plan future marketing programs. They also use research to monitor a program's effectiveness by analyzing the number of consumers using a product or purchasing it more than once. In addition, they use marketing research to keep an eye on the competition, track industry trends, and measure customer satisfaction.

Sometimes you need to gather *primary data* (data that are gathered for a specific purpose or for a specific research project). Primary data can be collected by observation, focus groups, surveys or questionnaires, and experiments. Other times you can use *secondary data,* or existing data that were collected for another purpose. Secondary data can be obtained from company sales analysis reports, publications, journals, research services, and a variety of materials available on the Internet. When using secondary data, remember that researchers have biases, statistics can be twisted, and respondents' answers depend both on the kinds of questions asked and on the technologies used to conduct the survey. Also, it's always a good idea to confirm statistics and limit your research to reliable sources. Be careful to collect the right data and use that information appropriately.

Marketing surveys are a common way of gathering data directly from consumers.

Coca-Cola's experience with new Coke is a classic example of how marketing research can lead a company astray when data are not used correctly. In an effort to stem the growth of archcompetitor Pepsi, Coca-Cola conducted extensive taste tests to find a cola taste consumers liked better than either Coke or Pepsi. On the basis of this research, the company launched New Coke, replacing the 100-year-old Coca-Cola formula. New Coke simply did not sell, and Coca-Cola had to mount an expensive marketing effort to salvage the brand. At the same time, the public outcry drove the company to bring back the original formula, renamed Coke Classic.

What went wrong? First, researchers focused only on taste and failed to look at the emotional attachment consumers had to the traditional Coke soft drink. Second, many of the people who participated in the test did not realize that old Coke would be taken off the shelf. If the company had asked the right questions, the rocky course of New Coke's introduction might have been smoother.[43]

Limitations of Marketing Research

Marketing research is simply one of the tools used by managers to understand the market. It is not a substitute for judgment, and used inappropriately, it can be the source of expensive mistakes. Sure you need data. But in the end, it's a healthy dose of intuition that leads you to invent something special.

Consider media mogul Barry Diller. He forged ahead with Fox Broadcasting even though surveys said there was no need for another network. Diller notes: "We become slaves to demographics, marketing research, and focus groups. We produce what the numbers tell us to produce. And gradually, in this dizzying chase, our senses lose feeling and our instincts dim, corroded with safe action."[44] Although marketing research can suggest, in a narrow way, what people might prefer or dislike today, it is seldom a good predictor of what will excite consumers in the future.

Consider Sony. The Walkman is one of the most successful consumer products of the 1980s, yet it was greeted by skepticism during the prototype test.[45] Even FedEx and CNN were met with public naysaying. So was the minivan and its subsequent enhancements. When Ford asked prospective minivan buyers how many doors they would be satisfied with, about 70 percent said three doors. So Ford continued to build vans with three doors. Meanwhile, either ignorant of or unimpressed with the Ford survey, Chrysler decided to offer a fourth-door option. It was a hit. Today 70 percent of Chrysler vans are so equipped, whereas Ford and other manufacturers are scrambling to catch up.[46]

Is It True?

Market research is too expensive for small and midsize companies.

Companies today are learning that one of the best ways to understand what customers want is to stay in constant communication with them. It seems that traditional marketing research—measuring whether customers are a little more or a little less pleased with you than they were last year—has outlived its usefulness. Although focus groups, consumer surveys, and other marketing research tools for probing consumers wants and needs can be useful, they are limited. Frequently they are administered in artificial settings that do not accurately represent the marketplace.

Virtual Reality

Three-dimensional modeling (also known as virtual reality) allows the marketer to quickly and inexpensively re-create the atmosphere of an actual retail store on a computer screen.

Here's how it works: Consumers can view shelves stocked with any kind of product, pick up the package from the shelf by touching its image on the monitor, turn the package so it can be examined from all sides, and move the product to the shopping cart—as they do in a physical store. Meanwhile, the computer records (1) the amount of time the consumer spends shopping in each product category and examining the package and (2) the quantity of products purchased and in which order.

BEST OF THE WEB

Shop with Virtual Reality

See why virtual reality is a valuable tool for marketing research. Visit the Simulation Research Web site and learn about Visionary Shopper. Shop 3-D shelves. Discover why companies are using virtual reality to test consumers' reactions to price changes, new package designs, new products, new shelf layouts, and more. Imagine the possibilities of this new marketing tool. You'll be seeing a lot more of it in the future. http://www.simulationresearch.com

The advantages of virtual reality research over traditional marketing research methods include realistic settings; quick setup; easy reconfiguration of brands, pricing, and shelf space; fast and error-free data collection; low costs and flexibility; and the ability to test new concepts before incurring manufacturing or advertising costs. For example, when Goodyear Tire wanted to expand its distribution to general merchandise outlets (previously available only in company-owned retail stores), Goodyear used a series of virtual re-

THINKING ABOUT ETHICS

Your Right to Privacy versus the Marketing Databases

Imagine, you're sorting through your mail at home when you come across a postcard touting an upcoming sale at the store where your bought a shirt last week. That's funny, you think. You never gave the clerk your address. There's only one explanation. The store probably got it through your credit-card number. How? Even though credit-card providers don't release that information, independent companies will provide it for a fee. And marketers really do need that address because customized mailings are the cornerstone of a sound one-to-one marketing program.

In fact, getting consumer data is probably easier than you think. Privacy experts estimate that you are profiled in at least 25, and perhaps as many as 100, databases. Marketers can follow every aspect of your life. Consider this: Your bank knows your account balance, where you used to bank, and your mother's maiden name. Your government knows how much money you made last year, the kind of car you own, and how many speeding tickets you've gotten. This list goes on and on, from video stores to insurance companies.

Unknowingly, through things you do every day—getting your car washed, going to the grocery store, ordering a sweater from a catalog—you leave fingerprints that give marketers crucial information. Plus every time you enter your name in some blank registration field on the Web, or even click on a Web site, all sorts of data are being collected about you. By depositing "cookies" on your hard drive, Web sites can follow your path and keep track of the sites you recently visited. This information is stored in a "cookie file" in your browser so that the next time you drop by the same Web site, the server picks up your footprint and gathers more information that can be shared with advertisers.

Of course, there's nothing unethical about maintaining a database, and there's certainly nothing unethical about using a computer to manage the database. The ethical problems arise when marketers buy, borrow, rent, or exchange information, usually without your knowledge or permission. Most of the time, you won't even know that your records are being seen or used by others, people you never imagined would or should be able to put together a big file on your life.

ality simulations to assess consumer brand-name loyalty and product-line pricing strategies. The simulations even identified which of Goodyear's competitors posed the greatest threat to its business. Virtual reality simulations are also being used by vending machine companies to record a consumer's second choice when their preferred brand is "temporarily out-of-stock." In short, the possibilities of virtual reality testing are limitless—offering greater insight into consumer buying behavior than traditional marketing research.[47]

The Visionary Shopper system creates a simulated shopping environment that lets researchers test consumer reactions to packaging and other marketing variables.

Database Marketing

Most companies today rely on data when making marketing decisions. In fact, customer relationships like the ones Helen and Marty Shih established with the Asian Americans are a key source of customer data. Even though relationship and database marketing are related, they are not the same. Relationship marketing focuses on maintaining two-way lines of communication between the company and the customer. **Database marketing** is the tool for recording those customer interactions. The underlying principle of database marketing is simple: All customers share certain common needs and characteristics, but each has his or her own twist. If you collect information on the key attributes of your customers, you can develop composites of target customers by combining several of these attributes. Then once you learn more about your customers, you can customize messages to them and deepen their loyalty (see Exhibit 12.8).[48]

database marketing
Process of building, maintaining, and using customer databases for the purpose of contacting customers and transacting business

Many companies today use database marketing to win new customers. For example, Kimberly Clark, manufacturer of Huggies diapers, purchases lists of expectant mothers from doctors and hospitals and then sends these mothers-to-be magazines and letters. Later, after the baby is born, the company sends each mother a coded coupon that allows Huggies to

That's the first question: Who should have the right to see your records? The Selective Service Administration once wanted to find men of draft age who hadn't yet registered. Among other databases, they bought a list of names and birthdays from an ice cream parlor, a list developed as a promotion to recognize children's birthdays in some special way. In fact, for as little as a nickel, marketers can find out who you are, where you live, how much you earn, and what you like to buy.

Here's the second question: Should you have the right to know who wants your records and be able to refuse access? What happens when you apply for health insurance and you're asked to sign a statement that allows the insurer to search a medical-records database for your history and to provide information on you to others? Despite some state laws, a lot of personal information about U.S. citizens can still be disclosed, information that may embarrass people or in some other way have a negative impact on their lives. In fact, inaccurate or incomplete information is routinely used to determine whether someone should be hired, insured, rented to, or given credit.

A debate is raging between marketers and those who are concerned about privacy. On the one hand, privacy advocates argue that people should have the right to be left alone. On the other hand, marketers argue that they should have the right to freedom of speech, the right to inform customers about their offers. Thus the ultimate dilemma: Does a marketer's needs and freedom of speech outweigh the consumer's right to privacy? Some argue that although the freedom of speech is guaranteed in the U.S. Constitution, the right to privacy is not. As the number of comprehensive databases continues to grow, this issue promises to be a central topic in marketing.

QUESTIONS FOR CRITICAL THINKING

1. Should a marketer selling low-cost long-distance telephone service be allowed to look at your telephone records?
2. When researchers ask respondents to answer questions about family, friends, or neighbors, are they invading the privacy of those not present?

EXHIBIT 12-8

Database Marketing

Here are the four ways to achieve good relationship marketing by using a customer database.

Four Commandments to Achieve Effective Database Marketing

Commandment #1: Identify Your Customers
- Build a customer database
- Add relevant information
- Continually update

Commandment #2: Learn More About the Customers Who Drive Your Business
- Profile your customers
- Develop predictive behavioral models
- Invest marketing resources in high-value customers

Commandment #3: Tailor Individual Messages to Individual Customers
- Focus on their needs
- Provide relevant information
- Begin a dialogue

Commandment #4: Deepen Customer Loyalty
- Communicate regularly
- Involve customers in the marketing function
- Up-sell, cross-sell, and begin again

track which mothers have tried the product.[49] Likewise, Allstate uses database marketing to amass huge amounts of data about applicants (credit reports, driving records, claims history) in order to swiftly price a customer's insurance policy. And Ritz Carlton enters all customer requests, comments, and complaints into a database that now contains individual profiles of more than 500,000 guests. By accessing these profiles, employees at any Ritz Carlton hotel can accommodate the individual tastes of its customers from anywhere in the world.[50]

Database marketing not only enables companies to interact with customers in a truly personalized manner, but it allows companies to monitor changes in customer purchase patterns, alerting them to the possibility of defecting customers. In addition, companies can monitor repeat purchases to determine the success of new-product launches and to reward repeat buyers. Perhaps the biggest benefit of database marketing is the ability to use the data gathered in strategic marketing planning and decision making, the topic of Chapter 13.

Summary of Learning Objectives

1. **Explain what marketing is.**
   Marketing is the process of planning and executing the conception, pricing, promotion, and distribution of ideas, goods, and services to create exchanges that satisfy individual and organizational objectives.
2. **Describe the four utilities created by marketing.**
   Form utility is created when companies turn raw materials into finished goods desired by consumers. Time utility is created by making the product available when the consumer wants to buy it. Place utility is created when a product is made available at a location that is convenient for the consumer. Possession utility is created by facilitating the transfer of ownership from seller to buyer.
3. **Clarify how technology is shaping the marketing function.**
   Technology is making it possible to mass-customize products. It is making it easier to conduct a dialogue with customers and build long-term relationships. It is providing marketers with new ways to learn about consumer preferences and buying behavior. Finally, it is opening up new shopping alternatives while creating new marketing opportunities and challenges.
4. **List the benefits of delivering quality products and superior customer service.**
   Delivering quality products backed with good customer service improves customer satisfaction, enhances customer loyalty, decreases marketing costs, and increases profits. These benefits can give companies a competitive advantage in the marketplace.

5. **Define market segmentation and review the five factors used to identify segments.**
   Market segmentation is the process of subdividing a market into homogeneous groups in order to identify potential customers and to devise marketing approaches geared to their needs and interests. The five most common factors used to identify segments are demographics, geographics, psychographics, geodemographics, and behavior.
6. **List five factors that influence the buyer's purchase decision.**
   The purchase decision is influenced by the buyer's culture, social class, reference groups, self-image, and situational factors.
7. **Discuss how marketing research helps the marketing effort, and highlight its limitations.**
   Marketing research can help companies set goals, develop new products, segment markets, plan future marketing programs, evaluate the effectiveness of a marketing program, keep an eye on competition, and measure customer satisfaction. On the other hand, marketing research is a poor predictor of what will excite consumers in the future, and it can be ineffective—especially when conducted in an artificial setting.
8. **Distinguish between relationship marketing, database marketing, and one-to-one marketing.**
   Relationship marketing is the practice of building long-term satisfying relationships with customers. It focuses on two-way communication. Database marketing is the tool for recording customer interactions and customer data. One-to-one marketing treats customers individually. It requires a thorough understanding of a customer's preferences, which are entered into a detailed customer information file or database.

On the Job: Meeting Business Challenges at She's Florists

Customer by customer, Helen and Marty Shih built a business empire serving the huge multicultural Asian American market. While Helen continued to push flowers to customers, Marty began telemarketing other services to this rapidly growing market. After all, having a database of Asian American immigrants, knowing their language, and understanding their cultural differences, the Shihs could make their blossoming database pay off. So Marty Shih founded the Asian Business Co-op, an Asian buying club that negotiates discounts on products and services for its members.

For instance, by entering into a joint venture with Sprint, the co-op sold special discount long-distance services to the Asian community. Of course, the growth of the partnership was helped by the fact that Asian Americans make three times more international calls than other ethnic groups in the United States. Soon Marty entered into relationships with other service providers: DHL Air Express, New York Life Insurance Company, Service Master, Lucent Technologies, United Van Lines, and Pearle Vision—to name a few. It seemed that the Shihs' not-so-little database (currently 1.5 million names) was a gold mine of opportunity for companies looking for new business. And Marty was their bridge—repackaging and customizing products and services and selling them to Asian Americans at a substantial discount.

At the heart of the co-op were the 550 telemarketers who understood the diverse Asian culture and collectively spoke six different languages—Mandarin, Cantonese, Korean, Japanese, Vietnamese, and Tagalog (spoken in the Philippines). Asian immigrants (most of whom did not speak English) needing advice on dealing with immigration officials or perhaps help in understanding a bill, could call the Asian American 411 (at 1–800–777-Club) and get whatever information they requested—for free. After all, Marty knew that they would eventually buy something. Meanwhile, each caller was added to the company's database. With over 1,200 new immigrants calling daily, the Shihs decided to sell the flower shops and concentrate on the more profitable telemarketing business.

Today the Asian American Association (founded in 1995 as an offshoot of the co-op) comprises 13 companies and has branches across the United States. The 550 informed telemarketers sit ready at computer banks and phones to address the financial, health, insurance, travel, and other personal concerns and needs of Asian Americans, while moving well over $200 million in merchandise annually and bringing the association over $25 million in annual revenue. The association has become a center of social, cultural, educational, and political life for Asian Americans. With over 1.5 million members, the list of offerings keeps expanding. The more the telemarketers learn about the callers, the better the association can serve them.

Headquartered in a 65,000-square-foot building in El Monte, California, Marty and Helen Shih have come a long way from that single street corner flower stand. Still, many challenges lie ahead. With services aimed mostly at recent immigrants, the

Shihs must find new ways to keep customers once they become more assimilated into the American culture. Plus, it's not easy to market to this diverse group. After all, a person who is Chinese is not Japanese is not Korean or Thai. And that makes it especially difficult to convey a single marketing message. But, "we always keep thinking big," says Marty. With over 500,000 people visiting the association's Web site daily, there's a blooming opportunity out there.

Your Mission: Marty Shih hires you to help develop strategies for the Asian American Association's future. Using your knowledge of marketing and customer service, decide how the company should respond to the following issues. Some of these issues have more than one good answer, so be sure you can defend the answer you choose.

1. Even though the Shihs have dedicated their business to serving the needs of the Asian American market, competition isn't standing still. Other businesses sell similar products—perhaps not customized for this group, but often at comparable prices and quality. What advice would you give the Shihs on how to compete?
   a. The Shihs should focus on beating the competition with the lowest prices. Even though the Asian American Association sells many products that customers can acquire elsewhere, low prices will keep their customers loyal.
   b. Increasingly today's busy customers have limited time for shopping, so convenience has become important. The telephone makes it easy for customers to check on their accounts and to check on the progress of their orders. The Shihs must ensure that telephone agents provide courteous and high-quality service and that they always have updated customer information.
   c. To keep the company growing, the Shihs should concentrate on creating more sales and enhancing their database to make a better match between what customers really want and the products their telemarketing agents sell.
2. Technology has played a key role in the Shihs' success ever since the early days of the business when Marty and Helen developed their first primitive database. Now database technology and computer networking have advanced, and technology costs have decreased dramatically. Many firms are now able to compete more effectively by installing sophisticated sales and service systems. Even though technology costs have come down, the Asian American Association's budget is limited. Would you recommend spending more money on technology now, or would you suggest holding off on technology spending until your competition catches up?
   a. The Shihs have spent wisely in the technology area and have clearly established leadership in marketing to the Asian American community. The Asian American Association should refrain from technology spending now and focus instead on upgrading customer-service staff and back-shop operations.
   b. Telemarketing tools have become very sophisticated. Agents who normally handle service calls from customers can now place outward calls as well—selling more products during times when service call volumes are low. Marty and Helen Shih can help improve agent productivity by implementing these telemarketing tools.
   c. Selling is the key to ongoing success. Even though the Shihs' database has served them well, they should develop new approaches to matching customer preferences with company products. The Asian American Association should invest more in database technology.
3. Marty is deeply committed to the Asian American community. The Shihs' early success is due to their ability to communicate and empathize with fellow immigrants from China. But today Asian Americans are highly fragmented in many ethnic groups, including Chinese, Japanese, Filipino, and Korean, making it difficult to get across a single marketing message. Because Asian Americans are joining the American "melting pot," selling along purely ethnic lines will be more difficult in the future. Would you advise Marty to continue focusing primarily on Asian Americans or to seek more diversity in the customer base?
   a. The Asian American population in the United States surged by more than a third from the early to mid-1990s. Moreover, Asian Americans tend to have higher incomes than the population at large. It makes sense to continue focusing on the important Asian American segment.
   b. The Asian American population is fragmented, and research indicates that this ethnic group responds positively when addressed in its own language. At the same time Marty should anticipate the "melting pot" effect and start developing plans that will attract non-Asian customers as well.
   c. The melting pot will prevail, and Marty should start aggressively marketing his services to non-Asian members. Because of the size of the Asian American Association and its mighty purchasing power, Marty can offer reasonably priced products to all consumers regardless of their ethnic background.
4. Having an extensive database can be a huge marketable asset. Imagine what some businesses would do to get their hands on the Asian American Association's membership file. Some might even pay the association a handsome amount. The Shihs are constantly bombarded with offers to rent or purchase the information on their database. Which alternative do you think would best serve the Asian American Association in the long run?
   a. Make the database available to other organizations (even political ones), but charge a high price for its use—after all, it's unique. This could be a tremendous source of revenue for the Asian American Association on a continual basis.

b. Don't lease or sell the database; rather continue to develop alliances with companies to market their products through the association—even though members might be able to find a better deal on their own.

c. Don't sell or lease the database as a list; rather, focus on collecting even more customer information in order to generate detailed analytical reports on the consumer buying behavior of Asian Americans. Of course, because individual names would not be included, it would be fine to publish or sell this summary information to organizations for a sizable fee.[51]

Key Terms

behavioral segmentation (369)
buyer's market (360)
cause-related marketing (359)
cognitive dissonance (370)
consumer buying behavior (370)
consumer markets (372)
database marketing (375)
demographics (368)
exchange process (359)
form utility (359)
geodemographics (369)
geographic segmentation (368)
market (367)
market segmentation (368)
marketing (358)
marketing concept (360)
marketing research (372)
need (359)
organizational market (371)
place marketing (359)
place utility (360)
possession utility (360)
psychographics (368)
relationship marketing (361)
sellers' markets (360)
time utility (360)
transaction (359)
utility (359)
wants (359)

Questions

For Review

1. How has marketing evolved over time?
2. Why are customers less loyal today?
3. How does organizational buying differ from consumer buying?
4. What factors influence the consumer when making purchasing decisions?
5. What is the difference between primary and secondary data?

For Analysis

6. Why do companies segment markets?
7. Why is it important to build relationships with customers?
8. What are some of the challenges electronic shopping poses to marketers?
9. How are companies using the Internet as a marketing tool?
10. How can companies use databases in their marketing efforts?

For Application

11. How might an airline use relationship and database marketing to improve customer loyalty?
12. How might a company use virtual reality simulations to test-market consumer acceptance of a new-age beverage product like Snapple or Fruitopia?

A Case for Critical Thinking ■ Homebuilder Finds a Profitable Way to Satisfy Customers

A home is the most complex purchase most consumers will ever make. The decision spans the entire spectrum of behavioral influences, from legal and practical factors to social and emotional ones. Whether traditional and cozy or sleek and futuristic, whether practical or extravagant, homes reflect their owners' sense of style, activities, and personal values. Because of this deep connection with self-image and lifestyle, many buyers want their homes to be unique, to have special touches that meet their personal needs and distinguish them from all other houses in the neighborhood.

Unfortunately, this desire to create unique houses collides with the cold realities of homebuilding economics. Customized houses cost more money, and the more customized a house, the more it's likely to cost. The reasons range from the cost of hiring an architect to draw up plans to the cost of builders buying specialized materials in small quantities. For the vast majority of new-home buyers, creating a one-of-a-kind masterpiece is simply too expensive. In the typical suburban planned neighborhood, one or more homebuilders offer a few different models from which buyers can choose. Builders can construct these models quickly and cost effectively, but the result is often cookie-cutter houses that look nearly identical. Consumers who'd love to have a unique house built to satisfy their dreams and demands can look up and down the street and find other people with practically the same house. It's a little like showing up for a party in some splendid new outfit, only to find a dozen other people wearing the same thing—except that you're stuck with your house for years, not just for an evening.

In this buyer frustration, homebuilder Donald Horton saw a business opportunity. He realized that it doesn't take much to give most buyers a sense of uniqueness. It could be a marble entryway to impress guests, an enlarged kitchen window to let parents keep a better eye on their children playing in the yard, or a whirlpool bathtub in the master bedroom. Horton offers perhaps ten basic home models in each of his developments; then he lets people make choices about how to customize from those standardized starting points. Horton still gets much of the cost efficiency of mass production, and buyers get to feel a little more special about their new homes. In contrast, many cost-conscious builders calculate their costs for each model down to the penny and refuse to budge when buyers ask for changes.

Options such as whirlpool baths and fancy windows have a strong emotional pull for buyers, who often don't think twice about the additional cost. If they do think about the cost, a smart salesperson can remind them that over the life of the typical 30-year mortgage, a few indulgences barely create a financial blip. Adding a $1,000 whirlpool bath to a $200,000 house with a 10 percent, 30-year mortgage, for instance, works out to less than $.30 a day. For $5 a day, you could add about $17,000 worth of custom goodies—enough to add a lot of personal touches to a standard-issue structure.

Being flexible enough to let consumers add all these options pays off handsomely for Horton. First, the profit margin on options is often higher than on the basic structure of the house, so the more options people buy, the higher Horton's profit margin. Second, letting people choose the personal details often leads to faster sales. The faster he can sell homes, the less money he has tied up in inventory.

Having the flexibility to respond to customers' unique requests looks like good business to Horton. His company's profit margin is more than twice that of his nearest competitors, and sales continue to grow. He'd be the first to tell you that listening to customers is just basic good business.

1. How does Donald Horton apply the marketing concept?
2. Because of his willingness to customize the details, would Horton be able to attract all home buyers, regardless of price category? Why or why not?
3. How does Horton's flexibility relate to the definition of quality used in this chapter? Identify at least three other consumer purchase choices that, like houses, reflect the buyer's self-image and lifestyle.
4. Before building your dream home, why not check out the existing homes for sale in your area. Go to the USA Home Show Web site <http://www.usahomeshow.com> and click on *American Home Show*, then click on *here*. Select a state, city, area, and community. Enter the required search criteria and find the homes for sale that match your criteria. Be sure to click on *more information* and *map it!* to see the details.
   a. How easy was it to find a listing of homes in your area?
   b. Click back to the home page and click on the *Mover's Toolkit*. If you are moving to a different city, use the salary calculator to compare the cost-of-living differences. Will it cost more or less to live in your new city?
   c. What other types of information and links could be added to this Web site that might be helpful for a potential home buyer?

Building Your Business Skills

Select a small local retail store where you frequently shop. Based on your familiarity with its products and customers, prepare a brief report summarizing the following:

- Define the store's "typical" customer, describing age, income level, gender, activities, interests, lifestyle, and so on.
- Does this store focus on a specific market microsegment or niche? If so, describe it.
- Does this store maintain a relationship with its customers? How?
- Do you periodically receive targeted communication from this store? Is it personalized?

As directed by your instructor, share your findings with the members of your class in a brief presentation.

Keeping Current Using *The Wall Street Journal*

From recent issues of *The Wall Street Journal*, select an article that describes in some detail a particular company's attempt to build relationships with its customers (either in general or for a particular product or product line).

1. Describe the company's market. What geographic, demographic, behavioral, or psychographic segments of the market is the company targeting?
2. How does the company hold a dialogue with its customers? Does the company maintain a customer database? If so, what kinds of information does it gather?
3. According to the article, how successful has the company been in understanding its customers?
4. Learning about population trends is one way companies plan ahead. Go to the U.S. Census Bureau online population reports <http://www.census.gov/population/www/> and click on *Social and Demographic Characteristics Data.* Click on the *Population Profile* and view it using HTML. Review the material on *National Population Trends* and *National Population Projections.*
   a. Briefly summarize current demographic trends in the U.S. population.
   b. How are these trends expected to change?
   c. How could a company use this information to plan its marketing programs? What types of demographic information might it want to gather into a customer database?

Exploring the Best of the Web

Fasten Your Seatbelt, page 362

Today's consumer has all the information he or she needs to make a smart purchase. Go to Car Smart <http:www.carsmart.com/autoadvr.htm> to answer these questions.

1. Check out the *Auto Buying Tips.* Scroll down to the bottom of the page, click on *Invoice Pricing Reports,* and then click on *View the Sample Report.* How is this information useful to consumers?
2. Visit several of the *Manufacturers' Sites.* Which manufacturers make it easy to contact their customer-service department? For those who don't, how might they improve? Were you asked to fill out information? How might the company use this information?
3. Do you think car manufacturers and dealers like smart consumers? Why or why not?

Place These Data In Your Marketing Toolbox, page 369

Learning about consumer demographics is one of the first steps in developing an effective marketing program. To answer these questions, go to American Demographics Marketing Tools <http://www.marketingtools.com>.

1. Review the publications *American Demographics* and *Marketing Tools.* Read some of the articles. How might these journals be helpful to marketers? Which journal has the most useful information? Why?
2. Scroll down to *Hot Links to Useful Government and Commercial Sites.* Jump directly to the Bureau of Labor Statistics (BLS) *Consumer Expenditure* data. Click on the *FAQs.* What is the Consumer Expenditure Survey and how is it used?
3. Go back to the home page, and click on the *Standard Bulletin.* Using the latest year of information, click on the *Composition of Consumer Unit.* Review the table. How much did the "typical husband and wife only" spend on food away from home? On which three food categories did they spend the most? How much did they spend on entertainment? Go back and review some of the other tables. How do data like this help marketers?

Shop with Virtual Reality, page 374

See the power of virtual reality marketing research. Go to Simulation Research at <http://www.simulationresearch.com>. To answer these questions, click on *Learn More About Visionary Shopper.*

1. How does virtual reality consumer research work, and what are some of the benefits of using it over other marketing research techniques?
2. Why is virtual reality an effective way to test your pricing strategies? *(Go to Price Tests)*
3. Why would a company want to test a consumer's response to a product being "unavailable"? *(Go To Substitution Tests)*

Answers to "Is It True?"

Page 362. False. The Web makes it easy for customers to find you *if* they're already looking for you. Web addresses are like 800 numbers—fantastic for people who are already looking for you, but not a first point of contact with most customers.

Page 366. True.

Page 373. False. Good market research does not have to be expensive. A recent study by *Inc.* magazine found that customers are the best source of market research for new products and services. Nearly 40 percent of the 173 CEOs surveyed spend less than $1,000 on a market research project.

CHAPTER 13

PRODUCT AND PRICING DECISIONS

OBJECTIVES

After studying this chapter, you will be able to

1. Outline the ten steps in the strategic marketing planning process
2. Identify the four basic components of the marketing mix
3. Specify the four stages in the life cycle of a product
4. Describe the six stages of product development
5. Identify four ways of expanding a product line
6. Cite three levels of brand loyalty
7. Discuss the functions of packaging
8. List seven factors that influence pricing decisions

On the Job On the Job

ON THE JOB: FACING A BUSINESS CHALLENGE AT STARBUCKS

Brewing Up Success Nationwide

Have you had your coffee yet today? If so, did you open a can of Folgers and brew it yourself, or did you hand $2 to a barista and ask for a "single tall skinny mocha no whip with extra cocoa"? More and more coffee drinkers are getting their daily dose of java from Starbucks Coffee Company. Founded in 1971, Starbucks originally sold its trademark dark-roasted coffee beans in a few Seattle stores. But everything changed when current chairman and CEO Howard Schultz took over in 1987. Schultz envisioned selling gourmet coffee beverages in hip neighborhood coffee bars like the ones he saw on every corner while vacationing in Italy. He wanted Starbucks to be a meeting place where people could exchange ideas and escape from everyday hassles. And from day one he wanted to go national.

Schultz focused on building a competitive advantage through a loyal, well-trained labor force that delivers consistently superior products and service. He also fostered a company commitment to employer responsibility, environmental stewardship, passion for coffee, and integrity in customer relations. His efforts paid off. In a decade, Starbucks grew to over 1,100 stores in 22 states and 3 foreign countries. In the United States, Starbucks literally changed the definition of "a good cup of coffee." Loyal customers are described as "religious" about the product. In fact, Starbucks is so highly regarded that the company is leveraging its reputation with brand extensions. Bottled coffee beverages, ice cream, music CDs, and a coffee-laced beer now bear the Starbucks logo and are available on grocery store shelves. In addition, the company receives hundreds of joint venture proposals for new products every week.

But even though the success of Schultz's vision has led to unprecedented opportunities, it has also created new challenges. Rapid expansion has led some consumers to view Starbucks as a corporate villain that rides into town, throws down a lump of cash to get the best locations, and then drives the local cafés out of business. Locals fear that a Starbucks on the corner means the loss of a community's unique character. Brand extensions also raise new concerns. Although initial products have proven successful, they run the risk of diluting Starbucks' core identity as a premium coffee company. The company also faces the challenge of keeping quality consistent as the company continues to grow. Starbucks sets customers' expectations high, and it must continue to meet those expectations to stay ahead of new competitors that enter the market almost daily.

These concerns weighed heavily on the minds of Schultz's marketing team as Starbucks celebrated its twenty-fifth birthday. Team members were developing a new marketing strategy that they hoped would establish Starbucks' image and assure its future success nationwide. If you were on that team, what would you do to maintain Starbucks' leadership position? How would you evaluate the potential of new products? How would you define your target markets? What image would you want consumers to have of Starbucks, and how would you maintain that image as the company continues to grow?[1]

STRATEGIC MARKETING PLANNING

Successful marketing rarely happens without careful planning. *Strategic marketing planning* is a process that involves examining your current marketing situation, assessing your opportunities, setting your objectives, and developing a marketing strategy to reach those objectives (see Exhibit 13.1). The purpose of strategic marketing planning is to help you identify and create a competitive advantage, something that sets you apart from your rivals and makes your product more appealing to customers.[2] Most companies document the results of their planning efforts in a document called the *marketing plan*. Here's a closer look at the process.

Examining Your Current Marketing Situation

Examining your current marketing situation includes reviewing your past performance (or how well each product is doing in each market where you sell it), evaluating your competition, assessing your internal strengths and weaknesses, and analyzing the external environment. The complexity of this step depends on the complexity of your business. Whereas a giant multinational firm such as Xerox or British Petroleum has to review the performance of dozens of product lines and geographic divisions, a small business may have only a handful of products to think about.

Reviewing Your Past Performance Unless you're starting a new business, your company has a history of marketing performance. Maybe your sales have slowed down in the past year, maybe you've had to cut prices so much that you're barely earning a profit, or maybe things are going quite well and you have lots of cash to spend on new marketing activities. Reviewing where you are and how you got there is a critical step in planning, because you can't fix problems or build on your strengths unless you know what they are.

Evaluating Your Competition An essential ingredient in any marketing plan is knowing your competition. If you own a Burger King franchise, your success obviously depends on what McDonald's and Wendy's do. To some extent, you are at the mercy of Taco Bell, KFC, Pizza Hut, and other restaurants as well. On any given day, your customers might decide to satisfy their hunger in any number of ways—they might even fix themselves a sandwich. A successful marketing plan identifies sources of competitive advantage you might have and builds a marketing program around them.

Keep in mind that your competition isn't always the obvious product or store next door. In fact, it might not even exist yet. For example, laundry detergent manufacturers

STAGE 1	STAGE 2	STAGE 3
Current Marketing Situation • Review past/current performance • Evaluate competition • Examine internal strengths and weaknesses • Analyze external environment	**Opportunities and Objectives** • Assess your opportunities • Set your objectives	**Marketing Strategy** • Segment your market • Choose your target market • Position your product • Develop your marketing mix

EXHIBIT 13.1

The Strategic Marketing Planning Process

Strategic marketing planning involves three steps: Evaluating your current marketing situation, analyzing your opportunities, and then developing your marketing strategy.

would be smart to recognize that their competition might someday be ultrasonic washing machines. If perfected, these machines will wash clothes with little or no detergent.

Examining Your Internal Strengths and Weaknesses Various marketing opportunities require differing financial resources, production capabilities, distribution networks, managerial expertise, and promotional capabilities. Before you can develop a marketing strategy, you must decide whether your business should (1) limit itself to those opportunities for which it possesses the required strengths or (2) challenge itself to reach higher goals by acquiring and developing new strengths.

Understanding your strengths and weaknesses is especially important when evaluating the merits of global expansion. Selling products overseas requires managerial expertise and financial resources in addition to the ability to adjust your operation to accommodate different cultures, customs, legal requirements, and product specifications. Even selling on the Internet requires technological expertise and commitment. After all, placing a Web site on the Internet does not automatically guarantee you a competitive advantage.

Analyzing the External Environment Economic conditions, the natural environment, social and cultural trends, laws and regulations, technology—all have a profound impact on a firm's marketing options. The external environment can create entirely new markets, destroy old markets, and generally present an endless parade of problems and opportunities for marketers.

ECONOMIC CONDITIONS Marketers are keenly aware of the importance of such broad economic trends as gross domestic product, interest rates, inflation, unemployment, personal income, and savings rates. In tough times, consumers postpone the purchase of expensive items like major appliances, automobiles, and homes. They cut back on travel, entertainment, and luxury goods. Conversely, when the economy is good, consumers open their pocketbooks and satisfy their pent-up demand for higher-priced goods and services.

NATURAL ENVIRONMENT Changes in the natural environment can affect marketers, both positively and negatively. Interruptions in the supply of raw materials can upset even the most carefully conceived marketing plans. Floods, droughts, and cold weather can affect the price and availability of many products as well as the behavior of target customers.

SOCIAL AND CULTURAL TRENDS Planners also study the social and cultural environment to determine shifts in consumer values. If social trends are running against a product, the producer might need to increase its advertising budget to educate consumers about the product's benefits. Alternatively, it might modify the product to respond to changing tastes.

LAWS AND REGULATIONS Like every other function in business today, marketing is controlled by laws at the local, state, national, and international levels. From product design to pricing to advertising, virtually every task you'll encounter in marketing is affected in some way by laws and regulations. For example, the Nutritional Education and Labeling Act of 1990 forced food marketers to include standardized nutritional labels on their products. Although this requirement cost manufacturers (both large and small) millions of dollars, it was a bonanza for the laboratories that conduct food testing.

TECHNOLOGY When technology changes, so must your marketing approaches. Look at Encyclopaedia Britannica. It didn't take long for new computer technology to almost wreck this 229-year-old publishing company with annual sales of $650 million. After all, with books costing $1,500, weighing 118 pounds, and taking 4.5 feet of shelf space, consumers opted for the competitors' $99 to $395 CD-ROM versions that talk and play moving pictures.[3]

Chapter 12 discusses technology and the changing marketplace in depth. Keep in mind, however, that marketers must not only keep on top of today's technology but also be able to envision the technology of tomorrow. For example, Coke has 800,000 vending machines in Japan alone, and each one has a computer chip in it. Consider the competitive advantage Coke will have when this chip is used to record the number of cans left, the number of times a button was pressed for an item out of stock, and the time of day when purchases are highest. Coke might even be able to calculate the optimal product mix per machine.[4]

Vending machines have a computer chip in them to record consumer preferences.

Assessing Your Opportunities and Setting Your Objectives

Once you've reviewed your performance, evaluated your competition, examined your internal strengths and weaknesses, and analyzed the external environment, the next step is to assess your opportunities. Successful companies are always on the lookout for new opportunities, which can be divided into four groups: (1) selling more of your existing products in current markets, (2) creating new products for your current markets, (3) selling your existing products in new markets, and (4) creating new products for new markets.[5] These four groups are listed in order of increasing risk; trying new products in unfamiliar markets is usually the riskiest choice of all.

Once you have your opportunities in mind, you can set your marketing objectives. Good objectives are specific and measurable. Establishing a goal to "increase sales in the future" is not a good objective; it doesn't say by how much or by what date. On the other hand, a goal to "increase sales 25 percent by the end of next year" provides a clear target and a reference against which progress can be measured. Objectives should also be challenging enough to be motivating. As Mitchell Leibovitz of the Pep Boys auto parts chain says: "If you want to have ho-hum performance, have ho-hum goals."[6] A common marketing objective is to achieve a certain level of **market share,** which is a firm's portion of the total sales in a market.

market share
Measure of a firm's portion of the total sales in a market

Developing Your Marketing Strategy

Using your current marketing situation and your objectives as your guide, you're ready to develop your **marketing strategy,** which consists of choosing your *target markets* and the *position* you'd like to achieve in those markets, and developing a *marketing mix* to help you get there. A firm's **marketing mix** (also referred to as the *four Ps*) consists of product, price, distribution (or place), and promotion (see Exhibit 13.2). This chapter discusses the first two elements—product and price. Chapter 14 discusses distribution (place), and Chapter 15 discusses promotion.

marketing strategy
Overall plan for marketing a product

marketing mix
The four key elements of marketing strategy: product, price, distribution, and promotion

Choosing Your Target Markets Chapter 12 discusses market segmentation, niches, one-to-one marketing, and consumer buying behavior as part of the process of understanding consumers. Once you've segmented your market, the next step is to decide which *target segments* or **target markets** you'll focus on.

target markets
Specific groups of customers to whom a company wants to sell a particular product

How do you decide which market segments to focus your efforts on? In some cases the answer will be obvious, such as when you don't have the necessary technological skills or financial power to enter a market segment. In other cases, you'll have the resources to compete in a number of segments but not enough resources to compete in all of them. Consider Apple's early decision against licensing the Macintosh operating system for computer clones. That decision kept Apple computers priced too high to successfully compete in the general business market, and Apple is now paying the price.[7] Marketers often use criteria to narrow their options to a few market segments. These criteria can include size of segment, number and strength of competition already in the segment, sales and profit potential, compatibility with company's resources and strengths, costs, growth potential, and risks.[8]

EXHIBIT 13.2

The Marketing Mix

The right decisions about product, price, distribution, and promotion yield the marketing mix that best meets the needs of customers.

DECISION AREA	COMPONENT	DEFINITION
Product	The product	The set of tangible and intangible attributes of the good, service, person, or idea that is being exchanged
	Brand name	Portion of a brand (words, letters, or numbers) that may be expressed orally
	Packaging	The activities that involve designing and producing the container or wrapper for a product
	Services	Activities, benefits, or satisfactions that are offered for sale or are provided in connection with the sale of goods
	Warranty	A manufacturer's promise that the product is fit for the purpose intended
	Postexchange servicing	Activities, such as warranty services, that ensure customer satisfaction
Price	Pricing	Activities concerned with setting the price of a product
	Discount	A reduction from the asked price of a product
Distribution (place)	Channels of distribution	The route taken by a product as it moves from the producer to the final consumer
	Physical distribution	The physical movement of goods from the point of production to the point of consumption
Promotion	Advertising	Nonpersonal communication that is paid for by an identified marketer to promote a product or service
	Personal selling	Person-to-person communication between a marketer and members of the market.
	Public relations	Any communication created primarily to build prestige or goodwill for an individual or an organization
	Sales promotion	Promotional activities other than advertising, personal selling, and publicity that stimulate consumer purchases and dealer effectiveness

positioning
Promotional strategy intended to differentiate a good or service from those of competitors in the mind of the prospective buyer

Positioning Your Product Regardless of the segmentation and targeting selections you make, your next step will be to stake out the position you'd like to occupy in the mind of buyers and potential buyers. **Positioning** your product is the act of designing your company's offering and image so that it occupies a meaningful and distinct competitive position in your target customers' minds. For example, one auto company might choose to differentiate its cars on durability, whereas its competitors may choose to emphasize comfort or fuel economy. Most companies position their products by choosing among several differentiating product factors, including features, performance, quality, durability, reliability, style, design, and customer service such as ordering ease, delivery and installation methods, and customer support. Besides product factors, companies also differentiate their products on the basis of price, distribution, and promotion (see Exhibit 13.3).[9] Keep in mind that whether you're content to follow in someone else's footsteps or you're aiming for the top, the position you choose to occupy drives your product, brand, and pricing strategies.

MARKET LEADERS Here are some current strategies companies use to position their products as market leaders:

- *Freeware.* America Online gives its software away for free. So does Netscape. Id gives away an abbreviated but functioning version of its Cro-Magnon game in spite of spending over $2 million to develop it. Why? Id hopes players will like the game

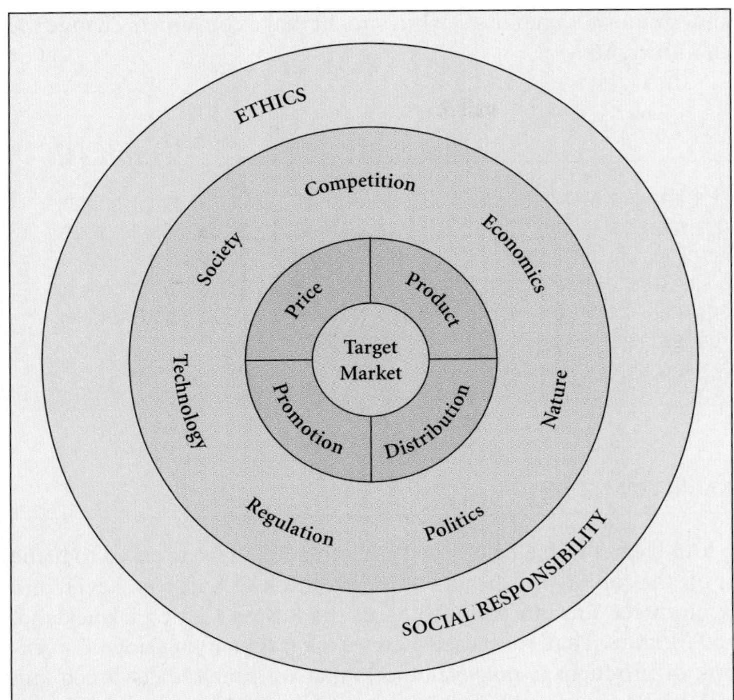

EXHIBIT 13.3

The Marketing Environment

When positioning products in your target markets, you need to take into consideration the four marketing mix elements plus the external environment.

and be willing to pay for the full version at a later date. Of course, getting to first position by earning zero dollars in revenue is an unsustainable position. Sooner or later companies have to make sales. Netscape did. By giving away its Web Navigator, the company lured thousands of independent software developers to design Web pages that work best with Navigator. And the company's revenues went from zero to $55 million in 26 months.[10]

- *Switching costs.* Learning new software takes a lot of time and money. Autodesk knows this. By investing your time in learning its AutoCAD software, the company is hoping that you won't switch to a competitor's product too swiftly—even if the competitor's product is in some ways superior.[11]
- *Copy cats.* Dial succeeds in the marketplace by walking in the footsteps of others. Rather than spending big bucks on researching and developing new products, it lets other companies develop new products and educate consumers about the benefits. Then it copies them.[12] And Dial isn't the only one. Consider Mentadent, the first toothpaste with baking soda and peroxide. After Chesebrough pumped $65 million into its initial launch, both Crest and Colgate came out with their own versions, stealing market share and pushing Mentadent back to third place.[13]

ALTERNATIVES TO FIRST POSITION Even though most companies would like to be first in the minds of their target segments, the simple fact is that they are not. So what should you do if you're not at the top? You have three choices. First, you can try to dislodge the leader in a direct competitive assault. Second, you can acknowledge that the leader already has that position and try to find a comfortable position lower down the chain. Price is a common way to do this, when companies present themselves as lower-cost alternatives to the leader. Third, you can try to change the way the market thinks about the product category by emphasizing product differences, benefits, or usage. For example, mouthwashes have traditionally competed on the basis of effectiveness, but some brands have started to tout plaque-removal capabilities, which might make consumers change the way they think about mouthwashes.

BEST OF THE WEB

Fetch It!

Thinking about starting a new business? You'll need to do a lot of research to plan your marketing strategies. In fact, there's a pile of information on the Internet waiting for you to explore. One of the best ways to start your Internet research is with a search engine. But which search engine should you use? Not all of them link you to the same information. Try *Dogpile*. It's the search engine for search engines. Enter your search strategy, and then tell Arfie to "go fetch."
http://www.dogpile.com

PRODUCT MANAGEMENT

Products are one of the four elements in a firm's marketing mix. If you were asked to name three popular products off the top of your head, you might think of Snickers, Levi's, and Pepsi—or three similar products. You might not think of the Boston Celtics, Disneyland, or the television show *60 Minutes*. That's because when we're on the buying side of an exchange, we tend to think of products as *tangible* objects that we can actually touch and possess. Basketball teams, amusement parks, and TV programs provide an *intangible* service for our use or enjoyment, not for our ownership; nevertheless, they are products just the same.

Types of Products

product
Good or service used as the basis of commerce

From a marketing standpoint, a **product** is anything offered for the purpose of satisfying a want or need in a marketing exchange. Marketers have a variety of ways to categorize products. You wouldn't market a garden tractor the same way you'd market accounting services; the buyer behavior, product characteristics, market expectations, competition, and other elements of the equation are all different. The two most common product categorizations involve the degree of tangibility and the product's use.

Tangible and Intangible Products It's convenient to group products as tangible goods or intangible services and ideas, but in reality, things aren't quite so simple. Nearly all products are combinations of tangible and intangible components. Some products are predominantly tangible, whereas others are mostly intangible; however, most products like Intuit's software programs fall somewhere between these two extremes. Even though you are purchasing Quicken, in most cases you're basing your purchase decision on the additional service features that come with the software—like online banking capabilities, direct stock portfolio updates, Web site links, customer assistance, and so on.

The *product continuum* graphically indicates the relative amounts of tangible and intangible components in a product (see Exhibit 13.4). Political ideas are an example of products at the intangible extreme, whereas salt and sugar represent the tangible extreme. Starbucks cafés fall somewhere in the middle because customers get both tangible and intangible components (coffee and service). Auto repair, on the other hand, can range all over the continuum, depending on the particular problem being repaired.

As the product continuum indicates, service products have some special characteristics that affect the way they are marketed. The most important of these is the fundamental intangibility of services. You can't usually show a service in an ad, demonstrate it

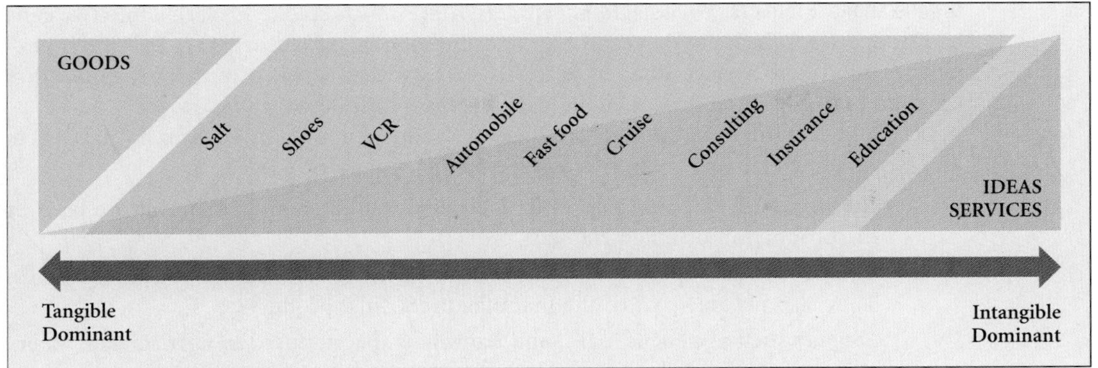

EXHIBIT 13.4

The Product Continuum

Products contain both tangible and intangible components; predominantly tangible products are called goods, and predominantly intangible products are considered services.

for customers before they buy it, or give customers anything tangible to show for their purchase. Successful services marketers often compensate for intangibility by using tangible symbols or by adding tangible components to their products. Prudential Insurance uses the Rock of Gibraltar in its logo and talks about having "a piece of the rock." Gibraltar is a symbol of solid stability, and Prudential wants you to think the same about its services.

Another unique aspect of service products is *perishability.* Services cannot usually be created in advance and stored until people want to buy them. That's why you schedule an appointment at the doctor's office and why your computer class meets at a specific time. Service perishability often presents big challenges in terms of staffing, pricing, and other management issues. For instance, movie theaters try to shift some of the customer demand from the busy evening and weekend times by offering cheaper tickets during the day.

Consumer Products Chapter 12 discusses the different buying behaviors of organizational and consumer markets. Even though some products are sold to both markets, those known as *consumer products* are sold exclusively to consumers. Most marketing specialists divide the broad category of consumer products into four subgroups, according to the approach people take when shopping for them.

- *Convenience products* are the goods and services that people buy frequently, without much conscious thought. They include inexpensive items like toothpaste, soda, razor blades, dry cleaning, film developing, and photocopying.
- *Shopping products* are fairly important goods and services that a person doesn't buy every day: a stereo, a computer, a suit, an interior decorator, or a college. Such purchases require more thought about price, features, quality, or reputation. These brand differences prompt comparison shopping.
- *Specialty products* are things like Chanel perfume, Brooks Brothers suits, and Suzuki violin lessons—particular brands that the buyer especially wants and will seek out, regardless of location or price. Not all specialty products are expensive, however. Consider your own shopping behavior when you purchase a six-pack of soda: If you're like many people, you want only your favorite brand, and you won't readily accept a substitute.
- *Unsought goods* are products that the consumer does not normally think of buying. These include life insurance, cemetery plots, and new products that the consumer must be made aware of through advertising.[14]

Is It True?

Some 51 percent of all tires are sold to women.

Organizational Products *Organizational products,* or products sold to firms, fall into two general categories (which are based on cost and life span). *Expense items* are relatively inexpensive goods and services that are generally used within a year of purchase. Those that are more expensive and have a longer useful life are considered *capital items.*

Aside from dividing products into expense and capital items, organizational buyers and sellers often classify products according to their intended usage.

- *Raw materials* like iron ore, crude petroleum, lumber, and chemicals are used in the production of final products.
- *Components* like spark plugs and printer cartridges are similar to raw materials. They also become part of the manufacturers' final products.
- *Supplies* such as pencils, nails, and lightbulbs that are used in a firm's daily operation are considered expense items.
- *Installations* such as factories, buildings, power plants, airports, production lines, and semiconductor fabrication machinery are major capital projects.
- *Equipment* includes less expensive capital items like desks, telephones, and fax machines that are shorter lived than installations.
- *Business services* range from simple and fairly risk-free services such as landscaping and cleaning to complex services such as management consulting and auditing.

The Product Life Cycle

product life cycle
Four basic stages through which a product progresses: introduction, growth, maturity, and decline

Few products last forever. Most products go through a **product life cycle,** passing through four distinct stages in sales and earnings: introduction, growth, maturity, and decline (see Exhibit 13.5). As the product passes from stage to stage, various marketing approaches become appropriate.

The amount of time that elapses during any one of the stages depends on customer needs and preferences, economic conditions, the nature of the product, and the manufacturer's marketing strategy; however, most product life cycles today are shrinking dramatically. The proliferation of new products, changing technology, globalization, and the ability to quickly imitate your competitor is pushing and pulling products through their life cycles at a much faster pace. In fact, the president of GTE describes this pace as instantaneous: "Companies are marketing products that are still evolving, delivered to a market that is still emerging, via technology that is changing on a daily basis."[15]

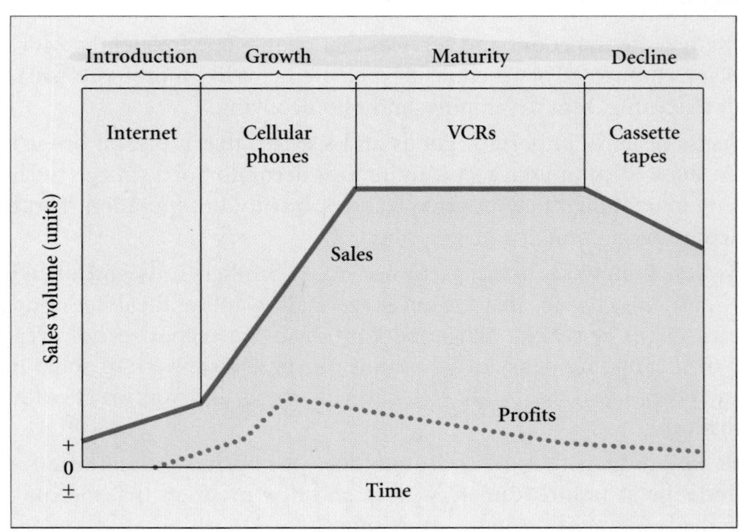

EXHIBIT 13.5

Stages in the Product Life Cycle

Almost all products and product categories have a life cycle like the one shown by the curve in this diagram. However, the duration of the life cycle varies widely from product to product. A business must introduce new products periodically to balance sales losses as older products decline.

Consider electronics. The life cycles for electronic products are now recorded in months. At Panasonic, consumer electronic products are replaced with new models on a 90-day cycle.[16] Hewlett-Packard purposely shortens the life cycles of its own products by bringing out better and cheaper technologies in the printer market. The company is feasting on itself by manufacturing low-priced ink-jet printers that compete against its high-priced laser printers.[17] Why would a company do this? Smart companies know that if they don't cannibalize their own products, someone else will do it for them.

Some product life cycles are so short these days that entirely new product categories approach commodity status within a year or two; that is, they become mass produced and lose their specialty status. Look at carbonated fruit drinks. As one new-age beverage distributor put it, "You can build a viable business around creating new-age beverage brands as long as you don't try to sustain them. When their term has passed, let them go, and be ready with the next one."[18] In fact, with increasing product customization, product life cycles effectively shrink to zero.

Introduction The first stage in the product life cycle is the *introductory stage,* during which the producer tries to stimulate demand. Typically, this stage involves an expensive advertising and promotional campaign, plus research-and-development costs. Products in the introductory phase generally require large investments to cover the costs of developing the product, building distribution systems, and educating the public about the product's benefits. The producer isn't likely to make a great deal of profit during this phase and, in many cases, won't make any profit for some time to come. Still, these costs are a necessary investment if a product is to succeed.

Growth Next comes the *growth stage,* marked by a rapid jump in sales—and, usually, in the number of competitors—as the introductory effort starts paying off. As the product enters the growth phase, competition usually increases and the struggle for market share begins, creating pressure to maintain large promotional budgets and reduce prices. This competitive warfare is expensive, and often the small, weak firms do not survive. For the remaining participants, prices stabilize, and as sales volume increases, per-unit costs decline. The combination of stable prices and lower costs creates better profits, and producers begin to reap the rewards of their investment.

Maturity During the *maturity stage,* sales begin to level off or show a slight decline. Competition increases and market share is maximized—making further expansion difficult. The maturity phase is typically the longest phase in the product life cycle, and the costs of introduction and growth have diminished. Companies count on the profits generated by mature-phase products to fund development of new products, so they work hard to keep mature products competitive.

Some companies extend the life of a mature product by broadening its appeal or making minor improvements. Even Barbie got a face lift. By spinning out Totally Hair Coiffable Barbie, Barbie Businesswoman, and Teen Talk Barbie, Mattel moved Barbie back into the number one position. Likewise, when Cheez Whiz sales leveled off, the marketers at Kraft Foods decided not to let their product fade into the sunset. With the help of a $6 million advertising budget, they began promoting Cheez Whiz as a cheese sauce for the microwave oven, and sales climbed 35 percent.[19]

Barbie dolls continue to be big sellers year after year by delivering an image of growth and glamour.

Decline Although maturity can be extended for many years, eventually most products enter the *decline phase,* when sales and profits begin to slip and eventually fade away. Declines occur for several reasons: changing demographics, shifts in popular taste, product competition, and advances in technology. When a product reaches this phase, the company must decide whether to keep the product or discontinue it and focus on developing newer items.

New-Product-Development Process

Suppose your company decides to develop a new product. Where do you begin? Many companies ask that question all the time. In fact, the possibility of developing a big winner is so alluring that U.S. companies spend billions of dollars a year trying to create new products or improve old ones.[20]

In reality, however, most new products are not really new at all; only about 5 percent are true innovations.[21] The rest are variations of familiar products, created by changing the packaging, improving the formula, or modifying the form or flavor. For example, when Kraft took its decade-old Crystal Light powdered fruit drink, added water, and packaged it in fancy plastic bottles, sales of the reinvented brand swiftly surpassed those of Coke's lavishly launched Fruitopia.[22]

Nevertheless, coming up with a winning product is not an easy task. That's because many competitors are likely to get the same idea at the same time. So the victory often goes to the company with the best *product-development process*—the series of stages through which a product idea passes (see Exhibit 13.6). As noted by MIT researcher and journalist Michael Schrage: Effective *prototyping* (or turning an idea into a working model) may be the most valuable competitive advantage an innovative organization can have.[23]

Consider Sony. The company's competitors can take 6 to 10 months to turn an idea into a prototype, but on average Sony takes only 5 days.[24] This faster development time is possible because innovative companies like Sony, Hewlett-Packard, and 3M use cross-functional teams to push new products through development and onto the market.

How many of the new products created each year will endure? Nobody knows for sure, but the odds are that most new products will disappear within a few years. According to one authority, less than 1 percent of new product introductions will be around in five years; some will vanish within six months; others will never make it to market.[25] That's because not all ideas become new products. Some are killed midstream because they do not meet the exit criteria that specify what needs to be accomplished before a product moves from one stage into the next. Here are the six stages of the new-product-development process:

- *Generation.* The first step in the product-development process is to come up with ideas that will satisfy unmet needs. Customers, competitors, and employees are often the best source of new-product ideas. In fact, employees at 3M can spend up to 15 percent of their time working on a new-product idea without management's approval.[26]

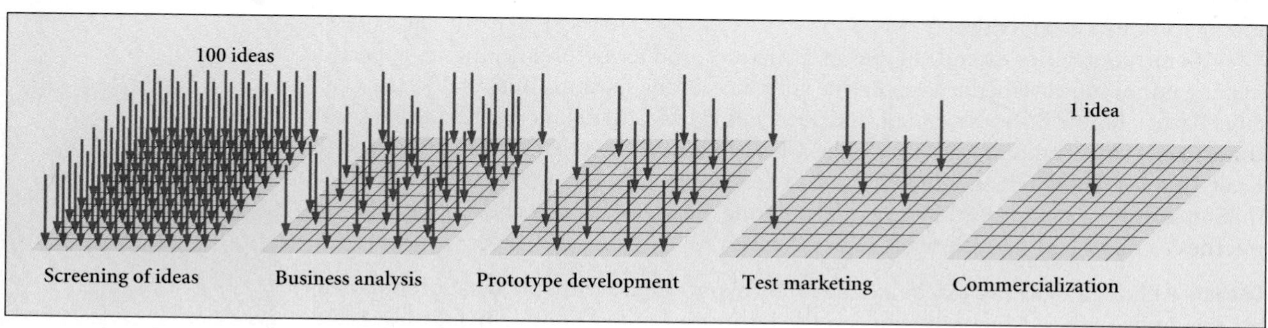

EXHIBIT 13.6

The Product-Development Process

For every hundred ideas generated, only one or two salable products may emerge from the lengthy and expensive process of product development.

- *Screening.* From the mass of ideas suggested, the company culls a few that appear to be worthy of further development, applying broad criteria such as whether the product can use existing production facilities and how much technical and marketing risk is involved.
- *Business analysis.* A product idea that survives the screening stage is subjected to a business analysis. At this point the question is: Can the company make enough money on the product to justify the investment? To answer this question, the company forecasts the probable sales of the product, assuming various pricing strategies. In addition, it estimates the costs associated with various levels of production. Given these projections, the company calculates the potential cash flow and return on investment that will be achieved if the product is introduced.
- *Prototype development.* At this stage the firm actually creates and tests a few samples, or *prototypes,* of the product, including its packaging. During this stage, the various elements of the marketing mix are put together. In addition, the company evaluates the feasibility of large-scale production and specifies the resources required to bring the product to market.
- *Test marketing.* During **test marketing,** the firm introduces the product in selected areas of the country and monitors consumer reactions. Test marketing makes the most sense in cases where the cost of marketing a product far exceeds the cost of developing it. There are some risks, however. Testing a new product in a supermarket may cost $1 million and take nine months or more, and it may give competitors a chance to find out about a company's newest ideas.[27]

test marketing
Product-development stage in which a product is sold on a limited basis—a trial introduction

- *Commercialization.* The final stage of development is **commercialization,** the large-scale production and distribution of those products that have survived the testing process. This phase (also referred to as a *product launch*) requires the coordination of many activities—manufacturing, packaging, distribution, pricing, and promotion. A classic mistake is letting marketing get out of phase with production by promoting the product before the company can supply it in adequate quantity. Many companies roll out their new products gradually, going from one geographic area to the next. This plan enables them to spread the costs of launching the product over a longer period and to refine their strategy as the rollout proceeds.

commercialization
Large-scale production and distribution of a product

Companies launch new products all the time. In fact, according to *New Product News,* consumer product companies launch more than 20,000 new items each year.[28] Sometimes they launch them because they have a terrific new concept, other times because they are following in the footsteps of their competitors. Regardless of the reason, most companies wind up with a long list of products to manage—each at a different stage in the product life cycle.

Product-Mix and Product-Line Decisions

Anticipating the impact of product life cycles, most companies continually add and drop products to ensure that declining items will be replaced by growth products. In this way, they develop a **product mix,** a collection of goods or services offered for sale. For example, the General Mills product mix consists of cereals, baking products, desserts, dairy products, side dishes, snack foods, and so on. Each of these components is a **product line,** a group of products that are similar in terms of use or characteristics. Using the same example, the General Mills snack-food line includes Bugles, Fruit Roll-Ups, Sweet Rewards Snack Bars, Pop Secret Popcorn, and more.

product mix
Complete list of all products that a company offers for sale

product line
A series of related products offered by a firm

Width and Depth of Product Mix Product mixes vary in terms of their width and depth. The simplest product mix is not really a mix at all, but rather a single product. However, most

UNDERSTANDING THE HIGH-TECH REVOLUTION

Back to the Drawing Board? With Computer-Aided Design, It's a Snap!

An artistic endeavor such as jewelry design sounds like a great example of traditional craftsmanship, using techniques handed down through the ages. Lately, however, these age-old techniques have been getting some contemporary high-tech help. Jewelry designers can now use computer models to simulate their designs before moving to the expensive and often time-consuming production stage.

If you've ever tried to create accurate three-dimensional (3D) drawings, you know how difficult it can be. Even if you do have the skill to draw a precise 3D picture, what if you (or your customer) would like to see the design from a different angle? You'd have to draw the whole thing all over again. Many people find it hard to visualize in three dimensions, and a customer's idea of what a new product will look like might be different from what you have in mind.

By creating a 3D model of your design on a computer first, you can move it around to look at all sides and change colors, dimensions, and shapes until the design is right. Dan Harding, of the renowned product-design firm Frogdesign, says that the computer gives him a "liquid model" that he can pull and twist and shape until he gets it just right.

RPD, a Boston firm, specializes in designing new products for other companies, and the firm uses models to show customers what products will look like—while it's still easy and inexpensive to make changes. Plus, the models help RPD transform a customer's idea into a

companies find that they need more than one product to sustain their sales growth (see Exhibit 13.7). When deciding on the width of its product mix, a company weighs the risks and rewards associated with various approaches. Some companies limit their product offerings to be economical: They can keep the production costs per unit down and also limit selling expenses to a single sales force. Other companies follow the philosophy that a broad product mix is insurance against shifts in technology, taste, and economic conditions.

READY-TO-EAT CEREALS	SNACK FOODS AND BEVERAGES	BAKING PRODUCTS AND DESSERTS	MAIN MEALS AND SIDE DISHES	DAIRY PRODUCTS
Total	Pop Secret Popcorn	Gold Medal Flour	Bac*Os	Yoplait Yogurt
Wheaties	Berry-Bears	Bisquick	Hamburger Helper	Colombo Frozen Yogurt
Raisin Nut Bran	Fruit Roll-Ups	Softasilk Cake Flour	Potato Buds	
Oatmeal Crisp	Nature Valley Granola Bars	Betty Crocker Cake Mixes	Skillet Chicken Helper	
Cinnamon Toast Crunch	Bugles Corn Snacks	Creamy Deluxe Frosting	Suddenly Salad	
Cheerios	Fruit by the Foot		Tuna Helper	
Kix	Sweet Rewards Snack Bars			
Cocoa Puffs				
Nature Valley Granola				

EXHIBIT 13.7

The Product Mix at General Mills

Selected products from General Mills show a product mix that is fairly wide but is of varying depth inside each product line.

finished design more faithfully, boosting customer satisfaction while minimizing expensive rework.

Another key advantage of using computers to design new products is speed. In many industries, from computer parts to clothes, companies must respond to changing customer demands quickly if they are to stay competitive. Computer modeling helped RPD reduce its typical design time from one month to five days.

Jewelry is just one of dozens of industries that have turned to high technology to improve the product-development process. The Boeing 777 jetliner was designed entirely on computers. From home appliances to spacecraft to commemorative coins, computers help product designers create more desirable products in less time. In fact, in many cases, computer-based product design is rapidly becoming necessary even to compete. As one leading designer put it, if you're not designing on computer by now, you're probably making a mistake.

QUESTIONS FOR CRITICAL THINKING

1. Besides saving time, how do companies benefit by using technology in the product-development process?
2. Identify whether the following are consumer or organizational products, and classify them according to their product subgroup: jewelry, Boeing 777, commemorative coins, computers, AutoCAD software, printer paper.

Product-Line Strategies Within each product line, a company once again confronts decisions about the number of goods and services to offer. For example, how many types of coffee should Starbucks offer or how many varieties of cheese should Kraft make? A full-line strategy involves selling a wide number and variety of products, whereas a limited-line strategy focuses on selling a few selected items.

Product lines have a tendency to grow over time as companies look for new ways to boost sales. A line can be expanded in a number of ways:

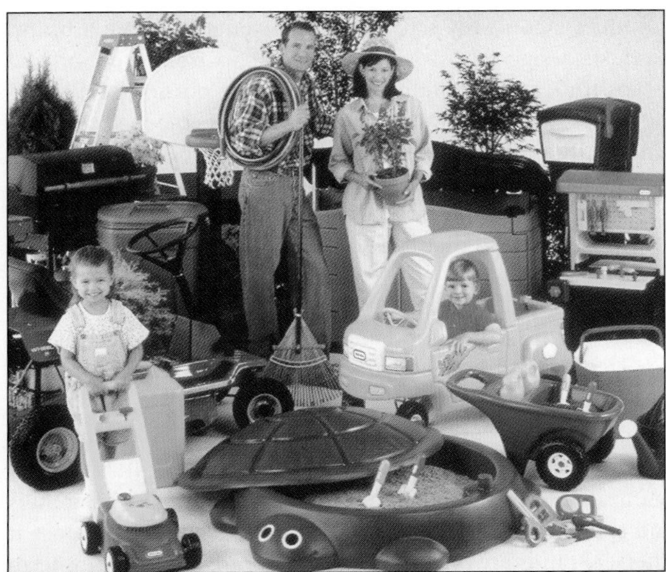

Rubbermaid's product mix includes a unique variety of product types, including mailboxes, garden hoses, bathroom accessories, toys for toddlers—even industrial-strength tool chests.

- *Line filling* is developing items to fill gaps in the market that have been overlooked by competitors or that have emerged as consumers' tastes and needs shift.
- *Line extensions* are new variations of a basic product, such as Tartar Control Crest.
- *Brand extensions* occur when the brand name for an existing product category is extended to a new category, as in the case of Jell-O Pudding Pops.
- *Line stretching* involves the addition of higher- or lower-priced items at either end of the current product line, thus extending its appeal to new economic groups.

In many cases, firms have expanded the range of their product offerings beyond what the world needs. After all, do we really need 31 varieties of Head and Shoulders shampoo or 52 varieties of Crest toothpaste? Procter & Gamble (P&G) has decided that the answer is no. After decades of spinning out new and improved this, lemon-freshened that, and extra-jumbo-sized the other thing, P&G has decided that it sells too many different kinds of stuff. So it's cutting back by trimming its product lines. P&G knows that thousands of supermarket products leave shoppers staggering down the aisles in sensory overload causing them to become immune to marketing messages, indifferent to brands, and suspicious of pricing. Even Nabisco acknowledges that its brand extensions are out of hand. So it's cutting new-product launches by 20 percent and taking some 15 percent of existing items out of production.[29]

BEST OF THE WEB

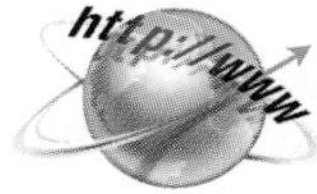

Be a Sharp Shopper

Put your marketing knowledge to practice. Visit the Sharper Image Web site and think like a marketer. Evaluate the company's product mix. What types of consumer products does this company sell? Who is its target market? Do the products have recognizable brand names? Which other stores carry this type of product? Be sure to read about the company's mission. And don't leave without checking out Emiglio the robot. Coffee anyone?
http://www.sharperimage.com

BRANDS, PACKAGING, AND LABELING

Regardless of what type of product a company sells, it usually wants to create a **brand** identity by using a unique name or design that sets the product apart from those offered by competitors. Jeep, Apple, Mossimo, and Bic are **brand names**, the portion of a brand that can be spoken, including letters, words, or numbers. McDonald's golden arches and the Nike swoosh are **brand marks,** the portion of a brand that cannot be expressed verbally. The choice of a brand name and any associated brand marks can be a success factor. Brand names and brand symbols may be registered with the Patent and Trademark Office as trademarks. A **trademark** is a brand that has been given legal protection so that its owner has exclusive rights to its use.

brand
A name, term, sign, symbol, design, or combination used to identify the products of a firm and differentiate them from competing products

brand names
Portion of a brand that can be expressed orally, including letters, words, or numbers

brand marks
Portion of a brand that cannot be expressed verbally

trademark
Brand that has been given legal protection so that its owner has exclusive rights to its use

Sometimes companies *license* or sell the rights to specific well-known names and symbols, and then manufacturers use these licensed labels to help sell products. Sales of licensed logo merchandise for U.S. sports franchises are pushing $7 billion a year. Such merchandise is also quite popular outside the United States and Canada.[30]

Brand Equity and Loyalty

A brand name is often an organization's most valuable asset because it provides customers with a way of recognizing and specifying a particular product so that they can choose it again or recommend it to others. "Brands are one of the strongest providers of long-term cash flow security," says the executive director of Interbrand. "If you calculate the capitalized value of Sara Lee, you'd probably find that about 70 percent of Sara Lee's value is in its brands."[31] This notion of value of a brand is also called *brand equity.*

Strong brands can also command a premium price in the marketplace, and it is often the only element of a product that competitors can't copy—although they sometimes try. The Levi's name is a strong brand. A pair of the company's flagship 501 blue jeans consists of about 2 yards of denim, 213 yards of thread, 5 buttons, and 5 rivets, and sells for an average price of $50.[32] Of course, just because consumers recognize the brand name is no guarantee they will buy the product. Surveys show that some of the best-known brands are among the least-respected products.[33]

Is It True?

Americans are loyal to their brand of soft drink.

Starbucks customers provide convincing evidence of the strength of **brand loyalty,** or commitment to a particular brand. Brand loyalty can be measured in degrees. The first level is **brand awareness,** which means that people are likely to buy a product because they are familiar with it, because they recognize it. The next level is **brand preference.** At this level, people purchase the product if it is available. However, they may be willing to experiment with alternatives if they cannot find it or even for some other reason. The ultimate brand loyalty is **brand insistence,** the stage at which buyers accept no substitute.

brand loyalty Commitment to a particular brand

brand awareness Level of brand loyalty at which people are familiar with a product—they recognize it

brand preference Level of brand loyalty at which people habitually buy a product if it is available

brand insistence Level of brand loyalty at which people will accept no substitute for a particular product

Brand Categories

Brands offered and promoted by a manufacturer such as Procter & Gamble are called **national brands.** Examples are Gatorade, Snickers, and Downy. **Private brands** are not linked to a manufacturer but instead carry a wholesaler's or retailer's brand. Sears DieHard battery and Kenmore appliances are examples of private brands.

In many product categories, the perceived difference between national and private brands has narrowed, prompting more and more consumers to make the switch to the often cheaper private brands. This trend isn't confined to the United States, either; private brands now account for 24 percent of all supermarket sales in France and 32 percent in Great Britain. Even in Japan in recent years, aggressive cost reductions on private label brands have caused many consumers to switch from well-known U.S. and Japanese national brands.[34]

national brands Brands owned by manufacturer and distributed nationally

private brands Brands that carry the label of a retailer or wholesaler rather than a manufacturer

Nevertheless, a company has to think carefully about the benefits before spending from $20 million to $40 million or more on a huge promotional campaign to establish a national brand name.[35] The cost of such a campaign may drive up the price of the product, making it possible for other companies to sell unbranded or lesser-known brand products at a substantially lower price.

As an alternative to branded products, some retailers also offer **generic products,** which are packaged in plain containers that bear only the name of the product. Generic products are most often standard rather than premium quality. They can cost up to 40 percent less than brand-name products because of uneven quality, plain packaging, and lack of promotion. Generic goods have found a definite market niche, as a look at your local supermarket shelves will confirm.

generic products Products characterized by a plain label, with no advertising and no brand name

Brand Strategies

Companies take various approaches to building brands. The traditional approach is to create a separate identity for each product a company sells so that if a problem develops with that product, the other items in the line will not suffer. For example, General Motors (GM) assigns different brand names to each of its line of cars such as Chevy Blazer, Pontiac Firebird, Cadillac Seville, and so on. Even if Cadillac sales begin to decline and lose favor, the other GM brands will not suffer. This approach has the added advantage of allowing a company to create separate product images for various market segments. The person who likes a Corvette and the person who wants a Cadillac are looking for completely different

GAINING THE COMPETITIVE EDGE

Choosing a Company Name: Distinguishing Yourself from the Competition

Across the United States each day, enterprises and businesses, large and small, are popping up like wildflowers after a spring rain—140,475 last year alone (according to Dun & Bradstreet). Eager for gaining a competitive edge in these hyper-cutthroat times, owners are laboring to come up with a name for their products and companies. Plus they're racing to stake out commercial territory on the Internet. Why?

WHAT'S IN A NAME?

Choosing a name may be the most important decision your company makes. It's everything. It's your calling card. It sets the tone for marketing and may shape your future opportunities. In fact, it's the one thing that your competition can't take away from you. So how do you make the right choice?

TIPS

Great names create an image for the product. They speak to the target market and often invoke visual images. Sunkist is one of the best names ever developed because it creates a warm, fresh image that works perfectly with the product. Another effective name is Lean Cuisine. It's memorable, and it says it all. A good name should:

- Speak directly to the product's target customers.
- Motivate consumers to buy the product or service.
- Stick in the consumer's mind. Think about your customers. What do you want the name to mean to them?
- Be distinctive enough to prevent its unauthorized use.
- Be distinguishable from the competition.

THE NAMING PROCESS

Long gone are the days when corporate executives picked product names at random—such as Germany's Gottlieb Daimler, who named his flagship car Mercedes after the daughter of a client. Today picking a name is a tricky business. Searching for an effective name means looking hard at your company's strategy; it can be frustrating, time consuming, and fraught with legal difficulties. Nonetheless, the naming process is crucial for a company of any size. When choosing a name be sure to do these things:

things, even though both want a General Motors car. Among more recent car introductions, Nissan, Toyota, and Honda all opted to create separate brand names for their luxury-car divisions (Infiniti, Lexus, and Acura, respectively). Mitsubishi and Mazda, on the other hand, decided to keep the company brand name for their luxury models.

family branding
Using a brand name on a variety of related products

Family Branding Although individual branding has its advantages, in the past few years an increasing number of companies have been using **family branding** (or using a brand name on a variety of related products) to add to their product lines. Frito-Lay, for example, launched Cool Ranch Doritos and Cajun Spice Ruffles, extending the brand by building on the reputations of regular Doritos Tortilla Chips and Ruffles potato chips. Of course, Frito-Lay isn't alone. Around 75 percent of new products introduced by the largest consumer food companies are brand extensions.[36]

Building on the name recognition of an existing brand enables companies to cut both costs and risks associated with introducing new products. However, there are limits to how far a brand name can be stretched to accommodate new products. Snickers ice cream bars, Rubbermaid feed bins (for farm use), and Dr. Scholl's socks and shoes worked as brand extensions, but Bic perfume, Rubbermaid computer accessories, and Playboy men's suits did not. The secret is in extending with products that fit the buyer's perception of what the brand stands for.[37]

co-branding
Partnership between two or more companies to closely link their brand names together for a single product

Co-Branding An increasingly popular way of strengthening your brand and product today is by combining forces with another company. **Co-branding** occurs when two or more

- *Find a flexible name for your company.* A good company name shouldn't simply describe what you do now. It should also describe what you hope to become in the future, and allow for a range of products and services to be rolled out over time.
- *Check for potential cultural conflicts. Rolls Royce Silver Mist is called Silver Shadow in Germany because* mist *in German means rubbish.*
- Keep it legible. Is it easy to spell, pronounce, and read? If your name is difficult to say or spell, it will work against you.
- *Keep it meaningful, friendly, and personalized. Names like* Yahoo!, *the Internet search firm, create an immediate emotional bond between consumer and company.*
- Know the law. The U.S. trademark system allows you to apply for and receive federal trademarks for names, and it can be confusing at best. You can also stake claims to names by registering them with your secretary of state. However, according to federal court rulings, "it's not the name on the secretary of state's list that counts, it's the name in the marketplace that matters from a legal perspective." So once you've decided on your name, use it! And if you're still stuck and can't find the right name, there's help out there for you.

Getting Help

Most global manufacturers use professional name-finding agencies before introducing a new product. Entering a market today is very expensive, and the more expensive the launch, the more important it is to get the name right. Fees for naming consultants can range from $20,000 to as high as $100,000. But considering what's at stake, it can be a small price to pay. After all, a good name may not help sell a bad product, but a bad name can ruin the sales of a good one.

Questions for Critical Thinking

1. Why is it important to choose a company name that is flexible?
2. What are the advantages of using professional agencies to assist you in naming your product or company?

companies team up to closely link their names together in a single product. A few examples of successful co-branding include Kellogg's Pop Tarts made with Smucker's jam, Nabisco Cranberry Newtons filled with Ocean Spray cranberries, Dreyer's ice cream flavored with Starbucks coffee, "Intel inside" computer cases, and Citibank packaged with American Airlines to form the AAdvantage credit card. Most companies who co-brand their products hope to reach new audiences. Others hope to tap into the equity of a particularly strong brand.[38]

Packaging

With annual sales of more than $50 billion, the packaging business is the third largest industry in the United States, providing everything from tin cans to airtight boxes.[39] Because most consumer buying decisions are made in the store, product manufacturers consider the money they pay for packaging well spent.[40] Effective packaging not only protects products from damage or tampering but also promotes a product's benefits through shape, composition, and design. Consider Coke. The relaunch of its traditional curved bottle in plastic has helped boost the company's earnings.[41]

Packages serve other purposes as well. They make products easier to display, attract customers' attention, and facilitate the sale of smaller products. Also, packages provide convenience. For example, today you can buy lettuce already washed, chopped, packaged, and ready to eat. In many cases, packaging is an essential part of the product

U.S. food labeling regulations require marketers to provide standardized nutrition information on their products.

itself. Consider microwave popcorn or toothpaste in pump dispensers. Innovative packages like these may give a company a powerful marketing boost, whereas a poor package may drive consumers away.

Labeling

Labeling is an integral part of packaging. Whether the label is a separate element attached to the package or a printed part of the container, it serves to identify a brand. Sometimes the label also gives grading information about the product or information about ingredients, operating procedures, shelf life, or risks.

The labeling of foods, drugs, cosmetics, and many health products is regulated under a variety of federal legislation. The Food, Drug and Cosmetic Act of 1938 gives the Food and Drug Administration the authority to monitor the accuracy of the list of ingredients on labels. For example, a fruit drink cannot be labeled and sold as a fruit *juice* unless it contains an established minimum fruit content. Labels are also regulated by the Fair Packaging and Labeling Act of 1966, which mandates that every label must carry the product name as well as the name and address of the manufacturer or distributor, and it must conspicuously show the net quantity. The Nutrition Education and Labeling Act of 1990 forced marketers to use standardized terms and amounts when they specify serving size, calories, fat content, and so on.[42]

Universal Product Codes (UPCs)
A bar code on a product's package that provides information read by optical scanners

In addition to communicating with consumers, labels may also be used by manufacturers and retailers as a tool for monitoring product performance. **Universal Product Codes (UPCs)** are those black stripes on packages that give companies a cost-effective method of tracking the movement of goods. Read by laser scanners, the lines of the code identify the product and allow a computer to record what happens to it. In addition to simply recording sales and reading prices, scanner data can help measure the effectiveness of promotional efforts, such as coupon programs and sale prices.

BEST OF THE WEB

Protect Your Invention

Got a winning product? Protect your invention by registering it with the U.S. Patent and Trademark Office. Visit its Web site and learn the basic facts about registering a patent or trademark. Find out how the process works and how much it costs. In fact, why not search its database first to see how many people already have a patent on your winning idea?
http://www.uspto.gov

PRICING STRATEGIES AND DECISIONS

Pricing is one of the most critical decisions a company must make because it's the only variable that ultimately generates income. In fact, pricing is sometimes the only thing that differentiates your product from your competitor's. And nothing affects sales more quickly than a change in price. Therefore, the stakes are often high. For example, if a company charges too much, it will make fewer sales; if it charges too little, it will sacrifice profits that it might have gained. How much is just right? The answer to that question depends on many variables.

Factors Affecting Pricing Decisions

A company's pricing decisions are influenced by a variety of internal and external factors. These factors include a firm's marketing objectives, government regulations, consumers' perceptions, manufacturing and selling costs, competition, consumer demand, and the needs of wholesalers and retailers who distribute the product to the final customer.

Marketing Objectives The first step in setting a price is to match it to the objectives you set in your strategic marketing plan. For example, you must consider whether your goal is to increase market share, increase sales, widen profit margins, promote a particular product image, or discourage competition altogether. For many years Chrysler had a lock on the minivan market and it depended heavily on profits from that market. So when management learned that its competitors might price their own minivans substantially below Chrysler's, the company sent a clear message: Chrysler would beat competitors' prices. The threat alone was enough to encourage competition to keep their prices in line.[43]

Sometimes pricing decisions are based on a desire to position a product as a premium brand. Remember, pricing is one of the four elements of a firm's marketing mix and is often used in conjunction with the other three elements to position a product. For example Rolex watches are positioned as premium watches. They are priced high to convey a superior image as well as to cover the higher costs associated with high-quality materials and advertising.

Government Regulations The U.S. government plays a big role in pricing, as do the governments of many other countries. In an effort to protect consumers and encourage fair competition, the U.S. government has enacted various price-related laws over the years, and all marketers need to be aware of their ramifications. Three important classes of pricing are regulated: (1) *price fixing*—when two or more companies supplying the same type of products agree on the prices they will charge, (2) *price discrimination*—the practice of unfairly offering attractive discounts to some customers but not others, and (3) *deceptive pricing*—pricing schemes that are considered misleading.

Price-Quality Relationship Another consideration when you're setting prices is the perception a price will elicit from the consumer. Generally speaking, when people go shopping, they have a rough price range in mind. If the item they seek is either too low or too high, they hesitate. An unexpectedly low price triggers fear that the item is inferior in quality, whereas an unexpectedly high price makes buyers question whether the product is worth the money.

Starbucks wants its coffee to be perceived as top quality, so it is generally priced above the market—that is, at prices higher that those of competitors. A premium price is also appropriate when the producer wants to appeal to a status-conscious buyer. The expense of owning a Rolls Royce is part of the automobile's appeal.

Pricing Strategies and Methods

Developing an effective price for your product is like a game of chess: Those who make their moves one at a time—seeking to minimize immediate losses or exploit immediate opportunities—will invariably be beaten by those who can envision the game a few moves ahead. In other words, every element in the marketing mix must be planned and coordinated to support an overall marketing strategy. Here are a few strategies that marketers use when setting their prices.

Cost-Based and Priced-Based Pricing Many companies today simplify the pricing task by using *cost-based pricing* (also known as cost plus pricing). They price their products by starting with the cost of producing a product or providing a service and then adding a markup to provide a profit. All the while, they keep an eye on competitors' prices, making sure not to exceed them. Although this strategy may ensure a certain profit, by setting a minimum price for a product, companies using such a strategy tend to sacrifice profit opportunity. In fact, recent thinking holds that cost should be the last item analyzed in the pricing formula, not the first. Instead, companies should use *priced-based pricing* and focus on an optimal price for a product or service by analyzing a product's competitive advantages, the users' perception of the item, and the target market.

By using this strategy, companies will force their costs down because they won't be able to artificially shield their operating inefficiencies. In fact, Japanese companies are notorious for setting their prices first and then forcing manufacturing to bring their costs in line so that appropriate margins can be maintained. This top-down approach allows you to maximize your profit dollars. Keep in mind that few businesses fail from overpricing their products, whereas many more fail from underpricing them.[44]

skimming
Charging a high price for a new product during the introductory stage and lowering the price later

penetration pricing
Introducing a new product at a low price in hopes of building sales volume quickly

Skimming and Penetration Often a company's pricing goals for a product vary over time, depending on the product's stage in its life cycle. During the introductory phase, the objective might be to recover development costs as quickly as possible. To achieve this goal, the manufacturer might charge a high initial price—a practice known as **skimming**—and then drop the price later, when the product is no longer a novelty and competition heats up. Alternatively, a company might try to build sales volume by charging a low initial price, a practice know as **penetration pricing.** Japanese companies practice penetration pricing when they are breaking into a new market. This approach has the added advantage of discouraging competition because the low price (which competitors would be pressured to match) limits the profit potential for everyone.

break-even analysis
Method of calculating the minimum volume of sales needed at a given price to cover all costs

variable costs
Business costs that increase with the number of units produced

fixed costs
Business costs that remain constant regardless of the number of units produced

break-even point
Sales volume at a given price that will cover all of a company's costs

Break-even Analysis Another approach to pricing involves cost. **Break-even analysis** enables a company to determine how many units of a product it would have to sell at a given price in order to cover all costs, or to break even.

Two types of costs are associated with producing a product: variable costs and fixed costs. **Variable costs** change with the level of production. They include raw materials, shipping costs, and supplies consumed during production. **Fixed costs** remain stable regardless of the production level. They include rent payments, insurance premiums, and real estate taxes. The total cost of operating the business is the sum of the variable and fixed costs.

The **break-even point** is the minimum sales volume the company needs in order to keep from losing money. Sales beyond the break-even point will generate profits; sales volume below the break-even amount will result in losses. You can determine the break-even point in units with this simple calculation:

$$\textit{Break-even point} = \frac{\textit{fixed costs}}{\textit{selling price per unit} - \textit{variable costs per unit}}$$

For example, if you wanted to price haircuts at $20 and you had fixed costs of $60,000 and variable costs per haircut of $5, you would need to sell 4,000 of them to break even:

$$\textit{Break-even point (in units)} = \frac{\$60{,}000}{\$20 - \$5} = 4{,}000 \textit{ units}$$

Of course, $20 isn't your only pricing option. Why not charge $30 instead? When you charge the higher price, you need to give only 2,400 haircuts to break even (see Exhibit 13.8). However, before you raise your haircut prices to $30, bear in mind that a lower price may attract more customers and enable you to make more money in the long run.

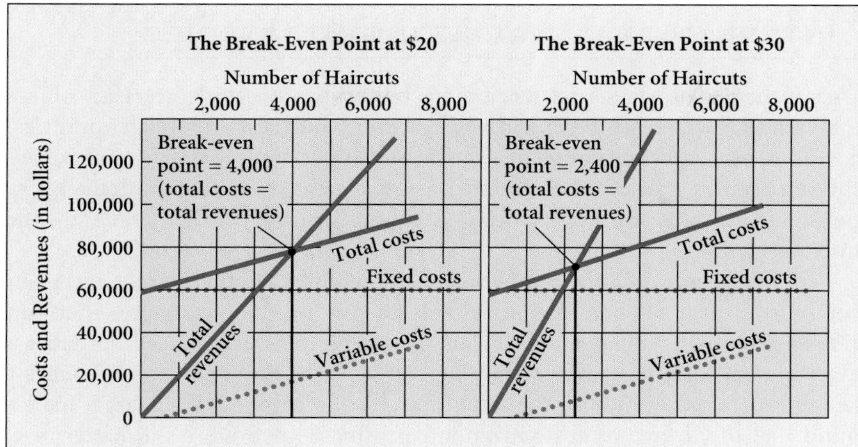

EXHIBIT 13.8

Break-Even Analysis

The break-even point is the point at which revenues will just cover costs. After fixed costs and variable costs are met, any additional income represents profit. The chart shows that at $20 per haircut, the break-even point is reached at 4,000 haircuts; charging $30 per haircut yields a break-even point at only 2,400 haircuts.

Break-even analysis by itself doesn't indicate exactly what price a company should charge; rather, it provides some insight into the number of units that will have to be sold at a given price to make a profit. It is especially useful when companies are trying to calculate the effect of running a special promotion, and it is frequently calculated by using spreadsheet software, which allows companies to plug in numbers under a variety of circumstances.

Discount and Value Pricing Everything seems to sell at a discount these days. With **discount pricing,** companies offer various types of temporary price reductions, depending on the type of customer being targeted and the type of item being offered. A trade discount is offered by the producer to the wholesaler or retailer, whereas a cash discount is a price reduction offered to people who pay in cash or who pay promptly.

discount pricing
Offering a reduction in price

Sometimes discounts get out of hand and can cause a price war between competitors. Price wars can have a devastating effect. Because they encourage customers to focus only on a product's pricing, and not its value or benefits, price wars can hurt a business for years. For instance, when is the last time you paid full fare to fly anywhere? Likewise, the practice of chronic price promotion can be counterproductive. Procter & Gamble recently abandoned its policy of chronic price promotion after concluding that the policy caused unusual purchasing patterns among its largest buyers that substantially increased the company's manufacturing and distribution costs.[45]

Another way firms discount their products is by *value pricing* them. They charge a fairly affordable price for a high-quality offering. Value pricing says that the price should represent a high-value offer to consumers. Toyota Camry is a value-priced car. Even though the Camry is expensive, it has many of the same features as the more expensive Lexus or BMW.

Electronic Pricing Electronic pricing, or the ability to publish your prices over the Internet, is changing the way many companies price their products. Essentially, electronic pricing is pushing us toward continually adjusting pricing and allowing businesses to price their goods or services according to today's marketplace—not according to what may or may not happen. Electronic pricing makes information immediately available to customers and allows businesses to keep prices current with little or no additional cost. It also gives business the ability to experiment with their pricing and determine what works best in a market without locking themselves into a long-term decision.

Is It True?

Less than 50 percent of outlet shoppers think the money they save at outlet stores is worth the extra travel time.

INTERNATIONAL MARKETING STRATEGIES

One of the biggest challenges faced today by companies selling overseas is understanding the various laws, regulations, and ways of doing business in foreign countries. Unstable governments, entry requirements, tariffs and other trade barriers, technology pirating, shifting borders, cultural differences, consumer preferences, foreign-exchange rates, traditions, and customs affect every decision you must make before marketing your products internationally.

Launching a product in other countries requires careful thought and planning. First you must identify the best foreign markets for your product or service. Then you must decide whether you will *standardize* your marketing mix—that is, sell the same product to everyone and use the same promotional strategies everywhere—or *customize* your marketing mix to accommodate the local lifestyles and habits of your target market. Keep in mind that the degree of customization can vary. Sometimes it's a matter of changing a product name or modifying the packaging. Other times customization can result in a completely different product for a foreign market.

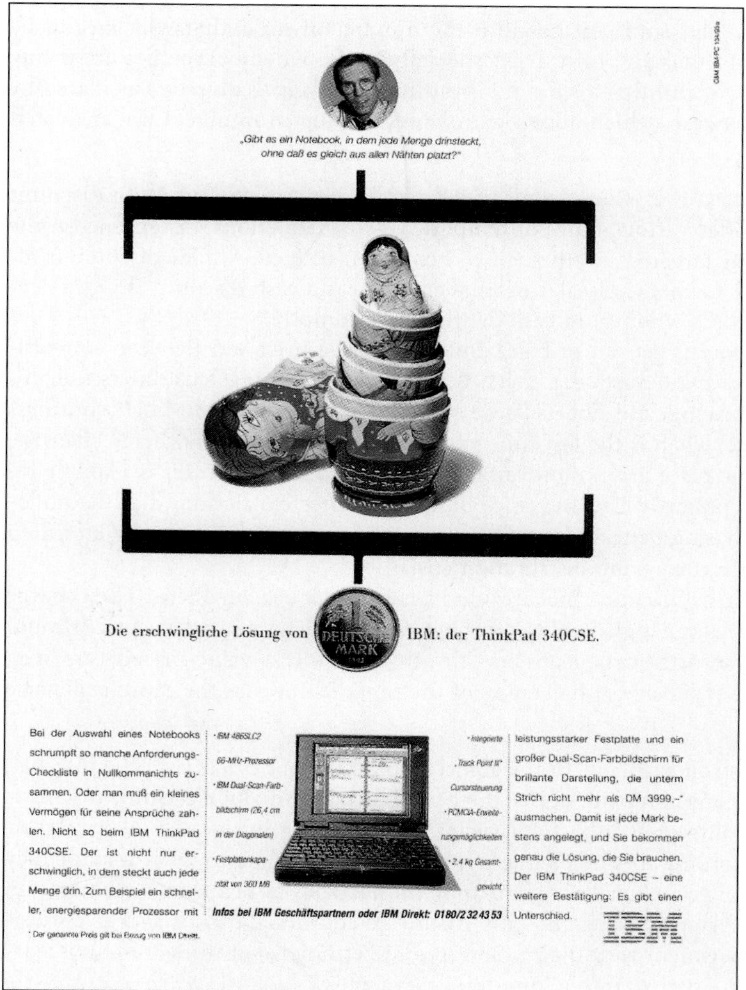

IBM markets its products worldwide. To appeal to different foreign markets, IBM customizes the language and theme of its advertising copy—just like this ad in German.

Of course, understanding the country's culture and regulations will help you make these important choices. But even the most successful U.S. companies sometimes blunder. Look at Disney. After losing $1 billion in Euro-Disney's first year of operation, the company realized that Paris was not Anaheim or Orlando. For example, French employees were insulted by the Disney dress code, and European customers were not accustomed to standing in line for rides or eating fast food standing up. So rather than continue alienating the Europeans, Disney switched from a standardized to a customized strategy by adjusting its marketing mix for Europeans. The company ditched its controversial dress code, authorized wine with meals, lowered admission prices, hired a French investor relations firm, and changed the name of the complex from Euro-Disney to Disneyland Paris to lure the French tourists.[46]

Similarly, other U.S. manufacturers have customized their products after learning that international customers are not all alike. For instance, Domino's learned that the British don't like delivery boys knocking on doors—they think it's rude. Heinz now varies its famous ketchup in different foreign markets—after discovering that consumers in Belgium and Holland use ketchup as a pasta sauce. In China Cheetos are cheeseless because the Chinese people don't really like cheese. Cheetos tested flavors like Peking duck, fried egg, and dog, trying to tempt Chinese palates. Even Ben and Jerry's most popular flavored ice cream—chocolate chip cookie dough—flopped in Britain because kids there didn't grow up sneaking raw cookie-dough batter from Mom.[47] On the other hand Starbucks is sticking with its global standardized product. Even though Japanese consumers haven't yet developed a taste for espresso drinks like caffe latte and caffe mocha, Starbucks is banking on its reputation to create a thirst for these new drinks.[48]

Summary of Learning Objectives

1. **Outline the ten steps in the strategic marketing planning process.**
   The ten steps in the strategic marketing planning process are reviewing your past performance, evaluating your competition, examining your internal strengths and weaknesses, analyzing the external environment, assessing your opportunities, setting your objectives, segmenting your market, choosing your target markets, positioning your product, and developing a marketing mix to satisfy that market.
2. **Identify the four basic components of the marketing mix.**
   The marketing mix consists of the four Ps: product, price, place (distribution), and promotion.
3. **Specify the four stages in the life cycle of a product.**
   Products move from the introductory phase through a growth phase; then they pass into maturity and eventually decline.
4. **Describe the six stages of product development.**
   The first two stages of product development involve generating and screening ideas to isolate those with the most potential. Promising ideas are analyzed to determine their likely profitability. Those that appear worthwhile enter the prototype development stage, in which a limited number of the products are created. In the next stage, the product is test-marketed to determine buyer response. Products that survive the testing process are then commercialized.
5. **Identify four ways of expanding a product line.**
   A product line can be expanded by filling gaps in the market, extending the line to include new varieties of existing products, extending the brand to new product categories, and stretching the line to include lower- or higher-priced items.
6. **Cite three levels of brand loyalty.**
   The first level of brand loyalty is brand awareness, in which the buyer is familiar with the product. The next level is brand preference, in which the buyer will select the product if it is available. The final level is brand insistence, in which the buyer will accept no substitute.
7. **Discuss the functions of packaging.**
   Packaging provides protection, makes products easier to display, and attracts attention. In addition, packaging enhances the convenience of the product and communicates its attributes to the buyer.
8. **List seven factors that influence pricing decisions.**
   Pricing decisions are influenced by a firm's marketing objectives, government regulations, consumer perceptions, manufacturing and selling costs, competition, consumer demand, and the needs of wholesalers and retailers who distribute the product to the final customer.

On the Job: Meeting Business Challenges at Starbucks

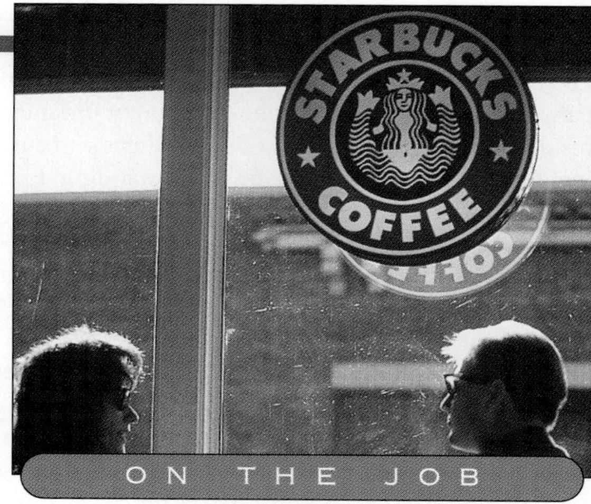

Starbucks entered its twenty-sixth year as the uncontested leader of the gourmet coffee market. The company had already experienced incredible growth, with sales approaching $700 million in 1996, and Schultz had plans to continue expanding, opening almost 900 new stores over the next several years. But the coming years would undoubtedly prove challenging. Competitors like The Second Cup, Seattle's Best Coffee, and Barnie's had expansion plans of their own. And many companies imitated Schultz's formula for success with the hope of beating Starbucks at its own game. The Starbucks marketing team had to be savvy to stay on top.

The team began by extensively researching both competitors' and Starbucks' stores. They brought in hidden cameras to document how well the employees knew their coffee, and they asked customers how they felt about the products, atmosphere, service, and coffee. The insights they gained became the foundation of their strategy.

As with all good marketing strategies, the heart of the plan was a vision of how they wanted to position Starbucks in the coffee market. In addition to remaining the quality leader, they wanted Starbucks stores to appear more like local cafés than a national chain and more like a sanctuary from daily stresses than just a take-out coffee store. Other goals included boosting stagnant sales in older stores, establishing a central focus for all Starbucks products, and developing national advertising that would convey a consistent image. Achieving these objectives required making changes in products, distribution, and promotion.

Over the years, Starbucks core products, coffee beans and beverages, had already undergone changes to meet customer preferences. But some merchandise, such as mugs and coffee makers, had been left untouched. Now new merchandise was planned for all stores. In addition, new food items were offered to attract customers throughout the day (because half the day's sales were typically made during the morning hours).

New products were targeted for grocery store distribution, including cold coffee drinks and ice cream novelties. However, the company was adamant about maintaining its identity through strict product standards. If a product wasn't fundamentally related to coffee and to Starbucks' core values, it wouldn't carry the Starbucks logo.

The retail distribution strategy had to address additional challenges. To combat the fears of certain communities about losing their uniqueness, Starbucks began designing new stores to reflect local cultures. For example, a store in Seattle's upscale Queen Anne neighborhood has a fireplace and large chairs that invite customers to linger and relax. The company also began redesigning older stores (where sales had begun to level off) in order to give them a more comfortable feel. To expand its market, Starbucks rolled out a nationwide line of specialty coffees to be sold exclusively in supermarkets. The company packaged the supermarket coffee uniquely but priced this new line of coffees to match prices at company stores, keeping the brand image high while discouraging café customers from purchasing Starbucks at the supermarket.

Even though product and distribution changes were important, a well-designed promotion strategy was the key to building a consistent image nationwide. Starbucks had always taken an undifferentiated approach to marketing. If a person was a coffee lover, that person was a potential Starbucks customer. And research shows that coffee lovers have an emotional tie to the beverage. It can even be a part of their self-identity. To capitalize on this, the marketing team focused on building a national campaign that didn't feel national. They wanted customers to build a personal identification with Starbucks products. So the advertisements they developed were down-to-earth and genuine, depicting Starbucks as a place to find peace in a hectic world. To counter arguments that the company is too pristine, Starbucks used ads that were somewhat unpolished, as though an art student had done them. In addition, the company began to experiment with "digital marketing" through a hip Web site that attempts to re-create the coffeehouse culture on the Internet.

Finally, to ensure high standards of quality and maintain what Schultz believes is Starbucks' biggest point of differentiation, the company reaffirmed its commitment to its employees. All Starbucks employees receive extensive training before they set foot behind a counter. They also receive progressive compensation, including full health benefits and stock options, even for part-time employees. As Schultz says, "The only way we're going to be successful is if we have the people who are attracted to the company and who are willing to sustain the growth as owners."

Only time will tell what the gourmet coffee market will be like when Starbucks turns 50. But by continuing to offer the best-quality coffee products in a comfortable environment, and by supporting the brand through innovative promotion, Howard Schultz expects Starbucks to remain on top of the bean hill.[49]

Your Mission: You have been hired as a marketing intern at Starbucks' Seattle headquarters. You are assigned to the staff of Scott Bedbury, senior vice president of marketing. Bedbury's staff has been developing strategies to increase sales and maintain a consistent company image as Starbucks grows. Your job is to research and help evaluate some of the options that are being considered. Use your knowledge of marketing concepts and your experience as a consumer to help you assess and develop effective marketing strategies.

1. Three weeks ago, one of Starbucks' main competitors, The Second Cup, started a promotion to win more business. Customers who buy a tall latte receive a scone or cookie for half price. As a result, Starbucks' weekly sales have dropped 4 percent in markets where the two companies compete. Three strategies have been proposed to deal with this situation. Make a case for the one you think is best.
   a. Initiate a counter-promotion that offers customers a free scone or cookie with any beverage purchase over $2. This is a better deal than what The Second Cup is offering, so it will bring in many more customers.
   b. Reduce the price of all coffee beverages by 10 percent. This will win back lost customers who are price-sensitive. It will also attract additional customers of The Second Cup and other competitors.
   c. Offer customers a card that entitles them to a free coffee beverage after they have purchased 10 beverages. This provides an incentive to customers while maintaining Starbucks' current price position.
2. Starbucks has been approached by a liquor manufacturer to bottle a coffee-flavored liqueur under the Starbucks name. The marketing team is evaluating how and where such a product might be sold. Protecting the Starbucks image is a major concern, but a coffee-flavored beer, produced in association with Redhook Brewery, has already been successfully introduced. Which of the following options would you recommend for marketing the coffee liqueur?
   a. Sell the liqueur under the Starbucks name in retail outlets such as liquor stores and grocery stores with liquor departments. This will ensure the widest possible distribution and will enhance Starbucks' brand awareness.
   b. Sell the packaged liqueur under Starbucks name only in Starbucks stores. This would establish it as an exclusive product, and a higher price could be charged. This plan requires obtaining liquor licenses for the stores.
   c. Sell the liqueur in retail outlets under the manufacturers name with Starbucks as a co-brand. The label would bear the manufacturer's name, but it would also say, "flavored with Starbucks coffee."
3. Market research indicates that 80 percent of all coffee is still purchased from grocery stores. Starbucks would like to get a chunk of that market. However, conventional grocery store distribution does not allow the company to offer truly fresh roasted coffee. At a strategy meeting, you are asked to comment on the following proposals. Which one has the most potential?
   a. Market Starbucks coffee beans under a different brand name. This will allow the company to reap the financial rewards of grocery store distribution without putting the Starbucks brand on the line.
   b. Spend money on developing a shelf package that will retain the coffee's fresh roasted flavor over a long period of time. At the same time, pay distributors to make sure packages are removed from the shelves after a certain expiration date.
   c. Open small Starbucks shops within grocery stores. The shops would be managed by the grocery stores, and Starbucks would supply them with fresh beans.
4. You are at a marketing team meeting. The group is kicking around ideas for a national advertising campaign with the hopes that one will stand out as the right theme to create a consistent image for the company. Which potential theme will be the most effective with Starbucks' broad target market?
   a. Starbucks as a place that represents the "spirit of thought." Ideas and solutions are found in Starbucks, just like in the coffeehouses of the 50s and 60s.
   b. Coffee as a passion and an inspiration. The focus is on the art of whole bean coffee, the romance of espresso, and Starbucks as an artisan of inspiration.
   c. Starbucks as a spirit of freedom and irreverence. The focus is on the Starbucks customer doing his or her own thing, just for the sake of doing it.

Key Terms

brand (398)
brand awareness (399)
brand insistence (399)
brand loyalty (399)
brand marks (398)
brand names (398)
brand preference (399)
break-even analysis (404)
break-even point (404)
co-branding (400)
commercialization (395)
discount pricing (405)
family branding (400)
fixed costs (404)
generic products (399)
market share (387)
marketing mix (387)
marketing strategy (387)
national brands (399)
penetration pricing (404)
positioning (388)
private brands (399)
product (390)
product life cycle (392)
product line (395)
product mix (395)
skimming (404)
target markets (387)
test marketing (395)
trademark (398)
Universal Product Codes (UPCs) (402)
variable costs (404)

Questions

For Review

1. What are the external environmental factors that affect strategic marketing decisions?
2. What growth opportunities might a business pursue?
3. What are the four main subgroups of consumer products?
4. What are some of the advantages and disadvantages of cost-based pricing?
5. How many books will a publisher have to sell to break even if fixed costs are $100,000, the selling price per book is $60, and the variable costs per book are $40?

For Analysis

6. Why are freeware and switching costs effective market leader strategies?
7. Why do businesses continually introduce new products, given the risks and the high rate of new-product failure?
8. Why are brand names important?
9. What are the various approaches to building brands? Explain the benefits of each.
10. How does electronic pricing help the marketing effort?

For Application

11. How might a company modify its pricing strategies during a product's life cycle?
12. As the international marketing manager for Naya bottled water, you are responsible for investigating the possibility of selling bottled water overseas. What are some of the product-related issues you should consider during your study?

A Case for Critical Thinking ■ Coffee, Tea, and On-Time Arrival: Turning Around Continental Airlines

Did you ever see a company succeed that didn't have a good product? Just ask Gordon Bethune. When this former Boeing VP took the helm as chairman and CEO of Continental Airlines on February 14, 1994, his product was in last place on everything—on-time performance, baggage handling, customer service—you name it. In fact employee morale was so low that maintenance workers tore the patches off their uniforms—ashamed to admit whom they worked for. Continental was a mess, going through ten CEOs in ten years.

WHAT CAUSED THE TURBULENCE?

As far back as 1978 Continental was striving to have the lowest costs in the industry. Having the lowest cost per available seat mile was the company's claim to fame—or route to disaster as it later learned. That's because in order to cut costs, Continental cut out things people wanted.

First it cut back on its frequent-flyer program because the company viewed it as too expensive. Then it removed food service from all flights under 2.5 hours—saving the company an extra $30 million per year. Continental even rewarded employees for giving poor service. For instance, pilots were given incentives to save fuel, so plane engines were set at economy cruise, causing numerous late arrivals. Also, all planes were cleaned in 20 minutes, regardless of the appearance of the cabin. And the company eliminated first-class service on a third of its domestic flights, converting those planes to Continental Lite—a new low-cost, short-haul subsidiary designed to compete with other low-fare airlines. Continental believed that by cutting costs and introducing lower "peanut fares" it could keep customers from leaving and even attract additional passengers.

But Continental's regular customers didn't quite see it this way. They got angry and took their business elsewhere. Continental lost 20 percent of its regular customers, not realizing that these business customers accounted for 40 percent of the company's revenue. Moreover, Continental was spending an additional $6 million a month to accommodate passengers who missed their connections because of the airline's late arrivals.

Continental was in the clouds. The company was flying on autopilot—flirting with bankruptcy for the third time. At least that was the flight plan until Bethune stepped onboard. Bethune took over on Valentine's Day, but he didn't bring candy or flowers. Instead, he brought a plan.

DESTINATION TURNAROUND

First Bethune capitalized on the airline's existing strengths and got rid of unprofitable efforts. He eliminated costly routes and targeted more "coats and ties" rather than "backpacks and flip-flops." Then he calmed the turbulence by changing the company's philosophy. No longer a low-cost finance-driven product, airline flights were now a market-driven product. "We decided that we would first provide a clean, safe, reliable airline with good on-time performance, and then compete on cost." After all, bringing costs down is easy. As Bethune saw it, the real challenge was to increase revenue. But he had no intention of doing it by himself, even if he was in the pilot's seat. Bethune knew that to turn this plane around he would need plenty of fuel. So he banked on the company's best resource—its employees.

Bethune burned the employee's manual and gave all personnel the authority to do their jobs the right way. To handle employee complaints and to take suggestions, Bethune established a 24-hour operations hot line—staffed by a pilot, a mechanic, and a flight attendant. Then he doubled the number of customer-service employees. He even sent his employees through training courses on interpersonal skills. And he lined their pockets with financial incentives. Each employee was given a $65 monthly bonus if the airline was rated among the top five carriers by the U.S. Transportation Department, or $100 a month extra if it was ranked number one.

Most important, Bethune listened to the customers, and he anticipated their needs. He brought back the frequent-flyer program, first-class service, and meals—including a growing assortment of specialty foods. Of course, serving customers onboard is one thing; getting them onboard is another. So Bethune increased product loyalty by changing the airline's frequent-flyer program to make it less restrictive. Then he updated the airline's automated ticket machines to give passengers complete control of their flight itineraries. He even rebuilt relationships with travel agents. Finally, he adjusted ticket prices to maximize revenue by recognizing what customers were willing to pay for, and he eliminated expenditures that did not add value.

SMOOTH LANDING

In less than two years, Bethune and his team flew Continental to the top. The airline had the best on-time flight performance, and it even recorded the fewest baggage-handling errors and customer complaints. Continental was named the top U.S. long-haul airline in 1995 by both J. D. Power and Associates and *Frequent Flyer* magazine. Now Bethune claims to be grabbing market share among business travelers from American and others. "We've been kicking their butts," boasts Bethune.

1. Explain the differences between turning around a tangible product like laundry detergent and an intangible product like Continental Airlines.
2. How did Bethune change Continental's marketing mix?
3. Who was Continental's target market prior to Bethune's leadership, and how did it change once he took over?
4. Visit Continental's corporate Web site at <http://www.flycontinental.com/corporate/>.
   a. What is the company's *Go Forward Plan*?
   b. What *Awards & Accolades* has the company earned recently?
   c. According to *D.O.T. Statistics,* how does Continental rank among major airlines?
   d. Scroll up and click on the *CO.O.L. Travel Specials.* Using your knowledge about perishability of services, why does Continental offer this e-mail service?

Building Your Business Skills

Examine the life cycle of a product you're familiar with. Locate an article in a magazine or book that describes the life cycle of that product. Note the factors affecting its introduction, its growth, and the strategies that have been used to maintain sales as it reached maturity. If this product has experienced a decline, identify the causes and describe the manufacturer's attempts to revive the product.

1. As directed by your instructor, prepare a brief presentation describing the life cycle of the product.
2. In a class discussion, identify the factors contributing to the various stages in your chosen product's life cycle. Compare them with those of products examined by other students. Identify common elements in the life cycles of all the products evaluated by class members.

Keeping Current Using *The Wall Street Journal*

Scan recent issues of *The Wall Street Journal* for an article related to one of the following:

- New-product development
- The product life cycle
- Pricing strategies
- Packaging

1. Does this article report on a development in a particular company, several companies, or an entire industry? Which companies or industries are specifically mentioned?
2. If you were a marketing manager in this industry, what concerns would you have as a result of reading the article? What questions do you think companies in this industry (or related ones) should be asking? What would you want to know?
3. In what ways do you think this industry, other industries, or the public might be affected by this trend or development in the next five years? Why?

4. Research some new-product developments that have changed the world. Visit the Inventure Place Web site at <http://www.invent.org> and click on the *National Inventors Hall of Fame.* Find the *Index of Inventions* and browse through them.
   a. Who invented air conditioning? Fiber optics? The magnetic resonance imaging (MRI) scanner?
   b. What is the purpose of this site and how are inventors selected?

Exploring the Best of the Web

Fetch It!, page 390

Say you're thinking about opening up a coffee café. Visit *Dogpile* at <http://www.dogpile.com> to find the best search engine to begin your industry, market, and product research. Log on to the site, enter *coffee* and *fetch it!* Click on some of the links provided. Be sure to check out *all* the search engines.

1. Which search engine(s) links you to the most industry-related information?
2. Which search engine(s) links you to the home pages of coffee retailers and suppliers?
3. Which search engine(s) links you to primarily local news, clubs, and nonindustry related sites?

Be a Sharp Shopper, page 398

Now that you are a sharp marketer, go to the Sharper Image Web site at <http://www.sharperimage.com>, and let's talk marketing.

1. Is the company's name a registered trademark?
2. What are the company's main product categories? Explore these categories. Is the product mix wide? Deep?
3. Describe this company's target market? How does the company use product features and price to position its products?

Protect Your Invention, page 402

Visit the U.S. Patent and Trademark Office at <http://www.uspto.gov> to learn about patents and trademarks.

1. Click on *General Information* and *Trademark Information.* Review the *Basic Facts About Registering a Trademark.*
   a. How do you establish trademark rights?
   b. Are you required to conduct a search for conflicting marks prior to applying with the Patent and Trademark Office (PTO)?
   c. Who may use the ® symbol?
2. Go back *Home* and click on *Libraries—PTDLs.* Go to *Frequently Asked Questions.* What do the terms *patent pending* and *patent applied for* mean?
3. Go back *Home* and click on *PTO Fees.* What is the basic filing fee for a patent?

Answers to "Is It True?"

Page 391 True

Page 399 False. Only 60 percent of soft drink consumers say they are strongly committed to their brand.

Page 405 False. Eighty-seven percent of outlet shoppers said that the savings they received at out let stores were worth the time, and 93 percent planned to shop there again.

CHAPTER 14

DISTRIBUTION

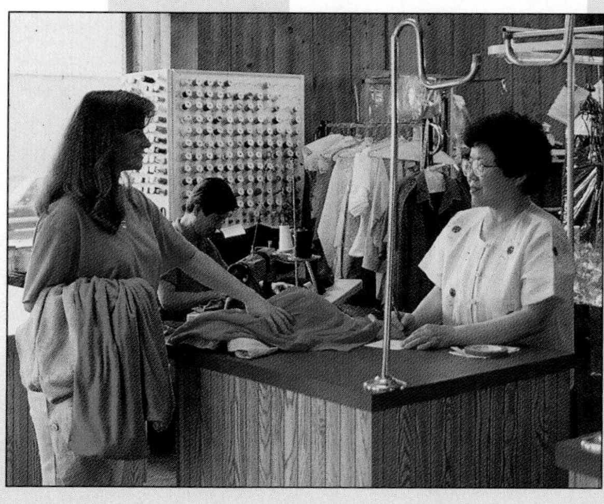

OBJECTIVES

After studying this chapter, you will be able to

1. List the eight functions performed by marketing intermediaries
2. Explain what a distribution channel is and discuss the major factors that influence channel design and selection
3. Differentiate between intensive, selective, and exclusive market-coverage strategies
4. Highlight the main advantage of a vertical marketing system and explain how it differs from a conventional marketing channel
5. Discuss how the Internet is influencing marketing channels
6. Explain what is meant by the wheel of retailing
7. Identify at least six types of store retailers and four types of nonstore retailers
8. Specify the activities included in physical distribution and list the five most common ways of transporting goods

On the Job On the Job

ON THE JOB: FACING BUSINESS CHALLENGES AT BLACK & DECKER

Power-Tool Maker Has a Remodeling Project of Its Own

Nolan Archibald had a bit of a mess on his hands. He had recently been promoted to chairman and CEO of Black & Decker, a multibillion-dollar power-tool manufacturer that was having profit problems and losing market share. Most troublesome, the company was generally annoying many of the wholesalers and retailers it relied on to sell products to consumers and construction professionals.

The company had developed a reputation for being arrogant, to put it mildly. In the words of a former Black & Decker employee, referring to Archibald's predecessors: "Management seemed to think it had the answer to every question and would generously impart its wisdom to the masses." Such an attitude nearly got Black & Decker kicked out of Wal-Mart, the largest retailer in the United States. Not the best plan for selling products, to say the least.

In addition, inventory shortages plagued retailers. If a Black & Decker product turned out to be popular with the public, retailers had a pretty good chance of running out of it because Black & Decker put a lot of emphasis on meeting its internal financial goals. The company restrained production toward the end of the year to make sure its inventory levels dropped quite low. This practice made Black & Decker's financial statements look good, but it was driving retailers away.

To make matters worse, Archibald's predecessors had recently purchased General Electric's entire line of small household appliances (at the time, the biggest brand transfer in history), and although the new line of products provided a strong stream of revenue, it gave Black & Decker yet another distribution headache. Before the acquisition, most Black & Decker products were sold through hardware stores, home-improvement centers, mail-order retailers, and discount stores. To be successful, small appliances had to be sold through department stores as well, and Black & Decker had little experience in this area. Unfortunately, the company tried to use the same approach it had used with power tools, which served only to alienate the department stores that had grown used to good treatment from General Electric.

How could Nolan Archibald repair the bad reputation that Black & Decker had gained with wholesalers and retailers? How could he combat the pressure from competitors who were trying to push Black & Decker off the shelf? How could he handle the new small appliances, given the company's lack of experience? In short, what steps could he take to ensure Black & Decker's survival and continued success?[1]

Developing a Distribution Strategy

Black & Decker's Nolan Archibald knew that having a great product was only half the battle. He had to figure out some way to balance inventory while regaining the support of wholesalers and retailers. Furthermore, he would have to find a way to distribute his small-appliance products to department stores.

Whether the product is a power tool, a haircut, toothpaste, or insurance, it needs to make its way from the producer to the ultimate user. A lot of work goes on behind the scenes to accomplish this task. **Distribution channels,** or *marketing channels,* are an organized network of firms that work together to get goods and services from producer to consumer. Distribution channels come in all shapes and sizes. Some channels are short and simple; others are complex and involve many people and organizations. An organization's decisions about which combination of channels to use—the **distribution mix**—and its overall plan for moving products to buyers—the **distribution strategy**—play major roles in the firm's success.

distribution channels
Systems for moving goods and services from producers to customers; also known as marketing channels

distribution mix
Combination of intermediaries and channels that a producer uses to get a product to end users

distribution strategy
Firm's overall plan for moving products to intermediaries and final customers

The Role of Marketing Intermediaries

Stop and think about all the products you buy: food, cosmetics, toiletries, clothing, sports equipment, airplane tickets, haircuts, gasoline, stationery, appliances, CDs, videotapes, books, magazines, and all the rest. How many of these products do you buy directly from the producer? If you're like most people, the answer is probably not many.

Most producers do not sell their goods directly to the final users—even though the Internet is making it easier to do so these days. Most producers lack the financial resources to carry out direct marketing. They work with **marketing intermediaries** (also called *middlemen*) to bring their products to market. In some cases, these "go-betweens" sell on behalf of the producers; in others, they actually own the products they sell to you.

marketing intermediaries
Businesspeople and organizations that channel goods and services from producers to consumers

Without these intermediaries, the buying and selling process would be an expensive, time-consuming experience (see Exhibit 14.1). Intermediaries are instrumental in creating three of the four forms of utility mentioned in Chapter 12: place utility, time utility, and possession utility. By transferring products from the producer to the customer, intermediaries ensure that goods and services are available at a convenient time and place. They also simplify the exchange process.

In addition, intermediaries perform a number of specific functions that make life easier for both producers and customers:

- *Providing a sales force.* Many producers like Black & Decker would find it expensive and inefficient to employ their own salespeople to sell directly to final customers. Instead, they rely on intermediaries to perform this function.
- *Providing market information.* Most intermediaries maintain databases that store valuable information about customer purchases—who buys, how often, and how much. They are close to the customer and spot trends in the marketplace long before producers catch wind of them.
- *Providing promotional support.* To boost their own sales, intermediaries design and distribute eye-catching store displays and use other promotional devices for some products, and they advertise other product lines.
- *Gathering an assortment of goods.* Intermediaries receive large shipments from producers and break them into more convenient units by sorting, standardizing, and dividing bulk quantities into smaller packages.
- *Stocking and delivering the product.* Most intermediaries maintain an inventory of merchandise that they acquire from manufacturers. By keeping this inventory,

EXHIBIT 14.1

How Intermediaries Simplify Commerce

Despite the common assumption that buying directly from the producer saves money, intermediaries actually reduce the price we pay for many goods and services. Intermediaries eliminate many of the contacts between producers and consumers that would otherwise be necessary. At the same time, they create place, time, and possession utility.

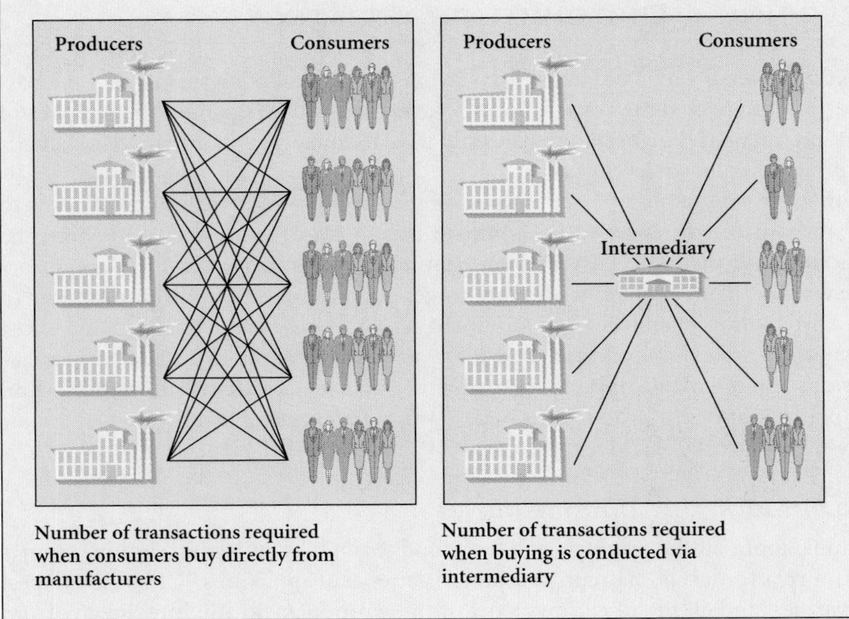

intermediaries can speed up the delivery of manufacturers' products to customers. Some intermediaries assume complete responsibility for transporting the goods to widely scattered buyers.

- *Assuming risks.* When intermediaries accept goods from manufacturers, they relieve producers of the risks associated with damage, theft, product perishability, and obsolescence.
- *Providing financing.* An intermediary that is much larger than the producers it represents can sometimes provide these producers with loans.
- *Buying.* Intermediaries match buyers and sellers. By handling a variety of goods, they reduce the number of transactions needed between the producer and consumer.

Types of Distribution Channels

The number and type of intermediaries involved in a distribution mix depend on the kind of product and the marketing practices of a particular industry. An arrangement that might be appropriate for a power-tool and appliance manufacturer like Black & Decker would not necessarily work for an insurance company, a restaurant, a steel manufacturer, or a movie studio. Important differences exist between the distribution channels for consumer goods, business goods, and services (see Exhibit 14.2).

Channel Levels Although most businesses purchase their goods directly from producers, channels for consumer goods generally have more than one level and are more complex. These channels can be categorized as follows:

- *Producer to consumer.* The most direct way to market a product is for the producer to sell directly to the consumer. This practice is becoming increasingly popular as producers use mail order, telemarketing, TV selling, and the Internet to sell their goods directly to consumers. A recent study predicts that 35 percent of U.S. con-

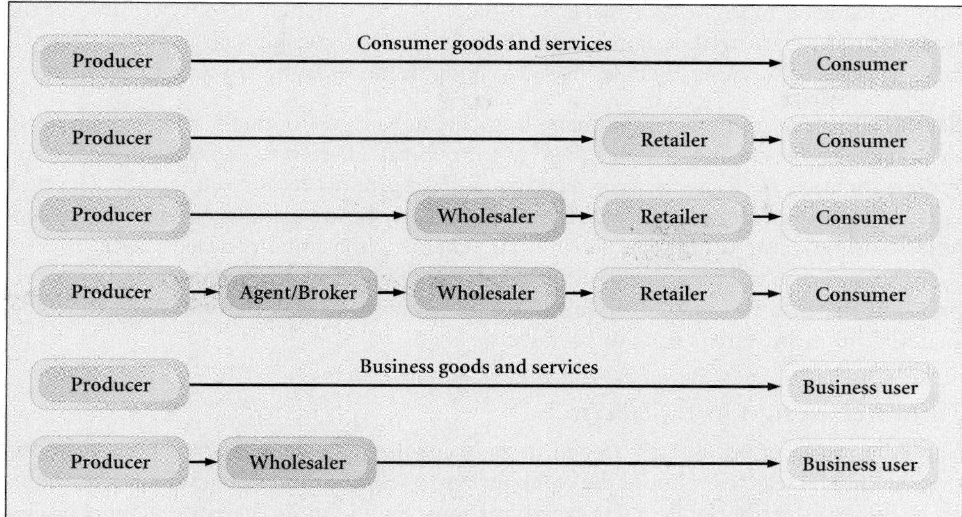

EXHIBIT 14.2

Alternative Channels of Distribution

Marketers of consumer goods, business goods, and services must analyze the alternative channels of distribution available and select the channel(s) that will best meet both the producer's marketing objectives and the consumer's needs.

sumers will purchase directly from producers via the Internet by 2005.[2] Some companies prefer to sell directly to the consumer because this approach gives them more control over pricing, service, and delivery. It also eliminates the intermediary's cut of the profit. The problem with direct distribution is that it forces producers to engage in a wide array of marketing functions, and not all producers are up to the task.

- *Producer to retailer to consumer.* Some producers sell their products to retailers, who then resell them to consumers. Automobiles, paint, gasoline, and clothing are typical of the many products distributed in this way. Giant retailers like Wal-Mart keep their costs down by buying directly from producers.
- *Producer to wholesaler to retailer to consumer.* The most common channel for consumer products is for the producer to sell to a wholesaler who in turn sells to a retailer. Most of the items you buy in supermarkets and drugstores are distributed through this type of channel. This approach is generally the most advantageous alternative for small producers who cannot afford to employ their own sales forces or delivery personnel.
- *Producer to agent/broker to wholesaler to retailer to consumer.* Another wholesaling level is typical in certain industries, such as agriculture, where specialists are required to negotiate transactions or perform such functions as sorting, grading, or subdividing the merchandise.

Channels for Service Goods Most services are distributed directly by the producer to the user because the nature of the service usually requires direct contact between the customer and the service provider. A hairstylist or lawyer, for example, would not be likely to use an intermediary to deal with clients. Some service businesses, however, do employ intermediaries. The travel industry uses agents to package vacations and sell tickets. Insurance companies market their policies through insurance brokers, and entertainers book engagements through agents who negotiate deals for them.

Technology provides an increasing number of options for the distribution of services as well. It allows the service provider to reach customers spread over a wide area.

Automated teller machines, for instance, allow a bank to distribute its services all over the world. Writers, industrial designers, advertising specialists, consultants, and other "knowledge workers" can deliver their services over long distances using computer networks.

reverse channels
Distribution channels designed to move products from the customer back to the producer

Reverse Channels Although most marketing channels move products from producers to customers, **reverse channels** move them in the opposite direction. The two most common reverse channels are those used for recycling and for product recalls and repairs. Recycling channels continue to grow in importance as consumers and businesses become more sensitive to solid-waste-disposal problems. The channels for some recycled goods, like returnable soft drink bottles, use traditional intermediaries—which in this case are retailers and bottlers. In other cases, recycling collection centers have been established to funnel material from consumers back to producers.

Is It True?

The United States does at least as well as other developed nations at recycling solid materials.

Channel Design and Selection

Should a producer sell directly to end users or rely on intermediaries? Which intermediaries should be selected? Should the company try to sell its products in every available outlet or limit its distribution to a few exclusive shops? Should more than one channel be employed? These are some of the critical decisions a company must make when designing and selecting its marketing channels. Keep in mind that it normally takes years to build an effective channel system, and when intermediaries are included, the producer must make a commitment to the middlemen. Once such commitments are made, it is difficult to change them. Therefore, management must choose its channels with an eye on the future as well as today.

Effective channel selection depends on a number of factors, some related to the type of product and the target market, others related to the company—its strengths, weaknesses, and objectives. In general, however, choosing one channel over another is a matter of making trade-offs among three factors: the number of outlets where the product is available, the cost of distribution, and the control of the product as it moves through the channel to the final customer.

Market Coverage Choosing the appropriate market coverage or the number of wholesalers or retailers who will carry the product depends primarily on the type of product. Inexpensive convenience goods or organizational supplies—such as bread, toothpaste, magazines, and pencils—sell best if they are available in as many outlets as possible. To achieve this type of **intensive distribution,** where the market is saturated with a product, a producer will almost certainly need a long distribution chain—that is, it will need wholesalers and many retailer types. Trying to cover every outlet without intermediaries would be a major undertaking, one that only the largest, best-financed producers could handle.

intensive distribution
Market coverage strategy that tries to place a product in as many outlets as possible

On the other hand, a different approach to market coverage might work better for a producer that specializes in shopping goods, such as apparel, appliances, or certain types of organizational products. When the buyer is likely to compare features and prices, the best strategy is usually **selective distribution,** in which a limited number of outlets are capable of giving the product adequate support. With fewer outlets, the distribution chain for shopping goods is generally shorter than it is for convenience goods.

selective distribution
Market coverage strategy that selects a limited number of outlets to distribute products

When a company produces expensive specialty or technical products, it may opt for direct sales or **exclusive distribution,** in which the product is available in only one outlet in each market area. Most car dealerships have exclusive distribution agreements with manufacturers. Here again, exclusive distribution normally involves simpler and shorter distribution systems.

exclusive distribution
Market coverage strategy that gives intermediaries exclusive rights to sell a product in a specific geographical area

Remember, many firms today use multiple channels to increase their market coverage and reach various target markets. Although some of these channels are primary and others are secondary, both are important. In fact, it's quite common for companies to sell their products through department stores, specialty stores, the Internet, mail-order catalogs, or some combination of these outlets.

Consider Goodyear Tire. Confronted by a need for better market coverage, Goodyear departed from its exclusive reliance on independent dealers and added a new marketing channel when it began selling its tires to Sears and Wal-Mart. Likewise Black & Decker has positioned its DeWalt brand of power tools in professional contractor channels and positioned its Black & Decker brand in hardware chains and home building centers.[3]

Cost Costs play a major role in determining a firm's distribution mix. It takes money to perform all the functions that are handled by intermediaries. Small or new companies often cannot afford to hire a sales force large enough to sell directly to end users or to call on a host of retail outlets. Neither can they afford to build large warehouses and distribution centers or buy trucks to ship their goods. These firms need the help of intermediaries who can spread the cost of such activities across a number of noncompeting products. With time and a larger sales base, a producer may build enough strength to take over some of these functions and reduce the length of the distribution chain.

Is It True?

For many products, distribution costs, including selling costs, can be as much as 30 to 40 percent of a product's cost.

Control Another important issue to consider when selecting distribution channels is control. Many manufacturers like to control how a product is sold and priced. A manufacturer cannot force intermediaries to promote and deliver the product aggressively. The longer the distribution chain, the more intermediaries there are, and the less control there is, because the manufacturer becomes increasingly distant from the ultimate seller.

For certain types of products, control is paramount because the firm's reputation is at stake. For instance, a designer of high-priced clothing might want to limit distribution to exclusive boutiques, because the clothing would lose some of its appeal if it were available in discount stores. Likewise, a company's entire merchandising strategy could be undercut if an intermediary sold some of the fashions to the wrong retailers. Producers of complex technical products like x-ray machines don't want their products handled by unqualified intermediaries who can't provide adequate customer service.

Other Factors Market coverage, cost, and control are the three big issues when selecting a distribution channel, but manufacturers must also take into account a host of other factors. These include the number of transactions, the dollar value of each transaction, the market's growth rate, the geographic concentration of the customers, and the buyer's need for service (see Exhibit 14.3).

International Channels Channel patterns differ widely from country to country. Sometimes even the simplest assumption doesn't apply when a company considers international distribution. Transportation, phone, and mail systems can differ. So do laws and regulations.

For example, if a U.S. company wants to market its goods in Austria, it has to abide by the export laws of the United States, the import and general business laws of Austria, and the applicable laws of any countries the goods pass through on the way. The complexities involved in distributing overseas are numerous. For example, when Kodak introduced a new line of copiers in Europe, the company established 13 separate companies, each with its own marketing channels, to sell copiers in 18 different countries.[4]

Channel Modification A producer must do more than design a good channel system. Channels must be periodically reviewed and modified to meet new conditions in the marketplace. Sometimes a company may switch channels if distribution becomes too difficult or too complex. Likewise, as a product advances through its life cycle, the company needs to modify its channel system to accommodate changes in the product's sales volume, selling support, and service requirements.

EXHIBIT 14.3

Factors Involved in Selecting Distribution Channels

The choice of distribution channel depends on the product, the customer, and the company's capabilities.

FACTOR	EXPLANATION
Number of transactions	When many transactions are likely, the channel should provide for many outlets, and several levels of intermediaries. If only a few transactions are likely, the number of outlets can be limited, and the channel can be relatively short.
Value of transactions	If the value of each transaction is high, the channel can be relatively short and direct, because the producer can better absorb the cost of making firsthand contact with each customer. If each transaction has a low value, a long channel is used to spread the cost of distribution over many products and outlets.
Market growth rate	In a rapidly growing market, many outlets and a long channel of distribution may be required to meet demand. In a shrinking market, fewer outlets are required.
Geographic concentration of market	If customers are clustered in a limited geographic area, the channel can be short, because the cost of reaching each account is relatively low. If customers are widely scattered, a multilevel channel with many outlets is preferable.
Need for service and sales support	Complex, innovative, or specialized products require sophisticated outlets where customers can receive information and service support; short, relatively direct channels are generally used. If the product is familiar and uncomplicated, the consumer requires little assistance; long channels with many self-serve outlets can be used.

THINKING ABOUT ETHICS

Changing the Channel

Roses are red,
Violets are blue.
We're changing the channel
And it might destroy you.

Greeting cards send some awfully sweet messages to their customers. But the types of messages some suppliers are sending their intermediaries these days are a bit more sour.

CARD SHARKS

When Hallmark recently introduced a new line of cards (Expressions from Hallmark) in mass market outlets, it angered the company's 8,200 independent card shops, and justifiably so. Hallmark had become a victim of one-stop shopping. It was losing market share against competing lines sold at discounters, supermarkets, and drugstores. Even though the company distributed its Ambassador card line to these retailers, this brand of greeting cards did not identify Hallmark as the producer. If you wanted a Hallmark-branded card, you had to buy it from an independent dealer. At least, that's the way it used to be.

Hallmark was between a rock and a hard place: Either the company could continue to watch its market share slip or it could abandon its reliance on the thousands of the specialty card shops that built its franchise. Hallmark bit the bullet. The company decided to sell Hallmark-branded cards to mass merchants. To placate the independents, the company launched a $175 million ad campaign to promote the Gold Crown retail stores. But many believe that this campaign won't be enough to save some mom-and-pop shops.

Channels (like products) have life cycles too. They emerge, grow, mature, and eventually wane over time. For example, warehouse clubs are already reaching maturity, as are malls and factory outlets. On the other hand, the Internet is opening up a wealth of new opportunities. Therefore, as a company manufactures new products or targets new markets, as new channels of distribution emerge, as technology improves, or as consumer buying behavior changes, the optimum distribution arrangement for a product is likely to change as well.

Vertical Marketing Systems

In a conventional marketing channel, wholesalers and retailers are independent of one another. Each firm essentially pursues its own objectives, although maximizing sales is usually a shared goal. In contrast, a **vertical marketing system (VMS)** is one in which the producer, wholesaler, and retailer act as a unified system to conduct distribution activities. The main advantage of a VMS is channel control.

vertical marketing systems (VMS)
Planned distribution channels in which members coordinate their efforts to optimize distribution activities

Vertical marketing systems vary in their level of formality. The most controlled form is the *corporate vertical marketing system,* in which a single firm handles production, wholesaling, and retailing functions. An example of this arrangement would be a firm like Walt Disney that sells its merchandise through company-owned retail stores. In some cases, the entire distribution chain is controlled by a single firm, but often the channel contains a mix of corporate-controlled and independently owned operations.

An *administered vertical marketing system* is a less formal arrangement in which one member of the distribution chain has enough power to influence the behavior of the others. The dominant company, known as the **channel captain,** performs functions that work to the mutual benefit of the entire chain. For instance, Toys 'R' Us dominates the toy

channel captain
Channel member that is able to influence the activities of the other members of the distribution channel

Fasten Your Seatbelts

Hallmark isn't the only one delivering bad news these days. When Circuit City offspring CarMax came to Atlanta, local auto dealers braced for the worst. CarMax threatened to do to car dealers what its corporate parent had done to mom-and-pop appliance shops: put them out of business.

First CarMax began luring buyers from other dealers by offering services few expected from a used-car dealer—like no-haggle prices, computer kiosks to search through the dealer's inventory, and money-back guarantees. Then Chrysler changed the channel. It allowed CarMax to sell new Chrysler, Plymouth, and Jeep vehicles, marking a major shift from the decades-old practice of local businesspeople owning dealerships. At a recent meeting between Chrysler officials and franchise dealers, some franchise dealers left in tears. But for others, it was like they all woke up. Now they are building new showrooms with children's play areas, kiosks, giveaways—all the perks.

In any competitive market, battles over distribution are almost assured. Multiple channels of distribution are becoming more commonplace. Aside from the specific legal and ethical issues involved, companies need to remain competitive. But what if doing so means putting others out of business?

Questions for Critical Thinking

1. Why do companies need to modify their marketing channel structures periodically?
2. What ethical issues surface when companies change their marketing channels?

This Liz Claiborne Outlet Store is part of a corporate vertical marketing system; both the store and the manufacturing operation that creates the clothes are owned by the same company.

industry. The company has developed computer software that spots emerging trends in toy sales. By passing this information on to toy manufacturers, Toys 'R' Us helps the industry balance its production volume.[5] The channel captain is often the manufacturer, as opposed to the retailer. Companies like Procter & Gamble, Kraft Foods, and Gillette are the dominant forces in the distribution of their products.

A *contractual vertical marketing system* is a compromise between a corporate system and an administered system. With this approach, the members of the channel are legally bound by a contractual agreement that spells out their respective responsibilities. Franchising is the most common form of the contractual vertical marketing system. Many of the world's best-known retail outlets, from McDonald's to Radio Shack, rely on franchising to cover attractive markets.

Channel Conflict

No matter how well a company designs and manages its channels, conflict is bound to arise. What causes channel conflict? Frequently it occurs when companies sell products in multiple channels, each of which is seeking an edge in the crowded marketplace. For instance, when Levi Strauss and Dr. Martens forayed into retail with company-owned stores, they danced around sensitive "turf war" issues, telling existing independent retailers that they weren't competing but rather "showcasing" the merchandise.[6] On the other hand, Viacom's Bill Fields wasn't quite as diplomatic. Shortly after Viacom purchased Blockbuster, Fields cut out its movie distributor and began purchasing videotapes directly from movie studios—a move some estimated would save the company $25 million a year.[7] Even Apple is breaking new ground by selling Mac computers directly over the phone and the Internet.[8]

Channel conflict can also occur when markets are oversaturated with channel intermediaries, when suppliers provide inadequate support, or when one channel member places its own success above the success of the entire channel. Consider Snapple. When Quaker Oats purchased Snapple for $1.7 billion, it got a bonus—350 independent distributors, many of whom had contracts giving them the lifetime right to distribute Snapple in an assigned territory. Of course, Quaker already had its own state-of-the-art distribution system for Gatorade. So rather than doubling up, it tried to make a deal. The Snapple distributors would acquire the right to sell Gatorade to small accounts in exchange for giving Quaker the right to sell Snapple in supermarkets. But the Snapple distributors balked. They were earning $4-per-case margins on Snapple—roughly double what they could make on Gatorade. So the distributors vetoed the deal, and it caused tremendous channel conflict. As one Snapple distributor put it: "Quaker didn't know our business." Eventually, Quaker encountered many other problems marketing Snapple and ultimately sold the brand for a $1.4 billion loss.[9]

Keep in mind that not all channel conflict is bad. Sometimes it can lead to a more dynamic adaptation to the changing environment. Therefore, the challenge is not to eliminate channel conflict but rather to manage it effectively so that it does not get out of hand and become dysfunctional. For instance, as new channels like the Internet emerge, producers must find ways to modify their current channel design, including these new channels, while accommodating the needs of older, valued channel members.

Amazon.com offers a selection of over 2.5 million books and can deliver your online order in a few days, because the company buys the bulk of its books directly from publishers—eliminating the middleman.

The Internet

The Internet is a sales, delivery, and repair channel of distribution. It moves forward and backward, and it's changing the way we market products. For instance, Amazon.com, Wal-Mart, and scores of other companies use the Internet to advertise and sell goods to consumers; Gateway 2000 uses the Internet to repair technical problems encountered by its customers; McAfee uses it to distribute software programs and upgrades to customers; and PointCast uses the Internet to transform your idle computer screen into a dynamic up-to-the-minute news wire.[10]

Some predict that the Internet, which allows manufacturers to bypass distributors and conduct business directly with end users, will lead to the demise of distribution channels as we know them. But this is speculation. Technology and the Internet will significantly change the way intermediaries do business in the future, but the multifaceted role intermediaries play is more important today than ever. No one can offer better coverage in a territory than an experienced intermediary who knows the market and has established long-term customer contacts.[11]

Change the Bloomin' Channel

BEST OF THE WEB

New outlets for selling floral arrangements are blossoming all over the Internet—from cyber flower shops to the real begonias. Competition is tough as florists try to distinguish themselves from the bloomin' lot. With Web sites like iflowers (sponsored by Phillip's 1-800-Florals), FTD and 1-800-Flowers no longer have a competitive advantage. In fact, customers visiting iflowers can send digital postcards and personalized messages and then follow the site's links to over 10,000 selected virtual Web sites offering free products, reference sources, live images, shareware, and multimedia tours. So what has all this got to do with romantic roses? Visit iflowers now, follow the links, and remember to think like a marketer.
http://www.iflowers.com

Choosing Intermediaries

Basically, intermediaries are of two main types: wholesalers and retailers. **Wholesalers** sell primarily to retailers, other wholesalers, and organizational users such as governments, institutions, and commercial operations (all of which either resell the product or use it in making products of their own). Wholesalers that sell to organizational customers are often called **industrial distributors** to distinguish them from wholesalers that supply retail outlets. Wholesalers seldom sell directly to the final user. **Retailers** sell to individuals who buy products for ultimate consumption—the final consumer. Retailers can operate out of a physical store (like a supermarket or department store), or they can sell goods without a store (by telephone, over the Internet, or by vending machine).

wholesalers
Firms that sell products to other firms for resale or for organizational use

industrial distributors
Wholesalers that sell to industrial customers, rather than to retailers

retailers
Firms that sell goods and services to individuals for their own use rather than for resale

Wholesale Intermediaries

Because wholesalers seldom deal directly with consumers, many people are unfamiliar with this link in the distribution chain. However, roughly 70 percent of all manufactured goods travel through wholesalers on the way to final customers.[12] Most U.S. wholesalers are independent wholesalers and can be classified as either *merchant wholesalers, agents,* or *brokers.*

merchant wholesalers
Independent wholesalers that take legal title to goods they distribute

full-service merchant wholesalers
Merchant wholesalers that provide a wide variety of services to their customers, such as storage, delivery, and marketing support

rack jobbers
Merchant wholesalers that are responsible for setting up and maintaining displays in a particular section of a retail store

limited-service merchant wholesalers
Merchant wholesalers that offer fewer services than full-service wholesalers; they often specialize in particular markets, such as agriculture

drop shippers
Merchant wholesalers that assume ownership of goods but don't take physical possession; commonly used to market agricultural and mineral products

agents and brokers
Independent wholesalers that do not take title to the goods they distribute, but may or may not take possession of those goods

branch office
Producer-owned marketing intermediary that carries stock and sells it; also called a sales branch

sales office
Producer-owned office that markets products but doesn't carry any stock

Types of Wholesale Intermediaries Roughly 80 percent of all wholesalers are **merchant wholesalers,** independently owned businesses that take legal title to merchandise and then resell it to retailers or organizational buyers. **Full-service merchant wholesalers** provide a wide variety of services to their customers, such as storage, selling, order processing, delivery, and promotional support. **Rack jobbers,** for example, set up displays in retail outlets, stock inventory, and mark prices on merchandise displayed in a particular section of a store. **Limited-service merchant wholesalers,** on the other hand, provide fewer services. Natural resources such as lumber, grain, and coal are usually marketed through a class of wholesaler called **drop shippers,** who take ownership but not physical possession of the goods they handle.

In contrast to merchant wholesalers, **agents and brokers** never take title to the products they handle, and they perform fewer services. Their primary role is to bring buyers and sellers together, and they are generally paid a commission (a percentage of the money received) for any transaction they handle. You are probably familiar with real estate agents, insurance brokers, and securities brokers. These agents and brokers match up buyers and sellers for a fee or commission, but don't take title to the property. Manufacturer's representatives are agents who sell several noncompeting products to customers in a specific territory and arrange for delivery of the products. By representing several manufacturers' products at once, the rep can achieve enough volume to justify the cost of a direct sales call.

Sometimes a manufacturer may decide to market its products through company-owned channels because the products are complex and require installation, servicing, or expertise. Two types of wholesale businesses that are owned by producers are *branch offices* and *sales offices.* A **branch office,** or *sales branch,* is an establishment that carries inventory and performs a full range of marketing and business activities. A **sales office,** on the other hand, often conducts the same range of marketing and business functions as a branch office but doesn't carry inventory.

The Changing Role of Wholesale Intermediaries A number of forces are changing the role of wholesale intermediaries today. Industry consolidations, intense competition, and new technology are just a few. Although small firms still predominate in wholesaling, some wholesalers are merging or banding together to form informal cooperatives. An increasing number of wholesalers today are adopting leading-edge technology to reengineer their businesses, enabling them to better serve suppliers on one end and customers on the other end.

Some wholesalers are redefining their function as marketing support businesses, whereas others are defining their primary function as improving customer satisfaction. Still others have decided that they are in the information business as well as the delivery business. As they see it, the customer's knowledge about a product's whereabouts is as important as safe delivery. By 2002, according to a recent industry report, 60 percent of wholesale distributors will earn a majority of their profits from post-sale services like information services, delivery, installation, warranty, and training.[13] In short, wholesalers today are beginning to view distribution activities as the means to this end—not the final objective.[14]

Store Retailers

In contrast to wholesalers, retailers are a visible element in the distribution chain. Today's retail stores include department stores, discount stores, off-price stores, warehouse clubs, factory outlets, specialty stores, category killers, supermarkets, hypermarkets, convenience stores, and catalog stores (see Exhibit 14.4). They sell everything from safety pins to Rolls-Royces and from hot dogs to haute cuisine. They compete on price, efficiency, customer service, store atmosphere, portfolio, and so on (see Exhibit 14.5).

Retailers provide many benefits to consumers. Some save people time and money by providing an assortment of merchandise under one roof. Others give shoppers access to goods and delicacies they might not be able to find on their own. Some retailers build traffic by diversifying their product lines, a practice known as **scrambled merchandising.** For example, you can rent movies, eat pizza, and buy clothes at the grocery store, and you can buy appliances, cosmetics, and toys at the drugstore. This makes it increasingly difficult to differentiate one retail store type from another. In fact, many retailers today look alike and sell the same products. Plus many discounters upgrade their operations to become more like department stores in appearance, merchandise, and price. This process of store evolution, know as the **wheel of retailing**, follows a predictable pattern: An innovative company with low operating costs attracts a following by offering low prices and limited service. Over time, management adds more services to broaden the appeal of the discount store, prices creep upward, opening the door for lower-priced competitors. Eventually, these competitors also upgrade their operations and are replaced by still other lower-priced stores.

scrambled merchandising
Policy of carrying merchandise that is ordinarily sold in a different type of outlet

wheel of retailing
Evolutionary process by which stores that feature low prices are gradually upgraded until they forfeit their appeal to price-sensitive shoppers and are replace by new competitors

Specialty Stores, Category Killers, and Discount Stores Although large multi-unit chain stores account for over half of all retail sales, many retail stores today are small **specialty stores**—which carry only particular types of goods.[15] The basic merchandising strategy of a specialty shop is to offer a limited number of product lines but an extensive selection of brands, styles, sizes, models, colors, materials, and prices within each line stocked. Specialty shops

specialty shops
Stores that carry only particular types of goods

TYPE OF RETAILER	DESCRIPTION	EXAMPLES
Department store	Offers a wide variety of merchandise under one roof in departmentalized sections and many customer services	Sears J. C. Penney Nordstrom
Discount store	Offers a wide variety of merchandise at low prices and few services	Kmart Wal-Mart
Off-price store	Offers designer and brand-name merchandise at low prices and few services	T.J. Maxx Marshall's
Warehouse club	Large, warehouse style store that sells food and general merchandise at discount prices. Some require club membership.	Sam's Club
Factory/retail outlet	Manufacturer-owned store selling discontinued items, overruns, and factory seconds	Nordstrom Rack Nike outlet store
Specialty store	Offers a compete selection in a narrow range of merchandise	Florsheim Shoes Williams Sonoma
Category killer	Type of specialty store focusing on specific products on giant scale and dominating retail sales in respective products categories	Office Depot Toys 'R' Us
Supermarket	Large, self-service store offering a wide selection of food and nonfood merchandise	Lucky Kroger
Hypermarket	Giant store offering food and general merchandise at discount prices	Super Kmart
Convenience store	Offers staple convenience goods, long service hours, quick checkouts	7-Eleven
Catalog store	Showroom that displays samples of catalog products—mostly at discount prices	Service Merchandise

EXHIBIT 14.4

Types of Retail Stores

When you think of retailers, stores such as J. C. Penney, The Gap, and Radio Shack probably come to mind. However, many other types of outlets fit the marketing definition. Here are some of the most common types of retail stores.

EXHIBIT 14.5

Retailing Strategies

Instead of trying to be all things to all people, retailers have begun to create special identities to respond to various target markets. Here are some of the most successful strategies.

STRATEGY	EXPLANATION
Value	Retailer offers greater overall value, lower prices than competitors. Holds down costs by eliminating alterations, delivery, exchanges, credit, gift wrapping. Stores are spartan; service is minimal.
Efficiency	Retailer caters to customers who have little time for shopping. Convenience stores are situated in handy locations, remain open long hours. Superstores offer one-stop shopping. Mail-order shopping, telemarketing, and TV shopping all allow customers to shop at home.
Service	Retailer emphasizes personal contact, expert assistance with purchase, postsale service.
Atmospherics	Retailer creates exciting shopping environment; caters to customer's fantasies with special effects such as theme décor, music, lighting, scents, special events, imaginative architecture.
Portfolio	Retailer has a mix of several outlets, each of which caters to a specific segment.

are particularly strong in certain product categories—books, children's clothing, fast food, or sporting goods, for example.

category killers
A discount chain that sells only one category of products

At the other end of the retail spectrum are the **category killers**—superstores that dominate a market by stocking every conceivable variety of a particular line of merchandise. Toys 'R' Us, Party City, Office Depot, and Barnes and Noble are category killers. These stores offer the consumer the widest selection of products, but according to Arthur Martinez, CEO of Sears, "There's some evidence that category killers have gotten too big, too overwhelming, too frightening, and too confusing to shop."[16] Unfortunately, Tandy found this out too late. Its Incredible Universe was an incredible flop. After only months of operation, Tandy pulled the plug on its 26 superstores, including all 17 Incredible Universe stores with over 184,000 square feet of every electronic product imaginable.[17]

discount stores
Retailers that sell a variety of goods below the market price by keeping their overhead low

On the other hand, **discount stores** offer a wider variety of merchandise, lower prices, and fewer services than category killers. And some are stopping category killers like Toys 'R' Us in their tracks. That's because toys account for only a fraction of a general discounter's

A "category killer" is a large retail store that tries to dominate in a particular product category. This Toys 'R' Us store in Paramus, New Jersey, is a good example.

business, so it can afford to cut its prices. But because toys are the only category at Toys 'R' Us, lowering prices hurts this category killer far more than it hurts a multiproduct discounter.

Look at giant discounter Wal-Mart. Since the early 1990s, Wal-Mart has expanded or opened over 300 supercenters with an average size of 181,000 square feet. Even Wal-Mart admits that it can sell groceries below cost because it compensates by selling other profitable merchandise. This discounting strategy has helped Wal-Mart become the second largest grocer in the United States—behind Kroger.[18]

Retail Trends and Challenges The average life cycle of a retail store today is considerably shorter than it used to be. It took 100 years for department stores to hit maturity, 10 years for warehouse stores, and now in just 5 to 6 years a new concept becomes tired. One of the reasons for this compressed cycle is the fact that there are too many stores. Today it is estimated that there are 20 square feet of retail space for every man, woman, and child in this nation, up from 14.7 square feet per person a decade ago.[19]

Even though some of this space will get transformed by the next wave of ideas, it is currently hurting the industry—especially because stores are aging and consumers are shopping less. A recent industry study indicates that the average time that consumers spend shopping has dropped 25 percent since 1982, and the average number of stores visited during a trip to the mall has also dropped by 32 percent.[20] In addition, nearly half of the more than 2,800 enclosed malls in the United States are 20 years old or older.[21] That's why some malls are being kept alive by extensive remodeling and others are becoming entertainment centers like the colossal Mall of America near Minneapolis. This mall is built around a full-scale amusement park, miniature golf course, nightclubs, restaurants, and movie complexes.[22] By adding entertainment, retailers hope people will visit the malls more frequently. After all, they worry that as new nonstore shopping possibilities emerge and grow, many consumers will elect the ultimate shopping convenience—to stay at home.

Explore the World of Retail

BEST OF THE WEB

Thinking about opening up a small retail store? Need some statistics? Find out what's hot in retail by visiting the National Retail Federation Web site. Plug in to *Industry Connections*. Read the *Washington Update*. Learn which government proposals might affect your retail business and how to do something about them. Opening a retail store is exciting—especially if you're prepared.
http://www.nrf.com

Nonstore Retailers

Consumers today can order clothing, electronics, and flowers from anywhere in the world and at any time of the day without visiting a store. Nonstore retailers include mail-order firms, automatic vending machines, telemarketers, door-to-door sales forces, and a variety of electronic retailer venues such as the Internet, interactive kiosks, and home shopping networks.

Although the overwhelming majority of goods and services is still sold through physical stores, nonstore retailing has been growing at a much faster rate than traditional store retailing. Some predict that as much as a third to a half of all general merchandise could soon be sold through nonstore retailing channels. Others predict that the increase in nonstore retailing will bring the demise of brick and mortar malls and their retail outlets.[23] Still, others aren't convinced. They see many benefits to Internet shopping (like 24-hour

GAINING THE COMPETITIVE EDGE

Smashing Pumpkins on the Produce Aisle? New Distribution Strategies Boost Sales

Starbucks did it. Dell did it. So did Charles Schwab, Home Depot, Dreyers, McAfee, PointCast, Amazon.com, The Body Shop, Taco Bell, and scores of others. They all took common products—coffee, computers, securities, hardware, ice cream, software, news, books, soap, and tacos—and found uncommon ways to get them to consumers.

THE ROAD TO RICHES

An often neglected route to growth, distribution has today become the road to riches for many companies. Consider Dreyers. Gary Rogers and William Cronk plunked down $1 million for the $6 million (sales) business and within a decade they literally drove the product to success. Truck by truck, region by region, they built a highly effective distribution strategy. Instead of going the conventional distribution route—dumping their ice cream in third-party warehouses to be delivered by independents—company sales reps used a company-owned refrigerated fleet to deliver ice cream directly to stores. And it paid off. With sales topping $791 million, their unconventional strategy has produced unconventional profits.

ROCKIN' RUTABAGA

But isn't stacking Mariah Carey CDs in the supermarket produce section taking uncommon distribution too far? Not according to Michael Rigby, owner of Fresh Picks. Rigby hopes to capture impulse buyers by outfitting supermarkets with CD racks, listening stations, and more than 400 titles of popular music. "Customers go into a supermarket with an open shopping list and a 100 percent intent to spend," notes Rigby. "Nobody I've ever spoken to comes out with exactly what they intended." Based on current trends in Europe where supermarket chains have plucked 12 percent of the music business in the United Kingdom and 50 percent in France, Rigby is rocking the distribution channels, and Tower Records might just become a victim. Of course if Rigby doesn't get the behemoth, maybe CDnow.com will.

NOWHERE MEN

No store. No catalog. No sales staff. Is this the future of retailing? A beige box sits on the floor, under a Formica-topped table. Wires connect the box (a $60,000 Sparc 20 workstation) to various disk drives. Every flash of a tiny red light indicates that somebody is in the store and shopping. Even though CDnow.com exists only in cyberspace—where commercial sites are popping up like mushrooms after the rain—this virtual business is grabbing market share in the brave new world of Internet commerce.

Instead of flipping through finite racks of ill-sorted CDs, this store's customers point and click, their orders filled by tapping the combined inventories of the company's distributors. But relying on intermediaries can be costly. That's why Amazon.com, the leading Internet bookseller, is changing its channels—again.

---

access), but they swiftly point out that shopping offers a tactile experience: People like to be around others; they like to see, feel, smell, and try out merchandise before they buy it.[24]

mail-order firms
Companies that sell products through catalogs and ship them directly to customers

Mail-Order Firms Examples of the most popular types of nonstore retailers are **mail-order firms.** These firms provide customers with a wide variety of goods ordered from catalogs and shipped by mail. Catalog shopping is a big business, and it's growing at around 7 percent annually. In 1996 U.S. consumers spent over $246 billion on mail-order goods and services, and businesses ordered another $145.6 billion worth through the mail.[25] Many of the most successful mail-order firms are more like specialty stores, focusing on a narrow range of merchandise; they include J. Crew, L. L. Bean, Lands' End, and Banana Republic, to name a few. Some companies use mail order to supplement and promote their base business, which is conducted primarily through retail stores. Others, such as Harry and David's Fruit-of-the-Month Club, rely almost entirely on mail-order sales. Still others, including J. Crew, view retail stores as a logical expansion from their mail-order businesses.[26]

IT'S A JUNGLE OUT THERE

Amazon.com is getting real. Company founder Jeffrey Beznos is modifying the company's "sell all, carry few" strategy by loosening ties to its distributor, Ingram Book Group. Beznos figures Ingram costs Amazon customers a couple of percentage points above the price of a book purchased directly from a publisher. So Amazon (whose revenues topped $43 million for the first half of 1997) will enlarge its warehouse capacity sixfold (stocking 200,000 to 300,000 titles) and buy the bulk of its books direct from publishers.

But doesn't this negate the one major cost advantage intrinsic to the virtual bookshop—minimal investment in bricks and mortar? Not according to Beznos. He sees effective distribution as the key success factor in online bookselling—"the iceberg below the waterline." So to get the books to customers faster and cheaper, he hired Richard Dalzell, the logistics whiz from Wal-Mart. Where does this leave Ingram Books? Like many distributors these days, they win some and lose some.

A MARRIAGE TURNED ROCKY

Turbulent. That's the best way to describe the tenuous relationship between companies and their distributors these days. It used to be that manufacturers made products and distributed them through a single channel: the old reliable dealer network. But with changing customer preferences, margin instability, increasing competition, rapid technological changes, and the emergence of alternative channels (such as the Internet, 800 numbers, catalogs, interactive TV), companies are increasingly bypassing their dealers, making them feel jilted, not to mention fearful for their future.

POINT, CLICK, AND SHIP

On the other hand, some suppliers don't see cutting out the middle guy as the best strategy. They feel that countervailing trends—shorter order cycle times, more frequent shipments, and continuous replenishment arrangements—may actually reinforce the distributor's position. After all, consumers accustomed to ordering products with a click of the mouse expect instant delivery of their purchases, intact and damage-free. So whether suppliers love 'em or leave 'em, it's a distribution revolution in the marketplace, and the role of the distributor is bound to change.

QUESTIONS FOR CRITICAL THINKING

1. Categorize the types of channels used by each of these four companies: Dreyers, Fresh Picks, CDnow.com, Amazon.com.
2. Using the same four companies, discuss the concept of making trade-offs (among market coverage, cost, and control) when choosing a firm's distribution mix.

Automatic Vending For certain types of products, vending machines are an important nonstore retail outlet. In Japan, soda pop, coffee, candy, sandwiches, and cigarettes are all commonly sold this way. From the consumer's point of view, the chief attraction of vending machines is their convenience: They are open 24 hours a day and may be found in a variety of handy locations such as college dormitories. On the other hand, vending-machine prices are usually no bargain. The cost of servicing the machines is relatively high, and vandalism is a factor. So high prices are required in order to provide the vending-machine company and the product manufacturer with a reasonable profit.

Direct Selling You are probably familiar with telephone retailing, or *telemarketing*. No doubt you have been called by insurance agents, newspaper circulation departments, and assorted nonprofit organizations, all trying to interest you in their goods, services, and causes. In 1996 U.S. consumers bought $168.6 billion worth of goods and services over the telephone.[27] Another form of direct selling is door-to-door sales where a large sales force calls directly on customers in their homes or offices to demonstrate merchandise, take orders,

BEST OF THE WEB

Visit a Virtual Store

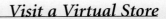

Virtual stores are an easy way to find what you are looking for. Try comparison shopping online. Visit Amazon.com, and Barnes & Noble online. Browse the subjects. Find your favorite author. Check out the reviews. Meet some of the authors. How do the two sites compare? Now review the Web sites from a marketer's perspective. What special features does a virtual store have? Why would consumers choose purchasing online over going to a bookstore? If you owned a small bookstore, how could you compete?
http:www.amazon.com
http:www.barnesandnoble.com

Is It True?

The average U.S. household receives between 350 and 400 telephone solicitations, and from 1,000 to 1,300 pieces of mail solicitation per year.

and make deliveries. The famous names in door-to-door selling—and its variant, the party plan—include Tupperware, Fuller Brush, Avon, and Electrolux. With more and more women working outside the home, this method of retailing is diminishing in importance.

Electronic Retailing We are only beginning to realize the potential of the Internet to deliver goods and services in the marketplace. Whether you call it electronic retailing, digital commerce, e-shopping, e-tailing, cybershopping, or virtual retail, the Internet is a borderless shopping environment where a shopper in London can browse through the newest offerings at a site in Los Angeles for products manufactured in Australia. Although electronic shopping is still in its infancy, predictions about its near-term potential vary wildly—from $7 billion to $20 billion in Internet sales.[28] Regardless of the magic number, one thing is certain: Hanging out a shingle on the Internet does not guarantee visitors, let alone sales. Those products that best fit the Internet will succeed. Those products that don't fit will fail.[29]

ELECTRONIC CATALOGS Electronic catalogs (catalogs on computer disk or published over the Internet) allow retailers to reach an enormous number of potential customers at a relatively low cost. Consider AMP, an electronics manufacturer in Harrisburg, Pennsylvania. The company was spending about $8 million to $10 million a year on its paper-based catalog, and as soon as it was shipped, some of the information was already out of date. So like many, AMP is switching to electronic catalogs. Experts predict a quick rise in business use of electronic catalogs on the Internet. Electronic catalogs provide an easy way to search for products as well as up-to-the-minute information.[30]

Some retailers are going full circle by linking their electronic catalogs with FedEx. Launched in 1996, FedEx's BusinessLink gives merchants custom software to create their own online catalogs that are housed on FedEx's computer. When customers place an order over the Internet, they are really communicating with an agent from FedEx who electronically transmits the order to merchants for fulfillment. Then FedEx sends a driver to pick up the merchandise and takes over from there. "We facilitate the electronic ordering on the front end and we facilitate the shipping and tracking on the back end," says one FedEx spokesperson.[31]

CYBERMALLS AND VIRTUAL STOREFRONTS A *cybermall* is a Web-based retail complex that houses dozens of *virtual storefronts* or Internet-based stores that sell everything from computer software to gourmet chocolates. Like their physical counterparts, these Internet storefronts rely on a lot of "walk-in" traffic. For instance, shoppers who come to the cybermall looking for a new CD might also click on the cyber shoe store. Besides exposure, another key advantage of a cybermall is that tenants do not have to create their own Web page or find a server to house it. Typically, the cybermall operator does all that for a sizable fee.[32] Some cybermalls specialize. For example, MelaNet's African Marketplace specializes in goods and services provided by African Americans.[33]

FedEx's BusinessLink software offers customers the ability to directly access an order-confirmation number and a package tracking number, and to determine the status of their shipments 24 hours a day.

TELEVISION AND INTERACTIVE SHOPPING Home shopping networks now ring up more than $3 billion in sales every year.[34] When Mark and Susan Scherr developed pump-a-present—a plastic device that allows users to gift wrap in a balloon any item that can pass through the device's 2.5-inch diameter—they swiftly sold 35,000 in just a few months on the QVC home shopping network. Prior to their debut on QVC, the couple had sold only 5,000 units in the previous $2\frac{1}{2}$ years using conventional channels.[35]

Perhaps the most exciting development under way in electronic retailing is the marriage of television and computer technologies, leading to interactive shopping. Home shopping networks allow customers to call in their orders after seeing merchandise on TV, but interactive TV goes one step further, allowing consumers to use a computer keyboard and modem to communicate directly with sellers (similar to video conferencing).[36] So far, interactive TV technology is in the very early stages, but services like SkyMall's e-commerce venture with LodgeNet are giving consumers new options for selecting and buying goods. Currently, guests in more than 250,000 hotel rooms can access a new video version of the popular SkyMall catalog without leaving their rooms and use the television to buy products from Hammacher Schlemmer, Sharper Image, Brookstone, and others.[37]

MANAGING PHYSICAL DISTRIBUTION

Physical distribution encompasses all the activities required to move finished products from the producer to the consumer (see Exhibit 14.6). It may not seem at first glance to be one of the most glamorous or exciting aspects of business, but it is definitely one of the most important. How important is physical distribution? Look at Compaq Computer. This company estimates that it once lost $500 million to $1 billion in sales because its laptops and desktops weren't available when and where customers were ready to buy them.

physical distribution
All the activities required to move finished products from the producer to the consumer

Many physical-distribution systems are burdened with duplication and inefficiency. For instance, a typical box of breakfast cereal can spend as long as 104 days getting from factory to supermarket, progressing haltingly through a series of wholesalers, distributors, brokers, diverters, and consolidators, each of which has a warehouse. That's why more and more companies are using physical distribution to gain a competitive advantage. Hard-pressed to knock out competitors on quality or price, companies are trying to gain an edge through their ability to deliver the right stuff in the right amount of time. In industry after industry, executives have been placing one item near the top of the corporate agenda: **logistics**—the planning and movement of goods and information throughout the supply chain.

logistics
The planning, movement, and flow of goods and related information throughout the supply chain

EXHIBIT 14.6

Steps in the Physical-Distribution Process

The phases of a distribution system should mesh as smoothly as the cogs in a machine. Because the steps are interrelated, a change in one phase can affect the other phases. The objective of the process is to provide a target level of customer service at the lowest overall cost.

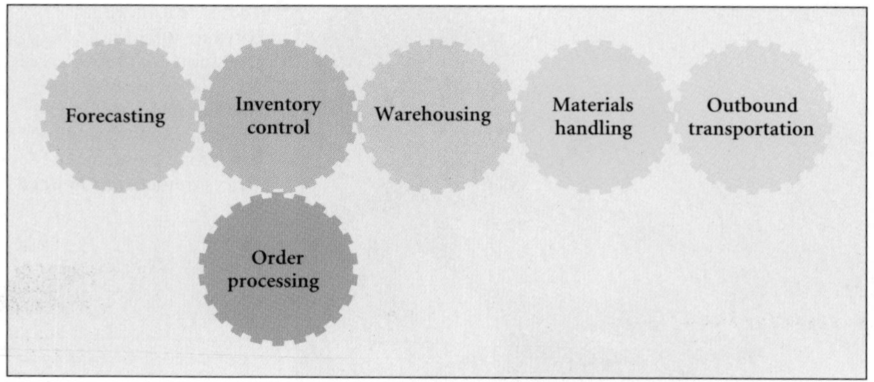

Long an unsung hero, logistics has suddenly become strategic.[38] For instance, PC Connection, a mail-order retailer of personal-computer hardware and software, uses physical distribution to maintain an edge in customer service. Computer owners can place orders as late as 3:00 A.M. and receive the goods later that same day, nearly anywhere in the United States. PC Connection achieves this remarkable level of service by maintaining a warehouse at the Ohio airport used by its shipping partner, Airborne Express. When an order arrives by phone or fax, the merchandise can be loaded on the next Airborne flight. This dedication to customer service pays off for PC Connection in increased sales and a loyal customer base.[39]

However, streamlining processes that traverse companies and continents is not an easy task, even though the payback can be enormous. In two years, National Semiconductor has cut its standard delivery time 47 percent, reduced distribution costs 2.5 percent, and increased sales 34 percent. How? By shutting down six warehouses around the globe and air-freighting its microchips to customers worldwide from a new distribution center in Singapore.[40]

Technology and Physical Distribution

Some of today's most advanced physical-distribution systems employ satellite navigation and communication, voice-input computers, machine vision, robots, onboard computer logbooks, and planning software that relies on artificial intelligence. Kansas-based trucking firm OTR Express operates almost as if it were a giant computer system that just happens to use trucks to get the job done. By using custom software to track everything from the location of trucks to the best places in the country to buy tires, OTR shows impressive profits while keeping the firm's prices competitive.[41]

Likewise FedEx fully exploits the benefits of technology to automate its services and provide superior customer service. The company's $180 million small-package sorting system processes over 400,000 packages an hour. Each parcel is scanned four times, weighed, and measured, and its digital image is recorded on computer. In addition, the company's world shipping software streamlines customer billing, reduces shipping paperwork, and allows customers to track their shipments over the Internet.[42]

customer-service standards Specifications for the quality of service that a firm will provide for its customers

Regardless of the technology a company uses, the key to success in managing physical distribution is to coordinate the activities of everyone involved, from the sales staff that is trying to satisfy demanding customers to the production staff that is trying to manage factory work loads. The overriding objective of all concerned should be to achieve a competitive level of **customer-service standards** (the quality of service that a firm provides for its customers) at the lowest total cost. Generally speaking, as the level of service improves, the

Computer technology, such as this Roadnet route-optimization software, is helping marketers locate new customers, simplify distribution routes, arrange efficient sales territories, and take other steps to boost profitability.

cost of distribution increases. A producer must analyze whether it is worthwhile to deliver the product in, say, three days as opposed to five, if doing so increases the price of the item.

This type of trade-off can be difficult to make because the steps in the distribution process are all interrelated. A change in one affects the others. For example, if you use slower forms of transportation, you reduce your shipping costs, but you probably increase your storage costs. Similarly, if you reduce the level of inventory to cut your storage costs, you run the risk of being unable to fill orders in a timely fashion. The trick is to optimize the *total* cost of achieving the desired level of service. This effort requires a careful analysis of each step in the distribution process in relation to every other step.

In-House Operations

The steps in the distribution process can be divided into in-house operations and transportation. The in-house steps in the process include forecasting, order processing, inventory control, warehousing, and materials handling.

Forecasting To control the flow of products through the distribution system, a firm must have an accurate estimate of demand. To some degree, historical data can be used to project future sales; however, the firm must also consider the impact of unusual events (such as special promotions) that might temporarily boost demand. For example, if Black & Decker decided to offer a special discount price on electric drills during September, management would need to ship additional drills to the dealers during the latter part of August to satisfy the extra demand.

order processing
Functions involved in preparing and receiving an order

Order Processing **Order processing** involves preparing orders for shipment and receiving orders when shipments arrive. It includes a number of activities, such as checking the customer's credit, recording the sale, making the appropriate accounting entries, arranging for the item to be shipped, adjusting the inventory records, and billing the customer. Because order processing involves direct interaction with the customer, it affects a company's reputation for customer service. Most companies establish standards for filling orders within a specific time period. PC Connection's guarantee of same-day shipping for orders received up to 3:00 A.M. is a good example.

Computers are playing an increasingly important role in processing orders. In some cases, customers and suppliers are connected electronically. Wal-Mart established a computerized ordering system between its warehouses and its suppliers.[43] Using a method called electronic data interchange (EDI), computers send and receive orders automatically—eliminating the need to exchange paper documents. Such systems can place orders automatically as stocks are depleted in stores.

Inventory Control In an ideal world, a company would always have just the right amount of goods on hand to fill the orders it receives. In reality, however, inventory and sales are seldom in perfect balance. Most firms like to build a supply of finished goods so that they can fill orders in a timely fashion. But how much inventory is enough? If your inventory is too large, you incur extra expenses for storage space, handling, insurance, and taxes; you also run the risk of product obsolescence. On the other hand, if your inventory is too low, you may lose sales when the product is not in stock. The objective of *inventory control* is to resolve these issues. Inventory managers decide how much product to keep on hand and when to replenish the supply of goods in inventory. They also decide how to allocate products to customers if orders exceed supply.

warehouse
Facility for storing inventory

distribution centers
Warehouse facilities that specialize in collecting and shipping merchandise

Warehousing Products held in inventory are physically stored in a **warehouse.** Warehouses may be owned by the manufacturer, by an intermediary, or by a private company that leases warehouses. Some warehouses are almost purely holding facilities in which goods are stored for relatively long periods. Other warehouses are known as **distribution centers** and serve as command posts for moving products to customers. In a typical distribution center, goods produced at a company's various locations are collected, sorted, coded, and redistributed to fill customer orders.

materials handling
Movement of goods within a firm's warehouse terminal, factory, or store

Materials Handling An important part of warehousing activities is **materials handling,** the movement of goods within and between physical-distribution facilities. One main area of concern is storage methods—whether to keep supplies and finished goods in individual packages, large boxes, or sealed shipping containers. The choice of storage method depends on how the product is shipped, in what quantities, and to which locations. For example, a firm that typically sends small quantities of goods to widely scattered customers wouldn't want to use large containers.

Materials handling also involves keeping track of inventory so that the company knows where in the distribution process its goods are located and when they need to be moved. At Helene Curtis' vast new distribution center in Chicago, goods are moved around almost magically. Computer-controlled forklift-trucks place packages on conveyers that laser-read the bar codes and send packages to their destinations. As a result, this $32 million facility has no paper order tickets or shipping tags, it has no logically ordered stacks of shampoo bottles or deodorant cans, and there aren't many people around either.[44]

Transportation

For any business, the cost of transportation is normally the largest single item in the overall cost of physical distribution (see Exhibit 14.7). However, it doesn't necessarily follow that a manufacturer should simply pick the cheapest available form of transportation. When a firm chooses a type of transportation, it has to bear in mind its other marketing concerns—storage, financing, sales, inventory size, and the like. The trick is to maximize the efficiency of the entire distribution process while minimizing its cost.

In fact, transportation may be an especially important sales tool. Think of it this way: All your teamwork and all your efforts to satisfy the customers are riding on the back of

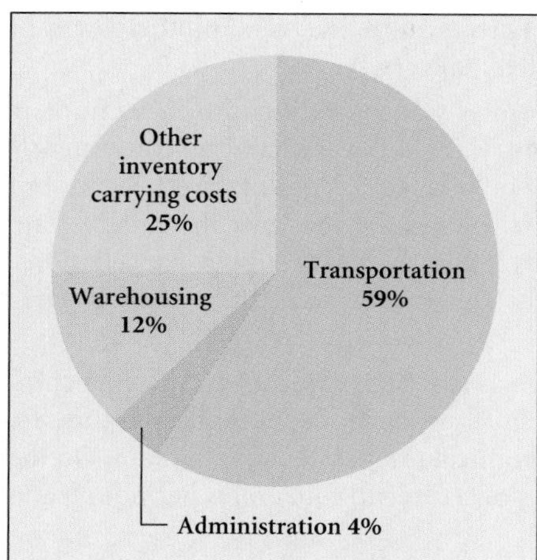

EXHIBIT 14.7

Physical-Distribution Costs

Although the cost of physical distribution varies widely by product, in some cases it adds as much as 20 percent to the retail price of an item. Transportation is the single biggest factor in physical-distribution costs.

a double-clutching, diesel-guzzling, steel-girded oversized vehicle that's rumbling down the highway while the rest of the economy sleeps. As PC Connection demonstrates, a firm that can fulfill its customers' needs more quickly and reliably than competitors gains a key advantage. Consider FedEx. This company maintains a competitive edge in global express transportation because the company offers customers real-time tracking of a package's whereabouts in addition to fast delivery.[45] Thus, it may be more profitable in the long run to pay higher transportation costs rather than risk the loss of future sales.

Companies that move freight are called *carriers,* and they fall into three basic categories: **Common carriers** offer their services to the general public, **contract carriers** haul freight for selected companies under written contract, and **private carriers** are company-owned systems that move their own company's products. Some firms use a combination, relying on common or contract carriers to help out when their own resources are stretched to the limit. In addition, specialized transportation companies help firms in particular areas of distribution. *Freight forwarders,* for instance, help improve shipping efficiency for many companies by pooling several small shipments bound for the same general location. Because of the high cost of international air and ocean freight, consolidation is particularly attractive when shipping goods overseas.

common carriers
Transportation companies that offer their services to the general public

contract carriers
Specialized freight haulers that serve selected companies under written contract

private carriers
Transportation operations owned by a company to move its own products and not those of the general public

There are five major modes of transportation. Each mode of transportation has distinct advantages and disadvantages. Sometimes companies use intermodal or a combination of multiple modes of transportation to complete a single long-distance movement of freight.

- *Truck.* Trucks are the most frequently used form of transportation for two reasons: (1) door-to-door delivery is convenient, and (2) operating on public highways does not require expensive terminals or right-of-way agreements (unlike transportation via air or rail). The main drawback of trucking is that trucks cannot carry all types of cargo cost effectively; for example, commodities such as steel or coal are too bulky.
- *Rail.* Railroads can carry heavier and more diverse cargo, and in fact they carry a larger volume of goods than any other mode of transportation. However, they have the big disadvantage of being constrained to railroad tracks, so they can seldom deliver directly to the customer.
- *Water.* The cheapest form of transportation, water is widely used for such low-cost bulk items as oil, coal, ore, cotton, and lumber. However, ships are slow, and ser-

vice to any given location is infrequent. Furthermore, like rail, another form of transportation is usually needed to complete delivery.

- *Air.* Although airplanes offer the fastest form of transportation, they have numerous disadvantages. Many areas of the country are still not served by conveniently located airports. Also, airplanes can carry only certain types of cargo because of size and shape limitations. Furthermore, airplanes are the least dependable and most expensive form of transportation. Weather may cause flight cancellations, and even minor repairs may lead to serious delays. However, when speed is paramount, air is usually the only way to go.
- *Pipeline.* For certain types of products, such as gasoline, natural gas, and coal chips or wood chips (suspended in liquid), pipelines are quite useful. Although they are expensive to build, they are extremely economical to operate and maintain. On the other hand, transportation via pipeline is slow (three to four miles per hour), and routes are not flexible.

Summary of Learning Objectives

1. **List the eight functions performed by marketing intermediaries.**
Marketing intermediaries provide a sales force, market information, and promotional support. They sort, standardize, and divide merchandise; and they also carry stock and deliver products. In addition, they assume risks, provide financing, and perform a preliminary buying function for users.
2. **Explain what a distribution channel is, and discuss the major factors that influence channel design and selection.**
A distribution channel is an organized network of firms that work together to get a product from a producer to consumers. Channel design and selection are influenced by the type of product; target market; company strengths, weaknesses, and objectives; desired market coverage; distribution costs; and desire for control.
3. **Differentiate between intensive, selective, and exclusive market-coverage strategies.**
With an intensive distribution strategy, a company attempts to saturate the market with its products by offering them in every available outlet. Companies that use a more selective approach to distribution choose a limited number of retailers that can adequately support the product. Firms that use exclusive distribution grant a single wholesaler or retailer the exclusive right to sell the product within a given geographic area.
4. **Highlight the main advantage of a vertical marketing system and explain how it differs from a conventional marketing channel.**
The main advantage of a vertical marketing system is channel control. In a vertical marketing system, the producer, wholesaler, and retailer act as a unified system to conduct distribution activities. By contrast, in a conventional marketing channel, wholesalers and retailers are independent.
5. **Discuss how the Internet is influencing marketing channels.**
The Internet is a sales, delivery, and repair marketing channel that moves forward and backward. Many companies are modifying their channel structures to include the Internet in their distribution mix, and such change is causing channel conflict. The Internet is the driving force behind the increased use of electronic catalogs and electronic storefronts for retail sales. It offers tremendous potential for direct marketing and interactive shopping.
6. **Explain what is meant by the wheel of retailing.**
Wheel of retailing is a term used to describe the evolution of stores from low-priced, limited-service establishments to higher-priced outlets that provide more services. As stores are upgraded, lower-priced competitors move in to fill the gap.
7. **Identify at least six types of store retailers and four types of nonstore retailers.**
Some of the most common types of store retailers are department stores, discount stores, specialty stores, supermarkets, convenience stores, and category killers. Common nonstore retailers are mail-order firms, vending machines, telemarketers, and virtual storefronts.
8. **Specify the activities included in physical distribution, and list the five most common ways of transporting goods.**
Physical distribution encompasses transportation and in-house activities such as forecasting, order processing, inventory control, warehousing, and materials handling. The five most common ways of transporting goods are trucks, railroads, ships, airplanes, and pipelines.

On the Job: Meeting Business Challenges at Black & Decker

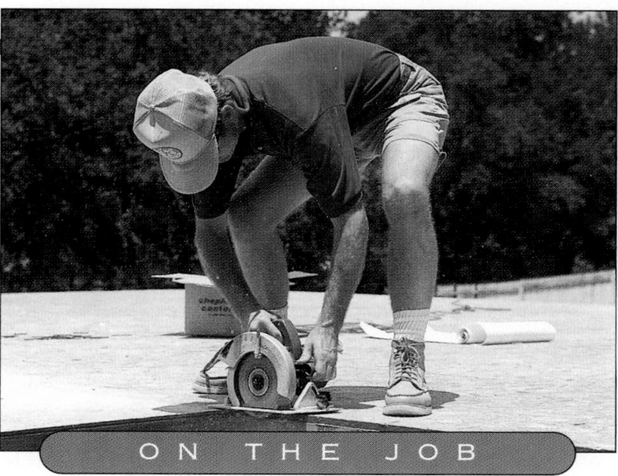

It's hard to say which is more impressive: the speed at which Nolan Archibald and his colleagues turned around the corporate culture or the thoroughness of the results. Black & Decker used to be a manufacturer driven by financial measurements; it is now well on its way to being Archibald's vision of a worldwide marketing powerhouse. The company's approach to managing its marketing channels is a central component of the new Black & Decker.

The change started with strategic planning, as it should. In Archibald's own words: "You analyze the problems that are unique to the company and the industry and then determine what the strengths and weaknesses are. Then you develop a plan to leverage the strengths and correct the weaknesses." Archibald and his colleagues made sure that marketing channels were a part of that strategic plan. Moreover, the new approach manages channels as a vital marketing resource, rather than simply as a pipeline for pumping products to customers.

The analysts who have observed Black & Decker's remarkable turnaround point out several aspects of channel management that have been a vital part of the success. The first change was simple but most important: more respect for marketing intermediaries. Black & Decker had a tough act to follow when it acquired General Electric's small-household-appliance line. Known as "Generous Electric" in some circles, GE went out of its way to be a good supplier. This effort included ample support of retailer promotions, deep inventories to prevent product shortages in the stores, and a general level of respect for the people and organizations on the front line. Black & Decker's efforts to improve relations started by emulating this regard for retailers.

Out of this new respect flowed assistance. Black & Decker took several important steps to help its channel partners. One of these was implementing a segmented channel strategy that focuses specialized sales assistance on the company's two major groups of customers: industrial or professional customers and retailers. This channel strategy allows Black & Decker to give each kind of intermediary the unique help it needs. Another key step was to train its sales force thoroughly, not only in mastering product performance but also in helping retailers with inventory management, purchasing, and in-store product displays. Also, the promotional budget was beefed up to help pull customers into retail stores.

Giving assistance is now mutual. Black & Decker established a number of dealer advisory panels, which retailers can use to give the company feedback on new products customers would like to see. By using its channel as a source of marketing-research information, Black & Decker benefits by getting a better picture of customer needs, and the retailers benefit by being able to deliver the right products.

Coordinated physical distribution is another change that helps both the company and its intermediaries. To better mesh its delivery systems with the needs of distributors and retailers, Black & Decker changed virtually every aspect of its physical distribution. This overhaul included new locations for distribution centers, modified transportation policies, and more powerful systems for managing and coordinating information.

Increasing the number of products held in inventory is another important step. Maintaining a deeper inventory gives retailers the confidence that they'll be able to keep up with demand, particularly during the Christmas shopping season, when many tools and small appliances are purchased.

Yet another element in Black & Decker's strategic plan is growth through acquisition, which has been tied closely to marketing channel management. The \$2.8 billion purchase of Emhart is a good example. Some observers criticized the move, which gave Black & Decker a big presence in hardware. However, the logic was clear after a second look: Some of Emhart's products (like lawn and garden tools, sprinkler systems, locks, and faucets) fit in perfectly with Black & Decker's existing consumer goods channels; other Emhart products mesh well with the industrial channels. The units of Emhart that didn't align with the existing marketing channels were put up for sale.

Black & Decker's dramatic turnaround is convincing evidence of the importance of managing marketing channels effectively. Its sales are growing in every channel of distribution it uses. In fact, the company is starting to be praised as a strong marketing organization that helps create demand for its retailers.

Your Mission: Nolan Archibald faces some tough issues in the selection and management of Black & Decker's marketing channels. However, he knows he can rely on you for help. In your role as the manager in charge of marketing channels, examine the following situations and make your recommendations from the available choices.

1. Archibald knows that marketing channels can perform a wide array of functions, ranging from gathering marketing information to providing physical distribution. He also knows that Black & Decker should identify the most crucial functions that the company would like to see its intermedi-

aries perform. He's asked you to identify these crucial functions. Which of the following combinations of marketing intermediary functions would be most important to Black & Decker?

a. Most of the vital channel functions required of intermediaries by Black & Decker occur after the sale. Keeping customers satisfied is an absolute necessity, and to do that, you need to be in direct contact. Black & Decker can't be there for every single customer. The functions of most interest here are providing product service and helping customers use products successfully.
b. Black & Decker's products are not terribly complicated, so customers don't need much help. The most important channel functions are at the beginning of the sales process, not at the end. Providing feedback from customers is the best place to start because market information like this is necessary if the company is going to design and manufacture the right products for its customers. With that information in place, the intermediaries should all have a say in Black & Decker's strategic planning process; after all, they are quite dependent on the decisions made during the company's planning process.
c. Alleviating discrepancies and matching buyers and sellers are definitely the most important tasks Black & Decker should ask of its channel partners. It simply isn't economical for the company to deliver individual products to each customer; marketing intermediaries need to fill the gap by rearranging quantities and assortments so that customers can get the right number and selection of products. Also, Black & Decker wouldn't necessarily know where to go to find potential customers, so it must rely on retailers to get the products to customers. Standardized transactions wouldn't hurt, either.

2. Customer service is, of course, a vital ingredient in all successful marketing transactions. Archibald knows this and realizes that customer service is not all that easy to define and execute in a multichannel system like the one Black & Decker relies on. Which of the following definitions of and approaches to customer service best fits the company's situation?
   a. Customer-service efforts focus on the final purchasers of the product. Black & Decker can accomplish this objective in several ways. The first is simply to make it easier to be successful with Black & Decker products. This step includes designing for ease of use, providing helpful user guides, and perhaps offering a toll-free number that customers can call with specific questions about using products. A second way to help customers might be to sponsor seminars at places like woodworking shows (for the power-tool and hardware lines) and home shows (for all three lines). For organizational customers in the power-tool segment, another way to help would be to send Black & Decker specialists to customer sites to help them solve specific problems.
   b. Black & Decker's real customers are the thousands of marketing intermediaries that buy and then resell its tools, appliances, and hardware. These are the customers that the company should worry about servicing. The intermediaries will, in turn, satisfy the final customers. Black & Decker can help the intermediaries in a number of ways, including promotions, pricing advice, product selection, and display help.
   c. The concept of customer service is irrelevant in this case because Black & Decker doesn't sell to final customers. It is the job of intermediaries to satisfy customers. That is, after all, the number one purpose of intermediaries and the reason they make money on the products manufactured by Black & Decker.
3. Black & Decker's engineers have developed a new tool that cuts concrete. Unfortunately, it doesn't really fit in the marketing channels that you already have in place, so it's time for you to design a new channel. Here are some important variables you'll need to consider:

   Customer type: Organizational, ranging in size from one-person contractors to multinational construction firms.

   Geography: Customers are all over the place; the geographic distribution roughly mirrors the population distribution, with concentrations in large cities and widely dispersed customers elsewhere.

   Market size: Big; the saw costs around $2,000, and Black & Decker expects to sell thousands every month; it makes sense to put a sizable investment into the distribution channel.

   Life cycle: Somewhere between the growth and maturity phases; most customers have a pretty good idea of how to use them and what they're all about.

   Support needs: These customers don't need a lot of help, but they do need to be assured of fast service when things go wrong; downtime is critical, and customers would prefer on-site delivery of loaner units in the event of a breakdown.

   On the basis of these variables, what's the best channel system for this product?
   a. Consider the purchase habits of the people likely to use these products. Even though they are industrial customers, they are human beings, after all. As such, they need to do personal shopping as much as the rest of us. Because of that, the best place to sell the concrete cutter is in retail stores where these customers do their other shopping. That way they can combine their personal shopping with their business shopping.
   b. The market is large and geographically diverse, and customers don't need much in the way of support. Therefore, mail order would be the perfect channel for this new product. It reaches every corner of the country, and it costs less because retail store space and salespeople are not needed.

c. This new product should be restricted to tool stores and masonry-supply stores that cater exclusively to professionals. These stores should be able to deliver superior customer service, including on-site delivery of replacement and loaner units. The biggest drawback of using this channel is that these outlets are not as widespread as homeowner-oriented retail stores, but professional builders in out-of-the-way locations are accustomed to a little travel time when it comes to shopping for tools and supplies.

4. A new product has just been designed by the small-home-appliance division. This new device is a combination coffee-bean grinder and espresso machine. What is the best channel system for this product? Here are some factors to consider, and this time consider the problem of product and brand image:

   Customer type: Consumer.

   Geography: Again, customers are all over the place, but they are concentrated primarily in and around large cities and, for the time being, are found mostly on the West Coast.

   Market size: Not terribly large because of the price, which is around $700; many people like espresso made from freshly ground coffee beans, but only the most avid connoisseurs are willing to pay that much for the quality and convenience of the combination grinder/coffeemaker.

   Life cycle: Espresso machines have been around for years, but their move into consumer markets is fairly new; in the past, most were sold to restaurants.

   Support needs: The machine is fairly easy to use and clean, and you don't expect much in the way of repair trouble, but some customers will initially need help and advice to brew the perfect demitasse of espresso.

a. Specialty kitchen stores, particularly those that cater to upscale urban consumers, would be the best choice. These stores carry other kitchen and household products of similar quality and price, so it's a natural that the new espresso machine will fit in here as well. The customers who shop at such stores enjoy buying quality products, and some like to boast that they purchase such goods only from specialty stores, never from department or discount stores.

b. No self-respecting connoisseur is going to buy an espresso machine from a manufacturer of power drills. Even the most astute channel selection isn't going to rescue this project; recommend to your managers that they abandon the product entirely or sell the design to another company. You'll need more than just a good marketing channel to make this miracle happen.

c. The existing channels are fine. A $700 coffee maker might look a little out of place in Kmart, but its presence will raise the image of the entire Black & Decker product family.[46]

Key Terms

agents and brokers (424)
branch office (424)
category killers (426)
channel captain (421)
common carriers (435)
contract carriers (435)
customer-service standards (432)
discount stores (426)
distribution centers (434)
distribution channels (415)
distribution mix (415)
distribution strategy (415)
drop shippers (424)
exclusive distribution (418)
full-service merchant wholesalers (424)
industrial distributors (423)
intensive distribution (418)
limited-service merchant wholesalers (424)
logistics (431)
mail-order firms (428)
marketing intermediaries (415)
materials handling (434)
merchant wholesalers (424)
order processing (433)
physical distribution (431)
private carriers (435)
rack jobbers (424)
retailers (423)
reverse channels (418)
sales office (424)
scrambled merchandising (425)
selective distribution (418)
specialty shops (425)
vertical marketing systems (VMS) (421)
warehouse (434)
wheel of retailing (425)
wholesalers (423)

Questions

For Review

1. What forms of utility do intermediaries create?
2. What are some of the main causes of channel conflict?
3. What is the difference between a wholesaler and a retailer?
4. What is the difference between a specialty store, a category killer, and a discount store?
5. What is the goal of inventory management?

For Analysis

6. How does the presence of intermediaries affect the price of products?
7. How does the length of the distribution chain tend to vary for convenience goods, shopping goods, and specialty goods?
8. How is the role of wholesalers changing?
9. What are some of the challenges that retailers are facing today?
10. What are the benefits of electronic catalogs?

For Application

For questions 11 and 12: Pretend that you own a small specialty shop in Chicago, "The Artisan," that sells hand-crafted wearables—sweaters, vests, jewelry, and so on.

11. What are some of the nonstore retail options you might explore to increase sales? What are the advantages and disadvantages of each?
12. Your hand-knit-sweater supplier has the capacity to expand her business. What alternative channel options might she explore? Which one would be the best for hand-knit sweaters?

A Case for Critical Thinking ■ Sears: From Turnaround to Transformation

Perhaps no one understands the challenges of the retail industry better than Arthur Martinez, Sears chief executive. After all, he's been in retailing for most of his career. And he's the man who brought Sears back from its near-death experience.

BACKGROUND

The outlook for Sears was grave. Sears stores were out of date, out of touch, and out of ideas to win back shoppers from rivals like Wal-Mart and J. C. Penney. With losses amounting to $3.9 billion, the company did not know what it was anymore—a department store, a discounter, a mass merchandiser, or a collection of specialty stores.

Believing they were in the dirty fingernails business of autos and hardware, Sears' managers saw nothing wrong with displaying intimate apparel on the same rack fixtures that were used to sell paint. Once hailed the most innovative company in U.S. economic history, Sears—like many retailers—was on the path to obsolescence. With the company dubbed a dinosaur by *Fortune* magazine, Martinez had his work cut out for him.

ACT 1: SLASHING THE WAY TO PROFITS

Even Martinez was surprised by the challenges that faced him in 1992. That's when he became the first outsider ever to head up Sears. His first assignment: Restore the health of Sears stores and pare the conglomerate to its rotten core.

Of course paring the conglomerate was easy. First Sears unloaded Allstate Insurance, Coldwell Banker real estate, Dean Witter brokerage, and the Discover credit card. With no time to waste, Martinez closed 113 unprofitable stores and cut 50,000 jobs. Then he sold the company's famous headquarters, the 110-story Sears Tower. And he terminated the Sears catalog, which some called the soul of Sears.

But Martinez knew that you can't shrink your way to greatness. He had to find a way to halt the free fall. Sears management was inbred and self-centered; it had lost focus. Believing that its core customers were guys, rather than women 25 to 54 years old, management didn't have a clue who its target customers should be. So Martinez chose one: the middle American mom. Then he recruited a new management team and set about his business.

ACT 2: THE SOFTER SIDE OF SEARS

Focusing on women customers, Martinez entered into an arrangement with Liz Claiborne to provide Sears with an exclusive private brand of women's clothes called "First Issue." Then he launched a $4 billion store renovation program and packed the remodeled aisles with women's apparel. Finally he redirected $1 billion of price promotion money to advertise "the softer side of Sears." It worked—and much faster than anyone dreamed possible.

The dinosaur turned into a cash cow. Earning $1.3 billion on revenues of $38.2 billion, Sears gained market share in virtually every category of merchandise. Even Martinez was amazed how marketing could make a difference in changing the consumer's perception of Sears. But he also knew that the retailing industry was in a state of turmoil. And his prior experience had taught him that the best retailers constantly reinvent themselves. Besides, Sears had some powerhouse brands—like Craftsman (the leading U.S. tool line), Kenmore (the number one appliance brand), DieHard, and of course Sears itself. So Martinez decided to transform the retailer into a top-echelon consumer brands and services company. But how?

ACT 3, SCENE 1: THE HARDER SIDE OF SEARS

Small stores. That was the answer. To get heavy-duty stuff like tools and auto parts to consumers, Sears would open small hardware stores—thousands of them—far from the shopping malls. And they would not even bear the Sears name. Pretty gutsy for a guy who revived the "Big Store."

Martinez had a mission—the harder side of Sears. Although he didn't expect to hammer Home Depot, he did expect to win over a few million shoppers that Home Depot didn't satisfy. He knew that many female customers were put off by the very thing that the category killers stand for: incredible selection. "These stores have gotten too big, too overwhelming, and too confusing to shop. Too frightening," notes Martinez. So he bought a chain of profitable hardware stores in California called Orchard Supply Hardware Stores, kept the name, and filled it with Sears Craftsman merchandise. And this too began to pay off.

ACT 3, SCENE 2: THE SERVICE SIDE OF SEARS

Martinez knew that Sears was bringing in $3 billion a year by calling on customers at home—to install their dishwashers, reface their kitchen cabinets, and even put roofs on their homes. But Sears was using a lot of independents to do the work. Service was inconsistent and the marketing was lousy. So he challenged Jane Thompson to transform an orphan operation into a $10 billion business by 2000. That's how Sears Home Services—a jumble of services from appliance repair to pest control—was born.

Sears Home Services would repair any appliances, even if you bought them somewhere else. And it would become the company's most promising growth vehicle. Martinez was on a roll. His company had just been rated the most innovative general-merchandise retailer. If he kept it up, Sears' transformation would be the kind of stuff they write about in future management texts—one of the most sweeping and surprising makeovers ever.

EPILOGUE

Meanwhile, back at his sixth floor office—many miles from that old black Sears Tower—Martinez is preparing for the monthly board meeting. He thinks about the issues that worry investors: (1) Sears stores in Canada and Mexico have been losing money for years, and expanding internationally is number 11 on Martinez's top 10 priority list; (2) uncollectible credit-card receivables have been rising and investors wonder whether new customers were really attracted by the revamped women's apparel and brand-name products or were shopping at Sears simply because it was easier to get credit; (3) store profit margins are mediocre and so is customer satisfaction; and (4) Sears' turnaround seems to have impressed Wall Street more than Main Street.

But these concerns are minor compared to Sears' big problem. The company is still stuck in retailing. Martinez knows that if his 821 "big" full-line stores ever get into an unhealthy situation again, it will be deadly. It would undercut the company's entire growth plan for small stores and service. In spite of Sears' success, the company is at a critical point in its journey. Martinez feels the need to accelerate the pace. He picks up a paperweight on his desk and stares at it. It reads: "Today's peacock is tomorrow's feather duster."

1. Using your knowledge about marketing channels, do you think the small store concept is a good idea? Why or why not?
2. Why is Sears Home Services the company's most promising growth vehicle?
3. Should global expansion be moved up on Martinez's priority list? Please explain.
4. Browse the Sears Web site at <http://www.sears.com>. Look at the company's products and services. Check out *Craftsman Online Shopping* and browse the tools. Review *Sears Home Services* and *The Softer Side of Sears.* From both a consumer and a company perspective, what advantages do electronic catalogs have over mail-order catalogs?

Building Your Business Skills

In a group of three or four students, select a consumer product with which you are familiar, and trace its channel of distribution. The product might be fresh foods, processed foods, cosmetics, clothing, or manufactured goods (ranging from something as simple as a fork to something as complex as a personal computer).

- For information, you might contact a business involved in the manufacture or distribution of the product, either by letter or by telephone. As an alternative, you could locate an article in a trade periodical that describes the channel of distribution for your chosen product.
- Examine the various factors involved in the distribution of the product, and prepare a brief summary of your findings. Consider the following:
  - The role of the intermediary in distribution
  - The type of distribution: intensive, selective, or exclusive
  - The amount of control the manufacturer has over the distribution process
  - The type of channel used in the distribution process and its influence on the cost of the product

Keeping Current Using *The Wall Street Journal*

Find an article in *The Wall Street Journal* describing changes in methods of distribution or distribution policies used by a company or several companies in the same industry. For example, have they changed from using an in-house sales force to using manufacturer's reps? Have they added local warehouses or centralized their distribution? Eliminated wholesalers and gone directly to dealers? Opened more company stores or eliminated independent retailers? Added a mail-order division to a retail operation or a retail operation to a mail-order firm? Changed discount policies or shipping methods? Closed stores in downtown areas and moved to malls? Added online ordering capabilities?

1. What changes in distribution have taken place? What additional changes, if any, are planned?
2. What were the reasons for the changes? How have population, lifestyle, financial, or other factors affected distribution in this industry?
3. If you were a stockholder in a company in this industry, would you be concerned about distribution-related changes hurting the company in the next five years? Why or why not?
4. View *The Wall Street Journal* Interactive Edition at <http://interactive.wsj.com> and *Take a Tour of the Interactive Edition.*
   a. How does the interactive edition differ from the paper edition? What additional features does it have?
   b. What is the *Personal Journal,* and how does it work?
   c. Do you think subscribers to *The Wall Street Journal* paper edition might also subscribe to the interactive edition? Why or why not?

Exploring the Best of the Web

Change the Bloomin' Channel, page 423

Visit the iflowers Web site (sponsored by Phillip's 1-800-Florals) at <http://www.iflowers.com>. Tour the site. Be sure to check out the catalog by clicking on *Order Flowers Online.*

1. How can a small, local flower shop compete with Web sites like this? What type of distribution channel is Phillip's 1-800-Florals?
2. From iflowers' home page, scroll down and click on *Infospace.com.* Why might an Internet flower shop feature a link like this?
3. From iflowers' home page, scroll down and click on links to other interesting *Free Sites.* Explore some of the sites on this page. How does the Internet assist companies in giving away products (or samples) for free? Why do companies do this?

Explore the World of Retail, page 427

Visit the National Retail Federation Web site at <http://www.nrf.com> to explore the world of retail.

1. Click on *Retail Information* and read about *Careers in Retailing.* What qualities should the ideal retail job seeker possess? What does a buyer or a department manager do?
2. Go back to the home page and read *About NRF.* What does this organization do? Why should a retailer join this organization?
3. Click on *Government Affairs.* Click on *Issues.* Read some of the current issues on the government's agenda. Why is it important for a small retailer to stay on top of these issues?

Visit a Virtual Store, page 430

Visit Amazon.com, the virtual bookstore at <http://www.amazon.com>. Browse the Web site. View the special features. Check out the reviews. Look for your favorite books and authors.

1. What are the advantages of a virtual store? What special features does Amazon.com offer consumers that you cannot find in a physical bookstore?
2. Do you find it easier or more confusing to shop in a virtual store? What do you like or dislike? Assuming that prices were the same at both a virtual and a physical store, why might consumers (with Internet access) be reluctant to buy from a virtual store?
3. Review the eight functions performed by marketing intermediaries. Which of these functions does Amazon.com perform? Cite some examples.

Answers to "Is It True?"

Page 418. False. The United States ranks last among Office for Economic Cooperation and Devel opment nations in recycling glass and is fifteenth in recycling paper. Germany and Japan reuse three times as much overall waste as the United States does.

Page 419. True.

Page 430. True.

15

CHAPTER 15

PROMOTION

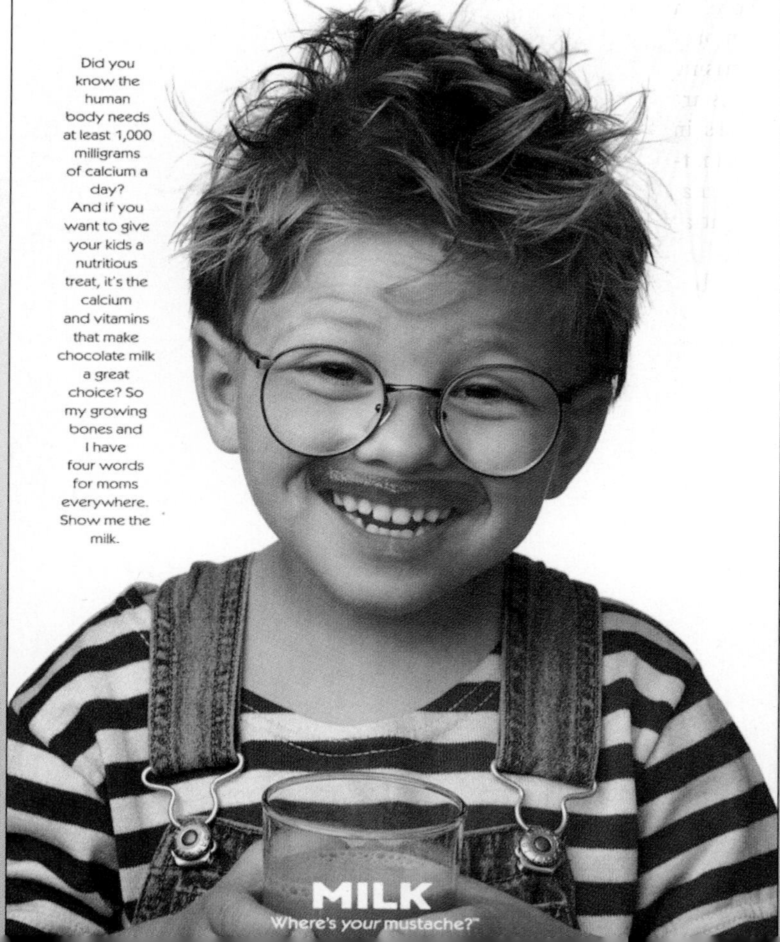

Did you know the human body needs at least 1,000 milligrams of calcium a day? And if you want to give your kids a nutritious treat, it's the calcium and vitamins that make chocolate milk a great choice? So my growing bones and I have four words for moms everywhere. Show me the milk.
MILK
Where's your mustache?

OBJECTIVES

After studying this chapter, you will be able to

1 Identify the five basic categories of promoti

2 Distinguish between push and pull strategi promotion

3 List the seven steps in the personal-selling process

4 Differentiate between institutional, product, competitive advertising

5 Define interactive advertising and discuss t challenge it presents to marketers

6 Discuss the difference between logical and emotional advertising appeals

7 Distinguish between the two main types of promotion, and give at least two examples

8 Explain the role of public relations in marke

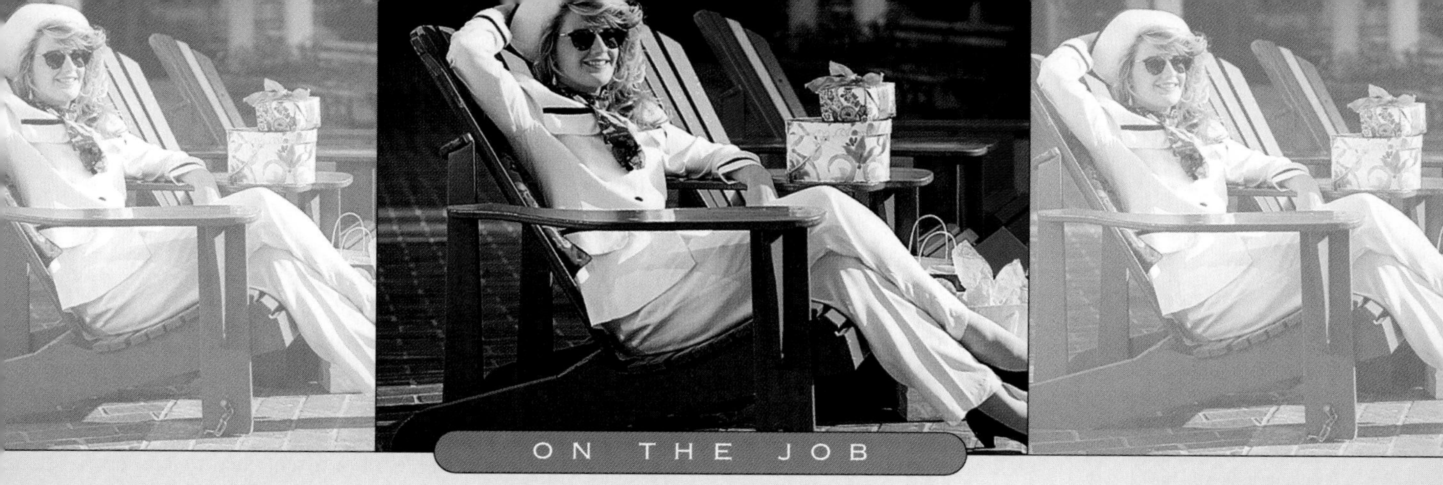

On the Job On the Job

ON THE JOB: FACING BUSINESS CHALLENGES AT IKEA

Opening the Door to Sales on Two Coasts

What's yellow and blue, as large as seven football fields, and filled from floor to ceiling with furniture? The answer, as millions of shoppers from Budapest to Burbank have learned, is an Ikea store. Based in Denmark, Ikea operates more than 139 warehouse-sized furniture stores in 28 countries. The retailer opens between five and ten outlets every year, and no two grand-opening advertising campaigns are exactly alike, because no two audiences are exactly alike. For instance, when Ikea opened stores in Elizabeth, New Jersey; Burbank, California; and Manhattan, New York; Ikea president Anders Moberg knew that the markets for each of these stores were as different as Coney Island hot dogs and avocado salad.

Ikea's international success has been anything but an overnight phenomenon. Founder Ingvar Kamprad came up with the company name in 1943 by combining his own initials with the first letter of his farm, Elmtaryd, and the first letter of his native parish, Agunnaryd (similar to a county in the United States). His first furniture showroom was in southern Sweden and featured bargain prices for simple but stylishly functional designs. However, it wasn't until he opened his Stockholm store, in 1965, that Kamprad put into practice the marketing concepts that now distinguish Ikea from its competitors: moderate prices, quality products, and a pleasant shopping environment.

Going to an Ikea store is like entering a home-furnishings paradise. Customers are invited to wander through each model room and measure, touch, even sit or lie down on any of the hundreds of furniture samples inside each 200,000-square-foot outlet. What's more, hungry shoppers can snack at the in-store cafe, and harried parents can leave their children at the in-store play area while shopping. Prices are low because customers select their own items and carry them home in flat-pack cartons, where they assemble the pieces using simple tools included with every purchase.

To enter these separate markets, Moberg knew that each store would need completely different ad campaigns. Plus, with real estate prices sky-high in Manhattan, Ikea would have to scale down the traditional superstore format to a more affordable size. If you were in Moberg's shoes, how would you use promotion to introduce Ikea to the target audiences in these separate markets? What advertising strategies would you use to develop ads to attract customers? How would you affordably merchandise 12,000 items at a pricey Manhattan location?[1]

THE PROMOTIONAL MIX

Ikea's Anders Moberg knows that effective promotions can make or break his plans to expand across the country. Of the four ingredients in the marketing mix (product, price, distribution, and promotion), promotion is perhaps the one most often associated with marketing. Although it is no guarantee of success, promotion does have a profound impact on a product's performance in the marketplace.

promotion
Wide variety of persuasive techniques used by companies to communicate with their target markets and the general public

promotional strategy
Statement or document that defines the direction and scope of the promotional activities that a company will use to meet its marketing objectives

What exactly is **promotion**? Although the term is defined in many ways, it is basically persuasive communication that motivates people to buy whatever an organization is selling—goods, services, or ideas. Promotion may take the form of direct, face-to-face communication or indirect communication through such media as television, radio, magazines, newspapers, direct mail, billboards, the Internet, and other channels. A company's **promotional strategy** defines the direction and scope of the promotional activities that will be implemented to meet marketing objectives.

Promotional Goals

persuasive advertising
Advertising designed to encourage product sampling and brand switching

reminder advertising
Advertising intended to remind existing customers of a product's availability and benefits

Promotional activities have three basic goals: to inform, to persuade, and to remind. *Informing* is the first promotional priority, because people cannot buy something until they are aware of it and understand what it will do for them. Potential customers need to know where the item can be found, how much it will cost, and how to use it. *Persuading* is also an important priority, because most people need to be encouraged to purchase something new or switch brands. Advertising that meets this goal is classified as **persuasive advertising.** If customers have never used the item before, they must be convinced that doing so will be beneficial. If they are using a competing brand, they must be persuaded to switch. *Reminding* the customer of the product's availability and benefits is also important, because such reminders stimulate additional purchases. The term for such promotional efforts is **reminder advertising.**

Informing, persuading, and reminding are the main goals of promotion, but a good promotional effort also seeks to achieve specific objectives. These include attracting new customers, increasing usage among existing customers, aiding distributors, stabilizing sales, boosting brand-name recognition, creating sales leads, differentiating the product, and influencing decision makers.

The variety of possible objectives highlights a key point about promotion in general and advertising in particular: Not all promotional efforts are designed to generate sales, at least not directly. That's why promotions experts think in terms of *communications objectives* and *sales objectives.* A communications objective is an interim step toward making a sale. It may be to make an audience aware of a new product or to change negative perceptions of a company. If accomplished, these objectives would probably lead to sales eventually, but the idea with such goals is to focus on a specific step in the process, not the final result.[2]

Promotional Ethics and Regulations

Although promotion serves many useful functions, critics argue that its goals are self-serving. Some contend that sellers use promotional tools to persuade people to buy unnecessary or potentially harmful goods like anti-aging creams, baldness "cures," sweetened cereals, liquor, and cigarettes. Others argue that promotion encourages materialism at the expense of more worthwhile values, that it exploits stereotypes, and that it manipulates the consumer on a subconscious level. Still others argue that the money spent on promotion could be put to better use inventing new products or improving the quality of existing items.

Some of these concerns are well founded, and abuses certainly do occur. However, some of the charges leveled at advertising don't stand up to serious logical analysis. Take the charge about *subliminal advertising,* the notion that advertisers hide manipulative visual or audio cues in ads. Critics claim that flashing brief targeted messages across a movie screen (although too short to be recognized at the conscious level) can induce consumers to purchase the promoted products. However, there is no objective evidence of the existence of this sort of trickery and little psychological evidence to suggest that it would work even if anyone were doing it.[3]

Public concern about potential misuse of promotion has led to the passage of government regulations that limit promotional abuses. The federal government's primary advertising watchdog is the Federal Trade Commission (FTC), which has developed some ground rules for promotion. One rule is that *all statements of fact must be supported by evidence.* This regulation includes words ("Lipton. The Only Naturally Decaffeinated Tea Bags") and demonstrations. Thus, companies cannot use whipped cream in a shaving-cream commercial to create an impression of a firm, heavy lather. Another rule is that *sellers must not create an overall impression that is incorrect.* In other words, they cannot claim that doctors recommend a product if doctors do not; nor can they present an actor who delivers the message dressed in a doctor's white jacket. Most states also regulate promotional practices by individual industries such as liquor stores, stock brokerages, employment agencies, and loan companies.

In response to growing concern and confusion among consumers and health professionals, the Food and Drug Administration and the U.S. Department of Agriculture developed sweeping guidelines and policies for advertising claims and product-label wording. For instance, the word *light* can now be used to describe a product only if it contains at least one-third fewer calories than the regular version of the product; *low calorie* means no more than 40 calories per standard-size serving. Similarly, the government now has specific definitions for such terms as *recyclable* and *biodegradable,* and advertisers can't use the terms if they can't meet federal guidelines.[4]

Many individual companies and agencies also practice self-regulation to restrain false and misleading promotion. The National Advertising Review Board, whose members include advertisers, agencies, and the general public, has a full-time professional staff that investigates complaints of deceptive advertising. If the complaint appears justified, the board tries to get the offending company to stop—even if it means referring the offender to proper government enforcement agencies.

Five Elements of Promotion

Within the framework of these guidelines, marketers use a mix of five activities to achieve their promotional objectives. The activities are personal selling, advertising, direct marketing, sales promotion, and public relations. These elements can be combined in various ways to create a **promotional mix** for a particular product or idea (see Exhibit 15.1).

promotional mix
Particular blend of personal selling, advertising, direct marketing, sales promotion, and public relations that a company uses to reach potential customers

Learn the Consumer Marketing Laws

BEST OF THE WEB

Thinking about advertising or marketing your product? There are some laws you'll need to obey. Visit the Federal Trade Commission (FTC) Web site and learn how this agency protects consumers against unfair and deceptive marketing practices. Do you know what the FTC's policies are on deceptive pricing, use of the word *free,* or use of endorsements and testimonials? Find out what it means to substantiate product claims such as "tests prove," or "studies show." Learn what the rules are for unsolicited telephone calls and telephone slamming before you telemarket your product. Tune in to the FCC now and avoid making some serious mistakes later.
http://www.ftc.gov

ACTIVITY	REACH	TIMING	FLEXIBILITY	COST/ EXPOSURE
Personal selling	Direct personal interaction with limited reach	Regular, recurrent contact	Message tailored to customer and adjusted to reflect feedback	Relatively high
Advertising	Indirect interaction with large reach	Regular, recurrent contact	Standard, unvarying message	Low to moderate
Direct marketing	Direct personal interaction with large reach	Intermittent, based on short-term sales objectives	Customized, varying message	Relatively high
Sales promotion	Indirect interaction with large reach	Intermittent, based on short-term sales objectives	Standard, unvarying message	Varies
Public relations	Indirect interaction with large reach	Intermittent, as newsworthy events occur	Standard, unvarying message	No direct cost

EXHIBIT 15.1

The Five Elements of Promotion

The promotional mix typically includes a blend of various elements. The "right" mix depends on the nature of the market and the characteristics of the item being sold. Over time the mix for a particular product may change.

personal selling
In-person communication between a seller and one or more potential buyers

advertising
Paid, nonpersonal communication to a target market from an identified sponsor using mass communications channels

direct marketing
Direct communication other than personal sales contacts designed to effect a measurable response

Is It True?

On average, children 6 to 12 years old watch 20 hours of television a week.

Personal selling involves direct, person-to-person communication, either face-to-face or by phone. The two primary advantages of personal selling are (1) It allows for immediate interaction between the buyer and seller, and (2) it enables the seller to adjust the message to the specific needs and interests of the individual customer. The chief disadvantage of personal selling is its relatively high cost.

Advertising consists of messages paid for by an identified sponsor and transmitted through a mass-communication medium. As we shall see later in the chapter, advertising can take many forms. Its chief advantage lies in its ability to reach a large audience economically. Advertising has several disadvantages, however, starting with the expense of creating an advertising campaign. Second, advertising can't always motivate customers to action as effectively as personal selling can. Finally, traditional forms of advertising can't provide direct feedback, as personal selling can, and they are also difficult to personalize.

As discussed in Chapter 13, newer forms of advertising—Internet and interactive TV—are overcoming many of these obstacles. What has traditionally been a one-way, passive medium is becoming interactive. Internet advertisements are targeted to specific groups of individuals, and technological advancements allow marketers to track not only the ads an individual clicks on but also how the individual interacts with each part of the ad.[5]

Direct marketing as defined by the Direct Marketing Association is any direct communication to a consumer or business recipient designed to generate (1) a response in the form of an order, (2) a request for further information, or (3) a visit to a store or other place of business for purchase of a specific product or service.[6] The principal vehicle for direct marketing is direct mail. However, other elements gaining importance in this promotional category include telemarketing, television infomercials, and electronic media. Chapter 14 discusses direct marketing as a form of distribution. Direct marketing is both a nonretail sales vehicle and a form of promotion. The focus in this chapter is on its promotional characteristics.

Sales promotion is the most difficult promotional element to define. That's because it includes a wide range of events and activities designed to stimulate interest in the product. Coupons, rebates, contests, in-store demonstrations, free samples, trade shows, and point-of-purchase displays all fall into this category.

sales promotion
Wide range of events and activities (including coupons, rebates, contests, in-store demonstrations, free samples, trade shows, and point-of-purchase displays) designed to stimulate interest in a product

Public relations is the final element in the promotional mix. It encompasses all the nonsales communications that businesses have with their various audiences. Part of the public relations effort covers general topics, such as responding to journalists' requests for information and helping local schools with educational projects. The other side of the public relations effort seeks to generate significant news coverage about the company and its products, and tries to encourage favorable reviews of products in newspapers and magazines and on radio and television programs.

public relations
Nonsales communication that businesses have with their various audiences (includes both communication with the general public and press relations)

Integrated Marketing Communications

Integrated marketing communications (IMC) is a strategy of coordinating and integrating all your communications and promotions efforts to provide customers with clarity, consistency, and maximum communications impact.[7] The basics of IMC are quite simple: communicating in one voice and one message to the marketplace.

integrated marketing communications (IMC)
Strategy of coordinating and integrating communications and promotions efforts with customers to ensure greater efficiency and effectiveness

When you consider all the ways that audiences can receive marketing messages today, the potential for consumer confusion is not all that surprising. Besides the old standards—billboards, radio, television, print ads in magazines, and direct-mail promotions—marketers are using faxes, e-mail, kiosks, electronic billboards, mentions in books and movies, and so on to deliver their messages to consumers. Coordinating these promotional vehicles is becoming more and more challenging. For example, salespeople may visit customers and say one thing about a product, whereas an ad campaign may say something different about the product. Fragmented messages not only reduce a promotion's effectiveness but also confuse buyers.

Consider this: What if Volvo suddenly decided to talk "speed" instead of "safety"? You can imagine the confusion it would cause, especially if some of the company's promotional material still featured the car as a safe, family vehicle whereas newer television commercials showed a Volvo speeding by BMWs on hairpin turns. Southwest Airlines uses IMC whenever it enters new markets. For example when the company offered new service to Baltimore, it had to communicate its low-fare, no-frills, high-frequency service to East Coast travelers who knew very little about the company. "We always start out with the public relations side in announcing inaugural services. Then we integrate government relations, community affairs, service announcements, special events, advertising, and promotion," says the president of Cramer-Krasselt, Southwest's ad agency. "We try to fire all guns at once so that by the time Southwest comes into the market, the airline already is part of the community."[8]

Properly implemented, IMC increases marketing and promotional effectiveness. Despite the benefits, however, many organizations find IMC difficult to implement. They discover that, over time, their promotional mixes develop into collections of disconnected efforts. Organizational resistance is the primary cause for IMC failure. Many marketing departments are accustomed to autonomy and see IMC as a threat to their resources and decision-making power. Besides, moving to an IMC approach requires new ways of organizing, planning, and managing all marketing functions, and some marketing departments are not up to the task.[9]

Outside advertising agencies are caught in the commotion as well. Many agencies are driven by their creative departments and they see little personal or professional reward in creating a magnificent in-store display. They want to do breakthrough, big-budget TV commercials that will earn them awards. Thus, although the client might need a direct-mail piece or a smashing trade brochure, these jobs are often relegated to entry-level marketing personnel.[10] In addition, few advertising agencies have specialized expertise in promotion through distribution channels. Still, in spite of these obstacles, the potential benefits of IMC are so valuable that the concept is fast becoming standard for everyone in the advertising and marketing professions.[11]

Promotional Strategies

Regardless of whether a company successfully adopts an integrated marketing approach, all firms must decide on the right blend of personal selling, advertising, direct marketing, sales promotion, and public relations. How do you decide on what constitutes the right blend? That's not an easy question to answer because many factors must be taken into account. Because most firms have limited resources, establishing a promotional budget is often the first step in developing a promotional strategy. Once the budget has been decided, firms take into account the many product- and market-related factors, the types of international approaches, and the desired market position to design the optimal promotional mix.

Product-Related Factors Various types of products lend themselves to differing forms of promotion. Simple, familiar items like laundry detergent can be explained adequately through advertising, but personal selling is generally required to communicate the features of unfamiliar and sophisticated goods and services such as office-automation equipment or municipal waste-treatment facilities. Direct, personal contact is particularly important in promoting customized services such as interior design, financial advice, or legal counsel. In general, consumer and organizational goods usually require differing promotional mixes.

The product's price is also a factor in the selection of the promotional mix. Inexpensive items sold to a mass market are well suited to advertising and sales promotion, which have a relatively low per-unit cost. At the other extreme, products with a high unit price lend themselves to personal selling because the high cost of a sales call is justified by the size of the order. Furthermore, the nature of the selling process often demands face-to-face interaction between the buyer and seller.

Another factor that influences both the level and mix of promotional activity is the product's position in its life cycle. Early on, when the seller is trying to inform the customer about the product and build the distribution network, promotional efforts are in high gear. Selective advertising, sales promotion, and public relations are used to build awareness and to encourage early adopters to try the product; personal selling is used to gain the cooperation of intermediaries. As the market expands during the growth phase, the seller broadens the advertising and sales-promotion activities to reach a wider audience and continues to use personal selling to expand the distribution network. When the product reaches maturity and competition is at its peak, the seller's primary goal is to differentiate the product from rival brands. Advertising generally dominates the promotional mix during this phase, but sales promotion is an important supplemental tool, particularly for low-priced consumer products. As the product begins to decline, the level of promotion generally tapers off. Advertising and selling efforts are carefully targeted toward loyal, steady customers.

push strategy
Promotional approach designed to motivate wholesalers and retailers to push a producer's products to end users

pull strategy
Promotional strategy that stimulates consumer demand, which then exerts pressure on wholesalers and retailers to carry a product

Market-Related Factors To some extent, the promotional mix depends on whether the seller plans to focus the marketing effort on intermediaries or final customers. If the focus is on intermediaries, the producer uses a **push strategy** to persuade wholesalers and retailers to carry the item. Personal selling and sales promotions aimed at intermediaries dominate the promotional mix. If the marketing focus is on end users, the producer uses a **pull strat-**

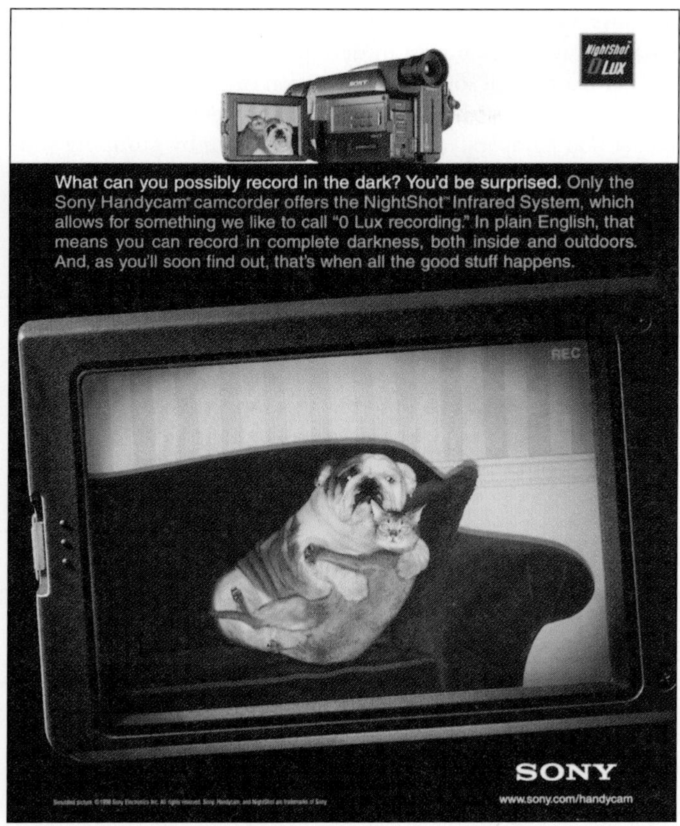

This product-oriented ad from Sony promotes the specific features of a single product.

egy to appeal directly to the ultimate customer, using advertising, direct mail, contests, discount coupons, and so on. With this approach, consumers learn of the product through promotion and request it from retailers, who respond by asking their wholesalers for it or by going directly to the producer.

Of course, most firms use a combination of push and pull tactics to increase the impact of their promotional efforts. Soda pop companies are notorious for this dual strategy. They offer their wholesalers special incentives or product discounts to persuade them to purchase extra inventory, while at the same time they carefully orchestrate a variety of consumer promotions (low prices, contests, and so on) to pull the product through the market.

The promotional mix is also influenced by the size and concentration of the market. In markets with many widely dispersed buyers, advertising is generally the most economical way of communicating the product's features. In markets with relatively few customers, particularly when they are clustered in a limited area, personal selling is a practical promotional alternative. Many marketers use a combination of methods, often relying on advertising and public relations to build awareness and interest, following up with personal selling to complete the sale.

When Heinz designs and promotes products like mayonnaise for the Russian market, it needs to take cultural context into account.

International Promotion Decisions Businesses operating in international markets face another layer of strategic and tactical decisions when it comes to promotion. The *global* and *local* approaches to international advertising represent two extremes. With the global approach, the advertiser tries to keep the strategy and tactics identical in every country, with necessary exceptions made for local laws and media. With the local approach, the advertiser allows its divisions or representatives in each country to design and implement their own advertising. Most international campaigns fall somewhere between these two extremes. Advertisers who opt for the regional approach strike a compromise between the efficiency of the global approach and the cost and complexity of the local approach by grouping similar countries together under a single campaign.

The Role of Positioning in Promotion The strategic importance of positioning is discussed in Chapter 13. Although promotion is just one aspect of the positioning process, it is certainly one of the most important. Consequently, positioning strategies should play a key role in the design of every company's promotional mix. The nature of a company's advertising, the type of salespeople it hires, its policy regarding coupons, its support for cultural events—decisions like these have a dramatic effect on the position that a company and its products will occupy in the minds of potential customers. Because so many things influence a product's position, successful businesspeople such as Ikea's Anders Moberg pay attention to the details, from the product selection to the lighting and decor in the stores.

PERSONAL SELLING

order getters
Salespeople who are responsible for generating new sales and for increasing sales to existing customers

creative selling
Selling process used by order getters, which involves determining customer needs, devising strategies to explain product benefits, and persuading customers to buy

By almost any measure, personal selling is the dominant form of promotional activity. Most companies spend twice as much on personal selling as they do on all other marketing activities combined, even though sales force automation is drastically changing the entire selling process.[12] Computers, telecommunication, hardware, and software—like online product configurators, proposal-generation systems, and order management systems—are relieving salespeople from nonproductive tasks, making the time they spend with customers more efficient and profitable.

For example, consider how Lou Adler's job has changed. As district manager for Chevrolet, he used to spend about 20 minutes configuring each vehicle order—and the process was far from foolproof. But today, it takes Adler less than 2 minutes to configure and price each vehicle—with virtually no errors. As a result, Adler can now spend more time marketing and consulting with customers.[13]

Types of Sales Personnel

From the general public's perspective, salespeople are salespeople. However, from a business perspective, salespeople play various roles depending on the size and organization of the company, the type of product it sells, and the nature of its customer base. In general, salespeople can be categorized according to three broad areas of responsibility: order getting, order taking, and sales support services. Although some salespeople focus primarily on one area of responsibility, others may have broader responsibilities that span several areas.

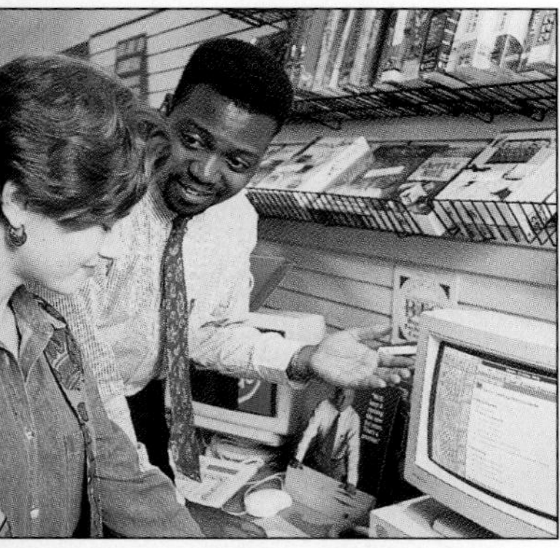

Today's professional salespeople are as much problem solvers and consultants as they are "salespeople" in the traditional sense.

Order Getters **Order getters** are responsible for generating new sales and for increasing sales to existing customers. Order getters can range from telemarketers selling bottled water and stockbrokers selling securities to engineers selling computers and nuclear physicists selling consulting services. Order getting is sometimes referred to as **creative selling,** particularly if the salesperson must invest a significant amount of time in determining what the customer needs, devising a strategy to explain how the product can meet those needs, and persuading the customer to buy. This type of creative selling requires a high degree of empathy, and the salesperson takes on the role of consultant in a long-term relationship with the customer.

Order Takers **Order takers** do little creative selling; they primarily process orders. Unfortunately, the term *order taker* has assumed negative overtones in recent years because salespeople often use it to refer to someone too lazy to work for new customers or actively close orders, or they use it to refer to someone whose territory is so attractive that he or she can just sit by the phone and wait for orders to roll in. Regardless of how salespeople use the term, order takers in the true sense play an important role in the sales function.

With the aim of generating additional sales, many companies are beginning to train their order takers to think more like order getters. You've probably noticed that nearly every time you order a meal at McDonald's and don't ask for French fries, the person at the counter will ask, "Would you like an order of fries to go with that?" Such suggestions can prompt customers to buy something they may not otherwise order.

order takers
Salespeople who generally process incoming orders without engaging in creative selling

Sales Support Personnel **Sales support personnel** generally don't sell products, but they facilitate the overall selling effort by providing a variety of services. Their responsibilities can include looking for new customers, educating potential and current customers, building goodwill, and providing service to customers after the sale. The three most common types of sales support personnel are missionary, technical, and trade salespeople.

sales support personnel
Salespeople who facilitate the selling effort by providing such services as prospecting, customer education, and customer service

Missionary salespeople are employed by manufacturers to disseminate information about new products to existing customers (usually wholesalers and retailers) and to motivate them to sell the product to their customers. Manufacturers of pharmaceuticals and medical supplies use missionary salespeople to call on doctors and pharmacists. They leave samples and information, answer questions, and persuade doctors to prescribe their products.

missionary salespeople
Salespeople who support existing customers, usually wholesalers and retailers

Technical salespeople contribute technical expertise and assistance to the selling function. They are usually engineers and scientists or have received specialized technical training. In addition to providing support services to existing customers, they may also participate in sales calls to prospective customers. Companies that manufacture computers, industrial equipment, and sophisticated medical equipment use technical salespeople to sell their products as well as to provide support services to existing customers.

technical salespeople
Specialists who contribute technical expertise and other sales assistance

Trade salespeople sell to and support marketing intermediaries. Producers such as Hormel, Nabisco, and Sara Lee use trade salespeople to give in-store demonstrations, offer samples to customers, set up displays, restock shelves, and work with retailers to obtain more shelf space. Increasingly, producers work to establish lasting, mutually beneficial relationships with their channel partners, and trade salespeople are responsible for building those relationships.

trade salespeople
Salespeople who sell to and support marketing intermediaries by giving in-store demonstrations, offering samples, and so on

The Creative Selling Process

Although it may look easy, creative selling is not a simple task. Of course, some sales are made in a matter of minutes. However, other sales, particularly for large organizational purchases, can take months to complete. Salespeople should follow a carefully planned process from start to finish.

Step 1: Prospecting **Prospecting** is the process of finding and qualifying potential customers. This step involves three activities: (1) *generating sales leads*—names of individuals and organizations that *might* be likely prospects for the company's product; (2) *identifying prospects*—potential customers who indicate a need or a desire for the seller's product; and (3) *qualifying prospects*—the process of figuring out which prospects have both the authority and the available money to buy. Those who pass the test are called **qualified prospects.**

prospecting
Process of finding and qualifying potential customers

qualified prospects
Potential buyers who have both the money needed to make the purchase and the authority to make the purchase decision

Step 2: Preparing With a list of hot prospects in hand, the salesperson's next step is to prepare for the sales call. Without this preparation, the chances of success are greatly reduced. Preparation starts with creating a prospect profile, which includes the names of key people, their role in the decision-making process, and other relevant information, such as the prospect's buying needs, motive for buying, current suppliers, income/revenue level, and so on.

Next, the salesperson decides how to approach the prospect. Possible options for a first contact include sending a letter or making a cold call in person or by telephone. For an existing customer, the salesperson can either drop by unannounced or call ahead for an appointment, which is generally preferred.

Before meeting with the prospect, the salesperson establishes specific objectives to achieve during the sales call. Depending on the situation, objectives can range anywhere from "getting the order today" to simply "persuading prospects to accept the company as a potential supplier." After establishing the objectives, the salesperson prepares the actual presentation, which can be as basic as a list of points to discuss or as elaborate as a product demonstration or multimedia presentation.

Step 3: Approaching the Prospect Whether the approach is by telephone, by letter, or in person, a positive first impression results from three elements. The first is an appropriate *appearance*—you wouldn't wear blue jeans to call on a banker, and you probably wouldn't wear a business suit to call on a farmer. Appearance also covers the things that represent you, including business cards, letters, and automobiles. Second, a salesperson's *attitude and behavior* can make or break a sale. A salesperson should come across as professional, courteous, and considerate. Third, a salesperson's *opening lines* should include a brief greeting and introduction, followed by a few carefully chosen words that get the prospect's attention and generate interest. The best way to get a prospect's attention is to focus on a benefit to the customer rather than on the product itself.

Step 4: Making the Presentation The most crucial step in the selling process is the presentation. It can take many forms, but its purpose never varies: to personally communicate a product message that will persuade a prospect to buy. Most sellers use one of two methods: The **canned approach** is a memorized presentation (easier for inexperienced sellers, but inefficient for complex products or for sellers who don't know the customer's needs). The **need-satisfaction approach** (now used by most professionals) identifies the customer's needs and creates a presentation to specifically address them.

canned approach
Selling method based on a fixed, memorized presentation

need-satisfaction approach
Selling method that starts with identifying the customer's needs and then creating a presentation that addresses those needs; this is the approach used by most professional salespeople

Step 5: Handling Objections No matter how well a presentation is delivered, it doesn't always conclude with an immediate offer that might move the prospect to buy. Often the prospect will express various types of objections and concerns throughout the presentation. In fact, the absence of objections is often an indication that the prospect is not all that interested. Many successful salespeople look at objections as a sign of the prospect's interest and as an opportunity to develop new ideas that will strengthen future presentations. Smart salespeople know that objections to price are often a mask for some other issue. They also know *not* to argue with the customer. If you do, you may prove how smart you are by winning the argument, but you will probably lose the sale.

Step 6: Closing So far, you haven't made a dime. You may have spent weeks or months to bring the customer to this point, but you don't make any money until the prospect decides to buy. This stage of the selling process, when you persuade the customer to place an order, is referred to as **closing.** How should you ask for the order? Closing techniques are numerous; among the more popular are the alternative proposal close, the assumptive close, the silent close, and the direct close. The *alternative proposal close* asks the prospect to choose between some minor details, such as method of shipment. With the *assumptive close,* you simply proceed with processing the order, assuming that the prospect has already decided to buy. Another alternative is the *silent close,* in which you finish your presentation and sit quietly, waiting for the customer to respond with his or her buying decision. Finally, many salespeople prefer the *direct close,* where you just come right out and ask for the order.

closing
Point at which a sale is completed

These closing techniques might strike you as tricks, and in the hands of unethical salespeople, some closing approaches certainly can be. However, the professional salesperson uses these techniques to make the selling process effective and efficient—not to trick people into buying when they aren't ready.

Step 7: Following Up Most salespeople depend on repeat sales and referrals from satisfied customers, so it's important that they follow up on all sales and not ignore the customer once the first sale is made. During this follow-up stage of the selling process, you need to make sure that the product has been delivered properly and that the customer is satisfied. Inexperienced salespeople may avoid the follow-up stage because they fear facing an unhappy customer. However, an important part of a salesperson's job is to ensure customer satisfaction and to build goodwill.

US West Cellular, for example, has its service representatives place "Welcome Aboard" calls to new subscribers to thank them for their business and to answer questions. The company has learned that when representatives call customers periodically, the customers perceive improvements in their cellular telephone service—even if there were no technical improvements to the service itself.[14]

Take an Idea Journey

BEST OF THE WEB

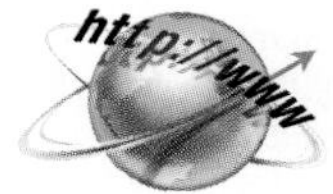

Looking for a way to market your product or service? Perhaps what you really need is a new marketing idea. How about 206 of them—many of which are quite unusual? Start your idea journey now by visiting the Sales and Marketing Management Web site. Learn some creative strategies for increasing your sales. Check out the tip of the week. Help solve a sticky management situation. Explore the list of resources for the sales and marketing professional. Follow the hot links. This journey never ends.
http://www.salesandmarketing.com

Advertising and Direct Marketing

Advertising is the lifeblood of every free-market economy. It creates product awareness and stimulates consumer demand. People who don't know a product won't buy it. Advertising not only determines what we buy, but it shapes our view of the world. It tells us which remedies to take for headaches and indigestion, how we should dress, and what we should eat. The power of advertising is the art of taking little and making it much.[15]

You have only to look around to agree with the estimate that the average person in this country is exposed to hundreds of advertising messages, perhaps as many as several thousand, every day.[16] It's a numbers game. If ads are shown to 10 million consumers, only a very small percentage will go to the store and buy the product. But if ads are shown continuously, year after year, an image is created and maintained.[17]

The prevalence of advertising underscores its many advantages. It is the form of promotion over which the organization has the greatest control. In an advertisement, you can say whatever you want, as long as you stay within the boundaries of the law and conform to the moral and ethical standards of the advertising medium and trade associations. Of the various forms of promotion, it is the best for reaching mass audiences quickly at a low per-person cost.

Little wonder then that businesses of all kinds spend large amounts of money on advertising. Together, the nation's 100 largest advertisers spend more than $52 billion a year on advertising.[18] The percentage of income that a company spends on advertising varies according to the product and the market. A cosmetics company like Esteé Lauder may spend 30 percent of total earnings to promote its products in a highly competitive market; a company that manufactures heavy industrial machinery may spend less than 1 percent. In most small businesses, the typical advertising budget is 2 to 5 percent of income.[19]

Besides the budget differences, small businesses also handle their advertising differently from larger organizations. For example, in small companies, advertising is often handled by someone in the sales or marketing department—or directly by the company president. Large advertising projects are typically outsourced to noncompany *advertising agencies* or firms of marketing specialists who assist companies in planning and preparing advertisements.

In contrast, larger companies often have enough personnel and resources to maintain a separate advertising department. Typically, internal advertising departments are responsible for establishing and maintaining an advertising budget, assisting the outside agency with developing advertising strategies, approving ad campaigns, and handling miscellaneous advertising functions not ordinarily performed by outside agencies. However, this division of responsibilities—both internally and externally—is becoming blurred as more companies adopt an integrated marketing approach using a variety of promotional vehicles and advertising media.

Types of Advertising

product advertising
Advertising that tries to sell specific goods or services, generally by describing features, benefits, and, occasionally, price

institutional advertising
Advertising that seeks to create goodwill and to build a desired image for a company rather than to sell specific products

Advertising can be divided into several categories. The most familiar type of advertising is **product advertising,** which tries to sell specific goods or services, such as Kellogg's cereals, Sega video games, or Esteé Lauder cosmetics. Product advertising generally describes the product's features and may mention its price.

Institutional Advertising **Institutional advertising,** on the other hand, is designed to create goodwill and build a desired image for a company rather than to sell specific products. Many companies are now spending large sums for institutional advertising that focuses on *green marketing,* creating an image of companies as corporate conservationists. Businesses tout their actions, contributions, and philosophies not only as supporting the environmental movement but as leading the way. Also known as *corporate advertising,* institutional advertising is often used by corporations to promote an entire line of products. At the same time, institutional ads serve to remind investors that the company is doing well.

advocacy advertising
Ads that present a company's opinions on public issues such as education and health

Institutional ads that address public issues are called **advocacy advertising.** Mobil and W. R. Grace are well known for running ads that deal with taxation, environmental regulation, and other issues. Advocacy advertising has recently expanded beyond issues in which the organization has a stake. Some companies now run advocacy ads that don't directly benefit their business, such as ads to project opinions and attitudes that support those of their target audiences. Clothing manufacturer Members Only has at times devoted its entire advertising budget to drug abuse awareness and voter registration.[20]

competitive advertising
Ads that specifically highlight how a product is better than its competitors

comparative advertising
Advertising technique in which two or more products are explicitly compared

Competitive versus Comparative Advertising You can argue that all advertising is competitive in nature, but the term **competitive advertising** is applied to those ads that specifically highlight how a product is better than its competitors. When two or more products are directly contrasted in an ad, the technique being used is **comparative advertising.** In some countries, comparative ads are tightly regulated and sometimes banned; that is clearly not the case in the United States. Indeed, the Federal Trade Commission started the ball rolling by encouraging advertisers to use direct product comparisons with the intent of better informing customers; 35 to 40 percent of all advertising in the United States is comparative.[21]

Comparative advertising is frequently used by competitors vying with the market leader, but it is useful whenever you believe you have some specific product strengths that are important to customers. Burger King used it on McDonald's, Pepsi used it on Coke, and car manufacturers from Ford to Toyota use it. This approach is bare-knuckle marketing, and, when done well, is effective. However, comparative advertising sometimes ends up getting neutralized by look-alike campaigns from the competition. Analgesics (painkillers) is one category cited as an example of comparative advertising taken too far. There are so many claims and counterclaims in this "ad war" that consumers can't keep it all straight anymore.[22]

National versus Local Advertising Finally, advertising can be classified according to the sponsor. **National advertising** is sponsored by companies that sell products on a nationwide basis. The term *national* refers to the level of the advertiser, not the geographic coverage of the ad. If a national manufacturer places an ad in only one city, the ad is still classified as a national ad. **Local advertising,** on the other hand, is sponsored by a local merchant. Its objective is to provide details about where a product can be found, at what price, and in what quantity. The grocery store ads in the local newspaper are a good example. **Cooperative advertising** is a financial arrangement whereby companies with nationally sold products share the costs of local advertising with local merchants and wholesalers. As a result, it is a cross between local and national advertising.

national advertising
Advertising sponsored by companies that sell products on a nationwide basis; refers to the geographic reach of the advertiser, not the geographic coverage of the ad

local advertising
Advertising sponsored by a local merchant

cooperative advertising
Joint efforts between local and national advertisers, in which producers of nationally sold products share the costs of local advertising with local merchants and wholesalers

Interactive Advertising **Interactive advertising,** or a two-way exchange between a merchant and a potential customer, is becoming the biggest challenge for advertisers today. For years advertisers produced a standard commercial and distributed it to the masses via TV, magazines, or newspapers. But the Internet, interactive TV, video screens on shopping carts, and free-standing kiosks are changing the nature of advertising from a one-way passive medium to a two-way marketing communication.

The biggest drawback of interactive advertising is that the marketer cannot control when the message is received. Consumers can choose to participate in the ad or to "exit." Consequently, the ads themselves must act as a "hook" to catch people's interest and get them to dig deeper. On the other hand, those who choose to participate are often more interested in the message—making it more effective. Plus interactive ads can transfer more information than can possibly be packed into a 30-second commercial.

interactive advertising
Customer-seller communication in which the customer controls the amount and type of information received

Advertising Appeals

Well-designed ads use a carefully planned appeal to whatever it is that motivates the target audience. Naturally, the best appeal to use depends largely on the target audience. By segmenting along lifestyles and other variables, advertisers try to identify which groups of people can be reached with various kinds of appeals.

Regardless of the specific nature of the appeal, all appeals fall into one of two general categories: logical or emotional. Some ads try to convince you with data, whereas others try to tug at your emotions to get their point across. Even with the most unemotional sort of product, however, emotions play a very big role. When selling to engineers and other technical people, some industrial and high-tech marketers assume that logic is the only way to go. However, people are people, and they all have hopes, fears, desires, and dreams, regardless of the job they have or the products they're buying.

Emotional appeals range from the most syrupy and sentimental to the downright terrifying. Fear appeals cover a broad range: personal and family safety, financial security, social acceptance, and business success or failure. Appeals to fear have to be managed carefully, however. Laying it on too thick can anger the audience or even cause them to block out the message entirely.[23] On the lighter side, some companies try to convince you of how good it will feel to use their products. Flowers, greeting cards, and gifts are among the products usually sold with a positive emotional appeal.

UNDERSTANDING THE HIGH-TECH REVOLUTION

Don't Touch that Dial! Interactive Advertising Battles for Your Attention

Whenever you see new computer or communications technology, you can safely assume that somebody, somewhere, is looking for ways to apply it to advertising. Technology is transforming the creation and transmission of just about every kind of traditional advertising, and it has opened up entirely new advertising possibilities. At the same time, however, advertisers may be unchaining a technological force that will turn much of the advertising business upside down.

First, the good news. Both print and broadcast advertising now benefit from the increased productivity and flexibility that technology brings. Take a basic magazine ad, for instance. Just a few years ago, the copywriter sat at a typewriter, and the art director mechanically pasted up typeset copy and whatever visual elements were in the ad. Making even a simple wording change was a slow, expensive process—and forget about anything complicated like moving a photo and surrounding copy.

Today the art director sits at a computer, imports photos and other visuals that have been digitally scanned, grabs the copywriter's words from another computer on the network, and then fits all the pieces together on the screen using a mouse. Photo in the wrong place? No problem; just pick it up with the mouse and move it. Client decides to change the wording of the headline at the last minute? Also not a problem; just type the new words right into the ad, which is sitting there on your screen. When everybody's satisfied, send the file over telephone lines to a service bureau that creates the photographic film ready to drop into a magazine.

For a television spot, computers help with everything from set design to special effects such as "morphing," a technique that seems to magically transform one product or

Now that he has more than enough money to qualify for credit cards and to require a staff of financial advisers, professional golfer Tiger Woods will join a cast of other American Express celebrity endorsers.

Price or Value Appeal Promising to give buyers more for their money is one of the most effective appeals you can use, particularly in terms of audience recall.[24] A value appeal can be accomplished in several ways: lowering the price and making people aware of the new price, keeping the price the same but offering more, or keeping the price and the product the same and trying to convince people that the product is worth whatever price you are charging.

Celebrity Appeal A popular ad approach is the use of celebrities. The theory behind these ads is that people will be more inclined to use products that celebrities use themselves and that some of the stars' image will rub off on the products they're holding. For instance, American Express recently signed Tiger Woods because the traits that characterize Woods—discipline, hard work, and preparation—are the pillars of American Express. "It's hard to visualize anyone he wouldn't appeal to," says the company president.[25]

Celebrity ads do have potential problems, however. First, consumers don't always find them convincing (or at least don't claim to find them convincing). In fact, one survey on the power of various advertising appeals ranked celebrity endorsements as the least convincing, as cited by 70 percent of the respondents. Another big problem is that the public's image of the celebrity can get tangled up with its image of the product, and if the star gets in trouble, the brand can get in trouble, too. Madonna, Mike Tyson, O. J. Simpson, Michael Jackson, and Jennifer Capriati are among celebrities who have lost endorsement contracts when aspects of their private lives became public news.

Is It True?

According to a recent survey of sports advertisers and agency executives, Michael Jordan is the most appealing athlete endorser in sports.

Sex Appeal Another old standby in the advertising world is selling with sex. The classic technique is to have an attractive, scantily attired model share the page or TV screen with the product. If the model's looks and pose somehow make sense, fine; if they don't, fine. The point is to have the audience associate the product with pleasure. Guess Jeans and

object into another. When you're ready to edit, digital editing systems make putting the pieces together as easy as moving paragraphs around in a word processor. Unlike the old system of splicing bits of film together and trying to synchronize the voices, music, and sound effects, these new systems let you work with all the parts on your computer screen; then they create a broadcast-quality videotape when you're finished. The technology gives you more creative flexibility and lets you get more done in less time.

Now for the potentially bad news. The emerging technology of interactive advertising puts the audience in control. With Web advertising, customers are no longer passive viewers, but have an unprecedented number of choices over the messages they receive. This means that traditional broadcast-style advertising won't be effective on the Internet because it dumps a one-way message on an audience with interactive capabilities.

Of course, the fact that consumers will actively participate in the sales process is a tremendous advantage. But getting them interested in the first place, and keeping them there will become the real challenge. To be effective, Internet ads must be entertaining; they must be fun, interesting, and offer valuable information. Otherwise, users will click on the "Exit" and cause the ad to disappear as quickly as it arrived.

QUESTIONS FOR CRITICAL THINKING

1. Technology also makes it easier to plagiarize by copying or importing someone else's text or artwork. How can companies discourage this?
2. What are some ways advertisers can keep consumers interested in an interactive Web ad?

Calvin Klein's Obsession perfume are well-known examples of this approach. The sex appeal has to be used with some caution, however. At the extremes, using sex as the appeal can keep an ad from running, when print or electronic media refuse to accept it for publication or broadcast. In addition, attempts to present a sexy image may cross the line, offending some readers and viewers as simply sexist, not sexy.[26]

The Elements of an Advertisement

All ads feature two basic elements. The first is **copy,** which is the verbal part of the ad, and the second is **artwork,** which is the visual part of the ad. For a magazine ad, the copy is the words you see on the page. For a radio or TV commercial, the copy is spoken by the actors.

copy
Verbal (spoken or written) part of an ad

artwork
Visual, graphic part of an ad

Many people have looked at an ad that has two sentences of copy and thought, "That looks easy. Anybody could crank out a couple of sentences." Alas, looks are deceiving. Writing ad copy is part art, part science, and part luck. Few people can do it well. Top copywriters are rewarded handsomely for their ability to create effective copy.

Ad copy has five fundamental purposes: getting the prospect's attention, stimulating the prospect's interest, building credibility for the product and the company, heightening the prospect's desire for the product, and motivating the prospect toward action.[27] Crafting words that can accomplish all these goals is no easy task. It requires good communication skills, a flair for language, and a thorough knowledge of both the product and the customer.

As powerful as good copy can be, it is usually enhanced by creative artwork. In fact, the artwork is sometimes much more prominent than the copy, with the visual images conveying most or all of the message. The arrangement of copy and artwork in an ad is referred to as the *layout.* Visual elements can be based on a variety of themes, including the product's own package, the product in use, product features, humor, before-and-after comparisons, visual comparisons with other products, and testimonials from users or celebrities.

Direct Marketing

Direct marketing is indeed an important element in the promotional mix. In 1997 more than 22.9 million workers were employed throughout the United States in direct-marketing activities. According to the Direct Marketing Association, revenues generated from direct marketing are expected to reach $1.9 trillion by 2002.[28] Three of the most popular direct-marketing categories are direct mail, telemarketing, and infomercials.

direct mail
Advertising sent directly to potential customers, usually through the U.S. Postal Service

telemarketing
Selling or supporting the sales process over the telephone

- *Direct mail.* The principal vehicle for direct marketing is **direct mail.** It includes both catalog sales and single items marketed through the U.S. Postal Service and private carriers. For many companies, mailing out letters, brochures, pamphlets, flyers, videotapes, diskettes, and other promotional items to customers and prospects is the most effective way to increase sales. But the high cost of printing and postage often limits the appeal of the direct-marketing campaign.
- *Telemarketing.* Another popular form of direct marketing is **telemarketing,** or selling over the telephone. Businesses and nonprofit organizations like telemarketing because it keeps selling costs down and is an efficient way to reach a great number of customers. Many customers like it because it saves them time.[29] Sometimes telemarketing is used by itself; in other cases, it is used to supplement door-to-door and other selling methods. Telemarketing can be broken down into two classes: *Outbound telemarketing* occurs when companies place *cold calls* to potential customers that have not requested a sales call; *inbound telemarketing* establishes phone lines for customers to call in to place orders. Outbound telemarketing can generate a lot of criticism because it interrupts family or business activities and can even pose a threat to safety by tying up a phone line needed in an emergency. Perhaps the worst abuse comes from computerized dialing systems that call numbers automatically and send a recorded message. Public pressure is leading some states to consider legislation that would regulate or even ban outbound telemarketing.[30]
- *Television infomercials.* These are long, informative commercials that have the appearance of regular programs. Although only one out of 40 infomercials turns a profit, some recent infomercials have been quite successful. For instance, "Ab" gadgets that made it easier for you to do sit-ups raked in over $250 million in sales from television and over $200 million in retail sales. And Ovation went from selling 2,000 ThighMasters per week to selling 75,000 per week in a 5-month period.[31]

media
Communications channels, such as newspapers, radio, and television

media plan
Written plan that outlines how a company will spend its media budget, including how the money will be divided among the various media and when the advertisements will appear

media mix
Combination of various media options that a company uses in an advertising campaign

Media Planning

To get the message to potential customers, suitable **media,** or channels of communication, must be chosen. The **media plan** specifies the advertising budget, establishes how the money will be divided among the various media, and indicates exactly when the advertisements will appear. The goal of the media plan is to make the most effective use of the company's advertising dollar.

The Media Mix The critical task in media planning is to select a **media mix,** the combination of print, broadcast, and other media for the advertising campaign. When selecting the media mix, the first step is to determine the characteristics of the target audience and the types of media that will reach the greatest audience at the lowest cost. The choice is also based on what the medium is expected to do (show the product in use, list numerous sale items and prices, and so on). The second step in choosing the media mix is to pick specific vehicles in each of the chosen media categories, such as individual magazines (*Time, Rolling Stone, Sports Illustrated*) or individual radio stations (a rock station, a classical station).

Media Buying Sorting through all the media is a challenging task. In fact, many advertisers rely on professional media planners to find the best combinations of media and to negotiate attractive terms. These planners use four important types of data in selecting their media buys. The first is **cost per thousand (CPM),** a standardized ratio that converts the total cost of advertising space to the more meaningful cost of reaching 1,000 people with the ad. CPM is especially useful for comparing media that reach similar audiences.

cost per thousand (CPM)
Cost of reaching 1,000 people with an ad

Two other decision tools are reach and frequency, which represent the trade-off between breadth and depth of communication. **Reach** refers to the total number of audience members who will be exposed to a message at least once in a given time period; it is usually expressed as a percentage of the total number of audience members in a particular population. **Frequency** is the average number of times that each audience member is exposed to the message; it is calculated by dividing the total number of exposures by the total audience population.

reach
Total number of audience members who will be exposed to a message at least once in a given period

frequency
Average number of times that each audience member is exposed to the message (equal to the total number of exposures divided by the total audience population)

The fourth decision tool is **continuity,** which refers to the period spanned by the media schedule and the timing of ad messages within the period evenly spread over the schedule or heavily concentrated in some periods. Obviously, within a fixed budget, a media plan cannot do everything: If it is important to reach a high percentage of a target group with significant frequency, the cost of doing so on a continuous basis may be prohibitive. Media planners often resort to airing messages in "waves" or "flights"—short periods of high reach and frequency that sacrifice continuity. This strategy is common in the travel industry, which crowds much of its annual media spending into the peak vacation seasons.

continuity
Pattern according to which an ad appears in the media; it can be spread evenly over time or concentrated during selected periods

Media Categories Advertising media fall into nine media categories: television, newspapers, direct mail, radio, yellow pages, magazines, business papers, outdoor, and miscellaneous (see Exhibit 15.2). Each medium has its own strengths and weaknesses for various advertising applications (see Exhibit 15.3). Other ways of bringing advertising messages to the public are limited only by the imagination. Free movie magazines are distributed in theater

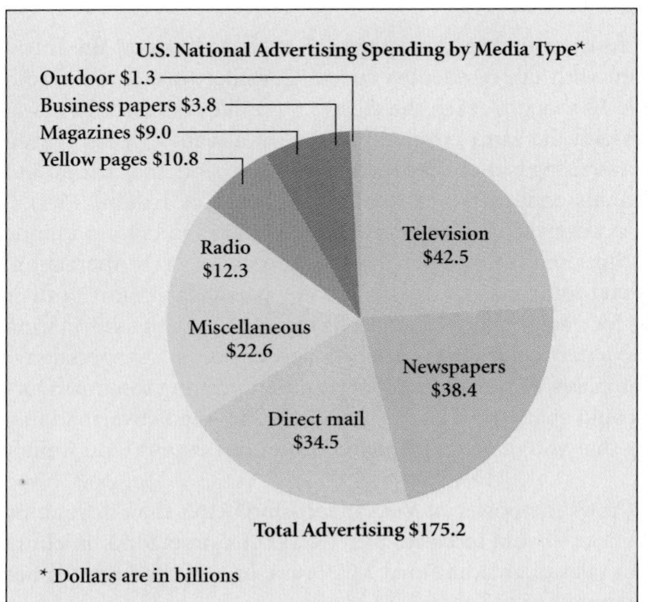

EXHIBIT 15.2

Advertising Expenditures

Despite downsizing, restructuring, and many changes in competitive marketing strategies, advertising is still being employed extensively by most marketers. U.S companies spent some $175.2 billion in advertising for 1996.

EXHIBIT 15.3

Advantages and Disadvantages of Major Advertising Media

When selecting the media mix, marketers attempt to match the characteristics of the media audience with the characteristics of the potential buyers. A typical advertising campaign involves the use of several media.

MEDIUM	ADVANTAGES	DISADVANTAGES
Newspapers	Extensive market coverage; low cost; short lead time for placing ads; good local market coverage; geographic selectivity	Poor graphic quality; short life span; cluttered pages; visual competition from other ads
Television	Great impact; broad reach; appealing to senses of sight, sound, and motion; creative opportunities for demonstration; high attention; entertainment carryover	High cost for production and air time; less audience selectivity; long preparation time; commercial clutter; short life for message; vulnerability to remote controls
Direct mail	Can deliver large amounts of information to narrowly selected audiences; excellent control over quality of message; personalization	High cost per contact; delivery delays; difficulty of obtaining desired mailing list; consumer resistance; generally poor image (junk mail)
Radio	Low cost; high frequency; immediacy; highly portable; high geographic and demographic selectivity	No visual possibilities; short life for message; commercial clutter; lower attention than television; easy to switch channels
Magazines	Good reproduction; long life; local and regional market selectivity; authority and credibility; multiple readers	Limited demonstration possibilities; long lead time between placing and publishing ads; high cost; less compelling than other major media

lobbies, commercial airlines carry in-flight advertising, and supermarkets run ads on their shopping bags and shopping carts. Companies are increasingly taking advantage of electronic media, marketing their products through the Internet. Moreover, technological advancements (such as in-home video carried by fiber optic lines) promise advertisers entirely new channels of communication.[32]

Web Advertising Key indicators from several sectors suggest that advertising on the Internet will become a mass medium with unprecedented speed. Consider this: It took radio 38 years, TV 13 years, and cable 10 years to reach the elusive 50 million household mark. But the Internet is on pace to reach the same coveted position in a scant 8 years.[33] Even though dollar for dollar, Web advertising is more expensive than television, magazines, and newspapers, revenue from Web ads continues to rise at a fast pace (see Exhibit 15.4).[34]

The biggest benefit of Web advertising is that it allows advertisers to tailor a unique pitch to the individual and at the same time gather information about each interaction. Companies can (1) track the exact information accessed by any particular visitor to their Web site, (2) develop a profile for each of their regular visitors, (3) present information that may be of special interest to a particular visitor, and (4) alert customers to special savings or remind them of past purchases. However, experts warn that pushing too much targeted information on the Net could spark a backlash. "There's a fine line between adding value and the consumer feeling that you're being intrusive," notes one expert with Jupiter Communications.[35]

Of course, no company knows the power of Web advertising better than Toyota. By slapping banner ads all over the Net, Toyota received over 152,000 requests for a brochure or video about a car—leading to sales of an additional 7,329 cars. In fact, the Internet, has become the number one lead generator for Toyota."[36]

MEDIA	COST	AUDIENCE	COST PER 1,000 CUSTOMERS
Television: 30-second spot, network news	$ 65,000	12,000,000	$ 5.42
Magazine: Full-page color ad, national weekly	135,000	3,100,000	43.55
Newspaper: Full-page ad, midsize city	31,000	514,000	60.31
World Wide Web: Online magazine, one-month placement	15,000	200,000	75.00

EXHIBIT 15.4

How Much Bang for the Buck?

Compared with TV and print, Web ads are pricey. But for some companies the ultra-niche targeting is worth it.

Make It a Banner Year

BEST OF THE WEB

Rev up traffic on your Web site by visiting the Website Promoters Resource Center (WPRC). Click on *Banner Advertising*, and then *Useful Resources*. Scroll down and go the *WPRC Library*. Tour the Web site. Take a crash course in banner advertising. Learn the dos and don'ts of online marketing. Find out how to optimize your Web site for search engine listings. Read the tip of the week and learn from the experience of others. Find out what's in a domain name. View some effective banner samples. Get some free advice and make it a banner year.
http://www.wprc.com

SALES PROMOTION

The fourth element of promotion, sales promotion, covers a wide variety of activities, including coupons, discounts, samples, contests, sweepstakes, and frequent-flyer programs. Depending on how one measures it, sales-promotion expenditures in the United States now appear to exceed those for advertising.[37] Sales promotion can be broken down into two basic categories: consumer promotion and trade promotion. Consumer promotion is aimed directly at final users of the product, whereas trade promotion is aimed at retailers and wholesalers. Although shoppers are more aware of consumer promotion, trade promotion actually accounts for a larger share of promotional spending.

Consumer Promotion

Consumer promotions include coupons, specialty advertising, premiums, point-of-purchase advertising, rebates, games and sweepstakes, special events, and other incentives. Such promotions are used to stimulate repeat purchases and to entice new users.

consumer promotions
Sales promotions aimed at final consumers

The biggest category of consumer promotion, **couponing,** aims to spur sales by offering a discount through redeemable coupons. Coupons work well in several situations, including stimulating trial of new products, reaching out to nonusers of mature products, encouraging repeat purchases, and reducing the price of products without having to enlist the cooperation of retailers. However, coupons have several drawbacks, and because of these drawbacks, many companies—including giants like Procter & Gamble—are starting

couponing
Distribution of certificates that offer discounts on particular items

GAINING THE COMPETITIVE EDGE

Web Ads Start to Click

Advertisers are rolling up their sleeves. There's a lot of hype about a medium that has yet to prove itself as an effective marketing tool. Yet the Net has come a long way. Not too long ago, Web site operators were wringing their hands over disappointing ad sales. But today industry experts predict that annual advertising revenues on the Web could soon reach $5 billion.

What's changed? Why is advertising on the Net starting to click? For starters, the sheer number of "Netizens" prowling the Web—some 50 million today—is becoming too large for companies to ignore. Some expect that number to put the Web on a fast track to coveted mass-media status. What's more, in the past two years, the Net has gone from being a haven for nerds and academics to a hangout for professionals, teenagers, and grandmothers alike. This rich demographic shift, coupled with technology that promises to make Net ads almost as much of a "must see" as those on TV, have finally turned the Web into a hip place to pitch.

At the same time, the buzz about how the Net's technology makes it possible to target specific customers is becoming a reality. Unlike a TV ad on say, *ER*, which is aimed broadly at the cool, thirtysomething crowd, a cyber promo can zero in on Netizens who live in a specific part of town, are female, and have shown an interest in certain topics or products. How? Much of this is done through a technology called "cookies," which are like electronic footprints that chronicle your movements on a particular Web site—what ads you saw or what you clicked on for more information. That information is stored in a "cookie file" in your browser, and the next time you drop by the same Web site, the server picks up your footprint and gathers more information that can then be shared with advertisers. Although privacy advocates fret about cookies, Web site operators insist they're not a problem because surfers can disable them.

Still, for all the hype, the world's fastest growing advertising segment is a murky area of unproved value. The biggest problem is that no one really knows how many people see an ad. Whereas a traditional broadcast ad can reach a passive audience of millions, a targeted pitch on a dedicated Web site is seen only by those who make the effort to go there. And, that's hard to track. Although it is possible to count the number of times a Web page has been accessed, that number tells you nothing about who stopped there, for how long, and whether it's a repeat visitor or a new one. And of course, audience size doesn't necessarily translate into effective advertising.

For one thing, Web advertising is crude and far from the standards for slick TV commercials. The static wallpaper-like appearance is a definite cyber-snore. But that is changing. Web advertising is borrowing pages from its broadcast counterpart by adding sound and animation. The next step will be *interstitials*—full-screen, in-your-face ads that pop up in the lag time between requesting a Web page and its appearance on the screen.

Is It True?

Less than 2 percent of coupons are actually redeemed.

point-of-purchase display Advertising or other display materials set up at retail locations to promote products to potential customers as they are making their purchase decisions

to wean shoppers off coupons. First, coupons are expensive: A lot of money is wasted on advertising and delivering coupons. Second, coupons have been accused of instilling a bargain-hunting mentality in many consumers; some customers won't purchase a product until a coupon is available.[38]

Another popular form of consumer promotions is a **point-of-purchase display** or a device for showing a product in a way that stimulates immediate sales. It may be simple, such as the end-of-aisle stacks of soda pop in a supermarket or the racks of gum and mints at checkout counters. On the other hand, it may be more elaborate, such as the "computers" Esteé Lauder uses to encourage consumers to buy the Clinique line. Point-of-purchase displays are becoming an important element of the integrated promotional mix—especially because studies show that in almost every instance, secondary displays significantly increase sales.[39]

Special-event sponsorship has become one of the most popular sales-promotion tactics. Thousands of companies spend a total of over $1 billion to sponsor 3,000 events ranging from golf to opera. The 1996 Summer Olympic Games in Atlanta drew over $100 mil-

Even though interstitials have more pizzazz than banner ads, some Netizens think animation can be downright irritating. That's why most companies are sticking with banners plastered across the top or bottom of a Web page, much like a billboard on the information highway. A click on one of these ads usually whisks you off to the Web site of that company, where more information can be found.

How effective is Web advertising? According to Parker Brothers—whose recent Web banner campaign brought over 100,000 visitors to its Trivial Pursuit game on the Internet—Web advertising "is a complete success." But others aren't as convinced. So while advertisers figure out how to make advertising work on the Web, the true winners—those who will gain a competitive edge through Web advertising—will be those who can apply new technology to advertising in a creative and innovative way.

POPULAR CYBERMARKETING TERMS

Cybermarketing Term	Explanation
Banner ad	Small, usually rectangular graphic, that appears on a Web site like a roadside billboard. Messages are often static. By clicking on the ad, users can make a quick trip to the advertiser's home page for more information.
Button ad	Small, square ad that is usually at the bottom of a Web page and contains less information than a banner ad—a company name, brand name, or subject matter. Clicking on the button takes you to the advertiser's home page for more information.
Click through	How often a viewer will respond to an ad by clicking on it.
Cookie	Information from a site that gets stored on a viewer's Web browser to help identify that particular person the next time he or she visits. Cookies allow companies to collect data on the user.
Cost per click (CPC)	The ad rate charged only if the Web surfer responds to a displayed ad.
Impressions	The total number of times an ad is displayed on a Web page.

QUESTIONS FOR CRITICAL THINKING

1. What are some of the main advantages of Web ads?
2. Should a company with a limited advertising budget use banner ads as a source for new business? Please explain.

lion alone from its largest corporate backers—Coke, Swatch, Anheuser Busch, AT&T, and GM, to name a few.[40]

cross-promotion
Jointly advertising two or more noncompeting brands

premiums
Free or bargain-priced items offered to encourage consumers to buy a product

specialty advertising
Advertising that appears on various items such as coffee mugs, pens, and calendars, designed to help keep a company's name in front of customers

Cross-promotion, which involves using one brand to advertise another noncompeting brand is another popular sales promotion vehicle. Examples include Tommy Lee Jones and Will Smith (*Men in Black*) playing alien-battling agents in their Bausch & Lomb Ray-Ban sunglasses, and McDonald's bundling HappyMeals with tiny Beanie Babies.[41] Of course, "Intel Inside," is one of the most successful cross-promotion campaigns ever. In just two years following the campaign's inception, awareness of the Intel chip went from roughly 22 percent of PC buyers to more than 80 percent.[42]

Other sales-promotion techniques include rebates, free samples, frequency programs like frequent-flyer miles, and **premiums,** which are free or bargain-priced items offered to encourage the consumer to buy a product. Contests and sweepstakes are also quite popular in some industries. Particularly when valuable or unusual prizes are offered, contests and sweepstakes can generate a great deal of public attention. **Specialty advertising** (on coffee mugs, pens, calendars, and so on) helps keep a company's name in front of cus-

The jerseys of bicycle racers are one of the many promotional vehicles used to promote WordPerfect software.

tomers for a long period of time. Advertisers constantly search for ways to display their names and logos. Need boxer shorts with the Domino's Pizza logo, ads made of chocolate, or Christmas ornaments with corporate logos? They're all available from specialty advertising firms.[43]

Trade Promotion

Sales-promotion efforts aimed at inducing distributors or retailers to push a producer's products are known as **trade promotions.** The usual lure is a discount on the price of the merchandise—a **trade allowance**—which enables the distributor or retailer to pass on a price cut to the ultimate consumer.

Many producers would like to see fewer trade allowances because they cut into producers' profit margins. However, according to one specialist, "trade allowances are like opium." Once retailers and distributors get used to receiving such allowances, they become addicted. In some product categories, up to 100 percent of all merchandise sold to retailers is sold on a trade deal.[44]

Trade allowances also create the controversial practice of **forward buying,** in which the retailer takes advantage of a trade allowance by stocking up while the price is low. Say that the producer of Bumble Bee tuna offers retailers a 20 percent discount for a period of 6 weeks. A retailer might choose, however, to buy enough tuna to last 8 or 10 weeks, which cuts into the producer's profit and increases the retailer's profit.

One of the best promotional tools for many industrial products is the **trade show,** a gathering where producers display their wares to potential buyers. Most of those who attend trade shows are hot prospects. According to one estimate, the average industrial exhibitor can reach 60 percent of all its prospects at a trade show, and some exhibitors do 25 percent or more of annual sales at a single show. Apart from attracting likely buyers, trade shows have the advantage of enabling a producer to demonstrate and explain the product and to compile information about prospects.[45]

In addition to trade allowances and trade shows, producers use several other trade promotion techniques, including display premiums, dealer contests or sweepstakes, and travel bonus programs, all designed to motivate the distributor or retailer to push the producer's merchandise.

trade promotions
Sales-promotion efforts aimed at inducing distributors or retailers to push a producer's products

trade allowance
Discount offered by producers to wholesalers and retailers

forward buying
Retailers' taking advantage of trade allowances by buying more products at discounted prices than they hope to sell

trade show
Gathering where producers display their wares to potential buyers; nearly every industry has one or more trade shows focused on particular types of products

PUBLIC RELATIONS

Public relations plays a vital role in the success of most companies, and that role applies to more than just the marketing of goods and services. Smart businesspeople know they need to maintain positive relations with their communities, investors, industry analysts, government agencies and officials, and the news media. All these activities fall under the umbrella of public relations. For many companies, public relations is the fastest growing element of the promotional mix.[46]

A good reputation is one of a business's most important assets. A recent study shows that companies with a good public image have a big edge over less respected companies. Consumers are more than twice as likely to buy new products from companies they admire, which is why smart companies work hard to build and protect their reputations. Denny's knows this. That's why it launched a $5 million advertising campaign to lure African American customers back following the settlement of two class-action discrimination lawsuits.[47]

Likewise, when PepsiCo began to hear reports of syringes and other dangerous objects in cans of Diet Pepsi during the summer of 1993, the company worked with the Food and Drug Administration to follow up on reports that the syringe stories may have in fact been hoaxes. After taking these actions, PepsiCo's president took to the airwaves on news programs and talk shows to explain that the company had been the victim of publicity and litigation seekers who had faked their claims.[48]

To build and maintain good reputations, many businesses place heavy emphasis on the coverage they receive in the media, both in general news media and in specialized media that cover specific industries. **Press relations** is the process of communicating with newspapers, magazines, and broadcast media. In the personal-computer industry, for example, manufacturers know that many people look to *ComputerWorld, PC, Byte,* and other computer publications as influential sources of information about new products. Editors and reporters often review new products and then make recommendations to their readers, pointing out both strengths and weaknesses. Companies roll out the proverbial red carpet for these media figures, treating them to hospitality suites at conventions, factory tours, and interviews with company leaders. When introducing products, manufacturers often send samples to reporters and editors for review, or they visit the media offices themselves.

press relations
Process of communicating with reporters and editors from newspapers, magazines, and radio and television networks and stations

The standard tools of press relations are the press release, or news release as it is sometimes called, and the press conference, or press briefing. A **press release** is a short memo sent to the media covering topics that are of potential news interest; some companies send video press releases to television stations.[49] Companies send press releases in the hope of getting favorable news coverage about themselves and their products. A **press conference** is arranged when companies have significant news to announce. Companies use press conferences in addition to press releases when the news is of widespread interest, when products need to be demonstrated, or when the company wants to be able to answer reporters' questions.

press release
Brief statement or video program released to the press announcing new products, management changes, sales performance, and other potential news items; also called a *news release*

press conference
Gathering of media representatives at which companies announce new information; also called a press briefing

Summary of Learning Objectives

1. **Identify the five basic categories of promotion.**
   The five basic categories of promotion are personal selling, advertising, direct marketing, sales promotion, and public relations.
2. **Distinguish between push and pull strategies of promotion.**
   In the push strategy, the producer "pushes" an item to distributors, who in turn promote the product to end users. The pull approach depends on stimulating enough consumer demand to "pull" a product through the distribution channel. Consumer products are more likely to rely on pull strategies; organizational products are more often pushed.
3. **List the seven steps in the personal-selling process.**
   The seven steps are prospecting (finding prospects and qualifying them), preparing, approaching the prospects, making the sales presentation, handling objections, closing, and following up after the sale has been made.
4. **Differentiate between institutional, product, and competitive advertising.**
   Institutional advertising promotes a company's overall image, not any particular products. Product advertising, however, emphasizes the products themselves. Competitive advertising emphasizes the differences between a product and its competitors.
5. **Define interactive advertising and discuss the challenge it presents to marketers.**
   Interactive advertising is a two-way exchange between a merchant and a potential customer. The biggest challenge it presents is that marketers cannot control when the message is received and consumers must actively choose to participate.
6. **Discuss the difference between logical and emotional advertising appeals.**
   You can view the difference between logical and emotional appeals as the difference between appealing to the head and appealing to the heart. Logical appeals try to convince the audience with facts, reasons, and rational conclusions. Emotional appeals, as the name implies, persuade through emotion—which can range from heart-warming tenderness to stark fear. It's important to remember, however, that nearly all ads contain a mixture of both logic and emotion; most just lean heavily in one direction or the other.
7. **Distinguish between the two main types of sales promotion, and give at least two examples of each.**
   The two main types of sales promotion are consumer promotion and trade promotion. Consumer promotions are

intended to motivate the final consumer to try new products or to experiment with the company's brands. Examples include coupons, cross-promotion, specialty advertising, premiums, point-of-purchase displays, and special events. Trade promotions are designed to induce wholesalers and retailers to stimulate sales of a producer's products. Examples include trade allowances, trade shows, display premiums, dealer contests, and travel bonus programs.

8. **Explain the role of public relations in marketing.** Because consumers and investors support companies with good reputations, smart companies use public relations to build and protect their reputations. They communicate with consumers, investors, industry analysts, and government officials through the media. They pursue and maintain press relations so that they can give effective press releases and hold effective press conferences.

On the Job: Meeting Business Challenges at Ikea

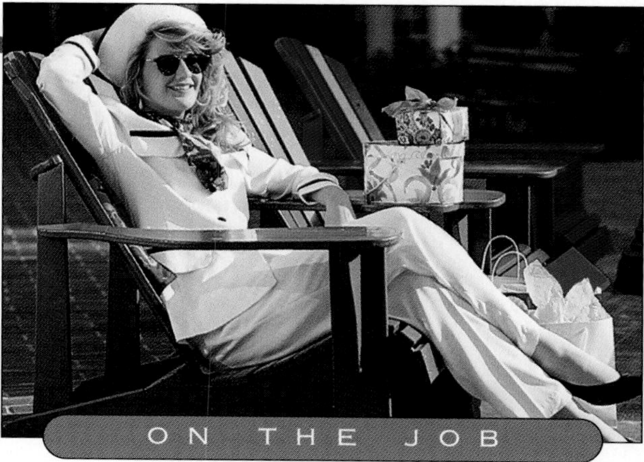

Introducing Ikea to entirely different markets—some 3,000 miles apart—was the promotional challenge facing Anders Moberg. Despite the success of the chain's first four U.S. outlets, Moberg knew that the grand openings in Elizabeth, New Jersey, and Burbank, California, were important stepping-stones to the heavily populated New York and Los Angeles metropolitan areas. The advertising had to build awareness of the store name and the retailing concept as well as attract store traffic. The Ikea president also realized that these grand-opening campaigns could not be clones; each had to be carefully tailored to its local audience.

The first store opening, in Elizabeth, was scheduled for May 23, 1990. To reach a target audience of young adults and families, the retailer launched an integrated marketing communications campaign of print, television, billboard, transit, and direct-mail advertising before the store opened. For instance, billboards on the New Jersey Turnpike teased motorists with cryptic messages. One billboard read, "On May 23, find a place to crash on the Jersey Turnpike." Print ads used lots of copy to explain the headline, "Why thousands will spend their Memorial Day vacation on the Jersey Turnpike." Topping off the ad blitz, Ikea mailed more than 1 million copies of its 200-page catalog to households within 40 miles of the new store.

While the preopening hoopla was going on, Ikea also kicked off a television campaign to support the chain's overall image. The commercials poked fun at the irritations of shopping at traditional furniture stores, such as high prices and delivery hassles. However, the campaign didn't take itself too seriously; its tag line was "It's a big country. Someone's got to furnish it." The two campaigns started people talking about Ikea, and they helped bring people—by the thousands—to the store on opening day. During the first hour the Elizabeth store was open, 3,000 people surged through the doors; by the end of the first day, 25,000 had visited the store.

Once the Elizabeth store was open, Moberg concentrated on the Burbank store opening. Sticking with a tongue-in-cheek creative approach, the retailer adjusted the media to the local market by relying more heavily on outdoor media, because southern California is car country. So for 6 weeks before the store opening, slightly irreverent teaser ads appeared on 1,600 billboards, buses, and transit shelters around Los Angeles. These intriguing outdoor ads were designed to start people talking about the campaign. Passersby might look at one poster, for example, and wonder what could possibly have "more mass appeal" than the Pope.

The suspense ended two weeks before the Burbank store opened, when Ikea added its store name and opening date to the posters. In addition to mailing catalogs to homes within an hour's drive, the retailer also used radio, television, newspaper, and magazine advertising to give more details about the outlet's products, services, and location. Once again, a brief but intense preopening campaign brought results: Burbank's first day was another blockbuster.

But the challenge Moberg faced in Manhattan years later was by and large his biggest. In order to successfully convert the big box concept to a much smaller 7,500-square-foot urban footprint, Ikea adopted a unique promotional format—a marketing outpost. The Manhattan store was designed as a stage—with a grid system that suspended lights and wooden panels that were easy to reconfigure. Like a theatrical production, every 6 to 12 weeks the store closes for about one week while the theme changes; product mix, walls, displays, figures, signage, video displays, lighting, and just about every other element is reconfigured. When the overhaul is complete, a "new" store emerges like

Ikea Entertains, or Ikea Plays, or Ikea Dines, or Ikea Sleeps—to name a few.

And by all indicators, the new marketing concept has been a smashing success. Still, Moberg isn't about to take the U.S. market for granted. He plans to boost advertising spending to fight competition from Ethan Allen and Pier 1. And Ikea is launching a new line of children's furniture—something few competitors specialize in. After all, it's a big country. Somebody's got to furnish it, and Anders Moberg is determined to see that Ikea gets the job.

Your Mission: Cynthia Neiman, the marketing manager of Ikea West, has hired you to work on advertising campaigns at the Burbank outlet. Your assignment is to battle competitors, to build store traffic, and to sell selected products. Use what you've learned about advertising to choose the best option in each situation:

1. Major competitor Pier 1 Imports recently started advertising its wide variety of international products. You wonder whether your audience will be tempted to try Pier 1 because it sells items from many countries, whereas Ikea sells mainly Scandinavian-inspired items. Which advertising strategy would best help you combat this competitive threat?
   a. Promote Ikea's key strengths, including huge product selection, without highlighting the store's Scandinavian emphasis.
   b. Promote the Scandinavian angle heavily to carve out a clear niche in buyers' minds.
   c. Ignore Pier 1 because it doesn't sell Scandinavian items.
2. After years of trying to sell European-sized beds, the chain recently switched to beds in standard U.S. sizes. Which headline do you think would play off the tone of Ikea's image advertising and entice people to the Burbank store to look at the new line of beds?
   a. "Now you can sleep with a Swedish king (or a queen, full, or twin)"
   b. "Now you can sleep in a bed designed in the land of the midnight sun"
   c. "Come see Ikea's new line of Swedish-style beds, the best of the Old World available in the New World"
3. Yet another competitor is Stor, which also offers a huge product selection and provides many of the same amenities as Ikea. Watching a television talk show, you notice a commercial inviting viewers to the grand reopening of the newly enlarged Stor outlet near your Burbank location. What should you do?
   a. Do nothing; it's not advertising special prices or special products, so you don't have to either. You can save your ad budget for other things.
   b. Double the number of times your existing television ads run during the next four weeks, when Stor is likely to be advertising most heavily. This will cost effectively keep the Ikea name in front of the target audience.
   c. Create new commercials showing how Ikea is superior to Stor in terms of prices, assortment, and customer service. This option is more costly than (b), but it's a good way to position Ikea as the market leader once and for all.
4. The average sale at the Burbank store isn't as high as at other Ikea outlets. How can you use advertising to increase the average sales amount?
   a. Show complete rooms of home furnishings rather than isolated pieces in your print ads. This will encourage customers to buy more than one of the items they see pictured so that they can get the same "finished" look at home.
   b. Advertise large assortments of lower-priced accessories. Because the items aren't expensive, shoppers will be encouraged to buy several.
   c. Show only expensive furniture in your ads. This approach will entice customers to buy those items, increasing the average sale amount.[50]

Key Terms

advertising (448)
advocacy advertising (456)
artwork (459)
canned approach (454)
closing (454)
comparative advertising (456)
competitive advertising (456)
consumer promotions (463)
continuity (461)
cooperative advertising (457)
copy (459)
cost per thousand (CPM) (461)
couponing (463)
creative selling (452)
cross-promotion (465)
direct mail (460)
direct marketing (448)
forward buying (466)
frequency (461)
institutional advertising (456)
integrated marketing communications (IMC) (449)
interactive advertising (457)
local advertising (457)
media (460)
media mix (460)
media plan (460)
missionary salespeople (453)
national advertising (457)
need-satisfaction approach (454)
order getters (452)
order takers (453)
personal selling (448)
persuasive advertising (446)
point-of-purchase display (464)
premiums (465)
press conference (467)
press relations (467)
press release (467)

product advertising (456)
promotion (446)
promotional mix (447)
promotional strategy (446)
prospecting (453)
public relations (449)
pull strategy (450)
push strategy (450)
qualified prospects (453)
reach (461)
reminder advertising (446)
sales promotion (449)
sales support personnel (453)
specialty advertising (465)
technical salespeople (453)
telemarketing (460)
trade allowance (466)
trade promotions (466)
trade salespeople (453)
trade show (466)

Questions

For Review

1. What are the three main goals of promotion?
2. What is integrated marketing communications?
3. What techniques do skilled salespeople employ when closing a sale?
4. What are the four chief criteria used in media buying?
5. What are some common types of consumer promotion?

For Analysis

6. What is the biggest advantage of personal selling over the other forms of promotion?
7. What factors should you consider when designing the optimal promotional mix?
8. How is automation changing the function of sales personnel?
9. How do advertisers determine the type of appeal to use in designing an ad, and why must they execute caution when using celebrity appeals?
10. What is the biggest problem with trade allowances from the producer's perspective?

For Application

11. If you were a realtor, how would you determine whether it's worth investing a significant amount of time in a particular prospect?
12. Assume you're a marketing manager for Ikea. How might you consider using each of the following types of advertising?
    a. product advertising
    b. institutional advertising
    c. advocacy advertising

A Case for Critical Thinking ■ America Online: Losing the Battles, but Winning the War

For the better part of 15 years, America Online (AOL) CEO and founder Steve Case has nurtured a vision. Back in the days when modems creaked along at 300 bits a second, when it took half an hour to download a small black-and-white photo, Case imagined a world where ordinary folk, like the ones he grew up with in Hawaii, would find real utility in connected computers. However, back then almost everyone considered Case's vision a perfectly ridiculous idea—except Case, of course.

In 1985 he founded a company that eventually became America Online, and he has jousted with the doubters ever since. Today, AOL connects millions of users to the Internet for a fee. The company categorizes Web sites and Internet information into Web Channels (similar to special TV stations) for travel, shopping, games, personal finance, and so on. By putting a frame around the Internet and world of information, AOL makes surfing the Net really, really easy, besides being fun and affordable. But for Steve Case, living his dream has been anything but easy.

It all started with a unique marketing approach—blanketing the countryside with diskettes containing AOL software. At trade shows, on magazine covers, in mailers, even on airplanes—you couldn't miss the free AOL disks. One analyst called this "marketing by carpet bombing." Although it took the company five years to attract a million subscribers, it only took two more years to double that. That's more than *The New York Times* and *Washington Post* have added during the last half-century. The Internet market changed overnight, and forever. Millions instantly recognized the value of getting online, and AOL was their first, best hope.

But enticing people with freeware and then charging them higher-than-market rates to hook into the Internet—even if AOL made it user-friendly—meant users might try a different service. So in 1996 AOL made its prices more competitive, and that's when the self-demolition derby began. First AOL changed its pricing structure to allow for unlimited access at a flat rate. Expecting 200,000 new customers, it attracted 500,000—in one month! Even though it had added modems in anticipation of increased demand, the surge quickly ate up the additional capacity, forcing AOL's already strained network to back up like a kitchen sink. Customers screamed. Frustrated users called the company America Onhold or America Offline—and for good reason. Attorney generals threatened to sue AOL for advertising a service it couldn't deliver. And AOL—forced to suspend its TV pitch for new subscribers—cut back on direct marketing and pumped an additional $100 million into its ailing network.

But the mess worsened. Case threw gasoline on the fire by publicly appealing to members to try to show some restraint during the peak evening hours. His appeal backfired. Skeptical users stayed on even longer, fearing that if they logged off, they wouldn't be able to get back on. Wall Street analysts argued that this was the sort of problem that would drive AOL users into the arms of other Internet firms, and the company's too-rich stock price collapsed—twice. Even though Case settled with the attorneys and state officials, it took him months to win back consumer confidence—not to mention a couple of hundred million dollars. "These guys flirted with disaster," says one industry expert. "Fortunately, they were smart enough to pull it out."

So how does AOL continue to do it? How does it continue to get new customers? "There's a Silicon Valley syndrome that is out of touch with what customers want," says Case. "Our market is everyone else." And internal research suggests "everyone else" could soon push AOL to 25 million members. Still, some wonder how AOL can compete with other Internet service providers. After all, people can access much of the same Internet information without having to go through a gatekeeper like AOL. With cheaper alternatives available, there's a limit to how much AOL can charge customers for this hand-holding. Which is why AOL is relying on advertising.

Case has decided that advertising revenue is the key to the online giant's future financial health. He wants advertising to account for at least 25 percent of revenue—an ambitious but perhaps attainable goal. After all, with a viewership that's now approaching that of ESPN, MTV, CNN, and a few others, if AOL fills that time with advertising, the power of the revenue generation machine is phenomenal. In addition to advertising, AOL is also banking on the growing business of selling products online and, of course, getting new subscribers. Firms such as 1–800-Flowers and bookseller Barnes & Noble pay a hefty fee for a direct line to AOL's growing audience. And AOL's deal with WorldCom in which AOL swallowed CompuServe (the nation's oldest online service) sent 2.6 million subscribers AOL's way.

In spite of this growth, the dirge goes on. First, critics point out that AOL has always been behind the technology curve. For instance, software for surfing the Web is revised about three times faster than AOL's software, and this technology gap can only get worse. Plus, AOL has a high turnover of subscribers. That's because for many, AOL serves as training wheels for the Net from which they eventually graduate. In fact, retaining customers will become even harder as phone companies, cable companies, Microsoft, and Netscape make it even easier to connect to the Internet, browse the Web, chat, and send e-mail without going though the suburban environment of AOL. In addition, customers could also be turned off by the increasingly intrusive ads, upon which AOL's flat-price business model now depends. Yet, despite all these challenges and the predictions of doomsayers over the years, Case's company has shown that it has at least the potential to thrive. The plain fact is that America Online has always been able to do what no one expects it to—survive.

1. AOL's pitch to sell subscriber phone numbers to its business partners for telemarketing purposes was met by customer fury, forcing AOL to back off. Should AOL be allowed to sell subscriber information to telemarketers? Please explain.
2. CompuServe had always been a more sophisticated Internet service provider, and AOL has always catered to the Internet novice. Now that AOL has acquired CompuServe, briefly explain how this presents a marketing challenge for AOL.
3. Raising subscriber rates is always a difficult company decision. How can public relations departments help decrease the potential for customer confusion and anger when a company raises its rates?
4. Log on to AOL's Web site <http://www.AOL.com> and browse the site. Click on some of the *Web channels* and learn how AOL makes Internet access easy.
   a. Why does AOL give away free hours to new users?
   b. Click on *Advertise With Us* and check out the *Products/Rates* for *Chat Room Banners.* Most people who use chat rooms have a common interest. Why would a company find this kind of advertising effective?

Building Your Business Skills

Select a product you're familiar with, and examine the strategies used to advertise and promote that product. Identify the media (print, television, radio, billboards, and so on) used to advertise the product. Consider the following:

- Where do the ads appear?
- Who is the target audience? Does the company attempt to appeal to a wide variety of people with differing ads?
- What creative theme or appeal is being used?
- Does the company make a large financial investment in advertising? For information

about advertising expenditures made by large companies, check the annual special issue of *Advertising Age,* "100 Leading National Advertisers."
- Is the company taking advantage of any emerging technologies for promotion, such as computer-interactive advertising?

In addition to your own observations, you might contact the manufacturer and interview a marketing representative regarding promotional strategies, or you might locate an article in a trade periodical that describes the promotional strategies for a specific product. Prepare a brief summary of your findings as directed by your instructor. Compare your findings with those of other students, and note any differences or similarities in the promotion of various products.

Keeping Current Using *The Wall Street Journal*

Choose an article from a recent issue of *The Wall Street Journal* that describes the advertising or promotion efforts of a particular company or trade association.

1. Who is the company or trade association targeting?
2. What specific marketing objectives is the organization trying to accomplish?
3. What role does advertising play in the promotion strategy? What other promotion techniques does the article mention? Are any of them unusual or noteworthy? Why?
4. Learn more about promotion techniques by visiting the Sales Marketing Network Web site <http://www.info-now.com/>, an information mall offering valuable sales and marketing information on demand. Click on *Promotion Marketing* and read about some promotional techniques.
   a. Does the company you researched in *The Wall Street Journal* article use any of these promotional techniques?
   b. What is point-of-purchase (POP) advertising, and why is it effective?
   c. Click on the *Core Overview: Definition & Statistics; Critical Issues; Books;* and so on. Why would an organization put together a Web site like this? How does it fund the site's costs? (Note: this Web site is free, but it requires initial site registration.)

Exploring the Best of the Web

Learn the Consumer Marketing Laws, page 447

Visit the Federal Trade Commission Web site <http://www.ftc.gov> and find out how this agency protects consumers.

1. What does the agency do and how does it serve the consumer?
2. Click on *Consumer Protection.* Read the *Advertising Policy Statements and Guidance on Deceptive Pricing.* Can you recall any instance of these rules being violated by a retail store you visited?
3. Go back to the *Consumer Protection* and click on *U.S. Consumer Gateway.* Click on *Technology.* Read the law on *Unsolicited Telephone Sales Calls.* What is the FCC's Do-Not-Call Rule?

Take an Idea Journey, page 455

Visit the Sales and Marketing Management Web site at <http://www.salesandmarketing.com>. Click on the *Article Index* and click on the *Table of Contents* (any year). Review the index of articles for several issues.

1. What are some of the recurring article themes for this magazine, and how might marketers benefit from this information?

2. Click on *Hot Links* and *Sales and Marketing.* Click on the hot link to *Idea Site for Business.* Review the *206 Marketing Ideas.* Review several of the idea groups. List five ideas that strike you as being innovative and ones that you might use as a future business owner. Compare your list to those of your fellow classmates.
3. Click on *Articles/Books Archive.* Review some of the articles. Many are good practical advice. List five valuable marketing tips highlighted in these articles. Share your list with those of your fellow classmates.

Make It a Banner Year, page 463

Go to Website Promoters Resource Center <http://www.wprc.com> and click on *Banner Advertising* to view two informative slide shows, click (1) *Beginner's Guide to Banner Advertising* and (2) *Effective Banner Design.* Now see how some of these principles are applied. View some effective banners at <http://wprc.com/pldb/all_banners.shtml>.

1. What are some of the advantages of banner advertising? What is the most common method used for banner ad pricing?
2. What are some effective tools in designing banners?
3. Practice your skills. Visit a related site, The Banner Generator at <http://www/coder.com/creations/banner>. Scroll down and *Make a Banner* of your own.

Part V: Mastering the Geography of Business ■ What's the Best Location for Your New Store?

You've probably heard the remark that the three most important things to look for when buying real estate are location, location, and location. The same basic concern applies to retail stores (although other factors certainly affect your chances of success). Where would you put a store in your city or town?

Assume you're going to start a new business (choose a computer store, restaurant, or service station). Outline the basic business you'd like to start, including target customers and the general goods or services you'll offer. Next, using a street map and the yellow pages, work through the following questions (if you're in a large city, you may want to restrict yourself to one particular section of the city):

1. Where do your target customers work, live, or travel regularly? For instance, if you've defined your business as an expensive restaurant, most of your customers are likely to come from business districts and affluent neighborhoods.
2. How will these people reach you? Can they walk? Will they have to drive? Will they use public transportation? Depending on the business you choose to start, you'll encounter different transportation needs. Think about how far people are willing to drive to eat at a special restaurant, shop at a computer store, or fill up at a service station.
3. Where do your competitors seem to be? You can get a good idea from the yellow pages. Identify the companies you'll compete with and mark their locations on your map. (Again, you may want to restrict the geographic scope of this project; you don't want to track down a thousand restaurants!) Narrow your location choices to two or three, and then visit each one if time permits. How does each area look and feel with respect to the type of business you want to start?
4. How easy will it be for others to get to your new business location? Check it out by logging on to MapBlast at <http://www.mapblast.com>. Enter the location for your desired business (as much information as you have) and generate the map. Now get *Driving Directions* from some main location points by entering their respective street locations and then clicking on *Drive.* Repeat for different locations. How easy will it be for customers to find you? Is the fast route different from the easy route? Read the *FAQs* and find out *What can I do with my map?* How do tools like these help with the marketing of your business?

Answers to "Is It True?"

Page 448. True.

Page 458. False. A recent survey of sports advertisers and agency executives named Tiger Woods the most appealing athlete endorser in sports, edging out basketball superstar Michael Jordan.

Page 464 True.

■ PART VI

Managing Information Systems and Accounting

CHAPTER 16

COMPUTERS AND INFORMATION TECHNOLOGY

OBJECTIVES

After studying this chapter, you will be able to

1. Distinguish between data and information and explain the characteristics of useful information
2. Identify the major ways companies use information systems
3. List seven common business computer applications
4. Describe the four classes of computers
5. Identify the major components of a computer system
6. Describe the primary components of computer networks
7. Explain the business uses of the Internet
8. Discuss the drawbacks to business computing

On the Job On the Job

ON THE JOB: FACING BUSINESS CHALLENGES AT AMERICAN EXPRESS

Information Has Its Privileges

Day after day, week after week, more than 30 million people around the world tell Harvey Golub all about themselves by the purchases they make on their American Express cards: what they eat, where they travel, when they are likely to buy luxuries, how busy their lifestyle is, and a host of other facts. That's the problem. They are giving him facts—tons of them. In a hotly competitive market, he couldn't afford to lose customer loyalty because of the inefficient management of information.

American Express used to have a microfiche system for storing images of transaction receipts, but processing the millions of pieces of paper for their return to cardholders was cumbersome and caused inaccuracies. Hundreds of employees were required to film receipts for storage, enter charge amounts into a mainframe computer for billing, sort receipts and match them with others in the same accounts, process billing statements, and insert the receipts and their corresponding statements into envelopes for mailing. Mistakes were made, and time was wasted. Some receipts were mangled. Account numbers were misread. Receipts were inserted into the wrong envelopes. Nearly 200 people were employed just to resolve errors that had been made during the initial processing—and those employees also had to shuffle piles of paper. Answering a cardholder's query about a single transaction could take hours while employees searched through long cartridges of film for a record of the appropriate receipt.

The cost of doing business this way was more than excess wages and low productivity. American Express did not grant credit for partial or late payment, so a "float" of cash had to be maintained to pay merchants for purchases while awaiting payment from cardholders. The longer it took to process receipts and to bill customers, the longer it took for American Express to get paid, which forced the company to keep more money in its float.

Even if the paper mountain could be flattened with a more efficient system, that would still leave the question of how to manage all those data describing the wants and behaviors of American Express cardholders. Golub's goal was to make American Express into a service-industry giant by offering a wide variety of services, from charge cards to financial planning to travel to entertainment. Those 30 million customers were telling Golub a lot about themselves, and he needed to use their data to gain a competitive advantage, build customer loyalty, and enter new markets. How could Golub get a grip on the mountain of paper? How could he transform the data into useful business information?[1]

Information and Computers in Today's Business Environment

We live in the Information Age; at no other time have data been so easily accessible and has information been so valuable. Harvey Golub and his management team at American Express recognize this. Like many managers, they are working hard to develop strategies for capturing and managing the data that flows through their company and for transforming the data into useful information. In business today, computer systems play a key role in such strategies. Computers and computer networks enable organizations to track, store, process, retrieve, and share information that can be leveraged to achieve competitive advantages. For example, Nike's ability to gather, manage, and utilize information about the various segments of the athletic shoe market has helped the company transform its sneakers into high-priced fashion goods.[2]

As computers become a more integral part of the business world, they change the way companies complete business transactions. In addition, computers create new business opportunities, new industries, and new companies. For instance, the development of the Internet has led to the emergence and rapid growth of companies like Netscape and America Online, as well as to the development of new positions such as *Webmaster*—someone who maintains a site on the Internet's World Wide Web. Computer technology can also increase competition. For example, many small companies can now compete with large companies on a global scale through strategic use of computer and communications technologies. This chapter explores in depth the roles that information and computers play in the workplace.

The Role of Information in Business

data
Recorded facts and statistics; data need to be converted to information before they can help people solve business problems

database
Collection of related data that can be cross-referenced in order to extract information

Every aspect of a business operation depends on the successful collection, storage, and application of information (see Exhibit 16.1). Information is a collection of **data**—recorded facts and statistics—that are relevant to a particular decision or problem. For example, the accounting department may have price and sales data for hundreds of different products. However, these data are not information until they are used to solve a problem, answer a question, or make a decision. When managers want to know the average monthly sales of products X, Y, and Z, they must cross-reference the data. This is often done by *querying* (asking questions of) a **database,** a collection of data that is usually stored in a computerized format. The answer managers receive constitutes information that they may use in developing strategies or making decisions (see Exhibit 16.2).

Information Applications Businesses both large and small rely on quality information for just about everything they do. Here's a quick overview of the many ways companies use information:[3]

- *Increasing organizational efficiency.* Companies from Wal-Mart to Reebok have made themselves more efficient through the smart use of information. For example, Dell Computer used information about its production requirements and its supplier capabilities to significantly reduce inventory. The company now keeps only 12 days of inventory on hand, which enables it to respond quickly to shifts in customer demand and supplier price changes.[4]
- *Staying ahead of competitors.* From gathering data on consumer trends to snooping out potential takeover targets, companies can use information to boost their competitive positions.
- *Finding new customers—and keeping current customers.* To find new customers, companies can use a variety of information sources, from newspaper stories to telephone directories. Once they have those customers in the fold, firms use information about customer needs and satisfaction levels to keep them coming back

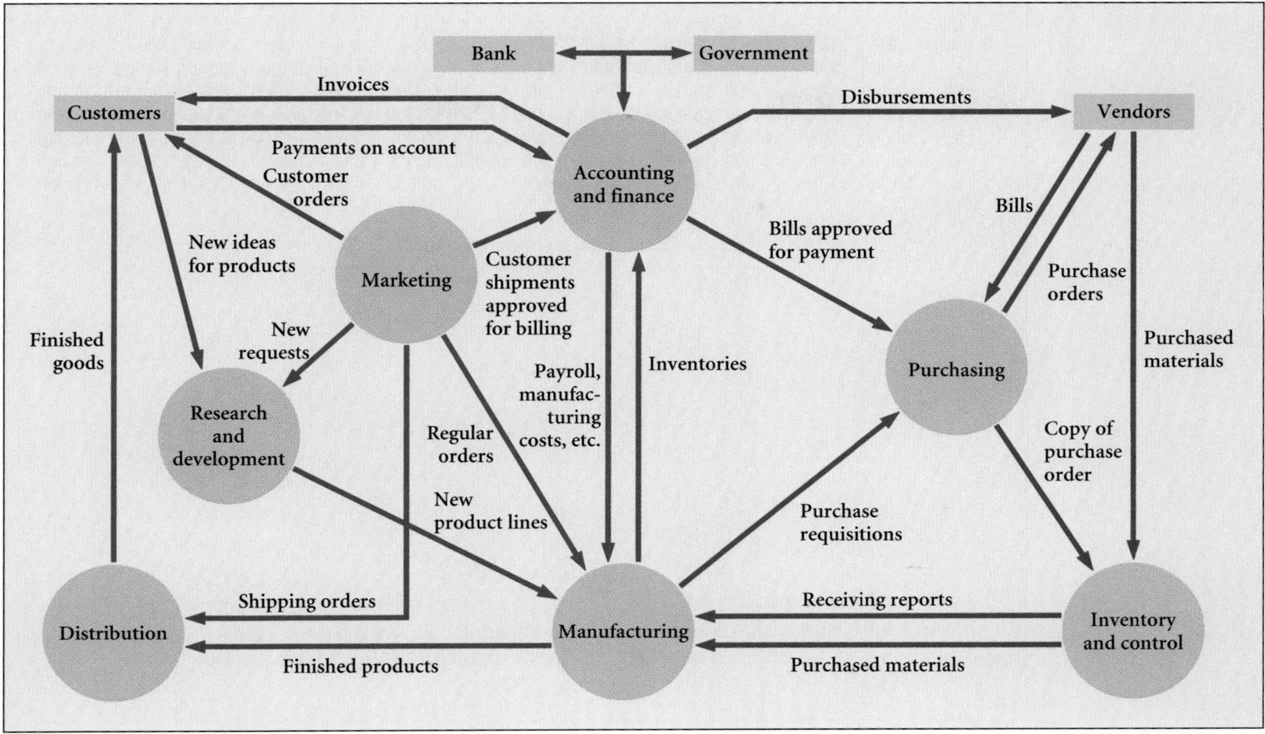

EXHIBIT 16.1

Information Flow in a Typical Manufacturing Company

Many kinds of manipulations and transfers of information support daily operations and decision making in a manufacturing company.

for more. For example, American Express analyzes purchasing patterns to identify new products that might interest customers.

- *Planning, organizing, leading, and controlling the organization.* Information is at the core of the management process, whether it's charting a new strategy, restructuring an organization, analyzing employee performance to determine salaries, or using process feedback to control a product line.

Information Management Every organization needs a system for collecting and managing data and information. In some companies, each department handles this task separately. But in the most progressive companies, departments integrate their systems to share any information that will help employees do their jobs better, build competitive advantages, and increase revenue. Consider U.S. Office Equipment. This distributor of photocopiers provides its sales representatives with even its most sensitive internal data. According to CEO Mark Challenger, "When all information is available—not just what the company wants them to have—[the sales reps] make much more intelligent decisions."[5]

Another example is Ernst & Young. The firm's thousands of consultants acquire vast amounts of knowledge in the course of their work with clients. Much of this knowledge can be used by other consultants within the company to solve problems and deliver more value to clients. To facilitate the sharing of this information, all Ernst & Young consultants receive a laptop computer and software that enables them to access company databases via the Internet from wherever they are working. Consultants can also access client information, industry background information, and templates for presentations. This constant sharing of information increases the productivity of Ernst & Young consultants as well as the quality of their work.[6]

Is It True?

Information management in the health-care industry is relatively inexpensive compared to the costs of treatment and medicine.

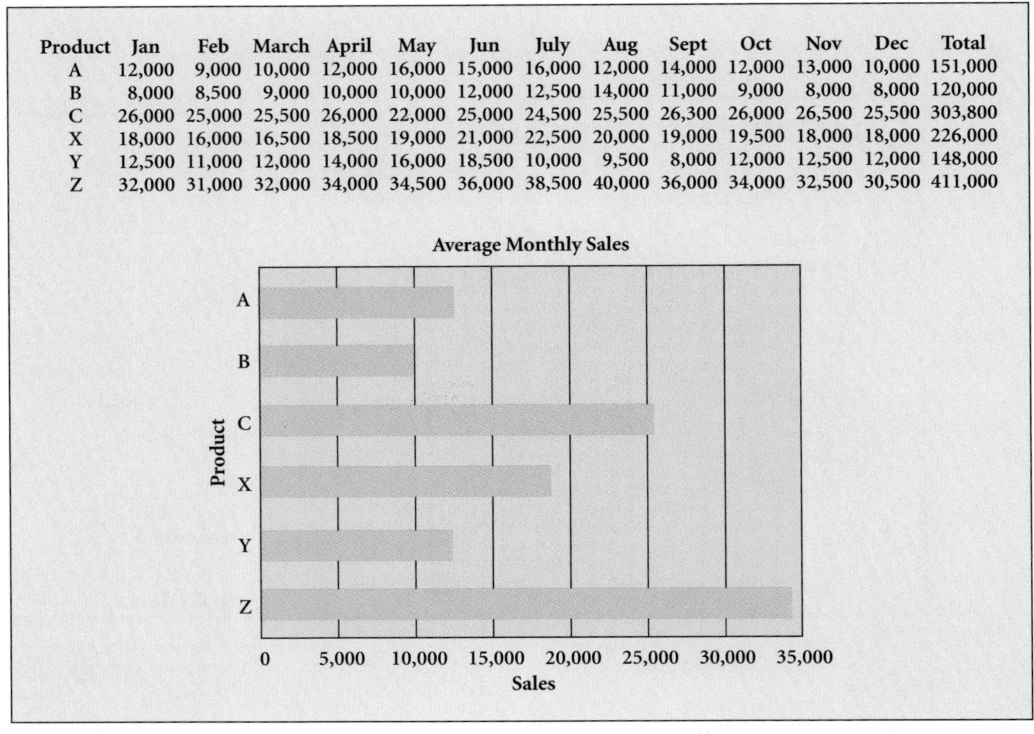

Product	Jan	Feb	March	April	May	Jun	July	Aug	Sept	Oct	Nov	Dec	Total
A	12,000	9,000	10,000	12,000	16,000	15,000	16,000	12,000	14,000	12,000	13,000	10,000	151,000
B	8,000	8,500	9,000	10,000	10,000	12,000	12,500	14,000	11,000	9,000	8,000	8,000	120,000
C	26,000	25,000	25,500	26,000	22,000	25,000	24,500	25,500	26,300	26,000	26,500	25,500	303,800
X	18,000	16,000	16,500	18,500	19,000	21,000	22,500	20,000	19,000	19,500	18,000	18,000	226,000
Y	12,500	11,000	12,000	14,000	16,000	18,500	10,000	9,500	8,000	12,000	12,500	12,000	148,000
Z	32,000	31,000	32,000	34,000	34,500	36,000	38,500	40,000	36,000	34,000	32,500	30,500	411,000

EXHIBIT 16.2

Data versus Information

The table represents sales data for a small company's six products. In this form, the data are just statistics that answer no particular question and solve no particular problem. Therefore, they are not considered information. When a manager queries the database to identify the average monthly sales for each product, she is asking for specific information. The sales data are used to generate the graph that illustrates the information she needs.

Of course, information is useful only in the hands of people who can act on it. A sales person doesn't need to know the salaries of other employees, and an administrative assistant in human resources typically doesn't benefit from seeing inventory control data. Therefore, a key element of information management systems is the ability to *filter* information: making sure that the *right information* reaches the *right people* at the *right time* in the *right form.*[7] Moreover, for information to be useful, it must be accurate, timely, complete, relevant, and concise.[8] Of course, information in the real world is rarely perfect, and managers must often make do with whatever information they can get. However, the closer information comes to meeting these five criteria, the more it will improve the management process.

chief information officer (CIO)
Top corporate executive with responsibility for managing information and information systems

Effective information management is of such strategic importance in business today that many companies now have a top-level executive, sometimes called the **chief information officer (CIO),** to handle the task. "More companies are seeing the value of information technology and how it can complement the business," says Kevin Keathley, CIO of telecommunications firm One Call Communications. "It's hard to imagine not having somebody in the role to facilitate that."[9]

The Role of Computer Systems in Business

As you can see, organizations depend on information to help them accomplish their goals. Imagine how much harder it would be for American Express to offer new services without knowing what customers want. Think of how much longer it would take Ernst & Young to provide solutions to its clients if employees were not able to share their knowledge easily. But how do organizations design and develop effective systems to manage information? First they must carefully plan what type of information to track and how it will be used, and then they must find the right computer hardware and software to collect, store, and process the information. The systems they use to meet those needs generally fall into two major categories: operations information systems and management information systems.[10] As Exhibit 16.3 illustrates, each category typically corresponds to business operations at specific levels of the organization.

Operations Information Systems Operations information systems include transaction processing systems, process and production control systems, and office automation systems. These systems typically support daily operations and decision making for lower-level managers and supervisors.

Much of the daily flow of data into and out of the typical business organization is handled by a **transaction processing system (TPS),** which takes care of customer orders, billing, employee payroll, inventory changes, and other essential transactions. For example, American Express uses TPSs to accept charges and to bill cardholders. Another example is the computer that an airline representative uses to assign you a seat on your flight. These TPSs interact with human beings. However, sometimes a TPS interacts directly with another computer system, as when a drugstore's computer senses the need for more products and transmits orders to a drug wholesaler's computers via electronic data interchange (EDI).

Operations information systems are also used to make routine decisions that control operational processes. **Process control systems** monitor conditions such as temperature or pressure change in physical processes. These systems use special sensing devices that take measurements, enabling a computer to make any necessary adjustments to the process.[11]

Production control systems are used to manage the production of goods and services by controlling production lines, robots, and other machinery and equipment. Chapter 8 discusses how computer-aided manufacturing can increase efficiency and improve

transaction processing system (TPS)
Computerized information system that processes the daily flow of customer, supplier, and employee transactions, including inventory, sales, and payroll records

process control system
Computer system that uses special sensing devices to monitor conditions in a physical process and makes necessary adjustments to the process

production control systems
Computer systems that manage production by controlling production lines, robots, and other machinery and equipment

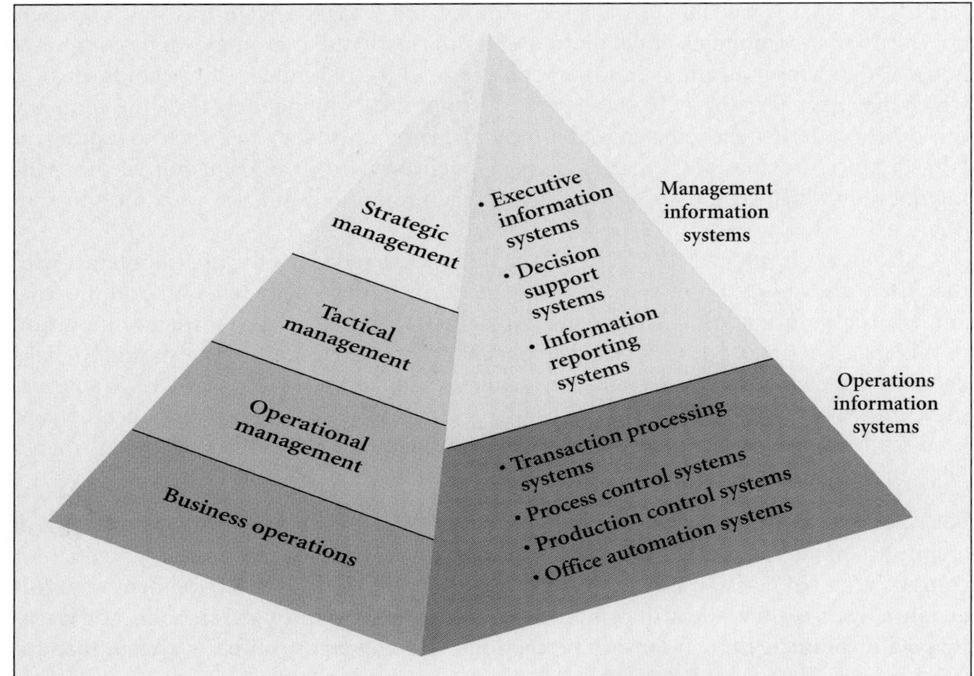

EXHIBIT 16.3

Information Systems and Organizational Levels

Managers and employees at the various levels of an organization rely on different types of information systems to help them accomplish their goals.

quality by automating production processes. In some cases, manufacturing software is linked with design software to automate the entire design-and-production cycle. For instance, an engineer designing a new component for a car engine can electronically transfer the design to the production department, which will then control a milling machine that automatically carves the part from a block of steel. This process involves the use of a CAD/CAM system.

office automation systems (OAS)
Computer systems that assist with the tasks that people in a typical business office face regularly, such as drawing graphs or processing documents

Office automation systems (OAS) include any type of operations information system that helps you execute typical office tasks. Whether the job is producing a report or calculating next year's budget, an OAS allows you to complete the task more efficiently by converting the process into an electronic format. Office automation systems range from a single personal computer with word-processing software to networks of computers that allow people to send e-mail and share work among computers.

management information system (MIS)
Computer system that supplies information to assist in managerial decision making

decision support system (DSS)
Information system that uses decision models, specialized databases, and artificial intelligence to assist managers in solving highly unstructured and nonroutine problems

data warehousing
Building an organized central database out of files and databases gathered from different functional areas, such as marketing, operations, and accounting

data mining
Sifting through huge amounts of data to identify what is valuable to a specific question or problem

Management Information Systems A **management information system (MIS)** is a computer-based system that provides managers with information and support for making effective decisions. An MIS usually supplies reports and statistics, such as monthly sales figures, employee records, and factory production schedules. In doing so, it often takes data from a transaction processing system and transforms them into useful information. In cases involving routine decision making—such as how many microchips to order to build a certain number of cellular phones—an MIS can go beyond simple report generation and provide answers to management questions.

Whereas a management information system provides structured, routine information for managerial decision making, a **decision support system (DSS)** assists managers in solving highly unstructured and nonroutine problems with the use of decision models, specialized databases, and even *artificial intelligence.* Through a process known as **data warehousing,** a DSS moves data from a variety of function-based files and databases—such as marketing, operations, and accounting—into a well-organized, central database. Managers from the different functional areas can then make complex queries that would not have been possible if the data had been spread throughout the organization.[12] In a process known as **data mining,** computer software sifts through huge amounts of data, identifying what is valuable to the specific query and what is not. In this way, managers are able to turn mountains of data into useful information. For example, in its data warehouse MCI Communications has marketing records on 140 million households, each of which may have as many as 10,000 separate attributes. By mining these data, the company can detect patterns that indicate which customers are most likely to switch to a different long-distance provider. MCI marketing personnel can use this information when deciding not only which customers to target for special promotions but also what incentives to offer current customers.[13]

Compared with an MIS, a DSS is more interactive (allowing the user to interact with the system instead of simply receiving information), and it usually relies on both internal and external information.[14] Group decision support systems are also a recent innovation in this area. They allow teams of people to work on problems simultaneously and to make decisions based on input from all team members. Similar in concept to a DSS is an **executive information system (EIS),** which helps executives make the necessary decisions to keep the organization moving forward. An EIS usually has a more strategic focus than a DSS, and it is used in the top ranks of the organization.

executive information system (EIS)
Similar to a decision support system, but customized to the strategic needs of executives

Other Business Computer Systems Business can also use computers to automate the work of architects, engineers, and other technical professionals. Perhaps the greatest potential for computers to aid decision making and problem solving lies in the development of **artificial intelligence**—the ability of computers to solve problems through reasoning and learning and to simulate human sensory perceptions.[15] One type of computer system that can

artificial intelligence
Ability of computers to reason, to learn, and to simulate human sensory perceptions

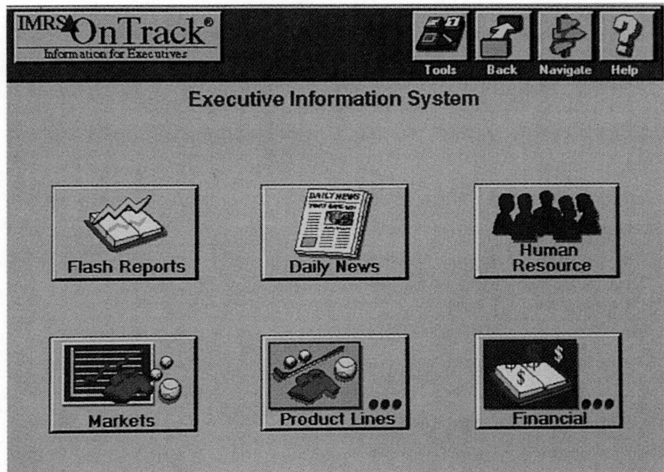

Executive information systems give top managers quick access to the information they need for decision making.

simulate human reasoning by responding to questions, asking for more information, and making recommendations is the **expert system.**[16] As its name implies, an expert system essentially takes the place of a human expert by helping less knowledgeable individuals make critical decisions. For instance, the troubleshooting methods used by an experienced auto mechanic could be programmed into an expert system. A beginning mechanic could describe a sick engine's symptoms to the system, which would then apply the expert mechanic's facts and rules to suggest which troubleshooting methods might reveal the cause of the problem. American Express uses an expert system to help with credit-card authorizations, a risky and time-consuming part of the credit-card business.

expert system
Computer system that simulates the thought processes of a human expert who is adept at solving particular problems

Consult an Expert

BEST OF THE WEB

By now you are aware of the huge number of federal laws with which businesses must comply. Making sure that they abide by all these laws can be a difficult task for managers, especially in small businesses where the cost of compliance is often higher than it is in large companies. However, through the use of an online expert system, the U.S. Department of Labor has made it easier for both employers and employees to understand their rights and obligations under labor laws such as the Family Medical Leave Act. The Employment Laws Assistance for Workers and Small Businesses (elaws) system asks a series of questions about the user's company. It then provides specific information about how the laws affect anyone working for that company. Because it provides easy access to free information, this expert system can save small businesses both time and money.
http://www.dol.gov

Several software companies have taken expert systems a step further by giving them the ability to suggest innovative solutions for problem solving. Drawing on their preprogrammed knowledge of inventive principles, physics, chemistry, and geometry, such systems have come up with solutions to problems that eventually lead to new product inventions. One example is a flash used in pocket cameras to eliminate "red eyes."[17]

A second advance in artificial intelligence to make its way into business is the **speech-recognition system.** Using computer software, a generic vocabulary database, and a

speech-recognition system
Computer system that recognizes human speech, enabling users to enter data and give commands vocally

microphone, speech-recognition systems enable the user to interact with the computer verbally. Today the average microcomputer can accept spoken words at speeds of up to 125 words per minute. Artificial intelligence techniques enable the computer to learn the user's speech patterns and update its vocabulary database continually. In this way, the system evolves, becoming more intelligent, versatile, and easy to use. Although most systems are still limited to a single user, some systems are able to recognize words spoken by anyone. Business uses for this technology include navigation (which uses voice commands in place of a mouse to open files, launch programs, and move around in document) and dictation (which enables the user to enter data verbally rather than through the keyboard).[18]

The Applications of Business Computing

Computers got their start in business doing accounting and financial tasks, and these operations remain a fundamental business application. In fact, nearly all the activities discussed in the next three chapters—accounting, banking and financial management, and securities markets—can be managed faster and more effectively with computers. In addition, computer applications in today's business world are almost limitless. Companies use them to set goals, hire employees, order supplies, manage inventory, sell products, store data, communicate with employees, and perform countless other tasks. Some of the most common applications are word processing, spreadsheets, desktop publishing, database management, business graphics, communications, and Internet publishing. The term *application* refers both to an actual task, such as preparing reports and memos, and to the *software* that is used to complete the task.

Word Processing Word processing is a fundamental business application of computers. Popular programs like Microsoft Word, WordPerfect, and MacWrite enable users to type, store, edit, and print documents for almost any purpose. Originally conceived of as an enhanced alternative to the typewriter, today's word processors go far beyond anything imaginable on a typewriter. For example, you can change the size and type of font in your document with just a few clicks of the mouse. If you perform the same tasks on a regular basis, such as preparing a weekly report or simply using repetitive keystrokes, you can create a *macro*—your own program within the word-processing software that will handle the task automatically. Another function called a *mail merge* can insert names into a generic form letter, giving the appearance that the letter is personalized. You've probably received promotional mailings that used this function. Word processors can also check your spelling, syntax, and sentence structure. However, one possible drawback to such advanced capabilities is that they may cause users to rely too much on the program's writing skills and not enough on their own. For example, a writer may use the word *their* when *there* was intended. A spelling checker program will not point out the problem because it recognizes both words.

spreadsheet
Program that organizes and manipulates data in a row-column matrix

Spreadsheets A **spreadsheet** is a program designed to let users organize and manipulate data in a row-column matrix (see Exhibit 16.4A). The intersection of each row-and-column pair is called a *cell,* and every cell can contain a number, a mathematical formula, or text used as a label. Among the spreadsheet's biggest strengths is the ability to quickly update masses of calculations when conditions change. For instance, if you have a spreadsheet that calculates profit sharing for your employees, and the profit-sharing percentage changes, you don't have to go through each employee's record and change the number by hand. You simply update the percentage in one place, and the spreadsheet will update all of the records for you (assuming you've programmed it to do so). Although spreadsheets were originally designed to replace the ledger books of accountants, businesspeople now use them to solve a wide variety of problems, ranging from statistical analysis to simulation models used in decision support systems.

1	Employee Name	Wage	Reg. Hours	OT Hours	Reg. Pay	OT Pay	Total Pay
2	Paula Chang	$12.00	40	6	$ 480.00	$ 108.00	$ 588.00
3	Lewis Bond	$10.50	32	5	$ 336.00	$ 78.75	$ 414.75
4	Mary Wright	$10.50	32	0	$ 336.00	$ -	$ 336.00
5	Wil Marquette	$11.75	40	2	$ 470.00	$ 35.25	$ 505.25
6	Tia Miller	$11.25	36	8	$ 404.00	$ 135.00	$ 540.00
7	Liz Reed	$10.85	40	0	$ 434.00	$ -	$ 434.00

EXHIBIT 16.4A

Sample Spreadsheet Analysis

Setting up a spreadsheet by hand takes time—especially to do the calculations. A spreadsheet program prepares the computer to accept values in preestablished spreadsheet cells. Paula Chang's hourly wage, for example, is entered in the cell where the "Paula Chang" row intersects the "Wage" column. A spreadsheet program also performs basic mathematical operations, given the proper instructions. To compute an employee's regular pay, the computer must multiply that employee's wage by his or her regular hours worked.

Desktop Publishing **Desktop publishing (DTP)** software goes a step beyond typical word processors by allowing designers to lay out printer-ready pages that incorporate artwork, photos, and a large variety of typographic elements. Together with scanners and other specialized input devices, publishing programs let businesspeople create sophisticated documents on their computers in a fraction of the time it once took. Rather than paying outside specialists to design and typeset marketing and advertising materials, many companies now use desktop publishing software to produce these items in-house. Flyers, brochures, user manuals, annual reports, and newsletters are just a few of the documents that can be produced in camera-ready formats that go directly to the print shop. Moreover, direct-to-press digital printers now make it possible to skip the print shop altogether. Although they aren't recommended for high-end work, they can save time and money in the printing of less important documents. However, it is important to keep in mind that using desktop publishing software and in-house printing devices does not instantly make one an expert designer or printer. Often the development of business materials is best left to professionals with the talent, training, and experience to do the job right.

desktop publishing (DTP) Ability to prepare documents using computerized typesetting and graphics-processing capabilities

Database Management As American Express's Harvey Golub knows, businesses often have massive amounts of data on their hands. This situation represents two important challenges: first, how to store all that information in a way that is safe yet accessible, and second, how to transform the data from a database into useful information as it is needed. The solution is **database management,** an application that uses software to create, store, maintain, rearrange, and retrieve the contents of databases.[19]

database management Creating, storing, maintaining, rearranging, and retrieving the contents of databases

Almost anywhere you find a sizable amount of data in electronic format, you'll find a database management program at work. Such programs help users produce useful information through its ability to look at data from various perspectives. Say that your business class of 100 students has quizzes every week, and that a helpful assistant logs all the quiz results into the computer every week, along with some basic data about each student. If your instructor wants to know how the class did on the last quiz, he or she can query the database for a printout of all 100 scores or for a simple average of the scores. To show how the class has done throughout the course, the instructor can mine the data to get a list of the weekly averages since the course began. The same can be done for a single student. If enough data were in the database, the instructor could look only at the scores of students who've taken courses in business before or of those students who are majoring in journalism. Alternatively, if the scores on one quiz were unexpectedly low, the instructor could compare your class's performance on that quiz with that of previous classes to see whether the quiz was too difficult. Even in this simple example, you can see that database management can provide a great deal of information from a single stack of data.

Business Graphics Businesspeople need to produce quite a variety of graphic materials including charts, graphs, tables, and diagrams. Together with specialized output devices such as plotters and color printers, business graphics software can produce overhead transparencies, 35 mm slides, posters, and signs. The graphic images created with these software packages can also be imported into publishing and word-processing programs for incorporation into documents and presentations.

In addition to software packages designed specifically for graphics applications, word-processing, spreadsheet, and desktop publishing software typically have some limited graphics capabilities built into them. This enables the user to create graphic elements without the use of a separate program. Exhibit 16.4B depicts two ways to graphically display data entered on a Microsoft Excel spreadsheet.

Communications Today computers play a central role in business communications. A computer can exchange information with other computers through communications software, which opens up an entirely new spectrum of business capabilities: *electronic mail,* or *e-mail,* enables users to transmit written messages in electronic format between computers; *bulletin board systems (BBS)* and *newsgroups* are electronic versions of traditional bulletin boards that allow users to exchange ideas, news, and other information; file transfer

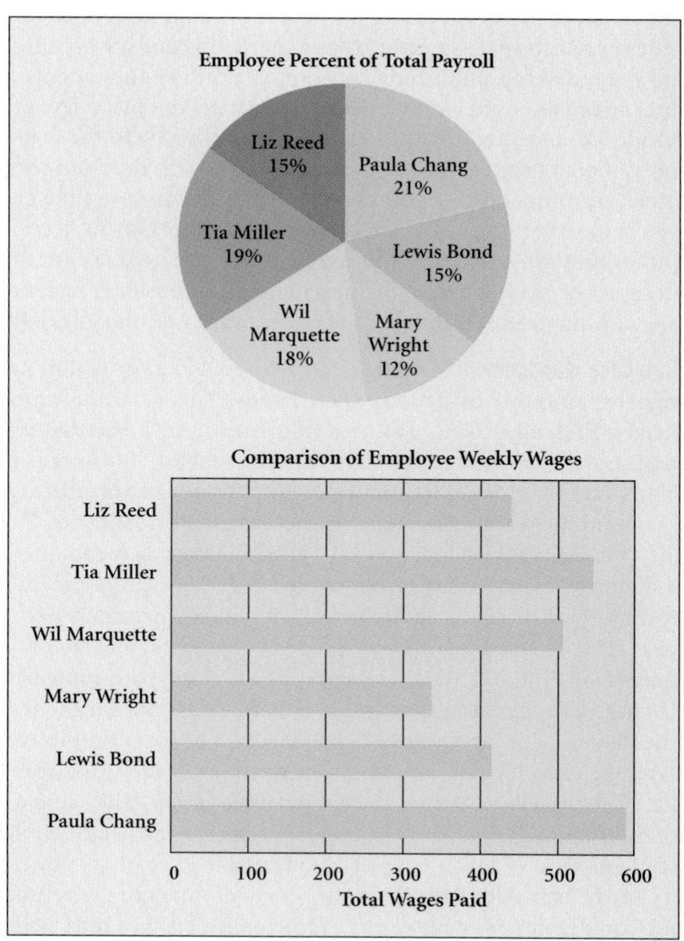

EXHIBIT 16.4B

The data entered on the payroll spreadsheet in Exhibit 16.4A can be presented graphically using Excel's built-in graphics function.

software enables the transfer of digital files—including data, programs, text, images, sounds, and videos—from one computer to another; and EDI systems permit computers to communicate with each other to handle transactions that used to require human intervention.[20] Computers can also send and receive faxes as easily as a fax machine if they have the right software and hardware. Furthermore, computers enable people in different locations to communicate face-to-face through video conferencing.

Communications software also gives business users access to an eye-popping array of business information services. Through the Internet, businesspeople can access a vast and growing variety of information in a fraction of the time it used to take. One example is *StatUSA,* a service of the U.S. Department of Commerce that provides international trade statistics and a variety of information ranging from trade leads to market research reports. Another is *The Wall Street Journal Interactive Edition,* an electronic version of the daily business newspaper that can deliver stock quotes, international news reports, and company information right to the user's desktop.

Internet Publishing A recent survey of over 3,400 executives by the American Management Association found that 60 percent of the companies represented in the study have home pages on the Internet. That number is expected to grow to over 80 percent by 2002.[21] Some companies pay many thousands of dollars to have pages designed and maintained by specialists. However, a variety of programs from companies like Corel, Adobe, and Microsoft now make it easy for someone with average computer skills to create a unique Web site. These programs use **hypertext markup language (HTML)** to format documents that can incorporate sound, graphics, and video with text. HTML documents are also able to *hyperlink* words, graphics, and images to other documents and images, enabling the reader to jump from document to document with a click of the mouse. These documents are then published on the World Wide Web or on a companywide intranet. At Silicon Graphics, almost all of the 11,000 employees publish their own Web pages on the company's intranet for the purpose of sharing vital information with each other.[22]

hypertext markup language (HTML)
An Internet publishing format that incorporates sound, graphics, and video with document text; HTML can also hyperlink documents together, making it easy for users to jump from one document to another

INFORMATION PROCESSING TECHNOLOGY

Now that you have an idea of the scope of computers in business, it's time to take a closer look at computers themselves. Today's computers can be grouped into four classes: mainframes, microcomputers, workstations, and supercomputers. Keep in mind that lines

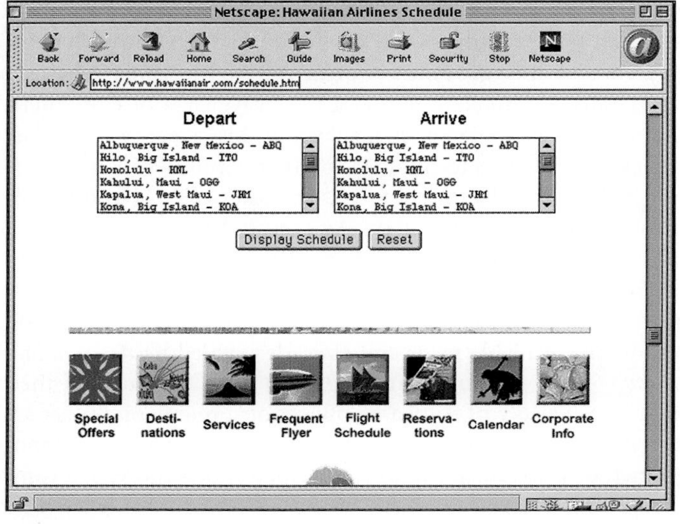

Hawaiian Airlines is one of many commercial airlines that now offer passenger reservations over the Internet. Not only is this a more convenient option for many customers, but it also reduces the number of reservations agents needed and increases the company's options for marketing its travel-related services.

between the various classes aren't always clear; technology continues to advance, and the computers in one class can start to behave like their higher-performing cousins in the next category.

Mainframe Computers

mainframe computer
A large and powerful computer, capable of storing and processing vast amounts of data

Until the late 1970s and early 1980s, the most common image of a computer was the **mainframe computer,** a large and powerful system capable of handling vast amounts of data. Those refrigerator-sized units that you've seen whirring away in computer rooms and on movie sets are mainframes. Mainframes are used to handle a variety of transaction processing tasks. They are especially useful when large-scale number crunching is involved, as with finance and accounting activities. Other common uses include controlling a manufacturing process in a factory, managing a company's payroll, and maintaining very large databases. Today's major mainframe manufacturers include IBM, Control Data, Hitachi, Siemens, Unisys, and Amdahl.[23]

Is It True?

The New York Stock Exchange is supported by 450 refrigerator-sized computers connected by 200 miles of fiber optic cable and costing more than $2 billion.

The traditional way for users to gain access to mainframe computing power is through *dumb terminals,* devices that look like desktop computers but that don't have the processing power to operate on their own. However, modern computer networks increasingly use stand-alone microcomputers to connect with mainframes.

As you'll read later in the chapter, many mainframes are being replaced by *client-server systems* composed of groups of smaller computers. However, an estimated 70 to 80 percent of the world's corporate data are still stored on mainframes. Moreover, organizations like Wells Fargo, J. C. Penney, Nationwide Insurance, the U.S. Food and Drug Administration, and Princeton University are discovering that their mainframe computers make excellent "Web servers." This means that the companies are able to use their existing mainframes to support the Internet applications that are becoming an increasingly important part of their business. These applications include sharing documents, sending and receiving e-mail, taking customer orders, and processing transactions.[24]

minicomputers
Smaller, less powerful, and less expensive mainframes; often referred to as midsize computers

Minicomputers are scaled-down versions of mainframes. They are smaller and more affordable, but they are also less powerful. The distinction between mainframes and minicomputers has become blurred in recent years to the point where the term *minicomputer* is seldom used anymore. Instead, smaller mainframes are commonly referred to as *midsize* or *midrange computers.*[25]

Microcomputers

microcomputer
Smallest and least expensive class of computers; often generally referred to as a personal computer

In the late 1960s, a mainframe computer costing over $1.5 million had less power than today's affordable microcomputers.[26] A **microcomputer,** often referred to generically as a *personal computer* or *PC,* represents the smallest and least-expensive class of computers. Apple and IBM were the first companies to make a big splash in this category in the late 1970s. Unlike Apple, IBM quickly licensed its technology to other computer manufacturers. The ensuing competition among manufacturers forced the price of IBM-compatible computers down, making them attractive to many users. As a result, IBM-compatible PCs are now the standard in most homes and offices, and Apple has only about a 5 percent share of the microcomputer market.[27]

Unlike large mainframes, a microcomputer is built around a single microprocessor. Computers in this category are now available in several sizes, designated by *desktop, laptop, notebook,* and even *palmtop* (for computers that fit in your hand). Because of their versatility, made possible by a huge variety of software applications, microcomputers are now common in homes as well as in both large and small businesses. The leading manufacturers of microcomputers include Compaq, Dell, IBM, and Apple, but hundreds of companies are fighting for a share of this market.

Workstations

The **workstation** marries the speed of midsize computers with the desktop convenience of microcomputers. Workstations are used primarily by designers, engineers, scientists, and others who need fast computing and powerful graphics capabilities to solve mathematically challenging problems. Workstations are just as "personal" as microcomputers, in that they are typically used by a single person. They also resemble microcomputers in appearance. However, workstations typically have large-screen, high-resolution (high-clarity) monitors, as well as devices that enable the user to create precision drawings and perform other specialized functions.

workstation
Class of computers with the basic size and shape of microcomputers but with the speed of traditional midsize computers; often used for design, engineering, and scientific applications

A typical application in this segment is the *computer-aided design (CAD)* function already discussed. An engineer for Rockwell International might use a CAD system on a workstation to design a part for the space shuttle. The system could perform such tasks as predicting responses to stress and calculating the amount of steel required to make the part. Three of the leading manufacturers of workstations are Sun Microsystems, Hewlett-Packard, and Digital Equipment Corporation (DEC).

Supercomputers

At about the same time that microcomputers were beginning to put computing capabilities into the hands of individual computer users, the engineering and scientific communities were growing increasingly frustrated with the limited ability of mainframes to process complicated mathematical models. Although mainframes were capable of processing huge amounts of data quickly, they were limited in the complexity of calculations they could perform. A scientific calculation might tie up a university's mainframe for days at a time. Therefore, computer designers began to develop what are now known as **supercomputers.**[28]

supercomputers
Computers with the highest level of performance, often boasting speeds greater than a trillion calculations per second

Supercomputers represent the leading edge in computer performance, and they are capable of handling the most complex processing tasks with speeds in excess of one trillion calculations per second. Seismic analysis, weather forecasting, complex engineering modeling, and genetic research are among the common uses of supercomputers. Virtual reality design simulators are another application. For instance, Caterpillar designs new tractors and earth movers using virtual reality that lets engineers see how the machines will look and operate before they ever build physical prototypes.[29] Still another application is the design of advanced graphics used to create the hair-raising special effects seen in Hollywood movies like *Titanic* and *Jurassic Park.*[30] As you might expect, only a handful of companies are in this arena; Silicon Graphics, which recently purchased industry leader Cray Research, has 50 percent of the supercomputer market.[31]

Special effects experts used the advanced graphics capabilities of supercomputers to bring dinosaurs back from extinction in *The Lost World.*

Computer Components

As you can see, an organization has many choices when selecting a computer system to manage its information and work processes. The first step in understanding what makes all these computers tick is distinguishing hardware from software. **Hardware** represents the tangible equipment used in a computer system, such as disk drives, keyboards, modems, and *integrated circuits* (small pieces of silicon containing thousands of transistors and electronic circuits). **Software** encompasses the programmed instructions, or applications, that direct the activity of the hardware.

hardware
Physical components of a computer system, including integrated circuits, keyboards, and disk drives

software
Programmed instructions that drive the activity of computer hardware

Hardware Whether it's a palmtop computer keeping track of your appointment schedule or a supercomputer modeling the structure of a DNA molecule, every computer is made up of a basic set of hardware components. Of course, the hardware in a supercomputer differs greatly from the hardware in a hand-held unit, but the concepts are similar. Hardware can be divided into four basic groups: input devices, the central processing unit, output devices, and storage (see Exhibit 16.5).

INPUT DEVICES Before it can perform any calculations, a computer needs data. These data can be entered through a keyboard, a mouse, a computerized pen, a microphone (for speech-recognition systems), or an optical scanner. With the growth of the Internet and *multimedia* computer applications, video cameras and digital cameras have also become increasingly important input devices.

central processing unit (CPU)
Core of the computer, performing the three basic functions of arithmetic (addition, etc.), logic (comparing numbers), and control/communication (managing the computer)

CENTRAL PROCESSING UNIT A computer's calculations are made in the **central processing unit (CPU),** which interprets and executes program instructions. The CPU performs the three basic functions of arithmetic, logic, and control/communication.[32] Actually, computer arithmetic is nothing more than addition; subtraction is performed through negative addition, multiplication is repeated addition, and division is repeated negative addition.[33] Computer logic is also a simple operation, nothing more than comparing two numbers. For example, a computerized ordering system at an office supply company might be programmed to offer a 10 percent discount on orders greater than $200. After the order has been placed, the computer will compare it to $200 and determine whether a discount is applicable. The control/communication function of the CPU keeps the computer working in a rational fashion. This function includes deciding when to accept data from the keyboard, when to perform arithmetic and logic operations, and when to display characters or graphics on the screen.

microprocessor
Advanced integrated circuit that combines most of the basic functions of a computer onto a single chip

In microcomputers the CPU consists of a single integrated circuit, known as a **microprocessor,** and some associated support circuitry. In workstations, mainframes, and supercomputers, the CPU can be either a single processing unit made of multiple integrated circuits or multiple processing units operating in parallel, a scheme known as

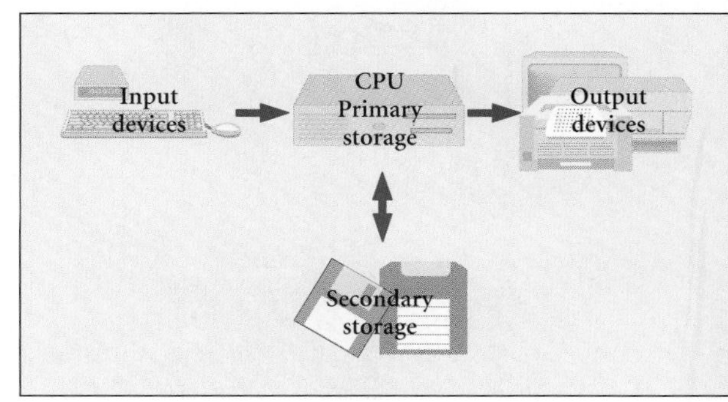

EXHIBIT 16.5

Hardware Elements in a Computer System

The primary elements of computer hardware are the central processing unit, input devices, output devices, and storage.

parallel processing. In such a setup, each processor takes one part of the problem—rather like ten students working on ten parts of an assignment at the same time.

parallel processing
Use of multiple processors in a single computer unit, with the intention of increasing the speed at which complex calculations can be completed

OUTPUT DEVICES Once the data have been successfully entered and the CPU has processed them, they won't be of any use unless they are sent back to the outside world. The first place a computer's output usually goes is the *display,* or monitor. The display acts in the same basic manner as a television, providing the user with text, graphics, or a combination of both. However, when you need a permanent record or when you need to share hard copy with someone, you will probably use a printer. Engineers and scientists also use *plotters,* output devices that use pens to reproduce a displayed image by drawing it on paper.

In addition, as with input devices, specialized equipment can provide output for particular applications. For example, a *projection panel* is a special display device that connects to your computer and sits on top of a regular overhead projector. These panels can display everything from regular computer screens to videotape from a VCR. When combined with presentation and *multimedia* software that use graphics, projection panels enable computer users to develop unique and impressive business presentations.

STORAGE Input, processing, and output complete the basic computing cycle, but this cycle can't happen without some form of storage for the data being processed and for the software that is in charge of the operation. A **primary storage device** stores data and programs while they are being used in the computer. This device usually involves a set of semiconductor components known as **random-access memory (RAM),** so called because the computer can access any piece of data in such memory at random. Computers use RAM for temporary storage of programs and data during input, processing, and output operations. Unless it is provided with special backup circuitry, RAM is erased when electrical power is removed from the computer. RAM's counterpart is called **read-only memory (ROM),** which uses special circuits for permanent storage. ROM keeps its contents even when power is cut off, and it cannot be accessed by the user for everyday data storage. ROM typically stores programs such as the start-up routines that computers go through when they are first turned on, which involves checking for problems and getting ready to go to work.

primary storage device
Storage for data and programs while they are being processed by the computer

random-access memory (RAM)
Primary storage devices allowing a computer to access any piece of data in such memory at random

read-only memory (ROM)
Special circuits that store data and programs permanently but don't allow users to record their own data or programs; a common use of ROM is for the programs that activate start-up routines when the computer is turned on

Ride the Technology Wave

BEST OF THE WEB

Computer technology advances at a dizzying pace. Today's industry standards in hardware and software can become dinosaurs almost overnight. This can be especially problematic for businesses that spend thousands, or even millions, of dollars on computer systems intended to improve productivity. Fortunately, a number of excellent resources are available on the Internet to help both businesspeople and home computer users stay on top of the advancing waves of technology. *PC Magazine Online* is one such resource. This Web site offers news on future technologies, reviews of current hot products, and hints for effective information and technology management, as well as hundreds of free software downloads. In business today, any extra information you can get about technology trends may become a competitive advantage.
http://www.zdnet.com/pcmag/

Secondary storage provides a permanent record of data and programs that aren't needed immediately, such as a report that you will modify in a month. The most common mechanism for secondary storage is the **disk drive,** which can be of four types: a hard disk drive, a floppy disk drive, a Zip drive, or a CD-ROM drive. Hard disk drives are usually

secondary storage
Computer storage for data and programs that aren't needed at the moment

disk drive
Most common mechanism for secondary storage, which can be of four types: a hard disk drive, a floppy disk drive, a Zip drive, or a CD-ROM drive

enclosed inside the computer and store data internally on rigid magnetic disks. Floppy disk drives, on the other hand, store data on removable magnetic disks. Although they are easily portable, floppy disks (also called diskettes) have very limited storage capacity. As a result, many businesses are now using Zip drives, which store data on magnetic Zip disks. With over 100 times the storage capacity of floppy disks, Zip disks are emerging as the ideal portable storage medium for **multimedia** computing (standard data combined with audio, computer animation, photography, and full-motion video). **CD-ROMs,** which are run on CD-ROM drives, are the clear choice for packaging multimedia software for retail sale. However, the high cost of CD-ROM recorders still makes it prohibitively expensive for most companies to use them as secondary storage devices.

multimedia
Computer activity that involves sound, photographic images, animation, and video in addition to traditional computer data

CD-ROMs
Storage devices that use the same technology as music CDs; popular because of their low cost and large storage capacity

Software The hardware components just described can be assembled to create impressive computer systems. However, the hardware isn't much good without software telling it what to do and how to behave. Software can be divided into three general categories: Systems software, application software, and computer languages.

SYSTEMS SOFTWARE Systems software is perhaps the most important software category because it includes **operating systems,** which control such fundamental actions as storing data on disk drives and displaying text or graphics on monitors. When you first turn on a computer, the operating system begins to direct the actions that enable the various hardware devices and software applications to interact in ways that are useful to you. A word-processing program can't read the disk or write text to the display by itself; it relies

operating systems
Class of software that controls the computer's hardware components

CD-ROMs are particularly useful for business applications that require the storage and retrieval of massive amounts of data, such as the millions of names on this nationwide telephone directory.

on the operating system to direct the computer's hardware and to manage the flow of data into, around, and out of the system.

For about 15 years, until the mid-1990s, the most popular operating system for use on PCs was MS-DOS, the software that made Microsoft a household word and Bill Gates a billionaire. In 1987 Microsoft introduced Windows, a **graphical user interface (GUI),** which made DOS and DOS-based applications more user-friendly. Instead of having to learn DOS commands, computer operators could use a mouse to point and click on various icons and menus. Today DOS has been replaced on many computers by Windows 95 and subsequent versions of Windows.

graphical user interface (GUI)
A user-friendly program running in conjunction with the operating system that enables computer operators to enter commands by clicking on icons and menus with a mouse

Other popular operating systems include IBM's OS/2, which runs on high-end microcomputers; UNIX, which runs on both microcomputers and mainframes and which enables a business to have several brands and classes of computers running the same software package; and Mac OS, which controls the operation of Apple microcomputers. (Mac OS was the first microcomputer operating system to use a graphical user interface.)

APPLICATION SOFTWARE **Application software** encompasses programs that perform specific user functions, such as word processing, database management, desktop publishing, and so on. Application software can be either *custom* (developed specifically for a single user or set of users and not sold to others) or *general purpose* (developed with the goal of selling it to multiple users). Commercially available general-purpose software products are commonly referred to as *packages,* as in a *word-processing package.* In today's business-software market, the array of software packages is vast, including products that can prepare books and newspapers, monitor the stock market, locate potential customers on a map, track employee records, and produce sales reports, to name just a few. One common commercial software package for business is Microsoft Office, which combines word processing, spreadsheet, presentation, database, e-mail, Internet, and scheduling software. Today's powerful microcomputers and workstations can perform **multitasking**—running more than one program at a time. This ability enables the user of a package like Office to run database, spreadsheet, word processing, and Internet software all at once and to switch back and forth between programs as needed.

application software
Programs that perform specific functions for users, such as word processing or spreadsheet analysis

multitasking
Running several programs at once and switching back and forth between them

COMPUTER LANGUAGES All software is created by another special class of software, **computer languages,** or sets of rules and conventions for communicating with a computer. Just as human beings communicate with each other using designated languages, we also communicate with computers using designated languages. The term **programming** describes the steps involved in giving a computer the instructions necessary to perform a desired task.

computer languages
Sets of programmable rules and conventions for communicating with computers

programming
Process of creating the sets of instructions that direct computers to perform desired tasks

Computer languages have evolved over the past several decades. The four language generations are machine language, assembly language, high-level languages, and fourth-generation languages.[35] As they have evolved, computer languages have become easier to work with. For example, high-level languages enable programmers to use a single command to accomplish the equivalent of several assembly-language commands. However, instead of replacing previous generations, each new generation of language builds on its predecessors. As a result, high-level languages must still be converted to assembly language, and then to machine language, before they can be run.

Fourth-generation languages (4GLs) have the benefit of allowing the programmer to give instructions to computers in a language that is remarkably similar to English, French, or another natural language. With the help of artificial intelligence technology, 4GLs like INTELLECT are being developed to be as easy to use as speaking in one's own native language.[36] As you might imagine, 4GLs are especially effective in programming database management software, in which users interact with the database by querying, or asking questions to be answered by the data it contains.

fourth-generation languages (4GLs)
Collective name applied to a variety of software tools that ease the task of interacting with computers; some let users give instructions in natural languages such as English

UNDERSTANDING THE HIGH-TECH REVOLUTION

Advanced Computer Technology: When Science Fiction Becomes Science Fact

Imagine darting among the skyscrapers of Los Angeles in a hang glider, exploring life forms on the bottom of an Antarctic lake, or touring the inside of a building that hasn't even been built yet. Sound impossible? Perhaps in the real world, but in the world of virtual reality, the impossible is commonplace. *Virtual reality* combines advanced hardware with computer graphics software to simulate the world we live in, hypothesize what the future will look like, or create a world of science fiction or fantasy.

Traveling in a virtual world requires some special equipment. First, a headpiece is worn to block out visual and audio sensations from the real world and to substitute 3D images and *holophonic* sounds. The images you see are displayed on two small video screens, one in front of each eye. When you turn your head, the computer shifts the view that you see. Second, a "data glove" containing fiber-optic sensors and cables enables you to grasp and move objects in the virtual world or execute commands by gesturing. The headpiece and data glove are each wired to powerful computers that record your movements and provide real-time feedback.

Although arcades use virtual reality to put the players into their video games, the technology has many business and scientific applications as well. For instance, Ford engineers use virtual reality to help them design the cars of the future, a Japanese department store lets customers tour a "virtual kitchen" when they plan custom-designed remodeling projects, and several telecommunications companies are experimenting with virtual reality as a tool for monitoring and maintaining their vast communications networks. Although this exciting technology is still in the early stages of its development, you can expect it to be used in many more applications in the future.

Other products of science fiction are also becoming science fact. Computers that are worn on the body may give a whole new meaning to the term *personal computer.* Engineers at Japan's NEC have redesigned standard computer components to fit into headsets, hang around

Although 4GLs make programming easier, the large number of instructions needed to create today's graphical user interfaces is still time consuming. To ease this burden, computer programmers have developed *visual programming,* which replaces text-based instructions with icons that represent objects or programming functions. One of the most popular visual languages for professionals and casual programmers alike is Microsoft's Visual BASIC.[37]

Still another recent advance in computer language is the introduction of the Java programming language by Sun Microsystems. Java enables tiny applications called "applets" to run over the Internet or an intranet. Rather than maintaining bulky software packages on a microcomputer's hard drive, an applet can be downloaded as it is needed to run a specific application. This development could lead to a future in which networks become the real insides of computers. Furthermore, programs written in Java can work on any operating system, so different versions of software would no longer need to be written for DOS, Windows, Mac OS, and UNIX, and users of different systems could share applications with ease. Computer giant IBM is convinced of Java's potential to revolutionize computing and is investing hundreds of millions of dollars in developing frameworks for Java applications and hardware for improved application performance.[38]

However, software companies currently offer few Java-based business applications such as spreadsheets, word processors, business graphics, or databases.[39] In addition, Microsoft and Intel have a strong interest in maintaining the current standard, in which desktop computers each contain an individual microprocessor and each run individual copies of Windows-based programs. Their combined market power constitutes a significant obstacle to widespread business acceptance of Java-based networks.

the neck, drape over the shoulders, and fasten around the waist, forearm, and wrist. In one possible application, a series of computer components worn in a headset, on the hands, and over the shoulders would allow paramedics to transmit diagnostic information to doctors at a hospital. Speech-recognition software, video, special body sensors, and satellite transmission capabilities would allow the doctors to see patients and diagnose their condition before they even arrive at the hospital. The doctors would then be able to give the paramedics emergency treatment instructions. Such wearable computers are already making their way into some workplaces.

Another type of computer technology, *biometrics,* looks more like something out of a James Bond movie. Before 007 is allowed to enter high-security areas, his hand or face is often scanned to ensure positive identification. This same technology is now being used in a growing number of applications. One example is Mr. Payroll, a check-cashing machine that's popping up in grocery and convenience stores. The machine makes a facial scan to ensure that only the proper owner of the check receives money from that account. Another example is found at the University of Georgia, where three-dimensional hand scanners are used instead of cards to admit students to dining halls. And in the future, ATM machines may scan the iris of your eye instead of asking you for a PIN number. As a method of identification, the iris is said to be even more telling than fingerprints. Although some people are concerned that biometrics technology is an invasion of privacy, many companies, including IBM, are banking on its widespread use in the future.

Questions for Critical Thinking

1. What other business applications can you think of where virtual reality technology might be used?
2. What are some ethical concerns that might be raised if biometrics technology becomes a common way of identifying customers?

Telecommunications and Computer Networks

It used to be that each piece of equipment in an office was self-contained. Even in the early years of business computing, the computer was used for word and data processing, the fax machine was used for transmitting data, the telephone was a device for communicating verbally, and the pager was for contacting people when they weren't near a telephone. Similarly, at home the computer, the television, the radio, and the telephone were all separate appliances that served individual purposes. However, all of these distinctions are now becoming blurred, thanks to advances in telecommunications and computer technology. For example, MCI Communications is no longer just a long-distance company; now it also offers cellular phone service, paging, and Internet access. In addition to offering all these services, Sprint is gearing up to offer movies and other television programming through partnerships with cable television companies. AT&T is going even further by offering high-speed *data communication* between computers via satellites.[40] In addition, computer users who have the right software and hardware can now have voice conversations over the Internet without incurring long-distance or cellular phone charges.

This linking of computers and communication devices is creating new opportunities for companies to accomplish their goals more efficiently and more effectively. For one thing, businesspeople can now easily stay in touch with their offices, their computers, their associates, and their families while they travel the world. It is also much easier for workers in remote locations to share work, ideas, and resources. What makes all of this possible are complex networks of linked computers and communication devices (see Exhibit 16.6).

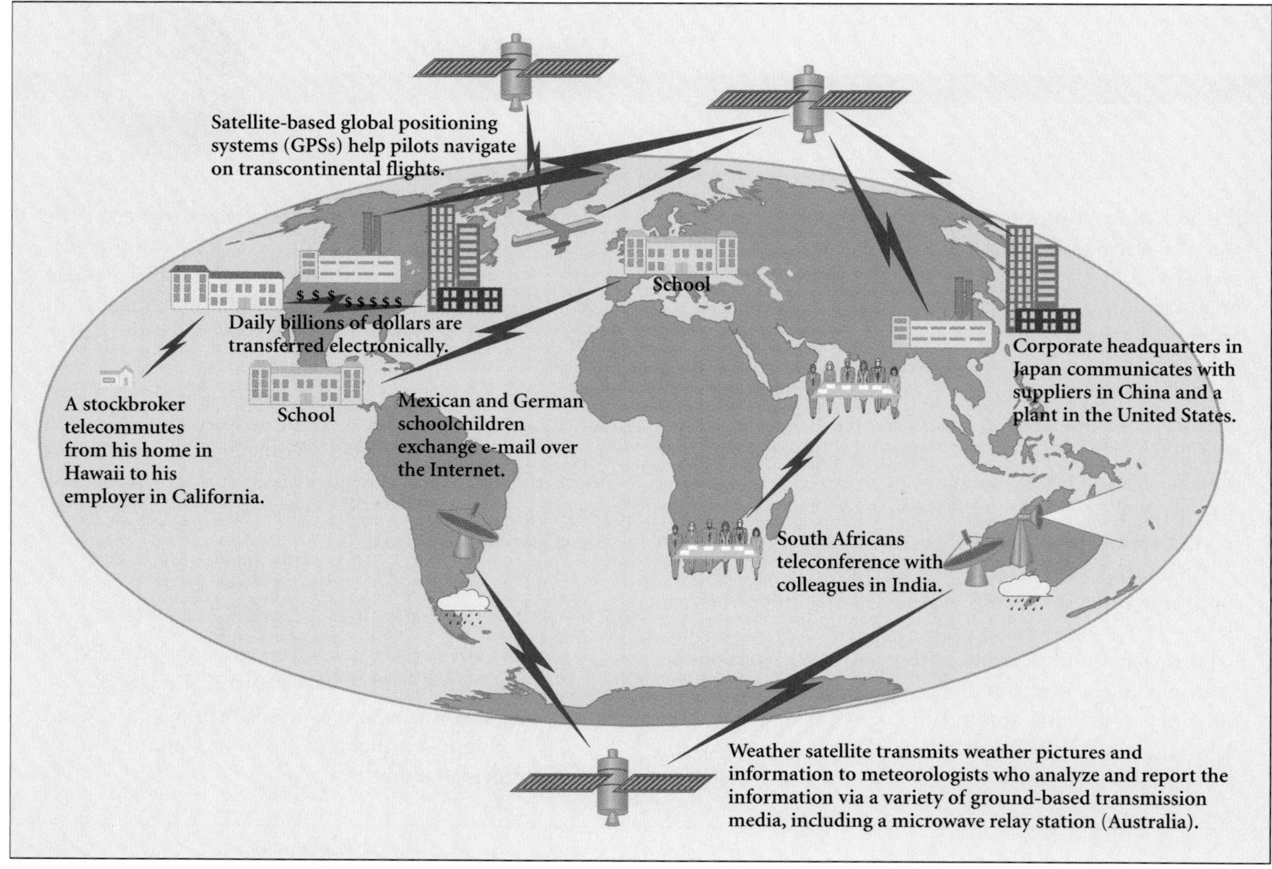

Satellite-based global positioning systems (GPSs) help pilots navigate on transcontinental flights.
School
Daily billions of dollars are transferred electronically.
Corporate headquarters in Japan communicates with suppliers in China and a plant in the United States.
A stockbroker telecommutes from his home in Hawaii to his employer in California.
School
Mexican and German schoolchildren exchange e-mail over the Internet.
South Africans teleconference with colleagues in India.
Weather satellite transmits weather pictures and information to meteorologists who analyze and report the information via a variety of ground-based transmission media, including a microwave relay station (Australia).

EXHIBIT 16.6

Our Shrinking World

Computer and communications networks are making the world smaller. We are now able to communicate and share work with people around the world as easily as if they were in the same room.

data communications
Process of connecting computers and allowing them to send data back and forth

network
Collection of computers, communications software, and transmission media (such as telephone lines) that allows computers to communicate

wide area network (WAN)
Computer network that encompasses a large geographic area

local area network (LAN)
Computer network that encompasses a small area, such as an office or a university campus

The Growth of Networks

The brief discussion of communications earlier in this chapter hinted at one of the most important issues in business computing: connecting multiple computers in one way or another and allowing them to exchange data, a process known as **data communications.** Data communications systems connect users to all sorts of information both inside and outside the organization, as well as to expensive resources such as supercomputers and high-speed laser printers. However, computers are not limited to data communications; audio and video communications between computers are also becoming increasingly common. How do they do it? Through networks.

In general, a **network** is a collection of hardware, software, and communications media that enables computers to communicate. Networks differ by the size of their geographic area. In a **wide area network (WAN),** computers at different geographic locations are linked through one of several transmission media. In contrast, a **local area network (LAN),** as its name implies, meets data communications needs within a small area, such as an office or a university campus. Exhibit 16.7 illustrates the three common network configurations. Note that some networks use a centralized host computer, whereas others employ a decentralized configuration.[41]

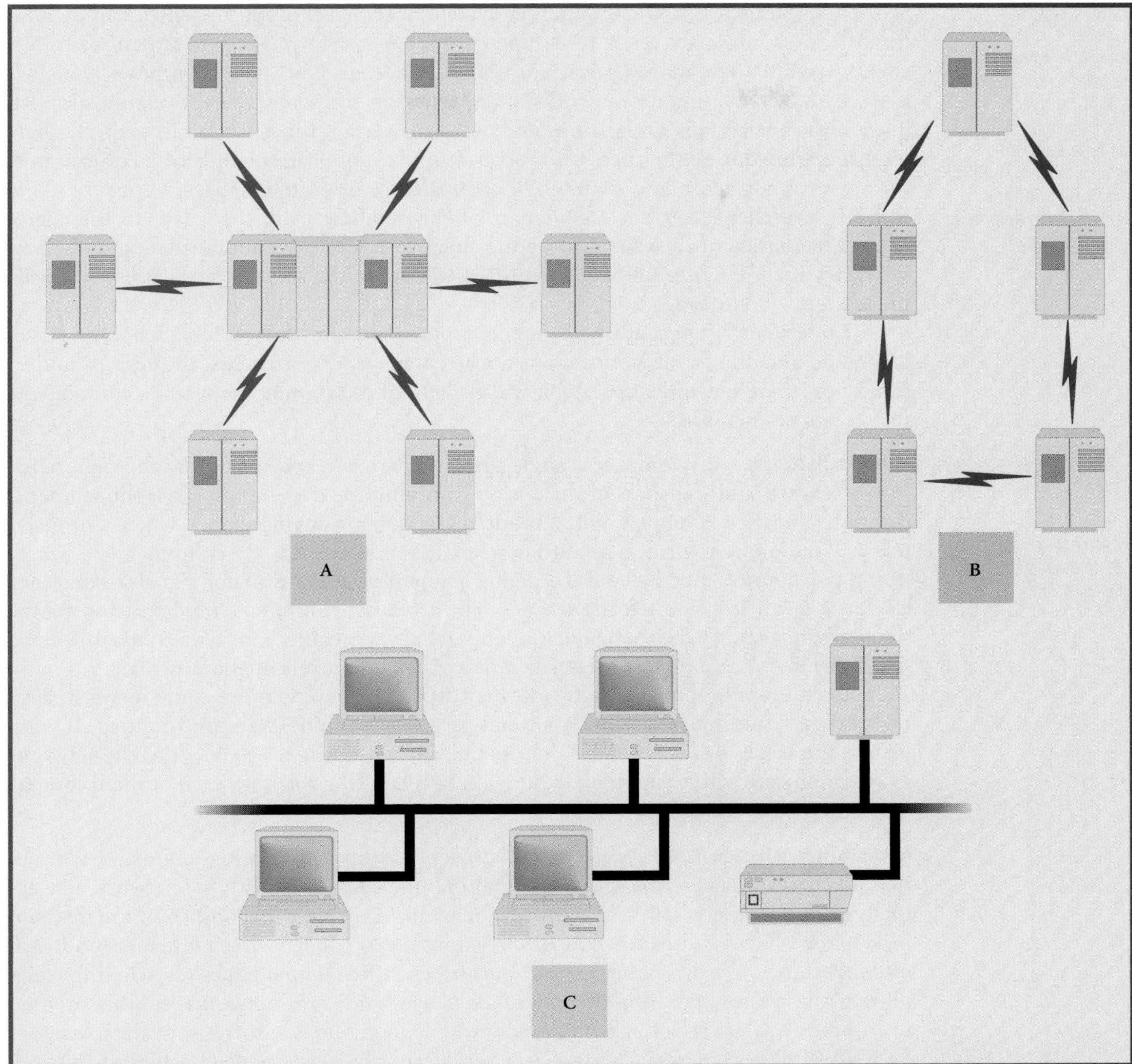

EXHIBIT 16.7

Network Configurations

There are three general types of network configurations or *topologies.* The star configuration (A) connects a centralized host computer to several other smaller computers. In this configuration, all communication between computers travels through the host. The ring configuration (B) connects similarly sized computers in a ring without the use of a host. Communications travel around the ring until they reach their destination computer. In a bus configuration (C), computers and peripheral devices (such as printers) are connected along a common cable called a *network bus.* Communication signals are broadcast to all nodes (connected devices) on the network, but only the destination node responds. Often, network configurations are actually hybrids of two or more of these configurations.

In the past, computer networks were highly centralized, usually consisting of a number of dumb terminals connected to a mainframe host. However, the affordability and power of today's microcomputers has led to the emergence of client/server networks

client/server system
Computer system design in which one computer (the server) contains software and data used by a number of attached computers (the clients); the clients also have their own processing capabilities, and they share certain tasks with the server, enabling the system to run at optimum efficiency

as the new standard. In a **client/server system,** a server computer—which can be anything from a microcomputer to a supercomputer—performs certain functions for its clients, such as data and applications software storage. The client computer, which is typically a microcomputer or workstation, relies on the server for processing support, but it also runs certain applications and performs certain functions on its own. By sharing processing duties, the client and server optimize application efficiency. For example, the server might store and maintain a centralized corporate database. Using *front-end software,* the client user downloads part of the database from the server to the client. The user can then process the data on the client computer without burdening the server. When finished, the user uploads the processed data to the server's *back-end software* for processing and storage.

More than 70 percent of all microcomputers are now linked to at least one server computer, and almost all workstations act as either servers or clients. In order to understand how these networks operate, it will be helpful to examine the various components that create the network.

modem
Hardware device that allows a computer to communicate over a regular telephone line

Network Hardware Any computer can be part of a network, provided it has the right hardware, software, and transmission media. To communicate over standard telephone lines, a computer must be equipped with a **modem** (modulator-demodulator), which can be either a stand-alone unit or a circuit board that is plugged into the computer. The transmitting computer's modem converts digital computer signals to analog signals so that they can be transmitted over telephone lines. The receiving computer's modem converts the signals from analog back to digital. Modems are always required for data transmission via telephone lines but are not necessarily required for other transmission media.

In addition to modems, networks may depend on several other components to keep the network running smoothly. Front-end processors, multiplexers, and routers all work behind the scenes to help the network operate efficiently and to enable different networks to communicate with each other. Exhibit 16.8 explains the role that each of these components plays in a network.

Network Transmission Media When people speak of a computer as being "online," they mean that it is part of a network. The "lines" that link the computers with the network may actually be one of several different transmission media. Currently the most common medium is telephone lines. These lines consist of two insulated copper wires twisted around each other. Because virtually all homes and businesses in the United States are wired for telephones, these lines have been the natural choice for wide area networks and the Internet.

However, the speed at which standard telephone lines can transmit data is rather limited. Therefore, many LANs use *coaxial cable* to achieve high-speed data transmission. Coaxial cable is the same type of wire used to bring cable channels to your television. Capable of transmitting data faster than telephone lines, some cable television companies now offer Internet access over their coaxial lines. This requires using a specially designed *cable modem.*[42]

fiber optic cable
Cable that transmits data as laser-generated pulses of light; capable of transmitting data at speeds of 2.5 billion bits per second without a modem

bandwidth
Maximum capacity of a data transmission medium

Standard telephone lines and coaxial cable transmit data as electrical signals. In contrast, **fiber optic cable** transmits data as laser-generated pulses of light at incredibly fast speeds. Transmitted data are measured in bits, and a standard phone line transmits up to 56,000 bits per second. However, a single strand of fiber optic cable can transmit 2.5 billion bits per second without the aid of a modem. Fiber optic cable now links the major countries and cities of the world for both voice and data transmission. However, because of the high cost involved, it will probably be quite a while before homes and businesses are linked by a universal fiber optic network. Instead, telephone companies are developing technologies to increase the data transmission capacity, or **bandwidth,** of common telephone lines.

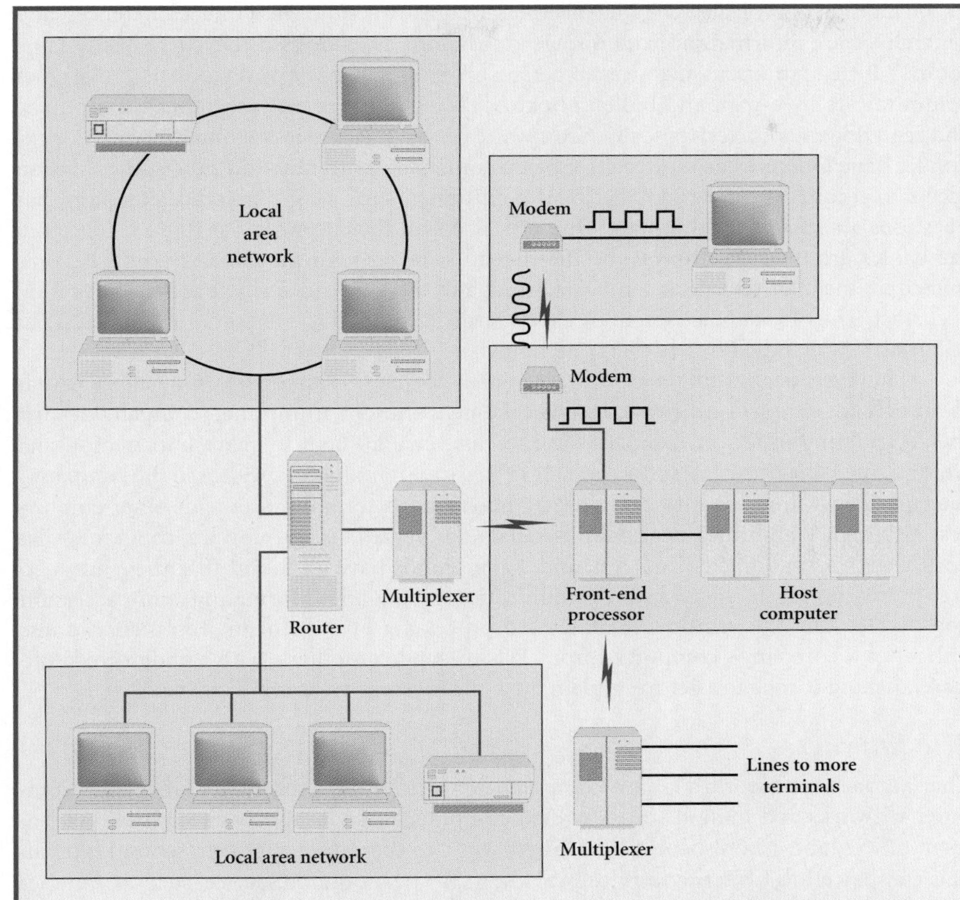

EXHIBIT 16.8

Hardware Components in Computer Networks

Computer networks often rely on several hardware components to help them transmit data more efficiently. The *front-end processor* establishes a link between the source of the transmission and the destination, thereby freeing up the host to take care of other processing duties. The *multiplexer's* job is to gather data from several low-speed devices, such as terminals and printers, and concentrate it for transmission over a single communications channel, saving both time and expense. *Routers* link networks that use different operating systems and communications protocols. When a message is sent from a computer in one network to a computer in an incompatible network, the router converts the message to the necessary protocol and routes it to its final destination.

Wireless communication offers an alternative to standard telephone, coaxial, and fiber optic lines. Just as humans can now communicate without wires via cellular telephones and pagers, so can computers send and receive data without being "hardwired" to a network. Instead, data are transmitted as microwave signals or radio signals to the receiving computer via stations located on mountains, towers, or tall buildings or by satellites orbiting the earth. **Wireless transceivers** are small devices attached to the computer that transmit and receive data. The mobility offered by this configuration is ideal for many applications.

wireless transceivers
Small hardware attachments that enable a computer to transmit and receive data

In the very near future, companies such as Motorola will offer satellite-based, high-speed data and voice transmission services to the entire world. This means that people in remote Indonesian islands or the rural villages of China and India, places where telephone service isn't even available yet, will be able to dial up distant relatives or access the Internet. Furthermore, Teledesic, a system of 840 satellites proposed by Bill Gates and cellular tycoon Craig McCaw, could offer multimedia Internet data transmission at speeds 1,000 times faster than a telephone line.[43] However, because such services will be costly, don't expect wired networks to become obsolete anytime soon.

workgroup computing
Computing arrangement in which teams can easily work together on projects

groupware
Software that enables users in different locations to share information, collaborate on projects, and perform other tasks together

Network Software The proliferation of networks has created the opportunity for **workgroup computing,** in which teams of employees can easily work together on any number of applications. Powerful software packages called **groupware,** such as Lotus Notes, enable users to collaborate on projects, schedule meetings, brainstorm, hold electronic conferences, and generally share information from dispersed locations as easily as if they were in the same room.[44] Instead of discussing ideas in person or sending hard-copy documents, colleagues communicate by e-mail and bulletin boards, access software on each other's computers, and send documents electronically. Groupware can even enhance customer service. For example, Banc One uses groupware to give customers of its transaction processing division access to records of processed checks. If a customer, such as an insurance company, has questions about a check that Banc One processed, all the customer has to do is log on to the bank's groupware setup on the Internet to scan through the check records. A computerized image of the check can be accessed, and the user can verify that its information is correct. The old manual system of check verification used to take seven to ten days, but it can now be handled in less than one hour.[45]

However, establishing a groupware system can be very expensive. One alternative is to launch an *intranet*—a private, Internetlike network. On an intranet, company departments and employees can launch Web sites that enable them to share information and work. Using Web-browsing software such as Netscape, employees can search the company's internal sites to find the information they need and to communicate with other employees. Although Web browsers are not as capable or versatile as groupware, companies like Lockheed Martin, Oracle, Chevron, and Tyson Foods have all found that their intranets are improving productivity and communication by making information more accessible and by reducing the printing, mailing, and processing of documents. Intranets can also link all of a company's computers, from PCs to supercomputers, with standardized software, making it much easier to implement a client/server system.[46]

The Internet

The *Internet* is the world's largest computer network. It links thousands of smaller computer networks and millions of individual computer users in homes, businesses, government offices, and schools worldwide. To get wired to the Internet, businesses and individuals can pay a local Internet service provider (ISP) or an online service, such as America Online, to connect them. These providers manage powerful Web servers that enable users to interface with other servers throughout the network. Organizations can also lease their own direct Internet access lines, which provide Internet access to every user wired to the organization's LAN.[47]

BEST OF THE WEB

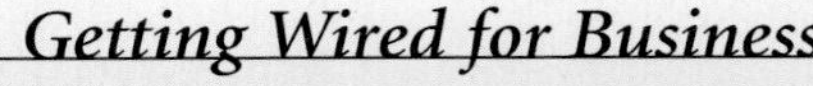

Everybody's making money on the Internet today, right? Well, not everybody. Although some companies have found the Internet to be a natural distribution channel for their products and services, many others are struggling to find ways to attract consumers to their Web sites and encourage surfers to spend their money online. Nevertheless, Internet commerce is expected to grow by leaps and bounds in the coming years as businesses refine their Net strategies and consumers get comfortable with online commerce. How can you learn the secrets of the successful Internet entrepreneurs? Check out the stories at *Wired.* One of the first magazines devoted to the Internet, *Wired* examines the impact of technology on business, culture, and life. You will find profiles of successful Internet companies, reviews of cutting-edge books, up-to-the-minute digital news, links to the Web's hottest sites, and online discussions with people who are blazing the trail for business on the Internet.
http:/wired.com/wired

The communication opportunities made possible by the Internet are changing the way companies around the world do business and the way people relate to one another. By one recent estimate, as many as 400 million e-mail messages are sent over the Internet each day.[48] Over the Internet, companies can find new partners, sell products, order supplies, invest funds, distribute information, and recruit employees without leaving the office or even picking up the phone. For example, General Electric is converting its entire supply chain from a paper-based system to the Internet. The complete parts procurement process, from soliciting contractor bids to ordering parts, will take place online. GE's lighting division has already shrunk the bidding process for spare parts from two weeks to one day.[49]

The World Wide Web, the graphical part of the Internet, is the place where a rapidly growing number of businesses are putting up Web sites to entice customers. Within a few months of opening shop on the Internet, Michigan florist Larry Grant was getting as many orders through that channel as he was through traditional means.[50] However, such success stories are still more the exception than the rule. In a recent survey of 1,100 Web-based businesses, only 31 percent claimed to be profitable. MCI Communications once thought an Internet shopping mall would do big business, but it has since closed the venture due to lack of consumer interest.[51] For now the most valuable use of the Internet is to communicate and share information; e-mail, research, and obtaining news and information are currently the top-ranked activities for users.[52] This situation is expected to change as more people begin to use the Internet and as new technology makes Internet transactions more secure. Experts have long cautioned consumers to be careful about giving out credit-card numbers over the Web where they are vulnerable to hackers (computer users skilled at electronically breaking into protected computer systems). However, Smart cards, electronic checks, digital IDs, and CyberCash—which are explained in Chapter 18—are just a few of the latest advances that are making it much safer for consumers to shop online. As a result, Internet commerce is expected to skyrocket over the next several years.[53]

Drawbacks to Business Computing

Computers are machines, and most machines can be used either well or poorly. Just as automobiles are both convenient and dangerous, computers can be both a help and a hindrance. A computer can greatly improve an employee's productivity, but it can also waste an employee's time. One study found that the average computer user wastes five hours a week not only waiting for programs to run, reports to print, and computer technicians to fix systems but also dealing with other computer-related problems such as lost files, disk crashes, and format and file incompatibilities.[54] In addition, computers create new ways for employees to shirk responsibility, such as playing computer games and surfing the Internet.

Perhaps the most significant problem businesses face as a result of computer technology is data security. Companies with valuable or sensitive information stored in a computer worry about competitors or thieves raiding the database simply by dialing in through a modem. Even firms that don't share their databases are subject to security breaches. In the mid-1990s, U.S. corporations spent more than $6 billion annually on network security. Even so, over 40 percent of 400 companies surveyed reported recent security break-ins, and the estimated annual cost of computer crime is as high as $10 billion.[55] The entire U.S. electronic infrastructure, including banks, financial markets, transportation systems, power grids, and telecommunication systems, could be vulnerable to attack. In one recent case, Russian hackers broke into Citibank's network and electronically stole $10 million.[56]

THINKING ABOUT ETHICS

Privacy in the Workplace: Whose E-Mail Is It, Anyway?

You just had a run-in with your boss and you're fuming. You have to vent your frustration to somebody, so you send an e-mail message to a co-worker in another department, telling her what a jerk your boss really is. You're safe because nobody will ever see it except for you and her, right? Think again. That "jerk" of a boss may be reading your e-mail.

As more and more companies link employees to the Internet, employee privacy in the workplace is becoming a bigger concern. In one survey, 22 percent of corporate executives admitted to reviewing communications between their employees, particularly computer files and electronic mail. In only a third of these cases were employees told ahead of time that managers would be taking a peek. Some managers contend that e-mail monitoring is necessary to maintain security and ensure productivity. However, many employees complain that such practices are an invasion of privacy.

One employee of Pillsbury filed a lawsuit when he was dismissed for what the company deemed "inappropriate and unprofessional comments." Pillsbury executives intercepted a message that the employee had sent to a co-worker containing unfavorable comments about his employers. A judge ruled that even if Pillsbury had made a promise of confidentiality, as the employee maintains, the company's actions did not invade the employee's privacy.

To protect themselves from such lawsuits, some companies, including Intel, Kmart, and Epson, have adopted formal policies to inform employees that the company reserves the right to review employee computer files and e-mail. On the other hand, companies such as Apple Computer have explicit policies that prohibit monitoring employee e-mail. Even when no such policy exists, 34 percent of executives say they find it unacceptable to look at employees' files or e-mail transmissions.

Do employers have legitimate security-related concerns that justify checking employee e-mail? As marketing director at VeriSign, an Internet security company in

Is It True?

More companies report financial losses as a result of information theft than they do for any other computer-related crime.

computer viruses
Computer programs that can work their way into a computer system and erase or corrupt data or programs

The average computer hacker is 13 to 14 years old, and experts say that the main reason they do it is for the challenge. However, computer crimes are also committed by disgruntled employees or by other organizations seeking trade secrets.[57] The FBI reports that more than $24 billion in proprietary information is being taken from companies like General Motors, Intel, and Hughes every year.[58] Thanks to the computer's ability to store information electronically, spies can steal information without physically taking anything, thereby leaving no trace of the theft. The Economic Espionage Act of 1996 imposes fines of up to $10 million and sentences of up to 15 years in computer theft cases involving espionage, but even so, companies must still take strong precautions to protect themselves.

Another critical security challenge is presented by **computer viruses,** hidden programs that can work their way into computer systems and erase or corrupt data and programs. For example, computers at National City Corporation, a mortgage lending firm, recently contracted a virus that shut down 3,000 of the company's servers and more than 8,000 workstations.[59] Computer viruses behave much like human viruses by invisibly attaching themselves to any computer data or programs that come into contact with them. Viruses can be spread by diskettes, electronic bulletin boards, or computer networks, including the Internet. There is no way to entirely stop the spread of computer viruses, because new ones are created all the time. However, a number of excellent "vaccine" programs exist that search for and destroy viruses and prevent new ones from infecting your computer system. You can reduce the chances of your system becoming infected by periodically scanning your hardware and software for viruses and by being very cautious about what programs and files you load onto your hard drive.

Mountain View, California, Anil Pereira likens e-mail to postcards sent through the mail—that is, they can easily be read as they travel from the sender to the receiver. If an e-mail sent to someone outside the company contained sensitive information such as trade secrets, it could jeopardize the company. However, a number of encryption programs now exist that will render an e-mail message unreadable until the receiver unscrambles it, thus acting as a sort of envelope. Although such programs require both the sender and the receiver to deal with certain commands and jargon, they can protect the company without the need for snooping.

Of course, e-mail encryption programs can only protect companies from individuals who spy on messages unbeknownst to the sender. Because the programs can be turned on and off by the user, they cannot stop a disgruntled employee from sending damaging information in order to get revenge on the company, a boss, or a coworker. Each company must decide for itself whether this possibility poses a threat significant enough to warrant monitoring employee communications. For those that believe it does, working to promote a more supportive, loyal, and trusting culture within the organization may be a better solution in the long run. First, employees will feel respected and valued, both of which can go a long way toward boosting teamwork and productivity while reducing the chance of sabotage. Second, managers won't have to waste valuable time reading what their employees send.

Questions for Critical Thinking

1. Would it be improper for a manager to read a sealed, handwritten note left on an employee's desk by another employee? Does this scenario differ from the exchange of e-mail between employees? Why or why not?
2. What types of companies or industries stand to suffer the most from breaches in security resulting from employee e-mail?

Summary of Learning Objectives

1. **Distinguish between data and information and explain the characteristics of useful information.**
   Data are recorded facts and statistics; information is created when data are arranged in such a manner as to be meaningful for a particular problem or situation. In order to be useful, information needs to be accurate, timely, complete, relevant, and concise, and it must reach the right people at the right time.
2. **Identify the major ways companies use information systems.**
   The chapter discusses five major categories: transaction processing; process and production control; office automation; design and engineering; and the managerial tasks of analysis, planning, and decision making as they relate to the company's various functional areas.
3. **List seven common business computer applications.**
   The seven common applications discussed in the chapter are word processing, spreadsheets, desktop publishing, database management, business graphics, communications, and Internet publishing.
4. **Describe the four classes of computers.**
   Mainframes represent the traditional notion of large and powerful computers. They are capable of processing and storing huge amounts of data. Smaller mainframes are called midsize computers, or minicomputers. Microcomputers, such as the Apple Macintosh and the IBM PC, are the smallest and cheapest computers. Workstations are a step up in price and performance; similar in size and shape to microcomputers, they approach or equal the performance of minicomputers. Supercomputers are the fastest and most expensive computers available today. They are often used for applications that rely on virtual reality.
5. **Identify the major components of a computer system.**
   Hardware and software are the two major aspects of a computer. Hardware includes input devices (such as keyboards), central processing units, output devices (such as printers), and primary and secondary storage. Software is divided into operating systems, application software, and computer languages.

6. **Describe the primary components of computer networks.** Networks are composed of hardware (such as modems, front-end processors, multiplexers, and routers), network transmission media (such as telephone lines, coaxial cable, fiber optic cable, microwave stations, and satellites), and network software (such as groupware and Web browsers).
7. **Explain the business uses of the Internet.** Businesses use the Internet to find new partners, sell products, order supplies, invest funds, distribute information, and recruit employees. Until recently, the primary power of the Internet has been in communicating and sharing information. However, Internet commerce is expected to boom as new users go online and Internet security improves.
8. **Discuss the drawbacks to business computing.** Computers enhance productivity in many ways, but they can also create new hassles and distractions for employees. For businesses, maintaining computer security (including guarding against hackers and viruses) poses an important problem.

On the Job: Meeting Business Challenges at American Express

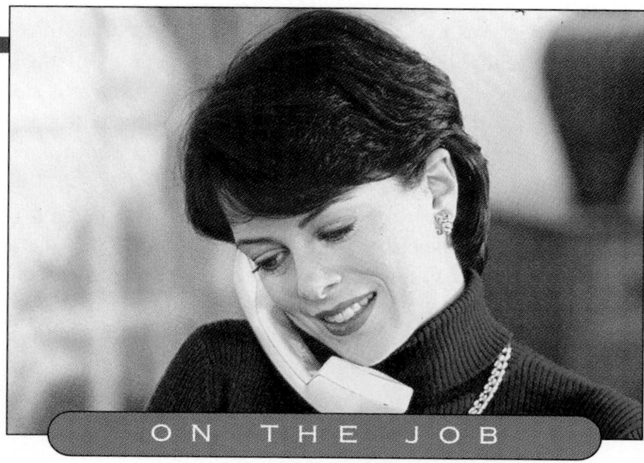

Harvey Golub has the distinct advantage of having one of the world's most advanced information management systems at his fingertips. It took the company 6 years and $80 million to create, but it provides a powerful set of competitive advantages.

Today more than 3 million charge receipts are received every day at American Express, and they are sent through a unique transaction processing system that converts data from paper into digitized images and then stores them on disk. All those pieces of paper are then shredded and buried in secret locations for security. Computers index and sort the digitized images according to billing cycle and ZIP code, collate the images with their appropriate billing statements, print more readable and useful copies of the images on perforated paper, and insert those sheets of paper with billing statements into envelopes, which are then presorted for mailing. All of this is done so quickly that 100,000 pages of billing statements are printed in only one hour at two processing sites in the United States. Customer queries can be processed within minutes now that the images are stored on optical disks.

Nearly 400 people were once employed only to process, correct, and retrieve the millions of paper receipts received each day, but they have been replaced by the transaction processing system, which is operated by three people who are able to do more work in less time and with greater accuracy. Billing costs have been reduced by 25 percent, with nearly half of the savings coming from a reduction in the cash American Express needs to have available to pay merchants for charged purchases.

The system has enabled the company to gain a competitive advantage in two ways. First, of the three major card companies, American Express is the only one that still returns copies of receipts to its customers for recordkeeping—a service that is especially useful for businesspeople. Second, Golub now knows his customers very well because the purchasing data on each receipt are transformed into useful information. Each cardholder is categorized and profiled according to 450 attributes derived from his or her purchasing patterns, age, gender, and other data. These continually updated portraits are augmented with surveys that are targeted to that cardholder's income and lifestyle.

All these data, and the information that can be derived from them, have allowed American Express to enter a booming business: direct-mail merchandising, which is now the company's fastest-growing subsidiary. This information has also prevented American Express from providing costly services to the wrong cardholders; for example, only holders of platinum cards are greeted with limousine service at airports. The information is also used to find new subscribers to magazines owned by the company's publishing subsidiary—periodicals that, again, are appropriate to each cardholder's lifestyle.

What began with a transaction processing system is now used to help Golub make better strategic decisions. He has a wealth of information useful in making decisions about new products, new services, new markets, and new ways to further innovate for a competitive advantage.

Your Mission: American Express is considered an industry leader in its use of technology, as evidenced by its unique transaction processing system. You are the CIO, responsible for considering tactical and strategic issues to ensure the best use of information throughout American Express subsidiaries, which include IDS Financial Services (a financial-planning firm) and Travel Related Services (American Express's best-known business, which includes the green, gold, and platinum American Express cards and the Optima card).

1. You know that organizing the right data is crucial to providing useful information to decision makers in the company. Assume that each of the following pieces of data is available to the people who make approval decisions for new customers for the classic green American Express card. Although you want to provide sufficient data, you don't want to overload the decision makers with irrelevant or unnecessary data. Which of the following pieces of data would be most useful for the card-approval decision?
   a. The applicant's past history with credit, specifically, whether or not the applicant pays bills on time
   b. The applicant's income, because people with more income are likely to use their cards more often, which increases American Express's revenue
   c. The applicant's educational background, so that you can pick the people who have graduated from the best universities
2. Suppose that several dozen customers called to complain about the system that delivers processed images of their receipts, not the actual receipts themselves. Your customer-service staff tried to convince them that the processed images contain the same data and information as the original and that, in fact, they offer even more. These customers are adamant, however; if they can't get the receipts back, they'll cancel their cards. What should you do?
   a. Explain to the customers that American Express needs to use the new system in order to stay competitive.
   b. For these customers only, circumvent the new system and provide them with their actual receipts.
   c. You hate to lose customers, but your calculations show that circumventing the system for these few customers will cost you more than the revenue that these customers represent. Thank them graciously for their past use of American Express cards, and explain that you won't be able to cater to their particular needs, that you hope they'll reconsider, and that you understand if they want to go ahead and turn in their cards.
3. Like nearly all other credit customers, American Express cardholders are concerned about database privacy. They worry that hackers will get access to their card numbers, and they fear that companies are building profiles of them that say more than they are comfortable revealing, such as what kinds of videos they like to rent or which hotels they prefer to stay in. How could American Express best calm the fears of its customers?
   a. The company should institute security measures to minimize the risk of people's breaking into its databases, but it can't restrict access so that employees are unable to access the data; in addition, the company should give customers a say in how their personal data are used and by whom.
   b. To be completely secure, the company should not use any of the data it collects, should never sell data to anyone, and should restrict access to a handful of top executives.
   c. Simply by using their cards, American Express customers forfeit their right to privacy, because there is no way to process a transaction without the customer's name being involved; if customers are worried about their privacy, they should use cash instead.
4. As an information-technology pioneer, American Express keeps a close eye on such developments as the Internet. Which of the following possibilities would you recommend as a potentially lucrative business for the Travel Related Services division?
   a. Mailing credit-card applications to everyone who uses the Internet.
   b. A "virtual reality" travel-agency service, in which vacation shoppers could experience the look and feel of various travel destinations before making their travel choices through American Express.
   c. An interactive Web site on the Internet that would provide computer users with a detailed look at each of the company's credit-and charge-card offerings, as well as its travel-planning services.[60]

Key Terms

application software (491)
artificial intelligence (480)
bandwidth (496)
CD-ROMs (490)
central processing unit (CPU) (488)
chief information officer (CIO) (478)
client/server system (496)
computer languages (491)
computer viruses (500)
data (476)
data communications (494)
data mining (480)
data warehousing (480)
database (476)
database management (483)
decision support system (DSS) (480)
desktop publishing (DTP) (483)
disk drive (489)
executive information system (EIS) (480)
expert system (481)
fiber optic cable (496)
fourth-generation languages (4GLs) (491)
graphical user interface (GUI) (491)
groupware (497)
hardware (488)
hypertext markup language (HTML) (485)
local area network (LAN) (494)
mainframe computer (486)
management information system (MIS) (480)
microcomputer (486)
microprocessor (488)

minicomputers (486)
modem (496)
multimedia (490)
multitasking (491)
network (494)
office automation systems (OAS) (480)
operating systems (490)
parallel processing (489)
primary storage device (489)
process control system (479)
production control systems (479)
programming (491)
random-access memory (RAM) (489)
read-only memory (ROM) (489)
secondary storage (489)
software (488)
speech-recognition system (482)
spreadsheet (482)
supercomputers (487)
transaction processing system (TPS) (479)
wide area network (WAN) (494)
wireless transceivers (497)
workgroup computing (497)
workstation (487)

Questions

For Review

1. Would employee records be considered data or information? Explain your answer.
2. Why do companies need information and information management systems?
3. What is the role of the chief information officer (CIO)?
4. How do transaction processing systems, management information systems, and executive information systems differ?
5. What are the purposes of data warehousing and data mining?

For Analysis

6. How has artificial intelligence been applied to business?
7. How are common computer applications used by businesspeople?
8. How do workstations differ from microcomputers and mainframes?
9. What are the functions of a central processing unit?
10. What characteristics distinguish fiber optic cable from standard telephone lines and coaxial cable?

For Application

11. If you were the CIO of a growing company and you were trying to decide whether to build a network that utilizes groupware or one that is intranet-based and uses Web browsing software, what factors would you need to consider?
12. You are CIO of a cosmetics firm, and the vice president of marketing asked you whether you thought the company should devote more resources to selling its skin-care products over the Internet. How would you respond?

A Case for Critical Thinking ■ High-Tech Time Bomb: The Spread of Computer Viruses—and Their Prevention

A competitor's raid on a database is only one security problem faced by information managers. Another potential nightmare is a wipeout of company data as a result of some unforeseen natural disaster such as an earthquake or flood. However, losses from this kind of catastrophe stand to be overshadowed by damage from computer viruses. Viruses are small fragments of software that make copies of themselves and spread those copies from computer to computer. Some viruses carry program instructions that can destroy data, damage computer hardware, or monopolize computer communications lines. Because so many computers are interconnected, viruses can spread quickly, infecting all the computers linked on a local area network and then spreading over the Internet to other computers and networks. One virus infected 350,000 computers in the United States and Europe.

According to Philip McKinney of Thumb Scan, a computer-security firm in Illinois, the first viruses were devised in the 1970s by software companies trying to protect their profits. Like published books, most commercial software is copyrighted, and the copyright holder has the right to sell the software or to give it away. Therefore, the first viruses were used to track the spread of programs being copied illegally in violation of copyright. The viruses never showed their presence, they just kept track of what computer systems they had passed through. Software authors who knew how to read them hoped that the virus programs could be used to trace the routes of the piracy.

Today viruses are often created by pranksters or vandals. Some hackers enjoy introducing viruses just to show how vulnerable computer systems are. Disgruntled employees or former employees, competitors, and creditors may also introduce viruses. Some viruses go to work corrupting data and programs immediately, whereas others are designed to act as time bombs, sitting quietly until a specified time and then activating themselves to wreak havoc.

Even viruses created accidentally or with no intent of harm can interfere with business by tying up computers and operators. Some viruses use a computer's CPU to copy themselves without restraint. The normal information-processing operations of a business slow as more and more of the computer's processing capacity and memory are used by the renegade programs. Operators must spend time removing viruses, checking to see whether programs or data have been destroyed, and rechecking to make sure that no new infections have taken hold.

One unintentional infection was caused by a Christmas message naively sent over a local network by a German student. The message automatically forwarded itself to everyone on each recipient's regular outgoing e-mail list. The message swamped the local network and eventually moved through interconnecting links to IBM's international network, attaching itself to every mailing list it contacted.

Besides originating in business networks, viruses sometimes spread through the electronic bulletin boards that allow computer users to share public domain (noncopyrighted) programs, or through programs and files downloaded from the Internet. Moreover, even though it is not possible to spread viruses by e-mail messages, they can be spread through e-mail attachments. Therefore, users should always think twice about opening attachments sent by people they don't know.

Just as with biological diseases, experts work hard to devise preventives for computer viruses. Several "vaccines" are now available to spot invading viruses and render them harmless. Some of the more popular programs include Norton Anti-Virus, VirusScan by McAfee Associates, and Dr. Solomon's Anti-Virus Toolkit from S&S International. Businesses from home-based sole proprietorships to IBM and the Internal Revenue Service now make such programs part of their collection of standard software. As systems analyst at George Washington University, Michael Peckman, recommends that computer-security tools be used in combination with safeguard practices that can limit the risk of virus infection. For example, using a write-protect tab on program disks prevents the addition of anything (including viruses) to a disk while it's being used in a disk drive. Furthermore, regularly backing up (copying) data and programs to disks or tapes that are safely stored at a distance provides a fallback if some virus causes destruction within the computer system.

Companies can take other precautions as well. For example, requiring users to enter a password limits access to the computer system by unauthorized personnel; an audit system allows a computer-system manager to track who accessed data, when the data were accessed, and what kinds of things were done to the data; policies that limit and control the movement of data, programs, and hardware among microcomputers within an organization can help control the spread of viruses; and restricting the use of public domain software, bulletin boards, and the Internet can also reduce the risk of infection.

1. Like the viruses that cause biological diseases, computer viruses come in many varieties with many "disease" strategies. They can even be designed to seek out various sites in the computer. What are some of the problems inherent in "vaccinating" computer systems against viruses?
2. Why might a bank go under after a computer disaster? If you were a bank president, how would you plan for such a disaster?
3. Some computer experts say that media coverage of computer viruses should be toned down or stopped because it only encourages publicity-seeking hackers to generate more viruses. What are some advantages and disadvantages of press reports about viruses?
4. The U.S. Department of Energy's Computer Incident Advisory Capability (CIAC) maintains a database of all known computer viruses at <http://ciac.llnl.gov/CIACVirusDatabase.html>. Explore this database to learn more about how specific viruses affect computer systems, and then answer the following questions. What does the "Edwin" virus do to PCs? What does "Jack the Ripper" do? What type of virus is "Omega"? What is the most effective way for a company to use the information in this database?

Building Your Business Skills

Select a local business that uses computer networks in its daily operations, and examine how those operations are affected by network technology. Contact a member of the management team, and ask how computer networks have changed the company. If that option isn't possible, locate an article in a periodical that describes the implementation of computer network in a particular business.

- Consider any changes or improvements in the efficiency of information processing that were made possible by the computer network. How have management-employee communications been affected? Has employee productivity increased or decreased? Is the company doing business over the Internet? Does the company engage suppliers or customers through an EDI system? What type of network software does the company use to support its activities? Have jobs been created or eliminated by the network?
- Prepare a brief written or oral summary of your investigation, as directed by your instructor. Compare the effects of computer network technology in the business you examined with those in businesses examined by other students.

Keeping Current Using *The Wall Street Journal*

Scan recent issues of *The Wall Street Journal* for an article showing how computers or other office-technology advances have helped a company improve its competitive advantage or its profitability.

1. What advantage did technology give the company?
2. Did the article mention any problems the company had implementing its new technology? What were they? Do you think the problems could have been avoided? How?
3. How do you think employees feel about this technology? How would you feel if your job required you to use it?
4. Search the Internet for information about other companies in the same industry that are also using this technology. You may try using several different search engines to find the best sources. Specific news sites include <http://www.brint.com/newswire.htm>, Newsbot at <http://www.hotbot.com/newsbot/index.html>, and Pathfinder at <http://pathfinder.com>. After reading the articles, explain whether these companies are using the technology as effectively as the company mentioned in *The Wall Street Journal*. In what ways are their experiences different? What factors contribute to this difference? What can the different companies learn from each other's experiences? Be sure to identify your sources of information.

Exploring the Best of the Web

Consult an Expert, page 481

Business owners, managers, and employees alike may find it easier to comply with labor laws thanks to the U.S. Department of Labor's "elaws" expert system. You can try it out yourself to get a better idea of how an expert system works. From the DOL's main Web page at <http://www.dol.gov>, click on *elaws: Employment Laws Assistance Tool,* and then select *Family Medical Leave Act Advisor.* Read the brief introductory pages and continue following the links to the expert system. Assume that you are an employer who wants to know whether the Family Medical Leave Act applies to you and what the valid reasons are for leave. Answer the expert system's questions as you like, but document each question and your response. Complete the exercises below as you respond to the system.

1. What information did the expert system provide you with after you responded to all of its questions? Is the information sufficient, or does it leave you with unanswered questions about the Family Medical Leave Act? Explain.
2. Return to the beginning of the expert system questions (use the back button on your Web browser). Begin another query, but this time respond to the system's questions differently (again, document your responses). How does the information you received this time differ from your first query?
3. Explore the capabilities of the elaws system by entering additional queries. For example, you might take the perspective of an employee who wants to know what rights and responsibilities are required by the Family Medical Leave Act. Overall, how do you rate this system's effectiveness in providing information? Do you find it easy to use? Is it comprehensive enough? Would you recommend the system to an employee or a small-business owner?

Ride the Technology Wave, page 489

PC Magazine Online can be a valuable resource for businesspeople who want to stay on top of the latest advances in computer technology. Knowing what is available today and what is coming in the future can end up saving a company money down the road. Take some time to explore the many resources at *PC Magazine Online* at <http://www.zdnet.com/pcmag/>, and then answer the following questions.

1. Click on one of the product categories under the *PC Labs Reviews* heading. Choose a product of interest to you, and review the attached article. Describe the product and its uses in your own words. How might the information supplied in this article be of use to a small-business owner who is looking to improve productivity, manage data more effectively, enhance employee communications, or establish a presence on the Internet? Would the information have different implications for a large organization?
2. From the main page, click on one of the products under the *First Looks* heading or the *Trends* heading, and review the attached article. Is this product a hardware or software product? What are the implications of this new product for business? What benefits does it offer? What are its limitations?
3. After exploring the Web site in more detail, use your impressions to write a short profile of the ideal user of *PC Magazine Online.* Is the user a corporate CIO, a small-business owner, a midlevel manager, or a home computer user?

Getting Wired for Business, page 498

Wired magazine was one of the first publications dedicated to examining the Internet's impact on business, culture, and life. If you are interested in doing business on the Net, or if you just want to learn more about what others are doing, this magazine is a great source of information. Visit the online edition of *Wired* at <http://www.wired.com/wired> and explore the site before answering the following questions.

1. Click on a link to a recent issue, and select an article to review that describes a current business development or trend on the Internet. Describe the trend in your own words, and explain the opportunities or threats it poses for the future of Internet commerce. How might current Internet-based businesses respond to this opportunity or threat? How might businesses that are not yet online respond?
2. Select an article that profiles a successful Internet business or entrepreneur. How did this person or business achieve success on the Internet? What obstacles had to be overcome? What challenges lie ahead, and how will this person or business meet them? What can other entrepreneurs or businesses learn from this success story?
3. Follow the link to *Hotwired* and explore the page's content. Cite at least three examples of information that would be useful to someone who is thinking of starting an Internet business or taking a current business online. What type of businessperson would benefit most from this information? A first-time entrepreneur? A seasoned manager? A small-business person? Explain.

Answers to "Is It True?"

Page 477. False. The cost of managing information such as patients' records, physicians' notes, test results, and insurance claims amounts to about one-third of the total cost of health care in the United States.

Page 486. True.

Page 500. False. More companies report financial losses from virus infection than from any other computer-related crime. Number two is laptop theft. Information theft ranks sixth.

CHAPTER 17

ACCOUNTING

OBJECTIVES

After studying this chapter, you will be able to

1. Describe the importance of accounting information to managers, investors, creditors, and government agencies
2. Identify two major reasons why the work of accountants is changing
3. State the basic accounting equation and explain the purpose of double-entry bookkeeping
4. Differentiate between cash basis and accrual basis accounting
5. Explain the purpose of the balance sheet and identify its three main sections
6. Explain the purpose of the income statement and the statement of cash flows
7. Explain the purpose of ratio analysis and list the four main categories of financial ratios
8. Explain how companies use what-if analysis and budgeting to plan for the future

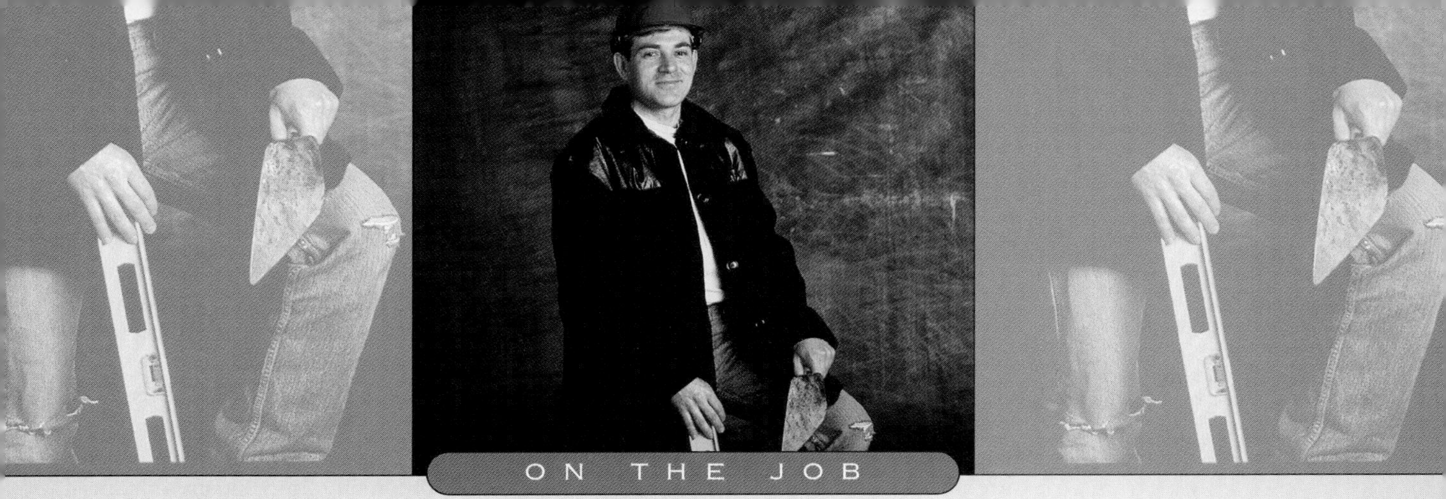

On the Job On the Job

ON THE JOB: FACING BUSINESS CHALLENGES AT THE CONCRETE DOCTOR

Counting on Heaven and Earth to Make a Sinking Buck

For years you could always catch Edward Weiner singing in the rain. In fact, each morning before he went to work, he would check the rain gauge outside his front door to see whether it was going to be a good day or perhaps a good month—as far as company sales and profits went. Weiner was president of U.S. Waterproofing (Milwaukee, Wisconsin). The company repaired leaky residential foundations, and raindrops were like pennies from heaven. Still, counting on mother nature for business made Weiner very nervous. He knew that sales could dry up for long periods of time. So he began looking for new ways to pump up business.

The idea for a different business occurred to Weiner while inspecting company job sites. He observed how customers' sidewalks and driveways were sometimes several inches lower than the adjacent stoops or garage floors they abutted. This was caused by poorly compacted soil, water infiltration, and voids below the concrete slabs. He had heard about a process called slabjacking where small holes were drilled into the concrete and a mud-like mortar was injected into the holes to stabilize the soil and lift the slab back to its original height. At one-third to one-half the cost of actual replacement, slabjacking was a cost-effective way of fixing the sinking mess. Weiner knew of only one company in the Chicago area that did this type of work—and it concentrated on larger, commercial projects. Weiner saw gold. He studied the market, found some investors, and before long, he launched The Concrete Doctor, Inc. (TCDI).

Like most new businesses, things got off to a slow start. But one day he discovered an out-of-state company slabjacking a huge section of pavement on a major roadway. Even a hard hat like Weiner knew a concrete opportunity when he saw one. The company was using the same process TCDI used for residential driveways, but on a much larger scale. Weiner pulled off the road and talked to the site's construction engineer for several hours. Then he went home, called the state department of transportation, and began reading just about anything he could find on road repair. He learned how jobs were awarded by the state, how to bid on state transportation projects, how to meet the state's prequalification requirements, and more.

For instance, Weiner learned that state construction jobs were awarded to responsible companies who submitted bids with the lowest project costs. So he studied years of public bidding records for previously awarded slabjacking jobs. Then he added up the published bid prices, subtracted the estimated costs, and calculated the potential profit margin per job. It was a numbers game. One that Weiner would have to master. He would have to develop accounting systems that would take the guesswork out of the bidding process by assigning costs to all the things that could go wrong—or perhaps right, if he got lucky.

If you were Edward Weiner, what types of accounting systems would you install to make sure you could track and predict your daily job costs? How would you charge each construction job for the costs of large machinery and equipment used for multiple projects? How might you use electronic spreadsheet programs like Microsoft Excel to help you refine your bidding process?[1]

THE NATURE OF ACCOUNTING

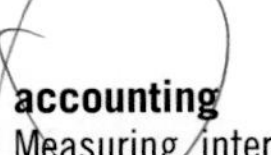

accounting
Measuring, interpreting, and communicating financial information to support internal and external decision making

bookkeeping
Record keeping, clerical phase of accounting

Like TCDI, companies today are demanding financial information that will allow them to make informed decisions in a rapidly changing business environment. **Accounting** is the system a business uses to identify, measure, and communicate financial information to enable others, inside and outside the firm, to make informed decisions.

During the accounting process, sales, purchases, and other transactions are recorded and classified into individual accounts. These accounts are later summarized in statements that make it possible to evaluate a company's past performance, present condition, and future prospects. Exhibit 17.1 presents the process for putting all of a company's financial data into standardized formats that can be used for decision making, analysis, and planning. Sometimes accounting is confused with **bookkeeping,** which is the clerical function of recording the economic activities of a business. Accounting includes bookkeeping but goes well beyond it in scope. Accountants design accounting systems, prepare financial statements, analyze and interpret financial information, prepare forecasts and budgets, provide tax services, and objectively evaluate financial statements.

Accounting is important to business for two reasons: First, it helps managers plan and control a company's operation. Armed with accounting information, managers are better equipped to make business decisions. Second, it helps outsiders evaluate a business. The outsiders who use accounting information have a variety of interests. Suppliers, banks, and other lenders want to know whether a business is credit worthy; investors and shareholders are concerned with a company's profit potential. Government agencies regulate and tax businesses; they are interested in a business's tax accounting. These users need information that is accurate, objective, consistent over time, and comparable to information

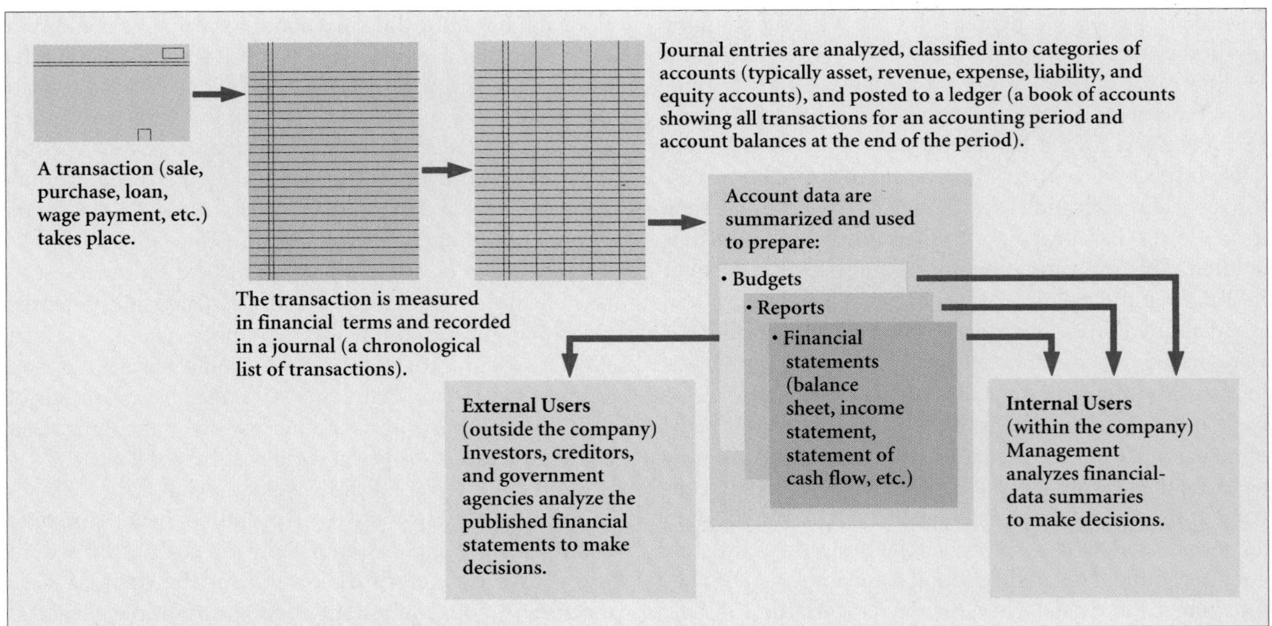

EXHIBIT 17.1

The Accounting Process

The traditional printed accounting forms are shown here. Today nearly all companies use the computer equivalents of these forms.

As part of a turnaround effort, Boston Chicken's ailing Boston Market chain is cutting some $40 million from its overall marketing budget, and is seeking to buy out its franchises to stem the sales decline at its 1,189 restaurants.

supplied by other companies. Thus published financial statements must be prepared according to **generally accepted accounting principles (GAAP),** basic standards and procedures that have been agreed on by the accounting profession.

generally accepted accounting principles (GAAP) Professionally approved standards and practices used by accountants in the preparation of financial statements

Even though published financial statements must comply with GAAP, they don't always tell the whole story. Consider Boston Market. This company reported lip-smacking-good earnings, while many of its franchises were hurting. But according to GAAP, franchisors are not required to disclose the operating results of their independent franchisees to the public—making it difficult to evaluate the financial soundness of the entire operation. After all, the biggest share of the Boston Market's revenues comes from franchise royalty fees (the amount franchisees pay the parent company for the privilege of using its name and goodwill) and from interest on large loans the company makes to its national network of franchisees, not from direct sales to customers.[2]

The Rules of Accounting

Who makes the rules of accounting? In the United States, the Financial Accounting Standards Board (FASB) controls the rule making. But some critics find their rules burdensome, incomprehensible, and unnecessary; moreover, they resent the board's resistance to international accounting standards.

Companies today sell their products all over the globe, and they operate there too. One issue facing accountants today is that different countries have different rules. Consider this: After Daimler-Benz listed on the New York Stock Exchange, the German car manufacturer reported a $370 million profit under German rules but a $1 billion loss under GAAP. Suppose you are an investor trying to evaluate whether to invest in a U.S. or foreign company. How do you account for these differences? How do you compare these investments? The need for international harmonization of accounting is growing lockstep with the globalization of business.

As a result, the International Accounting Standards Committee (IASC), founded in 1973, has established itself as the recognized body for the development of International Accounting Standards (IAS) for use in the presentation of financial statements. But there is a hitch. Although most big national stock exchanges allow foreign firms that list on them to report their financial results according to IAS, a few national regulators—including the Securities and Exchange Commission (SEC)—refuse to accept these standards. If a foreign firm wishes to list its shares on a U.S. stock exchange, it must publish a second set of accounts that are compatible with GAAP. Even though the New York Stock Exchange is desperate to lure more foreign firms, the SEC will not relax its position until the two separate rule-making authorities hammer out their differences over several troublesome rules—something the chairman of IASC intends to do.[3]

The Changing Accounting Profession

Of course rules aren't the only thing changing for today's accountants. In fact, the profession has been evolving for years. As the chairman of the American Institute of Certified Public Accountants (AICPA) put it: "now is the time for CPAs to be the architects of the accounting profession's future."[4] Today's accountant is a professional leader whose work activities include consulting, budgeting, forecasting, improving processes, planning for the future, evaluating performance, designing accounting and computer systems, and analyzing the profitability of products and customer groups.

Is It True?

To be an active member of the AICPA, you must pass the uniform CPA exam and pay an annual fee.

One of the forces driving this change is the availability of advanced technology: Electronic spreadsheets, faster computers, databases, and affordable computer programs make it possible to automate many accounting tasks and provide useful current reports and analytical detail. In fact, some companies like Bingo West, a manufacturer and distributor of bingo cards, are even using the Internet to set up interactive accounting systems. Customers at Bingo West can enter their own sales orders and generate invoices over the Internet, while the data they input update the company's accounting system.[5]

Advancements like these allow accountants to spend less time on routine number processing and more time analyzing and interpreting data and explaining their significance to managers. As one Hewlett-Packard finance manager put it: "We are not accountants, we are analysts and business partners."[6] Most accountants today are involved in company decision making and assist clients and managers in planning for the future. They must be able to convey technical messages to a nontechnical audience. In other words, accountants must be able to communicate effectively and relate comfortably to others outside their field.

certified public accountants (CPAs)
Professionally licensed accountants who meet certain requirements for education and experience and who pass a comprehensive examination

In addition, many accountants work on cross-functional teams, bringing the financial perspective to the decision-making process. This requires a strong business background and a variety of business skills, as listed in Exhibit 17.2. Of course, the AICPA has recognized this and has successfully persuaded over 30 states to increase the educational eligibility requirement to sit for the *CPA examination* from 120 to 150 semester hours. This exam is prepared by the AICPA and is a requirement for accountants to become **certified public accountants (CPAs).**

EXHIBIT 17.2

Ten Most Important Skills and Abilities for Accountants

Accountants are expected to have a thorough knowledge of basic accounting. Beyond the basics, accountants need excellent communication, interpersonal, analytical, and computer spreadsheet skills.

SKILLS AND ABILITIES
Analytical and problem-solving skills
Interpersonal skills
Listening skills
Use of computerized spreadsheets
Understanding the business
Writing skills
Familiarity with business processes
Understanding the relationship between balance sheet, income statement, and cash flow statement
Leadership skills
Understanding and preparing financial statements

Types of Accountants

Because outsiders and insiders use accounting information in different ways, accounting has two distinct facets. **Financial accounting** is concerned with preparing information for outsiders like stockholders, creditors, and the government; **management accounting** is concerned with preparing information for insiders like management and other company decision makers. The traditional distinction between financial accountants and management accountants is blurring, however, as all accountants become more involved in company operations and long-term planning. Nevertheless, accountants can choose whether they want to work as a *public accountant*—working for a variety of clients, or as a *private accountant*—working in a company, a government agency, or a nonprofit organization.

financial accounting
Area of accounting concerned with preparing financial information for users outside the organization

management accounting
Area of accounting concerned with preparing data for use by managers within the organization

Public Accountants

Public accountants are independent of the businesses, organizations, and individuals they serve. These accountants work for a variety of clients and they prepare financial statements, compute taxes, provide consultation for individuals and organizations, and evaluate the fairness of a company's financial statements. The investing public relies on the integrity of a company's financial statements and places great trust and confidence in the independence of public accountants whose detached position allows them to be objective and, when necessary, critical. Their reports are valuable to anyone who needs an unbiased picture of the financial standing of a particular business, such as creditors, shareholders, investors, and even government agencies. **Creditors** are people or organizations that have loaned money or extended credit to an individual or a business; those who borrow money are known as **debtors**. One way to assure the integrity and reliability of a company's financial statements is to conduct an **audit**—a formal evaluation of the fairness and reliability of financial statements.

public accountants
Professionals who provide accounting services to other businesses and individuals for a fee

creditors
People or organizations that have loaned money or extended credit

debtors
People or organizations that have to repay money they have borrowed

audit
Formal evaluation of the fairness and reliability of a client's financial statements

External Auditors *External auditors* are public accountants who work for an independent firm of accountants. They review clients' financial statements to determine whether the statements (1) have been prepared in accordance with the GAAP and (2) fairly present the financial position and operating results of the firm. Audit engagements provide outsiders with the highest level of assurance. Once an auditor completes an audit, he or she attaches a report summarizing the findings to the client's published financial statements. Sometimes these reports disclose an uncertainty that might materially affect the client's financial position, such as the bankruptcy of a major supplier, a large investment in obsolete inventory, or the discovery of costly environmental problems—an increasingly ethical dilemma.

For example, if an auditor finds certain environmental problems, under Canadian and U.S. regulations, the auditor is required to disclose these problems in the company's financial reports.[7] However, the cost of cleaning up environmental problems can vary, so accounting experts must make difficult decisions about how to estimate cleanup costs, how to explain the environmental problem, and how early to announce potential environmental problems. Wisconsin paper manufacturer Consolidated Papers has taken an unusually candid approach with respect to environmental problems. It discloses these problems (and sets aside money to cover cleanup costs) as soon as the company becomes aware of them.[8]

Many industries have unique regulations and reporting requirements. Some, like insurance, take years of experience to learn. Whenever possible, companies prefer to hire independent auditors who have strong backgrounds in their industry. This way auditors can make informed decisions when examining a company's financial reports. But auditor specialization has a downside. Auditors may become so close to the industry they specialize in that they may find themselves acting as an industry proponent rather than an independent, objective eye.

Consider the consequences: Over the past several years, huge judgments against independent accounting firms (for real or perceived audit problems) have had a profound impact on the profession. In fact, accounting firms have spent upward of $1 billion to settle civil lawsuits since the early 1990s.[9] Some big accounting firms are even dumping audit clients they deem to be high risk. They don't want to expose themselves to clients who will harm their reputations or generate costly litigation.[10] Given these disincentives, along with increased competition for the shrinking pool of clients as more and more companies merge, it's not surprising that many accounting firms are engineering a major transformation of their businesses away from auditing and toward less risky nonauditing services.[11]

Is It True?

Approximately two-thirds of the 50,000 students who take undergraduate accounting courses every year eventually work for public accounting firms.

Public Accounting Firms Ninety percent of companies whose stock (ownership shares) is publicly traded in the United States are audited by the world's five largest accounting firms: KPMG Peat Marwick, Arthur Andersen, Ernst & Young, Deloitte & Touche, and the largest firm (to be named) resulting from the merger between Price Waterhouse and Coopers & Lybrand.[12] These megafirms serve global customers, offer broader services, and provide one-stop shopping for clients. They've become multiline service organizations in which accounting and auditing are rapidly becoming secondary activities.[13]

BEST OF THE WEB

Size Them Up

Exactly how big are the big accounting firms? Why not size them up. Log on to the Ernst & Young Web site and learn about the many services this large accounting firm offers. With global locations, thousands of clients, a commitment to industry specialization, and experts in just about everything, this firm is a powerhouse. Be sure to visit with Ernie, its online business consultant. Did you think accountants only prepared financial statements and tax returns? Think again!
http://www.ey.com

In fact, many accounting firms (big or small) earn only half of their revenues from auditing and accounting services. At one time outside accountants served as the primary source of expertise on accounting and auditing issues. Today, however, many larger companies employ **internal auditors**—employees who investigate and evaluate their company's departments to determine whether they are operating efficiently, keeping accurate records, and complying with federal laws and regulations. Some public accounting firms have adjusted for this loss of business by establishing separate consulting business units—many of which now rank among the world's leading consulting firms.

internal auditors
Employees who analyze and evaluate the operation of company departments to determine their efficiency

As consultants, accountants design computer systems for businesses, advise management on a variety of business issues, establish employee benefit plans, and so on. These activities are often referred to as *management advisory services* (MAS), and have been especially valuable for small to midsize businesses that can't afford to staff a full-time finance department. For example, the accounting firm of Friedman & Fuller (Rockville, Maryland) offers its business clients specialized services in profit improvement, risk management, and systems training, and the accounting firm of Boulay, Hetmaker, Zibell & Company (Edina, Minnesota) specializes in mergers and acquisitions, technology, litigation support, and business valuations.

Some accountants are even expanding their services to include *personal financial plan-*

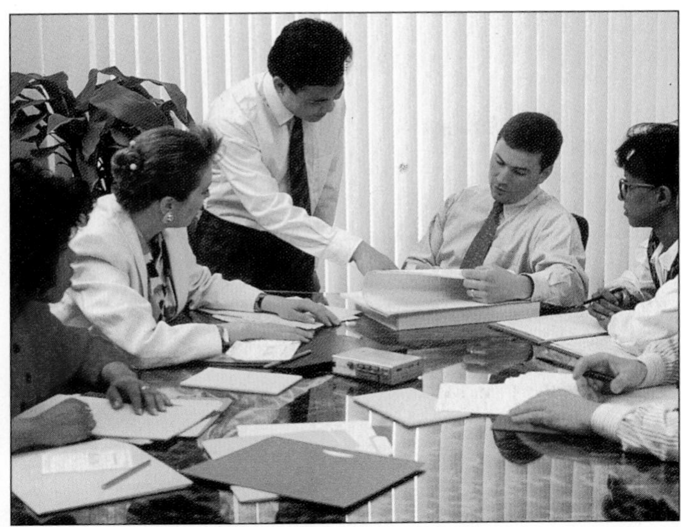

Accountants perform a variety of services for their clients beyond tax preparation and auditing. Many serve on strategic planning teams and help companies plan for the future.

ning (PFP) by assisting clients with their personal finances. In fact, personal financial planning is really an offshoot of income-tax planning, estate-tax planning, retirement planning, and profit sharing—services accountants have been providing for years.[14] However, as the role of accountants in the decision-making process increases and the need for industry specialization grows, the demand for the *traditional* services provided by public accountants (outside of the audit function) will continue to diminish. Even the chairman of the AICPA notes: "Users no longer want to look back—they want to look forward, and supplying forward-looking information is the kind of service businesses will be paying for in the future."[15]

Private Accountants

Of the 1.9 million accountants worldwide, only 35 percent are in public practice. The remaining 65 percent are, for the most part, **private accountants** (sometimes called corporate accountants) working for a business, a government agency (such as the Internal Revenue Service, a school, or a local police department), or a nonprofit corporation (such as a church, charity, or hospital).[16] Although many private accountants are CPAs, a growing number are **certified management accountants (CMAs)**, having passed a two-day exam (given by the Institute of Management Accountants) that is comparable in difficulty to the CPA exam.[17]

Some accountants specialize in different areas of accounting, such as **cost accounting** (computing and analyzing production costs), **tax accounting** (preparing tax returns and tax planning) or **financial analysis** (evaluating a company's performance and the financial implications of strategic decisions such as product pricing, employee benefits, and business acquisitions). Most company accountants, however, work together as a team under the supervision of the *controller,* who reports to the vice president of finance. Exhibit 17.3 shows the typical finance department of a large company. In smaller organizations like TCDI, the **controller** may be in charge of the company's entire finance operation and report directly to the president.

Many companies today are downsizing their accounting departments and are handling their work overflow by outsourcing special accounting projects to outside consulting firms. For example, the CPAs at Johnsson Reese Financial Solutions, a financial consulting firm in Chicago, work on special accounting projects for companies like Kraft Foods and Beatrice Foods.[18] In fact, at a recent gathering of 40 financial executives, accounting educators, and CPAs from leading institutions, the group agreed that outsourcing a com-

private accountants
In-house accountants employed by organizations and businesses other than a public accounting firm; also called corporate accountants

certified management accountants (CMAs)
Accountants who have fulfilled the requirements for certification as specialists in management accounting

cost accounting
Area of accounting focusing on the calculation of manufacturing and storage costs of products for use or sale in a business

tax accounting
Area of accounting focusing on tax preparation and tax planning

financial analysis
Process of evaluating a company's performance and analyzing the costs and benefits of a strategic action

controller
Highest-ranking accountant in a company, responsible for overseeing all accounting functions

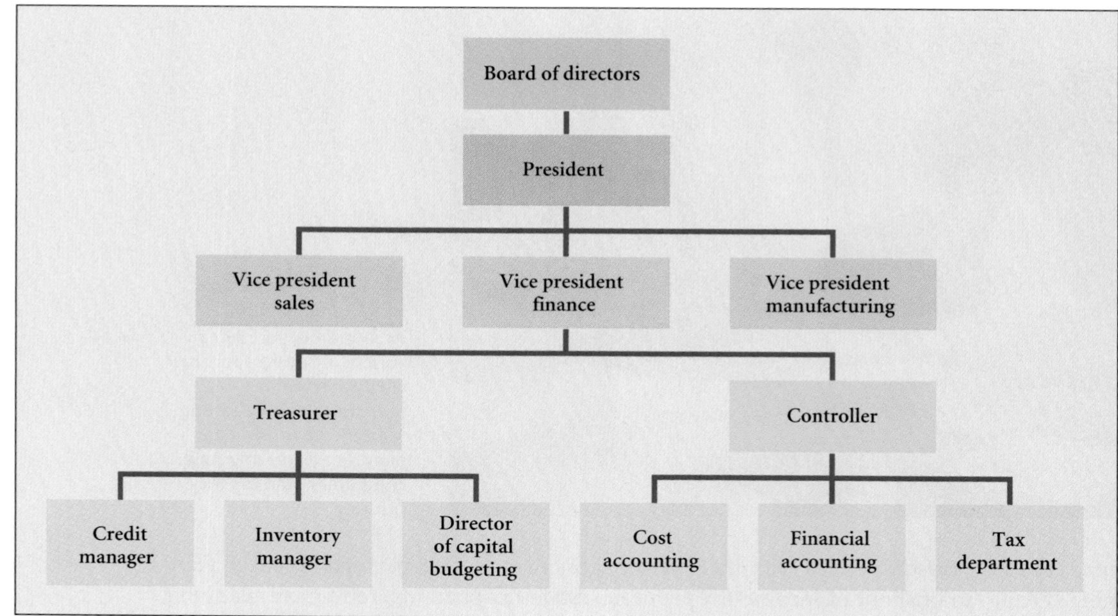

EXHIBIT 17.3

A Typical Finance Department

Here is a typical finance department of a large company. In smaller companies, the controller may be the highest ranking accountant and report directly to the president.

pany's finance functions will probably become more widespread in the future.[19] Regardless of who performs a company's accounting functions in the future, all accountants must master the fundamental principles of accounting. Knowing the rules of accounting is critical to an organization's financial health. Without rules and standards, there would be no consistencies for comparisons. Moreover, assessing a company's performance or the likelihood of continued success would be anyone's best guess.

KEY ACCOUNTING CONCEPTS

In their work with financial data, accountants are guided by three fundamental concepts: the *accounting equation, double-entry bookkeeping,* and *the matching principle.* All three remain central to the accounting process.

The Accounting Equation

assets
Anything of value owned or leased by a business

liabilities
Claim against a firm's assets by a creditor

owners' equity
Portion of a company's assets that belongs to the owners after obligations to all creditors have been met

For thousands of years, businesses and governments have kept records of their **assets**—valuable things they own or lease, such as equipment, cash, land, buildings, inventory, and investments. Claims against those assets are **liabilities** or what the business owes to its creditors—such as banks and suppliers. For example when a company borrows money to purchase a building, the lender or creditor has a claim against the company's assets. When it was said of ancient princes that they were "as rich as Croesus" (a wealthy king of Lydia), it was not just because they had much gold and grain. It was because they owned these treasures almost outright and had few debts or creditors' claims on their assets. In other words, wealth does not consist of assets alone. What remains after liabilities have been deducted from assets is **owners' equity:**

$$\text{Assets} - \text{Liabilities} = \text{Owners' equity}$$
$$\$100{,}000 - \$30{,}000 = \$70{,}000$$

Using the principles of algebra, this equation can be restated in a variety of formats. The most common is the simple **accounting equation,** which serves as the framework for the entire accounting process:

accounting equation
Basic accounting equation that assets equals liabilities plus owners' equity

$$\text{Assets} = \text{Liabilities} + \text{Owners' equity}$$
$$\$100{,}000 = \$30{,}000 + \$70{,}000$$

This equation suggests that either creditors or owners provide all the assets in a corporation. Think of it this way: If you were starting a new business, you could contribute cash to the company to buy the assets you needed to run your business or you could borrow money from a bank (the creditor) or both. The company's liabilities are placed before owners' equity in the accounting equation because creditors get paid first. After liabilities are paid, anything left over belongs to the owners or, in the case of a corporation, to the shareholders. As a business engages in economic activity, the dollar amounts and composition of its assets, liabilities, and owners' equity change. However, the equation must always be in balance; in other words, one side of the equation must always equal the other side.

Double-Entry Bookkeeping

To keep the accounting equation in balance, companies use a **double-entry bookkeeping** system that records every transaction affecting assets, liabilities, or owners' equity. For example, if a company purchases a $4,000 computer on credit, assets would increase by $4,000 (the amount of the computer) and liabilities would also increase by $4,000 (the amount you owe the vendor), keeping the accounting equation in balance. But if the company paid cash outright for the computer (instead of arranging for credit), then the company's *total* assets would not change because the $4,000 increase in equipment would be offset by an equal $4,000 reduction in cash. In fact, the company would just be switching assets—cash for equipment.

double-entry bookkeeping
Way of recording financial transactions that requires two entries for every transaction so that the accounting equation is always kept in balance

Even though computers do much of the tedious recording of accounting transactions like the one above, mastering fundamental principles of accounting such as double-entry bookkeeping is important because accountants must decide which accounts to increase or decrease, and they must understand what to do when transactions are recorded improperly. Once these individual transactions are recorded and then summarized, accountants review the resulting transaction summaries and adjust or correct errors, a key part of the process called **closing the books.** This process must be completed before the accountants can prepare financial statements.

closing the books
Transferring the net revenue and expense account balances to retained earnings for the period

The Matching Principle

The **matching principle** requires that expenses incurred in producing revenues be deducted from the revenue they generated during the same accounting period. This matching of expenses and revenue is necessary for the company's financial statements to present an accurate picture of the profitability of a business. Accountants match revenue to expenses by adopting the **accrual basis** of accounting, which states that revenue is recognized when you make a sale or provide a service, not when you get paid. Likewise, your expenses are recorded when you receive the benefit of a service or when you use an asset to produce revenue—not when you pay for it. Accrual accounting focuses on the economic substance of the event instead of the movement of cash. It's a way of recognizing that revenue can be earned either

matching principle
Fundamental principle requiring that expenses incurred in producing revenue be deducted from the revenues they generate during an accounting period

accrual basis
Accounting method in which revenue is recorded when a sale is made and expense is recorded when incurred

before or after cash is received and that expenses can be incurred when you receive a benefit (like a shipment or supplies) whether before or after you pay for it.

cash basis
Accounting method in which revenue is recorded when payment is received and expense is recorded when cash is paid

If a business runs on a **cash basis**, the company records revenue only when money from the sale is actually received. Your checkbook is an easy-to-understand cash-based accounting system: You record checks at the time of purchase and deposits at the time of receipt. Revenue thus equals cash received, and expenses equal cash paid. The trouble with cash-based accounting, however, is that it can be misleading. You can misrepresent expenses and income by the way you time payments. It's easy to inflate income, for example, by delaying the payment of bills. For that reason, few companies keep their books on a cash basis. In fact, manufacturers and retailers are required to use the accrual method.

depreciation
Accounting procedure for systematically spreading the cost of a tangible asset over its estimated useful life

Depreciation, or the allocation of the cost of a tangible long-term asset over a period of time, is another way that companies match expenses with revenue. During the normal course of business, a company enters into many transactions that benefit more than one accounting period—such as the purchase of buildings, inventory, and equipment. When you buy a piece of equipment or machinery, instead of deducting the entire cost of the item at the time of purchase, you depreciate it, or spread its cost over the asset's useful life (because the asset will likely generate income for years to come). If the company were to expense long-term assets at the time of purchase, the financial performance of the company would be distorted in the year of purchase as well as in all future years when these assets generate revenue.

FINANCIAL STATEMENTS

balance sheet
Statement of a firm's financial position on a particular date; also known as a statement of financial position

An accounting system is made up of thousands of individual transactions—debits and credits to be exact. After a while, these individual transactions accumulate, making it difficult for management to sort out what's going on. To simplify the picture, accountants prepare financial statements to summarize the transactions. Financial statements are tools for analyzing a business. They consist of three separate, yet interrelated reports: the *balance sheet,* the *income statement,* and the *statement of cash flows.* Together these statements provide information about an organization's financial strength and ability to meet current obligations, the effectiveness of its sales and collection efforts, and how well the company manages its assets. These reports can reveal opportunities and forewarn of pitfalls. In sum, they're indispensable.

In the following sections we will examine the financial statements of Computer Discount Warehouse (CDW), a mail-order reseller of brand-name personal computers (such as IBM, Toshiba, and Macintosh) and related computer products (such as software, printer cartridges, and scanners). The company mails over 54 million product catalogs annually to potential customers in the United States. As a result, CDW's 300 plus account executives receive up to 30,000 customer phone inquiries per day. Once a phone rings, it is up to the CDW account executive to determine the customer's needs, establish a relationship, and make a sale. In 1996 the company shipped over 1.3 million orders, amounting to over $927 million in sales—a 48 percent increase in sales from the prior year. Because of this tremendous growth and the increasing demand for new computer products, the company built a new 218,000-square-foot facility—doubling the size of its current facility. Keep these points in mind as we discuss the financial statements of CDW below.[20]

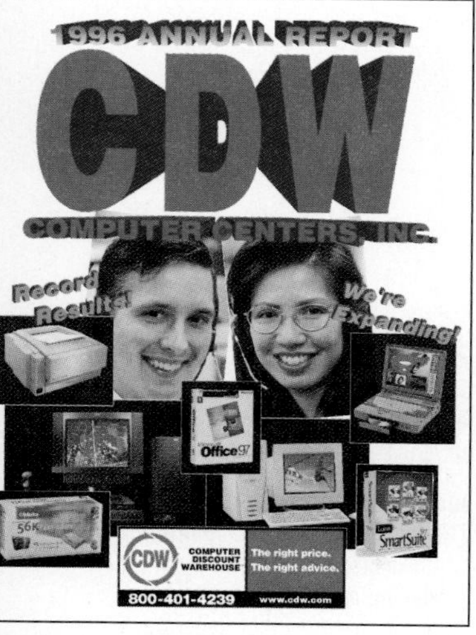

CDW has experienced continuous, rapid growth ever since the company was founded. In 1998, CDW was ranked among the largest 1,000 U.S. companies by *Fortune* magazine.

Balance Sheet

The **balance sheet**, also known as the statement of financial position, is a snapshot of a company's financial position on a particular date, like December 31, 1999. In effect it freezes all business actions and provides a baseline from which companies can measure change. This statement is called a balance sheet because it includes all elements in the accounting equation and shows the balance between assets on one side of the equation and liabilities and owners' equity on the other side. In other words, like the accounting equation, a change on one side of the balance sheet means changes elsewhere. Exhibit 17.4 is the balance sheet for CDW as of December 31, 1996.

Current Assets
Cash and other items that will or can be converted to cash within one year.

Fixed Assets
Long-term investments in buildings, equipment, furniture, and any other tangible property expected to be used in running the business for a period longer than one year.

Current Liabilities
Amounts owed by the company that are to be repaid within one year.

Long-Term Liabilities
Debts that are due a year or more after the date of the balance sheet.

Shareholders' Equity
Money contributed to the company for ownership interests, as well as the accumulation of profits that have not been paid out as dividends (retained earnings).

Computer Discount Warehouse

Balance Sheet
As of December 31, 1996
(rounded to nearest thousand)

ASSETS		
1. *Current Assets*		
Cash	$16,500	
Marketable Securities	58,500	
Accounts Receivable	61,300	
Inventory	41,500	
Miscellaneous Prepaid and Deferred Items	3,100	
Total Current Assets		$180,900
2. *Fixed Assets*		
Property and Equipment	$3,600	
Construction in Progress	8,600	
Other Assets		5,700
Total Fixed Assets		$17,900
Total Assets		198,800
LIABILITIES AND SHAREHOLDERS' EQUITY		
3. *Current Liabilities*		
Accounts Payable	$36,600	
Accrued Expenses	20,600	
Total Current Liabilities		$57,200
4. *Long-Term Liabilities*		$ 0
Total Liabilities		$57,200
5. *Shareholders' Equity*		
Common Stock		
(21,525 shares @ $.01 par value)	200	
Paid-in Capital	68,000	
Retained Earnings	73,400	
Total Owners' Equity		$141,600
Total Liabilities and Owners' Equity		$198,800

EXHIBIT 17.4

Balance Sheet for Computer Discount Warehouse

The categories used on Computer Discount Warehouse's year-end balance sheet are typical.

GAINING THE COMPETITIVE EDGE

How to Read an Annual Report

Spring is the time of year for bluebirds to sing, flowers to bloom, baseball players to take the field, and annual reports to pour off the printing presses. The nation's publicly traded corporations "tell all" in these financial reports to shareholders, but finding the important information in them isn't easy. The real story about the company's financial health is often buried in footnotes and dense tables. You'll need to know how to read annual reports in your career, whether you're thinking of investing in companies, becoming a supplier for them, or applying for a job with them. Thus, it's worth your while to consider the advice of *Newsweek* columnist Jane Bryant Quinn, who provided the following pointers in an ad created for International Paper Company as part of its "The Power of the Printed Word" campaign. Using as her example the annual report of the fictional Galactic Industries, Quinn tells you how to find the important information.

START AT THE BACK

First, turn back to the report of the certified public accountant. This third-party auditor will tell you right off the bat if Galactic's report conforms with "generally accepted accounting principles." Then go to the footnotes. Check to see whether earnings are up or down. If they're down only because of a change in accounting, maybe that's good! The company owes less tax and has more money in its pocket. If earnings are up, maybe that's bad. They may be up because of a special windfall that won't happen again next year. The footnotes often tell the whole story.

FIND OUT WHAT HAPPENED AND WHY

Now turn to the letter from the chairman. Usually addressed "to our shareholders," it's up front—and should be in more ways than one. The chairman's tone reflects the personality, the well-being of the company.

In this letter, the chairman should tell you how the company fared this year. But more important, the letter should tell you why. Keep an eye out for sentences that start with "Except for . . ." and "Despite the . . ." They're clues to problems.

LOOK FOR INSIGHTS INTO THE FUTURE

On the positive side, a chairman's letter should give you insights into the company's future and its stance on economic or political trends that may affect it. For example, look for what's new in each line of business. Is management getting the company in good shape to weather the tough and competitive years ahead?

Now—and no sooner—begin digging into the numbers!

One source is the balance sheet. It is a snapshot of how the company stands at a single point in time. On the top are assets—everything the company owns. Things that can quickly be turned into cash are current assets. On the bottom are liabilities—everything the company owes. Current liabilities are the debts due in one year, which are paid out of current assets.

The difference between current assets and current liabilities is working capital, a key figure to watch from one annual (and quarterly) report to another. If working capital shrinks, it could mean trouble. One possibility: The company may not be able to keep dividends growing rapidly.

LOOK FOR GROWTH HERE

Owners' or shareholders' equity is the difference between total assets and liabilities. It is the presumed dollar

In reality, however, no business can stand still while its financial condition is being examined. A business may make hundreds of transactions of various kinds every working day. Even during a holiday, office fixtures grow older and decrease in value, and interest on savings accounts accumulates. Yet the accountant must set up a balance sheet so that managers and other interested parties can evaluate the business's financial position as if it were static, rather than ever-changing.

calendar year
Twelve-month accounting period that begins on January 1 and ends on December 31

Every company prepares a balance sheet at least once a year, most often at the end of the **calendar year,** covering from January 1 to December 31. However, many business

value of what the owners or shareholders own. You want it to grow.

Another important number to watch is long-term debt. High and rising debt, relative to equity, may be no problem for a growing business. But it shows weakness in a company that's leveling out. (More on that later.)

The second basic source of numbers is the income statement. It shows how much money Galactic made or lost over the year.

Most people look at one figure first. It's in the income statement at the bottom: earnings per share. Watch out. It can fool you. Galactic's management could boost earnings by selling off a plant. Or by cutting the budget for research and advertising. (See the footnotes!) So don't be smug about earnings until you've found out how they happened—and how they might happen next year.

Check Net Sales First

The number you should look at first in the income statement is net sales. Ask yourself: Are sales going up at a faster rate than the last time around? When sales increases start to slow, the company may be in trouble. And ask yourself once more: Have sales gone down because the company is selling off a losing business? If so, profits may be soaring.

(I never promised you that figuring out an annual report was going to be easy!)

Get Out Your Calculator

Another important thing to study is the company's debt. Get out your pocket calculator, and turn to the balance sheet. Divide long-term liabilities by owners' or shareholders' equity. That's the debt-to-equity ratio.

A high ratio means the company borrows a lot of money to spark its growth. That's okay—if sales grow, too, and if there's enough cash on hand to meet the payments. A company doing well on borrowed money can earn big profits for its shareholders. But if sales fall, watch out. The whole enterprise may slowly sink. Some companies can handle high ratios; others can't.

Compare

That brings up the most important thing of all: One annual report, one chairman's letter, one ratio won't tell you much. You have to compare. Is the company's debt-to-equity ratio better or worse than it used to be? Better or worse than the industry norms? Better or worse after this recession than it was after the last recession? In company-watching, comparisons are all. They tell you if management is staying on top of things.

Each year, companies give you more and more information in their annual reports. Profiting from that information is up to you. I hope you profit from mine.

Questions for Critical Thinking

1. Why might a job applicant want to read a company's annual report before applying for a job with that company?
2. What types of valuable nonfinancial information might an annual report disclose to a potential supplier?

and government bodies use a **fiscal year,** which may be any 12 consecutive months. For example, a company may use a fiscal year such as June 1 to May 31 because its peak selling season ends in May. Its fiscal year would then correspond to its full annual cycle of manufacturing and selling. Some companies prepare a balance sheet more often than once a year, perhaps at the end of each month or quarter. Thus, every balance sheet is dated to show the exact date when the financial snapshot was taken.

fiscal year
Any 12 consecutive months used as an accounting period

By reading a company's balance sheet you should be able to determine the size of the company, the major assets owned, any asset changes that occurred in recent periods, how the company's assets are financed, and any major changes that have occurred in the company's debt and equity in recent periods. Most companies classify assets, liabilities, and owners' equity into categories like those shown in the CDW balance sheet.

Assets As discussed earlier in this chapter, an asset is something owned by a company that will be used to generate income. Assets can consist of cash, things you can convert into cash like investments, and equipment you need to make products or provide services. For example, CDW needs a warehouse and a sizable inventory in order to sell computer products to its customers. Most often, the asset section of the balance sheet is divided into *current assets* and *fixed assets.* **Current assets** include cash and other items that will or can become cash within the following year. **Fixed assets** (sometimes referred to as property, plant, and equipment) are long-term investments in buildings, equipment, furniture and fixtures, transportation equipment, land, and other tangible property used in running the business. Fixed assets have a useful life of more than one year.

current assets
Cash and other items that can be turned back into cash within one year

fixed assets
Assets retained for long-term use, such as land, buildings, machinery, and equipment; also referred to as property, plant, and equipment

Assets are listed in descending order by *liquidity,* or the ease with which they can be converted into cash. Thus current assets are listed before fixed assets. The balance sheet gives a subtotal for each type of asset and then a grand total for all assets. CDW's current assets consist primarily of cash, investments in short-term marketable securities such as money-market funds, accounts receivable (or the amounts due from customers), and inventory (such as computers, software, and other items the company sells to customers). Because the company leased its warehouse facility in 1996, the company's long-term assets consist of only a small amount of property and other miscellaneous assets. Take special note of the asset category "construction in progress." As the company pays the architect and builder for its new warehouse, the accountants record these payments as construction in progress. Once the construction is complete, the total amount spent (projected at $26 million) will be listed as a building and grouped with other property and equipment owned by the company.

Liabilities Liabilities come after assets because they represent claims against the company's assets, as shown in the basic accounting equation: *Assets* = *Liabilities* + *Owners' equity.* Liabilities may be current or long-term, and they are listed in the order in which they will come due. The balance sheet gives subtotals for **current liabilities** (obligations that will have to be met within one year of the date of the balance sheet) and **long-term liabilities** (obligations that are due one year or more after the date of the balance sheet), and then it gives a grand total for all liabilities.

current liabilities
Obligations that must be met within a year

long-term liabilities
Obligations that fall due more than a year from the date of the balance sheet

CDW's current liabilities consist of accounts payable or money it owes its suppliers (such as IBM and Toshiba) as well as money it owes for other miscellaneous services (such as electricity and telephone charges). Although highly unusual for a company this size, CDW has no long-term liabilities. The company is paying for the costs of its new facility with money it has saved over many years. By investing these accumulated earnings in short-term marketable securities, the company is able to earn interest on its funds until the money is needed for the new building.

Is It True?

More than 50 percent of corporate accountants never perform tax-related work for their jobs.

Another type of current liability is *accrued expenses* or expenses that have been incurred but for which bills have not yet been received. According to the matching principle, CDW records its expenses when the company receives the benefit of the service, not when the company pays for it. For example, CDW's account executives earn commissions on computer sales to customers. The company has a liability to its account executives once the sale is made, regardless of when a check is issued to the employee. CDW must record this liability because it represents a claim against company assets. If such expenses and their associated liabilities were not recorded, CDW's financial statements would be misleading and would violate the matching principle (because the commission expenses that were earned at the time of sale would not be matched to the revenue generated from the sale).

Owners' Equity The owners' investment in a business is listed on the balance sheet under owners' equity (or shareholders' equity for a corporation like CDW). Sole proprietorships list owner's equity under the owner's name with the amount (assets minus liabilities). Small partnerships list each partner's share of the business separately, and large partnerships list the total of all partners' shares. Shareholders' equity for a corporation is presented in terms of the amount of common stock that is outstanding, meaning the amount that is in the hands of the shareholders. The combined amount of the assigned or par value of the common stock plus the amount paid over the par value (paid-in capital) represents the shareholders' total investment. Roughly $68 million was paid into the corporation by CDW shareholders at the time these shares were issued.

Shareholders' equity also includes a corporation's **retained earnings**—the portion of shareholders' equity that is not distributed to its owners in the form of *dividends.* CDW's retained earnings amount to over $73 million. Most corporations like CDW keep or retain a portion of their earnings for future asset purchases. Sometimes they distribute some of the corporation's profits to shareholders in the form of **dividends.**

retained earnings
The portion of shareholders' equity earned by the company but not distributed to its owners in the form of dividends

dividends
Distributions of corporate assets to shareholders in the form of cash or other assets

income statement
Financial record of a company's revenues, expenses, and profits over a given period of time

revenues
Amount of sales of goods or services and inflow from miscellaneous sources such as interest, rent, and royalties

expenses
Costs created in the process of generating revenues

net income
Profit or loss earned by a firm, determined by subtracting expenses from revenues; also called the bottom line

cost of goods sold
Cost of producing or acquiring a company's products for sale during a given period

gross profit
Amount remaining when the cost of goods sold is deducted from net sales; also known as gross margin

operating expenses
All costs of operation that are not included under cost of goods sold

selling expenses
All the operating expenses associated with marketing goods or services

general expenses
Operating expenses, such as office and administrative expenses, not directly associated with creating or marketing a good or service

Income Statement

If the balance sheet is a snapshot, the income statement is a movie. The **income statement** shows how profitable the organization has been over a specific period of time, typically one year. It summarizes all **revenues** (or sales), the amounts that have been or are to be received from customers for goods or services delivered to them, and all **expenses,** the costs that have arisen in generating revenues. Expenses and income taxes are then subtracted from revenues to show the actual profit or loss of a company, a figure known as **net income**—profit or the *bottom line.* By briefly reviewing a company's income statements you should have a general sense of the company's size, trend in sales, major expenses, and the resulting net income or loss. Owners, creditors, and investors can evaluate the company's past performance and future prospects by comparing net income for one year with net income for previous years. Exhibit 17.5 is the 1996 income statement for CDW, showing a net income of $34 million. This is a 71 percent increase over the company's net income of $20 million from the prior year.

Expenses, the costs of doing business, include both the direct costs associated with creating or purchasing products for sale and the indirect costs associated with operating expenses. Whether a company manufactures or purchases its inventory, the cost of storing the product for sale (such as heating the warehouse, paying the rent, and buying insurance on the storage facility) is added to the difference between the cost of the beginning inventory and the cost of the ending inventory in order to compute the actual cost of items that were sold during a period—or the **cost of goods sold**.

As shown in Exhibit 17.5, cost of goods sold is deducted from sales to obtain a company's **gross profit**—a key figure used in financial statement analysis. In addition to the costs directly associated with producing goods, companies deduct **operating expenses,** which include both *selling expenses* and *general expenses.* **Selling expenses** are operating expenses incurred through marketing and distributing the product (such as wages or salaries of salespeople, advertising, supplies, insurance for the sales operation, depreciation for the store and sales equipment, and other sales-department expenses such as telephone charges). **General expenses** are operating expenses incurred in the overall administration of a business. They include professional services (accounting and legal fees), office salaries,

Revenue
Funds received from sales of goods and services to customers as well as other items such as rent, interest, and dividends. Net sales are gross sales less returns and allowances.

Cost of Goods Sold
Cost of merchandise or services that generate a company's income by adding purchases to beginning inventory and then subtracting ending inventory.

Operating Expenses
Generally classified as selling and general expenses. Selling expenses are those incurred through the marketing and distributing of the company's products. General expenses are operating expenses incurred in the overall administration of a business.

Net income
Profit or loss over a specific period determined by subtracting all expenses from revenues.

Computer Discount Warehouse

Income Statement
Year ended December 31, 1996
(rounded to nearest thousand)

1. *Revenue*		
Net Sales		$927,900
2. *Cost of Goods Sold*		
Beginning Inventory	$27,400	
Add: Purchases During the Year	819,500	
Cost of Goods Available for Sale	846,900	
Less: Ending Inventory	41,500	
Cost of Goods Sold		$805,400
Gross Profit		$122,500
3. *Operating Expenses*		$68,900
Net Operating Income		53,600
Other Income		$3,300
Net Income Before Taxes		$56,900
Less: Income Taxes		22,500
4. *Net Income*		$34,400

EXHIBIT 17.5

Income Statement for Computer Discount Warehouse

An income statement summarizes the company's financial operations over a particular accounting period, usually a year.

depreciation of office equipment, insurance for office operations, supplies, and so on. Operating expenses and income taxes are deducted from gross profit to compute the company's net income or loss (losses are shown in parentheses) for the period.

Statement of Cash Flows

statement of cash flows
Statement of a firm's cash receipts and cash payments that presents information on its sources and uses of cash.

In addition to preparing a balance sheet and an income statement, all public companies and many privately owned companies prepare a **statement of cash flows** to show how much cash the company generated over time and where it went (see Exhibit 17.6). The statement of cash flows reveals not only the increase or decrease in the company's cash for the period but also the accounts (by category) that caused that change. From a brief review of this statement you should have a general sense of the following: the amount of cash created or consumed by daily operations; the amount of cash invested in fixed or

Computer Discount Warehouse

Statement of Cash Flows
Year ended December 31, 1996
(rounded to nearest thousand)

Cash Provided by Operations*		
Net Income	$34,400	
Adjustments to reconcile net income to net cash provided by operating activities	(5,626)	
Net cash provided by operations		$28,774
Cash provided by and used in investing activities		
Purchase of property and equipment	(11,078)	
Purchase of securities	(111,482)	
Redemptions of securities	96,032	
Net cash used in investing activities		($26,528)
Net increase/decrease in cash		$2,246
Cash and cash equivalents at beginning of year		14,216
Cash and cash equivalents at end of year		16,462

*Note: Numbers in parentheses indicate cash outflows.

EXHIBIT 17.6

Statement of Cash Flows for Computer Discount Warehouse

A statement of cash flows shows a firm's cash receipts and cash payments as a result of three main activities—operating, investing, and financing—for a period.

other assets; the amount of debt borrowed or repaid; and the proceeds from the sale of stock or payments for dividends. In addition, an analysis of cash flows provides a good idea of a company's ability to pay its short-term obligations when they become due.

FINANCIAL ANALYSIS

Organizations and individuals use financial statements—balance sheets, income statements, and statements of cash flows—to spot problems and opportunities and to make business decisions. In other words, preparing financial statements, for many companies, is just the beginning of the accounting process. When analyzing financial statements, managers and outsiders try to evaluate a company's performance in relation to its previous performance, the economy as a whole, and the company's competitors, taking into account the methods the company uses as well as the effects of extraordinary or unusual items. These can include the sale of major assets; the purchase of a new line of products from another company; or local, regional, national, and international economic conditions, which have a significant influence on most industries and companies.

Consider the housing industry. When times are tough, people tend to put off buying a new house, and home builders' sales drop. Hard times may make even the best-run companies look weak. The converse is also true: Good times are likely to improve the earnings of even the worst-run businesses. When gauging a company's financial health, take into account these uncontrollable economic forces and then examine how the company has responded compared with its competitors. Sales growth may slow during a recession for all companies in an industry. However, a company that maintains large profit margins while its competitors struggle may be assumed to be doing well.

In order for companies to continuously improve the total quality of their products and customer service, managers and employees must gain a better understanding of both their operating costs and the operating functions that drive these costs. That's why companies like Motorola are applying the same total quality management standards to their financial functions as they do to their operational functions. By improving their accounting systems, they can close their books faster and spend more time analyzing their financial results.

Eliyahu Goldratt (respected theorist and author of *The Goal)* notes that in order for a company to be successful, it must increase the rate at which it generates cash while *simultaneously* reducing both inventory levels and operating expenses—something Goldratt labels as *throughput.*[21] However, before companies can reduce inventory levels and operating expenses, managers need to evaluate them and measure them. One way to do this is by restating key financial statement components into trends and ratios.

GAINING THE COMPETITIVE EDGE

Motorola: Applying TQM to Accounting Processes

How do you tell a $20 billion globalized company with 120,000 employees scattered over 30 nations to reduce the amount of time it takes to finalize its monthly accounting transactions (a process known as closing the books) from 8 days to 4? You just tell it. At least, that's what Motorola did.

WHY?

Every month companies must undergo what they refer to as the never-ending torture: the financial closing. It is the moment of truth when the books must balance. For years, it took Motorola's accountants eight working days to report the financial results of the prior month's financial activities to headquarters. This meant that by the time headquarters received the information, it was almost time to begin the process again, leaving no time for analysis. As a result, shareholders, customers, suppliers, corporate officers, board members, potential investors, and Wall Street analysts received monthly performance results long after the fact—something Motorola's management knew would have to change. Besides, the process was costing the company lots of money—almost 2.4 percent of sales.

But improving processes was not new to Motorola. Winner of the prestigious Malcolm Baldrige Quality Award, Motorola decided to apply the same total quality management standards to its financial reporting functions so that more time could be spent analyzing the results and less time producing them. So the company laid down the law: Shrink the month-end closing process from eight workdays to four, and make sure that the numbers submitted are the final numbers—no subsequent adjustments.

IT CAN'T BE DONE, CAN IT?

Of course, convincing the accountants was not an easy task. First management had to get people to stop saying, "It can't be done." Then it had to inspire each sector (that's Motorola's term for operating business unit) to look for ways to change how things were done—not for the sake of change, but to improve the sector. In fact, no one was told how to do the job; people were simply told to get it done so that a consolidated balance sheet could be on the CEO's desk by noon on the third day of the current fiscal month.

STREAMLINING THE PROCESS

Unfortunately, there were no secrets, tricks, or complex management strategy for the accountants to follow. Instead, each sector had to look for hundreds of 1 percent improvements the old fashioned way—with an awful lot of hard work. Errors became the clear target. The sectors found that the time they spent finding and correcting errors was a major factor in slowing them down. They discovered that the worst way to tackle errors was to wait until the month-end closing and then correct them. But first they had to know where they were coming from and how many there were. So they counted them, and they found that the entire company was recording about 10,000 errors a month.

Trend Analysis

The process of comparing financial data from year to year in order to see how they have changed is known as **trend analysis.** You can use trend analysis to uncover shifts in the nature of the business over time and to compare your company with others in its industry or with the economy as a whole. Most large companies provide data for trend analysis in their annual reports. Their balance sheets and income statements typically show three to five years or more of data (making comparative statement analysis possible); changes in other key items—such as revenues, income, earnings per share, and dividends per share—are usually presented in tables and graphs.

trend analysis
Comparison of a firm's financial data from year to year to see how they have changed

When you analyze trends, look closely to see whether the results have been distorted by inflationary trends. During the late 1970s, when the inflation rate was in double digits, every company in the United States could automatically increase its sales revenue by at least 10

Then they tried to figure out what was causing these errors and how they could prevent them without creating additional work. They examined their entire accounting process. They listed each accounting step on a yellow Post-it note and stuck the paper up on the wall, flowcharting the entire operation, and with maybe a hundred pieces of paper stuck to the wall, they asked: "Why is that step there? And why is that step here?" If no one could answer the question adequately, they ripped the note off the wall. Of course, each time they pulled a note down, it was like finding gold—less work, fewer steps. Even Motorola's vice president and controller admits that it wasn't a very sophisticated approach—but it worked.

As a result, they eliminated duplicate key punching of time cards, trimming the payroll function by two days. They also eliminated monthly reimbursement checks to employees for travel and entertainment by giving them company Visa cards. They even automated the receipt of inventory shipments from suppliers by using scanners, and they eliminated paper check writing by using electronic fund transfers. Of course these changes took a lot of time—three years in total. Then Motorola announced another quality/cycle-time stretch: a two-day close. But this time it took only two years before it was the standard operating procedure.

A Definite Competitive Advantage

Even Motorola executives admit that it took a long time for all sectors to buy into the initiative. But they acknowledge that empowering sectors to find their own workable answers was a positive step. Stressing creativity and not mandating solutions was a real plus, admits Bob Kleinkauf, Motorola's manager of financial management development. When one sector achieved seemingly effortless closings, others wanted to know why and emulated their success.

As a result of these changes, Motorola admits that the quality of its financial numbers is better than when it took the company longer. Moreover, it has reduced the company's annual cost of accumulating and disseminating financial data from 2.4 percent of sales to less than 1.3 percent—approaching the world-class standard of 1 percent. Besides saving money, these enhancements have benefited Motorola in other ways. Now with faster closings and fewer errors, the financial managers have more time to focus on analyzing trends and using the information to advise operating management. Not surprisingly, Motorola is acting on its next goal: a closing in one and one-half days. What's the advantage to Motorola? It would allow the company to release its numbers to investors sooner than other companies do—something they characterize as "a significant competitive edge."

Questions for Critical Thinking

1. Why did Motorola's management decide not to mandate solutions? Please explain.
2. Why is it important for financial information to be timely? Please explain.

percent annually without achieving any real improvement in its basic business. By simply raising prices to keep up with inflation, a company could give at least a superficial appearance of growth. When inflation slowed in the 1980s, many companies' sales growth slowed as well—not because their business was bad, but because the built-in inflation kicker had diminished.

To correct for this potential distortion, the Securities and Exchange Commission requires the largest public companies to supplement their financial statements with footnotes showing what their historical costs would look like when adjusted for inflation. Now that inflation has abated, the accounting profession has put this sort of inflation-adjusted accounting on the back burner. However, accountants may return to it if inflation rises again.

BEST OF THE WEB

Link Your Way to the World of Accounting

Often the best Web sites are the ones that link you to lots of others. Check out the Accountant's Home Page. It's a launching point for accountants. Got a question or two? You'll find the perfect link to resolve it. Meet the *Electronic Accountant.* Be sure to visit the *Small Business Exhibit Hall* to learn about accounting software packages for small businesses. And don't leave without checking out *CCH* for some late-breaking tax and business news. There's even some *Great Ideas for Teaching Accounting* your professor might be interested in.
http://computercpa.com

Ratio Analysis

ratio analysis
Use of quantitative measures to evaluate a firm's financial performance

Ratio analysis compares two elements from the same year's financial figures. They are called ratios because they are computed by dividing one number by another. This is in order to put companies on the same footing and enhance comparisons between different size companies and changing dollar amounts. For example, the amount of net income earned from sales of a large supermarket might be compared with the amount of net income earned from sales of a smaller grocery store by stating these comparisons as a percentage or ratio. Like trend analysis, ratio analysis reveals how the company's performance compares with that of similar companies in its industry. Every industry tends to have its own "normal" ratios, which act as yardsticks for individual companies.

Bankers are particularly interested in the financial results of the companies that have borrowed money from them. They regularly meet with company owners and executives to assess the borrower's financial performance through ratio analysis.

The importance of converting numbers into ratios can be explained by the following example: Suppose you wanted to know how well your favorite baseball player was performing this year. To find out, you would check his statistics—batting average, runs batted in (RBIs), hits, and home runs. You would probably also want to know how many hits, home runs, and RBIs the league leader has. In other words, to evaluate his performance, you need to rearrange the raw statistical data into formats that allow you to compare it with the competition, highlight historical trends, and develop key relationships, such as hits per times at bat or batting average.

Financial ratios do the same thing. They convert the raw numbers from the current and prior years' financial statements into ratios that highlight important relationships or measures of performance.[22] Just as baseball statistics focus on various aspects of performance (such as hitting or field percentage), financial ratios help companies understand their current operations and answer key questions: Is the inventory too large? Are credit customers paying too slowly? Can the company pay its bills? They also set standards and benchmarks for gauging future business by comparing a company's ratios with industry averages that show the performance of competition. Dun and Bradstreet, a credit rating firm, and Robert Morris Associates publish average financial figures and ratios for a variety of industries and company sizes.

Before reviewing specific ratios, consider two rules of thumb: First, avoid drawing too strong a conclusion from any one ratio. A baseball player's performance is measured by more than his batting average. Even though his batting average may be low, his RBIs may make him a valuable player in the lineup. Second, once ratios have presented a general indication, refer back to the specific data involved to see if the numbers confirm what the ratios suggest. In other words do a little investigating because statistics can be misleading. Remember, a player's batting average can be artificially quite high if he's had only a few times at bat. Financial ratios can be organized into the following groups: profitability, liquidity, activity, and leverage (or debt).

Profitability Ratios You can analyze how well a company is conducting its ongoing operations by computing **profitability ratios,** which show the state of the company's financial performance or how well it's generating profits. Three of the most common profitability ratios are **return on sales** or profit margin (the net income a business makes per unit of sales), **return on investment (ROI)** or return on equity (the income earned on the owner's investment), and **earnings per share** (the profit earned for each share of stock outstanding). Exhibit 17.7 shows how to compute these profitability ratios by using the financial information from CDW.

Liquidity Ratios **Liquidity ratios** measure the ability of the firm to pay its short-term obligations. As you might expect, lenders and creditors are keenly interested in liquidity measures. Liquidity can be judged on the basis of *working capital,* the *current ratio,* and the *quick ratio.* A company's **working capital** (current assets minus current liabilities) is an indicator of liquidity because it represents current assets remaining after the payment of all current liabilities. The dollar amount of working capital can be misleading, however. For example, it may include the value of slow-moving inventory items that cannot be used to help pay a company's short-term debts.

A different picture of the company's liquidity is provided by the **current ratio**—current assets divided by current liabilities. This compares the current debt owed with the current assets available to pay that debt. The **quick ratio,** also called the *acid-test ratio,* is computed by subtracting inventory from current assets and then dividing the result by current liabilities. This ratio is often a better indicator of a firm's ability to pay creditors than the current ratio because the quick ratio leaves out inventories—which at times can be slow moving and difficult to sell. Analysts generally consider a quick ratio of 1.0 to be reasonable whereas a current ratio of 2.0 is considered a safe risk for short-term credit.

profitability ratios
Ratios that measure the overall financial performance of a firm

return on sales
Ratio between net income and net sales; also known as profit margin

return on investment (ROI)
Ratio between the net income earned by a company and total owners' equity; also known as return on equity

earnings per share
Measure of a firm's profitability for each share of outstanding stock, calculated by dividing net income after taxes by shares of common stock outstanding

liquidity ratios
Ratios that measure a firm's ability to meet its short-term obligations when they are due

working capital
Current assets minus current liabilities

current ratio
Measure of a firm's short-term liquidity, calculated by dividing current assets by current liabilities

quick ratio
Measure of a firm's short-term liquidity, calculated by adding cash, marketable securities, and receivables, and then dividing that sum by current liabilities; also known as the acid-test ratio

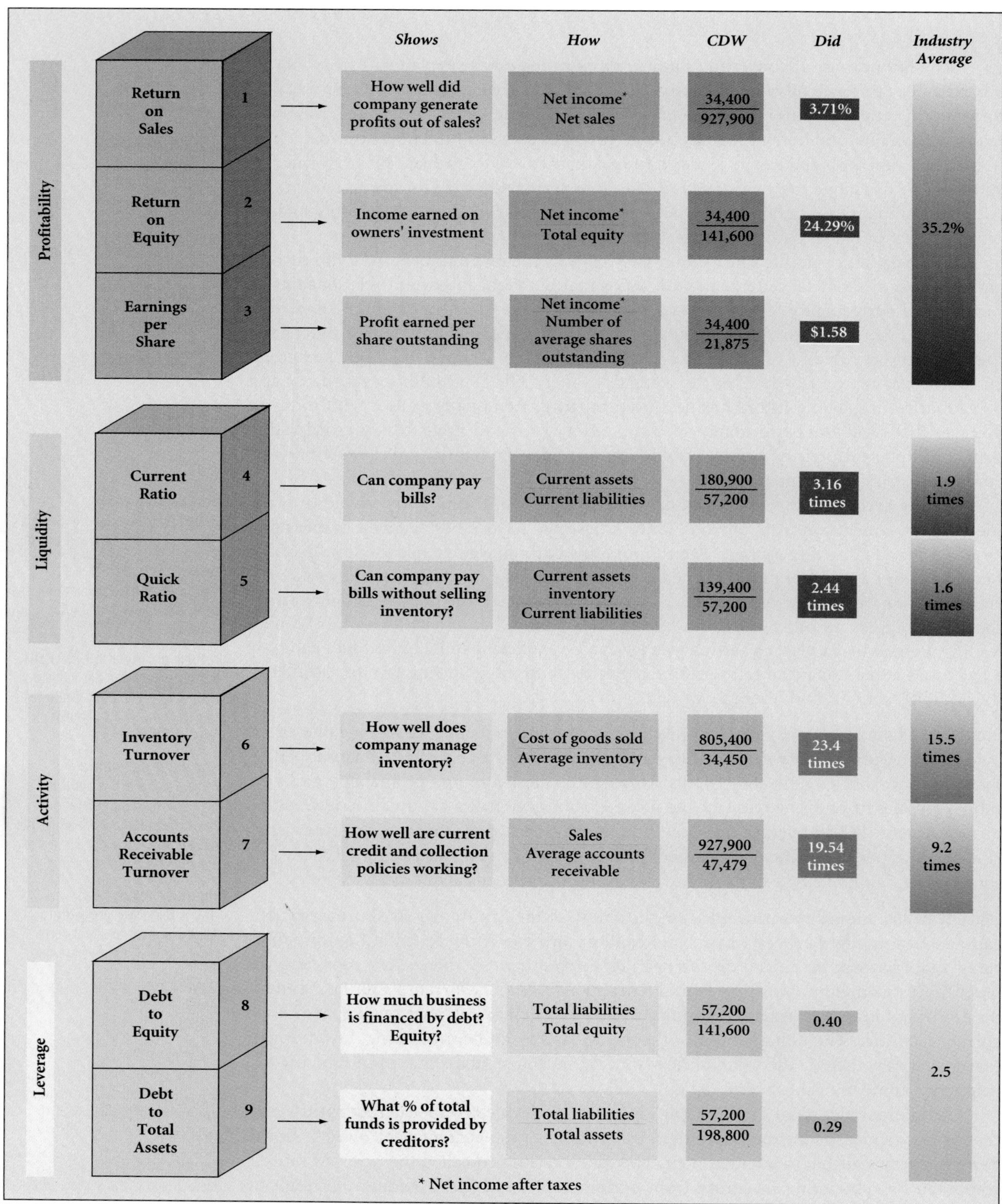

Shows
How
CDW
Did
Industry Average
Profitability
Return on Sales
1
How well did company generate profits out of sales?
Net income*
Net sales
34,400
927,900
3.71%
Return on Equity
2
Income earned on owners' investment
Net income*
Total equity
34,400
141,600
24.29%
35.2%
Earnings per Share
3
Profit earned per share outstanding
Net income*
Number of average shares outstanding
34,400
21,875
$1.58
Liquidity
Current Ratio
4
Can company pay bills?
Current assets
Current liabilities
180,900
57,200
3.16 times
1.9 times
Quick Ratio
5
Can company pay bills without selling inventory?
Current assets inventory
Current liabilities
139,400
57,200
2.44 times
1.6 times
Activity
Inventory Turnover
6
How well does company manage inventory?
Cost of goods sold
Average inventory
805,400
34,450
23.4 times
15.5 times
Accounts Receivable Turnover
7
How well are current credit and collection policies working?
Sales
Average accounts receivable
927,900
47,479
19.54 times
9.2 times
Leverage
Debt to Equity
8
How much business is financed by debt? Equity?
Total liabilities
Total equity
57,200
141,600
0.40
2.5
Debt to Total Assets
9
What % of total funds is provided by creditors?
Total liabilities
Total assets
57,200
198,800
0.29
* Net income after taxes

EXHIBIT 17.7

How Well Does This Company Stack Up?
Nearly all companies use ratios to evaluate how well the company is performing in relation to prior performance, the economy as a whole, and the company's competitors.

Exhibit 17.7 shows that both the current and quick ratios of CDW are well above these benchmarks and industry averages.

Activity Ratios A number of **activity ratios** may be used to analyze how well a company is managing its assets. The most common is the **inventory turnover ratio,** which measures how fast a company's inventory is turned into sales—generally speaking, the quicker the better because holding excess inventory can be expensive. When inventory sits on the shelf, money is tied up without earning interest; furthermore, the company incurs expenses for its storage, handling, insurance, and taxes. In addition, there is always a risk that the inventory will become obsolete before it can be converted into finished goods and sold. The firm's goal is to maintain enough inventory to fill orders in a timely fashion at the lowest cost.

activity ratios
Ratios that measure the effectiveness of the firm's use of its resources

inventory turnover ratio
Measure of the time a company takes to turn its inventory into sales, calculated by dividing cost of goods sold by the average value of inventory for a period

Keep in mind that it's difficult to judge a company by its inventory level. For example, lower inventories might mean one of many things: You're running an efficient operation; the right inventory is not being stocked; or perhaps your sales are booming and you need to increase your orders. Likewise, higher inventories could signal a decline in sales, careless ordering, or stocking up because of favorable pricing. The "ideal" turnover ratio varies with the type of operation. In 1996, CDW turned its inventory 23.4 times (see Exhibit 17.7). This is unusually high when compared to industry averages and may be a reflection of its need for larger warehouse space as well as increased sales efforts.

Another popular activity ratio is the **accounts receivable turnover ratio**—which measures how well a company's credit and collection policies are working by indicating how frequently accounts receivables are converted to cash. The volume of receivables outstanding depends on the financial manager's decisions regarding several issues, such as who qualifies for credit and who does not, how long customers have to pay their bills, or how aggressive the firm is in collecting its debts. Be careful here as well. If the ratio is going up, you need to determine whether that's because the company is doing a better job of collecting or because sales are rising. If the ratio is going down, it may be because sales are decreasing or because collection efforts are sagging. For example, in 1996 CDW expanded its sales generated from open credit terms to business customers. This resulted in a 52 percent increase in the balance of outstanding receivables, which is reflected in the company's accounts receivable turnover ratio of 19.5 times (see Exhibit 17.7).

accounts receivable turnover ratio
Measure of time a company takes to turn its accounts receivables into cash, calculated by dividing sales by the average value of accounts receivable for a period

Leverage or Debt Ratios You can measure a company's ability to pay its long-term debts by calculating its **debt ratios**, or leverage ratios. Lenders look at these ratios to determine whether the potential borrower has put enough money into the business to serve as a protective cushion for the loan. The **debt-to-equity ratio** (total liabilities divided by total equity) indicates the extent to which a business is financed by debt, as opposed to invested capital (equity). From the lender's standpoint, the lower this ratio, the safer the company, because the company has less existing debt and may be able to repay additional money it wants to borrow. However, a company that is conservative in its long-term borrowing is not necessarily well managed; often a low level of debt is associated with a low growth rate. The debt-to-equity ratio for CDW (as shown in Exhibit 17.7) is a very low 0.40 because the company does not have any long-term debt and has chosen to finance its growth through retained earnings and sales of common stock.

debt ratios
Ratios that measures a firm's reliance on debt financing of its operations (sometimes called coverage ratios)

debt-to-equity ratio
Measure of the extent to which a business is financed by debt as opposed to invested capital, calculated by dividing the company's total liabilities by owners' equity

Likewise the **debt-to-total-assets ratio** (total liabilities divided by total assets) also serves as a simple measure of a company's ability to carry long-term debt. As a rule of thumb, the amount of debt should not exceed 50 percent of the value of total assets. For CDW, this ratio is a very low 29 percent and again reflects the company's policy not to finance with long-term debt (see Exhibit 17.7). However, this ratio, like the others, is not a magic formula. Like grades on a report card, ratios are clues to performance. Managers, creditors, lenders, and investors can use them to get a fairly accurate idea of how a company is doing. But remember, one ratio by itself doesn't tell the whole story.

debt-to-total-assets ratio
Measure of a firm's ability to carry long-term debt, calculated by dividing total liabilities by total assets

BEST OF THE WEB

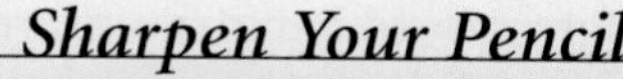

You never know what you'll find at a gallery these days. Art? Food? Videos? How about annual reports. And lots of them. So sharpen your pencil and start thinking like an accountant. Take a virtual field trip to the Annual Report Gallery. Check out 3Com, Boeing, MCI, and others. Be sure to view the *Award Winning Reports—The Real Works of Art.* You won't need a camera for this visit, but bring along your calculator.
http://reportgallery.com

FUTURE PLANNING

Suppose your company is considering changing the way it pays your sales force. Instead of paying a straight salary, the company would like to pay a base salary plus a commission because this will better motivate the salespeople to sell more product. How would you determine the best commission rate? Would this change cost the company more money? How could you guarantee that your sales force would benefit from this change? What if sales increased by 10 percent instead of the 20 percent you had projected? What if your commission structure was too high, and the company lost money? These are the types of questions accountants deal with frequently. Sometimes they are even more complex because there are more variables. Asking "what-if" questions is certainly not new. What is new, however, is the application of computing technology to the process.

What-If Analysis

With PC electronic spreadsheet programs like Microsoft Excel and Lotus 1-2-3, companies like TCDI can plan for the future by analyzing the costs and benefits of just about any decision using the firm's financial data as a starting point. Data-rich financial reports allow users to drill down from summary report data to more detailed transaction data for further investigative analysis. Typically, the accountant will enter these data into an electronic spreadsheet and manipulate the numbers by converting total costs to unit costs such as cost per passenger mile (for airlines) or cost per package delivered (for companies like FedEx). Consider this: American Airlines discovered that removing a single olive per salad could save the company $100,000 per year.[23] In fact, banks have gotten so good at computing their costs per unit of operations that they charge you for just about everything—including a service charge for counting that jar full of pennies. Once the financial data have been entered into the spreadsheet, the accountant will compute a range of outcomes using expected, best-case, and worst-case scenarios—such as unit costs will increase by 5 percent, 2 percent, or 10 percent. Using spreadsheet programs to build decision models is just one way that accountants use the financial data of a company to plan for a company's future. Another way to plan for the future is by monitoring cash and budgeting.

Cash Management and Budgeting

One of the biggest jobs that accountants handle is financial planning, which involves managing a company's cash and forecasting sales, costs, expenses, and profits. Because planning cash flow is strongly tied to an organization's needs and uses for money, it is discussed in detail in Chapter 18. Part of the cash management process includes developing a **budget,** a financial blueprint for a given period (often one year) that structures financial plans in a framework of estimated revenues, expenses, and cash flows. When most people hear the word *budget,* they usually think unpleasant thoughts because working out a

budget
Planning and control tool that reflects expected revenues, operating expenses, and cash receipts and outlays

Strong demand, higher fare levels, declining fuel prices, and lower distribution costs are the main factors contributing to increased profitability and record earnings for many major U.S. airlines. With strong balance sheets and costs under control, these airlines are better prepared to manage whatever turbulence may develop.

budget forces you to determine how much money will be coming in and how much will be going out. But budgeting can help you move from knowing how much you spend on things to controlling as well as planning your spending.

Companies prepare a master (or operating) budget—the overall estimate of revenues, costs, expenses, and cash flow—so that they can accomplish their objectives while controlling their costs. This master budget not only sets a standard for expenditures but also offers an integrated and detailed plan for the future. For example, by reviewing the budget of any airline you can determine whether the company plans on increasing its fleet of aircraft, adding more routes, hiring more employees, increasing employees' pay, or continuing or abandoning any discounts for travelers. No wonder companies like to keep their budgets confidential. Accountants provide much of the data for budget development and are frequently important members of the budget design team because preparing a budget requires a complete understanding of a company's operating costs.

Tomorrow's Finance Department

What will the corporate finance department look like in the twenty-first century? Will it be staffed by CPAs, MBAs, computer information specialists? These were some of the tough questions dealt with by 40 senior financial executives (from companies such as General Motors and Control Data), accounting educators (from schools such as Vanderbilt University and New York University), and CPAs (from accounting firms such as KPMG Peat Marwick, Price Waterhouse, and Arthur Andersen) during a two-day workshop sponsored by the AICPA. The goal of the workshop was to envision the future of the finance function in business, and thus help the institute prepare its members for the future. Although the participants certainly did not fully agree on the role of tomorrow's finance departments, they did reach a consensus on the following future scenarios:

- Transaction processing will become more automated than most in the profession think possible.
- Outsourcing of some finance management functions will become widespread.
- Managers will generally agree that no one financial report will meet everyone's needs.
- Data will no longer be stored separately by departments; instead, companies will create one central data warehouse, accessible companywide.
- Finance staff members will become information specialists.
- The title of CFO (chief financial officer) could become CAO (chief analytical officer) with a bigger role in modeling the whole business operation.

- The controller will no longer run the "backroom" accounting transactions "factory" but will take a more active role as business partner.

As one participant summed up the two-day workshop: "Times are changing. Today operating managers are telling us, 'Thanks very much, but the beans have already been counted. We need different information—information that will help us steer our business confidently into tomorrow.' We must be prepared for that change if we want to survive."[24]

Summary of Learning Objectives

1. **Describe the importance of accounting information to managers, investors, creditors, and government agencies.**
   Accounting information helps managers make business decisions and spot problems and opportunities; provides investors, suppliers, and creditors with the means to analyze a business; and supports the government's efforts to collect taxes and regulate business.
2. **Identify two major reasons why the work of accountants is changing.**
   The two principal reasons why the work of accountants is changing are the increasing demands by users for more information and the integration of technology into the accounting process.
3. **State the basic accounting equation and explain the purpose of double-entry bookkeeping.**
   Assets = *Liabilities* + *Owners' equity* is the basic accounting equation. Double-entry bookkeeping is a system of recording financial transactions to keep the accounting equation in balance.
4. **Differentiate between cash basis and accrual basis accounting.**
   Cash basis accounting recognizes revenue at the time payment is received, whereas accrual basis accounting recognizes revenue at the time of sale, even if payment is not made.
5. **Explain the purpose of the balance sheet and identify its three main sections.**
   The balance sheet provides a snapshot of the business at a particular point in time. Its main sections are assets, liabilities, and owners' equity.
6. **Explain the purpose of an income statement and the statement of cash flows.**
   The income statement reflects the results of operations over a period of time. The statement of cash flows shows how a company's cash was received and spent in three areas: operations, investments, and financing.
7. **Explain the purpose of ratio analysis and list the four main categories of financial ratios.**
   Financial ratios provide information for analyzing the health and future prospects of a business while allowing for comparisons between different size companies. Most of the important ratios fall into one of four categories: profitability ratios, liquidity ratios, activity ratios, and debt ratios.
8. **Explain how companies use what-if analysis and budgeting to plan for the future.**
   Companies use what-if analysis to analyze the costs and benefits of a particular decision. Companies use budgets to control costs and to plan for future spending.

On the Job: Meeting Business Challenges at The Concrete Doctor

The nation's highways were a mess. Between 1960 to 1975, highways were built in 15- to 20-foot jointed segments. It was the best technology at that time. Over the years, however, the heavy weight of trucks would cause these joints to break apart, disturbing the ground underneath. Slabjacking was an economical way to add years to the life of a sinking highway.

But breaking ground in this industry was harder than Weiner had imagined. TCDI was unsuccessful on its first six bid attempts. Then the company struck pay dirt. Within its first five years, TCDI landed its share of the jobs, hoisting annual revenue to over $1 million. The data from each completed job were entered into the company's computerized accounting system where they were later downloaded to financial spreadsheet models built by Weiner to eliminate the guesswork from the bidding process.

For instance, on one spreadsheet page he stored current payroll data: the hourly wage and benefit costs for workers in many states, plus other expenditures like payroll taxes and workers' compensation insurance. On a second page he stored operational cost data such as travel costs and room and board, which he used for bidding on out-of-state projects. On a third page he stored equipment costs, either the daily cost of renting equipment or the daily depreciation and maintenance costs of company-owned equipment—most of which was quite expensive. Then on a fourth page he stored job experience data, such as that DOT Project 70-97 took 37 days and 14 workers, drilling approximately 500 holes each day.

For each potential job, Weiner would run some 15 what-if scenarios, produce a range of outcomes, and factor these costs into his final bid price. For instance, what if the workers could drill only 400 holes a day instead of 500? What if they had to put in overtime? What if the necessary quantity of fly ash material increased by, say, 10 or 20 percent? Once the project began, TCDI's controller would prepare daily job cost-analysis reports. Weiner knew immediately whether he was on target or needed to contact his job supervisor to smooth out some bumps here and there.

Even though jobs kept pouring in, Weiner knew that sticking entirely to this business was risky. "You can only fix a road so many times; eventually it has to be replaced," notes Weiner. But roads weren't the only thing sinking. Soil stabilization and foundation repair were becoming big industries. Using similar concepts, TCDI expanded its business into geotechnical contracting: Steel piers were hydraulically pushed into the earth to stabilize and lift settled buildings. Sales exploded. By 1997 money was pouring in at a rate of $9 million a year.

One of TCDI's top projects was the renovation of Chicago's Orchestra Hall. TCDI was hired to find a way to support sections of a new balcony and stage. Only a handful of companies had the specialized equipment needed to work in high-density downtown areas; TCDI was one of them. When Weiner first heard about this project, he turned on his computer, ran the financial projections, and bid the project—as low as he could go. Even though Weiner isn't singing in the rain anymore (in fact, rainy days cost him a lot of money), there's a lot of singing going on at Orchestra Hall these days.

Your Mission: You have been hired as an independent contractor to work on a project-by-project basis to complete a variety of short-term financial-analysis and accounting projects for TCDI. Using your accounting knowledge and general business experience, select the best response to each situation.

1. In the process of closing the company books, you encounter a problematic transaction. One of the company's customers was charged twice for the same project materials, resulting in a $1,000 overcharge. You immediately notify the controller of this billing error, and her response is, "Let it go, it happens often." What should you do?
   a. Speak with the controller again, and if the matter is not properly resolved, drop it. Causing a stir would be unprofessional conduct, and besides, the error will probably be uncovered by the company's independent auditors.
   b. Notify the public accountants performing the current year's audit so that they can properly consult with management on their billing procedures.
   c. Speak with your controller again, and if the matter is not properly resolved, make an appointment to speak with her boss, Edward Weiner.
2. Weiner has asked you to research state wage rates and enter the updated information in his spreadsheet. He will use these data to estimate the cost of three new projects in out-of-state locations. Finding the data was easy, thanks to the Internet, and you completed the job in half the allocated time. However, one month later, you discover that you entered last year's data into the spreadsheet by mistake. Weiner has used the year-old data in the past three bids. What should you do?
   a. You checked it out, and each state is off by only 10 to 25 cents per hour. This shouldn't amount to very much. Ignore it, and correct it in the next quarterly update.
   b. Arrange a meeting with Weiner. Explain what happened, and offer to enter the correct costs, and compute the differences for the past three bids. Of course, because it was your error, you'll do this work without pay.
   c. Tell the company controller. She was responsible for checking your work. It's her headache now.
3. TCDI's controller has asked you to prepare a spreadsheet that will determine whether it is more economical (1) to lease several pieces of specialized equipment needed for five new projects or (2) to hire a company to custom make the equipment for TCDI. You think the assignment is a big waste of time—especially because you overheard that the equipment is needed ASAP and it will likely take one year to manufacture it. What should you do?
   a. You are only an independent contractor hired to work on a project-to-project basis. It is not your job to evaluate whether the projects assigned to you make sense. Do the work and bill the hours.
   b. Arrange to meet with Weiner. Explain that the project makes no sense and that you would be wasting the company's money to perform the analysis.
   c. Arrange to meet with the controller. Tell her you need some missing information to complete the assignment. Ask her how long it will take to manufacture this custom equipment. Explain your concerns before you start.
4. You have been asked to prepare next year's budget for TCDI. Which of the following information will you need to complete this assignment?
   a. Last year's detailed financial statements
   b. Current trends and lists of any extraordinary events that occurred last year
   c. Both (a) and (b)[25]

Key Terms

accounting (510)
accounting equation (517)
accounts receivable turnover ratio (531)
accrual basis (517)
activity ratios (531)
assets (516)
audit (513)
balance sheet (518)
bookkeeping (510)
budget (532)
calendar year (520)
cash basis (518)
certified management accountants (CMAs) (515)
certified public accountants (CPAs) (512)
closing the books (517)
controller (515)
cost accounting (515)
cost of goods sold (523)
creditors (513)
current assets (522)
current liabilities (522)
current ratio (529)
debt ratios (531)
debt-to-equity ratio (531)
debt-to-total-assets ratio (531)
debtors (513)
depreciation (518)
dividends (523)
double-entry bookkeeping (517)
earnings per share (529)
expenses (523)
financial accounting (513)
financial analysis (515)
fiscal year (521)
fixed assets (522)
general expenses (523)
generally accepted accounting principles (GAAP) (511)
gross profit (523)
income statement (523)
internal auditors (515)
inventory turnover ratio (531)
liabilities (516)
liquidity ratios (529)
long-term liabilities (522)
management accounting (513)
matching principle (517)
net income (523)
operating expenses (523)
owners' equity (516)
private accountants (515)
profitability ratios (529)
public accountants (513)
quick ratio (529)
ratio analysis (528)
retained earnings (523)
return on investment (ROI) (529)
return on sales (529)
revenues (523)
selling expenses (523)
statement of cash flows (524)
tax accounting (515)
trend analysis (527)
working capital (529)

Questions

For Review

1. What purpose does double-entry bookkeeping serve?
2. What is the matching principle?
3. What is the difference between an income statement, a balance sheet, and a statement of cash flows?
4. What is the difference between trend analysis and profitability analysis?
5. What are the three main profitability ratios, and how is each calculated?

For Analysis

6. Why is accounting important to business?
7. Why have many states increased the requirement to sit for the CPA examination from 120 to 150 semester hours?
8. What is the main advantage and disadvantage of auditors becoming industry specialists?
9. Why are the costs of fixed assets depreciated?
10. How has technology changed the jobs of accountants?

For Application

11. The senior partner of an accounting firm is looking for ways to increase the firm's business. What other services besides traditional accounting can the firm offer to its clients?
12. Besides saving costs, how might a company benefit from outsourcing some of its accounting functions?

A Case for Critical Thinking ■ Going to the Cleaners

After years of dreaming about owning your own business, you decide that a dry-cleaning business would be perfect. Luckily for you, two establishments happen to be for sale—at the same price and in equally attractive locations. You manage to get enough financial data to compare the year-end condition of the two companies, as shown in Exhibit 17.8. Study the numbers carefully; your livelihood depends on choosing wisely between the two.

EXHIBIT 17.8

Financial Data for Two Companies

December 31, 1998, year-end balance sheets.

	AJAX SERVICES, INC.	MALLARD CLEANERS, INC.
ASSETS		
Cash	$10,000	$ 25,000
Accounts receivable	2,000	4,000
Cleaning equipment	50,000	80,000
Office equipment	11,000	18,000
Supplies	22,000	34,000
TOTAL ASSETS	$95,000	$161,000
LIABILITIES AND OWNERS' EQUITY		
Accounts payable	$21,000	$ 38,000
Bank loans payable	49,000	68,000
Owners' equity	25,000	55,000
TOTAL LIABILITIES AND OWNERS' EQUITY	$95,000	$161,000
OTHER DATA		
Personal withdrawals from cash during 1998	$40,000	$ 38,000
Owners' investments in business during 1998	$16,000	$ 32,000
Capital balances for each business on January 1, 1998	$30,000	$ 12,000

1. What factors should you consider before deciding which company to buy? What additional data might be helpful to you? (Note that net income is implied.)
2. What questions should you ask about the methods used to record revenues and expenses?
3. On the basis of the data provided, which company would you purchase? Detail the process you use to make your decision.
4. Now that you're a small-business owner, don't get taken to the cleaners. Learn about the world of small business by visiting Inc. Online. Go to its Web site at <http://www.inc.com>.
   a. What types of information does this site have that is helpful for small-business owners like yourself?
   b. Click on the *Inc.500* minisite and take a *Statistical Tour.* Find out what keeps CEOs up at night. What's the number one worry?

Building Your Business Skills

Obtain a copy of the annual report of a business, and with three or four other students, examine what the report shows about finances and current operations. In addition to other chapter material, use the information in "How to Read an Annual Report" on pages 520–521 as a guideline for understanding the annual report's content.

- Consider the statements made by the CEO regarding the past year: Did the company do well, or are changes in operations necessary to its future well-being? What are the projections for future growth in sales and profits?
- Examine the financial summaries for information about the fiscal condition of the company: Did the company show a profit?
- If possible, obtain a copy of the company's annual report from the previous year, and compare it with the current report to determine whether past projections were accurate.
- Prepare a brief written summary of your conclusions.

Keeping Current Using *The Wall Street Journal*

Select an article from *The Wall Street Journal* that discusses the quarterly or year-end performance of a company that industry analysts consider notable for either positive or negative reasons.

1. Did the company report a profit or a loss for this accounting period? What other performance indicators were reported? Did the company's performance represent an improvement over previous accounting periods?
2. What, according to the article, was the significance of this performance? Did it match industry analysts' expectations, or was it a surprise?
3. What reasons were given for the company's improvement or decline in performance?
4. One way to determine whether the performance reported by a company is unique to that company or whether the entire industry is experiencing the same trends is to research that industry. All industries are assigned a specific industry code. Beginning in 1997 the Standard Industry Classification Codes (SIC) were replaced by a North American Industry Classification System (NAICS) for industries in Canada, Mexico, and the United States.
   a. Find the new NAICS coding system at <http://www.census.gov/epcd/www/naics.html>.
   b. Click on *NAICS and SIC Comparability Tables* and find the specific NAICS industry code(s) for your company. For example, if your company was Best Buy, then you would select *Retail Trade*, and then choose among the variety of retailers. What types of publications and agencies do you think might use these industry code classifications? (*Hint:* Go to the NAICS Web site <http://www.naics.com> and find *More About the NAICS.*)

Exploring the Best of the Web

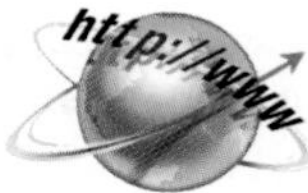

Size Them Up, page 514

Meet Ernie. Schedule a date with Ernst & Young's online business consultant at <http://www.ey.com> by visiting the *Idea Factory*. Scroll down until you find Ernie. Then scroll down for some information on *Trends by Size of Company*.

1. What is the biggest issue for companies with annual revenue under $50 million? Is it the same for companies in the $100 million to $200 million revenue range?
2. How is Ernie's online consulting an effective selling tool for Ernst & Young? If you were the owner of a small accounting firm, would online consulting make sense for a company your size?
3. Go back to the company home page and check out the *1040 Survival Kit*. Click on *Tips and Hints*, and click on *How to Avoid 25 Common Errors*. How is this advice helpful?

Link Your Way to the World of Accounting, page 528

The Accountant's Home Page is a launching pad for accountants searching for Internet resources. Explore this Web site <http://www.computercpa.com>.

1. As a business student, which of the links listed might you use in your studies? How?
2. Even if an accountant does not prepare tax returns for a living, it's always wise to remain current when it comes to taxes. Many new tax proposals affect business decisions. Go to Commerce Clearing House via the *CCH* link (under the Accounting-Software heading). Explore this site by clicking on *Federal and State Tax*. Enter the *Reception Room*. What does CCH do?
3. Take a virtual tour of its *Show Room* (get there from the home page). Click on the *Tax Research NetWork Demo*. Take the demo. How does CCH online assist accountants in keeping current?

Sharpen Your Pencil, page 532

Learning about different companies and industries is an important part of an accountant's job. Take a virtual field trip to the Annual Report Gallery at <http://www.reportgallery.com> to begin your journey to knowledge. Enter the *Viewing Library*, and click on the latest annual report for any company.

1. Learn some facts about the company.
   a. Where is it located?
   b. What does it do?
2. Click back and check out its latest annual report (*view electronically*).
   a. Find the *Chairman's Letter*. Was it a good year for the company? Why?
   b. Click on the *Financial Section* and find the *Auditor's Report*. Who are the company's auditors? Did the company get a clean audit report?
3. Check out the company's *Income Statement (Condensed Consolidated)*.
   a. By what percentage did its sales change from the prior year? (*Hint:* Use your calculator!)
   b. Using the knowledge you've gained from reading the company's annual report, what do you think contributed to this change? Read what management has to say by going to sections in the report where management analyzes the company's financial condition.

Part VI: Mastering the Geography of Business ■ Expanding the World of Computers

You are the president of a desktop publishing company that provides services to small businesses across the United States. You've risen to the top of a fragmented market by offering quality service at reasonable prices. One key to those reasonable prices has been your policy of hiring people who own home computers and are active users of their machines. These employees cost less for you to train, and they tend to keep up on current technology without much prodding from you. Part of the money you save on training goes back into better benefits and higher wages. In short, their personal interests overlap your business interests, so everybody wins.

An international business consultant has warned you not to expect the same scenario as you expand overseas. So far, computer companies have had less success penetrating the home market of many other countries, so you'll find fewer experienced home-computer users to hire as employees. In addition, businesses in some companies have not been as quick to adopt personal computers, so many people aren't getting on-the-job training either.

The strategy you've adopted for expansion is simple. Rather than change your business model and switch to more intensive (and expensive) employee training, you decide to expand only as quickly as the numbers of experienced computer users increase from country to country.

1. Find as much information as you can about home and business use of personal computers in the following countries:
   a. Japan
   b. Hong Kong
   c. India
   d. England
2. Now, strictly on the basis of your information about the home and business use of personal computers, decide the order in which you will expand into these countries.
3. Of course, as an international business owner you will be traveling to these countries frequently. Use the Internet to learn as much as you can about the customs and culture of each of the countries listed above. Start your journey by exploring Japan. Excite Travel by City.net is an excellent resource for travel information. Go directly to your destination at <http://www.city.net/countries/japan/>.
   a. Scroll down to *Travel and Tourism*, and click on *Japan Business Travel*, then click on *Doing Business*. Read about Japanese business customs and etiquette. How does doing business in Japan differ from doing business in the United States?
   b. Try exploring some other countries by going to the City.net home page <http://www.city.net/> and entering the country name under the search destination option. Be sure to notice the hot links to Internet sites with valuable information about geography, travel, education, newspapers, and even weather.

Answers to "Is It True?"

Page 512. False. Passing the CPA exam and paying a fee are only the first steps in joining this professional society. All members must fulfill mandatory continuing professional education (CPE) requirements. Members in public accounting must complete 120 hours of CPE course work over a three-year period. Members in private practice must complete 90 hours of CPE course work over a three-year period.

Page 514. False. Approximately two-thirds of the 50,000 students who take undergraduate accounting courses every year eventually work in business.

Page 522. True.

PART VII

Managing Financial Resources

CHAPTER 18

BANKING AND FINANCIAL MANAGEMENT

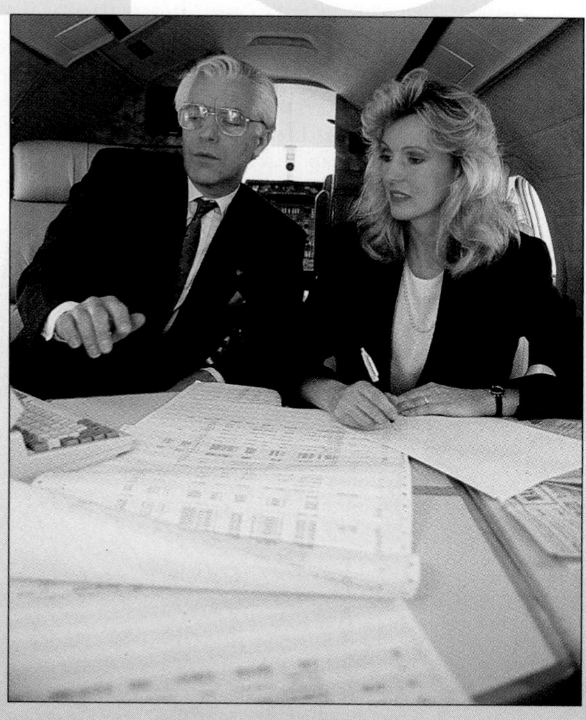

OBJECTIVES

After studying this chapter, you will be able to

1. Identify the responsibilities of a financial manager
2. Name the five main steps involved in the financial planning process
3. Cite three things financial managers must consider when selecting an appropriate funding vehicle
4. List the three major types of short-term debt and the three major types of long-term debt
5. Identify the main advantages and disadvantages public equity financing
6. Name the three functions and four characteristics of money
7. Cite the four ways the Federal Reserve System influences the money supply
8. Explain how the Internet is influencing the U.S. banking and monetary systems

On the Job On the Job

ON THE JOB: FACING BUSINESS CHALLENGES AT REMLIK

Finding Financial Fuel for a Food Firm

What filling food can boast no fat, high fiber, and only eight calories per ounce? The answer, as Jim Kilmer found out when he joined the Weight Watchers program, is spaghetti squash, a little-known vegetable that can be substituted for pasta. Relying on spaghetti squash and other healthful foods, Kilmer lost 62 pounds following the Weight Watchers program. Now he wanted to make spaghetti squash a key ingredient in his recipe for entrepreneurial success.

Kilmer had worked for H. J. Heinz, the parent company of Weight Watchers, for more than 13 years, including a stint as the product manager for Weight Watchers ice cream and frozen novelties, when Heinz eliminated a number of jobs, including his own. Kilmer gladly accepted severance pay and started his own food-manufacturing firm, which he called Remlik (Kilmer spelled backward). He considered many ideas, but he was particularly intrigued by the idea of selling prepared spaghetti squash.

From personal experience, he knew that foods low in calories but high in nutritional value weren't always the fastest or most convenient to cook. Preparing fresh spaghetti squash is a job that takes 30 minutes or more. Kilmer believed that people would flock to the refrigerator case to buy precooked spaghetti squash that was ready to be heated and sauced. To emphasize the cooked vegetable's similarity to pasta, he named his product Nature's Pasta.

One immediate problem was the product's shelf life: Refrigerated, precooked squash tended to spoil after seven days. Because his product had such a short shelf life, Kilmer would be forced to work out an especially speedy delivery system, and he would be limited to selling only to nearby stores. Finding a way to extend the squash's shelf life was essential if the company was to grow, but the cost of this research was beyond Kilmer's reach.

Expensive research wasn't his only financial concern. To avoid buying a manufacturing plant, Kilmer rented space and a part-time crew from a caterer. He kept costs low by buying used equipment and overhauling it himself. Rather than pay a salesperson, he visited grocery stores himself, persuading seven to buy the new product as a test. The initial sales were more than twice what he had expected. "I was giddy," he remembers. "But I woke up overwhelmed with the things I had to do to get through each day."

Working more than 80 hours a week to meet the unexpected demand wasn't enough. Where would Kilmer find the money to outfit a manufacturing plant, hire employees, and buy a large refrigerator truck? How could he finance the research he needed to extend the squash's shelf life? How would he pay his suppliers when the money from selling products didn't come in quickly enough?[1]

GOALS OF FINANCIAL MANAGEMENT

financial management
Effective acquisition and use of money

Jim Kilmer wants his new business to survive, but he's also looking ahead to expansion. The key to both of these efforts is money. Every company, from the little corner store to General Motors, worries about money—how to get it and how to use it. This area of concern, known as **financial management,** or finance, involves making decisions about alternative sources and uses of funds with the goal of maximizing the company's value. In order to make these decisions, financial managers, or those responsible for making these decisions, forecast and plan for the future, develop and implement the firm's financial plan, manage the company's cash flow, coordinate and control the efficiency of operations, decide on specific investments and how to finance these investments, raise capital needed to support growth, and interact with banks and capital markets. In smaller companies like Jim Kilmer's Remlik, the owner is responsible for the firm's financial decisions. In larger operations, however, financial planning is the responsibility of the finance department, which reports to a vice president of finance or chief financial officer (CFO). This department includes the accounting function. In fact, most financial managers are accountants.

Cash Flow Management

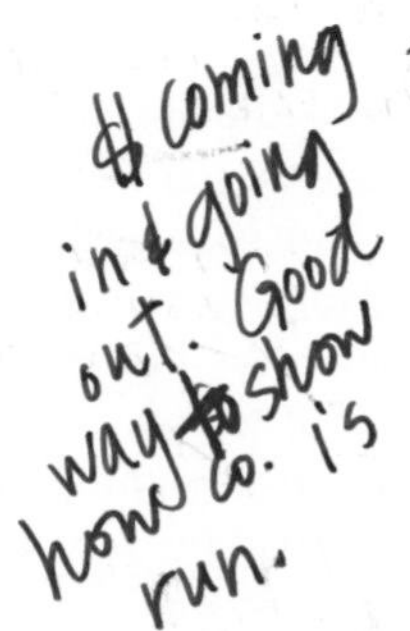

All companies need to pay their bills and still have some money left over to improve the business. Furthermore, a key goal of any business is to increase the value to its owners (and other stakeholders) by making it grow. Maximizing the owners' wealth sounds simple enough: Just sell a good product for more than it costs to make. Before you can earn any revenue, however, you need money to get started. Once the business is off the ground, your need for money continues—whether it's to see you through a slow season or to buy or renovate facilities and equipment, as Jim Kilmer needed to do.

financial plan
A forecast of financial requirements and the financing sources to be used

In accounting, you prepare income statements to determine the net income of a firm. In finance, however, you focus on cash flows. Although the firm's income is important, cash flows are even more important because cash is necessary to purchase the assets required to continue operations and pay dividends to shareholders. Cash flows are generally related to net income; that is, companies with relatively high accounting profits generally have relatively high cash flows, but the relationship is not precise. One way companies make sure they have enough money is by developing a **financial plan**, a document that shows the funds a firm will need for a period of time, as well as the sources and uses of those funds.

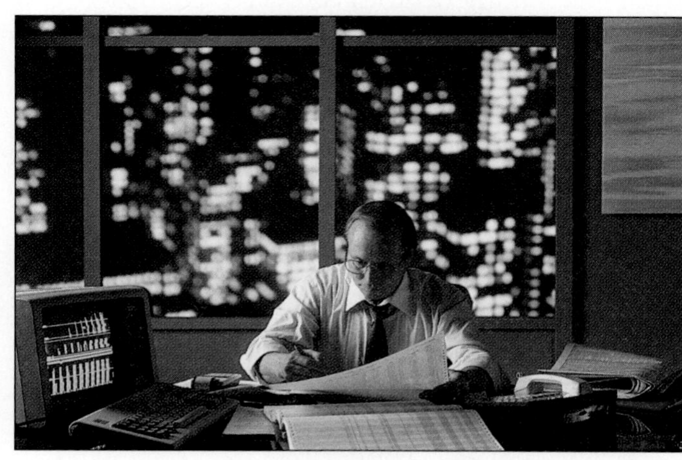

Financial managers help their companies determine how much money they need for operations and for expansion. They're also responsible for identifying the right combination of funding sources at the lowest cost.

Financial Planning

When you prepare a financial plan for a company, you have two objectives in mind: achieving positive cash flow and investing any excess cash flow to make your company grow. Most companies today use some type of computerized financial planning model to assist them with the financial planning process, which includes (1) estimating the flow of money into and out of the business, (2) determining whether cash flow is negative or positive and how to use or create excess funds, (3) choosing appropriate capital investments for continued growth, (4) selecting the optimal way to finance these investments, and (5) comparing actual results to projections to discover variances and take corrective action—a process known as **financial control**.

financial control
The process of analyzing and adjusting the basic financial plan to correct for forecasted events that do not materialize

Financial planning requires looking beyond the four walls of the company to answer questions such as: Is the company introducing a new product in the near future or expanding its market? Is the industry growing? Is the national economy declining? Is inflation heating up? Would an investment in new technology improve productivity?[2] Of course, one of the most important questions a financial manager must answer is whether to make *capital investments,* which ones, and how to finance those that are undertaken. This process is called **capital budgeting**.

capital budgeting
Process for evaluating proposed investments in select projects that provide the best long-term financial return

Capital Budgeting

Stockholders, of course, invest in public companies for more than just dividends. They're speculating on a company's ability to grow and compete. For that to happen, a company makes **capital investments,** major expenditures in long-term assets such as a new or renovated plant or new equipment. As with any major investment decision, an erroneous forecast of asset requirements can have serious consequences. If the firm invests too much in assets, it will incur unnecessarily heavy expenses. If it does not replace or upgrade existing assets on a regular basis, the assets will likely become obsolete. For example, old manufacturing equipment may be incapable of handling increasing capacities. This could eventually result in a loss of market share to competitors. For these important reasons, firms try to match capital investments with the company's goals. In other words, if the firm is growing, then projects that would produce the greatest growth rates would receive highest priority. However, if the company is trying to reduce costs, those projects that enhance the company's efficiency and productivity would be ranked toward the top. Because asset expansion frequently involves large sums of money and affects the company's productivity for an extended period of time, finance managers must carefully evaluate the best way to finance or pay for these investments.

capital investments
Money paid to acquire something of permanent value in a business

Before Mead Paper decided to build a mill in Phoenix City, Arizona the company used capital budgeting to determine the value of this capital investment.

FINANCING THE ENTERPRISE

Where can a firm obtain the money it needs? The most obvious source would be revenues—cash received from sales, rentals of property, interest on short-term investments, and so on. Another likely source would be suppliers who may be willing to do business on credit, thus enabling the company to postpone payment. Most firms also obtain money in the form of loans from banks, finance companies, or other commercial lenders. In addition, public companies can raise funds by selling shares of stock, and large corporations can sell bonds.

Firms use the money obtained from these sources to cover the day-to-day expenses of running the company such as meeting the payroll and buying inventory. Money is also needed to acquire new assets such as land, production facilities, and equipment (see Exhibit 18.1).

EXHIBIT 18.1

The Flow of a Company's Funds

Financial management involves both finding suitable sources of funds and deciding on the most appropriate uses for those funds.

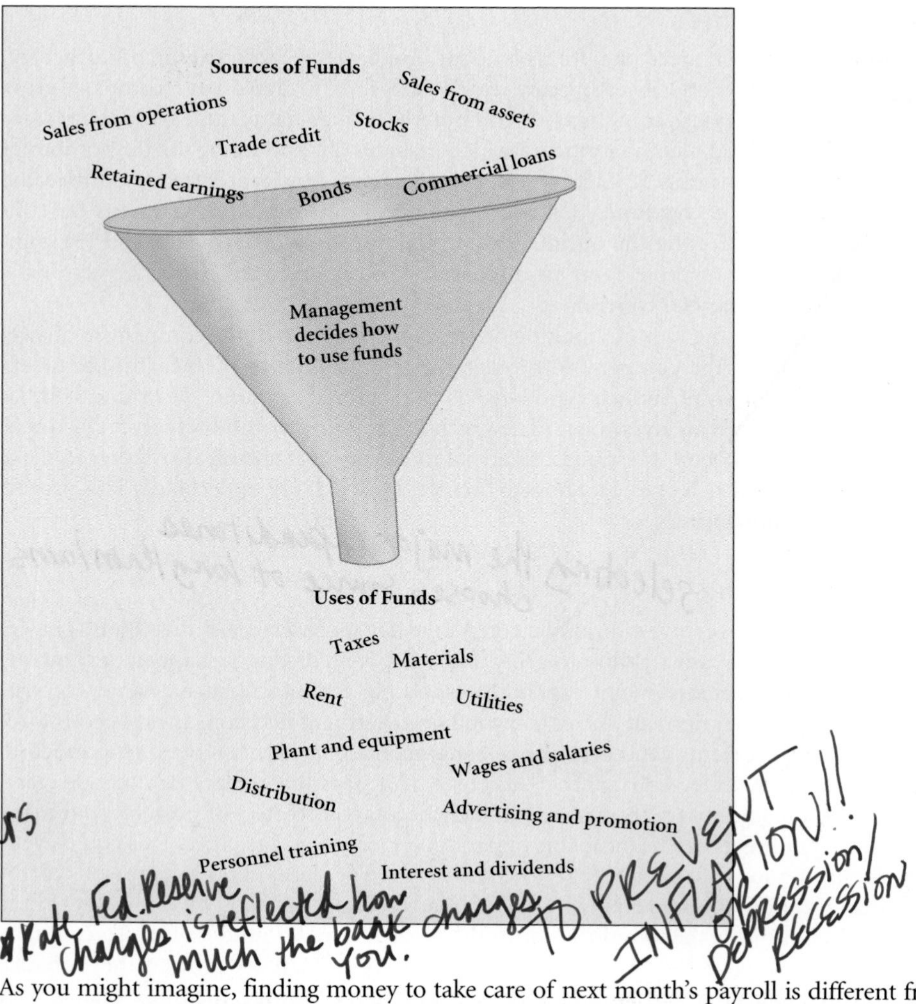

As you might imagine, finding money to take care of next month's payroll is different from arranging the financing for a new manufacturing plant that will be operational three years from now.

Cost of Capital

cost of capital
Average rate of interest a firm pays on its combination of debt and equity

Generally speaking, a company wants to obtain money at the lowest cost and least amount of risk. However, lenders and investors want to receive the highest possible return on their investment, also at the lowest risk. Therefore, a company's **cost of capital,** the price it must pay to raise money, depends on the risk associated with the company, the prevailing level of interest rates, and management's selection of funding vehicles.

Risk Lenders and investors who provide money to businesses expect their returns to be in proportion to the two types of risk they face: the quality and length of time of the venture. Obviously, the more financially solid a company is, the less risk investors face. However, time also plays a vital role. Because a dollar is worth less tomorrow than it is today, lenders need to be compensated for waiting to be repaid. As a result, long-term financing generally costs a company more than short-term financing.

prime interest rate (prime)
Lowest rate of interest charged by banks for short-term loans to their most credit-worthy customers

Interest Rates Regardless of how solid a company is, its cost of money will vary over time because interest rates fluctuate. The **prime interest rate (prime)** is the lowest interest rate offered on short-term bank loans to preferred borrowers. The prime changes irregularly and, at times, quite frequently: sometimes because of supply and demand; other times because the prime rate is closely tied to the **discount rate,** the interest rate Federal Reserve Banks charge on loans to commercial banks and other depository institutions. We will discuss the importance of the discount rate later in the chapter when we discuss the money supply.

discount rate
Interest rate charged by the Federal Reserve on loans to commercial banks and other financial institutions

Financial managers must take these interest rate fluctuations into account when making decisions. For instance, a financial manager planning a short-term project when the prime rate is 8.5 percent would want to reevaluate the project if the prime rose to 10 percent a few months later. Even though financial managers try to time their borrowing to take advantage of drops in interest rates, this option is not always possible. A firm's need for money doesn't always coincide with a period of favorable rates. At times, a company may be forced to borrow when rates are high and then renegotiate the loan when rates drop. Sometimes projects must be put on hold until interest rates become more affordable.

Mix of Funding Vehicles

Most companies can't grow without a periodic infusion of money. But in a world with limited financial resources, especially for business start-ups and small companies, cash-strapped business owners are typically forced to raise money a little bit at a time from a variety of people and institutions. Apart from timing their borrowing properly, financial managers may choose from an array of funding vehicles that are not mutually exclusive.

The selection process begins by trying to match a firm's financing needs with the characteristics of a particular funding vehicle. For instance, financial managers must first consider the purpose of the financing and whether it is for the short or long term. Then they must weigh the advantages and disadvantages of internal versus external financing. Finally, they must evaluate the merits of debt versus equity financing in light of their own needs and special circumstances. This selection process is further complicated by the fact that many sources of funding exist within these broader categories—each with its own special attributes. As a result, companies usually wind up with financing that resembles a patchwork quilt made up of different financing pieces. The following sections discuss each of these pieces.[3]

Short-Term versus Long-Term Financing One of the first things that a company must decide is whether the company's financing needs are for the short term or long term. **Short-term debt** is any debt that will be repaid within one year, whereas **long-term debt** is any debt that will be repaid in a period longer than one year. When deciding which vehicle is appropriate, companies are guided by the *matching principle*—the concept that the timing of a company's borrowing should roughly match the timing of its spending. In Chapter 17 we discussed how firms match their revenue to expenses to produce a more accurate picture of a company's performance. This concept also applies to financial management. If you borrow money for short-term purposes, you should plan to pay it back in that time frame so that the flow of money into and out of the business is balanced.

short-term debt
Borrowed funds used to cover current expenses (generally repaid within a year)

long-term debt
Borrowed funds used to cover long-term expenses (generally repaid over a period of more than one year)

Internal Financing Some companies use their excess cash to finance their growth. Using a company's own money has one chief attraction: No interest payments are required. For this reason, many companies accumulate excess earnings over a period of time instead of paying out dividends to shareholders. Some companies also raise money internally by selling assets that are no longer needed or obsolete.

MONITORING CASH FLOW Perhaps the best source of internal financing is the one most often overlooked—the daily monitoring of a company's *working capital accounts*—cash, inventory, accounts receivable, and accounts payable. How much cash do you carry in your

THINKING ABOUT ETHICS

Paying More for Less: The Dilemma of Tiered Lending

How is it possible to make so much money handing out billions of dollars to people who are less likely than others to hand it back? Easy: charge a lot more to compensate for the extra risk. Tiered lending does just that. But although banks and credit-card companies adjust loan rates based on a customer's risk, guess who is paying the price?

IS TIERED LENDING ETHICAL?

Banks say tiered lending is perfectly ethical. Shouldn't people who consistently pay their bills on time pay a lower interest rate than less responsible payers? It's no different than charging variable insurance rates based on your prior record—the greater the insurance risk, the higher the rate. However, critics point out that logic doesn't always add up. For instance, people who most need to borrow money are often turned down because they are considered a bad risk. It's a banking paradox. But that's changing.

WHY DO BANKS TAKE THE RISK?

Driven by intense competition for loan business and the 1977 Community Reinvestment Act (which requires banks to meet the credit needs of neighborhoods in which they do business—rich or poor, white or minority), banks have been relaxing loan standards and imposing tiered rates to compensate for lending to riskier borrowers. Banks recognize that the market for borrowers with less-than-stellar credit is large and lucrative—estimated at $65 million for auto loans alone. In fact, sub-prime customers will often pay between a third and a half more in interest than a more creditworthy borrower. Until recently, this market has been the province of finance companies like Household Finance and the Money Store. However, thanks to sophisticated computer models that can analyze enormous amounts of information, banks can identify borrowers who pose a greater risk of default and use this information to set loan fees and interest rates. Of course, lenders are prohibited from considering certain information, such as race, religion, or gender. But assessing risk can be subjective and at times discriminatory, especially because risk can be defined in many ways.

wallet? If you have more than you need to cover your immediate expenses, you're not thinking like an aggressive financial manager. Although excess cash might make you feel secure, it isn't earning any interest for you. An underlying concept of financial management is that all money should be used productively. A company can significantly improve its cash flow by using common-sense procedures such as controlling the level of raw materials and inventory, dispatching bills on a timely basis, shrinking accounts receivable collection periods, and paying bills no earlier than necessary.[4] In fact, electronic cash management or the ability to access bank account information online allows financial managers to move cash between accounts and pay bills on a daily basis, thus earning as much interest as possible on their cash reserves.[5]

INVESTING EXCESS CASH Sometimes companies find themselves with more cash on hand than they need. A seasonal business may experience a quiet period between the time when revenues are collected from the last busy season and the time when suppliers' bills are due. Department stores, for example, may have excess cash during a few weeks in February and March. A firm may also have excess cash if it is holding funds to meet a large commitment in the near future. It may be about to reach the next stage in the construction of a new plant, or it may be waiting for a special bargain on supplies. Finally, every firm keeps some surplus cash on hand as a cushion in case its needs are greater than expected.

Part of the financial manager's job is to make sure that this cash is invested so that it earns interest. The task is to find a good "parking place" for the funds, some sort of

GUESS WHO IS PAYING THE PRICE?

To prove the point, a market research firm conducted "blind tester" surveys in which minority and white applicants (essentially identical with respect to employment, income, assets, and credit histories) applied at 50 banking offices for mortgage loans on comparable properties. The survey results showed that in spite of similar qualifying information, the treatment received by the minority applicants differed. For example, not only did minority applicants wait longer to speak to a lending officer, but they received less detailed explanations of loan options, and they were told to anticipate longer approval times.

In fact, most borrowers do not know they can negotiate with a bank. As a result, minorities and women frequently pay higher rates and fees than other borrowers because loan officers often stereotype them as less astute and are allowed to charge fees and rates as high as they think the borrower will accept. Critics of tiered lending say that this saddles the poor, women, and minorities with punitive interest rates. They want banks to provide loan counseling and give borrowers an incentive to improve their credit records—something Chicago's Harris Trust and Savings Bank is already doing. But banks claim they are already being held to a higher standard than finance companies, which have been lending to less-than-perfect borrowers at higher rates for years. Although tiered lending isn't likely to go away, and neither is the controversy, it puts banks between a rock and a hard place: They are under pressure to lend more money to minorities and women, but by doing so they may have to charge a higher interest rate to the people who can least afford it.

QUESTIONS FOR CRITICAL THINKING

1. What steps can you take to find the best loan rate possible?
2. If performance counts, then why do some credit-card companies charge fees and higher rates to "perfect" users—those who pay their entire monthly balances on time?

investment that will yield the highest possible return but will create no problem if the firm needs to liquidate the investment for instant cash. A number of short-term investments, called **marketable securities,** meet these needs. These include investments in money-market funds or publicly traded stocks like IBM or Sears. They are said to be "marketable" because they can easily be converted back to cash. When selecting a portfolio of marketable securities, financial managers must make trade-offs between safety, liquidity, and maximum rate of return. Because marketable securities are generally viewed as contingency funds, most financial managers take a reasonably conservative approach to the management of these securities; that is, they invest in securities of solid companies or government securities—ones with the least amount of risk.

marketable securities
Stocks, bonds, and other investments that can be turned into cash quickly

External Financing Aggressive management of a company's cash flow can reduce reliance on outside funds. Keep in mind, however, that internal financing is not free; this money has an *opportunity cost.* That is, a company might be better off investing its excess cash in external opportunities such as another company's projects or stocks of growing companies, and borrowing money to finance its own growth. Doing this makes sense as long as you can earn a greater rate of return on borrowed money than the interest you pay. This concept is called **leverage** because the loan acts like a lever: It magnifies the power of the borrower to generate profits (see Exhibit 18.2). However, leverage works both ways: Borrowing may magnify your losses as well as your gains. Because most companies depend on some degree of external financing, the issue is not so much whether to use outside money; rather, it's a question of how much should be raised, by what means,

leverage
Technique of increasing the rate of return on an investment by financing it with borrowed funds

EXHIBIT 18.2

How Leverage Works

If you invest $10,000 of your own money in a business venture and it yields 15 percent (or $1,500), your return on equity is 15 percent. However, if you borrow an additional $30,000 at 10 percent interest and invest a total $40,000 with the same 15 percent yield, the ultimate return on your $10,000 equity is 30 percent (or $3,000). The key to using leverage successfully is to try to make sure that your profit on the total funds is greater than the interest you must pay on the portion of it that is borrowed.

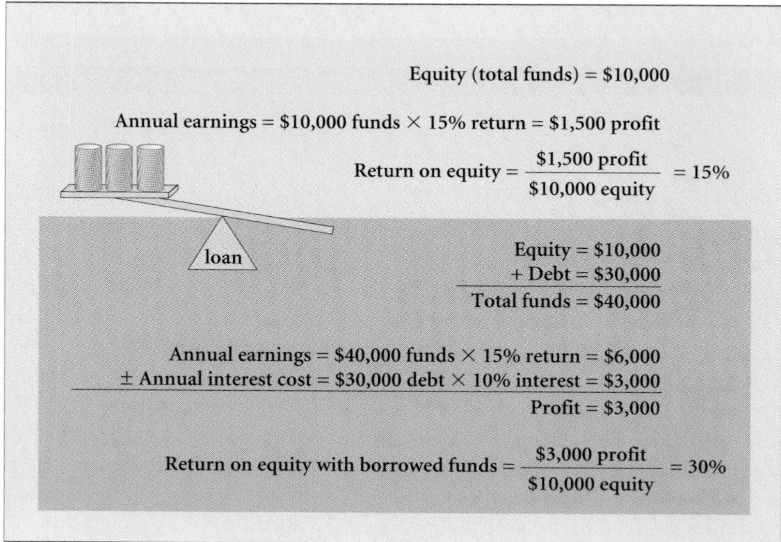
Equity (total funds) = $10,000
Annual earnings = $10,000 funds × 15% return = $1,500 profit
Return on equity = $1,500 profit / $10,000 equity = 15%
loan
Equity = $10,000
+ Debt = $30,000
Total funds = $40,000
Annual earnings = $40,000 funds × 15% return = $6,000
± Annual interest cost = $30,000 debt × 10% interest = $3,000
Profit = $3,000
Return on equity with borrowed funds = $3,000 profit / $10,000 equity = 30%

capital structure
Financing mix of a firm

and when. The answers to such questions determine the firm's **capital structure**, the mix of debt and equity.

Debt versus Equity Financing *Debt financing* refers to what we normally think of as a loan. A creditor agrees to lend money to a debtor in exchange for repayment, with accumulated interest, at some future date. Debt financing can be either short term or long term. One of the biggest benefits of debt financing is that the lender does not gain an ownership interest in your business and your obligations are limited to repaying the loan. On the other hand, equity financing describes an exchange of money for a share of business ownership—evidenced by a **stock certificate**. This form of financing allows you to obtain funds without incurring debt; in other words, without having to repay a specific amount of money at any particular time.

stock certificate
Document that proves stock ownership

When choosing between debt and equity financing, companies consider a variety of issues, including the amount of financing required; whether it is for the short or long term; the cost of the financing including interest, fees, and other charges; timing; economic conditions; marketability of the debt or securities; and desire for ownership control (see Exhibit 18.3). For example, small privately held companies seeking from $1 million to $5 million would probably not issue and sell securities to the public because of the high costs involved in issuing stock plus the cumbersome and costly federal registrations and filing requirements with the SEC. Likewise, a company that wants to retain ownership control would probably not consider equity financing because shareholders get an ownership interest. Still, companies must also take into account the disadvantages of debt financing—especially when interest rates are high and the amount required is large. For example, a company can sell stock and survive rough times by omitting dividend payments, but if it can't meet its loan and bond commitments, it could be forced into bankruptcy.

Sometimes companies get into trouble by taking on too much debt. For example when Quaker Oats unloaded Snapple for $300 million (after plunking down a whopping $1.7 billion to purchase the brand from its creators less than 3 years earlier), the company recorded a $1.4 billion loss on the sale. Analysts estimate that Quaker lost $1.6 million for every day it owned the brand because the net revenue generated from sales of the brand did not cover the costs of financing the acquisition.[6]

EXHIBIT 18.3

Debt versus Equity

The cost of debt is generally lower than the cost of equity, largely because the interest paid on debt is tax-deductible. However, too much debt can increase the risk that a company will be unable to meet its interest and principal payments.

CHARACTERISTIC	DEBT	EQUITY
Maturity	**Specific:** Specifies a date by which it must be repaid.	**Nonspecific:** Specifies no maturity date.
Claim on income	**Fixed cost:** Company must pay interest on debt held by bondholders and lenders before paying any dividends to shareholders. Interest payments must be met regardless of operating results.	**Discretionary cost:** Shareholders may receive dividends after creditors have received interest payments; however, company is not required to pay dividends.
Claim on assets	**Priority:** Lenders have prior claims on assets.	**Residual:** Shareholders have claims only after the firm satisfies claims of lenders.
Influence over management	**Little:** Lenders are creditors, not owners. They can impose limits on management only if interest payments are not received.	**Varies:** As owners of the company, shareholders can vote on some aspects of corporate operations. Shareholder influence varies, depending on whether stock is widely distributed or closely held.

Common Types of Short-Term Debt Financing

The primary purpose of short-term financing is to ensure that a company maintains its liquidity, or its ability to meet financial obligations (such as inventory payments) as they become due. Aside from internal financing, the three most common types of short-term financing are (1) **trade credit** (or open-account purchases) from suppliers allowing purchasers to obtain products before paying for them, (2) short-term commercial loans, and (3) **commercial paper**—short-term promissory notes of major corporations sold in minimum investments of $25,000 with a maturity or due date of 30 to 90 days.

Short-term financing can be secured or unsecured. **Secured loans** are those backed by something of value, known as **collateral,** which may be seized by the lender in the event that the borrower fails to repay the loan. The three main types of collateral are accounts receivable, inventories, and property such as marketable securities, buildings, and other assets. An **unsecured loan** is one that requires no collateral. Instead, the lender relies on the general credit record and the earning power of the borrower. To increase the returns on such loans and to obtain some protection in case of default, most lenders insist that the borrower maintain some minimum amount of money on deposit at the bank—a **compensating balance**—while the loan is outstanding.

One example of an unsecured loan is a working capital **line of credit,** which is an agreed-on maximum amount of money the bank is willing to lend the business during a specific period of time, usually one year. Once a line of credit has been established, the business may obtain unsecured loans for any amount up to that limit, provided the bank has funds. The line of credit can be canceled at any time, so companies that want to be sure of obtaining credit when needed should arrange a revolving line of credit, which guarantees that the bank will honor the line of credit up to the stated amount.

trade credit
Credit obtained by the purchaser directly from the supplier

commercial paper
An IOU, backed by the corporation's reputation, issued to raise short-term capital

secured loans
Loans backed up with something of value that the lender can claim in case of default, such as a piece of property

collateral
Tangible asset a lender can claim if a borrower defaults on a loan

unsecured loan
Loan requiring no collateral but a good credit rating

compensating balance
Portion of an unsecured loan that is kept on deposit at the lending institution to protect the lender and increase the lender's return

line of credit
Arrangement in which the financial institution makes money available for use at any time after the loan has been approved

BEST OF THE WEB

Plan Ahead

Start your personal financial planning now by using the tools at the Financenter. This Web site has loads of information on the best way to buy, finance, or refinance major assets such as cars and houses. Use the calculators to compute what it will take to pay off your credit-card balance. Find out whether you should consolidate your debts. Compute your available line of credit. Calculate how much money you can save by cutting your spending and investing the savings for ten years. Better hurry. You may be losing interest.
http://www.financenter.com

Common Types of Long-Term Debt Financing

When it comes to financing long-term projects—such as major construction, acquisitions of other companies, and research and development—most companies rely on a combination of internal and external funding sources. The three main sources of external debt funding are loans, leases, and bonds. Long-term loans are repaid over a period of one year or more and may be either secured or unsecured. The most common type of secured loan is a mortgage, in which a piece of property like a building is used as collateral. *Commercial banks*, or those accepting deposits and using these funds to make loans, traditionally made most of the long-term loans to businesses, but pension funds and insurance companies have increased the number of long-term corporate loans they make. Exhibit 18.4 shows some of the key factors lenders look for when analyzing the merits of a loan request.

lease
Legal agreement that obligates the user of an asset to make payments to the owner of the asset in exchange for using it

Rather than borrowing from a commercial lender to buy a piece of property or equipment, a firm may enter into a **lease,** under which the owner of an item allows another party to use it in exchange for regular payments. Leasing may be a good alternative for a company that has difficulty obtaining loans because of a poor credit rating. Creditors are

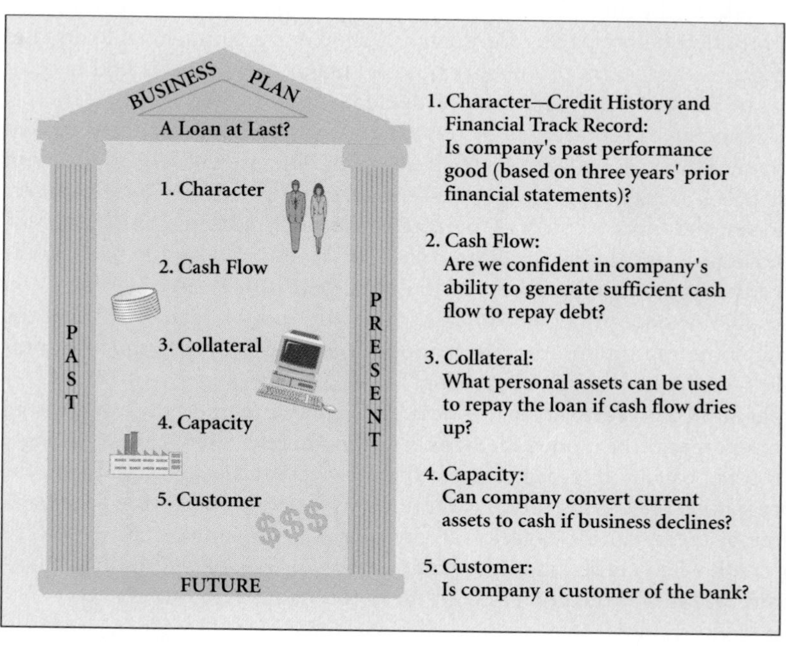

EXHIBIT 18.4

The 5 C's of Basic Lending

Lenders look at these five factors when analyzing the merits of a loan request.

more willing to provide a lease than a loan because, should the company fail, the lessor need not worry about a default on loan payments; it can simply repossess equipment it legally owns. Some firms use leases to finance up to 35 percent of their total assets, particularly in industries such as airlines, where assets are mostly large pieces of equipment.

When a company or a government needs to borrow a large sum of money, it may not be able to get the entire amount from a single source. Under such circumstances, it may borrow from many individual investors by issuing **bonds**—certificates that obligate the company (or government agency) to repay a certain sum, plus interest, to the bondholder on specific dates. Like stocks, bonds represent a major source of funds for corporations. Because bonds and stock issues of many corporations are traded on organized securities exchanges, both are covered in more depth in the next chapter.

bonds
Certificates of indebtedness that are sold to raise long-term funds for a corporation or government agency

Private Equity Financing

One of the biggest decisions a company must make is whether to achieve long-term financing through debt or equity. That's because financing with equity adds one more parameter to the decision—ownership control.

A key drawback of private equity financing is that investors will often require a discount on the actual market value of the securities purchased because of the risk inherent in owning a minority interest. In other words, they know that if they do not have voting control (over 50 percent of the voting stock), the inside stockholders can pay themselves exorbitant salaries or choose not to pay dividends. So in order to protect their interest, private investors frequently require board representation as part of the deal and sometimes place restrictions on future bank borrowings or dividend payments to common shareholders.[7]

On the other hand, there are many benefits to private equity financing. Sometimes firms choose this option because they are not ready to sell their stock on the open market. Another reason for choosing private equity financing might be that management does not want the pressure to produce annual earnings gains, especially when it might be in the shareholders' best interest to adopt strategies that could penalize short-term earnings in order to produce benefits in future years. This is especially true as companies try to restructure or reengineer their operations to be more competitive in the future by rightsizing their work force, selling their unprofitable business units, and writing off worthless assets. Corporate reengineering is one of the main reasons companies go private in *leveraged buyouts.*

Leveraged Buyouts In a **leveraged buyout (LBO)** a small group of equity investors (usually including current management) purchases the company with borrowed funds using the assets of the company they are buying to secure the loan. The debt is repaid with funds generated by the company's operations, and often, by the sale of some of its assets. Generally, the acquiring group plans to run the acquired company for a number of years, boost its sales and profits, and make it a stronger company. Naturally, the acquiring group expects to make a substantial profit from an LBO, and in most cases it earns this profit by selling the company at a later date for a higher price than the group paid for it. Still, the risks are great because, as discussed earlier, leveraging can magnify your losses as well as your gains.

leveraged buyout (LBO)
Situation in which individuals or groups of investors purchase companies primarily with debt secured by the company's assets

Look at Denny's. During the late 1980s Denny's restaurant chain underwent a series of leveraged buyouts. First the president took the company private by purchasing the company's public shares and saddling the company with $640 million in debt. Then TW Services borrowed $1.1 billion to buy the company, only to become the object of a hostile takeover bid that doubled the company's debt to $2.4 billion. This enormous amount of debt sucked up cash that should have gone to modernizing the restaurants. As a result,

After years of financial turmoil, a leveraged buyout of Denny's allowed the chain to refinance its enormous amount of debt and use the freed-up cash to modernize its restaurants.

customers began fleeing the restaurant in ever-rising numbers, affecting cash flow even further. Finally in 1991, Kohlberg Kravis Roberts, (the masters of LBOs) refinanced the mess and bought a 47 percent equity stake in the company. The refinancing freed up enough cash to spend $160 million to remodel the company-owned restaurants—resulting in a significant increase in store traffic and the first signs of a turnaround after a turbulent decade.[8] Montgomery Ward is another victim of leveraged buyouts. This company was forced to file for Chapter 11 bankruptcy protection in 1997 after negotiations to delay a $1.4 billion debt payment broke down.[9]

Private Financing Assistance Suppose you decide to seek private financing. Where would you find investors? How would you contact them? Many people use an investment banker, a venture capitalist, or even the Internet for assistance in finding private investors. Sometimes they even look for an angel.

venture capitalists
Investment specialists who provide money to finance new businesses or turnarounds in exchange for a portion of the ownership, with the objective of making a considerable profit on the investment; also called VCs

VENTURE CAPITALISTS **Venture capitalists** are investment specialists who raise pools of capital from private and institutional sources to fund ventures that have a high, rapid growth potential and a need for large amounts of capital. Venture capitalists, or VCs as they're called in entrepreneurial circles, do not simply lend money to a small business as a bank would. Instead they provide capital in return for an ownership interest (which may amount to half of the stock or more), and they frequently help run the business as well. In a typical scenario, the venture capital firm buys part of the company's stock at a low price and later on sells it to the investing public at a much higher price.

The problem with venture capital is that it's extremely hard to find and the price of financing through a venture capital firm is high. To catch the eye of a typical venture capitalist, you need a business with pizzazz that has the potential to reach $50 million in sales within 5 years and provides an annualized rate of return of 20 to 40 percent over 5 to 7 years.[10]

SMALL BUSINESS ADMINISTRATION If your business doesn't fit the profile of a high-powered venture capital firm, you might be able to raise money from one of the investment firms created by the Small Business Administration. Small Business Investment Companies (SBICs) and Special Enterprise Small Business Investment Companies (SESBICs), which finance minority-owned businesses, are similar in operation to venture capital firms, but they tend to make smaller investments and are willing to consider businesses that VCs may not want to finance.

ANGELS Wealthy individuals are one of the most promising sources of equity financing; however, finding rich friends or so-called angels may be difficult. According to *Inc.* magazine, more capital is invested by angel investors today than by venture capitalists. Aside from providing financing, angels can be a great source of business expertise. For instance, Bill Gates (chairman of Microsoft) is an angel. He has invested millions of dollars in biotech start-ups such as Darwin Molecular, which is trying to create artificial molecules that attack diseases.[11]

Public Equity Financing

Whenever the stock of a closely held corporation is offered to the public for the first time, the company is said to be *going public* and the initial shares issued are the company's *initial public offering* or IPO. Selling your stock to the public has several disadvantages: (1) The cost is high (ranging from $50,000 to $500,000) and the filing requirements with the SEC are burdensome; (2) offering your company's ownership for public sale does little good unless your business has sufficient investor awareness and appeal; (3) ownership control is lost; (4) management must be ready to handle the administrative and legal demands of widespread public ownership; and (5) nothing guarantees that the shares can be sold to the public at the initial target price.

Still, going public has many advantages, including increased liquidity (there is now a public market for your shares); voluntary dividend payments (unlike creditors, stockholders do not have to be repaid at a fixed rate or time); and enhanced visibility. In addition, it establishes a market value for the company. Keep in mind, however, that going public requires advance planning—sometimes as early as five years before your target date—because IPO candidates must have a history of solid and sustained growth, strong earning records, three to five years of audited financial reports, and solid management (including a strong board of directors).[12]

When Spring Street Brewing decided to offer its stock to the public for the first time, the company did not use traditional investment bankers or venture capitalists to market its stock. Instead the company sold its stock directly to the public—a practice known as a *direct public offering* or DPO.[13] The number of DPOs is steadily growing, thanks to the Internet, and DPOs are expected to become an increasingly popular funding option.

Although DPOs provide businesses with fresh capital for expansion at less than half the cost of an IPO, most companies still go the traditional IPO route mainly because DPO shares are not traded on public security exchanges. This makes it difficult for shareholders to find subsequent buyers for their shares. However, Spring Street Brewing took care of that. The company set up a digital stock exchange on the Internet to provide a market for its roughly 3,500 investors who originally purchased Spring Street's stock over the Internet. Oddly enough, not only did the SEC allow this digital stock exchange, but the SEC commissioner called it "terrific, innovative, and fantastic." Of course, Chapter 19 will point out that not all stockbrokers share in the SEC's enthusiasm.[14]

Even if you go the DPO route, there are still rules and regulations that a company must follow when selling securities privately. For example, Regulation D, Section 504 (also known as small corporate offering registrations, or SCOR) allows issues to raise up to $1 million every 12 months by registering with the state. Regulation A extends the size of the offering to $5 million but requires a registration with the Small Business Office of the SEC.[15]

THE NATURE OF MONEY

The bulk of this chapter has been devoted to discussing why a company needs money and the advantages and disadvantages of each financing alternative. Besides selecting an appropriate funding vehicle, a finance manager must also consider various external factors when planning for the firm's future. The remainder of this chapter will discuss these external factors, which include the forms and characteristics of money, how money is supplied and regulated, and the changing nature of the U.S. banking system.

Forms and Characteristics of Money

Money is anything generally accepted as a means of paying for goods and services. Before it was invented, people got what they needed by trading their services or possessions; in some primitive societies, this system of trading, or bartering, still prevails. However, barter is inconvenient and impractical in a modern industrial society, where many of the things we want are intangible or require the combined work of many people.

money
Anything generally accepted as a means of paying for goods and services

When the Phoenicians created money millennia ago, it was worth its weight in gold or silver or copper. But people grew tired of all that metal ripping holes in their pockets, and governments consolidated, becoming stable enough to earn the trust of their citizens. So paper IOUs were issued. Henry Ford Sr. once said that if the people of the nation actually understood our banking and monetary system, there would be a revolution the following morning. Perhaps he was referring to the fact that money is simply a representation of value and is built on faith.

To be an effective medium for exchange, money must have certain characteristics: It must be divisible, portable (easy to carry), durable, and difficult to counterfeit or secure, and it should have a stable value. When people lose faith in the value of their money, they begin to abandon it and look for different ways to store their wealth, such as precious metals. Additionally, money must perform three basic functions: First, it must serve as a medium of exchange—a tool for simplifying transactions between buyers and sellers. Second, it must serve as a measure of value so that you don't have to negotiate the relative worth of dissimilar items every time you buy something. Finally, money must serve as a temporary store of value—a way of accumulating your wealth until you need it.

BEST OF THE WEB

Tour the U.S. Treasury

Take a virtual tour of the U.S. Treasury. Visit the Learning Vault and find out how much paper currency is printed in one day or one year. Click on the Site Map and explore this Department from the inside out. Learn about the benefits of electronic funds transfer. Take the link to the Bureau of Engraving and Printing where you can play money trivia and get some money production figures. Discover how money gets into circulation. Find out whose picture was on the $500 bill. Bet you wish you had one!
http://www.ustreas.gov

credit cards
Plastic cards that allow the customer to buy now and pay back the loaned amount at a future date

debit cards
Plastic cards that allow the bank to take money from the user's demand-deposit account and transfer it to a retailer's account

smart cards
Plastic cards that include an embedded chip to store money drawn from the user's demand-deposit account and information that can be used for purchases

Credit, Debit, and Smart Cards Cash is dying. Money today is a plastic charge card and entries in a computer. Even though U.S. money is still based on the dollar currency, the form we carry and the way we get it is changing. For example, **credit cards**, plastic cards that entitle customers to make purchases now and repay the loaned amount later, are a significant source of credit for some, but for many they are simply payment devices. As a practical matter, it has become difficult to buy an airplane ticket or rent a car without a credit card. The vast bulk of mail-order and phone-order commerce depends on credit cards—or, more precisely, credit-card numbers.

In addition to credit cards, people can pay for purchases at many stores by using **debit cards,** plastic cards that are the mirror image of credit cards—that is, the cash value is deducted from your bank account and transferred to the retailer's account at the time of purchase. Debit cards are generally used for smaller purchases because using a credit card frequently requires a minimum dollar purchase. **Smart cards** are the next generation of debit cards. They allow you to load money and information (such as your credit-card number, frequent-flyer account numbers, or other personal information) onto a small computer chip embedded in the card. Once money is used up, you can add more by reloading it onto the microchip's memory.

Is It True?

About 18 percent of credit-card-holding families seldom pay off their credit-card balance.

Electronic Money Today institutions are wrestling with the implications of an emerging electronic third-wave substitute for coinage called electronic money, or e-cash. With e-cash, you'll no longer need to carry a wad of bills in your pocket or fumble for exact change. Instead, you might carry a plastic smart card with an embedded microchip, that stores your e-money. And, you'll be able to easily replenish your e-money over the phone, at a cash station, or even over the Internet. In fact, electronic money is really nothing more than debit and credit entries to your bank account, which moves along multiple electronic channels (such as the Internet).[16]

Security is one of the biggest obstacles that must be overcome before the electronic form of money is accepted as a safe way of doing commerce on the Internet. Without security, card numbers are vulnerable to being intercepted. Heavyweights VISA, MasterCard, Microsoft, Netscape, and IBM have all agreed on a Secure Electronic Transaction Standard

(SET) that will become the protocol for sending credit-card information and e-cash through the Internet. SET will work something like this: Consumers will receive digital certificates through their banks and keep them in "wallets" located on their Web browsers. When consumers make a purchase at a retailer's Web site, the amount will be requested from the wallet and the money will be sent back to the retail site in encrypted form. The retailer (which will not have access to the actual credit-card number) will then confirm the amount with the card issuer.[17]

International Monetary Systems

Perhaps you have traveled in Europe where you carried four, even five or more different currencies with you—each with a different exchange rate to the U.S. dollar. Converting currencies can be confusing and costly—especially when you are outside the geographic boundaries of the issuing country. But, if all goes according to plans, 11 European nations will soon join monetary forces to introduce a unified currency called the European Monetary Unit (EMU), or **euro** for short.[18] The euro will be a grab bag of European monies, and it could eventually challenge the dollar's role as the world's reserve currency. Additionally, the euro could bring about greater political integration, and it will allow people to travel from Berlin to Paris or Amsterdam to Rome without changing money.

euro
A planned unified currency to be used by European nations who meet certain strict requirements

You might ask why a country like Germany would want to give up its rock-solid deutsche mark for the risky new euro. Advocates of the new currency (which will be controlled by the European Central Bank) say the euro will make individual countries stronger through integration and thus more competitive globally. Critics, on the other hand, fear that besides losing control of their individual monetary policy, having a single European currency removes the devaluation safety valve currently in existence. For example, if Italy has poor economic times, it is reflected in the value of the lira, but Italy's economics do not *directly affect* Germany's deutsche mark, nor does Italy's economic problem escalate to become a global European problem.

Of course, because the 1992 Maastricht Treaty requires nations to pass a series of tough financial tests (including a long period of stability) in order to qualify for inclusion in the planned currency union, the likelihood of widespread devaluation is remote.[19] Still, even if the currencies of weaker countries are not included at first, one thing is certain: The euro will change the role individual governments play in regulating their money supply.

THE FEDERAL RESERVE SYSTEM

The Federal Reserve System was created in 1913 and is commonly known as the Fed. It is the most powerful financial institution in the United States, serving as the country's central bank. The Fed's primary role is to supply us with the "right" amount of money so that we avoid both recession and inflation. It also supervises and regulates banks and serves as a clearinghouse for checks.

The Fed is a network of 12 district banks that controls the country's banking system. The overall policy of the Fed is established by a seven-member board of governors in Washington, D.C. To preserve the board's political independence, the members are appointed by the president to 14-year terms, staggered at 2-year intervals. Although all national banks are required to be members of the Federal Reserve System, membership for state-chartered banks is optional. Currently the Fed oversees approximately 5,500 member banks, and it exercises regulatory power over all deposit institutions, whether they are members or not. The Federal Reserve System has three major functions: regulating the U.S. money supply, supplying currency, and clearing checks. The most important of these is regulating the money supply.

UNDERSTANDING THE HIGH-TECH REVOLUTION

Bytes, Bits, Banks, and Bucks: Money and the Internet

E-cash. Cyber-sheckels. Netchex. Call it whatever you want. It's the next logical extension of where the Internet is going. First the Internet changed how we find information and products. Now it's redefining how we will pay for them by allowing us to buy monetary bits (e-cash or electronic money) over the Internet, store them in a computer, and send them through cyberspace—just like e-mail.

HERE'S HOW IT WORKS

E-cash is the amount of money stored on a smart card—a plastic card with an embedded microcomputer chip—or loaded into your computer for online purchases. Linked with the holder's bank account, e-cash is downloaded from your bank account, debiting your bank account balance just like an ATM withdrawal. Once you make a purchase, the amount of your purchase is deducted from your e-cash balance. You can load more e-cash onto the smart card or into your computer at any time by using an ATM, a specially equipped telephone, or eventually even the Internet. In fact, future PCs and keyboards will be shipped with smart-card readers. As electronic commerce gains steam, this digital money will let you shop online, zapping money to merchants over the Internet. It will literally change the way business is done worldwide, and it could make our current monetary system obsolete.

CASHLESS, NOT BANKLESS

Consider this: In the physical world, it makes sense to use a medium of exchange that can be seen, felt, and carried. But in the wired world, electrons do better. Just as the postal service makes little sense in an e-mail world, moving money with armored trucks and transporting checks in chartered airplanes is equally arcane in a world where over 96 million U.S. households have telephones and over 37.5 million households have personal computers. Of course, you'll still need some "walking around" cash, but even that can be loaded on a smart card.

How will this affect the banks? Most banking experts agree that the role of banks in this new e-cash world will change: Some will die, a few will change enough to accommodate this new e-world, and new ones will emerge—like Integrion, a joint venture of IBM and a group of 15 large U.S. and Canadian banks (including Bank of America, Banc One, and Mellon Bank). Integrion will link consumers to accounts through the Internet and will provide a full range of financial services to its 60 million customers at the touch of a telephone button or the click of a mouse. Thus, in the e-world everyone will still need banking but not everyone will need a bank. That's because on a day-to-day basis almost all your financial transactions will take place

Regulating the U.S. Money Supply

currency
Bills and coins that make up the cash money of a society

checks
Written orders that tell the customer's bank to pay a specific amount to a particular individual or business

time deposits
Bank accounts that pay interest and require advance notice before money can be withdrawn

demand deposit
Money in a checking account that can be used by the customer at any time

The Fed's main job is to establish and implement *monetary policy,* which is a set of guidelines for handling the nation's economy and the money supply. In the United States today, the money supply consists of money outside the banking system or in the economy. It has three major components: (1) **currency** or money in the form of coins, paper, cashier's checks, money orders, and traveler's checks; (2) demand deposits, which are **checks** or written orders that direct the customer's bank to pay the stated amount of money to the check writer or someone else; and (3) **time deposits,** or accounts that pay interest and restrict the owner's right to withdraw funds on short notice. Savings accounts, certificates of deposit (CDs), and money-market deposit accounts are examples of time deposits. Because a time deposit is not payable on demand (although some money-market accounts offer limited check-writing privileges), it is less liquid than a **demand deposit**, which is available immediately (or on demand).

The Fed regulates the money supply to make certain that enough money and credit are available to allow the economy to expand. However, it must also be careful not to release too much money and credit into the economy at any one time because altering the money supply affects interest rates or the cost of money. For instance, when the money

electronically, including invoicing your customers, receiving their payments, and authorizing your own payments to suppliers and tax authorities. In fact, the only reason you would need a bank is to actually transfer and hold your funds—something other nontraditional financial institutions are already doing.

Even shopping for a loan could be done over the Internet. You could look for the best interest rates by submitting loan applications to, say, 50 institutions. After all, as a consumer, do you care whether the bank that lends you money is in your hometown, across the continent, or across the Pacific Ocean? Probably not. But governments do!

Governments, Geography, and Control

Today, geography determines much of what national and state banks can and cannot do. Governments want to be able to control their economies with monetary policy, but with e-cash, money can move beyond natural boundaries. In cyberspace, there are no physical boundaries and no clear indications of which country's laws apply. As a result, governments could lose control of their money supply. Free marketers contend that if U.S. government rules become burdensome, e-money players will simply shift their operations overseas. After all, if your bank won't lend you money due to tight credit or increased inflation, what's to stop you from borrowing from another country? Moreover, how will taxes be applied in cyberspace? With e-cash, the merchant could be in Guam and the buyer in Canada, whereas First Virtual's computers are located in Ohio. So whose sales tax do you pay?

These are just a few of the questions raised by the advent of e-cash. Other questions include: Who should be allowed to issue e-cash? Who will regulate those issuers? How do you ensure that payments made over the Internet will be secure? How will consumers be protected? How will regulators police money laundering and counterfeiting on private networks? Meanwhile, as regulators wrestle with these questions, technology will continue to remake the monetary system and redefine banking—something that banks actually started themselves when they invented the electronic clearinghouse system.

Questions for Critical Thinking

1. How could e-cash and debit cards improve a company's cash flow?
2. Which other industries (besides banking) would be negatively affected by an increased usage of e-cash? Please explain.

supply increases, there is more money to go around, and banks can charge lower interest rates to borrowers. However, complications may arise. An increased money supply may lead to more spending and a demand for goods that exceeds supply. When this happens, sellers can raise their prices (because of the increased demand), causing inflation. During inflationary periods, the dollars that borrowers repay to lenders have less purchasing power than they had when the loan was made. To offset this loss of purchasing power, lenders must add a certain percentage—corresponding to the rate of inflation—to the interest rates they would otherwise charge. So a growth in the money supply, if it fans inflation, may lead to higher interest rates.

Is It True?

Currency (coins, paper, cashier's checks, and traveler's checks) represents about 37 percent of all media of exchange in the United States.

Measuring the Money Supply Oddly enough, nobody knows precisely how much money there is in the money supply, although the federal government has a rough idea. When we measure the money supply, we look at various combinations of currency, demand deposits, and time deposits (see Exhibit 18.5). The narrowest commonly used measure of money, known as **M1,** consists of currency, demand deposits, and NOW accounts (interest-paying checking accounts that require a minimum balance). All the money defined as M1 can be used as a medium of exchange. **M2,** a broader measure of the money supply, includes M1 plus savings deposits, money-market funds, and small time deposits (less than

M1
That portion of the money supply consisting of currency and demand deposits

M2
That portion of the money supply consisting of currency, demand deposits, and small time deposits

EXHIBIT 18.5

The Total Money Supply

The U.S. Money Supply is measured at three different levels—M1, M2, and M3—with M1 being the narrowest measure. Here's a closer look at their components.

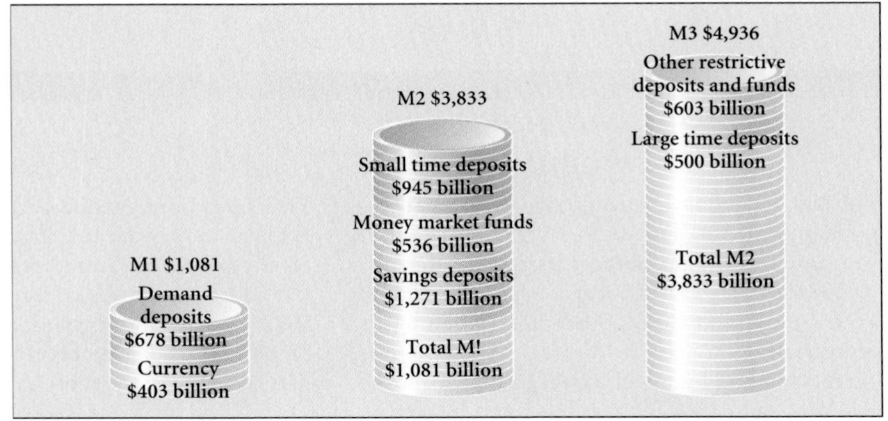

M3
That portion of the money supply consisting of M1 and M2 plus large time deposits and other restrictive deposits

Eurodollars
Dollars deposited in banks outside the United States

$100,000). **M3,** the broadest measure of the money supply, includes M2 plus large time deposits ($100,000 and above) and other restrictive deposits such as money-market funds held by institutional investors.

One reason it is difficult to measure the money supply is because a large number of dollars are deposited in banks outside the United States, commonly known as **Eurodollars**. It is estimated that two-thirds of the U.S. currency is currently abroad.[20] The major difference between a regular U.S. dollar and a Eurodollar is its geographic location. Because Eurodollars are outside the direct control of the U.S. monetary authorities, regulations such as federal insurance premiums and reserve requirements (which will be discussed later in this chapter) do not apply. As a result, the interest rate paid on Eurodollar deposits tends to be higher than domestic rates.

Influencing the Money Supply The Fed uses the following four basic tools to influence the money supply. Exhibit 18.6 summarizes the effects of using these tools.

reserve requirement
Percentage of a bank's deposit that must be set aside

CHANGING THE RESERVE REQUIREMENT The Fed requires all member banks and financial institutions to set aside *reserves,* sums of money equal to a certain percentage of their deposits. The Fed can change the **reserve requirement**, the percentage of deposits that banks must set aside, to influence the money supply. However, the Fed rarely uses this technique because a small change can have a drastic effect on the money supply. For example, by increasing the reserve requirement, the Fed can slow down the economy because

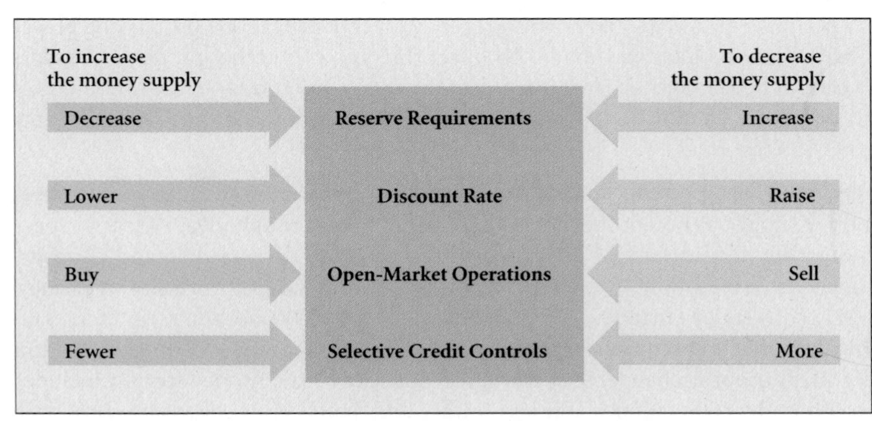

EXHIBIT 18.6

Influencing the Money Supply

The Federal Reserve manipulates the money supply in various ways as it attempts to stimulate economic growth and keep both inflation and interest rates at acceptable levels.

banks will have less money to lend to customers. Conversely, by reducing this requirement, it can boost the economy because banks will have more money available to lend to businesses and consumers (see Exhibit 18.7).

CHANGING THE DISCOUNT RATE Another way the Fed influences the money supply is by changing the *discount rate,* the interest rate it charges on loans to commercial banks and other depository institutions. When the Fed raises the discount rate, member banks generally raise the prime rate. This discourages loans, which in turn tightens the money supply and slows down economic growth. On the other hand, lowering the discount rate results in lower lending rates, which encourages more loans and fuels economic growth.

CONDUCTING OPEN-MARKET OPERATIONS The tool that the Fed uses most frequently to influence the money supply is the power to buy and sell government bonds (which are promises to repay a debt with interest). Because anyone can buy these government bonds on the open market, this tool is known as **open-market operations**. If the Fed is concerned about inflation, it can reduce the money supply by selling U.S. government bonds to the public. The money consumers use to buy these bonds is in effect taken out of circulation. Conversely, when the Fed wants to boost the economy it can buy back government bonds. This puts additional cash back into circulation, increasing the money supply.

open-market operations
Activity of the Federal Reserve in buying and selling government bonds on the open market

ESTABLISHING SELECTIVE CREDIT CONTROLS The Fed also has the authority known as **selective credit controls** to set the terms of credit for various kinds of loans. This includes the power to set *margin requirements,* the percentage of the purchase price that an investor must pay in cash when purchasing a stock or bond on credit. By altering the margin requirements, the Fed is able to influence the amount of money spent on stock market speculation.

selective credit controls
Federal Reserve's power to set credit terms on various types of loans

Supplying Currency and Clearing Checks

In addition to regulating the money supply, the Fed supplies currency to help keep the financial system running smoothly. For example, individual Federal Reserve Banks are responsible for providing member banks with adequate amounts of currency. The demand

Deposits	Reserves		Borrowers
$100.00	$20.00	$80.00	B
80.00	16.00	64.00	C
64.00	12.80	51.20	D
51.20	10.24	40.96	E
40.96	8.19	32.77	F
32.77	6.55	26.22	G
26.22	5.24	20.98	H

EXHIBIT 18.7

How Banks Create Money

Banks stay in business by earning more on interest from loans than they pay out in the form of interest on deposits; they can increase their earnings by "creating" money. When customer A deposits $100, the bank must keep some in reserve but can lend, say, $80 to customer B (and earn interest on that loan). If customer B deposits the borrowed $80 in the same bank, the bank can lend 80 percent of *that* amount to borrower C. The initial $100 deposit, therefore, creates a much larger pool of funds from which customer loans may be made.

for coins and paper money is seasonal. As you might expect, many people withdraw some of their savings from the banks in the form of cash during the winter holidays. The Federal Reserve has to supply the extra currency that banks need at such times.

Another function of the Federal Reserve is to act as a clearinghouse for checks. Here's how it works: In today's banking world, money consists of ledger entries on the books of banks or other financial institutions. A checking account, also known as a demand-deposit account, records deposits by the consumer and can be used, via the consumer's instructions in the form of a check, to make payments to third parties. Typically, a check is written by a consumer, authenticated by signature, and presented to a merchant, who may endorse it with a signature before presenting it to a bank for payment. If the merchant's bank and the consumer's bank are the same, it can simply transfer the funds on its ledgers from the consumer's account to the merchant's.

BEST OF THE WEB

Take a Field Trip to the Fed

Visit the Fed. Find out what the Board of Governors of the Federal Reserve System does. Read summaries of their regulations. Learn what "Truth in Lending" means or how to file a consumer complaint against a bank. Brush up on your credit-card knowledge. Do you know what a grace period is or how finance charges are calculated? Take a side trip to the Federal Reserve Banks. Don't leave without meeting Carmen Cents. She's at the FDIC and she has a wonderful tour planned for you.
http://www.bog.frb.fed.us/

Is It True?

The average American signs 270 checks in one year compared with 10 for the average German.

If the payer and the payee keep accounts at different banks, however, the payee bank presents the check for settlement to the payer's bank and receives funds in return through a settlement system. Banks use the Fed's automated check-processing system to clear checks drawn on banks outside their federal districts. This system allows banks to electronically transfer funds between accounts in different banks. Of course, not all checks are sent to the Fed for clearance. Many rural banks simply pay larger banks to perform this service for them. Transactions among banks in the same area are handled locally and then reported to the Federal Reserve, which charges and credits the appropriate accounts.

Exhibit 18.8 shows the steps involved in processing standard paper checks. Electronic

The Federal Reserve System functions as a clearinghouse for business and personal checks that are presented for payment at member banks throughout the United States.

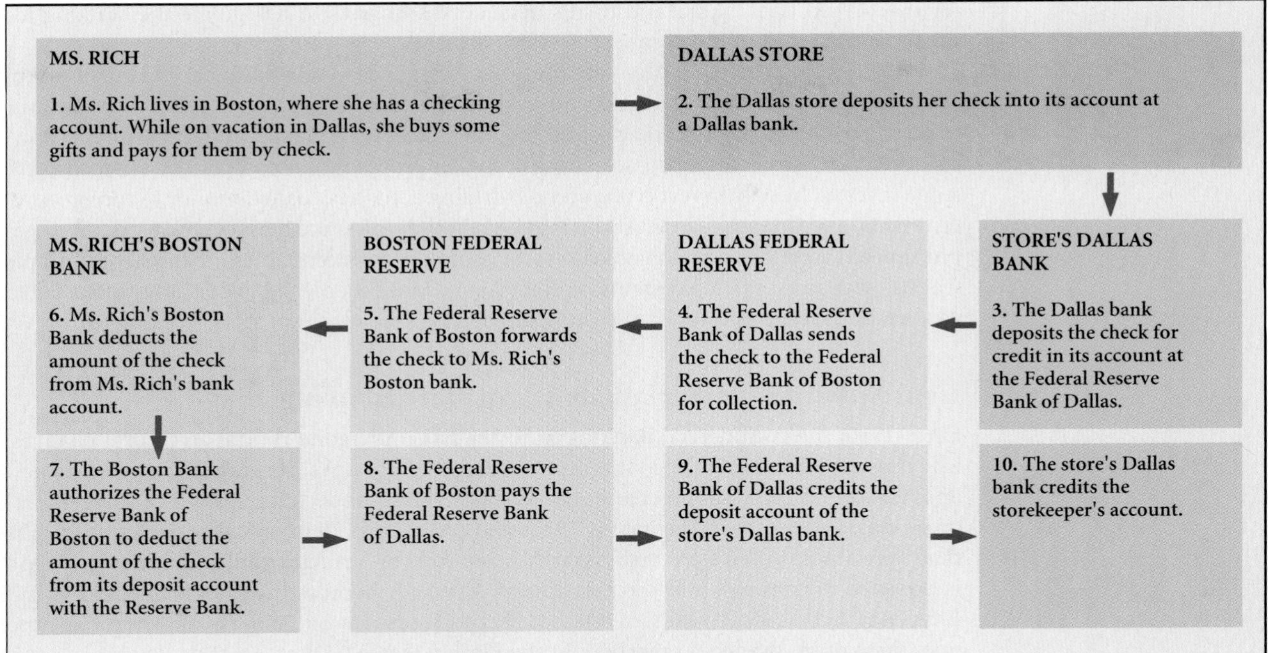

MS. RICH
1. Ms. Rich lives in Boston, where she has a checking account. While on vacation in Dallas, she buys some gifts and pays for them by check.
DALLAS STORE
2. The Dallas store deposits her check into its account at a Dallas bank.
STORE'S DALLAS BANK
3. The Dallas bank deposits the check for credit in its account at the Federal Reserve Bank of Dallas.
DALLAS FEDERAL RESERVE
4. The Federal Reserve Bank of Dallas sends the check to the Federal Reserve Bank of Boston for collection.
BOSTON FEDERAL RESERVE
5. The Federal Reserve Bank of Boston forwards the check to Ms. Rich's Boston bank.
MS. RICH'S BOSTON BANK
6. Ms. Rich's Boston Bank deducts the amount of the check from Ms. Rich's bank account.
7. The Boston Bank authorizes the Federal Reserve Bank of Boston to deduct the amount of the check from its deposit account with the Reserve Bank.
8. The Federal Reserve Bank of Boston pays the Federal Reserve Bank of Dallas.
9. The Federal Reserve Bank of Dallas credits the deposit account of the store's Dallas bank.
10. The store's Dallas bank credits the storekeeper's account.

EXHIBIT 18.8

How a Check Clears

The Fed processes more than 55 billion checks every year. In this example, a customer who lives in Boston pays by check for a purchase made in a Dallas store. The check passes through the Federal Reserve Banks in Dallas and Boston before reaching the customer's bank and the store's bank.

payments have a speed advantage over checks, and they are cheaper to process. On the other hand, paying by check allows the payer to benefit from the time between when the check is written and when funds are finally transferred from the account—a period of time called the *float.*

THE EVOLVING U.S. BANKING ENVIRONMENT

No matter where in the world you live, work, or travel, you'll find that a banking system has developed to provide individuals and businesses with a wide range of financial services. Before 1980 banks, finance companies, and other financial institutions operated within well-defined boundaries in a highly regulated environment. Commercial banks made business loans, thrifts lent money for home mortgages, investment banks underwrote corporate stock and bond issues, brokerage firms sold those securities, and insurance companies insured businesses and individuals. The government set a ceiling on the amount of interest that could be paid on savings accounts, which limited competition for depositors' dollars.

Deregulation and Competition

This highly regulated approach worked well until double-digit inflation hit the U.S. economy in the late 1970s. Depositors seeking higher returns increasingly moved their money out of banks and thrifts and into money market mutual funds offered by Merrill Lynch and other brokerage firms, which could offer higher interest rates because they were not regulated.[21] In turn, banks and thrifts persuaded Congress to deregulate the banking industry so that they could compete for deposits.

As a result, the Depository Institutions Deregulation and Monetary Control Act of 1980 was passed. This act deregulated banking and paved the way for financial institutions to offer a wider range of services—blurring the line between banks and other financial institutions. As banks and thrifts searched for higher profits in this competitive environment, some invested heavily in real estate and oil-drilling activities, loaned money to foreign governments, and financed company buyouts. Then the real estate market collapsed, oil prices plummeted, developers went bankrupt, and countries and companies hit hard by economic woes slowed or stopped payments on their loans. More than 1,000 banks and thrifts failed as a result of these and other risky investments.[22]

Consolidations, Branches, and Interstate Banking

Since 1980, the commercial banking industry has undergone radical structural changes. The most obvious evidence: a decline in the number of banks. Seeking strength, efficiency, and access to more customers and markets, U.S. banks undertook a series of mergers, acquisitions, and takeovers during the 1980s and early 1990s. In many cases, banks and thrifts that were about to fail were involuntarily taken over by stronger banks. This merger trend is expected to continue into the near future, especially because the Interstate Banking and Efficiency Act of 1994 removed the barriers to interstate banking by allowing banks to open or acquire branches anywhere in the United States.[23]

As a result of this legislation, customers can make deposits, cash checks, or handle any banking transaction in any branch of their banks, regardless of location. This easing of restrictions is especially convenient for travelers and for the 60 million people who live and work in metropolitan areas that cross state lines or move from one state to another. Of course, the banks benefit as well: BankAmerica, for example, was forced to operate separate banking systems in 10 states until this bill allowed it to bring all its banks under a single system, thereby maximizing operating efficiencies.[24]

Although some community banks, particularly the weaker ones, will be swallowed up in the continuing wave of consolidation, many are expected to remain viable institutions. In fact, some believe that small *community banks*—banks with less than $1 billion in assets and not part of a conglomerate—could fare the best in this evolving highly competitive and global environment. That's because community banks focus on developing personal relationships with customers and servicing local needs. "We're really focused on the community," says the president of Virginia National Bank. "We financed a lot of businesses that would not have been otherwise. It's good for the town, and it's good for us because we live here."[25]

In order to compete with community banks, many branches are also focusing on servicing individual customers' needs. For example, officials at Norwest's branch bank in Dodge Center, Minnesota, recently pulled its ATM out of the wall to encourage visits by its customers. Norwest officials say the key to their aggressive financial strategy is to merchandise a wide range of financial products, including mutual funds and insurance. The bank does so the old-fashioned way—by building relationships with customers via personal conversations rather than calls to 800 numbers.[26] Even giant Merrill Lynch is setting up a system that provides its 13,000 domestic brokers with a file on all of the business a client does with the firm, and it is making a big bet that in spite of the Internet, the individual still needs an adviser to sort through all the information out there—but at what price?[27]

Unfortunately, customers today are being nickel-and-dimed for these individual services. There are monthly fees, per-check charges, annual credit-card fees, monthly charges for debit cards, fees for using a teller, fees for using automated teller machines—or not using your ATM card often enough—fees for not maintaining a minimum balance, and maintenance fees for inactive savings accounts. Reportedly, the number of service fees has grown from 26 to 250 over the past 4 years. What's more, these fees are by no means uniform throughout the industry—or even from one side of town to the other.[28]

Consolidations aren't the only thing changing the banking industry. Increased competition from nontraditional institutions and foreign banks, new information technologies, declining processing costs, less restrictive government regulations, electronic banking, and the erosion of product and geographic boundaries have changed the entire financial services landscape. In fact, the old bundle of functions and services provided by banks is being repackaged.[29]

Services

The process of moving money from person to person and business to business is facilitated by a network of financial institutions that are frequently categorized by the services they provide. For example, deposit institutions accept deposits from customers or members and provide some form of checking account. They include commercial banks, thrifts (savings and loan associations and savings banks), and credit unions (financial cooperatives owned by the members or employees of a company or other group). Nondeposit institutions, which include insurance companies, pension funds, and commercial and consumer finance companies, provide a variety of other services. The traditional types of services, typical investments, and primary sources of funds for deposit and nondeposit institutions are listed in Exhibit 18.9. These include a variety of checking and savings accounts, loans, credit cards, safe-deposit boxes, tax-deferred individual retirement accounts (IRAs), discount brokerage services, wire transfers, and financial counseling. In addition, most banks provide low-cost traveler's checks and automatic overdraft protections for checking accounts when depositors write checks exceeding their account balances.

Today, many large commercial banks, along with smaller community banks, are becoming full-service financial supermarkets. The era of opening a simple passbook savings account is over. Even though the provisions of the Glass Steagall Act of 1933 prohibit banks from giving customers advice on stocks or underwriting them, banks are allowed to offer discount brokerage services and charge fees for security transactions. In fact, some banks now offer securities trading on the Internet. Banking-industry experts project that within two to three years, computerized banking could begin to make traditional banking business ancient history.

Electronic Banking More than one-third of all U.S. workers take advantage of **electronic funds transfer systems (EFTS)**—computerized systems for conducting financial transactions electronically. Many employers transfer wages directly from the company bank account to employee accounts. This saves both employer and employee the worry and headache of handling large amounts of cash.[30]

electronic funds transfer system (EFTS)
Computerized systems for performing financial transactions

Electronic banking also allows customers to withdraw money from their demand-deposit accounts using **automated teller machines (ATMs)** located all over the United States and around the world. These electronic banking machines permit banking transactions on a 24-hour basis by entering personal access codes. By linking their ATMs with regional, national, and international ATM networks, banks can offer you the convenience of drawing out cash from an account hundreds or thousands of miles from home. These machines allow customers to withdraw cash or make deposits, provide customers with up-to-the minute bank statements, and handle other simple banking transactions. Newer ATMs will make change and dispense stamps, traveler's checks, and movie tickets. Plus they will play a key role in implementing newer forms of money, such as the debit cards, smart cards, and electronic money discussed earlier in this chapter.[31]

automated teller machines (ATMs)
Electronic terminals that permit people with plastic cards to perform simple banking transactions 24 hours a day without the aid of a human teller

INSTITUTION	TYPICAL SERVICES	TYPES OF ACCOUNTS OFFERED TO DEPOSITORS	PRIMARY SOURCE OF FUNDS
		Deposit Institutions	
Commercial bank	• Personal loans • Business loans • Real estate, construction, and home mortgage loans	• Checking accounts • NOW accounts • Passbook savings accounts • Time deposits • Money market deposit accounts	• Customer deposits • Interest earned on loans
Savings and loan association (S&L)	• Bond purchases • Home mortgages • Construction loans	• Savings accounts • NOW accounts • Time deposits • Money market deposit accounts	• Customer deposits • Interest earned on loans
Savings bank	• Bond purchases • Home mortgages • Construction loans	• Savings accounts • NOW accounts • Time deposits • Money market deposit accounts	• Customer deposits • Interest earned on loans
Credit union	• Short-term consumer loans • Longer-term mortgage loans	• Share draft accounts • Savings accounts • Money market deposit accounts	• Deposits by members • Interest earned on loans
		Nondeposit Institutions	
Insurance company	• Corporate long-term loans • Commercial mortgages • Government bonds		• Premiums paid by policyholders • Earnings on investments
Pension fund	• Some commercial mortgages • Government bonds • Corporate securities		• Contributions by member employees and employers • Earnings on investments
Commercial and consumer finance company	• Short-term loans to businesses • Individual consumer loans		• Interest earned on loans • Sales of bonds • Short-term borrowings

EXHIBIT 18.9

Financial Institutions and Their Traditional Services

Listed here are the traditional services, sources, and uses of funds for financial institutions.

Loans Today, a California fruit grower can borrow from a Japanese bank to finance exports to France, while a Pennsylvania manufacturer can issue securities through a Swiss investment banker to finance a plant in Singapore. To remain competitive, major U.S. banks (such as BankAmerica, Bank One, and Wells Fargo) and nonbank financial-services companies (such as American Express and Merrill Lynch) are racing to set up or expand coast-to-coast lending operations by using direct mail, telemarketing, or nationwide sales forces to flush out customers.

Automated teller machines (ATMs) allow customers to perform certain bank transactions 24 hours a day in places other than a branch. This ATM, installed in the food court of a shopping mall, offers customers the convenience of banking where they shop.

Regardless, many U.S. businesses are turning to foreign banks as attractive sources of loans and expertise. Bank of Tokyo, for example, lends money to multinational corporations based in the United States, and it offers specialized services to help customers trade with Pacific Rim companies.[32] In fact, six of the ten largest banks in the world are Japanese-owned banks, including the world's largest bank (see Exhibit 18.10).[33]

This trend toward such worldwide linkages will continue at a fast pace as business loans are increasingly made by telephone, as approved credit lines are increasingly marketed by direct mail, and as loan applications are increasingly submitted on the Internet. In fact, many loan approvals today are not made at a banker's desk, but in sprawling computerized processing centers, lowering the cost of making loans from thousands to hundreds of dollars. The Internet costs little enough to put virtually all lenders (regardless of size or resources) on a relatively equal playing field, leading to more competition and narrower profit margins. Furthermore, the Internet offers special advantages in dealing with both loan customers and employees of the loan department. Loan officers, credit analysts, and even loan committees can readily communicate over great distances, bringing together a range of specialists' opinions to make the best decision.[34]

Bank	Country	Rank by Assets	1996 Assets (in millions)
Bank of Tokyo-Mitsubishi	Japan	1	$752,318
Deutsche Bank	Germany	2	575,693
Sumitomo Bank	Japan	3	513,718
Dai-Ichi Kangyo Bank	Japan	4	476,696
Fuji Bank	Japan	5	474,371
Sanwa Bank	Japan	6	470,336
ABN Amro Holdings	Netherlands	7	440,410
Sakura Bank	Japan	8	436,687
Industrial and Commercial Bank	China	9	435,723
HSBC Holdings	UK	10	405,031

EXHIBIT 18.10

The World's Largest Banks

Six of the ten largest banks in the world are from Japan.

Tomorrow's Bank

What is the role of traditional banks in this brave new electronic market? If a bank were built today, it might have no branches, no ATMs, and no employees. It wouldn't handle checks or dispense cash. It would be a software factory that lends money, processes transactions, and moves blips. It might be Microsoft Bank and Trust. Consider this: In October 1995, Security First National Bank (SFNB) became the world's first Internet-only bank and inaugurated a new era in banking—one without tellers, business hours, monthly statements, or a physical address. Today, with a staff of a dozen, SFNB serves customers in 50 states who have deposited money in their Internet accounts. Besides being an Internet bank, SFNB plans to expand into investment, insurance, and other corporate services.[35] But not all industry experts believe the Internet will replace traditional bank services. Although many banks are relying more heavily on the Internet as a means to provide customers with information, the actual delivery of services still takes place at banks themselves or over the telephone. Many banks see the Internet as an alternative delivery channel, but not as a replacement for their traditional outlets or customer communication systems.[36]

BANK SAFETY AND REGULATION

Everyone (including members of Congress and members of the financial community) worries about bank failure. As many as 9,000 U.S. banks failed during the Depression years from 1929 to 1934. Then from 1980 through 1990, 1,228 banks failed, and much of the thrift industry had to be salvaged by the largest taxpayer-financed bailout in history.[37]

In response to concerns about bank safety during the Depression years, the government established the Federal Deposit Insurance Corporation (FDIC) to protect money in customer accounts. Today FDIC insurance covers customers' funds on deposit with a particular bank to a maximum of $100,000. The FDIC collects insurance premiums from banks and sends the money to the Treasury, where it is put in the general fund to finance everything from defense needs to highway construction. When a bank fails, the Treasury borrows money in the financial markets on behalf of the FDIC, which keeps track of how much money it has collected and how much it has spent. Thus, the FDIC fund is really nothing more than a balance sheet.[38]

Keeping the FDIC funded is a prime concern, but paying for failures can be costly. Insurance premiums paid by banks skyrocketed 277 percent between 1989 and 1991 alone, and bankers warn that further increases might cause more bank failures.[39] Currently, healthy banks pay lower premiums than troubled banks, which gives problem banks a financial reason for improving their health. However, some are concerned that banks are overregulated and that even though the laws protect the safety of the institutions (thus protecting depositors), excessive regulation has hurt the efficiency of our capital markets—causing economic damage. They claim that the chief victims of this regulation are small businesses who must meet high standards for asset quality, loan documentation, and minimum earnings in order to qualify for loans. Whereas large companies can raise money by issuing bonds or commercial paper, small companies like Remlik depend on banks to provide the financing that allows them to grow and prosper.

U.S. authorities will have to balance bank regulations and safety with the need to remain economically competitive in international money markets. This will become even more important as the Internet, global communication, and intense competition continue to open up new resources for financing the enterprise.

Summary of Learning Objectives

1. **Identify the responsibilities of a financial manager.**
The responsibilities of a financial manager include forecasting and planning for the future, developing a financial plan, managing the company's cash flow, coordinating and controlling the efficiency of operations, deciding on specific investments and how to finance them, raising capital to support growth, and interacting with banks and capital markets.
2. **Name the five main steps involved in the financial planning process.**
When developing a financial plan, the financial manager estimates the flow of money into and out of the business; determines whether cash flow is negative or positive and how to use or create excess funds; chooses which capital investments should be made; selects the best way to finance these investments; and compares actual results to projections to discover variances and take corrective action.
3. **Cite three things financial managers must consider when selecting an appropriate funding vehicle.**
Finance managers must determine whether the financing is for the short term or the long term. They must analyze the advantages and disadvantages of internal versus external financing, and they must evaluate the merits of debt versus equity financing in light of their own needs.
4. **List the three major types of short-term debt and the three major types of long-term debt.**
The three major types of short-term debt are trade credit, loans, and commercial paper. The three major types of long-term debt are loans, leases, and bonds.
5. **Identify the main advantages and disadvantages of public equity financing.**
The main advantages are the increased financing, improved liquidity, voluntary dividend payments, and enhanced visibility; it also establishes a market value for the company. The main disadvantages are high costs, loss of ownership control, increased filing requirements, and increased public visibility.
6. **Name the three functions and four characteristics of money.**
Money functions as a medium of exchange, a measure of value, and a store of value. It must be divisible, portable, durable, and secure (or difficult to counterfeit).
7. **Cite the four ways the Federal Reserve System influences the money supply.**
The Fed regulates the money supply by changing reserve requirements, changing the discount rate, carrying out open-market operations, and setting selective credit controls.
8. **Explain how the Internet is influencing the U.S. banking and monetary systems.**
The Internet is a new channel of distribution that allows customers to shop for banking services anywhere in the world. It has made the banking environment highly competitive, redefined the types of services banks offer, and made it more difficult for governments to regulate and control their money supply.

On the Job: Meeting Business Challenges at Remlik

As sales of Nature's Pasta increased and Jim Kilmer stood on the brink of success, he learned the hard way that a new business needs money to grow—lots of money. From product research to storage space to transportation, everything costs more than the entrepreneur is prepared to spend. Nature's Pasta was being sold in 21 stores, including some Giant Eagle supermarkets, so Kilmer knew that his product was viable. Now the challenge was to obtain financing without going too far into debt or giving away too much control.

One of Kilmer's first steps was finding money for research to extend the shelf life of spaghetti squash. He solved this problem by applying for a research grant from the Ben Franklin Technology Center. Within a few months, the grant was approved—but for $50,000, not the $84,000 he had requested. Using the grant money, scientists at the Pennsylvania State University Food Science Department started work on the problem.

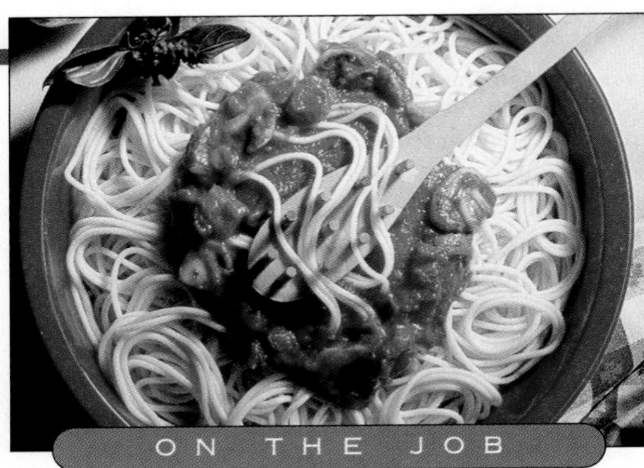

Next he had to find a way to fix his cash flow. Although he enjoyed a good profit margin, he found that collecting on his accounts receivable was a slow process. What's more, he had underestimated the storage and labor costs, so the money he did collect went right back out to pay urgent bills.

Fortunately, Kilmer had kept his bankers informed of his progress. "I had forwarded newspaper articles about me, called them often to tell them where I stood, and told them that by November I *might* need a loan," he says. Because the bankers were aware of his needs ahead of time and understood his plans, they were better able to evaluate his financial situation. The bank soon approved a $20,000 *demand loan,* which meant that Kilmer would pay interest but not have to repay the principal right away. Another advantage was that the loan did not have to be secured by his home or any of his other assets, so the bank wouldn't be able to take those assets from Kilmer if he didn't repay the loan.

Kilmer then began to search for investors who would put up $500,000 so that he could move his growing operation into a suitable plant. He found that few venture capital groups would invest in start-ups. So for help arranging additional financing and locating a plant site, he turned to the Fay-Penn Economic Development Corporation, a nonprofit organization. In the meantime, the cash crunch had become so severe that he had to temporarily shut down Remlik, even though the Penn State scientists had just succeeded in extending the shelf life of Nature's Pasta to 21 days.

Through Fay-Penn, Kilmer met several potential investors, and within a few months, he had negotiated a $500,000 deal that gave him the cash he needed. His investors gained partial ownership and seats on his board of directors, but Kilmer retained majority control of the company and the board.

With cash in hand, Kilmer started to pay himself a small salary. He also hired an office assistant to handle all of the administrative duties. Fay-Penn had found a suitable plant near Uniontown, but Kilmer needed more than $1 million to buy the plant and the production equipment. He applied for and received several low-interest loans from state agencies and other sources and then geared up for expansion throughout Pittsburgh—and beyond.

Your Mission: Jim Kilmer has hired you as chief financial officer of Remlik. You are responsible for financial planning and reporting for the company, and Kilmer relies on you for sound advice. Consider the following problems and select the best solution to each.

1. Sales have been strong and you have reported positive cash flow for six consecutive months. As you prepare to expand into two new markets, Kilmer asks your advice on what to do with the money. What is your best response?
   a. Tell him to immediately buy back some of the equity he sold when he started Remlik. This action will allow Kilmer to keep more of the money the company earns, rather than paying dividends to investors.
   b. Tell him to give himself and all of his key workers a raise, because they all have been drawing low salaries for many months.
   c. Tell him to invest in promotional activities that will build demand for Nature's Pasta in Pittsburgh and in the two new markets you will enter.
2. After expanding into two new markets, you need more cash to finance higher inventory levels because of the fast-growing demand. Which of the following ways of arranging short-term financing best suits your situation?
   a. Talk your supplier into letting you pay in 90 days instead of paying in 30 days so that you can buy more without having to pay for it right away. This way, by the time the bills come due, you will have collected your own accounts receivable.
   b. Talk your supplier into letting you sign a promissory note instead of paying cash for the next shipment. To persuade the supplier to agree, offer to pay a higher interest rate than you would pay to your bank.
   c. Talk a finance company into buying your accounts receivable at a discount. This strategy will relieve you of the problem of collecting when bills come due, and you will get cash that you can use to buy more squash when needed.
3. When Kilmer applies for a loan with the bank, which of the following would be the most important financial information for you to supply?
   a. How much of Remlik's revenue is devoted to repaying loans and how much is devoted to current operations
   b. Whether Remlik's cash flow is positive or negative, and what the company intends to do if cash flow is negative
   c. Both (a) and (b)
4. The bank where Remlik has its accounts and transacts most of its business was recently acquired by a larger, national bank. You have just received a note from the national bank's vice president stating that effective next month, all accounts will be charged check-handling fees plus teller-transaction fees. According to your calculations, this could cost Remlik over $500 per month. What should you do?
   a. Change banks. Investigate and find a bank that does not assess checking and transaction fees, especially because Remlik's business would be an attractive account at most smaller banks.
   b. Arrange a meeting with the new bank vice president and negotiate a deal where Remlik will keep a compensating minimum balance in a non-interest-bearing account at all times to cover the bank's costs for processing Remlik's checks and teller visits.
   c. Consider implementing an online banking system for Remlik even though it would require you to retrain your accounting manager and update all your financial systems.[40]

Key Terms

automated teller machines (ATMs) (563)
bonds (551)
capital budgeting (543)
capital investments (543)
capital structure (548)
checks (556)
collateral (549)
commercial paper (549)
compensating balance (549)
cost of capital (544)
credit cards (554)
currency (556)
debit cards (554)
demand deposit (556)
discount rate (545)
electronic funds transfer system (EFTS) (563)
euro (555)
Eurodollars (558)
financial control (543)
financial management (542)
financial plan (542)
lease (549)
leverage (547)
leveraged buyout (LBO) (551)
line of credit (549)
long-term debt (545)
M1 (557)
M2 (557)
M3 (558)
marketable securities (547)
money (553)
open-market operations (559)
prime interest rate (prime) (544)
reserve requirement (558)
secured loans (549)
selective credit controls (559)
short-term debt (545)
smart cards (554)
stock certificate (548)
time deposits (556)
trade credit (549)
unsecured loan (549)
venture capitalists (552)

Questions

For Review

1. What is the primary goal of financial management?
2. What types of projects are typically considered in the capital-budgeting process?
3. What are some of the advantages and disadvantages of private equity financing?
4. How do debit cards and smart cards work?
5. What is the main function of the Federal Reserve System?

For Analysis

6. How does the matching principle apply to financial management?
7. Why might the management or outside investors of a publicly traded company want to take the company private in a leveraged buyout?
8. How does the money supply affect the economy and inflation?
9. How has banking deregulation changed competition among financial institutions?
10. How can smaller community banks compete with large commercial banks?

For Application

11. The financial manager for a small manufacturing firm wants to improve the company's cash flow position. What steps can he or she take?
12. How might you prepare your company in advance for going public?

A Case for Critical Thinking ■ A Seller of Best-Sellers Goes Public

How does a nationwide bookseller finance a shift from small mall bookstores to huge discount stores? That was the challenge facing Leonard Riggio, chairman and CEO of Barnes & Noble. Riggio's New York–based company owned the B. Dalton, Doubleday, Scribner's, and Barnes & Noble book chains, which together sold more than $1 billion worth of books in a year. Already the company operated some 900 stores in shopping centers and downtown locations across 48 states.

Riggio saw that more and more of the book battles were being fought in "superstores," gigantic stores with up to 175,000 titles on the shelf (compared with 15,000 to 25,000 in the typical mall store). Where the mall stores had only about 3,000 square feet in which to sell books, superstores could sell books in spacious, attractive surroundings that ranged from roughly 10,000 to 40,000 square feet. Superstores had the space for a coffee bar or a children's corner (or both), which encouraged customers to stay for an hour or two. Also, once a superstore was open for a few years, it was more economical to operate than a mall store.

Superstores were the future, and Barnes & Noble was already operating more than 100 superstores, but its competitors weren't standing still. The Crown chain had more than 60 superstores, and the Borders chain had more than 44 superstores—and these rivals were expanding into more superstores. At the same time, independent booksellers were fighting back by offering specialized books and individualized customer service. In short, competition was becoming more intense.

To compete more effectively, Riggio planned to shut down some less productive mall bookstores and push ahead with a string of new superstores. Although Barnes & Noble's cash flow was strong, financing this rapid expansion required more long-term debt, which raised the amount of money spent on interest. Plowing so much money into expansion didn't help the company's profit picture: It posted a loss two years in a row. Despite the lack of profits, the CEO saw a brighter future ahead, and he was determined to stay on the road to fast expansion.

As he searched for another source of financing, Riggio tried an initial public offering of common stock in 1992. This offering was postponed because the market for new stocks wasn't favorable. By 1993, however, the market was more interested in new stocks, so the company went ahead and offered shares at $20 each, to be traded on the New York Stock Exchange. This initial public offering sold more than 9 million shares of common stock and raised more than $160 million. It also lowered the ratio of long-term debt to stockholders' equity, which improved the company's financial health.

As Riggio had forecast, superstores soon began bringing in an ever-larger share of Barnes & Noble's revenues, and they now account for a large percentage of the company's sales. Going public helped Riggio expand superstore operations, but it had another important consequence as well: It added shareholders to the list of company stakeholders. Although Riggio is the largest individual investor in Barnes & Noble, he still has to be sure that any actions he takes are in the best interests of his fellow shareholders. One measure of shareholder response to company actions is in the stock price, and Riggio is bound to watch this indicator as closely as his competitors follow the pace of his superstore expansion.

1. Why would Riggio choose to issue common stock rather than finance with long-term debt?
2. Each superstore has as many as 175,000 books in inventory. How does inventory affect cash flow?
3. Barnes & Noble also operates a virtual bookstore on the Internet. What are the cash flow benefits of operating a virtual bookstore?
4. Go to Hoovers online at <http://www.hoovers.com> and research the company's stock performance. Type in *Barnes & Noble, Inc.* and read about the company. Check out the latest earnings estimates and view the *Stock Master Chart.* How well has this company's common stock performed since the company went public?

Building Your Business Skills

When a new business is formed, its owners usually try to defray their initial expenses by obtaining a business loan. Call or write to a loan officer in a nearby financial institution or in a local Small Business Administration office to find out how a company qualifies for a small-business loan. Ask about the following:

- The materials that must be presented to show the company's credit worthiness
- How the loan approval process works
- What information is requested on the loan application
- The terms and conditions of such loans

As directed by your instructor, prepare a brief summary of the information you have obtained regarding the small-business loan policies of that financial institution. Compare your findings with the information obtained by other students. Are the terms and conditions of the various institutions similar? Are the loan approval processes similar? What do these differences mean for small businesses seeking loans from these institutions?

Keeping Current Using *The Wall Street Journal*

Choose a recent article from *The Wall Street Journal* that deals with the financing arrangements or strategies of a particular company.

1. What form of financing did the company choose? Did the article indicate why the company selected this form of financing?
2. Who provided the financing for the company? Was this arrangement considered unusual, or was it routine?

3. What does the company intend to do with the arranged financing—purchase equipment or other assets, finance a construction project, finance growth and expansion, or do something else?
4. Browse the Commercial Finance Online Web site at <http://www.cfol.com>. How does this Web site assist companies in finding financing?

Exploring the Best of the Web

Plan Ahead, page 550

Use the tools at Financenter at <http://www.financenter.com> to do some personal financial planning. Browse this Web site. It's full of information and handy calculators.

1. Click on *Credit Cards.* Calculate how much you will need to increase your monthly payments to in order to pay off your outstanding balance in 12 months. If your balance is $0, use these numbers: amount now owed $3,000; future monthly charges $300; future monthly payments $400; annual rate 18%; annual fee $50; desired months until payoff 12.
2. Go back home and click on *Credit Lines.* Calculate how large a line of credit you can obtain if the appraised value of your home is $200,000 with a $125,000 mortgage.
3. Go back home and click on *Autos.* Calculate whether you should finance or pay cash for your next car.

Tour the U.S. Treasury, page 554

Visit the U.S. Treasury Department Web site at <http://www.ustreas.gov>.

1. Go to the *Learning Vault* and click on *Savings Bonds.* What are U.S. savings bonds and where can you buy them? Go back to the *Learning Vault* and click on *Paper Currency.* Roughly how much currency is printed daily? How many $20 bills were printed last year?
2. Go back to the home page. Click on *Site Map.* Go to *Financial Management* and click on *Electronic Funds Transfer.* Get some information by clicking on *Commonly Asked Questions* and *Background.* What are some of the benefits of electronic funds transfer?
3. Go back to the *Site Map.* Click on *Treasury Bureaus* and visit the *Bureau of Engraving and Printing (BEP).* Click on *Facts and Trivia* and get some *Production Figures.* Scroll down and find out *how money gets into circulation.* What is the life expectancy of a $1 bill?

Take a Field Trip to the Fed, page 560

Visit the Fed at <http://www.bog.frb.fed.us/> and explore the U.S. Federal Reserve System.

1. Who is the current chairperson of the Federal Reserve System? How is he or she appointed?
2. Where are the Federal Reserve Banks located?
3. Click on the link to the *FDIC.* What does it mean when a bank has a sign that says "Insured by FDIC"?

Answers to "Is It True?"

Page 554. False. Actually about 28 percent of credit-card-holding families seldom pay off their credit-card balance. About 52 percent almost always pay off their balance, whereas the remaining 20 percent sometimes pay off their balance.

Page 557. True.

Page 560. True.

CHAPTER 19

SECURITIES MARKETS

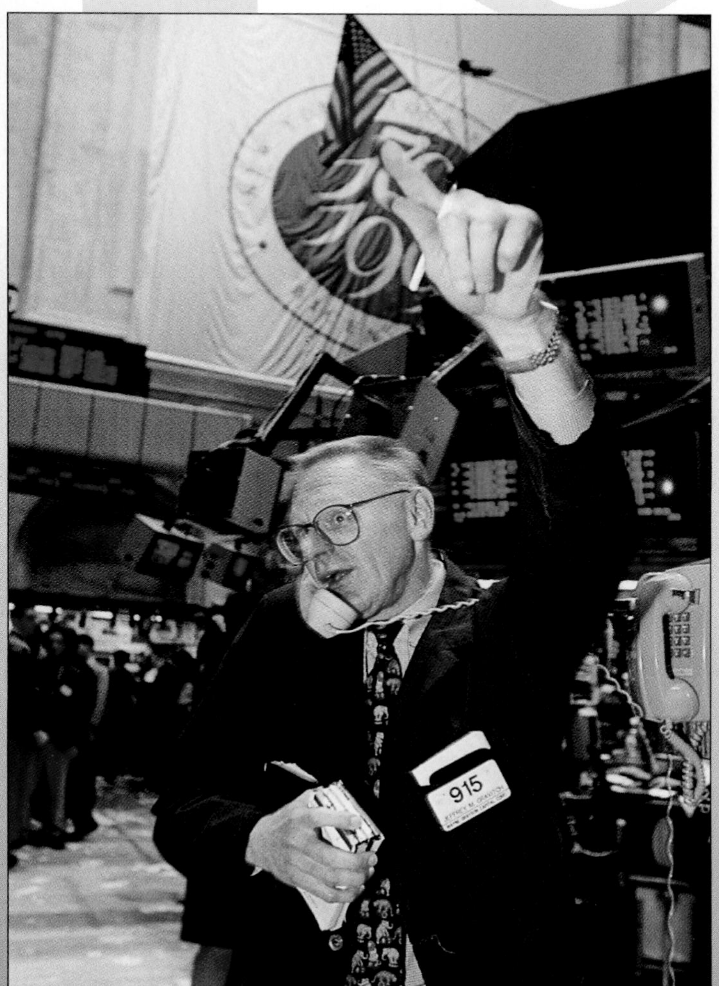

OBJECTIVES

After studying this chapter, you will be able to

1 Explain the differences between common stock, preferred stock, and bonds from an investor's perspective

2 Explain the safety and tax advantages of investing in U.S. government securities

3 Name five criteria to be considered when making investment decisions

4 Explain what mutual funds are and describe their main benefits

5 Describe the two types of security marketplaces and the challenges they are facing

6 Explain how the Internet is redefining the investment industry

7 Identify the two major broad market indexes and explain their differences

8 Explain how government regulation of securities trading tries to protect investors

On the Job On the Job

ON THE JOB: FACING BUSINESS CHALLENGES AT LANDES ASSOCIATES

Searching for Growth Beneath a Mountain of Debt

It was a heavy responsibility: managing millions of dollars invested by clients so that their wealth would continue to grow. Moreover, clients expected their wealth to grow regardless of prevailing economic or stock market conditions. As a vice president at Landes Associates (a Delaware-based investment management firm), William A. Francis could choose among a wide array of investments, including commodities futures, common and preferred stock, corporate and government bonds, and mutual funds. The challenge was knowing when to buy which products, how long to hold them, and when to sell them.

His challenge was made more difficult by the investment needs of his clients. Primarily wealthy individuals, these investors didn't need extra income. They wanted their investments to grow steadily and without a high degree of risk. Francis decided to avoid commodities, the riskiest of available investments. He also decided against preferred stock, corporate bonds, and government bonds, because such investments are usually designed to produce reliable income (something his clients didn't need). Finally, he ruled out mutual funds, because such funds are intended for small investors who lack the financial means to create their own portfolios. His analysis showed that the best investment for his clients would be common stocks.

To pick the right companies to invest his clients' money in, Francis had to know three things: (1) the major forces at work in the economy that could affect a particular industry or company, (2) the general investment climate of the securities markets, and (3) the performance of particular companies. Francis knew that purchasing stock isn't like buying products in a store, where prices are clearly marked and where value is relatively easy to recognize. Investors buy expectations. They are always asking: "What's going to attract other investors to this stock? Why should somebody else be willing to pay a higher price for this stock than I'm paying now?" The answer to both questions is the company's expected growth.

However, the recessionary economy of the early 1990s had slowed many a company's growth, which presented Francis with a tremendous challenge. He had to find the few companies worth investing in. Then he had to decide the best time to invest in them: immediately, after the economy improved, or once the stock market was on the way up. Finally, he had to determine the best time to sell stocks—both those his clients were currently invested in and those he would recommend. Where would Francis find the information he needed to make these decisions? How could he determine which companies his clients could invest in to make their wealth grow without undue risk? How would he know when to sell a client's stock?[1]

INVESTMENT CHOICES

As William Francis knows well, various investment instruments serve different purposes. Corporations issue stocks and bonds to finance business operations. Governments and municipalities issue bonds to raise money for federal, state, and local governments, and to fund public expenses—from national defense to road improvements. Investors purchase *securities*—stocks, bonds, options, futures, and commodities—to make money or to protect their investments. All these securities are traded in organized markets, and they are cyclical in their performance; that is, sometimes they rise in value, and sometimes they fall.

Stocks

Unlike debt, which must be repaid at a future date, stock or equity represents a "piece of the action." When a company raises capital by selling stock, it expands the ownership of the business. Shareholders receive a stock certificate as evidence of ownership. Each certificate shows the name of the shareholder, the number of shares of stock owned, and the special characteristics of the stock. Many stock certificates also bear a **par value**, a dollar value assigned to the stock used chiefly for bookkeeping purposes and sometimes used (for certain kinds of stock) to calculate dividends. This value should not be confused with a stock's *market value*, the price at which a stock currently sells, or its *book value*, the amount of net assets of a corporation represented by one share of common stock.

par value
Arbitrary value assigned to a stock that is shown on the stock certificate

The number of stock shares a company sells depends on the amount of equity capital the company will require and on the price of each share it sells. A corporation's board of directors sets a maximum number of shares into which the business can be divided. In theory, all these shares—called **authorized stock**—may be sold at once. What often happens, however, is that the company sells only part of its authorized stock. The part sold and held by shareholders is called **issued stock**; unsold stock is called **unissued stock**. A company may issue two classes of stock: preferred and common.

authorized stock
Shares that a corporation's board of directors has decided to sell eventually

issued stock
Authorized shares that have been released to the market

unissued stock
Authorized shares that are to be released in the future

preferred stock
Shares that give their owners first claim on a company's dividends and assets after paying all debts

Preferred Stock In spite of its name, preferred stock is far less popular as a funding vehicle than common stock. Holders of **preferred stock** get a preference in the payment of dividends and a priority claim (after creditors) on assets if the company goes out of business. However, in exchange for these benefits, they do not get voting privileges and they do not share directly in the success (or failure) of the business. For these reasons, dividends paid on preferred stock tend to be higher than those paid on common stock.

The amount of the dividend on preferred stock is shown on the stock certificate. It may be expressed either as a percentage of the par value or as a dollar amount. The dividend is set when the stock is issued; it is closely tied to market interest rates and will not change in the future. Therefore, if interest rates fluctuate, the market price of the preferred stock will go up or down to adjust for the difference between the market interest rate and the stock's dividend rate. Preferred stock is mostly owned by corporations because they receive a 70 percent tax break on stock dividends but do not receive the same break on bond interest income. So if the investing corporation receives $100,000 in dividend income in a year, it pays taxes on only $30,000 of that income.

Firms often issue preferred stock with special privileges. *Convertible preferred stock* can be exchanged at the shareholder's discretion for a certain number of shares of common stock issued by the company. Cumulative preferred stock has an additional advantage: If the issuing company suspends dividends because it is saving for equipment purchases or perhaps because cash flow is tight, the dividends on these shares will accumulate until shareholders have been paid in full.

Common Stock Most stock issued by corporations is **common stock,** securities that represent an ownership interest in a corporation. As part owners, shareholders get to elect the company's board of directors as well as vote on any major policies that will affect ownership—such as mergers, acquisitions, and takeovers. Another main advantage of common stock—in addition to receiving dividends—is that the profit that shareholders can enjoy isn't limited like it is for preferred stock. The value of the company's common stock goes up and down (depending on the company's success or failure). So if shareholders sell their stock in good times for more than they paid for it, they stand to pocket a handsome gain.

common stock
Shares whose owners have voting rights and have the last claim on distributed profits and assets

A special type of common stock is *targeted stock,* which refers to shares linked to the performance of one business unit of a public corporation. Targeted stock is riskier because if the unit is profitable, the corporation may pay a special dividend to its holders—but it can also choose not to pay a dividend if the money is needed for other corporate obligations. In other words, the corporation has the right to do what it wishes with the unit's assets, so holders of targeted stock may not benefit from the unit's success. From the corporation's perspective, targeted stock is a good way of showing market watchers and investors what a particular unit can do on its own—as if it were an independent company. The first targeted stock was issued by General Motors in 1984; the handful that have been issued since have had mixed performance.[2]

COMMON-STOCK DIVIDENDS After a company has paid all expenses and taxes out of revenues, its board of directors can pay a portion of what remains to investors in the form of dividends. There is no law that requires them to do so. The decision is up to the board of directors, who may decide—for good reasons—to omit the dividend or keep it to a minimum. In the case of a small, young company, for instance, the best course is usually to put all the profits back into the business. This practice enables the company to grow without using expensive outside financing. In the long run, the shareholders benefit more from the growth of the company and the resulting increase in the value of their stock than they do solely from the dividend.

On the other hand, large, well-established companies sometimes cut or omit dividends if profits decline. Dividends theoretically represent a share of the profits; when profits fall, there is less to share. The company hangs on to its cash in order to cover operating expenses. Unfortunately, shareholders not only lose out on their dividends in such situations but frequently lose out on the value of the stock as well—because when a big company cuts its dividend, it sends a message to investors that there may be financial problems, which causes the stock to fall, at least temporarily.

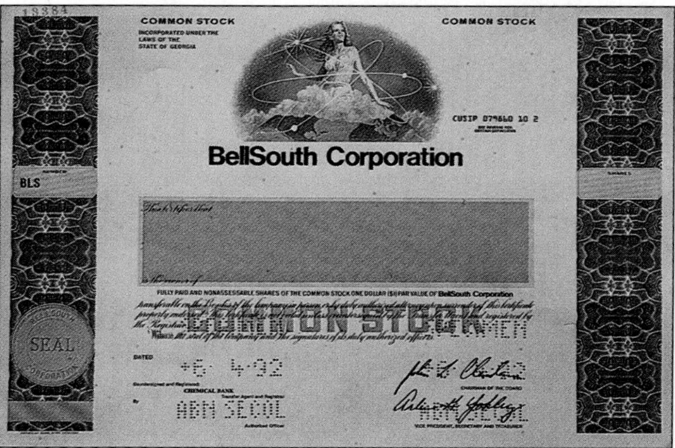

Stock certificates represent a share of ownership of a company.

Dividends may be paid in cash, but rapidly growing companies often issue dividends in the form of additional company stock. By doing so, they conserve the firm's cash for capital investment, research and development, and similar types of expenditures. In addition to paying a dividend, another option for increasing shareholder value is to repurchase outstanding common stock. This option reduces the amount of issued stock and increases the value of each share because fewer shares now have a piece of the same company value.

stock split
Increase in the number of shares of ownership that each stock certificate represents

STOCK SPLITS A dividend is not the only benefit a company can offer its common shareholders. Another alternative is a **stock split,** a procedure whereby the company doubles (or triples, or whatever) the number of shares that each stock certificate represents. Companies generally use a stock split to reduce the price per share of a high-priced stock, making it more affordable to investors. Keep in mind, however, that although a stock split may double a company's issued shares, the market value of each share is cut in half because the total value of the company does not change. In a two-for-one stock split, for example, a company with 1 million issued shares selling for $50 per share would double the number of shares outstanding to 2 million, giving each shareholder two shares instead of one. Initially, these 2 million shares would each be worth only $25 (representing the same total market value of $50 million).

Corporate Bonds

When you look in the business section of your daily newspaper, you'll see that the stock market gets most of the attention. The bond market, which is actually several times larger, operates with less fanfare, even though nearly as many individual investors own bonds as own common stock.[3] For years bonds quietly earned interest for investors, but that changed during the 1980s when the junk bond market ballooned and then burst. Corporations all across the United States found themselves in default on their bond issues.

denomination
Face value of a single bond

principal
Amount of a debt, excluding any interest

secured bonds
Bonds backed by specific assets

mortgage bonds
Corporate bonds backed by real property

debentures
Corporate bonds backed only by the reputation of the issuer

convertible bonds
Corporate bonds that can be exchanged at the owner's discretion into common stock of the issuing company

Bond Attributes All bonds have a **denomination,** the amount of the loan represented by one bond. Bonds sold by corporations are usually available in $1,000 denominations, but they also come in denominations of $5,000, $10,000, $50,000, and $100,000. A bond usually shows the date when the full amount of the bond, or the **principal,** must be repaid. Bonds typically have maturity dates of 10 years or more.

Like loans, corporate bonds may be either secured or unsecured. **Secured bonds** are backed by specific company-owned property (such as airplanes or plant equipment) that will pass to the bondholders if the issuer does not live up to the terms of the agreement. **Mortgage bonds** are one type of secured bonds. They are backed by real property that's owned by the issuing corporation. **Debentures** are unsecured bonds, backed only by the corporation's promise to pay. Because debentures are riskier than other types of bonds, they pay higher interest to the investor. Only firms with extremely sound financial reputations can find buyers for their debentures. **Convertible bonds** can be exchanged, at the investor's option, for a certain number of shares of the corporation's common stock. Because of this feature, convertible bonds generally carry lower interest rates. Two factors determine the price of a bond: its interest rate and its degree of risk.

BOND INTEREST RATES A bond provides interest, stated in terms of an annual percentage rate but usually paid at 6-month intervals. For example, the holder of a $1,000 bond that pays 8 percent interest due January 15 and July 15 could expect to receive $40 on each of those dates. A look at the financial section of any newspaper will show that some corporations sell new bonds at an interest rate two or three percentage points higher than that offered by other companies. Yet the terms of the bonds seem similar. These variations in interest rates reflect the degree of risk associated with the bond.

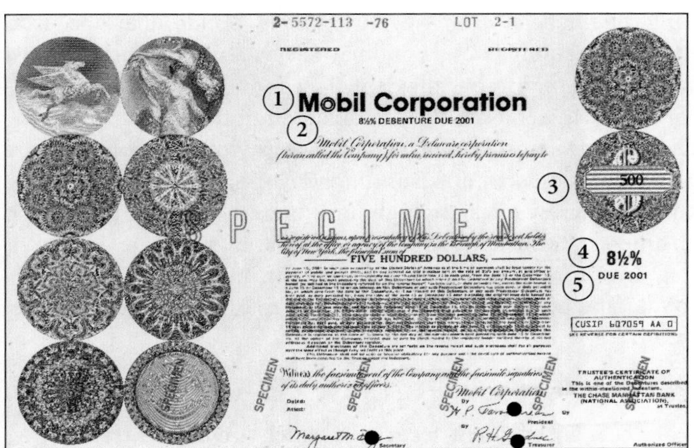

Mobil Corporation Bond Certificate

1. Name of corporation issuing the bond
2. Type of bond (debenture)
3. Face value of the bond
4. Annual interest rate (8.5%)
5. Maturity date (due 2001)

Degree of Risk Some bonds are riskier than others. For example, corporations with excellent prospects of earning enough money in future years to pay both the interest and the principal at maturity have a lower degree of risk to the investor than a new corporation with no prior earnings history. Bond-rating agencies such as Standard & Poor's (S&P) or Moody's rate bonds on the basis of the financial stability of issuing companies. Bonds that are rated investment grade are considered the safest bonds for investors. Bonds rated below investment grade are popularly known as **junk bonds.** To compensate for their risk, junk bonds must pay higher-than-market interest rates to attract investors. Exhibit 19.1 shows that the least risky corporate bonds are rated AAA (S&P) and Aaa (Moody's). Because many institutional investors are restricted to investment-grade securities, a rating below BBB (S&P) means that a company will have a harder time trying to sell its bonds.

Is It True?

Coupon bonds are bonds sold at a discount.

junk bonds
Bonds that pay high interest because they are below investment grade

Retirement of Debt A company that sells bonds must repay its debt to the bondholders. Normally, this is done when the bonds mature—say, 10, 15, or 20 years after the bond is issued. The cost of retiring the debt can be staggering because bonds are generally issued in quantity—perhaps thousands of individual bonds in a single issue. To ease the cash flow burden of redeeming its bonds all at once, a company sometimes issues *serial bonds,* which mature at various times, as opposed to *term bonds,* which mature all at the same time.

S&P	INTERPRETATION	MOODY'S	INTERPRETATION
AAA	Highest rating	Aaa	Prime quality
AA	Very strong capacity to pay	Aa	High grade
A	Strong capacity to pay; somewhat susceptible to changing business conditions	A	Upper-medium grade
BBB	More susceptible than A rated bonds	Baa	Medium grade
BB	Somewhat speculative	Ba	Somewhat speculative
B	Speculative	B	Speculative
CCC	Vulnerable to nonpayment	Caa	Poor standing; may be in default
CC	Highly vulnerable to nonpayment	Ca	Highly spectulative; often in default
C	Bankruptcy petition filed or similar action taken	C	Lowest rated; extremely poor chance of ever attaining real investment standing
D	In default		

EXHIBIT 19.1

Corporate Bond Ratings

Standard & Poor's Corporation and Moody's Investors Service are the two primary companies that rate the safety of corporate bonds. As ratings decline, investors take on more risk, so they are compensated with higher interest rates.

sinking fund
Account into which a company makes annual payments for use in redeeming its bonds in the future

Another way of relieving the financial strain of retiring many bonds all at once is to set up a **sinking fund.** When a corporation issues a bond payable by a sinking fund, it must set aside a certain sum of money each year to pay the debt. This money may be used to retire a few bonds each year, or it may be set aside to accumulate until the issue matures.

With most bond issues, a corporation retains the right to pay off the bonds before maturity. Bonds containing this provision are known as *callable bonds,* or *redeemable bonds.* If a company issues bonds when interest rates are high and interest rates fall later on, it may want to pay off its high-interest bonds and sell a new issue at a lower rate. However, this feature carries a price tag: Investors must be offered a higher interest rate to encourage them to buy callable bonds. The portion of the percentage rate that is above market rates is actually a "call premium."

Government Securities

The least risky investments are U.S. government securities, which are of two basic types: those backed by the U.S. Treasury and those backed by agencies of the government. State and local governments also raise money through bond issues. Although government securities pay less interest than corporate bonds, they do provide advantages in terms of safety and tax consequences.

Treasury bills
Short-term debt issued by the federal government; also referred to as *T-bills*

Treasury notes
Debt securities issued by the federal government that mature within 1 to 10 years

Treasury bonds
Debt securities issued by the federal government that mature in 10 to 30 years

Federal Government Issues The three principal types of U.S. government issues are **Treasury bills** for short-term debt, **Treasury notes** for debt obligations of 1 to 10 years, and **Treasury bonds** for long-term debt. All three are generally the most liquid investments available; you do not have to hold them until maturity because they are traded in an organized market.

Treasury bills (also referred to as T-bills) come in maturities of 13 weeks, 26 weeks, or 52 weeks. Unlike many other income-oriented investments, T-bills do not pay interest. Instead, they are sold at a discount from their face value and then redeemed at full face value when they mature. The difference between the purchase price and the redemption price is, in effect, interest. T-bills require a minimum investment of $10,000. Treasury notes and Treasury bonds, which have maturities of 1 to 30 years, are available for a minimum investment of $1,000. Twice a year they pay a fixed amount of interest, which is exempt from state and local income taxes.

U.S. savings bonds
Debt instruments sold by the federal government in small denominations

municipal bonds
Debt issued by a state or a local agency; interest earned on municipal bonds is exempt from federal income tax and from taxes in the issuing jurisdiction

U.S. savings bonds are nonmarketable debt instruments issued by the U.S. government, available in denominations ranging from $50 to $10,000. Series EE, 30-year savings bonds are issued by the Treasury at 50 percent of face value. You must hold a EE bond for at least six months. Interest rates on EE bonds vary and interest is credited at the first of every month. It is not paid or taxed federally, however, until you actually redeem the bond. Once the bond's face value equals its redemption value, the bond continues to earn interest, but only until the bond's final maturity date (30 years).[4]

general obligation bonds
Municipal bonds backed by the issuing agency's general taxing authority

revenue bonds
Municipal bonds backed by revenue generated from the projects financed with the bonds

capital gains
Difference between the price at which a financial asset is sold and its original cost (assuming the price has gone up)

Municipal Bonds **Municipal bonds** are issued by states, cities, and special government agencies to finance public services such as schools, transportation, and airports. They come in two forms, general obligation bonds and revenue bonds. Governments pay off their principal and interest obligations to the buyers of **general obligation bonds** through tax receipts. The principal and interest on **revenue bonds** are paid from the revenues raised by the issuer. For example, revenue bonds issued by a city airport are paid from revenues raised by the airport's operation.

To encourage investment, the federal government doesn't tax the interest that investors receive from municipal bonds. Also, many states do not tax the interest paid on bonds issued by governments within those states. However, **capital gains**—the return made by selling a security for a price that is higher than its purchase price—are taxed at both the federal and state levels.

Other Investments

Stocks and bonds are the most common marketable securities available for investors. However, other securities have been developed. For the most part, options, futures, derivatives, commodities, and their variations are used by money managers and savvy traders. In recent years, some of these securities, particularly options, have been used more by individual investors.

Options and Financial Futures A **stock option** is the purchased right—but not the obligation—to buy or sell a specified number of shares of a stock at a predetermined price during a specified period. Options can be used for wild speculation, or they can be used to **hedge** your positions—that is, partially protect against the risk of a sudden loss. By trading options, the investor doesn't have to own shares of stock in a company—only an option to buy or sell those shares. Investors who trade stock options are betting that the price of the stock will either rise or fall. The cost of buying an option on shares of stock is only the premium paid to the seller, or the price of the option.

stock option
Contract allowing the holder to buy or sell a given number of shares of a particular stock at a given price by a certain date

hedge
To make an investment that protects the investor from suffering loss on another investment

All options fall into two broad categories: *puts* and *calls.* Exhibit 19.2 explains the rights acquired with each type of option. **Financial futures** are similar to options, but they are legally binding contracts to buy or sell a financial instrument (stocks, Treasury bonds, foreign currencies) for a set price at a future date.

financial futures
Legally binding agreements to buy or sell financial instruments

Derivatives Stock options and financial futures contracts are *derivative investments.* That means their price at any given time is derived from or linked to the performance of an underlying asset (like a stock), the performance of a financial market, or current interest rates. Derivatives have become increasingly popular in recent years as corporations look for new and better ways to manage financial and operating risks.

Every business needs to expose itself to risks in order to seek profit. But companies are in business to take some risks and avoid others. Consider the case of an airline that has an opportunity to buy the rights to serve a new route from Chicago to London. The expected return on that investment might be about 25 percent, but the chance of an outright loss might be 35 percent. The airline is in the business of trying to profit from the new route, so it makes sense to expose itself to the risk of uncertain demand for seats on this route—even if the fear of losing money keeps its executives awake at night.

However, the airline's goal is not to try to profit from fluctuations in currency exchange rates, so the company would probably minimize its exposure to dollar/sterling rate

RIGHT	BUYER'S BELIEF	SELLER'S BELIEF
	CALL OPTION	
The right to buy the stock at a fixed price until the expiration date.	Buyer believes price of underlying stock will increase. Buyer can buy stock at a set price and sell it at higher price for a capital gain.	Seller believes price of underlying stock will decline and that the option will not be exercised. Seller earns a premium.
	PUT OPTION	
The right to sell the stock at a fixed price until the expiration date.	Buyer believes price of underlying stock will decline and wants to lock in a fixed profit. Buyer usually already owns shares of underlying stock.	Seller believes price of underlying stock will rise and that the option will not be exercised. Seller earns a premium.

EXHIBIT 19.2

Options

All options fall into two broad categories: puts and calls.

fluctuations. To compensate for this added risk, top management might be able to reshape the risk by selling an investor an option on the share of the profits from the new route. Why would the airline do this? Although the expected return on this investment might fall from 25 percent to 20 percent when the cost of the option is figured in, the additional income from the sale of the option might be enough to lower the potential loss from 35 to 10 percent—something the airline could live with.

By using derivatives properly, a company is not creating new exposures to outside risk but adjusting the exposures it already has. Nevertheless, some derivatives can be so complex and risky that even the people who design them are not completely sure of the risks involved for either the buyer or seller. That's why successful companies develop policies that define which kinds of derivatives are appropriate for the particular exposure they are protecting; moreover, they must clearly understand the risks associated with using derivatives.[5]

commodities
Raw materials used in producing other goods

Commodities For the investor who is comfortable with risky investments, nothing compares with speculating in **commodities**—raw materials and agricultural products, such as petroleum, gold, coffee beans, pork bellies, beef, and coconut oil. Commodities markets originally sprang up as a convenience for buyers and sellers interested in trading the actual commodities. A manufacturer of breakfast cereals, for example, must buy wheat, rye, oats, and sugar from hundreds of farmers. The easiest way to arrange these transactions is to meet in a forum where many buyers and sellers come to trade. Because the commodities are too bulky to bring to the marketplace, the traders buy and sell contracts for delivery of a given amount of these raw materials at a given time.

Trading contracts for immediate delivery of a commodity is called *spot trading,* or *cash trading.* Most commodity trading is for future delivery, usually months in advance, sometimes a year or more; this is called trading commodities futures. The original purpose of futures trading was to allow producers and consumers of commodities to hedge their position, or protect themselves against violent price swings. For example, farmers might sell futures contracts calling for delivery of some of the wheat they expect to have grown by harvest time to bakers who expect to use the flour milled from that wheat to bake bread. By selling before the crop is in, farmers get operating capital—as well as the assurance that they'll get a certain fixed price for their crops, even if prices collapse later. The bakers, on the other hand, can buy some of the supplies they expect to use and be assured that no matter how bad the crop is or how high the price goes, they'll have enough wheat to stay in business.

Today speculators play an important role in the commodities markets, doing most of the trading and increasing the liquidity of the market. Hoping to profit as prices rise

On an average day nearly 1 million futures and options are traded on the Chicago Mercantile Exchange (CME). Each trader at the CME acts as buyer and seller, communicating with hand signals and by shouting bids to buy and offers to sell.

and fall, they voluntarily assume the risk that the hedger tries to avoid. In reality, however, 75 percent of the people who speculate in commodities lose money in the long run.[6] Even seasoned veterans have been known to lose literally millions of dollars within a few days. Despite the risks, many investors see speculation in commodities as a way to reach higher returns.

INVESTORS AND INVESTING

Whether you are a corporation or an individual, investing means putting your money to work to earn more money. Done wisely, it can help you meet your financial goals. But investing means you have to make decisions about how much you want to invest and where to invest it. To choose wisely, you need to know what options you have and what risks they entail.

Institutional and Private Investors

Two types of investors buy and sell marketable securities (investments that can easily be converted to cash): institutions and individuals. **Institutional investors**—such as pension funds, insurance companies, investment companies, banks, and colleges and universities—dominate U.S. securities markets. Institutional investors buy and sell securities in large quantities, often in blocks of at least 10,000 shares per transaction. A study by the Securities Industry Association found that institutions and large securities firms constitute nearly 82 percent of all trading on the New York Stock Exchange, whereas individual investors account for only 18 percent.[7]

institutional investors
Companies that invest money entrusted to them by others

Institutions hire professional money managers to handle their accounts, and these managers increasingly use computers to make instantaneous trades based on hundreds of financial and economic factors. Quants, short for quantitative analysts, use statistics, mathematics, and advanced computer technology to analyze investments and estimate earnings. Because institutions have such large pools of money to work with, their investment decisions have a major impact on the marketability of a company's shares as well as the overall behavior of the securities markets.

Investment Objectives

Many investors seek the highest **yield** or return to supplement their income. Yield on a stock is calculated by dividing stock dividends by its market price. Some investors want to make a large profit in a short period of time. Others may be looking for a long-term steady return to fund retirement activities or provide money to send their children to college. In general, people make investment decisions on the basis of five criteria: *income, growth, safety, liquidity,* and *tax consequences.*

yield
Income received from securities, calculated by dividing dividend or interest income by market price

If an investor wants a steady, reasonably predictable flow of cash, he or she will seek an investment that provides fixed or dividend income. Fixed income investments include certificates of deposit, government securities, corporate bonds, and preferred stocks. A retired person wanting to supplement Social Security or pension benefits would be a customer for this type of investment.

Many investors are concerned with wealth accumulation, or growth. Their objective is to maximize capital gains. **Growth stocks** are issued by younger and smaller companies that have strong growth potential. These companies normally pay no dividends because they reinvest earnings in the company to expand operations. High-growth stocks attract a breed of investors who buy stocks with rapidly accelerating earnings and sell them on the tiniest of disappointments over a company's prospects. For this reason, they are considered the most *volatile* in the market—that is, their stock prices tend to rise more quickly, but they can fall just as quickly.

growth stocks
Equities issued by small companies with unproven products or services

speculators
Investors who purchase securities in anticipation of making large profits quickly

blue-chip stocks
Equities issued by large, well-established companies with consistent records of stock price increases and dividend payments

Safety is another concern. Generally, the higher the potential for income or growth, the greater the risk of the investment. **Speculators** are investors who accept high risks in order to realize large capital gains. Of course, every investor must make some kind of trade-off. This is true for all investments. Government bonds are safer than corporate bonds, which are safer than common stocks, which are safer than futures contracts, which are safer than commodities.

Blue-chip stocks are the stocks of established corporations like IBM that have paid sizable dividends consistently for years and that have periodically raised their dividends as profits increased. These are considered to be conservative equity investments because, in addition to the dividends they pay, their prices tend to rise slowly over longer periods, and they are generally less susceptible to sudden drops in the market. For example, the common stock of a major, established corporation such as Wal-Mart is safer than the stock of a start-up technology company. This assumption doesn't mean that Wal-Mart's stock will never decline in value, but it does mean that Wal-Mart's stock is more likely to climb in price and provide dividends over a longer period than the stock of a small technology company with an unproven product.

Still, experts caution that investors who stick only to the safest instruments face the risk that their holdings will not provide the good returns characteristic of riskier investments.[8] In fact, Exhibit 19.3 shows that stocks have historically outpaced inflation and provided better returns than government bonds and T-bills.

When selecting investments, experts consider two additional factors: liquidity and tax consequences. Liquidity is the measure of how quickly an investor can change an investment into cash. For example, common stock is more liquid than real estate; most financial assets can be changed into cash within a day. Some, like certificates of deposit, can be cashed in before maturity, but only after paying a penalty. All investors must consider the tax consequences of their decisions. Historically, dividend and interest income have been taxed heavily, and capital gains have been taxed relatively lightly. In addition, the income from most government securities is not taxed at the federal level, and the income from most municipal securities is not taxed at state levels.

Keep in mind that before you get too caught up in focusing on your own assessment of a specific security, you need to understand what other investors are thinking. You may

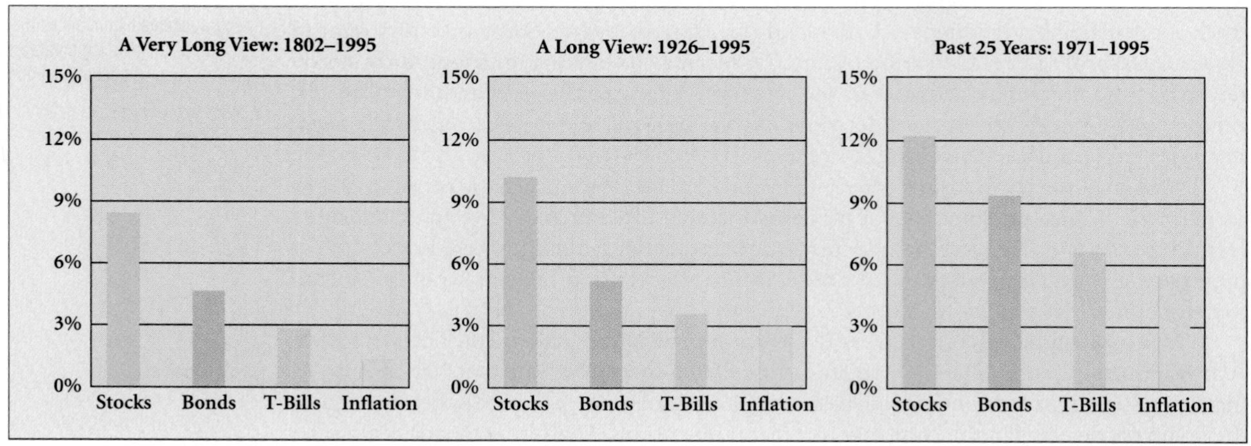

EXHIBIT 19.3

Century of Investing

Stocks have returned far more over time than government bonds and U.S. Treasury bills, and they have soundly outpaced inflation.

see an abundance of value, or substantial growth potential, but if other investors don't share your view, your insights won't do you much good. The market is a voting machine, whereon countless individuals register choices—sometimes based on reason and sometimes based on emotion.[9] One way to protect against the risk of making a poor decision is to diversify, or spread your investments around.

Investment Portfolio

No single investment instrument will provide income, growth, and a high degree of safety. For this reason, all investors—whether institutions or individuals—build **investment portfolios,** or collections of various types of investments. Money managers and financial advisers, like William Francis, are often asked to determine which investments should be in an investor's portfolio and to buy and sell securities and maintain the client's portfolio. Sometimes they must structure a portfolio to provide a desired **rate of return**, the percentage of gain or interest yield on investments.

investment portfolios
Assortment of investment instruments

rate of return
Percentage increase in the value of an investment

A major concern for these managers is **diversification**—reducing the risk of loss in a client's total portfolio by investing funds in several different securities so that a loss experienced by any one will not hurt the entire portfolio. One way to diversify is by investing in securities from unrelated industries and a variety of countries. Another way is by allocating your assets among different investment types. Both of these goals can be accomplished by investing in mutual funds.

diversification
Assembling investment portfolios in such a way that a loss in one investment won't cripple the value of the entire portfolio

Asset Allocation Managing a portfolio to gain the highest rates of return while reducing risk as much as possible is known as **asset allocation.** A portion of the portfolio might be devoted to cash instruments such as money-market mutual funds, a portion to income instruments such as government and corporate bonds, and a portion to equities (mainly common stock). The money manager then determines how much each portion should be, on the basis of economic and market conditions—not an easy task. If the economy is booming and the stock market is performing well, the money manager might take advantage of the good environment by shifting 75 percent of the total portfolio into stocks, 20 percent into bonds, and 5 percent into cash. If the economy turns bad, the stock market heads downward, and inflation heats up, the money manager might readjust the portfolio and invest 30 percent in stocks, 40 percent in short-term government securities, and 30 percent in cash. This adjustment helps protect the value of the portfolio during poor investment conditions.[10]

asset allocation
Method of shifting investments within a portfolio to adapt them to the current investment environment

Mutual Funds Many investors reduce their risk by buying shares of **mutual funds,** financial organizations that pool money drawn from many investors to buy diversified portfolios of stocks, bonds, government securities, gold, or other marketable securities. These funds are particularly suited to small investors who do not have the time or experience to search for investment opportunities.

mutual funds
Pools of money raised by investment companies and invested in stocks, bonds, or other marketable securities

Load funds require investors to pay a one-time small percentage of their investment as a commission to the brokers who sell those funds. The most common types of loads are front end (assessed when you purchase the fund) and back end (assessed when you sell the fund). Funds without any sales charges are known as no-load funds. Two of the biggest discount brokerages—Charles Schwab and Fidelity—now offer their investors no-load mutual funds that combine stock and bond funds from dozens of mutual fund families.[11]

Various funds have different investment priorities. Among the more popular mutual funds are **money-market funds,** which seek good returns by investing in short-term securities such as commercial paper, certificates of deposit, Treasury bills, and other liquid investments. *Growth funds* invest in stocks of rapidly growing companies. *Income funds* invest in securities that return high dividends and interest. *Balanced funds* diversify by allocating their investments among common stocks, preferred stocks, and bonds. *Sector funds,* also known

money-market funds
Mutual funds that invest in short-term securities

as specialty or industry funds, focus on investing in companies within a particular industry. *Global funds* invest in foreign and U.S. securities, whereas *international funds* invest strictly in foreign securities. Because of the potential for growth, many investment advisers recommend global and international funds for individual investors, so these funds are becoming more popular. *Index funds* buy stocks in the companies included in a specific market average or index such as the S&P 500. When you buy shares in the S&P 500, for example, you're buying a small piece of the 500 companies it represents. Today, nearly every stock market in the world—from Tokyo to Trinidad and Tobago—has its own index. In addition, Morgan Stanley Group, Salomon, and Goldman Sachs have each created global stock indexes.

Investment companies offer two types of mutual funds. An *open-end fund* issues additional shares as new investors ask to buy them. In essence, the fund's books never close. The number of shares outstanding changes daily as investors buy new shares or redeem old ones. These shares aren't traded in a separate market. *Closed-end funds,* on the other hand, raise all their money at once by distributing a fixed number of shares that trade much like stocks on major exchanges. As soon as a certain number of shares are sold, the fund closes its books.

BEST OF THE WEB

Invest Wisely, Don't Be a Fool

Here's a fun securities Web site you can fool around at for a while. Visit the Motley Fool and don't be afraid to ask a foolish investment question or two. Roll up your sleeves and do a little work on your own. Discover the strategies, ideas, and information needed to make investment decisions at Fool School. Learn the 13 steps to investing foolishly and how to value stocks, plus much more. Take a journey through the balance sheet and find out why cash is king.
http://www.fool.com

Security Marketplaces

Where do you buy securities? When Wall Street was in its infancy, investors could buy stocks "over the counter," as though they had walked into a store for a loaf of bread. Around 1817 the New York Stock Exchange (NYSE) board organized an indoor market for trading securities. Since the advent of that market, investors must work through a broker, who places the order with a central clearinghouse for trading in that type of security. But that's all changing.

After 200 years of trading being dominated by the New York Stock Exchange, technology is restoring some of the "over-the-counter" feeling from the past by letting investors trade through their brokers on-screen (via computer). Because of the Internet and the ability to make direct contacts between buyers and sellers, the mechanisms of investing as well as the types of the investments will change significantly in the next few years. According to Stephen Eckett, author of *Investing Online,* "no industry will be more greatly affected by the Internet than the investment industry."[12]

New Issues and the Secondary Market

Some companies are so small that their common stock is not actively traded—it is owned by only a few people, usually the firm's managers. However, the stock of most larger public companies are traded on a stock exchange. These companies and their stocks are said to be *listed.*

Stocks and bonds are bought and sold in two kinds of marketplaces: primary markets and secondary markets. In Chapter 18, we discussed that often a company requires more capital than can be generated from retained earnings, so it issues new or additional equity shares. Newly issued shares or IPOs are sold in the **primary market**. Once these shares are issued, subsequent owners buy and sell these shares in the organized **secondary market** known as **stock exchanges**.

primary market
Market where firms sell new securities issued publicly for the first time

secondary market
Market where subsequent owners trade previously issued shares of stocks and bonds

stock exchanges
Location where traders buy and sell stocks and bonds

Security Exchanges

Security or stock exchanges are marketplaces for stocks and bonds. Investors can trade securities in two types of secondary marketplaces: auction exchanges (the traditional marketplace) and dealer exchanges. In an **auction exchange,** all buy and sell orders (and all information concerning companies traded on that exchange) are funneled onto an auction floor. There, buyers and sellers are matched by a **stock specialist,** a member of a brokerage firm who occupies a post on the trading floor and conducts all the trades in a particular stock. The specialist's job is to oversee the transaction. For instance, they can halt trading if buying or selling imbalances occur, thereby preventing a stock's price from plunging without adequate cause.[13]

auction exchange
Centralized marketplace where securities are traded by specialists on behalf of investors

stock specialist
Intermediary who trades in a particular security on the floor of an auction exchange; "buyer of last resort"

The process for buying and selling securities is different in **dealer exchanges,** primarily because no central place exists for making transactions. Instead, all buy and sell orders are executed through computers by **market makers,** registered stock and bond representatives who sell securities out of their own inventories and who are spread out across the country—in some cases, even around the world.

dealer exchanges
Decentralized marketplaces where securities are bought and sold by dealers out of their own inventories

market makers
Dealers in dealer exchanges who sell securities out of their own inventories so that a market is always available for buyers and sellers

Stock Specialists The primary problem that auction exchanges confront is that the auction process itself is rapidly becoming antiquated. In an auction exchange transaction, stock specialists occupy a post on the trading floor and conduct all the trades in a particular stock. When brokers send their buy and sell orders to the exchange, specialists match them up by acting as an auctioneer. Specialists must fill small public orders before handling large institutional trades, thus ensuring that the small trader gets a fair shake.

One of the most important duties of specialists is to act as the buyer or seller if one can't be found. This means that specialists will buy or sell for their own accounts out of their own inventory of stocks. However, they are not required to fund all unmatched orders at any time. As good as this arrangement may sound for investors who want to bail out of a free-falling stock, it doesn't work well in highly volatile markets. For example, during the dramatic market sell-off on October 27, 1997—when the market plunged 554 points, or 7.2 percent—specialists were forced to buy countless stocks for which there were no buyers.[14]

The inability of specialists to cover all stock sales is becoming a major problem because of **program trading,** in which institutional investors use computer programs to buy and sell diversified collections, or "baskets," of shares. Program trading has a number of variations, but the most common approach involves **arbitrage,** the age-old practice of buying something in one market and simultaneously selling its equivalent in another market at a higher price (and pocketing the difference). For these trades to work best, large blocks of stock must be traded instantaneously without causing stock prices to fluctuate sharply. If prices change too much too quickly, the gains that program traders expect may not materialize.

program trading
Automated securities transactions using computer programs to buy or sell large numbers of securities in response to price changes exceeding predetermined amounts

arbitrage
Simultaneous purchase in one market and sale in a different market with a profitable price or yield differential

By serving as "buyers and sellers of last resort," specialists have traditionally prevented prices from making sharp swings. However, institutional investors doubt that specialists will be able to continue doing so as trading in huge quantities becomes more common. Conceivably, if stock prices fall too much, specialists could run out of capital and be unable to buy stocks from program traders in a rush to sell.[15]

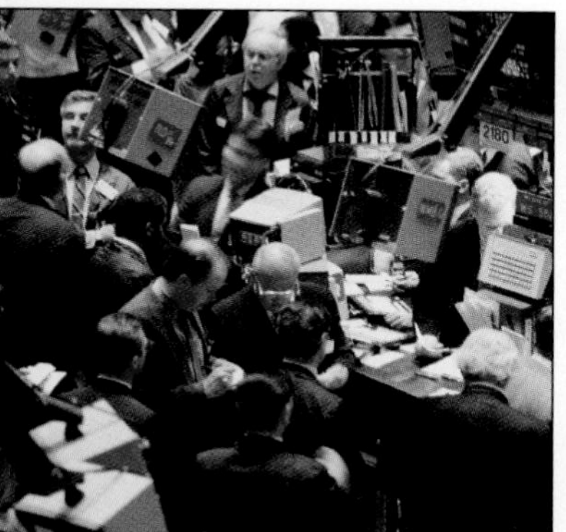

Once a buy or sell order for stocks listed on auction exchanges are fulfilled, brokers must initial each other's order slips. Within minutes, the transaction is reported back to the brokerage houses and to the two customers.

Auction Exchanges In order for a company to list its stock on an auction exchange, it must become a member of that exchange. In addition, it must meet certain listing requirements that relate to the size of the company's net income, the number of shares outstanding, and the total market value of all outstanding shares of the company's stock—its *market capitalization.* The size qualification increases as one moves from the regional exchanges to the larger New York Stock Exchange. For example, as of 1998, the minimum requirement for listing on the American Stock Exchange was 500,000 shares with a total minimum capitalization value of $3 million, whereas a listing on the NYSE required 1.1 million shares with a total minimum capitalization value of $40 million.[16]

The NYSE, also known as the "Big Board," is the largest and most widely known of the auction stock exchanges in the United States. The stocks and bonds of more than 3,000 companies, whose combined market values exceed $9.4 trillion, are traded on the exchange's floor.[17] Options, futures, and closed-end funds are also traded there. For all of its importance, however, the NYSE is feeling competitive pressure from many directions. More than half of the NYSE-listed stocks can also be bought and sold at one or more of the regional exchanges that include the Pacific, Boston, Philadelphia, and Chicago exchanges. The regional exchanges handle the stocks of many large corporations, as does the American Stock Exchange (AMEX), the world's second largest auction marketplace. Because it costs less to trade on the regionals, institutional investors often use them to trade stocks listed on the Big Board. In addition, more than half of all the stocks around the world are traded outside the United States.[18]

BEST OF THE WEB

Stock Up at the NYSE

Tour the New York Stock Exchange. Visit the trading floor and learn about the hectic pace of trading. Find out why having a seat for $1 million doesn't necessarily mean you'll have a chance to sit down. Listen in on a stock transaction and discover how a stock is bought and sold. Learn how investors are protected and how unusual stock transactions are spotted. Get the latest market information as well as a historical perspective of the Exchange. Don't leave without checking out your favorite stock price. Maybe it's time to sell.
http://www.nyse.com

Foreign and International Exchanges New York was once the center of the financial world; today the Tokyo Stock Exchange is second only to the NYSE, followed closely by stock exchanges in London, Frankfurt, Paris, Toronto, and Montreal. In recent years, companies listed on foreign exchanges have produced large gains for investors around the world. In fact, the head global strategist at ING Baring in London predicts that by 2010, emerging markets such as Brazil, China, and India will account for about 45 percent of the total value of all stocks traded in the world, up from 15 percent.[19]

Investing in foreign equities can be problematic, however, because most exchanges around the world require less information from listed companies than U.S. exchanges do, so investors can't easily evaluate a potential investment.[20] Moreover, regulatory standards are looser in overseas markets, which can complicate the process of obtaining good information or enforcing legal rights.[21]

over-the-counter (OTC) market
Network of dealers who trade securities that are not listed on an exchange

NASDAQ The biggest threat to all auction exchanges comes from dealer exchanges—in particular the **over-the-counter (OTC) market.** Instead of a single trading floor where transactions occur, the OTC market consists of a network of registered stock and bond representatives across the country who are linked by a nationwide computer network called **NASDAQ (National Association of Securities Dealers Automated Quotations).**

NASDAQ (National Association of Securities Dealers Automated Quotations)
National over-the-counter securities trading network

NASDAQ has grown so much that it now represents a total market value of $1.95 trillion—second only to the NYSE ($8.7 trillion).[22] One reason for NASDAQ's growth is that its listing requirements are substantially lower than those of other exchanges, making it easier for small, growing companies to list on this exchange. In addition, NASDAQ has been a computerized trading system from the beginning, giving it a head start in creating a global, 24-hour securities exchange—which is what many market experts expect will be common in the next decade. Consequently, NASDAQ frequently surpasses the NYSE in average daily trading volume even though the total value of shares traded on the NYSE still vastly exceeds the value of shares traded on the NASDAQ.[23]

Nevertheless, NASDAQ has its problems. Investors must trade only with dealers that charge them a markup or spread—something critics say needlessly costs investors billions of dollars. To avoid the spread, some investors are turning to trading sites on the Internet or trading through electronic forums like Instinet Crossing Network or Postit. Both of these national services match buyers and sellers at certain times of the day for trades based on closing NYSE prices.[24] Even the president of NASDAQ suspects that the Internet "will have a huge impact" on his market, so he's pushing NASDAQ to roll out a broad array of online services. Still, there are some lines he is not ready to cross—like trading online.[25]

Trading Procedures

For the present—even if you trade online—all trades must be executed by a securities broker. A **broker** is an expert who has studied the intricacies of the market and has passed a series of examinations on buying and selling securities. Landes Associates's William Francis is a broker and investment adviser.

broker
Individual registered to sell securities

Orders to Buy and Sell When you place a buy or sell order, you must specify the parameters of your order. A **market order** gives the broker the go-ahead to make the trade at the best price that can be negotiated at the moment. A **limit order** specifies the highest price at which you are willing to buy, or the lowest price at which you are willing to sell. Limit orders are good for one day only. You can also place an **open order,** which instructs the broker to leave the order open until canceled by the investor.

If you have special confidence in your stockbroker's ability to judge the trend of market prices, you may place a **discretionary order,** which gives the broker the right to buy or sell the security at his or her discretion. In some cases, discretionary orders can save you from taking a loss, because the broker may have a better sense of when to sell a stock. If the broker's judgment proves wrong, however, you cannot hold him or her legally responsible for the consequences.

market order
Authorization for a broker to buy or sell securities at the best price that can be negotiated at the moment

limit order
Market order that stipulates the highest or lowest price at which the customer is willing to trade securities

open order
Limit order that does not expire at the end of a trading day

discretionary order
Market order that allows the broker to decide when to trade a security

Margin Trading You might want to leverage an investment to magnify the potential for capital gains through **margin trading.** Instead of paying for the stock in full, you borrow money from your stockbroker, paying interest on the borrowed money and leaving the stock with the broker as collateral. In Chapter 18 we discussed that the Federal Reserve Board sets *margin requirements,* dictating the percentage of the stock's purchase price that the customer must place on deposit with the broker. For many years, the margin on most stock trades has been set at 50 percent.

However, buying on margin increases risk. If the price of a stock falls, investors have to give the broker more money to increase collateral or the broker will sell your stock. Such forced sales can cause prices to fall even further, triggering a vicious circle of sales and margin calls.[26]

margin trading
Borrowing money from brokers to buy stock, paying interest on the borrowed money, and leaving the stock with the broker as collateral

UNDERSTANDING THE HIGH-TECH REVOLUTION

Cyber-Trading Lures Savvy Investors: Will Brokers Become Obsolete?

Ed Harrison could be Merrill Lynch's worst nightmare. Harrison is a small investor who makes several stock trades a week. But you won't find him using a full-service broker or even a conventional discount broker. Instead, Harrison trades over the Internet using an online broker, and he pays peanuts compared to the $160 commission he used to pay his traditional broker for similar trades.

WILL WALL STREET BE CAUGHT FLAT-FOOTED?

Of course, not everyone is happy that the Internet has arrived on Wall Street. Over time, the Internet could fundamentally restructure the brokerage business and grab the active traders who are the Street's best customers. The situation is similar to the mid-1980s, when Charles Schwab shook up the big full-service brokers such as Merrill Lynch by offering discount commissions. Likewise, traditional brokers could face a similar challenge from the new wave of online brokers, such as E*Trade at <http://www.etrade.com>. "What Schwab did to the full-service firms, online brokers will do to Schwab and the full-service firms," notes the president of Fidelity Brokerage Group. "The Internet is a big threat to the current system. I think the full-service firms are worried about it." After all, trading online is easy.

HOW DO INVESTORS TRADE ONLINE?

Here's how it works. First you mail in vital stats about yourself and a check for $1,000 to cover the minimum balance. Then the firm assigns you a password and you're ready to roll. With a mere click of a mouse you can execute stock transactions, personalize a page to see the market snapshots you prefer, and even assemble and track dummy portfolios of stock. Once your order gets sucked into the firm's computers, it is sent through the clearing broker to the NYSE, NASDAQ, or other markets. Many users hope that the Internet will eventually allow them to bypass both the broker and the exchange in the future.

But for now, cyberbrokerages such as E*Trade are content with gobbling up technically proficient investors who in the past used discount brokers for low-cost trade executions. E*Trade estimates that 70 percent of its customers are defecting from discount brokers, 20 percent from full-service brokers, and 10 percent from other types of financial firms. And Cambridge, Massachusetts–based Forrester Research expects growth in online trading to soon reach 10 million accounts. Although the president of NASDAQ suspects that the Internet will have a huge impact on his market, he is not ready to offer direct online trading without brokers. "We don't want to compete with our members, and it ignores the complexities of being in the brokerage business"—even if it is destined to change.

ARE BROKERS OBSOLETE?

If you can get information and trade over the Internet, why do you need a broker? Traditional brokers claim

short selling
Selling stock borrowed from a broker with the intention of buying it back later at a lower price, repaying the broker, and pocketing the profit

Short Selling **Short selling** is selling stock that is borrowed from a broker in the hope of buying it back later at a lower price. When the borrowed stock is returned to the broker, the investor keeps the price difference. Selling a stock short is something done by an investor who is pessimistic. Suppose you think a company's stock will decline in the near future. You borrow shares of the stock that are selling for $30 per share and then sell short, pledging to deliver the shares you do not own back to the broker from whom you borrowed them. When the stock's price has sunk to say $15 per share, you buy the stock on the open market and make $15 a share profit (minus transaction costs).

Selling short is not without its risks. If you had waited for the stock's price to go even lower than $15 a share, you might have wound up owing your broker money. For instance, if instead of declining, the stock climbed to say $32, you would have had to buy it at that price; after paying the costs of broker's commissions and interest charges, you would have lost over $2 per share.

that the Internet can't replace a flesh-and-blood broker's counsel. "We find investors want ongoing advice and service," notes the executive vice president of Smith Barney. "As investors' portfolios become larger, people have less time to make investment decisions and have to rely more on financial advisers to make those decisions for them." But when it comes to tapping the Internet investment crowd, Chistos Cotsakos, president of E*Trade, thinks Wall Street hasn't a clue. "Commissions are too high, brokers are overpaid, and the technology stinks."

Although the early success of Internet firms has pushed many traditional brokers into the Internet game, they are being reactive, not proactive. Discounters like Schwab have established Internet trading services (e.Schwab) and have cut commissions by 25 percent. In addition, they are being forced to offer more research and value-added services just as their full-service competitors do. Even Merrill Lynch clients can now trade 24 hours a day through a toll-free telephone number, and the company is considering the once unimaginable possibility of offering direct, online trading.

Will Wall Street Go Cybertrade?

E*Trade isn't too concerned about the big brokers. That's because the major firms have a huge stake in the status quo. They charge high commissions that support an array of services, sprawling networks of brokers, offices, and research staffs. And with so much invested in old-fashioned systems, most Wall Street firms can't come close to E*Trade's cost per trade, which Cotsakso estimates at one-quarter that of the typical discount firm.

Of course, with low barriers to entry to the online market and the potential for fierce competition, Cotsakso isn't taking any chances. E*Trade is working on enhancements to cement its customer relationships—such as customized screens that include personalized tickers that track a customer's stock portfolio. In addition, the firm is looking to challenge Wall Street on other fronts such as underwriting stock offerings—even if the Wall Street firms try to shut E*Trade out. "I think some of that will happen at first," says Cotsakos. "But there will be one that will take the risk. Then two. Then three. Then the wall will come down." Cotsakos insists the handwriting is on the wall for Wall Street's army of brokers. "The days of the $100,000 broker are coming to an end."

Questions for Critical Thinking

1. What are some value-added services that traditional brokers can provide to customers to keep their business?
2. How can online brokerages like E*Trade cement their customer relationships besides personalized tickers and stock underwritings?

Cost of Trading As an investor, you pay **transaction costs** for every buy or sell order, to cover the broker's commission and the taxes on a sale. Commissions vary with the size of the trade: The fewer the shares traded, the more it costs; the more the shares traded, the less the cost per share. Most trades are executed in *round lots* (minimum groups of 100 shares). Fewer than 100 shares are traded in odd lots. So if you want to sell 150 shares of a stock, the brokerage actually makes two trades, one of 100 shares and another of 50 shares. Trading in odd lots is more expensive for the broker and the investor.

The nature of the brokerage house also affects transaction costs. **Full-service brokerages,** such as Merrill Lynch, provide research and financial management services such as investment counseling and planning. As a result, the commissions they charge are higher than those charged by **discount brokerages,** which often provide nothing more than a service to buy or sell. However, the early success of online securities brokers such as E*Trade

transaction costs
Costs of trading securities, including broker's commission and taxes

full-service brokerages
Financial-services companies with a full range of services, including investment advice, securities research, and investment products

discount brokerages
Financial-services companies that sell securities but give no advice

with rock-bottom transaction costs is pushing traditional brokers into the Internet game and redefining their services.

Trading Online Some people envision that in the near future the Internet could serve as a virtual stock exchange that will allow you to bypass not only the traditional brokers, but the exchanges as well. This means that intermediaries such as stockbrokers must add some value in some other way if they are to be useful to customers. Even Charles Schwab believes that online electronic services will shape the future of finance. So Schwab is moving his firm up-market, away from straight execution and toward providing more valuable services such as investment planning and performance analysis.[27]

How big will online investing be? Experts predict that online trading will grow considerably—from over 1.5 million accounts today to more than 10 million in the near future.[28] In addition, they predict that technology will give rise of a new class of brokerage firms: neither full-service nor discount, but mid-tier brokers who will provide 90 percent of the value offered by full-service firms, at a fraction of the cost. To accomplish this, mid-tier brokers will employ a new class of investment adviser—a professional with technical skills in place of the sales skills needed by traditional brokers.

This investment adviser will gather enough basic information about individual customers to assist them in forming their own financial plan. Because most customers do not have time to review and analyze the financial news themselves, these professionals will do it for them by using technology to cull and consolidate investment news, quotes, and research.

Analysis of the Financial News

Individual stocks are bought and sold every business day, and their values fluctuate minute to minute, hour to hour, day to day, depending on what buyers and sellers think of each company's investment potential. Investors, brokers, and others who trade stocks are careful to follow the thousands of bits of information that affect each company, its stock, and the economy (everything from revenues and profits to interest rates and currency exchange rates). Here are some of the sources of information they use.

Emotions fly high as traders like this one react to the October 23, 1997 Hong Kong stock market crash where the Hang Seng Index plummeted by nearly 10.5 percent, bringing its total losses in one week to more than 23 percent.

Sources of Information

When you're a serious investor, you continually research financial markets. No single source of information is the best, but a good place to start would be the daily reports on stocks, bonds, mutual funds, government securities, commodities, and financial futures in major city newspapers. Other sources of financial information include newspapers aimed specifically at investors (such as *Investor's Daily* and *Barron's*) and general-interest business publications that not only follow corporate developments but also report news and give hints about investing (such as *The Wall Street Journal, Forbes, Fortune,* and *Business Week*). Standard & Poor's, Moody's Investor Service, and Value Line also publish newsletters and special reports on equities, bonds, and mutual funds. These publications can often be found in large libraries, and most maintain Web sites on the Internet.

In fact, the Internet is leveling the playing field for small investors because today they can get the following information for free: quotes on stocks, bonds, mutual funds, and stock market indexes; world market conditions; business and financial news; company information and earnings estimates; Wall Street analysts' opinions; and economic data. But analyzing all this information can be overwhelming and tricky. That's because stock prices can drop quickly in reaction to news of war, sudden political changes, and other important events—but they can also bounce back within hours or days. For example, when the Hong Kong stock market dropped 23 percent in one week in October 1997, the U.S. markets swiftly responded with a record one-day drop of 7.2 percent, triggering two market shutdowns to safeguard against a repeat performance of the 1987 crash. However, on the next day, the market dramatically reversed itself, rising 4.7 percent on a record volume of 1.1 billion shares.[29]

Make a Pile of Money

BEST OF THE WEB

Visit the E-Investor Network. This premier investor resource center provides the most comprehensive access to online trading, investor forums, financial news, securities, research, corporations, and market changes. E-investor links you to over 2,000 financial Web sites including international and domestic exchanges, online trading, brokerage firms, mutual funds, investment advice, and more. Talk with industry professionals or money managers, and stay ahead of the game. Learn how to make a pile of money by visiting E-Investor now.
http://www.einvestor.com

Broad Market Indicators and Economic News

Stocks go up and down for many reasons: Someone needs money; someone thinks the price is too high; someone is covering an option or balancing her portfolio; someone got a tip from his barber; and so on.

Equity investors always want to know whether now is the time to buy or sell. If investors are buying low and selling high—that is, if they are counting on making a profit from rising prices because they are optimistic and believe business is improving—then Wall Street is said to be in a **bull market,** one characterized by a long-term trend of rising prices. Conversely, if investors are selling short—that is, if they are counting on making profits from falling prices because they are pessimistic and believe business is getting worse—then Wall Street is said to be in a **bear market,** one characterized by a long-term trend of falling prices.

bull market
Rising stock market

bear market
Falling stock market

How might you determine whether you should be bullish or bearish? First, look at the broad movements in the markets (see Exhibit 19.4). Has a bull market gone on maybe too long, which would suggest that stocks are overvalued and a *correction* might be imminent? If so, the market will correct itself downward, sometimes slowly and other times quickly, as it did when the Asian market turmoil extended to U.S. markets on October 27, 1997. Second, watch the volume of shares traded each day. If the stock market is down on heavy volume (that is, if prices are moving downward and a lot of trading is going on), you might conclude that investors are trying to sell before prices go down further—a strong bearish sign.

Is It True?

The terms *bull market* and *bear market* are derived from the way those animals attack a foe, because bears attack by swiping their paws downward and bulls toss their horns upward.

The most common way investors determine whether the market is bullish or bearish is to watch **market indexes** and averages, which use the performance of a representative sampling of stocks, bonds, or commodities as a gauge of activity in the market as a whole. Institutional investors can tie the performance of their investments to the overall performance of the market by *indexing,* which involves building a portfolio of securities that are selected because together they reflect the profile of the market as a whole.

market indexes
Measures of security markets calculated from the prices of a selection of securities

Dow Jones Industrial Average The most famous average is the Dow Jones Industrial Average (DJIA), which tracks the prices of 30 blue-chip stocks traded on the NYSE—each one representing a particular sector of the economy. The DJIA is the barometer that captures the headlines: It's what people talk about in the office and on the golf course; it's the number quoted on the nightly news and remembered when the market takes a dive. Even though the average has become a historical touchpoint, some find our fascination with an industrial average puzzling—especially in an economy where the majority of the nation's

GAINING THE COMPETITIVE EDGE

Using the Wired World of Investment Information

When Chris Winter wants to check out profitability trends for a high-tech company, he doesn't call his broker. Instead, he logs on to the Internet and gets the information he needs in a matter of minutes. Thanks to the growth of the Internet, individual investors like Winter have an abundance of raw data and research at their fingertips to help them evaluate potential investments.

The Internet has also made it possible for small businesses like Zap Power Systems of Sebastapol, California (maker of batteries for electrically powered bikes and scooters) to directly promote its stock offerings to a wide range of investors. Keep in mind, however that direct or independent stock offerings do not have a third-party broker or dealer standing behind the company to objectively evaluate the stock's offering price. This leaves the door wide open to fraud—something the Securities and Exchange Commission (SEC) is trying to monitor and control. For example, before the SEC shut down Comparator Systems (a marketer of a fingerprint comparison system), the company had a market capitalization of $1 billion even though its entire inventory was in three rented lockers. Much of the reason for the stock's rise was small investors making unsolicited purchases through discount brokerage houses on hot Internet tips. That's why it's important to do some research before deciding on an investment.

DON'T BE A VICTIM

Check how well the security or index has performed over the past year or longer. Get a description of the company. Learn something about the people running the company. Ask yourself: What is their prior management track record? Then decide on how much confidence you should put in their claims. Review the company's financial statements for the past three years and any documents it has filed with the SEC such as S1s, which often disclose insiders selling stock. Be sure to get third-party information. Use your computer to check quotes; check the status of financial markets worldwide; view performance charts of a security or index; find out how many Wall Street analysts are recommending purchase of the company's stock; find out what Wall Street expects the company to earn this year and next year; find out what top economists expect the business climate to be like this year. And of course, compare the stock to industry averages by looking at its net profit margin, return on net worth, cash flow per share, price-earnings ratio, ratio of price to book value, and five-year average annual earnings growth.

CLICK BEFORE YOU LEAP

The amount of useful information available online is staggering. One of the best ways to begin your information journey is to use one of the Internet search engines such as AltaVista, Excite, Yahoo!, Infoseek, or Lycos. However, to really burrow into a company's background you can check out the sites listed in the table on page 593 or check out a company's Internet site. Some companies are even offering individuals the same quality, information they give to institutions. Keep in mind, however, that surfing the World Wide Web for investment information can be maddeningly slow and frustrating—especially if you're not sure where to look. But, with a little practice, you'll find that once you learn your way around, getting investment information online can be fast and remarkably rewarding.

QUESTIONS FOR CRITICAL THINKING

1. Why is it important to learn about the company's management before investing in the company's stock?
2. Many companies today have direct stock-purchase plans. These programs let you buy stock directly from the company, saving the broker's commission. Aside from commission savings, what are some of the advantages and disadvantages of buying any stock directly from the issuing company?

Internet Information Sites for Security Investors

Site/Address	Information
SEC's EDGAR FILINGS <http://www.sec.gov/edgarhp/htm>	10-Ks, 10-Qs, and other SEC mandatory corporate filings including disclosures
NEW YORK STOCK EXCHANGE <http://www.nyse.com>	Information on companies listed on the NYSE
MORNINGSTAR MUTUAL FUNDS ON DEMAND <http://www.morningstar.net>	Compendium of unbiased mutual fund data and market news
STOCKMASTER <http://www.stockmaster.com>	Current stock quotes plus graphical performance compared to S&P 500
ZACKS INVESTMENT RESEARCH <http://www.zacks.com/docs/free.html>	Forecasted company earnings based on poll of analysts
BLOOMBERG PERSONAL <http://www.bloomberg.com>	Updates for markets around the world and highlights from Bloomberg news
DR. ED. YARDENI'S ECONOMICS NETWORK <http://www.yardeni.com>	Economic data and indicators
INVESTORNET <http://www.researchmag.com>	Database of over 9,000 stocks with links to news, charts, and analyses
STANDARD & POORS <http://www.stockinfo.standardpoor.com>	Company information and stock lists
STOCK SMART <http://www.stocksmart.com>	Decision-making tools previously available only to big-time investors
CHARTER MEDIA'S BRIEFING SERVICE <http://www.briefing.com>	News on stock, bond, and foreign exchange markets, and the economy
POINTCAST NETWORK <http://www.pointcast.com>	Customized news reports you can broadcast on your PC as a screen saver
INVEST-O-RAMA <http://www.investorama.com/>	Links to about 2,000 investment-related Web sites
NETWORTH <http://www.networth.galt.com>	Database of 5,000 mutual funds by 20 criteria
NORTH AMERICAN SECURITIES ADMINISTRATORS <http://www.nasaa.org>	Allow you to register a complaint about a broker

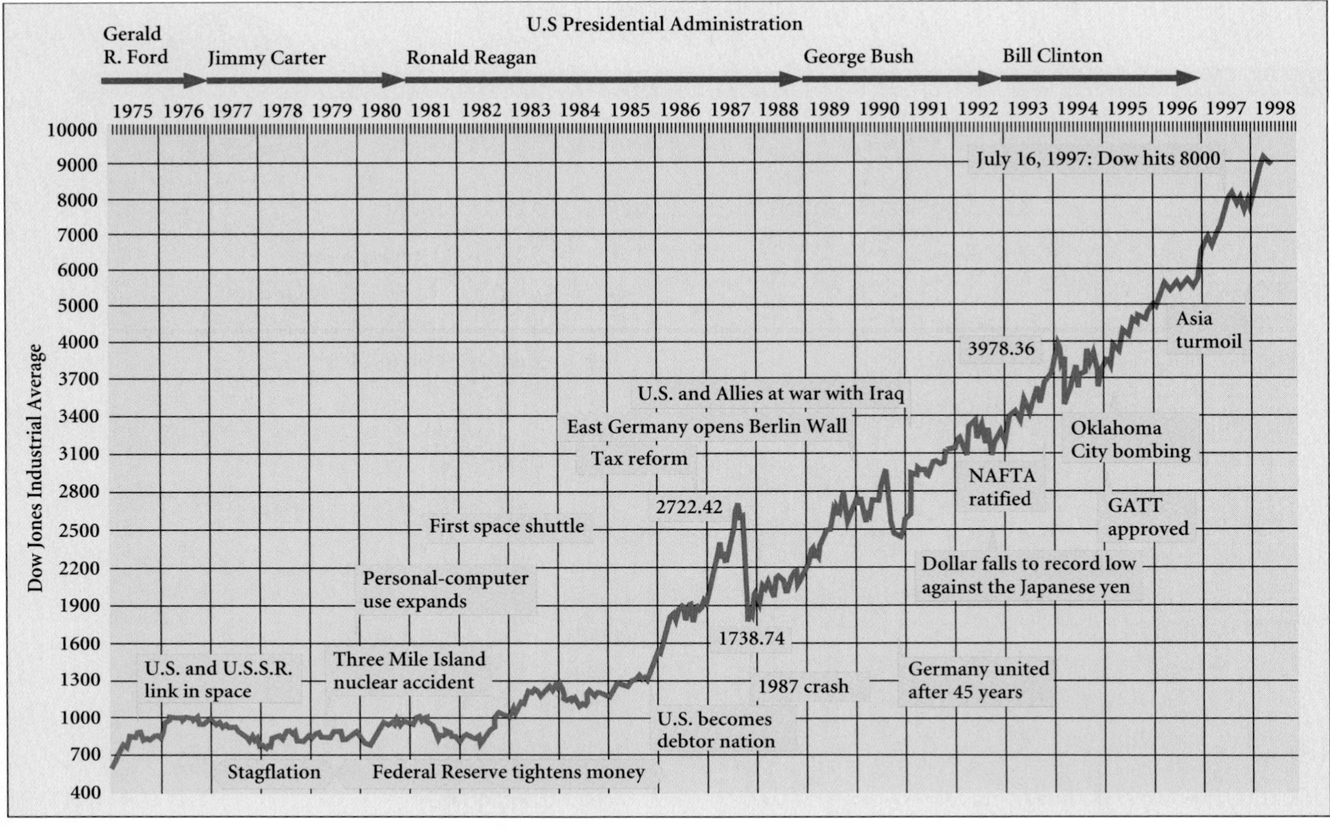

EXHIBIT 19.4

The Stock Market's Ups and Downs

The performance of the stock market is affected by the state of the economy and other world events. The peaks and valleys on this chart represent swings in the Dow Jones Industrial Average, the most widely used indicator of stock prices.

workers provide services rather than assemble manufactured goods. But in recent years, that has been corrected by replacing DJIA stocks U.S. Steel, Manville, and American Brands with service firms Walt Disney, American Express, and McDonald's.

Critics say the Dow is too narrow and too susceptible to violent short-term swings. They argue that it doesn't have the right stocks, and that it has a funny way of giving more weight to higher-priced shares even though they may not be as large or profitable. Why is the Dow price-weighted rather than market-weighted? The answer partly lies in the technology of Charles Dow's day: He needed something that was easy to figure with paper and pencil. In fact, he probably never imagined a market-weighted index.

Certainly, you can chart the market's gyrations on plenty of indexes that are more sophisticated than the Dow. But advocates say the Dow is exactly what it's supposed to be. It does not purport to measure the entire stock market, only 30 blue-chip stocks. In fact, if the Dow didn't already exist, no one would bother to invent it. In order to keep the index historically significant, *The Wall Street Journal* editors (guardians of the Dow) keep changes in the index's component stocks to a minimum. Most substitutions have

Is It True?

IBM was one of the DJIA star performers from 1940 to 1980, a period during which the DJIA rose from roughly 100 to almost 1,000.

EXHIBIT 19.5

The DJIA First Hundred Years

These companies were included in the Dow Jones Industrial Average when it celebrated its 100-year anniversary on May 24, 1996. Some have been in and out several times. Only General Electric was in the Dow at its inception.

COMPANY	IN DJIA SINCE
Allied Signal, Inc. (formerly Allied Chemical & Dye)	1925
Alcoa (formerly Aluminum Co. of America)	1959
American Express	1982
AT&T (formerly American Telephone & Telegraph)	1919–1928; 1939
Bethlehem Steel	1928
Boeing	1987
Caterpillar	1991
Chevron (formerly Standard Oil of California)	1924–1925; 1930
Coca-Cola	1932–1935; 1987
Disney	1991
Du Pont	1924–1925; 1935
Eastman Kodak	1930
Exxon (formerly Standard Oil Co. New Jersey)	1928
General Electric (in DJIA at inception)	1896–1898; 1899–1901; 1907
General Motors	1915–1916; 1925
Goodyear Tire and Rubber	1930
International Business Machines (IBM)	1932–1939; 1979
International Paper	1956
McDonald's	1985
Merck	1979
Minnesota Mining and Manufacturing	1976
J. P. Morgan	1991
Philip Morris	1985
Procter & Gamble	1932
Sears, Roebuck	1924
Texaco	1916–1924; 1925
Union Carbide	1928
United Technologies (formerly United Aircraft and Transport)	1930–1932; 1933–1934; 1939
Westinghouse	1916–1925; 1928
F. W. Woolworth	1924

Shaded companies replaced on 3/13/97 with Hewlett-Packard, Johnson & Johnson, Travelers Group, and Wal-Mart.

arisen because of mergers or company failures. Exhibit 19.5 is a list of the 30 companies in the DJIA at the Dow's 100-year anniversary. Only General Electric was in the DJIA at its inception (in 1896).[30]

Other Indexes Virtually no institutional investors compare their performance with the Dow. Instead they use the Standard & Poor's 500 Stock Average (S&P 500) because it is more representative of the entire market. The S&P 500 tracks the performances of 500 company stocks, so it can't be thrown off by fluctuations in just a few. Born in 1956, this index has done a good job of reflecting the decline in basic manufacturing, the rise of technology, and the state of smaller U.S. corporations. However, because the index is weighted by market value, big companies have far more weight in the index than do small companies. In fact the 10 largest stocks drive 19 percent of the index.[31]

Investors also use other indexes to evaluate market performance. These include the Dow Jones Utility Average of 15 utility stocks; the Dow Jones Transportation Average of 20 transportation stocks; the New York Stock Exchange Composite Index; the NASDAQ Index; and the 7,000 stocks in the imprecisely named Wilshire 5000 Index, which covers all the stocks traded on the New York and American Stock Exchanges, plus actively traded NASDAQ stocks. The most widely followed indicators for commodities are the Dow Jones commodity indexes, which cover spot and futures trading. Dow Jones also publishes bond averages. In short, there are many indexes to watch and no one index that satisfies all investors under all circumstances.

Interpreting the Financial News

Watching indexes and analyzing specific stocks can be as simple as opening up the morning newspaper. For example, you might pick 20 companies that appeal to you and begin to track their daily performance. Whether you use the newspaper, publications, Internet, or other sources of information to do your research, understanding the codes used in these sources and their significance will help you interpret the performance of a specific stock. Exhibit 19.6 is a sample of a stock exchange report in a daily newspaper, showing high and low prices for the past 52 weeks, the number of shares traded (volume), and the change from the closing price of the day before.

Although stock prices are currently quoted in fractions as small as 1/16, most exchanges will soon begin quoting stock prices in dollars and cents (decimals). Advocates argue that the shift could save investors more than $1 billion annually because smaller pricing increments could narrow the difference between the price at which stocks are bought and sold from 6.25 cents (the decimal equivalent of 1/16) to a penny. By narrowing the difference, or spread, between the price at which a trader is willing to buy a stock (the "bid" price) and the lowest price at which another investor is willing to sell (the "asked" price), the trader will make less profit per trade and this savings will be passed on to investors.[32]

❶		❷	❸	❹	❺	❻	❼	❽		❾	❿
52-WEEK HI	52-WEEK LOW	STOCK	SYM	DIV	YTD %	PE	VOL 100S	HIGH	LOW	CLOSE	NET CHG.
38	13 1/4	**CompUSA**	CPU	...	...	28	5976	32 1/2	30 3/4	32 1/2	1 3/4
57 1/2	24 13/16	CompASC	CA	0.04	0.1	69	7028	54 3/4	52 9/16	54 9/16	+1 9/16
87 3/4	57 7/8	CompScs	CSC	...	...	27	4820	83 7/16	82 11/16	82 13/16	−1 1/16
49 3/8	16 9/16	CompTsks	TSK	0.05	0.1	39	271	36	35 3/16	35 3/16	−3/8

1. **52-Week High/Low**: Indicates the highest and lowest trading price of the stock in the past 52 weeks, adjusted for splits. New issues begin at the date of issue. Stocks are quoted in 1/16 of a dollar.
2. **Stock:** The company's name abbreviated (Comp USA, Computer Assc. Intl., Computer Sciences, Computer Task Group). A capital letter usually means a new word. For example, CompScs is Computer Sciences. Boldface names are those issues whose price changed by 5 percent or more if their previous closing price was $2 or higher.
3. **Symbol:** Symbol on the New York Stock Exchange Ticker Tape.
4. **Dividend:** Dividends are usually annual payments based on the last quarterly or semiannual declaration. Special or extra dividends or payments are identified in footnotes. Not all stocks pay dividends.
5. **Yield:** The percentage yield shows dividends as a percentage of the share price.
6. **PE:** Price-to-earnings ratio, calculated by taking the last closing price of the stock and dividing it by the earnings per share for the latest four quarters.
7. **Volume:** Trading volume in 100-share lots. A listing of 5976 means 597,600 shares were traded during the day. A figure preceded by a "z" is the actual number of shares traded.
8. **High/Low:** High and low price of the stock for the day.
9. **Close:** Closing price of the stock.
10. **Net change:** Change in price from the close of the previous trading day.

Common Stock Footnotes: **d**—new 52 week low; **n**—new; **pf**—preferred; **s**—stock split or stock dividend of 25 percent or more in previous 52 weeks; **u**—new 52 week high; **v**—trading halted on primary market; **vi**—in bankruptcy; **x**—ex dividend (the buyer won't receive a recently declared dividend, but the seller will).

EXHIBIT 19.6

How to Read a Newspaper Stock Quotation

To the uninitiated, the daily stock quotations in the newspaper look like a mysterious code. However, the code, when broken, yields a great deal of information on the performance of a particular stock.

Aside from the price, another item of information included in stock listings for the major exchanges is the **price-earnings ratio,** or **p/e ratio** (also known as the price-earnings multiple), which is computed by dividing a stock's market price by its *prior* year's earnings per share. Say that Acme stock sold for $20 a share last year and earned $2 per share. The price-earnings ratio would be 20 divided by 2 or 10. Because the p/e ratio is calculated on the prior year's earnings, it is a trailing ratio and has no predictive value. Some investors calculate a forward p/e ratio, which uses expected year earnings in the ratio's denominator.

price-earnings ratio (p/e ratio)
Stock's current market price divided by issuer's annual earnings per share; also known as the price-earnings multiple

Although a high forward p/e ratio is a positive sign of investors' happy expectations, it also makes a stock especially sensitive to the slightest whisper of bad news. That's why you should always examine a company's ratio relative to those of other companies in its industry. If the p/e ratio is significantly below the industry norm, you may conclude either that the company is having problems or that it is an undiscovered gem whose stock may soon go up in price.

Many newspapers carry a report of bond trading on the major exchanges (see Exhibit 19.7) as well as price quotations for mutual funds, commodities, options, and government securities. Exhibit 19.8 illustrates a mutual fund listing. When reading bond prices, remember that the high and low are given as a percentage of the bond's face value. For example, a $1,000 bond shown closing at 65 actually sold at $650.

REGULATION OF SECURITIES TRADING

Since the early days of stock trading, state governments have tried to control the way stocks are bought and sold. Even though almost every state has its own laws governing securities trading, the federal government has the leading role in investment regulation (see Exhibit 19.9). For example, to protect investors against failing brokerage houses, Congress established the Securities Investor Protection Corporation (SIPC). The SIPC is not a part of the federal government; its operations and insurance fund are financed by the securities industry. It provides up to $500,000 worth of insurance against fraud or bankruptcy for each investor who buys and leaves securities for safekeeping with a brokerage house, and it provides up to $100,000 worth of insurance for cash left with a brokerage house. The SIPC does not cover commodities contracts or limited-partnership investments, nor does it protect against losses from declines in the price of securities.

❶ BONDS	❷ CUR YLD	❸ VOL	❹ CLOSE	❺ NET CHG
Chryslr 10.95s17	10.1	10	108¼	−⅛
ClrkOil 9½04	9.8	45	97⅜	−⅛
ClevEl 8⅜ 12	10.2	79	82¼	+¼
Coastl 9¾ 03	9.4	35	104⅛	+1⅛
Coeur 7s02	cv	12	110	−3½

1. **Bonds:** Name of company, such as Clark Oil, and bond description, such as 9½ percent bond maturing in 2004
2. **Current Yield:** Annual interest on $1,000 bond, divided by its purchase price. For example using Clark Oil 9½: $95÷$973.75=0.09756 or approximately a 9.8 percent yield. The abbreviation "cv" indicates a bond that is convertible into shares of common stock at a specific price
3. **Volume:** Number of $1,000 bonds traded that day
4. **Close:** Price at the close of last day's business
5. **Net Change:** Change from previous day's closing price

EXHIBIT 19.7

How to Read a Newspaper Bond Quotation

Many newspapers carry bond quotations in addition to stock quotations. Prices represent a percentage of a bond's face value, which is typically $1,000.

EXHIBIT 19.8

How to Read a Newspaper Mutual Fund Quotation

A mutual fund listing shows the net asset value of one share (the price at which one share is trading) and the change in trading price from one day to the next.

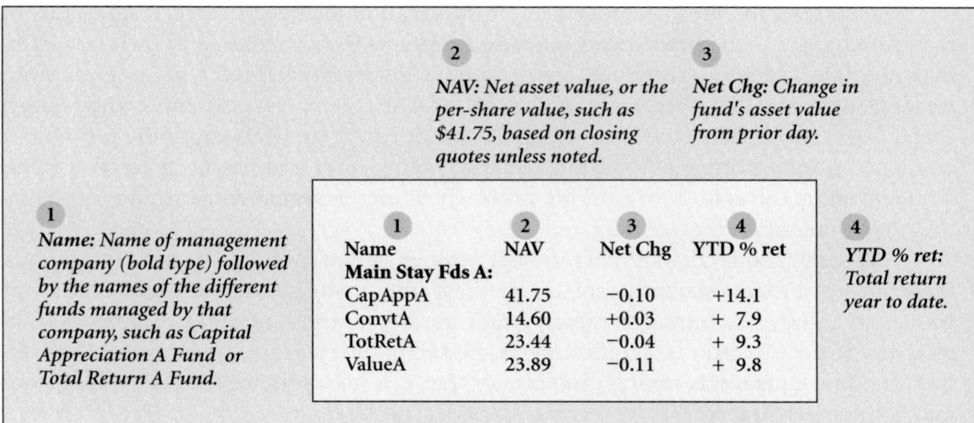
2
NAV: Net asset value, or the per-share value, such as $41.75, based on closing quotes unless noted.
3
Net Chg: Change in fund's asset value from prior day.
1
Name: Name of management company (bold type) followed by the names of the different funds managed by that company, such as Capital Appreciation A Fund or Total Return A Fund.
4
YTD % ret: Total return year to date.

Name (1)	NAV (2)	Net Chg (3)	YTD % ret (4)
Main Stay Fds A:			
CapAppA	41.75	−0.10	+14.1
ConvtA	14.60	+0.03	+ 7.9
TotRetA	23.44	−0.04	+ 9.3
ValueA	23.89	−0.11	+ 9.8

EXHIBIT 19.9

Major Federal Legislation Governing the Securities Industry

Although you have no guarantee that you'll make money on your investments, you are protected by laws against unfair securities trading practices.

LEGISLATION	DATE	EFFECT
Securities Act	1933	Known as the Truth in Securities Act; requires full disclosure of relevant financial information from companies that want to sell new stock or bond issues to the general public
Securities Exchange Act	1934	Created the Securities and Exchange Commission (SEC) to regulate the national stock exchanges and to establish trading rules
Maloney Act	1938	Created the National Association of Securities Dealers to regulate over-the-counter securities trading
Investment Company Act	1940	Extended the SEC's authority to cover the regulation of mutual funds
Amendment to the Securities Exchange Act	1964	Extended the SEC's authority to cover the over-the-counter market
Securities Investor Protection Act	1970	Created the Securities Investor Protection Corporation (SIPC) to insure individual investors against losses in the event of dealer fraud or insolvency
Commodity Futures Trading Commission Act	1974	Created the Commodity Futures Trading Commission (CFTC) to establish and enforce regulations governing futures trading
Insider Trading and Securities Fraud Act	1988	Toughened penalties, authorized bounties for information, required brokerages to establish written policies to prevent employee violations, and made it easier for investors to bring legal action against violators
Securities Market Reform Act	1990	Increased SEC market control by granting additional authority to suspend trading in any security for 10 days, to restore order in the event of a major disturbance, to establish a national system for settlement and clearance of securities transactions, to adapt rules for actions affecting market volatility, and to require more detailed record keeping and reporting of brokers and dealers
Private Securities Litigation Reform Act	1995	Protected companies from frivolous lawsuits by investors: limited how many class-action suits can be filed by the same person in a 3-year period, and encouraged judges to penalize plaintiffs that bring meritless cases

In general, government regulation of securities trading, as well as industry self-regulation, is designed to ensure that investors receive information that is as accurate as possible, and that no one artificially manipulates the market price of a given stock. Today trading in stocks and bonds is monitored by the Securities and Exchange Commission (SEC), and trading in commodities is supervised by the Commodity Futures Trading Commission (CFTC). In addition, the SEC works closely with the stock exchanges and the National Association of Securities Dealers (NASD) to police transactions on the exchanges in order to maintain the integrity and credibility of the system.

To be listed on an exchange, a company must file registration papers and reports, in addition to fulfilling certain requirements. Plus, traders must conform to the rules of the exchange, many of which are designed to protect investors. The magnitude of these filing requirements keeps the SEC very busy indeed. Every year the SEC screens over 15,200 annual reports, 40,000 investor complaints, 14,000 prospectuses (a legal statement that describes the objectives of a specific investment), and 6,500 proxy statements (a shareholder's written authorization giving someone else the authority to cast his or her vote).

Although the securities industry has mushroomed in the past ten years, the SEC has not expanded its staff as rapidly.[33] Like many other regulatory agencies with a heavy work load and a limited staff, the SEC tries to focus its efforts where they will do the most good. It concentrates on a few big cases and urges brokerage houses and securities exchanges to police themselves.

One of the SEC's top priorities is to crack down on *insider trading*, in which a few people with access to nonpublic information (say, a pending merger) buy or sell a company's stock before the information can become public and before the price can change in reaction to the news. But monitoring insider information and securities fraud has become increasingly difficult now that stock promoters have cheap global access to millions of investors through the Internet. As a result, NASD is developing an Internet search engine to find phrases such as "too good to be true," and monitor securities chat forums for fraudulent or misleading information.[34]

Although the SEC has so far won praise for its attempts to keep pace with new challenges brought by the Internet, the commissioner of the SEC is uncertain how much longer traditional regulation can ride this whirlwind. The range of issues that must be resolved include: Are firms required to regularly sweep the Internet to patrol for online abuses by their employees? Can proxy materials be delivered through the Internet? Can agents close deals online with digital signatures? Who has jurisdiction of a Web site with a server in France that reaches investors in the United States? Like all major regulatory issues, the good intentions, politics, and selfish goals quickly get tangled.[35]

Summary of Learning Objectives

1. **Explain the differences between common stock, preferred stock, and bonds from an investor's perspective.**
   Stocks are ownership shares investors buy in a corporation. Bonds are loans investors make to corporations and governments. Common stockholders can vote and share in the company's profits and losses through dividends and capital gains or losses whereas preferred shareholders get a fixed return on their investment and a priority claim on assets after creditors. Bondholders get a fixed return. They do not vote or share in profits or losses.
2. **Explain the safety and tax advantages of investing in U.S. government securities.**
   U.S. government securities, including those backed by the U.S. Treasury and those backed by agencies of the government, are relatively safe because the government and its agencies are unlikely to default on interest payments.

Interest from Treasury notes and Treasury bonds is exempt from state and local income taxes.

3. **Name five criteria to be considered when making investment decisions.**
Investors should consider the income, growth, safety, liquidity, and tax consequences of alternative investments.
4. **Explain what mutual funds are and describe their main benefits.**
Mutual funds are pools of money drawn from many investors to buy diversified portfolios of stocks, bonds, and other marketable securities. The primary benefit is that investors gain greater diversification from buying a share in a mutual fund than from investing the same money in the stock of one company.
5. **Describe the two types of security marketplaces and the challenges they are facing.**
Auction exchanges funnel all buy and sell orders into one centralized location. This process is rapidly becoming antiquated, and specialists are finding it difficult to serve as "buyers of last resort"—especially with higher volume trades. Dealer exchanges are decentralized marketplaces in which dealers are connected electronically. They are under attack from investors who no longer want to pay the spread—the fees dealers earn on the trade.
6. **Explain how the Internet is redefining the investment industry.**
The Internet allows investors to get an abundance of securities information that was previously available only to brokers. As a result, it is changing the function of brokers and in many cases restructuring their business. It has spurred the growth of online brokers and lowered the commission costs to investors. And some think it is paving the way for a virtual stock exchange in the future where brokers and exchanges will not be needed.
7. **Identify the two major broad market indexes and explain their differences.**
The Dow Jones Industrial Average tracks the prices of 30 blue-chip stocks. It is a barometer, not a predictor of performance. It gives more weight to higher priced shares. The Standard & Poor's 500 includes the prices of stocks in 500 large and small companies, which are selected to represent the performance of all U.S. corporations. The index is weighted by market value, giving bigger companies more weight in the formula.
8. **Explain how government regulation of securities trading tries to protect investors.**
It tries to prevent fraud in the securities markets by requiring companies to file registration papers, fulfill certain requirements, and file periodic information reports so that investors receive accurate information. Regulations also try to monitor the use of insider information and police fraudulent manipulation of securities.

On the Job: Meeting Business Challenges at Landes Associates

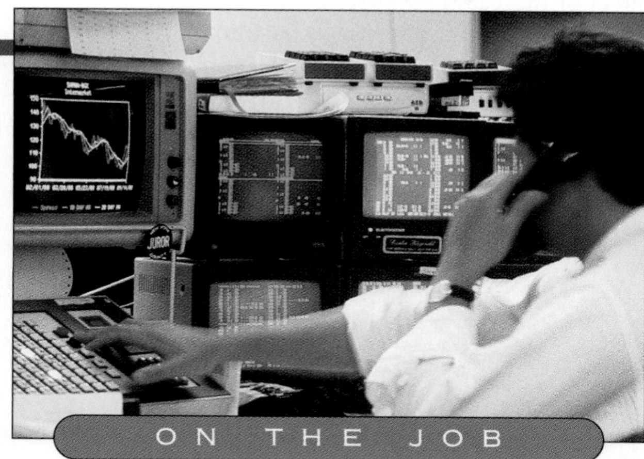

William A. Francis had to understand the economic trends that affected the stock market. However, no matter how well the economy fared, no matter whether the stock market was moving up or down, his objective remained the same: to steadily increase the wealth of his clients over time. He knew that speculating for a quick gain could lead to an even quicker loss.

Therefore, Francis had to know how *not* to invest. He didn't want to invest in companies just because they were fascinating or just because they were big. Biotechnology might be exciting, but it had yet to realize its promise. Until it did, investing in biotechnology companies carried a heavy risk. As for big firms, a $60 billion giant usually has less growth potential than a company worth $6 million (a 10 percent gain would require $6 billion for the giant firm, but only $600,000 for the smaller one). Neither did Francis want to invest in companies that were unsure of their business. Corporations that are in the headlines tend to be those that are continually changing focus, management structure, or business plans, and their potential is generally uncertain. Well-managed companies that stick to their business might attract less press, but the news is usually much better.

So just what was Francis looking for in a company? Most important, Francis wanted to see companies developing a particular competitive advantage. Whether they developed it through their product, their customer service, or their market share wasn't important, as long as the advantage gave the company a sustainable growth potential. A software firm might specialize in the types of products that businesses are expected to need in the coming years, or a major retailer might be expanding into lucrative new markets. In addition, Francis wanted to see companies that had positive track records: at least two years of rising productivity, falling costs, low debt, and consistent spending for research and development.

Francis was in search of the few companies that were still pursuing long-term growth. He needed information about products and services that were relatively new. He wanted to know about companies that held great promise. He needed information about which companies were satisfying their customers and increasing sales. Even though the times had changed, his methods of searching had not. He turned to business publications such as *The Wall Street Journal, Investor's Daily, Barron's, Business Week, Fortune,* and *Forbes.* He also read industry publications and studied statistical profiles found in *Standard & Poor's Stock Guide* and in Value Line.

To determine when to sell a stock, Francis needed the same information. The only difference was that instead of looking for growth potential, he looked for the likelihood that growth would slow down enough to affect stock prices. Before selling a stock, he asked three questions: (1) Are the stocks, in general, overvalued? (2) Are the profit margins ("the blood pressure of the company") beginning to drop? (3) Is the company making any unnecessary strategic changes? A yes answer to all three questions signaled Francis to consider selling. After all, he invests his clients' money in common stock to realize capital gains, not capital losses.

Your Mission: You have just been hired as an investment adviser at Landes Associates. In addition to your assignment to bring new clients into the firm, you have been assigned to manage a certain number of existing accounts. They include investors who are interested in both growth and income, who are more conservative and less conservative, and who all seek good value in their investments. Your job is to successfully manage the investments for all these clients.

1. A new client has come to you seeking safe income from a long-term investment. Which of the following would be the best investment for her needs?
   a. Buying U.S. Treasury bonds
   b. Short-selling common stocks
   c. Buying debentures
2. One of your best clients is thinking about buying stock in General Motors. He asks for your opinion. Before you give him an answer, you need to find out for yourself whether it's a good investment. What sources would you use to find the latest, most accurate, and most objective information about GM's current business and future prospects?
   a. *Car and Driver* and *Consumer Reports* magazines
   b. Automotive-industry reports and *Standard & Poor's Stock Guide*
   c. GM's annual and quarterly reports
3. A friend has asked you for some advice. She has a small amount of money to invest and is looking for a diverse portfolio of stocks and bonds, mainly for long-term capital gains. Which would be the best investment?
   a. A mutual stock fund of common stocks and a mutual bond fund of corporate and government bonds
   b. Selected individual common stocks and an investment in both long-term and short-term government bonds
   c. Individual common stocks and a mutual bond fund of corporate bonds
4. You have to buy a new battery for your car one Saturday, so you decide to visit the new auto parts store that just opened on the corner. When you enter the store, you notice how busy the store is, how large the store's selection of auto parts is, and how well customers (including you) are being served. As you're paying for your battery, you recall reading about the company that owns and operates this chain of auto parts stores—an article that complimented the company's management and its business strategy. You also believe that, with the economy in its current status, more people will be repairing their old cars rather than buying new ones. On the basis of these observations, you think this company might make a good investment, but you aren't sure. What would be the best way for you to find out?
   a. Study the company's annual and quarterly reports.
   b. Research the company and the industry in business and industry publications.
   c. Both (a) and (b)[36]

Key Terms

arbitrage (585)
asset allocation (583)
auction exchange (585)
authorized stock (574)
bear market (591)
blue-chip stocks (582)
broker (587)
bull market (591)
capital gains (578)
commodities (580)
common stock (575)
convertible bonds (576)
dealer exchanges (585)
debentures (576)
denomination (576)
discount brokerages (589)
discretionary order (587)
diversification (583)
financial futures (579)
full-service brokerages (589)
general obligation bonds (578)
growth stocks (581)
hedge (579)
institutional investors (581)
investment portfolios (583)
issued stock (574)
junk bonds (577)

limit order (587)
margin trading (587)
market indexes (591)
market makers (585)
market order (587)
money-market funds (583)
mortgage bonds (576)
municipal bonds (578)
mutual funds (583)
NASDAQ (National Association of Securities Dealers Automated Quotations) (587)
open order (587)
over-the-counter (OTC) market (586)
par value (574)
preferred stock (574)
price-earnings ratio (p/e ratio) (597)
primary market (585)
principal (576)
program trading (585)
rate of return (583)
revenue bonds (578)
secondary market (585)
secured bonds (576)
short selling (588)
sinking fund (578)
speculators (582)
stock exchanges (585)
stock option (579)
stock specialist (585)
stock split (576)
transaction costs (589)
Treasury bills (578)
Treasury bonds (578)
Treasury notes (578)
unissued stock (574)
U.S. savings bonds (578)
yield (581)

Questions

For Review

1. What are the differences between a Treasury bill, a Treasury note, and a U.S. savings bond?
2. What is the difference between a general obligation bond and a revenue bond?
3. What is an institutional investor?
4. What is a p/e ratio, and what does it signify to an investor?
5. What is the function of the Securities Investor Protection Corporation?

For Analysis

6. Why might a company's board of directors decide not to pay a cash dividend, and what effect might this have on the company's stock price?
7. Why might an investor who owns 1,000 shares of XYZ Corporation sell an option on those shares? Who might buy that option?
8. What are some of the ways an investor can diversify investments to reduce risk of loss?
9. How does a load mutual fund differ from a no-load mutual fund?
10. When might an investor sell a stock short? What risks are involved in selling short?

For Application

11. If an investor wants a steady, predictable flow of cash, what types of investments should she seek and why?
12. When placing an order to buy a security, under what circumstances would you place each of the following orders: market, limit, open, and discretionary?

A Case for Critical Thinking ▪ The Price of Success

Tom Stemberg knew his idea for a chain of office-supply superstores called Staples was a good one. So good that it wasn't long before clones like Office Depot and Office Club were also ringing in profits at the register. In order to remain competitive, Stemberg knew that he had to stake out his territory fast. He needed to expand quickly. He needed money. So he decided to take Staples public.

With both Office Depot and Office Club already trading on the stock exchanges, Stemberg did his homework, chose a team of investment bankers, and answered endless questioning by lawyers, bankers, and accountants. After all, they wanted reassurance that they were not misrepresenting the tiniest detail to investors. Then Stemberg and the bankers packed up their paperwork and went on a 17-day road show to present the company to potential investors. The presentations were absolutely packed. It was clear that Staples was a hot IPO.

With perfect market conditions and demand outstripping supply, the investment bankers set the initial price of the stock at $13 to $15 per share, raised it to $18, and finally nudged the price up to $19 per share. "You want the price of the stock to be set high so that as much money as possible is raised," notes Stemberg. "But, it can't be so high that the share price falls after the first day of trading." Of course, this was not a problem for Staples. The stock was immediately bid up by enthusiastic investors, surpassed $23, and closed at $22—18 percent above the offering price. The grueling work paid off. Staples raised $61.7 million.

Like most fast-growing companies, Staples stock was quickly awarded a high price-earnings (p/e) multiple based on investors' high expectations. However, this also makes a stock especially sensitive to even the slightest whisper of bad news. That's because high-growth characteristics attract a breed of investors who will sell the shares on the tiniest disappointment over a company's prospects—making a stock highly volatile. Any slight concerns are multiplied and magnified—something Stemberg would learn the hard way.

It began when David Childe, an analyst with San Francisco–based Robertson Stephens & Co., issued a three-page report cutting his earnings estimates for companies in the superstore industry. The news surprised Staples' management. Instead of alerting Staples to his change in opinion (the customary procedure), Childe simply faxed the report out to institutional investors—claiming that Staples would not be able to crack the California market with profitable stores. Then he recommended that investors not only sell the stock, but sell short—in other words, bet on the stock falling. With Staples stock already under pressure—falling from $25.50 to $16.00 in less than 3 months—the stock fell another 15 percent following Childe's report.

The pattern of negative reports containing often-faulty reasoning continued for a month or two. Childe gave Staples no chance to respond to his extrapolations. He even began issuing reports that his estimates were based on company "guidance," when in fact the company had provided none. He continued to recommend selling Staples stock, but even worse, he took his story to the media. CNBC aired a story about Office Depot and Staples. "It might as well have been called *Beauty and the Beast*," notes Stemberg. According to the story, Office Depot was in a lovely position—essentially without any competitors invading its territory—whereas a big chunk of Staples stores were about to suffer an assault from OfficeMax. Childe was not only referenced in the story, he seemed to be the only source for it.

Unfortunately, being wrong didn't alter Childe's stance. When he first recommended selling Staples short, it was at $13 per share. But in spite of his recommendation, the stock continued to rise. By 1992, it was trading at about $30. Stemberg's strategy of ignoring Childe to focus on Staples' business seemed to be paying off—at least for the short term. But, in the spring of 1993, Stemberg was shocked again—this time by Dan Dorfman, a reporter for *USA Today*. After telling Dorfman (off the record) that Staples would not be hurt by OfficeMax's expansion because good real estate locations were hard to find plus Staples planned to grab market share by lowering prices, Dorfman published a column stating that Staples would "get slammered." He even quoted Stemberg and made him look like a buffoon. And he ignored Staples' requests for correction.

In the end, Stemberg learned a lesson the hard way—that is, don't try to control what is out of your control. Instead of focusing his efforts on the bad press, Stemberg chose to focus his efforts on managing the company. And it paid off. By the end of fiscal 1992, store sales were up 16 percent and Staples stock rose to $33.50. By the end of fiscal 1995, the stock had risen 124 percent above the 1992 level, adjusted for stock splits. And in 1996 Staples offered to buy Office Depot for nearly $3.5 billion, but the Federal Trade Commission blocked the merger on the grounds that it would violate antitrust laws and lead to higher prices. Meanwhile, Childe eventually left Robertson Stephens & Co. And Dorfman left *USA Today* to become a columnist for *Money* but resigned from the magazine in 1996 because he refused to divulge his sources for other stories to *Money*'s editors.

1. What are some of the qualities a company should look for when selecting an investment banker?
2. What steps can a company take to prevent misinformation about the company's past performance and future prospects?
3. Why is it important for a public company to build good working relationships with analysts and reporters?
4. Visit Staples' Web site at <http://www.staples.com> and click on *About Staples, Inc.* Click on *Facts & Financial Highlights.* Scroll down to the Financial highlights.
   a. How well has the company performed since 1992? Are the company's financial figures and operating statistics trending in the same direction? Why is that important?
   b. Go back and click on *Press Releases, Quote Server and SEC Filings.* Take the link to the Business Wire World, and click on *Staples Company Profile in Hoover's Online.* Click on the *Stock Master Stock Chart.* How is Staples' stock performing relative to the S&P 500? Is it the same? better? worse?
   c. Using the company's p/e ratio and the current stock price, calculate the company's earnings per share.

Building Your Business Skills

Using this chapter as a resource, investigate the world of securities markets by interviewing a stockbroker. The interview may be conducted either by phone or in person. Prepare for the interview by drafting a list of eight to ten questions about current and expected trends in stock and bond prices, methods of working with clients, selection of appropriate investments to meet investors' objectives, and other issues that interest you. Then, as requested by your instructor, write a brief report describing the results of your interview, or give a three-minute oral report to the class.

Keeping Current Using *The Wall Street Journal*

You have $10,000 to invest. Using as much information as your instructor recommends, select a well-known company traded on the New York Stock Exchange, American Stock Exchange, or NASDAQ. Assignment: Begin a stock-transaction journal. On the first page, record the company's name, the stock exchange abbreviation, the exchange on which it is traded, the 52-week high and low, the price-earnings ratio, and your reasons for selecting this stock.

- *Buying.* On the first day of the project, record the number of shares purchased (whole shares only), the price per share, the total purchase price (number of shares × price/share), the commission paid on your purchase (assume 1 percent of the purchase price), and today's Dow Jones Industrial Average. Now add the commission paid to the purchase price to get your *total purchase cost.*
- *Monitoring.* Record and chart the closing price of your stock each day, and plot it on a graph. Scan *The Wall Street Journal* or other publications regularly for articles on your company to include in your journal. Note any major developments that may affect your stock.
- *Selling.* In this exercise, you select the best time to sell as long as it meets two requirements: You must sell on or before the day designated by your instructor, and (if your instructor wishes) you must notify your instructor on the day you sell your stock. (This means that you'll probably need to sell on a day that your class meets—unless your instructor posts a sign-up sheet that you can use on other days.) On the day you sell your stock, record the following information: the selling price (the closing price/share that day), the number of shares sold, the total sales price (the number of shares × selling price/share), the commission paid on the sale (assume 1 percent of the total sales price), and that day's Dow Jones Industrial Average. Now subtract the commission paid from the total sales price to arrive at your *sales proceeds.*
- *Analysis.* Subtract your total purchase cost from your sales proceeds to arrive at your *net gain* or *net loss.*

1. How well did your investment do? Use the articles you collected during this project to relate recent developments to the performance of your stock.
2. How did it compare with gains or losses in the Dow Jones Industrial Average during this period?
3. How close was the selling price to the stock's 52-week high or low?
4. Visit the Dow Jones Indexes Web site at <http://averages.dowjones.com/>. Click on *Dow Jones Averages* and *Continue.* Browse the site. Read some interesting details about the Dow Jones Averages. Click on *Dow Jones Industrial Average* and *DJIA Facts.* Read the facts and review the *Index Comparisons.*
   a. How well has the DJIA performed relative to other stock market indexes?
   b. Is the DJIA an effective daily measure of the stock market performance or is it a better long-term indicator? Explain your answer.

Exploring the Best of the Web

Invest Wisely, Don't Be a Fool, page 584

It's OK to fool around at this Web site for a while. In fact, you may learn a thing or two about investing in stocks. Browse the Motley Fool at <http://www.fool.com>.

1. Get some answers to your not-so-foolish questions by clicking on *Fool FAQ.* Pick three items you would like to learn more about and click on them. What did you learn? How helpful was this advice?
2. Go to Fool School and read about *Valuing Stocks.* Take *A Journey Through the Balance Sheet* and discover why cash is king. Because you learned about most of this stuff in Chapters 17

and 18, brush up on the components a bit and then jump to *working capital.* Why is working capital important?

3. What is market capitalization? What does the working capital to market capitalization ratio show you?

Stock Up at the NYSE, page 586

Tour the New York Stock Exchange at <http://www.nyse.com> and learn how the exchange operates.

1. Click on *Education* and *You & The Investment World.* Click on *How the NYSE Operates* and page through the text. What does it mean to keep securities in "street name"?
2. Click on *Investor Protection* (far left section of screen, under NYSE) and then learn about *Regulating the Market.* What is Stock Watch? List some of the steps involved.
3. Get a *Historical Perspective* of the Exchange (far left section of screen, under NYSE). What percentage of value did the Dow lose from 1929 through 1932?

Make a Pile of Money, page 591

Learn how to make a pile of money. Log on to the E-Investor Network at <http//www.einvestor.com> and browse this site.

1. Click on the *Financial Site Directory.* Scroll down to the General Investing drop-down box and select *Reference.* Scroll down and click on *Young Investor*; register and pick your guide. Browse a bit, then go to the *Library* and click on the *Basics.* Read about *Different Investments for Different Goals.* What are some of the things you need to ask yourself before selecting a mutual fund?
2. Go back to the site's home page and *Mutual Funds.* Select *Fund Analysis* and click on *The Mutual Funds Investor's Center* at <http://www.mfea.com.> At the Education Center click on *Basics of Mutual Fund Investing.* Then click on *How to Read a Prospectus.* Review the information. What are the three most important items to look for in any prospectus?
3. Go back to the E-Investor and click on *Exchanges, Orgs. & Govt.* Select *Government.* Scroll down and click on the *Securities and Exchange Commission* at <http://www.sec.gov>, *Edgar Database,* and *Edgar Form Definitions.* Scroll down to the 1934 Act Registration Statements. Which companies must register under this act? What is form 10K? 10Q?

Part VII: Mastering the Geography of Business ■ Monitoring the World Markets

The Dow Jones Industrial Average (DJIA), the Standard & Poor's 500, the Wilshire Index—these and other such stock market indexes provide good indications of where U.S. markets are headed. Unfortunately, they aren't much help for markets in other countries. You can find similar indexes in all the other major industrialized countries of the world; perhaps the best known of these is Japan's Nikkei index.

Understanding the composition of a market index is vital (1) to interpret the index's movement up or down and (2) to compare it with the DJIA or other U.S. indexes. Select one of the following stock market indexes and answer the questions that follow:

- Nikkei (Japan)
- DAX (Germany)
- FT-SE (Britain)
- CAC (France)
- Hang Seng (Hong Kong)
- Straits Times (Singapore)
- All Ordinaries (Australia)[37]

1. Does the index have more or fewer companies than the DJIA? Than the S&P 500?
2. Over the last five or ten years, how has your chosen index performed, compared with the DJIA?
3. Does the index appear to represent the stock market as a whole or just one sector?
4. Go to the Financial Network Web site at <http://www.cnnfn.com> to view the latest performance of world markets. Click on *Markets, World Markets,* and compare the performance of the following market indexes: Hong Kong's Hang Seng, Tokyo's Nikkei 225, Frankfort's DAX,

and Paris's CAC 40. Then scroll down and click on *U.S. Markets* to see how the U.S. markets are performing.

a. Do you spot any trends or patterns?
b. The October 1997 Hong Kong market crash sent shock waves around the world. Read about this crash and its effect on world markets at <http://cnnfn.com/specials/asiamarket>. Click on the *Hong Kong Crash* (logo) plus *Asia troubles strike Dow.*
c. Now do some Web surfing on your own to find out what happened to the U.S. stock markets on October 27, 1997. Try the Dow Jones Index's Web site at <http://averages.dowjones> and drill down to get some facts. Then step back in time (ten years earlier) to Black Monday (October 19, 1987). Read about that historic event at <http://cnnfn.com/markets/crash>. Why was Monday so black?

Answers to "Is It True?"

Page 577. False. Coupon bonds mean interest-paying bonds. Not too long ago every bond had coupons attached to it. About every six months, bond owners would take a scissors to the bond, clip the coupon, and present it to the bond issuer (or a bank) for payment. Today most bonds are registered in the owner's name and interest is mailed.

Page 591. False. Long ago "bearskin jobbers" were known for selling bearskins that they did not own (in other words, the bears had not yet been caught). This was the original source of the term *bear.* It describes short sellers—speculators who sold shares they did not own, betting that the stock price would drop. Because bull and bear baiting once was a popular sport, "bull" was understood as the opposite of "bear." In other words, bulls were those people who bought in the expectation that a stock price would rise, not fall.

Page 594. False. In 1939 IBM was ejected from the DJIA to make room for AT&T. Over the next four decades, AT&T's share price slightly doubled. During that same period, IBM's stock split 29 times and racked up a cumulative price gain of 22,000%. IBM was brought back into the DJIA in 1979, but by then its banner years were behind it.

The Environment of Business

COMPONENT CHAPTER A

GOVERNMENT REGULATION, TAXATION, AND BUSINESS LAW

BUSINESS AND GOVERNMENT

Over the years, the United States has accumulated laws and regulations that help resolve disputes between businesses, individuals, and communities. Although the United States is philosophically committed to the free-enterprise system, and even though its economy is shaped primarily by market forces, the government has often stepped in to solve specific problems. In many ways, a company's success hinges on its ability to understand the law and to manage its relations with the government.

The process of managing government relations is complicated by the fact that more than one government must be dealt with. In addition to worrying about Uncle Sam, a business has to consider local, county, state, and possibly foreign governments, all imposing specific and sometimes conflicting laws and restrictions. Moreover, each government body interacts with business in a variety of ways. On Monday, a business may deal with the government as supporter, partner, or customer; on Tuesday, it may clash with the government over regulations; on Wednesday, it may interact with the government on a tax matter; and on Thursday, it may be involved in legal actions of a criminal or civil nature, as defined by the government.

Government as Supporter, Partner, and Customer

Although it often seems that business and government are adversaries, the opposite is true. One of government's chief objectives is to foster business prosperity, as a nation's, state's, or locality's economic health depends on the success of individual companies. When businesses make a profit and create jobs, citizens benefit.

Government support for business takes several forms:

- *Promoting economic growth.* The federal government tries to keep the economy growing at a steady pace by adjusting monetary (money supply) policy. At the same time, all governments affect the economy through their fiscal (taxing and spending) policies. Theoretically, these actions help the economy avoid high inflation and severe recessions, both of which are harmful to business. By smoothing out the economic cycle, the government creates a climate that is good for business.
- *Promoting foreign trade.* The federal government also helps promote business by negotiating international treaties and trade agreements, such as

NAFTA and GATT. Although these trade agreements do not benefit all business, and may actually hurt some, they are created with the goal of helping U.S. companies as a whole to compete and operate more efficiently. The government also arranges "trade missions" in which U.S. business leaders accompany high-ranking government officials on visits to foreign countries for the express purpose of promoting U.S. business interests. In some cases, state and federal agencies step in to help with specific business deals.

- *Supporting and subsidizing business.* Governments operate countless programs that are specifically designed to help businesses. One of governments' most valuable functions is simply providing information and training through agencies such as the U.S. Department of Commerce. Today the U.S. government publishes a wide variety of helpful information for business owners on the Internet. Governments also provide direct loans, loan guarantees, and subsidies of various types. For companies trying to develop new technologies and new products, some of the federal government's 700 research labs will help, too.[1]
- *Maintaining the infrastructure.* By building roads, bridges, dams, airports, harbors, and the like, governments indirectly help businesses distribute their products. In addition, governments own and operate power plants that provide energy for business operations. Moreover, public schools provide companies with a supply of educated labor.
- *Buying industry's products.* Federal, state, and local government agencies spend almost $1.5 trillion for goods and services provided by private industry.[2] Government procurements range from army uniforms and delivery trucks to consulting services and computers. These procurements involve companies of every size and description.

The U.S. government is a major customer for General Dynamics, whose engineers are shown here testing a cruise missile.

Government as Watchdog and Regulator

Although the United States has one of the "freest" free-market systems in the world, various government bodies regulate and monitor nearly every aspect of business to one degree or another. This section discusses two major areas in which government regulates business activities: competition and stakeholder rights. Sometimes these areas overlap. For instance, laws designed to promote competition often have the ultimate goal of protecting consumers. In addition, over time the government has regulated and deregulated a number of specific industries, as you'll see at the end of this section.

Promoting Competition In most sectors of the economy, state and federal regulators work to ensure that all competitors have an equal chance of producing a product, reaching the market, and making a profit. By setting ground rules and establishing basic standards of proper business behavior, government helps prevent conflicts and facilitates the workings of the economic system. Laws concerning competition make up a huge and complex body of government regulation.

When regulators figure that the public can be best served by limiting competition in certain industries, they will consider restricting entry into those markets. However, in most industries, the government prefers to set ground rules that enable many companies to compete. Over the last century or so, a number of regulations have been established to help prevent individual companies or groups of companies from gaining control of markets in ways that restrain competition and/or harm consumers. Some of the earliest government moves in this arena occurred from 1890 to the beginning of World War I. That period saw the passage of such landmark pieces of legislation as the Sherman Antitrust Act, the Clayton Antitrust Act, and the Federal Trade Commission Act, which generally sought to rein in the power of a few huge companies such as Standard Oil. These companies, usually referred to as the *trusts* (hence the label *antitrust legislation,* which you read about in Chapter 1), had financial and management control of a significant number of other companies in the same industry. The trusts thus controlled enough of the supply and distribution in their respective industries to muscle smaller competitors out of the way.[3]

The Sherman Act got the regulatory ball rolling, and the Clayton Act added specific restrictions against **interlocking directorates,** or boards of directors made up of board members from competing firms; the practice of acquiring large blocks of competitors' stock; and discriminatory prices. The Clayton Act also restricted **tying contracts,** which attempt to force buyers to purchase unwanted goods along with goods actually desired. For example, Microsoft has been charged by the Justice Department with threatening to terminate contracts that allow computer makers to install Windows 95 on their computers if those companies do not also install Microsoft's Internet Explorer.[4]

In 1914 the Federal Trade Commission Act set up a watchdog group, the FTC, to monitor activities that might be unfair. The FTC's authority was later expanded to cover practices that harmed the public even if they didn't harm competitors, such as marketing unsafe products.

Following the Great Depression of the 1930s, the rise of giant retailing firms prompted small retailers to turn to the federal government for protection against the chains, which were able to negotiate big price discounts from suppliers. The government responded by passing the Robinson-Patman Act, which, among other things, made it illegal for manufacturers to sell the same product to two customers at different prices if that would stand in the way of free competition.

Frito-Lay, which commands over 50 percent of the U.S. market for salty snacks, was recently investigated by the Justice Department for allegedly using its market power to muscle out competitors on grocery store shelves.

Laws regulating competition continue to grow and evolve as the economy itself evolves. A key area of concern to regulators involves mergers and acquisitions. Such deals must pass government approval, and approval won't be granted if regulators think a deal will restrain competition. For example, the FTC did not approve a proposed merger between Office Depot and Staples, the top two office-supply superstores, because it felt that competition would suffer as a result of the new company's market power.[5]

Regulators also keep an eye on changes in technology that might give companies an unfair advantage and on the ability of large companies to control technological development. For example, the Justice Department recently launched an investigation of Intel, which makes the microprocessors found in a large majority of microcomputers. The department is concerned that Intel withholds technical information as well as allotments of its popular Pentium chips from companies that don't purchase exclusively from Intel.[6]

Protecting Stakeholders As we discussed in Chapter 3, businesses have many stakeholders, including employees, consumers, investors, and society as a whole. Although almost every business exists to serve one or more of these stakeholders, often the interests of other stakeholders are neglected in the process. For example, managers who are too narrowly focused on generating wealth for shareholders might not spend the funds necessary to create a safe work environment for employees or to reduce waste. On the other hand, by withholding information about the company's financial performance, managers may hamper the ability of investors to make solid decisions, which could limit investors' returns. As a result, government has passed many laws and established several regulatory agencies that protect consumers, employees, shareholders, and the environment from the potentially harmful actions of business. The Occupational Safety and Health Administration (OSHA), the Equal Employment Opportunity Commission (EEOC), the Securities and Exchange Commission (SEC), and the Environmental Protection Agency (EPA) are just a few examples of the federal regulatory agencies that most companies must deal with. In addition, the Nutrition Education and Labeling Act of 1990, the Fair Credit Reporting Act, the Americans with Disabilities Act, and the Clean Air Act represent only a fraction of the laws that most businesses must adhere to.

Regulating and Deregulating Specific Industries In addition to these regulations, another layer of regulations applies to specific industries. From mining to retailing and banking to advertising, government officials keep tabs on companies to ensure fair competition, safe working conditions, and generally ethical business practices. For instance, the Federal Aviation Administration (FAA) sets rules for the commercial airline industry, the Federal Reserve Board and the Treasury Department look after the banking industry, and the Federal Communications Commission (FCC) oversees telephone services and radio and television broadcasts.[7] Some lawmakers and citizens have recently called upon the FCC to also regulate Internet development and content more closely. However, top FCC officials have emphatically stated their belief that passing laws to regulate the Internet would be a mistake. Opponents of Internet regulation scored a huge victory in 1997 when the Supreme Court struck down the Communications Decency Act—a law signed in 1996 that prohibited the transmission of "indecent" material on the Internet—on the grounds that the act restricted the constitutional right to freedom of speech.[8]

In past years, some industries were under very strict government control. In the most extreme cases, regulators decided who could enter an industry, what customers they had to serve, and how much they could charge. The telecommunications, airline, and banking industries fell under such control until the 1970s and 1980s, when a wave of *deregulation,* the abandonment or relaxation of existing regulations, opened up competition (see Exhibit A.1). Consider the telecommunications business. In 1982 the federal government broke AT&T up into seven local telephone companies and one long-distance provider. The move allowed other companies like MCI and Sprint to compete for long-distance telephone business, and price emerged as a key competitive issue.[9] However, deregulation wasn't all bad for AT&T, as it freed up the company to pursue other businesses besides telephone services.

The telecommunications industry was further deregulated in 1996 to allow long-distance carriers to enter local telephone markets, thus ending the seven local telephone companies' monopolies. The Telecommunications Reform Act of 1996 also deregulated the cable television industry, enabling telephone companies and others to compete for cable television viewers.

Deregulation sometimes produces problems, as industries used to government protection and stability struggle to compete. In one three-year period following deregulation, the U.S. airline industry lost more money than it had earned it its entire existence, dating all the way back to the Wright brothers. The lack of price controls set off a frenzy of discounting, and some companies simply could not remain profitable. More recently, deregulation of the cable television industry has caused the price of cable service in the United States to rise rather than fall. One reason is that head-to-head competition for existing cable TV companies may take a while to develop; cable is an extremely expensive business to enter, prompting several telephone companies to abandon their plans of offering video programming. At the same time, the government is phasing out the price controls it once placed on cable companies. The result is the continued dominance of the cable market by a few companies that are enjoying fewer and fewer restrictions. One consumer group has even asked Congress to freeze cable television rates.[10] On the average, however, deregulation is good for consumers. Adjusting for inflation, airfares have decreased by almost one-third since 1978, and long-distance rates have been cut by about 50 percent since 1984.[11]

Understanding the Impact of Government Regulation It would be hard to overstate the complexity of business regulation. As Exhibit A.2 shows, even the production of a fast-food hamburger requires compliance with many specifications. Not only do thousands of federal rules and regulations restrict what companies can do, but the individual states often have overlapping and conflicting rules on the same subjects. Many companies resent the struggle of dealing with 50 "little Washingtons," referring to the rules enacted by every state. On top of that, doing business outside the United States means complying with regulations in other countries. For example, the Treaty on European Union (Maastricht Treaty) contains laws to "protect the health, safety, and economic interest of consumers" in the European Union.[12]

Regulations keep lots of employees busy in large companies—just keeping track of new regulations is a big job by itself—and they can be an extreme burden to small companies that lack the resources of their larger cousins. Many businesses are challenging the need for rules that cost both time and money but produce no real benefits. For example, the EPA requires companies that use flammable substances to file a report with the local fire department so that firefighters are aware of any hazards they might encounter in the event of a fire. Although this requirement can help firefighters to do their jobs better and more safely, some gas station owners question the necessity of telling the fire department that there is gas on the premises. The government has responded by eliminating 16,000 pages of "superfluous rules" from the Code of Federal Regulations. Moreover, regulatory agencies like OSHA, the EPA, and the Food and Drug Administration (FDA) have begun to ease up on certain restrictions. Perhaps even more significantly, the Small Business

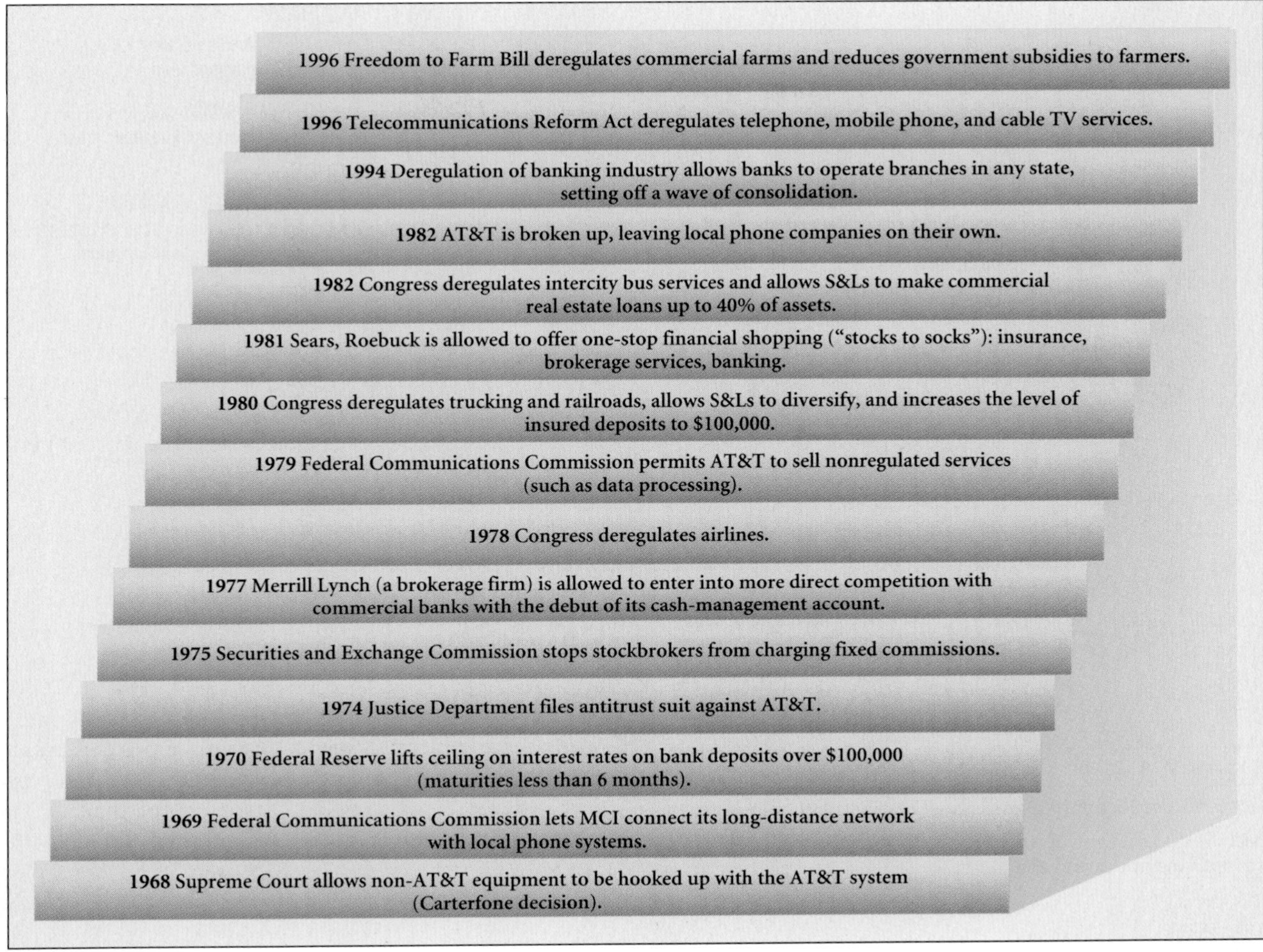

1996 Freedom to Farm Bill deregulates commercial farms and reduces government subsidies to farmers.
1996 Telecommunications Reform Act deregulates telephone, mobile phone, and cable TV services.
1994 Deregulation of banking industry allows banks to operate branches in any state, setting off a wave of consolidation.
1982 AT&T is broken up, leaving local phone companies on their own.
1982 Congress deregulates intercity bus services and allows S&Ls to make commercial real estate loans up to 40% of assets.
1981 Sears, Roebuck is allowed to offer one-stop financial shopping ("stocks to socks"): insurance, brokerage services, banking.
1980 Congress deregulates trucking and railroads, allows S&Ls to diversify, and increases the level of insured deposits to $100,000.
1979 Federal Communications Commission permits AT&T to sell nonregulated services (such as data processing).
1978 Congress deregulates airlines.
1977 Merrill Lynch (a brokerage firm) is allowed to enter into more direct competition with commercial banks with the debut of its cash-management account.
1975 Securities and Exchange Commission stops stockbrokers from charging fixed commissions.
1974 Justice Department files antitrust suit against AT&T.
1970 Federal Reserve lifts ceiling on interest rates on bank deposits over $100,000 (maturities less than 6 months).
1969 Federal Communications Commission lets MCI connect its long-distance network with local phone systems.
1968 Supreme Court allows non-AT&T equipment to be hooked up with the AT&T system (Carterfone decision).

EXHIBIT A.1

The Steps in Deregulation

The move toward deregulation started slowly in the late 1960s, gained momentum in the 1970s and 1980s, and continued throughout the 1990s. Although the immediate results of deregulation are not always favorable, consumers and the economy usually benefit in the long run.

Regulatory Enforcement Fairness Act was passed in 1996 to allow small businesses to sue federal agencies for failing to adequately evaluate the impact of a new regulation on small businesses or for imposing excessive fines.[13]

Although they may find some regulations costly and inconvenient, this doesn't mean that businesses universally dislike regulations. The antitrust laws, for instance, make it possible for many small companies to compete with larger ones. In addition, some regulations designed to help consumers also help businesses by encouraging an honest business environment. When the Chinese government imposed rules for accuracy and scientific supportability on medical advertising, legitimate marketers were pleased. Kenny Ho of the Dentsu, Young & Rubicam ad agency explained that the new rules will help stop dishonest advertising and allow his clients to compete more effectively.[14]

Government as Tax Collector

From road repair to regulation, running a government is an expensive affair. To fund government operations and projects, cities, counties, states, and national governments levy a variety of revenue-raising taxes: personal and corporate income taxes, property taxes, and sales taxes—to name a few. In addition, governments also levy

Enriched bun: Must contain at least 1.8 mg of thiamine, at least 1.1 mg of riboflavin, and at least 8.0 but no more than 12.5 mg of iron

Meat: Must be fresh or frozen chopped beef without added water, binders, or extenders; must be inspected before and after slaughter and at boning, grinding, fabrication, and packaging stages

Growth promoters: Must not be used beyond the time specified by law

Pesticides: No more than 5 parts of the pesticide DDT per million parts of fat in the meat

Fat: No more than 30 percent fat content

Pickle slices: Must be between 1/8 and 3/8 inch thick

Tomatoes: Must be mature but not overripe or soft

Lettuce: Must be fresh, not soft, overgrown, burst, or ribby; no sulfites may be used to preserve a fresh appearance

Cheese: Must contain at least 50 percent milk fat and, if made with milk that is not pasteurized, must be cured for 60 or more days at temperature of at least 35°F

Ketchup: To be considered grade A fancy, must flow no more than 14 cm in 30 seconds at 20°C (69°F)

Mayonnaise: May be seasoned or flavored as long as the substances do not color it to look like egg yolk

EXHIBIT A.2

Government Regulations Affecting Fast-Food Hamburgers

Each of the government-imposed specifications shown here is intended to ensure that fast-food burgers are both nutritious and safe to eat.

regulatory taxes such as *excise taxes* and *customs duties* to encourage or discourage taxpayers from doing something.

Like any typical regulatory structure, tax laws have developed in a hodgepodge fashion over many years. Entire segments of accounting and legal professions have sprung up to help companies and individuals cope with their interpretation and compliance. As you know, filing a tax return can be a hair-pulling experience. Some corporations today file tax returns that are several feet thick or more. The following descriptions include the primary tax issues that affect businesses.

- *Individual and corporate income taxes.* Individual (personal) income taxes have been the federal government's largest single source of revenue and a major source of state revenue as well.[15] On the federal level, personal income is currently taxed at a graduated tax rate, which means that as your taxable income increases, so does the rate at which you pay tax. Some businesses—like partnerships and sole proprietorships—include the profits generated from their operations in their personal income tax returns. These entities pay income tax at individual income tax rates. Only corporations pay federal income tax at corporate income tax rates. However, corporate profits distributed to individual shareholders (in the form of dividends) are taxed at individual income tax rates. In addition to federal income taxes, many states and local governments also levy income taxes on both corporations and individuals.
- *Tax credits and deductions.* A **tax credit** is a direct (dollar-for-dollar) reduction in the amount of income tax that an individual or corporate taxpayer owes. By contrast, a **tax deduction** is a reduction in the amount of income on which tax must be paid. Tax credits and deductions are frequently granted by a government body in return for engaging or not engaging in selected activities. For instance, many state and local governments grant

tax credits to businesses to encourage them to locate in their area. The U.S. government also grants tax credits for activities such as hiring people from selected population groups, increasing investments in research, or using recycled motor oil.[16]

- *Property taxes.* Both business and individual property owners pay property taxes on the land and structures they own. In some communities, taxes are assessed on the market value of this property. In addition, property owned by businesses (commercial property) is usually taxed at a higher rate than houses and farms. As a result, businesses often pay a larger portion of a community's property tax.
- *Sales taxes.* In most states and in some cities, merchandise sold at the retail level is subject to a sales tax. Even though wholesale businesses are exempt from paying a sales tax on merchandise they buy for resale to other businesses, all businesses are indirectly affected by the sales tax: It ultimately increases the price of a product to the consumer. Sales tax is collected by retail businesses on purchases made by their customers, and then forwarded to the government, which adds further administrative expense for the retailer.
- *Excise taxes.* A number of items, including gasoline, tobacco, and liquor, are subject to **excise taxes**—regulatory taxes intended to help control potentially harmful practices ("sin taxes") or to help pay for public services that are used by the taxpayers. For example, the gasoline tax is used to fund road-building projects. Federal excise taxes are also levied on certain services of national scope, such as air travel and telephone calls. Income from federal excise taxes must be used for a purpose related to the tax.
- *Custom duties.* Products brought into this country are often subject to import taxes, or **customs duties.** These regulatory taxes are selective; they vary with the product and its country of origin. Designed to protect U.S. businesses against foreign competition, customs duties have the effect of raising the price of imports to a level comparable to the price of similar U.S.-made merchandise. Customs duties have been used with increasing frequency as a weapon in foreign policy; the products of friendly nations are often taxed at lower rates than those of indifferent or openly hostile countries.

Business's Influence on Government

Given the impact that government has on business, it is not surprising that business has responded by trying to influence government in various ways. One of the most common approaches is to create **lobbies,** groups of people who try to persuade legislators to vote according to the groups' interests. Industry associations such as the American Bankers Association and the American Medical Association are typically involved in lobbying. Although the members of such associations are competitors, they often have common objectives when it comes to government action. Consider the banking industry, which successfully lobbied Congress to block a bill that would have specified that credit-card payments be considered paid as soon as they are postmarked, rather than when the banks receive them.[17] The nation's largest business lobbying group is the Chamber of Commerce of the United States, which spends about $15 million a year on lobbying. Some of its pet causes include a balanced federal budget and lower corporate taxes.[18]

Businesses also try to influence government by donating money to politicians. Campaign laws strictly limit businesses' ability to donate money directly to candidates; however, they may funnel contributions through **political action committees (PACs).** Through a PAC, a company can solicit contributions from its employees and then allocate the money to various campaigns. In addition to operating company PACs, many companies also work through trade-association PACs. Opponents of PACs complain that these committees corrupt the

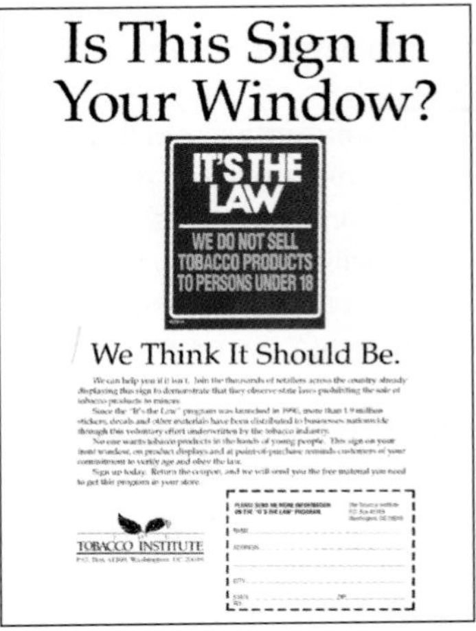

The Tobacco Institute, an industry association representing tobacco companies, wants retailers to take a clear stand on selling to minors.

democratic process, favor incumbents, and drive up the cost of campaigning for everyone. Some employees dislike PACs because they feel pressured to contribute, yet they have little say in how their money will be allocated.[19]

A recent report by the Center for Responsive Politics shows that PACs tend to shift their contribution habits based on which party is in power, rather than on ideology. In 1994, when the Democrats controlled Congress, business PACs gave 51 percent of their funds to Democrats and 49 percent to Republicans; in 1996, after control of Congress had shifted to the Republicans, the percentage of PAC funding received by Republicans in Congress also shifted to 70 percent.[20] In the late 1990s, campaign finance reform has been a hot topic in Washington, although little action has been taken to restrict contributions to political candidates thus far.

The U.S. Legal System

One of the most pervasive ways that government affects business is through the legal system. The law protects both businesses and individuals against those who threaten society. It also spells out accepted ways of performing many essential business functions—along with the penalties for failing to comply. In other words, like the average person, companies must obey the law or face the consequences. Although this fact limits a company's freedom, it also provides protection from wrongdoers.

Sources of Law

The U.S. Constitution, including the Bill of Rights, is the foundation for our laws. Because the Constitution is a general document, laws offering specific answers to specific problems are constantly embellishing its basic principles. However, law is not static; it develops in response to changing conditions and social standards. Individual laws originate in various ways: through legislative action (*statutory law*), through administrative rulings (*administrative law*), and through customs and judicial precedents (*common law*). To one degree or another, all three forms of law affect businesses. In addition, companies that conduct business overseas must be familiar with **international law,** the body of principles, customs, and rules that govern the relationships between sovereign states and international organizations and persons.[21] Successful global business requires an understanding of the domestic laws of trading partners as well as established international trading standards and legal guidelines.

Statutory Law Without Congress, there would be no federal **statutory law,** which is law written by legislative bodies. The Constitution, in fact, specifically grants the Senate and the House of Representatives the right "to regulate commerce." States also have legislative bodies that write statutory laws applicable within their boundaries. However, state laws can vary considerably, presenting problems for companies that do business in several states.

The differences in statutory laws between states are mitigated somewhat by the **Uniform Commercial Code (UCC).** A code is a comprehensive, systematic collection of statutes in a particular legal area.[22] The UCC provides a nationwide standard in many issues of commercial law, such as sales contracts, bank deposits, and warranties. The UCC has been adopted in its entirety in 49 states and the District of Columbia, and about half of it has been adopted in Louisiana.

Administrative Law Once laws have been passed by a state legislature or Congress, an administrative agency or commission typically takes responsibility for enforcing them. That agency may be called on to clarify a regulation's intent, often by consulting representatives of the affected industry. The administrative agency may then write more specific regulations, which are considered **administrative law.** For example, the FTC issues regulations and enforces statutory laws concerning such deceptive trade practices as unfair debt collection and false advertising. Governmental agencies cannot, however, create regulations out of thin air—they must be linked to specific statutes to be legal.

Administrative agencies also have the power to investigate corporations suspected of breaking administrative laws. A corporation found to be misbehaving may agree to a **consent order,** which allows the company to promise to stop doing something without actually admitting to any illegal behavior. For example, Gerber Products recently signed a consent order issued by the FTC that prohibits the company from making false claims about doctors recommending its baby food.[23]

As an alternative, the administrative agency may start legal proceedings against the company in a hearing presided over by an administrative law judge. For instance, the Securities and Exchange Commission required KPMG Peat Marwick to go before an administrative law judge to answer to charges that the company violated the SEC's auditor independence rules when it audited the client of a former KPMG-affiliated company.[24] During such a hearing, witnesses are called and evidence is presented to determine the facts of the situation. The judge then issues a decision, which may impose corrective actions on the company. If either party objects to the decision, the party may file an appeal to the appropriate federal court.[25]

Common Law **Common law,** the type of law that comes out of courtrooms and judges' decisions, began in England many centuries ago and was transported to the United States by the colonists. It is applied in all states except Louisiana (which follows a French model). Common law is sometimes called the "unwritten law" to distinguish it from legislative acts and administrative-agency regulations, which are written documents. Instead, common law is established through custom and the precedents set in courtroom proceedings.

Despite its unwritten nature, common law has great continuity, which derives from the doctrine of ***stare decisis*** (Latin for "to stand by decisions"). What the *stare decisis* doctrine means is that judges' decisions establish a precedent for deciding future cases of a similar nature. Because common law is based on what has gone before, the legal framework develops gradually.

In the United States, common law is applied and interpreted in the system of courts (see Exhibit A.3). Common law thus develops through the decisions in trial courts, special courts, and appellate courts. The Supreme Court, or the highest court of a state when state laws are involved, sets precedents for entire legal systems. Lower courts must then abide by those precedents as they pertain to similar cases.

In all but six states, business cases are heard in standard trial courts. However, many corporations are pushing for the establishment of a network of special business courts. Advocates say that the special nature of business legal disputes requires experienced judges who understand business issues. They also feel that a system of business courts would go a long way toward reducing the

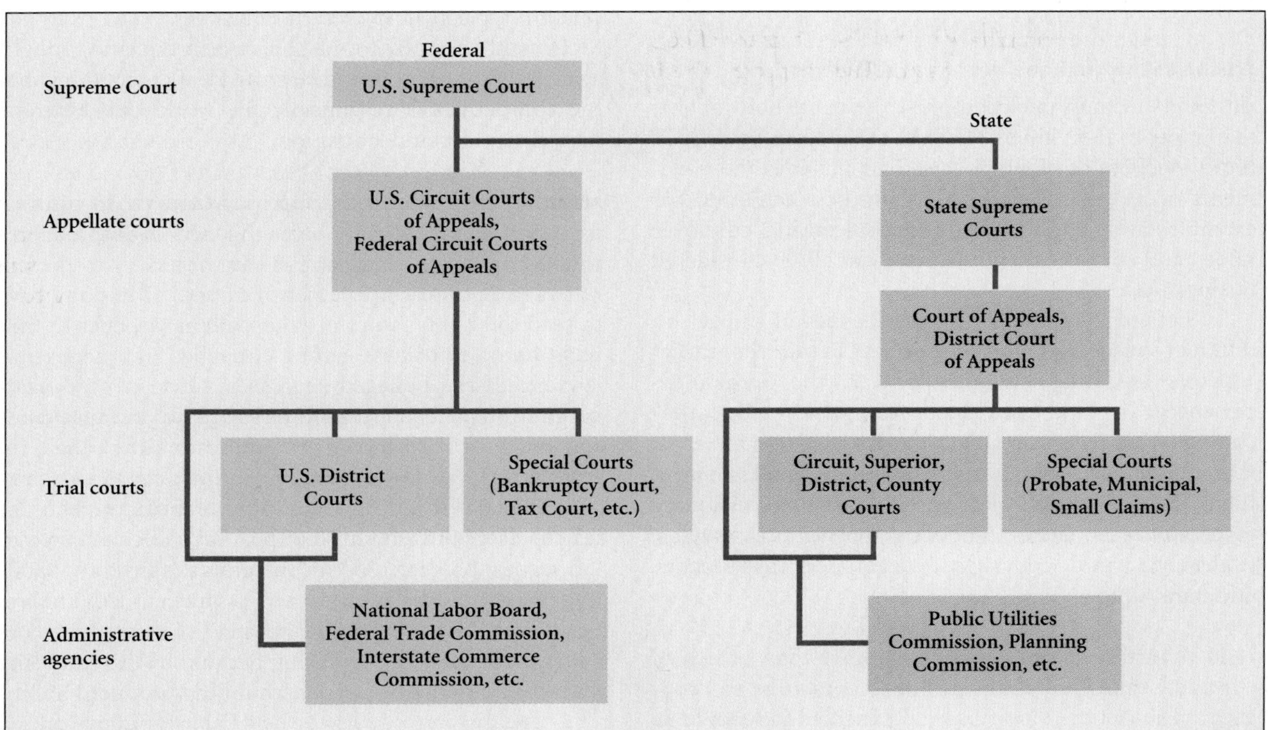

EXHIBIT A.3

The U.S. Court System

A legal proceeding may begin in a trial court or an administrative agency (examples of each are given here). An unfavorable decision may be appealed to a higher court at the federal or state level. (The court of appeals is the highest court in states that have no state supreme court; some other states have no intermediate appellate court.) The U.S. Supreme Court, the country's highest court, is the court of final appeal.

expense and unpredictability of business litigation. However, opponents say that business courts are likely to favor local companies in disputes involving out-of-state litigants. Moreover, they say that the courts are likely to come under the influence of powerful business special-interest groups. It remains to be seen whether more states establish special business courts, but at least nine are currently considering it.[26]

In legal proceedings, common law, administrative law, and statutory law may all be applicable. If they conflict, statutory law generally prevails. However, the three forms of law overlap to such an extent that the differences between them are often indistinguishable. For instance, if you bought what you thought was a goose-down coat and then found out that it was actually filled with reprocessed polyester, you could sue the coat manufacturer for misrepresentation. Although the basis for this suit is an old concept in common law, it has also been incorporated in state and federal legislation against fraudulent and misleading advertising, which is further interpreted and enforced by the Federal Trade Commission.

Business-Related Law

Although business must comply with the full body of laws that apply to individuals, a subset of laws can be defined more precisely as **business law.** This includes those elements of law that directly affect business activities. For example, laws pertaining to business licensing, employee safety, and corporate income taxes can all be considered business law.

Different laws have varying degrees of impact on different businesses and industries. Recall the earlier example regarding the imbalance in the burden experienced by large and small companies when they comply with federal regulations. For the remainder of this chapter, we will examine in more detail some of the specific categories of laws affecting business, including torts; contracts; agency; property transactions; patents, trademarks, and copyrights; negotiable instruments; and bankruptcy.

Torts A **tort** is a noncriminal act (other than breach of contract) that results in injury to a person or to property.[27] The victim of a tort is legally entitled to some form of financial compensation, or **damages,** for his loss and suffering. This compensation is also known as a *compensatory damage award.* In some cases, the victim may also receive a *punitive damage award* to punish the wrongdoer if the misdeed was glaringly bad. You may have heard about cases of excessively high punitive damage awards, such as the $4 million punitive judgment against BMW for retouching a car with paint damage and selling it as new, or the $1.2 million awarded a former Home Depot worker after a jury found that she was sexually harassed and unfairly terminated. However, a recent Cornell University study found that punitive damages are awarded in only about 6 percent of cases nationwide, and that the majority of them are commensurate with compensatory damage awards.[28] Such cases involve tort law, which covers both intentional torts and negligence.

INTENTIONAL TORTS An **intentional tort** is a willful act that results in injury. For example, accidentally knocking a ball through someone's window while you're playing softball is a tort, but purposely cutting down someone's tree because it obscures your view is an intentional tort. Note that *intent* in this case does not mean the intent to cause harm; it is the intent to commit a specific physical act. Some intentional torts involve communication of false statements that harm another's reputation. If the communication is in writing or on television, it is called *libel*; if it is spoken, it is *slander.*[29] For example, McDonald's recently won a libel case in England brought against two activists who distributed leaflets claiming that the company was responsible for worldwide environmental damage and starvation.[30]

NEGLIGENCE AND PRODUCT LIABILITY In contrast to intentional torts, torts of **negligence** involve a failure to use a reasonable amount of care necessary to protect others from unreasonable risk of injury.[31] You don't have to read too many issues of your daily newspaper to find mention of a business getting entangled in a negligence lawsuit. Cases of alleged negligence often involve **product liability,** which is a product's capacity to cause damages or injury for which the producer or seller is held responsible. For example, over 200 health-care workers have sued Johnson & Johnson and other manufacturers of latex medical gloves because of health problems linked to lubricating powder used on the gloves.[32] Product-liability lawsuits cost business owners as much as $150 billion every year.[33] In addition to the sheer costs of these lawsuits, such cases are perplexing because of the confusing and often conflicting laws surrounding product liability.

A company may also be held liable for injury caused by a defective product even if the company used all reasonable care in the manufacture, distribution, or sale of its product. Such **strict product liability** makes it possible to assign liability without assigning fault. It must only be established that (1) the company is in the business of selling the product, (2) the product reached the customer or user without substantial change in its condition, (3) the product was defective, (4) the defective condition rendered the product unreasonably dangerous, and (5) the defective product caused the injury.[34]

Although few people would argue that individual victims of harmful products are entitled to some sort of compensation, many people question whether such strict interpretation of product-liability laws is good for society. Many individuals try to take advantage of the system by filing "frivolous" lawsuits. The large compensatory, and sometimes punitive, damages that plaintiffs are awarded makes it difficult for many companies to obtain product-liability insurance at a reasonable price. As a result, manufacturers have withheld products from the market that might otherwise benefit society. Although Congress passed a bill in 1996 that restricted the amounts of compensatory and punitive damages awarded in product-liability suits, the bill was vetoed by President Clinton, who felt that it was too restrictive and would have a negative impact on consumers. Nonetheless, the issue continues to be a priority with lawmakers.[35]

Contracts Broadly defined, a **contract** is an exchange of promises between two or more parties that is enforceable by law. Many business transactions—including buying and selling products, hiring employees, purchasing group insurance, and licensing technology—involve contracts. Contracts may be either express or implied. An **express contract** is derived from the words (either oral or written) of the parties; an **implied contract** stems from the actions or conduct of the parties.[36] Iris Kapustein learned the hard way how important contracts can be in the business world. When she first started her trade show management and consulting firm, Iris operated on the principle of "my word is my bond." But after losing $15,000 to clients who didn't pay, she adopted a new principle: All clients must sign contracts, and all contracts supplied by clients must be reviewed by her attorney.[37]

ELEMENTS OF A CONTRACT The law of contracts deals largely with identifying the exchanges that can be classified as contracts. The following factors must usually be present for a contract to be valid and enforceable:

- *An offer must be made.* One party must propose that an agreement be entered into. The offer may be oral or written, but it must be firm, definite, and specific enough to make it clear that someone intends to be legally bound by the offer. Finally, the offer must be communicated to the intended party or parties.
- *An offer must be accepted.* For an offer to be accepted, there must be clear intent (spoken, written, or by action) to enter into the contract. An implied contract arises when a person requests or accepts something and the other party has indicated that payment is expected. If, for example, your car breaks down on the road and you call a mobile mechanic and ask him or her to repair it, you are obligated to pay the reasonable value for the services, even if you didn't agree to specific charges beforehand. However, when a specific offer is made, the acceptance must satisfy the terms of the offer. For example, if someone offers you a car for $18,000, and you say you would take it for $15,000, you have not accepted the offer. Your response is a *counteroffer,* which may or may not be accepted by the salesperson.
- *Both parties must give consideration.* A contract is legally binding only when the parties have bargained with one another and exchanged something of value, which is called the **consideration.** The relative value of each party's consideration does not generally matter to the courts. In other words, if you make a deal with someone and later decide you didn't get enough in the deal, that result is not the court's concern. You entered into the deal with the original consideration in mind, and that fact is legally sufficient.[38]
- *Both parties must give genuine assent.* To have a legally enforceable contract, both parties must agree to it voluntarily. The contract must be free of fraud, duress, undue influence, and mutual mistake.[39] If only one party makes a mistake, it ordinarily does not affect the contract. On the other hand, if both parties make a mistake, the agreement would be void. For example, if both the buyer and seller of a business believed it was profitable, when in reality the business was operating at a loss, their agreement would be void.
- *Both parties must be competent.* The law gives to certain classes of people only a limited capacity to enter into contracts. Minors, people who are senile or insane, and in some cases those who are intoxicated cannot usually be bound by a contract for anything but the bare necessities: food, clothing, shelter, and medical care.
- *The contract must not involve an illegal act.* Courts will not enforce a promise that involves an illegal act. For example, a drug dealer cannot get help

from the courts to enforce a contract to deliver illegal drugs at a prearranged price.

- *The contract must be in proper form.* Most contracts can be made orally, by an act, or by a casually written document; however, certain contracts are required by law to be in writing. For example, the transfer of goods worth $500 or more must be accompanied by a written document. The written form is also required for all real estate contracts.

A contract need not be long; all these elements of a contract may be contained in a simple document (see Exhibit A.4). In fact, a personal check is one type of simple contract.

CONTRACT PERFORMANCE Contracts normally expire when the agreed-to conditions have been met, called *performance* in legal terms. However, not all contracts run their expected course. Both parties involved can agree to back out of the contract, for instance. In other cases, one party fails to live up to the terms of the contract, a situation called **breach of contract.** The other party has several options at that point:

- *Discharge.* When one party violates the terms of the agreement, generally the other party is under no obligation to continue with his or her end of the contract. In other words, the second party is discharged from the contract.
- *Damages.* A party has the right to sue in court for damages that were foreseeable at the time the contract was entered into and that result from the other party's failure to fulfill the contract. The amount of damages awarded usually reflects the amount of profit lost and often includes court costs as well.
- *Specific performance.* A party can be compelled to live up to the terms of the contract if money damages would not be adequate.

UOP, a petroleum-processing technology company, recently sued Andersen Consulting for breach of contract after computer systems installed by Andersen failed to deliver the results promised. UOP hopes to recover financial losses it claims resulted from the faulty systems and inadequate consultation.[40]

In the past, most businesspeople negotiated informally with each other when there were contract problems. In recent years, however, companies have increasingly resorted to litigation to solve problems. Not surprisingly, this tendency has increased the costs of doing business. In response, some companies are now experimenting with alternatives to the courtroom, including independent mediators who sit down with the two parties and try to hammer out a satisfactory solution to contract problems, and mandatory arbitration, in which an impartial arbitrator or arbitration panel hears evidence from both sides and makes a legally binding decision. However, mandatory arbitration has come under fire by consumer groups because it can wipe out a customer's right to sue. For example, Gateway 2000 includes a clause in the purchase agreement documents it ships with every computer stating that any dispute or controversy arising from an agreement to purchase a Gateway 2000 product "shall be settled exclusively and finally by arbitration." Moreover, the courts have ruled that failure to read such documents constitutes acceptance of Gateway's terms. Although some consumers prefer to use alternative dispute resolution, those who do not wish to waive their right to sue are advised to read the fine print of all contracts and purchase agreements. The same applies to employment and service contracts.[41]

The band entitled XYZ agrees to provide entertainment at the Club de Hohenzollern on April 30, 1999 between 8:30 P.M. and midnight.

The band will be paid $500.00 for its performance.

Signed on the date of

February 19, 1999

Violetta Harvey

Violetta Harvey,
Manager,
Club de Hohenzollern
and

Ralph Perkins

Ralph Perkins,
Manager, XYZ

EXHIBIT A.4

Elements of a Contract

This simple document contains all the essential elements of a valid contract.

WARRANTIES The Uniform Commercial Code specifies that everyday sales transactions are a special kind of contract (although this provision applies only to tangible goods, not services), even though they may not meet all the exact requirements of regular contracts. Related to the sales contract is the notion of a **warranty,** which is a statement specifying what the producer of a product will do to compensate the buyer if the product is defective or if it malfunctions. Warranties come in several flavors. One important distinction is between *express warranties,* which are specific, written statements, and *implied warranties,* which are unwritten but involve certain protections under the law. Also, warranties are either *full* or *limited.* The former obligates the seller to repair or replace the product, without charge, in the event of any defect or malfunction, whereas the latter imposes restrictions on the defects or malfunctions that will be covered. Warranty laws also address a number of other details, including giving consumers instructions on how to exercise their rights under the warranty.[42]

Agency These days it seems that nearly every celebrity has an agent. Basketball players hire agents to get them shoe commercials and handle their contract negotiations; authors' agents sell manuscripts to the publishers that offer the largest advances; actors' agents try to find choice movie and television roles for their clients. These relationships illustrate a common legal association known as **agency,** which exists when one party, known as the *principal,* authorizes another party, known as the *agent,* to act on his or her behalf in contractual matters.[43]

All contractual obligations come into play in agency relationships. The principal usually creates this relationship by explicit authorization. In some cases—where a transfer of property is involved, for example—the authorization must be written in the form of a document called **power of attorney,** which states that one person may legally act for another (to the extent authorized).

Usually, an agency relationship is terminated when the objective of the relationship is met or at the end of a period specified in the contract between agent and principal. It may also be ended by a change of circumstances, by the agent's breach of duty or loyalty, or by the death of either party.

Property Transactions Anyone interested in business must know the basics of property law. Most people think of property as some object they own (a book, a car, a house). However, **property** is actually the relationship between the person having the rights to any tangible or intangible object and all other persons. The law recognizes two primary types of property: real and personal. **Real property** is land and everything permanently attached to it, such as trees, fences, or mineral deposits. **Personal property** is all property that is not real property; it may be tangible (cars, jewelry, or anything having a physical existence) or intangible (bank accounts, stocks, insurance policies, customer lists). A piece of marble in the earth is real property until it is cut and sold as a block, when it becomes personal property. Property rights are subject to various limitations and restrictions. For example, the government monitors the use of real property for the welfare of the public, to the point of explicitly prohibiting some property uses and abuses.[44]

Two types of documents are important in obtaining real property for factory, office, or store space: a deed and a lease. A **deed** is a legal document by which an owner transfers the *title,* or right of ownership, to real property to a new owner. A lease is used for a temporary transfer of interest in real property. The party that owns the property is commonly called the landlord; the party that occupies or gains the right to occupy the property is the tenant. The tenant pays the landlord, usually in periodic installments, for the use of the property. Generally, a lease may be granted for any length of time that the two parties agree on.

Patents, Trademarks, and Copyrights If you invent a product, write a book, develop some new software, or simply come up with a unique name for your business, you probably want to prevent other people from using or prospering from your **intellectual property** without fairly compensating you. Several forms of legal protection are available for your creations. They include patents, trademarks, and copyrights. Which one you should use depends on what you have created. Having a patent, copyright, or trademark still doesn't guarantee that your idea or product will not be copied. In fact, experts say that U.S. companies lose $200 billion a year to counterfeiters.[45] However, they do provide you with legal recourse when your creations are infringed upon.

PATENTS A patent protects the invention or discovery of a new and useful process, an article of manufacture, a machine, a chemical substance, or an improvement on any of these. Issued by the U.S. Patent Office, a patent grants the owner the right to exclude others from making, using, or selling the invention for 17 years. After that time, the patent becomes available for common use. On the one hand, patent law guarantees the originator the right to use the discovery exclusively for a relatively long period of time, thus encouraging people to devise new machines, gadgets, and processes. On the other hand, it also ensures that rights to the new item will be released eventually, allowing other enterprises to discover even

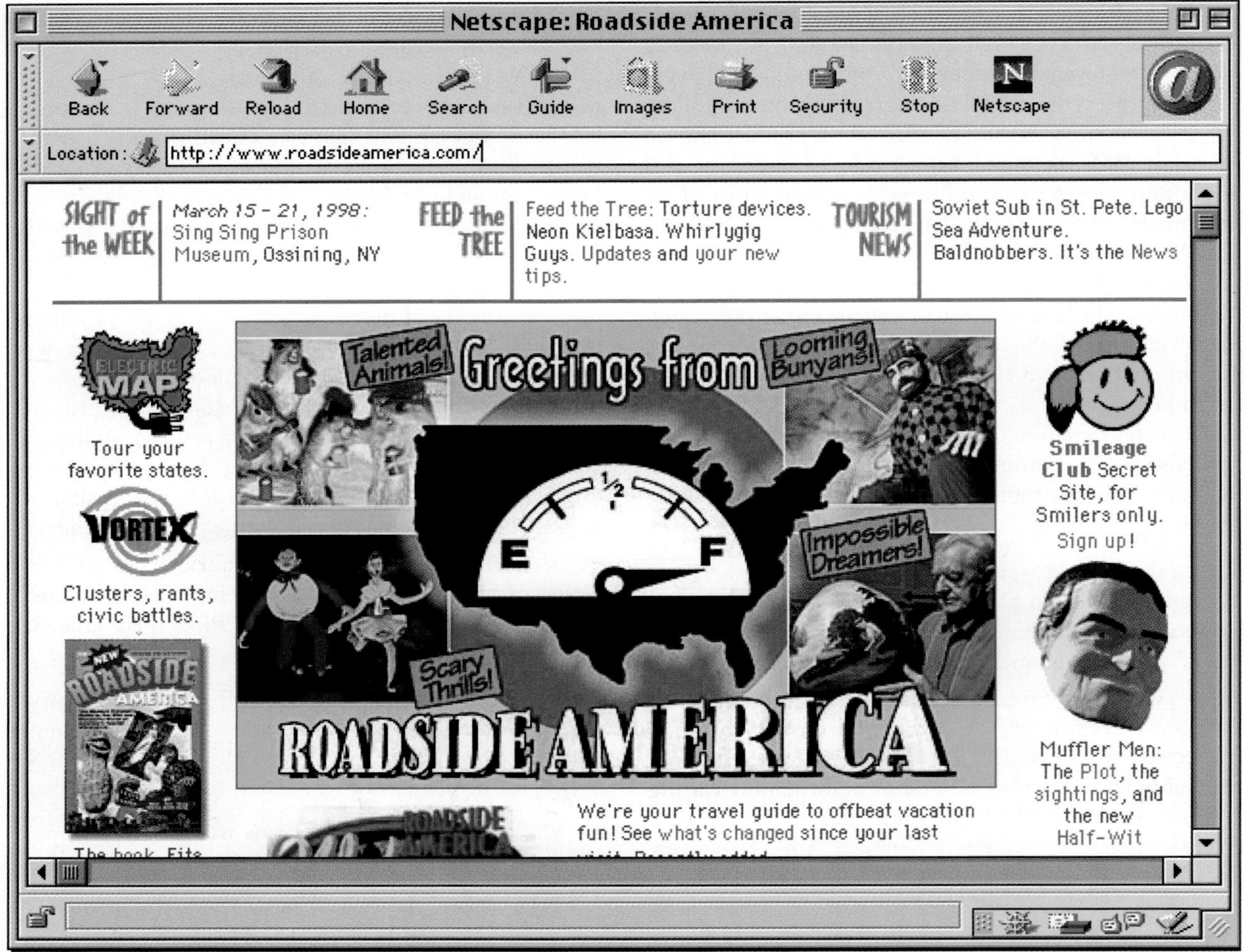

Roadside America and other companies that publish information on the World Wide Web often copyright the information and have guidelines for how it may be used.

more innovative ways to use it. As you might imagine, the number of software patents issued has skyrocketed since the early 1990s. However, you might be surprised to know that the greatest number of software patents by far are held by IBM, a company known more for its market power in computer hardware.[46]

TRADEMARKS A trademark is any word, name, symbol, or device used to distinguish the product of one manufacturer from those made by others. A service mark is the same thing for services. McDonald's golden arches are one of the most visible of modern trademarks. Brand names can also be registered as trademarks. Examples are Exxon, Polaroid, and Chevrolet.

If properly registered and renewed every 20 years, a trademark generally belongs to its owner forever. Among the exceptions are popular brand names that have become generic terms, meaning that they describe a whole class of products. A brand-name trademark can become a generic term if the trademark has been allowed to expire, if it has been incorrectly used by its owner (as in the case of Borden's ReaLemon lemon juice, which the Federal Trade Commission ruled was being used by Borden to maintain a monopoly in bottled lemon juice), or if the public comes to equate the name with the class of products, as was the case with zipper, linoleum, aspirin, Xerox, and many other brand names.

COPYRIGHTS Copyrights protect the creators of literary, dramatic, musical, artistic, scientific, and other intellectual works. Any printed, filmed, or recorded material can be copyrighted. The copyright gives its owner the exclusive right to reproduce (copy), sell, or adapt the work he or she has created. Copyright law covers reproduction by photocopying, videotape, and magnetic storage.

The Library of Congress Copyright Office will issue a copyright to the creator or to whomever the creator has granted the right to reproduce the work. (A book, for example, may be copyrighted by the author or the publisher.) Copyrights issued after 1977 are valid for the lifetime of the creator plus 50 years. Copyrights issued through 1977 are good for 75 years.

Copyright protection on the Internet has become an especially important topic as more businesses and individuals publish Web sites. Technically, copyright protection exists from the moment material is created. Therefore, anything you post on a Web site is protected by copyright law. However, loose Internet standards and a history of sharing information via the Net has made it difficult for some users to accept this. Experts suggest including copyright and trademark notices on Web pages that contain protected material, including a link on each page to a detailed copyright notice that explains what users can and cannot do, and placing disclaimers on all pages that contain links to other sites to ensure that no warranties or endorsements are made.[47]

Negotiable Instruments Whenever you write a personal check, you are creating a **negotiable instrument,** a transferable document that represents a promise to pay a specified amount. (*Negotiable* in this sense means that it can be sold or used as payment of a debt; an *instrument* is simply a written document that expresses a legal agreement.) In addition to checks, negotiable instruments include certificates of deposit, promissory notes, and the commercial paper you read about in Chapters 18 and 19. To be negotiable, an instrument must meet several criteria:[48]

- It must be in writing and signed by the person who created it.
- It must have an unconditional promise to pay a specified sum of money.
- It must be payable either on demand or at a specified date in the future.
- It must be payable either to some specified person or organization or to the person holding it (the bearer).

You can see how a personal check meets these criteria—when you write one, you are agreeing to pay the amount of the check to the person or organization to whom you're writing it.

Bankruptcy Even though the U.S. legal system establishes the rules of fair play and offers protection from the unscrupulous, it can't prevent most businesses from taking on too much debt. The legal system does, however, provide help for businesses that find themselves in deep financial trouble. **Bankruptcy** is the legal means of relief for debtors (either individuals or businesses) who are no longer able to meet their financial obligations.[49]

Voluntary bankruptcy is initiated by the debtor; *involuntary bankruptcy* is initiated by creditors. The law provides for several types of bankruptcy, which are commonly referred to by chapter number of the Bankruptcy Reform Act. In a Chapter 7 bankruptcy, the debtor's assets will be sold, and the proceeds will be divided equitably among the creditors. Under Chapter 11 (which is usually aimed at businesses but does not exclude individuals other than stockbrokers), a business is allowed to get back on its feet and continue functioning while it arranges to pay its debts.[50] For the steps involved in a Chapter 11 bankruptcy, see Exhibit A.5.

By entering Chapter 11, a company gains time to cut costs and streamline operations. Many companies emerge from Chapter 11 as leaner, healthier organizations. Creditors often benefit too. If the company can get back on its financial feet, creditors may be able to retrieve more of the money they are owed. Consider Carson Pirie Scott & Co. The Milwaukee-based department store chain entered Chapter 11 in 1991 with an $800 million mountain of debt. Today the company is out of bankruptcy, virtually debt free, and bringing in $1 billion a year in revenue.[51] However, filing for bankruptcy is an extremely risky venture and should not be pursued lightly. Bankruptcy can damage a company's or individual's credit rating and reputation for a long time to come. It should never be used as a tactic to avoid paying creditors.

Step 1: All current legal proceedings against the firm are halted. A decision is made to either liquidate or reorganize the firm, based on the value of the firm's assets. If liquidation is chosen, the firm's assets are transferred to a trustee, who sells them to pay the firm's debts. If reorganization is chosen, go to step 2.

Step 2: The courts may appoint a trustee to operate the firm, or current management may continue to operate it. A reorganization plan is developed either by current management, by the trustee, or by a committee of creditors. When plan is developed, go to step 3.

Step 3: Creditors and shareholders vote on the reorganization plan. Plan is ratified if (1) at least one-half of creditors vote in favor and if their claims against the company represent at least two-thirds of total claims; (2) at least two-thirds of shareholders approve the plan; and (3) the plan is confirmed by the court. When plan is ratified, go to step 4.

Step 4: The plan guarantees creditors new securities, and sometimes cash, in exchange for dismissal of their claims. With the firm discharged from its debts, it is free to start anew without the weight of past failures.

EXHIBIT A.5

Steps in Chapter 11 Bankruptcy Proceedings

Chapter 11 bankruptcy may buy a debtor time to reorganize finances and continue operating. However, using this device to evade financial obligations is extremely risky from a legal standpoint, and declaring bankruptcy may severely damage the reputation and credit rating of a firm or an individual.

Questions

For Review

1. What are the major areas in which governments regulate business?
2. In what ways does deregulation benefit consumers? Do all businesses benefit from deregulation? Explain.
3. Explain the difference between a sales tax and an excise tax.
4. How can political action committees benefit business? Why are they controversial?
5. What are the three types of U.S. laws and how do they differ? What additional laws must global companies consider?

For Analysis

6. What is precedent and how does it affect common law?
7. What is the difference between negligence and intentional torts?
8. What does the concept of strict product liability mean to businesses?
9. Why is agency important to business?
10. What is the advantage of declaring Chapter 11 bankruptcy? What is the disadvantage?

For Application

11. If you wrote a poem or short story and published it on your own Web site, would your work be protected under copyright law? What steps should you take to make sure your work is not stolen or misused?
12. As the owner of a small manufacturing firm, why might you be in favor of a law limiting the amount of compensatory and punitive damages awarded in product-liability lawsuits? Why might you be against such a law?

Chapter Glossary

administrative law Rules, regulations, and interpretations of statutory law set forth by administrative agencies and commissions

agency Business relationship that exists when one party (the principal) authorizes another party (the agent) to enter into contracts on the principal's behalf

bankruptcy Legal procedure by which a person or a business that is unable to meet financial obligations is relieved of debt

breach of contract Failure to live up to the terms of a contract, with no legal excuse

business law Those elements of law that directly influence or control business activities

common law Law based on the precedents established by judges' decisions

consent order Settlement in which an individual or organization promises to discontinue some illegal activity without admitting guilt

consideration Negotiated exchange necessary to make a contract legally binding

contract Legally enforceable exchange of promises between two or more parties

customs duties Fees imposed on goods brought into the country; also called import taxes

damages Financial compensation to an injured party for loss and suffering

deed Legal document by which an owner transfers the title, or ownership rights, to real property to a new owner

excise taxes Taxes intended to help control potentially harmful practices or to help pay for government services used only by certain people or businesses

express contract Contract derived from words, either oral or written

implied contract Contract derived from actions or conduct

intellectual property Intangible personal property, such as ideas, songs, trade secrets, and computer programs, that are protected by patents, trademarks, and copyrights

intentional tort Willful act that results in injury

interlocking directorates Situation in which members of the board of one firm sit on the board of a competing firm

international law Principles, customs, and rules that govern the international relationships between states, organizations, and persons

lobbies Groups who try to persuade legislators to vote according to the groups' interests

negligence Tort in which a reasonable amount of care to protect others from unreasonable risk of injury is not used

negotiable instrument Transferable document that represents a promise to pay a specified amount

personal property All property that is not real property

political action committees (PACs) Groups formed under federal election laws to raise money for candidates through employee contributions

power of attorney Written authorization for one party to legally act for another

product liability The capacity of a product to cause harm or damage for which the producer or seller is held accountable.

property Rights held regarding any tangible or intangible object

real property Land and everything permanently attached to it

stare decisis Concept of using previous judicial decisions as the basis for deciding similar court cases

statutory law Statute, or law, created by a legislature

strict product liability Liability for injury caused by a defective product when all reasonable care is used in its manufacture, distribution, or sale; no fault is assigned

tax credit Direct reduction in the amount of income tax owed by a person or business; granted by a government body for engaging or not engaging in selected activities

tax deduction Direct reductions in the amount of income on which a person or business pays taxes

tort Noncriminal act (other than breach of contract) that results in injury to a person or to property

tying contracts Contracts forcing buyers to purchase unwanted goods along with goods actually desired

Uniform Commercial Code (UCC) Set of standardized laws, adopted by most states, that govern business transactions

warranty Statement specifying what the producer of a product will do to compensate the buyer if the product is defective or if it malfunctions

COMPONENT CHAPTER B

RISK MANAGEMENT AND INSURANCE

PROTECTION AGAINST RISK

All businesses face the potential for loss. Fire, lawsuits, accidents, natural disasters, theft, illness, disability, and death are common occurrences that can devastate any business—large or small—if they are not anticipated and prepared for in advance. Of course, managers cannot guard against every conceivable threat of loss. Still, they know that in any given situation, the greater the number of different outcomes that may occur, the greater their company is at *risk.*

Understanding Risk

Risk is a daily fact of life for both businesses and individuals. Most businesses accept the possibility of losing money in order to make money. In fact, it prompts people to go into business in the first place. Although the formal definition of **risk** is the variation in possible outcomes of an event based on chance, it's not unusual to sometimes hear the term used to mean exposure to loss. This second definition is helpful, because it explains why people purchase **insurance**, a contractual arrangement whereby one party agrees to compensate another party for losses. By purchasing insurance, companies contractually transfer the risk of loss to an insurance firm.

Speculative risk refers to those exposures that offer the prospect of making a profit—like investments in stock. Because in most cases speculative risks are not insurable, the idea is to identify the risks, take steps to minimize them, and provide for the funding of potential losses. **Pure risk,** on the other hand, is the threat of loss without the possibility of gain. Disasters such as an earthquake or a fire at a manufacturing plant are examples of pure risk. Nothing good can come from an exposure to pure risk.

An **insurable risk** is one that meets certain requirements in order for the insurer to provide protection, whereas an **uninsurable risk** is one that an insurance company will not cover (see Exhibit B.1). For example, most insurance companies are unwilling to cover potential losses that can occur from general economic conditions like a recession. Such uncertainties are beyond the realm of insurance.

Sometimes uninsurable risks become insurable when enough data become available to permit accurate estimation of future losses. For instance, insurers were

INSURABLE	UNINSURABLE
Property risks: Uncertainty surrounding the occurrence of loss from perils that cause 1. Direct loss of property 2. Indirect loss of property	Market risks: Factors that may result in loss of property or income, such as 1. Price changes, seasonal or cyclical 2. Consumer indifference 3. Style changes 4. Competition offered by a better product
Personal risks: Uncertainty surrounding the occurrence of loss due to 1. Premature death 2. Physical disability 3. Old age	Political risks: Uncertainty surrounding the occurrence of 1. Overthrow of the government 2. Restrictions imposed on free trade 3. Unreasonable or punitive taxation 4. Restrictions on free exchange of currencies
Legal liability risks: Uncertainty surrounding the occurrence of loss arising out of 1. Use of automobiles 2. Occupancy of buildings 3. Employment 4. Manufacture of products 5. Professional misconduct	Production risks: Uncertainties surrounding the occurrence of 1. Failure of machinery to function economically 2. Failure to solve technical problems 3. Exhaustion of raw-material resources 4. Strikes, absenteeism, labor unrest
	Personal risks: Uncertainty surrounding the occurrence of 1. Unemployment 2. Poverty from factors such as divorce, lack of education or opportunity, loss of health from military service

EXHIBIT B.1

Insurable and Uninsurable Risks

Insurance companies consider some pure risks insurable. They usually view speculative risks as uninsurable. (Some pure risks such as flood and strike are also considered uninsurable.)

once reluctant to cover passengers on airplanes, but decades of experience have made these risks predictable. Similarly, companies can now buy insurance against the prospect of a foreign country's seizing their overseas factories, mines, or offices. Generally speaking, a risk is insurable if it meets the following requirements:

- *The loss must be accidental and beyond the insured's control.* For example, a fire insurance policy excludes losses caused by the insured's own arson, but losses caused by an employee's arson would be covered.
- *The loss must be financially measurable.* Although the loss of an apartment building is financially measurable, the loss suffered by having an undesirable tenant is not.
- *A large number of similar cases must be subject to the same peril.* In order for the likelihood of a loss to be predictable, insurance companies must have data on the frequency and severity of losses caused by a given peril. If this information covers a long period of time and is based on a large number of cases or observations, the **law of large numbers** will usually allow insurance companies to predict accurately how many losses will occur in the future. For example, the death rate per 1,000 people in the United States has been calculated with great precision.
- *The risk should be spread over a wide geographic area.* Unless an insurance company spreads its coverage over a large geographic area or a broad population base, a single disaster might force it to pay out on all its policies at once. Consider Hurricane Andrew. This catastrophe caused over $16.3 billion in insured losses, the largest dollar amount of damage claims ever made on the insurance system from a single natural event. Even though all insured claims for the damage caused by Hurricane Andrew were honored, many insurers now restrict the amount of insurance they provide in Florida.[1]
- *The possible loss must be financially serious to the insured.* An insurance company could not afford the paperwork involved in handling numerous small **claims** (demands by the insured that the

insurance company pay for a loss) of a few dollars each; nor would a business be likely to insure such a small loss. For this reason many policies have a clause specifying that the insurance company will pay only that part of a loss greater than an amount stated in the policy. This amount, the **deductible,** represents small losses (like the first $250 of covered repairs) that the insured has agreed to absorb.

Managing Risk

If you own a home or a car, chances are you have purchased insurance to protect yourself from losses due to theft, accidents, fire, and so on. Although a loss from any one of these incidents would be a terrible tragedy, in most cases you would still be able to go to work and earn a living. But what would happen if your industrial plant burned to the ground? Where would your employees work? What would happen to all of your customers who were waiting for their orders to be delivered? Would they take their business elsewhere? Could your business survive?

Managing risk is an important part of running a business. The process of reducing the threat of loss from uncontrollable events and funding potential losses is called **risk management.** Those areas of risk in which a potential for loss exists are called **loss exposures,** and they fall under four headings: (1) loss of property (due to destruction or theft of tangible or intangible assets); (2) loss of income (either through decreased revenues or through increased expenses resulting from an accidental event); (3) legal liability to others, including employees; and (4) loss of the services of key personnel (through accidental injury or death).

In a large company, the function of establishing programs and policies to prevent and fund losses is typically performed by the *risk manager,* whose job has become increasingly complex and critical. Risk managers must understand the types of risk their company faces and develop methods for dealing with them. In short they must (1) decide whether to take on (assume) risk, or finance it by purchasing conventional insurance or establishing some form of self-insurance program; (2) implement a risk-management program that is cost effective and provides maximum risk protection; and (3) monitor and modify these choices as conditions change by setting standards for acceptable performance, comparing actual results with these standards, and modifying risk management techniques to comply more fully with them.

But what if you own a small company and cannot afford to hire a risk manager? Somebody still has to take care of "that insurance stuff." In most small companies, managers, even the company president, must perform at least some of these functions themselves. Experts recommend that all companies should ask these questions: What do I have? What can go wrong? What's the minimum I need to stay in business? And, what's the best way to protect the company's assets?[2] Furthermore, smart managers recognize that risk management is really everybody's job. Practically every employee can take steps to reduce his or her company's exposure to risk by preventing it or controlling it altogether. For instance, in its simplest form, this means fixing the loose step because sooner or later someone's going to trip over it.

Assessing Risk

One of the first steps in protecting against risk is identifying where it exists. Consider just one of the many loss exposures that a manufacturer of stuffed toys must face: First, the manufacturer must identify the ways a consumer (most likely a child) can be injured by a stuffed toy. Among numerous possibilities, the child might choke on button eyes, get sick from eating the stuffing, or have an allergic reaction to any material in the toy. Second, the company must identify any possible flaws in the production or marketing of the toy that might lead to one of these injuries; for example, a child may have an allergic reaction to the toy if its materials are not carefully tested for allergenic substances, if impurities enter the toy during manufacture, or if the toy is not properly packaged (allowing foreign substances to reach it). Third, the manufacturer must analyze these possibilities in order to predict product-liability losses accurately.

Sometimes it is impossible to identify all the ways a product might cause injury or property damage. Look at Mattel. It voluntarily took its Cabbage Patch Kids Snacktime Kids Dolls off the shelves after enduring a rash of complaints that the doll not only chomped intended plastic food but munched on children's hair and fingers as well. At least one lawsuit was filed against Mattel and Wal-Mart asking for $25 million on behalf of a 9-year-old girl whose hair was reportedly chewed to the scalp. After offering a $40 cash refund to each consumer for the return of approximately 500,000 dolls, Mattel learned its lesson the hard way. It had plenty of product-liability insurance; it did not have product recall insurance.[3]

Controlling Risk

Once you've assessed your potential risk, the next step is to try to control it. Here are some of the *risk-control techniques* managers use to minimize an organization's losses:

- *Risk avoidance.* A risk manager might try to eliminate completely the chance of a particular type of loss. With rare exceptions, such risk avoidance is not practical. The stuffed-toy manufacturer could avoid being sued for a child's allergic reaction by not making stuffed toys, but, of course, the company would also be out of business.
- *Loss prevention.* A risk manager may try to reduce (but not totally eliminate) the *chance* of a given loss by removing hazards or taking preventive measures. Security guards at banks, warnings on medicines and dangerous chemicals, and safety locks are examples of loss prevention.
- *Loss reduction.* A risk manager may try to reduce the *severity* of the losses that do occur. Examples include installing overhead sprinklers to prevent extensive damage during a fire, or paying the medical expenses of an injured consumer to reduce the punitive damages exposure and likelihood of litigation.
- *Risk-control transfer.* A risk manager may try to eliminate risk by transferring to some other person or group either (1) the actual property or activity responsible for the risk or (2) the responsibility for the risk. For example, a firm can sell a building to eliminate the risks of ownership.

Avoiding accidents and injuries through such measures as protective clothing is an important step in managing corporate risk.

Financing Risk

Of course, not all risk is controllable. Whereas some companies choose to fully accept the financial consequences of a loss themselves—especially when the potential loss costs are small or can be financed by the company itself—others choose to finance it. *Risk financing* determines when and by whom the costs of losses are borne.

Shifting Risk to an Insurance Company By purchasing insurance, companies transfer the risk of loss to an outside insurance company that agrees to pay for certain types of losses.

BASIC INSURANCE CONCEPTS Insurance is an intangible good; a contingent promise to be delivered in the future. When companies purchase insurance, they transfer a group's (but not an individual's) predicted losses to an insurance pool. The pool combines the cost of the potential losses to be financed and then redistributes them back to the individuals exposed (in advance) by charging them a fee known as a **premium.**

Actuaries determine how much income insurance companies need to generate from premiums by compiling statistics of losses, predicting the amount they will have to pay in claims over a given period, and calculating the amount needed to cover these expenses plus any anticipated operating costs. Keep in mind that insurance companies don't count on making a profit on any particular policy, nor do they count on paying for a single policyholder's losses out of the premium paid by that particular policyholder. Rather, the insurance company pays for a loss by drawing the money out of the pool of funds it has received from all its policyholders in the form of premiums (see Exhibit B.2). In this way, the insurance company redistributes the cost of predicted losses from a single individual to a large number of policies.

One of the most challenging activities in an insurance company is underwriting new business. **Underwriters** review the insurance applications and either accept them at an appropriate rate or reject them. In recent years, some insurance companies have begun experimenting with computerized expert systems to supplement, and in some cases replace, company underwriters. However, because many underwriting decisions are based on an appraisal of the applicant's past moral behavior, these systems generally are reserved for small, routine cases.[4]

PRIVATE INSURANCE COMPANIES In its simplest form, the idea of insurance is probably as old as humankind. Since the days of the cave dweller, groups of people have banded together to help one another in times of trouble. They have stored food in years of plenty so

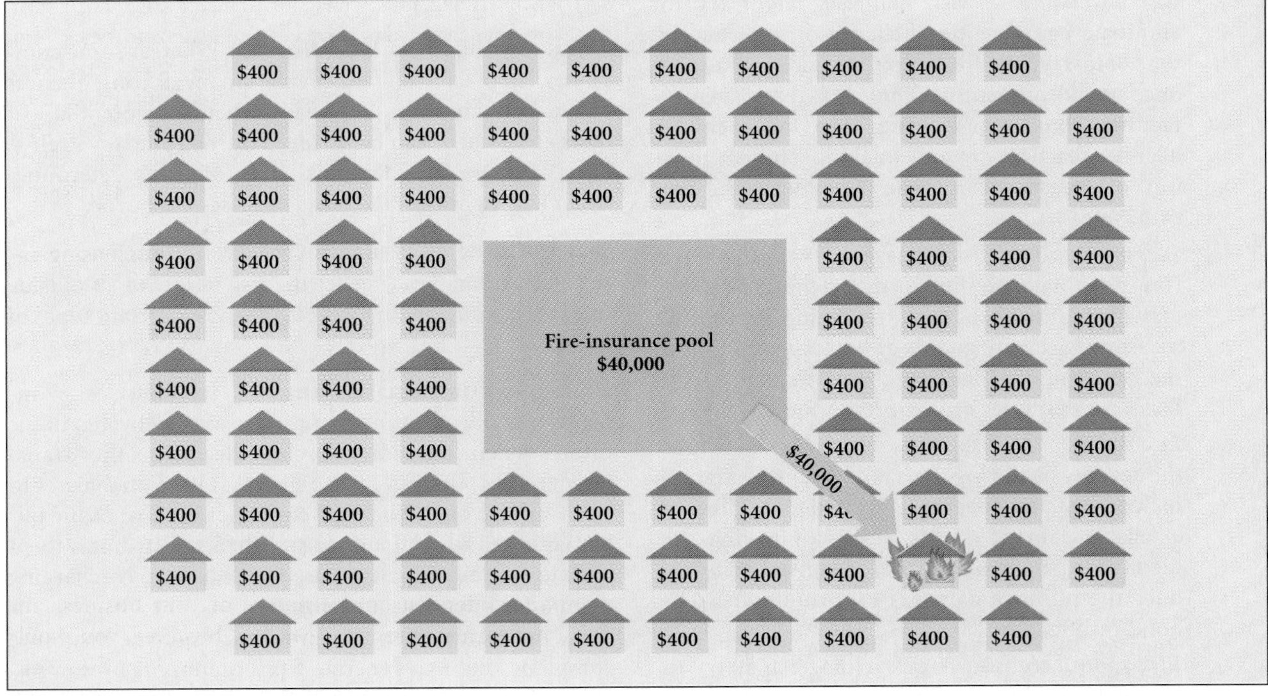

EXHIBIT B.2

How Insurance Works

An insurance company covers the cost of a policyholder's loss out of the premiums paid by a large pool of policyholders. Thus, if 100 policyholders pay $400 each to insure against fire damage, the insurance company can afford to compensate one policyholder who actually suffers fire damage with $40,000.

that they would have something to draw on during years of famine. If their neighbor's house burned, they helped rebuild it, with the tacit understanding that the favor would be returned if they were ever in need. Over the years, the informal cooperation between neighbors gradually became institutionalized. Mutual-aid societies were formed, and dues were collected from the members for use in emergencies. Ultimately, modern insurance companies emerged, with professional management.

Thousands of private insurance companies are currently doing business in the United States; most are either *stock* or *mutual* companies.[5] All private insurance companies are regulated by state law. A **stock insurance company** is similar to all other profit-making corporations; shareholders (who need not be policyholders) receive dividends or capital gains on their investment in the company. A **mutual insurance company** is a nonprofit cooperative owned by its policyholders. Excess income may be returned to the policyholders, either in the form of dividends or as a reduction in their insurance premiums.

Self-insuring Against Risk Self-insurance is becoming an increasingly popular method of insuring against risk. Because self-insurance plans are not subject to state regulation, mandates, and premium taxes (typically 2 percent), companies that use self-insurance often save quite a bit of money. Deciding to **self-insure** with a liability reserve fund means putting aside a certain sum each year to cover predicted liability losses. Unless payments to the self-insurance fund are calculated scientifically and paid regularly, a true self-insurance system does not exist.

Keep in mind that self-insurance differs greatly from "going bare" or having no reserve funds. Self-insurance implies an attempt by business to combine a sufficient number of its own similar exposures to predict the losses accurately. It also implies that adequate financial arrangements have been made in advance to provide funds to pay for losses should they occur.

Nevertheless, some losses are unpredictable. Companies that self-insure often set aside a revenue or self-insurance contingency fund to cover any unexpected or large losses. That way, if disaster strikes, companies won't have to borrow funds to cover their losses, or be forced out of business.

Setting aside enough money to cover catastrophes in a small company is virtually impossible, however. Consequently, some companies solve this problem by joining cooperatives or *risk-retention* groups, collections of companies that band together to self-insure. Look at Zebra Technologies, a maker of industrial printers. Randy Whitchurch, Zebra's CFO, is just the kind of hardheaded business executive who is giving big insurance companies headaches these days. Tired of paying hefty insurance premiums, Whitchurch joined a cooperative of about 20 businesses that insure themselves, slashing Zebra's annual insurance bill from $140,000 to $95,000.[6]

Most companies that self-insure, however, protect themselves from disaster by purchasing excess insurance from commercial insurers called *stop-loss insurance.* This additional insurance is designed to cover losses that would exceed a company's own financial capabilities. Unfortunately, some companies are using self-insurance to avoid state regulation. They are establishing qualified self-insurance plans but purchasing enough stop-loss insurance to actually shift the risk right back to a private insurance company. This virtually eliminates their loss exposure while allowing them to escape state regulation and costly mandates. Meanwhile, recent efforts by state legislatures and the National Association of Insurance Commissioners (NAIC), a private, nonprofit association of state insurance commissioners, to curb these shams are meeting strong opposition from small businesses. That's because small businesses can't afford to absorb the proposed $20,000 minimum payout per employee before stop-loss insurance kicks in.[7]

Most self-insurers protect themselves from disasters by purchasing stop-loss insurance.

Still, self-insurance is not for everyone. For example, consider health insurance. When the number of employees covered by a self-insured health plan drops below 50, one or two major illnesses can suddenly make a big difference. Experts advise that companies should consider self-insurance plans only if they are prepared to handle the worst-case scenario (usually the point at which stop-loss insurance kicks in), and that self-insurance should be used only as a long-term strategy. That's because in some years the cost to self-insure will be lower than the cost of commercial insurance, whereas in other years it will be higher. In the long run, however, statistics show that the good and bad years should average out in the employer's favor.[8]

TYPES OF BUSINESS INSURANCE

If you were starting a business, what types of insurance would you need? To some extent, the answer to that question would depend on the nature of your business and your potential for loss. In general, however, you would probably want to protect yourself against these four types of loss exposures: loss of property, loss of income, liability, and loss of services of key personnel (see Exhibit B.3).

Some small business owners underestimate the importance of having adequate insurance. Take Eric Goodman. Shortly after Goodman got Wood Classics (a chair manufacturing business) off the ground, disaster hit. First, Goodman almost sliced off his thumb. But without health and disability insurance, he went though half his savings to cover medical expenses and loss of income. Then four years later, Goodman received another blow—this time a legal one. Wood Classics was sued for $3 million by an unhappy customer who claimed he injured himself by falling out of a chair he built from a Wood Classics' kit. Again, Goodman was underinsured. With only $1 million in liability insurance, Goodman settled the case and learned his lesson the hard way—for the second time. Today Wood Classics carries $5 million in liability insurance.[9]

Loss of Property

Property can be lost through a variety of causes, including accidental damage, natural disaster, and theft. Property can also be lost through employee dishonesty and nonperformance.

Loss Due to Destruction or Theft When a cannery in California ships jars of pizza sauce by a truck to New York, the goods face unavoidable risks in transit. One wrong turn could cover a whole hillside with broken glass and

RISK	PROTECTION
Loss of property	
Due to destruction or theft	Fire insurance Disaster insurance Marine insurance Automobile insurance
Due to dishonesty or nonperformance	Fidelity bonding Surety bonding Credit life insurance Crime insurance
Loss of income	Business-interruption insurance Extra-expense insurance Contingent business-interruption insurance
Liabililty	Comprehensive general liability insurance Automobile liability insurance Workers' compensation insurance Umbrella liability insurance Professional liability insurance
Loss of services of key personnel	Key-person insurance

EXHIBIT B.3

Business Risks and Protection

Here are some of the more widely purchased types of business insurance.

sauce, which would represent a sizable loss to the manufacturer. The canning factory itself is vulnerable to fire, flood, and (especially in California) earthquake.

Property insurance covers the insured for physical damage to or destruction of property and also for its loss by theft. When purchasing property insurance, the buyer has three coverage options: replacement cost, actual cash value, or functional replacement cost. **Replacement-cost coverage** means that the insurer promises to pay an amount equal to the full cost of repairing or replacing the property even if the property was old or run-down before the loss occurred. Because the insured is often better off after the loss, the premium for this type of coverage is generally quite expensive.

Actual cash value coverage assumes that the property that was lost or damaged was worth less than new property because of normal aging or use. Thus, the insurance company will pay the amount that allows the insured to return the property to its same state before the incident. Sometimes, however, it does not pay to restore a property to its same state because the replacement cost of a building is greater than its market value (as is often the case with older, inner-city structures). **Functional-replacement-cost coverage** allows for the substitution of modern construction materials such as wallboard instead of plaster to restore a property to a similar, functioning state.

Loss Due to Dishonesty or Nonperformance Dishonest employees and criminals outside the company pose yet another threat to business property and assets. Various ways exist for addressing this problem. One is a **fidelity bond,** which protects the insured business against dishonest acts committed by employees, such as embezzlement, forgery, and theft.

Another is a **surety bond,** a three-party contract where the surety (insurance company) is required to pay a second party (the obligee) if a third party (the principal) fails to fulfill an obligation to the obligee. By law, surety bonds are required in public construction projects in order to guarantee the performance of every contract and complete construction in a timely manner. Exhibit B.4 shows how a surety works. Say, for example, a contractor (the principal) fails to meet its obligation to a school board. The school board (the obligee) could collect from the insurance company (the surety) and use that money to pay a new contractor to finish the work. Surety bonds are also used to protect against fraud. For example, if a contractor substitutes lower-quality materials than those specified in the contract, the insurance company would be responsible for reimbursing the obligee for damages incurred.[10]

Consequential Loss Exposure

When disasters strike, like a fire or flood, property loss is only one part of the story. Disasters not only disrupt the

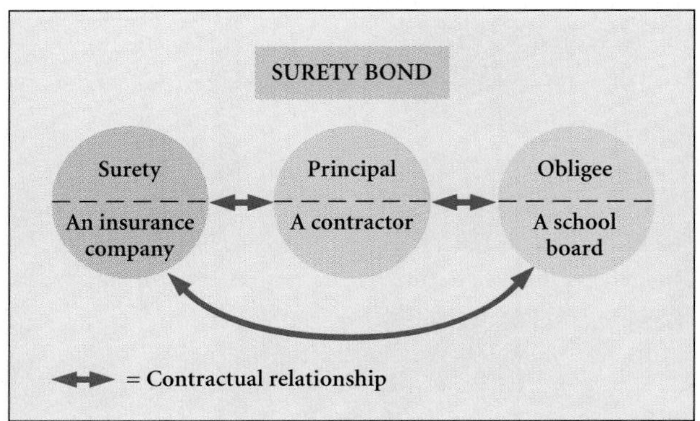

EXHIBIT B.4

Surety Bonding

The surety bond removes uncertainty from major construction projects by guaranteeing the contractor's performance.

business operation, but often they result in temporary shutdown, costing the company far more than the equipment repairs or replacement of damaged stock. That's because expenses continue—salaries, interest payments, rent—even though the company is not earning revenues. Disruption also results in extra expenses: leasing temporary space, paying overtime to meet work schedules with a reduced capacity, or buying additional advertising to assure the public that the business is still a going concern. In fact, a prolonged interruption of business could even cause bankruptcy.

For this reason, many companies carry *consequential loss insurance.* Available coverage includes **business-interruption insurance,** which protects the insured against lost profits and continuing expenses when a fire or other disaster causes a company to shut down temporarily; **extra-expense insurance,** which pays the additional costs of maintaining the operation in temporary quarters; and **contingent business-interruption insurance,** which protects against a company's loss of profit due to the misfortune of another business, such as a fire or other disaster that interrupts the operation of an important supplier, or the closing of an anchor store in the mall where the business is located.

Many companies discovered the value of business-interruption insurance when the Alfred P. Murrah Federal Building in Oklahoma City was bombed. Small firms in a 50-block area sustained about $500 million worth of damage from the explosion. However, Hogan Information Services, an Oklahoma City firm that collects nationwide credit-reporting information for companies and creditors, was closed for only 3 days following the explosion. That's because Hogan had purchased business-interruption insurance, and Kemper, Hogan's insurer, paid all the costs for relocating the company to another building, six blocks away.[11]

Liability Insurance

Liability insurance provides protection against a number of perils. **Liability losses** are financial losses suffered by firms or individuals held responsible for property damage or injuries suffered by others. In general, liability losses arise from three sources: First, an organization must pay legal damages awarded by a court to the injured party if they are found negligent; second, the costs of a legal defense can be quite expensive; third, the costs of loss prevention or identifying potential liability problems so they may be handled in an appropriate way can also add up. To accommodate theses various sources of liability, the insurance industry has created the following types of liability policies:

- *Commercial general liability.* This basic coverage automatically provides protection against all forms of liability not specifically excluded under the terms of the policy. Examples would be liability for operations on business premises, product liability, completed operations, and operations of independent contractors. When purchasing commercial liability insurance, the buyer has two options: An *occurrence-based liability policy* requires the carrier providing the insurance at the time the injury was sustained to pay the claim even if the claim is made 25 years after the policy expired; a *claims-made liability policy* obligates the insurer to pay for claims made against the insured only during the policy period and arising from incidents occurring after a date stated in the policy.[12]
- *Product liability.* Manufacturers of a product have a legal duty to design and produce a product that will not injure people in normal use. In addition, products must be packaged carefully and accompanied by adequate instructions and warnings so consumers may use them properly and avoid injury. If these duties are not fulfilled and result in an injured user, a potential for a product-liability lawsuit exists. **Product-liability coverage** protects insured companies from being threatened financially when someone claims

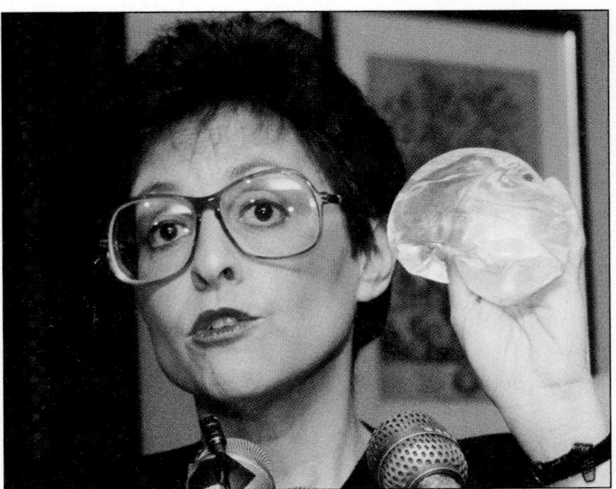

Author Karen Berger was one of the leading authorities in the recent product-liability debates over the safety of silicone breast implants.

that one of their products caused damage, injury, or death.

- *Automobile liability.* Many companies also carry insurance that specifically covers liability connected with any vehicles owned or operated by the company. Some states have **no-fault insurance laws,** which means that all parties involved in an automobile accident receive compensation for their injuries from their own insurer, regardless of who causes the accident. According to current no-fault plans, after some threshold of damage has been reached, the injured party may revert to the liability system to seek compensation for loss. In some cases this threshold is so low that the term *no-fault* hardly seems descriptive.[13]
- *Umbrella liability.* Because many liability policies have limits, or maximum amounts that may be paid out, businesses sometimes purchase **umbrella policies** to provide coverage after underlying liability policies have been exhausted. Sometimes an umbrella policy is called *excess liability insurance.* Because of the unknowns associated with this type of coverage, it is very expensive and sometimes unavailable.
- *Professional liability.* Also known as *malpractice insurance* or *errors and omissions insurance,* **professional liability insurance** commits an insurer to pay a designated amount if the insured becomes legally obligated to pay for damages resulting from providing or failing to provide professional services. Because this type of coverage protects professionals from financial ruin if sued by dissatisfied clients, it is very expensive.

Loss of Services of Key Personnel

Sometimes one executive or employee has expertise or experience that is crucial to the company's operation. If a business loses this key person by unplanned retirement, illness, disability, or death, the effect may be felt in lost income. **Key-person insurance** can be purchased by a company to protect itself against the financial impact of losing such a key employee under the circumstances described. Part of identifying the key-employee exposure is developing an estimate of where, at what cost, and how quickly a replacement may be hired and trained. For example, if a movie production company loses its main star during filming, even though the insurance proceeds may not solve the immediate problem of replacing the employee's services caused by death or disability, the insurance settlement may provide some additional time to develop a solution.

Types of Employee Insurance

Besides insuring their property and assets, most businesses provide group medical, disability, workers' compensation, and life insurance coverage for employees. Disease and disability may cost employees huge sums of money unless they are insured. In addition, death carries the threat of financial hardship for an employee's family. In some cases, the employer pays for these types of insurance in full; in other cases, employees pay part or all of the costs through a payroll deduction plan.

Health Insurance

Approximately 90 percent of the people who have private health insurance acquire their benefits as part of an employee benefit program. Employers providing group health insurance typically cover the employee and eligible dependents. Traditionally, group insurance includes health expense coverage as well as a coverage guaranteeing income in the event of a disabling illness or injury. Most group policies place limits on the amount they will pay for mental health and substance abuse claims. Exhibit B.5 lists the most common types of health expense coverage offered by employers.[14]

Disability income insurance, which replaces income not earned because of illness or accident, is often included as part of the health insurance package provided by employers. These policies are designated as either short or long term, depending on the period for which coverage is provided. Short-term policies are more common and provide a specific number of weeks of coverage (often 30), after a brief waiting or elimination period—a period that must elapse before an employee is eligible to receive insurance payments. The purpose of the elimination period is to exclude payments for minor illness. Long-term disability income, on the other hand, provides a number of years of protection after a substantial elimination period has elapsed (generally six months of continuous disability).

The amount of disability payment depends on whether the disability is partial or total, temporary or permanent, short term or long term. Generally, the amount received is offset by any disability payments received from Social Security. To encourage employees to return to work as soon as possible, some policies will continue partial payments if an employee is able to perform some type of

COMMON TYPES OF HEALTH INSURANCE

Basic medical	Health insurance designed to pay for most inpatient and some outpatient hospital costs
Major medical	Health insurance that protects the insured against catastrophic financial losses by covering expenses that exceed the coverage limits of basic policies
Disability income	Insurance designed to protect against the loss of short-term or long-term income while the insured is disabled as a result of an illness or accident
Medicare supplemental	Insurance that is designed specifically to supplement benefits provided under the Medicare program
Long-term care	Insurance designed to cover lengthy stays in long-term care facilities

EXHIBIT B.5

Common Types of Health Insurance

Here are five of the most common types of health insurance policies sold by insurers.

work, even if he or she is unable to maintain the same pace of career advancement or hours of labor per week.

Long-Term Care Insurance Many illnesses today require lengthy stays in long-term care (LTC) facilities like nursing homes. Conditions such as paraplegia, arthritis, mental illness, mental retardation, and respiratory disorders affect both young and old. In the past, many seniors relied on government aid (Medicaid) to foot their LTC bills. Recently signed legislation, however, requires seniors to virtually impoverish themselves before Medicaid pays for their nursing home stay. The Health Insurance Portability and Accountability Act has, in fact, sent all consumers and insurance companies a strong message: Individuals (not the government) are responsible for financing their own long-term care.[15]

Of course, if thinking about long-term care is the furthest thing from your mind, consider this: Long-term care isn't just for the aging. Surprisingly, 40 percent of those who receive LTC are between the ages 18 and 64, and the chances that you will need LTC in the future are almost 50 percent. With the cost of staying at a nursing home ranging from $40,000 to $80,000 annually, planning early makes good sense.[16]

The Increasing Cost of Medical Care Employers today typically pay a large portion of the premium costs of medical insurance for their employees; however, as costs rise, many employers are shifting more of the cost burden to employees by requiring them to pay a larger portion of their own premiums and larger deductibles. Small companies often get hit the hardest. Because their groups are smaller, premiums tend to be more costly, forcing some small companies to drop health insurance altogether.

Several factors have led to the escalating costs of health care. Some observers assert that the most significant factor is *cost shifting,* whereby hospitals and doctors boost their charges to private-paying patients and their insurers to make up for the shortfall in government reimbursements for their Medicare and Medicaid patients.[17] Other factors causing the escalation of insurance premiums include the high costs and increased use of medical technology like MRI scanners, the high costs of professional liability insurance, increased hospital operating costs, and costly state mandates like the one recently signed into law by the state of New York: This new mandate requires health insurance companies and HMOs to cover up to 15 chiropractic visits per year.[18] Remember, when hospitals and doctors increase their charges, and when states mandate certain benefit coverage, health insurance premiums go up.

Cost Containment Measures Most employers use cost containment measures to control the escalating costs of medical insurance. Some of the practices companies are implementing include preadmission testing (to qualify health insurance applicants), case management, second opinions, home health care, hospice care (long-term home care for the terminally ill), and generic drugs. Some companies are establishing worksite disease-prevention programs, referred to as "wellness programs" or "wellcare," because they know that keeping employees healthy reduces absenteeism and lowers health costs.

Johnson & Johnson's version of a wellness program is Live for Life: Employees volunteer for physical checkups to identify health risks, after which they participate in free, professionally run workshops to stop smoking, control weight, improve nutrition, reduce stress, and promote physical fitness. Other companies reward employees for maintaining healthy lifestyles with cash incentives.

Still other companies choose to contain their costs by joining **health maintenance organizations (HMOs),** which are comprehensive, prepaid, group-practice medical plans in which consumers pay a set fee (called a capitation payment) and in return receive most of their

Cutting health-care costs by improving employees' health is the goal of the Xerox Corporate Fitness Center.

health care at little or no additional cost. Because the capitation payment does not change with usage, HMOs shift the risk from the employer to the health-care provider. Unlike hospitals and doctors in private practice, who charge on a fee-for-service basis, HMOs charge a fixed fee with which they must cover all their expenses.

Critics of HMOs claim that because these doctors are forced to operate within each year's "subscription income," they have a strong incentive to limit treatment and to avoid costly hospitalization. On the other hand, advocates claim that HMOs not only lower health insurance costs but provide employees with preventive care. Certain HMOs (called "open HMOs") allow members the option of using hospitals and doctors outside the network. These variations are actually a form of **managed care** programs where employers (usually through an insurance carrier) set up their own network of doctors and hospitals that agree to discount the fees they charge in return for the flow of patients. Today, over 91 percent of firms with 1,000 or more workers and over 73 percent of small businesses offer some form of managed care programs.[19]

As an alternative to HMOs, some employers opt for **preferred-provider organizations (PPOs),** health-care providers that contract with employers, insurance companies, or other third-party payers to deliver health-care services to an employee group at a reduced fee. In most companies, employees are not required to use preferred providers, but they are offered incentives to do so—like reduced deductibles, lower co-payments, and wellcare. PPOs not only save employers money but also allow them to control the quality and appropriateness of services provided. However, employees are restricted in their choice of hospitals and doctors, and preventive services are generally not covered.

Workers' Compensation

Each year, thousands of workers die or are injured permanently because of job-related injuries. **Workers' compensation insurance** pays the medical bills of employees who are hurt or become ill as a result of their work. It covers loss of income by occupationally injured or diseased workers, full payment of medical expenses, and rehabilitation expenses for these workers. Plus it provides death benefits to the survivors of any employee killed on the job. In most cases, it covers both full- and part-time employees.

Workers' compensation insurance is required by U.S. law, and the benefits are enumerated in the workers' compensation statute. It can be obtained through adequate self-insurance in some states, from state funds in some states, and from a private insurer in most states. An employee who is temporarily disabled as a result of work-related injury receives weekly benefits. If the injury is fatal, dependents receive weekly payments for a specified period. In nearly all states, the weekly benefit rate for an injured worker is normally two-thirds of the employee's weekly wage.

Premiums for workers' compensation insurance are based on the employer's payroll and past experience. Thus, employers with relatively good safety results will pay lower workers' compensation insurance rates than employers with poor safety records. This approval rewards loss prevention and loss reduction efforts. Insurers also classify employers by industry, giving recognition to the fact that some industries involve more danger to workers than others. Thus an employer in a mining industry would pay higher rates than an employer in the food services industry. Although workers' compensation premiums have more than doubled in recent years, efforts to control escalating rates are finally paying off: A renewed focus on worker safety, narrower definitions of "work-related injuries," antifraud efforts, state reform legislation, and managed-care initiatives are beginning to drive rates down.[20]

Life Insurance

One of the most unfortunate circumstances that could strike a family would be the loss of its main source of income. Life insurance policies provide some protection against the financial problems associated with premature death by paying predetermined amounts to **beneficiaries** when the covered individual dies. Life insurance is the closest thing to a universal employee benefit: It is offered to roughly 90 percent of the employees in the United States.[21]

There are many different types of life insurance, and each is used for a variety of purposes. For example, *credit life insurance* is required by many lending institutions to guarantee that a mortgage or other large loan will be paid off in the case of the borrower's death.[22] Some life insurance policies provide a type of savings fund for retirement or other purposes by building a *cash value* from excess premiums. In some policies, owners can borrow against the cash value by paying interest to the insurer (sometimes at a lower rate than banks charge), and they can withdraw the accumulated cash value in one lump sum or in annual payments if they want to end the policy.

Term insurance, as the name implies, covers a person for a specific period of time—the term of the policy. If the insured outlives the period, no payment is made by the insurer, and the policy has no cash value. Group life insurance is term insurance that is commonly purchased by employers for their employees. Generally it may be renewed without the proof of insurability (also known as guaranteed renewable), but not past the age of 65.

Types of life insurance not usually provided by employers include whole life, variable, and universal. **Whole life insurance,** which is more expensive than term insurance, provides a combination of insurance and savings. The policy stays in force until the insured dies, provided that the premiums are paid. In addition to paying death benefits, whole life insurance accumulates cash value.

Variable life insurance was developed in response to the soaring inflation of the late 1970s and early 1980s. The difference between variable life insurance and whole life insurance is that variable is most often associated with an investment portfolio because the underlying investments are securities, and the policy owner has some investment choice. If the insured's investment decisions are good, the policy's cash value and death benefit (the amount paid at death) will increase. On the other hand, if the investments do poorly, the cash value may drop to $0 and the death benefit may decrease—although not below the original amount purchased (the face value) as long as the policy remains in force and accumulates cash value.

Universal life insurance is also a flexible policy. It allows the insured to buy term insurance and invest an additional amount with the insurance company. Premiums on a universal life insurance policy are used to fund, in essence, term insurance and a savings account. The accumulated premium payments produce a cash value that then earns two types of interest: a guaranteed interest rate specified in the contract and an excess interest rate if policy conditions are met. The interest that accumulates on the savings portion of the policy is pegged to current money-market rates (but generally guaranteed to stay above a certain level). Premium payments may vary too, depending on the insured's preferences and as long as cash value is large enough to fund the term insurance portion of the policy. Because of low market interest rates, this type of policy has lost popularity during the past few years.

Social Insurance Programs and Reform Efforts

When most people think of insurance, they think of the kind of insurance purchased from a private insurance company. Actually, the largest single source of insurance in the United States is the government, which accounts for nearly half of the total insurance premiums collected for all types of coverage combined. More than a quarter of the federal government's revenue comes from social insurance receipts.[23] Most social insurance programs are designed to protect people from loss of income, either because they have reached retirement age or because they have lost their jobs or become disabled. Unlike private insurance, which is voluntarily chosen by the insured, government-sponsored programs are compulsory.

Social Security Social Security was created by the federal government following the Great Depression of the 1930s. Officially known as Old-Age, Survivors, Disability, and Health Insurance, this program covers just about every wage earner in the United States.

The basic purpose of the Social Security program is to provide a minimum level of income for retirees, their survivors, and their dependents, as well as for the permanently disabled. The program also provides hospital and supplemental medical insurance—known as Medicare—for people age 65 and over. Social Security benefits vary, depending on a worker's average indexed monthly earnings and number of dependents. The program is funded by a payroll tax paid half by workers and half by their employers. In most cases, these taxes are automatically deducted from each paycheck. Self-employed people pay the full amount of the tax as part of their federal income tax liability. It's important to note that Social Security is not a needs-based program; every eligible person is entitled to the benefits of the system, regardless of his or her financial status.[24]

The future of Social Security is questionable. Experts predict that by 2015 annual payments by Social Security will exceed income by $57 billion, and that without reform, cumulative deficits through 2075 will total an astounding $160 trillion. Increased longevity and a low birth rate are the chief blames for this financial dilemma. In the past, the system worked because a far greater number of workers supported every retiree, and many potential beneficiaries died before collecting their first check. This is no longer the case.[25]

Several alternative solutions have been proposed to restore the system's financial stability. These include increasing the tax rate paid by employees and employers, subjecting more earnings of higher-paid workers to the tax, and subjecting all Social Security benefits to the federal income tax. Still, some argue that the only solution is to terminate the program and switch to a private pension system where people could invest their own money for their own retirement.

Unemployment Insurance Under the terms of the Social Security Act of 1935, employers in all 50 states finance special **unemployment insurance** to benefit employees who are unemployed. The cost is borne by employers. Currently, the unemployment insurance program is a joint federal-state program, with about 90 percent of the funding coming from the states.

The unemployment insurance program is designed to meet the peril of short-term unemployment caused by the business cycle and other factors over which workers have little control. Thus, an employee who becomes unemployed for reasons not related to performance is entitled to collect benefits—typically for 26 weeks. However, many workers today are exhausting their regular unemployment insurance benefits and applying for an additional 26 weeks of extended coverage. This is straining the system, and some redesign or reform will be required in the future if these trends continue.[26]

National Health Insurance The health-care crisis has employers and employees alike clamoring for reform, and the problem is getting more attention from Congress, which has been struggling with the issue for over a decade. Much of the debate on health-care reform focuses on the idea of *national health care*, which is generally interpreted as some form of centralized government support or control. One of the strongest motivations for national health care is the goal of providing coverage for people who either aren't covered by employer programs or can't afford to cover themselves. England, Canada, and many other countries have national health-care programs; however, many of these programs are struggling to stay afloat because of the need to increase taxes to pay for escalating health-care costs.

National health-care proposals have generally met with strong opposition in the United States for a variety of reasons. Some people want to let free-market forces drive the system; others believe the only way to get everyone covered is through government intervention. Some argue that a centralized, so-called single-payer system is the best way to make health care more efficient and more widely available, but opponents are skeptical that any government program—particularly one as massive as national health care—could ever be efficient. In fact, because of the huge amounts of money involved, any changes to the current system are likely to meet opposition from somebody, whether it's health-care professionals, insurance companies, taxpayers, employers, or employees.

It's difficult to predict where reform efforts will lead in the next few years, but several things are possible. The burden of coverage may shift from employers to the government, or it may continue to shift toward employees, who are increasingly expected to pay for more of their own coverage. The idea of *pooling*, in which groups of consumers, businesses, or communities band together to buy coverage, may spread. Many states are forging ahead with their own plans, not waiting to see if Congress can resolve the issue on a national level.[27] Nevertheless, a recent presidential advisory report filed by health-care industry experts bluntly states: "A health care system that leaves 41 million Americans without health coverage cannot adequately protect the rights of consumers." As one industry expert puts it, "Everybody thinks health reform has been there, done that, but that's just the problem. We've been there but we haven't done much at all."[28]

Challenges Facing the Insurance Industry

Aside from the soaring cost of medical care discussed earlier in this chapter, one of the biggest challenges facing insurance companies today is competition from outside the insurance industry. Although domestic demand for life, property, and casualty insurance is declining at a rate of about 10 percent annually, competition from banks for a share of this shrinking market is escalating. Large multinational and smaller retail banks are competing with insurance companies to sell mutual funds, retirement packages, life insurance, and other products, blurring the line between insurance and financial services.[29]

At the same time, some of the stronger insurance companies are swallowing up weaker ones at a record pace, to sell everything from tornado insurance to auto policies (see Exhibit B.6). Still other conglomerates

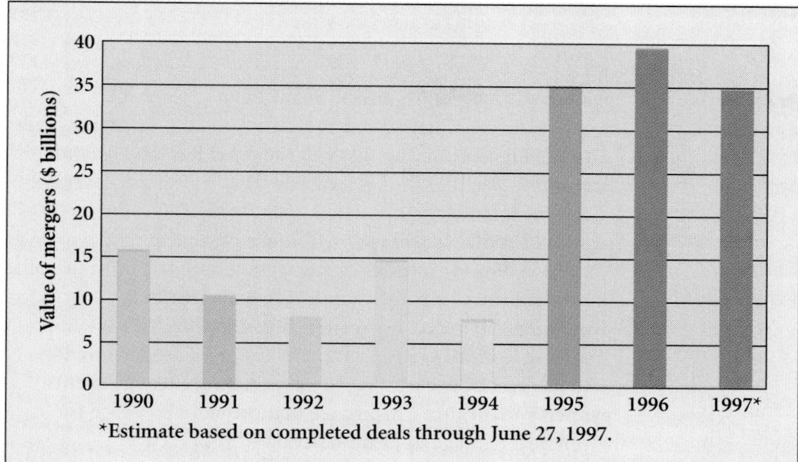

EXHIBIT B.6

Merger Mania

From 1995 through 1997, over $100 billion worth of mergers and acquisitions took place in the insurance industry. Larger companies gobbled up smaller ones in an often desperate effort to become profitable.

like Aetna are discovering that life, health, and property insurance are very different businesses; so they are streamlining their operations and narrowing their focus on only a few types of insurance and improved customer service.[30]

To respond to outside competition, industry consolidation, and the increasing popularity of self-insurance programs, many private insurance companies—large and small—are abandoning their old "take it or leave it" attitude. Companies like Cigna are bending over backward to tailor policies to fit the needs of their corporate clients, offering them greater flexibility in contract terms, negotiable deductibles, multiple-year contracts, and premium refunds.[31]

Some insurance companies are even using the Internet to provide customers with interactive account information. Today, over 15 million health plan members at Prudential have access to their medical and dental benefits information, claims history, lists of primary-care physicians, directions to doctors' offices, and insurance forms, at the touch of a keypad. Although Prudential's primary goal is to make health-care information as self-service as possible, it hopes that Web site visitors will also tap into the company's many other business services.[32]

Questions

For Review

1. What is the difference between pure risk and speculative risk?
2. What are the four types of loss exposure?
3. What are the five characteristics of insurable risks?
4. How can you control risk?
5. What is the difference between workers' compensation insurance and disability income insurance?

For Analysis

6. How do insurance companies calculate their premiums?
7. What is self-insurance and why is it becoming an increasingly popular risk financing technique?
8. Why is it a good idea to purchase consequential loss insurance?
9. What are some of the factors contributing to today's escalating health-care costs?
10. How does term insurance differ from whole life insurance?

For Application

11. If you were starting a new accounting practice with 15 employees, what types of insurance might you need?
12. One of your smaller clients is seeking your advice on ways he might lower or control his rising health insurance premium costs. Currently he offers his 25 employees a group health policy with few restrictions. What advice might you offer him?

Chapter Glossary

actual cash value coverage Property insurance in which the insurer pays for the replacement cost of property at the time of loss, less an allowance for depreciation

actuaries People employed by an insurance company to compute expected losses and to calculate the cost of premiums

beneficiaries People named in a life insurance policy who receive the proceeds of an insurance contract when the insured dies

business-interruption insurance Insurance that covers losses resulting from temporary business closings

claims Demands for payments from an insurance company due to some loss by the insured

contingent business-interruption insurance Insurance that protects a business from losses due to losses sustained by other businesses like suppliers or transportation companies

deductible Amount of loss that must be paid by the insured before the insurer will pay for the rest

disability income insurance Short-term or long-term insurance that protects an individual against loss of income while that individual is disabled as the result of an illness or accident

extra-expense insurance Insurance that covers the added expense of operating the business in temporary facilities after an event such as a fire or flood

fidelity bond Coverage that protects employers from dishonesty on the part of employees

functional-replacement-cost coverage Property insurance that allows for the substitution of construction materials to restore a property to a similar, functioning state

health maintenance organizations (HMOs) Prepaid medical plans in which consumers pay a set fee in order to receive a full range of medical care from a group of medical practitioners

insurable risk Risk for which an acceptable probability of loss may be calculated and that an insurance company might, therefore, be willing to cover

insurance Written contract that transfers to an insurer the financial responsibility for losses up to specified limits

key-person insurance Insurance that provides a business with funds to compensate for the loss of a key employee by unplanned retirement, resignation, death, or disability

law of large numbers Principle that the larger the group on which probabilities are calculated, the more accurate the predictive value

liability losses Financial losses suffered by a business firm or individual held responsible for property damage or injuries suffered by others

loss exposures Areas of risk in which a potential for loss exists

managed care Health care set up by employers (usually through an insurance carrier) who provide networks of doctors and hospitals that agree to discount the fees they charge in return for the flow of patients

mutual insurance company Nonprofit insurance company owned by the policyholders

no-fault insurance laws Laws limiting lawsuits connected with auto accidents

preferred-provider organizations (PPOs) Health-care providers offering reduced-rate contracts to groups that agree to obtain medical care through the providers' organization

premium Fee that the insured pays the insurer for coverage against loss

product-liability coverage Insurance that protects companies from claims for injuries or damages that result from use of a product the company manufactures or distributes

professional liability insurance Insurance that covers losses arising from damages or injuries caused by the insured in the course of performing professional services for clients

property insurance Insurance that provides coverage for physical damage to or destruction of property

pure risk Risk that involves the chance of loss only

replacement-cost coverage Property insurance in which the insurer pays for the full cost of repairing or replacing the property rather than the actual cash value

risk Uncertainty of an event or exposure to loss

risk management Process used by business firms and individuals to deal with their exposures to loss

self-insure Accumulating funds each year to pay for predicted liability losses, rather than buying insurance from another company

speculative risk Risk that involves the chance of both loss and profits

stock insurance company Profit-making insurance company owned by shareholders

surety bond Coverage that protects companies against losses incurred through nonperformance of a contract

term insurance Life insurance that provides death benefits for a specified period

umbrella policies Insurance that provides businesses with coverage beyond what is provided by a basic liability policy

underwriters Insurance company employees who decide which risks to insure, for how much, and for what premiums

unemployment insurance Government-sponsored program for assisting employees who are laid off for reasons not related to performance

uninsurable risk Risk that few, if any, insurance companies will assume because of the difficulty of calculating the probability of loss

universal life insurance Combination of a term life insurance policy and a savings plan with flexible interest rates and flexible premiums

variable life insurance Whole life insurance policy that allows the policyholder to decide how to invest the cash value

whole life insurance Insurance that provides both death benefits and savings for the insured's lifetime, provided premiums are paid

workers' compensation insurance Insurance that partially replaces lost income and that pays for employees' medical costs and rehabilitation expenses for work-related injuries

COMPONENT CHAPTER C

THE INTERNET AND BUSINESS SUCCESS

STRENGTHENING SUCCESS WITH THE INTERNET

What is this thing that is transforming the way we communicate and succeed in business? Simply put, the **Internet** is the world's largest computer network. Actually it is a network of many interlinked networks. Started in 1969 by the U.S. Department of Defense, the Internet is now accessible to individuals, companies, colleges, government agencies, and other institutions in countries all over the world. In 1985 some 1,900 individual computers were connected. By 1994 that number had grown exponentially to more than 3 million. Today more than 60 million people use the Internet regularly, and millions more are signing up every month. These users are able to visit over 200 million sites, turning their computers into global communication devices capable of accessing information and exchanging messages and computer files with other users anywhere in the world.[1]

The Internet is a voluntary, cooperative undertaking; no one individual, network, organization, or government owns the entire network. As with any group or community, however, the Internet has its own common practices, customs, conventions, and expectations, which are often referred to as "netiquette" (see Exhibit C.1). Although no Internet police enforce these "rules," you will find that fellow users can be pretty vocal when they detect inappropriate behavior. One of the best ways to learn about the rules and practices of an Internet group or Web site is to read the **frequently asked questions (FAQs).** This list provides answers to common questions and states any rules or unique site features.

The most widely used part of the Internet is the **World Wide Web (WWW** or **Web)**. Developed in 1990, the Web is a graphical system for accessing information using Internet technology. Its outstanding feature is **hypertext**—words or phrases that are colored or underlined and that enable you to jump from one Web document to another with a click of your mouse. In order to read these colorful pages you need a Web **browser,** software like Netscape Navigator or Microsoft's Internet Explorer. These Internet programs operate through a graphical user interface (GUI) rather than text commands, making it easier to search for, display, and save **multimedia** resources, such as graphics, text, audio, and video files.

What You Can Do on the Internet

Of course, you can't really get a picture of what the Internet is until you have a better idea of how you can use

DO'S	DON'Ts
Send e-mail about your company to people who have expressed interest in receiving it from you. Post commercial messages only in newsgroups that explicitly allow advertisements.	Send mass e-mail about your company's products and services to individuals or Internet newsgroups. Internet users often respond immediately with angry messages called flames. The volume of incoming flames has been known to overload the server of the offending company's Internet service provider (ISP), resulting in cancellation of the offender's account. Post questions and comments in discussion areas such as newsgroups, chat rooms, or mailing lists if your postings are not related to the group's subject matter.
Observe or "lurk" in a discussion area to get an idea about its subject matter before posting messages. Read the group's frequently asked questions (FAQs) to find out what type of material is appropriate. Give advice and make comments in discussion areas where you and your company can offer expertise.	Type entire messages or words in capital letters. This is the online equivalent of shouting.
Make sure your Web site is easy to navigate. If the user has to dig around too much to find information, you may lose a customer.	Overload your Web site—especially the home page—with an excessive amount of graphics. Graphics are eye-catching, but they can take a long time to appear on the user's computer screen, particularly at 28.8 bits per second or slower.
Be careful about using the e-mail "Reply All" button if your system has one. This button does not just mean reply to the sender; rather, it means reply to everyone that received a copy. Try using the "Forward" button instead. Keep e-mail messages and newsgroup postings short and relevant. Longer messages take more time to download.	Assume your e-mail messages are private. One day they could be subpoenaed or show up on the company bulletin board. Try not to write about someone unless you send that person a copy, because someone else might send them a copy for you.

EXHIBIT C.1

Do's and Don'ts On the Internet

The Internet has developed a unique culture—one that values personal privacy. Users are expected to conduct themselves with decorum. Your chances of incurring the wrath of fellow users will be minimized if you follow these basic do's and don'ts.

it. The following section explains several key Internet applications. You can also learn more about the Internet by taking the Internet tour at <http://www.globalvillage.com/gcweb/tour.html> and by visiting the Web site for this book at <http://www.phlip.morist.edu>.

Communicating on the Internet The original network that evolved into the Internet was designed to improve communication between scientists in the United States. Today communication remains one of the primary uses for the Internet. Different types of Internet communications include the following:

- *Sending and receiving e-mail.* Chapter 16 explains how e-mail (electronic mail) enables users to create, transmit, and read written messages entirely on computer. An e-mail document may be a simple text message, or it might include long and complex files or programs. In fact, if you can save a file on your computer, you can probably send it via e-mail.
- *Telnet.* **Telnet** is a class of Internet application program that allows you to connect with a remote host computer even though your computer is not a permanent part of the network that the host supports. This enables you to run a normal interactive session with other computers on the network as if you were sitting at an on-site terminal. For instance, you would use Telnet to access your county library's electronic card catalog from your home computer.[2]
- *Internet telephony.* It is now possible for Internet users to converse vocally over the Internet. Although the telephone has handled this job for decades, converting traditional voice calls to digital signals and sending them over the Inter-

Clicking on hypertext links (highlighted and underlined words) with your mouse allows you to jump from page to page. Images can also serve as links on the World Wide Web.

net is much less expensive than calling over standard analog phone lines. It can also be more efficient, allowing an organization to accommodate more users on a single line at once. Developers of this technology are still working out the bugs, but experts say that Internet telephony could capture 4 percent of U.S. telephone company revenues by 2004.[3]

Transferring Files Between Computers The **file transfer protocol (FTP)** is an Internet service that enables you to **download** files—that is, transfer data from the Internet into your computer.[4] Millions of useful files, including art, music, educational materials, games, maps, photos, software, and books are available on the Internet. When you download a file, the FTP software breaks down the file, transmits it, and reassembles it on your computer in a usable form.[5] Large files are often compressed or *zipped* into smaller packets to make them easier to transfer.

Participating in Discussion Groups Two forms of discussion groups are common on the Internet: *discussion mailing lists* and *Usenet newsgroups.* A **discussion mailing list** (of which there are more than 100,000) is made up of people with a common interest. You can subscribe by sending a message to the list's e-mail address. From then on, you will automatically receive via e-mail a copy of any message posted to that list by any other subscriber, and only other subscribers will see messages that you post. It's like subscribing to an electronic newsletter to which everyone can contribute.[6]

Usenet **newsgroups** differ from mailing lists in a

couple of key ways. First, whereas discussion mailing lists are accessed by e-mail, newsgroups are accessed by a newsgroup reader program in your Web browser. Think of a newsgroup as a *place* you visit to read posted messages, whereas a discussion mailing list *delivers* posted messages to you. Second, messages posted to a newsgroup can be viewed by anyone, and you can submit to and receive information from over 50,000 newsgroups. For example, the newsgroup <alt.business.misc> is a forum for small-business owners.[7] Once you subscribe, you can read messages posted by other subscribers and leave messages for other subscribers to read.

In addition to discussion mailing lists and Usenet newsgroups, many Internet users engage in **chat**—an online conversation in which any number of computer users can type in messages to each other and receive responses in real time.[8]

Searching for Information One of the most common uses of the Internet is to search for information. On the Web, you can locate current news articles and statistics; company information; tips for running a business, buying a home, or managing your finances; descriptions of products and services for sale; the latest buzz about your favorite entertainers; how and where to travel; and so on. The applications are almost endless, and the number of places to visit are growing daily. Fortunately, there are several excellent search tools available to help you find

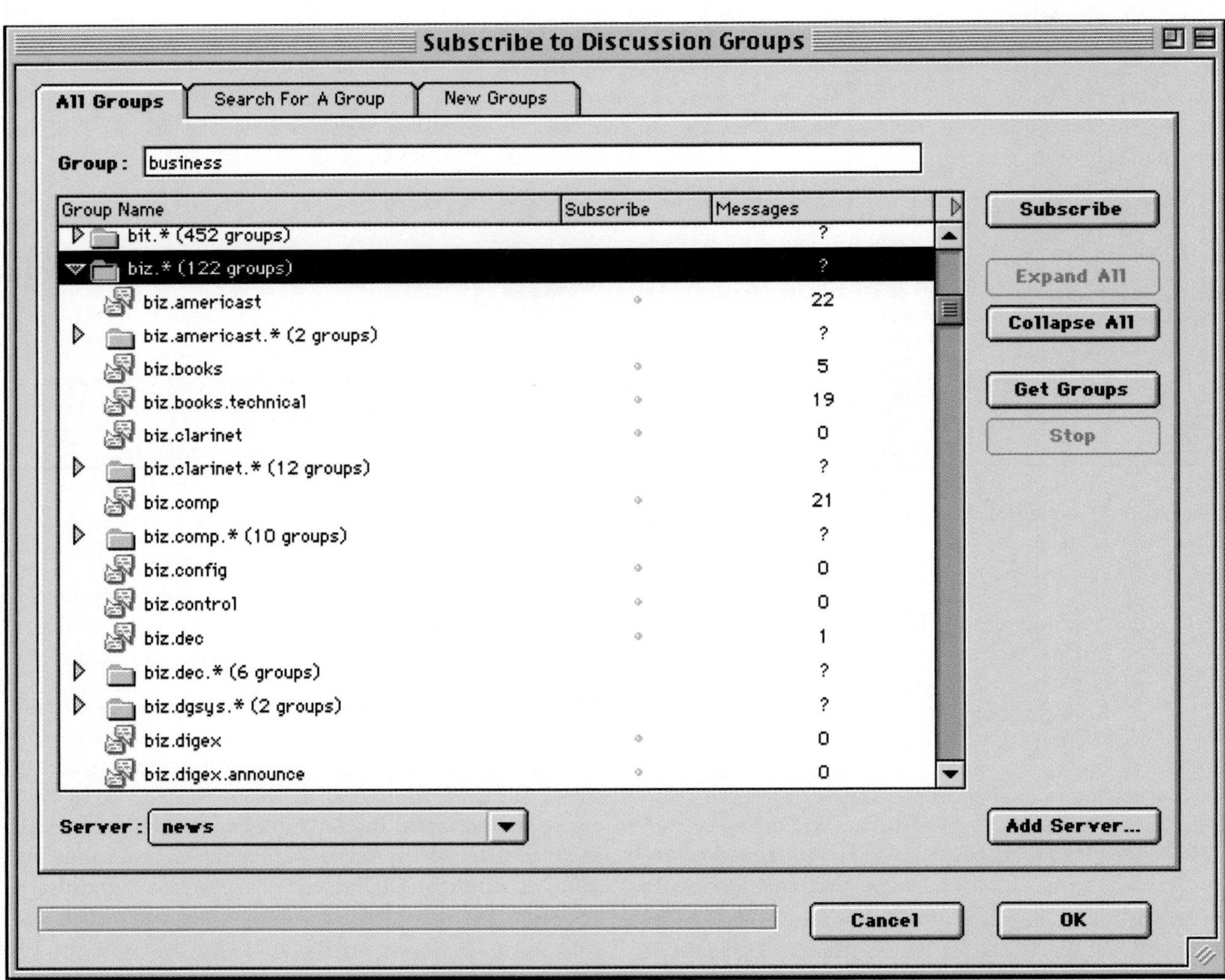

There are thousands of newsgroups on the Internet that let you express your thoughts on a particular topic and read what others have to say.

what you are looking for. These tools are discussed later in the chapter.

How Businesses Are Using the Internet

The Internet provides businesses with an unparalleled opportunity to improve their day-to-day operations and pursue markets beyond their borders. It has not only dramatically changed the way we do business but also created entirely new business opportunities in just about every industry. Here are some of the ways that businesses today are using the Internet:

- *Marketing and sales.* Chapters 12 through 15 provide numerous examples of how companies are using the Internet to test-market new ideas or products; distribute goods, services, and information; sell products online; provide customer support; and of course, advertise. In addition, companies are using the Internet to communicate with customers and develop relationships with them—both before and after the sale.

- *Communication and collaboration.* Chapter 7 elaborates on how businesses are using the Internet to keep departments, work groups, and individuals in close contact. Companies are using the Internet to exchange and search for information, to consult with experts and

China Expo is a Web page designed for English-speaking businesspeople to help them improve their effectiveness in China. The site has a wealth of information on topics such as culture, technology, economy, people, laws, and travel. Each one of these categories is broken down further into numerous subheadings, providing detailed information on each topic.

solve problems collaboratively, and to develop products jointly. In the next section, we will discuss how *intranets* are facilitating this communication function.

- *Globalization.* Throughout this textbook, you find examples of how companies are using the Internet to pursue markets all over the globe. Thanks to the Internet, individuals from Taiwan are doing business with others in Toronto, Moscow, and Michigan—easily and economically. Because access to the Internet is relatively cheap, even tiny companies can compete with larger organizations. In fact, no one knows how big or small you are on the Net.
- *Telecommuting and outsourcing.* Chapter 9 discusses how the Internet provides the flexibility for companies to employ staff anywhere. In some cases, employees who telecommute may meet face-to-face only occasionally. Because of its file transfer and e-mail capabilities, the Internet also facilitates the common practice of outsourcing work. For example, many U.S. companies outsource data entry in the Caribbean. Other companies outsource product design, logistics management, research and development, and even customer service across national borders.
- *Cost containment.* Recent studies have shown that businesses can save thousands of dollars using e-mail in lieu of some long-distance phone calls and postal deliveries. In addition, electronic catalogs published over the Internet can reach an enormous number of potential customers at a fraction of the cost of mail-order catalogs. But that's only the start. Businesses may soon be purchasing postage over the Internet, printing out the new e-stamp on a regular computer printer while addressing an envelope.[9] And even more impressive are companies like Amazon.com and CDnow.com, virtual companies that exist only on the Internet and save plenty of money on reduced overhead. That's because they don't need a large retail space to display their products or a sales staff to wait on customers. Plus they don't get stuck with last year's products. Even the banking industry is saving money by using the Internet. A recent study by industry experts found that a single bank transaction costs $1.08 at a branch bank, $.60 at an ATM machine, $.26 with PC banking, and only $.13 on the Internet.[10]
- *Information.* The Internet is rich in data, providing access to databases, books, manuals, training information, searchable databases, online expertise, and so on. In fact, some experts have compared the volume of information on the Internet to drinking from a fire hose. Many companies use the Internet to gather practical information about suppliers, competitors, and customers, and much of that information is free. Companies are also using the Internet to keep tabs on competition and stay up-to-date on business and industry trends.
- *Raising investment funds.* Chapter 19 discusses how companies are using the Internet to help them find private investors. Some are even selling their securities online—directly to the public; others are shopping for business loans online. Chapter 18 explains how online banking, electronic cash, and digital money will facilitate and expand the world of online commerce.
- *Employee recruitment.* Chapter 10 and Appendix I discuss how many companies recruit online by using their Web sites to highlight employment opportunities and convey an attractive image to prospective employees. Many job seekers use the Internet to search for job vacancies, research companies, communicate with potential employers, and post résumés.[11]

How Businesses Are Using Intranets

Not all Web sites are available to anyone cruising the Net. Some are reserved for the private use of a single company's employees and stakeholders. An **intranet** uses the same technologies as the Internet and the World Wide Web, but the information provided and the access allowed are restricted to the boundaries of a companywide computer network. In some cases, suppliers, distribution partners, and key customers may also have access, but the sensitive corporate data that resides on intranets are protected from unauthorized access through the Internet by security software called a **firewall,** a special type of gateway that controls access to the company's network. When anyone on the Internet tries to get into the internal web, the firewall requests a password and other forms of identification. Although people using an intranet can get out to the Internet, unauthorized people on the Internet can't get in.

One of the biggest advantages of an intranet is that it eliminates the problem of employees using different types of computers. On an intranet, all information is available in a format compatible with Macintosh, PC, or UNIX-based computers. This compatibility virtually eliminates the need to publish internal documents on paper because everyone can access the information electronically. Some companies have set goals of becoming "paperless." In fact, Owens-Corning Fiberglass planned no space for filing cabinets in its new headquarters (whereas filing cabinets took up 20 percent of the floor space in the old building). Other companies are looking at ways to open parts of their internal networks to customers and suppliers who have Internet connections. FedEx customers, for example, can already track their packages by logging on to the company's Web site, which is linked to the FedEx internal database.

Besides saving paper and floor space, an intranet can save a company money in the form of employee hours. Employees are able to find information much faster and easier by using a well-designed database on an intranet rather than digging through a filing cabinet. Other uses of intranets include scheduling meetings, setting up company phone directories, and publishing company newsletters. In fact, just about any information that needs to be shared among employees in the normal course of their business is a good candidate for an intranet. Although more sophisticated intranets are being developed daily, here are some basic business uses companies have for their intranets:

- *Policy manuals.* The most current version is always available to all employees without having to reprint hundreds of copies when policies change.
- *Employee benefits information.* Not only can you find out what your benefits are, but many companies have made it possible for employees using their intranet to reallocate the funds in their employee benefit plans.
- *Job openings.* New positions can be posted on an intranet, and current employees can submit job applications over an intranet as well.
- *Presentation materials used by marketing and sales departments.* Representatives can download sales and marketing materials at customer sites all over the world. Moreover, changes made by marketing representatives at company headquarters are immediately available to field salespeople.
- *Record keeping.* Company records are kept in one location and are accessible from anywhere on the company's intranet.

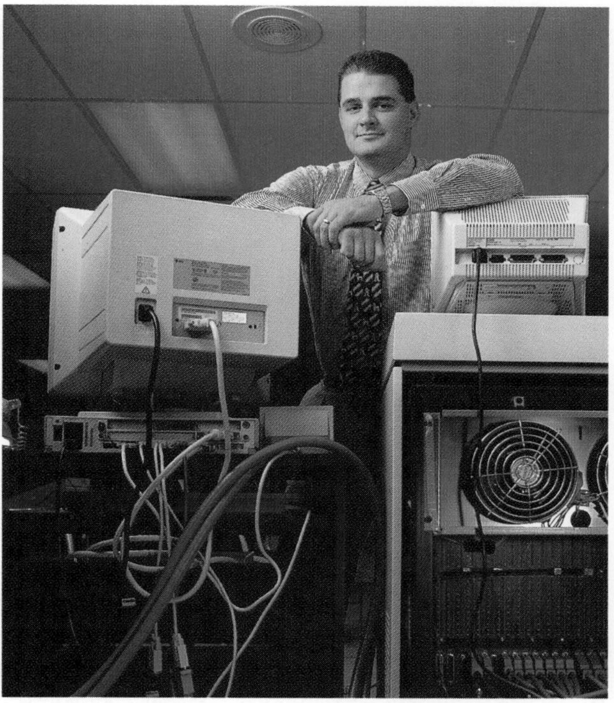

By using an Intranet, companies can distribute marketing materials and other information to their employees in the field quickly and easily.

- *Collaboration and development.* Ford Motor's 1996 Taurus was developed by engineers at design centers in Asia, Europe, and the United States, all communicating via Ford's intranet.[12]

How to Connect to the Internet

By now you'd probably like to know how you can connect to the Internet and start using all the great resources you've been reading about. Chapter 16 discusses how all computer networks depend on a combination of computer hardware, software, and communications media. Because almost every home and business is wired for telephone, most people access the Internet via standard telephone lines using a microcomputer (PC) equipped with a modem and sufficient memory to support Internet software. Those who use Internet telephony must also hook a microphone and speakers up to their computer.

The telephone line–modem combination is capable of transmitting data at a maximum speed of 56,000 bits per second. Coaxial cable, fiber optic cable, and digital wireless transmissions are much faster, but they are also more expensive, require specialized equipment, and are not available in all areas. For businesses demanding more

America Online is a popular online service. This gateway organizes Internet resources under a menu of specific topics.

speed, an **integrated services digital network** *(ISDN)* line offers a reasonable alternative. ISDN lines have a larger bandwidth than standard phone lines, carrying data at speeds of up to 1.5 million bits per second. They are widely available, and they require no modem. Even though the installation and monthly maintenance costs of an ISDN line are greater than those of a standard telephone line, the efficiencies gained in voice and data transmission can save a company time and money in the long run. Today many telecommuters use ISDN lines.[13]

Once you have the necessary hardware and transmission media, you will need software and a service connection. Many companies and colleges provide their employees and students direct Internet access through a designated Internet host connected to their local area networks (LANs). If such a system is not available to you, you can consider one of the following options. Your choice will depend on your own needs and comfort level.

- *Online services.* Commercial services such as America Online (AOL), CompuServe, and Prodigy are *gateways* that index many of the Net's most popular features into categories like travel, news, finance, sports, and entertainment. These services also enable users to send and receive e-mail and to access Usenet newsgroups, discussion mail lists, and the World Wide Web. The software necessary to access an online service is usually available free of charge to anyone who wishes to sign up.

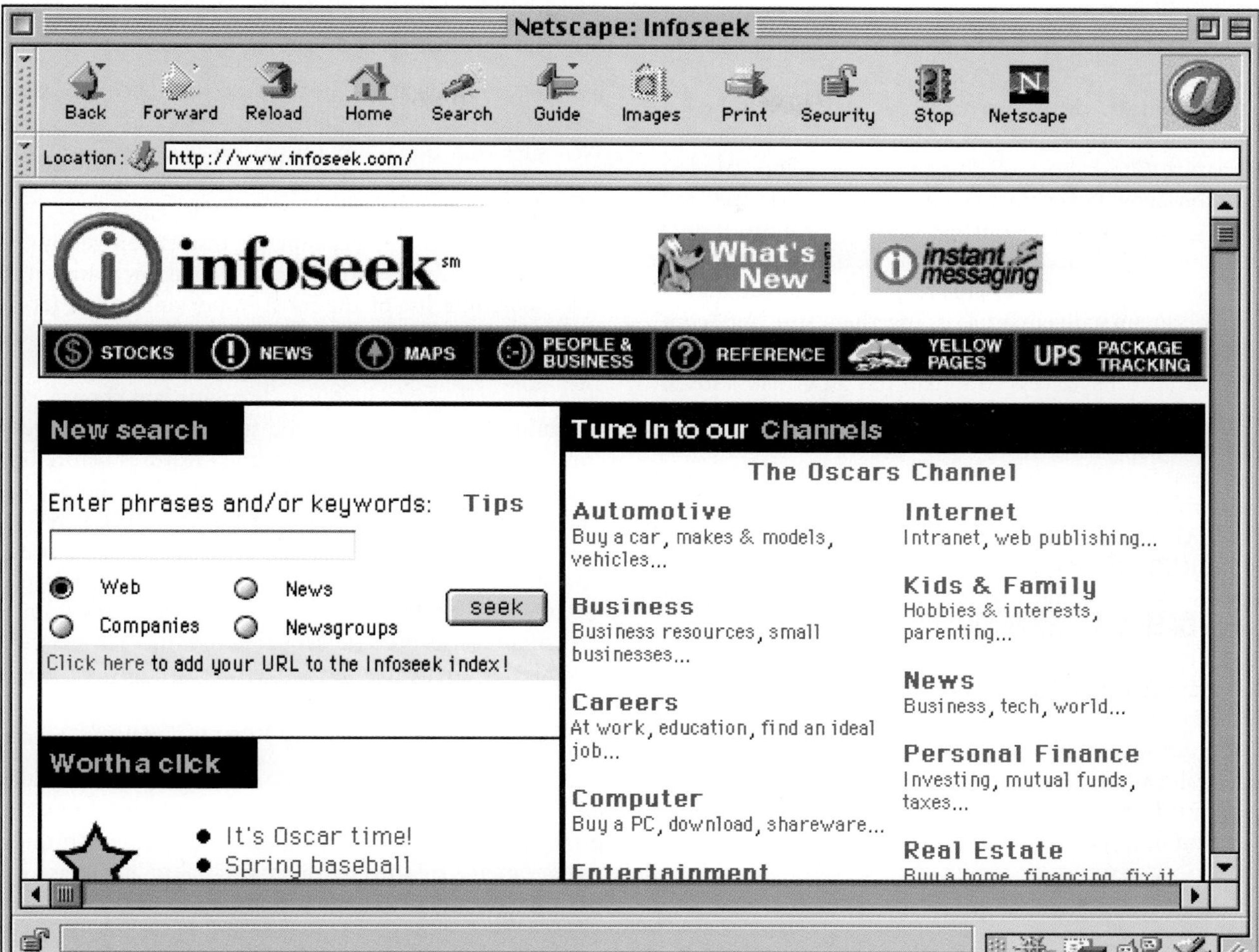

Infoseek has a reputation for consistently finding the most relevant Web sites. This search engine ranks sites by the proximity of the search terms to each other within the document. Extra features include stock updates, company profiles, Usenet searches, maps, and reference tools.

- *Internet service providers (ISPs).* When you dial into the host computers of an Internet service provider (ISP), you are directly connected to the Internet, not just a gateway. This connection gives you immediate access to any unrestricted site on the Net. ISP access requires an account with a service provider in your area (just look in the yellow pages) and software that supports direct Internet links, such as Netscape or Internet Explorer. Again, the software is typically free. Connection charges are comparable to those for an online service and may be calculated on either a flat monthly fee or on a per-use basis.

Searching for Information on the Internet

Chances are good that you'll find information on the Internet about almost any research topic. However, finding that information can be frustrating if you don't know how to look. You can access information on the Web in many ways. If you know the Web site's address, known as a **uniform resource locator (URL),** you can simply enter it in your browser software, beginning with **http:** (which is the abbreviation for **hypertext transfer protocol,** the communications protocol that allows you to navigate the Web).

Keep in mind that each Web site has a unique address, and each address contains a **domain name** that identifies the site's host. Consider Sun Microsystem's Internet address, <http://www.sun.com>. "Com" is the *top-level* domain name, indicating that the site is commercial in nature. Other top-level domain names include edu (education), gov (government), int (international), mil (military), net (network resources), and org (nonprofit organization). "Sun" indicates that Sun Microsystems is the host of the Internet site. This name is registered, and no other domain name may use it. Together, "sun" and "com" are known as the second-level domain name. In addition, anyone who has access to e-mail has an e-mail address, which is created by adding a user name to the domain name, separated by the @ symbol. For example, an employee at Sun Microsystems named Laura Dempsey might have the e-mail address *ldempsey@sun.com.*

Of course, you won't always have to remember all those URLs because just about every bit of information on the Web is **hyperlinked,** or *hot linked,* which means you can click on the highlighted word with your mouse to go to another Internet site automatically. Once you get to your new destination, you can **bookmark** the site by using a browser feature that places selected URLs in a file for quick access, allowing you to return to that site automatically at a later time. Plus you can navigate your trail backward or forward at any time by using the *back* and *forward* buttons on your browser software.

Search Strategies and Tips

Search engines are Internet research tools that can help you identify and screen resources. A search engine constantly travels the Web with a program called a spider or robot, indexing documents it finds on Web sites and placing these documents in a database. When you enter key words or phrases to be searched, the engine scans its database and returns all documents, or "hits," that contain the match. *Directories* (like Yahoo!) are similar to search engines, but they are created manually; submitted documents are reviewed and filed in an appropriate category (or categories). Because the internet is growing so fast, new search tools appear and existing ones become obsolete very quickly. Exhibit C.2 is a handy table of some of the currently well-known, commercially backed search engines and Web directories. Each engine has qualities that distinguish it from others. For a closer look at some of the features of these search engines visit the Web site *Search Engines Fact and Fun* at <http://searchenginewatch.internet.com/facts/major.html/>.

Narrowing Your Search The biggest drawback of using search engines is that they often pull up too many Web sites that don't contain the exact information you want. One way to narrow your search is by using **boolean operators** such as *AND, OR,* and *NOT.* Exhibit C.3 on page 651 explains the results you get by using boolean operators. Another way to narrow your search is by making a list of the most important search terms and key words, and by trying a variety of different key words in your search strategy.

Regardless of which search engine you choose, you will improve your results if you spend a few minutes becoming acquainted with the engine's features before initiating your search. Each engine has a "tips" or "help" page that explains which operators it uses, whether it recognizes misspellings, whether case sensitivity is supported, how it ranks pages for relevancy, and whether it is capable of searching from phrases. To achieve better results, you should also become acquainted with each engine's advanced search capabilities. Getting to know each engine's strengths and weaknesses at the start of your search can save you a lot of time and frustration later.[14]

Using Gopher Not all information on the Internet resides on the Web. **Gopher** is a text-based Internet-browsing program that allows you to locate information through a huge menu tree from which you select items as you narrow down to a specific topic. Gopher was developed at the University of Minnesota (home of the Golden Gophers) when the Internet was just beginning to take off. The university made Gopher available throughout the Internet, and today the program is used on thousands of Internet servers. However, as the files on Gopher servers are gradually converted to HTML files, Gopher (and its search tools) will become less important.[15]

Research Citations

The value of your research depends on the quality of the data it's based on. When it comes to choosing references, be selective. Remember, anyone with a modem, the right software, and access to a server can publish information on the Internet. Therefore, it is important to make certain that the information you access comes from reliable sources. The old saying, "You can't believe everything you read" is more true in the Internet age than ever before. Exhibit C.4 is a list of questions you should ask before citing data found on the Internet.

SITE	DESCRIPTION
	Major Search Engines and Directories
Alta Vista	<http://altavista.digital.com/> As of January 1998, this search engine claims to index nearly 200 gigabytes of data from millions of Web pages and articles from thousands of Usenet newsgroups. Searches in 25 different languages.
Excite	<http://www.excite.com/> All-purpose site loaded with options. Either search by keyword or browse by dozens of preselected subject categories (channels), with short abstracts for each match.
Fedstats	<http://www.fedstats.gov/search.html> Terrific service for data users and researchers. This one site simultaneously queries 14 federal agencies for specified statistics and numeric data. Either enter a search query or browse the index from A to Z. For a quick guide to all of this site's features, browse through the Site Map.
HotBot	<http://www.hotbot.com/> *Wired* magazine packs all kinds of searching possibilities into this site. Users may type in a simple query from the top screen, select a slightly narrower search in the *Look for* scroll box, specify date or location, or even request a SuperSearch, which provides templates for advanced features such as by date, media type, or location. If you're a news junkie, try their client program, NewsBot.
Infoseek	<http://www.infoseek.com/> Search with keywords, or just browse preselected categories. Users can also specify searches for Web sites, companies, news, or Usenet newsgroups. Some sites are listed with red checkmarks. These are Infoseek Select Sites, ones that have been reviewed and are recommended by Infoseek. Extra features include company profiles and stock quotes.
Lycos	<http://www.lycos.com/> One of the oldest of the major search engines, provides short abstracts for each match. Either search by keyword or browse several preselected subject categories. For the most popular sites on the Internet, see their Top 5% sites. Lycos can look for image and sound files, plus track your UPS packages too. Extra features include a city guide and stock finder.
Northern Light	<http://www.northernlight.com/> This newer search engine has two unique features: it actually categorizes returns by subject, plus it has a "special collection" of over 2 million documents (from about 2900 sources—including news wires, magazines, journals, books, and databases) that are not readily accessible to search engine spiders. Searching these special documents is free, but there is a small charge to view them.
WebCrawler	<http://www.webcrawler.com/> Either search the entire site or browse any of the preselected categories, including an excellent reference section. Like its owner, Excite, WebCrawler features many commonplace offerings.
Yahoo!	<http://www.yahoo.com> The oldest major Web site directory (as opposed to search engine), listing over 500,000 sites. Because it is a directory based on user submissions, it may not have some sites in its catalog that a crawler might find from searching the Web each day. But with a click, the query originally sent to Yahoo! is forwarded to any of the major search engines. For their latest additions to the index, check out their Weekly Picks. Extra features include sports and stock quotes.
	Multiple Search Sites—Metacrawlers
Dogpile	<http://www.dogpile.com/> Despite the silly name, just enter one query and this hound sniffs through dozens of FTP, Usenet, and Web sites. Dogpile allows the user to set the maximum time for waiting for results.
Mamma	<http://www.mamma.com/> Claiming to be the "Mother of All Search Engines," this multilegged spider queries the major search engines for fast results. To narrow results, specify searches or results by phrase or title.

SITE	DESCRIPTION
MetaCrawler	<http://www.metacrawler.com> One of the oldest services, this spider searches six different search engines simultaneously. There's also plenty of information on this site, including weather reports and apartment listings.
Metafind	<http://www.metafind.com/> Same as Dogpile, except that searches only go to search engines.
ProFusion	<http://www.designlab.ukans.edu/profusion/> Search this University of Kansas spider to retrieve only the "best" results from selected search engines. Specify specific search engines, or the fastest engines, or let the pros choose for you.
	Specialty Search Engines
Amnesi	<http://www.amnesi.com/> Can't remember the exact URL of a Web site? Tell Amnesi what you remember, and it will provide a list of sites it thinks match.
Deja News	<http://www.dejanews.com/> Search thousands of discussion groups found on Usenet from among the several categories or use keywords.
Education World	<http://www.education-world.com/> Over 50,000 sites of interest to educators, with the ability to narrow searches by appropriate grade level.
Forum One	<http://www.forumone.com> Allows you to search over 180,000 Web-based discussion forums.
HumanSearch	<http://www.humansearch.com/> Send in a question, and a team of volunteer researchers will try to find an answer—one located on or off the Web.
News search engines	If you are still looking for news using "normal" search engines, you'll find using the services listed below to be a much better way to search for the latest news stories from hundreds of sources on the Web: *News Tracker* <http://nt.excite.com>; *NewsBot* <http://newsbot.com>; *News Index* <http://newsindex.com>; *NewsHub* <http://newshub.com>; *Paperboy* <http://www.paperboy.net>; *TotalNews* <http://totalnews.com/>

EXHIBIT C.2

Best of Internet Searching

For searchers, well-known, commercially backed search engines generally mean more dependable results. These major search engines (and directories) are more likely to be well-maintained and upgraded when necessary, to keep pace with the growing Web. Most have simple or advanced search features, plus extras such as interactive maps, weather, travel information, phone and e-mail directories, and company profiles.

Information retrieved from the Internet may be cited in several formats. Here's an example of one popular way to list the cite reference:

> U.S. Department of Commerce, *Falling Through the Net: A Survey of the "Have Nots" in Rural and Urban America*, July 1995. <http://www.ntia.doc.gov/ntiahome/gfallingthru.html>. [accessed online 6 March 1998].

To keep up with formats for citing various types of electronic documents, check the citation guides at the University of Michigan's Internet Public Library <http://www.ipl.org/ref/QUE/FARQ/netciteFARQ.html>.

SEARCH OPERATOR	EFFECT	STRATEGY	RESULTS
AND	Narrows the results. Searches for records containing both of the words it separates. Words separated by AND may be anywhere in the document—and far away from each other.	Rock AND Roll	Music
OR	Broadens the results. This is a scattergun search that will turn up lots of matches and is not particularly precise. Searches for records containing either of the words it separates.	Rock OR Roll	Igneous rocks; Gemstones; Crescent rolls; Gymnastics; Music
NOT	Limits the results. Searches for records containing the first word(s) but not the second one.	Snow skiing NOT water skiing	snow skiing; cross-country skiing
NEAR	Proximity operator. Searches for words that all appear in a specified word range	Snow NEAR/2 Skiing	Specifies that skiing must be within 2 words of snow
ADJ	Adjacency operator. Searches for records where second word immediately follows first word (two words are next to each other).	Ski ADJ Patrol	Ski Patrol
?	Wildcard operator for single character; matches any one character.	Ski?	Skit; Skid; Skin; Skip
*	Wildcard operator for string of characters	Ski*	ski; skiing; skies; skill; skirt; skit; skinny; skimpy
""	Exact match. Searches for string of words placed within quotation marks.	"1997 budget deficit"	1997 budget deficit

EXHIBIT C.3

Improving Your Search Results

Computerized search mechanisms are based on Boolean logic, which uses the primary operators AND, OR, and NOT. Here are some strategies for better searches.

Does the source have a reputation for honesty and reliability?	Will the source's claims stand up to thoughtful scrutiny?
Is the source potentially biased?	Are the data up to date?
Where did the source get its information?	Are the data objective? Who collected the data, and how?
Can you verify the material independently?	What are the authors' qualifications and reputations?

EXHIBIT C.4

Choosing and Using Sources

Common sense will help you judge the credibility of the sources you plan to use for your research. Before selecting a piece of material, ask yourself these questions.

Questions

For Review

1. Who owns the Internet?
2. What are some of the primary uses of the Internet?
3. What are some of the ways businesses are using the Internet?
4. What does a search engine do, and how does it help you identify and screen resources?
5. Besides the World Wide Web, what else resides on the Internet?

For Analysis

6. What equipment and software do you need to connect to the Internet? Why might a company consider installing an ISDN line?
7. How do newsgroups differ from mailing lists?
8. In what ways can the Internet help companies reduce costs? What new costs does a company incur when it becomes wired to the Net?
9. What are some of the key benefits of company intranets?
10. How can you navigate the Web, and how can you keep from getting lost?

For Application

11. How is the Internet transforming the way we communicate and do business?
12. Your instructor has given you the assignment to write a research paper on the topic "graduating from college in four years." Using the Internet as a resource:
    a. What are some key words and phrases you might use in your search strategy?
    b. Using boolean operators, how might your narrow your search?
    c. What are some of the things you would need to consider when selecting your sources?

Chapter Glossary *

attachment A file transmitted with an e-mail message

bookmark A browser feature that places selected URLs in a file for quick access, allowing you to automatically return to the Web site by clicking on the site's name

boolean operators The term *boolean* refers to a system of logical thought developed by the English mathematician, George Boole. It uses the operators AND, OR, and NOT

browser Software, such as Netscape Navigator or Microsoft's Internet Explorer, that enables a computer to search for, display, and download the multimedia information that appears on the World Wide Web

chat A form of interactive communication that enables computer users in separate locations to have real-time conversations. Usually takes place at Web sites called chat rooms

cookie A string of numbers a Web site uses to identify visitors. The cookie can contain information about subscriptions and memberships to online services and other information

discussion mailing lists Similar to newsgroups, they allow people to discuss a common interest by posting messages, which are received by everyone in the group. Unlike newsgroups, people must subscribe to a mailing list to post and receive messages. Also called a listserv

domain name The portion of an Internet address that identifies the host and indicates the type of organization it is. For example: <http://www.sun.com> is the address for Sun Microsystems. The "com" part of the domain name reflects the purpose of the organization or entity (in this example, "commercial") and is called the *top-level* domain name. The "sun" part of the domain name, together with the top-level, is called the *second-level* domain name; it must be registered and is unique on the Internet

download Transmitting a file from one computer system to another. On the Internet, downloading a file means bringing data from the Internet into your computer

file transfer protocol (FTP) A software protocol that lets you copy or move files from a remote computer—called an FTP site—to your computer over the Internet. File transfer protocol is the Internet facility for downloading and uploading files

firewall Computer hardware and software that protects part or all of a private computer network attached to the Internet by preventing public Internet users from accessing it

flaming An e-mail message or a posting to a newgroup that's intended to insult, provoke, or irritate the recipient

*For the first, the last, and virtually every word or acronym you come across in the technology world, see Whatis.com, the online encyclopedia <http://www.whatis.com>. Clear explanations, pronunciation guides, and links to sites for further information make this site a valuable tool.

frequently asked questions (FAQs) A list of common questions about a particular subject such as a newsgroup or a Web site

Gopher A text-based Internet navigation program that uses a menu tree to search for subjects. Developed at the University of Minnesota and named after the school's mascot

home page The primary Web site for an organization or individual; the first hypertext document displayed on a Web site

hyperlink A hypertext code that automatically allows people to move from one document to another by clicking on the link with a mouse

hypertext Colored or underlined words on a Web page that transport you to an entirely different page when you click on them with your mouse

hypertext markup language (HTML) The software language used to create, present, and link pages on the World Wide Web

hypertext transfer protocol (HTTP) A communications protocol that allows people to navigate among documents or pages linked by hypertext and to download pages from the World Wide Web

integrated services digital network (ISDN) A communications system that allows people to connect to the Internet and send and receive data in digital form over telephone lines at much higher speeds than standard lines. Unlike modems, ISDN does not require computer data to be converted into analog voice signals

Internet A worldwide collection of interconnected networks that enables users to share information electronically and provides digital access to a wide variety of services

Internet service provider (ISP) A company that provides access to the Internet, usually via the public telephone network

intranet A private network, set up within a corporation or organization, that operates over the Internet and may be used to link geographically remote sites

multimedia Typically used to mean the combination of more than one presentation medium—such as text, sound, graphics, or motion video

newsgroups One or more discussion groups on the Internet where people with similar interests can post articles and reply to messages. Also called *Usenet* newsgroups. Unlike mailing lists that are accessed by e-mail, newsgroups are accessed by a newsgroup reader in your browser. Once you subscribe you can read messages posted by other subscribers and leave messages for other subscribers to read. Newsgroup discussions do not take place in real time

search engine A server-based application used to search large databases for selected words or phrases. Common search engines use key words to search for information on the World Wide Web

spam Unsolicited e-mail. From the sender's point-of-view, it's a form of bulk mail. To the receiver, it seems like junk e-mail

Telnet A way to access someone else's computer (the host computer), assuming you have permission, and to use that computer as if it were right on your desk. A Telnet command request looks like this: telnet the.libraryat.harvard.edu. The result of this fictitious request would be an invitation to log on with a user ID and a prompt for a password. If accepted, you would be logged in like any user who uses this computer every day

uniform resource locator (URL) Web address that gives the exact location of an Internet resource. It contains information about the server to be contacted and the method and path of access. Example: http://www.patriots.com

upload On the Internet, uploading a file means sending a file from your computer to the Internet

Usenet An electronic bulletin-board system through which newsgroups are transmitted

Web site A related collection of Web files that includes a beginning file called a home page. To get to a Web site, you use the URL address of the home page. From the home page, you can get to all other pages on the site

World Wide Web (WWW) A hypertext-based system for finding and accessing Internet resources such as text, graphics, sound, and other multimedia resources

SMALL BUSINESS 2000

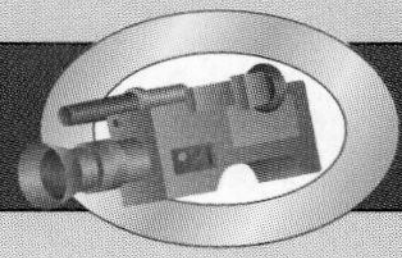

Part I Video Case: Jimmy Fand and the Tile Connection—Getting in on the Ground Floor

SMALL BUSINESS 2000

Jimmy Fand has built his business from the ground up—literally. A high school dropout in his native Colombia, Fand traveled extensively as a youth and ended up in New York City. After completing his education and working as a teacher, Fand moved with his growing family to Tampa, Florida. Today, Fand is the owner of The Tile Connection, the largest importer of ceramic tile in the United States. As is the case with many other entrepreneurs, Fand's inspiration for starting a business was the result of a simple observation. While shopping in Tampa for tile to install in his own home, Fand came to the conclusion that prices were too high and the selection was inadequate. Realizing that this situation represented a market opportunity, Fand began to import tile and set up his own distributorship in Florida.

Because Fand had earned a degree in geology, he possessed expertise that helped him as he searched the world for ceramic tile manufacturers that could satisfy his rigorous quality requirements. Fand understood that in order to carve out a niche for himself in the local market, he had to offer products that were truly superior. Fand's three criteria for suppliers are quality, availability, and price. Important tile-producing countries include Italy, Spain, Portugal, Colombia, and Brazil. Tile is also manufactured in the United States, but Fand could not find the types of tile he was looking for, nor could U.S. producers maintain a consistent supply of the quantities he needed at a competitive price. Fand buys only from manufacturers that are reliable and capable of meeting his quality standards. For example, after assessing nearly 1,000 tile producers in Italy and Spain alone, Fand concluded that fewer than one hundred factories were capable of meeting his standards.

Before starting The Tile Connection, Fand gained considerable experience and wisdom through his involvement in other business ventures. Fand has developed a set of principles that he has successfully applied at The Tile Connection. He knows that market research can give him an edge on competitors, and he endeavors to understand what styles of tile are likely to become popular with his customers. Fand has also learned that too much overhead can be fatal to a business and that proper money management and strict financial controls are crucial. Fand takes pride in the excellent credit rating that he has built up with his vendors. When buying goods abroad, many small importers are required to open a letter of credit (L/C), which is a document stating that a bank has substituted its credit worthiness for that of the importer. The manufacturers from whom Fand buys no longer require L/Cs. Such trust does not come automatically in a business relationship; it must be earned. Fand's philosophy is to pay bills on time. "That, to me, is sacred," Fand says. "That money doesn't belong to us; it belongs to the suppliers, who in turn need it to pay their employees." When paying, Fand makes sure that bank-to-bank transfers are carried out on the day the bills are due.

Strict attention to financial considerations is not Fand's only concern. Because his business is international in scope, he has to pay particular attention to the logistics of transporting fragile tile from his far-flung network of suppliers. Fand takes advantage of containerization, a modern form of transportation technology involving the use of steel trailers measuring 20 feet, 40 feet, or longer. To minimize breakage and protect the tiles, Fand requires that his manufacturers ship the tiles on special tilt-resistant pallets with special corner beads. Once the pallets are loaded in containers, the containers are sealed and transferred via truck or rail to a port in the country of manufacture. The tiles then make the trip to Tampa by oceangoing freighter. After a local customs broker clears the containers for entry into the United States, they are shipped to The Tile Connection's warehouse. There, Fand inspects each container to make sure the seals have not been tampered with.

In Fand's view, it is easier than ever to conduct business abroad. He notes that the United States is surrounded by friendly nations and that other countries are only hours away by airplane, or seconds away by telephone or fax machine. Still, many American business owners are reluctant to become importers or exporters. Some are held back by a lack of knowledge of market opportunities abroad. Or, they may simply have misconceptions about those markets. Fand explains, "The more we look for international places to deal with, the more chances of success we can have. We can sell our products to those people as well as buy their products and distribute them as I do." Many U.S. business owners speak only English and believe that is an obstacle for doing business abroad. Fand points out that the U.S. Commerce Department, local chambers of commerce, and private organizations have qualified translators available to facilitate business relationships.

Despite the fact that such resources are readily available, Fand knows from experience that it takes a major investment of managerial time to succeed in any business, especially an international one. "Prospective importers should be cautious about whom they deal with. Go to trade shows, meet manufacturers, and agents that represent the manufacturers as well. You need to do a lot of homework to find out which products you need to buy, and whether or not they are good products for your marketplace," Fand advises. Prospective importers must learn to identify and eliminate from consideration any factories that do not maintain quality controls. The other side of the equation for importers is understanding the needs of the local market and customers. Fand monitors the Florida market closely and attempts to stay ahead of competitors by anticipating the types and styles of tile that will be in demand.

Fand is proud of his business success, and he knows he has earned it himself through hard work. "I'm self-made," he says. "A lot of people are used to getting things for free, but only those who work hard for those things are able to appreciate them." But he also knows there are important things in life besides work. What does he value the most? He reflects, "The ability to be a human being. To think in terms of the needs of others. To create, to raise your family with very high standards, and to raise them with a high degree of education."

VIDEO CASE QUESTIONS

1. Briefly explain how The Tile Connection competes on price, quality, and innovation. Of these three, which one appears to be most important to Fand?
2. Why is it easier today for companies like Fand's to cross national borders? How can small businesses like The Tile Connection compete in the global economy with larger companies that have more resources?
3. Describe in two or three sentences Jimmy Fand's sense of social responsibility and what ethics means to him. You might pay particular attention to his philosophy on paying bills.
4. How did the force of supply and demand attribute to Fand's success? How can Fand stimulate demand should his stock of tile inventory grow too large?
5. Jimmy Fand indicates that there are resources available to small-business owners to help them expand globally. Identify one resource he discusses in the video.

SMALL BUSINESS 2000

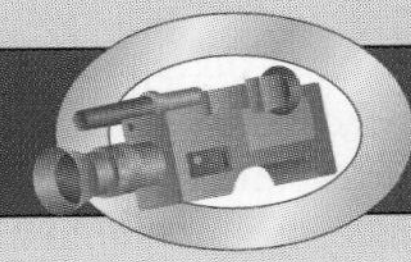

Part II Video Case: Buckeye Beans & Herbs—Shaping Semolina Without Spilling the Beans

SMALL BUSINESS 2000

Do you want to start a business? If so, Jill Smith has some advice for you. She says, "Know what you're going to do, be excited about it, and live it with a passion. Because if you don't have a passion for what you're doing, nobody else will have any interest in it." The business that Jill is passionate about is Buckeye Beans & Herbs. Started in a basement with a modest $1,000 investment, Spokane, Washington–based Buckeye Beans & Herbs had grown to a company that sells $8 million of all-natural soups, chili, bread mixes, and pasta each year. Along the way, Jill has drawn on her background as an artist to demonstrate how an innovative company mission statement, a well thought-out marketing strategy, an international scope, and family-oriented hiring policies can take a start-up along the right path to business success.

According to the company's mission statement, Buckeye Beans & Herbs is in business to make people smile. Jill explains, "Our belief is that cooking should be fun." For example, the first ingredient listed on a package of Buckeye Beans Soup is "a cup of good wine for the cook." That sense of good cheer also manifests itself inside the company. The plaque on Jill's door reads "Queen Bean," her husband, Doug, is the "bean boss," the head of accounting is a "bean counter," and every employee is treated like a "human bean." Doug notes that the mission statement is embodied in the company's "He-He Principle," which stands for "Humor, Education, Health, and Environment."

Savvy marketing has also been important to Jill's success. Jill is constantly seeking out and evaluating new opportunities to sell her products; she also spends time listening to customers. Both approaches have paid off, sometimes in unexpected ways. For example, to commemorate the state of Washington's centennial year, Jill created several special pasta shapes. One was modeled after the state symbol, an evergreen tree. That product flopped in the marketplace, but Jill displayed it at the annual food trade exhibition in New York. Visitors to the Buckeye Beans booth kept referring to the "Christmas tree" pasta. Jill seized the opportunity, and by year's end Buckeye Beans Christmas tree pasta had become a best-seller. Later on, other seasonal shapes were added, including hearts for Valentine's Day and rabbits for Easter.

Another marketing tactic is finding new channels of distribution and developing new products that will not take sales away from existing ones. Although Jill's original Buckeye Beans soup line sold at specialty food stores and through catalogs, it did not escape Jill's notice that many people still shop for food in supermarkets. Jill's instincts told her that these shoppers were looking for good-tasting, easy-to-cook alternatives to meat and potatoes. Jill created a new line with the brand name Aunt Patsie's Pantry, modeled on Jill's real-life aunt. According to the packages, "Aunt Patsie can't cook worth a darn," a lighthearted approach that was in sync with the sentiments of the typical supermarket customer.

Clearly, Jill sells more than just a product. She has found a way to add value to simple products like beans and pasta by creating a mystique that centers on who she is and what she does for her customers. In short, she sells a concept: the aroma in the house, the image of a family sitting at the table eating together. Jill says, "Our product goes beyond just a bag of beans. Sometimes I think we're as much an entertainment company as a product company." Jill's concept of entertainment, in turn, is perfectly suited to catalog marketing as a supplemental sales channel. The company has created catalogs featuring cartoon characters such as "Black Bean Bart" and "the Pinto Kid." As one company executive says, "Catalogs are just like magazines. A small business can take a catalog and create a company personally around it."

As was true in the Part I video case on The Tile Connection, another important consideration for Jill and Doug Smith is the international dimension of business. Whereas Jimmy Fand was concerned with importing, the issue at Buckeye Beans was exporting. When the Smiths tried to export their soups to Japan, they learned that Japan and other countries have tariffs and other barriers designed to hinder importation of certain types of food products. The Smiths got a boost by linking up with JETRO, the Japan External Trade Organization. The issue of trade between the United States and Japan has been a sensitive one in recent years. Specifically, there have been accusations that some segments of the Japanese market are closed to outsiders, even as Japan takes advantage of open access to the U.S. market. One of JETRO's basic functions is to help smooth the way for foreign companies such as Buckeye Beans & Herbs to do business in Japan. In addition to publishing numerous how-to guides, such as *Distribution in Japan* and *Negotiating with the Japanese*, JETRO sponsors trade missions to identify foreign products that have good prospects for finding market acceptance in Japan. JETRO's assistance was critical to the Smiths' efforts to bring Buckeye Beans to Japan.

Ultimately, after many months of slow but steady progress, Buckeye Beans is enjoying good market success in Japan. Because entering a foreign market can be such a time-consuming process, Doug Smith uses a cautionary tone when giving advice to prospective exporters. He notes, for example, that although many small-business owners want to sell internationally, they aren't, in fact, ready to do so. In some instances, for example, an oceangoing container may hold six months' worth of production from a small food manufacturer. But most foreign customers won't wait that long to get an order filled. Doug advises working with an export agent who'll take one or two pallets of a product at a time to help a small business get used to selling abroad.

Another interesting aspect of Buckeye Beans & Herbs is the emphasis on hiring family and friends. Doug's two sisters work for the company, as does Jill's brother. Doug cautions, though, that the approach may not work for others. "It comes back to values. What kind of a company is it, and what kind of a company do you want it to be? We're trying to create a different type of company." Jill echoes the thought, noting, "we are not only a value-added product company, we are a *values*-added, *people* company," emphasizing the *s* in the word *values.* There is plenty of evidence that the employees at Buckeye Beans & Herbs agree with the Queen Bean. Many have been offered higher pay at other companies but choose to stay at Buckeye. One reason, Doug says, is a flextime policy that offers employees more freedom and control over their own lives. For example, if employees need to spend time at home with a sick family member or want to work with Scout groups, their wishes can be accommodated. Summing up what she has accomplished, Jill says, "As an artist, we talk about 'the work that we do.' Businesspeople talk about '*going* to work.' It's a very different concept, but the two can mesh."

VIDEO CASE QUESTIONS

1. Entrepreneurs often possess certain qualities and attributes that contribute to their success. Briefly describe some of the entrepreneurial "success" qualities that Jill Smith possesses.
2. Explain what Jill Smith means when she says, "Sometimes I think we're as much an entertainment company as a product company." Why is "entertainment" important to Jill's customers?
3. Should Jill Smith consider the possibility of franchising Buckeye Beans & Herbs in order to expand into new markets? Why or why not? What are some of the advantages and disadvantages of this option? What are some new issues that Jill will face if the company franchises its stores?
4. What is JETRO? How can JETRO help companies like Buckeye Beans & Herbs succeed in reaching the Japanese market?
5. Small companies perform a number of important roles in the economy. Briefly describe how Buckeye Beans & Herbs contributes to the overall economy.

SMALL BUSINESS 2000

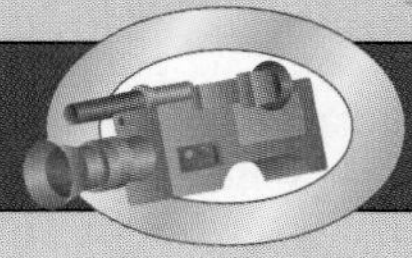

Part III Video Case: On Target Supplies and Logistics—The Amazing Story of Albert Black's $10 Million Paper Chase

SMALL BUSINESS 2000

Albert Black is a man with a mission. Even though he grew up in a government housing project in south Dallas, his parents gave him careful guidance and instilled in him a sense of confidence that helped prepare him for success in the business world. As a boy, Albert learned the value of hard work by mowing lawns. Albert's mother expected the best from her children; Albert credits his grandmother with teaching him to "treat people with Christian passion and look out for others." His father worked for many years as a doorman at a Dallas hotel and became acquainted with many prominent Dallas businesspersons. Albert's father encouraged the youth to set his sights on becoming a businessman, and Albert heeded that advice.

After attending college on a football scholarship, Albert borrowed money from friends and started On Target Supplies and Logistics. The company supplies printing and photocopy paper to Dallas-area businesses. Although running On Target Supplies was Albert's "day job," he also worked nights in the information systems department at Lone Star Gas. Over the course of ten years, the second job provided much-needed funding for On Target Supplies, and it also allowed Albert to become more familiar with the technology needs of large businesses that he hoped would one day be his customers. Albert recalls, "I had a goal. I would pick up a skill set, a management ability, a competency that I could take into my company and make it work. I managed information systems, I managed technology development, I managed customer satisfaction."

Today, Albert has 30 people on the payroll, and On Target generates $10 million in annual sales. Customers include Electronic Data Services, Texas Instruments, Southwestern Bell, and Texas Utilities. High visibility in the community is one reason Albert has attracted such an impressive roster of customers. Early on, Albert recognized the benefits of active participation with nonprofit organizations in the Dallas area. "We decided to get involved with communities, and provide leadership around town. By volunteering, we would get exposure and a chance to network while doing real good for the city of Dallas. Our goal was to make business friends that we could eventually call on and do business with."

Another reason for Albert's success is that he knows how to listen. For example, On Target is a supplier to Lone Star Gas where Albert once worked nights. At first, On Target's paper products moved from its loading dock to Lone Star's. Albert devised a strategy of just-in-time "desktop distribution" that added value to the supply chain by delivering boxes of paper directly to the persons who needed them. Albert's solution saves Lone Star time, money, and inventory expense. Albert explains, "I have the ability to listen, to plan, to present, to perform, to adjust. The flexibility of the supplier must be so demonstrated that it's continuously changing, and continuously adding value, and continuously redefining value for our customers."

In keeping with his desire to learn, Albert recently earned an MBA from Southern Methodist University. Albert also understands that he needs ongoing input from others if he is to take his company to the next level. On Target has a board of advisers made up of representatives from client companies. Albert has also formed a board of directors made up of professionals from the Dallas business community. John Castle, a senior executive at EDS, serves as chairman of the board of directors. "Our role is to serve as a sounding board. Albert brings his ideas and strategies, and we give him our perspective." Albert says, "John Castle felt that once On Target reached the $10 million mark, we needed more challenge and balance in our strategic direction." Albert acknowledges that initially he felt intimidated at the prospect of approaching Castle. He says, however, "Business leaders must have courage. We must get beyond that emotional feeling of being intimidated. We have to find common interests and build on those things to build a partnership."

Having tasted success for himself, Albert is driven to create jobs and make the American dream available to his employees. His purpose in building a business, he says, was to "hire people, improve the infrastructure of the inner city where we do business, pay taxes, provide leadership, and get rich along the way." He relishes the opportunity to dispel some myths about business and, in doing so, come to the attention of the broader business community. For example, On Target's success contradicts the myth that a small business cannot capitalize itself sufficiently to finance growth. Albert has also proven that a minority business can indeed put together the type of management team necessary to take advantage of market opportunities. Albert does not hesitate to become involved in the private lives of his employees. For example, On Target has a 401K plan and Albert encourages employees to maximize their tax-deferred retirement savings. He also encourages—even insists—that employees continue their educations.

Albert's promise to employees involves three things. First, they will earn an "educational" income. Albert believes in *open-book management*, a concept that has been featured in *Inc.* magazine and described by author John Case in *Open-Book Management: The Coming Business Revolution.* In a nutshell, the open-book approach calls for top management to share virtually all information with employees, including the contents of the company's financial statements. Employees at On Target know about the company's expense and revenue streams, as well as its cost of sales. At many companies, such information is not shared with rank-and-file employees. Albert wants his employees to learn enough so that they can eventually start their own businesses if they so desire. Second, On Target employees earn "psychological" incomes. As Albert explains, "I want you to feel good about what you do. You'll get a sense of esprit de corps, that together we can climb mountains and make a contribution every day." Finally, there is financial income. Albert's goal is to pay his employees salaries that exceed the industry average. He takes great personal pride in noting that, despite the fact that many of his employees come from humble beginnings like his own, the average annual salary of On Target's employees is about $30,000. "I've taken tax users and helped them become tax producers," he says.

VIDEO CASE QUESTIONS

1. Successful businesspeople must learn management fundamentals. How did Albert Black acquire the business skills he needed to start and operate his own business? Consider his education and experiential background as discussed in the video.
2. On Target devised a unique strategy for product distribution at Lone Star Gas. Identify the strategy and why it is an improvement over the previous method.
3. Managing a business as it grows presents special challenges. As On Target reached $10 million in sales, what did Albert Black do in order to assure proper guidance as the company grew?
4. Albert Black says his promise to employees involves three things. What are those three things identified in the video, and why are they important for On Target employees?
5. What is *open-book management,* and what role does it play at On Target? How does it fit in with Albert Black's philosophy?

SMALL BUSINESS 2000

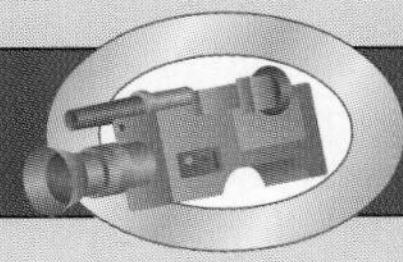

Part IV Video Case: Tom Gegax and Tires Plus—Making the Rubber Meet the Road

SMALL BUSINESS 2000 Tom Gegax is not the president of Tires Plus. He is the "head coach." Tires Plus does not have employees. It has "team members." The team members do not serve customers. They serve "guests." The company's operations manual is known as the "playbook." The simple act of using a special management vocabulary speaks volumes about Tom's business philosophy, which he sums up this way: "Take something that you believe is not being done well, and then go for it and make it better."

It's an approach that has served Tom well. He spent the early years of his career at Shell Oil and went from there to owning a few gas stations. Tom recalls, "I didn't feel that I had the know-how to make a big impact in, say, the computer industry." But he did recognize that, with the right management formula, selling tires could be a lot more profitable than selling gasoline. Tom and partner Don Gullett started with a mission that could be shared with others, found a niche, and relied on self-coaching. Tom explains, "Everybody wants to go out and manage others. But until you learn how to manage yourself, it's pretty hard to manage others." With that in mind, the partners built Tires Plus into a company with $100 million in annual sales and 70 stores located in the upper Midwest.

Tires Plus competes with some very well-known companies. For example, Goodyear Tire & Rubber has a national network of more than 2,500 independent dealers. Sears, Roebuck & Company is also an important competitor with its auto centers. Still, Tires Plus has carved out a niche for itself by offering a wide selection of brands, speedy service, and clean, modern stores. Moreover, Tom and Don have succeeded by creating a business environment that allows employees to gain the satisfaction that comes from providing products and services that people need while getting the chance to reap financial rewards.

Tom and Don try to hire people who buy into their philosophy. "We start by finding people who are trainable and can be motivated. Then we compensate them right—a "pay for productivity" situation. Third, you have to take care of them." Don continues, "We're looking for people who care about others. A good team member is one who is willing to sit back and explain something to a customer, who comes across as sincere." Team members who attend training sessions at Tires Plus University are treated to healthy doses of business philosophy from their head coach. With his intense gaze, piercing blue eyes, and fervent demeanor, Tom resembles a preacher. He reminds trainees, "If money is your focus, it doesn't work. What does work is taking care of our guests, and helping our teammates. When that occurs, the by-product of that is you'll make money. But don't try to make money." Tom admits that selling has gotten a tarnished reputation in some circles. But, in his view, "Selling is communicating. It's the ability to communicate with guests about what their needs are and whether we can fill those needs in a proper way." Tom believes that "People sense your purpose and if your purpose really is a greater good. If teammates feel you're serving them and caring about them, then they'll perform better. If guests perceive you care about them, sales will go up."

A period of personal growth following a divorce and a brush with cancer helped Tom fine-tune his business philosophy. He says, "As long as our lives seem to be going OK, we don't get on the path for personal growth. It often takes a wake-up call. I encourage my teammates to not wait for a wake-up call." In his search for personal growth, Tom found emotional teachers who could supplement what he had learned from spiritual and intellectual teachers. The world of sports was also an important source of inspiration for Tom's business model. Tom recalls, "I saw college basketball coaches on the sidelines. I said to myself, 'I like the way they're giving constant feedback.'" Tom recognized that language could play a big role in helping him motivate his employees by verbalizing what is expected of them. "People don't want to be managed," Tom says. "If you call them 'manager' every day, then they're going to manage. But if we call them 'coach,' then that gets in their mind as what we want them doing."

Tom's belief in the power of words and language is supported by some well-known management experts. For example, the use of a "special language" was identified by Tom Peters and Robert Waterman as an attribute of excellent companies in their classic book, *In Search of Excellence.* The Walt Disney Company, for example, is legendary for its innovative use of language. At Disneyland and other Disney theme parks, for example, employees are "cast members," the personnel department is known as "central casting," and employees who work with the public are "on stage." Although Tom is proud to have the words "head coach" on his business card, his enthusiasm for such unconventional language is not shared by everyone he meets. Tom once encountered former Chrysler Corporation chief Lee Iacocca at a professional meeting. After reading Tom's business card, Iacocca's response was, "What's the matter—don't you want to be a CEO?" Tom answered, "No, I want to be a Head Coach."

VIDEO CASE QUESTIONS

1. Is Tom Gegax a theory X-, Y-, or Z-oriented manager? Please explain and give examples.
2. Tom Gegax believes that language can play a special role in motivating employees. What are some of the specific things that he does to communicate effectively with employees?
3. Do you think Gegax's employees would ever vote to join a union? Why or why not?
4. Tom does not believe that money should be the most important motivator for Tires Plus team members. What other types of motivators are important to Tom?
5. How does Tires Plus University contribute to the success of the Tires Plus organization?

SMALL BUSINESS 2000

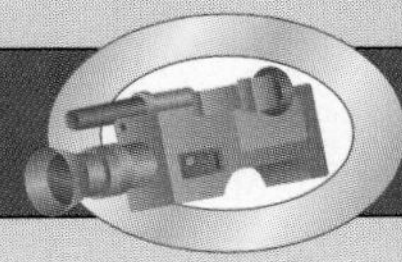

Part V Video Case: S.C.R.U.B.S.—How Nurse Calloway Keeps Them All in Stitches

SMALL BUSINESS 2000

For anyone who has worked in, or simply visited, a hospital or other health-care facility, they are a familiar sight: the ubiquitous green or blue baggy outfits worn by doctors, nurses, orderlies and technicians. Known as "scrub suits," or simply "scrubs," these two-piece outfits typically had v-neck, pullover tops with a patch pocket and draw-string trousers. For years, scrubs were purchased in mass quantities by hospitals and issued to employees who arrived at work in street clothes and changed in locker rooms. Scrubs were made from a cotton-polyester blend fabric designed to withstand the extremely high laundering temperatures that were believed to be necessary for thorough sanitation. A few years ago, however, studies began appearing that indicated that germs were not transmitted by health-care workers' clothing. Rather, it was found that the key to preventing the spread of infection was thorough handwashing. At roughly the same time, hospital administrators were coming under increased pressure to cut costs. One way of doing so was to transfer the responsibility for buying and laundering scrubs onto nurses and other staff employees. Employees began wearing their scrubs to work.

These events created a marketing opportunity for Sue Calloway. Sue had enjoyed sewing for most of her life, and continued to sew after fulfilling her lifelong ambition to become a nurse. Rather than buying scrubs like many other nurses, Sue sewed her own. However, hers were not at all like the standard-issue blue and green uniforms of old. She added some subtle styling touches and chose 100 percent cotton fabrics with bright colors and designs. When Sue began wearing her homemade scrubs to work in 1988, her friends asked where she had gotten them. Sue explained that she had made them herself. Sue recalls, "All my friends wanted them. I never said 'no,' and I just kept sewing and taking orders."

For several years, Sue continued to pursue nursing and sewed at home in her spare time. In 1992, Sue's husband Rocky encouraged her to quit sewing part time and turn her hobby into a full-time business. Today, Sue devotes all her time to the design and marketing of scrubs, surgical dresses, and other apparel items for health-care workers. Most of the actual sewing is outsourced to another company. Sue has registered the brand name S.C.R.U.B.S., which stands for "Simply Comfortable Really Unique Basic Scrubs." Her years of experience enable her to add whimsical touches to her products, such as S.C.R.U.B.S. featuring flying pigs. As Sue notes with a twinkle in her eye, "Sometimes when you work in a high-stress environment in a hospital, it's like, 'When pigs fly, I'll get to it.'"

Early on, Sue found a partner who could help steer S.C.R.U.B.S. in the right direction. Steve Epstein, a longtime family acquaintance, had extensive experience and expertise in the apparel industry. Steve convinced her that the high number of health-care professionals represented a significant opportunity. His conservative projection of how the business could grow exceeded Sue's expectations. To support the fledging venture, Sue, Rocky, Steve, and Steve's wife Ida borrowed money from their friends, used their credit cards, and sold their cars.

Although it was occasionally touch and go early on, Steve's projections, optimism, and confidence in Sue turned out to be justified. Not only was there a market to be tapped, but Sue had the right product for that market. As Steve explains, "The product is unique, it's different, and it addresses a genuine need in the community. There is a need for something fun in an otherwise morbid business." Tom Taylor, a health-care worker who lives in Marin County, California, is a loyal S.C.R.U.B.S. customer. "Patients really notice them," Tom says. "Nine out of ten say something, and patients who are in the hospital for extended stays have said they look forward to what I'm going to wear the next day." Tom adds, "I'm sort of putting on pajamas and tennis shoes to go to work instead of a suit and tie, so the only way I can be creative is with the material and patterns on my uniform."

In Steve's opinion, S.C.R.U.B.S. has succeeded because of sound business fundamentals. He says, "We are extremely quality conscious, we are customer service conscious, and we provide guarantees that make the purchase nonrisky to the customer." Rocky notes that the partners' motivation is not to get rich. "Here's a business that we enjoy doing, it does good for someone, and we can make a living at it." S.C.R.U.B.S. relies primarily on mail order to reach its customers, who today include dentists, veterinarians, and even teachers. The catalog strategy at S.C.R.U.B.S. is similar to that of Buckeye Beans in Part II in that it relies on compelling visuals and strong copywriting and storytelling to communicate details about the product. Melissa Holmes is responsible for creating copy that conveys a sense of how it feels to wear the company's fabrics. The company's original artwork was created by hand by a designer using pastel watercolors. As the company grew, however, the transition was made to computerized design.

In order to increase the cost efficiency of its mailings, Sue hired Kathy Murphy as marketing director. Kathy introduced more sophisticated marketing techniques such as market segmentation. Kathy explains, "Anybody who ever asked for one got a catalog every month. Anybody who ever bought got a catalog every month." Kathy is using a more targeted approach. She segments the customers in S.C.R.U.B.S.' database according to recency—whether they bought in the last 3 months, 4 to 6 months, 7 to 9 months; frequency—if they bought once, two times, four times; and how much money they spent. Kathy notes, "If they spent less than $25 and bought once, and it was a year ago, they're less likely to buy again than somebody who's spent $100, has bought four times, and has bought in the last 4 months." The more the customer tends to buy, the more catalogs he or she will receive. Financial considerations are also important. Kathy says, "I know before I mail what my breakeven is on the catalog. The breakeven takes into account the cost of producing the catalog and mailing it, the cost of fulfilling the order, the cost of the building that we're in, everybody's salary. I have to have a pretty good idea of how these people are going to respond before I mail it."

To generate inquiries and add to the company's database, Kathy places advertisements for S.C.R.U.B.S. in magazines. The ads contain postage-paid response cards. Card decks are another tool that Kathy likes; organizations that specialize in mail-order send packets of cards representing various businesses and products to specific lists such as "OB/GYN," "firemen and doctors," and so on. In mail order, "test and track" is the operative concept. "The beauty of mail order is that you can track everything," Kathy says.

Although mail order is currently the mainstay of S.C.R.U.B.S., Sue and Steve have targeted retail customers as critical elements in the company's growth strategy. Now that the company's first two store locations have proven to be successful, more are on the drawing board. However, Sue is still doing everything she can to retain the loyalty of her mail order customers. For example, each order is shipped with a postage-paid Priority Mail return envelope that customers can use to exchange return merchandise. How can a small business afford to make that kind of investment in returns? The key, Sue says, is to think long term. "That customer will order more in the future. Then you will make more on that customer. You have to build a strong connection and be there to serve that customer."

VIDEO CASE QUESTIONS

1. The essence of marketing is identifying needs and wants and taking advantage of opportunities. Explain how Sue Calloway found a need and filled it. What other factors contributed to Sue's initial success?
2. A company's marketing plan should focus on the marketing mix, also known as the "4Ps": product, price, place, and promotion. Give an example each of these marketing mix elements based on the information in the S.C.R.U.B.S. case.
3. Effective marketers understand the importance of market segmentation and target marketing. How does S.C.R.U.B.S. use a database to segment and target its market? How does the company add names to its database? Who represents the company's most important target market?
4. What efforts does Sue make to ensure customer satisfaction?
5. What other types of nonstore retail opportunities besides mail-order catalogs might Sue want to explore to grow her business, and why?

SMALL BUSINESS 2000

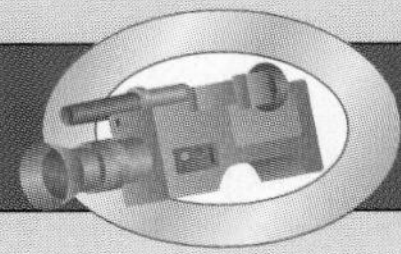

Part VI Video Case: SiloCaf—This Coffee Server Has All the Answers

SMALL BUSINESS 2000

At the Port of New Orleans, tradition meets technology at SiloCaf, an international forwarding company that imports and processes coffee beans for American roasters. The company's name reflects the fact that it occupies a facility once used for grain storage. Silocaf's chief is Frederico Pacorini, whose father established a coffee business in Italy in the 1920s. Upon learning that Port authorities planned to tear down the building, Frederico secured $20 million in financing from headquarters, bought the property, and installed a network of chutes, scales, and other mechanical equipment for processing coffee. Frederico also invested in a sophisticated information system (IS) that automates the operation.

SiloCaf was well positioned to capitalize on the explosive increase in coffee consumption in the United States during the 1990s. The Specialty Coffee Association of America (SCAA) predicts that, by the year 2000, there will be 10,000 coffee bars, cafes, and kiosks, compared with only about 200 in 1990. By the mid-1990s, employment in the specialty coffee industry included about 10,000 people who worked for roaster/retailers such as Starbucks and about 20,000 who worked for roasters. About 300 people were employed by importers such as SiloCaf.

The phenomenal growth of the coffee industry has been accompanied by increased sophistication among consumers. According to data compiled by the SCAA, per capita coffee consumption in the United States actually decreased from 2.68 cups a day to 1.75 cups between 1969 and 1989. However, purchases of specialty coffee—that is, coffee sold in whole-bean form rather than instant or ground coffee in jars or vacuum-packed cans—increased from $44 million to $1.5 billion. Coffee drinkers have come to expect consistent flavor and quality from their favorite brands. Learning about coffee means learning about geography, with beans imported from Central and South America, Africa, and Asia. But, because coffee is an agricultural product subject to variations in weather, soil chemistry, and growing conditions, achieving that consistency year in and year out is both a requirement and a challenge.

Computer technology allows Silocaf to blend 10 million pounds of coffee each week. Frederico notes, "If you think about trying to do this with people rather than technology, basically there would be no guarantee that we would be able to process four million bags of coffee each year." He continues, "Technology in a business like ours lets us make all the blends that we need and optimize the way we create blends. We have statistical reports for each scale that weighs the coffee." Computers are the basic building blocks for all the statistical process controls. Part of SiloCaf's is a network of fifteen personal computers for tracking the consistency of each scale. The blending process is complicated, with chutes sending coffee to different bins. Computer controls allow operators to stop one blend and start another one immediately. Any data input into one of the company's personal computers is then routed via the local area network (LAN) into the company's server. The LAN makes it possible for anyone at any PC to access data from the server; the server at SiloCaf is a "mid-range" IBM AS/400 that acts as the company's information warehouse.

For a small business like SiloCaf, a mid-range system provides plenty of computing power, but with a price range of $30,000 to $80,000, it costs much less than a mainframe computer. Even state-of-the-art computers become obsolete within 18 to 36 months, so SiloCaf's system will be expanded and upgraded on a regular basis. By continually investing in technology, company executives can keep costs down while increasing the volume of business. Says Frederico, "You can use technology to do things better, but you can't do things without technology anymore."

VIDEO CASE QUESTIONS

1. Explain the role that computer technology plays in quality control at SiloCaf. Why is quality control so important in the coffee industry today? Think about the dynamics of the coffee market explained in the video.
2. Because SiloCaf's operation is completely dependent on computer technology, recommend some technology precautions or safeguards the company should adopt on a regular basis to protect its operation. How might your recommendations prevent a technology crisis from occurring?
3. What types of data do you think SiloCaf's management team might want to access from the network server on a regular basis, and how would they use that data?
4. Whenever SiloCaf purchases new computer equipment, the company accountants depreciate the cost of the equipment over a 3-year period. Why do they do this?
5. One way SiloCaf manages to keep its cost under control is by using "what if" analysis to test and prepare for the financial impact of possible future events. What might be a few of the "what-if" questions SiloCaf's accountants might want to ask? Why?

SMALL BUSINESS 2000

Part VII Video Case: Financing a New Business—Cruising for Capital Down the Information Superhighway

SMALL BUSINESS 2000

Good financial management is vital to the success of any business enterprise. When starting small businesses, owners are often able to obtain financing based on their personal credit histories and assets. If companies have no previous credit history, owners are often required to personally guarantee the loan. The company may also be required to pledge inventory, property, plant, equipment, or accounts receivable as collateral. After a company establishes credit, the personal guarantee of the owner may no longer be necessary. Small businesses are often formed as corporations that are privately owned by one or a few individuals who own shares of stock. As a company grows, a key financing decision is whether to take the company public by selling shares through a public stock offering. Financing can also take the form of long-term debt such as bonds; it is also possible to fund growth out of retained earnings. The cost of these types of financing determines the company's cost of capital.

Bill Tobin is the founder of PC Flowers & Gifts, a successful online retailing venture that is the subject of the video case at the end of Part VIII. Bill's business career began when, at age eleven, he borrowed his mother's credit card, bought a lawn mower, and went door-to-door seeking customers in his neighborhood on Long Island. When he turned 16 and got his driver's license, Bill bought a car and expanded the reach of his business. By the time he graduated from college, he had fifty employees and a fleet of trucks. Over the next two decades, Bill reinvested his own money in several new businesses. He recalls, "When you take money from an investment banker or any other source you become an employee, and that felt very alien to me. I wanted to be the decision maker and not have to go back and ask permission." Because of the huge opportunities offered by the Internet, Bill is considering taking on a financial partner for the first time in his career. "All entrepreneurs must know that there's a time in the life cycle of a company or a product when you need a partner. The Internet is a perfect example: It's bigger than any company in the United States. I am now ready to take in a financial partner."

When Tom Gegax and partner Don Gullett wanted to start Tires Plus, they had to visit ten banks before they could finally secure a loan. The problem? Tom recalls, "They kept saying, 'No, you don't have experience.' Finally, the tenth bank was willing to take a risk with us." Now, Tom and Don finance growth at Tires Plus out of retained earnings with some financial assistance from tire manufacturers that are the company's suppliers. Tom has considered an initial public offering but prefers to keep his company private. Tom explains, "You can only keep your eye on two balls at a time: One is your customers, who are your guests, the other is your teammates. You better have your eye on those two balls. If you inject a third element and get lots of shareholders, you'll have to spend lots of time with them."

Sometimes new business ventures do attract outside investors from the start. When Howard Schultz bought Starbucks Coffee Company in 1987, it operated as a coffee roaster with eleven retail stores in the Seattle area. By 1993, there were 280 Starbucks stores across America, and sales revenue had grown from $1.3 million to more than $160 million. In 1992, Starbucks went public and sold 2.1 million shares at $14 per share. The stock price doubled within 2 years. Schultz and his original investors were rewarded handsomely, a fact that has not been lost on the local investment community. The success of Starbucks helped another Seattle entrepreneur, Dave de Varona, when he needed financing for a new restaurant venture. Dave explains, "Retail categories like ourselves are getting funded a lot faster by sophisticated investment groups because of Howard Schultz and Starbucks. Because of him, companies like ours are being noticed sooner. One of the major players in our investment group missed the Starbucks opportunity and doesn't want it to happen again." However, Dave cautions would-be entrepreneurs to master the vocabulary of finance before meeting with investors. "We didn't have terms like 'unilevel economics' or 'footprint,'" he recalls.

Obtaining start-up capital is only one financial issue that entrepreneurs face. Another concerns financial management of the ongoing firm. Keeping costs down is a must in a fledgling small business. Once a company has been viable for two or three years, bankers are more willing to establish a line of credit and make loans. There are a number of ways to keep costs down. One is outsourcing. Instead of investing in bricks and mortar and owning a production facility, a business owner may be able to subcontract some or all of the manufacturing work. Similarly, to help keep down payroll costs, outsourcing may involve hiring freelance designers, artists, or writers. Hiring right is another way to hold down costs; as Tom Gegax of Tires Plus explains, "We start by finding people who are trainable and can be motivated. Then we compensate them right—a "pay for productivity" situation. Third, you have to take care of them. Give them strokes and let them know when they're doing well, but also let them know when they're not doing things well and that they can do better."

A small business can also prosper if its owner stays tightly focused on market niches. "Stick with what you know" is one way of expressing it; as one small business owner puts it, "In niches there's riches." Bill Tobin says, "I'm always looking for a niche. When you're a small-business, you have to find the small niche and be the best at it and then grow the niche. The crumbs that fall off large corporate America's table are a big meal for a small company." Investments in state-of-the-art computer technology are necessary to keep a company on the cutting edge. It may involve point-of-sale cash register systems, sophisticated desk-top computers, or a network of PCs and a server. Whatever the particular technology needs of a small business may be, as one small business owner notes, "You can't do things without technology anymore."

VIDEO CASE QUESTIONS

1. Why are banks sometimes reluctant to provide financial support to individuals starting a business? Refer to the discussion about Tom Gegax and Don Gullet of Tires Plus in this case for help with the answer.
2. Small businesses often have to look far and wide for financing. What are some of the other sources of financing for small businesses besides banks?
3. Tom Gegax has considered selling shares to the general public through an initail public offering (IPO), but he does not want to do that. What is his reasoning? Do you agree with his philosophy?
4. Outsourcing is one of the financial management techniques identified in the case. What is outsourcing? How can it help a small business owner cut costs?
5. Another way to cut costs is by banking electronically. How does electronic banking improve a company's cash flow?

SMALL BUSINESS 2000

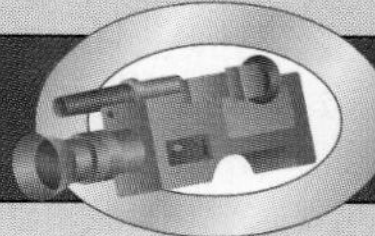

Part VIII Video Case: PC Flowers on the Net—It's a Blooming Business These Days

SMALL BUSINESS 2000 As the 20th century comes to a close, merchandise purchase transactions in cyberspace represent only about one percent of total retail sales revenues in the United States. Still, the dollar amount of those transactions is impressive: According to industry analysts, revenue from cybersales totaled $2.6 billion in 1997, up from $350 million in 1995. Although the Internet and the World Wide Web are household words now, that was not the case just a few years ago. Even so, by the late-1980s, Prodigy, CompuServe, and other subscription-based online services promised a tantalizing new interactive world of advertising and marketing distribution. Prodigy was launched in 1988 by two industry giants, computer maker IBM and retailer Sears, Roebuck & Company. Research indicated that the typical Prodigy subscriber household consisted of a married couple under 40 years of age with $70,000 in annual income. This profile was perfectly matched to the target market for entrepreneur Bill Tobin's new venture: Selling fresh flowers online.

Tobin had to fight to convince others that the time was ripe for what he calls "a new transactional paradigm." "Everybody said it couldn't be done. Everybody said it won't work," Tobin recalls. Even though Tobin had an impressive track record of business success, he did not succeed in convincing FTD's Board of Directors to support his idea for electronic ordering. Undeterred, Tobin bought a chain of florists, converted their offerings to digital format, and then played hardball: He informed the FTD network that he intended to launch an online service. If the FTD didn't cooperate with his efforts, he would sue on antitrust grounds. Needless to say, the FTD had a change of heart.

Tobin spent a year developing a technology infrastructure and order fulfillment process, then launched PC Flowers on Prodigy in 1989. It quickly became one of the most successful services on the system as subscribers used Prodigy to order floral arrangements—at an average price of $34—for delivery anywhere in the country through the FTD's electronic Mercury florist network. During 1990, its first full year on Prodigy, PC Flowers jumped from last place into the top ten among the 25,000 florists in the United States providing FTD services. Emboldened by that success, Tobin went to FTD with a new demand: To expand his strategic alliance with FTD by obtaining 5,000 square feet at the Mercury network, staffed with his people, and equipped with his software. His goal was to provide the highest level of customer service in the industry. Tobin notes that even the best FTD florist has a 5 to 7 percent documented error rate, while PC Flowers boasts an error rate of only .2 percent. To achieve that, Tobin bypasses 93 percent of the florists in the FTD network. He uses only the top 7 percent—approximately 2800 florists nationwide—who can meet his exacting standards.

Ironically, today Prodigy struggles for survival in an industry dominated by America Online. However, PC Flowers continues to prosper, and, thanks to the Internet, it can now serve customers worldwide. It has become, in Tobin's words, "the most comprehensive floral and gift service in the interactive world." One reason for Tobin's success is that he understands how dramatically different online retailing is from traditional retailing. He explains, "You must earn the right of the consumer to tell them about your message. You can't be as intrusive as traditional channels and means of advertising. This is a highly educated user. This is a consumer who is used to a laser-beam approach to what they want, a consumer who won't put up with a waste of his or her time. Online consumers are far more demanding than traditional consumers."

Shoppers are also savvy enough to know that many online retailers have lower overhead costs than retailers who have made substantial investments in "bricks and mortar." Therefore, Tobin points out, online shoppers expect lower prices. Another crucial difference is that online consumers have much more control than traditional consumers. Tobin describes this as "the sword of Damocles": If an online customer is unhappy with something, that dissatisfaction can be shared with millions of other online users with just a few keystrokes. To ensure the highest level of customer satisfaction, Tobin has designed PC Flowers with the best graphics and the best navigational tools in the industry. Another thing that online shoppers demand is security when they use credit cards to pay for their orders. Tobin is aware that the general public does not have a high degree of confidence in Internet security. However, most Internet retailers use highly effective forms of electronic encryption when uploading credit card information. Tobin insists that Internet transactions are more secure than traditional methods of using credit cards; for example, customers give out credit card information over the telephone.

Tobin's online enterprise boasts other state-of-the-art features, such as cutting-edge "push-pull" technology that changes screen images automatically without prompting from the online shopper. In 1994, Tobin expanded the scope of his business to include greeting cards, balloons, stuffed bears, gift baskets, and gourmet food items; his company is now known as PC Flowers & Gifts. Tobin's research told him that, in the United States, men don't sent flowers to other men, women don't send men flowers, and kids under age 13 don't get flowers. Tobin's response: Offer customers the opportunity to build balloon arrangements online that are delivered by the FTD network. Tobin also seeks out new value-added ways to market flowers. For example, he is capitalizing on the do-it-yourself trend by offering Superbatch, an assortment of cut flowers that is sent with a how-to video and booklet that allows individuals to create their own flower arrangements. Because Superbatch consists of flowers that represent overstock to growers, Tobin can offer customers a $90 retail value for about half price.

Despite the success Tobin has achieved to date, he still has ambitious plans for the future. Tobin says, "An entrepreneur is like a dog with a bone. He doesn't drop it until there's not a scrap of meat on it. He stays with it. He's focused. He's driven and cannot sleep, cannot eat until he accomplishes that goal." To get to the next level with his business, Tobin is ready to take on a strategic partner that will be able to provide the resources necessary to transform PC Flowers into an even bigger interactive shopping experience. Tobin hopes that PC Flowers' proven ability to attract customers will enable him to pass those customers on to other, less well-known Internet sites. Summing up his business philosophy, Tobin says, "An entrepreneur is one of the biggest gamblers in the world. But he gambles in an area where he figures he controls the odds, as opposed to the house controlling the odds." He continues, "I understand the Internet, and I understand where I want to go with it. The Internet gives me the opportunity to take my business forward into one hundred new areas. It's a wide-open, free-for-all highway—it's the autobahn of opportunity."

VIDEO CASE QUESTIONS

1. Bill Tobin believes that the Internet represents a "new transactional paradigm." What does he mean by this?
2. Why did the FTD board initially refuse to cooperate with Bill Tobin?
3. What are some of the key differences between online retailing and traditional retailing?
4. In the video, Tobin speaks of "the sword of Damocles." In what sense do online consumers wield this "sword"?
5. Shopping at PC Flowers Web site can be a culinary treat. With mouth-watering items like chocolate lace cookies, cheesecakes, and fancy cashews, some may be tempted to forget the flowers. Does it make sense to combine different products requiring different distribution systems on a single Web site? Why or why not?

APPENDIX I

CAREER GUIDE: THE EMPLOYMENT SEARCH

THINKING ABOUT YOUR CAREER

Getting the job that's right for you takes more than sending out a few letters and signing up with the college placement office. Planning and research are important if you want to find a company that suits you. Before you limit your job search to a particular industry or functional specialty, analyze what you have to offer and what you hope to get from your work.

Analyze What You Have to Offer

First, examine your marketable skills. One way is to jot down ten achievements you're proud of, whether they include learning to ski, taking a prizewinning photo, tutoring a child, or editing the school paper. Look carefully at each of these achievements. What specific skills did they demand? For example, leadership, speaking ability, and artistic talent may have been the skills that helped you coordinate a winning presentation to the college administration. As you analyze your achievements, you'll begin to recognize a pattern of skills. Which of them might be valuable to potential employers?

Second, examine your educational preparation, work experience, and extracurricular activities. What kinds of jobs are you qualified to do on the basis of your knowledge and experience? What have you learned from participating in volunteer work or class projects that could benefit you on the job? Have you held any offices, won any awards or scholarships, mastered a second language?

Third, take stock of your personal characteristics so that you can determine the type of job you'll do best. Are you aggressive, a born leader—or would you rather follow? Are you outgoing, articulate, great with people—or do you prefer working alone? Make a list of what you believe are your four or five most important qualities. Ask a relative or friend to rate your traits as well.

If you're having trouble figuring out your interests and capabilities, consult your college placement office or career guidance center. Many campuses administer a variety of tests designed to help you identify your interests, aptitudes, and personality traits. Although these tests won't reveal the "perfect" job for you, they'll help you focus on the types of work that best suit your personality.

Determine What You Want

Knowing what you *can* do is one thing. Knowing what you *want* to do is another. Many students are so accustomed to doing what parents, peers, and instructors expect that they've lost sight of their own values. Choosing a career is a decision you need to make on your own. Get advice and information from everyone you know (family, friends, teachers, professional acquaintances), but remember that you are the only one who can decide which career is best for you. Begin by finding out just what it is you want: the tasks you enjoy, the compensation you expect, and the work environment you prefer.

What Tasks Do You Enjoy? Basically, you need to decide what you'd like to do every day. If you have a limited range of experience, take part-time jobs, participate in work/

study programs, serve as an intern in your particular field, participate in study-abroad programs, do anything you can think of to broaden your career horizons. You can also talk to people in various occupations. When Nathan James was a sophomore in college, he thought he might enjoy a career in sales, marketing research, or advertising, but he didn't know enough about the working lives of people in those fields to make an intelligent choice. So he went to his school's alumni relations office and made a list of former graduates working in the three professions. After making a few phone calls, he knew a lot more. In fact, one alumnus—an account executive with an advertising agency—invited James to spend spring break shadowing him. That experience persuaded James to focus his courses on advertising. He's now interning with a prominent advertising agency in Philadelphia.[1]

Another way to learn about various occupations is to read about them. Your college library or placement office might be a good place to start. One of the liveliest books aimed at college students is Lisa Birnbach's *Going to Work.* Among other things, Birnbach describes test-driving cars for Ford and selling cosmetics at Bloomingdale's. Another useful source is the 13-volume *Career Information Center* encyclopedia of jobs and careers, which is arranged by industry. For each job title, there's a description of the nature of the work, entry requirements, application procedures, advancement possibilities, working conditions, earnings, and benefits.

Apart from looking at specific occupations, also consider general factors, such as how much independence you want on the job, how much variety you like, and whether you prefer to work with products, machines, people, ideas, figures, or some combination. Do you like physical work, mental work, or a mix? Do you prefer constant change or a predictable role?

What Compensation Do You Expect? Money and opportunities for advancement are also something to think about. Establish some specific compensation targets. What do you hope to earn in your first year on the job? What kind of pay increase do you expect each year? What's your ultimate earnings goal? Would you be comfortable with a job that pays on commission, or would you prefer a steady paycheck? What occupations offer the kind of money you're looking for? Are these occupations realistic for someone with your qualifications? Are you willing to settle for less money in order to do something you really love?

Next, consider your place within the company or profession. Where would you like to start? Where do you want to go from there? What's the ultimate position you would like to attain? How soon after joining the company would you like to receive your first promotion? Your next one? Once you have established these goals, ask yourself what additional training or preparation you'll need to achieve them.

What Work Environment Do You Prefer? Another factor to consider is the environment you want to work in. Start by thinking in broad terms about the size and type of operation that appeals to you. Do you like the idea of working for a small, entrepreneurial operation, or would you prefer to be part of a large company? How do you feel about profit-making versus nonprofit organizations? Are you attracted to service businesses or manufacturing operations? What types of products appeal to you? Do you want regular, predictable hours, or do you thrive on flexible, varied hours? Do you prefer to work from 9:00 A.M. to 5:00 P.M., or are you willing to work evenings and weekends, as in the entertainment and hospitality industries? Would you enjoy a seasonally varied job like education (which may give you summers off) or like retailing (with its selling cycles)?

Location can also be important. Would you like to work in a city, a suburb, or a small town? In an industrial area or an uptown setting? Do you favor a particular part of the country? Does working in another country appeal to you? Do you like working indoors or outdoors?

What about facilities? Is it important to you to work in an attractive place, or will simple, functional quarters suffice? Do you need a quiet office to work effectively, or can you concentrate in a noisy, open setting? Would you prefer to work at the company's headquarters or in a small field office? Do such amenities as an in-house gym or handball court matter to you? Is access to public transportation or freeways important?

Perhaps the most important environmental factor is the corporate culture. Would you be happy in a well-defined hierarchy, where roles and reporting relationships are clear, or would you prefer a less structured situation? What qualities do you want in a boss? Are you looking for a paternalistic organization or one that fosters individualism? Do you like a competitive environment or one that rewards teamwork?

Seeking Employment Opportunities

Once you know what you have to offer and what you want, you can start finding an employer to match. If you haven't already committed yourself to any particular career field, first find out where the job opportunities are. Which industries are strong? Which parts of the country are booming, and which specific job categories offer the best prospects for the future? Consult sources in several areas:

- *Business and financial news.* Subscribe to a major newspaper and scan the business pages every day. Watch some of the TV programs that focus on business such as *Wall Street Week,* and read the business articles in popular magazines such as *Time* and *Newsweek.* You might even want to subscribe to a business magazine such as *Fortune, Business Week,* or *Forbes.*
- *Library references.* For information about the future for specific jobs, see *The Dictionary of Occupational Titles* (U.S. Employment Service), *Occupational Outlook Handbook* (U.S. Bureau of Labor Statistics), and the employment publications of Science Research Associates. For an analysis of major industries, see the annual Market Data and Directory issue of *Industrial Marketing,* and look through Standard & Poor's industry surveys.
- *Journals, people, and associations.* Study professional and trade journals in the career fields that interest you. Also, talk to people in these fields; for names of the most prominent, consult *Standard & Poor's Register of Corporations, Directors and Executives.* Find recent books about the fields you're considering by checking *Books in Print.* You may be able to network with executives in your field by joining or participating in student business organizations, especially those with ties to real-world organizations such as the American Marketing Association or the American Management Association.

Once you've identified a promising industry and a career field, compile a list of specific organizations that appeal to you. You can put together a reasonable list by consulting several sources:

- *Directories of employers.* Directories such as *The College Placement Annual* and *Career: The Annual Guide to Business Opportunities* may be helpful. Write to the organizations on your list and ask for an annual report and any descriptive brochures or newsletters they've published. If possible, visit some of the organizations on your list, contact their personnel departments, or talk with key employees.
- *Local and major newspapers.* Businesses often advertise their products as well as their job openings in newspapers.
- *Trade and professional journals.* For information on journals in career fields that interest you, see *Ulrich's International Periodicals Directory.*
- *Agencies and offices.* Job listings can also be obtained from your college placement office, state employment bureaus, and private employment agencies.
- *Electronic services.* A source of growing importance to your job search is the Internet, or more specifically, the World Wide Web. The following section covers in detail ways to find employment on the Web. The fastest way to learn about a company is by visiting its Web site. If you land an important interview and you need information on a company fast, you can use a Web search engine to find the location of information about mission statements, product descriptions, annual reports, and job listings. The largest companies also post press releases and employee news.[2]

Seeking Employment on the Web[3]

The World Wide Web offers an amazing amount of employment information. Is the Web the answer to all your employment dreams? Perhaps . . . or perhaps not. But as the Web grows, the employment information it provides is constantly expanding. And you're fortunate, because you don't have to start from scratch like some intrepid adventurer. For helpful hints and useful Web addresses, you can turn to innumerable books, such as *What Color Is Your Parachute?* by Richard Nelson Bolles.

When you're dealing with the Internet, the one thing you can count on is rapid change. So exactly how using the Web will affect your job search depends on how well you prepare your job-search strategy, how many employers come to accept the Web as a source of potential employees, and how quickly the resources already available expand and adapt to the ever-changing Web environment. All major online services (such as America Online and CompuServe) already have areas for people seeking employment. The World Wide Web offers information not only from employers seeking applicants but also from people seeking work. You can use the World Wide Web for a variety of job-seeking tasks:

- *Finding career counseling.* Even when using the Web to locate particular job opportunities, you still need to analyze your skills and work expectations. For example, you can begin your self-assessment with the *Keirsey Temperament Sorter,* an online personality test. The Web offers you job-seeking pointers and counseling from online career centers, many of which are run by colleges and universities that put a lot of effort into creating interesting and helpful sites. Other career centers are commercial and can run the gamut from award winning to depressing. So make sure the advice you get is both useful and sensible. One good commercial site is Mary-Ellen Mort's *Job-Smart.*

- *Making contacts.* You can use the Web to locate and communicate with potential employers. One way to locate people is through Usenet newsgroups that are dedicated to your field of interest. Newsgroup members leave messages for one another on an electronic bulletin board and retrieve messages by visiting that Web site. You might also try listservs (or Internet mailing lists). These discussion groups are similar to Usenet newsgroups, except that the group mails each message to every member's e-mail address. Commercial systems such as Prodigy, America Online, and CompuServe have their own discussion groups (called Special Interest Groups, RoundTables, Clubs, or Bulletin Boards). These commercial groups are also devoted to a particular interest, but they make a profit from the time users spend using their services. Once you've located a potential contact, you can communicate quickly and nonintrusively by using e-mail to request information or to let an employer know you're interested in working for a particular company.
- *Researching employers' companies.* When looking for information about the companies you might want to work for, don't forget the Web. Even companies that don't yet have a home page are getting one, and many of them are including job listings on their Web site. By visiting a company's Web site, you can find out about its mission, products, annual reports, employee benefits, and job openings. You can locate company Web sites by knowing the URL (or Web address), by using links from other sites, or by using a search engine such as Alta Vista, Lycos, or Excite.
- *Searching for job vacancies.* In addition to visiting company home pages, you can find job vacancies at sites that list openings from multiple companies. Such online indexes include College Grad Job Hunter (offering links to organizations with entry-level jobs), Online Career Center (offering searchable information), Career Mosaic, America's Job Bank, CareerPath, Help Wanted USA, and many others. Of course, even the World Wide Web offers no central, unified marketplace, so plan on visiting hundreds of Web sites to learn what jobs are available. Also, remember that only a small percentage of jobs are currently listed on the World Wide Web. Employers generally prefer to fill job vacancies through the "hidden job market" (finding people without advertising, whether on the Internet or in newspapers).
- *Posting your résumé online.* You can post your résumé online either through an index service or on your own home page. To post your résumé on an Index service, you simply prepare the information to be input into the database and then transmit it by mail, fax, modem, or e-mail. When employers contact your index service, specifying all the key words to be found in qualifying résumés, your index service sends them a list of names along with résumés or background profile sheets. Finally, employers can decide whether to interview any of the people on the list. When posting your résumé on your own home page, you can retain a nicer looking format, and you can even include color photographs of yourself, links to papers you've written or recommendations you've received, and sound or video clips.

Using the World Wide Web to seek employment allows you to respond directly to job postings (without going through recruiters), post résumés (that have been tailored to match exactly the skills and qualifications necessary to fill a particular position), send résumés through e-mail (which is faster and less expensive than printing and mailing them), send focused cover letters directly to the executives doing the hiring, and quickly gain detailed information about your prospective employers. Moreover, most campus placement offices are retooling to help you take advantage of Web opportunities. But keep in mind just how many job openings are not listed on the Internet. The World Wide Web cannot replace other techniques for finding employment—it's just one more tool in your overall strategy.

For any job, your ultimate goal is an interview with potential employers. The fastest way to obtain an interview is to get a referral from someone you know. Some organizations recruit students for job openings by sending representatives to college campuses for interviews (usually coordinated by the campus placement office, which keeps files containing college records, data sheets, and letters of recommendation for all students registered for the service). Employers also recruit candidates through campus publications and the employment bureaus operated by some trade associations. Unsolicited résumés can be vital for obtaining interviews—just remember that for every 100 letters you send out, you can expect to get only about 6 interviews.[4]

Preparing Your Résumé

A **résumé** is a structured, written summary of a person's education, employment background, and job qualifications. It's a form of advertising, designed to help you get an interview. Your objective is to call attention to your best features and to downplay your disadvantages, without distorting or misrepresenting the facts.[5] A good résumé conveys seven specific qualities that employers seek. It shows that a candidate (1) thinks in terms of results, (2) knows how to get things done, (3) is well-rounded, (4) shows signs of progress, (5) has personal standards of excellence, (6) is flexible and willing to try new things, and (7) possesses strong communication skills. As you put your résumé together, think about how the format, style, and content convey these seven qualities.

Controlling the Format and Style

If your résumé doesn't *look* sharp, chances are nobody will read it carefully enough to judge your qualifications. So it's important to use a clean typeface on high-grade, letter-size bond paper (in white or some light earth tone). Make sure that your stationery and envelope match. Leave ample margins all around, and be certain any corrections are unnoticeable. Avoid italic typefaces, which can be difficult to read. If you have reservations about the quality of your typewriter or printer (dot-matrix printing is not suitable for most résumés), you might want to turn your résumé over to a professional service. To make duplicate copies, use offset printing or photocopying.

Lay out your résumé so that the information is easy to grasp.[6] Break up the text by using headings that call attention to various aspects of your background, such as your work experience and education. Underline or capitalize key points, or set them off in the left margin. Use indented lists to itemize your most important qualifications. Leave plenty of white space, even if doing so forces you to use two pages rather than one.

Pay attention to mechanics. Be sure that your grammar, spelling, and punctuation are correct. Because your résumé has only seconds to make an impression, keep the writing style simple and direct. Instead of whole sentences, use short, crisp phrases starting with action verbs. You might say, "Coached a Little League team to the regional playoffs" or "Managed a fast-food restaurant and four employees."

In general, try to write a one-page résumé. If you have a great deal of experience and are applying for a higher-level position, you may wish to prepare a somewhat longer résumé. The important thing is to give yourself enough space to present a persuasive but accurate portrait of your skills and accomplishments.

Tailoring the Contents

Most potential employers expect to see certain items in any résumé. The bare essentials are name and address, academic credentials, and employment history. Otherwise, make sure your résumé emphasizes your strongest, most impressive qualifications. It's up to you to combine your experiences into a straightforward message that communicates what you can do for your potential employer.[7] Think in terms of an image or a theme you'd like to project. Are you academically gifted? Are you a campus leader? A well-rounded person? A creative genius? A technical wizard? If you know what you have to sell, you can shape the elements of your résumé accordingly. Don't exaggerate, and don't alter the past or claim skills you don't have, but don't dwell on negatives, either. By focusing on your strengths, you can convey the desired impression without distorting the facts.

Choosing the Organizational Plan

Although you may want to include a little information in all categories, emphasize the information that has a bearing on your career objective and minimize or exclude any that is irrelevant or counterproductive. You focus attention on your strongest points by adopting the most appropriate organizational plan—chronological, functional, or targeted.

- *Chronological résumés.* The most traditional type of résumé is the **chronological résumé,** in which a person's employment history is listed sequentially in reverse order, starting with the most recent experience. When you organize your résumé chronologically, the "Work Experience" section dominates the résumé and is placed in the most prominent slot, immediately after the name and address and the objective. Under each listing, you describe your responsibilities and accomplishments, giving the most space to the most recent positions. If you're just graduating from college, you can vary the chronological plan by putting your educational qualifications before your experience, thereby focusing attention on your academic credentials. The chronological approach is especially appropriate if you have a strong employment history and are aiming for a job that builds on your current career path (see Exhibit I.1).

- *Functional résumés.* A **functional résumé** is organized around a list of skills and accomplishments, identifying employers and academic experience in subordinate sections. This pattern stresses individual areas of competence, and it's useful for people who are just entering the job market or those who want to redirect their careers or minimize breaks in employment. Exhibit I.2 illustrates how a recent two-year graduate used the functional approach to showcase her qualifications for a career in retail sales.

ROBERTO CORTEZ
5687 Crosswoods Drive
Falls Church, Virginia 22046
Home: (703) 987-0086 Office: (703) 549-6624

OBJECTIVE

Accounting management position requiring a knowledge of international finance

EXPERIENCE

March 1995 to present — Staff Accountant/Financial Analyst, Inter-American Imports (Alexandria, Virginia)

- Prepare accounting reports for wholesale giftware importer with annual sales of $15 million
- Audit financial transactions with suppliers in 12 Latin American countries
- Create computerized models to adjust accounts for fluctuations in currency exchange rates
- Negotiate joint-venture agreements with major suppliers in Mexico and Colombia

October 1991 to March 1995 — Staff Accountant, Monsanto Agricultural Chemicals (Mexico City, Mexico)

- Handled budgeting, billing, and credit-processing functions for the Mexico City branch
- Audited travel/entertainment expenses for Monsanto's 30-member Latin American sales force
- Assisted in launching an online computer system (IBM)

EDUCATION

1989 to 1991 — MBA with emphasis on international business
George Mason University (Fairfax, Virginia)

1985 to 1989 — BBA, Accounting
Universidad Nacional Autónoma de Mexico (Mexico City, Mexico)

INTERCULTURAL QUALIFICATIONS

- Born and raised in Mexico City
- Fluent in Spanish and German
- Traveled extensively in Latin America

References Available on Request
Résumé Submitted in Confidence

EXHIBIT I.1

Chronological Résumé

EXHIBIT I.2

Functional Résumé

Glenda S. Johns

Home: 457 Mountain View Road
Clear Lake, IA 50428
(515) 633-5971

School: 1254 Main Street
Council Bluffs, IA 51505
(712) 438-5254

OBJECTIVE

Retailing position that utilizes my experience

RELEVANT SKILLS

- Personal Selling/Retailing
  - Led housewares department in fewest mistakes while cashiering and balancing register receipts
  - Created end-cap and shelf displays for special housewares promotions
  - Sold the most benefit tickets during college fund-raising drive for local community center
- Public Interaction
  - Commended by housewares manager for resolving customer complaints amicably
  - Performed in summer theater productions in Clear Lake, Iowa
- Managing
  - Trained part-time housewares employees in cash register operation and customer service
  - Reworked housewares employee schedules as assistant manager
  - Organized summer activities for children 6–12 years old for city of Clear Lake, Iowa—including reading programs, sports activities, and field trips

EDUCATION

- AA, Retailing Mid-Management (3.81 GPA / 4.0 scale), Iowa Western Community College, June 1998
- In addition to required retailing, buying, marketing, and merchandising courses, completed electives in visual merchandising, business information systems, principles of management, and business math

WORK EXPERIENCE

- Assistant manager, housewares, at Jefferson's Department Store during off-campus work experience program, Council Bluffs, Iowa (winter 1997–spring 1998)
- Sales clerk, housewares, at Jefferson's Department Store during off-campus work experience program, Council Bluffs, Iowa (winter 1996–spring 1997)
- Assistant director, Summer Recreation Program, Clear Lake, Iowa (summer 1996)
- Actress, Cobblestone Players, Clear Lake, Iowa (summer 1995)

REFERENCES AND SUPPORTING DOCUMENTS

Available from Placement Office, Iowa Western Community College, Council Bluffs, Iowa 51505

- *Targeted résumés.* A **targeted résumé** is organized to focus attention on what you can do for a particular employer in a particular position. Immediately after stating your career objective, you list any related capabilities. This list is followed by a list of your achievements, which provide evidence of your capabilities. Employers and schools are listed in subordinate sections. Targeted résumés are a good choice for people who have a clear idea of what they want to do and who can demonstrate their ability in the targeted area (see Exhibit I.3).

Adapting Your Résumé to an Electronic Format

Although it was once considered unacceptable to fax a résumé to a potential employer, many executives now say they would indeed accept a résumé by fax if they've given no other specific guidelines.[8] What about sending

EXHIBIT I.3

Targeted Résumé

Erica Vorkamp

993 Church Street, Barrington, IL 60010
(312) 884-2153

Qualifications for Special Events Coordinator
for the City of Barrington

CAPABILITIES

- Plan and coordinate large-scale public events
- Develop community support for concerts, festivals, and entertainment
- Manage publicity for major events
- Coordinate activities of diverse community groups
- Establish and maintain financial controls for public events
- Negotiate contracts with performers, carpenters, electricians, and suppliers

ACHIEVEMENTS

- Arranged 1998's week-long Arts and Entertainment Festival for the Barrington Public Library, involving performances by 25 musicians, dancers, actors, magicians, and artists
- Supervised the 1997 PTA Halloween Carnival, an all-day festival with game booths, live bands, contests, and food service that raised $7,600 for the PTA
- Organized the 1995 Midwestern convention for 800 members of the League of Women Voters, which extended over a three-day period and required arrangements for hotels, meals, speakers, and special tours
- Served as chairperson for the 1996 Children's Home Society Fashion Show, a luncheon for 400 that raised $5,000 for orphans and abused children

EDUCATION

- BA, Psychology, Northwestern University (Evanston, Illinois), September 1979 to June 1984, Phi Beta Kappa

WORK HISTORY

- First National Bank of Chicago, June 1984 to October 1986, personnel counselor/campus recruiter; scheduled and conducted interviews with graduating MBA students on 18 Midwestern campuses; managed orientation program for recruits hired for bank's management trainee staff
- Northwestern University, November 1981 to June 1984, part-time research assistant; helped Professor Paul Harris conduct behavioral experiments using rats trained to go through mazes

résumés by e-mail and responding to job openings via the Internet? If employers advertise job openings online and provide an e-mail address for responses, sending your résumé by e-mail and responding via the Internet isn't only acceptable, it is preferable.

Large companies have been storing résumés in centralized databases for some time. Now, when employers look for potential employees, more and more of them are searching online databases as well as their own in-house files.[9] Depending on where you wish to apply and how you wish to be perceived, you may want to consider the unique characteristics of electronic résumés—those that are printed out but end up being scanned into a database and those that are sent to employers by e-mail or posted on the Internet.

Because many employers are lowering costs and increasing efficiency by maintaining and using database information, you may want to consider making even your paper résumé *scannable,* that is, able to be read by OCR scanners and digested by employers' computers. You can convert your traditional paper résumé into a scannable résumé in three steps (see Exhibit I.4):[10]

1. *Save your résumé as a plain ASCII text file.* ASCII is a common text language that allows your résumé to be read by any scanner and accessed by any computer. All word-processing programs allow you to save files as ASCII. However, this language does have its limitations. ASCII will not handle decorative or uncommon typefaces, underlining, italics, graphics, or shading. Stick to a popular Times Roman or Helvetica typeface, and use blank spaces to align text (rather than tabs). To help your résumé appear more readable, you might sparingly use an asterisk or a lowercase letter *o* to indicate a bullet. Be sure to use a lot of white space to allow scanners and computers to recognize when one topic ends and another begins.

Roberto Cortez
5687 Crosswoods Drive
Falls Church, Virginia 22046

Home: (703) 987-0086 Office: (703) 549-6624
RCortez@silvernet.com

KEY WORDS

Financial executive, accounting management, international finance, financial analyst, accounting reports, financial audit, computerized accounting model, exchange rates, joint-venture agreements, budgets, billing, credit processing, online systems, MBA, fluent Spanish, fluent German

OBJECTIVE

Accounting management position requiring a knowledge of international finance

EXPERIENCE

Staff Accountant/Financial Analyst, Inter-American Imports (Alexandria, Virginia)
March 1995 to present

o Prepare accounting reports for wholesale importer, annual sales of $15 million
o Audit financial transactions with suppliers in 12 Latin American countries
o Create computerized models to adjust for fluctuations in currency exchange rates
o Negotiate joint-venture agreements with suppliers in Mexico and Colombia

Staff Accountant, Monsanto Agricultural Chemicals (Mexico City, Mexico)
October 1991 to March 1995

o Handled budgeting, billing, credit-processing functions for the Mexico City branch
o Audited travel/entertainment expenses for Monsanto's 30-member Latin American sales force
o Assisted in launching an online computer system (IBM)

EDUCATION

MBA with emphasis on international business, George Mason University (Fairfax, Virginia) 1989 to 1991

BBA, Accounting, Universidad Nacional Autónoma de Mexico (Mexico City, Mexico) 1985 to 1989

INTERCULTURAL QUALIFICATIONS

Born and raised in Mexico City
Fluent in Spanish and German
Traveled extensively in Latin America

EXHIBIT I.4

Electronic Résumé

2. *Provide a list of key words.* Emphasizing certain words will help potential employers select your résumé from the thousands they scan. Because computers scan for nouns (rather than the active verbs you've included in your traditional paper résumé), you can provide those key nouns in a separate list and place it right after your name and address. These key words may or may not actually appear in your résumé, but they accomplish two things: They give potential employers a quick picture of you, and they show that you're sensitive to the requirements of the today's electronic business world. When choosing your key words, consider the following categories: job titles (staff accountant), job-related tasks (instead of "created a computerized accounting model" simply list "computerized accounting model"), skills or knowledge (Excel, fluent Spanish), degree(s) (MBA or master of business administration), major (accounting major), certifications (CPA), school (George Mason University), class ranking (top 20 percent), interpersonal traits or skills (intercultural experience, organized, proven leader, willing to travel, written and oral communication skills).
3. *Balance common language with current jargon.* To maximize matches (or *hits*) between your résumé and an employer's search, use words that potential employers will understand. For example, don't call a keyboard an input device. Also, use abbreviations sparingly, except for common ones like BA or MBA. At the same time, learn the important buzz words used in your field, and use them. Places to look for the most current trends include want ads in major newspapers like *The Wall Street Journal* and the résumés in your field that are posted online. Be careful to check and recheck the spelling, capitalization, and punctuation of any jargon you include, and use only those words you see most often.

Make sure your name and address are the first lines on the résumé (with no text appearing above or alongside your name). Also, particular sections are sometimes omitted from electronic résumés—special interests and references, for example.[11] To find out what employers expect to see, check online résumés in your field. If most of them list a career objective, then perhaps you should too. If you're mailing your résumé, you may want to send both a well-designed, traditional one and a scannable one.

Two other quick points. First, when sending your résumé to a public access area (such as a résumé database) or when posting it on your own home page, leave out social security numbers and other identification codes. You might also leave out the names of references and previous employers. Simply say that references are available on request, and refer to "a large accounting firm" or "a wholesale giftware importer" rather than naming companies.

Second, avoid attaching fully designed résumés to e-mail messages. Your audience will have to spend extra effort to open your résumé, and chances are that your résumé will be in a format that your audience can't read.

Preparing Your Application Letter

If you're like most job seekers, you'll send your résumé to as many employers as possible, because the chances of getting an interview from each inquiry are relatively slight. To make the process more efficient, use the same résumé repeatedly, and tailor your application for each potential employer by including a cover letter that projects your theme and tells what you can do for that specific organization. Like your résumé, your application letter is a form of advertising. You stimulate the reader's interest before showing how you can satisfy the organization's needs.

Let your letter reflect your personal style. Be yourself, but be businesslike too; avoid sounding cute, using slang, or designing a gimmicky layout. By doing your homework and showing that you know something about the organization, you'll capture the reader's attention and convey your desire to join the organization. The letter in Exhibit I.5 makes an impression by focusing on the employer's needs.

Following Up on Your Application

If your application letter and résumé fail to bring a response within a month or so, follow up with a second letter to keep your file active. This follow-up letter also gives you a chance to update your original application with any recent job-related information. Even if you have received a letter acknowledging your application and saying that it will be kept on file, don't hesitate to send a follow-up letter three months later to show that you are still interested. Sending such letters demonstrates that you are sincerely interested in working for the organization, that you are persistent in pursuing your goals, and that you continue upgrading your skills to make yourself a better employee—and it might just get you an interview.

EXHIBIT I.5

Application Letter

Glenda S. Johns

Home: 457 Mountain View Road, Clear Lake, IA 50428 (515) 633-5971
School: 1254 Main Street, Council Bluffs, IA 51505 (712) 438-5254

June 16, 1998

Ms. Patricia Downings, Store Manager
Wal-Mart
840 South Oak
Iowa Falls, Iowa 50126

Dear Ms. Downings:

You want retail clerks and managers who are accurate, enthusiastic, and experienced. You want someone who cares about customer service, who understands merchandising, and who can work with others to get the job done. When you're ready to hire a manager trainee or a clerk who is willing to work toward promotion, please consider me for the job.

Working as clerk and then as assistant department manager in a large department store has taught me how challenging a career in retailing can be. Moreover, my AA degree in retailing (including work in such courses as retailing, marketing, and business information systems) will provide your store with a well-rounded associate. Most important, I can offer Wal-Mart's Iowa Falls store more than my two years' of study and field experience. You'll find that I'm interested in every facet of retailing, eager to take on responsibility, and willing to continue learning throughout my career. Please look over my résumé to see how my skills can benefit your store.

I understand that Wal-Mart prefers to promote its managers from within the company, and I would be pleased to start out with an entry-level position until I gain the necessary experience. Do you have any associate positions opening up soon? Could we discuss my qualifications? I will phone you early next Wednesday to arrange a meeting at your convenience.

Sincerely,

Glenda Johns

Glenda Johns

Enclosure

INTERVIEWING WITH POTENTIAL EMPLOYERS

The best way to prepare for a job interview is to think carefully about the job itself. Approach job interviews with a sound appreciation of their dual purpose: The organization's main objective is to find the best person available for the job; the applicant's main objective is to find the job best suited to his or her goals and capabilities.

Organizations approach the recruiting process in various ways, so adjust your job search accordingly. In general, the easiest way to connect with a big company is through your campus placement office; the most efficient way to approach a smaller business is by contacting the company directly. In either case, once you get your foot in the door, you move to the next stage and prepare to meet with a recruiter during an **employment interview,** a formal meeting during which an employer and an applicant ask questions and exchange information to see whether the applicant and the organization are a good match.

Most employers conduct two or three interviews before deciding whether to offer a person a job. The first interview, generally held on campus, is the **preliminary screening interview,** which helps employers eliminate unqualified applicants from the hiring process. Those candidates who best meet the organization's requirements are invited to visit company offices for further evaluation. Some organizations make a decision at that point, but many schedule a third interview to complete the evaluation process before extending a job offer.

Because these three steps take time, start seeking interviews well in advance of the date you want to start work. It takes an average of 10 interviews to get one job offer. If you hope to have several offers to choose from, you can expect to go through 20 or 30 interviews during your job search.[12] Some students start their job search as early as nine months before graduation. Early planning is even more crucial during downturns in the economy because many employers become more selective when times are tough, and many corporations reduce their campus visits and campus hiring programs, which puts more of the job-search burden on you.

What Employers Look For

In general, employers are looking for two things: proof that a candidate can handle a specific job and evidence that the person will fit in with the organization. Every interviewer approaches these issues a little differently. Employers are usually most concerned with the candidate's experience, intelligence, communication skills, enthusiasm, creativity, and motivation.

- *Qualifications for the job.* When you're invited to interview for a position, the interviewer may already have some idea of whether you have the right qualifications, based on a review of your résumé. During the interview, you'll be asked to describe your education and previous jobs in more depth so that the interviewer can determine how well your skills match the requirements. In many cases, the interviewer will be seeking someone with the flexibility to apply diverse skills in several areas.[13]
- *Personality traits.* A résumé can't show whether a person is lively and outgoing, subdued and low-key, able to take direction, or able to take charge. Each job requires a different mix of personality traits, so the task of the interviewer is to find out whether a candidate will be effective in a particular job.
- *Physical appearance.* Clothing and grooming reveal something about a candidate's personality and professionalism. For example, for an interview with a conservative firm, it would probably be a big mistake to show up in blue jeans. Even in companies where interviewers may dress casually, it's important to show good judgment by dressing (and acting) in a professional manner. Interviewers also consider such physical factors as posture, eye contact, handshake, facial expression, and tone of voice.
- *Age.* Job discrimination against middle-aged people is prohibited by law, but if you feel your youth could count against you, counteract its influence by emphasizing your experience, dependability, and mature attitudes.
- *Personal background.* You might be asked about your interests, hobbies, awareness of world events, and so forth. You can expand your potential along these lines by reading widely, making an effort to meet new people, and participating in discussion groups, seminars, and workshops.
- *Attitudes and personal style.* Openness, enthusiasm, and interest are likely to impress an interviewer. So are courtesy, sincerity, willingness to learn, and a positive, self-confident style—all of which help a new employee adapt to a new workplace and new responsibilities.

What Applicants Need to Find Out

What things should you find out about the prospective job and employer? By doing a little advance research and asking the right questions during the interview, you can probably find answers to all the following questions and more:

- Are these my kind of people?
- Can I do this work?
- Will I enjoy the work?
- Is this job what I want?
- Does the job pay what I'm worth?
- What kind of person would I be working for?
- What sort of future can I look forward to with this organization?

How to Prepare for a Job Interview

It's perfectly normal to feel a little anxious before an interview. So much depends on it, and you don't know quite what to expect. Don't worry too much, however; preparation will help you perform well.

- *Do some basic research.* Learning about the organization and the job is important because it enables you to review your résumé from the employer's point of view.
- *Think ahead about questions.* Most job interviews are essentially question-and-answer sessions: You answer the interviewer's questions about your background, and you ask questions of your own to determine whether the job and the organization are right for you. By planning for your interviews, you can handle these exchanges intelligently (see Exhibit I.6). Of course, you don't want to memorize responses or sound overrehearsed.
- *Bolster your confidence.* By overcoming your tendencies to feel self-conscious or nervous during an interview, you can build your confidence and make a better impression. If some aspect of your background or appearance makes you uneasy, correct it or exercise positive traits to offset it, such as warmth, wit, intelligence, or charm. Instead of dwelling on your weaknesses, focus on your strengths so that you can emphasize them to an interviewer.
- *Polish your interview style.* Confidence helps you walk into an interview, and once there, give the interviewer an impression of poise, good manners, and good judgment. In the United States, you're more likely to be invited back for a second interview or offered a job if you maintain eye contact, smile frequently, sit in an attentive position, and use frequent hand gestures. These nonverbal signals convince the interviewer that you're alert, assertive, dependable, confident, responsible, and energetic.[14] Work on eliminating speech mannerisms such as "you know," "like," and "um," which might make you sound inarticulate. Speak in your natural tone, and try to vary the pitch, rate, and volume of your voice to express enthusiasm and energy.
- *Plan to look good.* The best policy is to dress conservatively. Wear the best-quality businesslike clothing you can, preferably in a dark, solid color. Avoid flamboyant styles, colors, and prints. Good grooming makes any style of clothing look better. Make sure your clothes are clean and unwrinkled, your shoes unscuffed and well shined, your hair neatly styled and combed, your fingernails clean, and your breath fresh. If possible, check your appearance in a mirror before entering the room for the interview. Don't spoil the effect by smoking cigarettes before or during the interview. Finally, remember that one of the best ways to look good is to smile at appropriate moments.
- *Be ready when you arrive.* For the interview, plan to take a small notebook, a pen, a list of the questions you want to ask, two copies of your résumé protected in a folder, an outline of what you have learned about the organization, and any past correspondence about the position. You may also want to take a small calendar, a transcript of your college grades, a list of references, and if appropriate, samples of your work. Be sure you know when and where the interview will be held. The worst way to start any interview is to be late. Then, once you arrive, relax. You may have to wait a little while, so bring along something to read or occupy your time (the less frivolous or controversial, the better).

How to Follow Up After the Interview

Touching base with the prospective employer after the interview, either by phone or in writing, shows that you really want the job and are determined to get it. It also brings your name to the interviewer's attention once again and reminds him or her that you're waiting to know the decision.

The two most common forms of follow-up are the thank-you message and the inquiry. These are generally handled by letter, but a phone call is often just as effective, particularly if the employer seems to favor a casual, personal style. Express your thanks within two days after the interview, even if you feel you have little chance for the job. Keep your message brief. Acknowledge the interviewer's time and courtesy, convey the idea that you continue to be interested, and then ask politely for a decision. If you're not advised of the interviewer's decision by the promised date or within two weeks, you might make an inquiry, particularly if you've received a job offer from a second firm and don't want to accept it before you have an answer from the first. Assume that a simple oversight is the reason for the delay, not outright rejection.

1. **Employers' Questions About College**
   What courses in college did you like most? Least? Why?
   Do you think your extracurricular activities in college were worth the time you devoted to them? Why?
   When did you choose your college major? Did you ever change your major? If so, why?
   Do you feel you did the best scholastic work you are capable of?
   Which of your college years was the toughest? Why?
2. **Employers' Questions About Employment and Jobs**
   What jobs have you held? Why did you leave?
   What percentage of your college expenses did you earn? How?
   Why did you choose your particular field of work?
   What are the disadvantages of your chosen field?
   Have you served in the military? What rank did you achieve? What jobs did you perform?
   What do you think about how this industry operates today?
   Why do you think you would like this particular type of job?
3. **Employers' Questions About Personal Attitudes and Preferences**
   Do you prefer to work in any specific geographic location? If so, why?
   How much money do you hope to be earning in 5 years? In 10 years?
   What do you think determines a person's progress in a good organization?
   What personal characteristics do you feel are necessary for success in your chosen field?
   Tell me a story.
   Do you like to travel?
   Do you think grades should be considered by employers? Why or why not?
4. **Employers' Questions About Work Habits**
   Do you prefer working with others or by yourself?
   What type of boss do you prefer?
   Have you ever had any difficulty getting along with colleagues or supervisors? Other students? Instructors?
   Would you prefer to work in a large or a small organization? Why?
   How do you feel about overtime work?
   What have you done that shows initiative and willingness to work?
5. **Students' Questions for Interviewers**
   What are this job's major responsibilities?
   What qualities do you want in the person who fills this position?
   Do you want to know more about my related training?
   What is the first problem that needs the attention of the person you hire?
   What are the organization's major strengths? Weaknesses?
   Who are your organization's major competitors, and what are their strengths and weaknesses?
   What makes your organization different from others in the industry?
   What are your organization's major markets?
   Does the organization have any plans for new products? Acquisitions?
   What can you tell me about the person I would report to?
   How would you define your organization's managerial philosophy?
   What additional training does your organization provide?
   Do employees have an opportunity to continue their education with help from the organization?
   Would relocation be required, now or in the future?
   Why is this job now vacant?

EXHIBIT I.6

Common Interview Questions

BUILDING YOUR CAREER

At one time in the United States, joining an organization meant you would most likely be employed with that same organization for life. You would start at the bottom step of the hierarchy and, through seniority, climb the ladder to success. Today the average person beginning a career in the United States will probably work in ten or more jobs for five or more employers before retiring. So getting a job after graduation is only one step toward building your career.[15]

Employers are seeking people who are able and willing to adapt to diverse situations, who thrive in an ever-changing workplace, and who continue to learn throughout their careers. Employers want team players with strong work records. So try to gain skills you can market in various industries. Join networks of professional colleagues and friends who can help you stay abreast of where your occupation, industry, and company are going. As you search for a permanent job that fulfills your career goals, take interim job assignments, consider temporary work or freelance jobs. Employers will be more willing to find (or even create) a position for someone they've learned to respect, and your temporary or freelance work gives them a chance to see what you can do. You might even consider starting your own business.

To better market yourself, consider keeping an employment portfolio now. Get a three-ring notebook and a package of plastic sleeves that open at the top. Collect anything that shows your ability to perform, such as classroom or work evaluations, certificates, awards, and papers you've written. A chef's apprentice may collect photographs of food presentations or ice sculptures. This employment portfolio accomplishes two things: First, employers are impressed that you're not just talking about what you've done. You have tangible evidence of your professionalism. Second, you can be more relaxed because your portfolio will let you discuss your skills and accomplishments more calmly and more enthusiastically.

At the least, work on polishing and updating your skills. While you're waiting for responses to your résumé or to hear about your last interview, take a computer course or use the time to gain some other educational or work experience that would be difficult to get while working full time. Have a plan, but be flexible and ready to take advantage of new opportunities. That's the way you'll build your career and achieve your career goals.[16]

Chapter Glossary

chronological résumé Most traditional type of résumé, listing employment history sequentially in reverse order so that the most recent experience is listed first

employment interview Formal meeting during which an employer and an applicant ask questions and exchange information to see whether the applicant and the organization are a good match

functional résumé Résumé organized around a list of skills and accomplishments, subordinating employers and academic experience in order to stress individual areas of competence

preliminary screening interview Meeting between an employer's representative and a candidate for the purpose of eliminating unqualified applicants from the hiring process

résumé Form of advertising that lists a person's education, employment background, and job qualifications in order to obtain an interview

targeted résumé Résumé tailored to meet the requirements of a particular employer, focusing attention on what the applicant can do for that employer in a particular position

APPENDIX II

RESEARCH, STATISTICAL ANALYSIS, AND REPORTS

Businesspeople use sophisticated information-gathering methods and interpretation techniques to get a clear view of many factors affecting the efficiency, productivity, and profits of their businesses. Production managers use statistics in quality control. Human resources managers may use statistics to ensure that test scores reflect the ability to do a job. Marketing managers do a lot of research, measuring the size of markets, the effectiveness of various marketing techniques, and the needs and desires of prospective customers. In accounting, audits are often conducted by analyzing in detail a representative group of accounts. Financial managers analyze the performance of their investment portfolios. Risk managers use statistics to determine risks. Without such research, managers might make some very costly errors.

BASIC RESEARCH

The first step in business research is to decide what needs to be studied. What precisely is the problem, and what are the possible answers? A production manager may know that the quality of a finished product is a problem, but she or he needs to make some educated guesses about the specific components or processes that are faulty in order to pursue solutions. The next step is to seek data that will prove or disprove the possible solutions.

Sources of Data

Staff people and all levels of managers need to know where and how to obtain data; it is an important business skill. They must also understand the two main ways to classify data: (1) according to where they are located and (2) according to the reason they were gathered.

Data grouped according to location are either internal data or external data. **Internal data** are those available in the company's own records—invoices, purchase orders, personnel files, and the like. **External data** are those obtained from outside sources, including government agencies—say, the Census Bureau—and nongovernment sources, such as trade associations and trade periodicals. Internal data are sometimes easier to obtain and more specific to the company, but outside sources often have better resources for gathering data on broad economic and social trends.

Data grouped by purpose are either primary or secondary. **Primary data** consist of information gathered for the study of a specific problem. **Secondary data** consist of information previously produced or collected for a purpose other than that of the moment. Sometimes the collection of secondary data is characterized as "library research." In business research, government and trade organizations are the major sources of secondary data.

Businesspeople usually examine secondary data first because these data often have three advantages over primary data:

- *Speed.* Secondary data sources, such as *A Guide to Consumer Markets,* put out by The Conference Board, provide information at a moment's notice.
- *Cost.* Collecting primary data may be an expen-

sive process. On the other hand, for the cost of membership in an organization, a business can have the results of all the group's research at its disposal.

- *Availability.* The owner of a business can hardly expect the owner of a competing firm to make information available. Trade associations and the government, on the other hand, collect information from all firms and make it available to everyone.

Secondary data do have some drawbacks, however. The information may be out of date, or it may not be as relevant as it first seems. The company or agency that collected the data may not be as impartial as it should be. Furthermore, the source may lack expertise: The survey may not be broad enough to cover the targeted geographic area or income group, or questions may be phrased in such a way that the respondents may guess the "correct answers"—that is, they may say what the researcher wants to hear.

Primary Research Techniques

The best way to overcome the disadvantages of secondary data may be to collect primary data through original research. Although primary data may also be collected ineptly, they are certain to be more relevant to the particular business's needs. To find answers to their questions and problems, businesses of all sizes and types use the following techniques: sampling, observation, survey, and experimentation.

Sampling A **sample** is a small part of a large group of people or items. (In statistical language, the group from which a sample is drawn is known as a *population* or *universe.*) Researchers use data collected from a properly selected sample to draw conclusions or to make forecasts about the population from which the sample was drawn, and they are able to do so because of the laws of probability.

PROBABILITY **Probability** is the likelihood, over the long run, that a certain event will occur in one way rather than in another way. For example, if you flip a coin, the likelihood of throwing heads is one-half, or 50 percent (because a coin has only two sides), and the likelihood of throwing tails is also 50 percent. In a series of 10 tosses, you would expect to throw heads about 5 times. You could throw heads 10 times, but that outcome would be unlikely.

How does a businessperson use probability in everyday operations? Suppose the manager of a department store found that out of every 1,000 letters from customers, about 50 letters, or 5 percent, were complaints. The manager would expect that on any day when 100 letters arrive from customers, about 5 of them will be complaints. Of course, there may be more or fewer complaint letters, but if the number suddenly increases to 20 or 30 and stays at that level for a few days, the manager might suspect a problem. Perhaps someone is tampering with the customer correspondence file; perhaps customers don't like something new or different in the store's operations. In either case, a sudden shift that contradicts probability will alert the manager.

Probability is the principle behind sampling. For instance, if 10 out of 100 finished products sampled Monday are found to be defective, it is probably safe to assume that 10 percent of the whole production run is defective, provided that the sample was selected to fairly represent the universe of finished products.

RANDOM SAMPLING The most common method of selecting a sample is **random sampling.** A group of items or individuals is chosen from a larger group in a way that gives all items or persons in the group an equal chance of being selected. Simple methods of random selection include drawing names from a hat, taking every hundredth product to come off the production line, and auditing every fifth financial report.

Imagine that a college bookstore in an urban area has ordered 1,000 T-shirts imprinted with the school's name. The T-shirt manufacturer may use sampling to determine whether clothing stores in that city would also like to stock the T-shirts. It is impractical for the manufacturer to call the 200 stores that, according to the yellow pages, carry this kind of merchandise. Instead, the manufacturer may call every twentieth shop listed. The 10 stores that would be called represent a random sample because they are listed alphabetically—not by size, location, type of customer, or any other factor that might affect their interest in the T-shirts. A good response from those 10 stores would indicate that many of the other 190 stores would be interested in the T-shirts too.

The major limitation of random sampling is that the population to be sampled has to be small enough and sufficiently concentrated geographically so that a list of all the names or items it includes is available or can easily be prepared. To draw a sample from all the clothing stores in the United States would be too large and expensive a task; other sampling techniques may be used in such instances. It's sufficient to note here that random sampling is most effective when used in limited populations.

Observation **Observation** is the technique of watching or otherwise monitoring incidents of the particular sort that the investigator wants to study. One example of observation would be an employer's using cameras and videotape to study the way employees do their work. Another example would be a municipal traffic department's using a counting mechanism to record the number of cars that use a given street; the department would then be able to determine whether the street should be widened or whether a traffic light should be installed.

Observation sounds simple enough, but deciding exactly what sort of activity should be measured can be difficult, especially when it comes to observing human behavior. For example, if the purpose of the research is to determine the level of procrastination among office workers, what behavior reveals procrastination? Is gazing into space a sign of procrastination, or is it a necessary pause to reflect and plan? Is someone who makes frequent trips to the water cooler procrastinating? Is the procrastinator the one who industriously writes ten relatively pointless memos instead of writing one important ten-page report?

Survey Businesses often need to know why employees or potential customers behave the way they do. The simplest way to find out is to ask them, and that's where **surveys** come in. To conduct a survey, investigators may mail a questionnaire (a list of questions) to the respondents (the people who answer the questions), or they may get their answers via face-to-face or telephone interviews. Respondents may be questioned once or a number of times. The biggest problems in doing surveys are selecting an appropriate sample and phrasing questions objectively.

Experimentation In an **experiment,** the investigator tries to find out how one set of conditions will affect another set of conditions by setting up a situation in which all factors may be carefully measured. An experiment differs from ordinary observation because the experimenter can deliberately make changes in the situation to see what effect each change has. The conditions that change are called **variables.** The changes that the experimenter makes deliberately are the **independent variables**; those that change in response are the **dependent variables.** In a taste test, for example, the independent variable would be the various brands sampled; the dependent variable would be the tasters' preferences for particular brands.

Experiments are often conducted in laboratories, where independent variables can be easily controlled. A scientist studying the effects of crowding on mice could, in the laboratory, control the size of the cages, the number of mice in each cage, and so on. On the other hand, some experiments may be performed in an ordinary social setting.

An experimenter usually tries to observe two separate groups made up of similar individuals who are randomly assigned to one group or the other. One group is exposed to a specific independent variable, and the other is not. (The group that is not exposed to the independent variable is called the control group.) To find out whether employees who undergo a certain type of training do better work, a personnel director might put one group of workers through on-the-job training only, while putting the other group through both on-the-job training and classroom training. After a suitable time in the actual work setting, the performance of the two groups of workers could be compared. If the group that underwent both classroom and on-the-job training was doing a significantly better job, the dual-training approach (the independent variable) might be considered worth the expense. However, if the control group (the group that received only on-the-job training) did better or if the two groups did equally well, the dual-training approach would not be considered advantageous.

STATISTICS

Some data obtained through primary and secondary research pertain to people's likes and dislikes, their opinions and feelings; other data are of a more factual nature. Factual data presented in numerical form are referred to as **statistics.** Examples of statistics include the batting averages of ballplayers, the number of highway deaths in a year, and the number of ice cream cones eaten in August. Statistics are often expressed as percentages—an inflation rate of 7 percent, for instance.

Businesspeople rely on statistical information because of its relative precision and analytical value. Although they must be able to understand such statistics, they do not really need to be statisticians. Today many microcomputer software packages are available that allow even those who have little experience with statistics to analyze and interpret data.

Analyzing Data

Raw data—lists and tables of numbers—are of little practical value by themselves. Instead, they must be manipulated to bring forward certain key numbers, such as averages, index numbers, and trends.

Averages One way to present data in an easily understood way is to find an **average,** a number typical of a group of numbers or quantities. A personnel manager may want to know the average wage of workers in each labor classification in order to make a forecast of future labor costs when a new union contract is negotiated. A marketing manager may want to know the average age of potential consumers of a new product in order to slant advertising toward that age group.

The most widely used averages are the mean, the median, and the mode. A single set of data may be used to produce all three. In Exhibit II.1, for example, the mean, median, and mode are different numbers, even though all three have been calculated on one week's performance by a sales force.

THE MEAN The statistic most often thought of as an average is the **mean,** the sum of all the items in a group divided by the number of items in the group. The mean is invaluable when comparing one item or individual with a group.

For example, if a sales manager wants to compare the performance of her salespeople during a certain week, the mean would give a simple figure for comparison. She would begin with the basic data in Exhibit II.1 and then divide total sales by the number of salespeople:

$$\frac{\$63{,}000}{9} = \$7{,}000 \text{ mean sales for the week}$$

Salesperson	Sales	
Wilson	$3,000	
Green	5,000	
Carrick	6,000	
Wimper	7,000	— Mean
Keeble	7,500	— Median
Kemble	8,500	
O'Toole	8,500	— Mode
Mannix	8,500	
Caruso	9,000	
Total	$63,000	

EXHIBIT II.1

Mean, Median, and Mode

The same set of data can be used to produce three kinds of averages, each of which has important business applications.

By this measure, Wimper's sales were average; the three .people with sales below $7,000 were below average; the five with sales above $7,000 were above average. If some of the salespeople needed to be cut, the sales manager could base decisions on figures like these.

The advantages of the mean are ease of comprehension and speed of computation. One disadvantage is that the mean gives a distorted picture when there is an extreme value. For instance, if Caruso's sales for the week were $27,000, the mean for the nine salespeople would be $9,000 ($81,000 divided by 9). Because eight of the nine salespeople would have sold less than the mean, this calculation would be of little help to the sales manager.

THE MEDIAN When items or numbers are arranged from lowest to highest, as in Exhibit II.1, it is possible to find the **median**—the midpoint, or the point at which half the numbers are above and half are below. With an odd number of items, the median may be arrived at by inspection. In Exhibit II.1, for example, the median is $7,500. Four figures are above it and four are below. With an even number of items—say, ten salespeople instead of nine—the midpoint would be the mean of the two central figures. The chief disadvantage of the median is that many people do not understand what it means. Moreover, it is cumbersome to arrange a large number of items in order of size.

With a limited number of items, the median is easy to find, and when items that are difficult to measure can be arranged in order of size, the median is a great timesaver. It also avoids the distortion caused by extreme val ues and thus gives a more accurate picture of the data. For example, if Caruso's sales were $27,000 instead of $9,000, the median would not be affected. If it were necessary to know the average amount spent on advertising by retail grocers, the figure used would probably be the median because the amounts spent by the big chains would not distort the average. In business, therefore, the median is a useful measure.

THE MODE The **mode** is the number that occurs most often in any series of data or observations. The mode answers the question, How frequently? or What is the usual size or amount? In the sales manager's study, the mode is $8,500.

One important use of the mode is to supply marketing information about common sizes of shoes and clothing. If you were the owner of a shoe store, you would not want to stock 4 pairs of every shoe size in each style. You might find that for every 40 pairs of size 8 sold, only 2 of size 12 were sold.

Like the median, the mode is not influenced by extreme values. The mode should not be used, however, when the total number of observations is small or when a large group is subdivided into many small groups. In such cases, a significantly repeated value may not exist, and there is no mode if a number does not appear more than once.

Index Numbers In business, it is often important to know how results in one period compare with those of another. To express this comparison conveniently, an index number is used. An **index number** is a percentage that represents the amount of fluctuation between a base figure, such as a price or cost at one period, and the current figure.

Say an oil company wants to keep an index on the number of workers it employs. It chooses as a base year 1996, when it employed 5,000 workers. In 1997 employment slipped to 4,900 workers. In 1998 it surged to 5,300. The index numbers for the years 1997 and 1998 are obtained by dividing the base-year figure into the current-year figure and then multiplying by 100 to change the resulting decimal into a percentage:

$$\frac{\textit{Current-year employment (1997)}}{\textit{Base-year employment}} = \frac{4{,}900}{5{,}000} = 0.98, \text{ or } 98\%$$

$$\frac{\textit{Current-year employment (1998)}}{\textit{Base-year employment}} = \frac{5{,}300}{5{,}000} = 1.06, \text{ or } 106\%$$

These figures tell us that employment was off 2 percent in 1997 but up 6 percent in 1998.

One of the best-known index numbers is the Consumer Price Index, which is used by economists to track inflation. Others include the Dow Jones Industrial Average (which gauges ups and downs in the stock market), the Index of Industrial Production, and the Wholesale Price Index.

Time-Series Analysis Managers must often determine whether the variations in business activity indicated by statistics have any regular pattern. Suppose that a department store's monthly index of sales shows an increase of 6 percent for December. Before the manager can decide whether to increase the number of sales clerks, the amount of inventory, and the advertising budget, he or she must know whether the increase in sales will continue into January and February and beyond.

Time-series analysis, also known as trend analysis, is the examination of data over a sufficiently long time so that regularities and relationships can be detected, interpreted, and used as the basis for forecasts of business activity. Such an analysis generally explains change in terms of three factors: seasonal variations, cyclical variations, and secular (or long-term) trends in business growth.

SEASONAL VARIATIONS A **seasonal variation** is a regular, predictable change over the course of a year. For instance, the demand for ice cream is always higher in August than in February. Two other examples are increased store sales durin the winter holidays and the rise in sales of swimsuits when the temperature rises.

Businesses can sometimes use knowledge of seasonal variations to open up new markets in slack seasons. Makers of tea, for example, noticed that tea drinking fell off sharply at the end of winter. However, they wanted to maintain a constant labor and sales force; they wanted to avoid hiring extra workers in peak seasons and laying off workers in slack periods. So they successfully promoted iced tea to keep sales (and thus production) more evenly distributed throughout the year.

CYCLICAL VARIATIONS Over a period of several years (often four), the economy goes through a fluctuation known as the business cycle, which is a familiar example of medium-term **cyclical variation.** The business cycle begins with prosperity, a period of high income and employment in which businesses grow and construction activity is high. Then follows a recession, during which income, employment, and production all fall. If sufficient corrective measures (usually by government regulation) are not taken, depression sets in. A depression is a radical drop in business activity with consequent high unemployment and frequent business failures. Generally, a depression is followed by recovery, characterized by a rise in production, construction, and employment. The cycle usually begins again. Government spending, wars, and inflation may temporarily disrupt this pattern, but eventually the cycle's phases are likely to return to normal.

An understanding of this cycle is important in financial management because investments yield various results in various economic climates. Cycles are also important in manufacturing and other capital-intensive businesses. Building an expensive new plant just before the economy hits a recession phase is dangerous because orders for the goods produced in it may not reach necessary levels for several years. If the plant is built at the tail end of a recession, however, the manufacturer will be ready to take advantage of the surge in demand that accompanies the recovery phase.

SECULAR TRENDS A **secular trend** (or *long-term trend*) is a pattern of growth or decline in a particular industry or in a national economy over a long period, usually 20 or 30 years. Secular trends may result from changes in population, availability of capital, new technology and production methods, consumer habits and spending patterns, and so on. One familiar secular trend has been the decline in the demand for rail travel since the development of the automobile and airplane. Another is the upward trend the drug companies have been enjoying because of increased interest in health care. Managers study secular trends to plan for the long term, to compare their company's growth with that of other firms in the same industry, and to set standards for their own performance.

Interpreting Data

As useful as key numbers are in making business decisions, more sophisticated techniques may produce even more valuable statistics. Assuming the data has been collected carefully, further calculations can reveal relationships between sets of data, suggest predictions, and help uncover the underlying factors that contribute to a wider range of findings. In effect, data analysis yields a picture; data interpretation yields a story.

One of the most common types of data interpretation is the calculation of a **correlation,** which is a relationship between two or more variables (changeable factors in a situation or experiment). Imagine that analysis has shown a decrease in worker productivity over the past year. It is possible, but not efficient, to think of all the variables that might have caused the change and then, one by one, construct experiments to test their relationship to the decrease. It costs far less and takes far less time to statistically compare the trends for all those variables with the trend in productivity to see whether any of them exhibit a similar pattern.

Correlations may be positive or negative. A **positive correlation** is one in which the trends travel in the same direction simultaneously. The decrease in productivity, for instance, may be positively correlated with workers' experience levels or with incentive pay scales; in other words, as experience levels or incentive pay scales go down, so does productivity. A **negative correlation,** on the other hand, is like a mirror image: The trends travel in opposite directions. If productivity goes down as the number of accidents goes up, the two variables are negatively correlated.

Correlations may point the way toward solutions, but remember that correlations do not indicate cause-and-effect relationships. They merely show that two variables change at the same time, not that change in one actually causes change in the other. Even though productivity drops when the number of accidents goes up, for instance, there is no evidence that accidents cause productivity declines or vice versa.

To predict or control business activity, it may be foolish to rely on a correlation without further interpretation. For example, a large department store noticed that its sales seemed to be positively correlated with the Dow Jones Industrial Average: An increase in the stock price index was regularly followed by a similar increase in the store's sales. After several years, however, the correlation suddenly turned negative: When the stock price index went up, store sales went down. Statisticians soon found the reason. The Dow Jones Industrial Average and the store's sales were both dependent variables related to a third variable, the state of the economy as a whole. When the economy started to decline, so did the store's sales (a positive correlation). However, the economy's health and stock prices were not so clearly correlated. Stock prices sometimes rose temporarily during periods of low prosperity. So the store managers realized that watching stock prices would not help them predict how well the business would do; there was no real cause-and-effect relationship between the two.

REPORTS

Even the most carefully planned and painstakingly prepared statistical research project may be a waste of time if the information is poorly presented. Written reports that highlight key research results must be clear and easy to follow. Tables and graphs help, and such visual aids may even be crucial to giving readers a clear picture of the situation.

Business-Report Format

A good business report has six parts:

- The *title* should be a brief description of the report as a whole rather than a catchy headline. The names of the authors and the date go under the title.
- The *introduction* should briefly state the subject of the report, the research techniques used, and the nature of the specific problem to be solved.

- The *conclusions*—the answers to the problem outlined in the introduction—should be presented concisely.
- *Recommendations*—suggestions on how the company might deal with the problem—should be practical, specific, and derived from the conclusions.
- The *body of the report* should present data to back up the conclusions and recommendations.
- *Appendixes* (which contain data not directly related to the problem), *notes* (which give additional information on points made in the body), and *sources* (which tell the reader where the information in the report was obtained) all go at the end of the report.

Sometimes the conclusions and recommendations follow the body of the report.

Tables and Diagrams

With all the graphics software available for computers, there is little reason not to present data in a form that has visual impact. Several types of diagrams are used to display relationships between data (see Exhibit II.2):

- A *line graph* is a line connecting points. Line graphs show trends, such as an increase in profits.
- A *bar chart* uses either vertical or horizontal bars to compare information. Because of its simplicity, the bar chart is frequently used in business reports.
- A *pictograph* is a variation of the bar chart, with symbols or pictures instead of bars used to represent data. Pictographs are good attention-getters, but using them can often mean sacrificing some accuracy.
- A *pie chart* is a circle divided into slices. The slices are labeled as percentages of the whole circle, or 100 percent. A pie chart provides a vivid picture of relationships, but it is not good for showing precise data.
- A *statistical map* shows both locations and quantities by variations in color, texture, or shading or by a concentration of dots. Like the pie chart, it

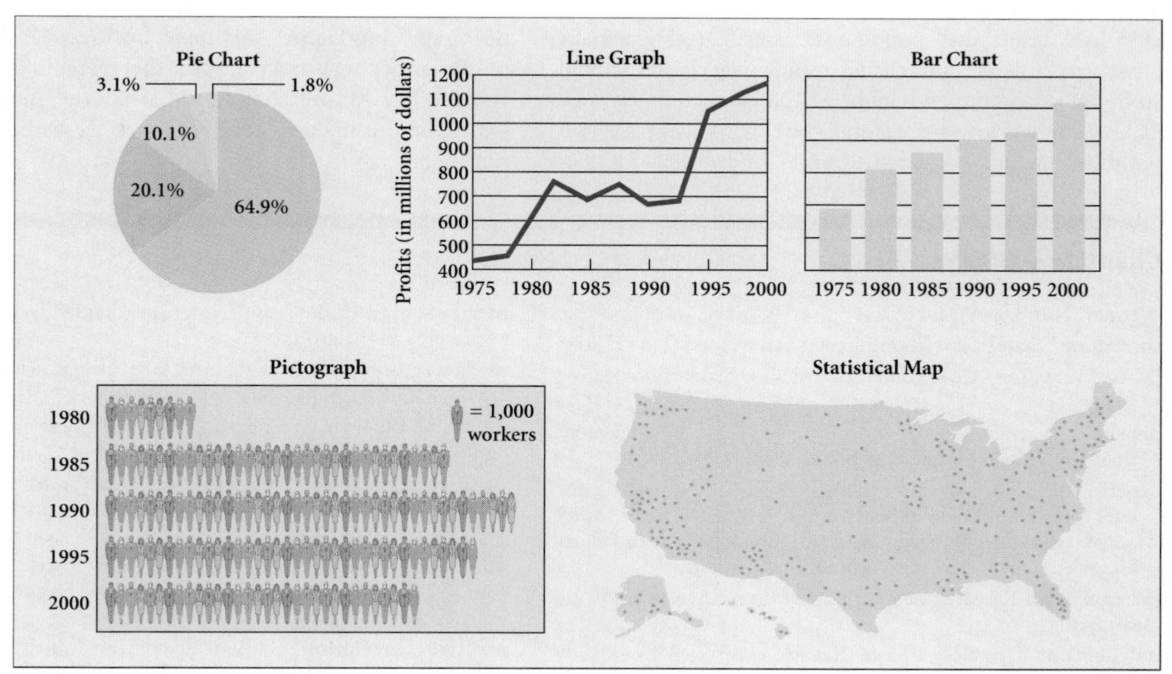

EXHIBIT II.2

Diagrams Used in Business Reports

These types of diagrams—pie chart, line graph, bar chart, pictograph, and statistical map—are most often used to present business data.

GROSS REVENUES BY SOURCE (IN THOUSANDS OF DOLLARS)				
Source of Revenue	*1995**	*1996*	*1997*	*1998*
Entertainment and recreation	445,165	508,444	571,079	643,380
Motion pictures	118,058	152,135	134,785	161,400
Consumer products and other	66,602	80,564	90,909	109,725
TOTAL REVENUES	629,825	741,143	796,773	914,505

*Reclassified for comparative purposes and to comply with reporting requirements adopted in 1992.
Source: Company Annual Reports, 1995, 1996, 1997, 1998.

EXHIBIT II.3

The Parts of a Table

All tables, whether long or short, simple or complicated, contain a title, column heads (across the top), line heads (down the left side), and entries to complete the matrix. They may also include footnotes and a source note.

shows general relationships better than it shows specifics.

A **table,** a grid of words and numbers, is commonly used to present data when there is a large amount of precise numerical information to convey. Exhibit II.3 shows the standard parts of a table.

Statistics and Honesty

Numbers don't lie, as the saying goes. However, it's also true that the people who collect and present numbers are not always as straightforward as they might be. Statistical findings are sometimes manipulated or juggled to make them appear in the best possible light. One of many such tactics is the use of precise, impressive-sounding statistics that may actually prove very little. An advertising agency may claim that half an ounce of an antiseptic killed 31,108 germs in a test tube in 11 seconds. However, an antiseptic that kills germs in a test tube may not work in the human body. Even if it does work in the human body, there may be so many thousands of germs in a comparable portion of the human anatomy that the ability to kill 31,108 is woefully inadequate.

Another juggling technique is the "shifting base." Suppose a store offers $10 Christmas gifts in October and urges customers to buy right away to save 50 percent. Save 50 percent of what? The store plans to increase the price to $20 in November, so the saving would be 50 percent of the coming markup, not of the advertised price. In neglecting to say what base the percentage was figured on, the store is being less than honest.

The people who misuse statistics cannot take all the blame, however. There are so many ways to analyze, interpret, and report numbers that judgment naturally becomes a big factor. Anyone in business (and, for that matter, any consumer) should, therefore, take some responsibility for understanding what the numbers are saying before making decisions that are based on those numbers.

Chapter Glossary

average Number typical of a group of numbers or quantities

correlation Statistical relationship between two or more variables

cyclical variation Change that occurs in a regularly repeating pattern

dependent variables Conditions or events in an experiment that change as the independent variables change

experiment Data-collection method in which the investigator tries to find out how one set of conditions will affect another set of conditions by setting up a situation in which all factors and events involved may be carefully measured

external data Research data acquired from sources outside the company

independent variables Events that are controlled by outside factors

index number Percentage used to compare such figures as prices or costs in one period with those in a base or standard period

internal data Research data that the company already has or an extract from some internal source

mean Sum of all the items in a group, divided by the number of items in the group

median Midpoint, or the point in a group of numbers at which half are higher and half are lower

mode Number that occurs most often in any series of data or observations

negative correlation Statistical relationship in which a change in one variable is associated with the other variable's change in the opposite direction

observation Technique of watching or otherwise monitoring all incidents of the particular sort that the investigator wants to study

positive correlation Statistical relationship in which an increase or decrease in one variable is associated with another variable's change in the same direction

primary data Facts gathered for the study of a specific problem

probability Likelihood, over the long run, that a certain event will occur in one way rather than in another way

random sampling Selecting a sample in a way that gives all items or persons in the larger group an equal chance of being selected

sample Small part of a large group

seasonal variation Regular, predictable change over a year's time

secondary data Facts previously produced or collected for a purpose other than that of the moment

secular trend Pattern of growth or decline in a particular business, industry, or economy that occurs over a long period of time—say, 20 or 30 years; also called a *long-term trend*

statistics Factual data that can be presented in numerical form

surveys Data-collection method in which the subjects are asked questions to determine their attitudes and opinions

table Grid for displaying relationships between words and numbers, particularly many precise numbers

time-series analysis Examination of data over a sufficiently long period so that regularities and relationships may be detected, analyzed, and used as the basis for forecasts; also known as *trend analysis*

variables Changeable factors in an experiment

REFERENCES

Notes

CHAPTER 1

1. Adapted from ANDREW KUPFER, "The Champ of Cheap Clones," *Fortune,* 23 September 1991, 115–120; JOSHUA HYATT, "Betting the Farm," *Inc.,* December 1991, 36–48; JODY H. J. HARNOIS AND DARIN L. PETERSON, "Quality Assurance Comes to Gateway 2000," *South Dakota Business Review,* September 1994, 9+; JUDY WARD, "Little Stock on the Prairie," *Financial World,* 17 January 1995, 52–55; MICHAEL BARRIER, "Entrepreneurs Who Excel," *Nation's Business,* August 1996, 18–28; BILL SNYDER, "Cash Cow," *PC Week,* 14 October 1996, A1–A3; MICHAEL WARSHAW, "Guts and Glory," *Success,* March 1997, 28–33; DANIEL KADLEC, "The Price of Freedom—How Gateway's Billionaire Founder Decided Not to Cash in with Compaq," *Time,* 19 May 1997, 60; PETER ELSTROM AND PETER BURROWS, "Can Gateway Round Up the Suits," *Business Week,* 26 May 1997, 132–136; JEFF BLISS, "Gateway Acquisition Target or Buyer," *Computer Reseller News,* 20 October 1997, 40; "Gateway 2000 Sees Productivity Increases and Cost Savings," *Training,* January 1998, S1; JERRY LANGTON, "Looking Out for Number One: Dell and Gateway 2000 Taught Steve Jobs How to 'Think Different' About Competition," *Computer Dealer News,* 19 January 1998, 28+; DAVID WATSON, "Gateway Seeks Greener Pastures for Direct Sales Operations," *Computer Dealer News,* 19 January 1998, 8+; "Gateway Opens Up Shop," *PC World,* February 1998, 274.

2. MICHAEL MOYNIHAN, *The Coming American Renaissance* (New York: Simon & Schuster, 1996), 58.

3. ROBERT L. HEILBRONER AND LESTER C. THUROW, *Economics Explained* (New York: Simon & Schuster, 1987), 27.

4. ROBERT L. HEILBRONER AND LESTER C. THUROW, *Economics Explained* (New York: Simon & Schuster, 1994 updated ed.), 250.

5. HEILBRONER AND THUROW, *Economics Explained,* 1994, 250.

6. LARRY DERFNER, "The Fight over Privatization: Netanyahu Has Pledged to End Israel's," *The Jewish Week,* 9 August 1996, 14+; PIERRE TRAN, "Air France Head Hopes for Privatization," *Reuters Business Report,* 8 June 1997, 6; NATHAN GARDELS, "Socialism Fate Awaits the Welfare State," *New Perspectives Quarterly,* 22 March 1996, 2.

7. CHRISTOPHER FARRELL, "The Triple Revolution," *Business Week/21st Century Capitalism,* Special 1994 Bonus Issue, 16–19.

8. MARK L. CLIFFORD, DEXTER ROBERTS, JOYCE BARNATHAN, AND PETE ENGARDIO, "Can China Reform Its Economy?," *Business Week,* 29 September 1997, 116–123; CARLA RAPOPORT, "China an Island of Calm in Asia's Stormy Economic Sea: Economists Tout Stable, High-Growth Economy," *Journal of Commerce and Commercial,* 4 February 1998, 1A; JAKE STRATTON, "The Straight and Narrow," *China Business Review,* January–February, 1998, 24; IAN JOHNSON AND KATHY CHEN, "China Unveils Bold Steps to Reform Economy; Ambitious Recapitalization Is Set for State Banks; Bureaucracy to Be Cut," *Wall Street Journal,* 2 March 1998, A15.

9. ROY ROWAN, "Trading Places," *Fortune,* 23 June 1997, 126–137; LOUIS KRAAR, "China's Hong Kong," *Fortune,* 26 May 1997, 86–94.

10. ROBERT PEAR, "In Bush Presidency, the Regulators Ride Again," *New York Times,* 28 April 1991, sec. 4, 5.

11. JAMES F. PELTZ AND ROBERT A. ROSENBLATT, "FTC Opposes Staples–Office Depot Merger," *Los Angeles Times,* 11 March 1997, D1; DAVID LAWSKY, "Government Wins Major Court Victory Against Staples," *Reuters Business Report,* 30 June 1997.

12. DAVID WHITFORD, "Sale of the Century," *Fortune,* 17 February, 1997, 92–100.

13. NANCY MILLMAN, "ADM Mole Begged to Quit FBI's Taping," *Chicago Tribune,* 8 September 1997, 1.

14. JOHN R. WILKE AND DON CLARK, "Federal Judge Orders Microsoft Not to Bundle Windows Browser," *Wall Street Journal Interactive Edition,* 12 December 1997, Online, 12 December 1997; JAMES V. GRIMALDI, "Judge for Microsoft Case Voted the Worst," *Seattle Times,* 4 December 1997, A1, A20; MARTIN WOLK, "FOCUS—As Microsoft Power Grows, so Do Legal Battles," Reuters Business Report, 7 October 1997, *Electric Library,* Online, 11 December 1997; PETER JENNINGS AND GINA SMITH, "Microsoft Releases New Web Browsing Software," *World News Tonight with Peter Jennings,* 30 September 1997, *Electric Library,* Online, 11 December 1997; ELIZABETH CORCORAN, "Deal: How Microsoft Settled," *Seattle Times,* 18 July 1994, A1; CAROLYN WHELAN, "Will Intel and Microsoft Lose Dominance?" *Electronic News,* 9 March 1998, 38+; ROBERT FALETRA, "It Can Be Dangerous," *Computer Reseller News,* 9 March 1998, 14.

15. MARTIN KASINDORF AND KEN FIREMAN, "The Clinton Budget/2002 Solution," *Newsday,* 7 February 1997, A4; GILBERT C. ALSTON, "Balancing the Federal Budget," *Los Angeles Times,* 14 February 1997, B8; JENNIFER OLDHAM, "The Budget Battle; Deficit and Debt: A Primer," *Los Angeles Times,* 6 January 1996, D1; BRIAN NAYLOR, JACKI LYNDEN, AND ROBERT SIEGEL, "House Budget Debate," *1997 National Public Radio,* 30 July 1997; "Following the Federal Dollar," *Los Angeles Times,* February 1998, 12; RAYMOND J. KEATING, "Playing Games with the Surplus," *Journal of Commerce and Commercial,* 20 January 1998.4A.

16. DAVID KIRKPATRICK, "Houston, We Have Some Problems," *Fortune,* 23 June 1997, 102–103.

17. BRIAN O'REILLY, "The Rent-a-Car Jocks Who Made Enterprise #1," *Fortune,* 28 October 1996, 125–128; FedEx Internet Home Page <http:\\www.fedex.com> (accessed 1 September 1997).

18. LESTER THUROW, *Head to Head* (New York: Warner Books, 1993).

19. MICHAEL GRECCO-SYGMA, "The Next Big Thing: A Bookstore?" *Fortune,* 9 December 1996, 169–170.

20. "Post-Capitalist Society," *Soundview Executive Book Summaries* 17, no. 3 (March 1995).

21. JAMES WILFONG AND TONI SEGER, *Taking Your Business Global* (New Jersey: Career Press, 1997).

22. THOMAS STEWART, "Brain Power," *Fortune,* 17 March 1997, 105–110.

23. ELIA KACAPYR, "The Well-Being Index," *American Demographics,* February 1996, 32–35.

24. World Competitiveness On-Line, Institute for Management Development, Lausanne, Switzerland, 1997 <http://www.imd> (accessed 1 September 1997).

25. MOYNIHAN, *The Coming American Renaissance,* 25.

26. MOYNIHAN, *The Coming American Renaissance,* 42–43.

27. STEPHEN B. SHEPARD, "The New Economy: What It Really Means," *Business Week,* 17 November 1997, 38–39.

28. MOYNIHAN, *The Coming American Renaissance,* 166–167; RON STODGHILL, "Workplace: Demographics: The Coming Job Bottleneck," *Business Week,* 24 March 1997, 184; "The Evolving Workplace; Home Edition," *Los Angeles Times,* 31 August 1997, B6.

29. NANCY MUELLER, "Wisconsin Power and Light's Model Diversity Program," *Training and Development,* 1 March 1996, 57; "Pathways & Progress—Corporate Best Practices to Shatter the Glass Ceiling [Part 13 of 20]," *Contemporary Women's Issues Collection,* 1 January 1996, 52; STEPHEN GREGORY, "Safety Glass Ceiling? Some Women Have Management Jobs with Automotive Firms but Industry Is Still Dominated by Men," *Los Angeles Times,* 19 January 1998, 26.

30. See note 1.

CHAPTER 2

1. CLINTON WILDER, "No Regrets for Holiday Inn," *Information Week,* 10 March 1997, 32; GENE SLOAN, "Hotel Chains Make a Big Move into India," *USA Today,* 16 May 1997, D9; "New Holiday Inn Hotel En Basto," *El Cronista,* 23 April 1997, 10, *Electric Library,* Online, 25 March 1997; ELIZABETH SHERIDAN, "Holiday Inn Closes South African Deal," *Hotel and Motel Management,* 7 October 1997, 6; "Holiday Inn to Double Crowne Plazas," *The Atlanta Journal and Constitution,* 28 February 1996, F3; KATHY BALOG, "U.S. Hotels Spin on Global Market," *USA Today,* 7 May 1996, E14; "Holiday Inn Expands Its Portfolio to Korea," *Hotel and Motel Management,* 22 July 1996, 22; "Holiday Inn Invests in Argentina," *La Nacion,* 28 July 1996, 14, *Electric Library,* Online, 21 July 1997; ROBERT SELWITZ, "Holiday Inn Spearheads Charge to Uruguay," *Hotel and Motel Management,* 3 July 1996, 12; ELAINE UNDERWOOD, "Innkeeper to the World," *Brandweek,* 9 November 1992, 14–19; "Holiday Inn Worldwide Brings Emmy Award-Winning Children's Game Show to Atlanta Halloween Weekend," *PR Newswire,* 9 October 1992; "Holiday Inn Worldwide Announces Management Changes," *PR Newswire,* 20 April 1992; "Holiday Inn Worldwide Brand Portfolio Strategy," *PR Newswire,* 10 March 1992; MEGAN ROWE, "Asia's Allure," *Lodging Hospitality,* October 1992, 51–52; MEGAN ROWE, "Holiday Inn: Fat and Sassy to Lean and Mean," *Lodging Hospitality,* July 1992, 24–26; FRANK GO AND VINCENT HEUNG, "Harnessing Environmental Analysis to Expand in Asia Pacific," *International Journal of Contemporary Hospitality Management* 7, no. 7 (1992): i–iv.

2. SUSAN DENTZER, "The Coming Global Boom," *U.S. News and World Report,* 16 July 1990, 22–28.

3. MICHAEL A. VERESPEJ, "An Abrupt Turnaround," *Investment World,* 15 April 1996, 62–66.

4. JOHN GREENWALD, "Get Asia Now, Pay Later," *Time,* 10 October 1994, 61; LEWIS M. SIMONS, "High-Tech Jobs for Sale," *Time,* 22 July 1996, 59.

5. MICHAEL E. PORTER, "The Competitive Advantage of Nations," *Harvard Business Review,* March–April 1990, 73–93; MICHAEL E. PORTER, *Competitive Advantage of Nations* (New York: Free Press, 1990), 71; "Developing Competitive Advantage," *Business Africa,* 1 April 1995, 47; JOHN H. FRAIR, "Competitive Advantage Through Performance Innovation in a Competitive Market," *Journal of Product Innovation Management,* January 1995, 33–42; KENNETH B. ACKERMAN, MICHAEL A. MCGINNIS, AND C. M. KOCHUNNY, "Who Provides Competitive Advantage?" *Transportation & Distribution,* January 1995, 66–86; ELISABETH FARRELL, "Flower Power," *Europe,* November 1993, 8–10.

6. "Government IT Plan Criticized in New Auditor General Report," *Computing Canada,* 1994, *Electric Library,* Online, 17 July 1997; LEO R. GOTLIEB, "How Information Technology Is

Reinventing Government," *CMA Magazine,* 1994, *Electric Library,* Online, 17 July 1997.

7. Nabil Adam et al., "Globalizing Business, Education, Culture Through the Internet," *Communications of the ACM,* February 1997, 115–121; James T. McKenna, "Internet Expands Global Competition," *Aviation Week & Space Technology,* 8 July 1996, 57.

8. "Intel Sets Up Subsidiary in India," *Newsbytes News Network,* 25 March 1997, *Electric Library,* Online, 17 July 1997; "Intel to Increase Investment in Philippines Factory," *Newsbytes News Network,* 12 January 1994, *Electric Library,* Online, 17 July 1997.

9. President, Proclamation, "World Trade Week, 1997," *M2 PressWIRE,* 22 May 1997, *Electric Library,* Online, 17 July 1997; James Toedtman, "Battle over U.S. Trade Fought Across 1,000 Fronts," *Newsday,* 1997, *Electric Library,* Online, 17 July 1997.

10. Amy Barrett, "It's a Small (Business) World," *Business Week,* 17 April 1995.

11. "Padgett Surveys Franchise/Small Business Sectors," *Franchising World,* March–April 1995, 46; John Stansworth, "Penetrating the Myths Surrounding Franchise Failure Rates—Some Old Lessons for New Businesses," *International Small Business Journal,* January–March 1995, 59–63; Laura Koss-Feder, "Building Better Franchise Relations," *Hotel & Motel Management,* 6 March 1995, 18; Carol Steinberg, "Franchise Fever," *World Trade,* July 1992, 86, 88, 90–91; John O'Dell, "Franchising America," *Los Angeles Times,* 25 June 1989, sec. IV, 1. Dan Morse and Jeffrey A. Tannenbaum, "Here We Go Again: Is the Success Rate for Franchises Really Sky-High?" *Wall Street Journal,* 17 March 1998, B2.

12. Brian Bremner et al., "Keiretsu Connections," *Business Week,* 22 July 1996.

13. Simons, "High-Tech Jobs for Sale," 59.

14. Anthony DePalma, "Economics Lesson in a Border Town," *New York Times,* 23 May 1996, C1; Joel Millman, "Asian Investment Floods into Mexican Border Region," *Wall Street Journal,* 6 September 1996, A10; Damon Darlin, "Maquiladora-ville," *Forbes,* 6 May 1996, 111–112.

15. "Foreign Investment in U.S. Reaches 54.4 Billion Dollars in 1995," *Xinhua News Agency,* 1996, *Electric Library,* Online, 17 July 1997.

16. "Re-engineering a Unilever Unit with HR Help," *Business Europe,* 20 March 1995, 7; David Teather, "Does Unilever's Move Mean Direct Success?" *Marketing,* 23 February 1995, 9; Floris A. Maljers, "Inside Unilever: The Evolving Transnational Company," *Harvard Business Review,* September–October 1992, 46–51.

17. Maria Mallory, "Wheels of Fortune," *U.S. News and World Report,* 4 March 1996, 49–50.

18. "Economic Trends: A New Twist in Trade Numbers," *McGraw-Hill Companies,* 1997, *Electric Library,* Online, 17 July 1997.

19. "Foreign Investment in U.S. Reaches 54.4 Billion Dollars in 1995."

20. "Bell South Waltzes Out of Australia to Colombia," *The Atlanta Journal and Constitution,* 1997, *Electric Library,* Online, 17 July 1997; "Bell South Seeking Stake in Nicaragua's Phone Company," *The Atlanta Journal and Constitution,* 1997, *Electric Library,* Online, 17 July 1997.

21. Miriam Jordan, "From the West, a Burst of Seed Money," *Wall Street Journal,* 13 March 1996, A1; Andrew Tanzer, "The Pacific Century," *Forbes,* 15 July 1996; Neil Weinberg, "Move Over, Japan," *Forbes,* 23 September 1996; "Foreign Direct Investment Soars with Business Globalization," *Xinhua News Agency,* 1996, *Electric Library,* Online, 17 July 1997.

22. *Big Emerging Markets: 1996 Outlook* (Washington D.C.: GPO, 1996).

23. David Holley and Sonni Efron, "Despite Bailout, South Koreans Remain Upbeat," *Los Angeles Times,* 7 December 1997, A1, *Electric Library,* Online, 14 January 1998; Stephen Vines, "South Korea to Sign Record $55 Billion IMF Bail-Out Package," *Independent,* 3 December 1997, 25, *Electric Library,* Online, 14 January 1998; Tom Petruno, "Reforms Seen as Key to Asia's Fiscal Recovery," *Los Angeles Times,* 30 November 1997, A1, *Electric Library,* Online, 14 January 1998; "Thailand Pledges to Strengthen Financial System, *Xinhua News Agency,* 15 October 1997, *Electric Library,* Online, 14 January 1998.

24. Robert J. Samuelson, "Trading with the Enemy," *Newsweek,* 1 April 1996, 41; Amy Borrus, Pete Engardio, and Dexter Roberts, "The New Trade Superpower," *Business Week,* 16 October 1995, 56–57; David A. Andelman, "Marco Polo Revisited," *American Management Association,* August 1995, 10–12; Greenwald, "Get Asia Now, Pay Later," 61; Simons, "High-Tech Jobs for Sale," 59.

25. Steven Greenhouse, "Trade Curbs: Do They Do the Job?" *New York Times,* 16 April 1992, C1, 20.

26. Todd G. Buchholz, "Free Trade Keeps Prices Down," *Consumers' Research Magazine,* 1995, excerpted from Todd G. Buchholz, *From Here to Economy: A Shortcut to Economic Literacy* (New York: Dutton Signet, 1995).

27. "Europe-Trade: The High Cost of Protection," *Inter Press Service English News Wire,* 20 October 1995, *Electric Library,* Online, 17 July 1997; "Japan's Protection Racket: How Much Do Barriers to Imports Cost Japanese Consumers?" *The Economist,* 1995, *Electric Library,* Online, 17 July 1997.

28. Buchholz, "Free Trade Keeps Prices Down," 1995.

29. Nick Cummings-Bruce and James Popkin, "Apparatchiks and Entrepreneurs," *U.S. News and World Report,* 14 February 1994, 23–25.

30. "U.S. Sanction Can Hardly Affect Mayanmar: Minister," *Xinhua News Agency,* 26 May 1997, *Electric Library,* Online, 17 July 1997; Joe Urschel, "Activists Make Inroads with U.S. Companies," *USA Today,* 29 April 1996, A1–A2.

31. Ellyn Ferguson, "Here Are Details of New Farm Law," *Gannett News Service,* 4 April 1996, S12.

32. "Saudi Arabia Hopes to Join WTO by 2002," *Reuters Business Report,* 3 August 1997, *Electric Library,* Online, 22 August 1997.

33. "U.S. Announces New Trade Enforcement Actions," *Xinhua News Agency,* 1 October 1996, *Electric Library,* Online, 17 July 1997.

34. Steve Holland, "China Decries Anti-Dumping Actions by U.S., E.U.," *Reuters,* 23 January, 1996, *Electric Library,* Online, 17 July 1997.

35. Roger Cohen, "After 7 Years, a Trade Accord: A Success, Although a Limited One," *New York Times,* 16 December 1993, C1,

C6; CLYDE H. FARNSWORTH, "Trade Focus Has Changed," *New York Times,* 28 May 1991, C1, C9.

36. SEELEY LODWICK, "Reviewing the World Trade Organization," *Choices: The Magazine of Food, Farm, & Resource Issues,* 1 January 1996, 29; BRUCE BARNARD, "WTO," *Europe,* November 1994, 22–23.

37. "APEC Ministers Commit to Sustainable Development," *Xinhua News Agency,* 11 June 1997, *Electric Library,* Online, 17 July 1997; FRED C. BERGSTEN, "An Asian Push for World-Wide Free Trade: The Case For APEC," *The Economist,* 6 January 1996, 62; "U.S. Must Press to Reduce Trade Barriers in Asia, Pacific, Congress Told," *Gannett News Service,* 1995, *Electric Library,* Online, 17 July 1997.

38. "Grand Illusions," *Economist,* 4 March 1995, 87; BOB DAVIS, "Global Paradox: Growth of Trade Binds Nations, but It Also Can Spur Separatism," *Wall Street Journal,* 20 June 1994, A1, A6; BARBARA RUDOLPH, "Megamarket," *Time,* 10 August 1992, 43–44; PETER TRUELL, "Free Trade May Suffer from Regional Blocs," *Wall Street Journal,* 1 July 1991, A1.

39. "Eurostat: Total EU GDP Up by 2.5 Percent in 1995," *Xinhua News Agency,* 5 February 1997, *Electric Library,* Online, 17 July 1997; WALTER LEA FILHO, "An Overview of Current Trends in European Environmental Education," *Journal of Environmental Education,* 1996, *Electric Library,* Online, 17 July 1997.

40. "Sweden Says EU Enlargement Outweighs NATO Expansion," *Xinhua News Agency,* 16 July 1996, *Electric Library,* Online, 17 July 1997.

41. JOEL RUSSEL, "NAFTA in the Real World," *Hispanic Business,* June 1996, 22–28; SCOT J. PALTROW, "NAFTA's Job Impact Slight, Study Says," *Los Angeles Times,* 19 December 1996, D3.

42. DAVID R. FRANCIS, "How NAFTA Impacts Flow of US Jobs South of Border," *Christian Science Monitor,* 24 March 1997, 1; ABID ASLAM, "Clinton Declares NAFTA a Winner," *Inter Press Service English News Wire,* 12 July 1997; CHRISTOPHER MARQUIS, "Poor Report Card Ammunition for Critics," *The Seattle Times,* 12 July 1997, A2; HELENE COOPER, "Labor Mismatch," *Wall Street Journal,* 21 March 1997, A1; "ASEAN Investment Area to Be Launched Next Year," *Xinhua News Agency,* 19 May 1997, *Electric Library,* Online, 17 July 1997, TOBY B. GOOLEY, "Truckers Identify Biggest Problems, Priorities Under NAFTA," *Logistics Management,* January 1998, 74; PETER FORD, "A Pact to Guide Global Investing Promises Jobs—But at What Cost?" *Christian Science Monitor,* 25 February 1998, 7; "The NAFTA Trash," *Christian Science Monitor,* 5 March 1998, 20+; GEORGE PEAFF, "Nafta Spurs Trade, Impact Debated," *Chemical & Engineering News,* 2 February 1998, 12+; CECILIA M. FALBE AND H. B. DIANNE, "MAFTA and Franchising: A Comparison of Franchisor Perceptions of Characteristics Associated with Franchisee Success and Failure in Canada," *Journal of Business Venturing,* March 1998, 151+; "Deep in the Heart of NAFTA: On the Border with Mexico, Economic Growth Is Curiously Lopsided," *Economist,* 28 February 1998, 31+.

43. EMERIC LEPOURTE, "Europe's Challenge to the U.S. in South America's Biggest Market," *The Christian Science Monitor,* 8 April 1997, 19; MARIO OSAVA, "Merocsur: Free Trade with Europe More Advantageous than FTAA," *Inter Press English News Wire,* 6 May 1997, *Electric Library,* Online, 17 July 1997; ROBERT MAYNARD, "At a Crossroads in Latin America," *Nation's Business,* April 1996, 38–39; GREGORY L. MILES AND LOUBNA FREIH, "Join the Caribbean Revolution," *International Business,* September 1994, 42–54; MATT MOFFETT, "Spreading the Gospel," *Wall Street Journal,* 28 October 1994, R12.

44. "Korea Chronology," *Christian Science Monitor,* 22 December 1997, Work & Money, *Electric Library,* Online, 12 January 1998.

45. CHRISTOPHER KOCH, "It's a Wired, Wired World," *Webmaster,* March 1997, 50–55.

46. MICHAEL R. CZINKOTA, ILKKA A. RONKAINEN, AND MICHAEL H. MOFFETT, *International Business,* 3d ed. (Fort Worth, Tex.: Dryden Press, 1994), 223.

47. JOSE LORIA, "Third World Urges Easing of Its Debt Load," *Reuters,* 13 January 1997, *Electric Library,* Online, 17 July 1997.

48. "Summit in Brief: Posh Economics of the Eight," *The Atlanta Journal and Constitution,* 22 June 1997, A5; JULIA MALONE, "Summit of the Eight: Yeltsin Gets Red-Carpet Entrée into Paris Club of Nations," *The Atlanta Journal and Constitution,* 21 June 1997, A1.

49. MARK ROBICHAUX, "Federal Export Programs Overlap Despite Changes," *Wall Street Journal,* 26 June 1991, B1.

50. "California Microwave Third Quarter: $.32 EPS; Order Up 19%," *Cambridge Telecom Report,* 1995, *Electric Library,* Online, 17 July 1997.

51. GARY M. WEDERSPAHN, "Exporting Corporate Ethics," *Global Workforce,* January 1997, 29–30; DANA MILBANK AND MARCUS W. BRAUCHLI, "Greasing Wheels," *Wall Street Journal,* 29 September 1995, A1; A7; BRIAN R. HOLLSTEIN, "Don't Do as the Romans Do," *Security Management,* February 1998, 56+.

52. JUSTIN MARTIN, "Mercedes: Made in Alabama," *Fortune,* 7 July 1997, 150–158; "The Soul of a New Mercedes," *Business Week,* 31 March 1997, 70; CHRIS CEDERGREN, "The Retail Shopping Experience," *Ward's Dealer Business,* February 1998, 19; TIM KEENAN, "Mercedes' Star Is Rising," *Ward's Dealer Business,* January 1998, 27.

53. TOM PETRUNO AND ART PINE, "Indonesian Currency Fall Deepens Asia Crisis," *Los Angeles Times,* 9 January 1998, A1, *Electric Library,* Online, 12 January 1998.

54. "Philippines Studying Russian Offer of MiG-29s," *Reuters,* 7 March 1997, *Electric Library,* Online, 17 July 1997.

55. FLORIS A. MALJIERS, "Inside Unilever: The Evolving Transnational Company," *Harvard Business Review,* September–October 1992, 46–51.

56. "Getting It Right in Japan," *International Business,* May–June 1997, 19.

57. See note 1.

CHAPTER 3

1. STACY PERMAN, "Levi's Gets the Blues," *Time,* 17 November 1997, 66, *Electric Library,* Online, accessed 22 January 1998; Greg Johnson, "Levi Strauss Is Trying to Give Its Product and Image a Better Fit," *Los Angeles Times,* 6 November 1997, D1, *Electric Library,* Online, 22 January 1998; DAVID CAY JOHNSTON, "At Levi Strauss, a Big Cutback, with Largess," *New York Times,* 4 November 1997, C1, C26; "Levi to Close 11 Plants, Cut a Third of Jobs," *Los Angeles Times,* 4 November 1997, D1, *Electric Library,* Online, 22 January 1998; JAMES BERNSTEIN, "Levi to Shut Plants, Cut 6,400 Jobs," *Newsday,* 4 November 1997, *Electric Library,*

Online, 22 January 1998; Greg Frost, "Focus: Levi Strauss to Lay Off 6,395 Workers," *Reuters Business Report,* 3 November 1997, *Electric Library,* Online, 22 January 1998; Stratford Sherman, "Levi's: As Ye Sew, So Shall Ye Reap," *Fortune,* 12 May 1997, 104, *Electric Library,* Online, 22 January 1998; John F. Dickerson et al., "Doing Well by Doing Good," *Time,* 20 May 1996, 43; William Beaver, "Levi's Is Leaving China," *Business Horizons,* March–April 1995, 35–40; Charles Garfield, "Ethics and Corporate Social Responsibility," *Executive Excellence* 12, no. 8 (August 1995): 5; Robert D. Haas, "Ethics in the Trenches," *Across the Board* 31, no. 5 (May 1994): 12–13; Robert Howard, "Values Make the Company: An Interview with Robert Haas," *Harvard Business Review* 68, no. 5 (September–October 1990): 133–144; Cherry Mill, "Using Principles to Win Respect," *Personnel Management* 26, no. 4 (April 1994): 19; Rhymer Rigby, "Jeans Genius," *Management Today,* November 1996, 56–60; Charlene Marmer Solomon, "Put Your Ethics to a Global Test," *Personnel Journal* 75, no. 1 (January 1996): 66–74; Erik Wohlgemuth, "Portrait of a Socially Responsible Company: Levi Strauss & Co.," *SRB Newsletters* 3, no. 2 (June 1995): 1; "Cape Town Fits Levi Strauss," *Cape Business News* (S.A.), May 1996, Online, 17 September 1997.

2. Douglas S. Barasch, "God and Toothpaste," *New York Times Magazine,* 22 December 1996, 28.

3. Ralph T. King, Jr., "Bitter Pill: How a Drug Firm Paid for a University Study Then Undermined It," *Wall Street Journal,* 25 April 1996, A1, A11.

4. John R. Boatright, *Ethics and the Conduct of Business,* 2d ed. (Upper Saddle River, N.J.: Prentice Hall, 1997), 35–39, 59–64, 79–86; Michael Barrier, "Doing the Right Thing," *Nation's Business,* March 1998, 32+; Michele Blecher, "Ethics and the CEO," *Hospitals and Health Networks,* 20 January 1998, 28+; John Mariotti, "The Death of Ethics," *Industry Week,* 5 January 1998, 68.

5. Manuel G. Velasquez, *Business Ethics: Concepts and Cases* (Upper Saddle River, N.J.: Prentice Hall, 1998), 87.

6. James R. Healey and Jayne O'Donnell, "Ford Recalls 8.7 Million Cars," *USA Today,* 26 April 1996, A1; James R. Healey and Jayne O'Donnell, "Record Shows Ford Concerned as Early as '90," *USA Today,* 26 April 1996, A1–A2.

7. Dawn-Marie Driscoll, W. Michael Hoffman, and Edward S. Petry, "Nynex Regains Moral Footing," *Personnel Journal,* June 1996, 147–156; "Business Ethics: Corporations Gearing Up to Do the Right Thing," *Los Angeles Times,* 16 April 1995, D6.

8. Susan Gaines, "Handing Out Halos," *Business Ethics,* March–April 1994, 20–24.

9. Marshal Glickman, "Green Plastics," *E Magazine,* 17 July 1996, 44; "Warm Plastic: Heartless Bankers? Maybe Not," *Business Week,* 30 January 1995, 8.

10. Florence Fabricant, "A Young Entrepreneur Makes Food, Not War," *New York Times,* 30 November 1996, sec. International Business, 21.

11. Judith Miller, "Push for Volunteerism Brings No Outpouring," *New York Times,* 23 September 1997, A10; William H. Miller, "Volunteerism: A New Strategic School," *Industry Week,* 1 September 1997, 13–16; Del Jones, "Good Works, Good Business," *USA Today,* 25 April 1997, B1.

12. See letters in *New York Times,* 25 August 1918, and *New York Herald,* 1 October 1918.

13. "Does It Pay to Be Ethical?" *Business Ethics,* March–April 1997, 14–16; Don L. Boroughs, "The Bottom Line on Ethics," *U.S. News and World Report,* 20 March 1995, 61–66.

14. Howard Rothman, "Interview: Amory Lovins," *Business Ethics,* March–April 1996, 34–36; Dale Kurschener, "5 Ways Ethical Business Creates Fatter Profits," *Business Ethics,* March–April 1996, 22; Ron Trujillo, "Good Ethics Pay Off," *USA Today,* 23 October 1995, B2.

15. Joyce Jones, "Doing Good While Doing Well," *Black Enterprise,* February 1996, 178–179; Jones, "Good Works, Good Business," B2.

16. Gil Adams, "Cleaning Up," *International Business,* February 1996, 32; Susan Moffat, "Asia Stinks," *Fortune,* 9 December 1996, 120–132; Pete Engardio, Jonathan Moore, and Christine Hill, "Time for a Reality Check in Asia," *Business Week,* 2 December 1996, 58–66.

17. Chris Bury and Ted Koppel, "The Ad Campaign and the Kyoto Summit," *ABC Nightline,* 9 December 1997, *Electric Library,* Online, 19 January 1998; Peter Passell, "Trading on the Pollution Exchange," *New York Times,* 24 October 1997, C1, C4; Julia Flynn, Heidi Dawley, and Naomi Freundlich, "Green Warrior in Gray Flannel," *Business Week,* 6 May 1996, 96.

18. Michael Castleman, "Tiny Particles, Big Problems: Our Air Is Cleaner, yet the Body Count Climbs," *Sierra,* 21 November 1995, 26; Stanley Kripper, Ann Mortifee, and David Feinstein, "New Myths for the New Millennium," *Futurist,* March 1998, 30+.

19. Michael Satchell, Betsy Carpenter, Kenan Pollack, "A New Day for Earth Lovers," *U.S. News and World Report,* 24 April 1994, 58–62; Kirk Spitzer, "Companies Divert Enough Waste to Fill Five Astrodomes," *Gannett News Service,* 2 November 1995, *Electric Library,* Online, 28 July 1997.

20. Satchell, Carpenter, and Pollack, "A New Day for Earth Lovers"; "Earth Day, Green—or Blue?" *Reputation Management,* May–June 1995, 9–15; Barbara Rosewicz, "Americans Are Willing to Sacrifice to Reduce Pollution, They Say," *Wall Street Journal,* 20 April 1990, A1.

21. "Money to Burn?" *The Economist* 345, 6 December 1997, *Electric Library,* Online, accessed 19 January 1998; Donna Beckley, "Industrial Pollution Still Haunts Hudson, Group Says," *Gannett News Service,* 24 September 1996, S12; Jim Bradley, "Buying High, Selling Low," *E Magazine,* 17 July 1996, 14–15; Brian Doherty, "Selling Air Pollution," *Reason,* 1 May 1996, 32–37; Bill Nichols, "Four Years of Work, Debate Produce First Phase of EPA's Cluster Rules," *Pulp & Paper,* 1998, 71+.

22. John Holusha, "Pulp Mills Turn Over a New Leaf," *New York Times,* 9 March 1996, 21–23.

23. Holusha, "Pulp Mills Turn Over a New Leaf."

24. Satchell, Carpenter, and Pollack, "A New Day for Earth Lovers."

25. Gregg Easterbrook, "Cleaning Up," *Newsweek,* 24 July 1989, 27–42.

26. David Brinkerhoff, "Honda Unveils Electric Car to Rival GM Version," *Reuters Business Report,* 3 January 1997, *Electric*

Library, Online, 28 July 1997; "Manhattan Beach Offers Free Charging for Electric Cars," *Los Angeles Times,* 27 March 1997, B5; ROTHMAN, "Interview: Amory Lovins," 34–36.

27. SATCHELL, CARPENTER, AND POLLACK, "A New Day for Earth Lovers."

28. EASTERBROOK, "Cleaning Up."

29. DAN CHARLES, "Industrial Symbiosis," *Morning Edition (NPR),* 31 July 1997.

30. SATCHELL, CARPENTER, AND POLLACK, "A New Day for Earth Lovers."

31. KIRK SPITZER, "Companies Divert Enough Waste to Fill Five Astrodomes," Gannett News Service *Electric Library,* Online, 28 July 1997.

32. CHAD DORN, "Nestlé's Full-time Approach to the Environment," *Candy Industry,* 1 September 1996, 18.

33. CHRIS BURRITT, "Fallout from the Tobacco Settlement," *Atlanta Journal and Constitution,* 22 June 1997, A14; JOLIE SOLOMON, "Smoke Signals," *Newsweek,* 28 April 1997, 50–51; MARILYN ELIAS, "Mortality Rate Rose Through '80s," *USA Today,* 17 April 1997, B3; MIKE FRANCE, MONICA LARNER, AND DAVE LINDORFF, "The World War on Tobacco," *Business Week,* 11 November 1996; RICHARD LACAYO, "Put Out the Butt, Junior," *Time,* 2 September 1996, 51; ELIZABETH GLEICK, "Smoking Guns," *Time,* 1 April 1996, 50; RICHARD WATERS, "Cigarette Makers Take to Web to Clear the Air," 2 March 1998, *Financial Times,* 1; CHRISTINE O. GREGOIRE, "The Benefits of the National Tobacco Settlement," *Nation's Cities Weekly,* 2 February 1998, 2; MATTHEW SCULLY, "Will Lawyers' Greed Sink the Tobacco Settlement?" *Wall Street Journal,* 10 February 1998, A18.

34. LAURA SHAPIRO, "The War of the Labels," *Newsweek,* 5 October 1992, 63, 66.

35. SANDRA BLOCK, "Discount Brokers Adopt Ethics Code," *USA Today,* 19 November 1996, B3; LEAH NATHANS SPIRO AND MICHAEL SCHROEDER, "Can You Trust Your Broker?" *Business Week,* 20 February 1995, 70–76.

36. KAREN FRIEFELD, "As Subtle as a Slap in the Face: New Ad Campaign Makes Certain Its Messages Are Absolutely Clear," *Newsday,* 21 May 1995, A56.

37. ROGER FILLION, "Law Could Curb Phone Company Use of Customer Data," *Reuters Business Report,* 23 October 1996, *Electric Library,* Online, 28 July 1997; BRUCE KNIGHT, "A New Casualty in Legal Battles: Your Privacy," *Wall Street Journal,* 11 April 1995, B1; THOMAS B. ROSENSTIEL, "Someone May Be Watching," *Los Angeles Times,* 18 May 1994, A1.

38. LESLIE MILLER, "AOL Won't Sell Phone Numbers," *USA Today,* 25 July 1997, A1; "Telemarket Deal Irks AOL Members," *Atlanta Journal and Constitution,* 24 July 1997, A1; FILLION, "Law Could Curb Phone Company Use of Customer Data"; KNIGHT, "A New Casualty in Legal Battles: Your Privacy"; ROSENSTIEL, "Someone May Be Watching."

39. ANNE FAIRCLOTH, "Denny's Changes Its Spots," *Fortune,* 13 May 1996, 133–142; NICOLE HARRIS, "A New Denny's—Diner by Diner," *Business Week,* 25 March 1996, 166–168; ERIC SMITH, "Not Paid in Full," *Black Enterprise,* April 1996, 16; MARK LOWERY, "Denny's New Deal Ends Blackout," Black Enterprise, 20 February 1995, 43; "Denny's Does Some of the Right Things," *Business Week,* 6 June 1994, 42; "Making Amends at Denny's," *Business Week,* 21 November 1994, 47.

40. "Supreme Court Rejects Challenges to California's Proposition 209," *Xinhua News Agency,* 3 November 1997, *Electric Library,* Online, 19 January 1998; GRAHAM WITHERALL, "A Job Well-Done?" *Hispanic Business,* April 1997, 36; CECILIA A. CONRAD, "California Torpedoes Affirmative Action," *Black Enterprise,* February 1997, 32.

41. SHARI CAUDRON, "Don't Make Texaco's $175 Million Mistake," *Workforce,* March 1997, 58–66; CONNIE AITCHESON, "Corporate America's Black Eye," *Black Enterprise,* April 1997, 109–111; ERIC L. SMITH, "Playing the Corporate Race Card," *Black Enterprise,* January 1997, 19; KURT EICHENWALD, "Texaco Punishes Executives for Racial Comments and Plans to Destroy Papers," *New York Times,* 7 November 1996, C2.

42. CAUDRON, "Don't Make Texaco's $175 Million Mistake," 58–66; MARIA ZATE, "The New Mindset," *Hispanic Business,* February 1997, 20–22; DOROTHY J. GAITER, "Eating Crow: How Shoney's, Belted by a Lawsuit, Found the Path to Diversity," *Wall Street Journal,* 16 April 1996, A1, 11.

43. ALAN FARMHAM, "Holding Firm on Affirmative Action," *Fortune,* 13 March 1989, 87, 88; DON MUNRO, "The Continuing Evolution of Affirmative Action Under Title VII: New Directions After the Civil Rights Act of 1991," *Virginia Law Review,* March 1995, 565–610; "Congress to Review Affirmative Action," *HR Magazine,* 4 April 1995, 12; "Affirmative Football," *Economist,* 14 January 1995, 78; ALFRED EDMOND, "25 Years of Affirmative Action," *Black Enterprise,* February 1995, 156–157.

44. AITCHESON, "Corporate America's Black Eye," 109–111; JEFFREY A. TANNENBAUM AND STEPHANIE N. MEHTA, "Bias at Single Store Can Taint Franchise Chain's Image," *Wall Street Journal,* 6 March 1997, B2; CHRISTIE DUGAS, "Redlining? Insurer's Policy Under Fire, Lawsuits Say Coverage Denied," *USA Today,* 27 January 1997, B1–2; ALLEN R. MYERSON, "At Rental Counters, Are All Drivers Created Equal?" *New York Times,* 18 March 1997, C1, C9; ELLEN NEUBORNE, "Avis Faces New Claims of Discrimination," *USA Today,* 5 March 1997, B1; ANNE KATES SMITH, "Does Coverage Depend on Color?" *U.S. News & World Report,* 9 October 1995, 85.

45. LINDA HIMELSTEIN AND STEPHANIE FOREST, "Breaking Through," *Business Week,* 17 February 1997, 64; "Study Says U.S. Women Make Workplace Gains," *Reuters Business Report,* 2 January 1997, *Electric Library,* Online, 28 July 1997; MARTHA GROVES, "Women Still Bumping Up Against Glass Ceiling," *Los Angeles Times,* 26 May 1996, D1.

46. RICHARD L. DAFT, *Management* 4th ed. (Fort Worth, Tex: Dryden Press, 1997), 462–463.

47. JOSEPH WHITE AND CAROL HYMOWITZ, "Broken Glass: Watershed Generation of Women Executives Is Rising to the Top," *Wall Street Journal,* 10 February 1997, A1, A6; ANDREA ADELSON, "Casual, Worker-Friendly, and a Moneymaker, Too: At Patagonia, Glass Ceiling Is Sky-High," *New York Times,* 30 June 1996, sec. Earning It, 8; JOAN S. LUBLIN, "Women at Top Still Are Distant from CEO Jobs," *Wall Street Journal,* 28 February 1996, B1, 12; "Firm's Diversity Efforts Even the Playing Field," *Personnel Journal,* January 1996, 56; HIMELSTEIN AND FOREST, "Breaking Through," 64–70; GROVES, "Women Still Bumping Up Against Glass Ceiling," D1, D5.

48. "Study Says U.S. Women Make Workplace Gains," *Reuters Business Report,* 2 January 1997, *Electric Library,* Online, accessed 28 July 1997.

49. "Europe: Ever Widening Pay Gap Between Men and Women," *WIN News,* 1 June 1995, 70.

50. Susan Crawford, "A Wink Here, a Leer There: It's Costly," *New York Times,* 28 March 1993, C17; Elizabeth Kolbert, "Sexual Harassment at Work is Pervasive, Survey Suggests," *New York Times,* 11 October 1991, A1, A11.

51. Warren Cohen, "The Long Road to a Model Workplace," *U.S. News and World Report,* 24 February 1997, 57; Leon Jaroff, "Assembly-Line Sexism," *Time,* 6 May 1996, 56–58.

52. Keith Hammonds, Wendy Zellner, and Richard Melcher, "Writing a New Social Contract," *Business Week,* 11 March 1996, 60–61; Aaron Bernstein, "Is American Becoming More of a Class Society?" *Business Week,* 26 February 1996, 86; Dawn Anfuso, "Strategies to Stop the Layoffs: Save Jobs," *Personnel Journal,* June 1996, 66–69.

53. Anne Carey and Tammi Wark, "USA Inc.," *USA Today,* 16 May 1996, B3.

54. Judith H. Dobrzynski, "Chicken Done to a Golden Rule," *New York Times,* 3 April 1996, C1, C3; Hammonds, Zellner, and Melcher, "Writing a New Social Contract," 60; Boroughs, "The Bottom Line on Ethics," 63–65.

55. Robert Pear, "U.S. Proposes Rules to Bar Obstacles to the Disabled," *New York Times,* 22 January 1991, A1, 12.

56. Kristin Downey Grimsley, "On-the-Job Deaths Decline to a 4-Year Low," *Los Angeles Times,* 9 August 1996, D3; *World Almanac Book of Facts* (Mahwah, N.J.: K-III Reference Corp., 1996), *Electric Library,* Online, 28 July 1997.

57. Nancy Lowther, "Curbing Workers' Comp Costs," *American Printer,* 1 November 1996, 52.

58. Wendy Bounds and Hilary Stout, "Sweatshop Pact: Good Fit or Threadbare?" *Wall Street Journal,* 10 April 1997, A2; Ellen Neuborne, "Nike to Take a Hit in Labor Report," *USA Today,* 27 March 1997, B1; William J. Holstein et al., "Santa's Sweatshop," *U.S. News and World Report,* 16 December 1996, 50–60; Stephanie Strom, "From Sweetheart to Scapegoat," *New York Times,* 27 June 1996, C1, C16; Nancy Gibbs, "Cause Celeb: Two High-Profile Endorsers Are Props in a Worldwide Debate over Sweatshops and the Use of Child Labor," *Time,* 17 June 1996; Ellen Neuborne, "Labor's Shopping List: No Sweatshops," *USA Today,* 5 December 1995, B1; Bob Herbert, "A Sweatshop Victory," *New York Times,* 22 December 1995, A15.

59. "Does It Pay to Be Ethical?" *Business Ethics,* March–April 1997, 15.

60. Jack Waggoner, "Joke's on Investors as Scams Abound: Hard Lessons in Shortcuts to Easy Street," *USA Today,* 23 May 1996, B1.

61. Suzanne Wooley, "The Hustlers Queue Up on the Net," *Business Week,* 20 November 1995, 146–148.

62. Robert Berner, "Sears Debt-Collecting Policy Was Ruled Illegal Twice by a Bankruptcy Judge," *Wall Street Journal,* 25 April 1997, A6; Chris Woodyard, "Sears to Refund Millions to Bankrupt Customers," *USA Today,* 11–13 April 1997, A1.

63. Ken Western, "Ethical Spying," *Business Ethics,* September–October 1995, 22; Boatright, *Ethics and the Conduct of Business,* 132–136.

64. Mark Sejvar, personal communication, 2 April 1998; "1-800-Jus-tice or 1-800-Rat-fink," *Reputation Management,* March–April 1995, 31–34; Margaret Kaeter, "The 5th Annual Business Ethics Awards for Excellence in Ethics," *Business Ethics,* December 1993, 26–29.

65. Kurt Eichenwald, "Blowing the Whistle, and Now Facing the Music," *New York Times,* 16 March 1997, sec. 3, 1; Laura Mansnerus, "Sounding the Trumpets for Whistle-Blowers," *New York Times,* 15 December 1996, sec. Earning It, 14; Susan Antilla, "Of Whistle-Blowers and Layoffs," *New York Times,* 9 October 1994, sec. Money, 11; Boatright, *Ethics and the Conduct of Business,* 114.

CHAPTER 4

1. "IBM Managed Messaging Offerings Expanded," *Corporate IT Update,* 1 July 1997, *Electric Library,* Online, accessed 14 August 1997; Cheryl Gerber, "IBM Sports a New Attitude," *Computerworld,* 28 July 1997, S5; "IBM Introduces Broad Array of Mobile and Wireless Services," *M2 PressWIRE,* 30 July 1997, *Electric Library,* Online, 14 August 1997; Gary Hoover, Alta Campbell, and Patrick J. Spain, eds., *Hoover's Handbook of American Business* (Austin, Tex.: Reference Press, 1994), 640–641.

2. "National Employment, Hours and Earnings," *Bureau of Labor Statistics,* <http://www.bls.gov> (Online, accessed 29 September 1997).

3. *Statistical Abstract of the United States: 1996* (Washington, D.C.: GPO, 1996), 410–411, 445.

4. *Statistical Abstract of the United States: 1996,* 56–59, 394, 396.

5. Courtland L. Bovée, Michael J. Houston, and John V. Thill, *Marketing,* 2d ed. (New York: McGraw-Hill, 1995), 301.

6. Felicity Barringer, "What America Did After the War: A Tale Told by the Census," *New York Times,* 2 September 1990, sec. 4, 5.

7. Michael Mandel et al., "How Long Can This Last?" *Business Week,* 9 May 1997, 30; "U.S. Manufacturers to Hold Jobs Steady—Survey," *Reuters Business Report,* 10 March 1997, *Electric Library,* Online, 14 August 1997.

8. Ralph C. Thomas, III, "The Next Frontier: Small Business Owners Launch Their Companies Into," *Minority Business Entrepreneur (MBE),* 30 April 1996, PG.

9. *Statistical Abstract of the United States: 1996,* 411.

10. *Statistical Abstract of the United States: 1996,* 553.

11. Ellyn Ferguson, "Here Are the Details of New Farm Law," *Gannett News Service,* 4 April 1996, S12, *Electric Library,* Online, 14 August 1997; Rachel Moskowitz and Drew Warwick, "The Job Outlook in Brief: 1994–2005," *Occupational Outlook Quarterly,* 1 March 1996, *Electric Library,* Online, 14 August 1997; *Statistical Abstract of the United States: 1996,* 784; "Farmers Speak Out," *Agri Marketing,* March 1995, 6; Owen Roberts, "I've Never Met So Many Real Farmers," *Agri Marketing,* February 1995, 20–22; Lamar James, "Farmers Appear to Be Dwindling," *Arkansas Gazette,* 4 August 1991, 10F; "U.S. Farmers Facing Uncertain Outlook," *Agra Europe,* 27 February 1998, M10+.

12. Sipo Kapumba, "Census Bureau Reports Large Increase in Asian, Pacific, America Indian, Alaska Native Business," *U.S. Newswire,* 1996, *Electric Library,* Online, 14 August 1997.

13. *Statistical Abstract of the United States:1996,* 533.

14. *Statistical Abstract of the United States: 1996,* 533.

15. JAMES W. CORTADA, "Do You Take This Partner," *Total Quality Review,* November–December 1995, 11.

16. MARCIA VICKERS, "How Tight Is the Know in Partnership Pacts?" *New York Times,* 8 June 1997, F9.

17. NEAL TEMPLIN, "Strange Bedfellows: More and More Firms Enter Joint Ventures with Big Competitors," *Wall Street Journal,* 1 November 1995, A1.

18. MICHAEL W. MILLER, "Race to Develop HDTV Narrows to Five Plans," *Wall Street Journal,* 24 March 1992, B1; PHILIP ELMER-DEWITT, "The Picture Suddenly Gets Clearer," *Time,* 30 March 1992, 54–55.

19. RUSS PARSONS, "Nuttier Than Before," *Los Angeles Times,* 13 August 1997, H2; JASON TERADA, "Citrus Group Marks 100th Anniversary," *Los Angeles Times,* 22 March 1997, B2.

20. "Fortune 500 Profits Up 23.3 Percent; GM Tops List," *Reuters Business Report,* 9 April 1997, *Electric Library,* Online, 18 August 1997.

21. VIVIEN KELLERMAN, "A Growing Business Takes the Corporate Plunge," *New York Times,* 23 July 1994, sec. Your Money, 31.

22. CHRISTOPHER OGDEN, ERYN BROWN, AND ALICIA HILLS MOORE, "Turning Points: Will Russia Turn Back the Clock?" *Fortune,* 10 June 1996, 81; JOYCE BARNATHAN AND BRUCE EINHORN, "China: The Party Is the Problem," *Business Week International,* 10 March 1997, 22; Bill JAVETSK ET AL., "Privatization: Europe Still Doesn't Get It," *Business Week International,* 24 March 1997, 16; "Bonn to Plug Budget Hole with 23 Billion Marks," *Xinhua News Agency,* 17 June 1997, *Electric Library,* Online, 14 August 1997; RHONDA COOK, "Prison Privatization: Sometimes Less Is Less," *Atlanta Journal and Constitution,* 2 May 1997, E4; "Miller Lauds Georgia's Privatization to U.S. Governors," *Atlanta Journal and Constitution,* 5 February 1996, A9.

23. JAMES FLANIGAN, "James Flanigan on Southern California; Q & A; How Power Deregulation Will Affect Consumers, Businesses," *Los Angeles Times,* 7 May 1997, D1.

24. MARTHA GROVES AND STUART SILVERSTEIN, "Levi Strauss Offers Year's Pay as Incentive Bonus," *Los Angeles Times,* 13 June 1996, A1.

25. JASPER L. CUMMINGS JR. AND SAMUEL P. STARR, "The Impact of the New S Corporation Revisions," *Journal of Taxation,* October 1996, 197–199.

26. BRAIN L. SCHORR, "LLCs: A New Form of Ownership," *Small Business Reports,* October 1991, 43–46; GEORGE LIVANOS, "LLCs: The Entity of the Future?" *CPA Journal,* March 1995, 66–67.

27. RICHARD A. BREALEY AND STEWART C. MEYERS, *Principles of Corporate Finance* (New York: McGraw-Hill, 1991), 317, 320.

28. RANA DOGAR, "Crony Baloney," *Working Woman,* January 1997; RICHARD H. KOPPES, "Institutional Investors, Now in Control of More Than Half the Share of U.S. Corporations, Demand More Accountability," *National Law Journal,* 14 April 1997, B5; JOHN A. BYRNE, "The Best and Worst Boards," *Business Week,* 25 November 1996, 82–84; ANTHONY BIANCO ET AL., "The Rush to Quality on Corporate Boards," *Business Week,* 3 March 1997, 34–35.

29. BARBARA ETTORRE, "Changing the Rules of the Board Game," *Management Review,* April 1996, 13–15; JOHN A. BYRNE, "Listen Up: The National Association of Corporate Directors' New Guidelines Won't Tolerate Inattentive, Passive, Uninformed Board Members," *Business Week,* 25 November 1996, 100; DOGAR, "Crony Baloney," 34–35; BYRNE, "The Best and Worst Boards," 82–84; BIANCO ET AL., "The Rush to Quality on Corporate Boards," 34–35.

30. MARTHA T. MOORE, "Firms Look Globally to Diversify Boards," *USA Today,* 4 December 1995, B7.

31. BYRNE, "Listen Up: The National Association of Corporate Directors' New Guidelines Won't Tolerate Inattentive, Passive, Uninformed Board Members," 100.

32. ROBIN SCHATZ, "ITT Dismantling the Conglomerate Giant to Divide Itself into Three Companies," *Newsday,* 14 June 1995, A37, *Electric Library,* Online, 21 January 1998.

33. MICHAEL ONEAL, BRIAN BREMNER, JONATHAN B. LEVINE, TODD VOGEL, ZACHARY SCHILLER, and DAVID WOODRUFF, "The Best and Worst Deals of the '80s," *Business Week,* 15 January 1990, 52.

34. STEVEN LIPEN, "Concentration: Corporations' Dreams Converge in One Idea: It's Time to Do a Deal," *Wall Street Journal,* 26 February 1997, A1, A8.

35. LIPEN, "Concentration: Corporations' Dreams Converge," A8.

36. CHARLES V. BAGLI, "A New Breed of Wolf Is at the Corporate Door," *New York Times,* C1; JOHN GREENWALD, "Come Together, Right Now," *Time,* 15 August 1994, 28.

37. STEVEN LIPEN, "In Many Merger Deals, Ego and Pride Play Big Roles in Which Way Talks Go," *Wall Street Journal,* 22 August 1996, C1; SAMUEL GREENGARD, "You're Next, There Is No Escaping Merger Mania!" *Workforce,* April 1997, 51–54; DENNIS KNEALE, JOHNNIE L. ROBERTS, AND LESLIE CAULEY, "The Undeal: Why the Mega-Merger Collapsed: Strong Wills and a Big Culture Gap," *Wall Street Journal,* 25 February 1994, A1, A4.

38. "WorldCom and MCI Announce $37 Billion Merger," *Cambridge Telecom Report,* 17 November 1997, *Electric Library,* Online, 21 January 1998.

39. BRUCE ORWELL AND KYLE POPE, "Relativity: Disney, ABC Promised 'Synergy' in Merger; So, What Happened?" *Wall Street Journal,* 16 May 1997, A1, A9; DON L. BOROUGHS, DAN MCGRAW, AND KEVIN WHITELAW, "Disney's All Smiles," *U.S. News and World Report,* 14 August 1995, 32–46.

40. MICHAEL J. MANDEL, CHRISTOPHER FARRELL, AND CATHERINE YANG, "Land of the Giants," *Business Week,* 11 September 1995, 34.

41. JEFFREY A. TANNENBAUM, "The Consolidators: Acquisitive Companies Set Out to 'Roll Up' Fragmented Industries," *Wall Street Journal,* 3 March 1997, A1; JOHN R. WILKE AND BRYAN GRULEY, "Merger Monitors: Acquisitions Can Mean Long-Lasting Scrutiny by Antitrust Agencies," *Wall Street Journal,* 4 March 1997, A1, A6; GREG FROST, "Western Resources Buying Kansas City P&L," *Reuters Business Report,* 7 February 1997, *Electric Library,* Online, 21 January 1998; BAGLI, "A New Breed of Wolf Is at the Corporate Door," C1; DAVID A. ANDELMAN, "The Urge to Merge," *Industry Week,* 33–34; DON L. BOROUGHS AND DAVID FISCHER, "Big!" *U.S. News and World Report,* 11 September 1995, 46–48; MANDEL, FARRELL, AND YANG, "Land of the Giants," 34.

42. LIPEN, "Concentration: Corporations' Dreams Converge," A8; MILT FREUDENHEIM, "Roche Set to Acquire Syntex," *New York Times,* 3 May 1994, C1.

43. AMEY STONE, DAVID LEONHARDT, AND WENDY ZELLNER, "You Don't Have to Be Ted Turner to Merge," *Business Week/Enterprise,* Summer 1996, ENT6.

44. HOOVER, CAMPBELL, AND SPAIN, eds., *Hoover's Handbook of American Business,* 282–283, 300–301, 560–561, 724–725.

45. JOANN S. LUBLIN, "'Poison Pills' Are Giving Shareholders a Big Headache, Union Proposals Assert," *Wall Street Journal,* 23 May 1997, C1; "Poison-Pill Plan Is Adopted Protecting Holders' Rights," *Wall Street Journal,* 10 March 1998, C7; "Directors' Clear 'Poison Pill' to Fight Hostile Takeovers," *Wall Street Journal,* 3 February 1998, B4+.

46. THOMAS MULLIGAN, "ITT Takes Starwood Offer," *Los Angeles Times,* 13 November 1997, D2, *Electric Library,* Online, accessed 21 January 1998; KATHLEEN MORRIS, "Behind the New Deal Mania," *Business Week,* 3 November 1997, 36.

CHAPTER 5

1. TOM DUFFY, "Baking Up Millions," *Self Employed Professional,* May–June 1997, 22–27; CAROLE MATTHEWS, "Grassroots Marketing," *Self Employed Professional,* May–June 1997, 22; GREGORY I. KRAVITT, *Creating a Winning Business Plan,* (Chicago, Ill.: Probus Publishing, 1993); MICHAEL FRIEDMAN, "Will Mrs. Smith's Acquisition Yield Array of Healthy Choice Desserts?" *Frozen Food Age,* April 1996, 5–6.

2. ELIZABETH MACDONALD, "Slim Pickings," *Wall Street Journal,* 22 May 1997, R6; STEPHANIE N. MEHTA, "Small Talk," *Wall Street Journal,* 23 May 1996, R28–R30.

3. "Matters of Fact," *Inc.,* April 1985, 32.

4. MEHTA, "Small Talk."

5. TIMOTHY D. SCHELHARDT, "David in Goliath," *Wall Street Journal,* 23 May 1996, R14.

6. DONNA FENN, "The Buyers," *Inc.,* June 1996, 46–52.

7. MARK ROBICHAUX, "Business First, Family Second," *Wall Street Journal,* 12 May 1989, B1.

8. RICK MENDOSA, "A Side Order of Success," *Hispanic Business,* August 1995, 48–50.

9. MACDONALD, "Slim Pickings"; MEHTA, "Small Talk"; SBA Web site, http:\\www.sbaonline.sba.gov> (accessed 16 September 1997).

10. JANICE CASTRO, "Big vs. Small," *Time,* 5 September 1988, 49; STEVE SOLOMON, *Small Business USA* (New York: Crown, 1986), 124.

11. LLOYD GITE AND DAWN M. BASKERVILLE, "Black Women Entrepreneurs on the Rise," *Black Enterprise,* August 1996, 73–74.

12. SHELLY BRANCH, "How Hip-Hop Fashion Won Over Mainstream America," *Black Enterprise,* June 1993, 111–120.

13. JOSHUA MACHT, "The Two Hundred Million Dash," *Inc. Technology 1997,* 16 September 1997, 48–55.

14. *Inc. Special Edition—The State of Small Business 1997,* 20 May 1997, 112; JAMES WILFONG AND TONI SEGER, *Taking Your Business Global* (Franklin Lakes, N.J.: Career Press, 1997), 84.

15. "Women-Owned Firms Grow in Number and Importance," *Nation's Business,* April 1996, 7; MARIA ZATE, "Leading the Charge," *Hispanic Business,* May 1996, 26; MARIA ZATE, "On a Course of Prosperity," *Hispanic Business,* April 1994, 50–56; WENDY ZELLNER, "Women Entrepreneurs," *Business Week,* 18 April 1994, 104–110; "Chicago's Top Women-Owned Firms," *Crain's Chicago Business,* 9 February 1998, 19; STEPHEN GREGORY, "Safety Glass Ceiling?" *Los Angeles Times,* 19 January 1998, 26.

16. CARRIE MASON-DRAFFEN, "Out on Her Own—Growing Numbers of Minority Women Take Business into Own Hands," *Newsday,* 3 August 1997, FO8.

17. MARIA ZATE, "Models of Efficiency," *Hispanic Business,* December 1995, 22–24.

18. RANDALL LANE, "Involuntary Entrepreneurs," *Forbes,* 3 June 1996, 81–82.

19. CAROLYN BROWN, "How to Make Your Ex-Boss Your Client," *Black Enterprise,* 30 April 1994, 95+.

20. "Outsourcing Provides Growth for IT Services Business," *Newsbytes News Network,* Online, 12 May 1997.

21. BRIAN O'REILLY, "The New Face of Small Business," *Fortune,* 2 May 1994, 82–88.

22. JOSEPH W. DUNCAN, "The True Failure Rate of Start-ups," *D&B Reports,* January–February 1994; MAGGIE JONES, "Smart Cookies," *Working Woman,* April 1995, 50–52+.

23. JANE APPLEGATE, *Succeeding in Small Business,* (New York: Plume/Penguin, 1992), 1.

24. WILFONG AND SEGER, *Taking Your Business Global,* 78–80.

25. LISA J. MOORE AND SHARON F. GOLDEN, "You Can Plan to Expand or Just Let It Happen," *U.S. News and World Report,* 23 October 1989, 78; JOHN CASE, "The Origins of Entrepreneurship," *Inc.,* June 1989, 56.

26. TOM RICHMAN, "Creators of the New Economy," *Inc.—Special Edition: The State of Small Business 1997,* 20 May 1997, 44–48.

27. ZELLNER, "Women Entrepreneurs," 104–110.

28. ROGER RICKLEFS, "Road to Success Becomes Less Littered with Failures," *Wall Street Journal,* 10 November 1989, B2.

29. ANDREW E. SERWER, "Trouble in Franchise Nation," *Fortune,* 6 March 1995, 115–128; ECHO MONTGOMERY GARRETT, "The Next Generation: Why Today's College Graduates Are Turning to Franchising," *Inc.,* January 1998, S2+; DAN MORSE AND JEFFREY A. TANNENBAUM, "Here We Go Again: Is the Success Rate for Franchises Really Sky-High?" *Wall Street Journal,* 17 March 1998, B2; ALBY GALLUN, "Franchise Owners Must Play by the Rules," *Business Journal-Milwaukee,* 23 January 1998, 9.

30. CAROLYN M. BROWN, "All Talk, No Action," *Black Enterprise,* September 1995, 60–64; "Franchising Fellowship," *Marketing Management* 4, no. 2 (Fall 1995): 4–6; ROBERTA MAYNARD, "The Changing Landscape," *Nation's Business,* January 1997, 54–55.

31. NICOLE HARRIS AND MIKE FRANCE, "Franchisees Get Feisty," *Business Week,* 24 February 1997, 65–66; ROBERTA MAYNARD, "Prospecting for Gold," *Nation's Business,* June 1996, 69–74; TIMOTHY BATES, "Survival Patterns Among Newcomers to Franchising," *Journal of Business Venturing,* March 1998, 133+; FRANCINE LAFONTAINE AND KATHRYN L. SHAW, "Franchising Growth and Franchisor Entry and Exit in the U.S. Market: Myth and Reality," *Journal of Business Venturing,* March 1998, 95+.

32. BUCK BROWN, "Franchisers Now Offer Direct Financial Aid," *Wall Street Journal,* 6 February 1989, B1.

33. CONSTANCE MITCHELL, "Franchising Fever Spreads," *USA Today,* 13 September 1985, 4B; JERRY WILKERSON, "Annual Franchise Survey Results Find Solid Business Growth in Store for '98," *Nation's Restaurant News,* 23 February 1998, 46+; CAROL WINSLOW, "Franchise Winners Prove That Not Only Big Is Beautiful," *Clinica,* 12 January 1998, 28+; REGINALD A. LITZ and

ALICE B. STEWART, "Franchising for Sustainable Advantage," *Journal of Business Venturing,* March 1998, 131+.

34. GREG BURNS, "Fast-Food Fight," *Business Week,* 2 June 1997, 34–36; AMY DUNKIN, "Franchising: A Recipe for Your Second Career?" *Business Week,* 4 March 1996, 128–129; "It May Be Fast, but Is It Good?" *Prepared Foods,* January 1998, 39.

35. JEFFREY TANNANBAUM, "To Pacify Irate Franchisees, Franchisers Extend Services," *Wall Street Journal,* 24 February 1995, B1–B2; DUNKIN, "Franchising: A Recipe for Your Second Career?"; ANDREW E. SERWER, "Trouble in Franchise Nation," *Fortune,* 6 March 1995, 115–128; JEFFREY A. TANNENBAUM, "Warning, Plaintiffs: Franchisee Status May Be Just a Start," *Wall Street Journal,* 3 February 1998, B2.

36. HARRIS AND FRANCE, "Franchisees Get Feisty"; FRANK HOY and SCOTT SHANE, "Franchising as an Entrepreneurial Venture Form," *Journal of Business Venturing,* March 1998, 91.

37. MAYNARD, "The Changing Landscape," *Nation's Business,* January 1997, 54–55.

38. ROBERTA MAYNARD, "Choosing a Franchise," *Nation's Business,* October 1996, 56–63.

39. "The 1990 Guide to Small Business," *U.S. News and World Report,* 23 November 1989, 78.

40. MARTHA E. MANGELSDORF, "Inc.'s Guide to 'Smart' Government Money," *Inc.,* August 1989, 51.

41. WILFONG AND SEGER, *Taking Your Business Global,* 20.

42. RONALEEN R. ROHA, "Big Loans for Small Businesses," *Changing Times,* April 1989, 105–109; "Small Loans, Big Problems," *Economist,* 28 January 1995, 73; ELIZABETH KADETSKY, "Small Loans, Big Dreams," *Working Woman,* February 1995, 46–49; REID RUTHERFORD, "Securitizing Small Business Loans: A Banker's Action Plan," *Commercial Lending Review,* Winter 1994–1995, 62–74.

43. ROHA, "Big Loans for Small Businesses," 105.

44. SUSAN HODGES, "Microloans Fuel Big Ideas," *Nation's Business,* February 1997, 34–35.

45. SCORE Internet site <http://www.score.org> (accessed 18 September 1997).

46. ROBERT MCGARVEY, "Peak Performance," *American Way,* July 1996, 56–60.

47. Data provided by the National Business Incubation Association, 153 South Hanover Street, Carlisle, PA 17013.

48. DAVID RIGGLE, "Great Places to Grow a Business," *In Business,* September–October 1990, 20–22.

49. J. TOL BROOME JR., "How to Write a Business Plan," *Nation's Business,* February 1993, 29–30; ALBERT RICHARDS, "The Ernst & Young Business Plan Guide," *R & D Management,* April 1995, 253; DAVID LANCHNER, "How Chitchat Became a Valuable Business Plan," *Global Finance,* February 1995, 54–56; MARGUERITA ASHBY-BERGER, "My Business Plan—and What Really Happened," *Small Business Forum,* Winter 1994–1995, 24–35; STANLEY R. RICH AND DAVID E. GUMPERT, *Business Plans That Win $$$* (New York: Harper & Row, 1985).

50. RICH AND GUMPERT, *Business Plans That Win $$$.*

51. LOUISE LEE, "A Company Failing from Too Much Success," *Wall Street Journal,* 17 March 1995, B1.

52. MEG WHITTEMORE, *Growth Opportunities in Franchising* (Washington, D.C.: International Franchise Association).

53. JOHN K. HAWKS, "Franchise?" *Business 96,* August–September 1996, 46–49.

54. ASSOCIATED PRESS, "Strange Case for California Pizza Kitchen," *Chicago Tribune,* 22 September 1997, B5.

55. WILFONG AND SEGER, *Taking Your Business Global,* 11.

56. WILFONG AND SEGER, *Taking Your Business Global,* 216–219.

57. *Inc. Special Edition—The State of Small Business 1997,* 20 May 1997, 121.

58. MCGARVEY, "Peak Performance."

59. JILL H. ELLSWORTH, "Staking a Claim on the Internet," *Nation's Business,* January 1996, 29; NICHOLAS DENTON, "Internet Changes the Game," *Financial Times,* 11 March 1998, 13; DAVE S. SMITH, "Our Friend Electric," *Marketing,* 29 January 1998, 28+; JERRY W. THOMAS, "The Brave New World of Internet Marketing," *Direct Marketing,* January 1998, 40+; "E-Commerce Comes of Age," *PC Week,* 9 March 1998, 16; PAT RYAN, "Securing Your Web Commerce Site," *InfoWorld,* 9 March 1998, 75+; TIM JACKSON, "Chains of Communication," *Financial Times,* 2 March 1998, 17

60. See note 1.

61. "United States of America," Microsoft® Encarta. Copyright © 1994 Microsoft Corporation. Copyright © 1994 Funk & Wagnall's Corporation.

CHAPTER 6

1. Adapted from THERESE POLETT, "WebTV to Unveil Major Upgrade, Melds TV and Internet," *Reuters Business Report,* 14 September 1997, *Electric Library,* Online, 28 November 1997; KATHY REBELLO, "Inside Microsoft," *Business Week,* 15 July 1996, 56–70; "How Bill Gates Sees the Future," *Fortune,* 28 June 1993, 10; T. R. REID, "The Future According to Gates: Reign and Sunshine for Microsoft," *Washington Post,* 9 March 1992, WB18; RICH KARLGAARD, "Bill Gates," *Forbes ASAP,* 7 December 1992, 63–64, 66, 70–72, 74; BRENTON R. SCHLENDER, "Bill Gates Sets a New Target," *Fortune,* 25 February 1991, 12–13; *Microsoft Corporation 1990 Annual Report,* 1–18; *Microsoft Corporation 1992 Annual Report,* 3–7; EVELYN RICHARDS, "A Hard-Nosed Businessman with a Certain Boyish Charm," *Washington Post,* 30 December 1990, H3; CARRIE TUHY AND GREG COUCH, "Software's Old Man Is 30," *Money,* July 1986, 54–55; BRENTON R. SCHLENDER, "How Bill Gates Keeps the Magic Going," *Fortune,* 18 June 1990, 82–86, 88–89; G. PASCAL ZACHARY, "Operating System: Opening of 'Windows' Shows How Bill Gates Succeeds in Software," *Wall Street Journal,* 21 May 1990, A1, A4; MARY JO FOLEY, "Boy Wonder: Microsoft's Bill Gates," *Electronic Business,* 15 August 1988, 54–56; D. RUBY, S. KANZLER, R. GLITMAN, AND T. POMPILI, "Can Microsoft Blend Blue Jeans and Gray Flannel?" *PC Week,* 21 October 1986, 57, 59, 72–74; "Microsoft's Network Is a Model for Corporate Communications Systems," *PC Week,* 21 October 1986, 73; RICHARD A. CHAFER, "The Growth of Microsoft," *Personal Computing,* June 1986, 29; JONATHAN B. ELEVEN, "Microsoft: Recovering from Its Stumble over 'Windows,'" *Business Week,* July 22, 1985, 107–108; ERIC NEE, "Interviews with Microsoft Executives," *Upside,* April 1995, 66, 87; "Why Microsoft (Mostly) Shouldn't Be Stopped," *Upside,* April 1995, 34–53; G. PASCAL ZACHARY, "The Once and Future Microsoft," *Upside,* April 1995, 16–32.

2. Richard L. Daft, *Management,* 4th ed. (Fort Worth, Tex.: Dryden, 1997), 8.

3. Stephen P. Robbins, *Managing Today* (Upper Saddle River, N.J.: Prentice Hall, 1997), 452.

4. Aimee L. Stern, "Management: You Can Keep Your Staff on the Competitive Track if You . . . Inspire Your Team with a Mission Statement," *Your Company,* 1 August 1997, 36, *Electric Library,* Online, 2 September 1997.

5. Daft, *Management,* 221–223, 260–262.

6. Richard Teitlebaum, "Tough Guys Finish First," *Fortune,* 21 July 1997, 82, *Electric Library,* Online, 2 September 1997; Neil Weinberg, "Shaking Up an Old Giant," *Forbes,* 20 May 1996, 80.

7. Kathryn M. Bartol and David C. Martin, *Management* (New York: McGraw-Hill, 1991), 268–272.

8. Daft, *Management,* 219–221.

9. Courtland L. Bovée, John V. Thill, Marian Burk Wood, and George P. Dovel, *Management* (New York: McGraw-Hill, 1993), 220; David H. Holt, *Management: Principles and Practices,* 2d ed. (Upper Saddle River, N.J.: Prentice Hall, 1990), 10–12; James A. F. Stoner, *Management,* 4th ed. (Upper Saddle River, N.J.: Prentice Hall, 1989), 15–18.

10. Robert L. Katz, "Skills of an Effective Administrator," *Harvard Business Review,* September–October 1974, reprinted in *Paths Toward Personal Progress: Leaders Are Made, Not Born* (Boston: Harvard Business Review, 1983), 23–35; Mike Dawson, "Leaders versus Managers," *Systems Management,* March 1995, 32; R. S. Dreyer, "Do Good Bosses Make Lousy Leaders?" *Supervision,* March 1995, 19–20; Michael Maccoby, "Teams Need Open Leaders," *Research-Technology Management,* January–February 1995, 57–59.

11. John V. Thill and Courtland L. Bovée, *Excellence in Business Communication* (Upper Saddle River, N.J.: Prentice Hall, 1997), 3.

12. Jolie Solomon, "Operation Rescue," *Working Woman,* May 1996, 57.

13. Daft, *Management,* 128; Bartol and Martin, *Management,* 17; Thill and Bovée, *Excellence in Business Communication,* 23.

14. Bartol and Martin, *Management,* 268–272; Ricky W. Griffin, *Management,* 3d ed. (Boston: Houghton Mifflin, 1990), 131–137.

15. Robbins, *Managing Today,* 72.

16. Judith H. Dobrzynski, "Yes, He's Revived Sears. But Can He Reinvent It?" *New York Times,* 7 January 1996, sec. 3, 1; Patricia Sellers, "Sears: The Turnaround Is Ending; the Revolution Has Begun," *Fortune,* 28 April 1997, 106–118.

17. Daft, *Management,* 59–61.

18. Michael Barrier, "When Big Still Seems Small," *Nation's Business,* October 1994, 75–77.

19. Brian S. Moskal, "Perception Is the Reality," *Industry Week,* 5 September 1994, 39.

20. Karen A. Edelman, "CEOs Take on Quality," *Across the Board,* September 1996, 56.

21. Moskal, "Perception Is the Reality," 40.

22. Bovée et al., *Management,* 680.

23. Michael A. Verespej, "Stability Before Growth," *Industry Week,* 15 April 1996, 12–16.

24. James R. Lackritz, "TQM Within Fortune 500 Corporations," *Quality Progress,* February 1997, 69–72; Dan Marcus, "Gain a Competitive Edge with TQM," *Modern Casting,* February 1998, 61.

25. David Sirota, Brian Usilaner, and Michelle S. Weber, "Sustaining Quality Improvement," *The Total Quality Review,* March–April 1994, 23; Joe Batten, "A Total Quality Culture," *Management Review,* May 1994, 61; Rahul Jacon, "More Than a Dying Fad?" *Fortune,* 18 October 1993, 66–72.

26. Lackritz, "TQM Within Fortune 500 Corporations," 69–72.

27. Daft, *Management,* 132–136; Bartol and Martin, *Management,* 172–173.

28. John A. Byrne, "Strategic Planning," *Business Week,* 26 August 1996, 52.

29. Daft, *Management,* 590.

30. Gary A. Yukl, *Leadership in Organizations,* 2d ed. (Englewood Cliffs, NJ: Prentice Hall, 1989), 9, 175–176.

31. Daft, *Management,* 498–499.

32. Michael A. Verespej, "Lead, Don't Manage," *Industry Week,* 4 March 1996, 58.

33. Stratford Sherman, "Secrets of HP's 'Muddled' Team," *Fortune,* 18 March 1996, 116–120.

34. Charles M. Farkas and Suzy Wetlaufer, "The Ways Chief Executive Officers Lead," *Harvard Business Review,* May–June 1996, 114.

35. Daft, *Management,* 494–497, 514–516.

36. Thomas Teal, "The Human Side of Management," *Harvard Business Review,* November–December 1996, 35–44; Verespej, "Lead, Don't Manage," 58.

37. Tim Stevens, "Dr. Feigenbaum," *Industry Week,* 4 July 1994, 16.

38. Jay Finegan, "Ready, Aim, Focus," *Inc.* March 1997, 44–55.

39. Stephen P. Robbins and David A. De Cenzo, *Fundamentals of Management,* 2d ed. (Upper Saddle River, N.J.: Prentice Hall, 1998), 55–56; James Waldroop and Timothy Butler, "The Executive as Coach," *Harvard Business Review,* November–December 1996, 113.

40. "The Advantage of Female Mentoring," *Working Woman,* October 1991, 104;

41. Bovée et al., *Management,* 86.

42. Michael Barrier, "Learning the Meaning of Measurement," *Nation's Business,* June 1994, 72–74.

43. Bovée et al., *Management,* 218–220.

44. William B. Werther Jr. and Keith Davis, *Human Resources and Personnel Management,* 4th ed. (New York: McGraw-Hill, 1993), 359–360; Daft, *Management,* 225–227.

45. Judy A. Smith, "Crisis Communications; The War on Two Fronts," *Industry Week,* 20 May 1996, 136; John F. Reukus, "Hazard Communication," *Occupational Hazards,* February 1998, 39+; Kim M. Gibson and Steven H. Smith, "Do We Understand Each Other?" *Journal of Accountancy,* January 1998, 53+.

46. Edward A. Robinson, "America's Most Admired Companies," *Fortune,* 3 March 1997, 68, *Electric Library,* Online, 2 September 1997; Susan Chandler, "Crisis Management: How TWA Faced the Nightmare," *Business Week,* 5 August 1996, 30; Kerri Selland, "Experts Say Corporations Ill-Prepared for Crises,"

Reuters, 23 July 1996, *Electric Library,* Online, 2 September 1997; THOMAS S. MULLIGAN, "TWA Garners Weak Marks for Crisis Management," *Los Angeles Times,* 20 July 1996, D1; TOM INCANTALUPO, "TWA's Image Polishing," *Newsday,* 23 July 1996, A49; MICHAEL SKAPINKER, "TWA Claws Its Way Back," *Financial Times,* 10 March 1998, 35; "Scrappy TWA Proves It Still Flies, but Can It Soar?" *Business Wire,* 12 March 1998, 31.

47. SELLAND, "Experts Say Corporations Ill-Prepared for Crises"; JOANNE R. PIERSALL, "Contingency Planning: Facing Disaster and Surviving," *Nonprofit World,* May–June 1993, 35–38; MARK HOFMAN, "Planning for Catastrophes," *Business Insurance,* 27 March 1995, 2.

48. See note 1.

CHAPTER 7

1. "Lexmark International Reports Record First-Quarter Operating," *Cambridge Work-Group Computing Report,* 28 April 1997, *Electric Library,* Online, accessed 18 September 1997; Marvin Mann, interview by PETER SCHACKNOW, *MSNBC Private Financial Network,* 18 June 1997, PATRICK FLANAGAN, "IBM One Day, Lexmark the Next," *Management Review,* January 1994, 38–44; MARY KATHLEEN FLYNN, "Inside Lexmark: A Taste of the New IBM?" *PC Magazine,* 25 February 1992, 30–31; PAUL B. CARROLL, "Culture Shock: Story of an IBM Unit That Split Off Shows Difficulties of Change," *Wall Street Journal,* 23 July 1992, A1, A5; "Lexmark: The Typing on the Wall," *Economist,* 3 October 1992, 74–75.

2. ROB GOFFEE AND GARETH JONES, "What Holds the Modern Company Together?" *Harvard Business Review,* November–December 1996, 134–145.

3. RICHARD L. DAFT, *Management,* 4th ed. (Fort Worth, Tex.: Dryden, 1997), 358.

4. KATHRYN M. BARTOL AND DAVID C. MARTIN, *Management* (New York: McGraw-Hill, 1991), 345.

5. STEPHEN P. ROBBINS, *Managing Today!* (Upper Saddle River, N.J.: Prentice Hall, 1997), 193; DAFT, *Management,* 320.

6. ANN MAJCHRZAK AND QIANWEI WANG, "Breaking the Functional Mind-Set in Process Organizations," *Harvard Business Review,* September–October 1996, 95–96.

7. STEPHEN P. ROBBINS AND DAVID A. DECENZO, *Fundamentals of Management,* 2d ed. (Upper Saddle River, N.J.: Prentice Hall, 1998), 201; DAFT, *Management,* 321.

8. ALAN WEBBER, "The Best Organization Is No Organization," *USA Today,* 13A, *Electric Library,* Online, accessed 25 September 1997; EVE TAHMINCIOGLU, "How GM's Team Approach Works," *Gannett News Service,* 24 April 1996, S11, *Electric Library,* Online, accessed 25 September 1997.

9. FRED R. DAVID, *Strategic Management,* 6th ed. (Upper Saddle River, N.J.: Prentice Hall, 1997), 225; BARTOL AND MARTIN, *Management,* 352.

10. JEANNE DUGAN, ALISON REA, AND JOSEPH WEBER, "The BW 50: Business Week's Performance Rankings of the S&P 500 Best Performers," *Business Week,* 24 March 1997, 80, *Electric Library,* Online, accessed 25 September 1997.

11. DAFT, *Management,* 325.

12. COURTLAND L. BOVÉE ET AL., *Management* (New York: McGraw-Hill, 1993), 285.

13. BARTOL AND MARTIN, *Management,* 370–371.

14. GARY IZUMO, "Teamwork Holds Key to Organization Success," *Los Angeles Times,* 20 August 1996, D9, *Electric Library,* Online, accessed 18 September 1997; DAFT, *Management,* 328–329; DAVID, *Strategic Management,* 223.

15. DAVID, *Strategic Management,* 223.

16. DAFT, *Management,* 329–333; DAVID, *Strategic Management,* 223–225; MAJCHRZAK AND WANG, "Breaking the Functional Mind-Set," 95–96.

17. JOHN A. BYRNE, "The Horizontal Corporation," *Business Week,* 20 December 1993, 76–81; "Is a Horizontal Organization for You?" *Fortune,* 3 April 1995, 96; RAHUL JACOB, "The Struggle to Create an Organization for the 21st Century," *Fortune,* 3 April 1995, 90–96.

18. DAFT, *Management,* 328–329, 332; DAVID, *Strategic Management,* 223; BARTOL AND MARTIN, *Management,* 376.

19. DAN DIMANCESCU AND KEMP DWENGER, "Smoothing the Product Development Path," *Management Review,* 1 January 1996, 36(6), *Electric Library,* Online, accessed 18 September 1997.

20. DIMANCESCU AND DWENGER, "Smoothing the Product Development Path," 36(6).

21. ROBBINS, *Managing Today!* 209; DAFT, *Management,* 333–336.

22. DAFT, *Management,* 340–343; ROBBINS, *Managing Today!* 213–214.

23. DONNA FENN, "Managing Virtual Employees," *Inc.,* July 1996, 91.

24. DAFT, *Management,* 340–343; ROBBINS, *Managing Today!* 213–214.

25. DAFT, *Management,* 352–353; RICHARDS, *Strategic Management,* 217; BARTOL AND MARTIN, *Management,* 357–358.

26. SAROJA GIRISHANKAR, "Integrator's Road to Success," *Communications Week,* 27 March 1995, 120, 125; DAFT, *Management,* 357–358.

27. THOMAS STEWART, "The Corporate Jungle Spawns a New Species: The Project Manager," *Fortune,* 10 July 1995, 179, *Electric Library,* Online, accessed 18 September 1997.

28. DAFT, *Management,* 284.

29. ROSS SHERWOOD, "The Boss's Open Door Means More Time for Employees," *Reuters Business Report,* 30 September 1996, *Electric Library,* Online, accessed 18 September 1997.

30. JEFFREY PFEFFER, "When It Comes to 'Best Practices'—Why do Smart Organizations Occasionally Do Dumb Things?" *Organizational Dynamics,* 1 June 1996, 33(12), *Electric Library,* Online, accessed 18 September 1997; LAMAR A. TREGO, "Reengineering starts with a 'clean sheet of paper,'" *Manage,* 1 July 1996, 17(4), *Electric Library,* Online, accessed 18 September 1997.

31. DAFT, *Management,* 338.

32. JAC FITZ-ENZ, "Measuring Team Effectiveness," *HR Focus,* 1 August 1997, *Electric Library,* Online, accessed 18 September 1997; STEVE ALEXANDER, "Reaping Team Rewards, *Computer World,* 1 February 1996, 55; PFEFFER, "When It Comes to 'Best Practices,'" 33(12); THOMAS A. STEWART AND JOYCE E. DAVIS, "Ideas & Solutions/The Leading Edge: Why Value Statements Don't Work," *Fortune,* 10 June 1996, 137+, *Electric Library,* Online, accessed 18 September 1997.

33. Daft, *Management,* 591; Robbins, *Managing Today!* 295.

34. "Microsoft Teamwork," *Executive Excellence,* 6 July 1996, 6–7.

35. Daft, *Management,* 594–595; Robbins and De Cenzo, *Fundamentals of Management,* 336; Robbins, *Managing Today!* 309.

36. Pfeffer, "When It Comes to 'Best Practices,'" 33(12).

37. Daft, *Management,* 594; Robbins and De Cenzo, *Fundamentals of Management,* 336.

38. Seth Lubove, "Destroying the Old Hierarchies," *Forbes,* 3 June 1996, 62–64.

39. Daft, *Management,* 594; Robbins and De Cenzo, *Fundamentals of Management,* 338; Robbins, *Managing Today!* 310–311.

40. Jenny C. McCune, "On the Train Gang: In the New Flat Organizations, Employees Who Want to be Competitive Must Be Versatile Enough to Perform a Variety of Tasks," *Management Review,* 1 October 1994, 57 (4), *Electric Library,* Online, accessed 18 September 1997.

41. Pfeffer, "When It Comes to 'Best Practices,'" 33(12).

42. Daft, *Management,* 596–598; Robbins and De Cenzo, *Fundamentals of Management,* 338; Robbins, *Managing Today!* 309–310; Robert Porter Lynch and Iain Sommerville, "The Shift from Vertical to Networked Integration," *Physician Executive,* 1 May 1996, 13(6), *Electric Library,* Online, accessed 18 September 1997.

43. Ellen Neuborne, "Companies Save, but Workers Pay," *USA Today,* 25 February 1997, B1; Daft, *Management,* 594; Robbins and De Cenzo, *Fundamentals of Management,* 338; Robbins, *Managing Today!* 310.

44. Richard Moderow, "Teamwork Is the Key to Cutting Costs," *Modern Healthcare,* 29 April 1996, 138.

45. David H. Freedman, "Culture of Urgency," *Forbes ASAP,* 13 September 1993, 25–26.

46. Daft, *Management,* 594.

47. Robbins and De Cenzo, *Fundamentals of Management,* 334–335; Daft, *Management,* 602–603.

48. Robbins, *Managing Today!* 297–298; Daft, *Management,* 604–607.

49. Daft, *Management,* 609–612.

50. Steven Crom and Herbert France, "Teamwork Brings Breakthrough Improvements in Quality and Climate," *Quality Progress,* March 1996, 39–41.

51. David, *Strategic Management,* 221.

52. Daft, *Management,* 612–615.

53. Neuborne, "Companies Save, but Workers Pay," B2; Charles L. Parnell, "Teamwork: Not a New Idea, but It's Transforming the Workplace," *Vital Speeches of the Day,* 1 November 1996, 46.

54. Robbins and De Cenzo, *Fundamentals of Management,*151.

55. Matthew Tallimer, "Legal Implications and Complications," *Total Quality Review,* September–October 1994, 11–12; William Roth and Thomas Smith, "The Little City That Could," *Total Quality Review,* September–October 1994, 18; Daft, Management, 615.

56. Jaesum Lee and Fredric Jablan, "A Cross-Cultural Investigation of Exit, Voice, Loyalty, and Neglect as Responses to Dissatisfying Job Conditions," *Journal of Business Communication* 23, no. 3 (1992): 203–208; Barron Wells and Nelda Spinks, "What Do You Mean People Communicate with Audiences?" *Bulletin of the Association for Business Communication* 54, no. 3 (1991): 100–102.

57. "Flying the Murky Skies at American," *Inside PR,* May–June 1993, 44.

58. James L. Heskett et al., "Putting the Service-Profit Chain to Work," *Harvard Business Review,* 167.

59. Elizabeth Conlin, "The Vital-Signs Assessment," *Inc.,* April 1993, 127.

60. Donald O. Wilson, "Diagonal Communication Links with Organizations," *Journal of Business Communication* 29, no. 2 (1992): 129–143.

61. Justin Martin and Amy Kover, "Tomorrow's CEOs: Meet Six Hot Young Managers Who Have What It Takes to Lead in the 21st Century," *Fortune,* 24 June 1996, 84.

62. Malcolm Groat, "The Informal Organization: Ride the Headless Monster," *Management Accounting,* 1 April 1997, 40(3), *Electric Library,* Online, accessed 24 September 1997; Fred Luthans, "Successful vs. Effective Real Managers," *Academy of Management Executive* 2, no. 2 (1988): 130.

63. Laurey Berk and Phillip G. Clampitt, "Finding the Right Path in the Communication Maze," *IABC Communication World,* October 1991, 28–32.

64. Sheree R. Curry, "Smart Managing: Stop the E-mail Madness! Cyberworld," *Fortune,* 26 May 1997, 195.

65. Alice LaPlante, "Still Drowning," *Computerworld,* 10 March 1997, 69+, *Electric Library,* Online, accessed 24 September 1997.

66. Richard F. Federic and James M. Bowley, "The Great E-mail Debate," *HR Magazine,* January 1996, 67–72.

67. Mike Bransby, "Voice Mail Makes a Difference," *Journal of Business Strategy,* January–February 1990, 7–10.

68. Harris Collingswood, "Voice Mail Hangups," *Business Week,* 17 February 1992, 46.

69. Andrew Kupfer, "Prime Time for Videoconferences," *Fortune,* 28 December 1992, 90–95.

70. Dimancescu and Dwenger, "Smoothing the Product Development Path," 36(6), *Electric Library,* Online, accessed 18 September 1997.

71. John V. Thill and Courtland L. Bovée, *Excellence in Business Communication* (Upper Saddle River, N.J.: Prentice Hall, 1997), 27–34.

72. See note 1.

CHAPTER 8

1. Adapted from *Harley-Davidson 1993 Annual Report*; Brian S. Moskal, "Born to Be Real," *Industry Week,* 2 August 1993, 14–18; Martha H. Peak, "Harley-Davidson: Going Whole Hog to Provide Stakeholder Satisfaction," *Management Review,* June 1993, 53–55; Gary Slutsker, "Hog Wild," *Forbes,* 24 May 1993, 45–46; Kevin Kelly and Karen Lowry Miller, "The Rumble Heard Round the World: Harleys," *Business Week,* 24 May 1993, 58, 60; James B. Shuman, "Easy Rider Rides Again," *Business Tokyo,* July 1991, 26–30; Holt Hackney, "Easy Rider," *Financial World,* 4 September 1990, 48–49; Roy L. Harmon and Leroy D.

Peterson, "Reinventing the Factory," *Across the Board*, March 1990, 30–38; John Holusha, "How Harley Outfoxed Japan with Exports," *New York Times*, 12 August 1990, F5; Peter C. Reid, "How Harley Beat Back the Japanese," *Fortune*, 25 September 1989, 155–164; Samer Iskandar, "Get a Life—Get a Harley," *Financial Times*, 31 January 1998, 12; Stephen Roth, "New Harley Plant Spotlights Training and Empowerment," *Kansas City Business Journal*, 9 January 1998, 3.

2. Roberta S. Russell and Bernard W. Taylor III, *Operations Management: Focusing on Quality and Competitiveness*, 2d ed. (Upper Saddle River, N.J.: Prentice Hall, 1998), 21.

3. Tad Tuleja, *The New York Public Library Book of Popular Americana* (New York: Stonesong Press, 1994), *Electric Library*, Online, 11 February 1998.

4. Justin Martin, "Are You as Good as You Think You Are?" *Fortune*, 30 September 1996, 143–144.

5. Larry E. Long and Nancy Long, *Introduction to Computers and Information Systems*, 5th ed. (Upper Saddle River, N.J.: Prentice Hall, 1997), 1997, AT 84.

6. Alex Taylor III, "How Toyota Copes with Hard Times," *Fortune*, 25 January 1993, 78–81.

7. Long and Long, *Introduction to Computers and Information Systems*, AT 84–85; Russell and Taylor, *Operations Management: Focusing on Quality and Competitiveness*, 255.

8. "IBM and Dassault Awarded Boeing CATIA Contract," *CAD/CAM Update*, 1 January 1997, 1–8, *Electric Library*, Online, 3 October 1997; Shawn Tully, "Can Boeing Reinvent Itself?" *Fortune*, 8 March 1993, 66–68, 72–73; Doris Jones Yang, "Boeing Knocks Down the Wall Between the Dreamers and the Doers," *Business Week*, 28 October 1991, 120–121.

9. Russell and Taylor, *Operations Management: Focusing on Quality and Competitiveness*, 211.

10. "CAD/CAM Industry Embracing Intranet-Based Technologies," *Computer Dealer News* 12 (28 November 1996): 21, *Electric Library*, Online, 3 October 1997.

11. Drew Winter, "C3P: New Acronym Signals Big Change at Ford," *Ward's Auto World* 32 (1 August 1996): 34, *Electric Library*, Online, 3 October 1997; Thomas Hoffman, "Ford to Cut Its Prototype Costs," *Computerworld*, 30 September 1996, 65, *Electric Library*, Online, 3 October 1997; Drew Winter, "Massive Changes Coming in Computer Engineering," *Ward's Auto World* 32 (1 April 1996): 34, *Electric Library*, Online, 3 October 1997.

12. Nicholas J. Aquilano, Richard B. Chase, and Mark M. Davis, *Fundamentals of Operations Management* (Chicago: Irwin, 1995), 75; Russell and Taylor, *Operations Management: Focusing on Quality and Competitiveness*, 257–258.

13. "Taiwan Signs Up Digital to Help Boost Productivity, *Newsbytes News Network*, 17 July 1996, *Electric Library*, Online, 3 October 1997; Pete Engardio, "A Worker Shortage Pinches Penang . . . So It's Time for a Skills Upgrade," *BusinessWeek International*, 5 May 1997, 4, *Electric Library*, Online, 3 October 1997; Al Morgan, "Canada's Strategic Sector for the 1990s," *Canadian Business Review*, 22 March 1994, 13, *Electric Library*, Online, 3 October 1997.

14. Moskal, "Born to Be Real," 14–18.

15. Russell and Taylor, *Operations Management: Focusing on Quality and Competitiveness*, 255–256.

16. John H. Sheridan, "Agile Manufacturing: Stepping Beyond Lean Production," *Industrial Week*, 19 April 1993, 30–33, 36–38, 40–41, 44, 46.

17. Brian McWilliams, "Re-engineering the Small Factory," *Inc. Technology*, no. 1 (1996): 44–45.

18. Roberta Maynard, "Striking the Right Match," *Nation's Business*, May 1996, 18.

19. John H. Sheridan, "The Agile Web: A Model for the Future?" *Industry Week*, 4 March 1996, 31–33.

20. John H. Sheridan, "Lessons from the Best," *Industry Week*, 19 February 1996, 16.

21. Neal M. Goldsmith and Ed Rosenfeld, "Shooting the Rapids—Business Process Reengineering Can Be a Wild Ride, but There Are a Number of Tools and Services Available to Help Companies Manage Change and Maximize Growth," *Information Week*, 25 November 1996, 65, *Electric Library*, Online, 3 October 1997; Sheridan, "Lessons from the Best," 16–17; Kathryn M. Bartol and David C. Martin, *Management* (New York: McGraw-Hill, 1991), 688.

22. Russell and Taylor, *Operations Management: Focusing on Quality and Competitiveness*, 501; Courtland L. Bovée et al., *Management* (New York: McGraw-Hill, 1993), 644.

23. Joseph G. Monks, *Operations Management, Theory and Problems* (New York: McGraw-Hill, 1987), 77–78.

24. Aquilano, Chase, and Davis, *Fundamentals of Operations Management*, 235–236.

25. Aquilano, Chase, and Davis, *Fundamentals of Operations Management*, 240–241.

26. Monks, *Operations Management, Theory and Problems*, 2–3.

27. Monks, *Operations Management, Theory and Problems*, 125.

28. Russell and Taylor, *Operations Management: Focusing on Quality and Competitiveness*, 291–292; Aquilano, Chase, and Davis, *Fundamentals of Operations Management*, 271–272; Richard L. Daft, *Management*, 4th ed. (Fort Worth, Tex.: Dryden, 1997), 718.

29. Russell and Taylor, *Operations Management: Focusing on Quality and Competitiveness*, 440.

30. Joseph P. Aleo, Jr., "Redefining the Manufacturer-Supplier Relationship," *Journal of Business Strategy*, September–October 1992, 12–13.

31. David Woodruff, Ian Katz, and Keith Naughton, "VW's Factory of the Future," *Business Week*, 7 October 1996, 52, 56.

32. Aquilano, Chase, and Davis, *Fundamentals of Operations Management*, 462.

33. Sheridan, "Lessons from the Best," 16.

34. Aquilano, Chase, and Davis, *Fundamentals of Operations Management*, 483–484; Russell and Taylor, *Operations Management: Focusing on Quality and Competitiveness*, 652–653.

35. Lawrence A. Berardinis, ed., "Factory Monitoring via the Internet," *Machine Design*, 20 March 1997.

36. Russell and Taylor, *Operations Management: Focusing on Quality and Competitiveness*, 712–733.

37. Patricia W. Hamilton, "Getting a Grip on Inventory," *D&B Reports*, March–April 1994, 32.

38. Marshall L. Fisher et al., "Making Supply Meet Demand in an Uncertain World," *Harvard Business Review*, May–June

1994, 84. "Mounting Demand, Dwindling Supply," *U.S. News & World Report*, 16 March 1998, 49; "50 Years Ago," *Forbes*, 9 March 1998, 253.

39. ROBERT O. KNORR AND JOHN L. NEUMAN, "Quick Response Technology: The Key to Outstanding Growth," *Journal of Business Strategy*, September–October 1992, 63.

40. JOHN A. BYRNE, "Never Mind the Buzzwords. Roll Up Your Sleeves," *Business Week*, 22 January 1996, 84.

41. DEL JONES, "Training and Service at Top of Winners' List," *USA Today*, 17 October 1996, 5B.

42. JUSTIN MARTIN, "Are You as Good as You Think You Are?" *Fortune*, 30 September 1996, 149–150.

43. AQUILANO, CHASE, AND DAVIS, *Fundamentals of Operations Management*, 140; RUSSELL AND TAYLOR, *Operations Management: Focusing on Quality and Competitiveness*, 131.

44. WILLIAM M. CARLEY, "Charging Ahead: To Keep GE's Profits Rising, Welch Pushes Quality-Control Plan," *Wall Street Journal*, 13 January 1997, A1, A6; NBC Boosts GE, *Television Digest*, 26 January 1998, 6.

45. RUSSELL AND TAYLOR, *Operations Management: Focusing on Quality and Competitiveness*, 131.

46. HUGH D. MENZIES, "Global Guide: Quality Counts When Wooing Overseas Clients," *Your Company*, 1 June 1997, 64, *Electric Library*, Online, 6 October 1997; MICHAEL E. RAYNOR, "Worldwide Winners," *Total Quality Management*, July–August 1993, 43–48; GREG BOUNDS, LYLE YORKS, MEL ADAMS, AND GIPSIE RANNEY, *Beyond Total Quality Management: Toward the Emerging Paradigm* (New York: McGraw-Hill, 1994), 87; RUSSELL AND TAYLOR, *Operations Management: Focusing on Quality and Competitiveness*, 115–116.

47. RAYNOR, "Worldwide Winners," 43–48; THEODORE R. MARRA, "The States of Excellence," *Total Quality Management*, July–August 1993, 27–31.

48. JONES, "Training and Service at Top of Winners' List," 5B.

49. FISHER ET AL., "Making Supply Meet Demand in an Uncertain World," 83–86.

50. KARL RITZLER, "A Mercedes Made from Scratch," *Atlanta Journal and Constitution*, 30 May 1997, S1, *Electric Library*, Online, 8 October 1997.

51. BARTOL AND MARTIN, *Management*, 307–308.

52. See note 1.

53. GARY HOOVER, ALTA CAMPBELL, AND PATRICK J. SPAIN, eds., *Hoover's Handbook of American Business 1994* (Austin, Tex.: Reference Press, 1994), 268–269, 712–713, 1092–1093; U.S. Bureau of the Census, *Statistical Abstract of the United States: 1993*, 113th ed. (Washington, D.C.: GPO, 1993), 750–751, 696–697.

CHAPTER 9

1. MARTIN EVANS, HUGH GUNZ, and R. MICHAEL JALLAND, "Alternatives to Downsizing," *Financial Post*, 27 April 1996; GILLIAN FLYNN, "A Satisfied Workforce Is in Hallmark's Cards," *Personnel Journal* 75, no. 1 (January 1996): 62; GILLIAN FLYNN, "Hallmark Cares: Sending a Quality of Life Message," *Personnel Journal* 75, no. 3 (March 1996): 50–61; BEVERLY GEBER, "The Bugaboo of Team Pay," *Training*, 32, no. 8 (August 1995): 25–34; SANDRA O'CONNELL, "Re-engineering: Ways to Do It with Technology," *HR Magazine* 39, no. 11 (November 1994): 40–46; THOMAS STEWART, "The Search for the Organization of Tomorrow," *Fortune*, 18 May 1992, 92–98; RICHARD WELLENS AND JULIE SCHULZ MURPHY, "Reengineering: Plug into the Human Factor," *Training and Development* 49, no. 1 (January 1995): 33–37.

2. RICHARD TOMKINS, "Cards Make a Hard Life Verse," *Financial Times*, 14 February 1998, 1; CALMETTA Y. COLEMAN, "Hallmark Campaign Focuses on Card Costs," *Wall Street Journal*, 12 February 1998, B6; RONALD ALSOP, "Hallmark Cards Creates Sympathy Card for Suicides," *Wall Street Journal*, 15 January 1998, A1.

3. DENNIS C. KINLAW, "What Employees See Is What Organizations Get,'" *Management Solutions*, March 1988, 38–41.

4. KERRY A. DOLAN, "When Money Isn't Enough," *Forbes*, 18 November 1996, 164.

5. CLAUDE S. GEORGE JR. *The History of Management Thought*, 2d ed. (Upper Saddle River, N.J.: Prentice Hall, 1972), 62–63; DANIEL A. WREN, *The Evolution of Management Thought*, 2d ed. (New York: Wiley, 1979), 70–75.

6. AARON LUCCHETTI, "Overdrive: An Auto Worker Earns More Than $100,000, but at a Personal Cost," *Wall Street Journal*, 1 August 1996, A1.

7. ABRAHAM H. MASLOW, "A Theory of Human Motivations," *Psychological Review*, July 1943, 370; *Motivation and Personality*, 2d ed. (New York: Harper & Row, 1970).

8. TIMOTHY D. SCHELLHARDT, "Company Memo to Stressed-Out Employees: 'Deal with It,'" *Wall Street Journal*, 2 October 1996, B1.

9. PATTI STANG AND BOB LAIRD, "Working Women's Motivators, *USA Today*, 12 February 1996, 1B.

10. JENNIFER BRESNAHAN, "The Elusive Muse," *CIO Enterprise*, 15 October 1997, 54.

11. FREDERICK HERZBERG, *Work and the Nature of Man* (New York: World, 1971).

12. DOUGLAS MCGREGOR, *The Human Side of Enterprise* (New York: McGraw-Hill, 1960).

13. RICHARD L. DAFT, *Management*, 4th ed. (Fort Worth, Tex.: Dryden, 1997), 60.

14. SUE SHELLENBARGER, "Work and Family: Enter the 'New Hero': A Boss Who Knows You Have a Life," *Wall Street Journal*, 10 February 1993, B1.

15. ELLEN NEUBORNE, "Temporary Workers Getting Short Shrift," *USA Today*, 11 April 1997, B1; ROBERT L. BODINE, "How to Find and Keep Good Contract Workers," *Training and Development*, February 1998, 54; CAROLYN GRIFFITH, "Building a Resilient Work Force," *Training*, January 1998, 54; JAMES WORSHAM, "Is Your Company Keeping Pace," *Nation's Business*, January 1998, 14; ANNE SHIHADEH-GOMMA, EDWARD W. ALLEN, JIM GREEN, "The Right Fit," *Risk Management*, January 1998, 37.

16. RON STODGHILL, "The Coming Job Bottleneck," *Business Week*, 24 March 1997, 184–185; MICHAEL MOSS, "Golden Years: For One 73-Year-Old, Punching Time Clock Isn't a Labor of Love," *Wall Street Journal*, 31 March 1997, A1, A8; RICHARD W. JUDY AND CAROL D'AMICO, *Workforce 2020* (Indianapolis: The Hudson Institute, 1997), 104.

17. JULIA LAWLOR, "Busters Have Work Ethic All Their Own," *USA Today*, 20 July 1993, 1B–2B.

18. RANDALL S. SCHULER, *Managing Human Resources,* 6th ed. (Cincinnati: South-Western College Publishing, 1998), 577.

19. JUDY AND D'AMICO, *Workforce 2020,* 53.

20. *Statistical Abstract of the United States: 1996* (Washington, D.C.: GPO, 1996), 58.

21. NIKHIL DEOGUN, "Top PepsiCo Executive Picks Family over Job," *Wall Street Journal,* 24 September 1997, B1.

22. ALEX MARKELS, "How One Hotel Manages Staff's Diversity," *Wall Street Journal,* 20 November 1996, B1.

23. JOSEPH F. MCKENNA AND BRIAN S. MOSKAL, "The Plight of the Seasoned Worker," *Industry Week,* 7 June 1993, 12–14, 18–19, 22.

24. DAVID A. THOMAS AND ROBIN J. ELY, "Making Differences Matter: A New Paradigm for Managing Diversity," *Harvard Business Review,* September–October 1996, 85; JOHN W. MILLIGAN, *Managing Diversity, U.S. Banker,* March 1998, 6.

25. JUDY AND D'AMICO, *Workforce 2020,* 21, 31–36, 39, 44.

26. RONALD B. LIEBER, "How Safe Is Your Job?" *Fortune,* 1 April 1996, 72.

27. SCHELLHARDT, "Company Memo to Stressed-Out Employees: 'Deal with It,'" B1.

28. BRIAN S. MOSKAL, "Company Loyalty Dies, a Victim of Neglect," *Industry Week,* 1 March 1993, 11–12.

29. N. R. KLEINFIELD, "The Company as Family No More," *New York Times,* 4 March 1996, A1.

30. T. J. LARKIN AND SANDAR LARKIN, "Reaching and Changing Frontline Employees," *Harvard Business Review,"* May–June 1996, 96.

31. JOHN GREENWALD, "Spinning Away," *Time,* 26 August 1996, 30–31.

32. DAFT, *Management,* 771.

33. GLENN BURKINS, "Technical Problems: Good Jobs Go Unfulfilled Amid Some Shortages of Skilled Workers," *Wall Street Journal,* 27 November 1996, A1, A7.

34. JAMES C. WETHERBE, *The World On Time* (Encino, Calif.: Knowledge Exchange, 1996), *Electric Library,* Online, 17 October 1997.

35. KAREN MATTHES, "Job Placement: Redefining the Fast Track," *Management Review,* November 1992, 5.

36. KLEINFIELD, "The Company as Family No More," A8.

37. BRUCE HOROVITZ, "CEOs May Need to Polish Their Public Image," *USA Today,* 21 February 1996, B1.

38. POLLY LABARRE, "Lighten Up!" *Industry Week,* 5 February 1996, 53.

39. DONALD J. MCNERNEY, "Employee Motivation: Creating a Motivated Workforce," *HR Focus* 73, 1 August 1996, 1, *Electric Library,* Online, 14 October 1997; JOHN W. HUNT, "A Salary Can't Buy Happiness," *Financial Times,* 11 March 1998, 13; RONALD B. LIEBER, "Why Employees Love These Companies," *Fortune,* 12 January 1998, 72+; ILANA DEBARE, "When Personal Problems Affect Job Performance," *San Francisco Chronicle,* March 23, 1998, B5.

40. BOB NELSON, "Dump the Cash, Load on the Praise," *Personnel Journal,* July 1996, 66.

41. SHARON NELTON, "Face to Face," *Nation's Business,* November 1995, 19–22.

42. BARBARA BRONSON GRAY, "Magic Motivators!" *Business 97,* December–January 1997, 54.

43. HELENE COOPER, "The New Educators: Carpet Firm Sets Up an In-House School to Stay Competitive," *Wall Street Journal,* 5 October 1992, A1, A6.

44. ADOLPH HAASEN AND GORDON F. SHEA, *A Better Place to Work* (New York: American Management Association, 1997), 19–20.

45. KRISTA OSTERTAG, "Motivating Employees—The Best Way to Motivate Your Most Prized Assets Is to Keep 'em Happy," *VarBusiness,* 1 February 1997, 99, *Electric Library,* Online, 14 October 1997.

46. CHARLENE MARMER SOLOMON, "Keep Them!" *Workforce,* August 1997, 49–51.

47. JOHN W. NEWSTROM AND KEITH DAVIS, *Organizational Behavior: Human Behavior at Work,* 9th ed. (New York: McGraw-Hill, 1993), 345.

48. LAURIE M. GROSSMAN, "Truck Cabs Turn into Mobile Offices as Drivers Take On White-Collar Tasks," *Wall Street Journal,* 3 August 1993, B1, B5.

49. TERRENCE E. DEAL, "Rally Your Troops," *Success,* March 1994, 44.

50. SCHULER, *Managing Human Resources,* 218.

51. BRESNEHAN, "The Elusive Muse," 52; KERRY A. DOLAN, "When Money Isn't Enough," *Forbes,* 18 November 1996, 164–170.

52. NICK RAVO, "Want a Day Off? Take It from the Bank," *New York Times,* 5 October 1997, BU8.

53. "USA Snapshots," *USA Today,* 20 November 1990, 1D.

54. GENEVIEVE CAPOWSKI, "The Joy of Flex," *Management Review,* March 1996, 13.

55. CHARLENE MARMER SOLOMON, "Flexibility Comes out of Flux," *Personnel Journal,* June 1996, 38–40; DON HEILMAN, "Flex Benefits Plans Can Save Money," *American City & County,* January 1998, 6.

56. BARBARA E. MILLER, "Reduce Your Work/Life Program," *Workforce,* June 1997, 84–90; CAPOWSKI, "The Joy of Flex," 13.

57. MELANIE WARNER, "Working at Home—The Right Way to Be a Star in Your Bunny Slippers," *Fortune,* 3 March 1997, 166; LIN GRENSING-POPHAL, "Employing the Best People—From Afar," *Workforce,* March 1997, 30–32.

58. KATHI S. ALLEN AND GLORIA FLYNN MOORMAN, "Leaving Home: The Emigration of Home-Office Workers," *American Demographics,* October 1997, 57–61; SHELLENBARGER, "Work and Family: Enter the 'New Hero.'" *Wall Street Journal,* 10 February 1993, B1.

59. "Tapping Employees' Insights to Expand Productivity," *Nation's Business,* November 1996, 13.

60. See note 1.

CHAPTER 10

1. Adapted from KIMBERLY SEALS MCDONALD, ERIN DAVIES, AND MARIA ATANASOV, "Your Benefits: You Know Your Salary, but You Don't Know What Your Job's Worth Until You Know," *Fortune,* 23 December 1996, 199, *Electric Library,* Online, 18 February 1998; ANITA BRUZZESE, "Johnson & Johnson Working with Community to Develop Home Care Programs," *Gannett News Service,* 28 March 1996, S12, *Electric Library,* Online, 18 February

1998; Lesley Alderman and Jeanhee Kim, "Your Worklife: Get the Most from Your Company Benefits," *Money,* 1 January 1996, 102, *Electric Library,* Online, 18 February 1998; Sally Roberts, "Balancing Work, Family," *Business Insurance,* 27 September 1993, 3, 20; Julie Cohen Mason, "Healthy Equals Happy Plus Productive," *Management Review,* July 1992, 33–37; Monica Battagliola, "Making Employees Better Health Care Consumers," *Business & Health,* June 1992, 22, 24, 26–28; "Changing a Corporate Culture," *Business Week,* 14 May 1984, 130–138; *The Johnson & Johnson 1990 Annual Report*; "Shrinking, Changing Labor Force Prompts Johnson & Johnson Family Issues Policies," *Employee Benefit Plan Review,* September 1989, 57–60; "What Makes Sales Forces Run?" *Sales & Marketing Management,* 3 December 1984, 24–26; Susan Dentzer, "Excessive Claims," *Business Month,* July 1990, 52–63; Evelyn Gilbert, "Benefits No 'Soft' Issue: J&J Official," *National Underwriter,* 10 December 1990, 15, 21; Christopher Power, "At Johnson & Johnson, a Mistake Can Be a Badge of Honor," *Business Week,* 26 September 1988, 126–128; Lee Smith, "J&J Comes a Long Way from Baby," *Fortune,* 1 June 1981, 58–66; Neal Templin, "Johnson & Johnson 'Wellness' Program for Workers Shows Healthy Bottom Line," *Wall Street Journal,* 21 May 1990, B1, B6; Barbara Scherr Trenk, "Corporate Fitness Programs Become Hearty Investments," *Management Review,* August 1989, 33–37; Michael A. Verespej, "A Ticket to Better Health," *Industry Week,* 4 February 1991, 24–25; Joseph Weber, "No Band-Aids for Ralph Larsen," *Business Week,* 28 May 1990, 86–87; Rhona L. Ferling, "Johnson & Johnson on How to Sell Wellness," *Financial Executive,* March/April 1995, 28.

2. Jennifer J. Laabs, "HR Pioneers Explore the Road Less Traveled," *Personnel Journal,* February 1996, 70.

3. Harvey Gittler, "Name Change Not Enough," *Industry Week,* 7 March 1994, 14.

4. Dale D. Buss, "Help Wanted Desperately," *Nation's Business,* April 1996, 16–17; U.S. Bureau of Labor Statistics, *Employment Statistics,* <www.bls.gov>, accessed 23 October 1997.

5. Richard W. Judy and Carol D'Amico, *Workforce 2020* (Indianapolis: The Hudson Institute, 1997), 69–73.

6. Judy and D'Amico, *Workforce 2020,* 81–85.

7. Lori Ionannou, "It's a Small World After All," *International Business,* February 1994, 82–84, 86–88.

8. John H. Sheridan, "Raising the Reading Curve," *Industry Week,* 20 November 1995, 31–32.

9. *Statistical Abstract of the United States: 1996* (Washington, D.C.: GPO, 1996), 403; Brian Tarcy, "Contingent Workers: Where's the Fit?" *Across the Board,* April 1994, 36–40; Peter T. Kilborn, "Part-Time Hirings Bring Deep Changes in U.S. Workplaces," *New York Times,* 17 June 1991, A1.

10. Timothy Egan, "A Temporary Force to be Reckoned With," *New York Times,* 20 May 1996, C1, C10; Jan Larsen, "Temps Are Here to Stay," *American Demographics,* February 1996, 26–31; Brenda Paik Sunoo, "From Santa to CEO—Temps Play All Roles," *Personnel Journal,* April 1996, 34–44; Max Messmer, "Strategic Staffing for the '90s," *Personnel Journal,* October 1990, 94.

11. John A. Byrne, "Has Outsourcing Gone Too Far?" *Business Week,* 1 April 1996, 26–28; Sana Siwolop, "Outsourcing: Savings Are Just the Beginning," *Business Week/Enterprise,* no date, ENT 24–ENT 25; Dale D. Buss, "Growing More by Doing Less," *Nation's Business,* December 1995, 18.

12. George Taninecz, "In Search of Creative Sparks," *Industry Week,* 4 December 1995, 43.

13. Ellen Neuborne, "Critics Say Paying Bounties Akin to Shooting Self in Foot," *USA Today,* 18 December 1996, B1–B2; Joann S. Lublin, "Rehiring Former Employees Has Its Pitfalls," *Wall Street Journal,* 30 December 1996, B1.

14. Buss, "Help Wanted Desperately," 16–18; Michael Barrier, "Hiring the Right People," *Nation's Business,* June 1996, 18–27.

15. Sheila M. Poole, "Hoping to Net That Ideal Job," *Atlanta Journal and Constitution,* 13 April 1997, H1, *Electric Library,* Online, 29 October 1997; "Oracle Leverages IntelliMatch and the Power of Its Own Web Technology to Fill Key Job Openings," *M2 PressWIRE,* 4 March 1997, *Electric Library,* Online, 29 October 1997; Julia King, "Point-and-Click Recruiting Falls Short," *Computerworld,* 10 February 1997, 1, *Electric Library,* Online, 29 October 1997; Alice M. Starcke, "Internet Recruiting Shows Rapid Growth," *HR Magazine* 41, 1 August 1996, 61, *Electric Library,* Online, 29 October 1997.

16. Audrey Arthur, "How Much Should Employees Know?" *Black Enterprise,* October 1997, 56; Anthony Ramirez, "Name, Résumé, References. And How's Your Credit?" *New York Times,* 31 August 1997, F8.

17. Robyn Meredith, "New Blood for the Big Three's Plants," *New York Times,* 21 April 1996, 3, 10.

18. Shari Caudron, "Hire for Attitude," *Workforce,* August 1997, supplement 21; Barrier, "Hiring the Right People," 24–25.

19. U.S. Department of Labor, *Prevalence of Drug Testing in the Workplace* (Washington, D.C.: GPO, 1996), *Electric Library,* Online, 29 October 1997.

20. "Drug Testing," *Wall Street Journal,* 19 March 1991, A1.

21. Catherine Yang, "Cheese It—the Boss," *Business Week,* 27 November 1995, 128.

22. Jonathan Segal, "When Norman Bates and Baby Jane Act Out at Work," *HR Magazine* 41 (1 February 1996): 31, *Electric Library,* Online, 30 October 1997; Jenny C. McCune, "Companies Grapple with Workplace Violence," *Management Review,* March 1994, 52–57.

23. Ellis Henican, "Nightmare at Saks Fifth Ave.," *Newsday,* 5 June 1996, A2, *Electric Library,* Online, 3 November 1997.

24. Randall S. Schuler, *Managing Human Resources* (Cincinnati: South-Western College Publishing, 1998), 386.

25. Tonia L. Shakespeare, "High-Tech Training, Wal-Mart Style," *Black Enterprise,* July 1996, 54.

26. Stephen Baker and Larry Armstrong, "The New Factory Worker," *Business Week,* 30 September 1996, 59–60.

27. Shakespeare, "High-Tech Training, Wal-Mart Style," 54; Charles Bermant, "For the Latest in Corporate Training, Try a CD-ROM," *New York Times,* 16 October 1995, C5.

28. Larry Stevens, "The Intranet: Your Newest Training Tool?" *Personnel Journal,* July 1996, 27; Lynn Anderson, "Building the High-Availability Intranet," *Computing Canada,* 23 February 1998, 40; Gerard Blanc, "The Intranet: First, Answer the Questions," *Computing Canada,* 23 February 1998, 37; "The Intranet Magna Carta," *Training and Development Journal,* January 1998, 54+; Sacha Cohen, "Knowledge Management's Killer Applica-

tion: Here's How an Intranet Can Wire Employees to Information and Knowledge Without Fragmenting a Company's Culture," *Training and Development Journal,* January 1998, 50+.

29. David Fischer and Kevin Whitelaw, "A New Way to Shine Up Corporate Profits," *U.S. News and World Report,* 15 April 1996, 54.

30. Philip R. Theibert, "Train and Degree Them Anywhere," *Personnel Journal,* February 1996, 29.

31. "UPS Management Training Program Helping Others," *New York Beacon,* 18 June 1997, PG, *Electric Library,* Online, 30 October 1997.

32. Stephen Dolainski, "Partnering with the (School) Board," *Workforce,* May 1997, 30; Max Messmer, "Steer Clear of the Skills Gap," *Personnel Journal,* March 1996, 48.

33. Bradely R. Schiller, *State Minimum Wage Laws: Youth Coverage and Impact* (Washington, D.C.: George Mason University, 1994), *Electric Library,* Online, 18 February 1998.

34. Schuler, *Managing Human Resources,* 508.

35. "The Boss's Pay," *Wall Street Journal,* 10 April 1997, R15; *Statistical Abstract of the United States: 1996* (Washington, D.C.: GPO, 1996), 425.

36. Janice Castro, "How's Your Pay?" *Time,* 15 April 1991, 40; John A. Byrne, "The Flap Over Executive Pay," *Business Week,* 6 May 1991, 90.

37. Joann S. Lublin, "Raising the Bar," *Wall Street Journal,* 10 April 1997, R1, R4.

38. Joseph B. White, "The 'In' Thing," *Wall Street Journal,* 10 April 1997, R10.

39. Kerry Hannon, "Variable-Pay Programs: Where the Real Raises Are," *Working Woman,* March 1994, 48–51, 72, 96.

40. Samuel Perry, "Intel Shares $820 Million Extra with Its Employees," *Reuters Business Report,* 11 February 1997, *Electric Library,* Online, 30 October 1997.

41. Jack Stack, "The Problem with Profit Sharing," *Inc.,* November 1996, 67–69; Ellen Neuborne, "Meeting Goals Just Got More Rewarding," *USA Today,* 15 October 1996, B1–B2; "Sharing the Wealth," *Ward's Auto World,* March 1998, 7.

42. Neuborne, "Meeting Goals Just Got More Rewarding," B1–B2.

43. Peter Passell, "Paid by the Widget and Proud," *New York Times,* 16 June 1996, F1.

44. Peter V. LeBlanc, "'Pay for Work': Reviving and Old Idea for the New Customer Focus," *Compensation & Benefits Review* 26 (1 July 1994), *Electric Library,* Online, 30 October 1997; Kevin J. Parent and Caroline L. Weber, "Case Study: Does Knowledge Pay Off?" *Compensation & Benefits Review* 26 (1 September 1994), *Electric Library,* Online, 30 October 1997; Earl Ingram, "Compensation: The Advantages of Knowledge-Based Pay," *Personnel Journal,* April 1990, 138–140.

45. Karen Jacobs, "The Broad View," *Wall Street Journal,* 10 April 1997, R10; Schuler, *Managing Human Resources,* 498–499.

46. Keith H. Hammonds, Wendy Zellner, and Richard Melcher, "Writing a New Social Contract," *Business Week,* 11 March 1996, 60; Don L. Boroughs, "The Bottom Line on Ethics," *U.S. News and World Report,* 20 March 1995, 63–65; Dawn Gunsch, "Benefits Leverage Hiring and Retention Efforts," *Personnel Journal,* November 1992, 91–92, 94–97.

47. Barbara Whitaker, "Partner Benefits Have a Surprising Lack of Takers," *New York Times,* 27 April 1997; Stephen Baker and Paul Judge, "Where IBM Goes, Others May Follow," *Business Week,* 7 October 1996, 39; Anne Underwood and Bruce Shenitz, "Do You, Tom, Take Harry . . . ," *Newsweek,* 11 December 1995, 84; David J. Jefferson, "Family Matters: Gay Employees Win Benefits for Partners at More Corporations," *Wall Street Journal,* 18 March 1994, A1, A6.

48. Pat Wechsler, "Firms Brace for Rising Health Costs," *USA Today,* 9 October 1997, 3B, *Electric Library,* Online, 30 October 1997; U.S. Census Bureau "Health Insurance Coverage: 1995," <www.census.gov>, accessed 30 October 1997.

49. Don L. Boroughs, "The Bottom Line on Ethics," *U.S. News & World Report,* 20 March 1995, 64.

50. Judy and D'Amico, *Workforce 2020,* 94–96, 103.

51. Bureau of Labor Statistics, "Employee Benefits Survey: Incidence of Defined Benefit Pension," <www.bls.gov/cgi-bin/surveymost>, accessed 30 October 1997; Roger Thompson, "The Threat to Pension Plans," *Nation's Business,* March 1991, 18–24.

52. Schuler, *Managing Human Resources,* 565–566.

53. Sarah Bowen, "Enough!" *Wall Street Journal,* 11 April 1996, R6.

54. Kerry Capell, "Options for Everyone," *Business Week,* 22 July 1996, 80–84; Bowen, "Enough!" R6.

55. *Workforce,* January 1997, supplement, 5; Barbara Presley Noble, "At Work: We're Doing Just Fine, Thank You," *New York Times,* 20 March 1994, 25.

56. U.S. Department of Social Security, "Reports Provide Detailed Picture of Impact of Maternity Legislation," *M2 PressWIRE,* 31 July 1997, *Electric Library,* Online, 30 October 1997.

57. "Workplace Briefs," *Gannett News Service,* 24 April 1997, *Electric Library,* Online, 30 October 1997; Julia Lawlor, "The Bottom Line," *Working Woman,* July–August 1996, 54–58, 74–76.

58. Jill Landauer, "Work/Family," *HR Focus* 74 (1 July 1997), *Electric Library,* Online, 30 October 1997.

59. Lawlor, "The Bottom Line," 56; Sue Shellenbarger, "Work and Family: Elderly Relatives Part of Relocation Deals," *Wall Street Journal,* 11 May 1994, B1.

60. Kathleen Murray, "The Childless Feel Left Out When Parents Get a Lift," *New York Times,* 1 December 1996, F12; Gillian Flynn, "Backlash," *Personnel Journal,* September 1996, 58–60.

61. Ellen Neuborne, "Firms Today Less Willing to Pay for Play," *USA Today,* 12 March 1997, B1.

62. Del Jones, "Firms Take New Look at Sick Days," *USA Today,* 8 October 1996, 8B.

63. Leslie Faught, "At Eddie Bauer You Can Work and Have a Life," *Workforce,* April 1997, 84.

64. Kerry A. Dolan, "When Money Isn't Enough," *Forbes,* 18 November 1996, 170.

65. "Perk Cutbacks in 90's," *USA Today,* 20 December 1995, B1; Joann S. Lublin and Joseph B. White, "Throwing Off Angst, Workers Are Feeling in Control of Careers," *Wall Street Journal,* 11 September 1997, A1, A6.

66. Alan R. Earls, "True Friends of the Family," *Computerworld,* 17 February 1997, 83, *Electric Library,* Online, 30 October 1997;

Robert Bryce, "Need an Extra Week Off? Visit the Company Store," *New York Times,* 16 July 1995, 10F.

67. Nancy Lowther, "Curbing Workers' Comp Costs," *American Printer,* 1 November 1996, 52; Glenn Whittington, "Workers' Compensation Legislation Enacted in 1997," *Monthly Labor Review,* January 1998, 23+.

68. Templin, "Johnson & Johnson 'Wellness' Program," B1.

69. "Wellness Works: Here's Why," *Wellness Councils of America Home Page,* <http://www.welcoa.org>, accessed 18 February 1998.

70. Michael J. Major, "Employee Assistance Programs: An Ideal Whose Time Has Come," *Modern Office Technology,* March 1990, 76.

71. "Company Chaplains a Booming Business," *Los Angeles Times,* 8 February 1997, B4; Barnaby J. Feder, "Ministers Who Work Around the Flock, *New York Times,* 3 October 1996, C1.

72. Gillian Flynn, "Heck No—We Won't Go!" *Personnel Journal,* March 1996, 37–43.

73. Timothy D. Schellhardt, "Off the Ladder," *Wall Street Journal,* 4 April 1997, A1, A4; Beverly Kaye and Caela Farren, "Up Is Not the Only Way," *Training & Development,* 1 February 1996, 48, *Electric Library,* Online, 30 October 1997, "Workplace Trends: Alternatives to Promotions," *Small Business Reports,* August 1991, 25–26; William McWhirter, "Major Overhaul," *Time,* 30 December 1991, 56–58.

74. Rodney Ho, "AT&T's Offer of $10,000 May Test Entrepreneurship of Laid-Off Workers," *Wall Street Journal,* 12 March 1997; David Fischer and Kevin Whitelaw, "A New Way to Shine Up Corporate Profits," 55.

75. Gillian Flynn, "Why Rhino Won't Wait 'til Tomorrow," *Personnel Journal,* July 1996, 36–39.

76. Shari Caudron, "Blow the Whistle on Employment Disputes," *Workforce,* May 1997, 50–57; Shari Caudron, "Angry Employees Bite Back in Court," *Personnel Journal,* December 1996, 32–37; Paulette Thomas, "Restructurings Generate Rash of Age-Bias Suits," *Wall Street Journal,* 29 August 1996, B1; Jay Finegan, "Law and Disorder," *Inc.,* April 1994, 64–71.

77. Laabs, "HR Pioneers Explore the Road Less Traveled," *Personnel Journal,* February 1996, 75.

78. Jennifer J. Laabs, "HR Pioneers Explore the Road Less Traveled," 70–78; Charlene Marmer Solomon, "HR in the Global Age: Managing Compensation," *Personnel Journal,* July 1995, 71–76.

79. See note 1.

CHAPTER 11

1. Adapted from Vicki Brown, "Saturn Workers to Keep Unique Contract," *San Diego Union Tribune,* 12 March 1998, C3; James Bennet, "Saturn, G.M.'s Big Hope, Is Taking Its First Lumps," *New York Times,* 29 March 1994, A1, A12; Phil Frame, "Saturn Status Report," *Automotive News,* 31 May 1993, 8; Lindsay Chappell, "UAW Beats the Drums for War on Saturn Labor Rules," *Automotive News,* 31 May 1993, 8; Liz Pinto, "Simplicity Is Key to Labor Tranquillity at Saturn," *Automotive News,* 7 September 1992, 42; Morgan O. Reynolds, "Unions and Jobs: The U.S. Auto Industry," *Journal of Labor Research,* Spring 1986, 103–126; William A. Nowlin, "Restructuring in Manufacturing: Management, Work, and Labor Relations," *Industrial Management,* November–December 1990, 5–9, 30; Anne B. Fisher, "Behind the Hype at GM's Saturn," *Fortune,* 11 November 1985, 34–49; Donald Ephlin, "Saturn's Strategic Role in Industrial Relations," *Survey of Business,* Summer 1986, 23–25; Alex Taylor III, "Back to the Future at Saturn," *Fortune,* 1 August 1988, 63–72; "GM–Auto Workers Saturn Contract," *Monthly Labor Review,* October 1985, 48–50; James B. Treece, "Here Comes GM's Saturn," *Business Week,* 9 April 1990, 56–62; Maralyn Edid, "How Power Will Be Balanced on Saturn's Shop Floor," *Business Week,* 5 August 1985, 65–66; Ben Fischer, "Finishing Out the Century," *Journal for Quality and Participation,* March 1991, 48–52; Doron P. Levin, "Reality Comes to G.M.'s Saturn Plant," *New York Times,* 14 November 1991, C1, C5; "Saturn Unit's Workers Pass Labor Pact by 72% to 28%," *Wall Street Journal,* 15 November 1991, A2; Jay C. Thomas, "Quality Wars: The Triumphs and Defeats of American Business," *Personnel Psychology,* Spring 1995, 182–185; David Mayes and Matthew N. Murray, "The Automobile Industry and the Economic Development of Tennessee and the Southeast: New Investment Has Increased Production Capacity," *Survey of Business,* Winter 1995, 41–52.

2. E. Edward Herman, *Collective Bargaining and Labor Relations,* 4th ed. (Upper Saddle River, N.J.: Prentice Hall, 1998), 12.

3. U.S. Bureau of Labor Statistics, "Union Members Summary," *Developments in Labor-Management Relations,* <www.bls.gov:80/newsrels.htm>, accessed 1 November 1997; International Labour Organization, "ILO Highlights Global Challenge to Trade Unions," *International Labour Organization 1997 Press Releases,* 4 November 1997, <www.ilo.org>, accessed 7 November 1997; International Labour Organization, *World Labour Report,* 4 November 1997, <www.ilo.org>, accessed 7 November 1997.

4. International Labour Organization, *World Labour Report.*

5. David Woodruff et al., "Labor's New Face in Europe," *Business Week,* 16 December 1996, 61–65; "Bashing the Unions," *The Economist,* 14 September 1996, 59–60; Sheryl WuDunn, "When Lifetime Jobs Die Prematurely," *New York Times,* 12 June 1996, C1, C6.

6. Aaron Bernstein, "Sweeney's Blitz," *Business Week,* 17 February 1997, 56–62; Marc Levinson, "It's Hip to Be Union," *Newsweek,* 8 July 1996, 44–45; James Worsham, "Labor Comes Alive," *Nation's Business,* February 1996, 16–24; Herman, *Collective Bargaining and Labor Relations.*

7. Woodruff et al., "Labor's New Face in Europe."

8. David Moberg, "Like Business, Unions Must Go Global," *New York Times,* 19 December 1993, sec. 3, 13.

9. Kathy Seal, "Unions Cross International Boundaries," *H&MM,* 3 March 1997, 3.

10. Lloyd G. Reynolds, Stanley H. Masters, and Colletta H. Moser, *Labor Economics and Labor Relations,* 11th ed. (Upper Saddle River, N.J.: Prentice Hall, 1998), 497; Indiana University News Bureau, "Trends in U.S. Labor Movement," *The Futurist,* January–February 1996, 44; Barbara Presley Noble, "Reinventing Labor: An Interview with Union President Lynn Williams," *Harvard Business Review,* July–August 1993, 115–125.

11. Thomas A. Kochan and Harry C. Katz, *Collective Bargaining and Industrial Relations* (Homewood, Ill.: Irwin, 1988), 165.

12. Bernstein, "Sweeney's Blitz," 59.

13. Martha Irvine, "Organizing Twentysomethings," *Los Angeles Times,* 7 September 1997, D5, *Electric Library,* Online, 13 November 1997.

14. Kochan and Katz, *Collective Bargaining and Industrial Relations,* 173.

15. Bernstein, "Sweeney's Blitz," 57.

16. Herman, *Collective Bargaining and Labor Relations,* 118.

17. Daniel Howes and Dave Phillips, "UAW: The Shrinking Union," *Gannett News Service,* 16 July 1997, *Electric Library,* Online, 10 November 1997.

18. Daniel Quinn Mills, *Labor-Management Relations,* 5th ed. (New York: McGraw-Hill, 1994), 366.

19. Zachary Schiller, "Reading, Writing, and Replacement Workers," *Business Week,* 23 September 1996, 125.

20. Herman, *Collective Bargaining and Labor Relations* 174–175.

21. Kochan and Katz, *Collective Bargaining and Industrial Relations,* 176, 238.

22. U.S. Department of Labor, Bureau of Labor Statistics, "Union Members Summary," *Developments in Labor-Management Relations,* 31 January 1997, <http://stats.bls.gov:80/newsrels.htm>, accessed 12 November 1997.

23. Paula B. Voos, ed., *Contemporary Collective Bargaining in the Private Sector* (Madison, Wisc: Industrial Relations Research Association, 1994), pp. 6–7, quoted in Herman, *Collective Bargaining and Labor Relations,* 146; "Strikes and Lockouts in U.S. Now on Rise," *New York Times,* 12 March 1987, A28.

24. Louis Uchitelle, "Blue-Collar Compromises in Pursuit of Job Security," *New York Times,* 19 April 1992, 1, 13.

25. Adrian Croft, "U.S. Labor Sees a Comeback with BART, UPS Strikes," *Reuters Business Reports,* 14 September 1997, *Electric Library,* Online, 11 November 1997; Kay S. Pedrotti, "Owens Plant in Fairburn Hit by Strike," *Atlanta Journal & Constitution,* 27 March 1997, G2, *Electric Library,* Online, 11 November 1997, Donald W. Nauss, "Ford-UAW Pact Would Create 2-Tier Pay Scale," *Los Angeles Times,* 18 September 1996, D1, *Electric Library,* Online, 11 November 1997.

26. U.S. Department of Labor, Bureau of Labor Statistics, *Employment Cost Index,* 28 October 1997, <http://stats.bls.gov/ecthome.htm>, accessed 14 November 1997; U.S. Department of Labor, Bureau of Labor Statistics, "Private Industry Union and Nonunion Workers," *Employment Cost Trends,* March 1997, <www.bls.gov>, accessed 10 November 1997.

27. Susan Benkelman, "Is Price Right?/Process, Politics of Powerful CPI," *Newsday,* 14 April 1997, A5, *Electric Library,* Online, 11 November 1997.

28. Edward Wasilewski Jr., "Bargaining Outlook for 1996," *Monthly Labor Review* 119, no. 11 (January 1996): 10 *Electric Library,* Online, 13 November 1997.

29. Gary W. Florkowski, "Profit Sharing and Public Policy: Insights for the United States," *Industrial Relations,* Winter 1991, 98.

30. Florkowski, "Profit Sharing and Public Policy," 98.

31. Reynolds, Masters, and Moser, *Labor Economics and Labor Relations,* 500–501.

32. David Lawder, "Chrysler, GM Strike Talks Slow," *Reuters Business Report,* 19 April 1997, Electric Library, Online, 11 November 1997; Robert L. Simison and Robert L. Rose, "In Backing the UAW, Ford Rankles Many of Its Parts Suppliers," *Wall Street Journal,* 13 February 1997, A1; Bill Vlasic, "What Labor Problem?" *Business Week,* 15 April 1996, 106–107; Jerry Flint, "The Dilemma," *Forbes,* 8 April 1996, 81–81; Bill Vlasic, "Bracing for the Big One," *Business Week,* 25 March 1996, 34–25.

33. Justin Fox, "The UAW Makes Nice," *Fortune,* 28 October 1996, 28–29; Bill Vlasic and William C. Symonds, "Sweet Deal," *Business Week,* 30 September 1996, 32–33.

34. Stuart Silverstein and Jeff Leeds, "Longshore Workers Seeking an Even Keel," *Los Angeles Times,* 2 September 1996, A1, *Electric Library,* Online, 13 November 1997.

35. Mills, *Labor-Management Relations,* 201.

36. "Green Flu Strikes Cookie Sales," *Time,* 3 February 1997, 42.

37. Reynolds, Masters, and Moser, *Labor Economics and Labor Relations,* 497.

38. Robert L. Rose and Carl Quintanilla, "McDonnell Follows Caterpillar Strategy," *Wall Street Journal,* 14 June 1996, A2; Barry Bearak, "After a Long Tug of War, Labor Slips," *Los Angeles Times,* 14 May 1995, A1, A14; "Caterpillar Offers UAW a New Contract Proposal," *Wall Street Journal,* 17 March 1998, A4; Robert L. Rose and Carl Quintilla, "Caterpillar Touts Its Gains as UAW Battle Ends," *Wall Street Journal,* 24 March 1998, A4; Frank Swoboda, "Caterpillar UAW at a Crossroads," *Washington Post,* 24 February 1998, D3.

39. Roanne Daniels, "Teamsters Officials Vote to End UPS Strike," *Reuters Business Report,* 19 August 1997, *Electric Library,* Online, 11 November 1997; "U.S. Teamsters Overwhelmingly Ratify UPS Contract," *Reuters Business Report,* 9 October 1997, *Electric Library,* Online, 11 November 1997; Paul Magnusson et al., "A Wake Up Call for Business," *Business Week,* 1 September 1997, 28–29; Aaron Bernstein, "At UPS, Part-Time Work Is a Full-Time Issue," *Business Week,* 16 June 1997.

40. *World Almanac and Book of Facts* (New York: Scripps Howard, 1989), 161.

41. Seal, "Unions Cross International Boundaries," 3, 38; Kathy Segal, "Unions Seek to Organize via Increased Boycotts," *H&MM,* 16 September 1996, 3, 25.

42. Steven A. Holmes, "Boycotts Rarely Affect the Bottom Line," *New York Times,* 15 November 1996, C2; Segal, "Unions Seek to Organize via Increased Boycotts," 3, 25.

43. Peter Szekely, "AFL-CIO Launches Unit to Organize Workers' Funds," *Reuters Business Report,* 24 September 1997, *Electric Library,* Online, 11 November 1997; Worsham, "Labor Comes Alive," 23.

44. Peter Szekely, "Unions Moving if Not Growing," *Reuters Business Report,* 1 September 1996, *Electric Library,* Online, 11 November 1997.

45. Aaron Bernstein, Amy Borrus, and Richard S. Durham, "Labor's Last Laugh," *Business Week,* 2 June 1997, 36–37.

46. Herman, *Collective Bargaining and Labor Relations,* 300; Milford Prewitt, "Unions Embrace New Tactics vs. Operators," *Nation's Restaurant News,* 13 May 1997, 1, 4+; Worsham, "Labor Comes Alive," 23.

47. Aaron Bernstein, "Big Labor Invites a Few Friends Over," *Business Week,* 21 April 1997, 44.

48. Levison, "It's Hip to Be Union," 44–45.

49. Eugene H. Methvin, "The Union Label: With the Level of Union Violence on the Rise, Congress Must, Again, Deal with the Courts," *National Review,* 29 September 1997, 47, *Electric Library,* Online, 11 November 1997; Anya Sacharow, "Walking the Line in Detroit," *Newspapers,* 22 July 1996, 8–13; Worsham, "Labor Comes Alive," 17.

50. Martin Kasindorf, "A Strike Against Replacement Hiring," *Newsday,* 9 March 1995, A20, *Electric Library,* Online, 11 November 1997.

51. Herman, *Collective Bargaining and Labor Relations,* 61; "NLRB Permits Replacements During Legal Lockout," *Personnel Journal,* January 1987, 14–15.

52. "Timex Closes Scottish Plant," *New York Times,* 30 August 1993, 2.

53. Greg Boeck, "Stern Hints That Owners Might Reopen Labor Deal," *USA Today,* 22 September 1997, 8C, *Electric Library,* Online, 11 November 1997.

54. David Field, "Airline Chief Has Become Key Figure in Labor Dispute," *USA Today,* 6 March 1997, B1, B2; Donna Rosato, "American Airlines Pilots Ask to Extend Deadline for Talks," *USA Today,* 18 March 1997, 2B, *Electric Library,* Online, 11 November 1997; David Field, "Clinton Unlikely to Act Unless Both Sides Ask," *USA Today,* 10 February 1997, 2A, *Electric Library,* Online, 11 November 1997.

55. Catherine Yang et al., "Low-Wage Lessons," *Business Week,* 11 November 1996, 108–110.

56. Dawn Anfuso, "Peer Review Wards Off Unions and Lawsuits," *Personnel Journal,* January 1994, 64; Daniel Seligman, "Who Needs Unions?" *Fortune,* 12 July 1982, 54+.

57. Robert L. Stimson and Robert L. Rose, "Divided Detroit: In Backing the UAW, Ford Rankles Many of Its Parts Suppliers," *Wall Street Journal,* 13 February 1997, A1, A5; Vlasic and Symonds, "Sweet Deal," 32–33.

58. Susan Chandler, "United We Own," *Business Week,* 18 March 1996, 96–100; Susan Carey, "Dear Airline: Thanks for Getting on My Nerves . . . and Quote Me!" *Wall Street Journal,* 20 March 1998, B1.

59. Peggy Stuart, "Labor Unions Become Business Partners," *Personnel Journal,* August 1993, 54–63.

60. James Worsham, "Labor's New Assault," *Nation's Business,* June 1997, 23.

61. Philip A. Miscimarra and Jeffrey C. Kauffman, "Keeping Teamwork Legal," *Small Business Reports,* May 1993, 16–20; Michael A. Verespej, "New Rules on Employee Involvement," *Industry Week,* 1 February 1993, 55–56.

62. Aaron Bernstein, "Meet the Al Dunlap of the Union Hall," *Business Week,* 17 February 1997, 62.

63. Aaron Bernstein, "Look Who's Pushing Productivity," *Business Week,* 7 April 1997, 72–75.

64. See note 1.

65. *Culturegram for the '90s: Egypt* (Provo, Utah: Brigham Young University, 1991).

CHAPTER 12

1. Carol Mauro-Noon, "Inspirational Odyssey—American Dream," *Success,* March 1997, 37–42; Damon Darlin, "Flower Power," *Forbes,* 22 April 1996, 102–108; Michael Barrier, "The Language of Success," *Nation's Business,* August 1997, 56+; Asian American Association <http://www.aan.net>, accessed 8 December 1997.

2. Gary Hamel, Video Lecture, *Lessons in Leadership,* Northern Illinois University, 23 October 1997.

3. "AMA Board Approves New Marketing Definition," *Marketing News,* 1 March 1985, 1.

4. Philip Kotler, *Marketing Management,* 9th ed. (Upper Saddle River, N.J.: Prentice Hall, 1997), 24.

5. Al Ries and Jack Trout, *The 22 Immutable Laws of Marketing* (New York: HarperCollins, 1994), 19–25.

6. Franklin S. Houston, "The Marketing Concept: What It Is and What It Is Not," *Journal of Marketing,* April 1986, 81–87; Michelle L. Smith, "One to One: Put the Customer in the Information Driver Seat, and Build Better Relationships," *Direct Marketing,* January 1998, 37+.

7. Roberta Maynard, "New Directions in Marketing," *Nation's Business,* July 1995, 25–26.

8. B. Joseph Pine II, Don Peppers, and Martha Rogers, "Do You Want to Keep Your Customers Forever?" *Harvard Business Review,* March–April 1995, 103–114.

9. Gary McWilliams, "Small Fry Go Online," *Business Week,* 20 November 1995, 158–164.

10. Ronald B. Lieber, "Storytelling: A New Way to Get Close to Your Customer," *Fortune* 3 (February 1997): 102–110.

11. Mary J. Cronin, *Doing More Business on the Internet* (New York: Van Nostrand Reinhold, 1995), 13.

12. Tim McCollum, "Making the Internet Work for You," *Nation's Business,* March 1997, 6–13; Mitch Wagner, "What E-Commerce Sites Need Most Is Common Sense," *Internet Week,* 16 March 1998, 48; "E-Commerce Comes of Age," *PC Week,* 9 March 1998, 16; Eric Lundquist, "Four Rules for Building Commerce Sites," *PC Week,* 9 March 1998, 154.

13. PC Week Executive Staff, "10 Who Dared to Be Different," *PC Week,* 6 January 1997, 21–31.

14. Maynard, "New Directions in Marketing."

15. Terry G. Vavra, "The Database Marketing Imperative," *Marketing Management,* 2, no. 1 (1993): 47–57.

16. Michael Treacy and Fred Wiersema, "The Discipline of Market Leaders," *Soundview Executive Book Summaries,* 15, no. 4 (April 1995), 1–4.

17. Suzanne Oliver, "Spoiled Rotten," *Forbes,* 15 July 1996, 70–73.

18. Bill Saporito, "What's for Dinner?" *Fortune,* 15 May 1995, 50–64; Robert F. Lusch, Deborah Zizzo, and James M Kenderdine, "Strategic Renewal in Distribution," *Marketing Management,* 2, no. 2 (1993): 20–27.

19. Ron Zemke and Dick Schaaf, *The Service Edge: 101 Companies that Profit from Customer Care* (New York: New American Library, 1989), 50.

20. Judy De Young and Grace Jidown, "Service Is Alive and Well," *Working Woman,* November 1997, 18–20.

21. William H. Davidow and Bro Uttal, *Total Customer Service: The Ultimate Weapon* (New York: Harper & Row, 1989), 8; Valarie A. Zeithaml, A. Parasuraman, and Leonard L. Berry, *Delivering Quality Service* (New York: Free Press, 1990), 9;

George J. Castellese, "Customer Service . . . Building a Winning Team," *Supervision,* January 1995, 9–13; Erica G. Sorohan and Catherine M. Petrini, "Dumpsters, Ducks, and Customer Service," *Training and Development,* January 1995, 9.

22. Thomas A. Stewart, "A Satisfied Customer Isn't Enough," *Fortune,* 21 July 1997, 112–113; Jacqueline Dulen and Jennifer Waters, "Sweet Success," *Restaurants & Institutions,* 1 March 1998, 64+; Michael Crom, "Satisfaction Is Not Enough," *Training,* January 1998, 6; Ronald B. Lieber, "Now Are You Satisfied?" *Fortune,* 16 February 1998, 161.

23. Frederick F. Reichheld, "Learning from Customer Defections," *Harvard Business Review,* March–April 1996, 56–69; Frederick F. Reichheld, "Loyalty and the Renaissance of Marketing," *Marketing Management,* 2, no. 4 (1994): 10–21; Michael Mueller, "FedEx Adds Shipping to Web," *PC Week,* July 1996, 100.

24. Davidow and Uttal, *Total Customer Service: The Ultimate Weapon,* 34–35.

25. David C. Edelman, "Satisfaction Is Nice, but Share Pays," *Marketing Management* 2, no. 1 (1993): 8–13.

26. Amy Cortese, "Here Comes the Intranet," *Business Week,* 26 February 1996, 76; Oliver Rist, "Push Power on the Intranet," *Internet Week,* 2 February 1998, 39; Lynn Anderson, "Building the High-Availability Intranet," *Computing Canada,* 23 February 1998, 40; Chris Dallas-Feeney, "Your Intranet: Dancing Icons or Enterprise Platform," *Telecommunications,* March 1998, S6+.

27. Lieber, "Storytelling: A New Way to Get Close to Your Customer."

28. Steve Schriver, "Customer Loyalty: Going Going . . ." *American Demographics,* September 1997, 20–23.

29. Janet Willen, "The Customer Is Wrong," *Business97,* October–November 1997, 40–42.

30. Treacy and Wiersema, "The Discipline of Market Leaders"; Michael Treacy and Fred Wiersema, "How Market Leaders Keep Their Edge," *Fortune,* 6 February 1995, 88–98.

31. Treacy and Wiersema, "The Discipline of Market Leaders"; Treacy and Wiersema, "How Market Leaders Keep Their Edge."

32. David Shani and Sujana Chalasani, "Exploring Niches Using Relationship Marketing," *Journal of Business and Industrial Marketing* 8, no. 4 (1993): 58–66; "Enterprise Finds Niches Within Niches," *Textile World,* February 1998, 35.

33. Larry Carpenter, "How to Market to Regions," *American Demographics,* November 1987, 45.

34. Michael J. Weiss, *The Clustering of America* (New York: Harper & Row, 1988), 41.

35. Shani and Chalasani, "Exploring Niches Using Relationship Marketing," 58–66.

36. Steven L. Goldman, Roger N. Nagel, and Kenneth Preiss, "Why Seiko Has 3,000 Watch Styles," *New York Times,* 9 October 1994, F9.

37. Justin Martin, "Give 'Em Exactly What They Want," *Fortune,* 10 November 1997, 283–285.

38. Don Peppers and Martha Rogers, *Enterprise One to One* (New York: Doubleday, 1997), 120–121.

39. "Some Cities See Gold in Those Water Bottles, May Turn to Their Own Taps," *Chicago Tribune,* 6 August 1997, sec. 1, 15.

40. Bruce Horovitz, "Malls Are Like, Totally Uncool, Say Hip Teens," *USA Today,* 1 May 1996, 1.

41. Courtland L. Bovée, Michael J. Houston, and John V. Thill, *Marketing,* 2d ed. (New York: McGraw-Hill, 1994), 188.

42. Michael H. Morris and Jeanne L. Holman, "Source Loyalty in Organizational Markets: A Dyadic Perspective," *Journal of Business Research* 16, no. 2 (1988): 117–131.

43. Pamela G. Hollie, "What's New in Market Research," *New York Times,* 15 June 1986, sec. 3, 19; Phyllis M. Thornton, "Linking Market Research to Strategic Planning," *Nursing Homes,* January–February 1995, 34–37; Oren Harari, "Six Myths of Market Research," *Management Review,* April 1994, 48–51.

44. Justin Martin, "Ignore Your Customer," *Fortune,* May 1995, 121–126.

45. Harari, "Six Myths of Market Research."

46. Robert Passikoff, "Loyal Opposition—The Limits of Customer Satisfaction," *Brandweek,* 3 March 1997, 17.

47. Raymond R. Burke, "Virtual Shopping: Breakthrough in Marketing Research," *Harvard Business Review,* March–April 1996, 120–131.

48. Harry S. Dent Jr., "Individualized Marketing," *Small Business Reports,* April 1991, 36–45.

49. Shani and Chalasani, "Exploring Niches Using Relationship Marketing."

50. Shani and Chalasani, "Exploring Niches Using Relationship Marketing"; Janet Novack, "The Data Miners," *Forbes,* 12 February 1996, 96–97; Peppers and Rogers, *Enterprise One to One,* 145–146.

51. See note 1.

CHAPTER 13

1. Jennifer Reese, "Starbucks: Inside the Coffee Cult," *Fortune,* 9 December 1996, 190–200; David Bank, "Starbucks Faces Growing Competition: Its Own Stores," *Wall Street Journal,* 21 January 1997, B1, B5; Matt Rothman, "Into the Black," *Inc.,* January 1993, 58–65; Bill McDowell, "Starbucks Is Ground Zero in Today's Coffee Culture," *Advertising Age,* 9 December 1996, 1, 49–50; Kim Murphy, "More Than Coffee," *Los Angeles Times Magazine,* 22 September 1996, 8–12, 29–30; Joan Voight, "Starbucks Taps Interactive Team to Craft On-line Coffee Culture," *Adweek,* 24 June 1996, 5; Laura Rich, "Starbucks AOL Area Launches New Ad Look," *Adweek,* 4 November 1996, 5; Jolie Solomon, "Not in My Backyard," *Newsweek,* 16 September 1996, 65–66; Marla Matzer, "Starbucks Restyles for 25th Bash," *Brandweek,* 16 September 1996, 1, 6; Karen Benezra and Betsy Spethmann, "Starbucks Rolls Big with Ice Cream Line," *Brandweek,* 1 April 1996, 7; Scott Bedbury and Rich Silverstein, "Brewing the Perfect Brand," *American Advertising,* Fall 1996, 12–15; Seanna Browder, "Starbucks Does Not Live by Coffee Alone," *Business Week,* 5 August 1996, 76; Alice Z. Cuneo, "Starbucks Readies Supermarket Invasion," *Advertising Age,* 9 June 1997, 1, 50; Michael Schrader, "Put Your Heart into It: How Starbucks Built a Company One Cup at a Time," *Nation's Restaurant News,* 2 February 1998, 26; Abraham McLaughlin, "Brewing a Tempest in a Coffee Cup," *Christian Science Moni-*

tor, 25 February 1998, 3; HAL KARP, "Worth More than a Hill of Beans," *Black Enterprise,* February 1998, 78.

2. MALCOLM H. B. MCDONALD, "Ten Barriers to Marketing Planning," *Journal of Product and Brand Management,* Fall 1992, 51–64; RUSH ECKDISH KNACK, "Inspiring the Troops," *Planning,* January 1998, 16+.

3. GARY SAMUELS, "CD-ROMs First Big Victim," *Forbes,* 28 February 1994, 42–44; RICHARD A. MELCHER, "Dusting Off the Britannica," *Business Week,* 20 October 1997, 143–146.

4. STAN DAVIS, "Business Wins, Organization Kills," *Forbes ASAP,* 7 April 1997, 49–50.

5. MALCOLM MCDONALD AND JOHN W. LEPPARD, *Marketing by Matrix* (Lincolnwood, Ill.: NTC, 1993), 10; H. IGOR ANSOFF, "Strategies for Diversification," *Harvard Business Review,* November–December 1957, 113–124; H. IGOR ANSOFF, *Corporate Strategy* (New York: McGraw-Hill, 1965).

6. ALEX TAYLOR III, "How to Murder the Competition," *Fortune,* 22 February 1993, 87, 90.

7. PETER BURROWS, "Luring Them Back to the Mac Aisle," *Business Week,* 25 November 1996, 156–158; LOUISE KEHOE, "Apple Seeks New Trails to Blaze," *Financial Times,* 4 September 1997, 18; DON CRABB, "Apple's Ads Show the Way Back to the Mac Platform," *MacWeek,* 16 February 1998, 24; CHARLES PILLER, "For Fans of Apple Computer, It Was a Keeper of a Week," *Los Angeles Times,* 12 January 1998, D4; "Apple Faces a Turning Point for the Mac," *MacWeek,* 5 January 1998, 3.

8. COURTLAND L. BOVÉE, MICHAEL J. HOUSTON, AND JOHN V. THILL, *Marketing,* 2d ed. (New York: McGraw Hill, 1995), 224.

9. PHILIP KOTLER, *Marketing Management,* 9th ed. (Upper Saddle River, N.J.: Prentice Hall, 1997), 294–297.

10. JAMES ALEY, "Give It Away and Get Rich," *Fortune,* 10 June 1996, 91–98.

11. ALEY, "Give It Away and Get Rich."

12. AMY BARRETT, "Dial Succeeds by Stepping in Bigger Footsteps," *Business Week,* 13 June 1994, 82–84.

13. ZACHARY SCHILLER, "The Sound and the Fluoride," *Business Week,* 14 August 1995, 48.

14. KOTLER, *Marketing Management,* 434.

15. GARY HAMEL, *Lessons in Leadership,* Northern Illinois University, 23 October 1997.

16. "Preparing for a Point to Point World," *Marketing Management* 3, no. 4 (Spring 1995): 30–40.

17. ALAN DEUTSCHMAN, "How HP Continues to Grow and Grow," *Fortune,* 2 May 1994, 90–100.

18. CHRISTOPHER CAGGIANO, "Brand New," *Inc.,* April 1997, 48–53.

19. RONALD ALSOP, "Giving Fading Brands a Second Chance," *Wall Street Journal,* 24 January 1989, B1; LISA BANNON, "She Reinvented Barbie, Now Can Jill Barad Do the Same for Mattel?" *Wall Street Journal,* 9 March 1997, A1, A8.

20. JACOB M. SCHLESINGER, "Firms Strive to Improve Basic Products," *Wall Street Journal,* 8 October 1985, B1.

21. "New Product Winners—And Losers," *In Business,* April 1985, 64.

22. YUMIKO ONO, "Kraft Searches Its Cupboard for Old Brands to Remake," *Wall Street Journal,* 12 March 1996, B1, B4.

23. TOM PETERS, "We Hold These Truths to Be Self-Evident," *Organizational Dynamics,* 1 June 1996, 27–32.

24. TOM PETERS, *Lessons in Leadership,* Northern Illinois University, 24 October 1997.

25. BRUCE HOROVITZ AND MELANIE WELLS, "Well-Known Products Try for Comeback," *USA Today,* 2 May 1995, B1.

26. L. D. DESIMONE, "How Can Big Companies Keep the Entrepreneurial Spirit Alive?" *Harvard Business Review,* November–December 1995, 183–184.

27. TONI MACK, "Let the Computer Do It," *Forbes,* 10 August 1987, 94.

28. ZACHARY SCHILLER, "Make It Simple," *Business Week,* 9 September 1996, 96–104.

29. SCHILLER, "Make It Simple."

30. ELIZABETH LESLY, "What's Next, Raiders' Deodorant?" *Business Week,* 30 November 1992, 65.

31. JIM KIRK, "Building Up the Brands," *Chicago Tribune,* 5 October 1997, B1, B4.

32. ROBERT LENZNER AND STEPHEN S. JOHNSON, "A Few Yards of Denim and Five Copper Rivets," *Forbes,* 26 February 1996, 82–87; LAURA RICH, "Levi's Easy Fit," *Adweek,* 16 February 1998, 38; SUZETTE HILL, "Levi Strauss Shrinks to Fit U.S. Market," *Apparel Industry Magazine,* January 1998, 32+.

33. RONALD ALSOP, "To Know a Brand Is Not to Love It," *Wall Street Journal,* 15 June 1988, 25.

34. PATRICK OSTER, GABRIELLE SAVERI, AND JOHN TEMPLEMANN, "The Eurosion of Brand Loyalty," *Business Week,* 19 July 1993, 22; YUMIKO ONO, "The Rising Sun Shines on Private Labels," *Wall Street Journal,* 26 April 1992, B1, B5; CYNDEE MILLER, "Big Brands Fight Back Against Private Labels," *Marketing News,* 16 January 1995, 1, 8+.

35. BILL SAPORITO, "Has-Been Brands Go Back to Work," *Fortune,* 28 April 1986, 124; CHRISTINE DONAHUE, "Marketers Restore Old Masters," *Adweek,* 14 September 1987, 4.

36. JOHN BISSELL, "What's in a Brand Name? Nothing Inherent to Start," *Brandweek,* 7 February 1994, 16.

37. STEVEN FLAX, "The Big Brand Stretch," *The Marketer,* September 1990, 32–35; MICHAEL MCDERMOTT, "Too Much of a Good Thing?" *Adweek's Marketing Week,* 4 December 1989, 20–25; TOM BUNDAY, "Capitalizing on Brand Extensions," *Journal of Consumer Marketing,* Fall 1989, 27–30; JOSHUA LEVINE, "But in the Office, No," *Forbes,* 16 October 1989, 272–273; IMOGENE MATTHEWS, "Renaissance: Investing in Brand Revival," *European Cosmetic Markets,* January 1998, 35+.

38. JAGDISH N. SHETH AND RAJENDRA S. SISODIA, "Feeling the Heat," *Marketing Management,* Fall 1995, 9–23.

39. "The Packaging Investment," *In Business,* March–April 1988, 40.

40. JACK G. VOGLER AND STEVEN LAWRENCE, "Packaging Better," *Boardroom Reports,* 1 June 1987, 10.

41. TOM LOWRY, "Coca-Cola Takes Shape from Bottle," *USA Today,* 16 July 1996, 3B.

42. EBEN SHAPIRO, "Food Labs Gaze Hungrily at Potential in Labeling Rules," *Wall Street Journal,* 10 December 1992, B2.

43. ROBERT J. CALVIN, "The Price Is Right," *Small Business Reports,* June 1994, 9–13.

44. THOMAS T. NAGLE, "Managing Price Competition, *Marketing Management,* 2, no. 1 (1993): 38–45; SHETH AND SISODA, "Feeling the Heat," 21.

45. NAGLE, "Managing Price Competition," 38–45.

46. "Disneyland Paris: How Beauty Became a Beast," *Reputation Management,* March–April 1995, 35–37.

47. TARA PARKET-POPE, "Custom-Made," *Wall Street Journal,* 26 September 1996, R22–R23.

48. NORIHIKO SHIROUZU, "Japan's Staid Coffee Bars Wake Up and Smell Starbucks," *Wall Street Journal,* 25 July 1996, B1, B13.

49. See note 1.

CHAPTER 14

1. JOSEPH WEBER, "Black & Decker Cuts a Neat Dovetail Joint," *Business Week,* 31 July 1989, 52–53; JANET MEYERS, "Black & Decker Ups Share in Hardware," *Advertising Age,* 24 July 1989, 28; REBECCA FANNIN AND LAURA KONRAD JERESKI, "Black & Decker Powers into Housewares," *Marketing & Media Decisions,* August 1985, 34–40, 109; BILL KELLEY, "Black & Decker Rebuilds," *Sales & Marketing Management,* June 1987, 49; CHRISTOPHER S. EKLUND, "How Black & Decker Got Back in the Black," *Business Week,* 13 July 1987, 86, 90; JAMES A. CONSTANTIN AND ROBERT F. LUSCH, "Discover the Resources in Your Marketing Channel," *Business,* July–September 1986, 19–26; PAULA SCHNORBUS, "B&D Turns on the Power," *Marketing & Media Decisions,* May 1988, 57–58, 62, 64; JOHN HUEY, "The New Power in Black & Decker," *Fortune,* 2 January 1989, 89–91, 94; "Winning Turnaround Strategies at Black & Decker," *Journal of Business Strategy,* March–April 1988, 30–33; "Black & Decker to Send Sales Specialists into Industrial and Construction Markets," *Industrial Distribution,* April 1987, 4; DEBORAH SCHONDORF, "Home Appliance Industry," *Value Line Investment Survey,* 20 March 1992, 128+; KURT KLEINER, "Black & Decker Takes Aim at Japanese with New Tool Line," *Baltimore Business Journal,* 7 February 1992, 3; DEBRA SPARKS, "Black & Decker: Back and Tougher," *Financial World,* 28 March 1995, 20–22; THOMAS JAFFE, "The Black & Decker Drill," *Forbes,* 13 March 1995, 188; "B&D Powers Up Tools," *Marketing,* 16 February 1995, 34; KELLEY HOLLAND, "Retooling," *Business Week,* 9 February 1998, 48.

2. IAN P. MURPHY, "Study Maps Course for Electronic Superhighway," *Marketing News,* 17 February 1997, 14.

3. AL MAGRATH, "Managing Distribution Channels," *Business Quarterly,* Spring 1996, 56+.

4. COURTLAND L. BOVÉE, MICHAEL J. HOUSTON, AND JOHN V. THILL, *Marketing,* 2d ed. (New York: McGraw-Hill, 1995), 406.

5. JOSEPH PEREIRA, "Toys 'R' Us: Big Kid on the Block, Won't Stop Growing," *Wall Street Journal,* 11 August 1988, B6; "Toys 'R' Us," *New York Times,* 13 March 1998, C19.

6. ALICE Z. CUNEO, "Levi Strauss Sizes the Retail Scene," *Advertising Age,* 23 January 1995, 4; ELAINE UNDERWOOD, "Store Brands," *Brandweek,* 9 January 1995, 23–27.

7. EBEN SHAPIRO, "Viacom Unit Moves to Cut a Distributor," *Wall Street Journal,* 16 August 1996, A3–A4.

8. PETER BURROWS, "A Peek at Steve Jobs' Plan," *Business Week,* 17 November 1997, 144–146; LEE GOMES, "Apple Plans Direct Sales over Internet," *Wall Street Journal,* 11 November 1997, A3, A6; PETER BURROWS, "Well, Steve, What'll It Be?" *Business Week,* 30 March 1998, 35; CHARLES PILLER, "Casting Jobs as Savior Is Premature," *Los Angeles Times,* 16 March 1998, D4; JERRY LANGTON, "Looking Out for Number One: Dell and Gateway 2000 Taught Steve Jobs How to 'Think Different' About Competition," *Computer Dealer News,* 19 January 1998, 28; OWEN EDWARDS, "Sects Crazed: By Resurrecting Steve Jobs, Apple May Have Seriously Endangered Its Cult Status," *Forbes,* 23 February 1998, 44; GREGORY QUICK, "Jobs Focuses on Apple's Future at Macworld Show," *Computer Retail Week,* 5 January 1998, 4+.

9. GREG BURNS, "Will Quaker Get the Recipe Right?" *Business Week,* 5 February 1996, 140–145; GREG BURNS, "Putting the Snap Back in Snapple," *Business Week,* 22 July 1996, 40.

10. KRISTIN DUNLAP GODSEY, "Big Thing—Point Cast Invented a New Medium, Now Let the Battle Begin," *Success,* April 1997, 41–48; SCOTT WOOLLEY, "The New Distribution," *Forbes,* 4 November 1996, 164–165.

11. JOSEPH CONLIN, "The Art of the Dealer Meeting," *Sales and Marketing Management,* February 1997, 76+.

12. JOSEPH WEBER, "It's 'Like Somebody Shot the Postman,'" *Business Week,* 13 January 1992, 82; LOUIS RUKEYSER, JOHN COONEY, AND GEORGE WINSLOW, *Louis Rukeyser's Business Almanac* (New York: Simon and Schuster, 1988), 649; STEVEN P. GALANTE, "Distributors Switch Strategies to Survive Coming Shakeout," *Wall Street Journal,* 20 July 1987, B21; *Statistical Abstract of the United States: 1989* (Washington, D.C.: GPO, 1989), 779.

13. "What Distributors Must Do to Survive," *Purchasing,* 19 June 1997, 51–54.

14. ROBERT F. LUSCH, DEBORAH ZIZZO, AND JAMES M. KENDERDINE, "Strategic Renewal in Distribution," *Marketing Management,* 2, no. 2 (1993): 20–29.

15. *Statistical Abstract of the United States: 1993* (Washington, D.C.: GPO, 1993), 538.

16. PATRICIA SELLERS, "Giants of the Fortune 5 Hundred: Sears: The Turnaround Is Ending; The Revolution Has Begun," *Fortune,* 28 April 1997, 106+.

17. JULIE SCHMIT, "Tandy Pulls Plug on 35 Superstores," *USA Today,* 31 December 1996, B1.

18. I. JEANNE DUGAN, "The Corporation: Strategies: Can Toys 'R' Us Get on Top of Its Game?" *Business Week,* 7 April 1997, 124; ZINA MOUKHEIBER, "The Great Wal-Mart Massacre, Part II," *Forbes,* 22 January 1996, 44–45.

19. WILLIAM J. HOLSTEIN AND KERRY HANNON, "They Drop Till You Shop," *U.S. News and World Report,* 21 July 1997, 51–52.

20. HOLSTEIN AND HANNON, "They Drop Till You Shop."

21. MICHELLE PACELLE, "The Aging Shopping Mall Must Either Adapt or Die," *Wall Street Journal,* 16 April 1996, B1, B14.

22. KENNETH LABICH, "What Will It Take to Keep People Hanging Out at the Mall," *Fortune,* 29 May 1995, 102–106.

23. PHILIP KOTLER, *Marketing Management,* 9th ed. (Upper Saddle River, N.J.: Prentice Hall, 1997), 567.

24. RICHARD A. FEINBERG, "Sobering Thoughts on Cybermalls, *Computerworld,* 14 April 1997, 35.

25. CHUCK JONES, "Cold Shoulders: Are Telemarketing and Door-to-Door Sales Doomed?" *Life Association News,* January 1998, 70+; SIMON FOSTER, "Looking Beyond the Telephone," *Marketing,* 22 January 1998, 21+; MICHAEL A. BROWN, "In Their

Ear: 21 Do's and Don'ts," *Direct,* January 1998, B6; VICTORIA GRIFFITH, "Telemarketing Hand-Ups," *Financial Times,* 19 January 1998, 15.

26. N. R. KLEINFIELD, "Even for J. Crew, the Mail-Order Boom Days Are Over," *New York Times,* 2 September 1990, sec. 3, 5; HOWARD RUDNITSKY, "Growing Pains," *Forbes,* 27 February 1995, 32; SIGMUND KIENER, "The Future of Mail Order," *Direct Marketing,* 15 February 1995, 17.

27. JONES, "Cold Shoulders: Are Telemarketing and Door-to-Door Sales Doomed?" 70+.

28. ZINA MOUKHEIBER, "Plus Ca Change," *Forbes,* 10 February 1997, 47; "Nonstore Retailing: Opportunity," *Footware News,* 18 November 1996, 13.

29. HEATHER PAGE, "Open for Business," *Entrepreneur,* December 1997, 51–53.

30. MARY BRANDEL, "On-line Catalogs Are Booting Up," *Computerworld Electronic Commerce Journal,* 29 April 1996, 5.

31. JAMES AARON COOKE, "Point, Click, and Shop," *Logistics Management,* February 1997, 70S+.

32. DANIEL S. JANAL, "Net Profit Now," *Success,* July–August 1997, 57–63.

33. TARIQ K. MUHAMMAD, "Marketing Online," *Black Enterprise,* September 1996, 85–88.

34. FRANK KOELSCH, *The Infomedia Revolution* (Canada: McGraw-Hill Ryerson, 1995), 214–216.

35. DALE D. BUSS, "Capturing Customers with TV Retailing," *Nation's Business,* February 1997, 29–31.

36. MICHAEL KRANTZ, "Enter the Interactive," *Adweek,* 13 June 1994, 38–40.

37. "SkyMall Opens Cyberspace Outpost," *Newsbytes News Network,* 3 October 1997.

38. RONALD HENKOFF, "Delivering the Goods," *Fortune,* 28 November 1994, 64–78.

39. *PC Connection Catalog* 4, no. 6B (1994): 2–3.

40. HENKOFF, "Delivering the Goods."

41. EDWARD O. WELLES, "Riding the High-Tech Highway," *Inc.,* March 1993, 72–85.

42. COLLEEN GOURLEY, "Retail Logistics in Cyberspace," *Distribution,* December 1996, 29; DAVE HIRSCHMAN, "FedEx Starts Up Package Sorting System at Memphis Tenn. Airport," *Knight-Ridder/Tribune Business News,* 28 September 1997, 928B0953; "FedEx and Technology—Maintaining a Competitive Edge," *PresWIRE,* 2 December 1996.

43. "Wal-Mart Computers Talk to Vendors," *Chain Store Age,* January 1985, 20.

44. RITA KOSELKA, "Distribution Revolution," *Forbes,* 25 May 1992, 54–61.

45. LINDA GRANT, "Why Fed Ex Is Flying High," *Fortune,* 10 November 1997, 155–160.

46. See note 1.

CHAPTER 15

1. RICHARD W. STEVENSON, "Ikea's New Realities: Recession and Aging Consumers," *New York Times,* 25 April 1993, sec. 3, 4; "Ikea Blasts into L. A. Marketplace with Record-Bashing Outdoor Blitz," *Adweek Western Advertising News,* 22 October 1990, 1, 4; CARA APPELBAUM, "How IKEA Blitzes a Market," *Adweek's Marketing Week,* 11 June 1990, 18–19; MICHAEL WINERIP, "Shopping Siren Sings This Song: IKEA! IKEA!" *New York Times,* 25 May 1990, B1; JUDITH NEWMAN, "Swede Deal," *Adweek,* 20 July 1992, 16; RANDALL ROTHENBERG, "Deutsch's Campaign for Ikea Furniture," *New York Times,* 4 May 1990, D17; MARY KRIENKE, "IKEA's Anders Moberg," *Stores,* January 1992, 98–100, 102; "Shoppers at IKEA Go Bonkers," *HFN The Weekly Newspaper for the Home Furnishing Network,* 9 January 1995, 8; MARIANNE WILSON, "Ikea's Moveable Feast," *Chain Store Age,* January 1996, 162–163; JENNIFER PELLET, "Ikea Takes Manhattan," *Discount Merchandiser,* October 1995, 22–23; JULIA FLYNN AND LORI BONGIORNO, "Ikea's New Game Plan," *Business Week,* 6 October 1997, 99–102.

2. COURTLAND L. BOVÉE, JOHN V. THILL, GEORGE P. DOVEL, AND MARIAN B. WOOD, *Advertising Excellence* (New York: McGraw-Hill, 1995), 177–182.

3. TIMOTHY E. MOORE, "Subliminal Advertising: What You See Is What You Get," *Journal of Marketing,* Spring 1982, 38–47; JACK HABERSTROH, "Can't Ignore Subliminal Ad Charges," *Advertising Age,* 17 September 1984, 3, 42, 44.

4. KEITH SCHNEIDER, "Guides on Environmental Ad Claims," *New York Times,* 29 July 1992, C3; JEANNE SADDLER, "FTC Issues a 'Green-Marketing' Guide to Help Prevent Deceptive-Ad Charges," *Wall Street Journal,* 29 July 1992, B5; NANCI HELLMICH, "Big Changes Proposed for Food Labels," *USA Today,* 6 November 1991, 1D.

5. FRANK KOELSCH, *The Infomedia Revolution* (Ontario: McGraw-Hill Ryerson, 1995), 284.

6. Direct Marketing Association, <http://www.the-dma.org/services1/libres-home1b.shtml>, accessed 23 November 1997.

7. BOVÉE, THILL, DOVEL, AND WOOD, *Advertising Excellence,* 16.

8. JENNIFER LAWRENCE, "Integrated Mix Makes Expansion Fly," *Advertising Age—Special Integrated Marketing Report,* 4 November 1993, S10–S12, UMI, 01634089.

9. JANET SMITH, "Integrated Marketing," *American Demographics,* November 1995, 62, UMI, 00253790.

10. DON E. SCHULTZ, "Some Agencies Find Dip in IMC Pool Too Cold," *Marketing News,* 28 April 1997, 9.

11. COURTLAND L. BOVÉE, MICHAEL J. HOUSTON, AND JOHN V. THILL, *Marketing,* 2d ed. (New York: McGraw-Hill, 1995), 539–540.

12. "Sales Costs Higher for Small Firms," *Small Business Reports,* November 1990, 18.

13. SHARI CAUDRON, "Sales-Force Automation Comes of Age," *IW Electronics and Technology,* 20 May 1996, 156–152; STANNIE HOLT, "Sales-Force Automation," *InfoWorld,* 23 March 1998, 29.

14. GEORGE R. WALTHER, "Reach Out to Accounts," *Success,* May 1990, 24.

15. KOELSCH, *The Infomedia Revolution,* 233.

16. KENNETH R. SHEETS, "3-D or Not 3-D? That's the Question for Advertisers," *U.S. News and World Report,* 25 January 1988, 59; authors' estimates; RICHARD KARPINSKI, "Microsoft, SGI Push 3-D Toward Web's Mainstream," *Internet Week,* 16 February 1998, 9.

17. KOELSCH, *The Infomedia Revolution,* 235.

18. "100 Leading National Advertisers," *Advertising Age,* 29 September 1997, S63.

19. "Down to Business, Chapter VII: Everything You Always Wanted to Know About Advertising—Cheap!" *Entrepreneur,* May 1985, 84.

20. "Not for Members Only," *Marketing Management,* 1, no. 4 (1993): 6–7; Herb Goldsmith, "Members Only Fashions a Unique Selling Strategy," *Journal of Business Strategy,* May–June 1989, 8–11.

21. Janet Neiman, "The Trouble with Comparative Ads," *Adweek's Marketing Week,* 12 January 1987, 4–5.

22. Neiman, "The Trouble with Comparative Ads," 4–5; Joseph B. White, "Ford Decides to Fight Back in Truck Ads," *Wall Street Journal,* 28 February 1989, B1, B6.

23. Paul Duke Jr. and Ronald Alsop, "Advertisers Beginning to Play Off Worker Concern over Job Security," *Wall Street Journal,* 1 April 1988, A11; Ronald Alsop, "More Food Advertising Plays on Cancer and Cardiac Fears," *Wall Street Journal,* 8 October 1987, 33; George E. Belch and Michael A. Belch, *Introduction to Advertising and Promotion Management* (Homewood, Ill.: Irwin, 1990), 186.

24. Thomas R. King, "Pitches on Value Stick in Consumers' Minds," *Wall Street Journal,* 4 June 1990, B1.

25. Richard Sandomir, "Tiger Woods Signs Pact with American Express," *New York Times,* 20 May 1997, C1.

26. Joshua Levine, "Fantasy, Not Flesh," *Forbes,* 22 January 1990, 118–120.

27. Courtland L. Bovée and William F. Arens, *Contemporary Advertising* (Homewood, Ill.: Irwin, 1989), 259–261.

28. Direct Marketing Association, <http://www.the-dma.org/services1/libres-home1b.shtml>, accessed, 23 November 1997.

29. Lynn Asinof, "Telemarketing Makes Rapid Strides at U.S. Corporations," *Wall Street Journal,* 21 July 1988, A1; Roger Reece, "The New Generation of Integrated Inbound/Outbound Telemarketing Systems," *Telemarketing,* March 1995, 58–65; Malynda H. Madzel, "Outsourcing Telemarketing: Why It May Work for You," *Telemarketing,* March 1995, 48–49; "Despite Hangups, Telemarketing a Success," *Marketing News,* 27 March 1995, 19.

30. Bovée, Houston, and Thill, *Marketing,* 475.

31. Steve Dworman, "Trends That Hurt Infomercials," *Target Marketing,* February 1997, 46, UMI, 08895333; Peter Bieler, "The ThighMaster Exerciser Bonanza," *Success,* July–August 1996, 59, UMI, 0201239482.

32. Hanna Rubin, "Home Video," *Adweek's Marketing Week,* 11 September 1989, 166, 168; Amy Zipken, "Direct Marketing," *Adweek's Marketing Week,* 11 September 1989, 228, 230; "Calculators on Shopping Carts Can Add Up to Good Business," *San Diego Union,* 23 December 1991, A22.

33. Internet Advertising Bureau, "Why Internet Advertising?" *Internet Advertising Bureau—Supplement to Adweek,* 5 May 1997, 9–16.

34. Ellen Neuborne, "Web Ads Start to Click," *Business Week,* 6 October 1997, 128–138.

35. Amy Cortese, "A Way Out of the Web Maze," *Business Week,* 24 February 1997, 95–108.

36. Neuborne, "Web Ads Start to Click."

37. "Sales Promotions—Annual Report 1989: Growing Up and Out," *Marketing & Media Decisions,* July 1990, 20–21.

38. Howard Schlossberg, "Coupons Likely to Remain Popular," *Marketing News,* 29 March 1993, 1, 7; Scott Hume, "Coupons Set Record, but Pace Slows," *Advertising Age,* 1 February 1993, 25; John Philip Jones, "The Double Jeopardy of Sales Promotions," *Harvard Business Review,* September–October 1990, 145–152; Laurie Petersen, "The Pavlovian Syndrome," *Adweek's Marketing Week,* 9 April 1990, P6–P7; Belch and Belch, *Introduction to Advertising and Promotion Management,* 524–526; Fiona Plant, "Smart Card Supersedes Coupons?" *International Journal of Retail & Distribution Management Retail Insights,* Spring 1995, xi; "Coupons—Still the Shopper's Best Friend," *Progressive Grocer,* February 1995, SS11; "Multiple Purchase Coupons Increase Face Value," *Food Institute Report,* 19 January 1998, 6+; Deena Amato-McCoy, "Smith's Casts Movie Coupons in Frequent-Shopper Program," *Supermarket News,* 19 January 1998, 23; Ronald Alsop, "More Merchants Play Retail Roulette to Woo Jaded Shoppers," *Wall Street Journal,* 22 January 1998, A1.

39. Lisa Z. Eccles, "Point of Purchase Advertising," *Advertising Age Supplement,* 26 September 1994, 1–6; Ed Liber, "The Show and Sell: Point-of-Purchase Materials Key to RTA Merchandising," *HFN: The Weekly Newspaper for the Home Furnishings Network,* 23 March 1998, 29.

40. Melanie Wells, "Marketing Capital of the World," *USA Today,* 22 July 1996, 1B–2B.

41. Jeff Jensen, "High Hopes for Men in Black, and Ray-Bans," *Advertising Age,* 14 April 1997, 1, 52; Richard Gibson and Calmetta Y. Coleman, "Teenie Beanie Babies Generate Great Big Buzz," *Wall Street Journal,* 11 April 1997, B1, B7.

42. Betsy Morris, "The Brand's the Thing," *Fortune,* 4 March 1996, 72–86.

43. Richard Gibson, "Latest in Corporate Freebies Try to Be Classy Instead of Trashy," *Wall Street Journal,* 7 August 1989, B4.

44. Monci Jo Williams, "Trade Promotion Junkies," *The Marketer,* October 1990, 30–33; Margaret Littman, "The Death of Advertising?" *Prepared Foods,* February 1992, 25; Anil Jagtiani, "How to Make Money on Trade Promotions," *Foods & Beverage Marketing,* February 1992, 21+; Michael McCarthy, "The Empire Strikes Back," *Adweek,* 24 February 1992, 1+; Al Urbanski, "Blame It on the Trade," *Food & Beverage Marketing,* January 1992, 28+; Betsy Spethmann, "Trade Promotion Redefined," *Brandweek,* 13 March 1995, 25–32; "Money Talk—Surprise, Surprise: Big Companies Pay More, but Tenure Doesn't Carry as Much Weight," *Food & Beverage Marketing,* January 1998, 16+.

45. "Trade Shows: An Alternative Method of Selling," *Small Business Reports,* January 1985, 67; Kate Bertrand, "Trade Shows Can Be Global Gateways," *Advertising Age's Business Marketing,* March 1995, 19–20.

46. Paul Holmes, "Public Relations," *Adweek's Marketing Week,* 11 September 1989, 234–235.

47. Melanie Wells, "Denny's Serves Up $5M Ad Campaign to Fix Racist Image," *USA Today,* 23 May 1997, B1.

48. Gerry Khermouch, "Pepsi Flack Attack Nips Hoax in the Bud," *Brandweek,* 21 June 1993, 5.

49. Cyndee Miller, "VNRs Are Still Hot, but They're Drawing Fire," *Marketing News,* 12 November 1990, 6.

50. See note 1.

CHAPTER 16

1. Adapted from Harvey P. Newquist, "AI at Amex," *AI Expert,* January 1993, 39–40; *American Express Annual Report, 1993;* Dennis Livingston, "American Express Reins in the Paper," *Systems Integration,* May 1990, 52–58; James A. Rothi and David C. Yen, "Why American Express Gambled on an Expert Data Base," *Information Strategy,* Spring 1990, 16–22; Patrick Lyons and Anthony Fabiano, "Using Expert System Technology to Foster Innovation," *Review of Business,* Fall 1990, 33–38; John Paul Newport Jr., "American Express: Service That Sells," *Fortune,* 20 November 1989, 80–94; Steve Fluty, "American Express Goes the Distance," *Inform,* January 1987, 34–36; Eva Kiess-Moser, "Customer Satisfaction," *Canadian Business Review,* Summer 1989, 43–45; "American Express: Focus on Management," *Incentive Marketing,* January 1989, 32–33; Jill Andresky Fraser, "James D. Robinson III: Member Since 1969," *Inc.,* September 1990, 159; Robert Teitelman, "Image vs. Reality at American Express," *Institutional Investor,* February 1992, 36+; Bruce Caldwell, "Amex's Data Center Shuffle: Unloading an Overbuilt Facility Has Proven Daunting," *Information Week,* 10 February 1992, 30+; Phil Britt, "Travelers Checks: An Uncertain Future?" *Savings & Community Banker,* March 1995, 31–34; Stephen E. Frank, "American Express Stages Its First Gain in Credit-Card Market Share in Decade," *Wall Street Journal,* 24 March 1998, A3+; Lisa Fickenscher, "Tough Job at Amex: Making Friends with Banks," *American Banker,* 12 March 1998, 1+; Jikki Tait, "Amex Tries to Tap Black Influence," *Financial Times,* 8 January 1998, 6.

2. Phillip B. Evans and Thomas S. Wurster, "Strategy and the New Economics of Information," *Harvard Business Review,* September–October 1997, 73.

3. Courtland L. Bovée, John V. Thill, Marian B. Wood, and George P. Dovel, *Management* (New York: McGraw-Hill, 1993), 572–578.

4. Laurence Zuckerman, "Do Computers Lift Productivity? It's Unclear, but Business Is Sold," *New York Times,* 2 January 1997, C15.

5. Thomas Petzinger Jr., "The Front Lines: Are You Still Clinging to Those Chestnuts of Business?" *Wall Street Journal,* 9 May 1997.

6. David Bank, "Know-It-Alls," *Wall Street Journal,* 18 November 1996, R28.

7. Larry Long and Nancy Long, *Computers,* 5th ed. (Upper Saddle River, N.J.: Prentice Hall, 1998), MIS 5.

8. Kathryn M. Bartol and David C. Martin, *Management* (New York: McGraw-Hill, 1991), 703–705.

9. Evelyn Ellison, "New Exec Title on the Rise," *Indianapolis Business Journal* 18 (15 September 1997) 27, *Electric Library,* Online, 2 December 1997.

10. Richard L. Daft, *Management,* 4th ed. (Fort Worth, Tex.: Dryden, 1997), 686.

11. Daft, *Management,* 687.

12. Long and Long, *Computers,* MIS 17–MIS 19; Daft, *Management,* 688.

13. John W. Verity, "Coaxing Meaning Out of Raw Data," *Business Week,* 3 February 1997, 134.

14. Bartol and Martin, *Management,* 709–710.

15. David Morse, ed., *CyberDictionary* (Santa Monica: Knowledge Exchange, 1996), 19; Long and Long, *Computers,* G1.

16. Long and Long, *Computers,* 21–22.

17. Paul C. Judge, "Artificial Imagination," *Business Week,* 18 March 1996, 60.

18. John Woram, "Feature: PC: Talk to Me!—Voice Recognition Is Starting to Make Some Noise," *Windows,* 1 November 1997, 208, *Electric Library,* Online, 2 December 1997; Walter S. Mossberg, "Dragon Systems Take a Giant Step in Speech Recognition," *Wall Street Journal,* 12 June 1997, B1; Long and Long, *Computers,* 137.

19. Donald H. Sanders, *Computers Today* (New York: McGraw-Hill, 1988), 406.

20. Larry Long and Nancy Long, *Introduction to Computers and Information Systems,* 5th ed. (Upper Saddle River, N.J.: Prentice Hall), CORE 191.

21. "U.S. Companies Becoming More Reliant on Internet," *Newsbytes News Network,* 10 April 1997, *Electric Library,* Online, 2 December 1997.

22. Michael C. Brandon, "From Need to Know to Need to Know," *Communication World* 13 (20 October 1996): 18, *Electric Library,* Online, 1 December 1997.

23. Gary Hoover, Alta Campbell, and Patrick J. Spain, eds., *Hoover's Handbook of American Business 1994* (Austin, Tex.: Reference Press, 1993), 161.

24. Mark Halper, "Bigiron.com: Why Merrill Lynch, J. C. Penney, Wells Fargo, and Others Turned Their Old Mainframe Computers into Hot Web Servers," *Forbes ASAP,* 2 June 1997, 38–39.

25. Long and Long, *Computers,* CORE 18.

26. Long and Long, *Computers,* CORE 18.

27. Kourosh Karimkhany, "Apple Advertisements Continue in National Newspapers," *Reuters Business Report,* 10 April 1997, *Electric Library,* Online, 2 December 1997.

28. Long and Long, *Computers,* CORE 19.

29. Gene Bylinksy, "The Digital Factory," *Fortune,* 14 November 1994, 92–110.

30. Randy Cerveny, "Making Weather in the Movies," *Weatherwise 49,* (1 December 1996): *35,* Electric Library, Online, 2 December 1997; Long and Long, *Computers,* CORE 19.

31. "Silicon Graphics Bids for Expansion," *USA Today,* 27 February 1996, *Electric Library,* Online, 2 December 1997.

32. Timothy Trainor and Diane Krasnewich, *Computers!* (New York: McGraw-Hill, 1989), 90.

33. Trainor and Krasnewich, *Computers!* 90–91.

34. Laurie Flynn, "CD-ROMs: They're Not Just for Entertainment," *New York Times,* 24 April 1994, F10; Nancy K. Herther, "CD-ROM at Ten Years: The Technology and the Industry Mature," *Online,* March–April 1995, 86–93.

35. James A. O'Brien, *Introduction to Information Systems,* 7th ed. (Burr Ridge, Ill.: Irwin, 1994), 95–97; Sanders, *Computers Today,* 501–517.

36. O'Brien, *Introduction to Information Systems,* 95–97.

37. Long and Long, *Computers,* CORE 81.

38. Kevin Maney, "Sun Rises on Java's Promise, CEO McNealy Sets Sights on Microsoft," *USA Today,* 14 July 1997, B1, *Electric Library,* Online, 2 December 1997; Deborah Gage and Edward F. Moltzen, "Gerstner's Plan: 2,000 Developers, Millions of Dollars for Java," *Computer Reseller News,* 2 June 1997, 5, *Electric Library,* Online, 2 December 1997; David Bottoms, "Sun Microsystems Inc.," *Industry Week,* 18 December 1995, 36–38; John W. Verity, "Meet Java, the Invisible Computer," *Business Week,* 4 December 1995, 82–83; Susan Headden, "The Glow of Success," *U.S. News and World Report,* 4 December 1995, 63–64.

39. Mark Halper, "Are Network Computers the Way to Go?" *Business Week Enterprise,* 13 October 1997, ENT 18; John Taschek, "Is There a Future for Network Computers?" *PC Week,* 16 March 1998, 56; Martin Banks, "Over-hyped, but Not Yet over Here," *Director,* February 1998, 69+; J. B. Miles, "Network Computers," *Government Computer News,* 9 February 1998, 43+; Dan Gillmor, "Cheap Hardware Boosts Network Computers," *Computerworld,* 26 January 1998, 105; James Geoffrey, "PC Users Won't Take NC for an Answer," *Network World,* 19 January 1998, 35+; Lisa DiCarlo, "Proponents Address NC Woes," *PC Week,* 19 January 1998, 10; Tom Foremski, "An Idea Whose Time Has Yet to Come," *Financial Times,* 7 January 1998, 8.

40. G. Christian Hill, "It's War," *Wall Street Journal,* 16 September 1997, R1, R4.

41. Portions of the following text on network components are adapted from Long and Long, *Introduction to Computers and Information Systems,* CORE 164–176.

42. Michael Krantz, "Wired for Speed," *Time,* 23 September 1996, 54–55; Michael Krantz, "The Biggest Thing Since Color?" *Time,* 12 August 1996, 42–43.

43. William J. Cook, "1997 A New Space Odyssey," *U.S. News and World Report,* 3 March 1997, 45–52.

44. Anne Field, "State of the Art," *Inc. Technology* no. 3 (1996): 39.

45. Bart Ziegler, "In the Net," *Wall Street Journal,* 18 November 1996, R21.

46. Joseph B. White, "Chrysler's Intranet: Promise vs. Reality," *Wall Street Journal,* 13 May 1997, B1; Brandon, "From Need to Know to Need to Know," 18, *Electric Library,* Online, 1 December 1997; George Taninecz, "The Web Within," *Industry Week,* 4 March 1996, 45–49.

47. David Morse, *Cyber Dictionary* (Santa Monica, CA: Knowledge Exchange, 1996), 151–152.

48. Jared Sandberg, "What Do They Do On-line?" *Wall Street Journal,* 9 December 1996, R8.

49. Zuckerman, "Do Computers Lift Productivity? It's Unclear, but Business Is Sold."

50. David C. Churbuck, "Dial-a-Catalog," *Forbes,* 10 October 1994, 126–130; John W. Verity, "The Internet: How It Will Change the Way You Do Business," *Business Week,* 14 November 1994, 80–88; Peter H. Lewis, "Getting Down to Business on the Net," *New York Times,* 19 June 1994, sec. 3, 1, 6; Paul Wiseman, "The Internet Snares More Businesses," *USA Today,* 7 July 1994, B1, B2; Albert Fried-Cassorla, "Successful Marketing on the Internet: A User's Guide," *Direct Marketing,* March 1995, 39–42; David Taylor, "Digital Dreaming: The Internet Marketing Primer," *Marketing Computers,* March 1995, 24, 36+.

51. William M. Bulkeley, "How Can You Make Money from the Web?" *Wall Street Journal,* 9 December 1996, R18; "Industry Pioneer Launches Company to Help Site Publishers Make Money on the Web," *PR Newswire,* 26 February 1998, 226SFTH002; Mark Halper, "(Almost) Making Money on the Web," *CIO,* 5 January 1998, S56+.

52. Sandberg, "What Do They Do On-line?"

53. Tariq K. Muhammad, "Electronic Commerce and the Future of Money," *Black Enterprise,* June 1997, 255–260; David Stipp, "The Birth of Digital Commerce," *Fortune,* 9 December 1996, 160; Bulkeley, "How Can You Make Money from the Web?"

54. Nina Munk, "Technology for Technology's Sake," *Forbes,* 21 October 1996, 280.

55. Richard Behar, "Who's Reading Your E-mail?" *Fortune,* 3 February 1997, 58–59; John Fantana, "Secure E-Mail Standards Wallow in Incompatability," *Internet Week,* 16 February 1998, 18; Steve Bass, "Survival Tips for E-Mail Junkies," *PC World,* March 1998, 286; Claudia Montague, "E-Mail by Request," *Marketing Tools,* March 1998, 28+.

56. M. J. Zuckerman, "Targeting Cyberterrorism," *USA Today,* 20 October 1997, 17A; Steve Lohr, "Feeling Insecure, Are We?" *New York Times,* 17 March 1997, C1.

57. M. J. Zuckerman, "FBI Takes on Security Fight in Cyberspace," *USA Today,* 21 November 1996, 4B; Payman Pejman, "Agents Now Rely on Systems, FBI Exec Says," *Government Computer News,* 16 March 1998, 6; Peyman Pejman, "FBI's Crime Net to Get a Face-Lift," *Government Computer News,* 16 March 1998, 1; Richard J. Koreto, "A CPA's Skills, an Agent's Badge," *Journal of Accountancy,* March 1998, 16+; Timothy Burger, "Plunging into the Computer Age," *LegalTimes,* 23 February 1998, 12; Thomas Ricks and John Simons, "FBI Probes Break-ins at Military Computers," *Wall Street Journal,* 26 February 1998, B8; Brian Duffy, "Crusader Brought FBI Surveillance into High-Tech Age," *Wall Street Journal,* 2 January 1998, 40.

58. Alan Farnham, "How Safe Are Your Secrets?" *Fortune,* 10 March 1997, 114.

59. James K. Wilcox, "Hacker Hints," *Working Woman,* June 1997, 11.

60. See note 1.

CHAPTER 17

1. Edward Weiner, chief operating officer, TCDI, personal communication, March 1998.

2. Eric Shrine, "The Squawk over Boston Chicken," *Business Week,* 21 October 1996, 64–72; "Profits and Loss," *Progressive Grocer,* July 1994, 112; Nelson D. Schwarz, "The Boston Chicken Problem," *Fortune,* 7 July 1997, 114–116; Louise Lee, "Booby Prize Goes to Boston Chicken," *Wall Street Journal,* 26 February 1998, 1.

3. Phillip L. Zweig and Dean Foust, "Corporate America Is Fed Up with FASB," *Business Week,* 21 April 1997, 108; H. D. Howarth, "Closing the GAAP," *CMA Magazine,* 1 September 1995, 3; "Interview with Dennis Beresford," *CFO,* May 1997,

49–54; "Global Accounting's Roadblock," *The Economist,* 27 April 1996, 79; Glenn Cheney, "New FASB Standard May Herald Reduced Disclosures," *Accounting Today,* 16 March 1998, 14+; "FASB Fighting Fire with Fire," *CFO Alert,* 2 February 1998, 1; Glenn Cheney, "FASB Chair Foresees Year of Global Developments," *Accounting Today,* 9 February 1998, 12+; Katherine M. Reynolds, "Proposed Legislation Allows Court Challenges of FASB Accounting Standards," *Bond Buyer,* 9 February 1998, 36.

4. John Von Brachel, "AICPA Chairman Lays the Foundation for the Future," *Journal of Accountancy,* November 1995, 64–67.

5. Robert H. Bellone, "Is Your Accounting Software Ready for the Internet," *Accounting Technology,* April 1997, 16–20; Neil Gross, Amy Cortese, and Steve Hamm, "Software Prognosis 1998," *Business Week,* 12 January 1998, 86+.

6. Institute of Management Accountants, 1994 Research Study.

7. Wayne Tusa, "A Proactive Approach to Environmental Risks," *Risk Management,* January 1994, 12–13; Dennis L. Kimmell, "Readings," *Internal Auditor,* June 1993, 16; JoAnn Longworth and Karen Montano, "Cleaning Up the Books," *CA Magazine,* June–July 1993, 55–58.

8. Bill Birchard, "The Right to Know," *CFO: The Magazine for Senior Financial Executives,* November 1993, 28–38.

9. Mark Maremont, "Bean Counters Get an Early-Warning System," *Business Week,* 9 December 1996, 68–69.

10. Elizabeth MacDonald, "More Accounting Firms Are Dumping Risky Clients," *Wall Street Journal,* 25 April, 1997, A2.

11. Ralph Saul, "Keeping the Watchdog Healthy," *Financial Executive,* November–December 1995, 10–13.

12. Jennifer Reingold and Richard A. Melcher, "Then There Were Four," *Business Week,* 3 November 1997, 37; Sallie L. Gaines, "KPMG and Ernst Call Off Merger," *Chicago Tribune,* 14 February 1998, B1, B3.

13. Paul Schneider, "Til Retirement Do Them Part," *Business Month,* July 1990, 14–15; "Less Is More Among the Bean Counters," *U.S. News and World Report,* 17 July 1989, 11; David Greising, Leah J. Nathans, and Laura Jereski, "The New Numbers Game in Accounting," *Business Week,* 24 July 1989, 20–21; "The Big Eight, Seven, Six . . .," *Time,* 17 July 1989, 77; Saul, "Keeping the Watchdog Healthy."

14. Susan Goodwin and Edward W. Younkins, "How the Expanding Scope of CPA Services Threatens Accountants' Claim to Independence," *Practical Accountant,* September 1990, 92–99; March Leepson, "Taking Off by the Numbers," *Nation's Business,* August 1987, 49; Tom Kennedy Smith, "The Changing Face of Accounting Services," *Corporate Report—Minnesota,* 1 August 1996, 61.

15. Von Brachel, "AICPA Chairman Lays the Foundation for the Future."

16. Robert Stuart, "Accountants in Management—A Globally Changing Role," *CMA Magazine,* 1 February 1997, 5.

17. Jack L. Smith, Robert M. Keith, and William L. Stephens, *Accounting Principles,* 4th ed. (New York: McGraw-Hill, 1993), 16–17.

18. Judith Crown, "Consultancy Tapping Skills of MBA Moms," *Crain's Chicago Business,* 27 September 1993; Barbara Marsh, "A Consulting Business Thrives by Hiring Mothers Part-Time," *Wall Street Journal,* 23 February 1994.

19. Stanley Zarowin, "The Future of Finance," *Journal of Accountancy,* August 1995, 47–49.

20. 1996 Annual Report of Computer Discount Warehouse.

21. Eliyahu Goldratt, *The Goal,* 2d ed. (Great Barrington, Mass.: North River Press, 1992), 297–302.

22. Frank Evans, "A Road Map to Your Financial Report," *Management Review,* October 1993, 39–47.

23. Stacy Perman, "Business: Welcome Aboard—Or Pay Up, Sit Up and Shut Up," *Time,* 24 February 1997, 48.

24. Stanley Zarowin, "The Future of Finance," *Journal of Accountancy,* August 1995, 47–49.

25. Edward Weiner, chief operating officer, TCDI, personal communication, March 1998.

CHAPTER 18

1. Adapted from Ronaleen R. Roha, "Starting a New Business: The Scary First Year," *Kiplinger's Personal Finance Magazine,* February 1993, 75–78, 80.

2. David H. Bangs Jr., *"Financial Troubleshooting,"* Soundview Executive Book Summaries 15, no. 5 (May 1993): 1–4.

3. Jill Andresky Fraser, "Capital Steps," *Inc.,* February 1996, 42.

4. Donald Ecker, "Managing Cash Flow to Increase the Bottom Line," *San Diego Business Journal,*16 January 1995, 18.

5. Jill Andresky Fraser, "Will Banking Go Virtual?" *Inc. Technology,* no. 3 (1996): 49–52; Teri Robinson, "Banks Hit Home—Web-based Banking Hits Home Like Few Other Technologies," *Internet Week,* 16 March 1998, 55; Jeffrey Marshall, "Internet Banking: How Far, How Fast?" *U.S. Banker,* March 1998, 66; Gregory Dalton, "Outside Help for Online Banking," *Information Week,* 16 March 1998, 85+; Nicolas Hammond, "Banking on a Secure Net," *Security Management,* February 1998, 69+; William Philips, "Catering to Diversity Customers," *ABA Banking Journal,* February 1998, S3+; Jeffrey Marshall, "Sensing a Gap in Knowledge About Home Banking and the Internet," *U.S. Banker,* January 1998, 42.

6. Bruce Horovitz and Chris Woodyard, "Quaker Oats' $1.4 Billion Washout," *USA Today,* 28 March 1997.

7. Lori Ioannou, "Need Money? Go Private," *International Business,* January 1995, 28–30.

8. Steve Brooks, "Nobody Said It'd Be Easy," *Restaurant Business,* 10 December 1994, 48.

9. Susan Chandler, "Tracing Trouble at Wards," *Chicago Tribune,* 13 July 1997, sec. 5, 1.

10. Caryn Brown, "The Best Ways to Finance Your Business, " *Black Enterprise,* June 1993, 270–278; Karen Gutloff, "Five Alternative Ways to Finance Your Business," *Black Enterprise,* March 1998, 81+.

11. Paul Carroll, "More High-Tech Entrepreneurs Turn to Angels, " *Wall Street Journal,* 20 May 1996, B1; "Who's Funding Today's Emerging Businesses?" *Inc.—Special Edition: State of Small Business 1997,* 20 May 1997, 118.

12. Roberta Maynard, "Are You Ready to Go Public?" *Nation's Business,* January 1995, 30–32.

13. Robert A. Mamis, "Face to Face—Andy Klein," *Inc.,* July 1996, 39–40.

14. MAMIS, "Face to Face—Andy Klein."

15. STEPHANIE GRUNER, "When Mom and Pop Go Public," *Inc.,* December 1996, 66–73.

16. JAMES GLEICK, "Dead as a Dollar," *New York Times Magazine,* 16 June 1996, 26–30; KELLY HOLLAND AND AMY CORTESE, "The Future of Money," *Business Week,* 12 June 1995, 66–78.

17. CRISTINA BRANDAO AND PIALI ROY, "The Next Internet," *Canadian Business* 69, no. 13 (Fall 1996): 50–58.

18. EDMUND L. ANDREWS, "Europeans Clear Remaining Hurdle to Currency Unit—11 Nations Pass the Test," *New York Times,* 28 February 1998, A1, B2.

19. EDMUND ANDREWS, "Dollar Soars as Europe Doubts Its Currency Plan," *New York Times,* 15 July 1997; JAY BRANEGAN, "Special Report: Here Comes the Euromark," *Time International,* 30 September 1996, 50; STEVE RATTNER, "Single Currency for Europe? Not So Fast," *Newsday,* 25 June 1997, A35; DAVID J. LYNCH, "Common Currency a Singular Issue in Europe," *USA Today,* 6 June 1997, 12B.

20. GENE KOPROWSKI, "The Money Changers: Digital Cash Innovators Talk Banks, Bits, Bytes and Bucks," *Forbes ASAP,* 26 August 1996, 68–74.

21. MICHAEL SICONOLFI, "Widening Reach: Merrill Lynch, Pushing into Many New Lines, Expands Bank Services," *Wall Street Journal,* 7 July 1993, A1, A9.

22. JOHN MEEHAN, "America's Bumbling Bankers: Ripe for a New Fiasco," *Business Week,* 2 March 1992, 86–87.

23. DONALD KORN, "Is Your Bank Robbing You Blind?" *Black Enterprise,* October 1996, 117–121.

24. ROBERT A. ROSENBLATT, "Border Crossing," *Los Angeles Times,* 5 June 1994, D1, D4.

25. MICHAEL ALLEN AND PETER PAE, "Feisty Small Fry: Despite the Mergers of Many Big Banks, Tiny Ones May Thrive," *Wall Street Journal,* 9 October 1991, A1, A7; PAMELA J. PODGER, "Bank Start-ups Draw Interest of Small Firms," *Wall Street Journal,* 28 December 1990, B1–B2; "Despite Changing Market, Banks Still Urge to Merge," *CFO Alert,* 30 January 1995, 1; STEVEN LIPIN AND TIMOTHY L. O'BRIEN, "Mergers Between U.S Banks Seem to Be Heating Up Again," *Wall Street Journal—Europe,* 23 February 1995, 11.

26. G. BRUCE KNECHT, "Norwest Corp. Relies on Branches, Pushes Service—and Prospers," *Wall Street Journal,* 17 August 1995, A9.

27. NANETTE BYRNES, "On the Cutting Edge," *Business Week,* 28 October 1996, 134–138.

28. KORN, "Is Your Bank Robbing Your Blind?"

29. PAIK SUNOO, "Racing Toward a New Horizon in Banking," *Personnel Journal,* September 1996, 28–36.

30. THOMAS MCCARROLL, "No Checks. No Cash. No Fuss?" *Time,* 9 May 1994, 60–61.

31. CONNIE GUGLIELMO, "Here Come the Super-ATMs," *Fortune,* 14 October 1996, 232–234.

32. LORI IOANNOU, "Friendly Invaders: Foreign Banks Score Big with U.S. Companies," *International Business,* November 1992, 29–30, 32; TERENCE PARE, "Why Banks Are Still Stingy," *Fortune,* 25 January 1993, 73–75.

33. "The World's 100 Largest Banks," *Wall Street Journal,* 18 September 1997, R27.

34. SAM ZUCKERMAN, "A Land of Plenty for Loans," *Business Week/Enterprise,* 24–25; PETER ROSE, " Lenders and the Internet," *Journal of Lending & Credit Risk Management,* 79, no. 10 (June 1997): 31–37.

35. "SFNB Makes One Year on the Frontline of Internet Banking," *ABA Banking Journal,* 88, no. 12 (December 1996): 62; RICHARD WATERS, "Increase in U.S. Bank Failures," *Financial Times,* 3 March 1998, 8.

36. PAUL NADLER, "Banking of the Net," *American Banker,* 161, no. 126 (2 July 1996): 6; "Forget all the Hype," *Banker,* 147, no. 853 (March 1997): 12.

37. JULIE STACEY, "USA Snapshots: Bank Failures," *USA Today,* 23 May 1991, 1B; FRED R. BLEAKLEY, "Bank Industry Had Dismal '90, Survey Shows," *Wall Street Journal,* 11 February 1991, A3, A6; KENNETH H. BACON, "Big Banks Would Get Vastly Broader Powers Under Treasury's Plan," *Wall Street Journal,* 6 February, 1991, A1–A4; STEPHEN LABATON, "Top U.S. Auditor Predicts Banks May Be Headed for Large Bailout," *New York Times,* 12 June 1991, A1, C3; LEONARD SILK, "The Argument over Banks," *New York Times,* 8 February 1991, D2; DAVID T. LLEWELLYN, "The Future Business of Banking," *Banking World,* January 1995, 16–19; RICHARD WATERS, "Increases in U.S. Bank Failures," *Financial Times,* 3 March 1998, 8.

38. WILLIAM M. ISAAC, "Wrong Time to Soak the Banks," *Wall Street Journal,* 29 January 1991, A16.

39. ASSOCIATED PRESS, "47% of Bankers Have Doubts About FDIC," *Arizona Republic,* 8 October 1991, 14; STEPHEN LABATON, "Bank Deposit Fund Nearly Insolvent, U.S. Auditor Says," *New York Times,* 27 April 1991, sec. 1, 31; STEPHEN LABATON, "Bank Fund Outlook Is Bleaker" *New York Times,* 28 June 1991, C1, C9.

40. See note 1.

CHAPTER 19

1. Adapted from WILLIAM A. FRANCIS, vice president, Landes Associates, Inc., Wilmington, Delaware, personal communication, 7 October 1991.

2. STEPHANIE STROM, "It's Called Targeted Stock: Shun It, Some Experts Say," *New York Times,* 12 July 1994, C1, C5.

3. JEFFREY B. LITTLE AND LUCIEN RHODES, *Understanding Wall Street,* 2d ed. (Blue Ridge Summit, Pa.: Liberty House, 1987), 128.

4. GORDON J. ALEXANDER, WILLIAM F. SHARPE, AND JEFFERY V. BAILEY, *Fundamentals of Investments,* 2d ed. (Upper Saddle River, N.J.: Prentice Hall, 1993), 540–542.

5. "Using Derivatives: What Senior Managers Must Know," *Harvard Business Review,* January–February 1995, 33–41; ROBERT CLOW, "Beyond the Scarlet Ledger," *Institutional Investor,* February 1998, 56+; TIMOTHY O'BRIEN, "Asia Woes Bring Derivatives Headaches," *International Herald Tribune,* 28 February 1998, 9+; ILANA POLYAK, "With Supply Tight, Money Market Funds Finding Derivatives Less of a Dirty Word," *Bond Buyer,* 3 March 1998, 1; ROBERT CLOW, "Creativity Returns," *Institutional Investor,* January 1998, 115+.

6. SUMNER N. LEVINE, ed., *The Dow Jones–Irwin Business and Investment Almanac* (Homewood, Ill.: Dow Jones–Irwin, 1988), 453.

7. William Power, "Small Investors Are Punier Than Many Think," *Wall Street Journal,* 28 March 1989, C1, C10; Jordan E. Goodman, "Small Investors Reach for Rising Rates," *Money,* March 1995, 63; T. Carter Hagaman, "A Sure-Footed Path for Small Investors," *Management Accounting,* January 1995, 14; Tam Pui-Wing, "Mutual Affection," *Wall Street Journal,* 4 February 1998, C29; J. R. Brandstrader, "Hanging Tough: Through Thick and Thin, Small Investors Bet Heavily on Stocks," *Barron's,* 12 January 1998, F24+.

8. Jonathan Clements, "For a Calmer Portfolio: Just Add a Little Risk," *Wall Street Journal,* 24 June 1994, C1.

9. Harvey Shapiro, "You Gotta Have a Style," *Hemispheres,* July 1997, 53–55.

10. Martin L. Leibowitz and Stanley Kogelman, "Asset Allocation Under Shortfall Constraints," *Journal of Portfolio Management,* Winter 1991, 18–23; Charles J. Cardona, "The Asset Allocation Decision," *ABA Banking Journal,* February 1998, 94+.

11. John Waggoner, "Schwab, Fidelity Face Off," *USA Today,* 3 June 1994, 1.

12. Stephen Eckett, managing director of Numa Financial systems, personal communication, July 1997.

13. Julie Bort, "Trading Places," *Computerworld,* 27 May 1996, 105+.

14. John Sullivan, "Manic Monday, Turnaround Tuesday," *Editor & Publisher,* 1 November 1997, 8+.

15. Craig Torres and William Power, "Big Board Is Losing Some of Its Influence over Stock Trading," *Wall Street Journal,* 17 April 1990, A1, A6.

16. Stephan D. Solomon, "So You Want to Go Public," *Inc.,* June 1997, 77.

17. New York Stock Exchange Web site, <http://www.nyse.com>, accessed 22 February 1998.

18. Catherine Friend White, "At Home in the Global Marketplace," *Business Ethics,* September–October, 1993, 39–40.

19. Michael R. Sesit, "Going Global," *Wall Street Journal,* 28 May 1996, R23–R24; Marla Dickerson, "Going Global by Going Online," *Los Angeles Times,* 11 February 1998, D1; Tom Stein, "Going Global," *Information Week,* 2 February 1998, 84+; Catherine Curan, "Going Global: Act Like a Local," *WWD,* 9 February 1998, 16+.

20. Catherine Friend White, "At Home in the Global Marketplace," *Business Ethics,* September–October 1993, 39–40.

21. Diana B. Henriques, "In World Markets, Loose Regulation," *New York Times,* 23 July 1991, C1, C6–7.

22. "Tough Love at NASDAQ," *Business Week,* 3 November 1997, 150–151.

23. Scot J. Paltrow, "New NYSE Chief Grasso Aims to Lure Foreign Firms," *Los Angeles Times,* 1 June 1995, 2.

24. "NASDAQ's Success Comes with a Price," *USA Today,* 19 September 1995.

25. "Challenges of the Financial Cybercop," *Institutional Investor,* April 1997, 99.

26. John R Dorfman, "Crash Courses," *Wall Street Journal,* 28 May 1996, R12–R13.

27. Andrew Freeman, "Fixing What Is Brokin," *Economist,* 26 October 1996, S10–S15.

28. Kimberly Weisul, "New Mid-Tier Brokers to Get 60% of On-line Trades," *Investment Dealers Digest,* 30 September 1996, 11.

29. Sullivan, "Manic Monday, Turnaround Tuesday"; Peter Stein and Darren McDermott, "Asian Market Turmoil Hits Hong Kong," *Wall Street Journal,* 24 October 1997, A1, A19.

30. Anita Raghavan and Nancy Ann Jeffrey, "What, How, Why—So What Is the Dow Jones Industrial Average, Anyway?" *Wall Street Journal,* 28 May 1996, R30; Kathy Kristof, "It Is the Most-Quoted Stock Index, but Is It the Best Market Barometer?" *Los Angeles Times,* 7 August 1994, D1; Jan M. Rosen, "Higher Still and Higher," *New York Times,* 22 March 1998, B2; Joel Shernoff, "Euro Changes Index Battle: Dow Jones Enters Struggle for Benchmark Supremacy," *Pensions & Investments,* 23 March 1998, 38; Subrara N. Chakravarty and Ashlea Eberling, "Dow Jones, Oh, the Pity of It," *Forbes,* 23 March 1998, 46+; Justin Martin, "As Customers Go, So Goes the Dow," *Fortune,* 16 February 1998, 168.

31. Jeffrey M. Laderman, "Why It's So Tough to Beat the S&P," *Business Week,* 24 March 1997, 82–88; Martin Sosnoff, "The Hit Parade," *Forbes,* 9 March 1998, 239; Sharon R. King, "Another Day, Another High," *New York Times,* 13 February 1998, D5.

32. Andrew Rice, "Taking Stock of Fractions/Bill Pushing Markets to Switch to Decimal Systems," *Washington Briefing,* 8 June 1997, A21; Vanessa O'Connell, "Conversion to Decimal System Stocks Could Prove a Boon to Small Investors," *Wall Street Journal,* 6 June 1997, C1; Angela Acquaye, "NYSE Goes to Decimals," *Black Enterprise,* December 1997, 54; Floyd Norris, "Fractions Seem Near Extinction on Wall Street," *New York Times,* 4 June 1997, C1, C10.

33. John Heine, deputy director of the office of public affairs, Securities and Exchange Commission, Washington, D.C., personal communication, December 1991; Susan Antilla, "Wall Street: A Watchdog from the Other Side," *New York Times,* 10 October 1993, C13.

34. Rebecca Buckman, "NASD Maps War on Claims on Internet," *Wall Street Journal,* 24 March 1997, B98W.

35. "Challenges of the Financial Cybercop," *Institutional Investor,* April 1997, 99.

36. Adapted from William A. Francis, vice president, Landes Associates, Inc., Wilmington, Delaware, personal communication, 7 October 1991.

37. Index names from Alan Chai, Alta Campbell, and Patrick J. Spain, eds., *Hoover's Handbook of World Business, 1993* (Austin, Tex.: Reference Press, 1993), 90–97.

COMPONENT CHAPTER A

1. Jacqueline Davidson and Barbara Ettorre, "Need R&D Help? Ask the Feds," *Small Business Reports,* May 1994, 48–54.

2. *Survey of Current Business* (Washington, D.C.: GPO, December 1997), D9.

3. Richard M. Steuer, *A Guide to Marketing Law: What Every Seller Should Know* (New York: Harcourt Brace Jovanovich, 1986), 4–6.

4. Steve Hamm, Susan B. Garland, and Owne Ullmann, "Going After Gates," *Business Week,* 3 November 1997, 34.

5. Michael Connor, "Office Depot to Increase Openings After Staples Deal Nixed," *Reuters Business Report,* 1 July 1997, *Electric Library,* Online, 11 December 1997; Michael Hirsh, "But Nary a Trust to Bust," *Newsweek,* 2 June 1997, 44–45.

6. Linda Himelstein, Andy Reinhardt, and Susan Garland, "Intel: The Feds Are Loaded for Bear," *Business Week,* 13 October 1997, 36; John R. Wilke, "FTC Expected to Clear Intel Purchase of Chip Maker Amid Continuing Probe," *Wall Street Journal,*" 13 January 1988, A4.

7. William C. Frederick, Keith Davis, and James E. Post, *Business and Society,* 6th ed. (New York: McGraw-Hill, 1990), 158.

8. "Hundt Calls Internet Key to Competition," *Newsbytes News Network,* 28 August 1997, *Electric Library,* Online, 11 December 1997; Susan Benkelman, "Free Cyberspeech/Ruling Strikes Indecency Law," *Newsday,* 26 June 1997, A5, *Electric Library,* Online, 12 December 1997; "FCC Paper Seeks to Limit Internet Regulation," *Newsbytes News Network,* 31 March 1997, *Electric Library,* Online, 11 December 1997.

9. "Ma Bell's Family Leaves Home, 1982," *Wall Street Journal,* 1 December 1989, B1; Laura Evenson, "MCI Cuts Intrastate Telephone Call Rates," *San Francisco Chronicle,* 9 January 1990, C1, C12.

10. P. J. Huffstutter, "PacBell Seeking Buyers for Its Cable TV System," *Los Angeles Times,* 13 November 1997, A1, *Electric Library,* Online, 12 December 1997; Elizabeth Sanger, "Congress Asked to Freeze Cable Rates," *Newsday,* 18 September 1997, A3, *Electric Library,* Online, 12 December 1997; David Lieberman, "Sky's Fall Lets Cable Fly," *USA Today,* 20 May 1997, 2B, *Electric Library,* online, accessed 12 December 1997.

11. Robert J. Samuelson, "The Joy of Deregulation," *Newsweek,* 3 February 1997, 39; Anne Millen Porter, "Four Things Buyers Should Know about Deregulation," *Purchasing,* 12 March 1998, 50+; Bruce W. Radford, "No Clamor, No Choice," *Public Utilities Fortnightly,* 1 January 1998, 4+; "Handling," *Air Cargo World,* February 1998, 2; Brigid Simmonds, "Deregulation Gets New Name," *Leisure Management,* February 1998, 19.

12. Nicholas Lansman, "Consumer Protection in the EU (Cosmetics and Toiletries Industry)," *Soap Perfumery & Cosmetics,* 69 (1 July 1996): 29, *Electric Library,* Online, 11 December 1997.

13. Vicki Torres, "Firms Push for Some Breathing Room," *Los Angeles Times,* 22 October 1997, D9, *Electric Library,* Online, 12 December 1997; Stephen Blakely, "Clean-Air Rules Encounter Turbulence," *Nation's Business* 85 (1 September 1997): 12, *Electric Library,* Online, 12 December 1997; Paul Sonali, "EPA's Browner Targets Big Polluters on New Air Rule," *Reuters Business Report,* 17 July 1997, *Electric Library,* Online, 12 December 1997; John M. Broder, "Deregulation Crusade Shifts to Compromise," *New York Times,* 31 January 1997, C1–C2; Mark Lewyn, "Fewer Strings Attached," *Business Week/Enterprise,* John Carey et al., "The Regulators Rein Themselves In," *Business Week,* 21 August 1995.

14. Kari Huus, "Look Out, Chinese Love Solution," *Advertising Age International,* 28 September 1992, I6.

15. *Survey of Current Business,* D8.

16. Internal Revenue Service, Form 1040 Instructions for 1993, 25.

17. Carl Weiser, "Lobbying: Players Say It's More Than Fat Cats, Money, Back-Room Deals," *Gannett News Service,* 4 June 1997, *Electric Library,* Online, 11 December 1997; Joyce James, "Making a Difference on the Hill," *Black Enterprise,* April 1998, 18; Jill Abramson, "The High Price of Love," *New York Times,* 15 March 1998, WK2; Steven Burns, "How to Ask for What You Want," *Legal Times,* 23 February 1998, S40.

18. Melinda Henneberger, "An Arm Twister's Dream Job," *New York Times,* 24 June 1997, C1.

19. Richard L. Berke, "Donors to Parties Sidestepped Rules," *New York Times,* 18 May 1991, B7.

20. William M. Welch, "PAC Money Plays Follow the Leader," *USA Today,* 25 November 1997, 9A, *Electric Library,* Online, 11 December 1997.

21. Bill Shaw and Art Wolfe, *The Structure of the Legal Environment: Law, Ethics, and Business,* 2d ed. (Boston: PWS-Kent, 1991), 635.

22. Shaw and Wolfe, *The Structure of the Legal Environment: Law, Ethics, and Business,* 146.

23. Bruce Ingersoll, "Claim by Gerber for Baby Food Was Simply Mush, FTC Alleges," *Wall Street Journal,* 13 March 1997, B15.

24. Elizabeth MacDonald, "SEC Alleges KPMG Violated Rules by Auditing Client of Former Affiliate," *Wall Street Journal Interactive Edition,* 5 December 1997, Online, 5 December 1997.

25. George A. Steiner and John F. Steiner, *Business, Government, and Society* (New York: McGraw-Hill, 1991), 149.

26. Mike France, "Order in the Business Court," *Business Week,* 9 December 1996, 138–140.

27. Thomas W. Dunfee, Frank F. Gibson, John D. Blackburn, Douglas Whitman, F. William McCarty, and Bartley A. Brennan, *Modern Business Law* (New York: Random House, 1989), 164.

28. Jacqueline Bueno, "Home Depot to Fight Sex-Bias Charges," *Wall Street Journal,* 19 September 1997, B5; Edward Felsenthal, "Punitive Awards Are Called Modest, Rare," *Wall Street Journal,* 17 June 1996, B2.

29. Bartley A. Brennan and Nancy Kubasek, *The Legal Environment of Business* (New York: McGraw-Hill, 1990), 183.

30. William Underhill, "A Pyrrhic McVictory," *Newsweek,* 30 June 1997, 52.

31. Brennan and Kubasek, *The Legal Environment of Business,* 184.

32. Joseph Weber and Mike France, "The Gloves Come Off over Latex," *Business Week,* 16 June 1997.

33. "Reasonable Product-Liability Reform," *Nation's Business,* 85 (1 September 1997): 88, *Electric Library,* Online, 12 December 1997; "Product-Liability Deadlock," *Business Week,* 12 January 1998, 51.

34. Dunfee et al., *Modern Business Law,* 569.

35. "Reasonable Product-Liability Reform," 88; Stephen Blakely, "Getting a Handle on Liability Coverage," *Nation's Business,* 85 (1 September 1997): 87, *Electric Library,* Online, 12 December 1997; John M. Broder, "Clinton Vetoes Bill to Limit Product-Liability Lawsuits," *Los Angeles Times,* 3 May 1996, A1, *Electric Library,* Online, 12 December 1997.

36. Dunfee et al., *Modern Business Law,* 236.

37. Ethan A. Blumen, "Legal Land Mines," *Business 96,* June–July 1996, 53.

38. Dunfee et al., *Modern Business Law,* 284–297; Brennan and Kubasek, *The Legal Environment of Business,* 125–127; Douglas Whitman and John William Gergacz, *The Legal Environment of Business,* 2d ed. (New York: Random House, 1988), 196–197; *The Lawyer's Almanac* (Upper Saddle River, N.J.: Prentice Hall Law & Business, 1991), 888.

39. Brennan and Kubasek, *The Legal Environment of Business,* 128.

40. Elizabeth MacDonald, "E-Mail Trail Could Haunt Consultant in Court," *Wall Street Journal,* 19 June 1997, B1.

41. Roy Furchgott, "Opposition Builds to Mandatory Arbitration at Work," *New York Times,* 20 July 1997, F11; Barry Meier, "In Fine Print, Customers Lose Ability to Sue," *New York Times,* 10 March 1997, A1, C7.

42. Steur, *A Guide to Marketing Law,* 151–152.

43. Dunfee et al., *Modern Business Law,* 745, 749.

44. Brennan and Kubasek, *The Legal Environment of Business,* 160; Whitman and Gergacz, *The Legal Environment of Business,* 260.

45. Mike France and Sana Siwolop, "How to Skin a Copycat," *Business Week/Enterprise,* ENT 4.

46. Ira Sanger, "Big Blue Is Out to Collar Software Scofflaws," *Business Week,* 17 March 1997, 34; "E-Commerce: Who Owns the Rights?" *Business Week,* 29 July 1996, 65.

47. Tariq K. Muhammad, "Real Law in a Virtual World," *Black Enterprise,* December 1996, 44.

48. Jerry M. Rosenberg, *Dictionary of Business and Management* (New York: Wiley, 1983), 340.

49. Ronald A. Anderson, Ivan Fox, and David P. Twomey, *Business Law* (Cincinnati: South-Western Publishing, 1987), 635.

50. Brennan and Kubasek, *The Legal Environment of Business,* 516–517.

51. Dale Kasler, "Carson's Department Store Chain Manager Stronger After Bankruptcy," *Gannett News Service,* 21 November 1994, *Electric Library,* Online, 12 December 1997.

COMPONENT CHAPTER B

1. "Hurricanes and the Insurance Crisis," *American Business Review,* 21 September 1997, 2+; Matt Walsh, "Deeper Pockets,"" *Forbes,* 26 September 1994, 42–44.

2. John S. DeMott, "Think Like a Risk Manager," *Nation's Business,* June 1995, 30–32.

3. Stephanie D. Esters, "Experts: Mattel Snacktime Doll May Spur Claims," *National Underwriter,* 20 January 1997, 33+.

4. Mark S. Dorfman, *Introduction to Risk Management and Insurance,* 6th ed. (Upper Saddle River, N.J.: Prentice Hall, 1998), 135–136.

5. "America's Insurers: No Thrift Crisis," *The Economist,* 20 April 1991, 78–82.

6. Joseph B. Treaster, "Protecting Against the Little Risks," *New York Times,* 31 December 1996, C1, C15.

7. Gary Sanders, "ERISA Preempts State Stop-loss Regulation," *Life Association News,* June 1996, 148+; Joseph B. Treaster, "Protecting Against the Little Risks," *New York Times,* 31 December 1996, C1, C15.

8. Laura M. Litvan, "Switching to Self-Insurance," *Nation's Business,* March 1996, 16–21; Joseph B. Treaster, "Protecting Against the Little Risks," *New York Times,* 31 December 1996, C1, C15; Matt Roush, "Worker's Comp Study Says Self-Insurance Is Cheaper," *Crain's Detroit Business,* 5 January 1998, 3+.

9. Mary Beth Grover, "Start-up Interruptus," *Forbes,* 17 June 1996, 184–185.

10. Dorfman, *Introduction to Risk Management and Insurance,* 357.

11. DeMott, "Think Like a Risk Manager."

12. Dorfman, *Introduction to Risk Management and Insurance,* 319–320.

13. Dorfman, *Introduction to Risk Management and Insurance,* 322–323.

14. Dorfman, *Introduction to Risk Management and Insurance,* 505.

15. Chuck Jones, "Long-term Care Contracts Are Now Tax Qualified," *Life Association News,* November 1997, 74+; Richard L. Peck, "We Have to Look at What 'Long-Term Care' Really Means," *Nursing Homes,* January 1998, 32+.

16. Nancy L. Breuer, "Uncle Sam No Longer Has His Hand Out," *Workforce,* July 1997, 84–88.

17. Sidney Marchasin, "Cost Shifting: How One Hospital Does It," *Wall Street Journal,* 9 December 1991, A10.

18. "Health Reform Continues on the State Level," *Employee Benefit Plan Review,* December 1997, 48–49.

19. Michael A. Morrisey and Gail A. Jensen, "Switching to Managed Care in the Small Employer Market," *Inquiry—Blue Cross and Blue Shield Association,* Fall 1997, 237–248.

20. Joseph Burns, "Don't Settle for Good with Workers' Comp," *Managed Healthcare,* November 1997, 58+.

21. *Employee Benefits* (Washington, D.C.: U.S. Chamber of Commerce, 1991), 28.

22. *1991 Life Insurance Fact Book, Update* (Washington, D.C.: American Council of Life Insurance, 1991), 4.

23. Martin Kasindorf and Ken Fireman, "The Clinton Budget/2002Solution," *Newsday,* 7 February 1997, A04; Mark R. Greene and James S. Trieschmann, *Risk and Insurance* (Cincinnati: South-Western Publishing, 1988), 81.

24. Dorfman, *Introduction to Risk Management and Insurance,* 524.

25. Doug Bandow, "Let Big Business Fix Social Security," *Fortune,* 8 December 1997, 56–60.

26. Oren Levin-Waldman, "Unemployment Insurance for a New Age," *Challenge,* March–April 1997, 110–120.

27. Barbara A. Grumet, "Health Policy Reform in America: Innovations from the States," *American Review of Public Administration* 24, no. 3 (1994): 331–332.

28. Steven Findlay, "Health Care Woes Are Long-time Companions," *Business and Health,* November 1997, 17+.

29. Bronwyn Fryer, "Agents of Change," *CIO,* 1 November 1997, 50–54.

30. Fryer, "Agents of Change."

31. KELLY HOLLAND AND TIM SMART, "Midlife Crisis for Insurers," *Business Week,* 18 September 1995, 137–138; Treaster, "Protecting Against Little Risks."

32. FRYER, "Agents of Change."

APPENDIX I

1. SEWELL WHITNEY, "On-Line Résumés Put Job Candidates in Line," *Advertising Age,* 7 March 1985, 48.

2. "Quick Click," *U.S. News and World Report,* 29 April 1996, 70.

3. Adapted from RICHARD NELSON BOLLES, *The 1997 What Color Is Your Parachute?* (Berkeley, Calif.: Ten Speed Press, 1996), 129–166; KAREN W. ARENSON, "Placement Offices Leave Old Niches to Become Computerized Job Bazaars," *New York Times,* 17 July 1996, B12; LAWRENCE J. MAGID, "Job Hunters Cast Wide Net Online," *Los Angeles Times,* 26 February 1996, 20; RICHARD VAN DOREN, "On-Line Career Advice Speeds Search for Jobs," *Network World,* 4 March 1996, 54; ALEX MARKELS, "Job Hunting Takes Off in Cyberspace," *Wall Street Journal,* 20 September 1996, B1, B2; MICHAEL CHOROST, "Jobs on the Web," *Hispanic,* October 1995, 50–53; ZANE K. QUIBLE, "Electronic Résumés: Their Time Is Coming," *Business Communication Quarterly,* 58, no. 3 (1995): 5–9; MARGARET MANNIX, "The Home-Page Help Wanteds," *U.S. News and World Report,* 30 October 1995, 88, 90; PAM DIXON AND SILVIA TIERSTEN, *Be Your Own Headhunter Online* (New York: Random House, 1995), 53–69.

4. CAROL M. BARNUM, "Writing Résumés That Sell," *MW,* September–October 1987, 11.

5. PAM STANLEY-WEIGAND, "Organizing the Writing of Your Résumé," *The Bulletin of the Association for Business Communication,* 54, no. 3 (September 1991): 11–12.

6. JANICE TOVEY, "Using Visual Theory in the Creation of Résumés: A Bibliography," *The Bulletin of the Association for Business Communication,* 54, no. 3 (September 1991): 97–99.

7. SAL DIVITA, "If You're Thinking Résumé, Think Creatively," *Marketing News,* 14 September 1992, 29.

8. JENNIFER J. LAABS, "For Your Information," *Personnel Journal,* August 1993, 16.

9. DIXON AND TIERSTEN, *Be Your Own Headhunter Online,* 75.

10. BRONWYN FRYER, "Job Hunting the Electronic Way," *Working Woman,* March 1995, 59–60, 78; JOYCE LANE KENNEDY AND THOMAS J. MORROW, *Electronic Resume Revolution,* 2d ed. (New York: Wiley, 1995), 30–33; MARY GOODWIN, DEBORAH COHN, AND DONNA SPIVEY, *netjobs: Use the Internet to Land Your Dream Job* (New York: Michael Wolff, 1996), 149–150; QUIBLE, "Electronic Résumés: Their Time Is Coming," 5–9; ALFRED AND EMILY GLOSSBRENNER, *Finding a Job on the Internet* (New York: McGraw-Hill, 1995), 194–197; DIXON AND TIERSTEN, *Be Your Own Headhunter Online,* 80–83.

11. QUIBLE, "Electronic Résumés: Their Time Is Coming," 5–9; GOODWIN, COHN, AND SPIVEY, *netjobs,* 149–150.

12. SYLVIA PORTER, "Your Money: How to Prepare for Job Interviews," *San Francisco Chronicle,* 3 November 1981, 54.

13. JOEL RUSSELL, "Finding Solid Ground," *Hispanic Business,* February 1992, 42–44, 46.

14. ROBERT GIFFORD, CHEUK FAN NG, AND MARGARET WILKINSON, "Nonverbal Cues in the Employment Interview: Links Between Applicant Qualities and Interviewer Judgments," *Journal of Applied Psychology,* 70, no. 4 (1985): 729.

15. LOUIS S. RICHMAN, "How to Get Ahead in America," *Fortune,* 16 May 1994, 46–51; BRUCE NUSSBAUM, "I'm Worried About My Job," *Business Week,* 7 October 1991, 94–97.

16. LEE SMITH, "Landing That First Real Job," *Fortune,* 16 May 1994, 58–60; RICHMAN, "How to Get Ahead in America," 46–51; RUSSELL, "Finding Solid Ground," 42–46.

Illustration and Text Credits

CHAPTER 1

8 Martin Kasindorf and Ken Fireman, "The Clinton Budget/2002 Solution," *Newsday*, 7 February 1997, A4.

10 Exhibit 1.2, From "21st Century Capitalism." Reprinted from *Business Week*, November 18, 1994 by special permission, copyright © 1994, McGraw-Hill, Inc., 194.

14 (Gaining the Competitive Edge): Adapted from David Kirkpatrick, "Intel's Amazing Profit Machine," *Fortune* 17 February 1997, 60-72; "Processor Prices Plunge," *Purchasing* 123, no 4 (September 1997): 59; Andy Santoni and Dana Gardner, "Intel Pursues Faster and Cheaper Processors," *InfoWorld* 19, no. 38 (September 1997): 6; Ken Yamada and Kelly Spang, "Intel's MMX Road Map," *Computer Reseller News*, 10 March 1997, 1, 219; Andy Reinhardt, Ira Sager, and Peter Burrows, "Intel," *Business Week*, 22 December 1997, 70-77.

15 Exhibit 1.4, Christopher Caggiano, "Will the Real Bootstrappers Please Stand Up?" *Inc.*, August 1995, 34; Mike Hofman, "Capitalism—A Bootstrappers' Hall of Fame," *Inc.*, August 197, 54-57.

18 Exhibit 1.5, Adapted from *The Information Please Almanac 1997* (Boston: Houghton Mifflin, 1997), 144-291.

21 (Exploring Global Business): Adapted from Regina Fazio Maruca, "The Right Way to Go Global," *Harvard Business Review*, March-April 1994, 135-145; Carl Quintanilla, "Despite Setbacks, Whirlpool Pursues Overseas Markets," *Wall Street Journal*, 9 December 1997, B4; Stephen S. Johnson, "In the Wringer," *Forbes*, 16 December 1996, 386+; Kevin Parker, "Heads in a Whirl," *Manufacturing Systems* 15, no. 4 (April 1997): 50-54; Joe Jancsurak, "Whirlpool: U.S. Leader Pursues Global Blueprint," *Appliance Manufacturer* 45, No. 2 (February 1997): G21; Deborah Duarte and Nancy Snyder, "From Experience: Facilitating Global Organizational Learning in Product Development at Whirlpool Corporation," *Journal of Product Innovation Management* 14, No. 1 (January 1997): 48-55.

23 Exhibit 1.6, Martha Groves, "Managing in the Next Millennium; Bracing for the 21st Century," *Los Angeles Times*, 25 March 1996, D2-D16.

26 (A Case for Critical Thinking): Adapted from Louis Hecht, corporate secretary, Molex, personal communication, May 1997; Matt Krantz, "Molex Inc.'s Fred Krehbiel," *Investor's Business Daily*, 7 January 1997, 1; Paul Conley, "Molex Sets Record-Breaking Global Pace," *Chicago Tribune*, 2 August 1996, 6. Dave Savona, "The Billion-Dollar Globetrotter," *International Business*, November 1995, 52-56; Robert Knight, "How Molex Inc. Connected in World Markets," *Chicago Enterprise*, July-August 1994, 24-27; Ronald E. Yates, "Firm's Growth Tied to Global Connections," *Chicago Tribune*, 6 February 1994, 8.

29 "Is It True?" D. Keith Denton and Charles Boyd, *Did You Know? Fascinating Facts and Fallacies About Business*, (Englewood Cliffs, N.J.: Prentice Hall, 1994), 13, 39, 43.

CHAPTER 2

32 Exhibit 2.1, *World Almanac and Book of Facts 1997* (Mahwah, N.J.: K-III Reference Corporation, 1997), 145.

35 Exhibit 2.2, Roger Ahrens, "Going Global," *International Business*, July-August 1996, 30.

38 Exhibit 2.3, Adapted from *Survey of Current Business* (Washington, D.C.: GPO, November 1997), Table F.1, 35.

39 Exhibit 2.4, Adapted from Christopher Farrell, Michael J. Mandel, Keith Hammonds, Dori Jones Yang, and Paul Magnusson, "At Last, Good News," reprinted from June 3, 1991, issue of *Business Week*, by special permission. Copyright © 1991 by McGraw Hill, Inc. Updated from *Survey of Current Business*, November 1992, 6-7; *Survey of Current Business* 73, no. 9 (September 1993): 7; *Survey of Current Business* 74, no. 9 (September 1994): 79; *Statistical Abstract of the United States: 1997* (Washington, D.C. GPO, 1997), Table 1292, 788.

40 Exhibit 2.5, Adapted from Sylvia Nasar, "U.S. Trade Benefits from War," *New York Times*, 13 March 1991, C1. Copyright © 1991 by The New York Times Company. Reprinted by permission; updated from *Statistical Abstract of the United States: 1997* (Washington, D.C.: GPO, 1997), Table 1292, 788-789.

41 Exhibit 2.6, *Big Emerging Markets: 1996 Outlook* (Washington, D.C.: GPO, 1996), <http://www.statusa.gov/itabems.htm > (accessed 17 July 1997).

45 Exhibit 2.7, Adapted in part from Clemens P. Work and Robert F. Black, "Uncle Sam as Unfair Trader," *U.S. News and World Report*, 12 June 1989, 42-44; Tod G. Buchholz, "Free Trade Keeps Prices Down," *Consumers' Research Magazine*, 1995, excerpted from Todd G. Buchholz, *From Here to Economy: A Short-cut to Economic Literary* (New York: Dutton Signet, 1995).

50 (Thinking About Ethics): Adapted from Marina Lakhman, "Mr. Gates Goes to Moscow," *New York Times*, 13 October 1997, C5-C6; Louis Kraar, "How Corrupt Is Asia?" *Fortune*, 21 August 1995, 26; Dave Savona, "Waging War on Pirates," *International Business*, January 1995, 42-47; Dana Milbank, "Greasing Wheels," *Wall Street Journal*, 29 September 1995, A1, A7; James Cox, "China's CD Pirates Flourish," *USA Today*, 19 February 1996, B4; Laurie Flynn, "New Piracy Feared in CD-ROM Software," 8 January 1996, C3; Craig Mellow, "Russia, Making Cash from Chaos," *Fortune*, 17 April 1995, 145-151; Joyce Barnatham, "The Gloves Are Coming Off in China," *Business Week*, 15 May 1995, 60-61; Michael Elliott, "Corruption," *Newsweek*, 15 November 1994; Michael Specter, "The Latest Films for Just \$2: Russia's Video Piracy Booms," *New York Times*, 11 April 1995, A1, A7; James Cox, "Siphoning U.S. Companies' Knowledge," *USA Today*, 16 February 1996, B1, B2; Karl Schoenberger, "Hong Kong's Secret Weapon," *Fortune*, 25 November 1996, 141-142; Marc Levinson, "The Big Game," *Newsweek*, 1 April 1996, 36-37; Douglas Pasternak and Gordon Witkin, "The Lure of the Steal," *U.S. News and World Report*, 4 March 1996, 45-48; Louis Kraar, "The Risks Are Rising in China," *Fortune*, 6 March 1995, 179-180; John Kimelman, "The Lonely Boy Scout," *Financial World*, Fall 1994, 50-51.

53 Exhibit 2.9, "Foreign Exchange Rates (Annual), *Federal Reserve Statistical Release*, 5 January 1998, online, 8 January 1998.

54 (Focusing on Cultural Diversity): Adapted from David Ricks, "How to Avoid Business Blunders Abroad," *Business*, April-June 1994, 3-11.

58 (A Case for Critical Thinking): Adapted from Frank McCoy, "Doing Business in South Africa," *Black Enterprise*, May 1995, 58-68; Karen Fawcett, "Challenges, Opportunities in South Africa, Americans Find Niche in a Developing Democracy,

Economy," *USA Today*, 22 May 1996, A7; Dominic Dhilwayo, "South Africa: Stainless Ambitions Thwarted," *African Business*, September 1997, 42; G.J. Rossouw, "Business Ethics in South Africa," *Journal of Business Ethics* 16, No. 14 (October 1997): 1539-1547.

61 "Is It True?" D. Keith Denton and Charles Boyd, *Did You Know? Fascinating Facts and Fallacies About Business* (Englewood Cliffs, N.J.: Prentice Hall, 1994), 44, 85, 104.

CHAPTER 3

66 Exhibit 3.1 Adapted from Thomas Donaldson and Lee E. Preston, "The Stakeholder Theory of the Corporation: Concepts, Evidence, and Implications," *Academy of Management Review* 20 (1995): 68; John R. Boatright, *Ethics and the Conduct of Business*, 2d ed (Upper Saddle River, N.J.: Prentice Hall, 1997), 361.

68 (Thinking About Ethics): Adapted from Robert Hauptman and Susan Motin, "The Internet, Cyberethics, and Virtual Morality," *Online*, March 1994, 8-9; Erin Gallaway, "A Matter of Ethics," *PC Week*, 3 February 1997, 97, 102; Margaret Mannix and Susan Gregory Thomas, "Exposed Online," *U.S. News and World Report*, 23 June 1997, 33; "When Cyberloafers Can Put You in Legal Danger," *Personnel Journal*, December 1996, 58; Samuel Greengard, "Privacy, Entitlement or Illusion," *Personnel Journal*, May 1996, 74-78.

81 Exhibit 3.5, *Statistical Abstract of the United States: 1997* (Washington, D.C.: GPO, 1997), Table 645, 410-411.

83 Exhibit 3.6, Adapted from *The Information Please Almanac 1997* (Boston: Houghton Mifflin, 1997), 55.

85 Exhibit 3.7, *The World Almanac and Book of Facts 1998* (New York: St. Martin's Press, 1997), 168; *Statistical Abstract of the United States, 1997* (Washington, D.C.: GPO, 1997), Table 685, 438; *Statistical Abstract of the United States: 1987* (Washington, D.C.: GPO, 1987), Table 664, 400.

88 (Exploring Global Business): Adapted from Marlene C. Piturro, "Just Say . . . Maybe," *World Trade*, June 1992, 87-88, 90-91; Kent Hodgson, "Adapting Ethical Decisions to a Global Marketplace," *Mangement Review*, May 1992, 53-57; Jeffrey A. Fadiman, "A Traveler's Guide to Gifts and Bribes," *Harvard Business Review*, July-August 1986, 122-136.

93 (A Case for Critical Thinking): Adapted from Africa Gordon, "Annual Donations Help Callers' Chats Do a World of Good," *USA Today*, 24 February 1997, B3; David Judson, "Call 'Bribe' Toll Free and Lobby Your Congress Members," *Gannett News Service*, 31 January 1996, *Electric Library*, online, accessed 28 July 1997; "Working Assets Green Power," *Working Assets Homepage*, <http://www.wald.com> (accessed 4 August 1997); "A Decade of Making a Difference," *Working Assets Homepage*, <http://www.wald.com> (accessed 4 August 1997); "Funding Social Change—A Decade of Difference," *Working Assets Homepage*, <http://www.wald.com> (accessed 4 August 1997); "The Flash Activist Network," *Working Assets Homepage*, <http://www.wald.com> (accessed 4 August 1997); "Citizens Actions—July 1997," *Working Assets Homepage*, <http://www.wald.com> (accessed 4 August 1997); Jane Gross, "Laura S. Scher: She Took One Look at the Age of Greed and Made a Quick Left," *New York Times*, 7 November 1993, sec. 3, 8: Ann Hornaday, "Making a Difference," *Working Woman*, February 1993, 31,34; James W. Cawley, "Phone Business Isn't All Business," *San Diego Union-Tribune*, 1 November 1992, I1-I2.

97 "Is It True?" D. Keith Denton and Charles Boyd, *Did You Know? Fascinating Facts and Fallacies About Business* (Englewood Cliffs, N.J.: Prentice Hall, 1994), 69, 208, 216.

CHAPTER 4

100 Exhibit 4.1, *The World Almanac and Book of Facts*, 1998 (Mahwah, N.J.: K-III Reference Corporation, 1997), 125.

101 Exhibit 4.2, Adapted from *Survey of Current Business* (Washington, D.C.: GPO, November 1997), Table B8, 132.

106 Exhibit 4.4, Reprinted with the permission of Simon & Schuster, Inc. from the Macmillan College text *The Legal Environment of Business*, 2d ed ., by Charles R. McGuire, Copyright © 1986, 1989 by Merrill Publishing, an imprint of Macmillan College Publishing Company, Inc., 216.

115 (Focusing on Cultural Diversity): Lori Lionnou, "It's a Small World After All," *International Business*, February 1994, 82-88.

116 (Thinking About Ethics): Adapted from Erick Schonfeld, "Have the Urge to Merge? You'd Better Think Twice," *Fortune*, 31 March 1997, 114-116; Phillip L. Zweig et al., "The Case Against Mergers," *Business Week*, 30 October 1995, 122-130; Kevin Kelly et al., "Mergers Today, Trouble Tomorrow?" *Business Week*, 12 September 1994.

118 Exhibit 4.7, Adapted from Charles V. Bagli, "Conditions Are Right for a Takeover Frenzy," *New York Times*, 2 January 1997, C3; Greg Steinmetz, "Mergers and Acquisitions Set Records, but Activity Lacked That 80s Pizazz," *Wall Street Journal*, 3 January 1995, R8.

126 (A Case for Critical Thinking): Adapted from Brent Bowers and Udayan Gupta, "Shareholder Suits Beset More Small Companies," *Wall Street Journal*, 9 March 1994, B1-B2; "High-Tech Industry Calls for Legislation to Stop Abusive Lawsuits," *U.S. Newswire*, 10 March 1997; David R. Sands, "Senate Vote Completes Override of Lawsuit-Reform Bill Veto," *Washington Times*, 1 January 1996, 12; U.S. Senate Subcommittee on Securities of the Committee on Banking, Housing, and Urban Affairs, *Ten Things We Know and Ten Things We Don't Know About the Private Securities Litigation Reform Act of 1995, Joint Written Testimony of Joseph A. Grundfest and Michael A. Perino*, Stanford Law School, 24 July 1997; "California Web Site Creates Electronic Courthouse," *Newsbytes News Network*, 9 December 1996; U.S. Senate Subcommittee on Securities Hearing on Abusive Shareholder Lawsuits, *Testimony of George Sollman, President and CEO Centigram Communications Corporation San Jose, California on Behalf of the American Electronics Association*, 2 March 1995, 104th Congress, American Electronics Association, 1997, on-line, 18 August 1997.

129 "Is It True?" Adapted from D. Keith Denton and Charles Boyd, *Did You Know? Fascinating Facts and Fallacies About Business* (Englewood Cliffs, N.J.: Prentice Hall, 1994), 3, 162, 218.

CHAPTER 5

133 Exhibit 5.1, Adapted from Carrie Dolan, "Entrepreneurs Often Fail as Managers," *Wall Street Journal*, 15 May 1989. Reprinted

by permission of The Wall Street Journal, © 1989 Dow Jones & Company, Inc. All Rights Reserved Worldwide, B1.

134 Exhibit 5.2, Adapted from John Case, "Disciples of David Birch" *Inc.*, January 1989, 41. Reprinted with permission, *Inc.* Magazine, January 1989. Copyright © 1989 Goldhirsch Group, Inc., 38 Commercial Wharf, Boston, Mass 02110.

135 Exhibit 5.3, *Inc. Special Edition—The State of Small Business 1997*, 20 May 1997, 114. Reprinted with permission of Inc. magazine, Goldhirsch Group, Inc., 38 Commercial Wharf, Boston, Mass 02110.

134 Exhibit 5.4, Adapted from Carol Lawson, "Life's Miraculous Transmissions," *New York Times*, 6 June 1996, B3; Nancy Rotenier, "La Tempesta," *Forbes*, 18 December 1995, 134-135; Anne Murphy, "Entrepreneur of the Year," *Inc.*, December 1995, 38-51; Christina F. Watts and Loyde Gite, "Emerging Entrepreneurs," *Black Enterprise*, November 1995, 100-110; Marc Ballon, "Pretzel Queen," *Forbes*, 13 March 1995, 112-113; Robet La Fanco, "Beach Bum Makes Good," *Forbes*, 19 June 1995, 80-82.

139 Exhibit 5.5, Adapted from Geoffrey N. Smith and Paul B. Brown, "Sweat Equity." Excerpted in *Macmillan Executive Summary Program*, December 1996, 3, 4.

139 Exhibit 5.6, <http://www.businessknowhow.com, (accessed 19 September 1997).

140 (Gaining the Competitive Edge): Adapted from Jay Finegan, "Unconventional Wisdom," *Inc.*, December 1994, 44-59; Alan J. Wax, "Range Wars," *Newsday*, 26 February 1996, C01; "Outback Shares Tumble on Weak Sales," *Reuters Business Report*, 1 October 1997, 4.

142 Exhibit 5.7, *Statistical Abstract of the United States 1994* (Washington, D.C.: GPO), 790; Marlal Dickeson, "Chain Reaction," *Los Angeles Times*, 5 September 1997, 1, 5; Roberta Maynard, "The Changing Landscape," *Nation's Business*, January 1997, 54-55.

144 Exhibit 5.8, Adapted from Alfred Edmond, Jr., "The B.E. Franchise Start-Up Guide," *Black Enterprise*, September, 1990, 75. Reprinted by permission of Earl G. Graves Publishing Co.

150 (Understanding the High-Tech Revolution): Adapted from Brian Hurley and Peter Birkwood, *A Small Business Guide to Doing Big Business on the Internet* (Vancouver, Canada: International Self-Counsel Press, 1996), 124-134.

155 (A Case for Critical Thinking): Adapted from Edward O. Welles, "There Are No Simple Businesses Anymore," *Inc.*, 16 May 1995, 66-79; Karen E. Carney, "Will the Family Business Survive?" *Inc.*, 17, no. 7 (May 1995): 70; Jill Andresky Fraser, "Innocents Abroad: Financial Strategies for Exporting," *Inc.*, 12, no. 5 (May 1990): 113-115.

159 "Is It True?" 1. L.A. Winokur, "Big Doubts—Small Business Isn't Necessarily a Stepping Stone to a Corporate Career," *Wall Street Journal*, 22 May 1997, R24. 2. *Inc. Special Edition—The State of Small Business 1997*, 20 May 1997, 111. 3. Roberta Maynard, "The Changing Landscape," *Nation's Business*, January 1997, 54.

CHAPTER 6

167 Exhibit 6.2, Adapted from Richard L. Daft, *Management*, 4th ed. (Fort Worth, Tex.: Dryden, 1997), 279, 282.

168 (Thinking About Ethics): Adapted from Andrew S. Grove, "What's the Right Thing? Everyday Ethical Dilemmas," *Working Woman*, June 1990, 16-18; John Case, "Honest Business," *Inc.*, January 1990, 59-65; Kenneth R. Andrews, "Ethics in Practice," *Harvard Business Review*, September-October 1989, 99-104.

169 Exhibit 6.3, Adapted from Courtland Bovée, et al., *Management* (New York: McGraw Hill, 1993), 678.

172 Exhibit 6.4, Adapted from *Management*, 2d ed, by Richard L. Daft, copyright © 1991 by The Dryden Press, reprinted by permission of the publisher. Based on information in Christie Brown, "Sweat Chic," *Forbes*, 5 September 1988, 130.

176 Exhibit 6.5, Adapted and reprinted by permission of *Harvard Business Review*, an exhibit from "How to Choose a Leadership Pattern" by Robert Tannenbaum and Warren H. Schmidt, May-June 1973. Copyright © 1973 by the President and Fellows of Harvard College, all rights reserved.

178 (Focus on Cultural Diversity): Adapted from Rob Goffee and Gareth Jones, "What Holds the Modern Company Together?" *Harvard Business Review*, November-December 1996, 133-134; Leah Beth Ward, "Diversity, It's About More Than Rice and Gender, Expert Says," *Gannett News Service*, 2 April 1996, S11, Electric Library, Online, accessed 26 September 1997; Ellen Neuborne, "Diversity Challenges Many Companies," *USA Today*, 18 November 1996, 10B; Ellen Neuborne, "NAACP Honors Procter & Gamble, Sara Lee," *USA Today*, 18 November 1996, 10B; Diversity at Microsoft, www.microsoft.com/diversity, (accessed 5 September 1997)).

181 Exhibit 6.7, Adapted from Courtland L. Bouvée et al., *Management* (New York: McGraw-Hill, 1993), 218-219.

186 (A Case for Critical Thinking): Adapted from Steve Kerr, interview by Richard M. Hodgetts, *Organizational Dynamics* (1 March 1996), 68, no.(12), *Electric Library*, Online, 10 September 1997; Anne Fisher, "The World's Most Admired Companies," *Fortune*, 27 October 1997, 220-228; John S. McClenahen, "Jack's Men," *Industry Week* 246, No. 13 (July 1997): 12-17; "A Blast from Neutron Jack," *Business Week*, 24 March 1997, 182; *General Electric 1993 Annual Report*, 3-5; "Jack Welch's Lessons for Success," *Fortune*, 25 January 1993, 86-89, 92-93; Linda Grant, "The Management Model That Jack Built," *Los Angeles Times Magazine*, 9 May 1993, 20+; James C. Hyatt and Amal Kumar Naj, "GE Is No Place for Autocrats, Welch Decrees," *Wall Street Journal*, 3 March 1992, B1, B10; Noel Tichy and Ram Charan, "Speed, Simplicity, Self-Confidence: An Interview with Jack Welch," *Harvard Business Review*, September-October 1989, 112-120; Stratford P. Sherman, "Today's Leaders Look to Tomorrow," *Fortune*, 26 March 1990, 30-32; Martha H. Peak, "Anti-Manager Names Manager of the Year," *Management Review*, October 1991, 7.

189 "Is It True?" Adapted from D. Keith Denton and Charles Boyd, *Did You Know? Fascinating Facts and Fallacies About Business* (Englewood Cliffs, N.J.: Prentice Hall, 1994), 11, 171, 197.

CHAPTER 7

198 Exhibit 7.5, Adapted from Fred R. DAvid, *Strategic Management*, 6th ed. (Upper Saddle River, N.J.: Prentice Hall, 1997), 224.

198 Exhibit 7.6, Adapted from *Time Warner 1993 Annual Report.*

199 Exhibit 7.8, Adapted from *Johnson & Johnson 1993 Annual Report.*

199 Exhibit 7.9, Adapted from *Quaker Oats 1993 Annual Report.*

202 (Gaining the Competitive Edge): Adapted from A.J. Vogel, "Reengineering," *Across the Board*, June 1993, 26-33; Thomas Vollmann, "Downsizing," *European Management Journal* 11, no. 1 (March 1993): 18-28; Ronald Henkoff, "Cost Cutting: How to Do It Right," *Fortune*, 9 April 1990, 40-53; Andrall E. Pearson, "Tough-Minded Ways to Get Innovative," *Harvard Business Review*, May-June 1998, 99-106; John H. Sheridan, "Aligning Structure with Strategy," *Industry Week*, 15 May 1989, 15-23; Patricia Sellers, "Pepsi keeps on Going After No. 1," *Fortune*, 11 March 1991, 62-70; Amanda Bennett, "Downsizing Doesn't Necessarily Bring an Upswing in Corporate Profitability," *Wall Street Journal*, 6 June 1991, B1; Joseph R. Mancuso and Lori Ioannou, "Trail Blazers: How Callaway Runs His Idea Factory," *Your Company*, 1 April 1997, 72; Jodi Wilgoren, "Wanted: Ideas to Save $220 Million; Reward: Lunch with the Mayor," *Los Angeles Times*, 1 March 1996, B3; Steven E. Gross, "When Jobs Become Team Roles, What Do You Pay For?" Compensation and Benefits Review, 20 January 1997, *Electric Library*, Online, 18 September 1997; Alex Markels and Matt Murray, "Slashed and Burned," *Wall Street Journal*, 14 May 1996, A1, A15.

206 Exhibit 7.11 Richard L. Daft, *Management*, 4th ed. (Fort Worth, Tex.: Dryden, 1997), 601.

210 (Understanding the High-Tech Revolution): Adapted from Melanie Warner, "Working at Home—The Right Way to Be a Star in Your Bunny Slippers," *Fortune*, 3 March 1997, 165+, *Electric Library*, Online, 25 September 1997; "A New National Survey Reports Sharp Rise in Telecommuting," *M2 PressWIRE*, 3 July 1997, *Electric Library*, Online, 25 September 1997; "KPMG Peat Marwick Launches Telecommuting Practice," *Newsbytes News Network*, 2 July 1997, *Electric Library*, Online, accessed 25 September 1997; Sheila McConnell, "The Role of Computers in Reshaping the Work Force," *Monthly Labor Review* 3, no. 3 (1 August 1996), *Electric Library*, Online, 25 September 1997; Lucas Spencer, "Staffing the Virtual Office," *Memphis Business Journal*, 20 November 1995, 1A, *Electric Library*, Online 18 September 1997; Kirk Johnson, "High-Tech Mobile Workers Transform Face and the Culture of Companies," *New York Times*, 8 February 1994, C19.

213 Exhibit 7.12, John V. Thill and Courtland L. Bovée, *Excellence in Business Communication*, 3rd ed. (Upper Saddle River, N.J.: Prentice Hall, 1997), 7.

221 (A Case for Critical Thinking): Adapted from John Fontana, "Top of the News: Chrysler Saves Big Online," *Communications Week*, 28 April 1997, 1+, *Electric Library*, Online, 25 September 1997; Jerry Flint, "Company of the Year: Chrysler," *Forbes*, 13 January 1997, 83-87; Robert Porter Lynch and Iain Somerville, "The Shift from Vertical to Networked Integration," *Physican Executive* 13 No. 6 (May 1996), *Electric Library*, Online, September 1997; Eve Tahmincioglu, "How GM's Team Approach Works," *Gannett News Service*, 25 April 1996, S11+, *Electric Library*, Online, 25 September 1997; Tim Keenan, "Snake Pit Suppliers: Viper Vendors Contribute Technology to New Coupe," *Ward's Auto World*, 134, no. 2 (1 March 1996), *Electric Library*, Online, 25 September 1997.

223 "Is It True?" 1. Sherwood Ross, "The Boss's Open Door Means More Time for Employees," *Reuters Business Report*, 30 September 1996, *Electric Library*, Online, accessed 18 September 1997. 2. Ellen Neuborne, "Why Teams Fail," *USA Today*, 25 February 1997. 3. S.C. Gwyne and John F. Dickerson, "Lost in the E-mail," Time, 21 April 1997, *Electric Library*, Online, 4 February 1998.

CHAPTER 8

231 Exhibit 8.2, Adapted from Roberta S. Russell and Bernard W. Taylor III, *Operations Management: Focusing on Quality and Competitiveness*, 2d ed. (Upper Saddle River, N.J.: Prentice Hall, 1998), 258.

232 (Understanding the High-Tech Revolution): Adapted from Gene Bylinsky, "The Digital Factory," *Fortune*, 14 November 1994, 92-110; John S. DeMott, "Look, World, No Hands!" *Nation's Business*, June 1994, 41-42; Ron Pidgeon, "Getting to Grips with High-Speed Product Handling," *Packaging Week*, 12 May 1994, 24-25.

237 Exhibit 8.3 Adapted from Courtland L. Bovée, et al., *Management* (New York: McGraw-Hill, 1993), 648; Roberta S. Russell and Bernard W. Taylor III, *Operations Management: Focusing on Quality and Competitiveness*, 2d ed. (Upper Saddle River, N.J.: Prentice Hall, 1998), 294.

243 Exhibit 8.5, Adapted from Courtland L. Bovée, et al., *Management* (New York: McGraw-Hill, 1993), 661.

244 Exhibit 8.6, Adapted from National Institute of Standards and Technology, *National Quality Program, Award Criteria*, <http://nist.gov/public_affairs/guide/qpage.htm> (accessed 11 February 1998).

245 (Exploring Global Business): Adapted from Richard W. Stevenson, "Auto Aristocrat Trims Down," *New York Times*, 8 March 1994, C1, C4; Brian S. Moskal, "The Rescue of the Gilded Lady," *Industry Week*, 17 January 1994, 15-16, 18.

248 Exhibit 8.8, Adapted from Gerald H. Graham, *The World of Business* (Reading, Mass.: Addison-Wesley, 1985), 199.

252 (A Case for Critical Thinking): Adapted from "Customer Service Is the Key to Supply Chain Excellence, According to KPMG," *M2PressWire*, 2 October 1997, *Electric Library*, Online, 6 October 1997; Herman Mehling, "Company Scores Big in Customer Support—Okidata Right on Track," *Computer Reseller News*, 29 September 1997, 53, *Electric Library*, Online, 6 October 1997; N. Craig Smith, Robert J. Thomas, and John A. Quelch, "A Strategic Approach to Managing Product Recalls," *Harvard Business Review*, September-October 1996, 104; Ronald Henkoff, "Service Is Everybody's Business," *Fortune*, 27 June 1994.

255 "Is It True?" Adapted from D. Keith Denton and Charles Boyd, *Did You Know? Fascinating Facts and Fallacies About Business* (Englewood Cliffs, N.J.: Prentice Hall, 1994), 166, 170, 183-184.

CHAPTER 9

262 Exhibit 9.3, Adapted from *Management*, 2d ed. by Richard L. Draft, copyright © 1991 by The Dryden press, reproduced by permission of the publisher.

265 Exhibit 9.4, U.S. Bureau of the Census, presented in Richard W. Judy and Carol D'Amico, *Workforce 2020* (Indianapolis: The Hudson Institute, 1997), 94.

267 Exhibit 9.5, Adapted from *Statistical Abstract of the United States: 1997* (Washington, D.C.: GPO, 1997), 397; *Statistical Abstract of the United States: 1987* (Washington, D.C.: GPO, 1987), 376; *Statistical Abstract of the United States: 1977* (Washington, D.C.: GPO, 1977), 388.

267 Exhibit 9.6, Richard W. Judy and Carol D'Amico, *Workforce 2020* (Indianapolis: The Hudson Institute, 1997), 109.

268 Exhibit 9.7, Patricia Arredondo, *Successful Diversity Management Initiatives* (Thousand Oaks, Calif.: Sage Publications, 1996), 18.

269 (Focusing on Cultural Diversity): Adapted from Dawn Gunsch, "Games Augment Diversity Training," *Personnel Journal*, June 1993, 78-83; Mary J. Winterle, "Toward Diversity, with Carrots and Sticks," *Across the Board*, January-February 1993, 50; "Diversity: Managing Diversity for Competitive Advantage," *Management Review*, April 1993, 6; Lena Williams, "Scrambling to Manage a Diverse Workforce," *New York Times*, 15 December 1992, A1, C2; Audrey Edwards, Suzanne B. Laporte, and Abby Livingston, "Cultural Diversity in today's Corporations," first appeared in *Working Woman* magazine. Copyright © 1991 by W.W.T. Partnership.

272 (Thinking About Ethics): Adapted from San Howe Verhovek, "Clash of Cultures Tears Texas City," *New York Times*, 30 September 1997, A10; Joseph D'Obrian, "Only English Speakers Need Apply," *Management Review*, January 1991, 41-45; Seth Mydans, "Pressure for English-Only Job Rules Stirring a Sharp Debate Across U.S.," *New York Times*, 8 August 1990, A12; L. Erik Bratt and Fred Alvarez, "English Only Memo Outrages Employees," *San Diego Union*, 15 September 1990, C1.

274 Exhibit 9.8, Adapted from Suzy Parker, "A Look at Statistics that Shape Your Finances," *USA Today*, 24 January 1990, 1B. Copyright 1990, *USA Today*, reprinted with permission.

275 Exhibit 9.9, Barbara Bronson Gray, "Magic Motivators," *Business97*, December-January 1997, 54.

284 (A Case for Critical Thinking): Adapted from Adolph Haasen and Gordon F. Shea, *A Better Place to Work* (New York: American Management Association, 1997), 13-21; Jessica Lee, "Approach Seems Flighty, but It Works," *USA Today*, 11 November 1996, 9B, *Electric Library*, Online, 18 October 1997; Kathy Balog, "Nuts!—Take It with a Grain of Sale," *USA Today*, 11 November 1996, 9B, *Electric Library*, Online, 18 October 1997; Donald J. McNerney, "Employee Motivation: Creating a Motivated Workforce," *HR Focus* 73 (1 August 1996): 1, *Electric Library*, Online, 18 October 1997.

287 "Is It True?" D. Keith Denton and Charles Boyd, *Did You Know? Fascinating Facts and Fallacies About Business* (Upper Saddle River, N.J.: Prentice Hall, 1994), 65, 204, 208.

CHAPTER 10

292 Exhibit 10.2, Adapted from Richard W. Judy and Carol D'Amico, *Workforce 2020* (Indianapolis: The Hudson Institute, 1997) 78, 80.

293 Exhibit 10.3, Adapted from Richard W. Judy and Carol D'Amico, *Workforce 2020* (Indianapolis: The Hudson Institute, 1997) 81-84.

295 Exhibit 10.4, Adapted from Louis E. Boone and David L. Kurtz, *Management*, 4th ed. (New York: McGraw Hill, 1992), 278. Reprinted by permission of the publisher.

298 Exhibit 10.5, Adapted from "The Interview Process," *Small Business Reports*, December 1987, 64.

300 (Thinking About Ethics): Adapted from Ellen Neuborne, "Putting Job Seekers to the Test," *USA Today*, 9 July 1997, 1B, *Electric Library*, Online, 30 October 1997; Joanne Kenen, "Experts Urge Limits to Genetic Tests in Workplace," *Reuters Business Report*, 30 March 1997, Electric Library, Online, 30 October 1997; Randall S. Schuler, *Managing Human Resources* (Cincinnati: South-Western College Publishing, 1998), 332; Jeffrey A. Mello, "Personality Tests and Privacy Rights," *HR Focus* 73 (1 March 1996): 22, *Electric Library*, Online, 30 October 1997; Alessandra Bianchi, "The Character-Revealing Handwriting Analysis," *Inc.*, February 1996, 77; U.S. Department of Labor, *Prevalence of Drug Testing in the Workplace* (Washington, D.C.: GPO, 1996), *Electric Library*, Online, 29 October 1997; Jennifer J. Laabs, "Balancing Spirituality and Work," *Personnel Journal*, September 1995, 67.

303 Exhibit 10.6 Adapted from Larry Stevens, "The Intranet: Your Newest Training Tool?" *Personnel Journal*, July 1996, p. 28. Copyright July 1996. Used with permission of ACC Communications Inc./*Personnel Journal* (now known as *Workforce*), Costa Mesa, Calif. All rights reserved.

304 (Understanding the High-Tech Revolution): Adapted from Lewis J. Perelman, "Kanban to Kan-brain," *Forbes ASAP*, April 1994, 85-95.

307 Exhibit 10.8, Adapted from "The Boss's Pay," *Wall Street Journal*, 10 April 1997, R15.

311 Exhibit 10.9, Adapted from Sarah Bowen, "Enough!" *Wall Street Journal*, 11 April 1996, R6.

312 Exhibit 10.10, Del Jones "Firms Take New Look at Sick Days" *USA Today*, 8 October, 1996, 8B. Copyright © 1996, USA TODAY. Reprinted by permission.

321 (A Case for Critical Thinking): Adapted from Charlene Marmer Solomon, "Big Mac's McGlobal HR Secrets," *Personnel Journal*, April 1996, 47-54; Gillian Flynn, "Can't Get This Big Without HR Deluxe," *Personnel Journal*, December 1996, 47-53; Amy Zuber, "'People—the Single Point of Difference'—Motivating Them," *Nation's Restaurant News* 31, no. 40 (October 1997): 114-116; Shelly Branch, What's Eating McDonald's? *Fortune*, 13 October 1997, 122-125; McDonald's Focuses on Similarities, *HRMagazine* 42, no. 7 (July 1997): 107.

323 "Is It True?" D. Keith Denton and Charles Boyd, *Did You Know? Fascinating Facts and Fallacies About Business* (Upper Saddle River, N.J.: Prentice Hall, 1994), 62, 119, 133.

CHAPTER 11

328 Figure 11.2, *The World Almanac and Book of Facts*, 1998 (Mahwah, N.J.: K-III Reference Corporation, 1997), 152.

330 Exhibit 11.3, U.S. Bureau of Labor Statistics, as reported in James Worsham, "Labor's New Assault," *Nation's Business*, June 1997, 22.

332 Exhibit 11.4, C.D. Gifford, Ed., *Directory of U.S. Labor Organizations*, 1996 Edition, Bureau of National Affairs (Washington, D.C.: GPO, 1996) p. 2, as presented in E. Edward Her-

man, *Collective Bargaining and Labor Relations*, 4th ed. (Upper Saddle River, N.J.: Prentice Hall, 1998), 82.

334 (Gaining the Competitive Edge): Adapted from Dana Milbank, "Labor Broadens Its Appeal by Setting Up Associations to Lobby and Offer Services," *Wall Street Journal*, 13 January 1993, B1, B4; John Hoerr, "What Should Unions Do?" *Harvard Business Review*, May-June 1991, 44-45; "Labor Letter," *Wall Street Journal*, 26 January 1991, A1; Dana Milbank, "Farm from the Mill," *Wall Street Journal*, 23 May 1991, A1.

338 Exhibit 11.8, U.S. Department of Labor, Bureau of Labor Statistics, *Compensation and Working Conditions* (Washington, D.C.: GPO, June 1991, June 1992, June 1993, June 1994); *The World Almanac Book of Facts*, 1998 (Mahwah, N.J.: K-III Reference Corporation, 1997), 109; *Employment Cost Trends*, *www.bls.gov* (online, accessed 8 January 1997); *Statistical Abstract of the United States*, 1994 (Washington, D.C.: GPO, 1994), 448.

345 (Exploring Global Business): Adapted from Randall S. Schuller, *Managing Human Resources* (Cincinnati: South-Western College Publishing, 1998), 649-652; Lloyd G. Reynolds, Stanley H. Masters, and Colletta H. Moser, *Labor Economics and Labor Relations* 11th ed. (Upper Saddle River, N.J.: Prentice Hall, 1998), 436-439; "Bashing the Unions," *The Economist*, 14 September 1996, 59.

352 (A Case for Critical Thinking): Adapted from Donald D. Tippett and Joseph Costa, "Labor Adversaries Bury the Hatchet," *Personnel Journal*, May 1996, 100-107; "People," *Aerospace Daily* 171, no. 58 (September 1994): 466; "Contracts," *Pittsburgh Business Times* 11, no. 14 (November 1991): 31; "Incumbents Picked by Air Force for AEDC O&M Contracts," *Aerospace Daily* 155, no. 9 (July 1990): 74; "SSI Services Receives $540 Million Contract from the Air Force," *Wall Street Journal*, 5 July 1990, A12.

355 "Is It True?" 1. D. Keith Denton and Charles Boyd, *Did You Know? Fascinating Facts and Fallacies About Business* (Upper Saddle River, N.J.: Prentice Hall, 1994), 141. 2. David Cay Johnston, "On Payday, Union Jobs Stack Up Very Well," *New York Times*, 31 August 1997, F1. 3. Margot Hornblower, "Picking a Fight," *Time*, 25 November 1996, 64.

CHAPTER 12

361 Exhibit 12.2, Courtland Bovée, Michael Houston and John V. Thill, *Marketing*, 2d ed (New York: McGraw Hill, 1994), 12.

362 Exhibit 12.3 Adapted from Mary J. Cronin, *Doing More Business On the Internet* (New York: Van Nostrand Reinhold, 1995), 61.

364 (Understanding the High-Tech Revolution): Adapted from Christine Bushey, "Interview with Peapod Founder John Furton," *MSNBC Business Video*, 13 August 1997; "How Peapod Is Customizing the Virtual Supermarket," *Harvard Business Review*, March-April 1995, 109; Larry E. Long, *Introduction to Computers and Information Systems* 5th ed. (Upper Saddle River, N:J: Prentice Hall, 1997), C24-C25; Kate Murphy, "Grocery Shopping in Cyberspace Means No Squeezing the Produce," *New York Times*, 12 May 1997, C4.

366 Exhibit 12.4, Joan O. Fredericks and James M. Salter, "Beyond Customer Satisfaction," *Management Review*, May 1995, p. 29.

367 Exhibit 12.5, Frederick Reichheld, "Loyalty and the Renaissance of Marketing" *Marketing Management*, 2 no. 4 (1994): 17. Reprinted by permission of American Marketing Association.

368 Exhibit 12.6, Adapted from William F. Schoell and Joseph P. Guiltinan, *Marketing: Contemporary Concepts and Practices*, 3d ed. (Boston: Allyn & Bacon, 1988), 215. Copyright © 1988 by Allyn & Bacon. Reprinted with permission; adapted from Samual C. Certo, Max E. .Douglas, and Stewart W. Husted, *Business*, 2d ed., Allyn & Bacon, 1988.

371 Exhibit 12.7, Courtland Bouvée, Michael Houston and John V. Thill, *Marketing*, 2d ed. (New York: McGraw Hill, 1994), 109.

374 (Thinking about Ethics): Adapted from Andrew L. Shapiro, "Privacy for Sale," *The Nation*, 23 June 1997, 11-16; Stephen M. Silverman, "Information Backlash," *Inc. Technology* no. 2, (1995): 27; R.C. Baker, Roge Dickinson, and Stanley Hollander, "Big Brother 1994: Marketing Data and the IRS," *Journal of Public Policy & Marketing* 5 (1986): 213; "Is Nothing Private?" *Business Week*, 4 September 1989, 74-82; "Privacy vs. Free Speech," *Direct Marketing*, May 1989, 42; Robert J. Posch, Jr., "Can We Have á la Carte Constitutional Rights?" *Direct Marketing*, July 1989, 76; Bruce Horovitz, "Marketers Tap Data We Once Called Our Own," *USA Today*, 19 December 1995, 1A-2A; Linda Himelstein, Ellen Neuborne, and Paul M. Eng, "Web Ads Start to Click," *Business Week*, 6 october 1997, 128-138.

376 Exhibit 12.8, Terry G. Varva, *Aftermarketing: How to Keep Customers for Life Through Relationship Marketing* (New York: McGraw Hill, 1995), 91.

382 "Is It True?" 1. Jade River Designs, *The 6 Myths of Web Marketing*, January 1998, <http://www.jaderiver.com/webmyth.html>. 2. and 3. D. Keith Denton and Charles Boyd, *Did You Know? Fascinating Facts and Fallacies About Business* (Upper Saddle River, N.J.: Prentice Hall, 1994), 28, 151.

CHAPTER 13

388 Exhibit 13.2, Adapted from Charles D. Schewe, From *Marketing Principles and Strategies* (New York: McGraw Hill, 1987), 35.

389 Exhibit 13.3, Adapted from Courtland Bovée, Michael F. Houston and John V. Thill, *Marketing*, 2d ed. (New York: McGraw Hill, 1994) 30.

391 Exhibit 13.4, Courtland Bovée, Michael F. Houston and John V. Thill, *Marketing*, 2d ed. (New York: McGraw Hill, 1994) 240, Exhibit 8.1

392 Exhibit 13.5, Adapted from Charles D. Schewe, From *Marketing Principles and Strategies* (New York: McGraw Hill, 1987), 294 Reprinted by permission of the publisher.

396 (Understanding the High-Tech Revolution): Adapted from "High-Tech Jewelry Design," *Industry Week*, 18 July 1994, 18; Jack R. Harkins, "Originality Sacrificed by CAD?" *Appliance Manufacturer*, June 1994, 11; Chris Williams, "Vibration Technology for Quality Products," Quality, June 1994, 26-28; Lisa Kempfer, "CAD Captures Creative Expression," *Computer-Aided Engineering*, June 1994, 28-34.

396 Exhibit 13.7, General Mills home page <http://www.generalmills.com (accessed 9 February 1998).

400 (Gaining the Competitive Edge): Adapted from David Gross, "The Name Game," *Hemispheres*, July 1997, 42-49; Ca-

cilie Rohwedder, "Global Products Require Name-Finders," *Wall Street Journal*, 11 April 1996, B6; Roberta Maynard, "What's in a Name," *Nation's Business*, September 1994, 54; "Packaging Your Business: How to Harness Image as Marketing Tool," *Small Business Success—Volume IX, Marketing* , 29-36.

410 (A Case for Critical Thinking): Adapted from "Continental Airlines: A Turnaruond Case Study," *Aviation Week & Space Technology*, 16 December 1996, S3-S30; Jonathan Burton, "Learning from the Customer," *Chief Executive*, March 1996, 58-59; Wendy Zellner, "Coffee, Tea—and On-Time Arrival," *Business Week*, 20 January 1997, 30; Keith L. Alexander, "Continental Airlines Soars to New Heights," *USA Today*, 23 January 1996, 4B; "Unisys Selected to Implement New Customer Loyalty System for Continental Airlines," *PressWire*, 4 August 1997, M2; Gillian Flynn, "A Flight Plan for Success," *Workforce*, July 1997, 73-78.

412 "Is It True?" 1. Gerry Myers, "Selling to Women," *American Demographics*, April 1996, 36-42. 2. D. Keith Denton and Charles Boyd, *Did You Know? Fascinating Facts and Fallacies About Business* (Upper Saddle River, N.J.: Prentice Hall, 1994), 151. 3. Caity Olson, "Outlet Stores Win Satisfied Consumers," *Advertising Age*, 11 July 1994, 33.

CHAPTER 14

416 Exhibit 14.1, Adapted from Theodore Beckman, William Davison, and W. Wayne Talarzyck, *Marketing*, 9th ed. (New York: Ronald Press, 1973), 307.

420 Exhibit 14.3, Adapted from Charles D. Schewe *Marketing Principles and Strategies* (New York: McGraw Hill, 1987), 399. Reprinted with permission of McGraw-Hill, Inc.

420 (Thinking About Ethics): Adapted from "Hallmark, a New Name in Mass Retailing," *Supermarket Business*, March 1997, 84; Daniel Roth, "Card Sharks," *Forbes*, 7 October 1996, 14; Julie Rygh, "Hallmark Cards Find Success with New Expressions Brand," *Knight-Ridder/Tribune Business News*, 31 August 1997, 831B0958; Earle Eldridge, "CarMax Not Alone in Its Field," *USA Today*, 18 June 1996, 8B; Earle Eldridge,"New Options Drive Hard Deal for Middle Man," *USA Today*, 13 December 1995, B1.

426 (Gaining the Competitive Edge): Adapted from Anthony Bianco, "Virtual Bookstores Start to Get Real," *Business Week*, 27 October, 1997, 146-148; Seith Lubove, "The Berserk-ley Boys," *Forbes*, 14 August 1995, 42-43; John Grossman, "Nowhere Men," *Inc.*, June 1996, 63-69; Peter Newcomb, "Peanut Butter and Pearl Jam," *Forbes*, 10 February 1997, 152; Ronald Henkoff, "Growing Your Company: Five Ways to Do It Right," *Fortune*, 25 November 1996, 78-88; Christine Bushey, "One-On-One Interview with Gary Dreyfuss, CEO of Dreyers Grand Ice Cream," *MSNBC Private Financial Network*, 18 July 1997; Kristin Dunlap Godsey, "Big Thing—Point Cast Invented a New Medium, Now Let the Battle Begin," *Success*, April 1997, 11-18; William C. Copacino, "The Changing Role of the Distributor," *Traffic Management*, February 1994, 31.

428 Exhibit 14.5, Adapted from Charles D. Schewe *Marketing Principles and Strategies* (New York: McGraw Hill, 1987), 435-436. Reprinted with permission of McGraw-Hill, Inc.

435 Exhibit 14.7, Adapted from Thomas A. Foster, "Logistics: Our Economy's Engine," *Chilton's Distribution*, July 1991, 6-14.

440 (A Case for Critical Thinking): Adapted from Patricia Sellers, "Giants of the Fortune 500: Sears: The Turnaround Is Ending; The Revolution Has Begun, Arthur Martinez's Idea Is to Sell Sears' Powerhouse Brands—To Anybody, Anywhere, Any Way He Can. Instead Of," *Fortune*, 28 April 1996, 106+; De'Ann Weimer, "Put the Comeback on My Card," *Business Week*, 10 November 1997, 118-119; Arthur C. Martinez, "Transforming the Legacy of Sears," *Strategy and Leadership*, July-August, 1997, 30-35; John Greenwald, "Reinventing Sears," *Time*, 23 December 1996, 52-56; Kim Ann Zimmerman, "Sears Sets Internet Selling," *HFN The Weekly Newspaper for the Home Furnishing Network*, 13 October, 1997, 12; Patricia Sellers, "Sears' Big Turnaround Runs into Big Trouble," *Fortune*, 16 February 1998, 34.

443 "Is It True?" 1. D. Keith Denton and Charles Boyd, *Did You Know? Fascinating Facts and Fallacies About Business* (Upper Saddle River, N.J.: Prentice Hall, 1994), 76. 2. Rita Koselka, "Distribution Revolution," *Forbes*, 25 May 1992, 54-61. #. Chuck Jones, "Cold Shoulders: Are Telemarketing and Door-to-Door Sales Doomed?" *Life Association News*, January 1998, 70+.

CHAPTER 15

458 (Understanding the High-Tech Revolution): Adapted in part from Don L. Boroughs, "New Age Advertising," *U.S. News and World Report*, 10 July 1995, 38-39; Courtland L. Bouvée, John V. Thill, George P. Dovel, and Marian B. Wood, *Advertising Excellence* (New York: McGraw-Hill, 1995), 277-283, 320-326.

461 Exhibit 15.2, *Advertising Age*, 29 September 1997, S63. Copyright, Crain Communications Inc., 1997.

463 Exhibit 15.4, *Newsweek*, April 1, 1996. © 1996, Newsweek Inc. All rights reserved. Reprinted by permission.

464 (Gaining the Competitive Edge): Adapted from "Net Population Breaks 50 Mil Mark," *Newsbytes News Network*, 2 October 1997, Online, 11 March 1998; Ellen Neuborne, "Web Ads Start to Click," *Business Week*, 6 October 1997, 128-138; Katie Hafner and Jennifer Tanaka, "This Web's for You," *Newsweek*, 1 April 1996, 74-76; "The State of Small Business," *Inc. Special Issue*, 20 May 1997, 111; Joag Levins, "In Search of Internet Business," *Editor and Publisher*, 8 February 1997, 4-6; Michael Krantz, "The Medium Is the Measure," IQ, 25 September 1995, 20-24; Joe Serino, "Return of the Best Seller—Trivial Pursuit Attracts New Converts on the Web," I*nternet Advertising Bureau—Supplement to Adweek*, 5 May 1997, 60.

470 (A Case for Critical Thinking): Adapted from Joshua Cooper Ramo, "How AOL Lost the Battles but Won the War," Time, 22 September 1997, 46; "America (and Everyone) Online," *The Economist*, 13 September 1997, 18; Tom Dellecave Jr., "America Offline," *Sales and Marketing Management* March 1997, 5; Gene Koprowski, "AOL CEO Steve Case," *Forbes*, 7 October 1996, 94; Cathy Taylor, "AOL: in Self-Defense," *Mediaweek*, 4 November 1996; Anya Sacharow, "AOL Says Ouch," Brewster, 20 January 1997, 8; David S. Jackson, "AOL Buys Some Time," Time, 10 February 1997, 50: Rory J. Thompson, "AOL—Not Dead Yet," *Informationweek*, 26 May 1997, 12; "AOL Bows to Criticism over Selling Members' Phone Numbers," *Direct Marketing*, October 1997, 6; Thomas Petzinger Jr., "Gunning for Growth," *Wall Street Journal*, 24 January 1997, B1; Eric Nee, "AOL Is Falling All Over Itself," *Upside*, April 1997, 20; Stewart

Alsop, "A Few Kind Words for America Online," *Fortune*, 17 March 1997, 159.

473 "Is It True?" 1. Nancy Webster, "Winnowed Kids' TV Field Still Drawing Big Bucks," *Advertising Age*, 10 February 1997, 28. 2. Jeff Jensen, "Woods Outpaces Jordan in Endorser Poll," *Advertising Age*, 12 May 1997, 18. 3. Raju Narisetti, "Many Companies Are Starting to Wean Shoppers Off Coupons," *Wall Street Journal*, 22 January 1997, B1, B10.

CHAPTER 16

463 Exhibit 16.1, Reprinted with the permission of Simon and Shuster, Inc. from the Macmillan College text *Systems and Design: A Case Study Approach*, 2d ed. by Robert J. Thierauf and George W. Reynolds, Copyright © 1986 by Merrill Publishing, an imprint of Macmillan College Publishing Company, Inc., 69.

479 Exhibit 16.3, Adapted from James A. O'Brien, *Introduction to Information Systems*, 7th ed. (Burr Ridge, Ill.: Irwin, 1994), 25.

492 (Understanding the High-Tech Revolution): Adapted from Saul Hansell, "Is This an Honest Face?" *New York Times*, 20 August 1997, C1; Larry Long and Nancy Long, *Introduction to Computers and Information Systems*, 5th ed. (Upper Saddle River, N.J.: Prentice Hall, 1997), AT116-AT117; Larry Long and Nancy Long, *Computers*, 5th ed. (Upper Saddle River, N.J.: Prentice Hall, 1998) CORE 88.

494 Exhibit 16.6, Adapted from Larry Long and Nancy Long, *Introduction to Computers and Information Systems*, 5th ed. (Upper Saddle River, N.J.: Prentice Hall, 1997), CORE 7.

495 Exhibit 16.7, Adapted from Larry Long and Nancy Long, *Introduction to Computers and Information Systems*, 5th ed. (Upper Saddle River, N.J.: Prentice Hall, 1997), CORE 173-174.

497 Exhibit 16.8 Adapted from Larry Long and Nancy Long, *Introduction to Computers and Information Systems*, 5th ed. (Upper Saddle River, N.J.: Prentice Hall, 1997), CORE 165-168

500 (Thinking About Ethics): Thomas E. Weber, "Should Only the Paranoid Get E-Mail Protection?" *Wall Street Journal*, 25 September 1997, B10; Leslie Miller, "On the Internet, Virtually No Privacy," *USA Today*, 30 May 1996, 6D; Patrice Duggan Samuels, "Who's Reading Your E-Mail? Maybe the Boss," 12 May 1996, F11; Frank Jossi, "Eavesdroppers in Cyberspace," *Business Ethics*, May-June 1994, 22-25.

504 (A Case for Critical Thinking): Adapted from Reid Goldsborough, "For PCs, a Little Maintenance Goes a Long Way," *Personal Computing*, 24 July 1997, *Electric Library*, Online, 3 December 1997; David Hakala, "Faux Viruses," *Newsday*, 6 July 1997, A37, *Electric Library*, Online, 3 December 1997; Stephen H. Wildstrom, "Out, Out, Damned Virus," *Business Week*, 22 July 1996, 19; Eliot Marshall, "The Scourge of Computer Viruses," *Science*, 8 April 1988, 133-134; Philip Elmer-DeWitt, "Invasion of the Data Snatchers!" *Time*, 26 September 1988, 62-67; Asra Q. Nomani, "Byteing Back: Bug Busters Devise Electronic Vaccines for Computer Viruses," *Wall Street Journal*, 17 June 1988, 1.

507 "Is It True?" 1. Phillip B. Evans and Thomas S. Wurster, "Strategy and the New Economics of Information" *Harvard Business Review*, September-October 1997, 72. 2. Raju Narisetti, Thomas E. Weber, and Rebecca Quick, "How Computers Calmly Handled Stock Frenzy," *Wall Street Journal*, 30 October 1997, B1. Tim McCollum, "Computer Crime," *Nation's Business*, November 1997, 19.

CHAPTER 17

512 Exhibit 17.2, From Gary Siegel and Bud Kulesza, "The Practice of Management Accounting," *Management Accounting*, April 1996, 20.

519 Exhibit 17.4, 1996 Annual Report for Computer Discount Warehouse.

520 (Gaining the Competitive Edge): Adapted from Manual Schiffres, "All the Good News That Fits," *U.S. News and World Report*, 14 April 1986, 50-51.

524 Exhibit 17.5, 1996 Annual Report for Computer Discount Warehouse.

525 Exhibit 17.6, 1996 Annual Report for Computer Discount Warehouse.

526 (Gaining the Competitive Edge): Adapted from Barbara Etorre, "How Motorola Closes Its Books in Two Days," *Management Review*, March 1995, 41-44; Stanley Zarowin, "Motorola's Financial Closings: 12 'Nonevents' a Year," *Journal of Accountancy*, November 1995, 59-63; Michael G. Winston, "Leadership of Renewal: Leadership for the 21st Century," *Business Forum* 22, no. 1 (Winter 1997): 4; "Tough at the Top," *Economist* 338, no. 7947 (January 1996): 47.

530 Exhibit 17.7, 1996 Annual Report for Computer Discount Warehouse.

539 "Is It True?" 1. AICPA, http://www.aicpa.org.2. Jerry G. Kreuze and Gale E. Newell, "A Strategy for Improving the Quality of Entry-level Management Accountants," *Journal of Education for Business*, 1 August 1996, 334. 3. Institute of Management Accountants, http://www.rutgers.edu/Accounting/raw/ima., Table 1-1 "Work Activities in Original Order."

CHAPTER 18

546 (Thinking About Ethics): Adapted from Christine Dugas, "Tiered Lending Adjusts Rates to Each Customer," *USA Today*, 16 November 1995, 1A; Andrew Brimmer, "The Cost of Bank Bias," *Black Enterprise*, July 1992, 43; Adam Zagorin, "Sub-Prime Time," *Time*, 4 November 1996, 67-68; Ilyce Glink, "Where to Look for Money Now," *Working Woman*, October 1994, 56-60.

550 Exhibit 18.4, Adapted from J. Tol Broome Jr., "A Loan at Last," *Nation's Business*, August 1994, 40-42; Maria Zate, "Put Away the Bootstraps," *Hispanic Business*, July 1994, 38-42.

556 (Understanding the High-Tech Revolution): Adapted from Amy Cortese, "Information Processing: Electronic Commerce: The Ultimate Plastic," *Business Week*, 19 May 1997, 119; Howard Anderson, "Showdown over E-cash," *Upside*, January 1996, 25-36; Kelly Holland and Amy Cortese, "The Future of Money," *Business Week*, 12 June 1995, 66-78; Adam Zagorin, "Cashless, Not Bankless," *Time*, 23 September 1996, 52; Gene Koprowski, "The Money Changers: Digital Cash Innovators Talk Banks, Bits, Bytes and Bucks," *Forbes ASAP*, 26 August 1996, 68-74; Jill Andresky Fraser, "Will Banking Go Virtual?" *Inc. Technology* no 3 (1996): 49-52; Saul Hansell, "It's Coming: Your Pocket Cash on a Plastic Card," *New York Times*, 10 April 1996, C1; James Gle-

ick, "Dead as a Dollar," *New York Times Magazine*, 16 June 1996, 26; Howard Anderson, "Money and the Internet: A Strange New Relationship," *IEEE Spectrum*, February 1997, 74-76.

558 Exhibit 18.5, Adapted from *Statistical Abstract of the United States, 1997* (Washington, D.C.: GPO, 1997), 521.

565 Exhibit 18.10, "The World's Largest Banks," *Wall Street Journal*, 18 September 1997, R27.

569 (A Case for Critical Thinking): Adapted from Myron Magnet, "Let's Go for Growth," *Fortune*, 7 March 1994, 60-72; Richard Phalon, "A Bold Gamble," *Forbes*, 28 February 1994, 90-91; *Barnes & Noble 1993 Annual Report*; Stephanie Strom, "Barnes & Noble Goes Public: Vol. 2," *New York Times*, 3 September 1993, C1, C2; John Mutter, "A Chat with Bookseller Len Riggio," *Publishers Weekly*, 3 May 1992, 33-38.

571 "Is It True?" 1. *Statistical Abstract of the United States: 1997* (Washington, D.C.: GPO, 1997), Table 800, 520. 2. *Statistical Abstract of the United States: 1997* (Washington, D.C.: GPO, 1997), 508. 3. James Gleick, "Dead as a Dollar," *New York Times Magazine*, 16 June 1996, 26-30.

CHAPTER 19

582 Exhibit 19.3, Karen Damato, "The Bottom Line," *Wall Street Journal*, 28 May 1996, R10.

588 (Understanding the High-Tech Revolution): Adapted from Hal Lux, "On the Net with E*Trade," *Institutional Investor*, January 1997, 23; Thomas Hoffman, "Online Brokers Drive Industry Changes," *Computerworld*, 14 April 1997, 77; Leah Nathans Spiro and Linda Himelstein, "With the World Wide Web, Who Needs Wall Street," *Business Week*, 29 April 1996, 120-121; John Wyatt, E*Trade: Is This Investing's Future?" *Fortune*, 3 March 1997, 190-192; Theresa Carey, "Surf's Up," *Barron's*, 17 March 1997, 33-34; "Challenges of the Financial Cybercop," *Institutional Investor*, April 1997, 99.

592 (Gaining the Competitive Edge): Adapted from Gretchen Morgenson, "Don't Be a Victim," *Forbes*, 2 June 1997, 42-43; Kimberly Weisul, "As Direct Public Offerings Grow, So Does Concern About Due Diligence," *Investment Dealers Digest*, 19 May 1997, 12; Randy Myers, "The Wired World of Investment Information," *Nation's Business*, March 1997, 58-60; Joseph Garber, "Click Before You Leap," *Forbes*, 24 February 1997, 162; Jim Ellis, "Getting the Net to Help Build Your Portfolio," *Business Week*, 15 July 1996, 92-93; Gary Weiss, "Web of Hype and Glory," *Business Week*, 16 June 1997, 108-110.

594 Exhibit 19.4, "A Big Test for Dow Jones Industrial's Long Bull Run," *Wall Street Journal*, 28 October 1997, C17; Standard & Poor's, Telescan, Inc. 1995; "A Centennial View: Dow Jones Industrial Average," *Wall Street Journal*, centennial edition, B15, and reprinted by permission of *The Wall Street Journal*, © 1991 Dow Jones & Company, Inc. All Rights Reserved Worldwide.

595 Exhibit 19.5, Adapted from "A Century of Investing—Ins and Outs, *Wall Street Journal*, 28 May 1996, R45-R51; Tom Petruno, "Dow Jones Shakes Up Its Index with Four Replacements," *Los Angeles Times*, 13 March 1997, D1.

602 (A Case for Critical Thinking): Thomas G. Stemberg, *Staples for Success*, Chapter 8, <http://www.Staples.com> (accessed 7 September 1997).

606 "Is It True?" 1. The Invetment FAQ Web site <http://www.investment-faq.com/articles/bonds-zero.html>. 2. The Investment FAQ Web site, <http://www.invest-faq.com/articles/triv-bull-bear.html>. 3. Nancy Ann Jeffrey, "A Century of Investing," *Wall Street Journal*, 28 May 1997, R42.

CHAPTER A

612 Exhibit A.2, Based on information from *Code of Federal Regulations*, Titles 9, 21, Pts. 100-69, 200-N, Superintendent of Documents, (Washington, D.C.: GPO), 1994.

615 Exhibit A.3, Adapted from Bartley A. Brennan and Nancy Kubasek, *The Legal Environment of Business* (New York: Macmillan, 1988), 24; Douglas Whitman and John Gergacz, *The Legal Environment of Business*, 2d ed. (New York: Random House, 1988), 22, 25.

622 Exhibit A.5, Adapted from Richard A. Brealely and Stewart C. Myers, *Principles of Corporate Finance* 4th ed. (New York: McGraw-Hill, 1991), 761-765.

CHAPTER B

631 Figure B.4, Adapted from Mark S. Dorfman, *Introduction to Risk Management and Insurance*, 6th ed. (Upper Saddle River, N.J.: Prentice Hall, 1998), 357.

633 Figure B.5, Adapted from Mark S. Dorfman, *Introduction to Risk Management and Insurance*, 6th ed. (Upper Saddle River, N.J.: Prentice Hall, 1998), 479.

637 Figure B.6 Adapted from Chris Farrell, "Risky Business," *Working Woman*, September 1997, p. 40.

CHAPTER C

640 Exhibit C.1, Tim McCollum, "Making the Internet Work for You," *Nation's Business*, March 1997, 6-13; US West, "A Guide to Using and Managing Today's Communications Technology, 1997.

649 Exhibit C.2, <http://searchenginewatch.internet.com/facts/major.html> [accessed 11 March 1998]; Getting Started—What You Need to Know to Begin Using the Internet," *Fortune Technology Buyer's Guide*, Winter 1998, 232-230.

651 Exhibit C.4, Adapted from Courtland L. Bovée and John V. Thill, *Business Communication Today*, 5th ed. (Upper Saddle River, N.J.: Prentice Hall, 1998), 485-491.

Photo Credits

CHAPTER 1

Opposite page 1 Jeff Zaruba/The Stock Market
1, 24 Randy Hampton/Black Star
4 Cary Wolinsky/Stock Boston
6 Courtesy The Bowing Company
11 David Barber/PhotoEdit
13 David Young-Wolff/PhotoEdit
20 Spencer Grant/PhotoEdit

CHAPTER 2

30 Anthony Cassidy/Tony Stone Images
31, 56 Justine Hill
34 R. Ian Lloyd
37 Reuters/Patrick de Noimont/Archive Photos
43 Greg Girard/Contact Press Images Inc.
48 Lee Celano Photography

CHAPTER 3

62 Jon Riley/Tony Stone
63, 90 Chris Craymer/Tony Stone Images
67 Marilynn K. Yee/New York Times Permissions
70 Donigny/REA/SABA Press Photos, Inc.
84 Marissa Roth/New York Times Permissions
89 Courtesy Aveda

CHAPTER 4

98 Jeffrey Sylvester/FPG International
99, 123 Churchill & Klehr Photography
103 Les Moore/Uniphoto New York
107 Frank Siteman/Monkmeyer Press
111 Elena Rooraid/PhotoEdit
121 Lawrence Migdale/Photo Researchers, Inc.

CHAPTER 5

130 Michael Newman/PhotoEdit
131, 153 Larry Dunn/Larry Dunn Photography
133 William Johnson/Stock Boston
136 Moto Photo/Excel Professional Services, Inc.
143 Bob Daemmrich/Stock Boston
144 Courtesy Alphagraphics, Inc.
146 Richard Howard Photography

CHAPTER 6

160 Gabe Palmer/The Stock Market
161, 183 Uniphoto New York
162 Courtesy GE Media Services Group
166 James Lukoski/James Lukoski Photography
170 Courtesy L.L. Bean
176 John Abbott Photography
182 Courtney Kelly/Gamma-Liaison, Inc.

CHAPTER 7

190 Jon Feingersh/The Stock Market
191, 218 Courtesy Lexmark International
196 Jamie Tanaka
205 Michael Newman/PhotoEdit
209 Peter Menzel/Stock Boston
215 Steve Niedorf/The Image Bank
216 Michael Newman/PhotoEdit

CHAPTER 8

224 Dick Luria/FPG International
225, 250 Oli Tennent/Tony Stone Images
229 Courtesy Ford Motor Company, Detroit
236 Andy Sachs/Tony Stone Images
240 Paul Chesley/Photographers/Aspen, Inc.
242 Peter Menzel/Stock Boston
243 Jo Rottger/VISUM Fotoreportagen Gmbh

CHAPTER 9

256 Uniphoto New York
257, 281 Michael Newman/PhotoEdit
260 Robert Holmgren Photography
264 Courtesy Pacific Crest Outward Bound School
271 Courtesy Hewlett-Packard Company

CHAPTER 10

288 Stephen Simpson/FPG International
289, 319 Uniphoto New York
296 Crandall/The Image Works
309 Courtesy Eddie Bauer Co.
313 Mark Graham/New York Times Permissions
317 Nicholle Benijveno/Matrix International

CHAPTER 11

325, 350 Robin Landholm Photography
335 Karl Mantyla/Solidarity Magazine
347 Courtesy United Airlines/WHQAD

CHAPTER 13

397 Courtesy Rubbermaid Incorporated

CHAPTER 14

414, 437 Bob Daemmerich/Stock Boston
423 Courtesy Roadnet Technologies, Inc.
429 Steve Winter/Black Star

CHAPTER 15

445, 468 Denise de Luise/Zephyr Pictures
458 AP/Wide World Photos

CHAPTER 16

474 David Joel/Tony Stone Images
481 Courtesy Information Management Resources, Inc.

CHAPTER 17

508 Gabe Palmer/The Stock Market
514 Terry Vine/Tony Stone Images
518 Courtesy Computer Discount Warehouse

CHAPTER 18

540 Uniphoto New York
541, 567 Zephyr Pictures
542 Gabe Palmer/The Stock Market
543 Clemer/Zuma Press
561 David Wells/The Image Works
565 Cathlyn Melloan/Tony Stone Images

CHAPTER 19

572 AP/Wide World Photos
573, 600 Dono Spiro/Tony Stone Images

CHAPTER A

608 Ken Whitmore/Tony Stone Images
614 Courtesy The Tobacco Institute

CHAPTER B

627 Philip Habib/Tony Stone Images
629 Susan Holtz
632 Reuters/Corbis-Bettmann
634 Ken Kerbs/DOT Pictures

CHAPTER C

645 Uniphoto New York

GLOSSARY

A

absolute advantage Nation's ability to produce a particular product with fewer resources per unit of output than any other nation

accountability Obligation to report results to supervisors or team members and justify outcomes that fall below expectations

accounting Measuring, interpreting, and communicating financial information to support internal and external decision making

accounting equation Basic accounting equation that assets equals liabilities plus owners' equity

accounts receivable turnover ratio Measure of time a company takes to turn its accounts receivables into cash, calculated by dividing sales by the average value of accounts receivable for a period

accrual basis Accounting method in which revenue is recorded when a sale is made and expense is recorded when incurred

acquisition Combination of two companies in which one company purchases the other and assumes control of its property and liabilities

activity ratios Ratios that measure the effectiveness of the firm's use of its resources

administrative skills Technical skills in information gathering, data analysis, planning, organizing, and other aspects of managerial work

advertising Paid, nonpersonal communication to a target market from an identified sponsor using mass communications channels

advocacy advertising Ads that present a company's opinions on public issues such as education and health

affirmative action Activities undertaken by businesses to recruit and promote women and minorities, based on an analysis of the work force and the available labor pool

agency shop Workplace requiring nonunion employees who are covered by agreements negotiated by the union to pay service fees to that union

agents and brokers Independent wholesalers that do not take title to the goods they distribute, but may or may not take possession of those goods

analytic system Production process that breaks incoming materials into various component products and divisional patterns simultaneously

application software Programs that perform specific functions for users, such as word processing or spreadsheet analysis

arbitrage Simultaneous purchase in one market and sale in a different market with a profitable price or yield differential

arbitration Process for resolving a labor-contract dispute in which an impartial third party studies the issues and makes a binding decision

artificial intelligence Ability of computers to reason, to learn, and to simulate human sensory perceptions

artwork Visual, graphic part of an ad

assembly line Series of workstations at which each employee performs a specific task in the production process

asset allocation Method of shifting investments within a portfolio to adapt them to the current investment environment

assets Anything of value owned or leased by a business

auction exchange Centralized marketplace where securities are traded by specialists on behalf of investors

audit Formal evaluation of the fairness and reliability of a client's financial statements

authority Power granted by the organization to make decisions, take actions, and allocate resources to accomplish goals

authorization cards Sign-up cards designating a union as the signer's preferred bargaining agent

authorized stock Shares that a corporation's board of directors has decided to sell eventually

autocratic leaders Leaders who do not involve others in decision making

automated teller machines (ATMs) Electronic terminals that permit people with plastic cards to perform simple banking transactions 24 hours a day without the aid of a human teller

automation Process of performing a mechanical operation with the absolute minimum of human intervention

B

balance of payments Sum of all payments one nation has made to other nations minus the payments it has received from other nations during a specified period of time

balance of trade Relationship between the value of the products a nation exports and those it imports

balance sheet Statement of a firm's financial position on a particular date; also known as a statement of financial position

bandwidth Maximum capacity of a data transmission medium

barriers to entry Factors that make it difficult to launch a business in a particular industry

bear market Falling stock market

behavior modification Systematic use of rewards and punishments to change human behavior

behavioral segmentation Categorization of customers according to their relationship with products or response to product characteristics

bill of materials List of all parts and materials in a product that are to be made or purchased

blue-chip stocks Equities issued by large, well-established companies with consistent records of stock price increases and dividend payments

board of directors Group of people, elected by the shareholders, who have the ultimate authority in guiding the affairs of a corporation

bonds Certificates of indebtedness that are sold to raise long-term funds for a corporation or government agency

bonus Cash payment in addition to the regular wage or salary, which serves as a reward for achievement

bookkeeping Record-keeping, clerical phase of accounting

both inside and outside the organization

boycott Union activity in which members and sympathizers refuse to buy or handle the product of a target company

branch office Producer-owned marketing intermediary that carries stock and sells it; also called a sales branch

brand A name, term, sign, symbol, design, or combination used to identify the products of a firm and differentiate them from competing products

brand awareness Level of brand loyalty at which people are familiar with a product—they recognize it

brand insistence Level of brand loyalty at which people will accept no substitute for a particular product

brand loyalty Commitment to a particular brand

brand marks Portion of a brand that cannot be expressed verbally

brand names Portion of a brand that can be expressed orally, including letters, words, or numbers

brand preference Level of brand loyalty at which people habitually buy a product if it is available

break-even analysis Method of calculating the minimum volume of sales needed at a given price to cover all costs

break-even point Sales volume at a given price that will cover all of a company's costs

broadbanding Payment system that uses wide pay grades, enabling the company to give pay raises without promotions

broker Individual registered to sell securities

budget Planning and control tool that reflects expected revenues, operating expenses, and cash receipts and outlays

bull market Rising stock market

business Activity and enterprise that provides goods and services that an economic system needs

business agent Full-time union staffer who negotiates with management and enforces the union's agreements with companies

business cycle Fluctuations in the rate of growth that an economy experiences over a period of several years

business plan A written document that provides an orderly statement of a company's goals and how it intends to achieve those goals

buyer's market Marketplace characterized by an abundance of products

C

calendar year Twelve-month accounting period that begins on January 1 and ends on December 31

canned approach Selling method based on a fixed, memorized presentation

capacity planning A long-term strategic decision that determines the level of resources available to an organization to meet customer demand

capital The physical, human-made elements used to produce goods and services, such as factories and computers; can also refer to the funds that finance the operations of a business

capital budgeting Process for evaluating proposed investments in select projects that provide the best long-term financial return

capital gains Difference between the price at which a financial asset is sold and its original cost (assuming the price has gone up)

capital-intensive businesses Businesses that require large investments in capital assets

capital investments Money paid to acquire something of permanent value in a business

capital structure Financing mix of a firm

capitalism Economic system based on economic freedom and competition

cash basis Accounting method in which revenue is recorded when payment is received and expense is recorded when cash is paid

category killers A discount chain that sells only one category of products

cause-related marketing Identification and marketing of a social issue, cause, or idea to selected target markets

CD-ROMs Storage devices that use the same technology as music CDs; popular because of their low cost and large storage capacity

cellular layout Method of arranging a facility so that parts with similar shapes or processing requirements are processed together in work centers

central processing unit (CPU) Core of the computer, performing the three basic functions of arithmetic (addition, etc.), logic (comparing numbers), and control/communication (managing the computer)

centralization Concentration of decision-making authority at the top of the organization

certification Process by which a union is officially recognized by the National Labor Relations Board as the bargaining agent for a group of employees

certified management accountants (CMAs) Accountants who have fulfilled the requirements for certification as specialists in management accounting

certified public accountants (CPAs) Professionally licensed accountants who meet certain requirements for education and experience and who pass a comprehensive examination

chain of command Pathway for the flow of authority from one management level to the next

channel captain Channel member that is able to influence the activities of the other members of the distribution channel

checks Written orders that tell the customer's bank to pay a specific amount to a particular individual or business

chief executive officer (CEO) Person appointed by a corporation's board of directors to carry out the board's policies and supervise the activities of the corporation

chief information officer (CIO) Top corporate executive with responsibility for managing information and information systems

client/server system Computer system design in which one computer (the server) contains software and data used by a number of attached computers (the clients); the clients also have their own processing capabilities, and they share certain tasks with the server, enabling the system to run at optimum efficiency

closed shop Workplace in which union membership is a condition of employment

closing Point at which a sale is completed

closing the books Transferring the net revenue and expense account balances to retained earnings for the period

co-branding Partnership between two or more companies to closely link their brand names together for a single product

coaching Helping employees reach their highest potential by meeting with them, discussing problems that hinder their ability to work effectively, and offering suggestions and encouragement to overcome these problems

code of ethics Written statement setting forth the principles that should guide an organization's decisions

cognitive dissonance Anxiety following a purchase that prompts buyers to seek reassurance about the purchase; commonly known as buyer's remorse

cohesiveness A measure of how committed the team members are to their team's goals

collateral Tangible asset a lender can claim if a borrower defaults on a loan

collective bargaining Process used by unions and management to negotiate work contracts

commercial paper An IOU, backed by the corporation's reputation, issued to raise short-term capital

commercialization Large-scale production and distribution of a product

commissions Payments to employees equal to a certain percentage of sales made

committee Team that may become a permanent part of the organization and is designed to deal with regularly recurring tasks

commodities Raw materials used in producing other goods

commodity business Business in which products are undifferentiated and price becomes the chief competitive weapon; usually applied to basic goods such as minerals and agricultural products

common carriers Transportation companies that offer their services to the general public

common stock Shares whose owners have voting rights and have the last claim on distributed profits and assets

communism Economic system in which all productive resources are owned and operated by the government, to the elimination of private property

comparable worth Concept of equal pay for jobs that are equal in value to the organization and require similar levels of education, training, and skills

comparative advantage Nation's ability to produce certain items more efficiently and at a lower cost than other items, relative to other nations

comparative advertising Advertising technique in which two or more products are explicitly compared

compensating balance Portion of an unsecured loan that is kept on deposit at the lending institution to protect the lender and increase the lender's return

compensation Money, benefits, and services paid to employees for their work

competition Rivalry among businesses for the same customer

competitive advantage Ability to perform in one or more ways that competitors cannot match

competitive advertising Ads that specifically highlight how a product is better than its competitors

computer-aided design (CAD) Use of computer graphics and mathematical modeling in the development of products

computer-aided engineering (CAE) Use of computers to test products without building an actual model

computer-aided manufacturing (CAM) Use of computers to control production equipment

computer-integrated manufacturing (CIM) Computer-based systems that coordinate and control all the elements of design and production, including CAD and CAM

computer languages Sets of programmable rules and conventions for communicating with computers

computer viruses Computer programs that can work their way into a computer system and erase or corrupt data or programs

conceptual skills Ability to understand the relationship of parts to the whole

conglomerate mergers Combinations of companies that are in unrelated businesses, designed to augment a company's growth and diversify risk

consortium Group of companies working jointly to promote a common objective or engage in a project of benefit to all members

consumer buying behavior Behavior exhibited by consumers as they consider and purchase various products

consumer markets Individuals or households that buy goods or services for personal use

consumer promotions Sales promotions aimed at final consumers

consumerism Movement that pressures businesses to consider consumer needs and interests

contingency leadership Adapting the leadership style to what is most appropriate, given current business conditions

contingency plans A blueprint for actions the company can take to cope with unforeseen events

continuity Pattern according to which an ad appears in the media; it can be spread evenly over time or concentrated during selected periods

contract carriers Specialized freight haulers that serve selected companies under written contract

controller Highest-ranking accountant in a company, responsible for overseeing all accounting functions

controlling Process of measuring progress against goals and objectives and correcting deviations if results are not as expected

convertible bonds Corporate bonds that can be exchanged at the owner's discretion into common stock of the issuing company

cooperative advertising Joint efforts between local and national advertisers, in which producers of nationally sold products share the costs of local advertising with local merchants and wholesalers

cooperatives Associations of people or small companies with similar interests, formed to obtain greater bargaining power and other economies of scale

copy Verbal (spoken or written) part of an ad

corporation Legally chartered enterprise having most of the legal rights of a person, including the right to conduct business, to own and sell property, to borrow money, and to sue or be sued; owners of the corporation enjoy limited liability

cost accounting Area of accounting focusing on the calculation of manufacturing and storage costs of products for use or sale in a business

cost of capital Average rate of interest a firm pays on its combination of debt and equity

cost of goods sold Cost of producing or acquiring a company's products for sale during a given period

cost-of-living adjustment (COLA) Clause in a union contract ensuring that wages will rise in proportion to inflation

cost per thousand (CPM) Cost of reaching 1,000 people with an ad

countertrade Trading practice in which local products are offered instead of cash in exchange for imported products

couponing Distribution of certificates that offer discounts on particular items

craft unions Unions made up of skilled artisans belonging to a single profession or practicing a single craft

creative selling Selling process used by order getters, which involves determining customer needs, devising strategies to explain product benefits, and persuading customers to buy

credit cards Plastic cards that allow the customer to buy now and pay back the loaned amount at a future date

creditors People or organizations that have loaned money or extended credit

crisis management System for minimizing the harm that might result from some unusually threatening situations

critical path In a PERT network diagram, the sequence of operations that requires the longest time to complete.

cross-functional teams Teams that draw together employees from different functional areas

cross-promotion Jointly advertising two or more noncompeting brands

currency Bills and coins that make up the cash money of a society

current assets Cash and other items that can be turned back into cash within one year

current liabilities Obligations that must be met within a year

current ratio Measure of a firm's short-term liquidity, calculated by dividing current assets by current liabilities

customer divisions Divisional structure that focuses on customers or clients

customer-service standards Specifications for the quality of service that a firm will provide for its customers

D

data Recorded facts and statistics; data need to be converted to information before they can help people solve business problems

data communications Process of connecting computers and allowing them to send data back and forth

data mining Sifting through huge amounts of data to identify what is valuable to a specific question or problem

data warehousing Building an organized central database out of files and databases gathered from different functional areas, such as marketing, operations, and accounting

database Collection of related data that can be cross-referenced in order to extract information

database management Creating, storing, maintaining, rearranging, and retrieving the contents of databases

database marketing Process of building, maintaining, and using customer databases for the purpose of contacting customers and transacting business

dealer exchanges Decentralized marketplaces where securities are bought and sold by dealers out of their own inventories

debentures Corporate bonds backed only by the reputation of the issuer

debit cards Plastic cards that allow the bank to take money from the user's demand-deposit account and transfer it to a retailer's account

debt ratios Ratios that measures a firm's reliance on debt financing of its operations (sometimes called coverage ratios)

debt-to-equity ratio Measure of the extent to which a business is financed by debt as opposed to invested capital, calculated by dividing the company's total liabilities by owners' equity

debt-to-total-assets ratio Measure of a firm's ability to carry long-term debt, calculated by dividing total liabilities by total assets

debtors People or organizations who have to repay money they have borrowed

decentralization Delegation of decision-making authority to employees in lower-level positions

decertification Process employees use to take away a union's official right to represent them

decision making Process of identifying a decision situation, analyzing the problem, weighing the alternatives, choosing and implementing an alternative, and evaluating the results

decision support system (DSS) Information system that uses decision models, specialized databases, and artificial intelligence to assist managers in solving highly unstructured and nonroutine problems

delegation Assignment of work and the authority and responsibility required to complete it

demand Buyer's willingness and ability to purchase products

demand curve Graph of relationship between various prices and the quantity demanded at each price

demand deposit Money in a checking account that can be used by the customer at any time

democratic leaders Leaders who delegate authority and involve employees in decision making

demographics Study of statistical characteristics of a population

denomination Face value of a single bond

departmentalization Grouping people within an organization according to function, division, matrix, or network

departmentalization by division Grouping departments according to similarities in product, process, customer, or geography

departmentalization by function Grouping workers according to their similar skills, resource use, and expertise

departmentalization by matrix Assigning employees to both a functional group and a project team (thus using functional and divisional patterns simultaneously)

departmentalization by network Electronically connecting separate companies that perform selected tasks for a small headquarters organization

depreciation Accounting procedure for systematically spreading the cost of a tangible asset over its estimated useful life

deregulation Removal or relaxation of rules and restrictions affecting businesses

desktop publishing (DTP) Ability to prepare documents using computerized typesetting and graphics-processing capabilities

direct mail Advertising sent directly to potential customers, usually through the U.S. Postal Service

direct marketing Direct communication other than personal sales contacts designed to effect a measurable response

discount brokerages Financial-services companies that sell securities but give no advice

discount pricing Offering a reduction in price

discount rate Interest rate charged by the Federal Reserve on loans to commercial banks and other financial institutions

discount stores Retailers that sell a variety of goods below the market price by keeping their overhead low

discretionary order Market order that allows the broker to decide when to trade a security

discrimination In a social and economic sense, denial of opportunities to individuals on the basis of some characteristic that has no bearing on their ability to perform in a job

disinflation Economic condition in which the rate of inflation declines

disk drive Most common mechanism for secondary storage; includes both hard disk drives and floppy disk (diskette) drives

dispatching Issuing work orders and schedules to department heads and supervisors

distortion Misunderstanding that results from a message passing through too many links in the organization

distribution centers Warehouse facilities that specialize in collecting and shipping merchandise

distribution channels Systems for moving goods and services from producers to customers; also known as marketing channels

distribution mix Combination of intermediaries and channels that a producer uses to get a product to end users

distribution strategy Firm's overall plan for moving products to intermediaries and final customers

diversification Assembling investment portfolios in such a way that a loss in one investment won't cripple the value of the entire portfolio

diversity initiatives Company policies designed to enhance opportunities for minorities and promote understanding of diverse cultures, customs, and talents

divestiture Sale of part of a company

dividends Distributions of corporate assets to shareholders in the form of cash or other assets

double-entry bookkeeping Way of recording financial transactions that requires two entries for every transaction so that the accounting equation is always kept in balance

drop shippers Merchant wholesalers that assume ownership of goods but don't take physical possession; commonly used to market agricultural and mineral products

due process System of procedures and mechanisms for ensuring fair treatment on the job

dumping Charging less than the actual cost or less than the home-country price for goods sold in other countries

E

earnings per share Measure of a firm's profitability for each share of outstanding stock, calculated by dividing net income after taxes by shares of common stock outstanding

ecology Study of the relationships between living things in the water, air, and soil, their environments, and the nutrients that support them

economic system Means by which a society distributes its resources to satisfy its people's needs

economies of scale Savings from manufacturing, marketing, or buying large quantities

electronic data interchange (EDI) Information systems that transmit documents such as invoices and purchase orders between computers, thereby lowering ordering costs and paperwork

electronic funds transfer system (EFTS) Computerized systems for performing financial transactions

electronic mail (e-mail) Communication system that enables computers to transmit and receive written messages over telephone lines or other electronic networks

embargo Total ban on trade with a particular nation or in a particular product

employee assistance program (EAP) Company-sponsored counseling or referral plan for employees with personal problems

employee benefits Compensation other than wages, salaries, and incentive programs

employee stock-ownership plan (ESOP) Program enabling employees to become partial owners of a company

employment at will Employer's right to keep or terminate employees as it wishes

entrepreneurs People who accept the risk of failure in the private enterprise system

equilibrium price Point at which quantity supplied equals quantity demanded

ergonomics Study of how tasks, equipment, and the environment relate to human performance

ethical dilemma Situation in which both sides of an issue can be supported with valid arguments

ethical lapse Situation in which an individual makes an unethical decision

ethics Study of standards of conduct and individual choices based on rules, values, and moral beliefs

euro A planned unified currency to be used by European nations who meet certain strict requirements

Eurodollars Dollars deposited in banks outside the United States

exchange process Act of obtaining a desired object from another party by offering something of value in return

exchange rate Rate at which the money of one country is traded for the money of another

exclusive distribution Market coverage strategy that gives intermediaries exclusive rights to sell a product in a specific geographical area

executive information system (EIS) Similar to a decision support system, but customized to the strategic needs of executives

expenses Costs created in the process of generating revenues

expert system Computer system that simulates the thought processes of a human expert who is adept at solving particular problems

exporting Selling and shipping goods or services to another country

external communication network Communication channels that carry information in and out of the organization

F

factors of production Basic inputs that a society uses to produce goods and services, including natural resources, labor, capital, and entrepreneurship

family branding Using a brand name on a variety of related products

featherbedding Practice of requiring employees to be kept on the payroll for work they don't do or for work that isn't necessary

fiber optic cable Cable that transmits data as laser-generated pulses of light; capable of transmitting data at speeds of 2.5 billion bits per second without a modem

financial accounting Area of accounting concerned with preparing financial information for users outside the organization

financial analysis Process of evaluating a company's performance and analyzing the costs and benefits of a strategic action

financial control The process of analyzing and adjusting the basic financial plan to correct for forecasted events that do not materialize

financial futures Legally binding agreements to buy or sell financial instruments at a future date

financial management Effective acquisition and use of money

financial plan A forecast of financial requirements and the financing sources to be used

first-line managers Those at the lowest level of the management hierarchy, who supervise the operating employees and implement the plans set at the higher management levels; also called supervisory managers

fiscal policy Use of government revenue collection and spending to influence the business cycle

fiscal year Any 12 consecutive months used as an accounting period

fixed assets Assets retained for long-term use, such as land, buildings, machinery, and equipment; also referred to as property, plant, and equipment

fixed costs Business costs that remain constant regardless of the number of units produced

fixed-position layout Method of arranging a facility so that the product is stationary and equipment and personnel come to it

flat organizations Organizations having a wide span of management and few hierarchical levels

flexible manufacturing system (FMS) Production system using computer-controlled machines that can adapt to various versions of the same operation

flextime Scheduling system in which employees are allowed certain options regarding time of arrival and departure

floating exchange rate system World economic system in which the values of all currencies are determined by supply and demand

forecasting Making educated assumptions about future trends and events that will have an impact on the organization

foreign direct investment (FDI) Investment of money by foreign companies in domestic business enterprises

foreign exchange Trading one currency for the equivalent value of another currency

foreign sales corporations (FSCs) Tax-sheltered subsidiaries of U.S.-based corporations that engage in exporting

form utility Consumer value created by converting raw materials and other inputs into finished goods and services

formal communication network Communication network that follows the official structure of the organization

forward buying Retailers' taking advantage of trade allowances by buying more products at discounted prices than they hope to sell

fourth-generation languages (4GLs) Collective name applied to a variety of software tools that ease the task of interacting with computers; some let users give instructions in natural languages such as English

franchise Business arrangement in which a small business obtains rights to sell the goods or services of the supplier (franchisor)

franchisee Small-business owner who contracts for the right to sell goods or services of the supplier (franchisor) in exchange for some payment

franchisor Supplier that grants a franchise to an individual or group (franchisee) in exchange for payments

free-market system Economic system in which the way people spend their money determines which products will be produced and what those products will cost

free rider Team member who doesn't contribute sufficiently to the group's activities because members are not being held individually accountable for their work

free trade International trade unencumbered by restrictive measures

frequency Average number of times that each audience member is exposed to the message (equal to the total number of exposures divided by the total audience population)

full-service brokerages Financial-services companies with a full range of services, including investment advice, securities research, and investment products

full-service merchant wholesalers Merchant wholesalers that provide a wide variety of services to their customers, such as storage, delivery, and marketing support

functional teams Teams whose members come from a single functional department and that are based on the organization's vertical structure

G

gain sharing Plan for rewarding employees not on the basis of overall profits but in relation to achievement of goals such as cost savings from higher productivity

Gantt chart Bar chart used to control schedules by showing how long each part of a production process should take and when it should take place

general expenses Operating expenses, such as office and administrative expenses, not directly associated with creating or marketing a good or service

general obligation bonds Municipal bonds backed by the issuing agency's general taxing authority

general partnership Partnership in which all partners have the right to participate as co-owners and are individually liable for the business's debts

generally accepted accounting principles (GAAP) Professionally approved standards and practices used by the accountants in the preparation of financial statements

generic products Products characterized by a plain label, with no advertising and no brand name

geodemographics Method of combining geographic data with demographic data to develop profiles of neighborhood segments

geographic divisions Divisional structure based on location of operations

geographic segmentation Categorization of customers according to their geographic location

givebacks Concessions made by union members to give up promised increases in wages or benefits in order to enhance the company's competitive position

glass ceiling Invisible barrier of subtle discrimination that keeps women out of the top positions in business

goal Broad, long-range target or aim

golden parachute Generous compensation packages guaranteed to executives in the event that they lose their jobs after a takeover

goods-producing businesses Businesses that produce tangible products

government-owned corporations Corporations formed and owned by a government body for a specific public purpose

grapevine Communication network of the informal organization

graphical user interface (GUI) A user-friendly program running in conjunction with the operating system that enables computer operators to enter commands by clicking on icons and menus with a mouse

grievances Employee complaints about management's violating some aspect of a labor contract

gross domestic product (GDP) Dollar value of all the final goods and services produced by businesses located within a nation's borders; excludes receipts from overseas operations of domestic companies

gross national product (GNP) Dollar value of all the final goods and services produced by domestic businesses, including receipts from overseas operations; excludes receipts from foreign-owned businesses within a nation's borders

gross profit Amount remaining when the cost of goods sold is deducted from net sales; also known as gross margin

groupware Software that enables users in different locations to share information, collaborate on projects, and perform other tasks together

growth stocks Equities issued by small companies with unproven products or services

H

hardware Physical components of a computer system, including integrated circuits, keyboards, and disk drives

hedge Making an investment that protects the investor from suffering loss on another investment

high-growth ventures Small businesses intended to achieve rapid growth and high profits on investment

holding company Company that owns most, if not all, of another company's stock but that does not actively participate in the management of that other company

horizontal coordination Coordinating communication and activities across departments

horizontal mergers Combinations of companies that are direct competitors in the same industry

hostile takeovers Situations in which an outside party buys enough stock in a corporation to take control against the wishes of the board of directors and corporate officers

human relations Interaction among people within an organization for the purpose of achieving organizational and personal goals

human resources Organization's employees

human resources management (HRM) Specialized function of planning how to obtain employees, oversee their training, evaluate them, and compensate them

hygiene factors Aspects of the work environment that are associated with dissatisfaction

hypertext markup language (HTML) An Internet publishing format that incorporates sound, graphics, and video with document text; HTML can also hyperlink documents together, making it easy for users to jump from one document to another

I

importing Purchasing goods or services from another country and bringing them into one's own country

incentives Cash payments to employees who produce at a desired level or whose unit (often the company as a whole) produces at a desired level

income statement Financial record of a company's revenues, expenses, and profits over a given period of time

incubators Facilities that house small businesses during their early growth phase

individual rights Philosophy used in making ethical decisions that aims to protect rights guaranteed by a legal system or by moral norms and principles

industrial distributors Wholesalers that sell to industrial customers, rather than to retailers

industrial unions Unions representing both skilled and unskilled employees from all phases of a particular industry

inflation Economic condition in which prices rise steadily throughout the economy

informal organization Network of informal employee interactions that are not defined by the formal structure

injunction Court order prohibiting certain actions by striking workers

insider trading Employee's or manager's use of unpublicized information gained in the course of his or her job to benefit from fluctuations in the stock market

institutional advertising Advertising that seeks to create goodwill and to build a desired image for a company rather than to sell specific products

institutional investors Companies that invest money entrusted to them by others

integrated marketing communications (IMC) Strategy of coordinating and integrating communications and promotions efforts with customers to ensure greater efficiency and effectiveness

intensive distribution Market coverage strategy that tries to place a product in as many outlets as possible

interactive advertising Customer-seller communication in which the customer controls the amount and type of information received

internal auditors Employees who analyze and evaluate the operation of company departments to determine their efficiency

internal communication Communication among employees within an organization

interpersonal skills Skills required to understand other people and to interact effectively with them

intrafirm trade Trade between global units of a multinational corporation

inventory Goods kept in stock for the production process or for sales to final customers

inventory control System for determining the right quantity of various items to have on hand and keeping track of their location, use, and condition

inventory turnover ratio Measure of the time a company takes to turn its inventory into sales, calculated by dividing cost of goods sold by the average value of inventory for a period

investment portfolios Assortment of investment instruments

ISO 9000 Global standards set by the International Organization for Standardization establishing a minimum level of acceptable quality

issued stock Authorized shares that have been released to the market

J

job analysis Process by which jobs are studied to determine the tasks and dynamics involved in performing them

job description Statement of the tasks involved in a given job and the conditions under which the holder of the job will work

job enrichment Reducing work specialization and making work more meaningful by adding to the responsibilities of each job

job sharing Splitting a single full-time job between two employees for their convenience

job specification Statement describing the kind of person who would be best for a given job—including the skills, education, and previous experience that the job requires

joint venture Cooperative partnership in which organizations share investment costs, risks, management, and profits in the development, production, or selling of products

junk bonds Bonds that pay high interest because they are below investment grade

just-in-time (JIT) system Continuous system that pulls materials through the production process, making sure that all materials arrive just when they are needed with minimal inventory and waste

justice Philosophy used in making ethical decisions that aims to ensure the equal distribution of burdens and benefits

K

knowledge-based pay Pay tied to an employee's acquisition of skills; also called skill-based pay

L

labor federation Umbrella organization of national unions and unaffiliated local unions that undertakes large-scale activities on behalf of their members and that resolves conflicts between unions

labor-intensive businesses Businesses in which labor costs are more significant than capital costs

labor unions Organizations of employees formed to protect and advance their members' interests

laissez-faire leaders Leaders who lead by leaving the actual decision making up to employees

layoffs Termination of employees for economic or business reasons

lead time Period that elapses between the ordering of materials and their arrival from the supplier

leading Process of guiding and motivating people to work toward organizational goals

lease Legal agreement that obligates the user of an asset to make payments to the owner of the asset in exchange for using it

leverage Technique of increasing the rate of return on an investment by financing it with borrowed funds

leveraged buyout (LBO) Situation in which individuals or groups of investors purchase companies primarily with debt secured by the company's assets

liabilities Claim against a firm's assets by a creditor

licensing Agreement to produce and market another company's product in exchange for a royalty or fee

lifestyle businesses Small businesses intended to provide the owner with a comfortable livelihood

limit order Market order that stipulates the highest or lowest price at which the customer is willing to trade securities

limited liability companies (LLCs) Organizations that combine the benefits of S corporations and limited partnerships without the drawbacks of either

limited partnership Partnership composed of one or more general partners and one or more partners whose liability is usually limited to the amount of their capital investment

limited-service merchant wholesalers Merchant wholesalers that offer fewer services than full-service wholesalers; they often specialize in particular markets, such as agriculture

line-and-staff organization Organization system that has a clear chain of command but that also includes functional groups of people who provide advice and specialized services

line of credit Arrangement in which the financial institution makes money available for use at any time after the loan has been approved

line organization Chain-of-command system that establishes a clear line of authority flowing from the top down

liquidity The level of ease with which an asset can be converted to cash

liquidity ratios Ratios that measure a firm's ability to meet its short-term obligations when they are due

local advertising Advertising sponsored by a local merchant

local area network (LAN) Computer network that encompasses a small area, such as an office or a university campus

locals Relatively small union groups, usually part of a national union or a labor federation, that represent members who work in a single facility or in a certain geographic area

lockouts Management tactic in which union members are prevented from entering a business during a strike in order to force union acceptance of management's last contract proposal

logistics The planning, movement, and flow of goods and related information throughout the supply chain.

long-term debt Borrowed funds used to cover long-term expenses (generally repaid over a period of more than one year)

long-term liabilities Obligations that fall due more than a year from the date of the balance sheet

M

M1 That portion of the money supply consisting of currency and demand deposits

M2 That portion of the money supply consisting of currency, demand deposits, and small time deposits

M3 That portion of the money supply consisting of M1 and M2 plus large time deposits and other restrictive deposits

macroeconomics Study of the economy as a whole

mail-order firms Companies that sell products through catalogs and ship them directly to customers

mainframe computer A large and powerful computer, capable of storing and processing vast amounts of data

management Process of coordinating resources to meet organizational goals

management accounting Area of accounting concerned with preparing data for use by managers within the organization

management by objectives (MBO) A motivational tool whereby managers and employees work together to structure personal goals and objectives for every individual, department, and project to mesh with the organization's goals

management information system (MIS) Computer system that supplies information to assist in managerial decision making

management pyramid Organizational structure comprising top, middle, and lower management

managerial integrator Manager who coordinates activities of several functional departments but belongs to none

mandatory retirement Required dismissal of an employee who reaches a certain age

mandatory subjects Topics that must be discussed in collective bargaining

manufacturing resource planning (MRP II) Computer-based system that integrates data from all departments to manage inventory and production planning and control

margin trading Borrowing money from brokers to buy stock, paying interest on the borrowed money, and leaving the stock with the broker as collateral

market People or businesses who need or want a product and have the money to buy it

market indexes Measures of security markets calculated from the prices of a selection of securities

market makers Dealers in dealer exchanges who sell securities out of their own inventories so that a market is always available for buyers and sellers

market order Authorization for a broker to buy or sell securities at the best price that can be negotiated at the moment

market segmentation Division of total market into smaller, relatively homogeneous groups

market share Measure of a firm's portion of the total sales in a market

marketable securities Stocks, bonds, and other investments that can be turned into cash quickly

marketing Process of planning and executing the conception, pricing, promotion, and distribution of ideas, goods, and services to create and maintain relationships that satisfy individual and organizational objectives

marketing concept Approach to business management that stresses customer needs and wants, seeks long-term profitability, and integrates marketing with other functional units within the organization

marketing intermediaries Businesspeople and organizations that channel goods and services from producers to consumers

marketing mix The four key elements of marketing strategy: product, price, distribution, and promotion

marketing research Collection and use of information for marketing decision making

marketing strategy Overall plan for marketing a product

mass customization Producing customized goods and services through mass production techniques

mass production Manufacture of uniform products in great quantities

master limited partnership (MLP) Business partnership that acts like a corporation, trading partnership units on listed stock exchanges; if 90 percent of income is passive, MLPs are taxed at individual rates

matching principle Fundamental principle requiring that expenses incurred in producing revenue be deducted from the revenues they generate during an accounting period

material requirements planning (MRP) Method of getting the correct materials where they are needed, on time, and without carrying unnecessary inventory

materials handling Movement of goods within a firm's warehouse terminal, factory, or store

mechanization Use of machines to do work previously done by people

media Communications channels, such as newspapers, radio, and television

media mix Combination of various media options that a company uses in an advertising campaign

media plan Written plan that outlines how a company will spend its media budget, including how the money will be divided among the various media and when the advertisements will appear

mediation Process for resolving a labor-contract dispute in which a neutral third party meets with both sides and attempts to steer them toward a solution

mentor Experienced manager or employee with a wide network of industry colleagues who can explain office politics, serve as a role model for appropriate business behavior, and help other employees negotiate the corporate structure

merchant wholesalers Independent wholesalers that take legal title to goods they distribute

merger Combination of two or more companies in which the old companies cease to exist and a new enterprise is created

microcomputer Smallest and least expensive class of computers; often generally referred to as a personal computer

microeconomics Study of specific entities in the economy, such as households, companies, or industries

microprocessor Advanced integrated circuit that combines most of the basic functions of a computer onto a single chip

middle managers Those in the middle of the management hierarchy; they develop plans to implement the goals of top managers and coordinate the work of first-line managers

minicomputers Smaller, less powerful, and less expensive mainframes; often referred to as midsize computers

minorities In a social and economic sense, categories of people that society at large singles out for discriminatory, selective, or unfavorable treatment

mission statement A statement of the organization's purpose

missionary salespeople Salespeople who support existing customers, usually wholesalers and retailers

modem Hardware device that allows a computer to communicate over a regular telephone line

monetary policy Government policy and actions taken by the Federal Reserve Board to regulate the nation's money supply

money Anything generally accepted as a means of paying for goods and services

money-market funds Mutual funds that invest in short-term securities

monopolistic competition Situation in which many sellers differentiate their products from those of competitors in at least some small way

monopoly Market in which there are no direct competitors so that one company dominates

morale Attitude an individual has toward his or her job and employer

mortgage bonds Corporate bonds backed by real property

most favored nation (MFN) trading status A privilege granted by the United States that greatly simplifies and reduces import duties levied on goods from certain countries

motivating Instilling employees with a desire to do the job and to perform at their peak

motivation Force that moves someone to take action

motivators Factors of human relations in business that may increase motivation

multimedia Computer activity that involves sound, photographic images, animation, and video in addition to traditional computer data

multinational corporations (MNCs) Companies with operations in more than one country

multitasking Running several programs at once and switching back and forth between them

municipal bonds Debt issued by a state or a local agency; interest earned on municipal bonds is exempt from federal income tax and from taxes in the issuing jurisdiction

mutual funds Pools of money raised by investment companies and invested in stocks, bonds, or other marketable securities

N

NASDAQ (National Association of Securities Dealers Automated Quotations) National over-the-counter securities trading network

national advertising Advertising sponsored by companies that sell products on a nationwide basis; refers to the geographic reach of the advertiser, not the geographic coverage of the ad

national brands Brands owned by manufacturer and distributed nationally

national competitive advantage Ability of a nation's industries to be innovative and move to a higher level of technology and productivity

national union Nationwide organization made up of local unions that represent employees in locations around the country

natural resources Land, forests, minerals, water, and other tangible assets usable in their natural state

need Difference between a person's actual state and his or her ideal state; provides the basic motivation to make a purchase

need-satisfaction approach Selling method that starts with identifying the customer's needs and then creating a presentation that addresses those needs; this is the approach used by most professional salespeople

net income Profit or loss earned by a firm, determined by subtracting expenses from revenues; also called the bottom line

network Collection of computers, communications software, and transmission media (such as a telephone lines) that allows computers to communicate

networking Making and using contacts

norms Informal standards of conduct that guide team behavior

not-for-profit organization Firm whose primary objective is something other than returning a profit to its owners

not publicly traded corporations Corporations that withhold their stock from public sale; also called closed corporations

O

objective Specific, short-range target or aim

office automation systems (OAS) Computer systems that assist with the tasks that people in a typical business office face regularly, such as drawing graphs or processing documents

oligopoly Market dominated by a few producers

open-market operations Activity of the Federal Reserve in buying and selling government bonds on the open market

open order Limit order that does not expire at the end of a trading day

open shop Workplace in which union membership is voluntary and employees need not join or pay dues

operating expenses All costs of operation that are not included under cost of goods sold

operating systems Class of software that controls the computer's hardware components

operational objectives Objectives that focus on short-term issues and describe the results needed to achieve tactical objectives and strategic goals

operational plans Plans that lay out the actions and the resource allocation needed to achieve operational objectives and to support tactical plans; usually defined for less than one year and developed by first-line managers

order getters Salespeople who are responsible for generating new sales and for increasing sales to existing customers

order processing Functions involved in preparing and receiving an order

order takers Salespeople who generally process incoming orders without engaging in creative selling

organization chart Diagram showing how employees and tasks are grouped and where the lines of communication and authority flow

organization structure Framework enabling managers to divide responsibilities, ensure employee accountability, and distribute decision-making authority

organizational culture A set of shared values and norms that support the management system and that guide management and employee behavior

organizational market Customers who buy goods or services for resale or for use in conducting their own operations

organizing Process of arranging resources to carry out the organization's plans

orientation Session or procedure for acclimating a new employee to the organization

outsourcing Subcontracting work to outside companies

over-the-counter (OTC) market Network of dealers who trade securities that are not listed on an exchange

owners' equity Portion of a company's assets that belongs to the owners after obligations to all creditors have been met

P

par value Arbitrary value assigned to a stock that is shown on the stock certificate

parallel processing Use of multiple processors in a single computer unit, with the intention of increasing the speed at which complex calculations can be completed

parent company Company that owns most, if not all, of another company's stock and that takes an active part in managing that other company

participative management Sharing information with employees and involving them in decision making

partnership Unincorporated business owned and operated by two or more persons under a voluntary legal association

pattern bargaining Negotiating similar wages and benefits for all companies within a particular industry

pay for performance Accepting a lower base pay in exchange for bonuses based on meeting production or other goals

penetration pricing Introducing a new product at a low price in hopes of building sales volume quickly

pension plans Company-sponsored programs for providing retirees with income

performance appraisal Evaluation of an employee's work according to specific criteria

permissive subjects Topics that may be omitted from collective bargaining

perpetual inventory System that uses computers to monitor inventory levels and automatically generate purchase orders when supplies are needed

personal selling In-person communication between a seller and one or more potential buyers

persuasive advertising Advertising designed to encourage product sampling and brand switching

physical distribution All the activities required to move finished products from the producer to the consumer

picketing Strike activity in which union members march before company entrances to persuade nonstriking employees to walk off the job and to persuade customers and others to cease doing business with the company

piecework system Compensation system that pays employees a certain amount for each unit produced

place marketing Marketing efforts to attract people and organizations to a particular geographic area

place utility Consumer value added by making a product available in a convenient location

planning Establishing objectives and goals for an organization and determining the best ways to accomplish them

point-of-purchase display Advertising or other display materials set up at retail locations to promote products to potential customers as they are making their purchase decisions

poison pill Defense against hostile takeovers that makes the company less attractive in some way to the potential raider

pollution Damage or destruction to the natural environment caused by human activities

positioning Promotional strategy intended to differentiate a good or service from those of competitors in the mind of the prospective buyer

possession utility Consumer value created when someone takes ownership of a product

preferred stock Shares that give their owners first claim on a company's dividends and assets after paying all debts

premiums Free or bargain-priced items offered to encourage consumers to buy a product

press conference Gathering of media representatives at which companies announce new information; also called a press briefing

press relations Process of communicating with reporters and editors from newspapers, magazines, and radio and television networks and stations

press release Brief statement or video program released to the press announcing new products, management changes, sales performance, and other potential news items; also called a news release

price-earnings ratio (p/e ratio) Stock's current market price divided by issuer's annual earnings per share; also known as the price-earnings multiple

primary market Market where firms sell new securities issued publicly for the first time

primary storage device Storage for data and programs while they are being processed by the computer

prime interest rate (prime) Lowest rate of interest charged by banks for short-term loans to their most credit-worthy customers

principal Amount of a debt, excluding any interest

private accountants In-house accountants employed by organizations and businesses other than a public accounting firm; also called corporate accountants

private brands Brands that carry the label of a retailer or wholesaler rather than a manufacturer

private carriers Transportation operations owned by a company to move its own products and not those of the general public

private corporations Companies owned by private individuals or companies

privatization Trend to substitute private ownership for public ownership

problem-solving teams Informal teams of 5 to 12 employees from the same department who meet voluntarily to find ways of improving quality, efficiency, and the work environment

process control system Computer system that uses special sensing devices to monitor conditions in a physical process and makes necessary adjustments to the process

process divisions Divisional structure based on the major steps of a production process

process layout Method of arranging a facility so that production tasks are carried out in separate departments containing specialized equipment and personnel

product Good or service used as the basis of commerce

product advertising Advertising that tries to sell specific goods or services, generally by describing features, benefits, and, occasionally, price

product divisions Divisional structure based on products

product layout Method of arranging a facility so that production proceeds along a line of workstations

product life cycle Four basic stages through which a product progresses: introduction, growth, maturity, and decline

product line A series of related products offered by a firm

product mix Complete list of all products that a company offers for sale

production Transformation of resources into goods or services that people need or want

production and operations management (POM) Coordination of an organization's resources for the manufacture of goods or the delivery of services

production control Planning, routing, scheduling, dispatching, and following up on production so as to achieve efficiency and high quality

production control systems Computer systems that manage production by controlling production lines, robots, and other machinery and equipment

production efficiency Minimizing cost by maximizing the level of output from each resource

production forecasting Estimating how much of a company's goods and services must be produced in order to meet future demand

profit Money left over after expenses and taxes have been deducted from revenue generated by selling goods and services

profit sharing System for distributing a portion of the company's profits to employees

profitability ratios Ratios that measure the overall financial performance of a firm

program evaluation and review technique (PERT) Planning tool that managers of complex projects use to determine the optimal order of activities, the expected time for project completion, and the best use of resources

program trading Automated securities transactions using computer programs to buy or sell large numbers of securities in response to price changes exceeding predetermined amounts

programming Process of creating the sets of instructions that direct computers to perform desired tasks

promotion Wide variety of persuasive techniques used by companies to communicate with their target markets and the general public

promotional mix Particular blend of personal selling, advertising, direct marketing, sales promotion, and public relations that a company uses to reach potential customers

promotional strategy Statement or document that defines the direction and scope of the promotional activities that a company will use to meet its marketing objectives

prospecting Process of finding and qualifying potential customers

protectionism Government policies aimed at shielding a country's industries from foreign competition

proxy Document authorizing another person to vote on behalf of a shareholder in a corporation

proxy fight Attempt to gain control of a takeover target by urging shareholders to vote for directors favored by the acquiring party

psychographics Classification of customers on the basis of their psychological makeup

public accountants Professionals who provide accounting services to other businesses and individuals for a fee

public relations Nonsales communication that businesses have with their various audiences (includes both communication with the general public and press relations)

publicly traded corporations Corporations that actively sell stock on the open market; also called open corporations

pull strategy Promotional strategy that stimulates consumer demand, which then exerts pressure on wholesalers and retailers to carry a product

purchasing Acquiring the raw materials, parts, components, supplies, and finished products needed to produce goods and services

pure competition Situation in which so many buyers and sellers exist that no single buyer or seller can individually influence market prices

push strategy Promotional approach designed to motivate wholesalers and retailers to push a producer's products to end users

Q

qualified prospects Potential buyers who have both the money needed to make the purchase and the authority to make the purchase decision

quality A measure of how closely a product conforms to predetermined standards and customer expectations

quality assurance System of policies, practices, and procedures implemented throughout the company to create and produce quality goods and services

quality control Routine checking and testing of a finished product for quality against an established standard

quality of work life (QWL) Overall environment that results from job and work conditions

quasi-government corporations Public utilities having a monopoly to provide basic services

quick ratio Measure of a firm's short-term liquidity, calculated by adding cash, marketable securities, and receivables, and then dividing that sum by current liabilities; also known as the acid-test ratio

quotas Fixed limits on the quantity of imports a nation will allow for a specific product

R

rack jobbers Merchant wholesalers that are responsible for setting up and maintaining displays in a particular section of a retail store

random-access memory (RAM) Primary storage devices allowing a computer to access any piece of data in such memory at random

rate of return Percentage increase in the value of an investment

ratification Process by which union members vote on a contract negotiated by union leaders

ratio analysis Use of quantitative measures to evaluate a firm's financial performance

reach Total number of audience members who will be exposed to a message at least once in a given period

read-only memory (ROM) Special circuits that store data and programs permanently but don't allow users to record their own data or programs; a common use of ROM is for the programs that activate start-up routines when the computer is turned on

recession Period during which national income, employment, and production all fall

recruiting Process of attracting appropriate applicants for an organization's jobs

relationship marketing Focus on developing and maintaining long-term relationships with customers, suppliers, and distributors for mutual benefit

reminder advertising Advertising intended to remind existing customers of a product's availability and benefits

reserve requirement Percentage of a bank's deposit that must be set aside

responsibility Obligation to perform the duties and achieve the goals and objectives associated with a particular position

résumé Brief description of education, experience, and personal data compiled by a job applicant

retailers Firms that sell goods and services to individuals for their own use rather than for resale

retained earnings The portion of shareholders' equity earned by the company but not distributed to its owners in the form of dividends

return on investment (ROI) Ratio between the net income earned by a company and total owners' equity; also known as return on equity

return on sales Ratio between net income and net sales; also known as profit margin

revenue bonds Municipal bonds backed by revenue generated from the projects financed with the bonds

revenues Amount of sales of goods or services and inflow from miscellaneous sources such as interest, rent, and royalties

reverse channels Distribution channels designed to move products from the customer back to the producer

right-to-work laws Laws giving employees the explicit right to keep a job without joining a union

robots Programmable machines that can complete a variety of tasks by working with tools and materials

roles Behavioral patterns associated with certain positions

routing Specifying the sequence of operations and the path the work will take through the production facility

S

S corporation Corporations with no more than 75 shareholders that may be taxed as a partnership; also known as a subchapter S corporation

salaries Fixed weekly, monthly, or yearly cash compensation for work

sales office Producer-owned office that markets products but doesn't carry any stock

sales promotion Wide range of events and activities (including coupons, rebates, contests, in-store demonstrations, free samples, trade shows, and point-of-purchase displays) designed to stimulate interest in a product

sales support personnel Salespeople who facilitate the selling effort by providing such services as prospecting, customer education, and customer service

scheduling Process of determining how long each production operation takes and then setting a starting and ending time for each

scientific management Management approach designed to improve employees' efficiency by scientifically studying their work

scrambled merchandising Policy of carrying merchandise that is ordinarily sold in a different type of outlet

secondary market Market where subsequent owners trade previously issued shares of stock and bonds

secondary storage Computer storage for data and programs that aren't needed at the moment

secured bonds Bonds backed by specific assets

secured loans Loans backed up with something of value that the lender can claim in case of default, such as a piece of property

selective credit controls Federal Reserve's power to set credit terms on various types of loans

selective distribution Market coverage strategy that selects a limited number of outlets to distribute products

self-directed teams Teams in which members are responsible for an entire process or operation

sellers' market Marketplace characterized by a shortage of products

selling expenses All the operating expenses associated with marketing goods or services

service businesses Businesses that provide intangible products or perform useful labor on behalf of another

Service Corps of Retired Executives (SCORE) SBA program in which retired executives volunteer as consultants to assist small businesses

setup costs Expenses incurred each time a producer organizes resources to begin producing goods or services

sexism Discriminating against a person on the basis of gender

sexual harassment Unwelcome sexual advance, request for sexual favors, or other verbal or physical conduct of a sexual nature within the workplace

shareholders Owners of a corporation

shark repellent Direct takeover defense in which the company's board requires a large majority of voting shares to approve any takeover attempt

shop steward Union member and employee who is elected to represent other union members and who attempts to resolve employee grievances with management

short selling Selling stock borrowed from a broker with the intention of buying it back later at a lower price, repaying the broker, and pocketing the profit

short-term debt Borrowed funds used to cover current expenses (generally repaid within a year)

sinking fund Account into which a company makes annual payments for use in redeeming its bonds in the future

skimming Charging a high price for a new product during the introductory stage and lowering the price later

slowdown Decreasing employee productivity to pressure management

small business Company that is independently owned and operated, is not dominant in its field, and meets certain criteria for the number of employees and annual sales revenue

smart cards Plastic cards that include an embedded chip to store money drawn from the user's demand-deposit account and information that can be used for purchases

social audit Assessment of a company's performance in the area of social responsibility

social responsibility The idea that business has certain obligations to society beyond the pursuit of profits

socialism Economic system characterized by public ownership and operation of key industries combined with private ownership and operation of less vital industries

software Programmed instructions that drive the activity of computer hardware

sole proprietorship Business owned by a single individual

span of management Number of people under one manager's control; also known as span of control

specialty advertising Advertising that appears on various items such as coffee mugs, pens, and calendars, designed to help keep a company's name in front of customers

specialty shops Stores that carry only particular types of goods

speculators Investors who purchase securities in anticipation of making large profits quickly

speech-recognition system Computer system that recognizes human speech, enabling users to enter data and give commands vocally

spreadsheet Program that organizes and manipulates data in a row-column matrix

stakeholders Individuals or groups to whom business has a responsibility

standardization Uniformity in goods or parts, making them interchangeable

standards Criteria against which performance may be measured

start-up companies New ventures

statement of cash flows Statement of a firm's cash receipts and cash payments that presents information on its sources and uses of cash.

statistical process control (SPC) Use of random sampling and control charts to monitor the production process

statistical quality control (SQC) Monitoring all aspects of the production process to see whether the process is operating as it should

stock Shares of ownership in a corporation

stock certificate Document that proves stock ownership

stock exchanges Location where traders buy and sell stocks and bonds

stock option Contract allowing the holder to buy or sell a given number of shares of a particular stock at a given price by a certain date

stock option plan Program enabling employees to purchase a certain amount of stock at a discount after they have worked for the company a specified length of time or after the company's stock reaches a specific market price

stock specialist Intermediary who trades in a particular security on the floor of an auction exchange; "buyer of last resort"

stock split Increase in the number of shares of ownership that each stock certificate represents

strategic alliance Long-term relationship in which two or more companies share ideas, resources, and technologies in order to establish competitive advantages

strategic goals Goals that focus on broad organizational issues and aim to improve performance

strategic plans Plans that establish the actions and the resource allocation required to accomplish strategic goals; usually defined for periods of two to five years and developed by top managers

strike Temporary work stoppage by employees who want management to accept their union's demands

strikebreakers Nonunion workers hired to replace striking workers

subsidiary corporations Corporations whose stock is owned entirely or almost entirely by another corporation

supercomputers Computers with the highest level of performance, often boasting speeds greater than a trillion calculations per second

supply Specific quantity of a product that the seller is able and willing to provide

supply chain management Integrating all of the facilities, functions, and processes associated with the production of goods and services, from suppliers to customers

supply curve Graph of relationship between various prices and the quantity supplied at each price

synthetic system Production process that combines two or more materials or components to create finished products; the reverse of an analytic system

T

tactical objectives Objectives that focus on departmental issues and describe the results necessary to achieve the organization's strategic goals

tactical plans Plans that define the actions and the resource allocation necessary to achieve tactical objectives and to support strategic plans; usually defined for a period of one to three years and developed by middle managers

tall organizations Organizations having a narrow span of management and many hierarchical levels

target markets Specific groups of customers to whom a company wants to sell a particular product

tariffs Taxes levied on imports

task force Team of people from several departments who are temporarily brought together to address a specific issue

tax accounting Area of accounting focusing on tax preparation and tax planning

team A unit of two or more people who share a mission and collective responsibility as they work together to achieve a goal

technical salespeople Specialists who contribute technical expertise and other sales assistance

technical skills Ability and knowledge to perform the mechanics of a particular job

technology Knowledge, tools, techniques, and activities used in the production of goods and services

telecommuting Working from home and communicating with the company's main office via computer and communication devices

telemarketing Selling or supporting the sales process over the telephone

temps Temporary teams that exist outside the formal organization hierarchy and are created to achieve a specific goal

tender offer Invitation made directly to shareholders by an outside party who wishes to buy a company's stock at a price above the current market price

termination Act of getting rid of an employee through layoffs or firing

test marketing Product-development stage in which a product is sold on a limited basis—a trial introduction

Theory X Managerial assumption that employees are irresponsible, unambitious, and distasteful of work and that managers must use force, control, or threats to motivate them

Theory Y Managerial assumption that employees like work, are naturally committed to certain goals, are capable of creativity, and seek out responsibility under the right conditions

Theory Z Human relations approach that emphasizes involving employees at all levels and treating them like family

time deposits Bank accounts that pay interest and require advance notice before money can be withdrawn

time utility Consumer value added by making a product available at a convenient time

top managers Those at the highest level of the organization's management hierarchy; they are responsible for setting strategic goals, and they have the most power and responsibility in the organization

total quality management (TQM) Comprehensive, strategic management approach that builds quality into every organizational process as a way of improving customer satisfaction

trade allowance Discount offered by producers to wholesalers and retailers

trade credit Credit obtained by the purchases directly from the supplier

trade deficit Negative trade balance created when a country imports more than it exports

trade promotions Sales-promotion efforts aimed at inducing distributors or retailers to push a producer's products

trade salespeople Salespeople who sell to and support marketing intermediaries by giving in-store demonstrations, offering samples, and so on

trade show Gathering where producers display their wares to potential buyers; nearly every industry has one or more trade shows focused on particular types of products

trade surplus Positive trade balance created when a country exports more than it imports

trademark Brand that has been given legal protection so that its owner has exclusive rights to its use

trading blocs Organizations of nations that remove barriers to trade among their members and that establish uniform barriers to trade with nonmember nations

transaction Exchange between parties

transaction costs Costs of trading securities, including broker's commission and taxes

transaction processing system (TPS) Computerized information system that processes the daily flow of customer, supplier, and employee transactions, including inventory, sales, and payroll records

transactional leaders Leaders who excel at creating an efficient organization and motivating employees to meet expectations

transfer payments Payments by government to individuals that are not made in return for goods and services

transformational leaders Leaders who possess the ability to inspire long-term vision, creativity, and change in their employees

Treasury bills Short-term debt issued by the federal government; also referred to as T-bills

Treasury bonds Debt securities issued by the federal government that mature in 10 to 30 years

Treasury notes Debt securities issued by the federal government that mature within 1 to 10 years

trend analysis Comparison of a firm's financial data from year to year to see how they have changed

trusts Monopolistic arrangements established when one company buys a controlling share of the stock of competing companies in the same industry

two-tier wage plan Compensation agreement in which new employees are put on a wage scale lower than that of veteran employees

U

union shop Workplace in which the employer may hire new employees at will, but where the employees are required to join the union after a probationary period

unissued stock Authorized shares that are to be released in the future

Universal Product Codes (UPCs) A bar code on a product's package that provides information read by optical scanners

unlimited liability Legal condition under which any damages or debts attributable to the business can also be attached to the owner because the two have no separate legal existence

unsecured loan Loan requiring no collateral but a good credit rating

U.S. savings bonds Debt instruments sold by the federal government in small denominations

utilitarianism Philosophy used in making ethical decisions that aims to achieve the greatest good for the greatest number

utility Power of a good or service to satisfy a human need

V

variable costs Business costs that increase with the number of units produced

venture capitalists Investment specialists who provide money to finance new businesses or turnarounds in exchange for a portion of the ownership, with the objective of making a considerable profit on the investment; also called VCs

vertical marketing systems (VMS) Planned distribution channels in which members coordinate their efforts to optimize distribution activities

vertical mergers Combinations of companies that participate in different phases of the same industry (i.e., materials, production, distribution)

vertical organization Structure linking activities at the top of the organization with those at the middle and lower levels

virtual teams Teams that use communication technology to bring geographically distant employees together to achieve goals

vision A viable view of the future that is rooted in but improves on the present

voluntary export restrictions (VERs) Self-imposed limits on the amount of certain goods a country exports

W

wages Cash payment based on the number of hours the employee has worked or the number of units the employee has produced

wants Things that are desirable in light of a person's experiences, culture, and personality

warehouse Facility for storing inventory

wheel of retailing Evolutionary process by which stores that feature low prices are gradually upgraded until they forfeit their appeal to price-sensitive shoppers and are replace by new competitors

white knight Friendly buyer who agrees to take over a company to prevent a raider from taking it over

wholesalers Firms that sell products to other firms for resale or for organizational use

wide area network (WAN) Computer network that encompasses a large geographic area

wireless transceivers Small hardware attachments that enable a computer to transmit and receive data

work rules Policies set during collective bargaining that govern what type of work union members will do and the conditions under which they will work

work sharing Slicing a few hours off everybody's workweek and cutting pay to minimize layoffs

work specialization Specialization in or responsibility for some portion of an organization's overall work tasks; also called division of labor

worker buyout Distribution of financial incentives to employees who voluntarily depart, usually undertaken in order to shrink the payroll

workgroup computing Computing arrangement in which teams can easily work together on projects

working capital Current assets minus current liabilities

workstation Class of computers with the basic size and shape of microcomputers but with the speed of traditional midsize computers; often used for design, engineering, and scientific applications

wrongful discharge Firing an employee with inadequate advance notice or explanation

Y

yield Income received from securities, calculated by dividing dividend or interest income by market price

NAME/ORGANIZATION/ BRAND/COMPANY INDEX

K

L

M

N

SUBJECT INDEX

Q

R

U

MESCON, BOVÉE, THILL • BUSINESS TODAY • NINTH EDITION

PRENTICE-HALL, INC.

YOU SHOULD CAREFULLY READ THE TERMS AND CONDITIONS BEFORE USING THE CD-ROM PACKAGE. USING THIS CD-ROM PACKAGE INDICATES YOUR ACCEPTANCE OF THESE TERMS AND CONDITIONS.

Prentice-Hall, Inc. provides this program and licenses its use. You assume responsibility for the selection of the program to achieve your intended results, and for the installation, use, and results obtained from the program. This license extends only to use of the program in the United States or countries in which the program is marketed by authorized distributors.

LICENSE GRANT You hereby accept a nonexclusive, nontransferable, permanent license to install and use the program ON A SINGLE COMPUTER at any given time. You may copy the program solely for backup or archival purposes in support of your use of the program on the single computer. You may not modify, translate, disassemble, decompile, or reverse engineer the program, in whole or in part.

TERM The License is effective until terminated. Prentice-Hall, Inc. reserves the right to terminate this License automatically if any provision of the License is violated. You may terminate the License at any time. To terminate this License, you must return the program, including documentation, along with a written warranty stating that all copies in your possession have been returned or destroyed.

LIMITED WARRANTY THE PROGRAM IS PROVIDED "AS IS" WITHOUT WARRANTY OF ANY KIND, EITHER EXPRESSED OR IMPLIED, INCLUDING, BUT NOT LIMITED TO, THE IMPLIED WARRANTIES OR MERCHANTABILITY AND FITNESS FOR A PARTICULAR PURPOSE. THE ENTIRE RISK AS TO THE QUALITY AND PERFORMANCE OF THE PROGRAM IS WITH YOU. SHOULD THE PROGRAM PROVE DEFECTIVE, YOU (AND NOT PRENTICE-HALL, INC. OR ANY AUTHORIZED DEALER) ASSUME THE ENTIRE COST OF ALL NECESSARY SERVICING, REPAIR, OR CORRECTION. NO ORAL OR WRITTEN INFORMATION OR ADVICE GIVEN BY PRENTICE-HALL, INC., ITS DEALERS, DISTRIBUTORS, OR AGENTS SHALL CREATE A WARRANTY OR INCREASE THE SCOPE OF THIS WARRANTY.

SOME STATES DO NOT ALLOW THE EXCLUSION OF IMPLIED WARRANTIES, SO THE ABOVE EXCLUSION MAY NOT APPLY TO YOU. THIS WARRANTY GIVES YOU SPECIFIC LEGAL RIGHTS AND YOU MAY ALSO HAVE OTHER LEGAL RIGHTS THAT VARY FROM STATE TO STATE.

Prentice-Hall, Inc. does not warrant that the functions contained in the program will meet your requirements or that the operation of the program will be uninterrupted or error-free.

However, Prentice-Hall, Inc. warrants the diskette(s) on which the program is furnished to be free from defects in material and workmanship under normal use for a period of ninety (90) days from the date of delivery to you as evidenced by a copy of your receipt.

The program should not be relied on as the sole basis to solve a problem whose incorrect solution could result in injury to person or property. If the program is employed in such a manner, it is at the user's own risk and Prentice-Hall, Inc. explicitly disclaims all liability for such misuse.

LIMITATION OF REMEDIES Prentice-Hall, Inc.'s entire liability and your exclusive remedy shall be:

1. the replacement of any diskette not meeting Prentice-Hall, Inc.'s "LIMITED WARRANTY" and that is returned to Prentice-Hall, or **2**. if Prentice-Hall is unable to deliver a replacement diskette that is free of defects in materials or workmanship, you may terminate this agreement by returning the program.

IN NO EVENT WILL PRENTICE-HALL, INC. BE LIABLE TO YOU FOR ANY DAMAGES, INCLUDING ANY LOST PROFITS, LOST SAVINGS, OR OTHER INCIDENTAL OR CONSEQUENTIAL DAMAGES ARISING OUT OF THE USE OR INABILITY TO USE SUCH PROGRAM EVEN IF PRENTICE-HALL, INC. OR AN AUTHORIZED DISTRIBUTOR HAS BEEN ADVISED OF THE POSSIBILITY OF SUCH DAMAGES, OR FOR ANY CLAIM BY ANY OTHER PARTY.

SOME STATES DO NOT ALLOW FOR THE LIMITATION OR EXCLUSION OF LIABILITY FOR INCIDENTAL OR CONSEQUENTIAL DAMAGES, SO THE ABOVE LIMITATION OR EXCLUSION MAY NOT APPLY TO YOU.

GENERAL You may not sublicense, assign, or transfer the license of the program. Any attempt to sublicense, assign or transfer any of the rights, duties, or obligations hereunder is void.

This Agreement will be governed by the laws of the State of New York.

Should you have any questions concerning this Agreement, you may contact Prentice-Hall, Inc. by writing to:

Director of New Media
Higher Education Division
Prentice-Hall, Inc.
1 Lake Street
Upper Saddle River, NJ 07458

Should you have any questions concerning technical support, you may write to:

New Media Production
Higher Education Division
Prentice-Hall, Inc.
1 Lake Street
Upper Saddle River, NJ 07458

YOU ACKNOWLEDGE THAT YOU HAVE READ THIS AGREEMENT, UNDERSTAND IT, AND AGREE TO BE BOUND BY ITS TERMS AND CONDITIONS. YOU FURTHER AGREE THAT IT IS THE COMPLETE AND EXCLUSIVE STATEMENT OF THE AGREEMENT BETWEEN US THAT SUPERSEDES ANY PROPOSAL OR PRIOR AGREEMENT, ORAL OR WRITTEN, AND ANY OTHER COMMUNICATIONS BETWEEN US RELATING TO THE SUBJECT MATTER OF THIS AGREEMENT.